BUSINESS LAW AND STRATEGY

Sean P. Melvin
Elizabethtown College

David Orozco
Florida State University

F. E. Guerra-Pujol
University of Central Florida

BUSINESS LAW AND STRATEGY

Published by McGraw-Hill Education, 2 Penn Plaza, New York, NY 10121. Copyright © 2021 by McGraw-Hill Education. All rights reserved. Printed in the United States of America. No part of this publication may be reproduced or distributed in any form or by any means, or stored in a database or retrieval system, without the prior written consent of McGraw-Hill Education, including, but not limited to, in any network or other electronic storage or transmission, or broadcast for distance learning.

Some ancillaries, including electronic and print components, may not be available to customers outside the United States.

This book is printed on acid-free paper.

1 2 3 4 5 6 7 8 9 LWI 24 23 22 21 20

ISBN 978-0-07-802382-8 (bound edition)
MHID 0-07-802382-3 (bound edition)
ISBN 978-0-07-761468-3 (loose-leaf edition)
MHID 0-07-761468-2 (loose-leaf edition)
ISBN 978-1-264-22842-3 (instructor's edition)
MHID 1-264-22842-2 (instructor's edition)

Executive Portfolio Manager: *Kathleen Klehr*
Product Developers: *Jaroslaw Szymanski; Allie Kukla*
Marketing Manager: *Claire McLemore*
Content Project Managers: *Lori Koetters; Angela Norris*
Buyer: *Sandy Ludovissy*
Design: *Egzon Shaqiri*
Content Licensing Specialist: *Beth Cray*
Cover Image: *©valterZ/Shutterstock*
Compositor: *SPi Global*

All credits appearing on page or at the end of the book are considered to be an extension of the copyright page.

Library of Congress Cataloging-in-Publication Data

Names: Melvin, Sean P., author. | Orozco, David, author. | Guerra-Pujol, F.
  E., author.
Title: Business law and strategy / Sean P. Melvin, Elizabethtown College,
  David Orozco, Florida State University, F. E. Guerra-Pujol, University
  of Central Florida.
Description: New York, NY : McGraw Hill Education, [2021] | Includes index.
Identifiers: LCCN 2019041962 | ISBN 9780078023828 (hardcover) |
  ISBN 9780077614690 (ebook)
Subjects: LCSH: Commercial law—United States.
Classification: LCC KF889.85 .M45 2021 | DDC 346.73/065—dc23
LC record available at https://lccn.loc.gov/2019041962

The Internet addresses listed in the text were accurate at the time of publication. The inclusion of a website does not indicate an endorsement by the authors or McGraw-Hill Education, and McGraw-Hill Education does not guarantee the accuracy of the information presented at these sites.

mheducation.com/highered

Dedication

For Joseph P. Melvin (1926–2009).

S.P.M.

For Lydie, who stood by my side.

D.O.

For Francisco and Oilda.

F.E.G.P.

For our students: past, present, and future.

The Authors

about the authors

Courtesy of Sean P. Melvin

Sean P. Melvin is an associate professor of business law at Elizabethtown College (Pennsylvania), where he served as department chair for eight years, won the Delta Mu Delta Outstanding Teacher of the Year award, and received several Faculty Merit awards for teaching and scholarship. Prior to his appointment at Elizabethtown, he was an assistant professor of business at a large state university where he taught in both the undergraduate and MBA programs. Before his academic career, Professor Melvin was a corporate lawyer in a large Philadelphia-based law firm and went on to become vice president and general counsel at a publicly traded technology company.

Professor Melvin is the author or co-author of eight books (including five textbooks), has contributed scholarly and professional articles and case studies to over two dozen publications, and is a member of the Academy of Legal Studies in Business (ALSB). His article "Case Study of a Coffee War" was selected as Best International Case Study at the 86th annual ALSB conference.

Courtesy of David Orozco

David Orozco is an associate professor of legal studies at Florida State University's College of Business. Professor Orozco has won several teaching awards and enjoys writing about law, ethics, legal strategy, and compliance. He has authored dozens of articles in top law reviews and peer-reviewed journals. He is a member of the Academy of Legal Studies in Business (ALSB) and serves on the editorial board of *American Business Law Journal*. He also maintains an active presence on Twitter @ProfessorOrozco.

Courtesy of F. E. Guerra-Pujol

F. E. Guerra-Pujol teaches business law at the University of Central Florida (UCF), where he also serves as faculty editor of *The Pegasus Review,* UCF's undergraduate research journal. Prior to his appointment at UCF, he was an associate professor at the Pontifical Catholic University School of Law in Ponce, Puerto Rico, and practiced business and tax law with a large Latin American law firm. Professor Guerra-Pujol received his BA from UC Santa Barbara and his JD from Yale Law School.

Professor Guerra-Pujol has published refereed articles, book chapters, and other scholarly works on the law and ethics of strategic decision making and is a member of the Academy of Legal Studies in Business (ALSB). He is currently writing a book titled *Alternate Legal Worlds* exploring law from a science fiction perspective.

FROM THE AUTHORS

Legal strategies act as a springboard for businesses to gain competitive advantages, identify opportunities to reach goals, and create value in the firm. Business managers are increasingly tasked with understanding the basics of legal strategy and recognizing which strategies tie into their business needs and influence their decision making. Because today's students are tomorrow's business managers and owners, empowering them with knowledge of business law and the basics of legal strategy provides a strong foundation for their future success in the business world.

There is a growing body of research and desire for more legal strategy in the business curriculum. *BUSINESS LAW AND STRATEGY* addresses those issues by bringing a fresh and accessible approach to the business law course. It differentiates itself from current text offerings for the business law course by weaving strategy as a defining thread throughout the tried-and-true business law course topics, giving today's students the tools they need as future business managers and owners to incorporate legal strategy as they make business decisions.

Each chapter opens with a brief description of the content within a strategic context, giving students focus as they begin their study of the core business law topics covered in the chapter. The strategy focus continues through the chapter with a generous use of engaging and current cases, workplace examples, and explanations through a strategic problem-solving and critical thinking lens. Each chapter concludes with a business scenario and thought-provoking questions that solidify students' understanding of the black-letter law within a strategy context.

The text's engaging and student-centered approach reinforces chapter material with the use of information chunking, dynamic pedagogical features that bridge the gap between theory and practice, and the use of exercises designed to improve critical thinking skills. The content includes carefully selected law cases with a blend of new-economy and old-economy organizations and brands.

BUSINESS LAW AND STRATEGY covers all the traditional topics in the business law course, ensuring students are well versed in those areas, including CPA-related topics required for accounting majors. The writing style is accessible and colloquial, and it makes generous use of examples and vignettes written in the active voice.

Furthermore, a robust technology suite of products supports the text content with online assignments and activities emulating common business situations in which students can actively explore the consequences of various actions and sharpen their strategic thinking skills.

To sum up, *BUSINESS LAW AND STRATEGY* is unique in approach and comprehensive in coverage.

- Cutting-edge cases blend landmark and new-economy companies.
- It has a strategic approach that appeals to business students.
- Pedagogical features center on strategy, critical thinking, and reinforcement. They are scalable, assignable, and flexible with auto-grading of some features.

TEACHING FEATURES RELATED TO STRATEGY AND CRITICAL THINKING

©valterZ/Shutterstock

Thinking Strategically

Thinking Strategically chapter openers Chapter-opening text provides students with a brief overview of chapter content with a strategy context in mind.

Thinking Strategically exercises In keeping with the text's strategy approach, each chapter integrates an exercise intended to introduce students to the intersection between law and strategy. These exercises help students think of the law as a part of business decision making rather than as a book of rules. Each *Thinking Strategically* exercise begins with a real-world legal dilemma faced by an individual or business. Through a series of multiple-choice questions and a critical thinking exercise, students work through various strategic considerations from the topics covered in the chapter.

Document-Based Review Exercises (DBREs)

After each unit, instructors may assign a multistep *Document-Based Review Exercise* (DBRE) designed to help students connect the various topics covered in a single unit. DBREs challenge students to analyze significant evidence such as legal documents, periodicals, data, and photos or editorial cartoons that are related to strategic legal dilemmas. These exercises encourage students to think critically and strategically and connect several concepts and sources when they prepare their answers.

- First, students read several open-ended *framing questions* and begin to formulate answers based on material they have learned in the text.
- Second, students read four to six *excerpts* from legal documents (e.g., a statute, a court case, or a contract), data (e.g., charts, graphs, tables), and a historic photo/editorial cartoon or pertinent image with the framing questions in mind.
- Third, students answer several *multiple-choice questions* to assess their knowledge of the relationship between the documents and the material they learned from the textbook or in class.
- Fourth, students answer a series of *short-answer/fill-in-the-blank questions* designed to reinforce the relationship between several different legal concepts from the same unit (e.g., agency law and negligence).
- Finally, instructors have the option to assign one or more longer essay questions for either assessment or reinforcement. A rubric is also included for each question.

The DBREs are a part of Connect, McGraw-Hill's digital platform for assignment and assessment. DBREs include both auto-graded questions and questions that require manual grading. The DBREs' multipart format permits instructors to customize which portions of the DBREs they would like to assign.

Capstone Case Studies

Capstone Case Studies center on three *business case studies* of actual corporations that faced corporate crises with legal, strategic, and ethical implications and their managements' responses. Students reread concept summaries from specific previous chapters; then, with an eye toward proactive law, they study a narrative of facts of the case, dynamics of the marketplace, and important trends of the time. Discussion questions are grouped by topical subject matter such as contracts, liability, administrative agency regulation, and criminal law. Strategic considerations and questions are integrated into each *Capstone Case Study.* The *Capstone Case Study* feature also provides a short exercise that can be used for writing assignments, small-group work, or class discussion.

OVERVIEW AND OBJECTIVES

Two years after opening their family-owned coffee bean roastery, Jim and Annie Clark had become accustomed to long workweeks and bootstrap financing. By 1997, their Black Bear Micro Roastery was finally growing, and the Clarks were hopeful that their new specialty

THE BLACK BEAR MICRO ROASTERY

Jim and Annie Clark were native New Englanders who shared a passion for coffee and an entrepreneurial spirit. After three years of research, they launched Black Bear Micro Roastery in 1995 with a mission of creating a unique methodology for roasting gourmet

Law, Ethics, and Society

Located in appropriate places throughout the text, the *Law, Ethics, and Society* feature ties together current issues of law and ethics and presents them in a societal context. For example, this feature integrates with the material in the "Torts and Products Liability" chapter to consider the use of product liability statutes by families of the Sandy Hook massacre to sue manufacturers of AK-47s. In some chapters, the feature ends with a set of questions for assignment or discussion. The use of this feature will also help instructors satisfy accreditation standards.

LAW, ETHICS, AND SOCIETY

Wells Fargo Ghost Accounts Scandal

In 2016, regulators announced that Wells Fargo employees secretly created millions of unauthorized bank and credit card accounts, without their customers knowing it, in some cases dating as far back to 2011. The fake accounts earned the bank unwarranted fees and allowed Wells Fargo employees to boost their sales figures and profit as a result. A consulting firm hired by Wells Fargo found that bank employees opened more than 1.5 million deposit accounts that may not have been authorized.

Consequently, Wells Fargo was fined more than $185 million by various regulators. The company's CEO John Stumpf was forced to resign, and 5,300 employees were fired. In the process, the company's reputation took a large hit, its stock market valuation fell, and the company must address multiple lawsuits from shareholders and those injured by the company's actions.

Discussion Questions

1. What role does a compliance department have in promoting a culture of ethics within an organization?
2. After the Wells Fargo scandal erupted it was discovered that unreasonable and strict sales quotas contributed to the pressure managers faced to create ghost accounts. What ethical duties do senior executives have to ensure this kind of sales pressure does not result in illegal or unethical activity?

Carefully Selected Case Law

The touchstones of every business law textbook are the cases. The authors use a careful selection process to include cases chosen for relevance, ease of understanding, clarity, and general appeal to students. The case law is a blend between landmark cases (e.g., *Palsgraf v. Long Island Railroad*) and cutting-edge cases featuring brands that connect with today's learners (e.g., *Facebook* and *Uber*).

To make the case material as accessible as possible, the text deploys a hybrid format for reporting cases. Students are provided with:

- a two- to three-paragraph summary of the relevant case facts;
- a short statement on the issue and ruling;
- narrowly tailored excerpts from the actual opinion, chosen to help students understand one or more key points in the case related to the material in the text;
- several case questions for reinforcement; and
- a designated critical thinking question that challenges students to think more globally about relationships between law, public policy, logic, and social responsibility.

TEACHING FEATURES RELATED TO REINFORCEMENT

At the Beginning of Each Chapter

- *Thinking Strategically Opener* Each chapter in this textbook features a Thinking Strategically chapter opener and a Thinking Strategically problem-solution format at the end of the chapter to help students understand law and strategy in a real-world context.
- *Learning Objectives Checklist* Dynamic learning objectives allow for assessment tied to AACSB Standards and Bloom's Learning Taxonomy.
- *Chapter Overview* A one-paragraph introduction previews the contents of the chapter and piques students' interest in the subject matter.

Throughout the Textbook

- *Takeaway Concepts* Each major section of each chapter features a bullet-pointed summary that features "takeaways" designed to help students focus on big-picture concepts.
- *Flowcharts, Tables, and Charts* Generous use of visual learning techniques appear throughout to help students process text concepts and black-letter law.
- *Quick Quiz* A four- to five-question feature throughout the text, the Quick Quiz provides students an opportunity to apply black-letter law and case law to short, practical situations and to check their work before moving on in the text.

At the End of Each Chapter

- *Thinking Strategically Exercise* A Thinking Strategically exercise begins with a real-world legal dilemma faced by an individual or business. Through a series of multiple-choice questions and a critical thinking exercise, students work through various strategic considerations from the topics covered in the chapter.
- *Key Terms* An end-of-chapter alphabetical listing of important terms/explanations that are bolded in the text reinforces the chapter's new terminology.
- *Case Summaries* Two to five brief case summaries (one or two paragraphs) are included along with a heading for each that indicates its general topic reference to the chapter as well as several questions about the case.
- *Chapter Review Questions* Short self-check multiple-choice and true/false questions with answers and explanations offer a quick review of key concepts and terminology.

OTHER PROGRAM FEATURES

Connect

McGraw-Hill Connect® is a highly reliable, easy-to-use homework and learning management solution that utilizes learning science and award-winning adaptive tools to improve student results. Connect assignment types include a variety of auto-gradable options that provide students with instant feedback and progress tracking. Interactive applications like decision generators, video cases, and timelines require students to apply key concepts to scenarios. Concept check questions and the test bank offer opportunities to assess students' mastery of key content.

Connect's Business Law Application-Based Activities (ABAs)

Application-based activities for business law provide students valuable practice using problem-solving skills to apply their knowledge to realistic scenarios. Students progress from understanding basic concepts to using their knowledge to analyze complex scenarios and solve problems. Application-based activities have been developed for the topics most often taught (as ranked by instructors) in the business law course. These unique activities are assignable and auto-gradable in Connect.

Mariusz Szczawinski/Alamy Stock Photo

SmartBook® 2.0

Available within Connect, SmartBook 2.0 is an adaptive learning solution that provides personalized learning to individual student needs, continually adapting to pinpoint knowledge gaps and focus learning on concepts requiring additional study. SmartBook 2.0 fosters more productive learning, taking the guesswork out of what to study, and helps students better prepare for class. With the ReadAnywhere mobile app, students can now read and complete SmartBook 2.0 assignments both online and off-line. For instructors, SmartBook 2.0 provides more granular control over assignments with content selection now available at the concept level. SmartBook 2.0 also includes advanced reporting features that enable instructors to track student progress with actionable insights that guide teaching strategies and advanced instruction, for a more dynamic class experience.

Ancillaries

A turnkey instructor package with chapter PowerPoint presentations, a test bank, teaching notes, and lecture outlines provides a basic foundation upon which to build classroom presentations.

Business Law Newsletter

McGraw-Hill Education's monthly business law newsletter, *Proceedings,* is designed specifically with the business law educator in mind. *Proceedings* incorporates "hot topics" in business law, video suggestions, an ethical dilemma, teaching tips, and a "chapter key" that cross-references newsletter topics with the various McGraw-Hill Education business law textbooks. *Proceedings* is delivered via e-mail to business law instructors each month. Please visit successinhighered.com/businesslaw/ for the latest edition.

Roger CPA Review

McGraw-Hill Education has partnered with Roger CPA Review, a global leader in CPA Exam preparation, to provide students a smooth transition from the accounting classroom to successful completion of the CPA Exam. While many aspiring accountants wait until they have completed their academic studies to begin preparing for the CPA Exam, research shows that those who become familiar with exam content earlier in the process have a stronger chance of successfully passing the CPA Exam. Accordingly, students using these McGraw-Hill materials will have access to sample CPA Exam multiple-choice questions and task-based simulations from Roger CPA Review, with expert-written explanations and solutions. All questions are either directly from the AICPA or are modeled on AICPA questions that appear in the exam. Task-based simulations are delivered via the Roger CPA Review platform, which mirrors the look, feel, and functionality of the actual exam. McGraw-Hill Education and Roger CPA Review are dedicated to supporting every accounting student along their journey, ultimately helping them achieve career success in the accounting profession. For more information about the full Roger CPA Review program, exam requirements, and exam content, visit www.rogercpareview.com.

Writing Assignments

As part of a larger set of learning activities that provide students with core course content as well as opportunities to practice the skills they need to develop, the new MH writing assignment toolset offers faculty the ability to assign a full range of writing assignments to students (both manual-scoring and auto-scoring) with just-in-time feedback. You may set up manually scored assignments in a way that students can

- automatically receive grammar and high-level writing feedback to improve their writing before they submit their project to you;
- run Originality checks and receive feedback on "exact matches" and "possibly altered text" that includes guidance to properly paraphrase, quote, and cite sources to improve the academic integrity of their writing before they submit their project to you.

The new writing assignment will also have features that allow you to assign milestone draft (optional), easily re-use your text and audio comments, build/score with your rubric, and review your own Originality report of student work.

In addition, you may choose from a set of auto-scored, short-answer questions that allow you to add lower-stake writing activities to your course without adding significant grading and feedback to your workload; these promote critical thinking/conceptual understanding of course content and provide students with instantaneous feedback.

AACSB

McGraw-Hill Education is a proud corporate member of AACSB International. The authors of *Business Law and Strategy* understand the importance and value of AACSB accreditation and recognize the curricular guidelines detailed in the AACSB standards for business accreditation by connecting selected questions in the test bank to the general knowledge and skill guidelines in the AACSB standards.

The statements contained in *Business Law and Strategy* are provided only as a guide for the users of this textbook. The AACSB leaves content coverage and assessment within the purview of individual schools, the mission of the school, and the faculty. Although *Business Law and Strategy,* and the teaching package, make no claim of any specific AACSB qualification or evaluation, we have within *Business Law and Strategy* labeled selected questions according to the AACSB general knowledge and skill areas.

Instructor's Manual

The Instructor's Manual is designed to be an effective course management tool and an integral part of the turnkey approach used throughout the supplementary material package. The features and format are intended to give instructors maximum flexibility to determine and produce high-quality course content. The IM also has a special "Day One" section addressing important fundamental course decisions for instructors who are new to the course.

PowerPoint Presentation

Each chapter has a PowerPoint presentation that offers additional support by providing detailed teaching notes, particularly for more complex topics.

Test Bank

The test bank allows instructors to custom-design, save, and generate tests. The test bank includes multiple-choice, true-false, fill-in-the-blank, and essay questions for every chapter in the text. To help instructors meet the requirements of AACSB, each question is tagged with the corresponding chapter learning objective and applicable AACSB categories.

Test Builder in Connect

Available within Connect, Test Builder is a cloud-based tool that enables instructors to format tests that can be printed or administered within an LMS. Test Builder offers a modern, streamlined interface for easy content configuration that matches course needs, without requiring a download.

Test Builder allows you to:

- access all test bank content from a particular title.
- easily pinpoint the most relevant content through robust filtering options.
- manipulate the order of questions or scramble questions and/or answers.
- pin questions to a specific location within a test.
- determine your preferred treatment of algorithmic questions.
- choose the layout and spacing.
- add instructions and configure default settings.

Test Builder provides a secure interface for better protection of content and allows for just-in-time updates to flow directly into assessments.

Tegrity: Lectures 24/7

Tegrity in Connect is a tool that makes class time available 24/7 by automatically capturing every lecture. With a simple one-click start-and-stop process, you capture all computer screens and corresponding audio in a format that is easy to search, frame by frame. Students can replay any part of any class with easy-to-use, browser-based viewing on a PC, Mac, iPod, or other mobile device.

Educators know that the more students can see, hear, and experience class resources, the better they learn. In fact, studies prove it. Tegrity's unique search feature helps students efficiently find what they need, when they need it, across an entire semester of class recordings. Help turn your students' study time into learning moments immediately supported by your lecture. With Tegrity, you also increase intent listening and class participation by easing students' concerns about note taking. Using Tegrity in Connect will make it more likely you will see students' faces, not the tops of their heads.

Assurance of Learning Ready

Many educational institutions today are focused on the notion of *assurance of learning,* an important element of some accreditation standards. *Business Law and Strategy* is designed specifically to support your assurance of learning initiatives with a simple, yet powerful solution. Each test bank question for *Business Law and Strategy* maps to a specific chapter learning objective listed in the text. You can use our test bank software, Test Builder, or Connect to easily query for learning objectives that directly relate to the learning objectives for your course. You can then use the reporting features of Test Builder to aggregate student results in similar fashion, making the collection and presentation of assurance of learning data simple and easy.

You're in the driver's seat.

Want to build your own course? No problem. Prefer to use our turnkey, prebuilt course? Easy. Want to make changes throughout the semester? Sure. And you'll save time with Connect's auto-grading too.

65%
Less Time Grading

Laptop: McGraw-Hill; Woman/dog: George Doyle/Getty Images

They'll thank you for it.

Adaptive study resources like SmartBook® 2.0 help your students be better prepared in less time. You can transform your class time from dull definitions to dynamic debates. Find out more about the powerful personalized learning experience available in SmartBook 2.0 at **www.mheducation.com/highered/ connect/smartbook**

Make it simple, make it affordable.

Connect makes it easy with seamless integration using any of the major Learning Management Systems—Blackboard®, Canvas, and D2L, among others—to let you organize your course in one convenient location. Give your students access to digital materials at a discount with our inclusive access program. Ask your McGraw-Hill representative for more information.

Padlock: Jobalou/Getty Images

Solutions for your challenges.

A product isn't a solution. Real solutions are affordable, reliable, and come with training and ongoing support when you need it and how you want it. Our Customer Experience Group can also help you troubleshoot tech problems—although Connect's 99% uptime means you might not need to call them. See for yourself at **status. mheducation.com**

Checkmark: Jobalou/Getty Images

Effective, efficient studying.

Connect helps you be more productive with your study time and get better grades using tools like SmartBook 2.0, which highlights key concepts and creates a personalized study plan. Connect sets you up for success, so you walk into class with confidence and walk out with better grades.

Study anytime, anywhere.

Download the free ReadAnywhere app and access your online eBook or SmartBook 2.0 assignments when it's convenient, even if you're offline. And since the app automatically syncs with your eBook and SmartBook 2.0 assignments in Connect, all of your work is available every time you open it. Find out more at **www.mheducation.com/readanywhere**

"I really liked this app—it made it easy to study when you don't have your textbook in front of you."

- Jordan Cunningham, Eastern Washington University

No surprises.

The Connect Calendar and Reports tools keep you on track with the work you need to get done and your assignment scores. Life gets busy; Connect tools help you keep learning through it all.

Calendar: owattaphotos/Getty Images

Learning for everyone.

McGraw-Hill works directly with Accessibility Services Departments and faculty to meet the learning needs of all students. Please contact your Accessibility Services office and ask them to email accessibility@mheducation.com, or visit **www.mheducation.com/about/accessibility** for more information.

Top: Jenner Images/Getty Images, Left: Hero Images/Getty Images, Right: Hero Images/Getty Images

acknowledgments

We owe a great deal of gratitude to the professionals at McGraw-Hill Education. Although many worked diligently with us in developing this book over several years, we are especially grateful for the skills and experience of the *Business Law and Strategy* team. Our Managing Director Tim Vertovec provided expert guidance and a steady hand in navigating stormy publishing waters. Our Executive Portfolio Manager Kathleen Klehr was a tireless advocate for the project and helped us to become market-savvy as we developed ideas into chapters and digital features. Jaroslaw Szymanski and Allie Kukla, the product developers, and Lori Koetters and Angela Norris, the content project managers, helped us to stay focused and prioritize our work. We owe the entire team special thanks for their patience, flexibility, and industriousness. Professors Constance Bagley and Robert Bird were two pioneers of legal strategy who provided inspiration for a textbook that integrated strategy.

Throughout the development of this book, we have been privileged to have the candid and valuable advice of our reviewers and focus groups. Our reviewers provided us with priceless suggestions, feedback, and constructive criticism. The depth and sincerity of their reviews indicate that they are a devoted group of teacher-scholars. The content of the book was greatly enhanced by their efforts.

Ross Allen
Rutgers University-Camden

Thomas Anthony
Central Michigan University

Valeriya Avdeev
William Patterson University

Colleen Baker
University of Oklahoma-Price College of Business

Jennifer Barger Johnson
University of Central Oklahoma

Louis Benedict
Bowling Green State University

Neil Benjamin
Howard Community College

Curtis Blakely
Ivy Tech Community College of Indiana

Justin Blount
Stephen F. Austin State University

William Bradley
Azusa Pacific University

Carol Brady
Milwaukee Area Technical College

H. Neil Broder
Kean University; Fairleigh Dickinson University

Diana Brown
Sam Houston State University

Elizabeth Brown
Bentley University

Joan Bukowski
Erie Community College

Mary Allison Burdette
Emory University

Debra Burke
Western Carolina University

Stacey Callaway
Rowan College of South Jersey

Elizabeth Cameron
Alma College

Thomas Cavenagh
North Central College

Machiavelli Chao
University of California Irvine

Larry Covell
Jefferson Community College

Patrick Creehan
Flagler College-St. Augustine

Howard Davidoff
Brooklyn College

Mark DeAngelis
University of Connecticut-Storrs

Gustavo Demoner
West Los Angeles College

Timothy Durfield
Citrus College

Frank Edgar
Christopher Newport University

Phillip Entzminger
Western Illinois University

Ronald Feinberg
Suffolk County Community College

Greg Finley
Clark College

Gina Firenzi
Foothill College

Chantalle Forgues
Plymouth State University

Richard Fountain
University of West Florida

Linda Fried
University of Colorado-Denver

Anthony Gabel
Fort Hays State University

Ken Gaines
East West University

Suzanne Gradisher
University of Akron

Shelly Grunsted
University of Oklahoma-Norman

Richard Guertin
Orange County Community College

Frank Harber
Indian River State College-Central

Charles Hartman
Cedarville University

Francis Hatstat
Bellevue College and Cascadia College

Cloyd Havens
Azusa Pacific University

Heidi Helgren
Delta College

Christie Highlander
Southwestern Illinois College

John Holden
Oklahoma State University

Thomas Hughes
University of South Carolina

Jill Jasperson
Utah Valley University-Orem

Robert Johnson
College of the Canyons

Judy Kalisker
Boston University

Michael King
Wake Tech Community College

Sharee Laidlaw
Salt Lake Community College

Patricia Laidler
Massasoit Community College

Eduardo Landeros
San Diego Mesa College

Sondi Lee
Camden County College

Richard Lewis
Los Angeles City College

Lucas Loafman
Texas A&M University-Central Texas

Ivan Lowe
York Technical College

Marty Ludlum
University of Central Oklahoma

Trina Lynch-Jackson
Ivy Tech Community College-Lake County

Jessica Magaldi
Pace University

Tanya Marcum
Bradley University

Michael Mass
American University

Caz McChrystal
University of Wisconsin-Stevens Point

Catherine McKee
Mt. San Antonio College

Elizabeth McKinley
San Jacinto College South

Paul McLester
Florida State College at Jacksonville

George McNary
Creighton University

Russell Meade
Husson University

Susan Mitchell
Des Moines Area Community College

Michael Molesky
Michigan State University-East Lansing

Jennifer Morton
Ivy Tech Community College-Lawrenceburg

Tonia Murphy
University of Notre Dame

J. Haskell Murray
Belmont University

Ben Neil
Towson University

LaToya Newell Burke
Bethune-Cookman University

Rebecca Nieman
San Diego Mesa College

Susanne Ninassi
Marymount University

William Padley
Madison Area Technical College

Jeffrey Penley
Catawba Valley Community College

Kyle Post
Tarleton State University

Tara Radin
George Washington University

Joey Robertson
Sam Houston State University

Karen Rush
Campbellsville University

Amber Ruszkowski
Ivy Tech Community College

Israel Salazar
St. Edward's University

Debra Schoenfeld
Montana State University Billings

Sarah Shepler
Ivy Tech Community College

Cherie Ann Sherman
Ramapo College of New Jersey

Lance Shoemaker
West Valley College

David Spatt
Johnson & Wales University

Michael Speck
Tulsa Community College Metro Campus

Kurt Stanberry
University of Houston Downtown

Nicole Stowell
University of South Florida-St. Petersburg

Laura Sullivan
Sam Houston State University

Scott Taylor
Moberly Area Community College

DeLyse Totten
Portland Community College

Martha Troxell
Indiana University of Pennsylvania-Indiana

Russell Waldon
College of the Canyons

Dennis Wallace
University of New Mexico

Deborah Walsh
Middlesex Community College-Lowell MA

Michael Warshaw
Monmouth University

Doug Waters
Washtenaw Community College

Thomas Webb
State University of New York-Erie

Shallin Williams
Tri-County Technical College-Pendleton

W. Ray Kwame Williams
Rutgers Business School-Newark

Peter Wirig
Anne Arundel Community College

Kim Wong
Central New Mexico Community College-Main

brief contents

table of contents

CHAPTER 41 Employment Discrimination   742

UNIT SEVEN
Regulatory Environment of Business   773

CHAPTER 42 Torts and Products Liability   774

UNIT ONE   Fundamentals of the Legal Environment of Business

CHAPTER 1

Legal Foundations and Thinking Strategically

 THINKING STRATEGICALLY

Law interacts with business in many different ways and on many different levels. In fact, because the law often has gaps or gray areas, because legal compliance is so costly, and because laws are not always enforced evenly, the legal environment of business is essentially a *strategic* environment. Each chapter in this textbook features a *Thinking Strategically* chapter opening and a *Thinking Strategically* problem-solution format at the end of the chapter to help you understand law and strategy in a real-world context. In this chapter's *Thinking Strategically,* we discuss the four major types of legal strategies used in business.

Learning Objectives

After studying this chapter, students who have mastered the material will be able to:

1-1   Articulate a working definition of law and explain its origins.

1-2   Categorize various laws and articulate the functions of law and legal systems.

1-3   Explain the importance and benefits of legal awareness for business owners and managers in creating strategy and adding value to a company and the role of counsel in decision making.

1-4   Differentiate between and provide examples of primary and secondary sources of American law.

1-5   Apply the legal doctrine of stare decisis in a business context.

CHAPTER OVERVIEW

We've designed the material and features in this textbook to make studying the law more *manageable* by examining legal issues in the business environment in short chapters with rich hypothetical examples, real-world cases, and reinforcement exercises. We also have integrated legal strategy into the materials and illustrate how legal awareness and strategy impact managerial decision making. This chapter lays out important touchstones for understanding the legal process and identifying legal issues that arise in the business environment. We begin with definitions, categories, and sources of law, then discuss how to understand legal cases and the importance of the doctrine of stare decisis. Then we analyze methods available to business owners and managers that use strategic lenses to limit risk, incorporate the law into business planning, and add value to their companies.

INTRODUCTION TO LAW

The term **law** has been defined in a variety of ways throughout recorded history. A generally accepted generic definition of the law is a *body of rules of action or conduct prescribed by controlling authority and having legal binding force.*[1] When studying law in any context, it is important to think of the law in broad terms. While many think of the law in terms of stacks of neatly bound volumes of codes in a library, this is only one component of a much larger body of law. Law may be set down in a written code as prescribed by an elected legislative body, or it may take the form of judicial decisions and actions of government agencies. While there are many sources of American law, the common characteristic of the current state of law is that it creates *duties, obligations,* and *rights* that reflect accepted views of a given society. Whereas much of the origins of the law dealt with issues related to ownership of property, modern legal doctrines have evolved into a relatively complex system of principles and protections. Most importantly, the law provides a mechanism to resolve disputes arising from those duties and rights and allows parties to enforce promises in a court of law. Law is often classified by subject matter so that one refers to certain rules regarding agreements as *contract law* or certain laws that regulate rights of employees as *employment law.*

LO 1-1

Articulate a working definition of law and explain its origins.

CATEGORIES OF LAW

Because the body of American law is so vast and diverse, it is sometimes helpful to break down the law into broad categories based on classifications related to a particular legal function or a right afforded by law. It is important to note that these classifications are not mutually exclusive. One particular act or transaction may be classified in more than one legal category. For example, suppose that a party to a contract breaks her promise to the other party (known as a *breach of contract*). The remedy for the breach may depend on the legal classification of contracts as *civil law.* At the same time, one party may have rights classified as *substantive law,* which are derived from a source of *statutory law.* Table 1.1 sets out the various categories of law and provides examples.

LO 1-2

Categorize various laws and articulate the functions of law and legal systems.

TABLE 1.1	Categories of Law	
Category of Law	**Purpose**	**Examples**
Criminal	Protection of society; the violation of criminal laws results in penalties to the violator such as fines or imprisonment.	Homicide, robbery, theft
Civil	To compensate parties (including businesses) for losses as a result of another's conduct.	Negligence that causes a personal injury
Substantive	Provide individuals with rights and create certain duties.	A state law that permits you to recover losses in a shipping contract
Procedural	Sets a structure and rules for pursuing substantive rights.	A state law that sets out a time period during which an injured party must file a lawsuit to recover losses
Public	Derived from some government entity (state or federal legislature/executive) and administrative regulations (state or federal administrative agencies).	Federal statutes (Patent Act) or state statutes (Business Corporation Law)
Private	Binding between two parties even though no specific statute or regulation provides for the rights of the parties.	Contract for services

---

[1]*Black's Law Dictionary.*

Remember that these categories are *not* mutually exclusive. For instance, a driver who is intoxicated and injures a pedestrian in an accident has committed both a criminal act (driving while intoxicated), for which he can be prosecuted by authorities, and a civil wrong (negligence), for which he can be sued by the injured party to recover any losses suffered as a result of the injury (medical bills, etc.). The criminal law prohibiting driving while intoxicated is a statutory/public law as well.

Language of the Law

In order to maximize the value of interaction between business owners/managers and attorneys, a basic understanding of legal terminology is useful. Business law students face the task of learning legal syntax at the same time they are learning how to apply the legal doctrines in a business context. This is analogous to learning complicated subject matter in a foreign language, yet it is manageable with careful study. Legal terms are sometimes referred to as *jargon* or *legalese,* but having a working knowledge of some common legal terminology is an important step to mastering the material. Although much of the language of the law has Latin roots, the terminology is primarily a combination of Latin, early and modern English, and French. The vocabulary of American law is drawn from the various cultures and events that shaped American history. To facilitate your understanding of legal expression, important legal terms are highlighted throughout the text, summarized at the end of each chapter, and featured alphabetically in the glossary. The authoritative source for legal terms is **Black's Law Dictionary**, first published in 1891. There are also several websites that provide definitions and examples of legal terminology. See Connect for legal terminology websites.

Functions of Law

The most visible day-to-day function of the law is to provide for some system of order that defines rules of conduct and levies punishment for violation of those rules. However, recognizing a uniform system of laws serves many other purposes. Recorded law was initially a collection of rules made by powerful tribal chieftains; it was intended to perpetuate the chieftains' domination and authority and had little consideration for the rights of individuals. Over the better part of three millennia, the purpose of law evolved substantially to ensure consistency and fairness. In the United States, lawmakers have increasingly embraced legal mechanisms, such as antidiscrimination laws, to help promote equality and justice in society, especially in education and the workplace. The law also sets out a system for resolving disputes by providing a basis for deciding the legal interests and rights of the parties. For purposes of studying the impact of law on business, it is important to recognize that the law also serves as an important catalyst for commerce by promoting *good faith dealing* among merchants and consumers and giving some degree of *reliability* that can be considered in business planning and commercial transactions.

TAKEAWAY CONCEPTS Categories of Law

- A generally accepted generic definition of the law is a body of rules of action or conduct prescribed by controlling authority and having legal binding force.
- Laws fit into one or more broad categories based on classifications related to a particular legal function or a right afforded by law. One particular act or transaction may be classified in more than one legal category.

(continued)

- Legal terms are sometimes referred to as jargon or legalese, but having a working knowledge of some common legal terminology is an important step to mastering the material.
- In a business context, law serves as an important catalyst by (1) promoting good faith dealing among merchants and consumers and (2) providing reliability that can be used in business planning.

LAW IN CONTEXT: BUSINESS AND STRATEGY

LO 1-3

Explain the importance and benefits of legal awareness for business owners and managers in creating strategy and adding value to a company and the role of counsel in decision making.

Developing legal insight by understanding the fundamentals of legal theory and how they may impact business is only a first step in learning how legal decisions should be made in a business context. The next step involves learning to *apply* legal theories in practice and recognizing that having legal awareness may present opportunities for proactive business planning, which empowers business owners and managers to limit liability, gain a competitive edge, and add value to the business. Relying exclusively on attorneys to drive the legal decision-making process in the context of business is expensive and involves the significant risk that a decision will be made without sufficient knowledge of business operations, objectives, and current economic realities. Instead, studies and research indicate that when managers work *cooperatively* with their attorneys, the results contribute to better strategic business decisions that add value to the business.[2]

Business Swimming in a Sea of Law: Defining Strategy

As Harvard Business School professor Constance Bagley noted in her touchstone legal strategy book, "business is swimming in a sea of law,"[3] and the need for business owners and managers to deploy legal resources in business planning has never been greater. Consider the current regulatory trends:

- *Navigating increased U.S. and foreign regulation* (e.g., regulation of financial markets through Dodd-Frank).
- *Varying international regimes in trade and intellectual property* (e.g., World Intellectual Property Organization versus developing nations).
- *Stiffer penalties for noncompliance* (e.g., Google was recently fined US$2.7 billion by the European Union for manipulating search results).
- *Increased officer and director liability* (e.g., liability for data breaches and cybercrime).
- *Substantial increase in attorney-directors* for U.S.-based corporate boards from 2000 (23%) to 2009 (48%).[4]

Using Strategy in Legal Decisions

Law interacts with business in many different ways and on many different levels. In this section, we focus on the big picture, on the strategic nature of these complex and multifaceted interactions. In fact, because legal rules often have gaps or gray areas, because legal compliance is costly, and because laws are not always perfectly enforced, the legal

---

[2]R.C. Bird, "Pathways of Legal Strategy," *Stanford Journal of Law, Business & Finance* 14, no. 1 (fall 2008), pp. 1–41.

[3]C.E. Bagley, *Winning Legally: How Managers Can Use the Law to Create Value, Marshal Resources, and Manage Risk* (Boston: Harvard Business Review Press, 2005).

[4]R.C. Bird and D. Orozco, "Finding the Right Corporate Legal Strategy," *MIT Sloan Management Review,* no. 56 (fall 2015), pp. 81–85.

environment of business in the real world is essentially a strategic environment. Generally speaking, a strategy refers to a *plan of action.* Strategies are helpful when one is operating under conditions of uncertainty. Because of various real-world factors—such as limited resources, opportunistic behavior, and asymmetrical information—the legal environment is full of uncertainty: Laws are not always obeyed; nor are laws always enforced. This uncertainty regarding the level of legal compliance and the level of legal enforcement opens up many types of legal strategies, strategies business leaders often pursue as they compete for customers and market share. For convenience, we will classify legal strategies into four major categories: (1) *noncompliance,* (2) *avoidance,* (3) *prevention,* and (4) *value creation* or *legal competitive advantage.*

The end of each chapter features a *Thinking Strategically* exercise. These exercises examine strategic opportunity through learning how other companies have used these strategies. Then you'll be challenged to put legal strategy into practice with a short exercise.

Role of Counsel

Although this textbook emphasizes understanding legal issues in the context of business decision making, this is not to suggest that an attorney's role in this process is diminished—quite the opposite. The content, features, and exercises contained in this textbook emphasize that working closely with a business attorney results in business opportunities, reduced costs, and limitation of risk and liability. Attorneys, particularly in a business context, may also be referred to as **counsel**. Business owners and managers work with counsel on a variety of matters. For larger companies or companies that have extraordinary regulatory burdens (such as complying with securities or patent laws), counsel may very well be a part of the executive or midlevel management team. These attorneys are referred to as *in-house counsel* and usually have the title "general counsel" at the executive management level (e.g., vice president and general counsel). Depending on the size and complexity of the company, the general counsel may also supervise one or more attorneys, usually with the title "associate counsel." Additionally, the general counsel may also serve as a corporate officer of the company, called the *secretary,* who is responsible for record keeping and complying with notice and voting requirements for the board of directors.[5] The general counsel is also responsible for selecting and supervising lawyers from outside law firms when a particular field of expertise is needed, such as a trial lawyer (also called a *litigator*).

The majority of companies, however, rely on attorneys employed by *law firms* for their legal needs. These attorneys devote a significant amount of their professional time to advising businesses on issues such as formation, governance, labor and employment laws, regulatory agency compliance, legal transactions (such as an acquisition), intellectual property (such as trademarks or patents), and other legal issues important to business operations. These attorneys (known as *business lawyers* or *corporate lawyers*), rarely if ever appear in court or perform other tasks that are associated with lawyers in the minds of the general public. Indeed, the law has become increasingly complex and specialized. Therefore, it is not unusual to need more than one attorney's advice when facing a significant legal issue such as an employment discrimination lawsuit or when obtaining financing for a corporation from the general public through the sale of stock. Law firms vary greatly in size, from one or just a few lawyers in a local or regional practice to firms that have hundreds of lawyers spread throughout the globe. In a business context, law firms bill clients based on an hourly rate that is tied to an individual lawyer's experience, her reputation in the field, and the market being served (with large cities that are the center of business operations having higher rates).

---

[5]The legal structure of corporations and other business entities is discussed in detail in Unit Four.

- Learning to apply legal awareness in practice involves recognizing opportunities for proactive business planning, limiting liability, gaining a competitive edge, and adding value to the business.
- Companies that have extraordinary regulatory burdens (such as complying with securities or patent laws) typically employ *in-house counsel* and usually have the title of *general counsel* at the executive management level. However, the majority of companies rely on attorneys employed by *law firms* for their legal needs.

PRIMARY SOURCES AND LEVELS OF AMERICAN LAW

American law is composed of a unique blend from various sources based on U.S. historical roots. Fundamentally, much of American law is derived from English legal doctrines that came with the English settlers of the colonies. In the United States, modern law regulating businesses and individuals is generally a combination of **constitutional law**, **statutory law**, **common law**, and **administrative** (regulatory) **law** at the federal, state, and local levels. These sources of law are known as *primary sources* of law and may work in conjunction with one another or independently.

LO 1-4

Differentiate between and provide examples of primary and secondary sources of American law.

Constitutional Law

Constitutional law is the foundation for all other law in the United States and is the supreme law of the land. It functions in tandem with other sources of law in three broad areas: (1) establishing a *structure* for federal and state governments (including qualifications of certain offices and positions) and setting rules for amending the constitution; (2) granting specific *powers* for the different branches of government; and (3) providing *procedural protections* for U.S. citizens from wrongful government actions.

Constitutional law is different from other sources of law primarily in terms of *permanence* and *preemption*. In terms of permanence, a constitution is thought to reflect the basic principles of a particular society and should be amended only in extraordinary cases and only when a majority of its constituents agree over a certain period of time. Preemption in this context means that constitutional law is supreme over other sources of law such as state statutes. In Case 1.1, the U.S. Supreme Court applies a provision of the U.S. Constitution in the context of a dispute between a local government and a property owner.

CASE 1.1 Kelo et al. v. City of New London, Connecticut, et al., 545 U.S. 469 (2005)

FACT SUMMARY Kelo moved to the Fort Trumbull area of New London, Connecticut, in 1997. She made extensive improvements to her house, which she prized for its coastal ocean view. New London had experienced decades of economic decline, which led a state agency to designate the city a distressed municipality. These conditions prompted state and local officials to target for economic revitalization New London and the Fort Trumbull area where Kelo lived. The New London Development Corporation (NLDC), a private nonprofit entity, was established to assist the city with economic development. In February 1998, the pharmaceutical company Pfizer Inc. announced that it would build

(continued)

a $300 million research facility on a site within the Fort Trumbull area.

The NLDC's Fort Trumbull development plan aimed to leverage Pfizer's relocation and encompassed seven parcels to include: a waterfront conference hotel, pedestrian river walk, restaurants, shopping, marinas, parking, and office space. The city council approved the plan in January 2000 and authorized the NLDC to acquire property by exercising eminent domain in the city's name. The NLDC successfully negotiated the purchase of most of the real estate in the 90-acre area, but its negotiations with Kelo and a few other holdouts failed.

In December 2000, Kelo and the other petitioners brought this action in the New London Superior Court. They claimed that the taking of their properties would violate the public use restriction of the Fifth Amendment of the U.S. Constitution, which states: "[N]or shall private property be taken for public use, without just compensation." Ultimately, the case made it to the U.S. Supreme Court.

SYNOPSIS OF DECISION AND OPINION The U.S. Supreme Court affirmed the Connecticut Supreme Court and allowed the NLDC to take Kelo's property in exchange for just compensation. The Court's previous interpretations of the public use wording in the Constitution encompasses public purposes to accommodate changing social needs such as economic revitalization. The Court granted high levels of deference to the carefully formulated revitalization plan put forth by the NLDC.

WORDS OF THE COURT: Public Purpose
"Two polar propositions are perfectly clear. On the one hand, it has long been accepted that the sovereign may not take the property of *A* for the sole purpose of transferring it to another private party *B*, even though *A* is paid just compensation. On the other hand, it is equally clear that a State may transfer property from one private party to another if future use by the public is the purpose of the

taking; the condemnation of land for a railroad with common-carrier duties is a familiar example. Neither of these propositions, however, determines the disposition of this case. As for the first proposition, the City would no doubt be forbidden from taking petitioners' land for the purpose of conferring a private benefit on a particular private party . . .

[T]his Court long ago rejected any literal requirement that condemned property be put into use for the general public. Indeed, while many state courts in the mid-19th century endorsed use by the public as the proper definition of public use, that narrow view steadily eroded over time. Not only was the use by the public test difficult to administer (*e.g.*, what proportion of the public need have access to the property? at what price?), but it proved to be impractical given the diverse and always evolving needs of society . . . The disposition of this case therefore turns on the question whether the City's development plan serves a public purpose. Without exception, our cases have defined that concept broadly, reflecting our longstanding policy of deference to legislative judgments in this field . . .

Those who govern the City were not confronted with the need to remove blight in the Fort Trumbull area, but their determination that the area was sufficiently distressed to justify a program of economic rejuvenation is entitled to our deference."

Case Questions

1. Is it ethical to place a city's redevelopment project on hold by behaving strategically as a real estate holdout? Note that Kelo's house was initially appraised at $78,000 and after five years of litigation the City paid her $442,000 as just compensation for taking her property.

2. What competing interests is the court trying to balance in this case? Did the Court strike the right balance? Explain.

3. *Focus on Critical Thinking:* Could an alternative solution have been reached in this case? Explain.

Note that constitutional law exists at both the federal and state level because each state has its own constitution that is the highest source of law within the state's borders (so long as it is not inconsistent with federal law). States tend to amend their constitutions more frequently than is the case with the U.S. Constitution. Constitutional issues that impact businesses include Congress's powers to regulate interstate commerce; the creation of legal protections for intellectual property (such as patents and copyrights); the protection of certain forms of commercial speech from unwarranted government regulation; limitations on a state's authority to tax products and services in commerce; and powers of the executive, legislative, and judicial branches to regulate business activity. Constitutional law is discussed in detail in Chapter 3, "Business and the Constitution."

Statutory Law

Statutory law is created by a legislative body and approved or disapproved by the executive branch of government. The U.S. Congress is the exclusive legislative body for the passage of federal law. When Congress is drafting a federal statute, but has not yet passed it or had the executive branch's concurrence, it is known as a *bill.* On the *federal level,* the president is the executive and may either sign a bill into law (thereby adopting it as a statute) or veto (reject) the bill. If the president vetoes the bill, Congress can override the veto and make the bill into a statute with a two-thirds majority vote.

At the *state level,* the state legislature (called by different names in different states, such as the *General Assembly*) passes statutes that regulate such areas as motor vehicle laws, business corporation and partnership laws, and other traditional state matters. The governor (as executive) has authority to sign a state bill into law or to exercise other rights as laid out in the state constitution. Statutes at the *local level* are called **ordinances** (sometimes referred to as *local regulations*). Ordinances generally regulate issues such as zoning (regulating where certain businesses, such as factories, may be located) or impose health and safety regulations on local merchants such as restaurants.

One of the biggest challenges courts face when interpreting a statute is applying the law in a context that did not exist at the time the statute became law. In Case 1.2, a federal trial court applies a 1986 law outlawing money laundering in the context of digital currency on the notorious (and now-defunct) Silk Road online marketplace.

CASE 1.2 United States v. Ulbricht, 31 F. Supp. 3d 540 (S.D.N.Y. 2014)

FACT SUMMARY In February 2014, a federal grand jury indicted Ross Ulbricht, also known as Dread Pirate Roberts (Ulbricht), for, among other things, conspiracy to launder money obtained from illegal activities. Prosecutors alleged that Ulbricht was engaged in narcotics trafficking, computer hacking, and money laundering conspiracies by designing, launching, and administering a website called Silk Road as an online marketplace for illicit goods and services. Silk Road was designed to operate like eBay: (1) a seller would electronically post a good or service for sale; (2) a buyer would electronically purchase the item; (3) the seller would then ship or otherwise provide to the buyer the purchased item; (4) the buyer would provide feedback; and (5) the site operator (i.e., Ulbricht) would receive a portion of the seller's revenue as a commission. Ulbricht, as the alleged site designer, made the site available only to those using Tor, a software and network system that allows for anonymous, untraceable Internet browsing. He allowed payment only via bitcoin, an anonymous and untraceable form of digital currency. Thousands of transactions allegedly occurred over the course of nearly three years—sellers posted goods when available; and buyers purchased goods when desired.

Ulbricht filed a motion to dismiss the indictments based on a number of theories. Ulbricht argued that he could not be guilty of money laundering because the use of bitcoins did not fit into the statute's requirement that money laundered be a result of a "financial transaction." Because bitcoins are not monetary instruments, transactions involving bitcoins cannot form the basis for a money laundering conspiracy. He supported his argument by noting that the IRS has announced that it treats virtual currency as property and not as currency.

(continued)

SYNOPSIS OF DECISION AND OPINION The U.S. District Court ruled against Ulbricht. The court rejected Ulbricht's theory that use of bitcoins is not a financial transaction. The court noted that because bitcoins carry value and act as a medium of exchange, they fall into the meaning of financial transaction in the money laundering statute. Because bitcoins may be exchanged for legal tender, be it U.S. dollars, euros, or some other currency, they can be an instrument in money laundering.

WORDS OF THE COURT: Plain Meaning of Statute "Put simply, 'funds' can be used to pay for things in the colloquial sense. Bitcoins can be either used directly to pay for certain things or can act as a medium of exchange and be converted into a currency which can pay for things. Indeed, the only value for Bitcoin lies in its ability to pay for things—it is digital and has no earthly form; it cannot be put on a shelf and looked at or collected in a nice display case. Its form is digital—bits and bytes that together constitute something of value. And they may be bought and sold using legal tender . . . The money laundering statute is broad enough to encompass use of Bitcoins in financial transactions. . . . Congress intended to prevent criminals from finding ways to wash the proceeds of criminal activity by transferring proceeds to other similar or different items that store significant value. . . . There is no doubt that if a narcotics transaction was paid for in cash, which was later exchanged for gold, and then converted back to cash, that would constitute a money laundering transaction. . . . One can money launder using Bitcoin."

Case Questions

1. Why did Ulbricht point out that the IRS treats bitcoins as property?

2. Does the fact that Ulbricht created Silk Road have any bearing on the court's decision?

3. *Focus on Critical Thinking:* Is the court interpreting the statute or filling in a gap that exists in a statute? If Congress had wanted to include digital currency in its definition of financial transactions, why didn't it do so by naming it specifically in the statute or in an amendment to the law? Did the court overreach in this case by trying to decipher the intent of Congress?

Aftermath: A jury found Ulbricht guilty on all counts, including money laundering. On May 29, 2015, Ulbricht was sentenced to life in prison and ordered to forfeit nearly $184 million.

Administrative Law

While statutory law stems from the authority of the legislature and common law is derived from the courts, administrative law is the source of law that authorizes the exercise of authority by *executive branch* agencies and *independent* government agencies. Federal administrative law is largely authorized by statutes and the Constitution, and rules for applying the law are articulated and carried out by *administrative agencies.* Pursuant to congressional mandates, these agencies are empowered to administer the details of federal statutes and have broad powers to impose regulations, make policy, and enforce the law in their designated area of jurisdiction. For example, the U.S. Environmental Protection Agency (EPA) is charged with drafting regulations that carry out the broad mandates set out by Congress in the Clean Air Act (among many others) to reduce air pollution. The EPA sets regulations and imposes restrictions on some industries to help accomplish that goal. The EPA is also empowered to enforce those regulations. Courts are highly deferential to agency decisions involving how and when an agency enforces a regulation. Detailed coverage of this source of law and administrative agencies is featured in Chapter 43, "Administrative Law."

Common Law

Common law is essentially law made by the courts; that is, law that has not specifically been passed by the legislature but is based on the fundamentals of previous cases that had similar facts. The notion of applying the law of previous cases to current cases with substantially similar circumstances is called **precedent**. Common law is composed of established

TABLE 1.2 Laws That Impact Business

Type of Law	Source(s)	Level(s)
Negligence (tort)	Statutory and common law	Primarily state
Employment discrimination	Primarily statutory and administrative	Primarily state and federal, some local
Copyright	Statutory and administrative	Federal
Contracts for sale of goods	Statutory	State
Contracts for services	Primarily common law	State
Bankruptcy	Statutory and administrative	Federal
Securities law (selling company stock to the public)	Statutory and administrative	Federal and state
Zoning ordinances	Statutory	Local
Taxes	Statutory and administrative	Federal, state, and local

principles of law based on a just resolution of disputes between parties, which also sets a specific standard for other courts to follow when the same dispute arises again.

The U.S. system of common law is deep-seated in British common law. The largest industrialized nations using the common law in some form include the United States, the United Kingdom, Canada, and Australia (i.e., former colonies of Britain). Other countries, such as Japan, use a *civil law* system that requires courts to adhere to a strict interpretation of a legislatively established code or regulation. While civil law still recognizes the general notion of precedent, its role is substantially reduced in a civil law system. The power of courts to establish law in matters not specifically addressed by the code is very limited in civil law countries.

Some of the specific laws covered in this textbook that impact business owners and managers are featured in Table 1.2.

Law versus Equity

Early English courts were classified under the king's authority as either *courts of law*, which applied existing laws and rules strictly, or *courts of equity*, which applied the rule of fairness when application of technical rules resulted in an injustice. Most modern American courts are combined courts of law and equity. However, we still use the terms *law* and *equity* when describing the appropriate *measure of judicial action* intended to compensate an injured party in a civil lawsuit. These measures are known as **remedies**. Remedies at law generally take the form of *money damages*: A court orders the wrongdoer to pay another party a certain sum of money to compensate for any losses suffered as a result of the wrongdoer's conduct. However, in some cases, a party will not be fully or even partially compensated through money damages. In such a case, a court may award **equitable relief** instead of (or in addition to) a remedy at law. The most common forms of equitable relief include an *injunction* or *restraining order* (a judicial order requiring a party to cease a certain activity) and *specific performance* (an order requiring a party to carry out her obligations as specified in a contract).

To understand this concept in a business context, suppose that Maxwell enters into a valid written agreement with Book Barn to purchase a first edition of *The Old Man and the Sea,* autographed by Ernest Hemingway, for $25,000. Maxwell leaves the store to obtain a certified check from his bank. When he returns one hour later, the owner of Book Barn refuses to sell him the book because he has received a phone call from another buyer offering $30,000.

In this case, Maxwell may file a lawsuit for Book Barn's failure to live up to the agreement (known as *breach of contract*[6]), but he has not suffered an out-of-pocket loss because

---

[6]Breach of contract is covered in detail in Chapter 11, "Breach and Remedies."

he never had the opportunity to present Book Barn with the check. However, Maxwell could seek a *remedy at equity* from a court, where he would request an injunction to prevent Book Barn from selling the book to another buyer until the court can hear the case. If Maxwell wins the case, he may seek an order of *specific performance* whereby the court orders Book Barn to transfer ownership of the book to Maxwell in exchange for the $25,000 price as specified in the agreement between the parties. Maxwell would likely be awarded these equitable remedies because the legal remedies available to him are not adequate to address his injury.

In Case 1.3, a state appellate court considers whether an equitable remedy is appropriate in a breach of contract case.

CASE 1.3 Wilcox Investment, L.P. v. Brad Wooley Auctioneers, Inc. et al., 454 S.W.3d 792 (Ark. Ct. App. 2015)

FACT SUMMARY Wilcox Investment Limited Partnership (Wilcox) entered into a contract with Brad Wooley Auctioneers, Inc. (Auctioneers) to market and sell approximately 333 acres of real property owned by Wilcox in Arkansas. It was to be an "absolute" auction, meaning that the property would be sold to the highest bidder regardless of price. As the date of the auction approached, Wilcox expressed reservations about the auction to Auctioneers but decided to go through with the auction because Auctioneers agreed to cancel the auction if the bidder turnout was low. Only four bidders attended the sale. Wilcox did not attend but was represented by two of his children and his attorney. According to Wilcox, Auctioneers agreed to postpone the sale. Auctioneers disputed that it agreed to halt the sale. In any case, Auctioneers started the bidding, and Shollmier was declared the highest bidder with a bid of $235,000. Wilcox, contending that the property was appraised in excess of $950,000, refused to complete the sale.

Shollmier sued Wilcox, asking the court for a remedy of specific performance to compel Wilcox to proceed with the sale. Auctioneers also filed suit to recover its commission. Wilcox argued that the sale was void because Shollmier engaged in collusion with Auctioneers during the bidding process. The jury found that Wilcox and Auctioneers entered into a contract to sell the real property at absolute auction to the highest bidder, that Shollmier was the highest bidder, and that Wilcox breached the auction contract and the purchase agreement. The court accordingly ordered Wilcox to convey the property to Shollmier. Wilcox appealed, arguing in part that specific performance was not an appropriate remedy.

SYNOPSIS OF DECISION AND OPINION The Court of Appeals of Arkansas affirmed the jury's verdict in favor of Shollmier and Auctioneers. The court reasoned that there was no evidence of collusion and rejected Wilcox's argument that the auction contract was void. The court held that Auctioneers had no duty to halt the auction and that Shollmier's bid was made in good faith and not in conjunction with Auctioneers. Because money is not an adequate remedy, specific performance is appropriate.

WORDS OF THE COURT: Specific Performance Appropriate "In his response . . . Wilcox argued that there was a disputed issue of whether the Auctioneers breached their duty by continuing the sale after perceiving collusion . . . [The trial] court found that this issue was not material to Wilcox's claims against the Auctioneers but that it would be dispositive on Shollmier's claim for specific performance against Wilcox. We now know from the final judgment that the issue of collusion was impliedly resolved against Wilcox by the jury in finding that Wilcox breached the purchase agreement."

Case Questions

1. Why wasn't money an adequate remedy in this case?

2. What does Wilcox mean when he alleges that Shollmier engaged in collusion?

3. *Focus on Critical Thinking:* How could Wilcox have prevented the property from being sold below the appraised price at auction?

Secondary Sources of Law

When interpreting statutory law or applying judicially created law, courts also look to **secondary sources** of law. In the business context, the most important secondary sources of law are (1) a collection of uniform legal principles focused in a particular area of traditional state law called ***Restatements of the Law***,[7] and (2) various sets of **model state statutes**[8] drafted by legal experts as a model for state legislatures to adopt in their individual jurisdictions. The purpose behind these secondary sources of law is to increase the level of uniformity and fairness across courts in all 50 states. The secondary sources of law also feature commentary and examples to help guide courts in applying the law. However, secondary sources of law have *no independent authority* or legally binding effect. State legislatures and courts are free to adopt all, adopt part of, or reject secondary sources of law.

 QUICK QUIZ Source of Law

What is/are the source(s) and level(s) of law that govern the following business transactions?

1. American Hardware Supply enters into an agreement with a retail home improvement chain to supply the chain with certain inventory.
2. Whitney wishes to apply for a patent for a device he invented.
3. Marshall is considering raising money for his business by selling stock in the company.
4. Bio-Tech Inc. ran out of cash and cannot pay its debts as they become due. Management seeks protection from creditors.
5. Barnum wishes to bring his famous horse show into town and plans to stage it in a residential area of the city.

Answers to this Quick Quiz are provided at the end of the chapter.

TAKEAWAY CONCEPTS Primary Sources and Levels of American Law

- Primary sources of law include constitutional law, statutory law, administrative law, and common law at both the federal and state levels.
- Constitutions have two primary functions: (1) to prescribe the basic structure and powers of a particular government body and (2) to protect certain rights of individuals and businesses from government encroachment.

(continued)

---

[7]*Restatements of the Law* were originally developed by a group of law professors, judges, and lawyers composing the American Law Institute (ALI). Restatements are continuously revised. When the ALI publishes a revision, the new version is referred to by name and edition; for example, the second edition of the contracts restatements is called *Restatements (Second) of Contracts*. The areas covered by the Restatements that are included in this textbook are: contracts, property, agency, torts, and foreign relations law.

[8]Uniform Model Laws are developed by the National Conference of Commissioners on Uniform State Laws (NCCUSL). The primary focus of the model laws was commerce, and the NCCUSL drafted the Uniform Commercial Code (UCC), which has been adopted in some form by every state except Louisiana. The UCC provides a comprehensive set of rules and principles intended to increase reliability and predictability in business transactions.

- Statutory law is created by a legislative body and approved or disapproved by the executive branch. Common law is law made by appellate courts and is based on the fundamentals of previous cases that had similar facts. Administrative law is the source of law that regulates the exercise of authority by administrative agencies.

- Secondary sources of law include the *Restatements of the Law* and sets of model statutes such as the Uniform Commercial Code (UCC); secondary sources have no independent authority, nor are they legally binding.

- *Law* and *equity* are terms describing the appropriate measure of judicial action intended to compensate an injured party in a civil lawsuit. These measures are known as *remedies*.

STARE DECISIS AND PRECEDENT

LO 1-5

Apply the legal doctrine of stare decisis in a business context.

The **doctrine of stare decisis**, one of the most important concepts in American law, is the principle that similar cases with similar facts and issues should have the same judicial outcome. This allows individuals and businesses to have some degree of confidence that the law will remain reasonably constant from year to year and court to court. Once an appellate court has decided a particular case, the decision becomes a **case precedent**. The principle of stare decisis requires all *lower courts,* such as trial courts, to follow the case precedent, meaning that any similar case from that point in time onward would be decided according to the precedent. Trial courts apply precedent by making use of key statements from earlier judicial opinions, known as the *holding* of the case. Note that the court system and how appellate courts form precedent are covered in detail in Chapter 4, "The American Judicial System, Jurisdiction, and Venue."

Stare Decisis and Business

To understand the importance of stare decisis in the business environment, consider how understanding the legal impact of a certain course of action can create opportunities for business planning. Suppose Jackson is in charge of managing the acquisition of certain assets from another company. One important aspect of such a transaction is how the acquisition will be *taxed.* If Jackson's company enters into an agreement with Main Street Industries (MSI) to acquire certain assets from MSI, how will the transaction be treated by the Internal Revenue Service (IRS)?[9] This, of course, is a key factor in determining the price of the transaction and planning for allocation of the tax burden between buyer and seller. How can the parties structure the transaction to ensure that the taxation represents the parties' intent? Ultimately, because stare decisis is a deeply rooted concept that applies to all laws, Jackson need only learn how the IRS has treated similar transactions in the past and how courts have ruled on the IRS's interpretation and actions in applying the law. If a certain transaction has been taxed in a certain way in the past, the doctrine of stare decisis dictates that if Jackson structures her transaction in a similar fashion, her transaction will be taxed in the same way. Having sufficient legal certainty about the transaction's taxation impact allows the parties to proceed with negotiating and structuring a mutually acceptable agreement.

However, strict adherence to precedent and the doctrine of stare decisis has a significant drawback: It doesn't allow for evolving societal standards of behavior or expectations. On a case-by-case basis, courts sometimes justify departing from precedent on the basis that technological or societal changes render a particular precedent unworkable. In Landmark Case 1.4, a state appellate court considers the question of when to abandon standing precedent.

---

[9]The IRS is the federal government's tax agency.

LANDMARK CASE 1.4 Flagiello v. Pennsylvania Hospital, 208 A.2d 193 (Pa. 1965)

FACT SUMMARY Flagiello, a patient at Pennsylvania Hospital ("the Hospital"), sued the Hospital claiming it was negligent in maintaining certain conditions on hospital property that resulted in her injuring her ankle. The ankle injury was unrelated to the original reason for Flagiello's admission to the Hospital. A Pennsylvania state trial court dismissed the lawsuit without trial because established state common law clearly exempted charitable institutions, such as the hospital, from any liability related to its negligence (called the *charitable immunity doctrine*). Flagiello appealed on the basis that (1) she was a paying patient and (2) the charitable immunity doctrine was outdated given the fact that most charity hospitals now received funding from state and local governments.

SYNOPSIS OF DECISION AND OPINION The Pennsylvania Supreme Court ruled in favor of Flagiello. Although the court acknowledged the important role of stare decisis, it also pointed out that the doctrine is not intended to apply when societal norms dictate otherwise. In this case, the court noted that other states had abandoned the charitable immunity doctrine as no longer necessary and that public benefit and fairness demanded that injured parties who are entitled to recover for their losses be allowed to pursue a negligence action against a charitable institution.

WORDS OF THE COURT: Limits of Stare Decisis "Stare decisis channels the law. It erects lighthouses and [flies] the signals of safety. The ships of

jurisprudence must follow that well-defined channel which, over the years, has been proved to be secure and trustworthy. But it would not comport with wisdom to insist that, should shoals rise in a heretofore safe course and rocks emerge to encumber the passage, the ship should nonetheless pursue the original course, merely because it presented no hazard in the past. The principle of stare decisis does not demand that we follow precedents which shipwreck justice.

"Stare decisis is not an iron mold into which every utterance by a court, regardless of circumstances, parties, economic barometer and sociological climate, must be poured, and, where, like wet concrete, it must acquire an unyielding rigidity which nothing later can change."

Case Questions

1. If Flagiello had been a burglar who was breaking into the medical supply cabinet instead of a patient when she injured her ankle, would the court have been willing to abandon the charitable immunity doctrine? Why or why not?

2. Do you agree with Flagiello's argument that the hospital should not have immunity from liability because she was a paying patient? Should standards of care be based on a patient's financial resources?

3. *Focus on Critical Thinking:* Does this case mean that stare decisis may be discarded whenever a judge perceives that following precedent will "shipwreck justice"?

TAKEAWAY CONCEPTS Stare Decisis and Precedent

- The doctrine of stare decisis, one of the most important concepts in American law, is the principle that similar cases with similar facts and issues should have the same judicial outcome.
- Once an appellate court has decided a particular case, the decision becomes a case precedent.

Four Categories

Earlier in this chapter, we began our discussion about the importance of capitalizing on the opportunities presented by the intersection of business, law, and strategy. Recall that we classified legal strategies into four major categories: (1) noncompliance, (2) avoidance, (3) prevention, and (4) value creation, or legal competitive advantage. Now we take a closer look at these strategies with some examples.

Strategy #1—Noncompliance: One possible legal strategy in an uncertain and competitive environment is noncompliance. Simply put, noncompliance consists of openly disregarding or flouting the law. But why would a business firm ever openly choose noncompliance as its legal strategy? Why risk flouting the law? Put crudely, in cost-benefit terms, when the costs of compliance are greater than the costs of noncompliance, it might actually pay to break the law.

Consider the market for overnight delivery and other shipping services in New York City, a highly lucrative and competitive industry. Instead of fully complying with burdensome parking regulations, it's a "dirty little secret" that shipping companies like FedEx, UPS, and even the United States Postal Service have openly adopted a noncompliance strategy: These firms write the costs of parking infractions into their business model, paying millions of dollars annually for the parking fines that their delivery trucks incur in New York City in order to effectively compete for the lucrative Gotham market.[10]

Critical Thinking Question: In your view, is the non-compliance strategy always unethical?

Strategy #2—Avoidance: When business firms decide to create legal loopholes or exploit gray areas in the law, they are essentially adopting an avoidance approach to law, a legal strategy that is frequently used in the business world. Before proceeding, notice that avoidance is technically not the same as noncompliance. Strictly speaking, the avoidance approach views legal compliance as a cost to be minimized; hence a company using an avoidance strategy takes steps to minimize its costs of legal compliance. By way of example, a familiar—and controversial—illustration of the avoidance approach is the decision to relocate overseas or outsource certain activities to another jurisdiction in order to avoid burdensome and costly local regulations.

Consider one of the biggest corporate megadeals of this decade: Pfizer's $160-billion merger with the Irish drug company Allergan. Pfizer, a U.S. company, was the world's 48th largest company before the merger. The parties structured this deal as a tax inversion; in other words, Pfizer will reconstitute itself as an Irish company in order to lower its U.S. tax burden.

In sum, companies are likely to adopt an avoidance strategy when they see a law as a costly obstacle or burdensome impediment that is interfering with their desired business goals.[11]

Critical Thinking Questions: From an ethical perspective, what do you think of Pfizer's tax inversion strategy? Is an avoidance strategy unethical?

Strategy #3—Prevention: Simply put, the prevention strategy consists of identifying potential legal risks to one's business and taking deliberate and proactive measures to minimize those risks *before* the risks materialize. In other words, business leaders adopting a preventive legal approach work directly with legal counsel in order to anticipate potential legal pitfalls their business may confront and then attempt to devise effective legal solutions ahead of time.

The widespread use of legal disclaimers in many types of consumer contracts provides a good example of the prevention strategy. For example, have you ever entered a spicy food contest? Increasingly, restaurateurs have used liability waivers to prevent any liability based on some physical injury that accompanies a potentially hazardous food item such as a "ghost pepper." According to the *Journal of Emergency Medicine*, one man was hospitalized for 23 days with a tear in his esophagus after participating in a ghost-pepper-eating contest.

At Mikey's Late Night Slice in Columbus, Ohio, the "Fiery Death with Hate Sausage" is a pizza loaded with a mix of the hottest peppers. However, customers can

[10]Andrew J. Hawkins, "Parking Tickets: All in the Cost of Doing Business," *Crain's New York Business,* May 26, 2013.

[11]James Surowiecki, "Why Firms Are Fleeing," *The New Yorker,* Jan. 11, 2016.

Need to sign a waiver when you order pizza?
FoodCollection

this fundamental question. Briefly, there are two types of business strategies a firm may follow in order to outperform its rivals. One strategy is lower cost; the other is differentiation. Here, let's focus on the strategy of differentiation.

From a legal perspective, one major method of differentiating one's business and creating durable forms of value is through intellectual property law. A great example of legal competitive advantage is Google's popular search engine algorithm, which was invented by Larry Page and Sergey Brin while they were graduate students at Stanford.

The original patent for their search engine algorithm (US 6,285,999) contains a detailed description of their first algorithm and also lists Stanford University as the "assignee" or legal owner of their important invention. Subsequently, however, Page and Brin left Stanford and founded their own private search engine company. They also continued to refine and improve their search engine algorithm over the years, but now, instead of using patent law to protect their rights to their search engine algorithm, they have opted to keep their world-famous algorithm a trade secret. In other words, no one but Larry Page and Sergey Brin know the exact details of how the Google search engine works.

Another form of legal competitive advantage occurs through lobbying efforts (i.e., when companies lobby legislatures like Congress to enact laws protecting their businesses from competition). One of the most notorious examples of this form of legal competitive advantage is the Walt Disney Company's efforts to protect its intellectual property rights in Mickey Mouse, perhaps the most iconic cartoon character of all time. Mickey is quite possibly the world's most famous personality; according to market researchers, his 97 percent recognition rate in the United States edges out even Santa Claus! *Forbes* even dubbed him "the world's richest fictional billionaire," placing his estimated worth to Disney at $5.8 billion per year.

In any case, in the words of one commentator, "Disney has done everything in its power to make sure it retains the copyright on Mickey . . . Every time Mickey's copyright is about to expire, Disney spends millions lobbying Congress for extensions, and trading campaign contributions for legislative support. With crushing legal force, they've squelched anyone who attempts

only try it once they've signed a three-page waiver outlining dangers and safety precautions, like how to wash skin and eyes, and agreeing to "disclaim, release and relinquish any and all claims, actions and lawsuits."[12]

Critical Thinking Exercise: Do you use Facebook, Twitter, Instagram, or some other social networking site? Look up the "terms of use" of one of these websites and try to find at least one disclaimer or other limitation of liability clause.

Strategy #4—Value Creation (or "Legal Competitive Advantage"): Last but certainly not least, business leaders can use the law creatively and strategically not only to minimize costs and risks but also to create new sources of value as well as generate new streams of revenue. We refer to this form of legal strategy as *value creation* or "legal competitive advantage" to acknowledge that law can often be a source of competitive advantage.

How can a business outperform its competitors? The concept of competitive advantage attempts to answer

---

[12] B. Parkin, "Want to Try Our Insanely Spicy Pizza with 'Hate Sausage': First Sign a Waiver," *The Wall Street Journal*, Jan. 17, 2018.

FIGURE 1.1   Money Spent on Lobbying by Disney

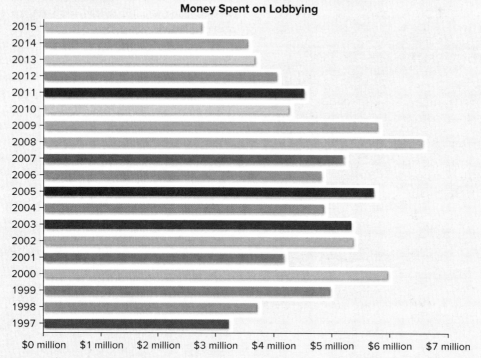

Money Spent on Lobbying

Adapted from Crockett, Zachary. "How Mickey Mouse Evades the Public Domain," *Priceonomics*, Jan. 7, 2016; data from OpenSecrets.org

to disagree with them." Figure 1.1 gives you some idea as to how much of its resources Disney expends on lobbying efforts in order to maintain its competitive advantage.[13]

Critical Thinking Questions: Have you ever created any form of intellectual property? What was it? Did you create it on your own, or is there a possibility that someone else has rights to it as well?

[13]Joseph Menn, "Whose Mouse Is It Anyway?" *Los Angeles Times,* Aug. 22, 2008.

KEY TERMS

Law p. 3   A body of rules of action or conduct prescribed by controlling authority and having legal binding force.

Criminal laws p. 3   Laws designed to protect society that result in penalties to the violator such as fines or imprisonment.

Civil laws p. 3   Laws designed to compensate parties for money lost as a result of another's conduct.

Substantive laws p. 3   Laws that provide individuals with rights and create certain duties.

Procedural laws p. 3   Laws that provide a structure and set out rules for pursuing substantive rights.

Public laws p. 3   Laws derived from a government entity.

Private laws p. 3   Laws recognized as binding between two parties even though no specific statute or regulation provides for the rights of the parties.

Black's Law Dictionary p. 4   The leading legal dictionary.

Counsel p. 6   Another name for an attorney.

Constitutional law p. 7   The body of law interpreting state and federal constitutions.

Statutory law p. 7   The body of law created by the legislature and approved by the executive branch of state and federal governments.

Common law p. 7   Law that has not been passed by the legislature, but rather is made by the courts and is based on the fundamentals of previous cases with similar facts.

Administrative law p. 7   Refers to both the law made by administrative agencies and the laws and regulations that govern the creation, organization, and operation of administrative agencies.

Ordinances p. 9   Local statutes passed by local legislatures.

Precedent p. 10   When courts apply the law of a previous case to current cases with similar facts.

Remedies p. 11   Judicial actions, which can be monetary or equitable, taken by courts that are intended to compensate an injured party in a civil lawsuit.

Equitable relief p. 11   A type of remedy, including injunctions and restraining orders, that is designed to compensate a party when money alone will not do, but instead forces the other party to do (or not do) something.

Secondary sources p. 13   Sources of law that have no independent authority or legally binding effect but can be used to illustrate a point or clarify a legal issue.

Restatements of the Law p. 13   A collection of uniform legal principles focused in a particular area of the law, which contains statements of common law legal principles and rules in a given area of law.

Model state statutes p. 13   Statutes drafted by legal experts to be used as a model for state legislatures to adopt in their individual jurisdictions in order to increase the level of uniformity and fairness across courts in all states.

Doctrine of stare decisis p. 14   The principle that similar cases with similar facts under similar circumstances should have similar outcomes.

Case precedent p. 14   The opinion of an appellate court, which is binding on all trial courts from that point in time onward so that any similar case would be decided according to the precedent.

CASE SUMMARY 1.1 U.S. v. Alvarez 567 U.S. 709 (2012)

First Amendment

The Stolen Valor Act of 2005 made it a federal crime for an individual to falsely claim they had received military decoration or honors. The penalty for false claims about the Congressional Medal of Honor was enhanced to include up to one year in prison. The law was passed largely in response to media stories about public officials who had exaggerated or lied about their military record during their campaign or while in office. Alvarez was an individual who served as a board member of a municipal water district board in Claremont, California. During one public meeting of the board, Alvarez introduced himself and mentioned facts about his past, including that he had served as a marine, was wounded, and had received the Congressional Medal of Honor. None of these representations were true. Alvarez was charged with violating the Stolen Valor Act and pleaded guilty, but he reserved the right to challenge the constitutionality of the law based on the First Amendment upon appeal. The U.S. Court of Appeals for the Ninth Circuit struck the statute down as unconstitutional. The government appealed to the U.S. Supreme Court, arguing that because Alvarez's statements were false, the speaker is not entitled to First Amendment protection.

CASE QUESTIONS

1. In what ways does this case illustrate the concepts of constitutional *permanence* and *preemption*?
2. Is the link between the statute and the government's interest enough to satisfy any constitutional scrutiny? Why or why not?
3. Could Congress have crafted a different law that would have survived a constitutional challenge? How?

CASE SUMMARY 1.2 Sokoloff v. Harriman Estate Development Corp., 754 N.E.2d 184 (N.Y. 2001)

Equity and Fairness

Sokoloff purchased land in the Village of Sands Point, New York. In anticipation of building a home, he hired Harriman to provide preconstruction services, including the creation of architectural and landscaping plans. Sokoloff paid Harriman a $10,000 retainer fee and a total of $55,000 for creating and filing the architectural plans with the village. However, when it came time to build the home, Harriman estimated the cost to be over $1.8 million. Sokoloff, finding this amount to be exorbitant, decided to get quotes from other builders, based on the plans Harriman designed. However, Harriman said that the plans could not be used to construct the home unless he was the builder.

CASE QUESTIONS

1. Can Harriman withhold the plans from Sokoloff?
2. What legal theories or maxims would a court consider in deciding this case?
3. How should the court rule and why?

CASE SUMMARY 1.3 Jones v. R. R. Donnelley & Sons Co., 541 U.S. 369 (2004)

Statute of Limitations

The U.S. Congress enacted a statute providing for a four-year statute of limitations for any cause of action arising out of an act of Congress enacted after 1990. Jones, an African-American employee of R. R. Donnelley & Sons Co. (Donnelley), was denied a transfer to one of Donnelley's other plants when his plant closed. Moreover, while an employee for Donnelley, Jones was subjected to a hostile work environment and various acts of discrimination. Jones, an Illinois citizen, wishes to sue Donnelley for violating federal antidiscrimination statutes. It has been three years since Jones worked for Donnelley, and Illinois has a two-year statute of limitations.

CASE QUESTIONS

1. Which statute of limitation governs and why?
2. Will Jones be able to sue Donnelley?

CASE SUMMARY 1.4 Kauffman-Harmon v. Kauffman, 36 P.3d 408 (Sup. Ct. Mont. 2001)

Equitable Remedies

Kauffman created a corporation to hold certain assets in a manner intended to minimize tax liability. After creation of the corporation, a judgment was entered against Kauffman as a result of a lawsuit against him. In order to avoid paying the judgment, Kauffman transferred all of his stock into his spouse's name. His spouse eventually transferred ownership of the stock to several Kauffman children. Several years later, a dispute developed between the children concerning the stock, and Kauffman intervened by filing a claim with the trial court requesting that all stock be transferred back to him on the basis that he was the rightful owner of the stock and that the transfer was nothing more than a temporary trust. The children contended that Kauffman is not the equitable owner of the stock and is not entitled to relief due to the clean hands doctrine.

CASE QUESTIONS

1. Should the court apply the clean hands doctrine here? Why or why not?
2. Do the children have clean hands? Didn't they accept the stock to help their father perpetrate fraud?

1. The U.S. Congress passes a law imposing criminal penalties on executives at corporations who engage in banking fraud. The law fits into which category(ies)?
   I. Public
   II. Private
   III. Statutory
   IV. Civil
      a. I only
      b. III only
      c. I and III
      d. III and IV
      e. I, II, and III

2. In the course of her day, Donnelly gives legal advice and prepares daily memorandums for the executive management team of a publicly traded technology company. The memos outline all current and potential legal challenges faced by the company, including the status of any securities compliance issues. She is a member of executive management and provides official record-keeping and certification procedures for the company's board of directors. Donnelly is likely to be:
      a. Vice president and general counsel at a technology company.
      b. A business attorney working in a law firm.
      c. A litigator working for a law firm.
      d. In-house intellectual property counsel.
      e. An assistant district attorney.

3. Constitutional law:
   I. Establishes a structure of government.
   II. Grants specific powers for the different branches of government.
   III. Provides procedural protection of citizens against wrongful government actions.
   IV. Allows executive branch and independent agencies to create and enforce regulations.
      a. I only
      b. II only
      c. I and III
      d. I, II, and III
      e. IV only

4. A state legislature passes a law that requires all licensed real estate brokers to have liability insurance. The law is a:
      a. Federal statute.
      b. State statute.
      c. Local ordinance.
      d. Federal administrative regulation.
      e. Constitutional amendment.

5. Generally speaking, legal strategy in business refers to a:
      a. Statute.
      b. Plan of action.
      c. Random occurrence.
      d. Lawyer transaction.
      e. Law firm.

6. The U.S. Constitution is a secondary source of law.
      a. True
      b. False

7. The U.S. Environmental Protection Agency is a federal administrative agency.
      a. True
      b. False

8. Precedent may be overruled only by the U.S. Supreme Court.
      a. True
      b. False

9. Legal decisions in the business context are made solely by corporate counsel.
      a. True
      b. False

10. One important function of law in the business environment is *reliability* for future business planning.
      a. True
      b. False

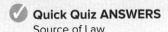
Quick Quiz ANSWERS
Source of Law

1. A contract issue governed by statutory (UCC) law at the state level.
2. A patent issue governed by statutory law at the federal level.
3. A securities issue governed by statutory and administrative law at the federal and state levels.
4. A bankruptcy issue governed by statutory and administrative law at the federal level.
5. A zoning issue governed by statutory law at the local level.

CHAPTER REVIEW QUESTIONS: Answers and Explanations

1. c. The fact that Congress passed the law makes it public (government-made) and a statute (legislative body). A law passed by Congress cannot be private, and because it carries criminal penalties, it cannot be categorized as civil.

2. a. Because her duties involve working for the same company on a variety of matters, *a* is the best answer. Answers *b* and *c* are wrong because law firm attorneys have multiple clients. Answer *d* is wrong because her duties are more general, and answer *e* is wrong because she is not a prosecutor.

3. d. The remaining are wrong because constitutional law has the functions listed in I, II, and III. IV is incorrect because it describes administrative law.

4. b. State legislatures pass state statutes. The remaining answers are incorrect because they are all sources of law where the state legislature has no role.

5. b. Legal strategy is a planning process. Answer *c* is incorrect because random is the opposite of strategy. Answers *a, d,* and *e,* are incorrect because they are nonsensical.

6. b. False. The U.S. Constitution is a primary source of law. An example of a secondary source would be the UCC and *Restatements.*

7. a. True. The U.S. EPA is an administrative agency charged with environmental rulemaking, enforcement, and adjudication.

8. b. False. Precedent may be overruled (and set) by any court of authority. Although the U.S. Supreme Court is a court of authority, it is not the *only* court of authority, which renders the statement false.

9. b. False. Managers are on the front lines of legal decision making, and most businesses do not have regular access or resources to contact corporate counsel.

10. a. True. Reliability allows business owners to plan transactions with a certain degree of assurance as to the legal impact of the transaction by understanding how similar transactions have been treated in the past.

CHAPTER 2

Business, Societal, and Ethical Contexts of Law

In this chapter you will learn how an entrepreneur or small business can engage a lawyer strategically when a much larger competitor unethically abuses the legal system to their advantage. The law and ethics are often closely related, however, in practice businesses may use the law in an unethical manner to achieve advantage over their competitors.

Learning Objectives

After studying this chapter, students who have mastered the material will be able to:

2-1	Analyze how business organizations, law, and ethics are related.
2-2	Identify the three main ethical decision-making regimes.
2-3	Analyze how corporate social responsibility (CSR) supports ethical decision making and identify the three views of corporate social responsibility.
2-4	Identify how values management supports ethical decision making.
2-5	Apply an ethical decision-making framework.
2-6	Identify the unique attributes of nonprofit and benefit corporations.

CHAPTER OVERVIEW

As will be discussed throughout this text, the law provides an important set of rules and guidelines that guide business decision making. Other important forces such as ethics and corporate social responsibility likewise guide business decision making and have a profound impact on the law. It is imperative, therefore, that informed and responsible business managers obtain a solid understanding of the relationship between business, law, and ethics to engage in sound decision making. The failure to engage in this reflective practice can lead to disastrous results that may negatively impact a firm, its stakeholders, and society. To address these issues, this chapter will discuss the relationship between businesses, law, and ethics, and the various tools and frameworks that promote ethical decision making.

THE RELATIONSHIPS BETWEEN BUSINESS ORGANIZATIONS, LAW, AND ETHICS

LO 2-1

Analyze how business organizations, law, and ethics are related.

How do you decide between right and wrong? **Ethics** is the set of moral principles or core values for deciding between right and wrong. Ethics apply to our everyday decisions, including those undertaken on behalf of a business. Have you ever received too much money back when you paid for something in a store? Have you ever been tempted to call in sick to work when you just wanted a day off? Each of these scenarios presents an ethical dilemma, and you must decide what to do in each case based on your core values and sense of ethics.

Later in the chapter we will discuss the origins of ethics and some of the most well-accepted ethical decision-making regimes. In this section, we will review the broader consideration that involves the relationship between businesses, law, and ethics.

A comprehensive understanding of law and ethics starts with the overarching notion of justice. Broadly defined, justice is the maintenance or administration of what is fair.

A popular depiction of justice since antiquity is captured in the image at right. This symbol has three elements that are meant to embody fundamental notions of justice as an arbiter of legal disputes. First, justice should apply equally to all. To justice, it does not matter if the individual is rich or poor, famous or not. In a just system, legal principles apply equally to all parties regardless of their position in society or wealth.

Second, justice has an enforcement mechanism to impose penalties and ensure compliance and fidelity to the law. A legal system that exists solely in theory without proper enforcement cannot adequately regulate behavior and exists as a fiction on paper rather than as a just and real system of law. You can have the best laws on the books, but without enforcement they will mean very little in practice.

A statue of Lady Justice.
©Jack R Perry/Getty Images

Third, justice equally considers opposing sides and weighs the merits of the competing arguments carefully and with due consideration. Just laws and outcomes must, therefore, balance competing interests to achieve a proportional outcome that is fair and balanced for the parties involved and those similarly situated.

 Quick Quiz The Elements of Justice

1. Match the various symbolic elements in the image with the three key attributes of justice. Do these symbols fully capture the meaning of justice's key attributes?

2. Are there any missing elements that should be added to the image?

Answers to this Quick Quiz are provided at the end of the chapter.

As an ideal, the law strives to encode basic notions of justice and fairness. For example, laws cannot be just if they are not made widely available for public consumption. It would be unfair and unjust to expect someone to comply with a law that was not made publicly available. In a business setting, it would be unfair to be held accountable for an offense many years after the injurious action allegedly occurred. To avoid this scenario, laws called *statutes of limitations* place a time limit on the ability of plaintiffs to pursue legal claims such as breach of contract.

In an ideal system, the law should always strive to achieve justice to derive the right outcome. In practice, however, this does not always occur because the overlap between ethics and the law is not always perfect as illustrated in the figure below.

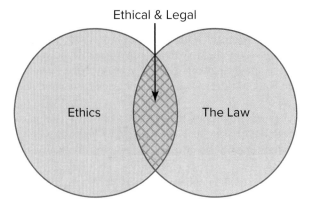

The relation between law and ethics.

At one extreme, an act might be ethical though not compelled by law. For example, in the United States, it is generally the case that an individual does not have an affirmative duty to go to someone's aid unless there is a legal duty to do so. If Marc is on a beach and sees Joe drowning beyond the breakers, Marc has no affirmative duty to go to Joe's rescue, or even call for help. Most people would agree that Marc has an ethical duty to try to help Joe in some way, for example, by alerting others nearby for help. In a business setting, a company may go above and beyond lax environmental regulations if it believes such actions are ethically required to ensure public safety and well-being.

Other acts are both ethical and mandated by law. For example, in some European nations, the scenario involving Marc and Joe would result in liability toward Marc if he does not try to alert authorities or seek help. In a business setting, regulations that protect employee safety and health and forbid child labor would be examples of laws that compel ethical behavior.

At another extreme, some actions are legal but unethical. For example, many large U.S. companies engage in what is called a *corporate inversion,* effectively merging the company with a foreign entity to avoid paying U.S. taxes. Until this tax loophole is closed through the enactment of federal legislation, it is entirely legal. Many would argue that although this strategy is perfectly legal, it violates the spirit of the law and is unethical because it exploits legal expertise to benefit large corporations and deprives society of general treasury revenues that could be used to fund public works and programs.

Ethics is a vital and unavoidable part of the tapestry that keeps society stitched together. For example, individuals and businesses often go above and beyond what the law requires. In the process, they may even decide to apply ethical **norms of behavior**, well-accepted standards of action given a particular circumstance, to resolve issues without resorting to the formal legal system. Even when the law provides specific types of relief, individuals and businesspeople sometimes forego a legal battle and instead choose to resolve the matter in a peaceful and amicable way outside of the formal legal system. Take the case of Julie and Sam, two adjoining property owners in a rural setting. Julie is a farmer and Sam is a cattle rancher. One day, Sam's cattle destroy the fence between their property and trespass onto Julie's farm, eating many of her valuable crops. It is likely that Sam will offer to compensate Julie for her loss in a fair manner without resorting to the legal system. For Sam, this is a natural course of action and the neighborly thing to do. In many cases, society maintains balance and order without law.[1]

---

[1]Robert C. Ellickson, *Order without Law: How Neighbors Settle Disputes* (Harvard University Press, 1994).

Enlightened businesspeople understand that companies are important actors within society and that this carries great responsibility to behave ethically. This responsibility often means businesses must act beyond what is required by the law. The following quote by Brad Smith, the president and chief legal officer of Microsoft Corporation, captures this idea:

> What is the right thing to serve our shareholders and our customers and our fundamental mission, which is about empowering people around the world? It starts with the law and then moves quickly to other things. If one tries to keep these things too separate, I think one can end up doing a disservice—not just to people who own the company as shareholders, but to the people who use our products and the world at large.[2]

TAKEAWAY CONCEPTS The Relationships between Business Organizations, Law, and Ethics

- Ethics is the set of moral principles or core values for deciding between right and wrong.
- Justice is the maintenance or administration of what is fair and has an important place within law and ethics.
- As an ideal, the law strives to encode basic notions of justice and fairness.
- The overlap between ethics and the law is not always perfect; some actions are ethical but not legally required, whereas others are legal but unethical.
- Parties sometimes apply ethical norms of behavior to resolve issues without resorting to the formal legal system.

ETHICAL DECISION-MAKING REGIMES

LO 2-2

Identify the three main ethical decision-making regimes.

Certain moral philosophies influence individuals' moral judgments and their preferred solutions to ethical dilemmas. **Morals** are generally accepted *standards* of right and wrong in a given society or community. These standards may be based on the law, one's religion, one's personal belief systems, or some combination of all three. From an applied perspective, ethics refers to having a *conscious system* in place for solving moral dilemmas. Individual approaches to thinking ethically may be based on several broad sources of ethical standards that stem from certain historical theories of morality. Although a close examination of moral philosophy is outside the scope of this textbook, it is essential to understand the main theoretical approaches to ethics and morality and how they can influence business decision making. In summary, there are three major ethical traditions: principles, consequences, and contracts.

Principles-Based Approach

The principles-based approach to ethics encompasses a large family of diverse moral theories, including theories based on religion, virtue, natural law, and universal moral duties. What these theories have in common is that they are all based on general or universal moral principles.

Religion   Ethical decisions that are made according to a set of established principles or standards such as *religious tenets* or codes—for example, the Koran (Islamic canonical law) or the Old Testament (Judeo-Christian tradition)—employ a principles-based approach.

---

[2]David Hechler, "Microsoft's Brad Smith Talks about Getting Kicked Upstairs," *Corporate Counsel*, Sept. 17, 2015.

These religious-based principles establish duties and are not subject to exceptions, but they may be tempered by other religious principles such as mercy and justice.

Virtue   Another principles-based approach to ethics is called *virtue ethics,* a tradition that goes back to Aristotle.[3] This ethical theory evaluates conduct based on whether it promotes good moral character. Moreover, according to Aristotle, for a person to become virtuous, she can't simply study what virtue *is;* she must actually do virtuous deeds.

Natural Law   In addition to religious-based principles, some philosophers claim that humans have certain *inherent* moral rights and duties that spring from their ability to reason and choose freely what they do with their lives. *Natural law* theory is a moral philosophy that certain rights and moral values are timeless, universal, and discoverable through human reason or, as the U.S. Declaration of Independence (1776) famously states:

> We hold these truths to be self-evident: that all men are created equal; that they are endowed by their Creator with certain unalienable rights; that among these are life, liberty, and the pursuit of happiness.

Historically, natural law refers to the use of reason to deduce universal and timeless rules of moral behavior. Although the natural law tradition goes back to the ancient Greeks and Romans, medieval theologian Thomas Aquinas (1225–1274) developed the most well-known theory of natural law. According to Aquinas, (1) natural law is given by God; (2) it is authoritative over all human beings; and (3) it is knowable through the use of reason.[4]

The Categorical Imperative   The great Prussian-born philosopher Immanuel Kant (1724–1804) developed a form of principles-based ethics, which he called *duty-based* ethics, in his famous and oft-cited work, *The Critique of Practical Reason.* According to Kant, one should act morally because it is the right thing to do, without any ulterior motive. In particular, Kant's approach to ethics is based on an inherent notion that humans should act from a sense of duty to human dignity. Kant theorized that *rights* imply *duties* and that the duty to respect the rights of others is paramount in acting morally. In the words of Kant:

> Act in such a way that you treat humanity, whether in your own person or in the person of any other, always at the same time as an end and never merely as a means to an end.

Moreover, the idea of the *categorical imperative* is a central theme in Kant's work. In summary, the categorical imperative is a moral test to help individuals decide right from wrong. Specifically, when considering whether a given action is right or wrong in the moral sense, Kant would ask, "What if everybody took that same action?" This Kantian question is sometimes called a *universalization* test. If everyone should act the same way (e.g., if everyone should tell the truth or keep their promises), then the action (promise-keeping; truth-telling) is moral. Kant further believed that the answers to this universal moral test are unconditional and absolute.

Consequences-Based Approach

The consequences-based approach emphasizes that the ethical course of action is the one that provides the greatest good (happiness) for the greatest number of people and has the least harmful consequences for the majority of the community. The approach stems from the **utilitarian** stream of moral philosophy.[5] Under this model, an action is ethically sound if it produces positive results or the least harm for the most people. Simply put, the course of action

---

[3]Aristotle, *Nicomachean Ethics,* trans. T.H. Irwin (Hackett Publishing Company, 1999).

[4]For a comprehensive overview of natural law theory, see Leo Strauss, *Natural Right and History* (University of Chicago Press, 1950).

[5]The founder of utilitarianism is the famous 18th-century philosopher Jeremy Bentham.

that results in the most benefits for the most individuals is the most ethical. By contrast, if an action impacts the majority of community members in a negative way, it is inherently unethical. Business owners and managers who employ a consequences-based approach seek to produce the greatest balance of good over harm for all who are affected, including owners, employees, customers, investors, and the community at large. Critics of utilitarianism argue that this approach amounts to using a mathematical formula to decide matters of morality.

Contract-Based Approach

Harvard philosopher John Rawls (1921–2002) developed a contract-based theory of ethics in his influential book, *A Theory of Justice* (1971). His approach is considered a contractarian one because Rawls imagines a world in which people must negotiate their own ethical rules and principles for themselves. What makes Rawls's particular theory so original, however, is his notion of the "original position," a hypothetical situation in which everyone negotiates from behind a "veil of ignorance." This veil blinds people to all facts about themselves:

> . . . no one knows his place in society, his class position or social status, nor does anyone know his fortune in the distribution of natural assets and abilities, his intelligence, strength, and the like. I shall even assume that the parties do not know their conceptions of the good or their special psychological propensities. The principles of justice are chosen behind a veil of ignorance.[6]

According to Rawls, ignorance of these details about oneself will lead people to negotiate a set of ethical principles that are fair to all. Why? Because if no one knows what his ultimate position in society will be, people negotiating from behind the veil of ignorance are not going to privilege any one class of people; instead, they will develop ethical rules and principles that treat all fairly. In particular, Rawls claims that individuals in the original position should adopt a *maximin* strategy that maximizes the prospects of the least well-off: "They are the principles that rational and free persons concerned to further their own interests would accept in an initial position of equality as defining the fundamentals of the terms of their association."[7]

Consider the ethical dilemmas presented in Case 2.1, where a California state appellate court decided if a punitive damages award should be upheld in a case involving ethics and managerial decision making.

CASE 2.1 Grimshaw v. Ford Motor Company, 119 Cal. App. 3d 757, 174 Cal. Rptr. 348 (1981)

FACT SUMMARY This was a personal injury tort case decided in Orange County, California, in 1978 and affirmed by a California appellate court in 1981. The lawsuit involved the safety of the design of the Ford Pinto automobile, manufactured by the Ford Motor Company. The jury awarded plaintiffs $127.8 million in damages, one of the largest ever granted at the time for a product liability and personal injury case.

During discovery, it was ascertained that Ford managers learned a troubling fact during crash tests involving the Pinto. They learned that the vehicle might, under certain conditions, explode due to a design flaw involving the positioning of the fuel tank.

(continued)

---

[6]John Rawls, *A Theory of Justice* (1971), p. 11.
[7]Ibid.

The explosion would likely cause deaths and serious burn injuries. Ford's managers considered the costs of fixing the design flaw and used a cost-benefit analysis to decide to go ahead with the flawed design. They set upon this course of action reasoning that it would cost less to pay injury claims than to redesign the vehicle.

The trial involved an accident where a 1972 Pinto sustained a rear-end impact and caught fire. This resulted in the death of the driver, Lily Gray, and severe injury to the passenger, Richard Grimshaw. The jury in the case awarded $125 million in punitive damages.

The images below represent the figures used in Ford's cost-benefit analysis and the design workaround that would have corrected the defect.

SYNOPSIS OF DECISION AND OPINION The California court of appeals upheld the trial court's award of punitive damages and ruled in favor of Grimshaw. The court rejected Ford's argument that it was entitled to a reversal of the trial court's award of punitive damages because there was no evidentiary support for a finding of malice or corporate responsibility for malice. The appellate court disagreed with Ford's arguments and affirmed the trial court's punitive damages award.

WORDS OF THE COURT: Malice as a Requirement for Punitive Damages in Product Liability Cases "The concept of punitive damages is rooted in the English common law and is a settled principle

WHAT'S YOUR LIFE WORTH?

Societal Cost Components for Fatalities, 1972 NHTSA Study

COMPONENT	1971 COSTS
FUTURE PRODUCTIVITY LOSSES	
Direct	$132,000
Indirect	41,300
MEDICAL COSTS	
Hospital	700
Other	425
PROPERTY DAMAGE	1,500
INSURANCE ADMINISTRATION	4,700
LEGAL AND COURT	3,000
EMPLOYER LOSSES	1,000
VICTIM'S PAIN AND SUFFERING	10,000
FUNERAL	900
ASSETS (Lost Consumption)	5,000
MISCELLANEOUS ACCIDENT COST	200
TOTAL PER FATALITY: $200,725	

Source: National Highway Traffic Safety Administration

$11 vs. A BURN DEATH

Benefits and Costs Relating to Fuel Leakage Associated with the Static Rollover Test Portion of FMVSS 208

Benefits
Savings:
 180 burn deaths, 180 serious burn injuries, 2,100 burned vehicles.
Unit Cost:
 $200,000 per death, $67,000 per injury, $700 per vehicle.
Total Benefit:
 180 × ($200,00) + 180 × ($67,000) + 2,100 × ($700) = $49.5 million.

Costs
Sales:
 11 million cars, 1.5 million light trucks.
Unit cost:
 $11 per car, $11 per truck.
Total cost:
 11,000,000 × ($11) + 1,500,000 × ($11) = $137 million.

–from *Ford Motor* Company internal memorandum: "Fatalities Associated with Crash-Induced Fuel Leakage and Fires"

Source: *The Ford Pinto Case – A Study in Applied Ethics, Business and Technology* edited by Douglas Birsch and John H. Fielder.

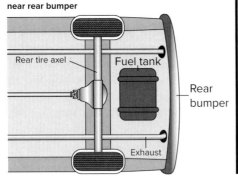
Rear of car design with fuel tank near rear bumper

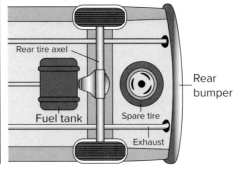
Rear of car design with fuel tank moved closer to mid-point of car

Source: *The Ford Pinto Case – A Study in Applied Ethics, Business and Technology* edited by Douglas Birsch and John H. Fielder.

(continued)

of the common law of this country. When our laws were codified in 1872, the doctrine was incorporated in Civil Code section 3294, which at the time of trial read: 'In an action for the breach of an obligation not arising from contract, where the defendant has been guilty of oppression, fraud, or malice, express or implied, the plaintiff, in addition to the actual damages, may recover damages for the sake of example and by way of punishing the defendant.'

. . .

"Ford argues that 'malice' as used in section 3294 and as interpreted by our Supreme Court in Davis v. Hearst (1911) 160 Cal. 143 [116 P. 530], requires animus malus or evil motive—an intention to injure the person harmed—and that the term is therefore conceptually incompatible with an unintentional tort such as the manufacture and marketing of a defectively designed product. This contention runs counter to our decisional law. As this court recently noted, numerous California cases after Davis v. Hearst, supra, have interpreted the term 'malice' as used in section 3294 to include, not only a malicious intention to injure the specific person harmed, but

conduct evincing 'a conscious disregard of the probability that the actor's conduct will result in injury to others.'

. . .

"The interpretation of the word 'malice' as used in section 3294 to encompass conduct evincing callous and conscious disregard of public safety by those who manufacture and market mass produced articles is consonant with and furthers the objectives of punitive damages. The primary purposes of punitive damages are punishment and deterrence of like conduct by the wrongdoer and others."

Case Questions

1. Which of the three major ethical decision-making traditions did the Ford managers apply in their decision, and how would the issue have been resolved had they applied the other two traditions?

2. How did ethics play a role in the court's assessment of malice and the jury's damage award?

3. *Focus on Critical Thinking:* Which ethical tradition would you have applied in this scenario?

TAKEAWAY CONCEPTS Ethical Decision-Making Regimes

- Morals are generally accepted *standards* of right and wrong in a given society or community, and they influence individuals' preferred solutions to ethical dilemmas.
- There are three major ethical traditions: principles, consequences, and contracts.
- Principals-based ethical theories are all based on general or universal moral principles such as religion, virtue, and natural law.
- A consequences-based approach emphasizes that the ethical course of action is the one that provides the greatest good (happiness) for the greatest number of people and has the least harmful consequences for the majority of the community.
- A contracts-based theory of ethics conceives a "veil of ignorance" that will lead people to negotiate ethical principles that are fair to all.

CORPORATE SOCIAL RESPONSIBILITY

While business ethics may be thought of as an application of ethics to the corporate sector and may be useful to determine responsibility in business dealings, **corporate social responsibility (CSR)** involves a broader-based identification of important business and social issues and a critique of business organizations and practices.

LO 2-3

Analyze how corporate social responsibility (CSR) supports ethical decision making and identify the three views of corporate social responsibility.

There are three schools of thought that define CSR in practice: the narrow view, the moderate view, and the broad view.

The Narrow View: "Greed Is Good"

Nobel Prize–winning economist Milton Friedman proposed that the only responsibility a business has is to maximize shareholder wealth (the *maximizing profits theory*).[8] Moreover, in his classic condemnation of the broad view of corporate social responsibility, Friedman further argued that managers who pursue social initiatives with corporate funds are violating their fiduciary duties to the owners of the corporation. This narrow view of CSR thus emphasizes a corporation's ethical duties to its shareholders. While individuals are free to act morally and behave in a socially responsible manner on their own time and with their own resources, managers are responsible solely to the shareholders to make as much profit as legally possible. As for society's well-being, the argument goes, the "invisible hand" of the market will end up producing the most benefits overall to society. According to Adam Smith's famous "invisible hand" metaphor, the common good is best served when people and businesses pursue not the common good, but rather their self-interest.

The Moderate View: Just Follow the Law

Advocates of a more moderate view of CSR emphasize the role that the government and regulatory agencies play in setting the outer limits of corporate social responsibility. According to this moderate or "government hand" view, it is the government's job to establish legal and regulatory guidelines for business because the government already represents the aggregate moral views of the public. Under this view, a business's ethical responsibility is to comply with the law and pursue objectives that are legal. The regulatory hands of the law and the political process, rather than Adam Smith's invisible hand, provide the basis for ethical decision making.

The Broad View: Good Corporate Citizenship and a Social License to Operate

Business organizations committed to a broad view of CSR aim to achieve commercial success in ways that honor ethical values and respect people, communities, and the natural environment in a sustainable manner while recognizing the interests of stakeholders. Stakeholders include investors, customers, employees, business partners, local communities, the environment, and society at large. The broad view of CSR also involves the notion of "corporate citizenship," which means a business should strive to promote the economic, legal, ethical, and philanthropic social responsibilities expected of it by its stakeholders. Furthermore, the broadest view of CSR is that corporations have a social responsibility to which profitability is secondary (the *moral minimum theory*). Indeed, some business ethicists argue that corporations are allowed to exist only because they serve some public good. These ethicists often invoke a set of societal expectations with the idea that corporations should conduct their business on such terms. Their starting point is socially defined goals rather than business objectives.

Business ethicists also invoke the concept of a **social license to operate**, which includes the demands on, and expectations for, a business that emerge from neighborhoods, environmental groups, community members, and other elements of civil society.[9] Businesspeople should realize that in some instances the conditions demanded by "social licensors" may be tougher than those imposed by regulation, resulting in a "beyond legal compliance" approach.

---

[8]Milton Friedman, "The Social Responsibility of Business Is to Increase Its Profits," *The New York Times Magazine*, Sept. 13, 1970.

[9]Neil Gunningham et al., "Social License and Environmental Protection: Why Businesses Go beyond Compliance," *Law & Social Inquiry* 29, no. 2 (April 2004), pp. 307, 321.

Others argue that CSR is in the public's interest and a company's self-interest *and* that a company does well by employing socially responsible principles in its business operations. In this way, CSR may be thought of as a form of enlightened self-interest because the long-term prosperity of a firm depends not on short-term profits but on societal well-being. In any case, an integral part of the broad CSR perspective is the focus on what some ethicists call the **triple bottom line**. Essentially, the triple bottom line emphasizes not only the conventional creation of economic value (profits), but also a company's creation (or destruction) of environmental and social value. The triple-bottom-line approach thus places a great deal more pressure on managers to perform, as it is not uncommon that these three sets of bottom-line issues conflict. It is not enough, then, for managers to aggressively pursue a social agenda; they must also not lose sight of financial goals and environmental performance.

Businesses are wise to apply CSR frameworks during litigation. In Case 2.2, The U.S. Trademark Trial and Appeal Board (TTAB), an administrative court of the U.S. Patent and Trademark Office (USPTO), hears a case involving a trademark owner's opposition to another company's trademark application.

CASE 2.2 Brooks Brothers Group, Inc., Opposer v. Bubbles by Brooks, LLC, Applicant, Opposition No. 91205596, in the U.S. Patent and Trademark Office and before the Trademark Trial and Appeal Board (2013)

FACT SUMMARY Amy Brooks, a cancer survivor from Minnesota, started her small home-based business, Bubbles by Brooks, which specializes in making soap and skin care products handcrafted and designed to reduce irritation as cancer patients go through therapy. Her sales at the time of this case amounted to a little less than $100,000 a year.

When Amy applied for a federal trademark for her business name, Brooks Brothers, the large clothing retailer, opposed her registration at the U.S. Trademark Office. The retailer's lawyers stated that "[although] 'Brooks' may be your surname, it does not give you the right to infringe on the Brooks Brothers trademark or otherwise compete with Brooks Brothers."

After a year of legal wrangling, Brooks Brothers withdrew its opposition to Amy's federal trademark application and she was finally able to register her mark.

SYNOPSIS OF DECISION AND OPINION The Trademark Trial and Appeal Board dismissed the case before reaching a decision in light of the settlement agreed upon by both parties.

Amy was fortunate to secure *pro bono* legal representation from a large law firm in her area that was willing to litigate on her behalf. During the proceedings, the law firm's attorneys working on her behalf filed a lengthy motion to the court requesting a ruling in Amy's favor. Facing a potentially adverse ruling, and a lengthy and potentially embarrassing case, Brooks Brothers settled and withdrew their opposition to Amy's use and application of the trademark "Bubbles by Brooks."

WORDS OF THE COURT: Opposition Dismissed "In view of the stipulation filed June 13, 2013, the opposition is dismissed with prejudice."

Case Questions

The Federal Rules of Civil Procedure, which govern the rules for federal litigation, state that the rules "should be construed, administered, and employed by the court and the parties to secure the just, speedy, and inexpensive determination of every action and proceeding."

1. In light of the Federal Rules of Civil Procedure, do parties have an ethical duty to refrain from lengthy litigation in certain cases?

2. Which CSR approach did the Opposer adopt in this case? How did this approach backfire from a strategic perspective?

3. *Focus on Critical Thinking:* Which CSR approach would you have chosen and why?

CSR and Litigation

Some companies apply a CSR lens when dealing with litigation. This approach may limit abusive litigation strategies initiated by lawyers who might be overly aggressive in their advocacy. For example, Walmart has specific internal CSR guidelines that instruct its attorneys to behave ethically during litigation and to:

- Honor the spirit, intent, and requirements of all rules of civil procedure and rules of professional conduct;
- Conduct themselves in a manner that enhances and preserves the dignity and integrity of the system of justice;
- Adhere to the principles and rules of conduct that further the truth-seeking process so that disputes will be resolved in a just, dignified, courteous, and efficient manner;
- Make reasonable responses to discovery request and not interpret them in an artificially restrictive manner so as to avoid disclosure of relevant and nonprivileged information;
- Make good faith efforts to resolve disputes concerning pleadings and discovery;
- Agree to reasonable requests for extension of time and waiver of procedural formalities when doing so will not adversely affect Walmart's legitimate rights; and
- Prepare and submit discovery requests that are limited to those requests reasonably necessary for the prosecution or defense of an action and not for the purpose of placing an undue burden or expense on another party.[10]

TAKEAWAY CONCEPTS Corporate Social Responsibility

- Corporate social responsibility (CSR) involves a broader-based identification of important business and social issues and a critique of business organizations and practices.
- There are three schools of thought that define CSR in practice: the narrow view, the moderate view, and the broad view.
- A narrow view of CSR emphasizes a corporation's ethical duties to its shareholders.
- Under a moderate view of CSR, a business's ethical responsibility is to comply with the law and pursue objectives that are legal.
- Businesses committed to a broad view of CSR aim to achieve commercial success in ways that honor ethical values and respect people, communities, and the natural environment in a sustainable manner while recognizing the interests of stakeholders.

LO 2-4

Identify how values management supports ethical decision making.

VALUES MANAGEMENT AND COMPLIANCE DEPARTMENTS

Business Ethics Challenges in Values Management

Business ethics in the workplace prioritizes moral values for the organization and ensures that employee and manager behaviors are aligned with those values. This approach is known as **values management**. Yet, despite evidence that embracing business ethics promotes

---

[10]Christopher J. Whelan and Neta Ziv, "Law Firm Ethics in the Shadow of Corporate Social Reponsibility," *Georgetown Journal of Legal Ethics* 26 (2013), p. 153.

TABLE 2.1　Challenges and Realities in Business Ethics

Challenge	Reality
Business ethics is unnecessary because it asserts the obvious: Act ethically.	The value of a code of ethics to an organization is its priority and focus with respect to certain ethical values in the company. Dishonesty takes a variety of forms. If an organization is confronting varying degrees of dishonesty (including more common examples such as office supply theft) or deceit in the workplace, a priority on honesty is very timely—and honesty should be listed in that organization's code of ethics.
Complying with the law is an organization's sole guide for ethical conduct.	While the law may operate as a baseline for ethical decision making, unethical acts may operate within the limits of the law (e.g., withholding information from superiors, casting revenue in favorable terms with a dubious basis for the projection, or spreading rumors). Illegal conduct sometimes has its genesis in unethical behavior that has gone unnoticed.
Ethics can't be managed.	Management inherently incorporates a value system. Strategic priorities (e.g., maximizing profit, expanding market share, cutting costs, etc.) can be very strong influences on ethical decision making. Workplace regulations and rules directly influence behaviors in a manner that improves the general good and/or minimizes potential harm to stakeholders.
Ethics is about philosophy and has little to do with the day-to-day realities of running a business.	Business ethics is a management discipline with a programmatic approach that includes several practical tools. Ethics management programs have practical applications in other areas of management as well.
Business ethics cannot be taught. It is religion, not management.	Altering people's values isn't the objective of an organizational ethics program. Managing values and *conflict* among them is the primary objective.

profitability and contributes to sound public policy, some business cultures are resistant to values management programs.

A useful approach to consider when deciding whether a manager or a company is acting in an ethical manner is to apply a "broadcast news test." Ask yourself, "How would I feel if the business decision was announced to the public on social media or the local and national news?" In today's social media environment, very little goes unnoticed or unreported, so it might be even more appropriate to ask how one would feel if a video of a major decision went viral. Table 2.1 lists common challenges and possible responses to business ethics and values management.

Common Traits of Effective Values Management

One way business organizations implement values management is by developing codes of ethics and an ethical vision to guide the decisions and behavior of their employees and managers. (Think of Google's widely known "Don't be evil" policy.) Such values management programs can also include extensive training and monitoring protocols, depending on the organization's command structure, but at a minimum, every business organization should consider developing a code of ethics to provide guidance in ethical dilemmas. A comprehensive code of ethics and conduct would cover various areas of business activity detailed further in Table 2.2.

An effective values management program places a duty on all employees to report violations of law or the company's code of ethics to a superior manager, in-house legal counsel, or the company's compliance department. The best programs also provide either an anonymous hotline or a direct contact person to report any violations.

TABLE 2.2 Contents of a Comprehensive Code of Ethics and Conduct

Topics	Specific Areas of Discussion
The workplace	Equal opportunity and diversity; anti-harassment; health and safety; substance abuse
Gifts, favors, and conflicts of interest	Receiving gifts or favors; insider trading; working outside the company
Use of company assets and data safeguarding	Personal data privacy; use of company assets; protecting company information; careful communications
Product quality, safety, and environmental matters	Product quality and safety; protecting the environment
Competition and antitrust law	Relations with competitors; relations with suppliers, dealers, and other customers
International business practices	Export controls and prohibited transactions; foreign corrupt practices; money laundering

Although ethicists have various views on how an ideal ethical organization should operate, effective values management programs share the following common traits:

- Management articulates a clear vision of ethics and moral integrity through all levels of the organization.
- Management's vision of ethics and integrity is implemented at all levels of the decision-making process within the organization.
- The reward systems, policies, and practices of the organization are aligned with management's vision of ethics and integrity.
- Above all, responsibility is seen as individual rather than collective in that individuals are encouraged to assume personal responsibility for the actions and decisions of the organization.

As with any management practice, the best outcome is behavior that is consistent with the organization's values and ethical vision. The best ethical values and intentions are meaningless unless they generate fair and just behaviors in the workplace. Employees at all levels within a company need to react to business situations in a fair and consistent manner.

Complaints and lawsuits frequently arise when employees, job applicants, or customers are treated, or are perceived as being treated, unfairly. One of the primary benefits of a code of ethics or a code of conduct is that such codes provide employees with rules and ideals they can universally follow. When a company is dealing with a diverse population of employees, common sense is not always common and the concept of right and wrong is not always easily agreed upon. Written codes can provide a central source of inspiration and guidance to ensure uniform conduct. That is why practices that generate lists of ethical values, or codes of ethics, must also generate policies, procedures, and training that translate those values into appropriate behaviors.

Compliance Departments

Several high-profile corporate scandals, such as those at Wells Fargo discussed below, have significantly damaged corporate reputations, triggered lawsuits, and led to increased regulations. These mishaps typically result in significant financial losses and employees being fired and, in some cases, going to jail. In light of the heightened public scrutiny on business activity, many

The Society of Corporate Compliance and Ethics (SCCE) is a leading compliance trade organization that offers training, certification, and publications committed to improving the quality and acknowledgment of the compliance industry. For more information about this society visit: https://www.corporatecompliance.org/

Wells Fargo Ghost Accounts Scandal

In 2016, regulators announced that Wells Fargo employees secretly created millions of unauthorized bank and credit card accounts, without their customers knowing it, in some cases dating as far back to 2011. The fake accounts earned the bank unwarranted fees and allowed Wells Fargo employees to boost their sales figures and profit as a result. A consulting firm hired by Wells Fargo found that bank employees opened more than 1.5 million deposit accounts that may not have been authorized.

Consequently, Wells Fargo was fined more than $185 million by various regulators. The company's CEO John Stumpf was forced to resign, and 5,300 employees were fired. In the process, the company's reputation took a large hit, its stock market valuation fell, and the company must address multiple lawsuits from shareholders and those injured by the company's actions.

Discussion Questions

1. What role does a compliance department have in promoting a culture of ethics within an organization?
2. After the Wells Fargo scandal erupted it was discovered that unreasonable and strict sales quotas contributed to the pressure managers faced to create ghost accounts. What ethical duties do senior executives have to ensure this kind of sales pressure does not result in illegal or unethical activity?

organizations have spent significant resources building their internal compliance departments in the hopes that this will prevent the next great scandal.

A **compliance department** is a unit within the organization that is staffed by lawyers and nonlawyers. These departments help an organization follow rules and regulations and maintain the company's overall culture and spirit of values and ethics. Having a well-staffed and resourced compliance department is an important step toward implementing a values management program.

TAKEAWAY CONCEPTS Values Management and Compliance Departments

- Values management prioritizes moral values for the organization and ensures that employee and manager behaviors are aligned with those values.
- One way business organizations implement values management is by developing codes of ethics.
- A compliance department is a unit staffed by lawyers and nonlawyers that helps an organization follow rules and regulations and helps maintain the company's overall culture and spirit of ethics.

ETHICAL DECISION MAKING: A MANAGER'S PARADIGM

LO 2-5

Apply an ethical decision-making framework.

It is not uncommon for business ethics to be portrayed as a matter of resolving conflicts in which one option appears to be the clear choice. Case studies that present situations where an employee is faced with whether or not to lie, steal, cheat, abuse another, break terms of a contract, and so on are too simplistic. Ethical dilemmas faced by managers are often complex, with no clear ethical choice. The use of a paradigm in a flowchart (see Figure 2.1) can help business owners apply ethical decision making more consistently.

Serious ethical lapses can occur at every level within an organization. In Case 2.3, The U.S. House of Representatives prepares a lengthy staff report on the activities leading up to the bankruptcy of MF Global, a major commodities broker, and their mishandling of customer accounts.

FIGURE 2.1   Ethical Decision Making

1. Define the dilemma →
How and when did the dilemma occur? What were the underlying reasons for the conflict?

2. Identify impact →
Which primary and secondary stakeholders will be affected? How will these stakeholders be affected?

3. Apply standards →
What is the legal impact of the dilemma? What values and ethical principles has the organization set out for guidance? What are the consequences of action or inaction?

4. Develop choices and discuss impact with various constituencies →
Which choice results in the most benefit to stakeholders? Will any of the choices result in harm to stakeholders? What are the level and severity of the harms? Which choice upholds the values of the organization?

5. Implement, evaluate, and monitor →
How can this decision be implemented with greatest attention to all stakeholders? Under what circumstances are you willing to make an exception to your decision? How could this company avoid this dilemma in the future?

CASE 2.3 U.S. House of Representatives Staff Report on MF Global Prepared for the Subcommittee on Oversight and Investigations—Committee on Financial Services

FACT SUMMARY In 2010, former New Jersey governor and Goldman Sachs CEO John Corzine agreed to take the helm of MF Global. He quickly transformed the beleaguered brokerage firm into a trading powerhouse and full-service investment bank. This strategy, however, required a risky business model. To finance growth, Corzine decided to invest heavily in the sovereign debts of struggling European countries. These investments carried significant default and liquidity risks. When the financial crisis in Europe caused losses in MF Global's European investments, the company filed for bankruptcy. Due to mismanagement and faulty internal risk controls, $1.6 billion in customer accounts went missing during the process, triggering various lawsuits and a congressional investigation.

SYNOPSIS OF DECISION AND OPINION The report severely criticized Mr. Corzine's actions and suggested his actions may have violated the company's internal controls and various state and federal investment laws.

The Congressional Report provided several recommendations to policymakers, including launching additional investigations by federal regulators into the potentially illegal activities undertaken at MF Global and strengthening regulations in the financial services industry.

WORDS OF THE STAFF REPORT: Default Risks
"In order to generate much-needed revenue to fund MF Global's transformation, Corzine decided to invest heavily in the sovereign debt of struggling European countries. These investments carried significant default and liquidity risks . . . As Corzine built the company's European bond portfolio, counterparty margin demands became a major draw on MF Global's cash reserves, further exacerbating the company's liquidity strain.

"These risks were compounded by the atmosphere that Corzine created at MF Global, in which

(continued)

no one could challenge his decisions. He hired his former gubernatorial chief of staff, Bradley Abelow, to serve as the company's COO. When Michael Roseman, the company's CRO [Chief Risk and Compliance Officer], disagreed with Corzine about the size of the company's European bond portfolio, Corzine directed Roseman to report to Abelow rather than to MF Global's board of directors. This change effectively sidelined the most senior individual charged with monitoring the company's risks and deprived the board of an independent assessment of the risks that Corzine's European RTM [repurchase-to-maturity] trades posed to MF Global, its shareholders, and its customers."

Case Questions

1. What evidence existed that MF Global lacked a values management plan and that a culture of ethics was lacking at the company?

2. Why did the board allow Mr. Corzine to reassign the chief risk officer's reporting to the chief operating officer? Would you have allowed that to occur as a board member? Explain.

3. *Focus on Critical Thinking:* Put yourself in Corzine's position when the chief risk officer voiced concern related to investment risk. Apply the ethical decision-making framework in Figure 2.1 and discuss how you would address each step.

TAKEAWAY CONCEPTS Ethical Decision Making: A Manager's Paradigm

- Ethical dilemmas faced by managers are often complex, with no clear ethical choice.
- A decision-making flowchart or paradigm can help business owners and managers apply ethical decision making more consistently.
- A decision-making paradigm may include: (1) defining the dilemma; (2) identifying the impact; (3) applying standards; (4) developing choices and discussing the impact with stakeholders; and (5) implementing, evaluating, and monitoring the choices made.

COMMUNITY-BASED NONPROFIT AND BENEFIT CORPORATIONS

LO 2-6

Identify the unique attributes of nonprofit and benefit corporations.

State laws that govern corporations do not require managers to adopt the narrow "greed is good" view of CSR in which the sole responsibility of business is to maximize shareholder wealth. In fact, Delaware, a popular forum for corporate law, explicitly states that managers may consider nonshareholder interests in scenarios such as a merger as long as there is some rational connection to providing value to shareholders.[11] Delaware, like many other states, therefore explicitly approves of the broader view of CSR that takes multiple stakeholders into account.

Nonetheless, alternative business organizational forms have emerged to allow managers to pursue other social ends that de-emphasize shareholder profit maximization. Community-based nonprofits and benefit corporations are two types of entities that facilitate the creation of enterprises with a social purpose as their driving goal.

---

[11]*Revlon, Inc. v. MacAndrews & Forbes Holdings, Inc.,* 506 A.2d 173, 176 (Del. 1986) ("[W]hile concern for various corporate constituencies is proper when addressing a takeover threat, that principle is limited by the requirement that there be some rationally related benefit accruing to the stockholders.")

A **community-based nonprofit** is typically a tax-exempt entity created for the purpose of serving the community. Any surplus earnings that remain are reinvested in activities that achieve the company's social mission. These entities lack shareholders and are typically governed by a board of directors. Amnesty International, Habitat for Humanity, and the Red Cross are examples of large, well-known nonprofit corporations.

A new type of hybrid organizational entity called a **benefit corporation** has been authorized by the majority of states. A benefit corporation resembles a traditional for-profit corporation, and its directors and officers operate the business with the same authority as in a traditional corporation. The main difference is directors and officers in a benefit corporation are required to consider the impact their decisions have on shareholders, society, and the environment. In a traditional corporation, shareholders judge the company's financial performance. Shareholders in a benefit corporation, on the other hand, judge performance based on the company's social, environmental, and financial performance. Benefit companies are, therefore, for-profit companies that consider additional stakeholders, morals, or missions in addition to making a profit for shareholders. A few examples of well-known benefit corporations include Etsy, Kickstarter, and Patagonia.

TAKEAWAY CONCEPTS Community-Based Nonprofit and Benefit Corporations

- Alternative business organizational forms have emerged to allow managers to pursue other social ends that de-emphasize shareholder profit maximization.
- A community-based nonprofit is typically a tax-exempt entity created for the purpose of serving the community.
- Directors and officers in a benefit corporation are required to consider the impact their decisions have on shareholders, society, and the environment.

THINKING STRATEGICALLY

Patently Unfair Behavior?

OVERVIEW: Sitting at his desk one evening in Chicago, Dan Brown (Brown) struggled to regain his composure after hearing 30 people would be laid off from his contracted manufacturing plant in Pennsylvania. Mr. Brown couldn't help but feel terrible about the production shortage that caused the layoffs. His company, LoggerHead Tools, LLC (LoggerHead Tools) had not produced the material forecast it was expected to meet.

Brown is the owner and founder of LoggerHead Tools (www.loggerheadtools.com). A prolific inventor and designer, in 2001 he watched his son struggle to remove a nut with a pair of pliers. Out of fear his son would strip the bolt, Brown came up with his design for a new device that would do away with wrenches and pliers that stripped bolts before they could be loosened. If successful, this tool would replace the

©Tribune Content Agency LLC/Alamy

multitude of wrenches and pliers necessary to tackle nuts and bolts of varying sizes, saving consumers money and storage space.

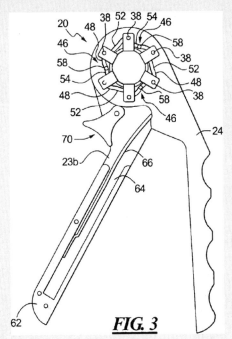

FIG. 3

The Bionic Wrench® Utility Patent Design and Bionic Wrench® Product Photograph
Source: United States Patent and Trademark Office

Craftsman Max Axess Locking Wrench
McGraw-Hill Education

Brown applied for a patent for his wrench in 2004. His Bionic Wrench® design applies equal pressure to a nut or bolt on all flat sides. In May 2005, utility patent US 6,889,579 B1 was issued to Brown for his invention. He then contracted Penn United Technologies, Inc., to handle the made-in-the-U.S.A. manufacturing and assembly of his wrench. In 2008, even in the midst of the recession, the Bionic Wrench generated sales of almost $11 million. Fifty employees at Penn United were employed on assembly lines devoted solely to the Bionic Wrench.

The product was distributed through QVC, Canadian Tire, Costco, Amazon, Ace Hardware, True Value, Menards, Sears, and others.

PROBLEM: In 2009, LoggerHead Tools entered into a contract with Sears for the sale of 15,000 units. Sears sold out of their entire stock of Bionic Wrenches during the 2009 Christmas season. The following year, Sears raised its forecast to 75,000 units and once again sold out during the Christmas season. In 2011, Sears took a major step and placed an order of 300,000 Bionic Wrenches under the stipulation that LoggerHead refrain from entering into any deal with their direct competition, Lowe's and Home Depot. LoggerHead agreed, and Sears received 300,000 units. Later, Sears reassigned the buyer in charge of the LoggerHead account

to another department. In early 2012, the departing buyer for Sears wrote the following e-mail to Brown:

> I just want you to know that your partnership with us is **VERY** important and that is not going to change. The biggest "To Do" right now is the bionic wrench for DRTV [direct response television]. With a new buyer on board, I will be working side by side with her on the launch.

After a meeting in February 2012, Sears placed an order for only 73,000 units for the upcoming Father's Day weekend. Having not received a renewed commitment for 300,000 units, LoggerHead sent Sears a revised pricing breakdown that reflected an increase in the price per unit due to the low volume. Brown made clear in this correspondence that without Sears's commitment to LoggerHead's required product volume, they would explore options with other direct competition retailers, including Lowe's and Home Depot. In May 2012, LoggerHead received a Christmas forecast for 213,519 units from Sears; however, within a month, the forecast was revised to less than 3,000 units. Blindsided by the sudden decrease in forecasted demand, Brown sent several e-mails seeking elaboration from

Sears. A formal answer was never given as to why the forecast decreased so dramatically.

In September 2012, in preparation for the Christmas season, Sears released the Craftsman Max Axess Locking Wrench. To manufacture the competing Max Access wrench, Sears contracted with Apex, an offshore manufacturer based in China. In a matter of months, and to Brown's great dismay, a new direct competitor to the Bionic Wrench had emerged.

Eventually, Brown would learn that Sears's position with respect to his patent was that it would be unenforceable since it was anticipated (not novel and obvious) by a patent issued in 1957 for wire crimping. He could expect that if he brought a federal patent infringement suit against Sears, they would try to use this 1957 patent to invalidate his patent. Brown had cited the 1957 patent as prior art during the examination stage at the U.S. Patent Office, so he felt this argument was dubious.

STRATEGIC SOLUTION: Contingency-based Litigation
Brown was left with a business-altering decision on his hands. Sensing that his business and intellectual property were at risk, he decided to pursue litigation against Sears. The average cost of a jury trial for a patent infringement lawsuit ranges between $970,000 and $5.9 million in legal fees.[12] Unable to finance this significant legal expense, Brown partnered with a contingency-based law firm that would collect one-third of any jury award or settlement in exchange for absorbing the entire cost of litigation. In 2017, after nearly five years of delays and legal maneuvering, a jury returned a verdict in favor of Brown and awarded him $6 million in damages.[13]

---

[12]American Intellectual Property Law Association (AIPLA), 2013 Report of the Economic Survey.

[13]Brigid Sweeney, "Sears Ripped Off Local Tool Maker, Jury Rules," *Crain's Chicago Business*, May 16, 2017.

Spotlight on "Efficient Patent Infringement" A business may strategically disregard a patent owner's rights and engage in something called *efficient infringement*. This is a business calculation whereby a business applies a cost-benefit analysis and decides it will be cheaper to infringe patented technology than to license the technology and pay a royalty to the patent owner. The costs of this strategy may involve litigation expenses, an out-of-court settlement, or a court-imposed reasonable royalty on the use of the infringing technology. Some view this practice as abusive because it may favor large companies that can afford to defend patent lawsuits and leverage the high costs, length, and uncertainty of the legal system to the detriment of smaller companies such as start-ups and family businesses.

QUESTIONS

1. Did Sears behave unethically? What tradition of ethics did Sears appear to follow?
2. What ethical arguments would support Sears's actions?
3. What ethical arguments support LoggerHead Tools's actions?
4. Was justice achieved in this case?
5. Is it fair to have to spend five years and millions of dollars to resolve a patent dispute of this nature?
6. How would you have achieved an ethical resolution to this issue?

KEY TERMS

Ethics p. 25   The set of moral principles or core values for deciding between right and wrong.

Norms of behavior p. 26   Well-accepted standards of action given a particular circumstance.

Morals p. 27   Generally accepted *standards* of right and wrong in a given society or community.

Utilitarian p. 28   An ethical framework whereby an action is ethically sound if it produces positive results or the least harm for the most people.

Corporate social responsibility (CSR) p. 31   A broad-based identification of important business and social issues and a critique of business organizations and practices.

Social license to operate p. 32   The demands on, and expectations for, a business that emerge from neighborhoods, environmental groups, community members, and other elements of civil society.

Triple bottom line p. 33   A CSR approach that emphasizes not only the conventional creation of economic value (profits), but also a company's creation (or destruction) of environmental and social value.

Values management p. 34   A system of business ethics in the workplace that prioritizes moral values for the organization and ensures that employee and manager behaviors are aligned with those values.

Compliance department p. 37   A unit within the organization staffed by lawyers and nonlawyers that helps an organization follow rules and regulations and maintain the company's culture of values and ethics.

Community-based nonprofit p. 40   A tax-exempt entity created for the purpose of serving the community.

Benefit corporation p. 40   A corporation whose performance is based on social, environmental, and financial performance.

CASE SUMMARY 2.1 Dodge v. Ford Motor Co., 204 Mich. 459, 170 N.W. 668 (1919)

Stakeholders' Interests and Corporate Social Responsibility

Henry Ford, majority shareholder of the Ford Motor Company, announced that rather than pay a special dividend to the company's shareholders, he was going to reinvest the accumulated earnings in order to expand the company and hire more workers. He stated, "My ambition is to employ still more men, to spread the benefits of this industrial system to the greatest possible number, to help them build up their lives and their homes. To do this we are putting the greatest share of our profits back in the business." He further indicated that he wished to lower the price of the Model T car to make it more accessible to the general public. Two minority shareholders, John and Horace Dodge, sued to require payment of the dividend. The Michigan Supreme Court upheld management's right to make decisions for the benefit of the company (the business judgment rule, discussed in Chapter 30, "Corporations: Formation and Organization"); however, the court said

that "the corporation is a business, not a charity," and found for the Dodges because Henry Ford's decision was to benefit the public instead of shareholders.

CASE QUESTIONS

1. Should a corporation act solely to maximize shareholder wealth? How should a corporation balance corporate social responsibility with shareholder interests?
2. Which moral philosophy approach describes Henry Ford's stated actions? Explain
3. Although not an issue at trial, the Dodge brothers used their dividends to build their own company, Dodge Brothers Company (Dodge Motors), which was later sold to, and became a part of, Chrysler Motors. Many historians speculate that Henry Ford was actually trying to slow down the formation of the Dodge brothers' new company. If Henry Ford's alleged motive was true, was he acting in an ethical manner?

CASE SUMMARY 2.2 *In re* High-Tech Employee Antitrust Litigation, U.S. District Court, Northern District of California 11-cv-2509 (2013)

Litigation and Ethics

In 2011, high-tech workers in Silicon Valley filed a class action antitrust suit against employers Apple Inc., Google Inc., Intel Corp., and Adobe Systems Inc. The complaint alleged that these high-tech companies agreed to not poach each other's workers, thus limiting

employees' job mobility and artificially limiting their salaries. Noncompete contracts are unenforceable in California, so this human resources collusion strategy was used as an alternative to prevent high-tech workers from departing to compete at other large companies. The trial court denied the companies' motion to dismiss the case; shortly before trial, a settlement was reached between the parties for $415 million.

CASE QUESTIONS

1. Was it ethical for these high-tech companies to agree not to hire each other's employees? Explain.

2. Is it ethical to use legal means such as noncompete contracts to prevent workers from leaving to join another business? How is this case different?

3. Which CSR view did the tech companies adopt in this case?

4. Which CSR view would you apply to this issue, and how would it be resolved under your view?

CASE SUMMARY 2.3 *In re* Volkswagen "Clean Diesel" Marketing, Sales Practices, and Products Liability Litigation, U.S. District Court, Northern District of California MDL No. 2672 CRB (2017)

Values Management Plan

Volkswagen AG has agreed to pay $175 million to plaintiffs' lawyers representing U.S. drivers in litigation involving an emissions cheating scandal. Volkswagen pleaded guilty to separate criminal charges and admitted to using software that made it appear that its autos were complying with emissions requirements. The lawyers' fees are on top of a $14.7 billion deal struck between Volkswagen, government agencies, and 475,000 drivers of diesel vehicles. A group of 22 court-appointed plaintiffs' lawyers from around the country represented consumers in litigation that was consolidated in U.S. District Court in San Francisco.

CASE QUESTIONS

1. How would a values management plan have avoided the legal liability at Volkswagen?

2. Several individuals were charged with criminal violations in this case. Who should face criminal prosecution and why?

3. What should be the punishment for Volkswagen employees who engaged in illegal acts?

4. Why do individuals risk facing legal liability on behalf of their employers?

CASE SUMMARY 2.4 Goswami v. American Collections Enterprise, Inc., 377 F.3d 488 (5th Cir. 2004)

Ethics in Debt Collection

American Collections Enterprise, Inc. (ACEI) is a debt collection company that contracted with Capital One bank to provide debt collection services. Under the terms of the collection agreement, Capital One assigned delinquent accounts to ACEI for collection, and ACEI collected these debts on a contingent fee basis. Under the collection agreement, Capital One gave ACEI the authority to settle any of its accounts at a discount according to a set formula. Pooja Goswami owed approximately $900 on her Capital One credit card and failed to make her payment. Capital One then referred her debt to ACEI for collection on March 20, 2001, and ACEI pursued Goswami's delinquent account. The debt

collection letter offered to settle the outstanding balance due with a 30 percent discount off the balance owed and stated that no other offers would be forthcoming. Unbeknownst to Goswami, ACEI actually had authority to settle for up to a 50 percent discount under the terms of ACEI's agreement with Capital One. The Fair Debt Collection Act prohibits misleading statements by debt collectors.

CASE QUESTIONS

1. Is the letter misleading?

2. Is it unethical to tell a partial truth as ACEI did here?

3. Is failure to disclose a fact the same as telling a lie?

Corporate Social Responsibility

In 2007, Countrywide was the largest provider of home mortgage loans in the world. Countrywide specialized in so-called subprime mortgage loans that allowed homebuyers with relatively low credit scores the opportunity to qualify for a mortgage by paying a higher interest rate along with a monthly premium to insure the loan in case of a default. One of Countrywide's mortgages featured "teaser rates" that made initial payments artificially low. Nearly 50 percent of Countrywide's customers ended up defaulting within one year of when the teaser rate adjusted upward. Several customers filed complaints with regulatory authorities contending that Countrywide never disclosed that the payments would increase so dramatically and applicants relied on Countrywide's judgment that they could afford the loan.

CASE QUESTIONS

1. Does Countrywide have an ethical obligation to not make risky loans?
2. Does Countrywide have an ethical obligation to verify the income of its loan applicants?
3. What ethical duties do applicants have when applying for a loan?

CHAPTER REVIEW QUESTIONS

1. The principles-based approach to ethics encompasses the following theories, except:
   a. Religion.
   b. Virtue.
   c. Consequences-based approach.
   d. Categorical imperative.
   e. Natural law.

2. Introducing a new pharmaceutical drug that will save millions of lives but injure a few individuals through negative side effects is an example of:
   a. Virtue.
   b. Categorical imperative.
   c. Natural law.
   d. Consequences-based approach.
   e. Contracts-based approach.

3. The CEO of X Corp. believes that the primary responsibility of the corporation is to increase profits for its shareholders. This CEO adopts:
   a. A narrow view of CSR.
   b. A moderate view of CSR.
   c. A broad view of CSR.
   d. Natural law.
   e. Virtue.

4. The CEO of X Corp. believes that the primary responsibility of the corporation is to increase financial, environmental, and social value. This CEO adopts:
   a. A narrow view of CSR.
   b. A moderate view of CSR.
   c. A broad view of CSR.
   d. Natural law.
   e. Virtue.

5. A(n) _____ helps an organization follow rules and regulations and maintains the company's overall culture and spirit of values and ethics.
   a. Finance department
   b. Marketing department
   c. Board of directors
   d. Compliance department
   e. Accounting department

6. One way that business organizations implement values management is by developing quarterly reports.
   a. True
   b. False

7. Disregarding constituencies is an aspect of an ethical decision-making paradigm.
   a. True
   b. False

8. A community-based nonprofit does not have any shareholders.
   a. True
   b. False

9. Directors and officers in a benefit corporation are required to consider the impact their decisions have on shareholders, the environment, and society.
   a. True
   b. False

10. If a company is interested in maximizing the triple bottom line, the best type of entity to achieve that goal is likely to be a benefit corporation.
    a. True
    b. False

 Quick Quiz ANSWERS
Lady Justice

1. The blindfold is meant to capture the idea of justice as applying equally to all. Justice is blind and does not care if the parties are rich or poor, powerful or famous. The sword symbolizes the enforcement of justice. The scales represent balance and the fact that justice considers and weighs the competing arguments. These symbols adequately convey these fundamental attributes of justice, and this powerful symbol has endured since antiquity.

2. Wings could be added to represent swift justice. Justice delayed is not justice.

CHAPTER REVIEW QUESTIONS: Answers and Explanations

1. **c.** Religion, virtue, the categorical imperative, and natural law all follow universal or general moral principles. In contrast, the consequence-based approach only looks at the results of an action to determine if it has ethical value.

2. **d.** The consequences-based approach justifies an action that maximizes the good for the many and minimizes the harm to the few.

3. **a.** The narrow view of CSR views profit maximization as the sole responsibility of business.

4. **c.** The broad view of CSR emphasizes financial, social, and environmental value.

5. **d.** The compliance department helps an organization follow rules and regulations and maintains the company's overall culture and spirit of values and ethics.

6. **b. False.** A code of ethics is one way a company can implement values management.

7. **b. False.** An aspect of the ethical decision-making paradigm is to discuss the impact with various constituencies.

8. **a. True.** Community-based nonprofits do not have shareholder owners.

9. **a. True.** Directors and officers in a benefit corporation are required to consider the impact their decisions have on shareholders, the environment, and society.

10. **a. True.** In a benefit corporation, directors and officers must consider the impact their decisions have on the triple bottom line, including profits, society, and the environment.

CHAPTER 3

Business and the Constitution

In this chapter we will consider the structure and main provisions of the United States Constitution in a strategic light, for the Constitution establishes the "rules of the game" and also precommits the federal government into respecting the rights of the people and business firms by establishing in writing a set of fundamental rights and procedural protections.

Learning Objectives

After studying this chapter, students who have mastered the material will be able to:

3-1   Understand the structure of the Constitution and the strategic system of checks and balances.

3-2   Identify the main powers of each branch of the federal government.

3-3   Describe the broad scope of Congress's power to regulate commerce under the Commerce Clause.

3-4   Identify the individual rights and guarantees protected by the Bill of Rights.

3-5   Define due process and equal protection.

3-6   List the methods and steps for amending the Constitution.

3-7   Compare and contrast two major theories of constitutional interpretation: originalism and the living Constitution.

CHAPTER OVERVIEW

The United States Constitution is the world's oldest surviving constitution.[1] It is also one of the shortest and most flexible national charters in the world. But what does the Constitution do, and why is it so important? In brief, the Constitution confers broad but well-defined powers on the federal government, and

---

[1] The U.S. Constitution was drafted in 1787 and ratified in 1789. The second-oldest constitution in continuous use is Norway's, which took effect in 1814. See Zachary Elkins, Tom Ginsburg, and James Melton, *The Endurance of National Constitutions* (2009), p. 219.

at the same time, it also imposes limits on those powers by establishing many individual rights and protections. In this chapter students will learn:

- The structure of the Constitution and the strategic system of checks and balances.
- The main powers granted to the three branches of the federal government.
- The fundamental constitutional rights and protections set forth in the Bill of Rights and the Fourteenth Amendment.
- How the Constitution can be amended.
- Two major theories of constitutional interpretation: originalism and the living Constitution.
- The strategic nature of the Constitution: constitutions as two-sided commitment devices.

STRUCTURE OF THE CONSTITUTION

The original United States Constitution was drafted in 1787 and consists of a preamble and seven separate articles. The Constitution also contains 27 subsequent amendments. The first ten of these amendments are referred to as the *Bill of Rights.*

The preamble lists the main goals of the Constitution: a more perfect union, justice, domestic tranquility, national defense, general welfare, and liberty. The first three articles of the Constitution establish a strong federal government consisting of three separate but coequal branches—Congress, the president, and the federal courts—while the first ten amendments to the Constitution set forth a number of individual rights and fundamental protections, such as freedom of speech, the right to keep and bear arms, and the privilege against compulsory self-incrimination. Table 3.1 provides a summary of the original U.S. Constitution.

Before proceeding any further, let's consider two unique structural features of the original 1787 Constitution. One is federalism; the other is separation of powers. These are two of the most important concepts in constitutional law, as both of these structural features create an overall strategic system of checks and balances.

Federalism

A federal system consists of two distinct levels of government—a central or national government as well as multiple regional governments. The U.S. Constitution thus exemplifies

LO 3-1

Understand the structure of the Constitution and the strategic system of checks and balances.

TABLE 3.1	Overview of the Original Seven Articles of the 1787 Constitution
Article I	Establishes the legislative branch (a bicameral Congress composed of the House of Representatives and the Senate); sets qualifications for members of Congress; grants congressional powers (lawmaking).
Article II	Establishes the executive branch (president); sets qualifications for the presidency; grants executive powers (enforcement of laws).
Article III	Establishes the judicial branch, including a Supreme Court; grants certain judicial powers.
Article IV	Establishes the relationship between the states and the federal government; describes the power of Congress over territories and the admission of new states into the Union.
Article V	Describes the process for amending the Constitution in the future.
Article VI	Establishes the Constitution and federal law as the supreme law of the land; authorizes the national debt (Congress may borrow money); requires public officials to take an oath to support the Constitution.
Article VII	Lists the requirements for ratification of the Constitution.

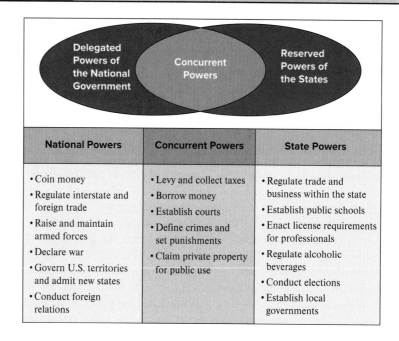

FIGURE 3.1	The Relationship between the Powers of Government

National Powers	Concurrent Powers	State Powers
• Coin money • Regulate interstate and foreign trade • Raise and maintain armed forces • Declare war • Govern U.S. territories and admit new states • Conduct foreign relations	• Levy and collect taxes • Borrow money • Establish courts • Define crimes and set punishments • Claim private property for public use	• Regulate trade and business within the state • Establish public schools • Enact license requirements for professionals • Regulate alcoholic beverages • Conduct elections • Establish local governments

the principle of **federalism**: It divides power along a vertical dimension between the federal government and the states. Moreover, the Constitution allocates some specific powers exclusively to the federal government, such as the power to declare war. Other powers are reserved to the states, such as the police power (i.e., the residual power to protect the health, safety, and welfare of the public). Yet other powers are shared by both levels of government, such as the power of taxation. Figure 3.1 uses a Venn diagram to illustrate the relationship between the powers of government.

Separation of Powers

The principle of **separation of powers** refers to the creation of multiple power centers within a single level of government. The U.S. Constitution, for example, creates three separate and coequal branches of the federal government—the legislative branch (Congress), the executive branch (the president), and the judicial branch (the federal courts)—and it divides power horizontally among them. Separation of powers thus divides power along a horizontal dimension.

Strategic Digression: Checks and Balances Why is the overall structure of our constitutional system divided into two levels (state and federal), and why is the federal level divided into three coequal branches? In short, this complex structure of overlapping powers creates a strategic system of *checks and balances*. Each level of government—and each branch within each level of government—can use its powers to monitor the other levels and branches of government. This concept was famously explained by James Madison in Federalist Paper No. 51:

> Ambition must be made to counteract ambition. The interest of the man must be connected with the constitutional rights of the place. . . . If men were angels, no government would be necessary. If angels were to govern men, neither external nor

FIGURE 3.2   The American System of Checks and Balances

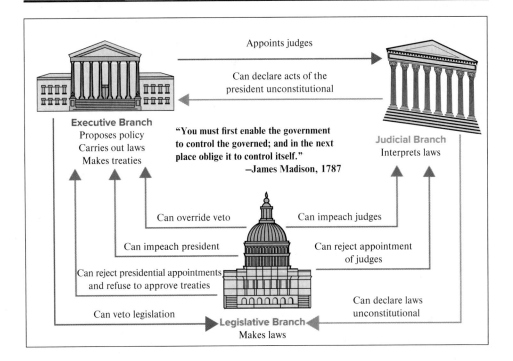

Appoints judges

Can declare acts of the
president unconstitutional

Executive Branch
Proposes policy
Carries out laws
Makes treaties

"You must first enable the government
to control the governed; and in the next
place oblige it to control itself."
—James Madison, 1787

Judicial Branch
Interprets laws

Can override veto

Can impeach judges

Can impeach president

Can reject appointment
of judges

Can reject presidential appointments
and refuse to approve treaties

Can veto legislation

Can declare laws
unconstitutional

Legislative Branch
Makes laws

internal controls on government would be necessary. In framing a government which is to be administered by men over men, the great difficulty lies in this: you must first enable the government to control the governed; and in the next place oblige it to control itself.[2]

In other words, no branch of government has a monopoly on power. Instead, each branch has sufficient powers to carry out its duties, but at the same time, each branch may exercise its respective powers to ensure that the other branches do not exceed their authority under the Constitution. Figure 3.2 provides an illustration of how these checks and balances work.

OVERVIEW OF FEDERAL POWERS

LO 3-2

Identify the main powers of each branch of the federal government.

The federal government is divided into three coequal branches, and each branch is assigned a specific set of powers.

The Congress (Article I)

Among other things, Article I of the Constitution establishes the House of Representatives and the Senate, provides a method for impeaching the president and federal judges, and delegates a finite and specific set of enumerated powers to Congress. These delegated powers, many of which are designed to promote a national economy, are listed in **Article I, Section 8** of the Constitution. For example, among the enumerated powers delegated to Congress are the power to regulate commerce, the power to lay and collect taxes, the power to borrow money, the power to coin money, the power to enact bankruptcy laws, and the power to establish copyright and patent laws. (Copyrights and patents are discussed more extensively in Chapter 50, "Intellectual Property.") In addition to these enumerated powers, Congress has the residual power to make all laws "necessary and proper" for carrying out its enumerated powers under the Necessary and Proper Clause.

[2]*The Federalist,* No. 51.

Article I of the Constitution also imposes strict limits on the powers of Congress in particular. Article I, Section 9, of the Constitution prohibits Congress from enacting an ex post facto law or bill of attainder and from granting any titles of nobility. An *ex post facto* law is one that retroactively declares someone's action to be criminal after it was committed, while a *bill of attainder* is a legislative act declaring a person or group of persons guilty of some crime. Moreover, Article I, Section 10 imposes additional limits on the powers of the states, prohibiting them from emitting their own currencies or from enacting any law impairing the obligation of contracts.

The President (Article II)

Article II of the Constitution vests general "executive power" in the president. As the chief executive of the United States and the commander-in-chief of the armed forces, the president has the power to enforce the laws made by Congress, the power to conduct foreign relations and negotiate treaties with other countries, and the power to appoint federal judges (subject to Senate approval).

In furtherance of their general power to enforce federal law, presidents often issue executive orders. Broadly speaking, an **executive order** is a presidential command or directive addressed to an officer or agency of the federal government. Although there is no constitutional provision that explicitly mentions executive orders, Congress often delegates discretionary power to the president to carry out a federal statute. In cases where there is no express congressional delegation, courts have upheld the president's power to issue executive orders based on Article II's general grant of constitutional power to the executive branch to carry out federal laws. Below is a recent example of an important executive order: President Donald J. Trump's executive order dated January 30, 2017, on "Reducing Regulations and Controlling Regulatory Costs."

EXECUTIVE ORDER

- - - - - - -

REDUCING REGULATION AND CONTROLLING REGULATORY COSTS

By the authority vested in me as President by the Constitution and the laws of the United States of America, including the Budget and Accounting Act of 1921, as amended (31 U.S.C. 1101 *et seq.*), section 1105 of title 31, United States Code, and section 301 of title 3, United States Code, it is hereby ordered as follows:

Section 1. Purpose. It is the policy of the executive branch to be prudent and financially responsible in the expenditure of funds, from both public and private sources. In addition to the management of the direct expenditure of taxpayer dollars through the budgeting process, it is essential to manage the costs associated with the governmental imposition of private expenditures required to comply with Federal regulations. Toward that end, it is important that for every one new regulation issued, at least two prior regulations be identified for elimination, and that the cost of planned regulations be prudently managed and controlled through a budgeting process. . . .

DONALD J. TRUMP

THE WHITE HOUSE,
January 30, 2017.

The Federal Courts (Article III)

Article III of the Constitution vests judicial power in one Supreme Court and in inferior federal courts established by Congress. (The organization and structure of the federal court system are discussed in more detail in Chapter 4, "The American Judicial System, Jurisdiction, and Venue.") In addition, Article III establishes the jurisdiction of the federal courts. (*Jurisdiction* is the legal authority of a court to decide a specific case. This concept is discussed more extensively in Chapter 4.)

One of the most important principles in constitutional law is the doctrine of **judicial review**, the principle that courts have the implicit authority to invalidate state or federal laws that are in direct conflict with the Constitution. This power is not enumerated in the text of the Constitution; instead, it was established by the Supreme Court in the landmark case of *Marbury v. Madison.*[3] In *Marbury,* President Thomas Jefferson had refused to deliver a commission appointing William Marbury as justice of the peace, a controversial last-minute appointment made by the outgoing president, Jefferson's rival John Adams. Although Mr. Marbury eventually lost his case, the Supreme Court ruled that when there is a conflict between a provision of the Constitution and a provision of ordinary law, courts have the authority to declare the challenged law unconstitutional because the Constitution is the supreme law of the land.

Because of its sweeping importance, *Marbury v. Madison* has been subject to intense analysis, justification, and criticism. Defenders of *Marbury* argue that judicial review is an indispensable part of the overall system of checks and balances established in the Constitution. Critics, by contrast, argue that the Supreme Court simply gave itself the power of judicial review. Most of the criticism of the *Marbury* opinion is derived from the fact that the Constitution does not expressly authorize the courts to invalidate statutes and that such a power is not mentioned in any preratification debates or in advocacy publications such as the *Federalist Papers.*

Although *Marbury* was decided over 200 years ago, it is still considered good precedent, and federal and state courts regularly cite this case as a source of authority for the power to invalidate a law or governmental action that is inconsistent with the Constitution. Over the better part of two centuries, the Supreme Court has further defined its self-declared power of judicial review, including the power of federal courts to review state court decisions to the extent that such decisions involve federal law or federal constitutional issues.

REGULATION OF COMMERCE

One of the most significant sources of Congress's powers is its enumerated power to regulate commerce under the **Commerce Clause** (Article I, Section 8, Clause 3). In full, the Commerce Clause states:

> The Congress shall have Power to regulate Commerce with foreign Nations, and among the several States, and with the Indian Tribes.

This express textual power to regulate *interstate* and foreign commerce (i.e., commerce among the states and commerce between the United States and foreign nations) is thus the fundamental source of Congress's commerce power. Not only does the text of the Constitution give Congress the enumerated power to regulate commerce, many leading cases decided by the U.S. Supreme Court have interpreted the scope of the Commerce Clause in very broad terms.

LO 3-3

Describe the broad scope of Congress's power to regulate commerce under the Commerce Clause.

---

[3] 5 U.S. 137 (1803).

Scope of the Commerce Power

Simply put, because almost every activity potentially affects commerce in some way or another, Congress can use its commerce power strategically to regulate almost any aspect of business. Specifically, the Supreme Court has held that Congress has the authority to regulate all persons and products in the flow of commerce, including:

- *channels* of interstate commerce, such as canals, highways, and railways;
- *instrumentalities* of interstate commerce, such as vehicles used in shipping products; and
- *persons and articles* moving in interstate commerce, such as passengers, finished goods, and raw materials.

Furthermore, even when an activity is noncommercial or a purely *intrastate* or local one (i.e., taking place within a single state's borders), the Supreme Court has ruled that Congress still has the power to regulate such noncommercial or local activity if the activity in the aggregate produces a *substantial economic effect* on interstate commerce. By way of example, in the leading case of *Wickard v. Filburn,*[4] the Supreme Court held that a crop cultivated for private consumption in one state was sufficiently related to *interstate* commerce under the aggregate economic effect test.

Negative Commerce Clause

The Commerce Clause not only has a "positive" aspect to it, one granting broad powers to Congress to regulate interstate and foreign commerce; it also has a "negative" or "dormant" side, imposing limits on the general police powers of the states. This facet of Congress's commerce power is commonly referred to as the *Negative Commerce Clause* or *Dormant Commerce Clause:* Even when Congress has not enacted legislation, the mere existence of congressional commerce powers under Article I, Section 8 of the Constitution restricts the states from *discriminating* against or *unduly burdening* interstate commerce.

States often regulate commerce and business activities that cross into their borders. Often, these state laws are just a pretext to protect local business firms from out-of-state competition. As a general rule, a state is free to regulate such cross-border commerce if two conditions are met: (1) The state law must be a *legitimate* effort to regulate the health, safety, or welfare of its residents, and (2) the state law must not discriminate against or impose an undue burden on out-of-state businesses.

Suppose, for example, that the Texas legislature enacts a law requiring all non-Texas-bred beef sold in Texas to undergo a health inspection and out-of-state ranchers to pay an inspection fee. The legislature justifies this inspection and fee on the basis that the law is protecting its citizens from diseased beef. In reality, however, the law was most likely enacted to protect Texas cattle ranchers from out-of-state ranchers. A federal court would likely strike down the law because it discriminates against out-of-state ranchers. Furthermore, the inspection fee and the inspection process could be viewed as unreasonably burdening interstate commerce.

The Commerce Clause Today

In recent times, the Supreme Court has attempted to impose some outer limits on Congress's extensive and far-reaching commerce powers. For example, when Congress enacted the Affordable Care Act in 2010 (the ACA, commonly called "Obamacare"), the law contained a controversial provision known as the "individual mandate," which required all persons to purchase health insurance or pay a penalty to the IRS. (An *individual*

---

[4]317 U.S. 111 (1942).

mandate is a requirement by law for designated persons to purchase or otherwise obtain a good or service.) Some business groups challenged the ACA's individual mandate in federal court, arguing that Congress did not have the power to compel people to engage in commerce. This issue was eventually resolved in the landmark case of *National Federation of Independent Business v. Sebelius.*[5] Although a narrow 5–4 majority of the justices held that the ACA's individual mandate was a constitutional exercise of Congress's power to tax, a different 5–4 majority held that the mandate exceeded Congress's power to regulate commerce.

Likewise, in cases where a regulated activity is purely *noncommercial* (such as when Congress passes a criminal statute unrelated to commerce), the Supreme Court has used increased levels of scrutiny to be sure that the activity that Congress seeks to regulate has a sufficient nexus (connection) to some legitimate economic interest. In *U.S. v. Lopez,*[6] for example, the Supreme Court used its judicial review power to invalidate the Gun-Free School Zones Act of 1990, which made it a federal crime to possess a gun within a certain distance from a school. By a narrow 5–4 margin, the Supreme Court declared the Gun-Free School Zones Act was beyond the commerce powers of Congress because gun possession was a noncommercial activity. The significance of this decision, however, remains to be seen. After the Court struck down the law in *Lopez,* Congress turned around and reenacted the exact same law, simply adding a finding of fact that gun possession in schools affected economic productivity by making it more difficult for students to obtain an education.

Five years after the *Lopez* case was decided, the Supreme Court invalidated another federal statute on the same grounds. In *U.S. v. Morrison,*[7] a narrow 5–4 majority of the Supreme Court struck down the Violence Against Women Act (VAWA), which gave victims of gender-motivated violence the right to sue their abusers in federal court for money damages. Once again, however, Congress brushed aside the Court's ruling and simply reauthorized the exact same law, this time making exhaustive findings of fact that detailed the cumulative economic effect of gender-motivated crimes.

THE BILL OF RIGHTS

LO 3-4

Identify the individual rights and guarantees protected by the Bill of Rights.

The **Bill of Rights** refers to the first ten amendments to the United States Constitution and is just as important as the original Constitution. The rights and privileges codified in the Bill of Rights are built upon those found in several earlier historic documents, including the Virginia Declaration of Rights of 1776, the English Bill of Rights of 1689, and the Magna Carta of 1215. These amendments were designed to address a wide variety of objections raised by the Anti-Federalists, who initially opposed ratification of the Constitution.

At first glance, the Bill of Rights appears to contain an extensive list of unrelated individual rights and privileges, such as the right to bear arms and the privilege against compulsory self-incrimination. But deep down there is a common thread that ties all these disparate rights and protections together: *strategic precommitment.* In brief, the Bill of Rights is designed to impose limits on the powers of the federal government by enumerating in writing ahead of time a specific set of guarantees and individual rights.

Also, the amendments contained in the Bill of Rights originally applied only to the federal government, but the door for their application upon the states was opened following ratification of the Fourteenth Amendment in 1868. Since then, both federal and state courts have used the Fourteenth Amendment to apply portions of the Bill of Rights to state and

---

[5]567 U.S. 519 (2012).

[6]514 U.S. 549 (1995).

[7]529 U.S. 598 (2000).

local governments. Although this process of extending the Bill of Rights is known as *incorporation,* it is not to be confused with the process of incorporating a business firm. (Business incorporation is discussed in Chapter 30, "Corporations: Formation and Organization.")

First Amendment (Freedom of Speech, Assembly, and Religion)

> Congress shall make no law respecting an establishment of religion, or prohibiting the free exercise thereof; or abridging the freedom of speech, or of the press; or the right of the people peaceably to assemble, and to petition the Government for a redress of grievances.

The First Amendment is perhaps the most famous provision in the entire Constitution. Designed to protect individual liberty in three overlapping domains—religion, speech, and association—the First Amendment also illustrates three deeper points about constitutional law: (1) The protections in the Bill of Rights apply against the government, not against private business firms; (2) the words of the Constitution often require interpretation; and (3) all three branches of government are engaged in this interpretative work. Let's consider each of these basic points in turn:

1. Most of the provisions of the Constitution and the Bill of Rights apply to governmental entities, not to private businesses. The importance of this first point cannot be overstated. It means that the First Amendment applies only to government employers; it doesn't apply to nongovernmental entities, regardless of whether those entities have government funding or contracts. As a result, private employers are free under the First Amendment to fire employees for attending a white supremacist rally or for posting hateful speech on the Internet. Private employers, however, are bound by various state and federal employment statutes. These laws ban discrimination based on race, religion, sex, national origin, age, disability, and various kinds of labor-union-related activity, but they don't ban discrimination based on political affiliation. (Employment laws are discussed in more detail in Chapter 40, "Employment Regulation and Labor Law.") As an aside, it is worth noting that a minority of states do ban discrimination based on political activity, especially off-the-job political activity.[8]

2. The words of the Constitution and the Bill of Rights often require interpretation. The First Amendment, for example, poses many interpretive problems and puzzles. What constitutes an "establishment" of religion? What is "speech"? Who decides whether an assembly is peaceable or not? The definition of *speech,* for example, was expanded significantly in a series of 20th- and 21st-century court decisions extending the First Amendment to anonymous speech, campaign financing, pornography, and school speech. These rulings also defined a series of exceptions to First Amendment protections. Commercial speech, for example, receives less protection under the First Amendment than political speech, and is therefore subject to greater regulation. (To avoid getting bogged down in the minutiae of Supreme Court case law, commercial speech and advertising are discussed in more detail in Chapter 44, "Consumer Protection.")

3. The last point is one that is often neglected by law professors, lawyers, and judges: The Supreme Court is not the only branch of government with the power to interpret the meaning of the Constitution or enforce its provisions. As a coequal branch of government, Congress, too, has a say in these matters. Consider religious liberty, a fundamental right protected under the First Amendment. In 1993, Congress enacted the Religious Freedom Restoration Act[9] to ensure that interests in religious freedom are protected. In addition,

---

[8]See, e.g., Eugene Volokh, "Private Employees' Speech and Political Activity: Statutory Protection against Employer Retaliation," 16 *Texas Review of Law & Politics* 295 (2012).

[9]Pub. L. No. 103-141, 107 Stat. 1488 (November 16, 1993), codified at 42 U.S.C.§§ 2000BB-200BB-4.

many states have enacted local religious freedom restoration acts that apply to state governments and local municipalities. Among other things, the federal Religious Freedom Restoration Act declares that a religiously neutral law can burden a person's exercise of religion just as much as one that was intended to interfere with religion, and therefore the law provides that the "Government shall not substantially burden a person's exercise of religion even if the burden results from a rule of general applicability." (The full text of the federal RFRA law is available here: http://www.prop1.org/rainbow/rfra.htm.)

KEY POINT

Is hate speech protected under the Constitution?

Historically, the government has had a dismal track record when it comes to protecting speech rights. The same Congress that proposed the First Amendment, for example, also enacted the infamous Alien and Sedition Acts, federal laws that punished speech that was critical of the government. During the Civil War, Abraham Lincoln issued executive orders punishing speech that was critical of his wartime presidency, and during both world wars, presidents Woodrow Wilson and Franklin D. Roosevelt used the Espionage Act of 1917 to punish speech that was critical of the government's war efforts.

But in the landmark case of *Brandenburg v. Ohio,*[10] the Supreme Court unanimously decided that the government cannot punish inflammatory speech unless that speech is "directed to inciting or producing imminent lawless action and is likely to incite or produce such action." Clarence Brandenburg was a leader of the Ku Klux Klan in Ohio. At a public rally, he urged his racist followers to join a march to Washington, D.C., to protest the presence of Jews and African-Americans in the government. He was prosecuted and convicted under an Ohio law that made it a crime to advocate the overthrow of the government.

Brandenburg's criminal conviction, however, was reversed by the Supreme Court of the United States. Inflammatory speech, or what today we would call "hate speech," is protected under the First Amendment, unless one's speech seeks to immediately incite others to commit a lawless action. This "imminent lawless action" test—known as the *Brandenburg* rule—has consistently been upheld by the courts since its articulation. After all, the whole purpose of the First Amendment is to protect speech that we hate and don't want to hear; speech that we love needs no protection.

Commercial Speech   The most common form of commercial speech—ways in which business entities communicate with the public—is advertising through print, television, radio, and the Internet. Traditionally, advertising has received little or no First Amendment protection, but the Supreme Court has gradually increased the constitutional protections for advertising.

In *Virginia State Board of Pharmacy v. Virginia Citizens Consumer Council,*[11] the U.S. Supreme Court held that purely commercial speech (speech with no political implications whatsoever) was entitled to partial First Amendment protection so long as the speech was truthful and concerned a lawful activity. In the Virginia case, the Court struck down a state law that prohibited pharmacists from advertising prices for prescription drugs. Given that the information banned by the statute was limiting the free flow of information to consumers, the Court held that such regulation violated the First Amendment.

Four years after the Virginia case, the Court expanded its analytical framework for deciding when regulations of commercial speech are constitutional. Specifically, in *Central*

---

[10]395 U.S. 444 (1969).

[11]425 U.S. 748 (1976).

Hudson Gas v. Public Service Commission,[12] the Court created a four-part test that subjects government restrictions on commercial speech to a form of intermediate-level scrutiny:

- *Part One:* So long as the commercial speech concerns lawful activities and is not misleading, the speech qualifies for protection under the First Amendment. If the speech is entitled to protection, then the government's regulation must pass the final three parts of the Central Hudson test in order for the restriction to be lawful.
- *Part Two:* The government must show that it has a substantial government interest in regulating the speech.
- *Part Three:* The government must demonstrate that the restriction directly advances the government's interest.
- *Part Four:* The government's restriction must be not more extensive than necessary (not too broad) to achieve the government's asserted interest.

Advertising and Obscenity Regulation   Sometimes commercial speech runs afoul of governmental attempts to ban or regulate materials it deems obscene. However, obscenity regulation of commercial speech is subject to the same scrutiny as any other government regulation of commercial speech. For example, a federal appellate court ruled that a state agency's decision to effectively prohibit a corporation's use of a certain label on its beer products, which the agency deemed offensive, violated the business owner's commercial speech rights. In that case, *Bad Frog Brewery, Inc. v. N.Y. State Liquor Authority,*[13] the U.S. Court of Appeals for the Second Circuit held that the labels on the brewery's beer bottles, which depicted a cartoon frog making a vulgar gesture, were protected commercial speech under the First Amendment. In particular, the court ruled that the New York State Liquor Authority failed to demonstrate the agency's asserted interest of protecting children from vulgarity when it denied Bad Frog's application to use the labels in New York on the basis that the labels were offensive. Because the labels were not misleading and did not concern an unlawful activity, the labels were a protected form of commercial speech and any government regulation must conform with the requirements set out in the four-part Central Hudson case. Ruling in favor of Bad Frog, the court remarked that a state must demonstrate that its commercial speech limitation is part of a substantial effort to advance a valid state interest, "not merely the removal of a few grains of offensive sand from the beach of vulgarity."

Second Amendment (Arms)

> A well regulated Militia, being necessary to the security of a free State, the right of the people to keep and bear Arms, shall not be infringed.

The English jurist Sir William Blackstone described the right to bear arms as an auxiliary right, one supporting the primary natural rights of self-defense and resistance to oppression and the civic duty to act in defense of one's country. The Second Amendment, which ostensibly protects the right to keep and bear weapons, is perhaps the most controversial amendment in the entire Constitution. For its part, the Supreme Court has ruled that the right to bear arms belongs to individuals, while also ruling that the right is not unlimited and does not prohibit all regulation of either firearms or similar devices.

In *District of Columbia v. Heller,*[14] the Supreme Court handed down a landmark decision that held the amendment protects an individual's right to possess and carry firearms. In *McDonald v. Chicago,*[15] the Court expanded the scope of the right to bear arms,

---

[12]447 U.S. 557 (1980).

[13]134 F.3d 87 (2d Cir. 1998).

[14]554 U.S. 570 (2008).

[15]561 U.S. 742 (2010).

expressly holding that the Due Process Clause of the Fourteenth Amendment incorporates the Second Amendment against state and local governments. Yet, despite these recent Supreme Court decisions interpreting the meaning of this language, the debate between gun control and gun rights continues.

Third Amendment (Housing of Soldiers)

Although the Third Amendment is rarely mentioned or studied today, it is one of three separate amendments in the Bill of Rights protecting private property rights. Along with the Fifth Amendment, which prohibits the government from taking private property without "just compensation," and the Fourth Amendment, which protects one's property and person from unreasonable searches and seizures, the Third Amendment prohibits the government from housing soldiers in private homes without the homeowner's consent.

> No Soldier shall, in time of peace be quartered in any house, without the consent of the Owner, nor in time of war, but in a manner to be prescribed by law.

Fourth Amendment (Search and Seizure)

The Fourth Amendment prohibits unreasonable searches and seizures. It requires governmental searches and seizures to be conducted only upon issuance of a warrant, judicially sanctioned by "probable cause," supported by oath or affirmation, and to particularly describe the place to be searched and the persons or things to be seized. Although the warrant requirement is most often thought of in the context of police agents, the Fourth Amendment applies to all government agents.

> The right of the people to be secure in their persons, houses, papers, and effects, against unreasonable searches and seizures, shall not be violated, and no Warrants shall issue, but upon probable cause, supported by Oath or affirmation, and particularly describing the place to be searched, and the persons or things to be seized.

Under the Fourth Amendment, search and seizure (including arrest) should be limited in scope according to specific information supplied to the issuing court, usually by a law enforcement officer who has sworn by it.

Broadly speaking, Fourth Amendment case law deals with three central questions: (1) how to enforce Fourth Amendment rights; (2) what government activities constitute a "search" or "seizure"; and (3) what situations do not require a warrant.

The Exclusionary Rule The main way the Fourth Amendment is enforced is by the judge-made *exclusionary rule.* This rule holds that evidence obtained in violation of the Fourth Amendment is generally inadmissible in criminal trials. In addition, evidence discovered as a result of an illegal search or seizure may also be inadmissible as "fruit of the poisonous tree," unless such evidence would have been discovered by legal means.

What Is a Search or Seizure? Courts have developed the following guidelines for determining what constitutes a *search* or a *seizure* under the Fourth Amendment:

- *Physical searches.* A search occurs when a governmental employee or an agent of the government violates an individual's reasonable expectation of privacy. A dog-sniff inspection, for example, is invalid if the inspection violates one's reasonable expectation of privacy.
- *Physical seizures of persons.* A seizure of a person, within the meaning of the Fourth Amendment, occurs when a person is not free to ignore the police and leave at will. Specifically, two elements must be present to constitute a seizure of a person. First, there must be a show of authority by the police officer or government agent. The presence of handcuffs or weapons, the use of forceful language, and physical contact are strong indicators of such authority. Second, the person being seized must submit to the

authority. Thus, an individual who ignores an officer's request and walks away has not been seized for Fourth Amendment purposes.

■ *Physical seizures of property.* A seizure of private property, within the meaning of the Fourth Amendment, occurs when there is some meaningful interference with an individual's possessory interests in the property. However, in some circumstances, warrantless seizures of objects in plain view may not constitute seizures. Also, when executing a search warrant, an officer might be able to seize an item observed in plain view even if it is not specified in the warrant.

■ *Electronic searches and seizures.* In recent years, the applicability of the Fourth Amendment to electronic searches and seizures has generated a significant amount of litigation and has received much attention from the courts. Many electronic search cases involve determining whether law enforcement can search a company-owned computer that an employee uses to conduct business. Although the case law is split, the majority of courts have held that employees do not have a legitimate expectation of privacy to information stored on a company-owned computer.

Exceptions to the Warrant Requirement To obtain a warrant, the government must first demonstrate **probable cause** to a judge or magistrate that the proposed search or seizure is justified under the law. The judge or magistrate must then consider the *totality of circumstances* and determine whether to issue the warrant.

Courts, however, have created many exceptions to the warrant requirement. To begin with, the government does not need a warrant if there are "exigent circumstances" and if it is acting with probable cause and obtaining a warrant is impractical. Other well-established exceptions to the warrant requirement include consensual searches, searches incident to a valid arrest, seizures of items in plain view, and brief investigatory stops. Investigatory stops must be temporary, and the questioning during the stop must be for a limited purpose and conducted in a manner necessary to fulfill the purpose of the stop.

Moreover, not every search or seizure raises a Fourth Amendment issue. The Fourth Amendment only protects against searches and seizures *conducted by the government* or pursuant to governmental direction. Surveillance and investigatory actions taken by private persons, such as private investigators, suspicious spouses, or nosy neighbors, are not governed by the Fourth Amendment.

Also, the Fourth Amendment does not apply against governmental action unless the target of the search can show that he has a reasonable expectation of privacy in the place to be searched or the thing to be seized. The U.S. Supreme Court has explained that what "a person knowingly exposes to the public, even in his own home or office, is not a subject of Fourth Amendment protection . . ." But what one seeks to preserve as private, even in an area accessible to the public, may be constitutionally protected.

Applying this principle, the Supreme Court has ruled that individuals generally maintain a reasonable expectation of privacy in their bodies, clothing, and personal belongings. Likewise, homeowners possess a privacy interest that extends inside their homes and in the curtilage immediately surrounding the outside of their homes, but not in the "open fields" and "wooded areas" extending beyond the curtilage. Automobile owners have a reasonable expectation of privacy in the cars they own and drive, though the expectation of privacy is less than a homeowner's privacy interest in his home.

Furthermore, courts have held that a business owner's expectation of privacy in commercial property is less than the privacy interest afforded to a private homeowner. This expectation is particularly attenuated in commercial property used in "closely regulated" industries, such as airports, railroads, restaurants, and liquor establishments, where business premises may be subject to regular administrative searches by state or federal agencies for the purpose of checking compliance with health, safety, or security regulations.

Lastly, public records, published phone numbers, and other matters readily accessible to the general public enjoy no expectation of privacy. Similarly, courts have held that individuals do not possess an expectation of privacy in their personal characteristics. Thus, the police may require individuals to give handwriting samples and voice exemplars—as well as hair, blood, DNA, and fingerprint samples—without complying with the Fourth Amendment's warrant requirement.

Fifth Amendment (Procedural Fairness and Property Rights)

At first glance, the Fifth Amendment appears to contain a collection of disparate rights. Among other things, it requires that felonies be tried only upon indictment by a grand jury; it protects individuals from being compelled to be witnesses against themselves in criminal cases; and it prohibits double jeopardy (i.e., acquittals are final). The Fifth Amendment also contains a separate Due Process Clause as well as an implied equal protection requirement (*Bolling v. Sharpe*[16]). Finally, the Amendment requires that the power of eminent domain be coupled with "just compensation" for those whose property is taken.

> No person shall be held to answer for a capital, or otherwise infamous crime, unless on a presentment or indictment of a Grand Jury . . . ; nor shall be compelled in any criminal case to be a witness against himself; nor be deprived of life, liberty, or property, without due process of law; nor shall private property be taken for public use, without just compensation.

Despite these disparate provisions, the common thread that ties them all together is the need to place limits ahead of time on the exercise of government power. In particular, this amendment is about procedural fairness and property rights. Since we will discuss due process more extensively later in this chapter and talk about criminal procedure in detail in Chapter 45, "Criminal Law and Procedure," here we focus on the protection of property rights.

Although the government (state and federal) has the power of eminent domain—the power to take private property for "public use"—the *Takings Clause,* the last clause of the Fifth Amendment, limits the power of eminent domain by requiring that "just compensation" be paid when private property is taken for public use. (The just compensation provision of the Fifth Amendment did not originally apply directly to the states, but since 1897, federal courts have held that the Takings Clause applies to the states.[17])

Sixth Amendment (Criminal Trials)

The Founding Fathers were worried that the federal government might one day abuse its enumerated powers under the Constitution to jail leaders of the opposition, so they made sure that all criminal defendants would have the right to a speedy and public trial before an impartial jury. This amendment also requires the government to inform criminal defendants of the actual charges against them and give them the opportunity to cross-examine government witnesses, the opportunity to call their own defense witnesses, and the opportunity to be represented by a lawyer.

> In all criminal prosecutions, the accused shall enjoy the right to a speedy and public trial, by an impartial jury of the State and district wherein the crime shall have been committed, . . . and to be informed of the nature and cause of the accusation; to be confronted with the witnesses against him; to have compulsory process for obtaining witnesses in his favor, and to have the Assistance of Counsel for his defence.

So, whether a criminal defendant is Edward Snowden (accused of espionage) or the notorious Mexican drug lord Joaquín "El Chapo" Guzmán (accused of drug trafficking), former North Carolina senator and vice presidential candidate John Edwards (accused of bribery and corruption) or Demetrius "Big Meech" Flenory (the reputed leader of the Black Mafia Family), he is entitled to these basic protections.

---

[16]347 U.S. 497 (1954).

[17]See *Chicago, Burlington & Quincy Railroad Co. v. City of Chicago,* 166 U.S. 226 (1897).

Seventh Amendment (Civil Trials)

In Suits at common law, where the value in controversy shall exceed twenty dollars, the right of trial by jury shall be preserved, and no fact tried by a jury, shall be otherwise re-examined in any Court of the United States, than according to the rules of the common law.

Today, whenever a private litigant brings a lawsuit for money damages (beyond nominal damages) in federal court, he or she has a constitutional right to a jury trial. In civil cases brought by private individuals against corporations or against the government, this amendment confers a huge strategic advantage in favor of the plaintiff (the party bringing the lawsuit and requesting an award of money damages), because the Seventh Amendment means that the facts of the case will be decided by a jury of the plaintiff's peers.

The Seventh Amendment proclaims the right to a jury trial in most federal civil cases. This amendment also affirms the fundamental distinction between judges and juries in federal courts. Although judges are empowered to decide questions of law, in federal cases juries get to decide questions of fact, and a jury's determination regarding the facts of a case may not be reviewed or overturned by a judge.

In addition, this amendment refers to the **common law**. The common law is a body of law developed by judges that encompasses many traditional areas of law, including property, contract, and torts, just to name a few. Broadly speaking, when a case presents a question of law, a judge is required by the principle of stare decisis to look to past decisions of relevant courts. Stare decisis, the linchpin of the common law system, is the principle that like cases should be decided alike, so if a similar dispute has been resolved in the past, the judge is bound to follow the reasoning used in the prior decision. (Common law and stare decisis are discussed in more detail in Chapter 1, "Legal Foundations and Thinking Strategically.")

Eighth Amendment (Bail, Fines, and Punishments)

Excessive bail shall not be required, nor excessive fines imposed, nor cruel and unusual punishments inflicted.

The Eighth Amendment prohibits the federal government from imposing excessive bail, excessive fines, or cruel and unusual punishments. (The U.S. Supreme Court has ruled that this amendment's Cruel and Unusual Punishment Clause also applies to the states.[18])

This amendment, however, does not define what "excessive" is or what constitutes a "cruel and unusual" punishment. That task of definition is left up to the federal courts. Also, what is interesting about this amendment is that it shows that federal judges are not above the law. Not only does this amendment limit Congress's powers when it is enacting criminal statutes; it also limits the powers of federal judges when they are exercising their sentencing powers in criminal cases.

Ninth Amendment (Unenumerated Rights)

The enumeration in the Constitution, of certain rights, shall not be construed to deny or disparage others retained by the people.

The Bill of Rights contains a short list of constitutional rights, but no list, however comprehensive, can ever be fully complete. The Ninth Amendment thus states a fundamental rule of constitutional construction: The federal government may not infringe or take away any rights belonging to the people, regardless of whether those rights are specifically listed or enumerated in the Constitution. Concrete examples of this principle include the right to vote or the right to personal privacy. Just because these basic rights are not explicitly stated anywhere within the four corners of the Constitution or in the Bill of Rights does not mean that the government is authorized to take these unenumerated rights away.

---

[18]See *Louisiana ex rel. Francis v. Resweber,* 329 U.S. 459 (1947).

Tenth Amendment (Federalism and Popular Sovereignty)

The Tenth Amendment embodies the structural principle of federalism, the idea that the United States contains two separate sources of political power: the states and the federal government. In our dual system, there are two levels of government in a single political system: a central or "federal" government as well as multiple regional governments. The Tenth Amendment and the original Constitution exemplify this federal approach. The Constitution creates a national (federal) government, but it also recognizes the preexisting political sovereignty of a finite number of coequal states.[19]

> The powers not delegated to the United States by the Constitution, nor prohibited by it to the States, are reserved to the States respectively, or to the people.

Before concluding our review of the Bill of Rights, it is also worth noting that the last two words of the original Bill of Rights are "the people." In other words, in addition to affirming the structural principle of federalism, the Tenth Amendment also reaffirms the revolutionary principle of *popular sovereignty,* the natural law idea that governments must be based on the consent of the governed.

TAKEAWAY CONCEPTS The Bill of Rights

First	Freedom of religion. Freedom of speech; freedom of the press. Right to assemble and petition the government.
Second	Right to keep and bear arms.
Third	No quartering of soldiers in private houses.
Fourth	The right to be secure against unreasonable searches and seizures.
Fifth	Grand jury presentment or indictment in criminal cases. No double jeopardy. Privilege against self-incrimination. Due process. No takings without just compensation.
Sixth	Right to speedy and public criminal trials and to an impartial jury. Right to cross-examination and to call witnesses in one's defense. Right to assistance of counsel.
Seventh	Right to a jury trial in most federal civil cases.
Eighth	Rule against excessive bail and excessive fines. Rule against cruel and unusual punishments.
Ninth	Rule of construction: The enumeration of rights in the Constitution is not exhaustive.
Tenth	Federalism: Those powers not delegated to the federal government are retained by the states. Popular sovereignty: Powers not delegated to the government are retained by the people.

---

[19]Originally, the United States consisted of 13 colonies. Today, the United States consists of 50 states, the District of Columbia, and insular territories such as Guam, Puerto Rico, and the U.S. Virgin Islands.

DUE PROCESS AND EQUAL PROTECTION

In addition to the many rights and protections enshrined in the Bill of Rights, the Constitution also protects a person's right to due process and to equal protection of the laws. Due process and equal protection are the most basic rights established in our Constitution; indeed, the right to due process can be traced all the way back to the Magna Carta of 1215, while the right to equality is the animating principle in Abraham Lincoln's historic Gettysburg Address. In a nutshell, the right to due process is designed to protect one's life, liberty, and property; the right to equal protection guarantees equality before the law.

In addition, both the right to due process and the right to equal protection apply not just to individuals but also to "legal persons," such as corporations, LLCs, and other business entities. Moreover, because due process (life, liberty, and property) and equal protection (equality before the law) are so fundamental to our constitutional order, we devote an entire section to these constitutional guarantees.

Due Process

Both the Fifth and the Fourteenth Amendments to the Constitution declare that no person shall be deprived "of life, liberty, or property, without due process of law." At a minimum, due process means two things: (1) Laws must not be vague, overly broad, or arbitrary; and (2) the government (state and federal) must provide reasonable notice, afford a neutral hearing, and provide a meaningful opportunity to present evidence before any official action is taken that would adversely affect an individual or business.

Broadly speaking, due process has two facets—procedural and substantive:

- **Procedural due process** requires that any government decision to take life, liberty, or property must be made using fair procedures. Specifically, the government must give a person reasonable notice, a fair hearing, and an opportunity to be heard.
- **Substantive due process** limits the ability of government to interfere with individual liberty. At a minimum, laws enacted by the government must be published for public inspection and must be specific enough so that a reasonable person would understand ahead of time how the law applies. Put another way, laws that are vague or overly broad are unconstitutional under the substantive due process doctrine.

The 2010 movie, *The Social Network,* contains an informal illustration of the principle of due process. In the opening scenes of the movie, Harvard sophomore Mark Zuckerberg is accused of hacking into Harvard's computers and breaching Harvard's cybersecurity. When he is called before Harvard's Administrative Board (Harvard's internal student conduct committee) to answer for his wrongful behavior, he is duly notified of the charges against him and given an opportunity to defend himself. Although Harvard is not a governmental entity, the idea of due process or fair procedures is so fundamental that it permeates many aspects of the business world and our daily lives.

Equal Protection

The Equal Protection Clause, which is set forth in the Fourteenth Amendment to the Constitution, prohibits state governments from denying their citizens equal protection of the laws. (After the Fourteenth Amendment was enacted in 1868, the U.S. Supreme Court subsequently held that the right to equal protection applies against the federal government as well.) Fundamentally, **equal protection** requires the government to treat people who are similarly situated equally. This requirement, however, does not mean that everyone must be treated in exactly the same way. When enacting legislation, the government may create constitutionally permissive *categories* and may treat each category differently, but at a minimum, persons within each category must be treated the same.

Suppose, for example, that you attend a state college or university. Do all students pay the same tuition? Most likely the answer is no. In-state residents generally pay less tuition than out-of-state students, justified by the fact that in-state students (or their parents) pay taxes that help support the school while out-of-state students' tax revenues stay in their home states. Accordingly, this classification between in-state and out-of-state students is permissible. A state college or university cannot, however, decide to charge different rates based on the students' different home states (one rate for Delaware, a second for California, a third for Iowa, etc.). Also, charging different rates based on race, religion, or national origin would not be constitutionally valid regardless of a student's state of residence.

Standards of Review

Courts generally use one of three levels of judicial review in cases involving due process and equal protection claims:

- **Rational basis test.** Under this level of judicial review, the government need only show that (1) its action advanced a *legitimate* government objective (such as health, safety, or welfare) and (2) the action was in some way related to the government's objective. Government actions that fall into this category include almost every economic regulation and tax-related law.

- *Intermediate scrutiny.* Under this intermediate standard, courts will uphold a government action as constitutional if the government can prove that (1) the action furthers an *important* government objective and (2) the action is *substantially related* to the government's objective. A relatively small number of cases fall into this category, such as cases involving gender discrimination.

- **Strict scrutiny.** When a government action impairs a fundamental constitutional right or is based on a "suspect" classification (i.e., race, national origin, or religious beliefs), courts will tend to apply a *strict scrutiny* standard in deciding whether to uphold the government action. Under this strict standard, courts will uphold the law only if (1) the government's objective is *compelling,* (2) the means chosen by the government to advance that objective are *narrowly tailored* or necessary to achieve that compelling end, and (3) no *less restrictive alternatives* exist. This is a high standard to meet. As a practical matter, when courts classify a government action as belonging in the strict scrutiny category, they are signaling that the government action is likely to be ruled unconstitutional.

Returning to our analysis of equal protection, whenever the government creates a category based on a suspect classification, courts will apply the *strict scrutiny* standard of judicial review. Specifically, courts have held that any government action based on race, religion, or national origin is automatically considered a *suspect* classification, thus triggering strict scrutiny. Courts have also held that government actions restricting the right to vote, access to the courts, or the right to interstate travel are subject to the strict scrutiny standard as well.

In the domain of substantive due process, courts often distinguish between ordinary laws and laws that burden a fundamental right. When a law restricts a fundamental right, the government must have compelling interest to justify its action, and the law must be narrowly tailored to accomplish its stated objective. Fundamental rights include the right to interstate travel, the right to privacy, voting rights, and all First Amendment rights.

In situations not involving fundamental rights, a law or governmental action does not run afoul of substantive due process if it is rationally related to any legitimate government purpose, including health, safety, and welfare. Legislation must be fair and reasonable in content and must further a legitimate governmental objective. Only when government conduct is arbitrary, or shocks the conscience, will it rise to the level of violating substantive due process. Under this "rational relation test," almost any business regulation will be upheld as reasonable.

Quick Quiz Due Process and Equal Protection

Are these laws unconstitutional?

1. Assume that a driver's license is a liberty interest or a form of property. If a driver is arrested for DUI, may his driver's license be automatically suspended without any notice or a hearing? Why is the government constitutionally required to provide some sort of opportunity for a driver to object before the government can suspend his license?

2. Suppose a city enacts a local ordinance making it illegal to "wander or stroll around from place to place at night without any lawful purpose or object." How might such a law be challenged on constitutional grounds?

3. Suppose a state enacts a law requiring all public and private institutions of higher learning in the state to charge the same tuition to in-state and out-of-state students. Would such a law be unconstitutional?

Answers to this Quick Quiz are provided at the end of the chapter.

TAKEAWAY CONCEPTS Due Process and Equal Protection

- There are two types of due process: procedural due process and substantive due process.

- Procedural due process means that any government decision to take life, liberty, or property must be made using fair procedures. Specifically, the government must give a person reasonable notice, a fair hearing, and an opportunity to be heard. Substantive due process means that laws must not be vague, overly broad, or arbitrary.

- Equal protection requires the government to treat people who are similarly situated equally.

- Courts generally use one of three levels of review in cases involving due process or equal protection.

- Most government actions, including almost every economic regulation and tax-related law, are reviewed using the rational basis test: The government need only show (1) that its action advanced a *legitimate* government objective (such as health, safety, or welfare) and (2) that the action was in some way related to the government's objective.

- In some cases, such as classifications based on gender discrimination, courts will use an intermediate standard of scrutiny: Courts will uphold a government action as constitutional if the government can prove that (1) the action furthers an *important* government objective and (2) the action is *substantially related* to the government's objective.

- Strict scrutiny is the most stringent standard of judicial review: Whenever a government action impairs a fundamental constitutional right or is based on a suspect classification, courts will uphold the law only if (1) the government's objective is *compelling,* (2) the means chosen by the government to advance that objective are *narrowly tailored* or necessary to achieve that compelling end, and (3) no *less restrictive alternatives* exist.

AN IMPORTANT DIGRESSION: AMENDING THE CONSTITUTION

LO 3-6

List the methods and steps for amending the Constitution.

The Constitution has only been amended 27 times since its ratification in 1789. This dearth of amendments is not by accident, for the framers intentionally made it very difficult to amend the Constitution. Specifically, under Article V of the Constitution, a constitutional amendment requires two separate steps, *proposal* and *ratification,* along with the approval of supermajorities at each step.

The first step in the amendment procedure consists of proposing an amendment. Amendments may be proposed either by Congress—with a two-thirds vote in both the House of Representatives and the Senate—or by a constitutional convention of states called for by two-thirds of the legislatures of the states. (In case you're wondering, only one constitutional amendment—the Twenty-first Amendment, proposing the repeal of Prohibition—has been proposed via constitutional convention.)

The second step consists of ratification. To become part of the Constitution, an amendment must not only be proposed; it must also be ratified by either the legislatures of three-quarters of the states or by state ratifying conventions in three-quarters of the states. (In all, 33 amendments have been proposed, but only 27 of these proposed amendments have formally been ratified.) The vote of each state (to either ratify or reject a proposed amendment) carries equal weight, regardless of a state's population or length of time in the Union.

Figure 3.3 presents a simple infographic explaining the various procedures for amending the Constitution.

Although this cumbersome two-step amendment procedure is simple and straightforward, it's unclear whether Article V itself can be amended. This conundrum is known as the *problem of self-amendment.*[20]

INTERPRETING THE CONSTITUTION: ORIGINALISM VERSUS THE LIVING CONSTITUTION

LO 3-7

Compare and contrast two major theories of constitutional interpretation: originalism and the living Constitution.

Because the original Constitution and the Bill of Rights are succinct documents consisting of many general provisions and concepts, such as "speech," "arms," "property," "due process," and "equal protection," the meanings of these provisions and concepts are often open

---

FIGURE 3.3 | Amending the Constitution

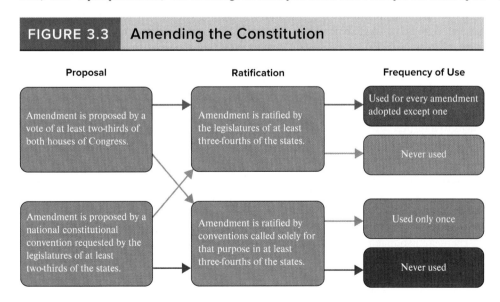

Proposal	Ratification	Frequency of Use
Amendment is proposed by a vote of at least two-thirds of both houses of Congress.	Amendment is ratified by the legislatures of at least three-fourths of the states.	Used for every amendment adopted except one
		Never used
Amendment is proposed by a national constitutional convention requested by the legislatures of at least two-thirds of the states.	Amendment is ratified by conventions called solely for that purpose in at least three-fourths of the states.	Used only once
		Never used

---

[20]See, e.g., F. E. Guerra-Pujol, "Goedel's Loophole," 41 *Capital University Law Review* 637 (2013).

to interpretation, especially when applied to a specific set of facts. In general, there are two competing theories of constitutional interpretation: originalism and the living Constitution. We discuss each theory in detail below.

Originalism

One approach to the problem of constitutional interpretation are theories of **originalism**, an umbrella term for interpretative methods that subscribe to the "fixation thesis," the notion that the meaning of the words of the Constitution is fixed and stable until and unless those provisions are formally amended under Article V. Broadly speaking, originalists believe there is an identifiable original intent or original public meaning, contemporaneous with the ratification of the Constitution (or constitutional amendment), and that this original intent or original meaning should govern its subsequent interpretation. Originalists have developed two approaches to discovering the meaning of the Constitution:

- the *original intent theory,* which holds that interpretation of a written constitution is (or should be) consistent with what was meant by those who drafted and ratified it; and
- the *original meaning theory,* which is the view that interpretation of a written constitution should be based on what reasonable persons living at the time of its adoption would have understood the ordinary meaning of the text to be.

Today, originalism is popular among most political conservatives, and this approach is most prominently associated with the late justice Antonin Scalia as well as justices Clarence Thomas, Samuel Alito, and Neil Gorsuch.

The Living Constitution

The other major approach to constitutional interpretation is called the **living Constitution** theory, the claim that the meaning of the Constitution is not fixed or static but rather dynamic and flexible. The living Constitution approach is known by a wide variety of labels and epithets, including *judicial pragmatism, flexible construction,* and *judicial activism,* but the main idea is that the Constitution is not a fossil; instead, it is a living, breathing, and evolving thing.

Perhaps the best way to appreciate the living Constitution theory of interpretation is with a simple example. Article I, Section 8 of the Constitution authorizes Congress to raise armies and maintain a navy, but it does not mention anything about aviation or outer space. Moreover, no amendment to the Constitution specifically mentions aircraft or spaceships. Nevertheless, no reasonable person would dispute Congress's power under the Constitution to establish an air force command or a space exploration agency such as NASA.

In addition, some supporters of the living Constitution argue that the living Constitution is more consistent with the original understanding of the framers of the Constitution than originalism is, because the framers purposefully wrote the Constitution in broad and flexible terms to create a dynamic and living document and authorize future generations of judges to interpret the Constitution in a flexible and pragmatic way.

Figure 3.4 presents the book covers of works written by Justice Breyer and the late Justice Scalia explaining their competing approaches to constitutional interpretation.

TAKEAWAY CONCEPT Interpreting the Constitution

There are two major theories of constitutional interpretation: originalism and the living Constitution. Originalism is the conservative view that the meaning of the Constitution is fixed and stable. With this view, the only way of changing the Constitution is by formally amending it under Article V. The living Constitution is the progressive view that the meaning of the Constitution is dynamic and flexible.

FIGURE 3.4   Books by Justices Breyer and Scalia

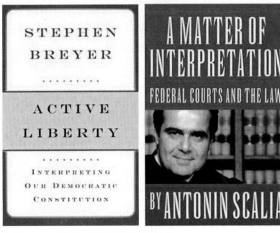

Both images: ©Roberts Publishing Services

THINKING STRATEGICALLY

©valterZ/Shutterstock

The Constitution as a Commitment Device

PROBLEM: Constitutions pose a deep puzzle. The original United States Constitution and Bill of Rights were drafted and ratified centuries ago. Why should people today treat the Constitution or Bill of Rights as having any continuing legal, political, or moral force? Or, in the words of Judge Richard Posner, "Everyone who voted for the Constitution is long dead, and to be ruled by the dead hand of the past is not self-government in any clear sense."[21]

STRATEGIC SOLUTION: The Constitution can be viewed in strategic terms as a two-sided **commitment device**: (1) It precommits future generations to respecting the legitimacy and basic structure of the government and (2) it precommits the government to respecting the rights of the people by establishing fundamental rights and protections.[22] The idea of a commitment device is, in turn, based on the strategic concept of *credible commitment,* or *precommitment.* In brief, this is a strategy in which a person or organization intentionally uses a commitment device in order to eliminate some of its choices or options *ahead of time.*[23] In military strategy, for example, an army can precommit to fight its adversary not only by crossing a bridge into enemy territory but also by burning the bridge after it is crossed! By eliminating the option of retreat, the advancing army signals to the other side that it is prepared to fight no matter what.

The same logic applies to the Constitution. For example, the Bill of Rights is designed to *precommit* the government to respecting the civil rights and property rights of the people, including business firms. By committing ahead of time to protect and preserve the rights of the people, the Bill of Rights sends a symbolic signal that the government is one of limited powers. But the idea of credible commitment in the Constitution goes much deeper than that. It also goes to the heart of democracy and the rule of law. Consider a pluralistic group of people with radically different political, moral, and religious beliefs. How can this group of people work together even though they disagree on such basic things as religion, politics, and morality? One way is by precommitting to the basic rules of the political game ahead of time. A constitution allows people to

[21]See R. A. Posner, *The Problems of Jurisprudence* (1990), pp. 137–38.

[22]See Stephen Holmes, "Precommitment and the Paradox of Democracy," in *Passions and Constraints: On the Theory of Liberal Democracy* (1995), pp. 134–77.

[23]See Chapter 2 of Thomas C. Schelling, *The Strategy of Conflict* (1960). See also Douglass C. North, *Journal of Institutional and Theoretical Economics* 149, no. 1 (Mar. 1993), pp. 11–23.

precommit not just to values but also to political procedures, such as popular representation, periodic elections, and judicial review.

The idea of credible commitment or precommitment is beautifully illustrated in the story of Ulysses and the Sirens.[24] According to this ancient legend, the Sirens had beautiful singing voices, but their songs were so enchanting and seductive that they would lure sailors toward dangerous rocks and cause them to shipwreck. Ulysses wanted to hear the beautiful songs of the Sirens, but he also wanted to avoid of the danger of shipwreck, so he made an agreement with the crew of his ship *before* they approached the Sirens. He ordered his men to tie him to the mast of the ship, and he ordered them to plug their ears with wax so they could not hear the songs themselves. This story is one of the earliest examples of a precommitment strategy. By having himself tied to the mast of his ship ahead of time, Ulysses was able to listen to the Sirens's beautiful songs and avoid the danger of shipwreck. Figure 3.5 depicts Ulysses's precommitment strategy.

In many ways, a constitution serves the same function as the lashes used to tie Ulysses to the mast of his ship. From a strategic perspective, the U.S. Constitution serves as a two-sided commitment device. On the one hand, the Constitution commits us to a strong federal government, one that is strong enough to solve national

---

[24]The legend of Ulysses and the Sirens was first recorded in Book XII of *The Odyssey* by Homer, available here: http://classics.mit.edu/Homer/odyssey.12.xii.html.

| FIGURE 3.5 | A Depiction of the Ancient Legend of Ulysses and the Sirens |

©Art Collection 3/Alamy

problems and create a level economic playing field for the entire nation. But at the same time, the Constitution also imposes limits on those federal powers by dividing power structurally (through federalism and separation of powers) and by establishing individual rights.

QUESTIONS

1. Can you think of other precommitment strategies used in the business world?

2. Have you ever used a precommittment strategy in your own life? Was it successful? Why or why not?

3. What are the relative advantages and drawbacks to using a precommitment strategy?

KEY TERMS

Federalism p. 50   The existence of a dual form of government in which there are two levels of government in a single political system: a central or "federal" government as well as multiple regional governments.

Separation of powers p. 50   The existence of multiple power centers within a single level of government.

Article 1, Section 8 p. 51   The main provision of the Constitution that enumerates the limited powers of Congress.

Executive order p. 52   An order made by the president that carries the full force of law; issued to enforce or interpret federal statutes and treaties.

Judicial review p. 53   The implied power of the courts to declare unconstitutional any law that is inconsistent with the Constitution.

Commerce Clause p. 53   That part of the Constitution that grants to Congress the power to regulate interstate and foreign commerce.

Bill of Rights p. 55   The first ten amendments to the United States Constitution.

Probable cause p. 60   A reasonable amount of suspicion supported by circumstances sufficiently strong to justify a belief that a person has committed a crime.

Common law p. 62   Law that has not been passed by the legislature, but rather is made by the courts and is based on the fundamentals of previous cases with similar facts.

Procedural due process p. 64   The idea that any government decision to take life, liberty, or property must be made using fair procedures; at a minimum, the government must give a person reasonable notice, a fair hearing, and an opportunity to be heard.

Substantive due process p. 64   The idea that laws must not be vague, overly broad, or arbitrary.

Equal protection p. 64   The idea that people who are similarly situated should be treated equally.

Rational basis test p. 65   Under the rational basis test, a government action is constitutional (1) if its action advances a *legitimate* government objective (such as health, safety, or welfare) and (2) if the action is in some way related to the government's objective.

Strict scrutiny p. 65   The most stringent standard of judicial review. Whenever a government action impairs a

fundamental constitutional right or is based on a suspect classification, courts will uphold the action only if (1) the government's objective is *compelling,* (2) the means chosen by the government to advance that objective are *narrowly tailored* or necessary to achieve that compelling end, and (3) no *less restrictive alternatives* exist.

Originalism p. 68   The conservative view that the meaning of the Constitution is fixed and stable. With this view, the only way to change the Constitution is by formally amending it under Article V.

Living Constitution p. 68   The progressive view that the meaning of the Constitution is dynamic and flexible.

Commitment device p. 69   Any method or manner of effectively reducing one's options or choices ahead of time.

CASE SUMMARY 3.1 Brown v. Board of Education II, 394 U.S. 294 (1955)

Judicial Enforcement of Equal Protection

In the landmark case of *Brown v. Board of Education,* 347 U.S. 483 (1954) (Brown I), the U.S. Supreme Court declared that racial segregation in public schools was a violation of the Equal Protection Clause of the Fourteenth Amendment. Many school districts, however, refused to comply with the Supreme Court's decision. The following year, in *Brown v. Board of Education,* 394 U.S. 294 (1955) (Brown II), the Supreme Court declared that the process of desegregation should occur

"with all deliberate speed," but the Supreme Court did not set a firm deadline or impose any specific penalties for noncompliance with its landmark 1954 decision.

CASE QUESTIONS

1. Why didn't the Supreme Court set a deadline or impose any penalties for noncompliance with its landmark desegregation decision?
2. In your opinion, does the Equal Protection Clause prohibit classifications on the basis of sexual orientation or gender identification?

CASE SUMMARY 3.2 Executive Order 10730 (Desegregation of Central High)

Executive Enforcement of Equal Protection

Three years after the Supreme Court's landmark desegregation decision in *Brown I,* nine African-American students—Minnijean Brown, Elizabeth Eckford, Ernest Green, Thelma Mothershed, Melba Pattillo, Gloria Ray, Terrence Roberts, Jefferson Thomas, and Carlotta Walls—attempted to integrate Central High School in Little Rock, Arkansas. On September 4, 1957, the

first day of school at Central High, an all-white mob gathered in front of the school, and Governor Orval Faubus deployed the Arkansas National Guard to restore order and prevent the black students from entering. In response to Faubus's action, a team of NAACP lawyers, led by Thurgood Marshall, petitioned a federal district court to issue an injunction preventing the governor from blocking the students' entry. When the nine students tried to enter the school a second time, a full-scale riot broke out and the nine students were again denied entry. Finally, after the mayor of Little Rock asked the federal government for help, President Dwight D. Eisenhower issued Executive Order 10730, placing the Arkansas National Guard under federal control and sending a thousand paratroopers from the 101st Airborne Division of the U.S. Army to help them restore order in Little Rock and allow the Little Rock Nine to attend Central High.

CASE QUESTIONS

1. Was President Eisenhower constitutionally required to send federal troops into Little Rock? Could a court have ordered him to do so?
2. If President Eisenhower had not sent federal troops into Little Rock, how would the federal courts have enforced the Supreme Court's desegregation decision?

CASE SUMMARY 3.3 Title IX

Legislative Enforcement of Equal Protection

Title IX is part of the United States Education Amendments of 1972, Public Law No. 92-318, 86 Stat. 235 (June 23, 1972), codified at 20 U.S.C. §§ 1681–1688. It states (in part): "No person in the United States shall, on the basis of sex, be excluded from participation in, be denied the benefits of, or be subjected to discrimination under any education program or activity receiving Federal financial assistance." For many years, women were not given the same academic or athletic opportunities that men were afforded. For example, prior to the enactment of Title IX, only 1 percent of collegiate athletic budgets went to female sports, and at the high school level, male athletes outnumbered female athletes 12.5 to 1. After Title IX was enacted, there was a 600 percent increase in the number of women playing college sports.

CASE QUESTIONS

1. What if Congress had never enacted Title IX? Could the federal courts or the president have prohibited discrimination in educational programs and activities? How?
2. What is the source of Congress's power to prohibit discrimination in educational programs and activities?

CASE SUMMARY 3.4 State v. DeAngelo, 930 A.2d 1236 (N.J. Supreme Ct. 2007)

Commercial Speech

During a labor dispute, a local labor union engaged in a public protest of what it claimed were unfair labor practices of a local business. As part of its protest, union members displayed a 10-foot inflatable rat-shaped balloon on a public sidewalk in front of the business involved in the dispute. A municipal ordinance banned all public displays of "balloon or inflated" signs except in cases of a grand opening. The union challenged the ordinance in court as an unconstitutional ban on commercial speech.

CASE QUESTIONS

1. Is the ordinance constitutional, or is it a valid (content-neutral) "time, place, and manner" regulation?
2. What level of scrutiny will a court apply to the ordinance?
3. What if it were an election year and the labor union had placed the inflatable rat-shaped balloon in front of the local chapter of the Republican Party or Democratic Party to protest either party's political platform?

Commerce Clause

In 2002, Congress passed the Body Armor Act that made it illegal for anyone who has been convicted of a violent felony to possess body armor. Cedrick Alderman was convicted of violating the statute, and he then challenged the law's constitutionality during appeal. Alderman contended that Congress had exceeded its authority because the law was not sufficiently related to interstate commerce.

CASE QUESTIONS

1. Is the Body Armor Act constitutional?
2. If Alderman purchased the body armor in the state where it was manufactured, how did his purchase affect "interstate" commerce?
3. Suppose Congress enacts a prospective law prohibiting all private persons from purchasing or owning body armor in the future. In your opinion, would such a law be constitutional?

CHAPTER REVIEW QUESTIONS

1. **Article I of the U.S. Constitution:**
   a. Protects freedom of speech.
   b. Contains the Supremacy Clause.
   c. Makes the president the commander-in-chief of the armed forces.
   d. Grants Congress the power to regulate commerce.
   e. Grants Congress the power to negotiate treaties.

2. **Article I of the U.S. Constitution does all of the following EXCEPT:**
   a. Establishes the Senate and House of Representatives.
   b. Outlines the powers of Congress in domestic and foreign affairs.
   c. Specifies the manner of impeachment.
   d. Grants Congress the power to regulate commerce.
   e. Establishes two methods of amending the Constitution.

3. **Article II of the U.S. Constitution:**
   a. Contains the Supremacy Clause.
   b. Establishes the powers of the president.
   c. Guarantees the right to keep and bear arms.
   d. Specifies the manner of impeachment.
   e. Grants Congress the power to regulate commerce.

4. **Article III of the U.S. Constitution:**
   a. Contains the Supremacy Clause.
   b. Establishes the powers of the president.
   c. Prohibits the quartering of soldiers in private houses.
   d. Establishes the judicial branch of the federal government.
   e. Specifies the manner of impeachment.

5. **Judicial review refers to:**
   a. The case or controversy requirement of Article III of the Constitution.
   b. The separation of powers among the three branches of government.
   c. The three standards of review used by courts in constitutional cases.
   d. The implied power of the courts to declare unconstitutional any law that is inconsistent with the Constitution.
   e. The implied power of the executive branch to veto Supreme Court decisions that are inconsistent with the Constitution.

6. **The Commerce Clause applies to interstate commerce as well as foreign commerce.**
   a. True
   b. False

7. **The Due Process Clause in the Bill of Rights declares that no state shall deny any person due process of law.**

   a. True

   b. False

8. **The privilege against compulsory self-incrimination is located in the First Amendment.**

   a. True

   b. False

9. **The right to assistance of counsel in criminal cases is guaranteed by the Sixth Amendment.**

   a. True

   b. False

10. **The text of the Equal Protection Clause of the Fourteenth Amendment prohibits Congress from discriminating on the basis of race, national origin, and other suspect categories.**

    a. True

    b. False

 Quick Quiz ANSWERS
Due Process and Equal Protection

1. This question involves procedural due process. Before the government can take any action depriving someone of his life, liberty, or property, it must provide him with reasonable notice and a hearing, and the government must give him the opportunity to object to the government's action.

2. Vague or overly broad laws could be struck down by the courts on substantive due process grounds. In this particular case, one could argue that the anti-panhandling law described here is too vague or overly broad, since it contains a blanket prohibition against all wandering and strolling at night, i.e., the law is overinclusive. Alternatively, one could argue that there is no rational relation between the government's objective (reducing panhandling on the streets) and "wandering or strolling at night," i.e., the law is underinclusive.

3. This question involves equal protection, the police power, and rational review. Here, the state is mandating equal treatment of in-state and out-of-state students, but does it have the power to impose this mandate on private colleges and private universities? States have broad police powers to protect the health, safety, and welfare of its residents, and courts will generally use the rational basis test to determine whether an economic regulation is constitutional. Here, the government will have to prove that its equal tuition mandate advanced a *legitimate* government objective (such as health, safety, or welfare) and that it was in some way related to the government's objective.

CHAPTER REVIEW QUESTIONS: Answers and Explanations

1. d. Article I grants Congress the power to regulate commerce. Answer *a* is incorrect because freedom of speech is protected under the First Amendment to the Constitution. Answer *b* is incorrect because the Supremacy Clause appears in Article VI of the Constitution. Answers *c* and *e* are incorrect because Article II, not Article I, makes the president the commander-in-chief of the armed forces and gives the president the authority to negotiate treaties.

2. e. Article V of the Constitution establishes the methods of amending the Constitution. Answers *a, b, c,* and *d* refer to provisions in Article I of the Constitution and are thus incorrect.

3. b. Article II establishes the powers of the president. Answer *a* is incorrect because the Supremacy Clause appears in Article VI of the Constitution. Answer *c* is incorrect because the right to bear arms is protected by the Second Amendment.

Answers *d* and *e* are incorrect because Article I, not Article II, specifies the manner of impeachment and grants Congress the power to regulate commerce.

4. **d.** Article III of the Constitution establishes the judicial branch of the federal government. The remaining responses are therefore incorrect.

5. **d.** Judicial review refers to the implied and inherent power of courts to declare unconstitutional those laws inconsistent with the Constitution. Answer *a* is incorrect because Article III does not refer to judicial review at all; answer *b* refers to the separation of powers; and answer *c* refers to the specific standards of review used by courts in constitutional cases. Answer *e* is incorrect because the president does not have the power to veto Supreme Court decisions.

6. **a. True.** The power to regulate commerce is an enumerated power that is explicitly granted to Congress in Article I of the Constitution, and the text of the Commerce Clause refers to both interstate and foreign commerce.

7. **b. False.** The text of the Due Process Clause in the Bill of Rights appears in the Fifth Amendment and refers only to Congress, not the states. As a result, the Due Process Clause in the Bill of Rights applies to the federal government. (The Due Process Clause in the post-Civil War Fourteenth Amendment, however, does refer to the states.)

8. **b. False.** The privilege against self-incrimination is protected by the Fifth Amendment, not the First.

9. **a. True.** The right to assistance of counsel is guaranteed by the Sixth Amendment.

10. **b. False.** The Fourteenth Amendment is directed toward the states, not Congress. The Equal Protection Clause of the Fourteenth Amendment thus prohibits the states (not Congress) from discriminating on the basis of race, national origin, and other suspect categories.

CHAPTER 4

The American Judicial System, Jurisdiction, and Venue

 THINKING STRATEGICALLY

As the economy creates more opportunities for businesses to enter new markets that cross state and national borders, the risk of being sued by an out-of-state or foreign party increases. In this chapter's *Thinking Strategically*, we discuss strategic use of contractual language, known as forum selection clauses, which addresses that potential threat.

Learning Objectives

After studying this chapter, students who have mastered the material will be able to:

4-1   Explain the roles of courts and the structure of the American judiciary.

4-2   Differentiate federal courts from state courts.

4-3   Identify the responsibilities of trial courts versus appellate courts.

4-4   Articulate how courts apply precedent.

4-5   Differentiate between subject matter jurisdiction versus personal jurisdiction.

4-6   Apply the minimum-contacts test in a cyber setting and describe the importance of the *Zippo* sliding scale.

4-7   Recognize how rules of venue affect the location of a trial.

CHAPTER OVERVIEW

Courts play an integral role in American law because they provide a forum to resolve disputes and because judicial decisions help shape or create legal doctrines. A fundamental knowledge of the function and structure of the judiciary helps business owners and managers weigh the strategic factors (e.g., costs, time) of resolving business disputes through courts. This chapter covers the role and structure of the American judicial system, the function and authority of state and federal courts, and the circumstances that determine whether a court has jurisdiction (the authority to hear a certain case).

ROLE AND STRUCTURE OF THE JUDICIARY

The American legal system is primarily structured around a set of federal and state **courts** that are collectively known as the **judiciary**. The judiciary has two primary roles. First, courts *adjudicate* disputes. This means that many courts are responsible for interpreting and applying the rules of law and principles of equity to settle legal cases and controversies. Second, certain courts exercise *judicial review*. In this role, these courts review decisions of lower courts and the actions of other branches of the government to be sure that the decisions and actions are consistent with existing law and that they comply with constitutional requirements. Which courts are authorized to hear which cases is determined by a set of legal principles collectively called **jurisdiction** and **venue**. These principles are discussed later in this chapter.

LO 4-1

Explain the roles of courts and the structure of the American judiciary.

STATE VERSUS FEDERAL COURTS

The U.S. court system has two separate structures that operate in tandem. **State courts** resolve matters dealing primarily with cases arising from state statutes, state common law, and state constitutional law. In some cases, state courts also apply federal constitutional provisions. **Federal courts** are concerned primarily with national laws, federal constitutional issues, and other cases that are outside the purview of state courts. It is important to note that not all courts have the *authority* to hear all cases.

State Courts

The majority of court cases filed in the United States are filed in state courts. All states have two levels of courts: **state trial courts** and **state appellate courts**.

State Trial Courts   When one party alleges a violation of some legal right or standard, the aggrieved party, called the **plaintiff**, may bring a lawsuit against the alleged violator, called the **defendant**, in a trial court. Trial courts are where cases are originally brought and heard. They are structured to adjudicate matters through an established procedure in which both parties present evidence, question witnesses, and articulate legal arguments about the case. Note that the role of trial courts is examined in the context of a civil lawsuit, known as *litigation,* in the next chapter.

The names of the courts vary widely from state to state. However, all state trial courts have either *general authority* to hear a case or *limited authority* to hear a particular type of case. Courts of general authority are organized into geographic districts (often divided by county or a set of contiguous counties) and hear many types of cases, including breach of contract, employment discrimination, personal injury, criminal cases, property disputes, and so forth. Courts of limited authority are often confined to a particular type of dispute such as family law matters (e.g., divorce or adoption cases) or probate courts (dealing with issues related to wills and trusts). Some states, notably Delaware, have courts devoted solely to issues relating to commercial law matters. Delaware calls these forums *chancery courts*.

It is important to remember that state trial court decisions are binding *only* on the parties involved in the dispute. Trial court decisions do not set precedent for future disputes or parties. Only appellate-level courts set precedent. Trial courts are often divided into those that hear civil matters, where one party seeks redress for a wrong committed by another party (such as a lawsuit for breach of contract), and those that hear criminal matters, where a party accused of a crime (such as theft) is put on trial.

Local Courts   For minor matters and cases with a dollar value that is relatively low (typically less than $10,000 depending on the state), states provide local courts known alternatively as *municipal courts, small-claims courts, justice-of-the-peace courts,* or *district justices*. Such courts provide local access to a court for the purpose of resolving relatively simple disputes on an expedited basis. These courts are sometimes referred to as *inferior* trial courts because states provide an automatic appeal for the losing party, usually to the state trial court, for decisions from local judges.

State Appellate Courts

After a trial court has rendered a decision, the losing party must decide whether to file an appeal in a state appellate court. Appellate courts are primarily concerned with reviewing the decisions of trial courts. Most states also have an intermediate appellate court, which is where the first appeal is filed. In some states, appeals to any appellate-level courts are *discretionary*. That is, the party requesting the appeal (known as the *petitioning* party or the *appellant*) files a document with the court petitioning for an appeal. Based on a variety of factors, the appellate court then decides whether to allow the appeal to be heard by the court. In other states, the losing party has an automatic right of appeal to the intermediate-level court but only a discretionary appeal to the highest court. If the appellate court denies an appeal, the trial court ruling is *binding* on the parties in that case.[1]

If the court grants an appeal, the appellate judges engage in the process of determining whether the trial was conducted in accordance with the legal rules and doctrines of that state. Appellate courts assess the lower court's decision by (1) reviewing lower court transcripts and rulings, (2) reading documents written by attorneys for each side articulating legal reasons why their side should prevail (known as *briefs*), and (3) sometimes allowing the attorneys to engage in *oral argument,* which requires the attorneys for the parties to appear in front of the appellate panel of judges to participate in an oral question and answer session on the legal issues in the case. The court focuses on such issues as the rulings of the trial judges, the admission of evidence, jury selection, and other factors that may have been a factor in the original trial's outcome. Note that appellate courts, except in rare cases, do *not* consider new evidence in their review. Using these methods, appellate courts determine whether an error was made at the trial level. In cases where the error is substantial enough, a court may reverse the decision of the trial court and send the case back to the trial court (known as **remand**).

The major distinction between state trial courts and state appellate courts is that appellate court decisions set *precedent* that is binding on all lower courts. Because one of the primary purposes of the law is to provide some degree of reliability and uniformity in adjudicating cases, trial courts are required to follow the rulings of appellate courts. In states where there is an intermediate-level appellate court, the highest court is often (although not always) called the *state supreme court*. A state supreme court's decision is final and binding on *all* courts in that state (including federal courts located in that state) so long as the decision does *not* involve a federal constitutional issue.

States vary as to how state trial court judges are selected. Some states elect all trial and appellate judges as part of their general elections; in other states, the governor appoints a judge, but the appointment is subject to review and rejection by the state legislature (typically the state senate). Some states use a hybrid method where local judges are elected and appellate court judges go through an appointment process.

Federal Courts

The federal government also operates a system of courts. The principal trial courts are the **U.S. District Courts**. Federal appellate courts are called **U.S. Courts of Appeals**. Because these courts are divided into circuits, federal appellate courts are frequently referred to as the *circuit courts of appeals*. Finally, the **U.S. Supreme Court**, the ultimate arbiter of federal law, reviews not only decisions of the federal courts but also state court decisions that involve some issue of federal law, such as applying a provision of the U.S. Constitution.

U.S. District Courts

District courts serve the same primary trial function as state trial courts, but they address issues involving federal matters such as federal statutes, regulations,

---

[1] In extraordinary cases, a petitioning party sometimes has the right to appeal to a higher court if the intermediate appellate court denies the appeal.

or constitutional issues. There is at least one federal district court in every state and one for the District of Columbia. Federal district courts also may decide certain matters involving *state law* when the parties are from different states and meet other jurisdictional requirements. These federal trial courts hear a variety of matters and render decisions that are binding only on the parties involved in the dispute. Some federal courts, such as the Bankruptcy Court, the Tax Court, and the Court of International Trade, specialize in certain areas of law.

Circuit Courts of Appeals   The 13 U.S. Courts of Appeals, each of which reviews the decisions of federal district courts in the state or several states within its circuit, are the intermediate appellate courts in the federal system. Two exceptions are the Court of Appeals for the District of Columbia, which decides cases originating in Washington, D.C., and the Federal Circuit Court of Appeals, which decides a variety of exclusively federal issues such as patent, copyright, and trademark cases or cases where the United States is named as a defendant. The Federal Circuit is said to have national jurisdiction because its authority is not confined to one particular circuit. As with state appellate courts, federal circuit courts of appeal set precedent, and their decisions are binding on all the states in that circuit. Appeals to the federal circuit courts of appeal are discretionary.

The circuits are divided geographically, as shown in Figure 4.1.

U.S. Supreme Court   The ultimate arbiters of federal law are the nine justices of the U.S. Supreme Court ("the Court"). Although the Court has both original[2] and appellate jurisdiction, the primary role of the Court is to finalize a legal decision on any given case. In addition to the Court's authority to decide an appeal from any federal circuit court of appeal, the Court also may exercise its appellate authority over state courts when a federal issue is involved. The Court also has the final authority on matters of interpretation of all federal law and the U.S. Constitution.

FIGURE 4.1	Map of the U.S. Circuits

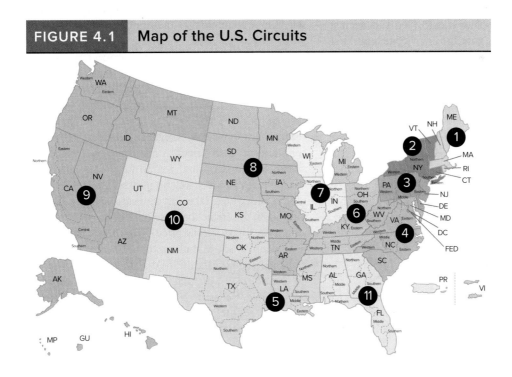

---

[2]The Court's original jurisdiction is limited to cases involving ambassadors and selected other public officials and those cases where the disputing parties are two states.

The bench of the U.S. Supreme Court including the "argument clock" used keep each side's argument to 30 minutes.
©Erik Cox Photography/Shutterstock

Of course, the Court's review is discretionary and, in fact, the odds of getting a case to the Court are very low. Typically, the Court grants only about 1 percent of the requests it receives to hear a case each year. An aggrieved party may petition the Court for an appeal using a petition for writ of certiorari that explains the basis for the appeal. Upon review, if four of the nine justices vote to hear the case, the parties in the case are then permitted to pursue the appeal.

Circuit Splits   While the Supreme Court is known to most of the country as the court that decides highly publicized and politically charged constitutional issues, more often cases are decided by the Court when the appellate courts have issued conflicting opinions. This conflict is called a *circuit split* or *conflict among the circuits*. For example, when several federal appellate courts disagreed whether state "no surcharge" laws (i.e., consumer statutes prohibiting merchants from charging credit card users an amount above the retail price) were lawful, the U.S. Supreme Court resolved the conflict. Case 4.1 gives us a look inside the Court's reasoning process.

CASE 4.1 Expressions Hair Design et al. v. Schneiderman, 137 S.Ct. 1144 (2017)

FACT SUMMARY   A New York state statute prohibits merchants from imposing a surcharge "on a holder who elects to use a credit card in lieu of payment by cash, check, or similar means." Several merchants covered under the statute filed suit against state officials arguing that the law violates the First Amendment by regulating how they communicate their prices. The trial court ruled in favor of the merchants, but the U.S. Court of Appeals for the Second Circuit reversed and vacated the trial court's order. Multiple other circuits, including the Eleventh Circuit and the Fifth Circuit, concluded that similar surcharge bans in other states directly target speech. Those courts held that since the government cannot identify a plausible governmental interest justifying the speech-based restrictions imposed by surcharge laws, they fail to withstand constitutional scrutiny. The U.S. Supreme Court accepted the case in order to resolve the conflict.

SYNOPSIS OF DECISION AND OPINION   The U.S. Supreme Court reversed the appellate court and ruled in favor of the merchants. They declared the law unconstitutional under the First Amendment because it unlawfully regulates speech. The Court pointed out that a surcharge ban is not like typical price regulation, which simply regulates the amount a store can collect. The law tells merchants nothing about the amount they are allowed to collect from a cash or credit card payer. Instead, it regulates how sellers may communicate their prices.

WORDS OF THE COURT: Communication of Prices   "The law tells merchants nothing about the amount they are allowed to collect from a cash or credit card payer. Sellers are free to charge $10 for cash and $9.70, $10, $10.30, or any other amount for credit. What the law does regulate is how sellers may communicate their prices. A merchant who wants to charge $10 for cash and $10.30 for credit may not convey that price any way he pleases. He is not free to say "$10, with a 3% credit card surcharge" or "$10, plus $0.30 for credit" because both of those displays identify a single sticker price—$10—that is less than the amount credit card users will be charged. Instead, if the merchant wishes to post a single sticker price, he must display $10.30 as his sticker price. Accordingly, while we agree with the Court of Appeals that [the statute] regulates a relationship between a sticker price and the price charged to credit card users, we cannot accept its conclusion that [the statute] is nothing more than a mine-run price regulation.

(continued)

In regulating the communication of prices rather than prices themselves, [the statute] regulates speech."

Case Questions

1. What was the primary theory of the merchants as to why the statute was unconstitutional?
2. Why is it important that the law "regulates how sellers may communicate their prices"?
3. *Focus on Critical Thinking:* Merchants argue that any credit card surcharge is simply passing along the fee that merchants pay to the credit card companies when a consumer uses a credit card. Do you find that argument compelling? Are there other examples of merchants passing along fees to consumers? Should the government be involved in regulating transactions between merchants and consumers? Why or why not?

Judicial Selection   All federal judges are selected via the appointment process. The president nominates candidates for federal trial and appellate courts, subject to review by the Senate. The Senate may either confirm or reject a judicial nominee. If a nominee is rejected, the president continues to nominate candidates until one is confirmed. Once confirmed, the nominee is sworn in as a federal judge and may only be removed from office by impeachment.

TAKEAWAY CONCEPTS Role and Structure of the Judiciary

- The primary roles of trial courts are to adjudicate disputes and resolve cases.
- The primary role of appellate courts is to review the decisions of trial courts.
- State courts generally handle matters dealing with state statutes, state common law, and state constitutional law.
- The majority of cases filed in the United States are filed in state courts.
- Federal courts are concerned primarily with national laws, federal constitutional issues, and other cases that are outside the purview of state courts.
- There are two levels of courts: (1) trial courts, where parties present their cases and evidence, and (2) appellate courts, which review the decisions of lower courts.
- Only appellate courts set precedent. The decisions of trial courts are binding only on the parties in the particular matter before the court.
- Federal trial courts are called *district courts*. Federal appellate courts are called *circuit courts of appeal*.
- The U.S. Supreme Court is the ultimate arbiter of federal law.

APPLYING PRECEDENT

As we've discussed, only courts of authority (appellate courts) set precedent. Recall from Chapter 1, "Legal Foundations and Thinking Strategically," that precedent springs from the doctrine of stare decisis (let the decision stand) and is a foundation of American law. This judicial power is also called *binding authority;* it requires a lower court to apply law as decided by a higher court with authority over the lower court. For example, the federal District Court of New Jersey is bound by the U.S. Court of Appeals for the Third Circuit because the District Court of New Jersey is in the Third Circuit's geographical boundaries. By the same token, the District Court of New Jersey is not bound by any *other* U.S. court of appeals decisions. On issues of state law, the highest appellate court in the state sets precedent for *all* lower courts.

LO 4-4

Articulate how courts apply precedent.

Persuasive Value

In cases where no binding authority exists on a particular legal issue, courts may look to decisions by either lower courts or appellate courts outside of their own geographic authority for reasoning they find to be *persuasive*. These are known as *cases of first impression*, and a court may consider the reasoning of courts of other jurisdictions that have dealt with the same or similar issues for their persuasive value.

Distinguishable Cases

If a lower court deviates from binding precedent on a settled legal issue, the court must justify its decision by articulating an essential *factual or legal difference* from the precedent case. To distinguish a case, a court shows that a prior case, cited as applicable to a pending case, is actually inapplicable due to an essential difference between the two cases.

TAKEAWAY CONCEPTS Applying Precedent

Concept	Effect	Example
Precedent established by court of authority	Binding on all lower courts in that jurisdiction.	U.S. Supreme Court decision on the First Amendment binding on all courts in the United States.
Case of first impression	Courts look to lower courts and courts outside their jurisdiction for persuasive reasoning.	Wyoming Supreme Court finds reasoning of Florida Supreme Court to be persuasive on an issue where no precedent is set.
Distinguishable	Factual or legal difference from precedent.	Trial court deviates from precedent because of a factual difference in cases.

LO 4-5

Differentiate between subject matter jurisdiction versus personal jurisdiction.

JURISDICTION

As noted earlier, it is important to understand that not all courts have the authority to hear all cases. The law sets out rules that govern which courts may decide certain cases. *Jurisdiction* is a court's authority to decide a particular case based on (1) who the parties are and (2) the subject matter of the dispute.

Jurisdiction and Business Strategy

The increasing integration of advanced technology in product and service delivery has made jurisdiction and venue important parts of business planning. As with all legal decisions that business owners and managers make, jurisdiction must be considered in a cost-benefit context.

Consider a dispute between two hypothetical companies, Ultimate Widget Corporation (UWC) and Knock Off Stores Inc. (Knock Off). Suppose UWC, a New York company, is considering suing Knock Off, a California company, over a trademark dispute. UWC management should consider the costs involved in pursuing the suit in a business context. In considering their strategy, UWC's management must consider (1) the total amount of the possible recovery from Knock Off; (2) the actual benefits UWC will reap from the prevention of Knock Off's use of the trademark; and (3) any alternative dispute resolution methods available.

If Knock Off is a small company and not likely to dilute the trademark in any of UWC's markets, it may not be worth the costs of litigation to sue UWC in their home state. Pursuing the infringement action would involve UWC's expense of traveling to California, hiring local counsel in California, and the lost hours of managers and other witnesses who would be required to travel to testify and be deposed for the case. However, if a New York court could possibly have jurisdiction over the dispute, that would change the dynamics of the cost-benefit analysis because the expenses of the suit would be markedly lower.

Overview of Jurisdiction

The origins of federal jurisdiction law are found in the U.S. Constitution, specifically, the Due Process Clause of the Fifth and Fourteenth Amendments. In essence, the Constitution prohibits the deprivation of a property interest (usually money damages) without a legal process being applied. While the origins of jurisdiction lie in the Constitution, appellate courts and legislatures have shaped the framework and rules used by modern courts to analyze jurisdiction questions.

Two-Part Analysis Jurisdiction requires a two-part analysis: A court must have both **subject matter jurisdiction** and **personal jurisdiction** (also known as *in personam jurisdiction*). Subject matter jurisdiction is the court's authority over the *dispute* between the parties, while personal jurisdiction is the court's authority over the *parties* involved in the dispute.

For example, suppose Baker is employed by Auto Parts Company (APC) to drive a delivery vehicle. One morning, Baker is on a delivery and due to his lack of care (called *negligence*),[3] he hits Cain, a pedestrian who is crossing the street in a designated public crosswalk located directly in front of the hotel where she is staying. Cain is severely injured and considers filing a lawsuit against Baker to reimburse her for losses she suffered as a result of the incident. However, Cain discovers that Baker is without assets and, in the state where the incident took place, the law provides that APC is responsible for Baker's actions. Consequently, Cain decides to pursue a lawsuit against APC.

Initially, Cain must decide in *which* court to file the lawsuit. She probably will have some choice, but it will be limited because the court selected must have jurisdiction over a case of this type of dispute (a negligence case) and over the defendant (APC). Cain will likely bring this suit in a *state* trial court because the jurisdiction of federal courts is limited in this type of case. Be sure to remember the basic facts of the Cain v. APC hypothetical case as it will be used throughout this section to illustrate various aspects of jurisdiction and venue.

Subject Matter Jurisdiction: Authority over the Dispute

Recall from the discussion at the beginning of this chapter that state and federal statutes define which courts have *general* jurisdiction and which have *limited* jurisdiction. State statutes give state trial courts subject matter jurisdiction on virtually all matters involving a state statute, state common law, or a state constitutional issue.

Federal district courts are limited by the Constitution and by federal statutes as to what types of cases they have authority to hear. In order for a federal court to have subject matter jurisdiction in a case, the issue generally must involve a **federal question** (e.g., some issue

---

[3]The legal term for such a lack of care is *negligence*. Negligence is discussed extensively in Chapter 42, "Torts and Product Liability."

arising from the U.S. Constitution, a federal statute or regulation, or federal common law). Federal courts also have *exclusive* jurisdiction over all cases where the United States is a **party** in the litigation. For example, a business that sues the Internal Revenue Service for a federal tax refund must pursue the matter in federal court because it involves the United States as a party named in the lawsuit.

Even if there is no federal question and the United States is not a party to the litigation, federal courts may have subject matter jurisdiction over cases involving parties from *two different states* (or if one party is from outside the United States), known as **diversity of citizenship**. An additional requirement that applies only in diversity of citizenship cases is that the amount in controversy must be more than $75,000. For example, if a dispute arises in which a business in New York sues a business in California for breach of contract for $80,000, the parties are said to be *diverse,* and a federal court sitting in New York or California would have subject matter jurisdiction in the case. Note that the amount in controversy requirement applies *only* when a court has jurisdiction via the diversity of citizenship requirement. In a diversity case, a federal court will be applying *state law* because the dispute is likely to involve issues governed by state statutes or common law.

 Quick Quiz Subject Matter Jurisdiction

Does a federal district court located in New Jersey have *subject matter* jurisdiction?

1. A New Jersey businessperson sues her in-state business partner for breach of contract that resulted in $40,000 in losses.
2. The U.S. Environmental Protection Agency sues a New Jersey corporation for cleanup costs under a federal statute that regulates local waste disposal.
3. A Pennsylvania resident sues a New Jersey corporation for an injury caused by the corporation's product resulting in $90,000 in unpaid medical bills.
4. A New Jersey corporation is sued by a New Jersey resident under the federal employment discrimination statutes.
5. A New Jersey resident sues the U.S. government in an appeal from the ruling of the U.S. Copyright Office.

Answers to this Quick Quiz are provided at the end of the chapter.

Recall the Cain v. APC hypothetical case from the beginning of this section. Assume that Cain is a resident of Massachusetts who was visiting Texas, where APC is headquartered, when the incident occurred. Cain would likely prefer to file the lawsuit in her home state so that she doesn't have to spend time and resources traveling to Texas several times for pretrial and trial tasks. Assuming that Cain's injuries were sufficiently severe to warrant damages exceeding $75,000, Cain may consider filing suit in the federal district court in Massachusetts. That court has subject matter jurisdiction because the parties are diverse and the amount in controversy has been satisfied. However, that is only the first part of the jurisdiction analysis. Once it has been determined that the federal district court in Massachusetts has subject matter jurisdiction, Cain must also clear another substantial jurisdictional requirement: *personal jurisdiction*.

Personal Jurisdiction

Personal jurisdiction is a court's authority over the *parties* in a legal dispute. In this context, a party may be either an individual or a business entity such as a corporation. Since 1877, in the landmark case *Pennoyer v. Neff*,[4] the U.S. Supreme Court has articulated a framework for the exercise of personal jurisdiction by lower courts with the objective of providing *fairness* to the parties and complying with federal constitutional requirements related to due process. Of course, courts have modified this framework as necessary based on the realities of industrial and technological advances in society. This framework is used to determine jurisdiction over the defendant by both that state's courts *and* federal district courts within that state. Typically, a jurisdiction analysis focuses on the *conditions* of the controversy and the *actions* of the defendant.

Out-of-State Defendants

A court uses a two-prong test to determine whether it has personal jurisdiction over a party who does not reside in the state in which the court is located. First, the court's jurisdiction must be authorized by a **state long-arm statute** that grants the court specific authorization over the defendant due to the defendant's conduct or other circumstances. As the name implies, long-arm statutes are intended to allow a court to "reach" into another state and exercise jurisdiction over a nonresident defendant. Typically, long-arm statutes provide for jurisdiction if an out-of-state defendant (1) transacts business within the state's borders, (2) commits a negligent act in that state that results in a loss to another party, or (3) owns property in the state.

The second prong requires a court to ensure that exercising jurisdiction over an out-of-state defendant meets the constitutional requirements of fairness and due process. This means that courts must consider the plight of the defendant who has been forced to defend a lawsuit in another state by taking into account the burden on the defendant. Courts examine two specific questions in deciding these fairness and due process issues.

Question No. 1: Does the defendant have some level of **minimum contacts** with the state, such as regularly shipping products to consumers in that state? If a defendant has continuous and systematic contact with a particular state, this will be sufficient to satisfy the minimum-contacts requirement.

Question No. 2: Has the defendant *purposefully availed* himself by some affirmative act directed to that specific state? Whether a company has purposely availed itself in a state was addressed by the U.S. Supreme Court in *Asahi Metal Industry Co., Ltd. v. Superior Court of California*.[5] When a company performs "some act by which [the company] purposefully avails itself of the privilege of conducting activities within the forum State, thus invoking the benefits and protections of its laws," then the availment test is met.

In Case 4.2, the U.S. Supreme Court applies the minimum-contacts test.

CASE 4.2 Goodyear Dunlop Tires v. Brown, 131 S. Ct. 2846 (2011)

FACT SUMMARY   Two 13-year-old boys from the state of North Carolina, Matthew Helms and Julian Brown, had traveled to France to participate in a soccer tournament. The two boys were involved in a bus wreck outside Paris on their way back to the airport and died of injuries suffered in the accident.

The parents of the boys believed the accident was due to a defective tire manufactured by a foreign subsidiary of the Goodyear Tire and Rubber Company (Goodyear USA) and sued the parent company and three of its foreign subsidiaries in a state court in North Carolina.

(continued)

---

[4]95 U.S. 714 (1877).

[5]480 U.S. 102 (1987).

Goodyear USA did not challenge personal jurisdiction, but the foreign subsidiaries argued that the North Carolina courts lacked jurisdiction over them and moved to dismiss the complaint for lack of personal jurisdiction. The trial court denied the motion, and the North Carolina Court of Appeals affirmed the trial court's decision in favor of Brown, ruling that a small percentage of tires manufactured by the foreign subsidiaries had entered the North Carolina market and that was sufficient minimum contacts. The Goodyear foreign subsidiaries then appealed to the U.S. Supreme Court.

SYNOPSIS OF DECISION AND OPINION The U.S. Supreme Court reversed the decision of the appellate court and ruled in favor of Goodyear. The Court concluded that specific jurisdiction was lacking in this case because the foreign subsidiaries' contacts with North Carolina were too limited. In addition, the Court also ruled that general jurisdiction over the foreign subsidiaries did not exist either. Specifically, the Court held that general jurisdiction is available to hold a corporation answerable for all claims within a state only if the corporation's contacts with the forum state are so continuous and systematic as to render the corporation "at home" in the forum state.

WORDS OF THE COURT: Continuous and Systematic Contacts "The Due Process Clause of the Fourteenth Amendment sets the outer boundaries of a state tribunal's authority to proceed against [an out-of-state] defendant. The canonical opinion in this area remains *International Shoe,* in which we held that a State may authorize its courts to exercise personal jurisdiction over an out-of-state defendant if the defendant has 'certain minimum contacts with [the State] such that the maintenance of the suit does not offend "traditional notions of fair play and substantial justice."' . . . North Carolina is not a forum in which it would be permissible to subject petitioners to [personal] jurisdiction. [The foreign subsidiaries of Goodyear USA] are in no sense at home in North Carolina. Their attenuated connections to the State . . . fall far short of 'the continuous and systematic general business contacts' necessary to empower North Carolina to entertain suit against them on claims unrelated to anything that connects them to the State.'"

Case Questions

1. Why didn't the parents of the boys in this case initiate their lawsuit against the foreign subsidiaries of Goodyear USA in a French court?

2. Does this decision mean that the boys' parents are without any legal recourse against Goodyear's foreign subsidiaries?

3. *Focus on Critical Thinking:* Why does the Court refer to the Due Process Clause in this decision? Also, should courts automatically deem a foreign subsidiary to share the "home" of its parent corporation for purposes of establishing personal jurisdiction over the foreign subsidiary?

Injurious Effect

Another important consideration that courts explore when analyzing personal jurisdiction is whether it was reasonably *foreseeable* that the defendant's actions would have an *injurious effect* on a resident of the court's state. This question is usually applied in the context of a dispute involving some *intentional* act by the defendant that results in an injury to an individual or business entity located in the court's state. The standard was set out by the U.S. Supreme Court in *Calder v. Jones.*[6] In *Calder,* the Court ruled that a California court had jurisdiction over a Florida corporation in a defamation case filed by actress Shirley Jones against a tabloid, the *National Enquirer.* Despite the fact that the tabloid had no physical presence or other contacts with California, the Court reasoned that jurisdiction was proper because the defendant knew, or should have known, that the defamatory article would have an injurious effect on the actress in California, where she lived and worked.

---

[6]465 U.S. 783 (1984).

This became known as the *Calder effects test* and is now an important part of a personal jurisdiction analysis. Note, however, that courts apply the test narrowly and only to cases involving intentional injurious acts (such as defamation).

In Case 4.3, a federal court uses the Calder effects test in a defamation case filed by a professional athlete.

Physical Presence

The physical presence of an out-of-state party in a particular state is generally an automatic basis for jurisdiction over the defendant by both that state's courts and federal trial courts

---

CASE 4.3 Clemens v. McNamee, 615 F.3d 374 (5th Cir. 2010)

FACT SUMMARY   In the summer of 2007, federal agents contacted Brian McNamee in connection with a federal investigation into the illegal manufacture and sale of performance-enhancing drugs in professional sports. McNamee was an athletic trainer who had worked for both the Toronto Blue Jays and the New York Yankees baseball clubs. After authorities convinced McNamee that they had sufficient evidence to convict him for injecting athletes with anabolic steroids, McNamee agreed to cooperate with investigators in exchange for immunity from prosecution.

During an interview with investigators, McNamee admitted that he had administered steroids to all-star pitcher Roger Clemens in both Toronto and New York. McNamee repeated this allegation to Major League Baseball investigators and to a reporter during an interview with *Sports Illustrated*. In 2008, Clemens, a citizen of Texas, filed a defamation suit against McNamee, a citizen of New York, in federal court based on diversity of citizenship. The trial court dismissed the complaint due to lack of personal jurisdiction over McNamee because his alleged defamatory statements were made outside Texas. Clemens appealed the decision.

SYNOPSIS OF DECISION AND OPINION   The Court of Appeals for the Fifth Circuit upheld the trial court's ruling in favor of McNamee and affirmed the dismissal of Clemens's defamation complaint. The court rejected Clemens's contention that jurisdiction was proper in a Texas court because he suffered harm from the defamation in Texas. The court analyzed McNamee's contacts with Texas in the context of the defamation claim and concluded that McNamee did not have sufficient minimum

contacts as required by the long-arm statute and due process. The court held that to support personal jurisdiction in a defamation claim, the forum must be the "focal point" of the story. Although the court acknowledged that the defamation may cause distress and damage to Clemens's reputation in Texas, it concluded that the alleged defamatory statement was inadequately directed to Texas to satisfy the minimum-contacts requirement.

WORDS OF THE COURT: Minimal Contacts and Injurious Effect   "In support of jurisdiction, Clemens points to the harm he suffered in Texas and to McNamee's knowledge of the likelihood of such damage in the forum. Yet under [previous case law], Clemens has not made a prima facie showing that McNamee made statements in which Texas was the focal point: the statements did not concern activity in Texas; nor were they made in Texas or directed to Texas residents any more than residents of any state. As such, the district court did not err in dismissing Clemens's suit for lack of personal jurisdiction over McNamee."

Case Questions

1. Why is due process relevant to the outcome of this case?

2. What is the practical implication of this decision? Does it mean that Clemens cannot bring suit for defamation in any court?

3. *Focus on Critical Thinking:* Why didn't Clemens sue McNamee in New York? Suppose McNamee claimed that he had injected Clemens with steroids in Texas. Would this admission change the outcome of this case? How?

---

within that state. In a business context, physical presence may include having an office, agent, or personnel (such as a sales team) located within the court's jurisdiction.

Many states have also passed specific statutes that give state courts personal jurisdiction over out-of-state residents who operate motor vehicles within the state for the narrow purposes of allowing a victim of an auto accident to pursue a claim against an out-of-state driver.

Voluntary

A court also has personal jurisdiction if the parties agree to litigate in a specific court. Voluntary personal jurisdiction applies when a nonresident party agrees to the jurisdiction of a particular court in a certain state. This voluntary jurisdiction is often done through a forum selection clause written in a contract between the parties. A *forum selection clause* is a contractual agreement that obligates the parties to litigate any dispute arising out of the contract in a particular court named in the clause. Essentially, the parties are agreeing to a forum ahead of time so that if any litigation involving that particular contract is instituted, both parties are obligated to litigate the dispute in a predetermined court.

The leading case involving a forum selection clause is *Carnival Cruise Lines v. Shute,*[7] in which the U.S. Supreme Court upheld a federal court's ruling that dismissed a personal injury claim by a resident of the state of Washington who had been a passenger on a Carnival Cruise Lines ship and had fallen during a guided tour of the ship. The Court concluded that the passenger ticket was a contract between the passenger and Carnival Cruise Lines and that the ticket contained a forum selection clause whereby the parties agreed to litigate any disputes in Miami, Florida (where Carnival's headquarters is located).

Recall our Cain v. APC hypothetical case introduced earlier in the chapter. Suppose Cain files her lawsuit in a federal district court in Massachusetts. In addition to establishing subject matter jurisdiction, she must also meet the court's standards for personal jurisdiction over APC. In this case, given the fact that the incident took place in Texas, it may be difficult for Cain to demonstrate APC's connection with Massachusetts unless APC owns property, maintains an office, regularly sends personnel to Massachusetts, or has some other regular and systematic connection with the state. In its jurisdiction analysis of the Cain v. APC matter, a federal court would first look to the Massachusetts long-arm statute and then to the constitutional requirements of due process and fairness, including APC's level of minimum contacts and purposeful availment in Massachusetts.

Forum selection clauses are common in technology licenses and social media agreements. Figure 4.2 is the forum selection clause from Facebook, and Case 4.4 provides us with a federal court's analysis of whether the clause is legally binding.

| FIGURE 4.2 | Facebook's Forum Selection Clause |

"You will resolve any claim, cause of action or dispute . . . you have with us arising out of or relating to [these terms of service] or Facebook exclusively in the U.S. District Court for the Northern District of California or a state court located in San Mateo County, and you agree to submit to the personal jurisdiction of such courts for the purpose of litigating all such claims."

---

[7]499 U.S. 585 (1991).

FACT SUMMARY Ricky Franklin received a series of unsolicited text messages from Facebook on his cell phone. (For example, one unsolicited text message read: "Today is Sara Glenn's birthday. Reply to post on her Timeline or reply to post 'Happy Birthday!'") Franklin sued Facebook in the United States District Court for the Northern District of Georgia, alleging that Facebook violated the Telephone Consumer Protection Act (TCPA), a federal law enacted in 1991, as well as Georgia law.

In response to Franklin's complaint, Facebook filed a motion to transfer venue, requesting that the district court enforce the forum selection clause in Facebook's terms of service (which every Facebook user must agree to when creating a Facebook account) and transfer the case to the federal district court in Northern California. Specifically, Facebook argued Franklin was contractually bound to Facebook's terms of service, which includes a forum selection clause requiring "any claim, cause of action or dispute (claim)" against Facebook must be brought exclusively in either "the U.S. District Court for the Northern District of California or a state court located in San Mateo County."

Franklin opposed Facebook's motion to transfer, arguing that his choice of forum was entitled to greater weight and that the forum selection clause in Facebook's terms of service was inapplicable to his case, since his complaint was not based on his own use of Facebook but rather on the transmission of unsolicited text messages.

SYNOPSIS OF DECISION AND OPINION The U.S. District Court for the Northern District of Georgia ruled in favor of Facebook and granted the motion to transfer. The court ruled that the forum selection clause in Facebook's terms of service was valid and applied to the facts of this case.

WORDS OF THE COURT: Presumptive Validity of the Forum Selection Clause "[Facebook's terms of service] governs the legal relationship between Defendant [Facebook] and millions of users of its website and related services. Because of this, the forum selection clause contained in [Facebook's terms of service] has been addressed by numerous courts in actions involving Defendant. The Court cannot identify a single instance where any federal court has struck down [Facebook's terms of service] as an impermissible contract of adhesion induced by fraud or overreaching or held the forum selection clause now at issue to be otherwise unenforceable due to public policy considerations. [Here, the court cites several other federal district court cases involving Facebook's forum selection clause.] The Court finds the reasoning of these cases persuasive, declines to depart from the great weight of persuasive authority on this question, and accordingly finds that Plaintiff [Ricky Franklin] has failed to overcome the presumptive validity of the forum selection clause on the basis of fraud, overreaching, or contravention of public policy."

Case Questions

1. Franklin had alleged in his complaint that the text messages he received from Facebook were unsolicited and thus not related to his own Facebook account. Given this allegation, did the court decide the case correctly?

2. In its order, the court refers to the "persuasive authority" of several district court decisions involving Facebook users in previous cases. Nevertheless, was the judge obligated as a matter of law to follow these previous decisions? Why or why not?

3. *Focus on Critical Thinking:* What if Franklin had posted the following "status update" on his Facebook account right after signing up for Facebook for the first time:

> I, Ricky Franklin, hereby agree to every provision in Facebook's terms of use, except for the forum selection clause. I do not agree to the forum selection clause because I live in Georgia and I want a court in Georgia to resolve any dispute I may have with Facebook in the future.

If Facebook had chosen not to deactivate or suspend Franklin's account after he had posted such a message to his Facebook account, would the forum selection clause still have been enforceable?

TAKEAWAY CONCEPTS Jurisdiction

	Federal Trial Courts	State Trial Courts
Personal jurisdiction	1. Residents and business entities located in the state where the federal trial court sits; or 2. Nonresidents with *minimum contacts* with the state in which the federal trial court sits; or 3. Nonresidents owning property in the state in which the federal trial court sits; or 4. Voluntary	1. Residents and business entities located in the state; or 2. Nonresidents owning property in the state; or 3. Nonresidents with *minimum contacts* with the state according to state long-arm statutes; or 4. Voluntary
Subject matter jurisdiction	1. Federal question; or 2. Is an involved party; or 3. Diversity of citizenship *and* amount in controversy is more than $75,000 (amount required only in diversity of citizenship cases)	State law matters (statutes, common law, state constitutional issues)

Minimum Contacts and the Internet

LO 4-6

Apply the minimum-contacts test in a cyber setting and describe the importance of the *Zippo* sliding scale.

The technology boom of the 1990s brought new challenges for courts grappling with the concept of minimum contacts in cyberspace. For example, suppose Copperfield is the principal owner of an advertising firm headquartered in New London, Connecticut. Hoping to attract new clients and generate new leads, Copperfield decides to develop a website with tips on running an effective marketing campaign that will be free to all Internet users who fill out a brief form with their contact information.

Does the fact that users from across the country could access Copperfield's website subject him to the jurisdiction of all 50 states? Because courts have held that advertising in a particular state may be a factor in determining whether minimum contacts exist, couldn't a *website* be the basis for those contacts as well? How does that square with the purposeful availment standard? Suppose Copperfield decided to start a subscription-based service and charge users to access the site? If Copperfield made downloads available to users for a fee, would that change your analysis? Is there any way that Copperfield can limit a court's authority over his firm's minimum contacts? Although the Supreme Court has yet to directly rule on minimum contacts in the context of cyberspace, the law developed thus far gives business owners and managers a relatively clear framework for answering the questions posed in the Copperfield hypothetical.

The *Zippo* Standard   In 1997, a federal district court in Pennsylvania generated the first comprehensive scheme for testing a minimum-contacts analysis of personal jurisdiction based on one party's use of the Internet in its business. Named after the parties in the case, this analytical model became known as the ***Zippo* standard**. Recall from the earlier discussion in this chapter that federal district courts are trial courts and thus do not set precedent. However, since the case was decided, at least six federal circuit courts of appeal have adopted the *Zippo* standard as the legal framework to be used by trial courts in determining personal jurisdiction when one party is asserting minimum contacts based on a certain level of Internet activity by the defendant.

The *Zippo* standard was established in *Zippo Manufacturing Company v. Zippo Dot Com, Inc.*[8] As one may imagine from its name, the case centers on a trademark infringement dispute between Zippo Manufacturing Company (Zippo), the famous lighter manufacturing company, and Zippo Dot Com (ZDC), an Internet news subscription service.[9] When Zippo sued ZDC, ZDC asked the court to dismiss the case claiming a federal court in Pennsylvania did not have personal jurisdiction because ZDC had no offices, agents, or property in Pennsylvania. Zippo argued that ZDC's sale of approximately 3,000 subscription-based memberships to residents of Pennsylvania satisfied both the state's long-arm statute and the constitutional fairness and due process requirements of minimum contacts.

In developing a framework for deciding the case, the court adopted a *continuum,* also called a *sliding scale,* approach for measuring the number of minimum contacts based on the interactivity of a website owner vis-à-vis the user. The court focused this test on the *level* and *nature* of interactivity between source and user that an individual or business transacted over the Internet. The court explained the continuum by using an illustration of three points along the scale: passive, interactive, and integral to the business model.

Passive   On one end of the continuum, a party with a passive website that provides information that could be accessed by any Internet user cannot be the *sole basis* for personal jurisdiction. The court analogized this type of website to a billboard advertisement and reasoned that such websites could not meet the purposeful availment standard and, thus, could not satisfy the minimum-contacts requirement.

Interactive   The middle of the continuum applies when a website provides users with some interactive function whereby users may exchange information, purchase products, download or upload material via the website, or engage in activity beyond merely viewing the content of the website. For cases that fall into this category, the court would be required to examine the interactivity more closely on a case-by-case basis with a focus on the *level* of interactivity and *commercial* nature of the website. For example, was the level of interactivity simply a product order form that could be downloaded, filled out, and faxed to the vendor? If so, the case may fall on the passive side of the scale and no minimum contacts exist. On the other hand, if the interactivity involved credit card purchases from a significant number of users in one particular state via the website or some subscription-based service provided by the website's owner, the case may fall on the active side of the scale, indicating that minimum contacts exist to the extent necessary for personal jurisdiction over the website's owner.

Integral to Business Model   At the other end of the continuum is a business where use of the website is an *integral part* of the business model and the website is used to accomplish commercial transactions with residents in the state of the court's jurisdiction. For example, Internet vendors such as Amazon.com or Netflix.com regularly transact business with residents of all 50 states (and beyond), and their business model depends almost exclusively on consumers interacting with their website, including financial transactions. In this case, the minimum-contacts and purposeful availment standards are met and personal jurisdiction is appropriate.

Ultimately, the court ruled that because ZDC contracted with 3,000 residents and seven Internet access providers all located in Pennsylvania, the purposeful availment standard was met, minimum contacts existed, and thus the federal court in Pennsylvania had personal jurisdiction over the case.

---

[8]952 F. Supp. 1119 (W.D. Pa. 1997).

[9]ZDC is now defunct.

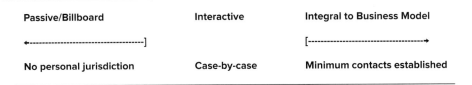

| FIGURE 4.3 | *Zippo* Sliding Scale Test |

Passive/Billboard	Interactive	Integral to Business Model
◄---------------------------------]		[-------------------------------------►
No personal jurisdiction	Case-by-case	Minimum contacts established

Figure 4.3 is an illustration of the *Zippo* sliding scale used by many courts to analyze minimum contacts via the Internet.

Adoption of the *Zippo* Standard Soon after *Zippo* was decided, several other courts began to use the same type of analytical framework. In 1999, the Fifth Circuit Court of Appeals became the first federal *appellate* court to expressly adopt the *Zippo* standard and also provided a useful application of the standard when the defendant had a website that involved some degree of interactivity. The case, *Mink v. AAAA Development LLC,*[10] involved a Texas resident (Mink) who sued an out-of-state company (AAAA) in a patent dispute. Although AAAA had no contacts at all with Texas, Mink alleged that AAAA's website was accessible to Texas residents and that conferred jurisdiction on Texas courts. The court ruled that no personal jurisdiction existed because the website was passive and only posted information about its products and services. Since then, the *Zippo* standard has been adopted by the majority of federal circuits as well as by *state* courts of authority in California, Minnesota, New York, Texas, and Washington.

In Case 4.5, a state appellate court applies the *Zippo* sliding scale test to determine personal jurisdiction.

CASE 4.5 Shisler v. Sanfer Sports Cars, Inc., 53 Cal. Rptr. 3d 335 (2006)

FACT SUMMARY Sanfer Sports Cars, Inc. (Sanfer) is an auto dealership located and incorporated in Florida. In its 32-year history, the overwhelming majority of cars sold by Sanfer were to residents of south Florida. Sanfer has never owned or leased property in California, has never advertised directly to residents of California, and has never intentionally focused on selling cars specifically to residents of California. However, Sanfer does maintain a website that is, naturally, accessible to any user in the world. The website was used by Shisler, a California resident, to locate a 2002 BMW M5 automobile. Shisler subsequently called and wrote Sanfer to inquire about price and delivery terms. The parties agreed on price, and Shisler purchased the car and arranged to have the car shipped from Florida to his home in California. When the car arrived in California, it was not as Shisler expected. After the parties failed to resolve the dispute, Shisler filed suit in California alleging deceptive trade practices. Sanfer requested that the California court dismiss the suit because it lacked personal jurisdiction over him. Shisler argued that Sanfer's maintenance of an interactive website that is used by California residents is sufficient minimum contacts to establish personal jurisdiction.

SYNOPSIS OF DECISION AND OPINION The California Court of Appeals held in favor of Sanfer and ruled that there was not enough contact with California or its residents. The court applied the *Zippo* sliding scale and concluded that the website did not target California residents and lacked interactive features. The court explained that creating a website, like placing a product into the stream

(continued)

---
[10]190 F.3d 333 (5th Cir. 1999).

of commerce, may be felt nationwide, but without more it is not an act purposefully directed toward the forum state. If it were, personal jurisdiction in Internet-related cases would almost always be found in any forum in the country, contrary to long-settled principles of personal jurisdiction.

WORDS OF THE COURT: Website as Basis for Jurisdiction   "In this case, defendant's Web site merely advertised its vehicles and (presumably) included a credit application. There is no evidence that files were exchanged via the Web site or that any business was actually conducted via the site. As plaintiff explained in his declaration, he "wrote to and phoned" defendant to get more information and to negotiate the purchase. Nor is there evidence that anything about the Web site specifically targeted California residents. Thus, defendant's maintenance of the Web site alone is insufficient to establish personal jurisdiction."

Case Questions

1. If Sanfer's website featured methods for purchasing items from the dealership via credit card, how would that change your analysis?

2. How is it possible to "target" residents of a particular state through a website? Have you ever seen an example?

3. *Focus on Critical Thinking:* Look up websites for merchants in your area. Are there any that potentially target residents of other states? What is the difference in format, language, and interactivity between these websites?

Criticism of the *Zippo* Standard

Despite the widespread adoption of the *Zippo* standard, some courts have rejected it as too vague. For example, the U.S. Court of Appeals has found that website interactivity alone is still not sufficient for jurisdiction. In *Snodgrass v. Berklee College of Music,*[11] the Seventh Circuit found that no general personal jurisdiction existed in Illinois for a music school in Massachusetts whose students and prospective students had thousands of online interactions and contacts on a regular and systematic basis. The court indicated that the interactivity alone, with evidence that they had targeted Illinois residents, was insufficient contact.

 Quick Quiz *Zippo* Standard

Would the court have personal jurisdiction under the *Zippo* standard?

1. Scanner Corp., a Maryland-based corporation with its principal place of business in Baltimore, creates and markets copyrighted photos of models that are used as background material on product packaging and picture frames. AP Picture Co. (AP) wrongfully appropriated hundreds of Scanner's photos and published them on its website, where members could pay to download them. AP received advertisement fees based on the amount of consumer traffic generated by the website. Scanner files suit in a Maryland court against AP and AP's Internet Service Provider, Megabites, a Georgia corporation with its principal place of business in Atlanta. Does the court have jurisdiction over Megabites?

2. Kristin, a resident of Hawaii, maintains a not-for-profit website from her home that offers information and opinions on commercial household movers. While the website does not charge for its usage, it does accept donations. Last summer, Kristin posted various derogatory and unflattering comments about Moving – U Inc. (MU) a New York corporation, one of which was in response to a user's question. Kristin asserted that MU was operating without the requisite legal authorization and insurance. If MU wishes to sue Kristin in a federal court in New York, does the court have personal jurisdiction?

(continued)

---

[11]559 Fed.Appx. 541 (7th Cir. 2014).

3. Natural Foods Inc. (Natural) is a Nevada-based firm that sells organic beef. Although it originally did business exclusively in Nevada through a small retail stand, Natural eventually created a website whereby customers throughout the United States could order beef to be shipped from Natural's ranch in Nevada to any city in the United States. When ordering, customers provided their billing and shipping addresses as well as credit card information and could sign up to receive newsletters. Johanna, a resident of Florida, ordered beef via Natural's website and became sick after eating the product. Johanna sues Natural in a federal district court in Florida under a variety of theories. Does Natural have sufficient contact for the Florida court to have personal jurisdiction over it?

4. Big Bank Securities Inc. (BBS) is a Delaware-based corporation, with its principal place of business in New York. BBS trades various securities for its own benefit and for its clients. Cheyenne Securities Investors Inc. (CSI) is a Wyoming-based corporation providing portfolio management for various clients. A trader for CSI contacted BBS through an instant messaging program used by investors. CSI offered to sell $15 million in bonds to BBS in response to an earlier inquiry. BBS agreed to buy the bonds and set a price and time for delivery of the bond instruments. The entire transaction was completed via the instant messaging system. The next day, CSI reneged on the sale claiming it believed BBS had insider information. CSI has no offices or agents in New York. Would New York state courts have personal jurisdiction over a BBS v. CSI lawsuit for breach of contract?

Answers to this Quick Quiz are provided at the end of the chapter.

TAKEAWAY CONCEPTS *Zippo* Standard

- The *Zippo* standard is a sliding scale approach for measuring the amount of minimum contacts a party has based on the interactivity of a website.

- Under the *Zippo* standard, passive websites that provide information alone that can be accessed by any Internet user do not provide a basis for personal jurisdiction. On the other hand, websites that are integral to the business model and used consistently for transactions do constitute minimum contacts.

- Websites used with some degree of interactivity are evaluated on a case-by-case basis. Websites that simply exchange information generally do not provide grounds for jurisdiction; those involving subscription services and other purposeful contact may provide the basis for minimum contacts and purposeful availment.

VENUE

LO 4-7

Recognize how rules of venue affect the location of a trial.

While jurisdiction requires an analysis of whether a court has authority over a particular case, venue is the legal concept that defines the most appropriate *location* for the trial. Two or more courts will sometimes have jurisdiction over the same matter, but it would be more appropriate from a fairness perspective to hear the case in a particular location. Many states have venue rules to determine where a case may be heard. Typically, state statutes provide that venue in a civil case is where the defendant resides or is headquartered, while in a criminal case the venue is ordinarily where the crime is committed. If a crime (or a criminal defendant) is very high profile, a defense attorney will ask for a *change of venue* to help select a jury from outside the area where the crime was committed, under the theory that the out-of-area jury will be more impartial and less influenced by the media.

To understand how venue may be important in a business context, suppose two Florida-based companies are involved in a breach of contract dispute and Beta sues Alpha. The transaction involved an order that took place over a website based in Florida. The order was shipped from Alpha's warehouse in Georgia to Beta's branch office in South Carolina. Although a number of state and federal courts may have jurisdiction over a dispute in this case given the contacts, a Florida court may decide that Florida is the best *venue* for the dispute to be litigated, because both parties have their principal office located there and presumably it is the most convenient forum for the parties. It is likely that the witnesses and records are in Florida as well. Note, however, that a state court cannot unilaterally declare that venue exists in *another* jurisdiction. Courts apply venue statutes to determine whether or not *their* court is the most appropriate venue.

 ## THINKING STRATEGICALLY

©valterZ/Shutterstock

PROBLEM: Perhaps the single greatest legal risk that all businesses face is the threat of litigation. Given the relative ease for a business to enter into markets that cross state and national borders, there is a real possibility of a lawsuit brought by an out-of-state or foreign plaintiff.

STRATEGIC SOLUTION: *Forum shopping* refers to a common strategic tactic by plaintiffs in civil litigation. It occurs when a plaintiff strategically selects the most favorable legal forum in which to initiate a lawsuit.

Forum shopping is often maligned and criticized, but it is a common legal strategy. In fact, forum shopping provides a good illustration of the *preventive* or risk-reduction legal strategy we saw at the end of Chapter 1, the proactive practice of anticipating potential legal risks to one's business and taking preventive measures to reduce or manage those risks.

A common legal strategy to address this risk is the use of well-drafted forum selection clauses in business agreements. Let's take a look at a real-world instance of this preventive legal strategy.

Consider a familiar website like Facebook. With over one billion active users, the threat of litigation is a daunting one. But to open a Facebook account in the first place, a user must agree to Facebook's *terms of service*. (You can check out Facebook's user agreement for yourself here: https://www.facebook.com/terms.) Among the many provisions in Facebook's user agreement is the following forum selection clause:

> You will resolve any claim, cause of action or dispute . . . you have with us arising out of or relating to this [user agreement] or Facebook exclusively in the U.S. District Court for the Northern District of California or a state court located in San Mateo County, and you agree to submit to the personal jurisdiction of such courts for the purpose of litigating all such claims.

In other words, since Facebook's corporate headquarters are located in Menlo Park, California (in San Mateo County), and since the closest federal trial court is located in nearby San José, California (in next-door Santa Clara County), if a Facebook user ever wants to sue Facebook for any reason, he or she must do so in Facebook's "backyard," so to speak. Moreover, notice how this legal strategy not only helps a giant firm like Facebook reduce its legal expenses by consolidating most of its litigation in northern California; it also guarantees Facebook "home-court advantage" in cases involving out-of-state plaintiffs!

Yes, the law is supposed to be applied impartially, and yes, courts are supposed to be fair and neutral, but in close cases, the benefit of securing the home-court advantage cannot be underestimated, especially in jury trials. Because the risk of litigation is a real one, businesses may take strategic measures—such as incorporating well-drafted forum selection clauses into their business agreements before any litigation ensues—in order to channel litigation toward a favorable legal forum or secure home-court advantage in the event of litigation.

QUESTIONS

1. Is forum shopping ethical?
2. Should courts enforce forum selection clauses in business to consumer contracts like the Facebook user agreement described here? Why or why not?
3. Suppose Facebook did not have a forum selection clause in its user agreement. Would Facebook be subject to the jurisdiction of every state court in the United States since it has millions of users in every state?

Court p. 76   A judicial tribunal duly constituted for the hearing and adjudication of cases.

Judiciary p. 76   The collection of federal and state courts existing primarily to adjudicate disputes and charged with the responsibility of judicial review.

Jurisdiction p. 77   The legal authority that a court must have before it can hear a case.

Venue p. 77   A determination of the most appropriate court location for litigating a dispute.

State courts p. 77   Courts that adjudicate matters dealing primarily with cases arising from state statutes, state common law, or state constitutional law.

Federal courts p. 77   Courts that adjudicate matters dealing primarily with national laws, federal constitutional issues, and other cases that are outside the purview of state courts.

State trial courts p. 77   The first courts at the state level before which the facts of a case are decided.

State appellate courts p. 77   State-level courts of precedent, concerned primarily with reviewing the decisions of trial courts.

Plaintiff p. 77   The party initiating a lawsuit who believes the conduct of another party has caused him to suffer damages.

Defendant p. 77   The party alleged by the plaintiff to have caused the plaintiff to suffer damages.

Remand p. 78   To send a case back to the lower court from which it came for further action consistent with the opinion and instructions of the higher court.

U.S. District Courts p. 78   Courts that serve the same primary trial function as state trial courts, but for issues involving federal matters.

U.S. Courts of Appeal p. 78   The intermediate appellate courts in the federal system frequently referred to as the *circuit courts of appeal,* consisting of 13 courts, each of which reviews the decisions of federal district courts in the state or several states within its circuit.

U.S. Supreme Court p. 78   The ultimate arbiter of federal law that not only reviews decisions of the federal courts but also reviews decisions of state courts that involve some issue of federal law.

Subject matter jurisdiction p. 83   The court's authority over the dispute between the parties.

Personal jurisdiction p. 83   The court's authority over the parties involved in the dispute.

Federal question p. 83   Some issue arising from the Constitution, a federal statute or regulation, or federal common law.

Party p. 84   A person or entity making or responding to a claim in a court.

Diversity of citizenship p. 84   When opposing parties in a lawsuit are citizens of different states or one party is a citizen of a foreign country, the case is placed under federal court jurisdiction if the amount in controversy exceeds $75,000.

State long-arm statute p. 85   State statute intended to allow a court to reach into another state and exercise jurisdiction over a nonresident defendant due to the defendant's conduct or other circumstances.

Minimum contacts p. 85   A defendant's activities within or affecting the state in which a lawsuit is brought that are considered legally sufficient to support jurisdiction in that state's courts.

***Zippo* standard** p. 90   The legal framework used by trial courts in determining personal jurisdiction when one party is asserting minimum contacts based on a certain level of Internet activity by the defendant.

CASE SUMMARY 4.1 Bickford v. Onslow Memorial Hospital Foundation, 855 A.2d 1150 (Me. 2004)

Personal Jurisdiction

Bickford, a resident of Maine, received hospital bills over a period of several months from Onslow Memorial Hospital, which had treated a relative of Bickford's ex-wife. Although Onslow eventually acknowledged that Bickford was not legally responsible for the bills, Onslow continued to pursue the debt through collection and reported the debt as delinquent to Bickford's credit agencies. Bickford filed suit against Onslow in a Maine state court alleging a violation of several consumer protection laws. Onslow is located in North Carolina and does not own property or have any agents in Maine.

CASE QUESTIONS

1. Does the Maine court have personal jurisdiction over Onslow?
2. Would any other jurisdiction have concurrent jurisdiction?

CASE SUMMARY 4.2 M/S Bremen v. Zapata Off-Shore Co., 407 U.S. 1 (1972)

Jurisdiction: Forum Selection Clause

Zapata, a Texas corporation, hired Unterweser, a German corporation, to provide a tugboat for pulling Zapata's oil rig. Unterweser prepared a contract, and Zapata signed the contract after making several changes. The contract contained a forum selection clause requiring that any disputes be litigated in an International Commercial Court in London. Zapata had not altered that part of the contract. Unterweser's tugboat departed from Louisiana pulling Zapata's oil rig, but while in international waters off the Gulf of Mexico, a storm arose that resulted in severe damage to the oil rig. Zapata instructed Unterweser to tow the rig to the nearest port in Tampa, Florida. Zapata then filed a lawsuit in the federal district court in Tampa for $3.5 million against Unterweser.

CASE QUESTIONS

1. Does the court in Tampa have jurisdiction? Why or why not?
2. Will the forum selection clause be enforced? Why or why not?

CASE SUMMARY 4.3 Mink v. AAAA Development LLC, 190 F.3d 333 (5th Cir. 1999)

Minimum Contacts

Mink, a Texas resident, had experience and expertise in the retail furniture business. He developed a computer program called the Opportunity Tracking Computer System (OTCS) that was designed to analyze information regarding retail furniture sales to pinpoint potential new leads for use in the furniture industry. Stark approached Mink to gauge interest in the possibility of marketing the OTCS software bundled with Stark's existing software through the use of Stark's marketing company called AAAA Development (AAAA). During the discussions, Stark allegedly shared Mink's ideas and information on the OTCS with Stark's AAAA business partner. AAAA was a Vermont corporation. Eventually, Mink filed suit in a federal district court in Texas against AAAA Development and its principals, alleging that they conspired to copy Mink's patent-pending OTCS system for their own financial gain. None of the defendants owned property or had any other contact in Texas. In the course of its business, AAAA maintained a website advertising its software products on the Internet. The site was available to all users, including residents of Texas, and Mink argued that the website alone was sufficient contact to warrant jurisdiction in Texas.

CASE QUESTIONS

1. Where does the AAAA website fall on the sliding scale of the *Zippo* standard?
2. As a practical matter, what happens to Mink's case now? May he refile it in another court?

CASE SUMMARY 4.4 Toys "R" Us, Inc. v. Step Two, S.A., 318 F.3d 446 (3d Cir. 2003)

Minimum Contacts via the Web and the *Zippo* Standard

Toys "R" Us is a Delaware corporation headquartered in New Jersey that owns and operates retail stores worldwide. In 1999, Toys "R" Us acquired Imaginarium Toy Centers, including the rights to various trademarks held by Imaginarium. Step Two, a corporation based in Spain, owns franchised toy stores operating under the Imaginarium name in several Spanish cities but does not maintain any offices or stores outside of Spain. Each corporation registered multiple e-mail addresses under the Imaginarium name. Step Two's sites were interactive and allowed users to purchase toys online, but the company would ship only within Spain. If users signed up for Step Two's electronic newsletter, they were prompted to enter personal information and were provided with a drop-down menu of various Spanish provinces to indicate their location. This menu did not accommodate mailing addresses within the United States, and Step Two maintains that it has never made a sale in the United States. Toys "R" Us claimed that it had evidence that a resident of New Jersey made two purchases via the website, but it conceded that these purchases were delivered to a Toys "R" Us employee in Spain, who then forwarded the items to the purchaser in New Jersey. Toys "R" Us filed a trademark infringement suit in a federal district court in New Jersey.

CASE QUESTIONS

1. Does the federal court in New Jersey have subject matter jurisdiction over this case?
2. Has Step Two purposefully availed themselves in New Jersey, thus having the requisite minimum contacts? Why or why not?
3. Analyze this case under both the *Zippo* and *Asahi* frameworks. Describe the analysis and potential outcome under each. Which is the correct test to use and why?

CASE SUMMARY 4.5 Estate of Weingeroff v. Pilatus Aircraft, 566 F.3d 94 (3d Cir. 2009)

Purposeful Availment

The legal representative of the estate of Weingeroff (Weingeroff), a passenger on a turboprop plane who was killed when the plane crashed near State College, Pennsylvania, brought a negligence and product liability lawsuit against Pilatus Air (Pilatus), the manufacturer of the plane. The plane crashed when approaching a small airport in Pennsylvania on a planned stop en route from Florida to Rhode Island. Weingeroff sued Pilatus in a federal district court situated in the Eastern District of Pennsylvania. Pilatus, a Swiss company, asked the court to dismiss the case for lack of personal jurisdiction. Pilatus claimed that they had no offices or agents in Pennsylvania, no commercial transactions with Pennsylvania residents, and no physical presence in the state that would constitute purposeful availment. Weingeroff pointed to evidence that (1) Pilatus had conducted a nationwide marketing campaign in the United States to sell its planes, which included Pennsylvania; and (2) Pilatus had purchased over $1 million in products, services, and equipment from Pennsylvania suppliers. The trial court ruled in favor of Pilatus and dismissed the suit for lack of personal jurisdiction.

CASE QUESTIONS

1. Who prevails and why?
2. Suppose the plane had crashed and injured a pedestrian on the ground. Would the victim be able to bring a case against Pilatus in a Pennsylvania (state or federal) court?

CHAPTER REVIEW QUESTIONS

1. Which of the following are primary roles of the judiciary?
   I. Judicial review
   II. Set policy
   III. Adjudicate disputes
   IV. Establish jurisdiction
      a. I and III
      b. II and III
      c. I, II, and III
      d. III and IV
      e. II, III, and IV

2. A state trial court has issued a ruling on a matter of a contract dispute between two parties. The ruling is binding on:
   a. All trial courts in that state.
   b. Only the parties in the case.
   c. Federal trial courts ruling on contract matters.
   d. All future parties in that state with a similar contract dispute.
   e. State trial courts and state appellate courts.

3. Which of the following are courts of authority (set precedent)?
   I. U.S. Court of Appeals
   II. U.S. District Court
   III. State appellate court
   IV. State trial court
   a. I and II
   b. II and III
   c. I, II, and III
   d. III and IV
   e. I and III

4. Rye, Inc., a manufacturer of sporting equipment based in New Hampshire, enters into an agreement with Sports R Us to supply 10,000 catcher's mitts. Sports R Us is a national retail chain of sporting goods stores based in Massachusetts. They also operate several store locations by leasing space in shopping centers throughout the northeast, including New Hampshire. Rye sues Sports R Us in the federal court in New Hampshire for breaking the contract. The federal court in New Hampshire has personal jurisdiction over Sports R Us primarily because of:
   a. Minimum contacts and purposeful availment.
   b. Voluntary jurisdiction.
   c. Injurious effects within the court's jurisdictional boundaries.
   d. Property ownership.
   e. The *Zippo* standard.

5. TechCo., a company based in Silicon Valley, California, files a lawsuit against its next-door neighbor claiming they violated the U.S. Patent Act. The court has subject matter jurisdiction because:
   I. Diversity of citizenship exists.
   II. The case involves a federal question.
   III. The United States is a party in the case.
   IV. The amount in controversy is more than $75,000.
   a. I only
   b. II only
   c. II and III
   d. I and IV
   e. IV only

6. Most states have an intermediate appellate court.
   a. True
   b. False

7. The U.S. Supreme Court has original and appellate jurisdiction.
   a. True
   b. False

8. A forum selection clause in a contract is unenforceable.
   a. True
   b. False

9. Some courts have rejected the *Zippo* standard as too vague.
   a. True
   b. False

10. Typically, the defendant chooses the venue for a trial.
    a. True
    b. False

 Quick Quiz ANSWERS
Subject Matter Jurisdiction

1. No, because there is no diversity or federal question.
2. Yes, because a government agency is a party to the litigation.
3. Yes, because there is diversity of citizenship with an amount exceeding $75,000.
4. Yes, because this is a federal issue involving a federal statute.
5. Yes, because the United States is a party to the litigation and a federal statute is at issue.

Zippo Standard

1. No. The court cannot exercise personal jurisdiction over Megabites. Their conduct is strictly passive and, thus, not sufficient for an exercise of jurisdiction. See generally *ALS Scan, Inc. v. Digital Service Consultants, Inc.,* 293 F.3d 707 (4th Cir. 2002).

(continued)

2. No. Regardless of the acceptance of donations or response to user questions, New York courts would not have jurisdiction for defamatory comments made outside of New York. The website in question here can be accessed by anyone in the world, and there is no evidence that Kristin was availing herself of the opportunity to directly conduct business in New York. See generally *Best Van Lines, Inc. v. Walker,* 490 F.3d 239 (2d Cir. 2007).

3. Yes. Considering the interactivity of its website and the fact that consumers can purchase products from it, courts in Florida could exercise jurisdiction over Natural Foods Inc.

4. Yes. A New York court would have jurisdiction because CSI was clearly attempting to do business in New York with BBS through the instant messaging system. CSI knowingly contacted BBS in order to initiate the transaction, which culminated in the sale of $15 million in bonds; thus, CSI had entered into New York to conduct business. See generally *Deutsche Bank Securities, Inc. v. Montana Board of Investments,* 850 N.E.2d 1140 (N.Y. 2006).

CHAPTER REVIEW QUESTIONS: Answers and Explanations

1. a. The primary responsibilities of the judiciary are to adjudicate disputes (trial courts) and engage in judicial review (appellate courts). The remaining answers are incorrect because courts do not set policy or establish jurisdiction (both are functions of other government units such as the legislature).

2. b. State trial courts are not courts of authority and cannot set precedent.

3. e. Only appellate courts have the authority to set precedent. Because the U.S. District Courts and the state trial courts are both *trial* courts, they do not have the authority to set precedent; therefore, the remaining answers are incorrect.

4. a. Although not based in New Hampshire, Sports R Us has continuous and systematic minimum contacts to the point where they have satisfied the purposeful availment requirement for personal jurisdiction.

5. b. Federal courts have subject matter jurisdiction in cases when (1) the United States is a party to the litigation; (2) the case concerns a federal question; and/or (3) diversity of citizenship exists (where the amount in controversy is more than $75,000). TechCo. is alleging a violation of a federal statute (U.S. Patent Act), so the case involves a federal question.

6. a. True. It is true that most states have a trial court, an intermediate appellate court, and a final appellate court.

7. a. True. The U.S. Supreme Court has original jurisdiction (e.g., cases involving ambassadors) and appellate jurisdiction (judicial review).

8. b. False. Forum selection clauses are presumptively valid (see Case 4.4: *Franklin v. Facebook*).

9. b. False. In *Snodgrass v. Berklee College of Music,* the court criticized the *Zippo* standard as too vague and determined that interactivity of a website alone is not the deciding factor.

10. b. False. Venue is the legal concept that defines the most appropriate location of a trial. Venue rules are prescribed by state statute.

CHAPTER 5

Resolving Disputes: Litigation and Alternative Dispute Resolution

©valterZ/Shutterstock

While a working knowledge of alternative methods for resolving disputes may provide an important strategic opportunity, consider the dilemma of business owners engaged in mostly low-cost transactions with various out-of-state vendors and customers. When disputes arise, a business may be at a distinct disadvantage because the amount in controversy is too low to justify even the least expensive form of dispute resolution. In this chapter's *Thinking Strategically,* we examine the use of online dispute resolution as a strategic solution to this predicament.

Learning Objectives

After studying this chapter, students who have mastered the material will be able to:

5-1 Explain the impact of using civil litigation as a method of resolving business disputes.

5-2 Name the stages of litigation and identify the characteristics and processes of each stage.

5-3 Identify the ways in which dispute resolution can be used in business planning.

5-4 List the methods of alternative dispute resolution (ADR) and describe potential advantages or drawbacks of using ADR.

CHAPTER OVERVIEW

Litigation and alternative dispute resolution (ADR) are essential parts of business planning and strategy. It is inevitable that businesses will need to resolve disputes with their customers, other businesses, and local, state, or federal government agencies. Whether those disputes can be resolved without recourse to costly litigation will significantly affect the company's bottom line. It is therefore imperative that managers understand their options and the advantages and disadvantages of ordinary civil litigation versus alternative methods of dispute resolution.

CIVIL LITIGATION

Civil litigation refers to dispute resolution processes of civil (noncriminal) cases in public courts of law. (The term *litigation* is sometimes used as a synonym for *trial,* but in reality the scope of litigation is much broader and includes pretrial as well as posttrial events.) There are many varieties of business litigation, including contract and employment disputes and lawsuits relating to negligence, bankruptcy, and intellectual property issues as well. Moreover, the odds that a business firm will become involved in litigation continue to go up. According to the U.S. Bureau of Justice Statistics, the total number of civil cases filed in state and federal courts now exceeds 30 million cases annually.[1]

LO 5-1

Explain the impact of using civil litigation as a method of resolving business disputes.

Impact of Civil Litigation Business Planning

Dispute resolution is a crucial part of business planning and strategy that requires a thoughtful cost-benefit analysis; that is, it is not a technical or purely legal matter to be delegated to attorneys. While legal counsel is an important source of information and advice, business managers and owners must make critical decisions regarding how to resolve disputes. Furthermore, business managers and owners have an ever-increasing number of options to resolve disputes within and outside the legal system, and each option has advantages and disadvantages.

To illustrate how dispute resolution may be used in business planning, suppose that Classic Retail Outlets, Inc. (CRO) enters into a contract with Sign Designs Company (SignCo). The contract calls for SignCo to design, manufacture, and install signage for several CRO locations. The parties agree on certain specifications and a payment of 50 percent when the contract is signed and 50 percent at the time of delivery. SignCo delivers a prototype of the new sign, but CRO management is unhappy with the design and claims that SignCo did not follow the specifications in the contract. SignCo agrees to work on a new prototype but delays the process for several months. Finally, SignCo submits a new prototype, but CRO again rejects the prototype, citing additional flaws in its design. In addition, so much time has passed that CRO has incurred the expense of installing temporary signs.

In this hypothetical example, a dispute is brewing between CRO and SignCo. At least two business problems still exist: (1) Despite the fact that 50 percent of the contract price has been paid to SignCo, CRO still needs a sign and now has expended more money than anticipated installing temporary signs; and (2) SignCo has devoted significant time and materials to the project and may believe that CRO is being unreasonable in its expectations. Business owners and managers have a host of options for resolving such disputes. CRO should consider the alternatives presented in Table 5.1 to resolve the dispute in the context of a cost-benefit analysis and business planning.

STAGES OF LITIGATION

LO 5-2

Name the stages of litigation and identify the characteristics and processes of each stage.

Litigation is most easily understood when broken down into stages. However, it is important to note that the timing of these stages may sometimes overlap.

Prelawsuit: Demand and Prelitigation Settlement Negotiations

When a dispute arises between two parties, one party typically will make an informal demand of the other party in which the principals (or their attorneys) lay out the basics of the dispute and demand a certain action. This usually leads to informal discussions.

---

[1] U.S. Bureau of Justice Statistics, "State Court Caseload Statistics," https://www.bjs.gov/index.cfm?ty=tp&tid=30.

Action	Potential Benefit(s)	Potential Costs	Threats
Lawsuit	Court-ordered resolution to have the deposit refunded and have SignCo pay additional damages to compensate for the cost of temporary signage.	Significant expenditures: legal fees; hard costs (such as travel and fees for experts); human resources costs when time must be devoted to litigation procedures; appellate costs.	Loss at trial or loss upon appeal. Legal fees may be higher than the final judgment amount awarded. Possible countersuit by SignCo. Permanent damage to business relationship. Potential for bad publicity.
Nonjudicial dispute resolution Arbitration, mediation, or hybrid form.	Enforceable resolution to have the deposit refunded and have SignCo pay additional damages to compensate for the cost of temporary signage.	Moderate range in legal fees, arbitration/ mediation fees; limited human resource expenditures; no chance of appellate fees (if binding).	Loss at arbitration that is not appealable (if binding). Win in arbitration, but still have to go to trial (if nonbinding). Potential damage to business relationship.
Informal settlement Cancel the contract, agree not to sue each other, and agree to a figure that (1) compensates CRO for the temporary signage and (2) allows a percentage of the total fee to compensate SignCo for time invested in the project.	Parties agree not to sue each other. Potential exists to preserve the business relationship. Time and talent are not used to prepare for dispute resolution methods.	Low range of legal fees; moderate human resources investment; no threat of litigation by SignCo.	Settlement negotiations may drag on and CRO must find a new vendor.
Revise contract, continue relationship Make contract expectations clearer and revise payments that compensate both parties for the loss.	Transaction is completed (perhaps even at a profit) and business relationship is preserved.	Low range of legal fees; moderate human resources.	Potential litigation by SignCo and potential for the new contract to generate yet another dispute.

In some states, it is necessary to make a formal demand before filing suit. The demand is often followed by an informal prelitigation settlement discussion involving the parties and their lawyers. If the issues are relatively simple, this can be a cost-effective way to resolve a dispute fairly. However, if the legal issues are more complex or the parties are antagonistic toward each other, the prelitigation discussion will simply act as notice that a party intends to file a lawsuit if an agreement cannot be reached.

Standing In order for one party to maintain a lawsuit against another party, she must have **standing** to sue. This means that the party asserting the claim: (1) must have suffered an *injury in fact;* (2) suffered harm that is *direct, concrete,* and *individualized;* and (3) articulates what *legal redress* exists to compensate for the injury. In a business context, most lawsuits involve economic interests and, therefore, most parties in commercial litigation have no trouble meeting the requirements for standing. In some cases, a court will allow many plaintiffs with the same injury to sue together as a *class action.*

Pleadings Stage

When the plaintiff is convinced that she wishes to file a lawsuit, the first steps involve the parties filing and answering documents that set out the basics of the dispute and alleged damages suffered. Specifically, a "pleading" is a document containing factual allegations that each party is required to file in a lawsuit. The specific format, deadlines, and requirements of each pleading are set forth in court rules known as the *Rules of Civil Procedure*.

Complaint and Summons   If informal attempts at resolution fail, formal action begins when the plaintiff initiates a lawsuit by filing a **complaint** with the local clerk of courts.[2] This sets the pleadings stage in motion, with both sides filing documents that set out the facts of the case, theories of liability, and any available defenses. At the same time, the plaintiff is typically required to arrange for service of the defendant with a **summons** along with a copy of the plaintiff's complaint. The summons is formal notification to the defendant that she has been named in a lawsuit and that an answer must be filed within a certain period of time. In some cases, the summons and complaint may be served by certified mail to the defendant. In other cases, a deputy sheriff or process server must deliver the documents in person.

Statutes and court rules impose time limits on the *litigants* (the adverse parties involved in litigation) requiring pleadings to be initiated within a set time frame. Failing to adhere to the timelines may result in the loss of any legal rights or defenses. The complaint sets out the plaintiff's version of the facts of the case, the damages that have been suffered, and why the plaintiff believes that the defendant is legally responsible for those damages. Court procedures prescribe how the complaint should be served upon the defendant to ensure timely notice of the claims asserted by the plaintiff.

Recall our hypothetical dispute between CRO and SignCo. In the event that CRO pursues litigation, Figure 5.1 sets out a sample complaint for the CRO v. SignCo case.

Answer   Once the defendant is served with the complaint, she must provide a formal **answer** within a prescribed time frame (normally within 20 days). The answer responds to each paragraph of the complaint. Often, the answer is simply a device for the parties to understand what issues they agree on and what issues will be in dispute at trial. If the defendant does not answer within the given time frame, she is said to *default* and generally will automatically lose the case without the benefit of trial. This is known as a *default judgment*. In Figure 5.2, SignCo sets out to answer CRO's complaint.

Counterclaim   If the defendant believes that the plaintiff has caused her damages arising out of the *very same* set of facts as articulated in the complaint, the defendant files both an answer and a **counterclaim** (in some states, this is called a *countersuit*). The counterclaim is similar to a complaint in that the defendant's allegations and theory of liability against the plaintiff are set out in the pleading. The plaintiff must now answer the counterclaim allegations by the defendant within a prescribed time period.

Cross-Claim   The defendant also may file a **cross-claim** to bring in a third party to the litigation. A cross-claim is filed when the defendant believes that a third party is either partially or fully liable for the damages that the plaintiff has suffered and, therefore, should be involved as an indispensable party in the trial.

---

[2]Although *clerk of courts* is a common title for the official designated to receive civil complaints, the actual title varies widely among the states.

Daniel J. Webster, Esquire
ID# 70665
1120 Liberty Place
Philadelphia, Pennsylvania 19124
Attorney for Plaintiffs

In the Pennsylvania Court of
Common Pleas of
Philadelphia County

CLASSIC RETAIL
OUTLETS, INC.

           Plaintiff,   :
                        :
            v.   :
                        :

SIGN DESIGNS COMPANY
           Defendant,   :
                        :
_____ :

<u>Complaint</u>
Civil Docket 20-4700

In this complaint, the plaintiff alleges as follows:

1. Plaintiff and defendant are both Pennsylvania business entities headquartered in Philadelphia, Pennsylvania.
2. Jurisdiction over the subject matter is proper under the Pennsylvania Code.
3. On July 1, 2019, plaintiff contracted with defendant for services related to the design and installation of exterior signage for several of plaintiff's retail outlet sites. The contract specified the appearance and features of the signs.
4. The contract called for plaintiff to pay $25,000 at the execution of the contract and $25,000 at the completion of defendant's services.
5. Plaintiff fulfilled their obligation under the contract by paying $25,000 to defendant on July 1, 2019.
6. On July 30, 2019, Troy Machir, a principal in the plaintiff company, met with Matthew Diller, a principal in the defendant company, to review a preliminary version of the designs that defendant had completed.
7. During that meeting, Machir expressed his dissatisfaction with the work done and pointed out several errors where defendant had failed to follow the specifications detailed in the original contract.
8. As a result of that meeting, Diller promised to begin the design process anew and adhere more closely to the specifications of the contract.
9. Over the next two months, Machir attempted to obtain another preliminary design from defendant by contacting Diller and others at the defendant company via telephone and e-mail.
10. Diller, nor anyone else at the defendant company, responded to these calls or e-mails.
11. On October 1, 2019, Machir met with Diller once again and Diller presented a revised version of the design.
12. At that meeting, Machir expressed continued dissatisfaction with the design and again pointed out that the design was not consistent with the specifications in the contract.
13. In addition, Machir pointed out several instances where the problems identified at their July meeting were not remedied. Diller again promised to fix the problems.
14. On October 15, 2019, Diller informed Machir that the defendant company could not follow the specifications in the contract at the price agreed to and that an additional fee of $20,000 would be necessary to complete the work.
15. Because of the delay caused by the defendant, plaintiff has had to expend $10,000 to erect temporary signage at its retail outlet sites.
16. The failure of Defendant Company to design a sign according to the specifications of the contract is a failure to perform its obligations under their agreement and constitutes a breach of contract.

    WHEREFORE, plaintiffs request judgment in the amount of $25,000 as refund of the deposit, plus $20,000 for the necessary temporary signage, plus statutory interest, and any other damages the court deems appropriate.

Dated: 1st day of October, 2020.

By:_____

Daniel J. Webster, Esquire
Attorney for the Plaintiff

Oliver W. Holmes, Esquire
ID# 40016
One Alpha Drive
Maintown, Pennsylvania 17022
Attorney for Defendants

In the Pennsylvania Court of
Common Pleas of
Philadelphia County

CLASSIC RETAIL
OUTLETS, INC.

       Plaintiff,   :

                :

        v.   :

                :

SIGN DESIGNS COMPANY

       Defendant,   :

                :

_____   :

Answer
Civil Docket 20-4700

In this answer, the defendant responds to plaintiff's complaint as follows:

1. Admitted.
2. Admitted.
3. Admitted.
4. Admitted.
5. Admitted.
6. Defendant has insufficient information to admit or deny.
7. Defendant has insufficient information to admit or deny.
8. Defendant has insufficient information to admit or deny.
9. Defendant has insufficient information to admit or deny.
10. Denied. Diller contacted Plaintiff Company several times during this period.
11. Defendant has insufficient information to admit or deny.
12. Defendant has insufficient information to admit or deny.
13. Defendant has insufficient information to admit or deny.
14. Defendant has insufficient information to admit or deny.
15. Defendant has insufficient information to admit or deny.
16. Paragraph 16 is a conclusion of law to which no answer is required.

    Defendant also denies any and all parts of the plaintiff's complaint not specifically mentioned in this Answer.

Dated: 20th day of October, 2020.

By:_____

Oliver W. Holmes, Esquire
Attorney for the Defendant

Motions   From the time the pleadings are filed, through discovery and trial, and even after the trial, parties to the litigation may file **motions**. A motion is a document filed by one party that requests court action in a matter pertaining to the litigation. Some of the more common motions are described in Table 5.2.

In Case 5.1, an appellate court reviews a summary judgment order of a trial court.

TABLE 5.2 — Motions Used during Litigation

Stage of Litigation	Motion	Request
Pretrial	To dismiss	To dismiss a case because of a procedural defect such as a court's lack of jurisdiction or failure to state a recognized legal theory in the complaint.
Pretrial	For summary judgment	To enter judgment in the requesting party's favor without a trial because no issues of fact are presented in the case and, thus, no jury trial is needed. The requesting party believes it should win as a matter of law.
Pretrial	To compel discovery	To issue a court order demanding that a party comply with a lawful discovery request.
Trial	To dismiss for mistrial	To stop the trial in progress and dismiss it because of some extraordinary circumstance resulting in prejudice against one side or the other (rare in civil litigation).
Posttrial	For judgment as a matter of law*	To reverse the verdict of the jury because no reasonable jury could have heard the evidence presented at trial and rendered such a verdict.

*Also called by some state courts a judgment *non obstante veredicto* (notwithstanding the verdict).

CASE 5.1 Hernandez et al. v. Yellow Transportation, 670 F.3d 644 (5th Cir. 2012)

FACT SUMMARY Hernandez was employed at Yellow Transportation (Yellow), a trucking company in Dallas, Texas. Hernandez brought a discrimination lawsuit against Yellow alleging that the employer maintained a hostile work environment. During discovery, Hernandez recounted that over a 10-year period he was subjected to several incidents of discrimination, including being called a racially derogatory name by a co-worker on one occasion and seeing a poster or letter that was derogatory toward Latinos. Hernandez also admitted that much of the harassment toward him was not based on race but on personal animus between co-workers in a gritty workplace environment. Yellow moved for summary judgment against Hernandez, arguing that since the record, taken as a whole, could not lead a rational trier of fact to find in Hernandez's favor, there was no genuine issue for trial. The trial court granted Yellow's motion for summary judgment, ruling that no genuine issue of fact existed. Hernandez appealed the summary judgment order.

SYNOPSIS OF DECISION AND OPINION The U.S. Court of Appeals for the Fifth Circuit upheld the lower court's ruling in favor of Yellow. The court ruled that Hernandez had not established the framework for a hostile work environment claim because he had not alleged personal racial harassment that was sufficiently severe or pervasive as to affect his employment. The court focused its analysis on evidence of harassment cited by Hernandez and concluded that the harassment was not based on race (or any other discriminatory classification) and did not rise to the level of a hostile work environment in which the harassment unreasonably interfered with his work performance. Concluding that Hernandez had failed to make a legal claim, the court held that the lower court had properly applied the standard for summary judgment in dismissing the case.

WORDS OF THE COURT: Summary Judgment "Summary judgment is proper if the pleadings and evidence show there is no genuine issue of material fact and the moving party is entitled to a judgment as a matter of law. [. . .] Hernandez had evidence of specific incidences of workplace hostility towards [other races, including] African-American employees. Nonetheless, such incidents were neither physically threatening or humiliating towards Hernandez, nor did the harassment unreasonably interfere with

(continued)

their work performance. Hernandez did not have evidence that the alleged non-race-based harassment was part of a pattern of race-based harassment. [. . .] The district court properly granted summary judgment as to Hernandez's claim of hostile work environment."

Case Questions

1. Shouldn't Hernandez be permitted to have his day in court? Why shouldn't this case go to trial?

2. Hernandez alleged he was the victim of race-based harassment, in part because of an anti-Latino poster that was located in the workplace. Isn't that what discrimination laws are supposed to prevent?

3. *Focus on Critical Thinking:* Given the court's reasoning, what are some examples of incidents that you think could have gotten Hernandez through the summary judgment stage? Have you ever experienced harassment in the workplace?

Discovery Stage

Once the initial pleadings are filed, most lawsuits move into the **discovery** stage, in which the parties attempt to collect evidence for trial. While it may make television shows and movies more interesting, surprise evidence may not be introduced at an actual trial. Discovery is the legal process for the orderly exchange of evidence. Each side has the right to know and examine the evidence that the other side has, including evidence that is both *inculpatory* and *exculpatory*.

Everything relevant to the dispute is discoverable. Unless the information is protected by a legal privilege, such as certain conversations between attorney and client, it must be produced in discovery if the information is relevant or could be useful in any way for resolving the dispute.

Methods of Discovery   The rules for exchanging information during discovery are set out in court procedures called the *Rules of Civil Procedure* and accomplished primarily by four methods: depositions, interrogatories, requests for production, and requests for admissions.

- **Depositions** are oral questions asked of a witness in the case. A deposition can be taken at a courthouse but is more commonly taken in the setting of a conference room at a law firm. Although there is a court reporter present to create a written record and the witnesses are under oath, no judge is present. Depositions may be taken from the plaintiff, the defendant, or any other witness in the case.

- **Interrogatories** are written questions to be answered by one of the litigants (plaintiffs or defendants) involved in the case. Generally, interrogatories involve questions about which the litigant does not have readily available knowledge. The litigant may need to review files, memoranda, transcripts, and so forth in order to properly answer the questions.

- **Requests for production** are aimed at producing specific items to help one party discover some important fact in the case. Requests for production usually are very wide in scope and might cover all documents, memoranda, reports, notes, calendars, videotape, audiotape, e-mail, computer hard drives, and so on. In a complex securities or banking fraud case, or one where many documents are involved, it is not uncommon for the parties to send a truckload of boxes containing materials that were requested by the other side.

- **Requests for admissions** are attempts to obtain information that furthers the objective of determining which facts are in dispute (and, thus, must be proved at trial) and which facts both parties accept as true. For example, one party may request that the other party admit the existence and date of a certain contract. If the other party refuses to admit those facts, witnesses must be called at trial to prove the existence and date of the contract.

Discovery provides crucial information, but it does have some important limits. One key issue for business owners and managers that may arise in the context of discovery includes an attempt by the opposing party to obtain legally protected business information (known as *trade secrets*[3]).

 QUICK QUIZ Discovery Techniques

A customer is injured after slipping on a wet floor in a retail store. What discovery technique(s) could he use to obtain the following evidence?

1. Photographs of the site that were taken by the store manager immediately after the fall.

2. Request from the plaintiffs for the defendants to concede that an employee had spilled water on the floor on the morning of the accident.

3. Statement of an employee as a witness who was in charge of keeping the floors clean.

4. Questions that will require the store's manager to look up calendars and logs to answer them accurately.

Answers to this Quick Quiz are provided at the end of the chapter.

Pretrial Conference

Several weeks before trial, the parties typically will attend a **pretrial conference** with the judge. The conference is generally held between the attorneys for the parties and the judge in the case, with no court reporter present. The pretrial conference is designed to accomplish two primary objectives. The first objective is to encourage *settlement*. A judge often can give a neutral, face-value view of the case and facilitate some negotiations between the two sides or eliminate any obstacles that have blocked negotiations, such as one party's refusal to discuss settlement. The second objective is for the court to resolve any outstanding motions, confirm that discovery is proceeding smoothly, and dispose of any procedural issues that have arisen during the pleadings or discovery stages.

Trial

If the case cannot be settled, the parties will eventually go to **trial**. The trial generally takes place in front of a judge as the *finder of law* and with a jury as the *finder of fact*. As the finder of law, the judge determines what evidence will be admitted, what witnesses may testify, what the jury will hear and not hear, and even what legal arguments the attorneys may present to the jury. The jury, as the finder of fact, determines whose version of the facts is more believable by examining the evidence and listening to the testimony of witnesses. In some cases, the judge will act as both the finder of fact and the finder of law at the same time. This is known as a **bench trial**.

Jury Selection and Opening Statements
The actual trial begins with **jury selection**. This is the process of asking potential jurors questions to reveal any prejudices that may affect their judgment of the facts. The questioning process is known as *voir dire*.[4]

---

[3]Trade secrets are covered extensively in Chapter 50, "Intellectual Property."

[4]Pronounced *vwar deer*, this is a permutation of a Latin word and a French word meaning "to speak the truth."

For a criminal trial, voir dire can be extensive and last for days or even weeks depending on the case. However, in civil litigation the voir dire process is not as extensive, and the jury will be seated (selected) in relatively short order. After the jury is selected, the attorneys present their theories of the case and what they hope to prove to the jury in **opening statements**.

Testimony and Submission of Evidence

After the opening statements, the plaintiff's attorney asks questions, known as **direct examination**, of the witnesses on the plaintiff's list. The defendant's attorney may then conduct **cross-examination** of the witnesses. The cross-examination is composed of questions limited to issues that were brought out on direct examination. The same process is repeated for the defendant's witnesses. Each side also uses its witnesses to introduce relevant evidence. Witnesses may be called upon to authenticate documents, verify physical evidence, or provide expert testimony accompanied by charts or graphs shown to the jury.

Closing Arguments and Charging the Jury

Once the testimony is completed and the evidence has been submitted to the jury, each attorney sums up the case and tries to convince the jury that her version of the case is more compelling. This is known as a **closing argument**. The judge then proceeds with the **charging of the jury** by giving the jurors instructions on how to work through the process of coming to a factual decision in the case. The judge also informs the jury that the standard of proof in a civil case is a **preponderance of the evidence**.

Deliberations and Verdict

After receiving the charge, jurors move to a private room and engage in **deliberations**. Although the jury is permitted to send questions to the judge or make other requests (such as a request to reexamine evidence), the jurors are alone in their deliberations, and the jury returns a decision known as the **verdict**. If the jury cannot agree on a verdict, this is known as a **hung jury**, and the litigants must start the process all over again with a new jury. Rules in state courts for civil litigation frequently do not require a unanimous verdict, so hung juries are rare in a commercial dispute.

Posttrial Motions and Appeals

As discussed earlier in this section, there may be posttrial motions in which the losing party tries to convince the original judge that the verdict was flawed. Finally, the losing party may appeal to a higher court. Appellate courts engage in judicial review to decide whether any errors were committed during the trial and also have the power to *reverse* or *modify* the decisions of trial courts.

Collecting the Judgment

Although the prevailing party may have received a court judgment stating what he is entitled to recover from the defendant, collecting judgments may be difficult, especially if the defendant's assets are tied up in nonliquid forms, such as real estate, or are exempt from claims of creditors through a bankruptcy filing. However, the law does afford the prevailing party some tools to collect the judgment. For example, some states allow a judgment to be collected through the garnishment of wages, whereby the defendant's employer is ordered by the court to pay part of the defendant's wages directly to the holder of the judgment. The holder of a judgment also becomes a creditor (typically called a *judgment creditor*) and has the right to pursue the defendant's assets to satisfy the debt owed. The rights and the regulation of creditors and debtors are discussed in detail in Chapter 24, "Creditors' Rights."

LO 5-3

Identify the ways in which dispute resolution can be used in business planning.

ALTERNATIVE DISPUTE RESOLUTION

Alternative dispute resolution (ADR) refers to nonjudicial methods by which disputes involving individuals or businesses are resolved outside of the federal or state court system through the help of third parties. The main methods of ADR include mediation and arbitration.

Recall the hypothetical dispute between Classic Retail Outlets (CRO) and Sign Designs Company (SignCo) at the beginning of this chapter. In this example, several forms of informal and formal dispute resolution may benefit CRO and SignCo. If CRO decides to file a lawsuit, the company's management will have to allocate significant resources in terms of legal fees and litigation costs. Equally important, CRO assumes several risks, including the risk of losing at trial. Even if CRO prevails, it may end up paying more in legal costs than it hopes to recover from SignCo in court. Moreover, any litigation will likely result in the dissolution of the business relationship between CRO and SignCo. Aside from those costs, time is wasted that could be spent on more productive activities, such as securing new business or executing existing business activities.

Given these risks of litigation, some of the potential advantages of ADR over litigation are as follows:

■ *Costs:* ADR could potentially cost a fraction of normal litigation costs. Depending on the location of the trial, trial attorneys may charge between $200 per hour in smaller markets to as much as $1,000 per hour in, for example, New York City. Although some of the more mundane work in litigation may be done by nonlawyer professionals (such as legal assistants or paralegals) at lower rates, legal fees accumulate quickly once a lawsuit commences and accelerate once discovery begins.

- *Preserving the business relationship:* Litigation is, by its nature, adversarial. Allegations and defenses may turn antagonistic and result in termination of a business relationship. ADR, particularly informal ADR (discussed next), is focused on preserving the business relationship as part of the dispute resolution process. Business owners and managers work carefully to build alliances among vendors, suppliers, retailers, advertisers, and many other businesses that add value. ADR can help preserve alliances and avoid unnecessary antagonism over a dispute.

- *Time:* The time spent in ADR is much less than the two- to three-year (or more) period normally associated with discovery, a civil jury trial, and possible appeal.

- *Expertise:* In some cases, the parties may choose an industry expert to help resolve their dispute. When a case is before a jury, there is an uncontrollable risk that the jury may have a difficult time grasping the details of a complex case. Even a highly competent judge conducting a bench trial may not have the background to fully understand the technical details and terminology involved in certain industry disputes. For example, knowing generally how to use a computer is very different from understanding the complexities of programming computer codes.

- *Privacy:* ADR methods are usually conducted in private with no public record required. This, in turn, reduces the risk of accidental disclosure of confidential business information through public court records. The privacy factor is also helpful in avoiding any unwanted publicity in the matter.

Informal ADR

Informal ADR often involves the parties negotiating face-to-face or through intermediaries to arrive at a mutually agreeable solution without the use of a formal process. It can take the form of (1) a settlement agreement, whereby one party agrees to a payment in exchange for the other party's promise not to sue, or (2) an agreement to cancel a contract or to revise an existing contract to better reflect the parties' obligations and needs. However, even when the parties agree to settle a case among themselves, courts still maintain oversight to ensure the integrity of the process.

In Case 5.2, an appellate court rules that settlements that did not yield any benefits for the plaintiffs, yet resulted in substantial fees for attorneys, could not be approved.

CASE 5.2 *In re* Subway Sandwich Marketing and Sales Practices Litigation, T. Frank, Objector; No. 16-1652 (7th Cir. 2017)

FACT SUMMARY In January 2013, an Australian teenager measured his Subway Footlong sandwich and discovered it was only 11 inches long. He photographed the sandwich alongside a tape measure and posted the photo on his Facebook page. Soon after the photo went viral, a number of lawsuits were filed across the United States against Subway for damages and injunctive relief under state consumer protection laws. The lawsuits were combined, and several plaintiffs sought class action certification.

During discovery, Subway established that its unbaked bread sticks are uniform, and the baked rolls rarely fall short of 12 inches. The minor variations that do occur are wholly attributable to the natural variability in the baking process and cannot be prevented. Nonetheless, Subway entered into a settlement agreement and implemented certain measures to ensure, to the extent practicable, that all Footlong sandwiches are at least 12 inches long. The settlement acknowledged, however, that even with these measures in place, some sandwich rolls will inevitably fall short due to the natural variability in the baking process. The parties also agreed to cap the fees of class counsel at $525,000. However, Theodore Frank (Frank),

(continued)

---

one of the class members, argued that the settlement enriched only the lawyers and provided no meaningful benefits to the class. The trial court preliminarily approved the settlement, and Frank appealed.

SYNOPSIS OF DECISION AND OPINION The U.S. Court of Appeals for the Seventh Circuit reversed the decision of the trial court and ruled in favor of Frank. The court held that the procedures required by the settlement do not benefit the class in any meaningful way and act only to benefit the class action lawyers. They reasoned that since there were no identifiable benefits to class members, the class should not have been certified, and the settlement should not have been approved.

WORDS OF THE COURT: No Meaningful Relief "A class settlement that results in fees for class counsel but yields no meaningful relief for the class is no better than a racket. If the class settlement does not provide effectual relief to the class and its principal effect is to induce the defendants to pay the class's

lawyers enough to make them go away, then the class representatives have failed in their duty . . . to fairly and adequately protect the interests of the class. . . . No class action settlement that yields zero benefits for the class should be approved, and a class action that seeks only worthless benefits for the class should be dismissed out of hand."

Case Questions

1. Why do you think the class representatives approved this settlement?

2. The plaintiff's counsel argued that the settlement did provide meaningful benefits to the class because Subway has bound itself to a set of procedures designed to achieve better bread-length uniformity. Is that a convincing argument? Why or why not?

3. *Focus on Critical Thinking:* Could there be *any* remedies that the court would find "meaningful"? If the Footlong sub was only 9 inches long, how would that impact the case? Is there a baseline as to how much a merchant can deceive a consumer?

FORMAL ADR METHODS

LO 5-4

List the methods of alternative dispute resolution (ADR) and describe potential advantages or drawbacks of using ADR.

The most common formal ADR methods are *arbitration, mediation,* and *expert evaluation.* Most state or federal courts require mediation or nonbinding arbitration prior to allowing certain civil lawsuits to go to trial. Typically, in a business context, ADR is invoked either via contract or by mutual agreement. In a contractual arrangement, the parties enter into a contract that contains a clause requiring the parties to submit any disputes to a specific alternative dispute resolution process (usually binding arbitration). These ADR clauses are commonly contained in contracts relating to employment, sale of goods, brokerage agreements (such as a stockbroker or online trading account), financing, and licenses to use software. By way of example, the terms of use for the popular social media website Instagram contain the following binding arbitration clause:

> . . . you agree that all disputes between you and Instagram . . . will be resolved by binding, individual arbitration under the American Arbitration Association's rules for arbitration of consumer-related disputes and you and Instagram hereby expressly waive trial by jury. . . .

In addition, many employment contracts require employees with job-related grievances to enter into binding arbitration and prohibit them from filing a civil lawsuit against the employer in a court of law. Should a work-related problem arise, employees often are surprised by such clauses, which they may have overlooked when signing the contract. Unless the terms of the arbitration clause are unfair, courts will enforce an arbitration award pursuant to such a clause.

Arbitration

One of the most common forms of ADR is **arbitration**. During arbitration, an individual *arbitrator* (or a panel of arbitrators) conducts a hearing between the parties in the dispute.

The hearing is similar to a court setting but is less formal, since there is no discovery and the rules of evidence do not apply. Parties seeking arbitration typically apply for an arbitrator through an ADR agency. The largest arbitration provider in the United States is the American Arbitration Association (AAA).

When the AAA receives an application for arbitration, it appoints a *tribunal administrator,* who coordinates the case and informs the parties of the procedures and rules of arbitration. Next, an arbitrator who is mutually agreed upon by the parties is appointed to the case. The arbitrator functions much like a judge would in a standard trial and in some states even has the power of subpoena (the ability to demand certain documents or witnesses). For arbitration cases, although an attorney is not required, parties in a business dispute often opt to be represented by counsel. An arbitration hearing resembles a trial in that there are opening statements, both parties present limited evidence and call a predetermined number of witnesses, both parties have the right of cross-examination, and both parties make closing arguments. Unless already mandated in a contract, at the beginning of the arbitration both parties agree to either binding or nonbinding arbitration. If binding, the arbitrator's decision is final unless both parties agree to have the case reopened.

Legally Mandated Arbitration   When the parties agree to an arbitration clause in a contract, this is known as a *private* arbitration. Additionally, some states and federal courts require (either by statute or a court-imposed procedure) that certain civil lawsuits go to nonbinding arbitration before proceeding to trial. Although this type of arbitration is nonbinding (i.e., the losing party has the right of automatic appeal to the trial court), the idea is to encourage the parties to settle before trial. The key advantage of legally mandated arbitration is that each side is able to present the case to a neutral party and the arbitrator's decision can be used as a starting point for settlement negotiations.

Federal Arbitration Act   The Federal Arbitration Act[5] (FAA) is a statute that requires state and federal courts to enforce arbitration awards. Specifically, the FAA states that "a written provision of . . . a contract evidencing a transaction involving commerce to settle by arbitration a controversy thereafter arising out of such a contract . . . shall be valid, irrevocable, and enforceable, save upon such grounds as exists at law . . . for the revocation of any contract."[6]

Congress enacted this law because many state and federal courts had previously invalidated arbitration clauses or overturned arbitration awards. This hostile view of arbitration led Congress to enact the FAA in order to make clear that arbitration was preferred over litigation as a method of dispute resolution so long as the parties agreed to an arbitration clause.

In addition, the FAA also identifies the following four grounds when courts may *set aside* the award of an arbitrator:

1. The arbitration involves some degree of corruption or fraud.
2. The arbitrator has exhibited inappropriate bias.
3. The arbitrator has committed some gross procedural error (such as refusing to hear relevant evidence) that prejudices the rights of one party.
4. The arbitrator has exceeded her explicit powers or failed to use them to make an appropriate final award.

Although the FAA does not spell out any specific procedure or format for arbitration, it does provide a means for enforcing both arbitration clauses and the decisions of arbitrators through the use of federal courts. In Case 5.3, the U.S. Supreme Court applies the FAA in the context of a class action arbitration.

---

[5]9 U.S.C. §§ 1 *et. seq.*
[6]9 U.S.C. § 2.

FACT SUMMARY American Express (Amex) entered into agreements with Italian Colors Restaurant (ICR) and other merchants that accept American Express credit cards. The agreement contains an arbitration clause requiring that all disputes between Amex and ICR be resolved through arbitration and prohibiting any claim from being arbitrated on a class action basis. Nonetheless, ICR and other merchants filed a class action suit against Amex, alleging violation of federal antitrust statutes. Amex moved to compel individual arbitration, but ICR argued that the clause was invalid because the cost of expert analysis necessary to prove their antitrust allegations would greatly exceed the maximum recovery for each individual merchant plaintiff. The trial court ruled in favor of Amex, but a federal court of appeals reversed the trial court's ruling and held that the clause was unenforceable because of the prohibitive cost structure. Amex appealed to the U.S. Supreme Court.

SYNOPSIS OF DECISION AND OPINION The U.S. Supreme Court ruled in favor of Amex. The Court held that the Federal Arbitration Act (FAA) does not permit courts to invalidate a contractual waiver of legal rights based solely on the grounds that a plaintiff's dispute resolution costs exceed any potential amounts to be recovered. The Court concluded that the FAA reflects the overarching principle that arbitration is a matter of contract and that courts have a responsibility to strictly enforce arbitration agreements according to their terms. The arbitration clause in the agreements between Amex and ICR and between AMEX and the other merchants must be enforced unless the FAA's mandate has been overridden by a contrary congressional command.

WORDS OF THE COURT: Congressional Intent "No contrary congressional command requires us to reject the waiver of class arbitration here. Respondents argue that requiring them to litigate their claims individually—as they contracted to do—would contravene the policies of the antitrust laws. But the antitrust laws do not guarantee an affordable procedural path to the vindication of every claim. Congress has taken some measures to facilitate the litigation of antitrust claims—for example, it enacted a multiplied-damages remedy. In enacting such measures, Congress has told us that it is willing to go, in certain respects, beyond the normal limits of law in advancing its goals of deterring and remedying unlawful trade practice. But to say that Congress must have intended whatever departures from those normal limits to advance antitrust goals is simply irrational."

Case Questions

1. Was the waiver of class action arbitration by the merchants truly voluntary? Why or why not?

2. If the costs of experts exceed the potential recovery amount in the absence of a class action, doesn't the arbitration clause in this case have the effect of shielding Amex from antitrust laws?

3. *Focus on Critical Thinking:* Why did the Court interpret the Federal Arbitration Act so strictly in this case? Should courts have more leeway when interpreting statutes?

Employment and Labor Arbitration

Arbitration clauses are a central issue in the context of employment and labor disputes. In these types of disputes, courts are highly deferential to a decision rendered by an arbitrator because an arbitration clause is the product of negotiations between employer and employee. In *Gilmer v. Interstate/Johnson Lane Corporation,*[7] the U.S. Supreme Court held that the FAA applies to arbitration clauses contained in employment contracts even when an employee brings suit against an employer for violating federal anti-discrimination laws.

---

[7]500 U.S. 20 (1991).

Labor unions negotiate a contract on behalf of their members called a *collective bargaining agreement* that frequently includes mandatory and binding arbitration. In *14 Penn Plaza LLC v. Pyett*,[8] the U.S. Supreme Court rejected a challenge by a union member to the legality of an arbitration clause in a union contract. The Court held that when a union negotiates an arbitration clause, it does not constitute an unconscionable or severable waiver of a union member's rights. In Case 5.4, a federal appellate court considers an appeal of a labor arbitration decision against star NFL quarterback Tom Brady surrounding a controversy dubbed by the media as "Deflategate."

CASE 5.4 National Football League Management Council v. Brady, No. 15-2801 (2d Cir. 2016)[9]

FACT SUMMARY On January 18, 2015, the New England Patriots and the Indianapolis Colts played in the American Football Conference Championship Game at the Patriots's home stadium to determine which team would advance to Super Bowl XLIX. During the game, officials from the National Football League (League) were prompted by a complaint from a Colts player to test all of the game balls for inflation level. Of 11 balls used by the Patriots, all 11 were underinflated and measured below the acceptable range established by League rules. Of the 4 balls used by the Colts, each tested within the permissible range.

The League retained a law firm to investigate the events, culminating in a 139-page report concluding that it was more probable than not that two Patriots equipment assistants were responsible for deflating the Patriots's game balls after the balls were examined by the referee. The report also concluded that Patriots quarterback Tom Brady had been at least generally aware of the deflation, and that it was unlikely that an equipment assistant would deflate game balls without Brady's knowledge and approval.

As a result of the report, the League notified Brady of his four-game suspension under the League's rules pursuant to its union contract governing players. Brady, through his union, appealed the suspension and asserted his union contract rights to an arbitration hearing. After 10 hours of testimony, including a revelation that Brady had ordered

his assistant to destroy the cell phone that he had been using since early November 2014 (a period that included the AFC Championship Game and the initial weeks of the subsequent investigation), Brady's suspension was upheld by the arbitrator. On appeal, a federal trial court vacated the decision on the basis that Brady had not been provided adequate notice that the suspension was within the League's range of punishments. The League appealed.

SYNOPSIS OF DECISION AND OPINION The U.S. Court of Appeals for the Second Circuit reversed the trial court's decision, ruled in favor of the League, and instructed the lower court to confirm the arbitration award. The court held that Brady had not met the high standard required for courts to vacate arbitration awards. This was particularly true when the arbitration was held pursuant to a union contract. The court rejected the trial court's conclusions about improper notice to Brady because it was outside the proper scope of a court's review in labor arbitration cases.

WORDS OF THE COURT: Deference to Arbitrator "The basic principle driving both our analysis and our conclusion is well established: a federal court's review of labor arbitration awards is narrowly circumscribed and highly deferential—indeed, among the most deferential in the law. Our role is not to determine for ourselves whether

(continued)

---

[8]129 S.Ct. 1456 (2009).

[9]The full name of this case is *National Football League Management Council and National Football League v. National Football League Players Association, on its own behalf and on behalf of Tom Brady, and Tom Brady*. It was condensed for the sake of clarity.

Brady participated in a scheme to deflate footballs or whether the suspension imposed by the [League] should have been for three games or five games or none at all. Nor is it our role to second-guess the arbitrator's procedural rulings. Our obligation is limited to determining whether the arbitration proceedings and award met the minimum legal standards. . . . These standards do not require perfection in arbitration awards. Rather, they dictate that even if an arbitrator makes mistakes of fact or law, we may not disturb an award so long as he acted within the bounds of his bargained-for authority."

Case Questions

1. Why did the court reject the trial court's conclusions?

2. What standard should a court apply in deciding whether to vacate a labor arbitration award?

3. *Focus on Critical Thinking:* The union contract permits the League's commissioner to serve as sole arbitrator in a disciplinary suspension appeal. Could this impact the impartiality of the arbitration? Why would the players' union agree to that provision in its contract with the League?

Mediation

Another common form of ADR is **mediation**. Mediation is becoming increasingly common as a cost-efficient form of dispute resolution primarily because mediation is relatively informal and does not require as much time or preparation as arbitration. A mediator is typically appointed in much the same manner as an arbitrator. In fact, in addition to arbitration services, the American Arbitration Association also provides mediation services.

The mediator is often, though not required to be, an attorney who is specially trained in the art of negotiation and paid an hourly rate or fixed fee for a certain period of time (usually per day or per mediation session). The mediator's task is to facilitate discussion, listening to each party's grievances and arguments and ensuring communication between the parties. The mediator's goal is to defuse any antagonism between the two parties and focus on working toward a mutually beneficial solution. Note, however, that in mediation no final decision is rendered, so if the parties are unable to reach an agreement, they must resolve their dispute using another method.

Mediation is sometimes required by statute or court procedure before a dispute can be brought to trial. As with legally mandated arbitration, the goal of legally required mediation is to allow the parties the opportunity to settle the case. Because much of the antagonism that surrounds a legal dispute is dissipated by the mediator's efforts, the process can help parties to see the dispute in a more even-tempered fashion. The ultimate goal is to work toward a mutually satisfactory resolution.

Expert Evaluation

For parties involved in a business dispute in which the issues are complex or related to the intricacies of a certain industry or profession, **expert evaluation** (neutral fact-finding) by an independent expert who can then recommend a settlement is an attractive alternative. The **expert evaluator** first reviews documents and evidence provided by each party that give a full description of the events and circumstances leading to the claim and the resulting loss. The evaluator then follows up with questions and sometimes takes statements from witnesses, if necessary. Drawing on her range of experience and expertise in the industry, the evaluator gives her opinion on the merits, puts a value on the claim, or recommends a settlement amount. The goal of this process is to facilitate a negotiated settlement without the expense and time required in a trial.

Other Forms of ADR

In some cases, parties to a dispute want to have the opportunity to settle the case through mediation, but they also want some degree of certainty in the event the mediation fails to produce a settlement. In those circumstances, parties may use a hybrid of mediation and arbitration. In this hybrid form, sometimes known as **med-arb**, both parties first submit to mediation for a set period of time (perhaps two business days). If the mediation fails, the process then moves to binding arbitration. The goal is to reach an agreement with the least amount of formality possible. If the dispute cannot be settled during mediation, arbitration is available as an automatic fallback.

Summary jury trials are used primarily in federal courts but have occasionally been used by state courts when there are complex issues to be litigated. An abbreviated half- to full-day trial is conducted before a jury, usually after discovery has been completed. Time limits may be set regarding each facet of the summary trial. No live expert testimony is presented, and the attorneys primarily conduct the proceeding through oral argument. Typically, no record is kept. A sitting or retired judge conducts the trial and issues a nonbinding advisory opinion.

Businesses may also use an ADR method called a **mini-trial**. Here, a condensed version of the case is presented to the top management from both sides. A neutral party, often an expert in the subject matter of the dispute, conducts the trial. The primary purpose of the mini-trial is to allow management from both sides to see and hear the facts and arguments, hopefully enabling them to engage in more fruitful negotiations and thus avoid litigation. The neutral party does not ordinarily render a decision, but he may be requested by the parties to provide his expert opinion as to the likelihood of the outcome should the matter proceed to trial.

TAKEAWAY CONCEPTS Alternative Dispute Resolution (ADR)

- The primary advantages of ADR are reductions in costs and time, the preservation of business relationships, the involvement of an expert neutral party, and privacy.
- ADR usually arises as a result of a contract between two parties that have agreed ahead of time to resolve any disputes using a certain ADR method, such as arbitration.
- The primary methods of ADR are arbitration, mediation, expert evaluation, or some hybrid of these three methods.
- In arbitration, the parties submit their dispute to one or more arbitrators and present evidence and limited witness testimony, and then a decision is made.
- Mediation is an attempt by a trained third party to bring the opposing parties to an agreement on a dispute by proposing possible solutions; however, no decision is made.
- The primary difference between arbitration and other methods of ADR is that arbitration provides the parties with a decision.

 THINKING STRATEGICALLY

©valterZ/Shutterstock

Online Dispute Resolution

PROBLEM: In situations involving small amounts of money, is there a way for a business to resolve relatively minor disputes in a cost-effective manner?

A business may be engaged in hundreds of relatively low-cost transactions per year with various out-of-state vendors such as suppliers, shipping companies, office supply stores, contractors, and the like. When disputes arise, a business may be at a distinct disadvantage and may lack bargaining position because the amount in controversy is too low to justify even the least expensive form of alternative dispute resolution. However, over an extended period of time these small losses add up to unnecessary liabilities, leaving managers with a difficult choice when faced with a dispute over a relatively low amount of money with an out-of-state vendor. Do they (1) invest in a dispute resolution method, despite the fact that the costs may very well exceed the benefits in that particular dispute, or (2) allow the losses to accumulate and potentially seek favorable tax treatment for writing off bad debt?

STRATEGIC SOLUTION: Attempt to use online dispute resolution (ODR).

Businesses are now capable of making small purchases from vendors across the globe quickly and conveniently. This renders traditional forms of ADR impracticable, given the reluctance to pay for an arbitrator or attorney and the fact that traveling to another location to settle a dispute often returns a sum less than the costs of travel. ODR has all of the advantages of traditional forms of ADR: The parties in question can avoid the expense and publicity of trial, plus an agreement usually is reached much faster.

Online technology is ideal for low-cost transactional disputes, such as a party seeking a refund for a defective product. Often these types of issues can be resolved using technology alone. For example, blind-bidding sites like ClickandSettle.com and Cybersettle.com offer an automated service where parties individually enter the price they are willing to pay or receive. The software evaluates these numbers and then sends each party a fair price based on their initial demand.

Another form of ODR is geared more toward complex transactions. For example, Square Trade proposes prewritten resolutions. For example, if you received a damaged shipment of goods, Square Trade offers a standard menu of solutions such as (1) replacement with an undamaged good, (2) return for a full refund, or (3) keep the merchandise with a partial refund. The parties may also fill in their own solution, but this guided approach helps the parties focus on a resolution to the dispute.

If direct negotiation fails to resolve the issue, Square Trade users can request a mediator for a $20 fee per participant plus a percentage fee if the dispute exceeds $1,000. At OnlineResolution.com, mediation fees range between $15 and $25. For disputes of more than $500, participants each pay between $50 and $150 per party per hour, based on the value under dispute.

Option 1: Online Mediation   Online mediation is a logical first step to settling disputes. Like traditional forms of mediation, online mediation is generally nonbinding. Parties present their positions to a mediator, who considers their arguments and attempts to negotiate a settlement. An advantage to online mediation is that dialogue is carried out via e-mail, so participants can submit responses at their convenience and can think out their replies rather than engage in what might be an antagonistic live hearing.

Option 2: Online Arbitration   Online arbitration is similar to traditional arbitration, except that all communications take place using the Internet. The arbitrator convenes the arbitration via live webcast and issues a decision based on the evidence presented. In an online setting, all communications, including the presentation of evidence, are supplied in electronic form: text, image, audio, or video. Participants in online arbitration agree in advance to abide by the arbitrator's decision and that the award may be enforced by an appropriate court. Following completion of the online arbitration, each participant typically completes a brief evaluation of the arbitrator and the process.

QUESTIONS

1. What are the primary advantages and drawbacks to online dispute resolution?
2. What kinds of disputes could *not* be resolved by online dispute resolution?
3. What are differences between online arbitration versus online mediation?

KEY TERMS

Civil litigation p. 102   A dispute resolution process in which the parties and their counsel argue their views of a civil controversy in a court of law.

Standing p. 104   Requirement for any party to maintain a lawsuit against another party necessitating that the party asserting the claim must have suffered an injury in fact and that harm must be direct, concrete, and individualized.

Complaint p. 105   The first formal document filed with the local clerk of courts when the plaintiff initiates a lawsuit claiming legal rights against another.

Summons p. 105   Formal notification to the defendant that she has been named in a lawsuit and that an answer must be filed within a certain period of time.

Answer p. 105   Defendant's formal response to each paragraph of the complaint.

Counterclaim p. 105   Filed when the defendant believes that the plaintiff has caused her damages arising out of the very same set of facts as articulated in the complaint.

Cross-claim p. 105   Filed when the defendant believes that a third party is either partially or fully liable for the damages that the plaintiff has suffered and, therefore, should be involved as an indispensable party in the trial.

Motion p. 107   A request by one party to the court asking it to issue a certain order (such as a motion for summary judgment). Motions may be made by either party before, during, and after the trial.

Discovery p. 109   Process for the orderly exchange of information and evidence between the parties involved in litigation (or in some cases arbitration) prior to trial.

Deposition p. 109   Method of discovery where a witness gives sworn testimony to provide evidence prior to trial.

Interrogatory p. 109   Method of discovery where one party submits written questions to the opposing party attempting to gather evidence prior to trial.

Request for production p. 109   A request aimed at producing specific items to help one party discover some important fact in the case.

Request for admissions p. 109   A set of statements sent from one litigant to an adversary, for the purpose of determining which facts are in dispute and which facts both parties accept as true.

Pretrial conference p. 110   A meeting between the attorneys for the parties and the judge in the case several weeks prior to trial, with the objectives of encouraging settlement and resolving any outstanding motions or procedural issues that arose during the pleadings or discovery stages.

Trial p. 110   Stage of litigation that occurs when the case cannot be settled, generally taking place in front of a judge as the finder of law and with a jury as a finder of fact.

Bench trial p. 110   Trial without a jury where the judge is both the finder of law and the finder of fact.

Jury selection p. 110   The process of asking potential jurors questions to reveal any prejudices that may affect their judgment of the facts.

Opening statements p. 111   Attorneys' presentation at the onset of the trial of their theory of the case and what they hope to prove to the jury.

Direct examination p. 111   The first questioning of a witness during a trial in which the plaintiff's attorney asks questions of the witnesses on the plaintiff's list.

Cross-examination p. 111   The opportunity for the attorney to ask questions in court, limited to issues that were brought out on direct examination, of a witness who has testified in a trial on behalf of the opposing party.

Closing arguments p. 111   Attorneys' summations of the case with the objective of convincing the jury of what theory to decide the case upon, occurring after testimony is completed and evidence has been submitted.

Charging of the jury p. 111   Instructions given by the judge to the jury explaining how to work through the process of coming to a factual decision in the case.

Preponderance of the evidence p. 111   The burden of proof used in civil cases, under which the fact finder need be convinced only that the defendant's liability was more likely than not to be true.

Deliberations p. 111   The process in which a jury discusses, in private, the findings of the court and decides by vote which argument of either opposing side to agree with.

Verdict p. 111   The final decision of a jury in a case.

Hung jury p. 111   A jury that cannot come to a consensus decision on which party should prevail in a case.

Arbitration p. 114   Method of alternative dispute resolution in which the parties present their sides of the dispute to one or more neutral parties who then render a decision; often involves a set of rules designed to move from dispute to decision quickly.

Mediation p. 118   Method of alternative dispute resolution in which a mediator attempts to settle a dispute by learning the facts of the matter and then negotiating a settlement between two adverse parties.

Expert evaluation p. 118   Method of alternative dispute resolution in which an independent expert acts as the neutral fact finder; particularly useful for parties involved in a business dispute where the issues are somewhat complex and related to the intricacies of a certain industry or profession.

Expert evaluator p. 118   The neutral fact finder in expert evaluation who reviews documents and evidence provided by each party and draws on her range of experience and expertise in the industry to offer an opinion on the merits and value of the claim and recommend a settlement amount.

Med-arb p. 119   Method of alternative dispute resolution whereby the parties begin with mediation and, if mediation fails in a fixed time period, the parties agree to submit to arbitration.

Summary jury trial p. 119   An abbreviated trial conducted before a jury and a sitting or retired judge at which attorneys present oral arguments without witness testimony and the decision is nonbinding.

Mini-trial p. 119   A condensed version of the case is presented to the top management from both sides, with an expert neutral party conducting the trial, allowing them to see and hear facts and arguments so more meaningful negotiations can take place.

CASE SUMMARY 5.1 Infinite Energy, Inc. v. Thai Heng Chang, 2008 WL 4098329 (N.D. Fla. 2008)

Request for Production

Chang was terminated from his employment at Infinite Energy, Inc., for allegedly leaking confidential information to competitors. Litigation ensued, and during discovery Infinite requested access to all of Chang's e-mail accounts. Although Chang turned over e-mails from his work account, he refused to turn over e-mails from his private Yahoo! account. Infinite claimed that the e-mails

were essential to its case, and Chang contended that the e-mails were confidential and unrelated to his employment and, therefore, not within the scope of discovery.

CASE QUESTIONS

1. Who prevails and why?
2. Is this information necessary for Infinite's case? Why or why not?

CASE SUMMARY 5.2 Bridgestone Americas Holding, Inc. v. Mayberry, 854 N.E.2d 355 (Ind. 2006)

Discovery

Mayberry filed a product liability action against Bridgestone alleging that tire tread separation caused a car accident that killed her son. During pretrial discovery, Mayberry sought the formula for the steel belt skim stock* on the tire in question. Bridgestone objected to these requests and moved for a court order to prevent disclosure of all trade secrets used to produce the tires, including the skim stock formula. Bridgestone claimed that the skim stock formula qualified as a trade secret

because (1) it frequently took several years to arrive at the detailed formula for a new rubber compound; (2) the steel belt skim stock formula represented one of the tire companies' most valuable assets and most closely guarded secrets; and (3) access to the recipes was very narrowly limited.

CASE QUESTIONS

1. If Bridgestone's formula for the tire were already known to its competitors, would they have been able to protect it from discovery? Why or why not?
2. Under what circumstances would potential harm of disclosure outweigh the need for the information in a trial?

---

*Skim stock is a specially formulated rubber component designed to provide adhesion between the rubber and steel cord, and between the belts and surrounding components, in a radial tire.

CASE SUMMARY 5.3 Massachusetts v. U.S. Environmental Protection Agency, 127 S. Ct. 1438 (2007)

Standing

The Commonwealth of Massachusetts sued the Environmental Protection Agency (EPA) for failing to properly enforce the Clean Air Act. The Commonwealth argued that the EPA's failure to strictly regulate greenhouse gases was causing a direct injury to its environment and citizenry. The EPA moved to dismiss the case based on the Commonwealth's lack of standing since they had not alleged an injury, causation, and redressability. The EPA argued that the injury of greenhouse gases was too

tenuous to claim as a direct injury. The Commonwealth countered that it has an interest in its land and coastline and that injury may be shown through erosion of the coastal property as water rises.

CASE QUESTIONS

1. Does a state have standing to sue a federal agency?
2. Is the erosion of a coastline an "injury" in the same context as injuries suffered in other types of cases (such as negligence or breach of contract)?

Arbitration Clauses and Public Policy

After the *Exxon Valdez* disaster, Exxon implemented a strict policy of testing its employees who served on tankers for drug and alcohol use. The policy allowed a manager to immediately discharge any employee who was intoxicated at the time of duty aboard the ship. Fris, an employee who boarded the ship while intoxicated, was discharged when his manager determined that he was unfit for work. However, Fris's union contract allowed him to appeal the discharge through an arbitration procedure. The arbitration panel ordered Fris reinstated, and Exxon filed suit in a federal court to have the arbitration set aside on the basis that the arbitration order violated public policy and would subject Exxon to liability should Fris act negligently while intoxicated. The Union argued that the court should give deference to the arbitration system articulated in the union contract.

CASE QUESTIONS

1. Who prevails and why?
2. In what way is this case similar to a case you read in this chapter?

Arbitration Clauses and Public Policy

Annette Phillips began working as a bartender at a Hooters restaurant in South Carolina in 1989. Five years later, Hooters initiated an alternative dispute resolution program among its employees. As part of that program, the company conditioned eligibility for raises, transfers, and promotions upon an employee's signing an agreement to arbitrate employment-related disputes including, among other issues, discrimination or sexual harassment claims. The agreement provided for binding arbitration in accordance with a standard set of rules that were created and administered by Hooters. In 1994 and again in 1995, Phillips signed the agreement but did not obtain a copy of the rules. In 1996, Phillips quit her job and refused to arbitrate based on the unfairness of the Hooters arbitration rules. Among the provisions she found to be unfair were:

- The requirement that arbitrators be selected exclusively from a list provided by Hooters.
- Hooters's rights to expand the scope of the arbitration, to move for summary dismissal, and to record the proceeding without any similar rights for the employee.
- Hooters's unilateral authority to bring an arbitration award to court in order to vacate or modify the award if the company could show that the panel had exceeded its authority.

After Phillips notified Hooters that she intended to file suit for sexual harassment and employment discrimination, Hooters filed suit to compel arbitration. The district court ruled in favor of Phillips and held that the arbitration clause was unenforceable and void because it was not a true meeting of the minds required for an enforceable agreement between the parties and that the clause was void as a matter of public policy. Hooters appealed.

CASE QUESTIONS

1. Who prevails and why?
2. Why do you think that Hooters chose to include a mandatory arbitration clause in its employment contracts?
3. Had Phillips been provided a copy of the rules when she signed the employment contract, would this change your analysis? Why or why not?

1. Food Mart Corporation is being sued by Adams for breach of contract related to her employment agreement with Food Mart. This is an example of:

   a. Criminal litigation.

   b. Mediation.

   c. Civil litigation.

   d. Civil arbitration.

   e. None of the above.

2. In order to have _____ to file a lawsuit, the party must have suffered an actual injury in fact.

   a. Authorization

   b. Standing

   c. Jurisdiction

   d. Status

   e. Impact

3. Raleigh is a customer at Outdoor World. He is injured while attempting to lift a heavy lawn ornament off a display shelf at the store. Raleigh sues Outdoor World claiming that the ornament was not sufficiently secured. If Raleigh wishes to obtain an oral statement from a witness who was at the scene of the incident, what is the appropriate method of discovery?

   a. Deposition

   b. Interrogatories

   c. Request for production

   d. Request for admission

   e. Request for interview

4. Burnett is being sued by his business partner over a dispute about profit distribution. Burnett contends that no issues of fact are present and he should win based on established legal precedent. He files a request that the court enter judgment in his favor without trial. Burnett's motion is:

   a. To compel litigation.

   b. To strike the judgment.

   c. For summary judgment.

   d. To compel discovery.

   e. To correct the record.

5. Which of the following could *not* occur in a bench trial?

   a. Opening statements

   b. Direct examination

   c. Cross-examination

   d. Closing arguments

   e. Charging the jury

6. One potential advantage of alternative dispute resolution is reduced costs.

   a. True

   b. False

7. Tomason and Roberts are in a dispute about the quality of Tomason's work, and Roberts has threatened a lawsuit. Instead, the parties agree to cancel the contract and agree to 50 percent of Tomason's fee as a settlement. This is an example of formal ADR.

   a. True

   b. False

8. Dialogue is carried out via e-mail and discussion boards through a neutral third party who is trained to negotiate a solution. This is an example of online mediation.

   a. True

   b. False

9. NewCo sues Consulting Partners for breach of contract. Because the amount of the claim is under $75,000, the state court rules require that the parties first have a mini-trial with a nonbinding decision by a neutral third-party attorney. This is a form of voluntary arbitration.

   a. True

   b. False

10. Under the Federal Arbitration Act, a court may set aside the award of an arbitrator if an arbitrator committed a gross procedural error that prejudiced the rights of one party.

    a. True

    b. False

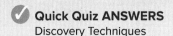

1. Request for production
2. Request for admissions
3. Deposition
4. Interrogatories

CHAPTER REVIEW QUESTIONS: Answers and Explanations

1. c. A breach of contract is a typical example of a dispute that is resolved through civil litigation. Answer *a* is wrong because a contract dispute is not a criminal matter. Answers *b* and *d* are wrong because the question asks about being sued, not about ADR.

2. b. An actual injury is necessary to have standing to maintain a lawsuit. Answer *a* is not a legal term in this context. Answer *c* is wrong because jurisdiction is not at issue. Answers *d* and *e* are incorrect statements of law.

3. a. A deposition is an oral interview of a witness that is recorded and considered sworn testimony. Answer *e* does not exist. The remaining answers are incorrect because they all seek a written document in one form or another.

4. c. A summary judgment motion is possible when no factual issues are in dispute and application of the law results in one party prevailing over the other without the necessity of a trial. The remaining answers are motions that are not related to issues of fact.

5. e. A bench trial is one where the judge is both finder of fact and finder of law and thus no jury is involved. The remaining answers are wrong because each of those phases still takes place in a bench trial.

6. a. True. Potential advantages to ADR include reduction in costs and time commitment.

7. b. False. When two parties negotiate a solution to a dispute that involves terms of settlement, this is a form of informal ADR and *not* a form of formal ADR (i.e., the parties never used any forums [such as mediation] to resolve the dispute).

8. a. True. When parties attempt to use a third party to negotiate a solution, this is a form of mediation. The key word is *negotiate*.

9. b. False. When court rules require parties to attempt to arbitrate claims prior to allowing the case to be brought in court, this is legally mandated arbitration because it is required by statute and not because the parties volunteered.

10. a. True. The FAA outlines four reasons for setting aside a private arbitration award by a court including when the arbitrator committed a gross procedural error that prejudiced the rights of one party under the statute.

UNIT TWO Contracts, Sales, and Leases

CHAPTER 6

Contracts: Overview, Definition, Categories, and Source of Law

 THINKING STRATEGICALLY

Contracts offer high degrees of flexibility for the contracting parties and this promotes creativity and value-creation. In this chapter you will learn how companies can strategically use contract law to increase market share and preserve competitive advantage over time.

Learning Objectives

After studying this chapter, students who have mastered the material will be able to:

6-1   Identify the basic definition and purpose of a contract.

6-2   List the basic elements of a valid contract.

6-3   Distinguish various ways that contracts can be classified.

6-4   Locate the basic structural items of a contract and compare legalese versus plain-English contract terms.

6-5   Identify the traits a strategically qualified attorney uses to assist with contracting.

CHAPTER OVERVIEW

Contracts are fundamental to business and a well-functioning market economy because they protect the expectations of parties who exchange value in commercial dealings. In business, upholding the promises and expectations captured within contracts minimizes risk and facilitates planning. Contracts allow businesses to budget, plan, coordinate, and allocate resources so they can deploy capital productively.

Contract law promotes these business objectives and is a flexible area of private law that encourages contracting parties to define their own terms and strike novel types of agreements. For example, Uber's ability to create and enforce novel contracts with drivers and its app users allows it to execute an innovative and successful business model as a ride-sharing technology company. The flexible nature of contracts encourages value creation and innovation.

This chapter will provide a broad overview of contracts and examine the definition, purpose, and elements of a contract as well as the various types of contracts and their basic structure.

THE NATURE AND APPLICATION OF CONTRACTS

LO 6-1

Identify the basic definition and purpose of a contract.

A **contract** is a legally enforceable promise or set of promises. Individuals have been exchanging promises in a business setting for thousands of years, and the law of contracts is one of the most ancient sources of law. The Code of Hammurabi, for example, is a Babylonian legal code that dates back to 1754 BC. Interestingly, nearly half of that ancient code deals with contract law.

Likewise, merchants in medieval Europe found themselves in need of a stable, uniform, and unbiased system of rules for deciding commercial disputes across borders and political boundaries. This led to the creation of the *lex mercatoria,* or merchant law, in medieval Europe, which facilitated trade across the region.

In the United States, there is a tradition of upholding and enforcing contracts by honoring **freedom of contract** principles. Under freedom of contract, parties are free to craft whatever bargains suit the parties' best interests and to structure the terms of the deal to best represent their intentions. Courts that support freedom of contract principles generally do not interfere with the contracting process, do not assess the wisdom of the deal, and will enforce valid contracts against parties absent evidence of fraud, mistake, oppression, or lack of legal purpose.

The U.S. Constitution reflects the important status of contracts in American society. For example, Article I, Section 10 of the Constitution limits government interference with contracts and says that "No State shall . . . pass any . . . Law impairing the Obligation of Contracts." Under the U.S. system of federalism created by the Constitution, contract law is primarily the domain of state law. Similar to the *lex mercatoria,* the U.S. common law process of judicial decision making has resulted in contract principles that are fair, are largely uniform, and facilitate trade across the various states. The ***Restatement (Second) of Contracts***, for example, is a model law that many state courts have adopted to govern contracts involving services or real estate. Likewise, every state has in whole or in part adopted the **Uniform Commercial Code**, a model code for the sale of all types of goods, new or used.

The Code of Hammurabi is one of the oldest legal texts known to exist. Nearly half of that code deals with contracts.
©Mariusz Jurgielewicz/123rf

Nonetheless, there are some differences in contract law between the states that impact businesses. For example, there is variance among the states in their levels of noncompete enforcement. A *noncompete contract* is a contract in which one party agrees not to compete with another. Most states require these agreements to further a legitimate business interest and be reasonable in length, geographical coverage, and scope. California, however, refuses to enforce noncompete contracts as a matter of public policy. Other states, like Florida, tend to uphold these contracts in favor of employers. Figure 6.1 illustrates the relative level of noncompete enforcement in 50 states.

> **Code of Hammurabi, Law 122:** "If anyone give another silver, gold, or anything else to keep, he shall show everything to some witness, draw up a contract, and then hand it over for safekeeping."

Just about every aspect of business relies on contracts to protect expectations and facilitate planning. Table 6.1 lists the different business functions that generate value and are referred to as the core **value chain activities** in most businesses. The table also provides examples of contracts commonly associated with these business activities.

Freedom of contract is an important principle in American contract law; however, it is not without limits. Ethics and public policy play equally important roles in contract law. For example, every contract is premised on the notion of **good faith** dealing. Good faith is widely recognized under the common law, and the UCC defines it as "honesty in fact and

Jimmy John's Use of Noncompete Agreements with Low-Wage Workers

Fast-food franchisor Jimmy John's became the target of public backlash when it became known that the company required sandwich makers and delivery drivers to sign broad noncompete agreements. The terms of these noncompete contracts were criticized as being overly broad and illegal, and for unfairly targeting low-wage workers. One of the most problematic terms in the contract states:

> Employee covenants and agrees that, during his or her employment with the Employer and for a period of (2) years after . . . he or she will not have any direct or indirect interest in or perform services for . . . any business which derives more than ten percent (10%) of its revenue from selling submarine, hero-type, deli-style, pita and/or wrapped or rolled sandwiches and which is located within three (3) miles

of either [the Jimmy John's location in question] or any such other Jimmy John's Sandwich Shop . . .

If these contracts were to be enforced, they would unduly restrict sandwich makers and delivery drivers from obtaining employment elsewhere. Due to the negative publicity, Jimmy John's publicly stepped away from attempting to enforce these unethical and overly restrictive agreements with its drivers and sandwich makers.

Discussion Questions

1. What was unethical about Jimmy John's use of a noncompete in this case?
2. What would be an example of an ethical use of a noncompete?
3. What is the risk of engaging in strategic business decision making that crosses the line into unethical activity?

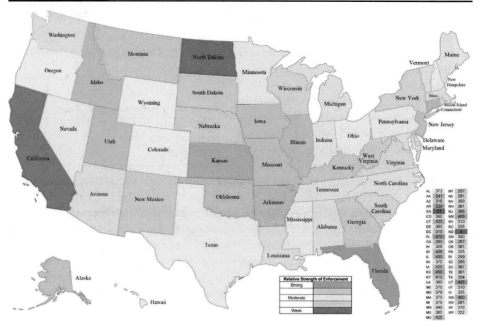

| FIGURE 6.1 | Enforcement of Noncompetes across All 50 States |

Source: Norman D. Bishara, 2011.

the observance of reasonable commercial standards of fair dealing."[1] If there is evidence of bad faith on either contracting party, this can lead to damages and remedies that are discussed in Chapter 11, "Breach and Remedies."

---

[1]UCC § 1-201.

TABLE 6.1 Contracts and the Value Chain Activities in Business

Business Activity	Transaction	Type of Contract
Research and development	A technology company hires an engineer as an outside contractor to develop inventions.	Invention assignment
Supply chain and logistics	An almond milk distributor chooses a company to manufacture, package, and label its beverage product.	Manufacturing and packaging agreement
Human resources	The board of directors hires a CEO to lead a company.	Employment agreement
Marketing	A sports team licenses its logo to an overseas apparel manufacturer.	License agreement
Distribution	A carmaker agrees to sell vehicles to an independent dealership.	Sales and distribution agreement
Sales	A sales representative negotiates a contract with a client.	Sales contract
Finance	A commercial bank extends a loan to a company.	Loan agreement

In Case 6.1, a federal appellate court decides whether a lender and borrower are required to negotiate in good faith after they signed an initial term sheet during the preliminary stages of negotiation.

CASE 6.1 Teachers Insurance and Annuity Association of America v. Tribune Co., 670 F. Supp. 491 (1987)

FACT SUMMARY Teachers Insurance and Annuity Association of America (TIAA) sued Tribune alleging that Tribune breached a commitment letter agreement for a 14-year, $76 million loan yielding 15.25%. During negotiations, Tribune had sought a loan that would allow them to employ off-balance-sheet accounting. TIAA sent Tribune a letter that included a term sheet with the major contract terms; however, the letter made no reference to loan conditions involving off-balance-sheet accounting. TIAA's letter stated that the final agreement was "contingent upon the preparation, execution and delivery of documents . . . in form and substance satisfactory to TIAA and to TIAA's special counsel . . ." and that the final loan documents would contain the "usual and customary" representations and warranties, closing conditions, other covenants, and events of default "as we [TIAA] and our special counsel may deem reasonably necessary to accomplish this transaction." The letter concluded by inviting Tribune to "evidence acceptance of the conditions of this letter by having it executed below by a duly authorized officer. . . ." The letter also stated that "[u]pon receipt by TIAA of an accepted counterpart of this letter, our agreement to purchase from you and your agreement to issue sell and deliver to us . . . the captioned securities, shall become a binding agreement between us."

Tribune signed and returned the letter and term sheet, adding that "our acceptance and agreement is subject to approval by the Company's Board of Directors and the preparation and execution of legal documentation satisfactory to the Company." Tribune's acceptance letter likewise made no mention of any off-balance-sheet accounting requirements. Before the final loan agreement was signed, however, Tribune's accountants expressed doubt that regulators would accept the off-balance-sheet nature of the proposed loan. Tribune then refused to enter into the final loan agreement and broke off further negotiations with TIAA.

TIAA alleged that Tribune breached an obligation to negotiate the final loan agreement in good faith. In response, Tribune argued that TIAA understood the loan was contingent upon the borrower's ability to employ off-balance-sheet accounting.

(continued)

SYNOPSIS OF DECISION AND OPINION   The trial court held that the term sheet and letter were binding on Tribune when it responded with its signed acceptance letter. It was important that neither the offer nor acceptance letters mentioned any off-balance-sheet loan requirements. Even though the parties had not settled on all the contract terms, the term sheet captured the most important and agreed-upon loan terms and created a duty on both parties to negotiate a final loan agreement in good faith. A binding preliminary agreement obligated the parties to negotiate in good faith with one another toward reaching a final contract.

WORDS OF THE COURT: Open Terms   "Tribune contends that the commitment letter agreement included so many open terms that it could not be deemed a binding contract. . . . The two page term sheet attached to the commitment letter covered the important economic terms of a loan. The fact that countless pages of relatively conventional minor clauses remained to be negotiated does not render the agreement unenforceable.

"[T]he reservation of [Tribune's] Board approval and the expressed 'contingen[cy] upon the preparation,

execution and delivery of documents' did not override and nullify the acknowledgement that a 'binding agreement' had been made on the stated terms; those reservations merely recognized that various issues and documentation remained open which also would require negotiation and approval. If full consideration of the circumstances and the contract language indicates that there was a mutual intent to be bound to a preliminary commitment, the presence of such reservations does not free a party to walk away from its deal merely because it later decides that the deal is not in its interest."

Case Questions

1. What factors did the court examine to decide if the parties intended to be bound to one another in a final loan contract?

2. How could Tribune have avoided breaching the good faith requirement imposed by the court?

3. *Focus on Critical Thinking:* Is it a good policy to impose a good faith requirement on parties when they are still negotiating a final contract? Explain.

 Quick Quiz Contracts in Context

1. Identify a successful company. What types of contracts do you think are most important to this company? How do contracts relate to the company's value chain activities? Explain.

2. Provide and discuss an example in which upholding freedom of contract might lead to an unjust or bad result.

Answers to this Quick Quiz are provided at the end of the chapter.

TAKEAWAY CONCEPTS The Nature and Application of Contracts

- A contract is a legally enforceable promise or set of promises.
- Contracts are fundamental to business and a well-functioning market economy because they protect the expectations of parties who exchange value in commercial dealings.
- Contract law promotes business objectives and is a flexible area of private law that encourages contracting parties to define their own terms and strike novel types of agreements.
- Contracts are vital to business because just about every aspect of business relies on contracts to protect expectations and facilitate planning.
- Every contract is premised on the notion of good faith dealing.

ELEMENTS OF A CONTRACT

A valid contract has four basic required elements: mutual assent, consideration, legality of purpose, and capacity. These elements are discussed in greater detail in the next two chapters.

LO 6-2

List the basic elements of a valid contract.

Mutual assent: The parties to a contract must indicate through words or behavior that they willingly agree to enter into a contract. A valid offer and acceptance is usually how parties demonstrate mutual assent.

Consideration: This element requires both sides to obtain something of value (legal benefit) and to give up something of value (legal detriment).

Legality of purpose: A contract must satisfy a legal purpose to be enforceable. Contracts that are contrary to existing laws or public policy are likely to be rendered unenforceable.

Capacity: Both parties to the contract must have the legal standing to enter into contracts. Individuals who are minors, mentally incapacitated, or intoxicated may lack the capacity to enter into contracts, which may result in a voidable contract.

The status of these four essential contract elements will determine whether a contract is valid, void, voidable, or unenforceable. Keep these definitions in mind as you continue your study of contract law.

Valid: When a contract has the required elements, it is called a **valid** contract.

Void: When an agreement lacks one of the required elements or has not been formed in conformance with the law from the outset, the contract is considered **void** (sometimes called void *per se*).

Voidable: A contract is **voidable** when the law gives one or more parties the right to cancel an otherwise valid contract under the circumstances.

Unenforceable: Although a contract may have all the required elements and be considered valid, it may be **unenforceable** because one party asserts a legal defense to performing the contract.

In Case 6.2, a federal appellate court decides the legality of purpose and status of Apple's e-book distribution contracts with book publishers.

CASE 6.2 United States v. Apple, Inc., No. 13-3741 (2d Cir. 2015)

FACT SUMMARY The publishing market in the United States is dominated by the six largest publishers of trade books, known as the "Big Six." Together, these companies publish many of the bestsellers in fiction and nonfiction. In 2010, their titles accounted for more than 90 percent of the *New York Times* bestsellers in the United States.

In 2007, Amazon launched the Kindle, a portable electronic device that allows consumers to purchase, download, and read e-books. Just two years later, Amazon was responsible for 90 percent of all e-book sales. Amazon followed a "wholesale" business model similar to the one used with print books, whereby publishers received a wholesale price for each e-book that Amazon sold. In exchange, Amazon could sell the publishers' e-books on the Kindle and determine the retail price.

Amazon departed significantly from the publishers' traditional business model in the sale of new releases and *New York Times* bestsellers. Rather than selling more expensive versions of these books upon release, Amazon set the Kindle price for these titles

(continued)

uniformly at $9.99. A vice president from Amazon described this as a "classic loss-leading strategy" designed to encourage consumers to adopt the Kindle device by discounting new releases and *New York Times* bestsellers. Members of the Big Six believed Amazon's lower-priced e-books would make it more difficult for them to sell higher-priced hardcover copies of new releases and would condition e-book readers to expect lower prices in general for all titles.

With the introduction of the iPad tablet, Apple decided it could compete with Amazon's Kindle in the e-book market. Under Apple's competing system, publishers would have the freedom to set e-book prices in Apple's iBookstore and would keep 70 percent of each sale. The remaining 30 percent would go to Apple as a commission. This is known in the industry as an "agency" model whereby the publisher sets the retail price that consumers pay for an e-book.

Apple communicated to publishers that e-book prices in the iBookstore needed to be comparable to those on Amazon's Kindle, expressing the view that it could not "tolerate a market where the product is sold significantly more cheaply elsewhere." Although Apple's agency model gave publishers control over pricing, it created the risk that the Big Six would sell e-books in the iBookstore at far higher prices than Kindle's $9.99 offering.

To solve this problem, Apple devised three strategies that were reflected in its contracts with the Big Six publishers. First, Apple would maintain "realistic prices" by establishing contractually fixed price caps for different types of books above Amazon's $9.99 price. Second, Apple contractually required each publisher to switch all other e-book retailers, including Amazon, to the agency model. Third, to avoid price competition with Amazon, Apple required the publishers to include a most-favored nation (MFN) clause in Apple's contract. This MFN clause required the publishers to offer any e-book in Apple's iBookstore for no more than what the same e-book was offered for elsewhere, including from Amazon.

SYNOPSIS OF DECISION AND OPINION

The Second Circuit appellate court affirmed the lower trial court decision, which found that Apple violated the Sherman Antitrust Act when it colluded and signed contracts with the Big Six publishers that resulted in higher e-book prices.

WORDS OF THE COURT: Express Collusion

"Apple understood that its proposed Contracts were attractive to the Publisher Defendants *only* if they collectively shifted their relationships with Amazon to an agency model—which Apple knew would result in higher consumer-facing ebook prices. In addition to these Contracts, moreover, ample additional evidence identified by the district court established both that the Publisher Defendants' shifting to an agency model with Amazon was the result of express collusion among them and that Apple consciously played a key role in organizing that collusion. [. . .]

"Apple offered each Big Six publisher a proposed Contract that would be attractive only if the publishers acted collectively. Under Apple's proposed agency model, the publishers stood to make *less* money per sale than under their wholesale agreements with Amazon, but the Publisher Defendants were willing to stomach this loss because the model allowed them to sell new releases and bestsellers for more than $9.99. Because of the MFN Clause, however, each new release and bestseller sold in the iBookstore would cost only $9.99 as long as Amazon continued to sell ebooks at that price. So in order to receive the perceived benefit of Apple's proposed Contracts, the Publisher Defendants had to switch *Amazon* to an agency model as well—something no individual publisher had sufficient leverage to do on its own. [. . .]

"Although the Sherman Act, by its terms, prohibits every agreement 'in restraint of trade,' [the Supreme] Court has long recognized that Congress intended to outlaw only unreasonable restraints. [. . .] By agreeing to orchestrate a horizontal price-fixing conspiracy, Apple committed itself to 'achiev[ing] [that] unlawful objective.'"

Case Questions

1. What is the legal status of Apple's contracts with the Big Six publishers after this decision (valid, void, voidable, or unenforceable)?

2. How would this case have been decided had the court applied freedom of contract as its primary deciding principle?

3. *Focus on Critical Thinking:* If you were Apple, how would you have strategically designed the contract with the Big Six publishers to enter the market legally and compete with Amazon?

TAKEAWAY CONCEPTS Elements of a Contract

- A valid contract has four basic requirements: mutual assent, consideration, legality of purpose, and capacity.
- The status of the four essential contract elements will determine if a contract is valid, void, voidable, or unenforceable.

TYPES OF CONTRACTS

LO 6-3

Distinguish various ways that contracts can be classified.

Contracts can be categorized by type of contractual commitment, source of law, level of explicitness, and the nature of the business relationships. These categories are not exclusive and may overlap.

Commitment in a contract relates to the required element of consideration. Recall that consideration requires both contracting parties to obtain something of value (incur legal benefit) and to give up something of value (incur legal detriment). In a **bilateral contract**, the legal detriment is incurred through the mutual promises the parties make to each other. For example, an employer promises to hire an employee in exchange for the employee's promise to satisfy the required job duties. Similarly, if you rent an apartment, your promise to pay the stipulated rent on a certain date in exchange for the landlord's promise to offer the unit at the agreed-upon monthly rent for the duration of the lease is also a bilateral contract.

In a **unilateral contract**, one party's legal detriment arises from its action or inaction rather than a promise. For example, a homeowner's promise to pay a contractor $10,000 to install a new roof on a specific date is a unilateral (promise-for-action) contract if and when the contractor installs the new roof on that date. The majority of business contracts are bilateral contracts: They are enforceable before the other party performs, and they facilitate planning ahead of the actual contract performance, which may or may not occur under a unilateral contract.

 Quick Quiz Bilateral versus Unilateral Contracts

Due to off-campus interviews with prospective employers, John anticipates missing several Business Law lectures during the semester. John would like to enter into a contract with his classmate, Susan, to obtain notes for the lectures he will miss.

1. How would John word the note-taking contract with Susan to structure it as a bilateral contract?

2. How would John word the note-taking contract with Susan to structure it as a unilateral contract?

Answers to this Quick Quiz are provided at the end of the chapter.

Contracts also can be categorized according to the applicable source of law. For example, contracts for services or real estate are governed by state common law and are referred to as **common law contracts**. Some examples of common law contracts include employment contracts, insurance contracts, rental agreements, licensing agreements, loans, and investment contracts. Contracts dealing with the sale of goods are governed by state UCC statutes and are referred to as **UCC sales contracts**. The purchase of inventory, raw materials, machinery, or finished goods would all involve UCC Sales contracts.

Contracts are also classified by their level of explicitness. **Explicit contracts** are those where the terms are explicitly defined by the parties, either orally or in writing. Some contracts are not enforceable unless they are in writing and satisfy a rule called the **statute of frauds**. The common law statute of frauds requires evidence of a written and signed contract for agreements that involve real estate, the payment of another's debt, or services that cannot be performed in less than one year. The UCC statute of frauds requires a written and signed contract when the sale of goods is worth more than $500. **Implied contracts**, on the other hand, lack explicit terms and are solely implied by the parties' behavior or through social custom.

For example, an apartment lease is typically an explicit agreement evidenced by a comprehensive contract with various detailed terms such as the amount of rent, length of the lease, payment due dates, security deposit, penalties, and other promises. The purchase of a textbook at a campus bookstore, on the other hand, is an implied contract. The act of entering the store, taking the book made available on the shelf, and paying at the cash register comprises an implied contract through the circumstances and the parties' behavior.

Businesses favor explicit, written contracts for various reasons. One reason is to reduce ambiguity in a "handshake" oral deal. This can prevent future misunderstandings and the risk that the other party will disavow the deal's existence. Oral contracts may be valid and enforceable as long as the statute of frauds does not apply and all the required contract elements are present; however, they are difficult to prove and enforce in court. Experienced businesspeople tend to work with legal counsel to negotiate the terms of their deals in writing to minimize risk and uncertainty.

Finally, contracts can be classified according to the nature of the business relationship between the parties. Some business relationships are based on short-term, impersonal interactions. These relationships are likely to yield what are known as **transactional contracts**. Other business relationships are long term and create strong interdependencies between the contracting parties. These relationships are likely to yield **relational contracts**. Due to the parties' stronger interdependence, relational contracts tend to place a higher value on ethical business norms such as trust, loyalty, reputation, and reciprocity.[2]

In Case 6.3, a trial court decides whether a handwritten agreement that was subsequently lost can provide the basis for a jury trial in a breach of contract case.

CASE 6.3 Dwayne D. Walker, Jr., v. Shawn Carter ("Jay Z") et al. (S.D.N.Y. 2016)

FACT SUMMARY Carter, Dash, and Burke co-founded the successful Roc-A-Fella hip-hop record label. Walker is an individual who claimed to have helped create Roc-A-Fella's logo. Starting with the commercial release of Carter's first full-length album, *Reasonable Doubt,* in 1996, Roc-A-Fella began using the logo and continued to use it thereafter.

According to Walker, Dash asked him how much he would charge for the creation of a logo, and Walker replied, "Five percent of everything that the logo is on and $3,500." According to Walker, Dash replied "[A]ll right, get it done," and the two "shook on it." After he created the logo, Walker went to Dash's home, where Carter and Biggs were present. After a negotiation, Walker and Dash "shook on" an agreement in which he would receive two percent royalties for the next 10 years after the first year of use of the logo, as well as $3,500 paid up front. Walker did not shake hands with either Carter or Biggs. At a later meeting, with only Walker and Dash

(continued)

---

[2]Ian R. Macneil, "Economic Analysis of Contractual Relations: Its Shortfalls and the Need for a 'Rich Classificatory Apparatus,'" *Northwestern University Law Review* 75, no. 6 (1981), p. 1018.

present, Walker claimed that he wrote the following on a piece of paper:

> I hereby Dwayne Walker received $3,500 as partial payment for creating the Roc-A-Fella logo in execution of Damon Dash as chief executive officer of Rock-A-Fella Records in which it's agreed if the logo is used after the first year, two percent for the next 10 years will be payable to Dwayne Walker.

Walker also claimed that Dash signed this handwritten agreement; however, Walker eventually lost the alleged handwritten contract. When he was paid $3,500 for the logo but did not receive any royalties, Walker sued for breach of contract.

SYNOPSIS OF DECISION AND OPINION In New York, a contract that cannot be performed in less than one year requires a written and signed agreement between the parties to be enforceable. Otherwise, there must be some basis such as testimony from witnesses to allege that a contract existed. Since the only testimony about the existence of the contract came from Walker, the court ruled against him and in favor of the defendants.

WORDS OF THE COURT: No Written Agreement "[Walker] does not present evidence of the existence of the writing sufficient to create a triable issue of material fact. Defendants do not admit to the existence of the writing and the testimony presented by [Walker] of the alleged writing is alternately contradictory, self-serving, and not based on first-hand knowledge. [Walker] can present no witnesses to the signing of the agreement . . .

"Furthermore, state courts in New York have rejected 'self-serving' testimony to show the existence of a writing. . . . Thus, [Walker]'s testimony here cannot prevent summary judgment: the alleged agreement is the type of agreement that must be in writing under New York's Statute of Frauds; any alleged writing has been lost; and [he] does not present evidence sufficient to create a genuine issue of material fact as to whether the writing actually ever existed."

Case Questions

1. What type(s) of contract did Walker enter into with the defendants?

2. If you were Walker, how would you have ensured that the contract would be upheld against the defendants?

3. *Focus on Critical Thinking:* Why do you think states like New York have rules that require certain contracts must be in writing to be enforceable? Is this a good rule? Whom does it favor?

Implied contracts or "handshake deals" can generate bad business and legal consequences. Consider the following excerpt from Gary Erickson, founder of Clif Bar & Company, regarding his trials and tribulations involving a distribution handshake deal that went sour during the early years of his company.

DON'T KILL THE LAWYERS

Although we couldn't afford to advertise much, we did create one ad for our big launch. We wanted to make our mark and differentiate ourselves from our main competitor. Doug and I created a print advertisement that read, "It's your body. You decide." The advertisement featured a photograph of the ingredients used in Clif Bar alongside a list of the ingredients used in PowerBar, making visual the stark difference between PowerBar's highly processed white powders and chemical-looking syrups and Clif Bar's whole grains, fruits, and natural sweeteners. Two days later PowerBar sued, claiming we misrepresented their product. They demanded $300,000—this before we'd sold a single bar! Since we'd photographed the actual list of ingredients, they didn't prevail, and we settled for the token sum of $5,000.

Another issue that got us involved with lawyers was distribution. We decided to use master distributors to launch the product, one for sport and bike outlets and another for the natural food industry. The sport distributor happened to be the same company that had employed me earlier. Both distributors did fine at first. One distributor, however, was unable to pay us for product and both wanted a bigger and bigger piece of Clif Bar. Their performance was also weakening and I felt the business would flatten if we didn't wrest control away from our distributors and operate in-house. But I'd made a huge mistake. Naively, I had entered major distribution agreements with handshake deals. I had given them too much control and now had no legal agreement to back up our position. We settled one relationship for under $100,000. I ended up in court with the other distributor, the bike company. We settled for $1.9 million, including attorneys' fees. Severing these ties cost us close to $2 million at a time when our annual sales were just over $2 million.

I want to encourage entrepreneurs to use legal counsel from day one. Over the years I've known many people starting new companies who shied away from hiring an attorney because they thought that they couldn't afford the fees. I know from sad experience that one three-hour meeting can save you a million dollars down the road. I've come to depend on legal counsel and trust it.

Source: G. Erickson, *Raising the Bar—Integrity and Passion in Life and Business: The Story of Clif Bar & Co.* Used with permission from John Wiley & Sons, Inc.

TAKEAWAY CONCEPTS Types of Contracts

- Contracts can be categorized by the type of contractual commitment, source of law, level of explicitness, and type of business relationships.
- A statute of frauds rule requires that certain contracts be signed and in writing to be enforceable.
- Businesses generally favor explicit written contracts to minimize risk.

LO 6-4

Locate the basic structural items of a contract and compare legalese versus plain-English contract terms.

BASIC CONTRACT STRUCTURE AND TERMINOLOGY

Contracts vary in their purpose, length, and quality of draftsmanship. A well-drafted contract avoids wordiness and overly technical **legalese** that is difficult to understand. Legalese is characterized by long, complex sentences written in a passive voice with many embedded clauses that employ obscure archaic terms such as "hereby," "sayeth," or "witnesseth." Consider the first contract provision below, written in legalese, compared to the plain-English equivalent that follows.

"This Agreement and the benefits and advantages herein contained are personal to the Member and shall not be sold, assigned or transferred by the Member."

vs.

"Membership is not transferable."[3]

The trend among contract drafters is to write in a clear, active voice that makes use of plain English whenever possible.

Regardless of the language used, many contracts follow a well-established structure and logical sequence. A considerable number of contracts include the following sections arranged in this order: preamble, recitals, definitions, clauses, termination conditions, and appendices.

Table 6.2 provides examples of various standard sections taken from a sales representative contract.

---

[3]A. Freedman, *The Party of the First Part—The Curious World of Legalese,* p. 35.

Contract Section	Description	Sample Language
Preamble	Identifies the name of the agreement, dates, and party names.	"Sales Representative Agreement"
Recitals	Explains why the parties are entering into the agreement.	"WHEREAS, the Company wishes to enter into a contract with the Representative for sales representation services for its products."
Definitions	Defines terms used by the parties.	"'Current existing sales accounts' means Kitchen-Craft, Mid-Continent Cabinetry, Norcraft Canada Corporation, Pro Link, and StarMark."
Clauses	Contains promises made by each party that comprise the exchange of value.	"All commissions calculated in accordance with Paragraph 5.1, above, shall be remitted to the Representative by the Company within 30 days of the Company's receipt of payment for products invoiced."
Termination	States the provisions that govern how and when the contract ceases to be in effect.	"This Agreement will automatically renew for a like period unless Representative or the Company gives notice of termination. This Agreement may be terminated at any time without cause by either party upon thirty (30) days' written notice to the other party."
Appendices	Contains supplementary materials, such as incentive compensation formulas or confidentiality agreements.	"Confidentiality and Nonsolicitation Agreement"

TAKEAWAY CONCEPTS   Basic Contract Structure and Terminology

- A well-drafted contract avoids legalese whenever possible.
- Most contracts follow a well-established structure and logical sequence.
- Many contracts include the following sections: preamble, recitals, definitions, clauses, termination conditions, and appendices.

DRAFTING CONTRACTS WITH A STRATEGICALLY QUALIFIED ATTORNEY

LO 6-5

Identify the traits a strategically qualified attorney uses to assist with contracting.

The quality of legal services provided by attorneys can vary considerably. Legally astute businesspeople should seek out the services of **strategically qualified attorneys** who have the skills and qualifications to work with managers to generate opportunities and value.[4] During the contracting process, strategically qualified attorneys view themselves as an important part of the deal-making process. These attorneys play an active role in helping the businessperson translate the important terms of the deal into the legal terms in a contract.[5]

A strategically qualified contracts attorney:

- Listens carefully to the business details of a transaction.
- Asks pertinent questions about the background and purpose of a transaction.

---

[4]Robert C. Bird and David Orozco, "Finding the Right Corporate Legal Strategy," *MIT Sloan Management Review* 56, no. 1 (2014), p. 81.

[5]Tina L. Stark, *Drafting Contracts: How and Why Lawyers Do What They Do* (2007).

- Understands the major risks involved.
- Works with you to assess major negotiating points.
- Translates legal terminology into business terminology.
- Appreciates the big picture, such as the importance of business relationships or reputation.
- Drafts customized contracts rather than relying on templates, legalese, and boilerplates.
- Solicits your input throughout the contract-drafting process.

To maximize the opportunities and value in a relationship with strategically qualified legal counsel, managers also need to contribute to that partnership and become legally astute. Legally astute managers have superior knowledge of the law as it relates to their business, realize that there are substantial gray areas in the law, and work proactively with legal counsel to find ethical and value-creating solutions to business challenges.[6] The failure to achieve legal astuteness may result in legal avoidance and a culture within an organization that views the law as a constraint rather than as a source of advantage.[7]

TAKEAWAY CONCEPTS Drafting Contracts with a Strategically Qualified Attorney

- Legally astute businesspeople seek out strategically qualified attorneys.
- Legally astute managers have superior knowledge of the law as it relates to their business, realize that there are substantial gray areas in the law, and work proactively with legal counsel to find ethical business solutions.

---

[6]Constance E. Bagley, "Winning Legally: The Value of Legal Astuteness," *Academy of Management Review* 33, no. 2 (2008), p. 378.

[7]Robert C. Bird and David Orozco, "Finding the Right Corporate Legal Strategy," *MIT Sloan Management Review* 56, no. 1 (2014), p. 81.

 THINKING STRATEGICALLY

©valterZ/Shutterstock

Ticketmaster's Strategic Contracts

PROBLEM: Ticketmaster is the leading live entertainment electronic ticketing service in a very competitive marketplace. How could Ticketmaster use contract law to increase its market share?

STRATEGIC SOLUTION: Ticketmaster designed and implemented unique contracts that make it extremely difficult for competitors to compete with Ticketmaster in this industry.

To understand how Ticketmaster strategically uses and leverages contract law, it is necessary to understand how the live entertainment industry operates and how Ticketmaster departed from the industry's traditional business model and contracting practices. First, it is important to assess the various players in the live entertainment industry, as depicted in the following industry value chain.

Traditionally, ticketing companies charged venues an *inside charge* for each ticket sold to fans. This was

normally limited by contract to $1 per ticket. The *convenience charges* assessed against fans were likewise kept at a minimum and retained by the ticketing company. These two relatively modest fees were the primary revenue sources for ticketing companies before Ticketmaster's arrival. Ticketmaster's pioneering model, however, challenged these practices and used contracts to preserve its competitive advantage.

First, Ticketmaster did away with the inside charge so that the venues would never have to pay to use Ticketmaster's service and technology. To earn profits, Ticketmaster negotiated with each venue the contractual right to obtain the complete and exclusive inventory of ticketing for all of the venue's live entertainment events for 3–5 years. In exchange for this major concession, Ticketmaster promised to assess convenience and order processing fees against the fans that would then be shared with the venue at a guaranteed percentage reflected in the written contract between Ticketmaster and each venue. The ticket receipt below demonstrates the two charges assessed by Ticketmaster against a ticket purchaser: the convenience charge and the order processing fee.

```
TOTAL TICKET PRICE  $      45.50
                         ------------
           SUBTOTAL  $      45.50
  CONVENIENCE CHRG   $      10.35
   CONV. CHRG TAX    $       0.52
 ORDER PROCESSING    $       3.15
                         ------------
       TOTAL CHARGE  $      59.52
```

At Ticketmaster, we strive to provide world-class service, one fan at a time.

The following contract term, standard among Ticketmaster's contracts, was negotiated between Ticketmaster and a county-owned venue in Florida:

Principal [the venue] shall be entitled to receive Ticket sales royalties from Ticketmaster with respect to each Convenience Charge and Processing Fee; all to the extent received (and not refunded) by Ticketmaster. The amount of the Royalties are as set forth below:

Type of Royalty	Amount of Royalty
Convenience charge	35% of the convenience charge
Processing fee	35% of the processing fee

This unique rebate model allowed Ticketmaster to contractually lock in all the major venues across the nation. Eventually, Ticketmaster signed similar rebate contracts with all the major promoters who represent the most popular artists. This locked in all the key industry players and prevented the venues from negotiating directly with the promoters.

QUESTIONS

1. What type(s) of contracts are used by Ticketmaster?
2. What is Ticketmaster's source of competitive advantage?
3. How did Ticketmaster use contracts to preserve its competitive advantage?
4. If you had a superior electronic ticketing technology, how might you compete against Ticketmaster?
5. Is it fair for companies to be able to use contracts such as these to preserve their market leadership position?
6. Can you think of other businesses that employ the "rebate model" that Ticketmaster used in the electronic ticketing industry? What role do contracts have in these industries?

KEY TERMS

Contract p. 129   A legally enforceable promise or set of promises.

Freedom of contract p. 129   A perspective where courts do not interfere with the contracting process, do not assess the wisdom of the deal, and enforce valid contracts against parties absent evidence of fraud, mistake, oppression, or lack of legal purpose.

Restatement (Second) of Contracts p. 129   A model law that many courts have adopted to govern contracts involving services or real estate.

Uniform Commercial Code p. 129   A model code for the sale of goods.

Value chain activities p. 129   The different business functions that generate value in most businesses.

Good faith p. 129   Honesty in fact and the observance of reasonable commercial standards of fair dealing.

Valid p. 133   When a contract has the required elements, it is called a valid contract.

Void p. 133   When an agreement lacks one of the required elements or has not been formed in conformance with the law from the outset, the contract is considered void.

Voidable p. 133   A contract is voidable when the law gives one or more parties the right to cancel an otherwise valid contract under the circumstances.

Unenforceable p. 133 Although a contract may have all the required elements and be considered valid, it may be unenforceable because one party asserts a legal defense to performing the contract.

Bilateral contract p. 135 A contract where the legal detriment is incurred through mutual promises the parties make to each other.

Unilateral contract p. 135 A contract where one party's legal detriment is incurred through the other party's action or inaction rather than through a promise.

Common law contracts p. 135 Contracts for services or real estate.

UCC sales contracts p. 135 Contracts dealing with the sale of goods.

Explicit contracts p. 136 Contracts where the terms are explicitly defined by the parties.

Statute of frauds p. 136 The law governing which contracts must be in writing in order to be enforceable.

Implied contracts p. 136 Contracts that lack explicit terms and are implied by the parties' behavior or through social custom.

Transactional contracts p. 136 Contracts involving business relationships based on short-term impersonal interactions.

Relational contracts p. 136 Contracts involving business relationships that are long term and create strong interdependencies between the contracting parties.

Legalese p. 138 Legal terminology that is characterized by long, complex sentences written in passive voice with many embedded clauses that employ obscure, often archaic, terms.

Strategically qualified attorneys p. 139 Attorneys who can work with managers to generate opportunities and create value.

CASE SUMMARY 6.1 Chambers v. Travelers Companies, 668 F.3d 559 (8th Cir. 2012)

Unilateral Contract

Chambers worked for Travelers as a managing director. Questions arose regarding her management style and effectiveness, and she was fired. Among her claims against Travelers, she claimed that she was due a bonus earned. In February 2007, Travelers provided Chambers a total compensation summary for the year that included a bonus of $30,000. The summary clearly stated that bonuses were at the discretion of Travelers. In September 2007, her boss provided Chambers a written performance review, giving her positive ratings in every performance category. The next month, in response to employee complaints, a climate survey was administered to the employees whom she supervised and it came back extremely negative. She was also found to have irregularities in various expense reports, and in January 2008, she was terminated. Chambers alleged that Travelers's failure to pay a $30,000 bonus for her work during 2007 breached a unilateral employment contract that she accepted by her performance.

CASE QUESTIONS

1. Suppose Chambers had performed her job well, the climate survey had come back positive, and no irregularities were found in her expense reports. If she had still been terminated due to cutbacks, could she have compelled Travelers to pay her the bonus?
2. Was Travelers's bonus statement in the compensation summary a unilateral offer that could be accepted by performance?

CASE SUMMARY 6.2 Biomedical Systems Corp. v. GE Marquette Medical Systems, Inc., 287 F.3d 707 (8th Cir. 2002)

Legality

GE Marquette Medical Systems (GE) contracted with Biomedical Systems Corp. to manufacture a new medical instrument based on technology owned by Biomedical. The contract required GE to obtain clearance from the Food and Drug Administration (the federal regulatory agency that oversees such medical devices) within 90 days in order to move ahead on the project. After this contract was signed, GE determined that obtaining this clearance was not a prudent path to reach its ultimate objective of having the product approved for selling to the public. Rather than seek the clearance required by the Biomedical contract, GE decided to pursue a different strategy with the FDA that took several years to complete. When Biomedical sued GE for breach of contract, GE defended on the basis that the clearance provision in the contract was a violation of FDA procedure and, thus, the term was illegal and the contract was void.

CASE QUESTIONS

1. Can a party make a unilateral judgment as to illegality on a term of the contract when there is no affirmative finding from a regulatory authority?
2. If GE had gone ahead with the clearance process and the FDA had told GE that it was not the proper procedure, would the contract be void for illegality?

CASE SUMMARY 6.3 Forest Park Pictures v. Universal Television Network, Inc., 683 F.3d 424 (2d Cir. 2012)

Informal/Implied Contracts

Forest Park formulated a concept for a television show called *Housecall,* in which a doctor, after being expelled from the medical community for treating patients who could not pay, moved to Malibu, California, and became a "concierge" doctor for the rich and famous. Forest Park created a written series treatment for the idea, including character biographies, themes, and story lines. It mailed this written material to Alex Sepiol, who worked for USA Network. A meeting was then held at which Forest Park explained its concept. It was common practice in the industry for writers and creators to pitch creative ideas to prospective purchasers with the object of selling those ideas for compensation. Sepiol admitted that before hearing the idea for *Housecall,* he had never heard of "concierge" doctors, or doctors who make house calls for wealthy patients, and "thought it was a fascinating concept for a television show."

The parties communicated for a week, and then no further contact occurred.

A little less than four years later, USA Network produced and aired a television show called *Royal Pains,* in which a doctor, after being expelled from the medical community for treating patients who could not pay, became a concierge doctor for the rich and famous in the Hamptons, an extremely affluent community on Long Island in New York. Forest Park had no prior knowledge of *Royal Pains,* did not consent to its production, and received no compensation from USA Network for the use of its idea for the show. Forest Park sued, claiming breach of contract.

CASE QUESTIONS

1. Who wins and why?
2. What allows Forest Park to argue that this is an implied contract?

CASE SUMMARY 6.4 Rochon Corp. v. City of Saint Paul, 814 N.W.2d 365 (Minn. Ct. App. 2012)

Void Contract

Rochon Corporation lost the municipal general-contract bidding contest to construct the Lofts at Farmer's Market for the city of St. Paul to Shaw-Lundquist Associates. When the city opened the sealed bids, Shaw-Lundquist appeared to be the clear winner. But Shaw-Lundquist discovered that it had bid $619,200 lower than it had intended due to a clerical error. Bidding instructions included the following: "A bid may not be modified, withdrawn, or canceled by the Bidder for a period of sixty (60) days following the time and date designated for the receipt of bids, and each Bidder so agrees in

submitting a bid." Nevertheless, the city allowed Shaw-Lundquist to change its bid, raising it to cover not only the $619,200 error but adding $89,211 more. Still, Shaw-Lundquist's raised bid was lower than Rochon's bid, and the city awarded Shaw-Lundquist the contract for $8,041,411. State common law long held that a contract entered into in violation of competitive bidding laws is void. The state supreme court had previously stated that a competitive bidding contract is void even "without any showing of actual fraud or an intent to commit fraud, if a procedure has been followed which emasculates the safeguards of competitive bidding."

CASE QUESTIONS

1. The city claimed that it benefited the public by allowing the bid change because it resulted in monetary savings for the city. Does this explanation justify the city's disregard of established precedent? Can the court of appeals disregard established state precedent?

2. Shaw-Lundquist was able to prove that its original bid was wrong due to a legitimate clerical error. Should this have mattered?

3. Why is it good policy to not permit amendments of bids in competitive bidding situations?

CHAPTER REVIEW QUESTIONS

1. **In the United States, courts have a tradition of upholding and enforcing contracts by honoring:**
   a. The Uniform Commercial Code.
   b. The common law.
   c. Freedom of contract principles.
   d. The *lex mercatoria.*
   e. None of the above are correct.

2. **Contracts apply to which of the following business activities?**
   a. Marketing
   b. Research and development
   c. Finance
   d. Human resources
   e. All of the above are correct

3. **_____ identifies the name of the agreement, dates, and party names in a contract.**
   a. Recitals
   b. Termination
   c. Preamble
   d. Appendices
   e. Definitions

4. **A valid contract requires:**
   a. Mutual assent.
   b. Consideration.
   c. Legality of purpose.
   d. Capacity.
   e. All of the above are correct.

5. **A written rental agreement is an example of a:**
   a. Common law contract.
   b. UCC contract.
   c. Explicit contract.
   d. A and C.
   e. B and C.

6. **When an agreement lacks one of the required elements or has not been formed in conformance with the law from the outset, the contract is considered void.**
   a. True
   b. False

7. **Joe tells Phil he'll pay Phil $20 if he mows the grass. Phil mows the grass. This is a bilateral contract.**
   a. True
   b. False

8. **Jill hands Peter a written contract. In the contract, Jill makes several promises to employ Peter as a sales representative for one year if Peter promises to perform the required job duties. This is a unilateral contract.**
   a. True
   b. False

9. **Contracts allow businesses to budget, plan, coordinate, and allocate resources productively.**
   a. True
   b. False

10. **Strategically qualified attorneys understand the major risks involved in a business deal.**
    a. True
    b. False

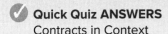
1. A sample company is Apple. For Apple, contracts related to human resources will be important to secure talent, creativity, and intellectual property rights. Manufacturing and distribution agreements will be important to source and deliver its products and software to consumers. Trademark licensing agreements will be important to exchange value and build the brand.

2. There are numerous examples where the presence of bad faith, oppression, or illegality might override freedom of contract. Courts have considered fraud and deceit to undo contracts, as well as public policy interests such as consumer protection. Courts and regulators may also limit freedom of contract to protect a weak or disadvantaged party.

Bilateral versus Unilateral Contracts

1. John agrees to pay Susan at a rate of $100 per class to take notes for lectures he misses. Susan agrees to take readable and concise notes and to turn them over to John upon payment.

2. John agrees to pay Susan at a rate of $100 per class if she will take notes for him on days that he misses classes.

CHAPTER REVIEW QUESTIONS: Answers and Explanations

1. c. Freedom of contract is a principle followed by U.S. courts to generally uphold contracts.

2. e. All of these business activities make use of contracts.

3. c. The preamble identifies the name of the agreement, dates, and party names in a contract.

4. e. A valid contract requires mutual assent, consideration, legality, and capacity.

5. d. A written rental contract is a service contract and has explicit terms negotiated by the parties, so it is both a common law and formal contract.

6. a. True. A void contract lacks one of the required elements or has not been formed in conformance with the law from the outset.

7. b. False. This contract is unilateral because the consideration involves a promise in exchange for action.

8. b. False. This contract is bilateral because the consideration involves a promise in exchange for another promise.

9. a. True. Contracts allow businesses to budget, plan, coordinate, and allocate resources productively.

10. a. True. Strategically qualified attorneys understand business risks.

CHAPTER 7

Mutual Assent: Agreement and Consideration

Understanding the requirements for an agreement to be legally binding allows business owners and managers to avoid uncertainty. As a practical matter, the contracting parties are generally free to negotiate specific terms or details unique to their business. This business reality also has a significant strategic aspect in terms of negotiation strategy. In this chapter's *Thinking Strategically,* we focus on advice from experts on how to develop an effective negotiation strategy.

Learning Objectives

After studying this chapter, students who have mastered the material will be able to:

7-1   Identify the broad underlying requirement of an enforceable contract.

7-2   List the requirements for a valid offer and explain how offers are terminated.

7-3   Articulate the rules for determining when acceptance is effective.

7-4   Apply the element of consideration in the context of contract formation.

7-5   Differentiate agreements that have consideration from those that do not.

CHAPTER OVERVIEW

Once you understand the basic framework and vocabulary of contract law that we covered in the previous chapter, the next step is to determine whether two (or more) parties' words or actions constitute a sufficient basis to form a legally enforceable contract. An agreement is legally binding if it meets certain *formation* elements set out in state common law and statutes. In this chapter, we discuss the first element, *mutual assent* (a two-part requirement consisting of a valid offer and acceptance), and the second requirement known as *consideration.* The remaining requirements are discussed in Chapter 8, "Capacity and Legality."

MUTUAL ASSENT

The broad underlying requirement of an enforceable contract is **mutual assent** (also referred to simply as *assent* or *agreement*). Typically, the parties reach mutual assent using a combination of *offer* and *acceptance.* In most cases, the *offeror* makes a valid offer to the *offeree,* who in turn must accept the offer in order for the parties to be bound by the agreement's terms. Typically referred to as a *meeting of the minds* because the parties have agreed to certain promises and obligations, mutual assent is the very root of any enforceable agreement.

REQUIREMENTS OF AN OFFER

LO 7-1

Identify the broad underlying requirement of an enforceable contract.

An **offer** is a *promise* or *commitment* to do (or refrain from doing) a specified activity such as selling a good at a certain price or offering to provide services at a given rate. An offer also is the expression of a willingness to enter into a contract by the offeror's promising an offeree that she will perform certain obligations in *exchange* for the offeree's counterpromise to perform. To take a simple example, suppose that Lewis offers to sell Williams a rare book for $1,000. In this case, Lewis is the offeror and is promising to perform through a transfer of ownership rights to the book so long as Williams, the offeree, counterpromises to perform by paying $1,000.

Objective Intent

LO 7-2

List the requirements for a valid offer and explain how offers are terminated.

The first step in determining whether a valid offer exists is analyzing the offeror's **objective intent** when making the offer. Was the offeror's intent to contract? To negotiate? Was the offer made as a joke? Courts use the parties' words and actions to decide whether a *reasonable person* would conclude that the offeror is serious in her intent to contract. If the terms of a serious offer to contract are reasonably certain, a valid offer is created and the offeree may then accept or reject the offer. It is important to note that it does not matter what the offeror actually intended. Rather, the objective test is what a reasonable person would believe the language and conduct, collectively referred to as *manifestations of intent,* mean in those circumstances. Otherwise, the offer is considered simply an offer to discuss or negotiate the terms of an agreement. For example, an e-mail from the owner of a computer retail store to a computer hardware wholesaler may contain the following language:

> I am interested in purchasing 10 new tablet computers. Please contact me about the price and delivery terms regarding the tablets.

This message does not express an immediate, objective intention to contract, and there is no definite offer of price, brand, or delivery terms. Rather, a reasonable person would look at this language as an *invitation to negotiate.* Under modern case law, the importance of the parties' intention, or lack of intention, to form a contract depends largely upon the context of the agreement. When an agreement is in the context of a business transaction, there is a strong presumption that the parties intended the agreement to be legally enforceable.

In Case 7.1, one of the most famous in American contract law, a state supreme court considers the circumstances of a transaction and the language of the parties in determining whether an offer involved an objective intent to contract.

CASE 7.1 Lucy v. Zehmer, 84 S.E.2d 516 (Va. 1954)

FACT SUMMARY W.O. Lucy (Lucy) was a farmer who knew A.H. Zehmer (Zehmer) for a period of 15 to 20 years. At one point during their relationship, Lucy offered to buy Zehmer's farm for $20,000, but Zehmer rejected the offer outright. Seven years later, Lucy met Zehmer at a restaurant and had a conversation over a period of hours while the two drank whiskey together. During this conversation, Lucy again offered to purchase Zehmer's farm.

According to the testimony at trial, the following exchange of words took place:

Lucy: I bet you wouldn't take $50,000 for that farm.

Zehmer: You haven't got $50,000 cash.

Lucy: I can get it.

Zehmer: But you haven't got $50,000 cash to pay me tonight.

(continued)

Eventually, Lucy persuaded Zehmer to put in writing that he would sell Lucy the farm for $50,000. Zehmer handwrote the following on the back of the pad: "We hereby agree to sell to W. O. Lucy the Ferguson Farm complete for $50,000.00, title satisfactory to buyer." Zehmer then signed as A. H. Zehmer and had his wife sign as Ida S. Zehmer. Before signing, the parties modified this writing several times and discussed terms over a period of 30 to 40 minutes. At the end of the evening, each party had signed the modified document that agreed to a sale of Zehmer's farm to Lucy for $50,000. The next day, Lucy believed that the contract was valid and proceeded to act accordingly by seeking financing for the purchase and checking title. However, Zehmer notified Lucy that he would not transfer title since no contract was formed. Rather, Zehmer had understood the whole transaction as a joke. At trial Zehmer testified that he "was high as a Georgia pine" while modifying and discussing the contract and that he was just "needling" Lucy because he believed Lucy could never come up with the money. Zehmer claimed that before he left the restaurant that night, he told Lucy that it was all a big joke, that the negotiations were just the "liquor talking." Zehmer claimed that he had not actually intended to sell the property, thus the contract lacked serious intent and was void.

SYNOPSIS OF DECISION AND OPINION   The court ruled that Zehmer was bound by the contract even if he had no actual (subjective) intent to sell the farm and may have been joking. The court used the objective standard in determining that a reasonable person would have construed Zehmer's actions and words as a serious intent to contract. The court held that evidence from the trial indicated that Zehmer took the transaction seriously and that Lucy was not unreasonable in believing that a contract was formed under the circumstances. The court made clear that actual mental intent is not required for formation of a contract.

WORDS OF THE COURT: Manifestation of Intent to Contract   "The appearance of a contract; the fact that it was under discussion for forty minutes or more before it was signed; Lucy's objection to the first draft; . . . the discussion of what was to be included in the sale . . . are facts which furnish persuasive evidence that the execution of the contract was a serious business transaction rather than a casual, jesting matter as the defendant now contends.

"An agreement or mutual assent is of course essential to a valid contract but the law imputes to a person an intention corresponding to the reasonable meaning of his words and acts. If his words and acts, judged by a reasonable standard, manifest an intention to agree, it is immaterial what may be the real but unexpressed state of his mind."

Case Questions

1. What factors does the court focus on when deciding whether Lucy's understanding of the contract formation was reasonable?

2. What facts could you change in this case that would result in the court determining that no contract existed?

3. *Focus on Critical Thinking:* Look at the check in Figure 7.1. Did a meeting of the minds actually occur here? Should words written on the back of a restaurant check be enough evidence to indicate objective intent? Why or why not?

FIGURE 7.1	Check from Ye Olde Virginnie Restaurant at Issue in *Lucy v. Zehmer*

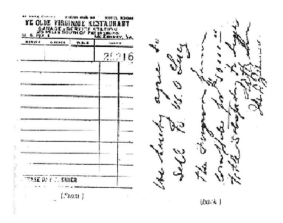

"We agree to sell to W.O. Lucy the Ferguson farm complete for $50,000, title satisfactory to buyer." *Signatures of the parties.*

Advertisements as an Offer

Most advertisements appearing in the mass media, in store windows, or in display cases are *not* offers. Rather, the law recognizes mass advertisements as an invitation for the consumer to make an offer to the seller to purchase the goods at a specified price. Frequently, these advertisements do not constitute an offer because they do not contain a specific commitment to sell. For example, suppose Big Time Appliance runs an advertisement in a local paper that misprints the ad as "Giant plasma screen TV for $10" instead of "$1,000." Ernest shows up at Big Time Appliance with a $10 bill and excitedly hands over the bill to a cashier, saying, "I accept your offer to sell me this television for $10." Big Time Appliance is not obligated to perform (i.e., sell the television for $10). The law recognizes Ernest's actions not as an acceptance of Big Time's offer but rather as an offer by Ernest to buy the television—which Big Time may accept or reject. Even a price tag on a product in the store is an invitation for the customer to make an offer and not an offer to sell at that price by the business.

Note that the preceding example is a contracts analysis. In the case of advertising, certain state consumer laws may apply to protect buyers against merchants acting in bad faith by using advertising as a "bait-and-switch" method (discussed in Chapter 44, "Consumer Protection").

Advertising as a Unilateral Offer The primary exception to the rule outlined above occurs when the advertisement is *specific* enough to constitute a unilateral contract. Advertisements that offer to sell a particular number of certain products at a certain price may constitute an offer. In the previous example, if the advertisement offered giant plasma televisions for $10 to the first 50 buyers on Friday, then the advertisement would be specific enough to constitute a valid offer requiring Big Time Appliance to sell as promised. Or if the advertisement invites the other party to accept in a *particular manner,* courts will treat this type of advertisement as a valid offer for a unilateral contract. Consider this example (based on a famous case called *Carlill v. Carbolic Smoke Ball Co.*[1] Anti-Flu Inc. sells an herbal inhaler device that it claims will prevent the flu as effectively as any flu vaccine. The company advertises, "We will pay $1,000 to anyone who uses the Anti-Flu herbal inhaler for two consecutive weeks and still contracts the flu." Pauline uses the device for two weeks (thereby accepting Anti-Flu's offer) and contracts the flu one day later. In this case, Anti-Flu would be obligated to perform its promise by paying the $1,000 sum because Anti-Flu's advertisement invited any party to accept the company's offer in a particular manner (by using the device).

In Case 7.2, an appellate court considers whether a television advertisement created an offer.

CASE 7.2 Leonard v. PepsiCo, Inc., 210 F.3d 88 (2d Cir. 2000) [affirming lower court decision and reasoning in 88 F. Supp. 2d 116 (S.D.N.Y. 1999)]

FACT SUMMARY Pepsi ran an advertisement on national television promoting its Pepsi Points program whereby consumers could obtain points by purchasing Pepsi products and then redeem the points for certain apparel and other items. An alternate way to accumulate points was to purchase them for a certain dollar amount.

The Pepsi advertisement opened with the morning routine of a high school student. The commercial was based on a *Top Gun* movie theme and depicted the student wearing a leather bomber jacket, a Pepsi T-shirt, and aviator sunglasses. For each item, the advertisement would flash the corresponding number of Pepsi points required to obtain the item. For example, when showing the actor with the aviator sunglasses, the advertisement featured the subtitle "Shades 175 Pepsi Points." The advertisement then showed a view of the cover of a Pepsi Stuff Catalog with a narration of "Introducing the new Pepsi Stuff Catalog" and the subtitle, "See details on specially marked packages." Finally, the

(continued)

---

[1] 1 Q.B. 256 (1893).

advertisement showed the student arriving at his high school in a Harrier fighter jet to the amazement of his friends and teachers. The student hops out of the jet and says, "Sure beats the bus." At this point, the subtitle flashed, "Harrier jet 7,000,000 Pepsi Points."

Leonard filled out the Pepsi Stuff order form (located in the catalog produced by Pepsi), but since there was no mention of the Harrier jet, Leonard simply wrote in the item on the order form and sent the order to Pepsi with a check for $700,000, the amount necessary to purchase the requisite points as stated in the advertisement. Pepsi refused to transfer title on the basis that no contract existed. The trial court ruled in favor of Pepsi. Leonard appealed, among other reasons, on the basis that the Pepsi advertisement was specific enough to constitute a valid offer of a unilateral contract through its advertisement.

SYNOPSIS OF DECISION AND OPINION The court ruled against Leonard. While acknowledging that certain advertisements could be an offer if the promise is clear, definite, and explicit, such was not the case here. The advertisement was not sufficiently definite because it reserved the details of the offer to a separate writing (the catalog).

WORDS OF THE COURT: Requirements for Advertisements as a Unilateral Offer "In the present case, the Harrier Jet commercial did not direct that anyone who appeared at Pepsi headquarters with 7,000,000 Pepsi Points on the Fourth of July would receive the Harrier Jet. Instead, the commercial urged consumers to accumulate Pepsi Points and refer to the catalog to determine how they could receive their Pepsi Points. The commercial sought a reciprocal promise, expressed through the acceptance of, and in compliance with, the terms of the Order Form. . . . [T]he catalog contains no mention of the Harrier Jet."

Case Questions

1. Are there any facts that support Leonard's primary argument as to why this commercial was a unilateral offer to contract?

2. Should a person seeing the television commercial reasonably believe that Pepsi would sell a $23 million Harrier jet for only $700,000?

3. *Focus on Critical Thinking:* If the wording on the catalog order form had allowed a consumer to write in the item (rather than check a box next to the item), would that have changed the outcome of this case?

TAKEAWAY CONCEPTS Valid Offers

The formation of a contract requires mutual assent, whereby the parties reach an agreement and a meeting of the minds.

- An agreement results from the offeror's making a valid offer and the offeree's accepting the terms of the offer and agreeing to be bound by its terms. This meeting of the minds may come from a true understanding or may be inferred through words and actions of the parties (objective intent).

- Advertisements generally are not considered an offer. Rather, they are an invitation for the consumer to make an offer to a seller of goods or services.

- For an offer to be valid, the parties must reach agreement on all of the essential terms of the agreement. An offer that is too vague or indefinite cannot be the basis for an agreement.

E-Contracts

About 190 million U.S. consumers—more than half the population—now shop online for products and services, according to a study by the data research firm Forrester.[2] Given the explosive growth of online retail transactions, a working knowledge of the law regarding

[2]Forrester Data: *Digital-Influenced Retail Sales Forecast, 2017 to 2022 (US).* Forrester, Nov. 14, 2017.

e-contracts can add a strategic advantage for businesses that depend on the web as a component of their business model. While traditional contract law principles still apply, courts have had to develop new applications and theories for electronic transactions. In this chapter, we discuss the enforceability of agreements that arise when computer users accept terms by (1) clicking on an "I agree" link *(click-wrap agreement)*, (2) downloading software *(browse-wrap agreement)*, or (3) opening the packaging of a product *(shrink-wrap agreement)*. Other aspects of e-contracts, such as the Uniform Electronic Transactions Act (UETA), are covered in future chapters in this section.

Click-Wrap Agreements

A *click-wrap agreement* is based on an Internet transaction where a website provider posts terms and conditions (such as their warranty terms or an arbitration clause) and the user clicks an "I Accept" button located on the web page of the purchase. In some cases, terms and conditions appear as soon as the user loads the website into her web browser. Courts have generally held click-wrap agreements to be enforceable. In *i.Lan, Inc. v. NetScout,*[3] a federal court held that a networking company that entered into a click-wrap agreement to purchase software was bound by a provision that severely limited the software manufacturers' liability in the event of a dispute.

However, click-wrap agreements are not automatically enforceable. In *Schnabel v. Trilegiant Corp.,*[4] a user who signed up for Trilegiant's service that provided discounts on sports memorabilia in exchange for a membership fee prevailed in his claim that an arbitration clause in Trilegiant's terms and conditions was *not* enforceable. In the *Schnabel* case, the contracting process required users to fill out an enrollment screen, then click on a "Yes" button agreeing that the vendor could transmit credit card data. The vendor followed up with an e-mail of terms and conditions, including a provision that all claims against Trilegiant had to be resolved through private arbitration. The court found that the contract was formed when Schnabel entered his information into the online enrollment screen. The court explained that the follow-up e-mail was not sufficient to add additional terms such as the arbitration clause because the terms and conditions were not shown on the enrollment screen.

Browse-Wrap Agreements

A *browse-wrap agreement* is one where the terms of an agreement are located on a website, but the user does not have the opportunity to click "I agree." Instead the terms are only posted via a hyperlink at the bottom of the page (or even on the next page). It is not necessary to click on the "Terms" link to use the website, so the user consents to the agreement simply by using the website. In a seminal case on browse-wrap agreements, a federal appellate court ruled that a user who downloaded software after checking an electronic box was not bound by a browse-wrap agreement where the reference to the existence of terms was located on a submerged screen.[5] Courts have held that a crucial factor in determining the validity of a browse-wrap agreement is whether the user was given *actual*

By clicking Sign Up, you agree to our Terms and that you have read our Data Use Policy, including our Cookie Use.

Sign Up   LOG IN INSTEAD

---

[3]183 F. Supp. 2d 328 (D. Mass 2002).

[4]697 F.3d 110 (2d Cir. 2012).

[5]*Specht v. Netscape Communications,* 306 F.3d 17 (2d Cir. 2002).

notice or *constructive notice* of the website's terms and conditions. One court explained the "notice" standard:

> [W]here a website makes its terms of use available via a conspicuous hyperlink of every page of the website but otherwise provides no notice to users nor prompts them to take any affirmative action to demonstrate assent, even close proximity of the hyperlink to relevant buttons users must click on—without more—is insufficient to give rise to [actual or] constructive notice.[6]

Shrink-Wrap Agreements

Shrink-Wrap Agreements   *Shrink-wrap agreements* are formed when a purchaser opens the packaging (thus the term *shrink-wrap*) after notification by the seller via a printed notice on the packaging or on a document included with the package. The notice provides that the purchaser agrees to the seller's terms by opening the package and/or keeping whatever is in the container (e.g., a box) for a certain period of time. For the most part, courts have held that such agreements are enforceable. This is true even if there is a notion that the purchaser never actually read the shrink-wrap terms before opening the package.[7] As one court has said: "Competent adults are bound by such documents, read or unread."[8]

Termination of an Offer

Once a valid offer has been terminated, the offeree may no longer accept the offer. Offers are terminated either through the actions of the parties or through operation of law.

Action of the Parties

An offer may be terminated by action of the parties in one of three ways: (1) **revocation** where the offeror revokes (withdraws) the offer prior to acceptance; (2) **rejection** where the offeree rejects the offer; and (3) **counteroffer** where the offeree rejects the original offer and proposes a new offer with different terms. Offers may also be terminated by **operation of law**.

Revocation   When the offeror decides to revoke (withdraw) the offer by expressly communicating the revocation to the offeree prior to acceptance, the offer is terminated by revocation. Revocation is consummated through an express repudiation of the offer (e.g., "I revoke my offer of May 1 to paint your office building for $1,000") or by some *inconsistent act* that would give reasonable notice from the offeror to the offeree that the offer no longer exists. For example, on Monday, Owner offers WidgetCo the nonexclusive opportunity to purchase a parcel of land for $100,000 with a deadline of Friday for responding. On Wednesday, WidgetCo learns that Owner has entered into a contract with ServiceCo for the land. On Thursday, WidgetCo calls Owner with an acceptance. No contract exists between Owner and WidgetCo because Owner's inconsistent acts were sufficient to give WidgetCo notice of the transaction. Note that a few states, notably California, do not follow the "receipt" rule, opting instead to make revocation effective upon dispatch of the revocation notice.

One important issue with revocation is the timing of the revocation. Most states follow the rule that revocation is effective only *upon receipt* by the offeree or the offeree's agent. For example, on Monday, Adams sends, via same-day courier, a letter of revocation to Bell's office. Bell's administrative assistant receives the revocation on that same day, but Bell is traveling in Japan and never actually sees the letter. On Wednesday, from his hotel room in Tokyo, Bell calls Adams and accepts Adams's initial offer. No contract exists because the revocation would be deemed effective upon receipt by Bell's administrative assistant. At that

---

[6]*Nguyen v. Barnes & Noble, Inc.*, 763 F.3d 1171, 1194 (9th Cir 2014).

[7]*M.A. Mortenson Co., Inc. v. Timberline Software Corp.*, 140 Wash. 2d 568 (2000).

[8]*Hill v. Gateway 2000, Inc.*, 105 F.3d 1147, 1150 (7th Cir 1997).

point, even though Bell had no *actual* knowledge of the revocation by Adams, the offer is revoked and Bell may no longer accept the offer.

Note that some offers are **irrevocable** (1) offers in the form of an **option contract**; (2) offers that the offeree partly performed or detrimentally relied on; and (3) so-called *firm offers* by a merchant under the UCC (firm offers under the UCC are discussed in Chapter 13, "Sales Contracts: Agreement, Consideration, and the Statute of Frauds").

Option Contracts

One way to make an offer irrevocable is for the offeror to grant the offeree an *option* to enter a contract. Typically, the offeror agrees to hold an offer open (not enter into a contract with another party) for a certain period of time in exchange for something of value (known as *consideration,* discussed later in this chapter). In the example discussed above, WidgetCo could have protected itself and enforced the "until Friday" deadline by entering into an *option* with Owner. If WidgetCo had paid Owner $1,000 to keep the offer to purchase the land open until Friday, Owner would now be obligated to keep the offer open and not entertain offers by third parties. However, if, at the end of Friday, WidgetCo hasn't communicated an acceptance of the offer to sell, Owner would keep the $1,000 and now be permitted to sell the property to another party.

Partial Performance and Detrimental Reliance

There are certain offers whereby the offeree may, prior to actual formation of the contract, take some action that *relies* on the offer; for example, the offeree begins to perform based on a unilateral offer. Recall that a unilateral offer is one in which the offer makes clear that acceptance can occur only through performance and not through a promise. This is known as *partial performance* and can render an offer temporarily irrevocable. For example, Burns offers Realtor a commission of 10 percent of the sales price if Realtor can find a buyer for the Burns Building for $500,000. Realtor spends funds to research and obtain potential buyer contact information and locates Walters, who is willing to accept the $500,000 offer to sell from Burns. Before any transaction takes place, Burns revokes his offer to Realtor and refuses to sell the property to Walters. Burns's revocation is *not effective.* Burns's promise to pay for a particular performance (a unilateral contract) was rendered irrevocable once Realtor performed by finding a buyer for the building.

An offer also may be rendered irrevocable if the offeree makes preparations prior to acceptance based on a reasonable reliance on the offer. This is known as **detrimental reliance**. For example, SubCo is a subcontractor for GeneralCo. GeneralCo relies on SubCo's bid in preparing to make an offer to renovate a commercial office complex. After GeneralCo is awarded the renovation contract, SubCo notifies GeneralCo that its bid was too low due to the poor business forecasting of one of SubCo's partners. Because it is no longer interested in the job, SubCo attempts to revoke its offer/bid. In this case, SubCo is *still required to perform* even at a loss. GeneralCo reasonably relied on SubCo's bid and would suffer a significant detriment based on this reliance. SubCo's offer became irrevocable once GeneralCo exercised reasonable reliance on the offer. Note that the UCC rules are different regarding counteroffers. The UCC rules for counteroffers are discussed in Chapter 13, "Sales Contracts: Agreement, Consideration, and the Statute of Frauds."

Rejection and Counteroffer

An offer is also terminated once the offeree either rejects the offer outright or makes a counteroffer by rejecting the original offer and making a new offer. Under the common law, the offeree's response operates as an acceptance only if it is the *precise mirror image* of the offer. If the response conflicts with the original offer even slightly, the original offer is terminated and the new offer is substituted. This principle is called the **mirror image rule**. Once the offeree has rejected the offer or made a counteroffer, her power of acceptance is terminated. For example, apply the mirror image rule to the following conversation:

Franz:	I will pay you $1,000 to paint the interior of our office building.
Josef:	I've seen your office; it is going to cost you more than that.
Franz:	How much more?
Josef:	I'll do it for $2,000.
Franz:	Ah, yes. Well, let's split it down the middle. I'll pay you $1,500.
Josef:	OK. I agree to do it for $1,500, but you must also supply the paint, brushes, ladder, tarps, cleaner, and other equipment I need.

Does a contract exist between Josef and Franz? Carefully examine the language of the parties. Josef made an outright rejection of Franz's first offer to paint the office for $1,000. Then Josef made an offer to paint the office for $2,000. Franz then rejected the offer via *counteroffer* and now has made a new offer for Josef to accept or reject his offer to pay $1,500 for the services. Although Josef starts out his response with "OK," he adds additional terms (Franz must supply the paint, etc.). Therefore, Josef rejected the offer because his acceptance was *not the mirror image* of Franz's offer. Despite the "OK" language, the law treats Josef's response as a counteroffer (and therefore a rejection). Franz's offer is now terminated, and *no* contract exists at this point. Of course, Franz is now free to accept or reject Josef's counteroffer.

Operation of Law

An offer may also be terminated by certain happenings or events covered by operation of law. Generally, these include (1) lapse of time, (2) death or incapacity of the offeror or offeree, (3) destruction of the subject matter of the contract before acceptance, and (4) supervening illegality.

Following the "offeror is the master of his offer" rule, the offeror will frequently attach some time limit on the offeree's power of acceptance. Once the time limit has expired, the offer is considered to have terminated via **lapse of time**. If, however, the offeror has not set a time limit, the offer will still expire after a *reasonable time*. Courts determine the "reasonable time period" for an acceptance by analyzing the circumstances that existed when the offer and attempted acceptance were made. When the offer involves a speculative transaction in which the subject matter is subject to sharp fluctuations in value, a reasonable time period will be considerably shorter. For example, Milton sends Dryden an e-mail: "I offer to sell you my private stock in Local Oil Company for $500 per share." Dryden waits one week, during which the price of oil skyrockets and Local Oil's stock rises to $700 per share. He then responds to Milton's e-mail: "I accept your offer of last week." In this case, Dryden would likely not be obligated to perform because the subject matter of the offer was so speculative that it dictated a short time period for expiration. On the other hand, if Milton wishes to sell Dryden a used lawn mower for $100, waiting one week would still be well within a reasonable time period for acceptance of the offer.

Death, Incapacity, Destruction, or Supervening Illegality   In the event that the offeror or the offeree either dies or becomes incapacitated before acceptance, the offer automatically terminates. Similarly, if the subject matter of the contract is destroyed before acceptance, the offer is considered terminated by operation of law. A supervening illegality occurs when changes in the law make a previously legal offer illegal. Suppose that on Monday Ben is walking past a gun shop and sees a sale sign on an AK-47 automatic assault rifle. When he asks the shopkeeper about the gun, he is assured that ownership of such a weapon is legal in the state and that the sale price is good until Saturday. On Wednesday, the state legislature passes a statute making the sale, ownership, and possession of the AK-47 a crime in the state. The gun shop's offer will immediately terminate due to the change in the law. Death, incapacity, destruction, and supervening illegality are all examples of what many courts refer to as *impossibility.*

ACCEPTANCE

A valid offer creates the power of **acceptance** for the offeree. An acceptance is the offeree's expression of agreement to the terms of the offer. An offeree typically communicates the acceptance in writing or orally but, in some cases, may accept via some action or conduct (as in a unilateral contract). So long as the offer is still in force (has not yet been terminated), the offeree may accept the terms of the offer, thereby forming an agreement.

Only the party or parties for whom the offer is intended has the power of acceptance and may accept. Suppose that during class, a professor says to a particular student, "I'll sell you my briefcase for $100." Only that student may accept, and no other student present in class has the power of acceptance. If instead the professor says, "I'll sell my briefcase for $100 to the first student in this class who accepts," then the power of acceptance is extended to the entire class, but not to the professor's students in other classes.

In order for agreement to exist, though, the offer has to be *properly* accepted by the offeree. Note that the offeror is considered the "master" of the offer and, therefore, has the power to terminate, modify its terms, or prescribe the method of acceptance of the offer *up and until the offer has been accepted* by the offeree. Once the offer has been terminated, the offeree has lost the power to accept and form an agreement. Under most circumstances, acceptance cannot be imposed or inferred from an offeree's silence after receiving an offer. Therefore, courts will not enforce a contract in which the offer states that failure to respond will be considered an acceptance of the offer.

LO 7-3

Articulate the rules for determining when acceptance is effective.

Acceptance of an Offer: The Mailbox Rule

The **mailbox rule** governs common law contracts and is a rule that determines when a contract is considered to be accepted by the offeree, thus depriving the offeror of the right to revoke the offer. In essence, the mailbox rule provides that the acceptance of an offer is generally effective upon dispatch of the acceptance when sent in a commercially reasonable manner (e.g., when the offeree places the acceptance in the mailbox, sends it by overnight mail, or faxes it) and not when the acceptance is received by the offeror. The time of acceptance depends on whether the offeror has specified a method of acceptance or not. Table 7.1 provides an illustration that summarizes the rules governing when acceptance is effective.

TABLE 7.1	When Is Acceptance Effective?	
Method Offeror Used to Make Offer	**Method Offeree Used to Accept**	**Rule**
Specified in offer *(e.g., "You must accept this offer via overnight mail").*	Used method specified by offeror, or a commercially reasonable substitute *(e.g., same-day courier).*	*Mailbox rule:* Acceptance effective upon dispatch by offeree.
Specified in offer.	Used slower method *(e.g., regular U.S. mail).*	Offer considered *rejected* and considered a counteroffer back to the original offeror.
Not specified in the offer *(e.g., "I offer to paint your office for $1,000").*	Used the same/faster method to accept than the offeror used to make the offer, or used a commercially reasonable method.	*Mailbox rule:* Acceptance effective upon dispatch by offeree.
Not specified in the offer.	Used a slower method than the offeror used to make the offer.	Acceptance effective upon *receipt* of acceptance by offeror.

For each transaction, does a contract exist? If yes, why, and what is the date of the contract? If no, why not?

PROBLEM 1

Day 1: Conley sent a fax to Raleigh's office: "We offer to provide you with widget-covering services for $1,000 per month for six months starting January 1."

Day 2: Raleigh sends a letter via U.S. mail to Conley: "I accept your offer of Day 1."

Day 3: Conley telephones Raleigh and tells him: "I revoke my widget-covering offer of Day 1." Upon hearing this, Raleigh states, "Too late, I already put my acceptance in the mailbox!"

Day 4: Conley receives Raleigh's letter of acceptance on Thursday.

PROBLEM 2

Day 1: BookCo's manager e-mails an offer to sell a rare first edition of *For Whom the Bell Tolls,* signed by Hemingway, for $50,000 to Rare Book Retailer (RBR).

Day 2: RBR receives the offer, prints out the e-mail, writes "ACCEPTED, one Hemingway book for $50,000, RBR Manager," and faxes BookCo the acceptance.

Day 3 (9:00 a.m.): BookCo's receptionist receives RBR's fax.

Day 3 (12:00 p.m.): BookCo's manager calls RBR to revoke her offer.

Day 3 (1:30 p.m.): The RBR acceptance fax is delivered to BookCo's manager.

PROBLEM 3

Day 1: On Monday, McGlyn mails an offer to Timothy.

Day 2: On Tuesday, McGlyn changes her mind and mails a revocation of the offer to Timothy.

Day 3: On Wednesday, while the revocation is in the mail, Timothy receives McGlyn's offer and immediately mails his acceptance.

Day 4: On Thursday, while the acceptance is in the mail, Timothy receives the revocation.

Day 5: On Friday, McGlyn receives Timothy's acceptance.

Answers to this Quick Quiz are provided at the end of the chapter.

Mistake

Over the course of a business life cycle, it is inevitable that a manager involved in a contract will make a **mistake** (or contract with a mistaken party). The law recognizes certain mistakes and provides a remedy intended to make the parties whole again. One famous legal commentator wrote that "mistake is one of the most difficult [doctrines] in the law, because so many men make so many mistakes, of so many different kinds, with so many varying effects."[9]

Generally, a mistake is defined in contract law as a *belief that is not in accord with the facts.* It is important to note that not *all* erroneous beliefs are classified as mistakes.

---

[9]*Corbin on Contracts,* Section 103.

A mistake is an erroneous belief about an *existing* fact, not an erroneous belief as to what will happen in the future. Erroneous beliefs about the future are covered by doctrines of impossibility and impracticability, which are discussed in Chapter 9, "Enforceability." Mistakes are classified as either *mutual* (both parties) or *unilateral* (one party).

A **mutual mistake** in which both parties hold an erroneous belief, may be the basis for *canceling* a contract (also called *avoiding* the contract). For the adversely affected party to cancel the contract, the mistake must concern a *basic assumption* on which the contract was made. For example, in *Raffles v. Wichelhaus*,[10] a landmark case on the doctrine of mistake, a court ruled in favor of a buyer of goods who mistakenly accepted goods not intended for him from a freight ship. The court held that the contract delivery terms (in particular, the name of the freighter ship) were ambiguous and the mutual misunderstanding resulted in a lack of mutual assent.

Other examples of mutual mistakes include mistakes as to the existence of the subject matter (e.g., parties agree to the sale of goods, but the goods were already destroyed by fire at the time of the contract) and the quality of the subject matter (e.g., parties agree to the sale of a rare first-edition book that turns out to be a second edition and not nearly as valuable). Courts will *not* generally consider market conditions (such as the fair market value of a piece of real estate) or financial ability (such as relying on one party's representation that she can receive adequate credit to purchase the real estate) as a mistake that allows a contract to be avoided.

In a **unilateral mistake** only one party has an erroneous belief about a basic assumption in the terms of the agreement. Courts are much less willing to allow a mistaken party to cancel a contract for a unilateral mistake than they are in the case of a mutual mistake. In fact, the general rule is that a unilateral mistake is not a valid reason to avoid a contract. However, if the nonmistaken party had reason to *know* of the mistake or his actions *caused* the mistake, a court will allow the mistaken party to avoid the contract. For example, General Contractor solicits bids from Cement Inc. in order to calculate a bid for a new construction project. Cement Inc. sends a letter offer with a clerical error that promises to provide $20,000 worth of cement for $2,000. General Contractor sends an e-mail accepting the $2,000 bid. A court would likely allow Cement Inc. to cancel the cement contract based on unilateral mistake. Note that courts are much less willing to allow a party to cancel a contract if the unilateral mistake is essentially an error in business judgment rather than a clerical error.

TAKEAWAY CONCEPTS Acceptance

- A valid offer creates the power of *acceptance* for the offeree. An acceptance is the offeree's expression of agreement to the terms of the offer.
- The mailbox rule provides that the acceptance of an offer is generally effective upon dispatch of the acceptance when sent in a commercially reasonable manner.
- A mistake is defined in contract law as a *belief that is not in accord with the facts.*

ADEQUACY OF CONSIDERATION

For a binding contract to exist, not only must there be agreement (i.e., offer and acceptance), but the agreement must be supported by consideration. **Consideration** is defined as the mutual exchange of benefits and detriments. In other words, each party receives something of value from the other, and each party gives up something of value (called *legal*

LO 7-4

Apply the element of consideration in the context of contract formation.

---

[10]159 Eng. Rep. 375 (1864).

detriment) to the other. This results in a **bargained-for exchange**. When someone goes to a store to purchase a sweater, the exchange of goods (the sweater) and cash paid is the contract consideration. When a homeowner hires someone to mow her lawn, the exchange of the cash paid and the service rendered (mowing the lawn) is the contract consideration. Suppose that a neighbor's teen throws a ball through your front window. You and your neighbor agree that if he pays for the cost of replacement, you'll promise not to sue him. Your promise is called **forbearance** and is valuable consideration. However, giving something up does not always create legal forbearance. What is forfeited must be a *legal right.* For example, suppose that nervous parents tell their 19-year-old daughter, a college freshman leaving home for the first time, that if she refrains from drinking alcohol for the entire year, they will give her $1,000. Even if she does forgo alcohol for the year, because a 19-year-old is not legally allowed to drink alcohol, she has not given up a legal right and thus has not provided valuable consideration.

Legal Detriment

Proper consideration requires that the parties suffer some type of detriment that the law recognizes as adequate. This is satisfied if the party promises to perform something that the party is not legally obligated to do (such as promising to sell your car for $5,000) or to refrain from doing something that the party had a right to do (such as waiving your rights to pursue a lawsuit when you have been injured). In one famous decision from 1891, an appellate court in New York held that one party's promise to abstain from the then-legal practices of drinking, smoking, and gambling until age 21, in exchange for a promise by his uncle to pay him $5,000,[11] was sufficient legal detriment for both parties and thus was an enforceable contract.[12] The nephew had given up a legal right that was sufficient to satisfy the legal detriment required (forbearance).

Amount and Type of Consideration

Consideration exchanged does not need to be of equal value. Ordinarily, in deciding the validity of consideration, courts will not look to the amount or type of consideration or the relative bargaining power of the parties (except in the rare case of a contract so burdensome on one party as to indicate unconscionability, discussed later). So long as some bargained-for exchange is contemplated, the contract will be deemed enforceable. For example, Sheila purchases a pair of designer shoes for $1,300. When her husband finds out, he is irate and demands that she return them. When she goes to the showroom to do so, the store will not accept the shoes because she has worn them outside on a sidewalk. If she files a lawsuit claiming that the value she paid was in excess of the cost of the shoes, the court won't care about the cost of the leather or the company's manufacturing costs; it will simply want to know whether Sheila voluntarily entered into the contract and understood that she was paying $1,300 for a pair of shoes.

Contracts may be based on **nominal consideration**, that is, consideration that is stated in a written contract even though it is not actually exchanged. Most courts have held that the consideration requirement is still met even if the nominal amount is never actually paid so long as the amount is truly nominal (such as $1). In *Bennett v. American Electric Power Services Corp.,*[13] a state appellate court ruled against an employee who had signed an employment agreement that assigned all of his rights for any invention made in the scope of employment to his employer "in consideration of the sum of One Dollar" even though

---

[11]Using the consumer price index rate to calculate the time value of money, this sum would be approximately $104,000 in today's dollars.

[12]*Hammer v. Sidway,* 124 N.Y. 538 (1891).

[13]2001 WL 1136150 (Ohio Ct. App. 2001).

the actual dollar was never paid. The court reasoned that the offer of employment to the employee in the contract was a sufficient bargained-for exchange.

AGREEMENTS THAT LACK CONSIDERATION

LO 7-5

Differentiate agreements that have consideration from those that do not.

If a party does or promises to do what she is already legally obligated to do, the law generally does not recognize this as a legal detriment and, thus, the contract is unenforceable. This is called the **preexisting duty** rule. One classic example is that a police officer cannot collect the reward for arresting a fugitive because the officer has a preexisting duty to find and arrest fugitives. More often, however, the preexisting duty rule applies in circumstances where one party claims he wishes to modify an existing contract because of unforeseen difficulties in performing his obligations. For example, Helsel contracts with Mullen to renovate Helsel's office building. During the renovation, Mullen discovers the costs of renovation will be more than he anticipated. Mullen threatens to walk off the job unless Helsel agrees to pay an amount higher than stated in the contract. Because Helsel's choices would be limited to either agreeing or hiring a new contractor and then suing Mullen, he consents to the price increase. Most courts would not enforce Helsel's promise to pay the additional amount because Mullen already had a preexisting contractual duty to perform for the original price.

The modern trend in the law recognizes a number of exceptions to the preexisting duty rule. For example, if a party who promises to do what she is already bound to do assumes additional duties, her undertaking of these duties is considered sufficient legal detriment. Also, courts may allow an exception in a case where certain circumstances were not reasonably anticipated by either party when the original contract was formed. For example, Waste Disposal Company (WDC) contracts with ManufactureCo to collect garbage from ManufactureCo's warehouse for one year. Six months into the agreement, WDC requests an additional $5,000 per month to provide this service because the ManufactureCo warehouse is now unexpectedly producing some hazardous material waste that must be removed using specially designed equipment. The parties then execute a modification to the contract, agreeing to the increase. One month later, ManufactureCo changes managers, and the new manager refuses to pay the additional sum, citing the preexisting duty rule. In this case, most courts would enforce the modification as an exception to the preexisting duty rule.

Illusory Promises

Even if a legal detriment is suffered by one party, that alone does not satisfy the consideration requirement. The bargained-for exchange aspect of consideration primarily distinguishes contracts from **illusory promises**. Some promises do not support a bargained-for exchange and will not support contractual consideration. Such promises are called *illusory promises.* Examples of illusory promises are (1) deathbed promises, in which you make a promise to a friend or loved one just prior to her death to comfort her; (2) promises of a gift, in which a promise is made but no reciprocal promise is exchanged; (3) promises of love and friendship; and (4) promises that by their terms are not binding. For example, a manager announces to his employees that each may have three personal days in December if he can get it approved by senior management. This is an illusory promise because neither the manager nor the company is bound by his statement. Since gift promises are not enforceable and contract promises are, it is important to understand the precise difference. A performance or return promise is "bargained for" only if it was exchanged for another promise.

Past Consideration

Another type of consideration that is not considered to meet the bargained-for exchange requirement is a promise made in return for a detriment previously made by the promisee. This is known as **past consideration** and it is not sufficient to meet the consideration requirement. Suppose that O'Connor has been working at her job for 40 years and is retiring. Her boss approaches her a week before her last scheduled day and tells her that because she has been such a faithful and effective employee for the past 40 years, on Friday, her last day, there will be a party and she will be presented with a gold watch. She gratefully thanks him and accepts the offer of a party and watch. On Thursday she is disappointed when informed that there will be no party and she will not receive a gold watch. Although the party and watch contract includes both an offer and an acceptance, it is *unenforceable* because it lacks consideration. O'Connor's contention that her 40 years of dedicated service is sufficient consideration is false because it is past consideration, performed prior to the current agreement. Thus, the offer of a party and watch is an offer of a gift and is not enforceable as a contract. Now suppose the company's employment manual, in force since she started work, states that employees receive a gold watch after 25 years of employment. In this case, O'Connor is entitled to the watch because she acted based on a promise made before she began performing.

Promissory Estoppel

If one party justifiably relies on the promise of another to her detriment, under certain circumstances the relying party may recover costs of the reliance from the promisor even though the original promise agreement lacked consideration. Under the theory of **promissory estoppel** a relying party may recover damages if (1) the promisor makes a promise that is *reasonable;* (2) the promisee *actually* relied on the promise (the promise must have induced the act) and suffered an injury; (3) the promisee's reliance was *reasonably foreseeable* to the promisor (what an objectively reasonable person would have foreseen under the same circumstances); and (4) principles of *equity and justice* (did each party act in good faith and fair dealing?) are served by providing compensation to the reliant party.

Estoppel and Employment   One particularly important aspect of promissory estoppel for managers is the promise of employment. Most commonly, this arises in a situation where an employer makes a promise of employment and then revokes the promise before the employee's start date (or soon thereafter). Typically, the employee would have left her previous position and potentially incurred moving expenses. In those cases, courts have held that the revocation of the employment-at-will promise before any consideration was exchanged triggers the doctrine of promissory estoppel, whereby the innocent party is entitled to damages. In promissory estoppel cases, courts frequently award damages equal to the out-of-pocket costs plus what the employee lost in quitting her job and declining employment elsewhere.

For example, suppose that Donatello is given a written offer of employment to work for Renaissance Architect Firm (RAF) for an annual salary of $50,000 to begin in 30 days. Donatello gives his current employer notice of his resignation and then moves 100 miles in order to be closer to RAF's headquarters. The day before Donatello shows up for work, RAF informs him that due to financial difficulties it can no longer honor its offer of employment. When Donatello attempts to regain his old employment, he is told that his position has been filled and there is no chance of rehiring him. Donatello cannot prevail on a breach of contract claim because no consideration was ever actually exchanged; therefore, the promise is not supported by consideration and not enforceable as a contract. However, a court would likely award Donatello damages based on promissory estoppel. RAF may be liable for damages related to Donatello's actions in reliance on RAF's promise, such as his moving expenses and compensation in connection with Donatello's resignation from his previous employer.

©valterZ/Shutterstock

What's Your Negotiation Strategy?

PROBLEM: The law of contracts specifies the minimum requirements for an agreement to be legally binding, but at the same time, contracting parties are generally free to negotiate the specific terms or details of their business agreements. In fact, when businesses are negotiating agreements with each other (business-to-business contracts) or with consumers (business-to-consumer contracts), the actual terms of their agreements will generally reflect the relative bargaining power and negotiation skills of the parties. This business reality, in turn, raises an important question: What is your negotiation strategy?

STRATEGIC SOLUTION: *Develop a negotiation strategy.*

Many best-selling books have been written about business negotiation skills, from Roger Fisher and William Ury's classic guide, *Getting to Yes,* to Charles Craver's *The Art of Negotiation in the Business World.* In reality, there is no one "right" way to negotiate a deal, but according to Barbara Buell, the Director of Communications of Stanford University's Graduate School of Business from 2001 to 2015, there are two practical pitfalls one should try to avoid when one is negotiating an agreement: "poor planning" and "thinking the pie is fixed."[14]

Good negotiators see negotiations as a cooperative activity and not as a zero-sum game (i.e., a noncooperative interaction with one clear winner and one clear loser). In other words, instead of haggling over a fixed pie, effective negotiators try to design mutually beneficial deals that result in positive gains to all the parties to the negotiation. Planning and preparation are of the essence in any negotiation. Effective negotiators know their bottom line or walk-away point before they enter into a negotiation. They also know what other options are available in the event a deal is not reached.

In the words of negotiation expert Keld Jensen, "Successful businesses have a strategy for virtually everything they do," whether it be research and development, marketing, or public relations.[15] Business negotiations are no exception to this rule. Negotiation permeates every aspect of our lives—not just business deals, but also family situations, legal disputes, and international conflicts. To develop your negotiation strategy, consider these guidelines:

---

[14]Barbara Buell, "Negotiation Strategy: Seven Common Pitfalls to Avoid," *Insights by Stanford Business,* Jan. 15, 2007.

[15]Keld Jensen, "What's Your Negotiation Strategy?" *Forbes,* Feb. 23, 2012.

- *Listen and understand the other party's issues and point of view.* The best negotiators actually listen to the other side in order to understand their key concerns and business objectives. Understanding the other side's perspective about what is important, what limitations they may have, and where they may have flexibility allows you to work toward a win-win solution.

- *Be prepared.* Review and understand the other party's business operations by reviewing its website and press releases, articles written about the company, and its social media outlets such as Facebook or Twitter. This information can be essential to learning about the background of the person and organization you are negotiating with and may provide insight into similar past deals.

- *Avoid the hard-nosed negotiator model.* Keep the negotiations professional and courteous. Establishing long-term relationships is consistent with the goals of every negotiation. A collaborative, positive tone in negotiations is more likely to result in progress to a closing.

- *Understand the deal dynamics.* Who has what advantages in the negotiation? Who wants the deal more? What timing constraints are at play? What alternatives does the other side have? Is the other side going to be getting a significant payment from you? If so, the leverage will tend to be on your side.

- *Start with a term sheet rather than negotiating a full agreement.* A term sheet is used to help the parties hammer out basic terms such as price, delivery terms, obligations of the parties, and other essentials before actually drafting the minutiae of a full contract. Term sheets are nonbinding and help to keep the transaction moving ahead.

- *Be ready to walk away.* This is easier said than done, but it is sometimes critical to get to a win-win situation. Know before you start what your walk-away terms are, and be prepared with data to back up why your term (e.g., price) is reasonable. If you are confronted with an ultimatum that you absolutely can't live with, be prepared to walk away. Be clear with the other party as to *why* you are walking away and that you are open to the possibility of future negotiation.

1. What other areas of daily life involve negotiation skills? Have you ever had to negotiate with a family member? A roommate? What was the outcome?

2. When you negotiate, do you see it as a cooperative exercise or as a zero-sum gain?

3. What role does ethics play in negotiation strategy?

KEY TERMS

Mutual assent p. 146   For the formation of a valid contract, the broad underlying requirement that the parties must reach an agreement using a combination of offer and acceptance and that the assent must be genuine.

Offer p. 147   A promise or commitment to do (or refrain from doing) a specified activity. In contract law, the expression of a willingness to enter into a contract by the offeror's promising an offeree that she will perform certain obligations in exchange for the offeree's counterpromise to perform.

Objective intent p. 147   For an offer to have legal effect, the requirement that, generally, the offeror must have a serious intention to become bound by the offer and that the terms of the offer must be reasonably certain.

Revocation p. 152   An action terminating an offer whereby the offeror decides to withdraw the offer by expressly communicating the revocation to the offeree prior to acceptance.

Rejection p. 152   An action terminating an offer whereby the offeree rejects the offer outright prior to acceptance.

Counteroffer p. 152   An action terminating an offer whereby the offeree rejects the original offer and proposes a new offer with different terms.

Operation of law (contracts) p. 152   Termination of an offer by the occurrence of certain happenings or events, which generally include lapse of time, death or incapacity of the offeror or offeree, destruction of the subject matter of the contract prior to acceptance, and supervening illegality.

Irrevocable offers p. 153   Offers that cannot be withdrawn by the offeror; include offers in the form of an option contract, offers that the offeree partly performed or detrimentally relied on, and firm offers by a merchant under the Uniform Commercial Code.

Option contract p. 153   Contract where offeror agrees to hold an offer open (not enter into a contract with another party) for a certain period of time in exchange for something of value.

Detrimental reliance p. 153   Situation in which the offeree acts, based on a reasonable promise made by the offeror, and would be injured if the offeror's promise is not enforced.

Mirror image rule p. 153   Principle stating that the offeree's response operates as an acceptance only if it is the precise mirror image of the offer.

Lapse of time p. 154   An event covered under operation of law in which a contract may be terminated once either the offeror's expressed time limit has expired or a reasonable time has passed.

Acceptance p. 155   The offeree's expression of agreement to the terms of the offer. The power of acceptance is created by a valid offer.

Mailbox rule p. 155   Principle stating that the acceptance of an offer is effective upon dispatch of the acceptance via a commercially reasonable means and not when the acceptance is received by the offeree; governs common law contracts.

Mistake p. 156   In contract law, an erroneous belief that is not in accord with the existing facts.

Mutual mistake p. 157   An erroneous belief held by both parties that concerns a basic assumption on which a contract was made.

Unilateral mistake p. 157   An erroneous belief held by only one party about a basic assumption in the terms of an agreement.

Consideration p. 157   The mutual exchange of benefits and detriments; for the formation of a valid contract, the requirement that each party receives something of value (the benefit) from the other and that each party gives up something of value (the legal detriment) to the other, resulting in a bargained-for exchange.

Bargained-for exchange p. 158   The aspect of consideration that differentiates contracts from illusory promises by holding that a performance or return promise is bargained for only if it was exchanged for another promise.

Forbearance p. 158   The giving up of a legal right as consideration in a contract.

Nominal consideration p. 158   Consideration that is stated in a written contract even though it is not actually exchanged.

Preexisting duty p. 159   A duty that one is already legally obligated to perform and, thus, that is generally not recognized as a legal detriment.

Illusory promise p. 159   A promise that courts will not enforce because the offeror is not truly bound by his vague promise or because a party cannot be bound by his promise due to the lack of a bargained-for exchange. Promises of gifts and deathbed promises are two examples.

Past consideration p. 159   A promise made in return for a detriment previously made by the promisee; does not meet the bargained-for exchange requirement.

Promissory estoppel p. 160   Theory allowing for the recovery of damages by the relying party if the promisee actually relied on the promise and the promisee's reliance was reasonably foreseeable to the promisor.

CASE SUMMARY 7.1 Arizona Cartridge Remanufacturers Association v. Lexmark, 421 F.3d 981 (9th Cir. 2005)

Mutual Assent/Acceptance

Lexmark is a manufacturer and distributor of ink cartridges for computer printers. It introduced a rebate plan called Return Program Cartridges whereby a consumer could receive a "prebate" (i.e., a discount upon purchase) on ink cartridges. This price discount was given in exchange for an agreement by the consumer not to tamper with the cartridge. The consumer simply had to agree to return the empty cartridge to Lexmark. The agreement was printed on the ink cartridge box, and Lexmark claimed that by opening the box the consumer agreed to the terms of the Return Program Cartridges program. A consumer group challenged Lexmark's program contending, among other things, that Lexmark could not enforce an agreement on the box because the consumer had never formally accepted the terms of Lexmark's offer.

CASE QUESTION

1. Can one party be deemed to accept an offer simply by opening a product box even if there is no evidence that the party *actually* read the terms?

CASE SUMMARY 7.2 Biomedical Systems Corp. v. GE Marquette Medical Systems, Inc., 287 F.3d 707 (8th Cir. 2002)

Mutual Assent

GE Marquette Medical Systems (GE) contracted with Biomedical Systems Corp. (Biomedical) to manufacture a new medical instrument based on technology owned by Biomedical. The contract required GE to obtain clearance from the Food and Drug Administration (the federal regulatory agency that covers such medical devices) within 90 days in order to move ahead on the project. After this contract was signed, GE determined that obtaining this clearance was not a prudent path to reach its ultimate objective of having the product approved for selling to the public. Rather than seek the clearance required by the Biomedical contract, GE decided to pursue a different strategy with the FDA that took several years to complete. When Biomedical sued GE for breach of contract, GE defended on the basis that the clearance provision in the contract was a violation of FDA procedure and, thus, there was no mutual assent.

CASE QUESTIONS

1. Can a party make a unilateral judgment as to mutual assent on a term of the contract when there is no affirmative finding from a regulatory authority?
2. If GE had gone ahead with the clearance process and the FDA had told GE that it was not the proper procedure, would there be a meeting of the minds?

CASE SUMMARY 7.3 Reed's Photo Mart, Inc. v. Monarch, 475 S.W.2d 356 (Tex. Civ. App. 1971)

Mistake

Reed owned a small photography store and purchased his price label products from Monarch. Over a period of years, Reed ordered no more than 4,000 labels at a time from Monarch. While preparing a new order form for labels, Reed was interrupted by a customer

(continued)

and wrote "4MM" on the order form instead of "4M." In the industry, *4M* means 4,000 labels, while *4MM* means 4 million labels. Reed sent the mistaken order to Monarch. Despite the course of past dealings and the fact that the maximum order that Monarch had ever received from a single customer was 1 million labels, Monarch proceeded to produce and deliver 4 million labels to Reed. Reed refused delivery and defended based on mistake.

CASE QUESTIONS

1. Who prevails and why?
2. Is this a unilateral or mutual mistake? What's the difference?

CHAPTER REVIEW QUESTIONS

1. **The concept of mutual assent is also called a/an:**
   a. Agreement of sorts.
   b. Meeting of the minds.
   c. Intent to negotiate.
   d. Void contract.
   e. Contract in rem.

2. **If the offeror revokes her offer before acceptance by the offeror, the offer is:**
   a. Terminated, by operation of law.
   b. Terminated, by action of the parties.
   c. Not terminated, because all offers are irrevocable.
   d. Not terminated, because the offeree is the master of her own offer.
   e. None of the above.

3. **The mailbox rule determines the effective date of the:**
   a. Acceptance.
   b. Revocation.
   c. Rejection.
   d. Postmark.
   e. Mutual assent.

4. **The night before his commencement ceremony, Leland's uncle promises to buy him a new car after he actually sees Leland receive his diploma. Leland gladly accepts. After the ceremony, Leland's uncle says, "Just kidding, no car!" Leland cannot prevail in a breach of contract claim because the agreement lacks:**
   a. Offer.
   b. Acceptance.
   c. Consideration.
   d. Legality.
   e. Mutual assent.

5. **Which of the following does *not* result in the termination of an offer?**
   a. Revocation
   b. Acceptance
   c. Rejection
   d. Death of the offeror
   e. Destruction of subject matter

6. **The party making an offer is called the offeree.**
   a. True
   b. False

7. **Objective intent is what a reasonable person would believe about the seriousness of an offer based on the language of the offer and the actions of the parties.**
   a. True
   b. False

8. **As a general rule, advertisements do not constitute an offer.**
   a. True
   b. False

9. **Only the offeror can terminate the offer.**
   a. True
   b. False

10. **If both parties hold an erroneous belief about a basic assumption in the contract, this may be the basis for canceling the contract as a mutual mistake.**
    a. True
    b. False

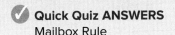

Quick Quiz ANSWERS
Mailbox Rule

PROBLEM 1

No contract. Conley still had the power to revoke the offer on Day 3 because Raleigh used a slower method (U.S. mail) to accept than Conley used to make the offer (fax). Therefore, Raleigh's acceptance could take effect only upon receipt of the acceptance by Conley. Because Conley did not receive the acceptance until Day 4, his revocation of Day 3 is effective and no contract exists.

PROBLEM 2

Contract exists on Day 2 upon dispatch (mailbox rule) because RBR used a reasonable method to accept (using fax to accept an e-mail offer is reasonable because both methods are similar in that they are relatively instantaneous when sending). When the offeror actually received the acceptance is irrelevant.

PROBLEM 3

Contract exists on Day 3 upon dispatch (mailbox rule) because Timothy used the same method to accept that was used to convey the offer. It is irrelevant that the revocation was already in the mail and equally irrelevant that the acceptance was received by McGlyn after Timothy had received the revocation.

CHAPTER REVIEW QUESTIONS: Answers and Explanations

1. b. Mutual assent is an offer and agreement and is referred to as a meeting of minds between the parties. The other answers are wrong because they are fictional terms.

2. b. Revocation results in a termination of an offer by action of the offeror. Answer *a* is wrong because revocation is not an operation of law termination. Answers *c, d,* and *e* are wrong because the offer is terminated.

3. a. The mailbox rule is used to determine when an acceptance is effective. Answers *b* and *c* are incorrect because they are results that are outside the mailbox rule. Answers *d* and *e* are unrelated to the mailbox rule.

4. c. This is an illusory gift promise that may be revoked even after acceptance. Leland suffered no burden, so the contract lacks consideration. The remaining answers are wrong because a legal offer was made and accepted, but no contract was formed.

5. b. Acceptance results in mutual assent. All other answers result in the termination of an offer.

6. b. False. The party making an offer is *not* called the offeree, rather the *offeror.*

7. a. True. Objective intent to offer is not what the party actually meant (that is subjective intent). Instead, it is what a reasonable person would believe under the circumstances.

8. a. True. As a general rule, advertisements do not constitute an offer unless it fits a certain unilateral contract offer model.

9. b. False. Offers may be terminated by actions of the parties or by operation of law.

10. a. True. In a mutual mistake, there is no mutual assent and therefore any agreement may be avoided.

CHAPTER 8

Capacity and Legality

 THINKING STRATEGICALLY

Promises are an essential feature of our daily lives and of most, if not all, business transactions. As a practical matter, however, not all promises are legally enforceable. Only those promises that meet certain conditions are enforceable. In this chapter we will consider two essential requirements for creating a legally enforceable promise: legal capacity and lawful purpose. In addition, in this chapter's *Thinking Strategically* we will consider the strategic use of forum selection clauses and choice of law clauses in business contracts and user agreements.

Learning Objectives

After studying this chapter, students who have mastered the material will be able to:

8-1 Articulate the legal requirement of capacity and identify the main categories of persons who do not have the full legal capacity to incur contractual duties.

8-2 Distinguish between bright-line rules (such as the age of majority) and flexible standards (such as the definition of mental competence).

8-3 Articulate the concept of legality, or lawful object.

CHAPTER OVERVIEW

In the previous chapter on mutual assent, we began to study the process of contract formation. In brief, to create a legally binding contract, the parties must agree to the same terms (mutual assent) and they must offer each other something of value (consideration). But these two elements are not enough to create a binding promise. In addition, the parties must have the legal capacity to make a contract, and the contract itself must be made for a lawful purpose. (See Figure 8.1 for the elements of a legally binding contract.) This chapter will spell out the legal requirements of

capacity and legality in some detail and identify some strategic aspects of the contracting process.

CAPACITY

Capacity is a legal doctrine used by courts to protect parties who may lack the ability to understand the terms of an agreement. In other words, before a party can be legally bound to a contract, he must have the *capacity* to understand and appreciate contract terms.[1] For example, minors, mental incompetents, and intoxicated

---

[1]See *Restatement (Second) of Contracts*, § 12.

FIGURE 8.1   The Elements of a Valid Contract

1. Agreement
2. Consideration
3. Contractual Capacity
4. Lawful Object

persons may lack the full legal capacity to make legally binding contracts.[2] Although persons in these categories lack the full capacity to contract, a promise made by such a person is merely *voidable*. In practice, a voidable contract is one that can later be affirmed or rejected by the person who lacked capacity at the time he made the contract. (By contrast, a void contract is not enforceable at all, because in the eyes of the law a void contract never existed.) Under this legal rule, the contract is enforceable against the party who is not to be protected by the capacity rule (i.e., the party contracting with a minor, with a mental incompetent, or with an intoxicated person). The rationale for this rule is to protect certain classes of persons against their own unwise acts, while at the same time allowing such persons to enforce contracts that will benefit them.

LO 8-1

Articulate the legal requirement of capacity and identify the main categories of persons who do not have the full legal capacity to incur contractual duties.

Minors

In general, the contracts of **minors** (persons younger than 18 years of age) are *voidable at their option*.[3] In most cases, a minor need not do any affirmative act in order to derive the benefit of this general rule of voidability. A minor may avoid his obligations under an *executory* or unperformed contract by merely doing nothing. In order to legally bind himself to an unperformed contract, the minor must *ratify* the contract upon reaching the age of majority (upon reaching his 18th birthday). **Ratification** includes any act that indicates that the minor intends to be bound by his promise; it can be expressed orally, in writing, or it can be implied. Ratification by implication occurs when the minor, after reaching majority, performs the contract (or begins performance)—for example, a minor obligated to repay a loan makes an installment payment after reaching majority.

When the contract has been performed or partially performed by the minor, he must take some action to avoid obligation under the contract. Such action is referred to as **disaffirmance**. The result will be to have the contract rescinded. As in any case of rescission, each party must return any consideration received from the other party. Therefore, when a minor disaffirms a contract, he must return whatever consideration he has received; otherwise, he will not be able to demand the consideration that he transferred to the adult party. An interesting question arises when the minor cannot return what he has received in consideration because he has squandered it. The majority of states would hold that the minor is still entitled to the return of the consideration with which he parted.

There is one major exception in which a minor may be held liable for consideration given to him under a contract. If the consideration is for "necessaries" or items necessary for the health and welfare of the minor, and the minor has consumed them, the minor will be liable for the reasonable value of such necessary items.

Case 8.1 involves Facebook's terms of use, the electronic contract Facebook users must agree to before they can open an

Which emoji would you choose to describe Case 8.1?

©solomon7/Shutterstock

---

[2]*Id.*

[3]See *Restatement (Second) of Contracts*, § 14.

account. Facebook allows minors as young as 13 to create their own accounts, which raises an intriguing legal question regarding the enforceability of Facebook's terms of use with respect to minors.

CASE 8.1 C.M.D. v. Facebook, Inc., unpublished opinion dated October 30, 2015 (9th Cir. 2015)

FACT SUMMARY   C.M.D. joined Facebook when he was a minor. Like many Facebook users, he posted many pictures to his Facebook account. When C.M.D.'s parents discovered that Facebook had used C.M.D.'s name and likeness in ads and other "sponsored content," they sued Facebook in federal court. They argued that Facebook had used C.M.D.'s name and likeness without his consent, since C.M.D. was still a minor when he signed up for Facebook. In response, Facebook requested that the district court judge dismiss C.M.D.'s lawsuit for failure to state a valid legal claim, arguing that C.M.D. had agreed to the terms of Facebook's standard user agreement, including the use of one's likeness in advertising, when he joined the social media site. The district judge granted Facebook's motion to dismiss. The parents of C.M.D. appealed to the Ninth Circuit Court of Appeals.

SYNOPSIS OF DECISION AND OPINION   The Ninth Circuit Court of Appeals ruled *against* C.M.D. in an unpublished memorandum opinion, affirming the decision of the district court judge to dismiss C.M.D.'s complaint. The appellate court ruled that minors have the ability to consent to contracts under California law and that none of the exceptions to this general rule applied to the facts of this case. The appellate court also concluded that C.M.D. had not disaffirmed or disavowed Facebook's user agreement, since he continued to use Facebook even after filing his lawsuit.

WORDS OF THE COURT: No Intention to Disaffirm the Contract   "Plaintiffs allege that their consent to Facebook's terms of service, which included a provision that gave Facebook the right to use their names and likenesses in advertisements, was . . . disaffirmed, and thus voided, under [California law]. . . . Plaintiffs did not disaffirm their contract. . . . While they may have intended to disaffirm the contract's advertising provision by filing their lawsuit, it is a longstanding and general rule of California law that 'a party cannot apply to his own use that part of the transaction which may bring to him a benefit, and repudiate the other, which may not be to his interest to fulfill.' *Babu v. Petersen*, 4 Cal. 2d 276, 286 (1935). By continuing to use facebook.com after bringing their action, Plaintiffs manifested an intention not to disaffirm the contract."

Case Questions

1. Would this case have been decided differently if C.M.D. had closed his Facebook account before filing his lawsuit against Facebook?

2. Section 4 of Facebook's terms of use states: "You will not use Facebook if you are under 13." (See: https://www.facebook.com/legal/terms.) Suppose C.M.D. had been younger than 13 when he opened his account and brought his lawsuit against Facebook. Would this case have been decided differently on these facts?

3. *Focus on Critical Thinking*: In a footnote, the appellate court stated: "This disposition is not appropriate for publication and is not precedent. . . ." Why did the court not want its decision to be published or to have the force of binding precedent?

Mental Competency

Like minors, **mental incompetents** are treated as having limited capacity to contract. This category covers not just obvious cases (such as mental disorders or dementia) but also temporary mental incompetence, such as people who are highly intoxicated, severely depressed, or under severe or traumatic pressure. The legal question is whether the person was lucid at the time he entered into the contract. Although there is no universally accepted definition, courts have held that a party who is lucid is one who is not suffering from delusion or confusion. In general, a person lacks capacity because of mental illness or defect if either (1) she is unable to understand the nature and consequences of the contract or (2) she is unable to act in a reasonable manner in relation to the transaction and the other party has reason to know of her condition.[4] For example, Oliver has Alzheimer's disease and enters into a contract with Wendell to sell 100 widgets for $1 per widget (the widget's fair market value). Oliver may avoid the contract even though the contract terms were fair and Wendell had no notice of Oliver's condition. This is true because Oliver has met the "unable to understand" criteria.

In a majority of states, contracts made by an incompetent are voidable, not void. If the incompetent party regains her mental capacity, or has a guardian appointed, she may ratify the contract. Note that the other party does not have the power to avoid the contract. However, many states classify a contract as void per se (not valid from the outset) if one party has been legally declared to be incompetent prior to entering into the contract.

In Case 8.2, a state's highest court considers a claim that a contract is void because one party does not have sufficient mental capacity.

CASE 8.2 Sparrow v. Demonico, Supreme Judicial Court of Massachusetts, 461 Mass. 322 (2012)

FACT SUMMARY A family dispute over ownership of what had been the family home in Woburn, Massachusetts, prompted Frances M. Sparrow (Sparrow) to file a complaint in a state trial court against her sister, Susan Demonico, and Susan's husband, David D. Demonico (Demonicos). Prior to trial, the parties resolved their differences by entering into a settlement agreement reached during voluntary mediation. However, when Sparrow attempted to obtain a court order to enforce the agreement, the Demonicos argued that the contract was void because Susan Demonico lacked the capacity to enter into the agreement. A trial court agreed with the Demonicos, ruling that the contract was void because it may have been the product of an emotionally overwrought state of mind and Susan was not able to understand in a reasonable manner the nature and consequences of her actions. The appellate court reversed the trial court's decision and issued an order enforcing the settlement agreement. The Demonicos appealed again and argued that Susan's withdrawal symptoms from the antidepressant drug Zoloft rendered her unable to act reasonably at the time of the agreement. They cited her behavior, such as the slurring of words, crying, and having to leave the room, as evidence that she was suffering from a mental breakdown on the day of the mediation. Sparrow countered that however upset Susan was during the mediation, it didn't rise to the level of incapacitation required under the law and that the Demonicos had produced no medical evidence or experts to support their claim about the Zoloft.

SYNOPSIS OF DECISION AND OPINION The Supreme Judicial Court of Massachusetts ruled in favor of Sparrow. Although the court ruled that a party could establish incapacity to contract without proof of a mental condition that is permanent, degenerative, progressive, or long standing, the court also held that any finding of incapacity must still be supported by medical evidence. According to the court, the proper inquiry as to the capacity to contract focuses on a party's understanding or conduct only at the time of the disputed transaction. In this case, the Demonicos failed to present medical evidence regarding a diagnosis that would have required her to take Zoloft, or the effect, if any, that ceasing to take the medication would have had on her medical or mental condition.

WORDS OF THE COURT: Evidence of Incapacity "We conclude that our evolving standard of contractual incapacity does not in all cases require proof that a party's claimed mental illness or defect was of some significant duration or that

(continued)

---

[4]*Restatement (Second) of Contracts*, § 15(2).

it is permanent, progressive, or degenerative; but, without medical evidence or expert testimony that the mental condition interfered with the party's understanding of the transaction, or her ability to act reasonably in relation to it, the evidence will not be sufficient to support a conclusion of incapacity . . . [T]here was no expert or medical testimony to explain the effect of Susan's experiences or behavior on her ability to understand the agreement, to appreciate what was happening, or to comprehend the reasonableness of the settlement terms or the consequences to her of authorizing the settlement. Without such medical evidence, there was no basis to conclude that Susan lacked the capacity to contract."

Case Questions

1. What does the court say was missing from the Demonicos's argument about capacity?

2. What factors went into the trial court's decision to void the settlement agreement?

3. *Focus on Critical Thinking*: Under the court's decision, are there any circumstances when medical evidence would not be necessary? If one party was acting in a bizarre manner, such as talking to oneself or making irrational statements, would that be sufficient to void a contract based on capacity? Does public policy require that medical evidence support all claims of incapacity?

Intoxicated Persons

Intoxication, whether it be through drugs or alcohol, can also affect capacity. Suppose that Oliver and Wendell were at a bar drinking heavily. Wendell writes on a cocktail napkin: "Because you bought me so many pints of beer, I will sell you 100 widgets for only five cents per widget." The next day Wendell sobers up and realizes what he did. Wendell may avoid the contract because he was so intoxicated that he was unable to act in a reasonable manner and because Oliver had reason to know of Wendell's condition. On the other hand, if Oliver and Wendell were drinking but neither was obviously impaired, their intoxication would likely have no effect on the validity of the contract. Remember that in *Lucy v. Zehmer* in Chapter 7, even though the parties had been drinking alcohol, the contract to sell Zehmer's farm was upheld because of objective intent. Courts will use an objective standard to determine whether a reasonable person would have believed that the intoxicated person had sufficient capacity to enter into an agreement.

TAKEAWAY CONCEPTS Capacity

- Contracts made by minors (not yet reached 18 years old) are usually voidable.
- Because such contracts are voidable, minors may choose to ratify (or affirm) their contracts during their minority or within a reasonable time after reaching the age of majority.
- Alternatively, minors may choose to disaffirm (avoid being bound by) their contracts during their minority or within a reasonable time after reaching the age of majority.
- A person lacks capacity because of mental illness or defect if either (1) she is unable to understand the nature and consequences of the contract or (2) she is unable to act in a reasonable manner in relation to the transaction and the other party has reason to know of her condition.
- Intoxication, whether it be through drugs or alcohol, can also affect capacity. Courts will use an objective standard to determine whether a reasonable person would have believed that the intoxicated person had sufficient capacity to enter into an agreement.

Does Caesar have capacity to enter into a contract?

1. Caesar, age 17, purchases a motorcycle from Brutus, a neighbor, for $1,000. The day after his 18th birthday, Caesar wants his money back from Brutus.
2. Caesar, recently diagnosed with Alzheimer's disease, enters into a contract to perform expert consulting services for Brutus. In fact, Caesar is not an expert.
3. Caesar and Brutus are drinking at a bar together and Caesar becomes heavily intoxicated. After paying a $200 bar tab, they enter into a contract for the sale of Caesar's warehouse building to Brutus for $1. The next day, Caesar wants to cancel the contract.
4. Caesar, who has been declared mentally incompetent, signs a contract with Brutus to provide Roman Widgets at the end of each year. After the first year, Caesar regains his competence and ratifies the Widget contract.

Answers to this Quick Quiz are provided at the end of the chapter.

BRIGHT-LINE RULES VERSUS FLEXIBLE STANDARDS

LO 8-2

Distinguish between bright-line rules (such as the age of majority) and flexible standards (such as the definition of mental competence).

Legal doctrines like capacity and mutual assent are not all cut from the same cloth. Some legal norms, such as speed limits, create clear-cut "bright lines" and are thus fairly easy to apply. (See Figure 8.2.) Other legal commands, such as the general exhortation to "drive with care," can be fuzzy or open ended. (See Figure 8.3.) Broadly speaking, open-ended standards are more flexible and less clear-cut than bright-line rules because standards provide a greater range of choice or discretion. For example, deciding whether an adult is intoxicated or **lucid** is often a judgment call based on a wide variety of contextual factors. Bright-line rules, however, are less flexible and much more rigid. The age of majority is a textbook example of a bright-line rule, because it is relatively simple and straightforward to determine whether a person has turned 18.

| FIGURE 8.2 | **Bright-Line Rule Example** | FIGURE 8.3 | **Flexible Standard Example** |

©karen roach/Shutterstock

©Alisha Arif/Alamy

TAKEAWAY CONCEPTS Bright-Line Rules versus Flexible Standards

- Bright-lines rules are clear-cut and easy to apply, such as determining whether a given person has reached the age of majority.
- Flexible standards are more like general guidelines. They provide a greater range of choice or discretion, such as deciding whether a given person was lucid when he made a contract.

LEGALITY

The right to contract is fundamental but not absolute. For a contract to be enforceable, it must meet the requirement of **legality**; that is, both the subject matter and the performance of the contract must be legal. Some contracts are specifically barred by statute, such as contracts related to illegal gambling, while other contracts are illegal because their terms violate some **public policy** objective, such as unreasonable restraint of trade. As a general rule, an illegal contract is automatically *void*, so neither party may enforce it against the other. This is true even when only one party's performance is illegal. For example, if Holmes promises to paint Cardozo's home in exchange for Cardozo's promise to smuggle 500 Cuban cigars into the United States in violation of federal law, then neither Holmes nor Cardozo may enforce the contract.

Statutes

As a general rule, a contract that violates a statute is unlawful and void and thus will not be enforced by the courts. If a statute (state or federal) declares that a specific type of contract is prohibited, such contract is absolutely void. For example, minimum wage laws restrict a person's freedom to contract for a lower wage.[5]

Public Policy

In addition to statutory limitations on the right to contract, courts have the power to declare certain types of contracts void on the grounds that they are contrary to public policy. *Public policy* is the common sense and conscience of the community extended and applied throughout the state to matters of public morals, health, safety, and welfare. This principle of law is based on the theory that one cannot lawfully do something that has a tendency to be injurious to the public or against the public good.

Contracts that bring about results that the law seeks to prevent are said to be unenforceable as "against public policy." The following list is not exhaustive but merely illustrative of the types of contracts that are deemed to be against the public interest:

- Agreements to unreasonably restrain trade or business. Reasonable restraints, such as a promise not to engage in business for a short time and in a small area, are not against public policy and are therefore enforceable.
- Agreements for the sale of, or traffic in, a public office (e.g., I contract with you for a price to use my political influence to get you appointed to a public office).
- Agreements by public officers to accept greater pay than is fixed by law for the performance of official duties (e.g., I offer a public official money to do something

---

[5]See *West Coast Hotel v. Parrish*, 300 U.S. 379 (1937).

that he already is required to do). Here the danger is that the public officer may not want to do his job in the future unless he gets extra pay.

- Agreements to procure government contracts by personal or political influence or corrupt means. Here the general rule is that if the fee is contingent upon receiving a contract, it appears that corrupt means or duress will be used, which is against the public interest.
- Agreements by or between public or quasi-public corporations that interfere with their public duty (e.g., two railroads might contract to do something in unison that might adversely affect their service to the public).

Case 8.3 involves the enforcement of a gambling contract.

CASE 8.3 Dorado Beach Hotel Corporation v. Jernigan, 202 So.2d 830 (Fla. Dist. Ct. App. 1967)

FACT SUMMARY Walter Alonzo Jernigan, a resident of Florida, was visiting Puerto Rico, where casino gambling is legal. He gambled at the Dorado Beach Hotel's casino, lost money, and then wrote a check out to the hotel for $6,000 to pay for his losses. When he returned to Florida, Jernigan placed a stop payment on the check. The hotel then sued Jernigan in a state court in Florida to collect this gambling debt. (For further background about this case, read about the history of the famed Dorado Beach Hotel here: http://www.travelandleisure.com/articles/puerto-ricos-dorado-beach-redone. Also, check out this obituary of the defendant, W. A. Jernigan: http://www.legacy.com/obituaries/nwfdailynews/obituary.aspx?pid=134360304. Mr. Jernigan was a lobbyist in Washington, D.C., on behalf of the aviation industry, and he was instrumental in securing the Apollo space rocket contract for North American Aviation, the biggest contract ever awarded by the U.S. government at the time.)

SYNOPSIS OF DECISION AND OPINION This case never went to a jury. Instead, the trial judge entered a summary final judgment in favor of Jernigan, holding that enforcement of a gambling debt would be contrary to public policy. The hotel appealed this decision to the District Court of Appeal of Florida, and the appellate court affirmed the decision of the trial judge. The hotel then appealed to the Supreme Court of Florida, but its appeal was dismissed without opinion.

Dorado Beach Hotel Casino Chip.
©Ebay

WORDS OF THE COURT: Public Policy "Dorado Beach Hotel Corporation has appealed from a summary final judgment denying it the right to collect a gambling debt in Florida. The sole question is, Can a gambling obligation valid in Puerto Rico where created be enforced in Florida?

"This State has consistently refused to permit gambling on non-spectator sports such as bookie parlors, football parlors, et cetera. Thus, the public policy of the State of Florida is well established that the State will condone certain selected forms of gambling, but it has likewise been established that the State will not lend its judicial arm to the collection of monies wagered in such enterprises not authorized by the law of the State of Florida. Although many efforts have been made to obtain legal sanction for wagering

(continued)

at gaming tables, such authorization has never been given; and should a citizen of the State of Florida lose at a gaming table in the State, clearly the operator could not collect through the judicial processes. It is our conclusion that this forum will not extend its judicial arm to aid in the collection of this type gambling debt whether the transaction giving rise to the loss arose in Nevada, Puerto Rico or Monte Carlo."

Case Questions

1. What if the defendant in this case had returned to Puerto Rico? Could the hotel have sued him again in a Puerto Rican court?

2. In your opinion, which party acted the least ethically in this case: the casino for allowing Jernigan to wager such large sums of money on credit or Jernigan for placing the stop payment on his check?

3. *Focus on Critical Thinking*: If you were the manager of the casino at the Dorado Beach Hotel when this case was decided, what steps, if any, would you take to reduce the risk of this scenario happening again?

Exceptions to the Nonenforcement Rule

As a general rule, courts will not enforce illegal bargains; instead, the law will leave the parties where it finds them. If the contract is executory (unperformed), neither party may enforce it. If the contract is executed (performed), a court will not permit rescission and recovery of what was given in performance. Where an agreement is illegal in part only, the part that is lawful may be enforced, only if it can be separated from the part that is illegal. If any part of the consideration that is given for a single promise is illegal and there is no possibility of separation, there can be no enforcement. If several considerations, one of which is bad, are given for several promises, and the legal consideration is by its terms apportioned to the legal promise, the legal part is enforceable. If two promises, one lawful and one unlawful, are given for a legal consideration, the lawful promise is enforceable.

There are some exceptions to this nonenforcement doctrine in which the court leaves the parties where it finds them. When a party to the contract is a member of the class of persons for whose protection the contract was made illegal, he may enforce it or obtain restitution. Examples include the following:

- When a person buys bonds that are illegal because they conflict with blue-sky laws (laws to protect against tricking people into buying the "blue sky"), the buyer can elect to enforce the contract.
- When an insurance policy is illegal because the company did not use an approved form, an insured under that policy can enforce the policy.
- When a party to an illegal contract repents and rescinds before any part of the illegal purpose is carried out, he may have restitution of the money or goods he has given in performance.
- When one party to the contract is not *in pari delicto* with the other (i.e., is not as guilty) because he was induced to enter into the bargain by fraud, duress, or strong economic pressure, he may have restitution of that which he has given in performance.

TAKEAWAY CONCEPTS Legality

- A contract should have a legal purpose.
- Legality is one of the elements of a valid contract.
- The subject matter or performance of a contract must not violate any laws or public policy.

When Do Nondisclosure Agreements Contravene Public Policy?

Since the *New Yorker* published a bombshell report in October 2017 detailing decades of alleged sexual harassment and assault by Hollywood producer Harvey Weinstein, dozens of women have come forward with similar claims against the movie mogul. In fact, over 60 women have accused Weinstein of inappropriate to potentially criminal behavior ranging from requests for massages to intimidating sexual advances to rape.

According to some reports, employees of Harvey Weinstein's company are required to sign contracts promising not to make statements that could harm the reputation of the firm or its top executives. And when female employees have sued Weinstein for harassment, he and his company have generally settled the claims confidentially—making payments conditional on the plaintiffs not talking about the details of their cases.

Confidentiality clauses have featured in many high-profile sexual harassment scandals. Venture capital firm Kleiner Perkins offered to settle former employee Ellen Pao's sexual harassment suit only if she signed an agreement limiting her freedom to talk about her experience. (She dropped her suit but declined to settle, saying she did not want to be silenced.) Fox News Channel likewise used confidentiality clauses in contracts with employees to protect its late chief Roger Ailes from sexual harassment claims.

New York Post cover story.
©Splash News/Alamy

Discussion Questions

1. Is it, or should it be, legal for employers to use confidentiality provisions to keep harassment claims secret?
2. Should public policy protect whistleblowers or victims of harassment who have signed confidentiality agreements?

THINKING STRATEGICALLY

©valterZ/Shutterstock

Forum Selection and Choice of Law Clauses

PROBLEM: Facebook has users across the United States and all over the world; at last count Facebook had over two billion active users around the world.[6] As a result, Facebook could potentially be sued anywhere. By way of example, the plaintiff in Case 8.1 was

[6]See Josh Constine, "Facebook Now Has Two Billion Users," *TechCrunch* (June 27, 2017), available at https://techcrunch.com/2017/06/27/facebook-2-billion-users/.

from Illinois, and he had originally sued Facebook in Illinois, not California. Thinking strategically, what can Facebook do to maintain its legal home-court advantage?

STRATEGIC SOLUTION: Facebook could include a forum selection clause in its standard user agreement. A forum selection clause is a contractual agreement that obligates the parties *ahead of time* to litigate any dispute arising out of the contract in a particular court named in the clause. As a result, if any litigation involving that particular contract is brought in the future, both parties are obligated to litigate the dispute in the court specified in the forum selection clause.

With this background in mind, consider Section 15(1) of Facebook's terms of use, which states in full:

> You will resolve any claim, cause of action or dispute (claim) you have with us arising out of or relating to this Statement or Facebook exclusively in the U.S. District Court for the Northern District of California or a state court located in San Mateo County, and you agree to submit to the personal jurisdiction of such courts for the purpose of litigating all such claims. The laws of the State of California will govern this Statement, as well as any claim that might arise between you and us, without regard to conflict of law provisions.

Thus, Facebook's forum selection clause provides a textbook illustration of legal strategy in action. Because Facebook's headquarters are located in San Mateo County in Northern California, where potential jurors might be more tech-friendly and less inclined to rule against a local firm, Facebook will likely enjoy a strategic home court advantage by requiring its users to agree ahead of time to the jurisdiction of a local court in Facebook's neck of the woods.

QUESTIONS

1. Are forum selection clauses ethical? Why or why not?
2. How would a forum selection clause figure into a cost-benefit analysis by a company? What are the costs of litigating in another state versus your home state?
3. Why is "home court" an advantage in a particular court? Don't all litigants have an equal chance at justice?

KEY TERMS

Capacity p. 166   For the formation of a valid contract, the requirement that both parties have the power to contract. Certain classes of persons have only limited powers to contract, including minors and those with mental incapacity.

Minors p. 167   Category of individuals who have limited capacity to enter into a contract; includes those younger than the majority age of 18. Until a person reaches his majority age, any contract entered into is voidable at the minor's option.

Ratification p. 167   Any act that indicates that a minor intends to be bound by his promise.

Disaffirmance p. 167   The taking of some affirmative action to avoid obligation under a contract; disaffirmance is required when a contract has already been performed or partially performed by the minor.

Mental incompetents p. 168   Category of individuals who have limited capacity to enter into a contract; includes anyone who is unable to understand the nature and consequences of the contract and anyone who is unable to act in a reasonable manner in relation to the transaction when the other party has reason to know of his condition.

Lucid p. 171   Sane; able to think clearly.

Legality p. 172   For the formation of a valid contract, the requirement that both the subject matter and performance of the contract must be legal.

Public policy p. 172   Part of the legality requirement for a valid contract; necessitates that the terms be consistent with public policy objectives.

CASE SUMMARY 8.1 Webster Street Partnership Ltd. v. Sheridan, 368 N.W.2d 439 (Neb. 1985)

Necessaries

Matthew Sheridan was a minor when he rented a second-floor apartment in Omaha, Nebraska, from Webster Street Partnership ("the Landlord"). After a couple of months, Sheridan was unable to pay the rent and decided to abandon the apartment and move back home with his parents. The Landlord sued to collect unpaid rents.

CASE QUESTIONS

1. Could the Landlord collect the unpaid rent from Sheridan?
2. In answering the above question, should it matter that Sheridan had chosen to voluntarily leave his parents' home, with the understanding that he could return whenever he desired? What if Sheridan had been an orphan with no home to go back to?

CASE SUMMARY 8.2 Faber v. Sweet Style Manufacturing Corporation, 242 N.Y.S.2d 763 (N.Y. Sup. Ct., Nassau County, 1963)

Bipolar Disorder

Faber was a businessman who was diagnosed with "manic-depressive disorder" or what we would now call *bipolar disorder*. Before he was diagnosed, he had purchased some commercial property during a manic phase. After his diagnosis, he sought to back out of the deal. In support of his argument that he lacked the capacity to make this deal, he testified that although he was ordinarily a frugal and cautious person, he purchased three expensive cars for himself, his son, and his daughter and that he began to drive at high speeds, take his wife out to expensive dinners, and discuss his sexual prowess with others.

CASE QUESTIONS

1. How should the court in this case determine whether Faber lacked the capacity to purchase the commercial property: by focusing on whether the terms of the deal were unreasonable under the objective standard, or by focusing on Faber's state of mind at the time he made the deal?
2. Unlike minors, a person with a psychological disorder can enter and exit his impaired state. How should courts determine whether individuals with mental disorders are mentally capable of entering into a contract?

CASE SUMMARY 8.3 Biomedical Systems Corp. v. GE Marquette Medical Systems, Inc., 287 F.3d 707 (8th Cir. 2002)

Legality

GE Marquette Medical Systems (GE) contracted with Biomedical Systems Corp. to manufacture a new medical instrument based on technology owned by Biomedical. The contract required GE to obtain clearance from the Food and Drug Administration (the federal regulatory agency that covers such medical devices) within 90 days in order to move ahead on the project. After this contract was signed, GE determined that obtaining this clearance was not a prudent path to reach its ultimate objective of having the product approved for selling to the public. Rather than seek the clearance required by the Biomedical contract, GE decided to pursue a different strategy with the FDA that took several years to complete. When Biomedical sued GE for breach of contract, GE defended on the basis that the clearance provision in the contract was a violation of FDA procedure and, thus, the term was illegal and the contract was void.

CASE QUESTIONS

1. Can a party make a unilateral judgment as to illegality on a term of the contract when there is no affirmative finding from a regulatory authority?
2. If GE had gone ahead with the clearance process and the FDA had told GE that it was not the proper procedure, would the contract be void for illegality?

CHAPTER REVIEW QUESTIONS

1. **The doctrine of capacity refers to:**

   a. The objective intention of the parties to create a valid contract.

   b. The subjective intention of the parties to create a valid contract.

   c. The physical ability of the parties to create a valid contract.

   d. The mental competence of the parties to create a valid contract.

   e. The willingness of the parties to create a valid contract.

2. **Sarah purchases a car from ACME Motors Inc. on her 16th birthday. Sarah's contract is:**

   a. Void.

   b. Valid.

   c. Voidable.

   d. Enforceable.

   e. Unconscionable.

3. **For the purposes of the validity of a contract, a person entering into a contract must be of sound mind:**

   a. Always.

   b. During the age of majority.

   c. Only at the time when he makes the contract.

   d. Only at the time when he enforces the contract.

   e. Both at the time of making as well as enforcement of the contract.

4. **Junior is 17 years old and has entered into an agreement to purchase a vintage 1968 Ford Mustang from his neighbor. Which of the following is true about the transaction?**

   a. The contract is automatically void.

   b. Junior has the right to void the contract until he turns 18.

   c. The contract lacks bargained-for consideration.

   d. No contract exists because there was no mutual assent.

   e. The contract is voidable unless ratified by Junior's parents or legal guardian.

5. **A contract entered into by a person who has been adjudged insane is:**

   a. Void.

   b. Valid.

   c. Voidable.

   d. Enforceable.

   e. Unconscionable.

6. **Minors may enter into legally binding contracts.**

   a. True

   b. False

7. **The doctrine of legality requires that both the subject matter and the performance of the contract be lawful.**

   a. True

   b. False

8. **An agreement between two competing gas station owners to fix their prices in order to drive a third gas station owner out of business is enforceable.**

   a. True

   b. False

9. **Cardozo enters into a contract with Holmes. While they were negotiating the contract, Cardozo was under the influence of a mind-altering drug, but Holmes had no reason to suspect it. In most states, the Cardozo-Holmes contract is voidable by either Holmes or Cardozo.**

   a. True

   b. False

10. **In the pilot episode of the critically acclaimed TV series *Breaking Bad,* high school chemistry teacher Walter White and his former student Jesse Pinkman join forces to manufacture and distribute a highly pure but illegal drug known as "crystal meth." In most states the informal partnership agreement between Walter White and Jesse Pinkman is enforceable.**

    a. True

    b. False

 Quick Quiz ANSWERS

Does Caesar have the capacity to contract?

1. Yes. Once Caesar turned 18 he ratified the contract and can no longer disaffirm it as a minor.

2. No. Because he is unable to understand the nature and consequences of the contract, Caesar does not have the capacity necessary to form a valid contract.

3. No. Because Caesar is unable to act in a reasonable manner in relation to the transaction and Brutus has reason to know of his intoxication, he does not have sufficient capacity to contract.

4. Yes. Be careful! Remember that in a majority of states contracts made by an incompetent are voidable, not void. If the incompetent party regains mental capacity, or has a guardian appointed, Caesar may ratify the contract and thus he has capacity to form a valid contract.

CHAPTER REVIEW QUESTIONS: Answers and Explanations

1. d. The doctrine of capacity refers to the mental competence of the parties to create a valid contract. Answers *a, b, c,* and *e* are incorrect because capacity does not have anything to do with a party's intention, physical ability, or willingness to enter into an agreement. Instead, capacity refers to one's mental ability to understand the terms of the agreement one is entering into.

2. c. Contracts involving minors are voidable by the minor due to lack of capacity until the age of majority. Answers *a* and *b* are wrong because contracts made by minors are merely voidable and not automatically void or automatically valid. Answer *d* is wrong because contracts involving minors cannot be enforced if disaffirmed by the minor, and answer *e* is wrong because such contracts are not automatically unconscionable.

3. c. A person entering into a contract must be of sound mind when he makes the contract. If he later becomes insane, his legal guardian may enforce the contract on his behalf. As a result, answers *a, b, d,* and *e* are incorrect.

4. b. Contracts involving minors are voidable by the minor (or guardian) due to capacity until the age of majority. Answer *a* is wrong because the contract is voidable at the minor's option, not automatically; answer *c* is wrong because

there was a bargained-for exchange; answer *d* is wrong because the parties had mutual assent; and answer *e* is wrong because the right to ratify or affirm the agreement belongs to the minor, not to his parents or legal guardian.

5. a. A contract made by someone who has previously been adjudged insane by a court of law is automatically void.

6. a. True. Minors may enter into contracts that are voidable.

7. a. True. The doctrine of legality or lawful purpose requires that *both* the subject matter and the performance of the contract be lawful.

8. b. False. An agreement in restraint of trade is literally a textbook example of an illegal agreement and is thus void and unenforceable.

9. b. False. Cardozo may have lacked capacity due to intoxication, but the contract is still valid so long as Cardozo is able to act in a reasonable manner in relation to the transaction and the other party has no reason to know of the intoxication.

10. b. False. Because both the subject matter and performance of this agreement are illegal, the partnership agreement is void under the doctrine of legality.

CHAPTER 9

Enforceability

THINKING STRATEGICALLY

©valterZ/Shutterstock

In order to be enforceable, promises must be the result of genuine assent. This chapter will consider a number of situations in which genuine assent might be lacking. In addition, because of their frequent use in many business transactions, we will consider as well the strategic problem of asymmetric information and the enforceability of confidentiality agreements and noncompete clauses in this chapter's *Thinking Strategically*.

Learning Objectives

After studying this chapter, students who have mastered the material will be able to:

9-1 Define the contract doctrine of enforceability.

9-2 Identify five types of "consent defects," situations in which genuine assent to a contract may be lacking.

9-3 Understand the strategic concept of asymmetric information, and distinguish between innocent misrepresentations and fraudulent misrepresentations in contracts.

9-4 Apply the contract defenses of duress, undue influence, and unconscionability.

9-5 Articulate when contracts must be in writing under the statute of frauds.

9-6 Explain how courts use the parol evidence rule to interpret contracts.

CHAPTER OVERVIEW

Not all promises are legally enforceable, and there is no legal obligation to perform one's promises in a contract unless the contract is both valid *and* enforceable. Once it has been established that a valid contract has been formed, the next step is to determine whether the contract is enforceable. In this chapter, we discuss the legal doctrine of enforceability, including the requirement of genuine assent and the scope of the statute of frauds.

ENFORCEABILITY OF CONTRACTS

If the parties have formed a valid contract, the legal analysis turns to the issue of **enforceability**. A contract is of little use if it is not enforceable in a court of law, so business firms must ensure that their contracts are not only properly formed but also legally enforceable. Specifically, even if the required elements of a contract (i.e., agreement, consideration, capacity, and lawful purpose) are present, the contract must be the product of genuine assent, and it must also be in writing under certain circumstances. First off, let's identify five situations in which genuine assent may be lacking, or five possible "consent defects": misrepresentation, fraud, duress, undue influence, and unconscionability.

CONSENT DEFECTS

For a contract to be enforceable, it must be the result of **genuine assent**. Without genuine assent, a promise made is not legally binding. A lack of genuine assent occurs in cases of (1) misrepresentation, (2) fraud, (3) duress, (4) undue influence, and (5) unconscionability. If any of these five "consent defects" are present, there is no genuine assent and the contract may not be enforceable.

From a strategic perspective, some of these consent defects may incentivize ex post strategic behavior in business transactions. Specifically, parties may try to invoke one or more of these consent defects to back out of their contracts. For instance, given the frequency of sales talks preceding many deals, given how common threats and bluffs are in business negotiations, and given that many business transactions involve the use of standard form contracts with boilerplate terms, there is always a risk that the other party may try to invoke the defense of misrepresentation, duress, or unconscionability to try to back out of an onerous deal.

MISREPRESENTATION AND THE STRATEGIC PROBLEM OF ASYMMETRIC INFORMATION

In contracts, *information asymmetry* refers to the problem of contracts in which one contracting party has more or better information than the other. Information asymmetries occur in many types of contracts[1] and often produce an imbalance of power in business transactions. Moreover, this imbalance can sometimes cause transactions to go awry. In contract law, a classic example of information asymmetry is **misrepresentation**, which occurs when one party to an agreement makes a promise or representation about a *material fact* that is not true. The common law recognizes two types of misrepresentation: innocent misrepresentations and fraudulent ones.

Innocent Misrepresentation

When one party to an agreement makes a promise or representation about a material fact that is not true, the other party may avoid the contract on the basis of misrepresentation, even if the misrepresenting party doesn't actually know that the promise or representation is false. Consequently, the defense is sometimes called *innocent misrepresentation,* which distinguishes it from *fraudulent misrepresentation* (discussed below).

For one party to avoid a contract on the basis of misrepresentation, he must prove (1) the misrepresented fact was *material* (i.e., it concerns a basic assumption in the agreement, or the false representation somehow changes the value of the contract); (2) he *justifiably relied* on the misstatement when forming an agreement (such as the price to be paid); and (3) the misrepresentation was one of *fact* and not just someone's opinion or

LO 9-1

Define the contract doctrine of enforceability.

LO 9-2

Identify five types of "consent defects," situations in which genuine assent to a contract may be lacking.

LO 9-3

Understand the strategic concept of asymmetric information, and distinguish between innocent misrepresentations and fraudulent misrepresentations in contracts.

mere puffing (e.g., "This building's roof is only five years old" is a verifiable fact, whereas "The roof is in great shape" is puffing).

Sometimes it is hard to distinguish between statements of fact and statements of opinion. In one famous case (see Case 9.1 below), a dance student sued her dancing school on the basis of misrepresentations by her instructor, who had frequently assured her that she had "excellent potential" for dance so long as she kept purchasing pricey lessons from the dancing school. Eventually, the student sought another teacher, who informed her that she had minimal dance aptitude and could barely detect a musical beat. The dance school argued that its advice was merely opinion and, therefore, could not be the basis for a misrepresentation claim. Nonetheless, the court ruled in favor of the student and reasoned that because the dancing school had "superior knowledge" on the subject, it had a duty to act in good faith in its contract transactions.

Fraud

When one party has engaged in conduct that meets the standards for misrepresentation and has *actual knowledge* that his representation is false, this conduct is classified as **fraudulent misrepresentation** (sometimes referred to simply as *fraud*). In other words, misrepresentation plus guilty knowledge (also known as *scienter*) equals fraudulent misrepresentation.

From a practical perspective, the main difference between misrepresentation and fraudulent misrepresentation is the legal remedy available to the aggrieved party. In cases of misrepresentation, the aggrieved party may avoid the contract but has only limited relief in terms of money damages because recovery in most states is limited to actual out-of-pocket damages. In cases of fraudulent misrepresentation, most states classify the contract as void and the aggrieved party is generally entitled to recover money damages for any losses incurred, plus additional damages for such things as loss of future profits. Some states go so far as to allow an award of **treble damages**, which are three times the amount of actual damages.

To better understand the difference between innocent and fraudulent misrepresentation, let's consider the following hypothetical example. LeBron negotiates to lease Kobe's house. During their negotiations, LeBron asks Kobe if his house has any toxic substances such as radon. (Radon is an invisible, naturally occurring gas that the Environmental Protection Agency has determined to be a risk factor for cancer.) Kobe replies that he has owned the building for 10 years and has never detected any radon or any other toxins. LeBron agrees to lease the property for $10,000 per month, but before moving in he finds out that radon is present in the basement and that it would cost $15,000 for a radon evacuation system to be installed. In this case, the radon was a material fact (it changed the value of the contract by $15,000), LeBron relied on that fact in calculating the price, and Kobe's representation was of a fact that turned out to be false. LeBron may, therefore, avoid the contract based on *innocent misrepresentation*.

Next, suppose that after LeBron cancels the contract, Kobe finds another party to buy the building (Melo). When Melo asks Kobe about the radon, Kobe gets nervous about the sale falling through and lies, saying, "As far as I know, there is no radon." Melo may thus avoid the contract on the basis of fraudulent misrepresentation because Kobe's statement fits the requirements for misrepresentation and, unlike in the earlier case, Kobe now has knowledge that his statement is false. Thus, Melo will also be entitled to additional money damages from Kobe for any losses that Melo incurs as a result of the fraudulent misrepresentation.

Figure 9.1 summarizes the main differences between *innocent* and *fraudulent* misrepresentations.

FIGURE 9.1 Innocent Misrepresentation versus Fraud

Difference Between Misrepresentation and Fraud	
Misrepresentation	**Fraud**
1. The person making the representation believes it to be true.	The person making the representation does not believe it to be true.
2. There is no intention to deceive the other party.	Here, the intention is to deceive the other party.
3. The aggrieved party can avoid the contract only and nothing else.	The aggrieved party can avoid the contract as well as claim the damages.

Strategic Digression: Concealment of Material Fact   Although many fraudulent misrepresentations arise out of affirmative promises, sometimes a fraudulent misrepresentation may occur when one party *conceals* a material fact. While parties do *not* have a general duty to disclose all information to each other, some courts have allowed the use of misrepresentation as a valid defense (1) when a party has asserted a half-truth that leads to an overall misrepresentation, (2) when one party takes an affirmative action to conceal the truth from the other party, or (3) when one party fails to correct a past statement that the other party subsequently discovers to be untrue. In addition, even in contractual situations where a party to a transaction owes no general duty to disclose facts within his knowledge or to answer inquiries respecting such facts, if he undertakes to do so he must disclose the *whole truth*. Consider Case 9.1 below.

CASE 9.1 Vokes v. Arthur Murray, Inc., 212 So.2d 906 (Fla. 1968)

FACT SUMMARY   Audrey E. Vokes, a widow of 51 years and without family, wished to become "an accomplished dancer." The defendant, J. P. Davenport, owned and operated a franchised Arthur Murray Dance Studio in Clearwater, Florida. One day, Vokes attended a "dance party" at Davenport's dancing establishment. Davenport complimented Vokes on her "grace and poise" and sold her eight half-hour dance lessons for $14.50. Over a period of 16 months, Davenport sold her 14 additional "dance courses," which she paid up front in cash. During this time, Davenport told Vokes that she was "rapidly improving and developing in her dancing skill"; that the additional lessons would "make her a beautiful dancer, capable of dancing with the most accomplished dancers"; and that she was "rapidly progressing in the development of her dancing skill and gracefulness." In all, Vokes signed 14 separate contracts titled "Enrollment Agreement—Arthur Murray's School of Dancing," totaling 2,302 hours of dancing lessons for a total cash outlay of $31,090.45. When she realized that her dancing had not improved, she sued Davenport and Arthur Murray, Inc.

(continued)

alleging that Davenport's representations to her "were in fact false and known by the defendant to be false and contrary to the plaintiff's true ability . . . but withheld from the plaintiff for the sole and specific intent to deceive and defraud the plaintiff and to induce her in the purchasing of additional hours of dance lessons." She also requested a refund "for that portion of the $31,090.45 not charged against specific hours of instruction given to the plaintiff." Davenport argued that his representations were statements of opinion, not statements of fact, and the trial court dismissed the case. Vokes appealed.

SYNOPSIS OF DECISION AND OPINION   The Court of Appeals for the Second District of Florida reversed the decision of the lower court. Although the court of appeals conceded that a misrepresentation, to be actionable, must be one of fact rather than one of opinion, the court identified several exceptions to this general rule: (1) where there is a fiduciary relationship between the parties, (2) where there has been some artifice or trick employed by the representor, (3) where the parties do not in general deal at "arm's length," or (4) where the representee does not have equal opportunity to become apprised of the truth or falsity of the fact represented.

WORDS OF THE COURT: Duty to Disclose   "It could be reasonably supposed here that [Davenport] had 'superior knowledge' as to whether [Vokes] had 'dance potential' and as to whether she was noticeably improving in the art of [dance]. And it would be a reasonable inference from the undenied averments of the complaint that the flowery eulogiums heaped upon her by [Davenport] as a prelude to her contracting for 1944 additional hours of instruction . . . proceeded as much or more from the urge to 'ring the cash register' as from any honest or realistic appraisal of her dancing prowess or a factual representation of her progress.

"Even in contractual situations where a party to a transaction owes no duty to disclose facts within his knowledge or to answer inquiries respecting such

FIGURE 9.2   An Arthur Murray Dance Studio

facts, the law is if he undertakes to do so he must disclose the *whole truth*. [Citation omitted.] From the face of the complaint, it should have been reasonably apparent to [Davenport] that her vast outlay of cash for the many hundreds of additional hours of instruction was not justified by her slow and awkward progress, which she would have been made well aware of if [he] had spoken the 'whole truth'."

Case Questions

1. Were Davenport's misrepresentations about Mrs. Vokes's dancing ability statements of *fact* or statements of *opinion*?

2. The court of appeals identified four exceptions to the general rule that only statements of fact are actionable as fraud. (See Synopsis of Decision and Opinion above.) Which of the four exceptions applies in this case?

3. *Focus on Critical Thinking:* In your opinion, why does the law make it so difficult for plaintiffs to prove fraudulent misrepresentation? Why isn't it enough just to show that a defendant's statements were false or deceptive, regardless of whether such statements are about matters of fact or opinion?

Quick Quiz Fraud versus Innocent Misrepresentation

For each transaction, does either fraud or misrepresentation exist?

1. Brittany buys a horse from Tex. She buys the horse because Tex tells her that the horse "runs like the wind." In fact, the horse can't run more than 50 yards without stopping to rest.

2. Hawkins is interested in buying Joan's home. He asks her if the roof leaks, and she truthfully answers that she's lived in the home for 13 years and the roof has never leaked. Three days later, it rains and the roof leaks. Hawkins returns a week later, Joan says nothing, and Hawkins purchases the home.

3. Paul bought a used car from John. John had turned back the odometer and changed public records to hide the fact that the car had been in three accidents. One year later, Paul sold the car to George. George bought the car because it had low mileage and public records showed no accidents.

4. Tony is selling his golf clubs. After Mel comes to look at them, he agrees to buy them and leaves for the bank to get cash. When he returns, he pays Tony and puts the golf clubs in his car. Tony and Mel shake hands, and Tony says, "You got a really good deal—these clubs once belonged to Tiger Woods." A week later, Mel discovers that Tiger Woods never owned or used the clubs.

5. Flo is selling her car. The car has an oil leak, so there is oil evident to anyone who looks at the engine. Just before Tom comes over to look at the car, Flo has the engine steam-cleaned. When Tom looks at the engine, it is spotless and he does not ask if it leaks oil.

6. Lisa needs a new battery for her car. The salesperson tells her that the Try-Hard battery is the best battery that money can buy. She always likes things that are the best, so she buys the battery. A week later she discovers that the Try-Hard battery is inferior and is not very well regarded by those who know car batteries.

Answers to this Quick Quiz are provided at the end of the chapter.

ADDITIONAL CONTRACT DEFENSES

In addition to misrepresentation, the common law recognizes several additional contract defenses, including duress, undue influence, and unconscionability. What do all of these contract defenses have in common? They manifest different ways in which genuine assent might be lacking during the formation stage of a contract.

Duress

If one party to a contract uses any form of unfair coercion to induce another party to enter into or modify a contract, the coerced party may avoid the contract on the basis of **duress**. Generally, the law recognizes three categories of duress: (1) violence or threats of a violent act, (2) economic threats such as wrongful termination or threats to breach a contract, and (3) threats of extortion or other threats whereby the other party has no meaningful choice.

Duress is one of the few areas of law that is based on the subjective belief of the parties. Regardless of the form or content of a threat, if a coerced party is able to prove that he is unusually timid or that he was in an unusually vulnerable state of mind when he acquiesced to the other party's threats, he may invoke the duress defense even if an ordinarily reasonable person would not have been intimidated by such threats.

LO 9-4

Apply the contract defenses of duress, undue influence, and unconscionability.

Moreover, the legal status of the underlying act that is being threatened is legally irrelevant to the issue of duress. Simply put, when one party threatens another with a given act, whether he would ordinarily have the legal right to perform that act is *irrelevant.* For example, suppose Bloom works for Joyce as an at-will employee, meaning that either party may terminate the employment at any time and for any reason, with or without cause. (Employment-at-will is discussed in detail in Chapter 39, "Employment at Will.") Joyce threatens to fire Bloom unless he agrees to sell his stock to Joyce for $5 per share. Bloom has no choice if he wants to keep his job, so he sells the stock to Joyce. A court will allow Bloom to avoid the contract based on this threat even though Joyce has a legitimate right to fire Bloom with or without just cause.

Undue Influence

The defense of **undue influence** gives legal relief to a party who has been induced to enter into a contract through the improper pressure of a trusted relationship. Undue influence allows the influenced party to avoid a contract when the court determines that the terms of the contract are *unfair* and the parties had some type of relationship that involved a *fiduciary duty* or some duty to *care* for the influenced party. For example, Edna is a caregiver for June, a wealthy widow who is confined to a wheelchair. Edna informs June that she can no longer be her caregiver unless June signs a contract to assign to Edna $50,000 worth of Microsoft stock. June cannot imagine being alone or finding another caregiver, so she goes ahead with the contract. In this case, a court would likely allow June to avoid the contract based on the undue influence that Edna had asserted over her.

Unconscionability

When an agreement is reached between two parties that have met the required elements and are not subject to the defenses discussed previously, the contract may still potentially be avoided on the grounds that one party suffered a grossly unfair burden that shocks the conscience. Recall from our discussion of consideration (see Chapter 7) that courts will generally not be inclined to weigh the amount and type of consideration to determine whether the exchange is objectively fair. While this doctrine remains true, the defense of **unconscionability** gives the court the tools to refuse to enforce a contract where the consideration is grossly unequal.

In *Waters v. Min Ltd.,*[2] an appellate court allowed one party to avoid a contract in which she signed over an annuity insurance contract with an immediate value in excess of $150,000 in exchange for a check for $50,000. The fully annuitized value of the contract would have been over $530,000. The court ruled that although there was a written contract that met the elements required under the law, the disparity of value in the exchange, along with other circumstances such as drug dependency and lack of legal advice, was "too hard of a bargain for a court [to enforce]." While courts apply this defense *very* narrowly, it remains a viable defense when one party has been induced to enter a contract through oppressive terms and no bargaining is possible. Thus, high-pressure sales tactics that mislead illiterate consumers may be one case in which a court would likely allow a party to avoid a contract.

Courts have also been suspicious of standardized, preprinted contracts, known as *adhesion contracts,* because there is an assumption that the nondrafter has not genuinely bargained for the terms of the agreement. For example, in *Henningsen v. Bloomfield Motors, Inc.,*[3] an appellate court held that the disclaimer of a warranty that was buried in small print in

---

[2]587 N.E.2d 231 (Mass. 1992).

[3]161 A.2d 69 (N.J. 1960).

a preprinted agreement to purchase a used car was *void* because the drafter had "gross inequity of bargaining position" and that an ordinary person would not be able to fully comprehend what legal rights he was giving up. Therefore, the court held that enforcement of the disclaimer was against public policy.

At the same time, it is worth noting that standard form contracts with boilerplate terms are very common in most consumer transactions. Are all such contracts to be deemed unconscionable? Is it possible to draw a principled or clear-cut line between standardized agreements that are enforceable and those that are unconscionable? Consider Case 9.2 below.

CASE 9.2 Williams v. Walker-Thomas Furniture Co., 350 F.2d 445 (D.C. Cir. 1965)

FACT SUMMARY Beginning in 1957, Ora Lee Williams, a mother of seven, purchased several home furnishings from the Walker-Thomas Furniture Company, located in Washington, D.C. At the time of making each purchase, she signed a standard form installment contract that contained the following boilerplate clause: "All payments now and hereafter made by [purchaser] shall be credited pro rata on all outstanding leases, bills, and accounts due the Company by [purchaser] at the time each such payment is made." The effect of this provision was to keep an outstanding balance on all items ever purchased by Williams, so if she ever defaulted on a single payment, the Walker-Thomas Furniture Co. would be able to repossess every item, regardless of how much had actually been paid off. In 1962, Williams purchased a record player from Walker-Thomas. When she fell behind on her payments for the record player, Walker-Thomas tried to repossess all the furniture sold to her since 1957. Williams objected and brought an action to prevent Walker-Thomas from repossessing the furniture that she had previously paid for, but the trial court dismissed her case, holding that the installment agreement was enforceable. Ms. Williams appealed.

SYNOPSIS OF DECISION AND OPINION In a landmark decision, the Court of Appeals for the District of Columbia reversed the decision of the lower court. Writing for the majority, Judge J. Skelly Wright applied the doctrine of unconscionability to the facts of the case and concluded that

genuine assent could be negated in circumstances involving "gross inequality of bargaining power." The court of appeals sent the case back to trial court to determine whether the installment contracts in this case were procured through unconscionable means.

WORDS OF THE COURT: Unconscionability "Unconscionability has generally been recognized to include an absence of meaningful choice on the part of one of the parties together with contract terms which are unreasonably favorable to the other party. . . .

"In many cases the meaningfulness of the choice is negated by a gross inequality of bargaining power. . . .

"The manner in which the contract was entered is also relevant to this consideration. Did each party to the contract, considering his obvious education or lack of it, have a reasonable opportunity to understand the terms of the contract, or were the important terms hidden in a maze of fine print and minimized by deceptive sales practices? Ordinarily, one who signs an agreement without full knowledge of its terms might be held to assume the risk that he has entered a one-sided bargain. But when a party of little bargaining power, and hence little real choice, signs a commercially unreasonable contract with little or no knowledge of its terms, it is hardly likely that his consent, or even an objective manifestation of his consent, was ever given to all the terms. In such a case the usual rule that the terms of the agreement are not to be questioned should be

(continued)

abandoned and the court should consider whether the terms of the contract are so unfair that enforcement should be withheld."

Case Questions

1. In your opinion, was the installment contract in this case unfair or unconscionable?

2. Should the bargaining power of the contracting parties be a relevant consideration in determining whether the weaker party's assent is genuine or not? Explain why or why not.

3. *Focus on Critical Thinking:* How relevant is an old case like *Williams v. Walker-Thomas Furniture Co.* today? By way of example, check out the standard terms of service of Facebook: www.facebook.com/terms.php. In your opinion, which provision in Facebook's terms of service is the most "unconscionable" one?

LO 9-5

Articulate when contracts must be in writing under the statute of frauds.

THE STATUTE OF FRAUDS

The **statute of frauds** refers to the law in each state governing which contracts must be *in writing* to be enforceable. As its name suggests, the main purpose of the statute of frauds is to prevent fraud by requiring that certain types of contracts have written evidence of their existence and terms. In particular, the statute of frauds applies to the following types of contracts: (1) contracts that involve the sale of land; (2) contracts that cannot be (i.e., are not able to be, by their terms) performed in under one year; (3) contracts to pay the debt of another (e.g., a loan surety); (4) contracts made in consideration of marriage (e.g., a prenuptial agreement); (5) contracts by the executor of a will to pay the debts of an estate with his own money; and (6) contracts for the sale of goods for $500 or more and lease transactions for goods amounting to $1,000 or more. Lawyers are taught to use the mnemonic "MY LEGS" to remember the list of contracts that fall under the statute of frauds and thus must be in writing. "MY LEGS" stands for *M*arriage, contracts for more than one *Y*ear, contracts for *L*and, *E*xecutor contracts, contracts for the sale of *G*oods over $500, and *S*urety contracts.

Below is a reprint of the original statute of frauds from the year 1677 AD.

> **Excerpt from the original statute of frauds enacted by Parliament during the reign of King Charles II:**
>
> *"And be it further enacted . . . That . . . no action shall be brought . . . to charge any person upon any agreement made upon consideration of marriage; or upon any contract or sale of lands, tenements or hereditaments, or any interest in or concerning them; or upon any agreement that is not to be performed within the space of one year from the making thereof; unless the agreement upon which such action shall be brought, or some memorandum or note thereof, shall be in writing, and signed by the party to be charged therewith, or some other person thereunto by him lawfully authorized."*
>
> Source: CHARLES II, c. 3, §4 (1677).

In other words, not all contracts must be in writing. Nor must a contract be in a prescribed format. For example, in one case,[4] a court held that an agreement on a brown piece of wrapping paper written in crayon between an art buyer and an artist was acceptable as an enforceable writing because it contained a signature, noted the quantity, and was supported by circumstances that indicated a contract with the artist for the sale of paintings. The one element that is uniformly required is a *signature of the party* against whom enforcement of the contract is sought.

---

[4]*Rosenfeld v. Basquiat,* 78 F.3d 184 (2d Cir. 1996).

CONTRACT INTERPRETATION AND THE PAROL EVIDENCE RULE

LO 9-6

Explain how courts use the parol evidence rule to interpret contracts.

In adjudicating disputes concerning the contents of a contract, courts use rules of interpretation to guide their analysis. The most important of these interpretation rules is the parol evidence rule. Before signing a written agreement, the parties typically engage in preliminary negotiations that involve discussions and perhaps documents, such as letters or memos, which are intended to help the parties come to an agreement. The **parol evidence rule** states that any writing intended by the parties to be the *final* expression of their agreement may not be *contradicted* by any oral or written agreements made prior to the writing. It's also important to note that the parol evidence rule does not bar admission of the preliminary documents when they are being used to determine the meaning that the parties intended concerning a particular term in the contract.

The parol evidence rule is not the only rule of interpretation used by courts in contract disputes. Sometimes contracts contain **ambiguous terms**. In such cases, these terms are construed by the court *against the interest* of the side that drafted the agreement. Courts may also *supply* a reasonable term in a situation where the contract is silent or has **omitted terms**.

TAKEAWAY CONCEPTS Genuine Assent

- For a contract to be enforceable, it must be the result of genuine assent.
- A lack of genuine assent occurs in cases of misrepresentation, fraud, duress, undue influence, and unconscionability.
- Misrepresentation applies only to statements of fact, not statements of opinion.
- Fraud requires guilty knowledge (i.e., knowledge that the misrepresentation is false).
- Not all contracts need to be in writing; the statute of frauds is the law in each state governing which contracts must be in writing to be enforceable.
- Courts rely on various rules of interpretation in disputes involving written contracts.

THINKING STRATEGICALLY

Enforceability of Confidentiality Agreements and Noncompete Clauses

PROBLEM: How do you protect your firm's trade secrets and business methods from employees who might depart from the company in the future and compete directly with their ex-employer?

STRATEGIC SOLUTION: One way of solving this problem is to "look forward and reason backward."[5] In other words, you should anticipate this risk by asking your employees to commit ahead of time not to reveal your secrets or compete against you when they leave the firm. Specifically, you could add a "nondisclosure" or *confidentiality* clause and a **covenant not to compete** (also called a *restrictive covenant*) to your firm's standard employment agreements. A confidentiality clause creates a confidential relationship between the parties and thus protects any type of confidential and proprietary information or trade secrets,[6] because the parties agree ahead of time not to disclose information covered by the agreement. Similarly, a covenant not to compete obligates one party not to compete with the other party for a specified period of time.

But there is a catch: Courts have historically subjected these contracts to close judicial scrutiny. This is not to say that covenants not to compete are unenforceable; rather, courts use a "reasonableness" test in determining the extent to which the covenant is enforceable. Even if a court finds that the terms of the covenant were unreasonable, most courts will opt to enforce the covenant to the extent required to protect the legitimate interests of the business instead of striking down the covenant completely.[7] For example, Jordan signs a noncompete agreement with Robert, her employer, whereby Jordan agrees not to contact any of

Robert's clients anywhere in the United States for two years after she has left Robert's company. After Jordan quits and starts her own firm, Robert finds out that Jordan has been contacting Robert's clients. Robert sues to enforce the covenant. If a court finds the covenant to be too broad, the covenant may be pared back by the court to, say, one year and a more limited geographic region. As a result, *restrictive covenant agreements should be narrowly tailored with the following requirements and standards in mind:*

Covenants not to compete most often arise out of either (1) the sale of a business, whereby the buyer is purchasing business assets, goodwill, and promises by the seller's principals not to compete with the buyer; or (2) as part of an employment agreement.

Sale of a business: In the context of the sale of a business, courts are willing to enforce such covenants, but they are often focused on the geographic area involved. If the covenant restriction is substantially broader than the area in which the buyer and seller are currently doing business, courts are often unwilling to enforce such an overly broad restriction.

Employment agreements: Covenants that are part of an employment contract (or an employment relationship) are subjected to a higher degree of scrutiny. Courts will generally permit the employment covenant to stand so long as it is designed to cover a recognized legitimate interest of the employer. Courts recognize an employer's interest in guarding *trade secrets* from being disclosed or used by an ex-employee. Employers also have a legitimate interest in ensuring that former employees do not act in a way that could *damage relationships* with their existing customers. Therefore, courts have permitted contracts that prevent ex-employees from soliciting (or even contacting) customers of the ex-employer for a certain period of time. However, these types of covenants must be *reasonable* in duration, subject matter, and geographic scope. Although these standards vary from industry to industry, the following general guidance regarding reasonableness is helpful:

- **Duration:** The higher the position of the employee, the longer the employer can restrict the employee. A sales staffer who quits after only one year will likely not be bound any more than one or two years, while the CEO of a corporation may

---

[5]Avinash K. Dixit and Barry J. Nalebuff, *Thinking Strategically* (Norton, 1991).

[6]A trade secret is a process, method, or data set (e.g., customer lists, formulas, etc.) that is not generally known and that gives a firm a competitive edge. Trade secrets are covered in depth in Chapter 50, "Intellectual Property."

[7]See *Restatement (Second) of Contracts,* § 184(2), Comment b, Illustration 2.

be bound in the range of five years or more. In any case, the duration must be no greater than is required for the protection of the employer while still considering the potential for undue hardship on the employee.

- **Subject Matter:** The restriction must be directly tied to the employee's work responsibilities. For example, if Foley works 10 years as an insurance agent for Garvey Insurance Agency, the restrictive covenant may cover only a competing interest of insurance sales. Thus, if Foley quits Garvey Insurance, starts a career as a golf instructor, and contacts customers he met while employed by Garvey, a court would not enforce a covenant to prevent this contact because any such restriction is too broad in terms of the scope of the subject.

Geographic Scope: Employers may limit the geographic area in which the employer conducts business, but the geographic region must not impose an undue hardship on the employee. While some companies may legitimately claim that they do business in all 50 states, courts are still reluctant to allow a restriction to be effective countrywide because that would require ex-employees to move abroad in order to comply with the covenant. On the other hand, a small manufacturing company in Philadelphia may wish to restrict its ex-engineering employees from competing within a radius of several miles of the city. This restriction would likely be seen as a protection of legitimate business interests without an undue burden to the employee.

QUESTIONS

1. Is it ethical for an employer to restrict an ex-employee's career prospects? Would you sign a noncompete clause upon starting a new job?
2. Should certain professions be exempt from use of a noncompete clause? Should physicians be restricted in where they can practice? Why or why not?

KEY TERMS

Enforceability p. 180   The ability of a properly formed contract to be enforceable in a court of law; determined by examining whether the contract is a product of genuine assent and is in writing (under certain circumstances).

Genuine assent p. 181   The knowing, voluntary, and mutual approval of the terms of a contract by each party; required for a contract to be enforceable.

Misrepresentation p. 181   Situation in which one party to an agreement makes a promise or representation about a material fact that is not true; basis for avoiding a contract.

Fraudulent misrepresentation p. 182   Situation in which one party has engaged in conduct that meets the standards for misrepresentation and that party has actual knowledge that the representation is not true; basis for avoiding a contract.

Treble damages p. 182   Triple damages; often awarded in fraud cases.

Duress p. 185   The use of any form of unfair coercion by one party to induce another party to enter into or modify a contract; basis for avoiding a contract.

Undue influence p. 186   A defense that gives legal relief to a party who was induced to enter into a contract through the improper pressure of a trusted relationship.

Unconscionability p. 186   A defense that may allow a party to potentially avoid a contract on the grounds that she suffered a grossly unfair burden that shocks the objective conscience.

Statute of frauds p. 188   The law governing which contracts must be in writing in order to be enforceable.

Parol evidence rule p. 189   Rule of contract interpretation stating that any writing intended by the parties to be the final expression of their agreement may not be contradicted by any oral or written agreements made prior to the writing.

Ambiguous terms p. 189   Contract terms that are vague and indefinite. In contract law, these terms are construed by the court against the interest of the side that drafted the agreement.

Omitted terms p. 189   Contract terms that are left out or absent. In contract law, courts may supply a reasonable term in a situation where the contract is silent.

Covenant not to compete p. 190   Type of contract in which one party agrees not to compete with another party for a specified period of time.

CASE SUMMARY 9.1 Professional Bull Riders, Inc. v. AutoZone, Inc., unpublished order and judgment dated August 15, 2005 (10th Cir. 2005)

Statute of Frauds

For many years, AutoZone, a Nevada corporation, was an official sponsor of the Bud Light Professional Bull Rider Series organized and conducted by Professional Bull Riders (PBR), a Colorado corporation. In late 2000, AutoZone verbally agreed to sponsor PBR events for a period of two additional years, from December 29, 2000, to December 31, 2002. At the same time, AutoZone and PBR agreed that AutoZone could terminate its sponsorship by giving notice in writing to PBR by August 15, 2001. In January 2002,

AutoZone notified PBR that it would not sponsor any PBR events in 2002. PBR then sued AutoZone for breach of contract.

CASE QUESTIONS

1. Could AutoZone use the statute of frauds as a defense in this case? Explain.
2. In your opinion, should the writing requirement set forth in the statute of frauds apply to all commercial agreements as a matter of sound public policy? Explain why or why not.

CASE SUMMARY 9.2 Alaska Packers' Association v. Domenico, 117 F. 99 (9th Cir. 1902)

Duress

The Alaska Packers' Association (APA) was a San Francisco–based manufacturer of Alaska canned salmon and the largest salmon packer in Alaska. In April 1900, it hired 21 seamen in San Francisco to work aboard one of its chartered vessels in Alaska. The seamen signed an agreement in which they were promised $60 each, plus two cents for each red salmon caught. When they arrived in Alaska, however, the seamen complained that the fishing nets they were provided were of poor quality, so they refused to continue working unless they were paid $100 each. Since the APA was unable to hire replacement fishermen in time, an agent of the APA in Alaska eventually agreed to the seamen's demands, but when the men returned to San Francisco

after completing their work, the APA refused to pay more than the originally agreed-upon amount of $60.

CASE QUESTIONS

1. In your opinion, is the second agreement in this case the product of genuine assent or the product of unjustified duress/coercion? Explain.
2. After season 4 of the hit HBO series show *The Sopranos,* actor James Gandolfini, who played lead character Tony Soprano, refused to appear in any further episodes of the show unless his salary was increased from $400,000 to $1 million per episode. In your opinion, was Mr. Gandolfini's threatened walkout a form of duress or undue influence? Explain why or why not.

CASE SUMMARY 9.3 Harley-Davidson Motor Co. v. PowerSports, Inc., 319 F.3d 973 (7th Cir. 2003)

Fraudulent Misrepresentation

PowerSports applied for a franchise license to operate a Harley-Davidson motorcycle dealership in Seminole County, Florida. Among other conditions, Harley-Davidson informed PowerSports that it does not allow

any of its dealerships to be publicly owned (i.e., to list its stock on a public stock exchange). PowerSports made certain representations about its business practices and procedures and assured Harley-Davidson that it would comply with Harley-Davidson's strict standards of quality and customer service. Based on these representations, Harley-Davidson awarded a franchise contract to PowerSports. However, just a few days later, Harley-Davidson discovered that PowerSports had taken significant steps to go public, which was inconsistent with Harley-Davidson's franchise contract. Harley-Davidson sued PowerSports for fraudulent misrepresentation, alleging that the representations made by PowerSports were false and demanding the rescission of the franchise contract, plus additional damages.

CASE QUESTIONS

1. In your opinion, were PowerSports's misrepresentations to Harley-Davidson "material"? Explain why or why not.
2. What if PowerSports had gone public three years after it was awarded the Harley-Davidson franchise contract? Could Harley-Davidson still sue for rescission? How about 10 years later?

CASE SUMMARY 9.4 Tafel v. Lion Antique Investments & Consulting Services, 773 S.E.2d 743, Supreme Court of Georgia (2015)

Unenforceability

Tafel Racing Team, Inc. (Tafel Racing) and Lion Antique Investments & Consulting Services, Inc. (Lion) entered into an agreement to purchase two Ferrari race cars. Pursuant to the agreement, Lion agreed to loan the race cars to Tafel Racing for use in the 2008 American Le Mans Series. Tafel Racing was obligated to purchase or sell the race cars 90 days after the conclusion of the 2008 American Le Mans Series. The plaintiff, James Tafel, Jr. (Tafel), is the former CEO of Tafel Racing. East Coast Jewelry (East Coast) agreed to purchase one of the Ferrari race cars for $700,000. Vladislav Yampolsky is a partial owner of East Coast. Although East Coast paid Tafel Racing $700,000, Tafel Racing did not deliver the car or refund East Coast's money. Tafel Racing filed a Voluntary Petition for Bankruptcy and listed Yampolsky as one of Tafel Racing's creditors holding unsecured nonpriority claims in the amount of $600,000. Tafel Racing also identified Tafel as a codebtor for each of Tafel Racing's creditors. At Yampolsky's request, Tafel executed a nonnegotiable promissory note in the principal amount of $600,000, plus $22,454.14 in interest, payable to Yampolsky. Tafel also executed a Deed to Secure Debt granting Yampolsky a security interest in Tafel's residence in Georgia. The note stated that it was "executed and delivered . . . in consideration of advances by Yampolsky to Tafel." Tafel, however, made no payments on the note. Yampolsky assigned his rights and interest in the note to Lion. Tafel claimed that the note was invalid and unenforceable. (*Hint:* Be sure to make a distinction between *Tafel Racing* and *Tafel.*)

CASE QUESTIONS

1. What defense can Tafel assert that would make the note unenforceable?
2. What must the note contain to make the note enforceable? Give an example.

CHAPTER REVIEW QUESTIONS

1. **The key difference between an innocent misrepresentation and a fraudulent misrepresentation is:**
   a. Puffing.
   b. Material fact.
   c. Guilty knowledge.
   d. Justified reliance.
   e. Monetary damages.

2. **The use of unfair coercion to force a party into a contract constitutes:**
   a. Duress.
   b. Undue influence.
   c. Misrepresentation.
   d. Unconscionability.
   e. Lack of genuine assent.

3. **To which of the following agreements does the statute of frauds apply?**
   I. **An option to purchase a parcel of land**
   II. **A promise to sell a used MacBook Pro for $1,000**
   III. **The donation of a new sailboat valued at $10,000**
   IV. **A 15-year mortgage instrument**

a. I and III

b. I, III, and IV

c. II, III, and IV

d. I, II, and IV

e. I, II, III, and IV

4. In a situation involving "gross inequality of bargaining power," which legal doctrine could a consumer use to challenge a standard form contract or boilerplate terms of service with shocking or totally one-sided terms?

a. Duress

b. Undue influence

c. Misrepresentation

d. Unconscionability

e. Lack of genuine assent

5. Which of the following does *not* fall within the statute of frauds?

a. A contract for a new car worth $25,000

b. An agreement to provide office cleaning services for a period of six months

c. A cosigner agreeing to guarantee a bank loan for her sister

d. An option contract to purchase a warehouse

e. A personal services agreement to provide consulting services for two years.

6. Julius enters into a contract for a 3-month consulting project with Augustus for $10,000 per month. This contract is subject to the statute of frauds.

a. True

b. False

7. Roscoe Jr. does not have sufficient credit to obtain an auto loan from the bank. His father, Roscoe Sr., agrees to act as a cosigner. The contract must be in writing.

a. True

b. False

8. The parol evidence rule requires a court to examine previous drafts of a contract in order to interpret it.

a. True

b. False

9. In order for a misrepresentation to be material, it must concern a basic assumption in the agreement or the misrepresentation must somehow change the value of the contract.

a. True

b. False

10. White enters into an employment contract with Gustavo only after Gustavo threatens to harm White's family. The contract is subject to the defense of fraud.

a. True

b. False

 Quick Quiz ANSWERS

Fraud versus Innocent Misrepresentation

1. No fraud or misrepresentation exists. This was sales talk (puffing), so Brittany has no course of action.

2. Joan is guilty of fraud. Even though she initially told the truth, the facts changed and her nondisclosure makes her liable for fraud.

3. John has committed a fraud against Paul by changing the mileage and accident records, two material facts in car negotiations. Paul committed a misrepresentation when he sold the car to George because, even though he had no knowledge of the true facts and did not intentionally conceal anything, the mileage and accident records were nevertheless false representations of material facts.

4. Tony's statement came after the contract had been executed, so Mel did not rely on Tony's statement when making the deal. (If the statement had been made during their negotiations and Mel was a huge Tiger Woods fan, it could be argued that the statement was an intentional falsehood of a material fact and therefore a fraud.)

5. Flo is guilty of fraud because she has concealed the material fact that the engine leaks oil.

6. No fraud or misrepresentation exists in this case. This sales talk constitutes puffing, so Lisa has no course of action.

(continued)

Statute of Frauds

1. Writing required. Promise to pay the debt of another.
2. Writing required. Real estate/land.
3. Careful! No writing required. Despite the high fee, the services can be performed in less than one year; thus, the contract is not subject to the statute of frauds requirements.
4. Writing required. A two-year contract for services that cannot be performed in less than one year.
5. Writing required. Even though the price is below $500, it is for the purchase of an interest in land.

CHAPTER REVIEW QUESTIONS: Answers and Explanations

1. c. Guilty knowledge, or *scienter,* is required to prove that a misrepresentation was intentional and thus constitutes fraud. Answer *a* is incorrect because it is not related to determining fraud, while answers *b, d,* and *e* are incorrect because they are common elements of fraud.

2. a. By definition, duress is the use of any form of unfair coercion by one party to induce another party to enter into or modify a contract. Answers *b, c,* and *d* are wrong because those doctrines do not apply to unfair coercion, while answer *e* is too general.

3. d. The statute of frauds does not apply to donations. The statute of frauds does apply to the sale of land (I), the sale of goods over $500 (II), and contracts that cannot be performed under one year (IV). Accordingly, answers *a, b, c,* and *e* are wrong because they include III, which refers to the donation of a good.

4. d. According to the landmark case of *Williams v. Walker Thomas Furniture Co.,* the doctrine of unconscionability could potentially apply to standard form contracts involving shocking terms and gross inequality of bargaining power. By contrast, answers *a, b,* and *c* are wrong

because those doctrines are not specific to boilerplate agreements, while answer *e* is too general.

5. b. The contract described in answer *b* can be performed in under one year. By contrast, answers *a, c, d,* and *e* do not fall under the statute of frauds.

6. b. False. Don't be fooled by the amounts involved. This is a service contract that will conclude in under one year. The contract does not have to be in writing.

7. a. True. Roscoe Sr. is promising to pay the debt of another and acting as a surety, and thus the contract is covered under the statute of frauds.

8. b. False. Under the parole evidence, any writing intended by the parties to be the final expression of their agreement cannot be contradicted by previous drafts/discussions.

9. a. True. Not all misrepresentations are material. To be material, the misrepresentation must involve a fundamental part of the contract or change the parties' responsibilities/value of the contract.

10. b. False. The defense is duress, not fraud.

CHAPTER 10

Performance

Contracts are strategic planning documents that can be used creatively in a variety of ways. For example, in this chapter's *Thinking Strategically* section, you will learn how businesses strategically use contract conditions to create incentives for high performing employees and manage the risks of employee under-performance.

Learning Objectives

After studying this chapter, students who have mastered the material will be able to:

10-1   Identify and categorize the three types of contract conditions.

10-2   Explain the doctrine of substantial performance and identify its effects on the contracting parties.

10-3   Describe the four ways contracting parties can discharge a contract through mutual agreement.

10-4   Describe the three ways contracting parties can discharge a contract through operation of law.

CHAPTER OVERVIEW

A central purpose of contract law is to provide a system that legally enforces the promises that are made willingly between contracting parties. As previously mentioned, contracts allow individuals and businesses to plan, budget, coordinate, and invest their capital in a productive manner. Once a valid contract has been entered into, the contracting parties usually seek to end or terminate their legal duties by performing as promised in the agreement. Honoring the agreed-upon promises is the most common and desirable method of terminating contracts since it preserves the parties' original expectations. However, there are several other ways to legally terminate

a contract. How and when a contract is legally terminated, known as **contract discharge**, will be the primary focus of this chapter.

THE NATURE AND EFFECT OF CONTRACT CONDITIONS

The fulfillment of mutual promises stipulated in a contract generally discharges contractual duties and legally terminates a contract. Sometimes, however, parties to an agreement wish to allocate or adjust a particular risk associated with performing a contract. This allocation of risk is sometimes shifted onto the other party by attaching an event, known as a *condition,* which can alter the performance obligations stipulated under the contract. These event-related conditions fall under three general categories: conditions precedent, subsequent, or concurrent.

LO 10-1

Identify and categorize the three types of contract conditions.

A **condition precedent** requires that an event must occur *before* performance under a contract is due. For example, suppose that Graham hires Frost as a sales representative. The parties agree to a base salary and other basic employment terms. In addition, Graham offers to pay Frost a $1,000 bonus *provided that* Frost secures 10 new customer accounts during his first 30 days as an employee. Frost is able to secure only 9 new accounts in that time period. In this case, Graham has no duty to perform and pay Frost $1,000 because his duty to pay the bonus was conditional on securing 10 new accounts. Since Frost did not meet the condition set in the agreement, Graham is discharged from his obligation to pay the bonus.

A **condition subsequent** stipulates an event that occurs after performance under the contract and discharges the parties' obligations. Examples of conditions subsequent include passing the bar exam or CPA exam or meeting some other licensing requirement within one year of beginning employment with a company. The ability to secure a zoning permit for a particular business use within 60 days of the date of a contract is another example. Conditions subsequent are frequently found in insurance contracts. For example, NewCo enters into a fire insurance contract with Big Carrier Inc. that specifies: "No lawsuit for recovery under this contract shall be valid unless the lawsuit is commenced within 12 months of the fire." A fire destroys NewCo's office, and the company files an immediate claim; however, Big Carrier refuses to pay based on an exclusion in the policy. NewCo takes no further action until 14 months after the fire and then files a lawsuit to recover damages under the policy. A court will dismiss NewCo's claim because Big Carrier is discharged from its obligation to pay, or even to litigate the dispute, by virtue of the time-period condition in the policy.

Conditions subsequent occur less frequently than other conditions; however, they have become more prevalent in senior executive employment contracts that include provisions known as *clawbacks.* A *clawback* contract provision allows the recovery of money already disbursed. This topic is discussed in Case 10.1.

A **condition concurrent** occurs when each party is required to render performance simultaneously. If Abel contracts with Betty to paint Abel's portrait, the parties may agree that Abel will pay the full price when Betty delivers the painting to him. If Betty fails to perform, Abel is no longer obligated to meet his obligation and may seek legal redress for any losses suffered as a result.

Unless clearly identified, the law typically assumes that both parties will render simultaneous performance under concurrent conditions. Also, modern contract law does not recognize any substantive difference between these categories of conditions. In fact, today most courts do not make any distinction between them. Rather, the law defines a condition broadly as "an event, not certain to occur, which must occur . . . before the performance under a contract becomes due."[1] Courts often enforce strict compliance standards for conditions. In *Luttinger v. Rosen,*[2] an appellate court ruled that a condition—namely, that a real estate buyer be able to obtain financing at a certain rate before going through with the purchase—must be strictly applied.

Table 10.1 summarizes the three types of conditions.

In Case 10.1, a federal appellate court analyzes whether an employer can "claw back" a bonus that has not yet been disbursed to a former employee if the employee violates a noncompete contract.

---

[1] *Restatement (Second) of Contracts,* §230.

[2] 316 A.2d 757 (Conn. 1972). The contract in question was conditional upon the buyer obtaining a mortgage at a rate not to exceed 8.5 percent. The only lending institutions in the area that would lend to the buyer charged 8.75 percent. Even after the seller offered to subsidize the loan so that the effective rate was 8.5 percent for the buyer, the court held that the buyer's duty to perform was discharged by failure of a condition.

TABLE 10.1 Conditions

Condition precedent	The condition must occur before performance is required.
Condition subsequent	The condition must occur after performance, otherwise the duty to perform is subsequently discharged.
Condition concurrent	Each parties' performance depends on the other's performance.

CASE 10.1 Lucente v. IBM, 310 F.3d 243 (2d Cir. 2002)

FACT SUMMARY Plaintiff Lucente worked for IBM for nearly 30 years before he retired in 1991 as the president of IBM's Asia Pacific Division. A major factor behind Lucente's retirement was his belief that he was being ousted from the company by the top leadership. While at IBM, Lucente participated in several incentive compensation plans from which he received stock options. These plans contained "forfeiture-for-competition" provisions that permitted IBM to cancel Lucente's unexercised stock options if he went to work for an IBM competitor after leaving IBM. In 1993, Lucente became the Vice President of Worldwide Sales and Marketing at Digital Equipment Corporation ("Digital"), an IBM competitor. Shortly afterward, IBM informed Lucente that his unexercised stock options were canceled as a result of his employment with Digital.

Lucente filed a complaint stating that IBM "breached, or has expressed an unequivocal intent to breach, its contractual obligations" under the incentive compensation plans. Lucente moved for summary judgment on his breach of contract claim, as well as IBM's counterclaim against him. The trial court found that IBM's noncompete associated with the clawback of Lucente's retirement benefits was unreasonable since Lucente had been involuntarily terminated. The trial court thus ruled in Lucente's favor on his breach of contract claim.

SYNOPSIS OF DECISION AND OPINION The appellate court overturned the trial court's decision. The appellate court's reversal was based on their application of the "employee choice doctrine." Under this doctrine, New York courts will enforce a noncompete without regard to its reasonableness if the employee quit and was afforded the choice between not competing and preserving contract

benefits versus competing and accepting the risk of forfeiting those benefits. The appellate court held that the trial court had disregarded important evidence suggesting that Lucente had voluntarily left IBM and that the question of whether he had been fired should have been left for a jury to decide.

WORDS OF THE COURT: Employee Choice Doctrine "New York courts will enforce a restrictive covenant without regard to its reasonableness if the employee has been afforded the choice between not competing (and thereby preserving his benefits) or competing (and thereby risking forfeiture). . . . This 'employee choice doctrine' assumes that an employee who elects to leave a company makes an informed choice between forfeiting a certain benefit or retaining the benefit by avoiding competitive employment. . . .

"Although New York courts have not sketched out every detail of the employee choice doctrine, three strokes are bold and clear. First, an employer can rely on the doctrine only if it can demonstrate its continued willingness to employ the party who covenanted not to compete. . . . Second, when an employee is involuntarily discharged without cause, the employer cannot invoke the benefits of the doctrine. . . . Third, the factual determination whether an employee was involuntarily terminated is generally not appropriate for summary judgment.

"Applying these standards to the present case, the district court's grant of summary judgment on Lucente's breach of contract claim was erroneous. In finding that Lucente had been involuntarily terminated by IBM (and therefore that the employee choice doctrine was inapplicable), the district court resolved numerous factual discrepancies in Lucente's favor. In so doing, the court usurped the jury's province as fact-finder. In

(continued)

concluding that Lucente was fired, the district court relied on selective and incomplete deposition testimony while ignoring substantial evidence that Lucente's departure from IBM was indeed voluntary. . . .

"The bedrock question in this case is whether Lucente quit or was fired. IBM contends that the district court's grant of summary judgment to Lucente on his breach of contract claim was erroneous because there are genuine issues of fact surrounding this question. We agree."

Case Questions

1. Was the clawback provision that allowed IBM to revoke Lucente's stock options designed as a condition precedent, subsequent, or concurrent? Explain.

2. Why are clawback provisions structured in this manner?

3. *Focus on Critical Thinking:* Should Lucente be able to keep the incentive compensation if he voluntarily quit and decided to compete against IBM? Explain.

TAKEAWAY CONCEPTS The Nature and Effect of Contract Conditions

- How and when a contract is legally terminated is known as *contract discharge.*
- Conditions are events that can alter the performance obligations stipulated under the contract.
- Conditions fall under three general categories: conditions precedent, subsequent, or concurrent.

DISCHARGING OBLIGATIONS THROUGH GOOD FAITH PERFORMANCE

LO 10-2

Explain the doctrine of substantial performance and identify its effects on the contracting parties.

If the promises to perform in a contract are not conditional, the duty to perform is absolute. Most frequently, parties agree on the terms and perform their contractual obligations in good faith to complete the contract. In this case, both parties have "discharged" their obligation to the other by performing their agreed-upon duties. Performance may also be accomplished by delivering products to an agreed-upon location, such as a warehouse. This is known as *tendering goods* and is discussed in detail in Chapter 15, "Performance and Cure in Sales Contracts."

Sometimes the parties to a contract may agree that either party may assign the rights of the contract to a third party. An **assignment** occurs when one of the contracting parties transfers their rights to another party. The original party with duties under the contract, however, must still perform as required under the contract. For example, DeLeo Agricultural Supply, Inc. contracts to supply peanuts to Jazzy Peanut Butter Co. Jazzy may assign the rights to receive peanuts under this contract to Nutty PBC, Inc. After this assignment, DeLeo would have to ship the peanuts to Nutty PBC.

As mentioned in Chapter 6, the law imposes an affirmative duty of good faith in performing contract obligations. In every contract, the parties have the duty of good faith and fair dealing in performance and enforcement.[3] Although the good faith requirement is ordinarily met by the parties' simply performing their obligations completely—a situation known as *perfect performance*—the law recognizes that there are some cases in which one party does *not* perform completely yet has still acted in good faith and is entitled to enforce the remaining obligations in the contract against the other party.

In some situations, the parties agree to terms of a contract and pursue good faith performance, but one party cannot render perfect performance. The law recognizes a party's good faith effort to *substantially perform* her obligations by allowing the **substantial performance** to

---

[3]*Restatement (Second) of Contracts,* § 205.

satisfy the requirements of the agreement and trigger the other party's obligation to perform. In order to prevail in a substantial performance case, the party trying to enforce the contract must show that she acted in good faith and that any deviation from the required performance was not **material**. In this context, *material* refers to some deviation from the contract that results in a substantial change in the value of the contract or that changes a fundamental basis of the agreement. Suppose that a retailer has contracted to purchase 500 pairs of jeans and 500 T-shirts from a clothing manufacturer. Despite a good faith effort, only the jeans and 400 T-shirts can be delivered. Since the delivered jeans and T-shirts can be sold without the missing 100 T-shirts, the missing T-shirts will not be material to the overall contract and the contract will be considered substantially performed.

Note that although the doctrine of substantial performance allows a party to meet her obligations in a contract through less-than-perfect performance, the innocent party is still entitled to collect *damages* to compensate for the imperfect performance. Generally, courts allow the substantially performing party to be paid the full amount of the contract price (or other performance due) *less* any costs suffered. Therefore, in the example discussed above, the clothing manufacturer will be paid only for the jeans and 400 T-shirts.

Case 10.2, known as the *Reading Pipe* case, has been used for decades as a guidepost to apply the doctrine of substantial performance.

CASE 10.2 Jacob and Youngs v. Kent, 129 N.E. 889 (Ct. App. N.Y. 1921)

FACT SUMMARY Kent contracted with Jacob and Youngs ("JY") for the construction of Kent's vacation home in upstate New York. The contract required JY to use "standard pipe of Reading manufacture." During construction, one of the JY subcontractors mistakenly used some pipe made by other manufacturers. Just before construction was complete, Kent's architect discovered the mistake and directed JY to remove the non-Reading pipe. However, the pipe was already sealed off and encased within the walls; thus, costly demolition would have been necessary to repair the mistake. JY claimed that the substitute pipe was the same in terms of quality, appearance, market value, and cost as the Reading pipe. Thus, JY completed the construction but refused to fix the pipe mistake. Kent refused to pay the remaining balance on the contract, and JY sued to recover the amount due.

SYNOPSIS OF DECISION AND OPINION The court ruled in favor of JY under the doctrine of substantial performance. In its opinion, the court focused on practical application to obtain fairness rather than a strict application of performance requirements and pointed out that trivial and innocent omissions may not always be a breach of a condition. Although there are limits to the substantial performance doctrine, in this case the omission of the Reading pipe was not the result of fraud or willfulness. Moreover, there was no evidence of substantial change in the value of the contract.

WORDS OF THE COURT: Difference in Value "Where the line is to be drawn between important and trivial cannot be settled by formula. . . . Nowhere will change be tolerated, however, if it is so dominant or pervasive as in any real or substantial measure to frustrate the purpose of the contract. . . . We must weigh the purpose to be served, the desire to be gratified, and the excuse for the deviation by the letter, and the cruelty of enforced adherence. . . .

"In the circumstances of this case, we think the measure of the allowance is not the cost of replacement, which would be great, but the difference in value, which would be either nominal or nothing."

Case Questions

1. A dissenting opinion in this case pointed out that JY's failure to use the correct pipe brand was grossly negligent and JY should bear the costs of reinstalling the Reading pipe. Does that strike you as convincing? Why or why not?

(continued)

2. If Kent had a vested interest in the use of Reading pipe (suppose Kent was the heir to the Reading pipe fortune), what condition could he have inserted in the agreement that would have ensured the use of Reading pipe?

3. *Focus on Critical Thinking:* The house was completed in June 1914 at a cost of $77,000. The owner inhabited the house and did not pay the remaining balance of $3,483 when he discovered the breach in March 1915. Do these facts influence your view of the case? Explain.

As indicated above, the doctrine of substantial performance applies to an immaterial contract breach. A nonbreaching party, however, may be discharged of its duties if the other party materially breaches the contract. The topic of a material breach is covered in greater detail in Chapter 11, "Breach and Remedies."

TAKEAWAY CONCEPTS Discharging Obligations through Good
Faith Performance

- If the promises to perform in a contract are not conditional, the duty to perform is absolute.
- The good faith requirement in contracts is ordinarily met by the parties' simply performing their obligations completely, a situation known as *perfect performance.*
- A party's good faith effort to substantially perform her obligations can satisfy the requirements of the agreement and trigger the other party's obligation to perform.
- A party trying to enforce the contract under substantial performance must show that he acted in good faith and that any deviation from the required performance was not material.
- Although substantial performance allows a party to meet its obligations in a contract through less-than-perfect performance, the innocent party is still entitled to collect damages to compensate for the imperfect performance.

DISCHARGE BY MUTUAL AGREEMENT

LO 10-3

Describe the four ways contracting parties can discharge a contract through mutual agreement.

Under the principles of freedom of contract, the parties may agree to mutually terminate their original contract using any of the following four methods.

Rescission

If neither party has fully performed, the parties may agree to cancel the contract. This cancellation is known as a **rescission**, and each party gives up rights under the contract in exchange for the release by the other party from performing their obligations. For example, Earl hires Peter to paint his office lobby for $1,000. The fee is payable in a lump sum upon Peter's completion of the entire lobby. After beginning work and painting one wall, Peter realizes that he vastly underestimated the time and supplies necessary to make the job profitable; he also now has another customer across town with a job where he could earn a profit. So long as Peter offers to rescind the contract and Earl accepts, the contract is canceled and Peter no longer has to perform. At the same time, despite the fact that Earl's lobby has been partially painted, Earl does not have to pay any sums due under the original contract.[4] It is important to note that rescission occurs only if both parties agree to rescind. A unilateral rescission, by only one party, is not permitted.

---

[4]Based on *Restatement (Second) of Contracts,* § 283, Illustration 1.

Accord and Satisfaction

In some cases, the parties to a contract agree to accept performance that is different from the originally promised performance. Under the doctrine of **accord and satisfaction**, one party agrees to render a *substitute performance* in the future (known as *accord*), and the other party promises to accept that substitute performance in discharge of the existing performance obligation. Once the substitute performance has been rendered, this acts as a *satisfaction* of the obligation. Note that discharge of the obligation occurs only when the terms of the accord are actually performed. If the accord performance is *not* rendered, the other party has the option to recover damages either under the original contract or under the accord contract. For example, in the Earl-Peter painting contract, suppose that Peter finishes the job but Earl does not have the $1,000 fee to pay Peter in one lump sum. Earl offers to pay Peter $1,100 in 60 days, and Peter accepts. The new agreement on payment terms is an *accord*. Once Earl has paid the $1,100 in 60 days, his accord will be *satisfied* and Peter will not be able to sue for any damages that he may have suffered as a result of Earl's failing to pay as originally agreed in the contract.[5]

The law of accord and satisfaction can have significant and sometimes unintended consequences in business. For example, say General Contractor Inc. (GCI) subcontracts with Windows-R-Us (WRU) to install specially designed windows, constructed by GCI, in a new office building for a total of $100,000 to be paid after services are completed. After WRU installs the windows, GCI notifies WRU that it is dissatisfied with the installation work. WRU claims that the windows were installed to industry standards and demands payment. GCI then sends a check for $50,000 (half of what is owed to WRU under the contract) to WRU's office. The check contains the endorsement "Payment in Full for Installation Services at the Office Center Site." If WRU deposits the check, this can have dire consequences. Most courts view depositing a check as an affirmative acceptance of the accord offer written on the check. When the check has cleared the bank's processing, it is considered a satisfaction of the accord agreement and WRU cannot sue for damages. The only way WRU might avoid an accord and satisfaction in this case is to return the check to GCI with a letter stating that the offer is rejected and demanding full payment under the original terms of the contract.

In Case 10.3, a federal appellate court discusses how an accord and satisfaction requires a good faith dispute of the amount in question.

CASE 10.3 McMahon Food Corp. v. Burger Dairy Co., 103 F.3d 1307 (7th Cir. 1997)

FACT SUMMARY   Burger Dairy Company ("Burger") sold milk products to McMahon Food Corporation ("MFC"), a Chicago distributor of dairy products. In February 1992, Burger's general manager, Richard L. Bylsma met with Frank McMahon to discuss MFC being in arrears for $58,518.41 ("the February debt"). McMahon disputed the debt; however, the parties agreed to continue to do business as they worked to resolve the issue. During this time, Larry Carter replaced Bylsma as Burger's general manager. Carter met with McMahon in June to discuss the February debt. According to Carter's notes, McMahon assured him that he had settled the February debt with Bylsma. When the two met, they went through the invoices dated February 15 through June 6, 1992. They determined that MFC owed a balance of $51,812.98. McMahon wrote a check to Burger for that amount and attached a voucher to

(continued)

---

[5]Since an accord does not discharge the previous contractual duty as soon as the accord is made, if Earl does not perform the accord agreement, Peter may recover damages from Earl under either the original contract obligation ($1,000 lump sum due upon completion) or under the accord agreement ($1,100 within 60 days of completion).

the check that stated "payment in full thru 6/6/92 - $51,812.98."

Later that day, Carter contacted Bylsma, who told Carter that he had never reached an agreement with McMahon about the February debt. Carter then called McMahon and told him that it was Burger's position that the February debt had not been settled. Burger eventually cashed McMahon's check and continued to bill McMahon for the outstanding February debt. MFC filed suit against Burger, asking the federal district court to issue a declaratory judgment that it had reached an accord and satisfaction relieving it of any debt to Burger. Burger countersued, seeking the money that it claimed MFC still owed. With the consent of the parties, the case was tried before a magistrate judge without a jury. The trial court found MFC in arrears and awarded Burger damages in the amount of $58,518.41, plus interest and costs.

SYNOPSIS OF DECISION AND OPINION The appellate court affirmed the lower trial court, stating that the trial court did not clearly err in concluding that MFC's first check marked "paid in full" did not create a satisfaction, because the accord it was meant to satisfy was obtained due to MFC's bad faith and deception.

WORDS OF THE COURT: Honest Dispute Required "Illinois courts . . . follow the common law of accord and satisfaction in holding that 'there must be an honest dispute between the parties as to the amount due at the time payment was tendered.' . . .

Consequently, under Illinois law, there can be no accord and satisfaction unless there was an 'honest dispute' between MFC and Burger at the time McMahon tendered the $51,812.98 check to Carter on June 17th. No such 'honest dispute' existed. . . .

"The trial court found that McMahon deliberately misled Carter, who had but recently been appointed to his position of general manager and did not know the specifics of his predecessor's dealings with MFC. McMahon did so, according to the court, by assuring Carter from the outset of their June 17th meeting that he had settled with Bylsma, the former general manager, all accounts prior to mid-February, 1992. . . . A trial court's conclusion that a party failed to act in good faith is a finding of fact which we reverse only for clear error.

"The debtor's mere refusal to pay the full claim does not make it a disputed claim. Where the refusal is arbitrary and the debtor knows it has no just basis, the payment of less than the full amount claimed does not operate as an accord and satisfaction even though it is tendered and received as such."

Case Questions

1. Had there been good faith, would cashing the check have created an accord and satisfaction? Explain.

2. How can a party prove that the disputed amount is a good faith disagreement?

3. *Focus on Critical Thinking:* What goals does the accord and satisfaction doctrine try to promote?

Substitute Agreement

The contracting parties also may discharge their obligations by replacing the original contract with a **substitute agreement**. The substitute agreement is generally used to compromise when two parties have a dispute as to performance of the contract and wish to amend its terms. The substituted agreement, unlike the accord agreement discussed above, *immediately* discharges any obligations under the original contract. For example, in the Earl-Peter painting contract, suppose that Earl and Peter enter into a substitute agreement whereby Earl agrees to pay $1,100 in 60 days so long as Peter agrees to extinguish the $1,000 debt immediately. If Earl does not perform (by paying), then Peter now has only one option: to recover damages under the *substitute agreement*. He cannot recover damages under the original agreement. Earl's obligation to pay the $1,000 sum at conclusion of the work was immediately discharged by the substitute agreement.

Novation

When the parties agree to substitute a third party for one of the original parties to the contract, the agreement may be discharged through **novation**. Essentially, a novation is a kind of substitute agreement that involves a substitute third *party* rather than a substitute promise.

A novation revokes and *discharges* all of the replaced party's obligations under the old contract. For example, in the Earl-Peter painting contract, suppose that Peter starts work and the next day he receives an offer from another customer for a major painting job. Peter proposes to Earl that Pablo (another painter who Peter knows does excellent work) complete the painting work under the original contract. If Earl agrees to allow Peter to substitute Pablo for the performance of the lobby-painting duties articulated in the original Earl-Peter contract, then a novation has occurred and Peter is now discharged from his obligation to perform the Earl-Peter contract. Earl is bound only by the new novation terms with Pablo.

TAKEAWAY CONCEPTS Discharge by Mutual Agreement

- Contract discharge may be made through mutual agreement.
- Discharge by mutual agreement may be made through rescission, accord and satisfaction, substituted agreement, or novation.
- Some courts require a good faith dispute concerning the amount in question to enforce an accord and satisfaction.

LO 10-4

Describe the three ways contracting parties can discharge a contract through operation of law.

DISCHARGE BY OPERATION OF LAW

Contract obligations also may be discharged through *operation of law*. Despite the fact that the parties have fulfilled the requirements to form a valid contract, the law provides a discharge under certain circumstances where fairness demands it. In some cases, after the parties have formed a contract, unexpected events occur that affect one party's ability to perform. In such cases, the law may allow the parties to be excused from performance under the contract. Courts analyze these special circumstances according to three separate doctrines: **impossibility**, **impracticability**, and **frustration of purpose**.

Impossibility

After the parties have entered an agreement, the contemplated performance of the obligations may become impossible and, therefore, may be subject to discharge. When encountering a situation in which one party is claiming impossibility, it is important for managers to understand that the impossibility must be *objective* (a reasonable person would consider the obligation impossible to perform) rather than *subjective* (one party decides unilaterally that performance is impossible) in order for the obligation to be discharged.[6] This can sometimes be a tricky distinction, and the modern trend of courts is against allowing impossibility as a defense unless it fits into one of four intervening events:

1. *Destruction* of the subject matter: A promises to sell B 1,000 widgets to be delivered on Tuesday. On Monday, a fire destroys the widgets. A is discharged from her obligation to provide the widgets.
2. *Death or incapacitation* of one of the parties to the contract:[7] A promises to paint B's portrait. Prior to the sitting date for the portrait, A becomes incapacitated. A is discharged from her obligation to paint the portrait.

---

[6]The Restatements, § 261, Comment c, distinguishes between the two standards by giving an example of objective impossibility ("the thing cannot be done") versus subjective impossibility ("I cannot do it").

[7]Note that unless a contract for services calls for *unique personal* services, it cannot be discharged via impossibility. The law contemplates that nonunique personal services should simply be delegated to another appropriate substitute party.

204   UNIT TWO | Contracts, Sales, and Leases

3. The *means of performance* contemplated in the contract cannot be performed: W, a wholesaler, agrees to sell R, a retailer, 5,000 widgets. Prior to the W-R contract, W contracted with M, a manufacturer, to supply him with 10,000 widgets. M halts production and cannot produce the widgets for W. W may be discharged from performance (unless the parties agreed otherwise about risk allocation).

4. Performance of the obligation has become *illegal* subsequent to the contract but prior to performance: Importer promises to buy 1,000 cigars from Producer, a manufacturer in the Dominican Republic. Subsequent to the agreement, but before Producer ships the cigars, Congress passes a federal statute imposing a complete trade embargo on the Dominican Republic. Importer and Producer are discharged from performance based on impossibility.

Sometimes performance is *temporarily impossible* for one or both parties. The illness of a party who is to perform unique personal services may prevent her from performing on the timeline contemplated by the parties. However, in most cases, an illness will not prevent the performance forever. The doctrine of impossibility operates to *suspend* (not discharge) the obligation to perform until the impossibility ceases. Note that an exception to this general rule occurs when, after the temporary impossibility ends, the performance is considerably more burdensome than it would have been if the parties had performed on time (i.e., the lapse of time affected the parties' abilities to perform). Courts then will allow the obligation of the burdened party to be discharged.

Sometimes parties add a clause that contemplates uncontrollable acts that will impede performance under the contract. These clauses are referred to as **force majeure**, or act of God, clauses. Riots, threats of terrorism, fires, earthquakes, wars, and embargoes are often mentioned in these clauses as events that will discharge the duties of the parties.

In Case 10.4, a state appellate court discusses the doctrine of impossibility in a construction case.

CASE 10.4 Holder Construction Group v. Georgia Tech Facilities, Inc., 282 Ga. App. 796 (2006)

FACT SUMMARY Holder Construction Group, LLC ("Holder") entered into a contract with Georgia Tech Facilities ("GTF") for the construction of the Georgia Tech Family Apartments project. Under this contract, Holder assumed the obligation to construct the project for a guaranteed maximum price. This is known as a *construction-manager-at-risk contract,* under which the construction manager is at risk for performance deficiencies, construction delays, and cost overruns. The parties also negotiated a force majeure clause that stated:

> If Construction Manager shall be unable to perform or shall be delayed in the performance of any of the terms and provisions of this Agreement as a result of (i) governmental preemption of materials in connection with a national emergency declared by the

Apartment building under construction.
©Slavapolo/Shutterstock

(continued)

President of the United States; (ii) riot, insurrection, or other civil disorder affecting performance of the Work; or (iii) unusual and extreme weather conditions constituting Acts of God, then, and in any such event, such inability or delay shall be excused, and the time for completing the affected portions of the Project shall be extended.

After construction on the project had begun, Holder experienced difficulties due to an increase in steel prices and the late delivery of steel materials. Because of these problems, Holder requested a 67-day time extension. GTF denied the request. Holder then filed a declaratory judgment action, arguing that it was entitled to an adjustment of more than $1 million in the contract price due to cost overruns and a time extension of no less than 63 days for completing the project.

The trial court granted summary judgment in favor of GTF, and Holder appealed the decision.

SYNOPSIS OF DECISION AND OPINION After reviewing the contract and its provisions allocating specific risks to the parties, the appellate court affirmed the trial court and allocated the risk of steel price increases and shipment delays to Holder.

WORDS OF THE COURT: Force Majeure Clause "It is undisputed that the late delivery of the steel was not the result of any of the causes stated in the 'Force Majeure' clause. The contract goes on to state that late deliveries of materials, for reasons other than those set out in the 'Force Majeure' clause, 'do not constitute reason for extending the Date for Final Completion' and it is the construction manager's responsibility to make adequate provision for this when scheduling the work. . . . Accordingly, under the contract, Holder bore the risk of the late delivery of the steel because it was not due to any of the reasons set out in the 'Force Majeure' clause. . . .

"Likewise, GTF was entitled to summary judgment on Holder's claim for damages due to the rise in steel prices. As the trial court held, the contract did not contain a [price] escalation clause, and Holder had already been paid from the construction contingency fund for this claim. . . . "

Case Questions

1. How might Holder have avoided the risk of bearing the unforeseen and significant increase in steel prices?

2. If you were Holder, how would you rewrite this contract to avoid liability in the future?

3. *Focus on Critical Thinking:* If the parties had left out the force majeure clause, how would the case have been decided?

Impracticability

There are certain agreements under which, although performance is not objectively impossible (as defined above), performance becomes extremely burdensome due to some unforeseen circumstance occurring between the time of agreement and the time of performance. If the burden is both *unforeseeable* and *extreme,* courts may allow the burdened parties' obligations to be discharged before performance.

Suppose that Ace Pools contracts with Homeowner to install an in-ground pool on her property. Ace is a small company but is profitable because it can complete two pools a week during the spring, summer, and fall seasons. It has installed numerous pools in the neighborhood without any complications. Prior to signing the contract, Ace does a preliminary test dig and finds no impediments to excavation. Once actual excavation begins, however, Ace discovers that 80 percent of Homeowner's property is solid rock beginning three feet below the surface. In order to successfully install the pool, explosives must be used, requiring a series of permits and the hiring of demolition experts. This will triple the contract cost and tie up Ace Pools for 30 days at the job site. If Homeowner does not want to pay the additional cost and Ace does not want to lose business by being at one site for 30 days, Homeowner and Ace may mutually agree to rescind the contract and end both of their obligations under the contract. But what if Homeowner decides that she wants the pool installed despite the increased time and cost? Can Ace be required to complete the contract? Ace will be able to claim that the impracticality of losing approximately eight jobs in order to complete this single job is too burdensome and will harm the company. Ace's past experience in the neighborhood and its preliminary experimental dig will be evidence that the burden caused by the rock was both unforeseen and extreme, excusing Ace from performance due to impracticability.

Frustration of Purpose

In some cases, events may occur that destroy a party's *purpose* in entering into the contract even though performance of the contract itself is not objectively impossible. When one party's purpose is completely or almost completely frustrated by such supervening events, courts will discharge that party from performance. Frustration of purpose may be used to discharge an obligation if, after the parties enter into an agreement, (1) a party's *principal purpose* is substantially frustrated without her fault; (2) some event occurs, when the *non-occurrence* of the event was a central assumption of both parties when entering into the contract; and (3) the parties have not otherwise agreed on who bears the risk of such an occurrence. Just as with impracticability, frustration of purpose requires the burdened party to show that the event was unforeseeable and extreme.

For example, suppose Padraig contracts with White Hall Inn to rent a room that faces Main Street for a period of two days. Padraig's intent is to have a balcony view of the street to see the St. Patrick's Day parade. One week before the parade is scheduled, White Hall sends Padraig a confirmation of the agreement:

> Confirmed: Balcony Room at White Hall Inn (Guaranteed view of Main Street) for Padraig. $200 per night (St. Patrick's Day Parade Special). Two days. $100 deposit due in 5 days—Balance due upon checkout.

Padraig signs the letter and sends it back with a $100 bill. Much to Padraig's dismay, the St. Patrick's Day Committee cancels the parade due to a last-minute regulatory problem in obtaining a permit. Padraig cancels his reservation. If Padraig sues for his $100 to be refunded (contending that his obligation has been discharged by virtue of frustration of purpose) and White Hall countersues for the $300 balance owed (contending that Padraig can still use the room even if there is no parade), who will prevail? It is likely that Padraig will prevail because the letter sent by White Hall *acknowledges* that the primary purpose of the contract is to have the balcony view of the parade. Assuming a court finds that the parade cancellation was reasonably unforeseeable, was not Padraig's fault, and was a basic assumption of the agreement, Padraig would prevail due to frustration of purpose.

Now consider an alternative situation in which the parties had agreed on risk allocation using language in the letter such as, "In the event that the St. Patrick's Day parade does not take place for any reason, the parties agree that Padraig will pay only 50 percent of the full price for the room whether he uses the room or not. Such amount shall be due on the checkout date." In that event, a court will very likely consider the parties to have bargained away any notion of frustration of purpose (or impossibility for that matter) as an event of discharge and, thus, enforce the agreed-upon terms.

The parties may also be discharged through operation of law when (1) a contract is unilaterally altered by a party (the other party is discharged from performing); (2) a contract is subject to relief of the Bankruptcy Code (the debtor is entitled to complete discharge from any contract once the bankruptcy filing has been approved by a court); or

(3) the statute of limitations (also known as the *statute of repose* in certain states), where state law imposes a time limit on enforcement of contract obligations, has expired. For example, in California a suit to enforce a written contract must be brought within four years from the date of breach.

 Quick Quiz Discharge of Obligations

Stephanie is a college student who rents an apartment near campus in Tampa, Florida. When she signed the lease, the apartment was well maintained and in compliance with all applicable local building, health, and safety codes. Midway through the lease, mold and mildew stains appear from within the walls due to faulty plumbing in violation of local ordinances. The Florida statute states that a "landlord at all times during the tenancy shall . . . [c]omply with the requirements of applicable building, housing, and health codes . . . "[8] If the landlord does not comply with this requirement, the statute states that: "Within 7 days after delivery of written notice by the tenant specifying the noncompliance [with any local ordinances] and indicating the intention of the tenant to terminate the rental agreement by reason thereof, the tenant may terminate the rental agreement."[9] Upon seeing the mold, Stephanie writes a letter to her landlord describing the problem and her intent to terminate the lease if the problem is not corrected in seven days. One week has passed and the landlord has failed to correct the problem.

1. Is Stephanie discharged from performing under the lease contract? Why?
2. Which type of discharge does this scenario most closely resemble?

Answers to this Quick Quiz are provided at the end of the chapter.

TAKEAWAY CONCEPTS Discharge by Operation of Law

- Discharge by operation of law may occur in cases of impossibility, impracticability, and frustration of purpose.
- Impossibility must be objective rather than subjective.
- Impossibility usually occurs due to the following: destruction of the subject matter; death or incapacitation of one of the parties to the contract; the means of performance contemplated in the contract cannot be performed; or performance of the obligation has become illegal.
- If the burden is both unforeseeable and extreme, courts may allow the burdened parties' obligations to be discharged due to impracticability.
- Frustration of purpose requires the burdened party to show that the event was unforeseeable and extreme.
- Allocating the risk of impossibility, impracticability, or frustration of purpose through contract terms can shift the burden of these risks onto a contracting party.

---

[8]Florida Statutes, Title VI, Ch. 83.51, Section 1(a).
[9]Florida Statues, Title VI, Ch. 83.56 Section 1.

Use of Conditions

PROBLEM: Employers often wish to provide incentives for its best performing employees, but want to allocate any financial risk (i.e., employee doesn't perform well or financial conditions prohibit an incentive) more evenly.

STRATEGIC SOLUTION: In this chapter we discussed how conditions impact obligations under a contract. The use of conditions in an employment contract often center on incentives. Consider the following fact scenario to help understand how conditions in employment contracts operate.

Jeffrey is a surgeon who works for a hospital practice group. As part of his physician employment contract with the hospital, Jeffrey is eligible to receive "Incentive Compensation." The language in his employment contract states:

> In addition to the salary set forth in the Physician's Employment Agreement, Physician shall also be eligible for incentive compensation, which will be based upon the following criteria:

> 1. Physician Practice Financial Performance

> Individual physician financial performance will be tracked. Physician-specific practice overhead and facility expenses will each be allocated to the physician practice. Physician will receive 50 percent of all receipts that exceed the total practice expenses. This compensation will not exceed $100,000 per year.

> 2. Employment

> Physician must be employed by Corporation at the conclusion of contract year to be eligible for incentive compensation.

After working diligently for one year, Jeffrey asks the hospital administrators about his year-end bonus under the incentive compensation plan. The hospital's chief financial officer replies, "Expenses during the year were very high and you did not qualify for a bonus; however, that could change next year."

QUESTIONS

1. What types of contract conditions are these two items? Explain.
2. When would Jeffrey have a valid breach of contract claim against the hospital? Explain.
3. Which particular contract terms worked against Jeffrey and why?
4. How would you rewrite the contract so that Jeffrey ensures his receipt of a bonus under the incentive plan?

KEY TERMS

Contract discharge p. 196   The subject of how and when a contract is legally terminated.

Condition precedent p. 197   A contract term that requires an event to occur before performance under a contract is due.

Condition subsequent p. 197   A contract term that discharges the parties' obligations if an event occurs after performance under the contract.

Condition concurrent p. 197   When each party is required to render performance simultaneously.

Assignment p. 199   When one of the contracting parties transfers their rights under the contract to another party.

Substantial performance p. 199   When one party fails to render perfect performance, yet they have acted in good faith and their breach is not material.

Material p. 200   Something that results in a substantial change in the value of the contract or that changes a fundamental basis of the agreement.

Rescission p. 201   When the parties agree to cancel the contract.

Accord and satisfaction p. 202   One party agrees to render a substitute performance in the future known as an accord, and the other party promises to accept that substitute performance to discharge the existing performance as a satisfaction.

Substitute agreement p. 203   When the contracting parties discharge their obligations by replacing the original contract with a new agreement.

Novation p. 203   When the parties agree to substitute a third party for one of the original parties to the contract.

Impossibility p. 204   When the contemplated performance of the obligations becomes objectively impossible and, therefore, is subject to discharge

Impracticability p. 204   Discharge arising when performance is not objectively impossible yet performance becomes extremely burdensome due to some unforeseen circumstance occurring between the time of agreement and the time of performance.

Frustration of purpose p. 204   When one party's purpose is completely or almost completely frustrated by supervening events, courts may discharge that party from performance.

Force majeure p. 205   A clause that contemplates uncontrollable acts that will impede performance under the contract.

CASE SUMMARY 10.1 Sechrest v. Forest Furniture Co., 264 N.C. 216 (N.C. 1965)

Impossibility

Sechrest Plywood Company contracted with Forest Furniture Company to sell it plywood bottoms for drawers that Forest would manufacture. After the contract was signed, Forest's warehouse, where it intended to make the drawers, was completely destroyed by a fire. Forest asserted that the contract was void due to impossibility. Sechrest argued that while the fire prevented Forest from manufacturing drawers, it did not prevent Forest from purchasing the plywood bottoms for which it had contracted with Sechrest. Therefore, Sechrest argued, the doctrine of impossibility did not apply.

CASE QUESTIONS

1. What are the standards for being discharged through impossibility?
2. Do they apply here? Why or why not?

CASE SUMMARY 10.2 1700 Rinehart, LLC v. Advance America, Cash Advance Centers, etc., 5D09-3759 (Fla. 5th DCA 2010)

Condition Subsequent

Rinehart entered into a commercial real estate lease contract with Advance America. The contract stated that the sole purpose of the rental was to operate a check-cashing facility. The contract also stated that if permits to operate a check-cashing facility could not be obtained within 90 days of executing the contract, the lease would be terminated. The language in the contract stated:

> In the event Tenant, after using best efforts, is unable to obtain all permits and approvals necessary for Tenant to open and operate its business in the Premises within ninety (90) days from the mutual execution of this Lease, Tenant shall have the right, upon written notice to Landlord, to terminate the Lease. . . .

The court affirmed the provision in the contract since the city did not provide a permit for operating a check-cashing facility on the property.

CASE QUESTIONS

1. The appellate court stated that the trial court had incorrectly applied the doctrine of frustration of purpose to this case. Explain why this was a mistake.
2. The landlord argued that the 90-day window applied to terminating the lease, not to obtaining a permit, and that the tenant had failed to terminate the lease within 90 days. Based on the language in the contract, is this persuasive?

CASE SUMMARY 10.3 Hearthstone, Inc. v. Dept. of Agriculture, CBCA 3725 (2015)

Commercial Impracticability

Hearthstone was awarded a timber sale contract from the Department of Agriculture and planned to use the timber to manufacture homes. After an economic downturn, Hearthstone sought an extension on the contract and a renegotiated price for the timber under a clause in the contract that allowed for price renegotiations due to increases in the price of timber. Eventually, Hearthstone failed to pay for the timber arguing commercial impracticability.

CASE QUESTIONS

1. Why should the doctrine of impracticability not be applied to this case?

2. What conditions would allow the parties to successfully argue impracticability?

CASE SUMMARY 10.4 Wooden v. Synovus Bank, A13A0876 Ga. App. (2013)

Novation

Wooden personally guaranteed the debts of Wooden Nickel Plantation, LLC, along with two other individuals. The company defaulted on its debt, and the bank that had extended the loan settled with the two other individuals. Wooden argued that this settlement created a novation with respect to his guarantee and relieved him of guaranteeing his portion of the debt.

CASE QUESTIONS

1. What is necessary to create a novation?
2. Do the facts here establish that a novation was created?

CASE SUMMARY 10.5 Ed Wolfe Construction, Inc. v. Richard Knight and Luann Knight, 2014 IL App (5th)

Substantial Performance

The Knights hired Wolfe Construction to repair the fire damage sustained in their home under a "fixed price contract" where the Knights agreed to pay for anything not covered by their homeowner's insurance policy. Wolfe completed 95 percent of the requested work but was then terminated by the Knights because they were dissatisfied with the work. Part of the dissatisfaction related to delays, which Wolfe attributed to the Knights requesting that the house be repainted when they did not like the color they had chosen. Similar issues arose involving cabinetry that had to be moved once it was installed and a concrete step that required redoing an entire concrete floor. Wolfe sued for the balance outstanding on the contract. The Knights countersued for breach of contract damages due to material breach.

CASE QUESTIONS

1. Is a contractor required to perform work perfectly? What is required of a contractor?
2. Do the facts in this case suggest Wolfe acted in good faith? Who should prevail in this case?

CHAPTER REVIEW QUESTIONS

1. **Which term refers to how and when a contract is legally terminated?**
   a. Rescission
   b. Force majeure
   c. Contract discharge
   d. Breach
   e. Novation

2. **All of the following are methods of discharge under mutual agreement, except:**
   a. Rescission.
   b. Accord and satisfaction.
   c. Novation.
   d. Substitute agreement.
   e. Impossibility.

3. **All of the following are methods of discharge under operation of law, except:**
   a. Impossibility.
   b. Impracticability.
   c. Frustration of purpose.
   d. Accord and satisfaction.
   e. Bankruptcy.

4. John and Lisa agree to substitute someone else to replace Lisa under the contract. This is known as a(n):

   a. Accord and satisfaction.

   b. Rescission.

   c. Novation.

   d. Substitute agreement.

   e. None of the above.

5. John has contracted to deliver his crops to Susan at a future date. A fire destroys all of John's crops and he is unable to perform under the contract. He might be discharged of his obligation due to:

   a. Impracticability.

   b. Frustration of purpose.

   c. Impossibility.

   d. Accord and satisfaction.

   e. Novation.

6. Courts may require a good faith dispute concerning the amount to enforce an accord and satisfaction.

   a. True

   b. False

7. John substantially performs his contract with Erin in good faith. Erin's contract duties are discharged and she is entitled to damages.

   a. True

   b. False

8. The doctrine of substantial performance applies when the breach is material and was made in bad faith.

   a. True

   b. False

9. The promise to retain an employee if the employee passes the CPA exam is an example of a condition subsequent.

   a. True

   b. False

10. The promise to award a bonus if a certain sales target is met is an example of a condition concurrent.

   a. True

   b. False

 Quick Quiz ANSWERS
Discharge of Obligations

1. Stephanie is discharged from performing under the lease. The statute gives her the right to terminate the lease since it imposes a mandatory obligation on the landlord to maintain the premises in accordance with all local health and safety ordinances. The statute is a public law that cannot be superseded by private contract.

2. This discharge most closely resembles the case of illegality and is an example of discharge by operation of law.

CHAPTER REVIEW QUESTIONS: Answers and Explanations

1. **c.** Contract discharge deals with how and when a contract is legally terminated.

2. **e.** Impossibility is a method of discharge by operation of law.

3. **d.** Accord and satisfaction is a method of discharge by mutual agreement.

4. **c.** Substituting someone else under the contract through mutual agreement is called a novation.

5. **c.** When an unforeseeable event destroys the subject matter of the contract, the parties may be discharged due to impossibility.

6. **a. True.** Some courts require a good faith dispute concerning the amount in question to enforce an accord and satisfaction.

7. **b. False.** Substantial performance does not discharge contract duties, but it does allow for damages.

8. b. False. Substantial performance applies when the breach was made in good faith and is immaterial.

9. a. True. This term stipulates an event that occurs after performance under the contract and discharges the parties' obligations, therefore it is a condition subsequent.

10. b. False. This condition requires that an event must occur *before* performance under a contract is due, therefore it is a condition precedent.

CHAPTER 11

Breach and Remedies

While business owners and managers should understand the legal impact of breaching a contract, as a practical matter a breach may also result in a significant business hardship to the innocent party. In this chapter's *Thinking Strategically,* we examine strategic legal methods that help reduce the risk of loss in the event one party suspects that the other party in a contract may breach their obligations in the near future.

Learning Objectives

After studying this chapter, students who have mastered the material will be able to:

11-1 Define breach of contract and differentiate between a material breach and a partial breach.

11-2 Explain the doctrine of anticipatory repudiation.

11-3 Identify the appropriate form of money damages for each type of breach.

11-4 Differentiate legal remedies from equitable remedies.

11-5 Explain the duty to mitigate damages.

CHAPTER OVERVIEW

This chapter continues our discussion of the law of contracts by focusing on the rights and duties of the parties when one party has failed to perform as promised. We start with the fundamentals of nonperformance, called a **breach**, and discuss the differences in the types of breach and learn why it is important. We then turn to alternatives for the nonbreaching party and examine the duty of a nonbreaching party to minimize their damages.

BREACH DEFINED

When a party to an agreement owes a duty to perform and fails to fulfill her obligation, she has *breached*

the contract. In cases where the breach is material (i.e., relates to a fundamental term of the contract or has an effect on the value of the contract), it is called a *total breach* and the nonbreaching party (also called the *innocent* party) is entitled to either suspend performance or be discharged from his obligations completely. The party that suffered the breach is also entitled to sue the breaching party in an attempt to recover losses suffered due to the breach. Money damage awards are one of the ways the law provides to compensate the nonbreaching party for losses suffered. In some cases, the nonbreaching party has not suffered an out-of-pocket loss and will instead turn to alternative methods. These compensation methods, called **remedies**, are discussed later in this chapter.

Partial Breach

There are some cases in which the breach is not material; this is sometimes referred to as a *partial breach*.[1] In such cases, the nonbreaching party may not be relieved from performing; however, the nonbreaching party may still recover damages related to the breach from the breaching party. Recall the *Jacob and Youngs v. Kent (Reading Pipe)* case from Chapter 10. In that case, the court decided that because the deviation from expected performance was not material, it was only a partial breach. Because the breach was partial, the court awarded the nonbreaching party damages equal to the difference in price between the Reading-brand pipe and the pipe actually used.

LO 11-1

Define breach of contract and differentiate between a material breach and a partial breach.

Anticipatory Repudiation

LO 11-2

Explain the doctrine of anticipatory repudiation.

After the parties have entered into an agreement but before performance has occurred, it sometimes becomes apparent that one party does not intend to perform as agreed. This may be apparent through the party's words or conduct. Under certain circumstances, the law provides an avenue of recovery for the nonbreaching party even *before* the non-performing party actually breaches the contract or even before the performance is due. For example, on December 15, Manager enters into an agreement with Consultant to provide operation-consulting services for a period of six months to commence January 2. On December 20, Manager is told to cut costs, so Manager contacts Consultant in an e-mail: "Dear Consultant: We don't require your services. Sorry. —Manager." At this point, Manager has not technically breached the contract because performance is not due until January 2. However, Consultant would still be entitled to sue immediately for damages (or other remedies if appropriate) under the doctrine of **anticipatory repudiation**, without waiting for the actual breach to occur on January 2. Anticipatory repudiation is also called *anticipatory breach*.

When one party uses unequivocal language (such as in the Manager-Consultant contract in the preceding paragraph) to repudiate, there is no question that the other may file suit immediately. Any threatened breach must be a material, or a total, breach (discussed earlier) for the nonbreaching party to exercise its right to claim an anticipatory repudiation. In cases where the language is more ambiguous or when conduct is the basis for determining the repudiation, the analysis is more complex. Modern courts have held that repudiation occurs in one of three ways:

- A statement by one party of her intent not to perform. Note that the statement must be such that a reasonable person would have believed that the promisor is quite unlikely to perform. Vague doubts about the statements are insufficient.
- An action by the promisor that renders her performance impossible. For example, A agrees to sell an office building to B with conveyance in 30 days. Several days later, B learns that A subsequently sold and conveyed the building to C. B may sue immediately for A's breach and need not wait the full 30-day period in the contract.
- Knowledge by the parties that one party may be unable to perform despite both parties' best efforts.

In Case 11.1, a state supreme court analyzes whether one party is entitled to damages after claiming anticipatory repudiation by another party.

---

[1]*Corbin on Contracts,* § 1374 (1963).

FACT SUMMARY In 2006, Ralph and Carolee Thomas ("the Thomases") signed a contract with Montelucia Villas, LLC ("Montelucia") for the construction of a custom villa for $3,295,000. As part of the purchase agreement, the Thomases made three installment deposits totaling $659,000, which represented 20 percent of the villa's purchase price. The remainder of the purchase price was due when the Thomases took title to the completed villa. The contract characterized the payments as "earnest money deposits." The contract also provided that Montelucia could retain the payments as damages if the Thomases breached the construction agreement.

On April 25, 2008, Montelucia notified the Thomases by letter that it had set the closing date of May 16 to transfer title to the villa in exchange for payment of the remainder of the purchase price from the Thomases. When the letter was sent, Montelucia did not have a certificate of occupancy for the property which the contract required as a condition for closing. The Thomases responded on May 6 with a letter stating that they would not close on May 16 and they were terminating the purchase contract, alleging that Montelucia had not performed and had violated Arizona statutes governing the sale of subdivided land. The Thomases' letter asked Montelucia to return the $659,000 in deposits. Montelucia did not respond to the letter or refund the deposits. Instead, it unsuccessfully attempted to obtain a certificate of occupancy for the property on May 8 and May 14. Montelucia ultimately obtained the certificate on August 27.

In February 2009, the Thomases sued to recover the deposits. Montelucia counterclaimed for breach of contract. Although the trial court ruled in favor of the Thomases, the court of appeals reversed and ruled that the Thomases had anticipatorily repudiated the contract by sending the May 6 letter. The Thomases appealed.

SYNOPSIS OF DECISION AND OPINION The Arizona Supreme Court reversed the decision of the court of appeals "and ruled in favor of the Thomases." The court "held" that although the doctrine of anticipatory breach could be applied in this case, damages for the nonbreaching party turned on whether Montelucia was ready, willing, and able to perform its obligations. Since there was a factual dispute as to whether Montelucia would have been able to perform, the court ordered that a trial court should determine whether Montelucia was able to close in accordance with the contract. If it was ultimately determined that Montelucia was ready, willing, and able to perform as required by the contract, the court would determine the appropriate remedy available to Montelucia under the contract.

WORDS OF THE COURT: Ready and Willing to Perform "An anticipatory repudiation is a breach of contract giving rise to a claim for damages and also excusing the necessity for the non-breaching party to tender performance. Yet, an anticipatory breach, by itself, does not entitle the injured party to damages. To recover damages, in addition to proving repudiation, the non-breaching party need only show that he would have been ready and willing to have performed the contract, if the repudiation had not occurred. Thus, a party's duty to pay damages for total breach by repudiation is discharged if it appears after the breach that there would have been a total failure by the injured party to perform his return promise."

Case Questions

1. Why did Montelucia claim that the May 6 letter was an anticipatory repudiation of the contract?

2. Is the fact that Montelucia ultimately obtained a certificate of occupancy important? Why or why not?

3. *Focus on Critical Thinking:* Ultimately, the villa was completed and the Thomases refused to pay. Were the Thomases trying to use a technicality in the law as a shield from contractual obligations?

TAKEAWAY CONCEPTS Breach Defined

- A breach of contract occurs when one party to an agreement fails to perform a promised obligation.
- Material breaches relate to a fundamental term of the contract, and the nonbreaching party may (1) suspend performance or (2) be discharged from any further obligations.
- In cases where the breach is not material *(partial breach),* the nonbreaching party may not be relieved from performing but may still recover damages related to the breach from the breaching party.
- Anticipatory repudiation/breach provides an avenue of recovery for the nonbreaching party *before* the nonperforming party actually breaches the contract or even before the performance is due.

REMEDIES AT LAW (MONEY DAMAGES)

For most contracts, the remedy at law will be **money damages** awarded by the court to the nonbreaching party. This is simply a legal mechanism for compelling the breaching party to compensate the innocent party for losses related to the breach. In a contract claim, money damages are primarily limited to (1) *compensatory* (also called *direct* or *actual*) *damages,* (2) *consequential damages,* (3) *restitution,* and (4) *liquidated damages.*

LO 11-3

Identify the appropriate form of money damages for each type of breach.

Compensatory Damages

Compensatory damages cover a broad spectrum of losses for recovery of *actual damages* suffered by the nonbreaching party. These damages are an attempt to put the nonbreaching party in the same position she would have been in if the other party had performed as agreed. This includes such sums as out-of-pocket damages and even potential profits that would have been earned if performance had occurred. For example, BigCo hires LowPrice to prepare BigCo's tax returns and financial statements in time for BigCo's shareholders meeting on March 1 for a fee of $5,000. On February 15, the principal of LowPrice notifies BigCo that she cannot prepare the returns because she has decided to switch careers and shut down the tax practice. BigCo must then hire HighPrice to prepare the documents. Because of the short timeline, HighPrice charges a fee of $12,000. BigCo is entitled to recover the difference between the price actually paid ($12,000) and the price that would have been paid if LowPrice had performed as originally agreed ($5,000). Thus, BigCo is entitled to $7,000 as compensatory damages (plus any additional out-of-pocket costs related to locating and hiring a new accounting firm).

Consequential Damages

Consequential damages compensate the nonbreaching party for *foreseeable indirect* losses not covered by compensatory damages. An aggrieved party is entitled to recover consequential damages if the damages are caused by unique and foreseeable circumstances beyond the contract itself. In order to recover consequential damages, the damages must flow from the breach (i.e., the damages were a consequence of the breach). For example, in the BigCo-LowPrice case discussed above, suppose that LowPrice had breached on the day before the tax returns were due and that BigCo needed the tax returns as documentation for a bank loan on that day. Because the tax returns were not ready until one month after the due date, the bank charged BankCo a delay fee and then raised the interest rate on the loan. These costs to BankCo are related to the unique circumstances (the tax returns were needed on a certain date) and were foreseeable (assuming LowPrice had reason to know of the bank loan).

The rules that limit damages for which a nonbreaching party may recover were set out in *Hadley v. Baxendale,*[2] a landmark case on consequential damages that has been followed almost universally by U.S. courts. The case involved Hadley, a 19th-century mill owner, who was forced to cease operations due to a broken crankshaft. The mill owner hired Baxendale to deliver the broken shaft to a repair shop in another city. Baxendale had no reason to know that the mill was shut down; in fact, it was common practice in the industry for mill owners to have a backup shaft for just such an occasion. Baxendale delayed delivery of the shaft, which resulted in additional days of shutdown for the mill and, thus, lost profits for Hadley. Hadley sued Baxendale for the lost profits as consequential damages. The court ruled in favor of Baxendale because Hadley had not shown that a reasonable person could have *foreseen* Hadley's ongoing damages. Because Hadley had not actually communicated the unique circumstances, Baxendale was not liable for the damages related to the delay.

Restitution

Restitution is a remedy designed to prevent *unjust enrichment* of one party in an agreement. In the event that one party is in the process of performing the contract and the other party commits a material breach, the nonbreaching party is entitled to rescind (cancel) the contract and receive fair market value for any services rendered. For example, BuildCo contracts with WidgetCo to build a new warehouse for WidgetCo's inventory. One-third of the way through construction, WidgetCo fails to make its payments on time and, therefore, materially breaches the contract. BuildCo rescinds the contract and may recover restitution equal to the fair market value of the work performed in a lawsuit against WidgetCo.

Liquidated Damages

Liquidated damages are damages that the parties agree to ahead of time. In situations where it might be very difficult to determine actual damages, parties may agree at the time of the contract that a breach would result in a fixed damage amount. Liquidated damages provisions are commonly used in license agreements (such as a software user's license), whereby the parties agree, for example, that a breaching party will pay $10,000 in the event of a breach caused by one party making unauthorized copies of the software. For such provisions to be enforceable, courts have held that a penalty clause (i.e., damages that are intended to penalize the breaching party rather than compensate the nonbreaching party) cannot be disguised as a liquidated damages clause. Although liquidated damages clauses are enforceable, the amount of harm caused by the breach must be impossible or difficult to estimate. The damages also must be directly related to the breach and be a *reasonable estimate* of the actual damages incurred.

In Case 11.2, a state appellate court parses the difference between liquidated damages and a penalty.

CASE 11.2 Bunker et al. v. Strandhagen, Court of Appeals of Texas, Third District, No. 03-14-00510-CV (2017)

FACT SUMMARY Bunker and the other appellants were physicians employed by American Anesthesiology of Texas, Inc. ("AAT") who comprise the practice group's advisory board ("board members"). Strandhagen and approximately 60 other physicians, including the board members, were partners

(continued)

---

[2]9 ExCh 341 (1854).

in Austin Anesthesiology Group ("AAG"). In 2011, those physicians sold their interests in AAG to AAT. In connection with that transaction, Strandhagen and the other physicians separately entered two other agreements: (1) individual employment agreements with AAT and (2) a separate internal operating agreement among themselves ("operating agreement") that, among other things, created an advisory board tasked with certain responsibilities within the practice group. AAT was *not* a party to the operating agreement.

Strandhagen's employment agreement with AAT specified the terms of her employment with AAT and provided for a seven-year term of employment. The operating agreement included a liquidated damages provision in the event that a physician's employment was terminated before the expiration of his or her employment term:

> [I]f a Physician's employment with the Company is terminated for any reason during the Initial Term other than termination without cause by the Company . . . then such a terminating Physician . . . shall promptly pay to the non-terminating Physicians . . . as liquidated damages, and not as a penalty, the amount set forth below. . . .

Strandhagen was terminated by AAT in year two of her seven-year employment term. The parties disputed whether she was terminated "without cause" by AAT under the employment agreement. The amount of damages applicable to the majority of the physicians, including Strandhagen, was $500,000, which would be owed, not to AAT, but to the other physician signatories to the operating agreement. Ultimately, each non-terminating physician would receive just under $10,000 in the event of breach.

"Strandhagen filed a motion with a Texas state trial court asking it to declare that the liquidated damages provision in the operating agreement was unenforceable because it amounted to a penalty. The court agreed with Strandhagen and the board members appealed."

SYNOPSIS OF DECISION AND OPINION   The Texas Court of Appeals reversed the decision of the trial court and ruled in favor of the board members.

The appellate court found that the trial court erred in two respects: (1) Proof of actual damages is not required if a liquidated damages provision is unreasonable on the face of a contract, and (2) the record did not conclusively demonstrate that the liquidated damages provision is a penalty as an unreasonable forecast of just compensation. The court ordered the case to be remanded back to the trial court.

WORDS OF THE COURT: Enforceability of Liquidated Damages   "Liquidated damages is a measure of damages that parties agree in advance will be assessed in the event of a contract breach. However, because the basic principle underlying contract damages is compensation for losses sustained due to breach and no more, courts may not enforce punitive contractual damages provisions. A liquidated-damages provision is unenforceable if it is actually a penalty for noncompliance rather than 'just compensation' for loss. . . . A liquidated-damages provision will be enforced if the court finds that (1) the harm caused by the breach is impossible or difficult to estimate and (2) the amount of liquidated damages is a reasonable forecast of just compensation. . . . Strandhagen concedes the first element, namely, that the harm caused by early termination was difficult to estimate at the time of contracting. [Moreover], the record does not conclusively demonstrate that the liquidated-damages provision is a penalty as an unreasonable forecast of just compensation."

Case Questions

1. Why did Strandhagen concede "that the harm caused by early termination was difficult to estimate at the time of contracting"?

2. What business reasons support the use of a liquidated damages clause in this case?

3. *Focus on Critical Thinking:* Liquidated damages clauses are everywhere. Can you find one in a software license agreement or terms of service agreement in any contracts that you have entered into? Did you know what liquidated damages were? Do most people?

Quick Quiz Money Damages

Ishmael is the owner of White Whale Ventures (WWV). Determine which category of money damages Ishmael is entitled to under the following scenarios:

1. WWV enters into a contract to deliver 10 harpoons to Local Marina for $100 per harpoon. One week after delivery, Local Marina's check for the harpoons is returned by Local Marina's bank for insufficient funds (a bounced check).

2. WWV develops software for devices used to detect fish in the deep sea. They license the software to Captain Ahab who proceeds to illegally copy the software for his friends. WWV's license agreement fixes damages at $10,000 in the event that a licensee illegally duplicates the software.

3. WWV enters into a contract with Ship Supplies Corporation (SSC) to manufacture specialized fishing equipment. Ishmael made clear that the equipment had to be delivered in time for the Annual Big Time Fishing Tournament because he intended to rent out the equipment to its customers. The day before the tournament, SSC notifies WWV it cannot complete the order until well after the tournament ended.

Answers to this Quick Quiz are provided at the end of the chapter.

TAKEAWAY CONCEPT Remedies at Law

Monetary damages can be (1) *compensatory*—direct losses from nonperformance; (2) *consequential*—indirect but foreseeable losses from nonperformance; (3) *restitution*—losses equal to the amount that the breaching party has been unjustly enriched by the nonbreaching party; or (4) *liquidated*—losses of a predetermined value according to the contract.

EQUITABLE REMEDIES

LO 11-4

Differentiate legal remedies from equitable remedies.

Although the usual remedy for a breach of contract is money damages, there are some instances when money damages are insufficient to compensate the nonbreaching party or when one party was unjustly enriched at the other party's expense. In these cases, a court may grant **equitable relief**. This relief comes primarily in the form of (1) *specific performance,* (2) *injunctive relief,* or (3) *reformation.*

Specific Performance

Specific performance is an equitable remedy whereby a court orders the breaching party to render the promised performance by ordering the party to take a specific action. This remedy is available only when the subject matter of the contract is sufficiently *unique* that money damages are inadequate. Therefore, specific performance is rarely available in a sale of goods case unless the goods are rare (such as a coin collection) or distinctive (such as a sculpture) enough that the buyer cannot reasonably be expected to locate the goods anywhere else.

One of the most common circumstances in which specific performance is awarded is in real estate contracts. Most courts consider each parcel of land to be sufficiently unique to trigger specific performance as a remedy. For example, Andrews agrees to sell Baker an office building in 30 days. At the closing, where conveyance of the title is to take place, Andrews breaches the agreement by refusing to sell the building. In this case, Baker cannot be completely compensated for the breach because Baker chose that building for its location, convenience, accessibility, appearance, and other important factors. Baker contracted for a unique parcel of real estate and is entitled to the benefit of the agreement for the same parcel. The court will require Andrews to *perform as promised* by conveying the property to Baker. However, if Andrews has already sold the property to a good faith buyer, then Baker may be awarded only money damages as a remedy.

Specific performance is also an appropriate remedy in a narrow category of personal service contracts in which the parties agree that a *specific individual*—who possesses a *unique quality* or expertise central to the contract—will perform the services. For example, if Marcel contracts with Constantine to paint Marcel's office lobby in whitewash and Constantine breaches, a court would not consider specific performance as an option because the work is not specialized enough. On the other hand, if the Marcel-Constantine contract requires that Constantine paint a special mural on the wall, that would be sufficiently unique to qualify for specific performance.

Injunctive Relief

A court order to refrain from performing a particular act is known as **injunctive relief**. In the Andrews-Baker office building contract, suppose that Andrews promises to sell the building to Baker in 30 days. Baker learns that Andrews is intending to breach the contract and sell the building to Dominguez for a higher price. In this case, both money damages and specific performance are inadequate because Baker still wants the building instead of compensation for the breach. Baker will ask the court to issue an injunction that would prevent the sale of the building to Dominguez as an equitable remedy consistent with the notion of putting the aggrieved party in the same position as he would have been if the other party had performed as agreed.

Reformation

When the parties have imperfectly expressed their agreement and this imperfection results in a dispute, a court may change the contract by rewriting it to conform to the parties' actual intentions. This contract modification is called **reformation**. For example, in the Andrews-Baker building contract, suppose Andrews's real estate broker accidentally deletes a decimal in the price, making it $10,000 instead of the parties' agreed-upon price of $100,000. At the closing, Baker gives Andrews the check for $10,000 and refuses to pay any more, citing the price in the contract. So long as there was a sufficient basis for believing the parties intended the price to be $100,000, a court may simply reform the contract. Andrews may then show that Baker breached the contract and request specific performance as an additional remedy.

TAKEAWAY CONCEPT Equitable Remedies

Equitable relief is given when monetary damages are insufficient; it takes the form of (1) specific performance, (2) injunctive relief, or (3) reformation.

DUTY TO MITIGATE

The law imposes an obligation on the parties in a contract to take appropriate steps to avoid incurring damages and losses. So long as a party can avoid the damages with reasonable effort, without undue risk or expense, she may be barred from recovery through a lawsuit. The rule preventing recovery for reasonably avoidable damages is often called the *duty to mitigate.* For example, Leonardo contracts with NewCo to design a new office building for NewCo. Midway through the design planning process, NewCo changes its management, notifies Leonardo that it believes that the design contract is invalid, and orders him to stop work. Despite this, Leonardo continues the design process, submits the final product to NewCo, and demands payment in full. In this case, it is likely that a court will not allow Leonardo to recover for any damages occurring after the NewCo stop order. Once Leonardo learned of NewCo's claim, he had an obligation to avoid the further damages incurred by his failure to stop the work even if NewCo's stop order breached the contract.

Managers may encounter a mitigation of damages issue when dealing with employees who claim that their employer breached an employment contract. If an employee has been wrongfully terminated, for example, that employee has a duty to seek new employment (of similar type and rank) if available in order to avoid damages resulting from the alleged breach by the employer.

In Case 11.3, a state supreme court considers whether a seller in a real estate transaction properly mitigated her damages.

CASE 11.3 Fischer v. Heymann, 12 N.E.3d 867 (Supreme Court of Indiana 2014)

FACT SUMMARY Michael and Noel Heymann ("the Heymanns") entered into an agreement to buy a condominium from Fischer for $315,000. The purchase agreement ("Agreement") authorized the Heymanns to terminate the contract if Fischer refused to fix any "major defect" discovered upon inspection but did not permit them to terminate if Fischer refused to perform "routine maintenance" or make "minor repair[s]." One week after signing the Agreement, the Heymanns demanded that Fischer fix an electrical problem after an inspection report revealed electricity was not flowing to three power outlets. The Heymanns considered this to be a "major defect" under the Agreement and conditioned their purchase on Fischer's timely response. Fischer failed to respond in the time frame set out in the Agreement contending the problem was not a major defect. When the Heymanns refused to complete the sale, Fischer put the condo back on the market and eventually sued the Heymanns for specific performance or, in the alternative, money damages.

Although the trial court rejected Fischer's claim, the Indiana Court of Appeals reversed the decision

and remanded the case back to the trial court to determine damages. On remand, the trial court concluded that Fischer fell short of exercising reasonable diligence in mitigating her damages when she listed the condo at an unreasonably high price from at least the beginning of 2007 to early 2011 and rejected a third-party offer to purchase the condo for $240,000 in February 2007 by making an unreasonably high counteroffer of $286,000. As a result, the trial court concluded she was only entitled to $93,972.18—the difference between the original $315,000 selling price and the $240,000 offer, plus all carrying costs, expenses, and attorney fees that accrued from the moment of breach until Fischer rejected the $240,000 offer. Fischer appealed arguing that she did everything possible to mitigate her damages.

SYNOPSIS OF DECISION AND OPINION The Indiana Supreme Court upheld the ruling in favor of the Heymanns and affirmed the trial court's conclusion that Fischer's award should be reduced because she failed to mitigate her damages. The court held that Fischer had a right to damages for the loss actually suffered as a result of the breach once the Heymanns breached the Agreement, but not to be placed in a better position than she would have been in had the contract not been broken. The court pointed out that Fischer's asking price was unreasonably high from 2007 to 2011. By the time Fischer finally sold the condo in November 2011, it had languished on the market for eight years. Two real estate agents testified they had never seen a property on the market for that length of time, and Fischer's own agent admitted she had never before listed a property for eight years.

WORDS OF THE COURT: Duty to Mitigate Damages "[T]he duty to mitigate damages is a common law duty independent of the contract terms that requires a non-breaching party [to] make a reasonable effort to act in such a manner as to decrease the damages caused by the breach. . . . The record also supports the trial court's finding that Fischer could have sold the condo for $240,000 in 2007. [A] third party, Joe Johnson, offered to purchase the condo for $240,000—the highest offer Fischer ever received after the Agreement with the Heymanns fell through. Fischer responded by making a counter-offer of $286,000, which Johnson rejected. The trial court heard testimony that Fischer 'overstated' the asking price by '[a] substantial amount,' and made an unreasonable counter-offer, particularly for a unit in 'an original non-updated condition.' . . . We affirm the trial court's conclusion that Fischer may receive only $75,000 in compensatory damages—the difference between the Heymann deal ($315,000) and the Johnson offer ($240,000)."

Case Questions

1. Was it reasonable for the Heymanns to consider the electrical problem a "major defect"? Why or why not?

2. Why did the court use the Johnson offer to help calculate Fischer's damages?

3. *Focus on Critical Thinking:* Much of the court's ruling turns on the fact that Fischer unreasonably held onto the property instead of selling it. Should the law impute knowledge of the real estate market to every seller? Wouldn't it have been difficult for Fischer to anticipate how far the value of her condo would fall in an extremely depressed housing market?

 THINKING STRATEGICALLY

Performance Assurances

PROBLEM: In a contract transaction, there may be a time when one party becomes wary about the other party's ability to perform. Perhaps this skepticism is based on the conduct of certain parties or on conversations with a vendor. What legal methods will help reduce the risk that the company will be left fighting other creditors in bankruptcy or suffer any further losses?

For example, suppose Whiteside agrees to purchase and develop five parcels of real estate from Greenside at a rate of one parcel every six months. Whiteside agrees to pay Greenside $75,000 per parcel *within one month* after the parcel has been developed and leased to a tenant. On January 10, Whiteside completes development of the first parcel; Whiteside pays Greenside $75,000 by check on February 10. In July, Whiteside develops a second parcel but fails to make the payment as agreed. As the end of August approaches with Whiteside still owing Greenside for the second parcel, Greenside faces a dilemma. While she wishes to preserve the potentially lucrative contractual relationship with Whiteside, she is also concerned that Whiteside may be having financial difficulties that may cause it to breach.

STRATEGIC SOLUTION: Greenside should seek *assurances of performance* about the past-due and future payments.

The common law provides both parties the right to demand assurances of performance from each other concerning performance.[3] When one party has

---

[3]*Restatements (Second) of Contracts,* § 251.

reasonable grounds to believe that the other will not perform, she has the right to demand that the other party give her written assurance that performance will take place as agreed. If that party does not provide adequate assurance of performance within 30 days, this failure will itself be considered a breach. Therefore, the demanding party may then suspend performance until she receives the requested assurance.

In the Whiteside-Greenside contract, suppose that one week prior to the date when the next parcel is scheduled to be developed, Greenside requests that Whiteside provide her with *written assurances* that (1) Whiteside will pay the amount due immediately and (2) Whiteside will continue to pay Greenside within the period as stated in the original contract. If Whiteside ignores the request or does not provide the requested assurances, Greenside then has the right to suspend performance and has no duty to deliver another parcel until she receives assurances from Whiteside. She preserves the contractual relationship until such time as the payment problems may be worked out to Greenside's satisfaction. At that point, the parties may continue in accordance with the original contract. However, if conditions are sufficient that Greenside reasonably believes that Whiteside intends to *renege* on its obligations in the contract, Greenside may cancel the contract and pursue legal remedies (such as a lawsuit to recover money damages) under the doctrine of *anticipatory repudiation*.

QUESTIONS

1. Can you think of conversations, words, or events that might lead one party to believe that the other party might breach in the near future?
2. Why do you think the law provides a right for one party to suspend performance based on lack of assurances?

KEY TERMS

Breach p. 214   Condition that exists when one party has failed to perform her obligation under a contract. If the breach is material, the nonbreaching party is excused from his performance and can recover monetary damages.

Remedies p. 214   Judicial actions, which can be monetary or equitable, taken by courts that are intended to compensate an injured party in a civil lawsuit.

Anticipatory repudiation p. 215   Doctrine under which, when one party makes clear that he has no intention to perform as agreed, the nonbreaching party is entitled to recover damages in anticipation of the breach rather than waiting until performance is due. Also called *anticipatory breach*.

Money damages p. 217   Sums levied on the breaching party and awarded to the nonbreaching party to remedy a loss from breach of contract.

Compensatory damages p. 217   Damages that are meant to make the injured party whole again. In contract law, they are an attempt to place the nonbreaching party in the position he would have been in had the contract been executed as agreed. Also called *direct* or *actual damages.*

Consequential damages p. 217   Foreseeable losses caused by the breach; may include lost profits.

Restitution p. 218   A remedy that restores to the plaintiff the value of the performance that he has already rendered to the breaching party and by which the breaching party has been unjustly enriched.

Liquidated damages p. 218   Damages that the parties expressly define in the contract and agree will compensate the nonbreaching party.

Equitable relief p. 220   A type of remedy, including injunctions and restraining orders, that is designed to compensate a party when money alone will not do, but instead forces the other party to do (or not do) something.

Specific performance p. 220   An equitable remedy whereby a court orders the breaching party to render the promised performance by ordering the party to take a specific action.

Injunctive relief p. 221   A court order to refrain from performing a particular act.

Reformation p. 221   Contract modification in which the court rewrites a contract to conform to the parties' actual intentions when the parties have imperfectly expressed their agreement and the imperfection results in a dispute.

Remedies

Steak 'n Shake restaurant chain entered a contract with Pepsi to replace King Cola with Pepsi in all its stores. Several issues surrounding the contract's execution strained the agreement, and Steak 'n Shake canceled the contract and refused to perform. Pepsi sued, and in court Steak 'n Shake insisted that Pepsi had no "legally cognizable" damages because all potential profits were purely speculative. Pepsi argued that it stood to gain from the contract and should be compensated for the breach even though damages could not be calculated exactly. The damages could be equal to what it reasonably stood to gain from the contract if not for Steak 'n Shake's breach.

CASE QUESTIONS

1. Should a court award damages to Pepsi even though the company admitted the damages could not be calculated exactly?
2. What other types of damages or relief could Pepsi seek?

Anticipatory Repudiation

DiFolco and MSNBC entered into a two-year employment agreement for DiFolco to work as a television commentator covering the entertainment industry. MSNBC had the right to terminate the agreement after the first year by giving DiFolco 60 days' advance notice. DiFolco's first eight months of employment were tumultuous, and she had several disputes with her supervisors over her assignments and working conditions. Through a series of e-mails, DiFolco complained to her supervisors about being forced off the air because of MSNBC's change in schedule and coverage. One of these e-mails indicated that DiFolco wished to have a meeting to discuss her exit from the shows and to give MSNBC ample time to replace her. In that same e-mail, however, DiFolco also wrote that she wanted to be part of the MSNBC team "for a long time to come." Nonetheless, MSNBC took these e-mails to mean that DiFolco intended to repudiate her contract and sent her a proposed separation agreement claiming that she had resigned. DiFolco filed a breach of contract action against MSNBC.

CASE QUESTIONS

1. Who prevails and why?
2. If you received an e-mail from an employee that concerned her "exit," would you believe she was quitting? Is the situation with DiFolco any different?

CHAPTER REVIEW QUESTIONS

1. A breach that relates to a fundamental term of the contract is called a _____ breach.
   a. Partial
   b. Important
   c. Total
   d. Substantial
   e. Bench

2. Which doctrine allows one party to pursue remedies before a breach has occurred?
   a. Anticipatory repudiation
   b. Specific performance
   c. Partial breach
   d. Equitable remedies
   e. First remedy

3. Which remedy compensates a nonbreaching party for foreseeable indirect losses?
   a. Consequential damages
   b. Specific performance
   c. Liquidated damages
   d. Compensatory damages
   e. Final damages

4. In cases where it is difficult to estimate actual damages in the event of a breach, the parties may agree to:
   a. Indirect damages
   b. Restitution
   c. Liquidated damages
   d. Future damages
   e. Approximate damages

5. Which duty requires the nonbreaching party to make reasonable efforts to act in such a manner as to decrease the damages caused by the breach?
   a. Care
   b. Mitigation
   c. Repudiation
   d. Performance
   e. Reasonableness

6. When a total breach occurs, the nonbreaching party may suspend performance or be discharged from its obligations completely.
   a. True
   b. False

7. Out-of-pocket losses are typically covered by compensatory damages.
   a. True
   b. False

8. Specific performance is one option for collecting damages as a remedy at law.
   a. True
   b. False

9. Injunctive relief is a court order to refrain from a particular act.
   a. True
   b. False

10. Mitigation of damages is a duty of the breaching party.
    a. True
    b. False

 Quick Quiz ANSWERS
Money Damages

1. **Compensatory**. Ishmael suffered a direct, out-of-pocket loss that qualifies for compensatory damages.
2. **Liquidated**. Commonly used in license agreements, the parties agree to damages ahead of time when it would be difficult to determine actual damages.
3. **Consequential**. Because SSC had direct knowledge that a delay would result in damages, Ishmael is entitled to collect indirect damages such as lost profit as a result of SSC's breach.

CHAPTER REVIEW QUESTIONS: Answers and Explanations

1. **c.** A total breach relates to a fundamental term of the contract or has an effect on the value of the contract.

2. **a.** After the parties have entered into an agreement but before performance has occurred, it sometimes becomes apparent that one party does not intend to perform as agreed. This may be apparent through the party's words or conduct.

3. **a.** Consequential damages allow recovery for damages that are unique and foreseeable beyond the contract itself. Answer *b* is incorrect because it is an equitable remedy. Answer *c* is incorrect

because liquidated damages are agreed to ahead of time. Answer *d* is incorrect because compensatory damages are for actual losses suffered.

4. c. Liquidated damages may be used if the amount of harm caused by the breach is impossible or difficult to estimate. The damages also must be directly related to the breach and a reasonable estimate of the actual damages incurred.

5. b. The rule preventing recovery for reasonably avoidable damages is often called the duty to mitigate.

6. a. True. The nonbreaching party is entitled to suspend performance.

7. a. True. Out-of-pocket damages are direct losses for which compensatory damages are appropriate.

8. b. False. Specific performance is an equitable remedy.

9. a. True. Injunctive relief is an equitable remedy.

10. b. False. Mitigation of damages is the duty of the nonbreaching party.

CHAPTER 12

Contracts for the Sale of Goods: Overview of Article 2

 THINKING STRATEGICALLY

©valterZ/Shutterstock

This chapter provides an overview of the Uniform Commercial Code (UCC), an important source of business law, and then introduces Article 2 of the UCC, which applies to contracts for the sale of goods. Broadly speaking, we shall see that the UCC is a strategic gap filler. It creates a series of standard default rules, and these rules help to promote commerce by filling potential gaps in business contracts. In addition, this chapter's *Thinking Strategically* will explain how a well-known strategic dilemma known as the Prisoner's Dilemma can arise in commercial transactions and will then explore a classic strategic solution: the shadow of the future.

Learning Objectives

After studying this chapter, students who have mastered the material will be able to:

12-1 Identify which types of contracts are governed by Article 2 of the UCC.

12-2 Articulate the fundamental purpose of UCC Article 2 in commercial transactions.

12-3 Explain what a default rule is and how default rules fill gaps in contracts.

12-4 Define *goods* and *merchants* under Article 2 of the UCC.

12-5 Distinguish between common law contracts and UCC contracts.

CHAPTER OVERVIEW

This chapter provides a general overview of Article 2 of the Uniform Commercial Code (UCC). In brief, Article 2 sets out a series of default rules that govern contracts involving the sale of goods. In this chapter, students will learn:

- The scope of Article 2 coverage.
- The fundamental purpose of UCC Article 2 in commercial transactions.

- The concept of default rules.
- The definition of "goods" and "merchants" under UCC Article 2.
- How contracts governed by the UCC differ from those governed by the common law.

INTRODUCTION TO THE UCC

The **Uniform Commercial Code (UCC)**, sometimes simply referred to as the *Code,* is a model statute published by the National Conference of Commissioners of Uniform State Laws (NCCUSL), a private organization.[1] The UCC is important because every state has now adopted all, or substantially all, of the provisions of the UCC.

Article 2 of the UCC governs contracts involving the sale of goods. In addition, the UCC contains a plethora of articles pertaining to other aspects of commercial law. Article 2A of the Code, for example, covers the *leasing* of goods. (Lease contracts are discussed in detail in Chapter 17, "UCC Article 2A: Lease of Goods.") In all, the UCC contains 11 separate articles. Article 1 sets forth general provisions that apply to the entire Code, while the remaining articles each deal with a different type of commercial transaction (see Figure 12.1).

This textbook is based on the current version of the model UCC. Because the model UCC entrusts each individual state to determine the precise wording of certain sections, you should always check your own state's commercial code for the most accurate information.

LO 12-1

Identify which types of contracts are governed by Article 2 of the UCC.

FIGURE 12.1   Uniform Commercial Code

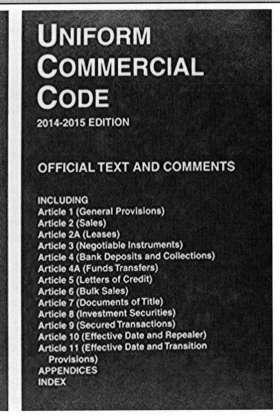

©Roberts Publishing Services

---

[1]The NCCUSL and other similar non-state organizations are discussed in more detail in Chapter 1.

TAKEAWAY CONCEPTS Introduction to the UCC

- The UCC is a model act containing 11 separate sections.
- Article 2 of the UCC governs contracts involving the sale of goods.

LO 12-2

Articulate the fundamental purpose of UCC Article 2 in commercial transactions.

PURPOSE OF ARTICLE 2 OF THE UCC

The underlying policy goal of Article 2 of the UCC is to promote commercial efficiency and the completion of business transactions. How? By providing simple and standardized procedures that merchants and consumers may rely upon in cases involving unforeseen contingencies. UCC Article 2, in particular, facilitates business transactions by providing merchants and consumers with a standard set of default rules for the sale of goods.

TAKEAWAY CONCEPT Purpose of Article 2 of the UCC

The underlying purpose of Article 2 of the UCC is to promote the completion of business transactions through the use of standard default rules covering unforeseen contingencies.

LO 12-3

Explain what a default rule is and how default rules fill gaps in contracts.

DEFAULT RULES

A default rule is a rule of law that is designed to fill "gaps" in business contracts, that is, unexpected or unforeseen situations that might occur after a deal is made. (See Figure 12.2 for a general overview of the gap-filling function of default rules.) As a result, default rules, like the rules contained in Article 2 of the UCC, help courts resolve problems that were not anticipated or addressed by the parties when they made their deal. If an unexpected problem does occur, courts will then apply those default rules to fill any gaps in a contract.

Default rules, however, can be modified by the parties at the time they enter into their contract. That is why they are called "default" rules. So, to sum up, a default rule applies to the parties to a transaction, unless the parties explicitly agree to override it with a different rule of their choosing. Default rules can thus be modified by agreement of the parties.

Contract law, for example, can be divided into two kinds of rules: *default rules* and *mandatory rules*. Whereas the *default rules* can be modified by agreement of the parties, *mandatory rules* will be enforced even if the parties to a contract attempt to override or modify them. One of the most important debates in contract theory concerns the proper role or purpose of default rules.

The idea of a default rule in contract law is sometimes connected to the notion of a *complete contract*. In contract theory, a complete contract fully specifies the rights and duties of the parties to the contract for all possible future states of the world. An incomplete contract, therefore, contains gaps. Most contract theorists find that default rules fill in the gaps in what would otherwise be incomplete contracts. This is often stated pragmatically as whether a court will imply terms in order to save a contract from uncertainty.

In the context of contracts for the sale of goods, Article 2 of the UCC should be thought of primarily as a strategic *gap filler* in cases where the parties have not otherwise agreed to specific terms. Typically, parties will enter into a **sales contract** after negotiating certain

FIGURE 12.2 | Default Rules

Default Rules

- **Gaps**: risks or circumstances that aren't specifically addressed in a contract

- **Default Rules**: rules applied by courts to fill gaps

Source: Prof. Dan Quint (University of Wisconsin, Madison).

terms. These terms, assuming they do not conflict with a UCC prohibition, are fully enforceable. The UCC mainly comes into play when the parties to a sales transaction have *not* expressly agreed on certain terms.

By way of example, suppose that Venus Williams manufactures tennis balls and Serena Williams distributes them to retail outlets. Further assume that Venus and Serena enter into an agreement for the sale of 1,000 Brand-A tennis balls at $1 per ball to be delivered to Serena's warehouse on Friday. However, the parties do not negotiate any terms other than price and delivery date. Suppose that Venus runs out of Brand-A tennis balls and ships 1,000 Brand-B tennis balls instead. Must Serena accept the goods? What are her options under the law? Suppose instead that the tennis balls are damaged in transit before they are delivered to Serena's warehouse. What are the parties' rights and responsibilities regarding the sale? Who will bear the risk of the loss? Because the parties have not specifically agreed on this contingency, they must turn to the UCC for the answers regarding those missing terms. We will study some specific default rules in the next few chapters.

TAKEAWAY CONCEPTS Default Rules

- Default rules are rules of law that apply to unforeseen contingencies—potential problems that the contracting parties did not anticipate when they drafted their contract.
- A default rule can be overridden or modified by the parties to a contract if they so choose.

UCC ARTICLE 2 COVERAGE AND DEFINITIONS

LO 12-4

Define *goods* and *merchants* under Article 2 of the UCC.

Article 2 of the UCC applies only to agreements for the *sale of goods.* The UCC defines **goods** as property that is (1) tangible (i.e., has a physical existence such as a laptop computer) and (2) movable from place to place. Therefore, real estate contracts or employment contracts are *not* covered by the UCC.

What about mixed contracts involving the sale of goods as well as the provision of some service? In general, courts have applied the "predominant purpose test" when dealing with mixed contracts. (See Figure 12.3 for a general overview of the predominant purpose test.) Under this test, courts must discern the main purpose or thrust of the contract; specifically, courts must determine whether the predominant purpose of the contract is the rendition of

FIGURE 12.3 | Scope of Article 2

Scope of Article 2

- Article 2
  - UCC §2-102; Article 2 applies to the sale of goods, things that are movable other than money and investment securities.
- Article 2A
  - Article 2A governs the leasing of goods.

In a mixed contract involving sales and services, the UCC will govern if the predominant purpose is the sale of goods, but the common law will control if the predominant purpose is the provision of a service.

a service, with goods only incidentally involved, or whether the main purpose of the contract is the transaction of a sale, with labor incidentally involved.

In addition, Article 2 contains special provisions that apply only to transactions involving *merchants.* The definition of **merchant** not only includes anyone who is *regularly engaged* in the sale of a particular good but also includes any person who employs a merchant as a broker, agent, or intermediary. The UCC imputes a certain level of knowledge and awareness to merchants and allows their transactions to proceed in an expedited manner without the necessity for safeguards intended for average consumers. For example, suppose that Acme Equipment sells a lawn tractor to Sanjay for $600. This sales agreement is subject to Article 2, but because Sanjay is a consumer, not a merchant, certain UCC requirements exist to protect Sanjay's interests in the sale. However, if Acme were a wholesaler and Sanjay the owner of a retail store, this would be a *merchant* transaction, which would trigger special business standards that are intended to allow parties to transact business unimpeded by any special consumer protections. What about contracts between merchants and consumers? In Landmark Case 12.1, a federal court of appeals applies Article 2 of the UCC to shrinkwrap licenses.

LANDMARK CASE 12.1 ProCD v. Zeidenberg, 86 F.3d 1447 (7th Cir. 1996)

FACT SUMMARY ProCD compiled information from more than 3,000 telephone directories around the world into a single, searchable computer database. (The database cost more than $10 million to compile and is expensive to keep current.) In addition to offering an expensive subscription service to the database over the Internet (designed for commercial clients), ProCD also offers a cheaper version of its database in the CD-ROM format to the general public for personal use. Each retail CD-ROM package includes a "shrinkwrap license." (Shrinkwrap licenses get their name from the fact that retail software packages are covered in plastic or cellophane "shrinkwrap.") One of the terms of ProCD's license prohibits the resale of the contents of the database. Matthew

(continued)

Zeidenberg purchased ProCD's consumer package of the database from a retail outlet in Madison, Wisconsin. He then formed Silken Mountain Web Services, Inc. and began to resell the information in the database over the Internet in contravention of the license.

SYNOPSIS OF DECISION AND OPINION

The District Court for the Western District of Wisconsin granted Zeidenberg's motion for summary judgment, holding that ProCD's shrinkwrap license was unenforceable because Zeidenberg did not consent to the terms on the interior of the package at the time of the purchase. The Seventh Circuit Court of Appeals, however, reversed the district court's holding with respect to the shrinkwrap license, holding that a database is a "good" and that shrinkwrap licenses in mass-market consumer transactions are enforceable under the Uniform Commercial Code.

WORDS OF THE COURT: Shrinkwrap Licences

"What then does the current version of the UCC have to say [about shrinkwrap licenses]? We think that the place to start is sec. 2-204(1): 'A contract for sale of goods may be made in any manner sufficient to show agreement, including conduct by both parties which recognizes the existence of such a contract.' A vendor, as master of the offer, may invite acceptance by conduct, and may propose limitations on the kind of conduct that constitutes acceptance. A buyer may accept by performing the acts the vendor proposes to treat as acceptance. And that is what happened. ProCD proposed a contract that a buyer would accept by *using* the software after having an opportunity to read the license at leisure. This Zeidenberg did. He had no choice, because the software splashed the license on the screen and would not let him proceed without indicating acceptance. So although the district judge was right to say that a contract can be, and often is, formed simply by paying the price and walking out of the store, the UCC permits contracts to be formed in other ways. ProCD proposed such a different way, and without protest Zeidenberg agreed. Ours is not a case in which a consumer opens a package to find an insert saying 'you owe us an extra $10,000' and the seller files suit to collect. Any buyer finding such a demand can prevent formation of the contract by returning the package, as can any consumer who concludes that the terms of the license make the software worth less than the purchase price. Nothing in the UCC requires a seller to maximize the buyer's net gains."

Case Questions

1. Is ProCD's license agreement a contract for the sale of goods or a contract for the provision of a service?

2. How would you classify Zeidenberg, as a merchant or a consumer?

3. *Focus on Critical Thinking:* Would the result of this case be the same under the common law instead of the UCC?

TAKEAWAY CONCEPTS Goods and Merchants

- The UCC defines goods as property that is (1) tangible and (2) movable from place to place.
- The UCC defines a merchant as one who is *regularly engaged* in the sale of a particular good, including any person who employs a merchant as a broker, agent, or intermediary.

Quick Quiz Scope of UCC Article 2 Coverage

Does UCC Article 2 apply to the following transactions?

1. Bob received a brand-new, six-foot Liquid Shredder surfboard for his 21st birthday, but he is so afraid of sharks that he decides to sell it on Craigslist for $99.

2. Jack owns a beautiful cottage on the beach. He lists his cottage on Airbnb to make some extra money, and he is so pleased with the results that he quits his day job and decides to convert his cottage into "Jack's Beach and Breakfast Inn" full time and make a living as an innkeeper.

3. Rosa is a computer science major with excellent computer coding skills. A local pizzeria hires Rosa to write the source code for their new website to advertise the sale of pizza and take pizza orders.

Answers to this Quick Quiz are provided at the end of the chapter.

UCC AND THE COMMON LAW

LO 12-5

Distinguish between common law contracts and UCC contracts.

Before concluding this chapter, it is important to distinguish between contracts governed by general principles of judge-made common law and those governed by the UCC because the legal rights and obligations of the parties to a contract under the common law differ from those under the UCC. Generally speaking, the common law applies to contracts involving the *provision of services,* while Article 2 of the UCC applies to contracts involving the *sale of goods.* (See Figure 12.4 for a general overview of the scope of Article 2.) This is a critical distinction for business owners and managers because the UCC preempts or displaces the common law when goods are being sold. Article 2, for example, relaxes some of the stricter common law contract requirements, such as the doctrine of consideration.

FIGURE 12.4	Scope of Article 2

The Scope of Article 2

- Governs contracts for sale of "goods."
- ◘ Article 2 preempts common law in sale of goods, but where Article 2 is silent, common law governs.

TAKEAWAY CONCEPT UCC and the Common Law

The requirements for common law contracts are stricter than the requirements for contracts for the sale of goods under Article 2 of the UCC.

©valterZ/Shutterstock

The Sale of Goods over the Internet and the Shadow of the Future

PROBLEM: You are planning a river-rafting adventure down the Colorado River and are considering buying a used canoe on eBay. You find a canoe you like for $99 and place your order, charging it to your debit or credit card or maybe making payment through a secure online payment system like PayPal. So, what's the problem?

In a nutshell, when you place your trust in someone, you may be opening yourself up to the possibility of being exploited or taken advantage of. Upon receiving payment, for example, the seller is supposed to ship the canoe to you. Yet, having received the money, the seller can either "cooperate" by shipping the canoe to you as promised, or she can "defect" by not sending the canoe or by sending a poorer-quality canoe than advertised.

In short, what guarantee do you have that the seller listed on eBay is real or that she will actually send you the product you ordered? How would you feel if you never received your order or if you received a different product instead? You can either trust the seller or wait for her to ship the canoe to you before you agree to pay for it. Of course, everything would be a lot easier if the buyer and the seller were able to trust each other. However, an Internet transaction produces a strategic dilemma: The buyer must trust that the seller will ship her the goods she ordered, and the seller must trust that the buyer will pay for the goods. Unless the parties are able to overcome this dilemma and trust each other, no deal will occur.

In general, a commercial transaction over the Internet is a strategic situation, where the outcome depends not only on your own choices but also on the choices of others. The essence of strategic thinking, therefore, is to always put yourself in the other player's shoes and try to figure out what he or she will do.

Notice how this simple eBay example can be modeled as a strategic two-player game. It involves just two parties, or "players": a potential buyer and a potential seller. Also note that this is a strategic situation because the outcome of the transaction depends on the decisions made by both parties. Specifically, the buyer must decide whether to send payment or not, and the seller must decide whether to ship the product

or not. There are thus four possible payoffs in our eBay example:

1. *Temptation to defect (T):* One party takes advantage of the other party. Upon receiving payment from the buyer, for example, the seller might be tempted to "defect" by taking advantage of the buyer—either by not sending the product or by sending a poorer-quality product than promised.

2. *Reward for mutual cooperation (R):* The parties do what they promise to do. Again, upon receiving payment from the buyer, the seller "cooperates" by shipping the product to the buyer as promised. Both sides benefit—the seller makes a sale, and the buyer gets a good deal.

3. *Punishment for mutual defection (P):* Fearing the other trading partner might defect, the parties refrain from engaging in any transaction at all. The seller loses out on a sale, and the buyer loses out on a good deal.

4. *Sucker's payoff (S):* The worst possible outcome is to be exploited, to cooperate when the other party defects. For example, the seller ships the product but never receives payment, or the buyer sends payment but never receives the product.

To sum up, in a "one-shot" strategic interaction like our eBay example—i.e., a scenario in which the parties will be dealing with each other only once—the "best" outcome is to take advantage of the other party. The second-best outcome is mutual cooperation, i.e., when both sides fully cooperate with each other by keeping their promises, because a mutually beneficial deal is better than no deal at all. The third-best outcome is mutual defection because both parties are worse off when no deal is made. The worst outcome, by far, is the sucker's payoff.

STRATEGIC SOLUTION: The *shadow of the future* is a critical strategic concept. It expresses the idea that we behave differently when we expect to interact with others repeatedly over time, or in the words of influential game theorist Robert Axelrod: "What makes it possible for cooperation to emerge [in a Prisoner's Dilemma] is the fact that the players might meet again. . . . The future can therefore cast a shadow back upon the present and thereby affect the current strategic situation."[2]

---

[2]Robert Axelrod, *The Evolution of Cooperation,* rev. ed., Basic Books (2006), p. 10.

The shadow of the future is also very important in commercial transactions over the Internet and in the business world generally. The possibility of future interaction allows players to escape strategic dilemmas by using conditional retaliation strategies. When the shadow of the future is visible to all, people can condition their behavior on the reputations of the other players. For example, on a massive Internet platform like eBay, the shadow of the future looms large every time a user posts feedback about his or her experience with a particular buyer or seller.

Each user's feedback is open and public for all users to see. A potential buyer can thus easily and quickly evaluate the reputation of a particular seller by clicking on his feedback profile. As the founder of eBay, Pierre Omidyar, explains in an early letter to all eBay users:

> By creating an open market that encourages honest dealings, I hope to make it easier to conduct business with strangers over the net. Most people are honest. And they mean well. Some people go out of their way to make things right. I've heard great stories about the honesty of people here. But some people are dishonest. Or deceptive. . . . But here, those people can't hide. We'll drive them away.

Protect others from them. This grand hope depends on your active participation. Become a registered user. Use our Feedback Forum. Give praise where it is due; make complaints where appropriate.[3]

Following eBay's lead, many online market platforms have implemented electronic reputation mechanisms that collect, process, and distribute large amounts of information about the past trading activities of the market participants. By emulating traditional word-of-mouth networks, these reputation mechanisms cast a large shadow over future transactions, thus promoting trust and trustworthiness among strangers.

QUESTIONS

1. Have you ever found yourself in a Prisoner's Dilemma situation, for example, a transaction in which the "temptation to defect" was strong? Describe the situation.

2. With reference to the UCC, how do the default rules contained in Article 2 of the UCC influence "the shadow of the future" in contracts for the sale of goods?

KEY TERMS

Uniform Commercial Code (UCC) p. 229   A model code for the sale of goods.

Sales contract p. 230   Agreement to transfer title to real property or tangible assets at a given price.

Goods p. 231   Tangible personal property that is movable at the time of identification to a contract of sale.

Merchant p. 232   One who is regularly engaged in the sale of a particular good, including anyone who employs a merchant as a broker, agent, or intermediary.

CASE SUMMARY 12.1 Advent Systems Ltd. v. Unisys Corp., 925 F.2d 670 (3d Cir. 1991)

Predominant Purpose

Advent Systems Limited was engaged primarily in the production of software for computers. As a result of its research and development efforts, Advent had developed an electronic document management system, a process for transforming engineering drawings and similar documents into a computer database. Unisys Corporation decided to market a document management

system in the U.S. market. Advent and Unisys signed a "Distribution Agreement" in which Advent agreed to provide the software making up the document systems to be sold by Unisys. Advent was also obligated to provide sales and marketing materials and manpower as well as technical personnel to work with Unisys employees in building and installing the document systems. Unisys, however, later decided to develop its own

---

[3]See Pierre Omidyar, "Founder's Letter," posted on Feb. 26, 1996, available at http://pages.ebay.com/services/forum/feedback-foundersnote.html.

document system and terminated the agreement with Advent. As a result, Advent sued Unisys for breach of contract. Although the trial court ruled that the UCC did not apply to this transaction, the court of appeals reversed, holding that the software developed by Advent was a good and not a service:

> Computer programs are the product of an intellectual process, but once implanted in a medium are widely distributed to computer owners. An analogy can be drawn to a compact disc recording of an orchestral rendition. The music is produced by the artistry of musicians and in itself is not a 'good,' but when transferred to a laser-readable disc becomes a readily merchantable commodity. Similarly, when a professor delivers a lecture, it is not a good, but, when transcribed as a book, it becomes a good.

CASE QUESTIONS

1. Do you find the court's analogy between music and software persuasive? Why
2. In your opinion, would the agreement still have been classified as a transaction involving the sale of goods if Advent had not yet developed its software at the time it entered into its agreement with Unisys, or would it have been classified as the provision of a service?

CASE SUMMARY 12.2 3L Communications LLC v. Merola, 2013 WL 4803532, Court of Appeals of Tennessee (2013)

Who Is a Merchant?

3L Communications (3L) is a merchant that sells high-end optical telecommunications equipment. Jodi Merola is a sole proprietor doing business as "NY Telecom Supply" (Merola). In summary, 3L entered into an agreement with Merola to purchase five optical circuit boards. Merola shipped the circuit boards via Federal Express, with the balance of $35,090 due on delivery in the form of a cashier's check. The circuit boards arrived at 3L's office and were paid for as agreed, but upon further inspection of the boards, 3L discovered that they were damaged. 3L immediately contacted Merola and notified her that the boards were unusable. In response, Merola provided shipping instructions and an account number to be used for returning the goods. 3L followed the shipping instructions and, two weeks later, 3L sent an e-mail message to Merola regarding the refund for the boards. Merola responded that she had not received the returned boards. 3L then supplied Merola with tracking information from the carrier that indicated that the boards had been delivered two weeks earlier. After Merola stopped responding to 3L inquiries, 3L filed suit to recover its $35,090 payment. Among other things, Merola argued that she was not a "merchant" for purposes of the UCC because she operated as a sole proprietor out of her home.

CASE QUESTIONS

1. Is Merola a merchant under the UCC? Why or why not?
2. Either way, should someone who has minimal business experience or education be held to the standard of a merchant?

CHAPTER REVIEW QUESTIONS

1. The Uniform Commercial Code (UCC) has been adopted by _____ states.
   a. All fifty
   b. Forty-nine
   c. Forty-eight
   d. Forty-seven
   e. Zero, because the UCC is part of the common law

2. Article 2 of the UCC governs _____ contracts, while Article 2A governs _____ contracts.
   a. Lease; sales
   b. Sales; lease
   c. Service; sales
   d. Sales; service
   e. Service; lease

3. A default rule is a:
   a. Standard industry practice.
   b. General commercial norm.
   c. Rule established by the common law.
   d. Rule of law that can be overridden by the parties to a contract.
   e. Rule of law that cannot be overridden by the parties to a contract.

4. UCC Section 2-105 defines _____ as "all (tangible) things . . . which are movable at the time of identification to the contract for sale."

   I. Goods
   II. Fixtures
   III. Services
   IV. Property

   a. I
   b. II
   c. I and II
   d. I, II, and III
   e. I, II, III, and IV

5. To resolve contract issues in cases in which a tangible good is mixed with something intangible (such as a service) most courts employ some variation of the _____ test.
   a. User-friendly
   b. Substantial performance
   c. Commercial impracticality
   d. Commercial practicality
   e. Predominant purpose

6. The purpose of Article 2 of the UCC is to promote fairness and justice for all.
   a. True
   b. False

7. Default rules can be modified by the parties at the time they enter into their contract.
   a. True
   b. False

8. Article 2 of the UCC displaces the common law when goods are being sold.
   a. True
   b. False

9. The UCC was enacted by Congress in order to promote uniform commercial rules for all 50 states.
   a. True
   b. False

10. In addition to contracts for the sale of goods, Article 2 of the UCC applies to real estate deals and employment contracts.
    a. True
    b. False

 Quick Quiz ANSWERS
Scope of UCC Article 2 Coverage

Article 2 of the UCC applies to the first scenario described in the Quick Quiz but not to the last two scenarios for the following reasons.

1. Although most courts would not classify Bob as a merchant (assuming the sale of the surfboard is a one-time deal), the transaction described in this scenario involves the sale of a good.

2. Even though Jack might be considered a merchant, he is not engaged in the sale of goods, since the rental of property does not classify as a sale of goods.

3. Even though the website itself will be used to advertise the sale of pizza and take pizza orders, Rosa is providing a service under the predominant purpose test.

CHAPTER REVIEW QUESTIONS: Answers and Explanations

1. **b.** Answer *a* is correct because every state has now adopted some version of the UCC. Answers *b, c,* and *d* are therefore incorrect. Answer *e* is incorrect because the UCC is a model act, not a common law source of law.

2. **b.** Article 2 of the UCC governs sales contracts, while Article 2A governs lease agreements.

3. **d.** A default rule is a rule of law that can be overridden by the parties to a contract. Answers *a* and *b* do not refer to default rules. Answer *c* is incorrect because not all common law rules are default rules; some are mandatory rules. Answer *e* is incorrect because it describes a mandatory rule.

4. **a.** UCC § 2-105 defines goods as "all (tangible) things . . . which are movable at the time of identification to the contract for sale." Answers *b, c, d,* and *e* are incorrect because Article 2 by its own terms applies to goods, not to property per se, and does not apply to fixtures or services.

5. **e.** Courts use the predominant purpose test to resolve contract issues in cases in which a tangible good is mixed with something intangible. Answer *a* is not a legal test, while choices *b, c,* and *d* are incorrect.

6. **b. False.** The ideals of justice and fairness are too broad; instead, the main purpose of Article 2 of the UCC is to promote commercial efficiency and the completion of business transactions.

7. **a. True.** By definition, default rules can be modified by agreement of the parties.

8. **a. True.** Article 2 of the UCC applies to agreements for the sale of goods and displaces the common law in this area.

9. **b. False.** The UCC is, in fact, a model statute published by a private organization called the National Conference of Commissioners of Uniform State Laws (NCCUSL).

10. **b. False.** Article 2 of the UCC applies only to agreements for the sale of goods.

CHAPTER 13

Sales Contracts: Agreement, Consideration, and the Statute of Frauds

THINKING STRATEGICALLY

©valterZ/Shutterstock

This chapter delves deeper into the gap-filling rules of Article 2 of the Uniform Commercial Code and explores a strategic scenario known as "the battle of the forms," a legal dilemma that arises in many business-to-business relationships.

Learning Objectives

After studying this chapter, students who have mastered the material will be able to:

13-1 Identify the elements required under the UCC to create an agreement for the sale of goods.

13-2 Compare and contrast the element of consideration under the common law and under UCC Article 2.

13-3 Explain the term *battle of the forms*.

13-4 Articulate when sales contracts must be in writing and specify what the writing must contain to be enforceable under the statute of frauds.

CHAPTER OVERVIEW

This chapter focuses on the sale of goods and Article 2 of the Uniform Commercial Code (UCC). Because Article 2 sets out the rules that govern contracts involving the sale of goods, it is important for business owners and managers to understand how UCC rules are applied. In this chapter, students will learn:

- The elements required under the UCC for the formation of an agreement for the sale of goods.
- Consideration under the common law and under UCC Article 2.
- The significance of the battle of the forms.
- When contracts for the sale of goods must be in writing.

FORMATION OF AGREEMENT FOR SALE OF GOODS

Recall that the UCC aims to promote the completion of business transactions. Accordingly, the formation elements for a sales contract are easier to meet and do not require the same level of intent that is required for common law contracts. Specifically, Article 2 lowers the bar for the formation of sales contracts by allowing an enforceable agreement to arise "in any manner sufficient to show agreement" between the parties.[1] As a result, the UCC allows a contract to be enforced based on (1) past commercial conduct, (2) correspondence

---

[1]UCC § 2-204(1).

or verbal exchanges between the parties, and (3) industry standards and norms. In fact, the parties need not even establish a definite time of formation, so long as the conduct of the parties indicates some basis for a reasonable person to believe a sales contract *exists*. For example, if a contractor says he will purchase 2,000 studs from a lumberyard if the supplier can provide them tomorrow, it may not be necessary for the lumberyard to send a return letter. Rather, it can accept by performance. If the delivery truck simply appears at the contractor's yard the next day with 2,000 studs, there has probably been an offer and a reasonable manner of acceptance. There is a binding contract.

LO 13-1

Identify the elements required under the UCC to create an agreement for the sale of goods.

Firm Offers by Merchants

If the seller is a merchant and promises in a signed writing to keep an offer for the sale of goods open for a period of time, under UCC Article 2 this action creates a **firm offer** that is irrevocable. The firm offer will only last for the period of time stated in the offer. If, however, no time period for the offer to remain open is stated, it will stay open for a maximum of three months. An example of a firm offer in writing might read as follows: "The seller agrees to offer 100 units of furniture for a price of $50 per unit, with this offer good for 60 days." The time limit for a firm offer can be exceeded by issuing a new firm offer after the first one expires or by entering into an option contract.

To sum up, a firm offer is created under Article 2 of the UCC when a merchant offers to buy or sell goods with an explicit promise, in writing, that the offer will be held open for a certain time period. In general, the UCC provides that the offer can be irrevocable for a maximum period of three months. Moreover, this offer is binding on the offeror even if the offeree has paid no consideration. By contrast, if the offeree has paid consideration tied to the offer, such a transaction would be classified as an *option contract* and not a firm offer.

Offers with Open Terms

Sometimes merchants wish to engage in a sales transaction, but the parties overlook or are unsure about some key element of the contract, such as quantity, delivery, payment terms, or even the price of the goods. The missing provisions, known as **open terms**, are entirely acceptable under the UCC so long as there is evidence that the parties intended to enter into a contract and the other terms are sufficiently articulated to provide a basis for some appropriate remedy in case of breach. The UCC's approach toward open terms is a great example of its *gap-filling* role. The UCC fills gaps in the parties' contract by providing a variety of answers based on what terms are missing.

A Word about Quantity

While quantity is generally a *required* term in contracts for the sale of goods (i.e., necessary to create an enforceable sales contract), there are two important exceptions to this general rule. First, quantity *may* be an open term if the buyer agrees to purchase *all* of the goods that a seller produces (known as an **output contract**). In this case, the seller has given up the right to sell the goods elsewhere. Second, when the buyer agrees to purchase all or up to an agreed amount of what the buyer needs for a given period (known as a **requirements contract**), a court will generally enforce that agreement despite the missing quantity. For example, suppose that Builder wishes to purchase small pine trees from Grower for use at one of Builder's commercial office complex sites. If Builder agrees to purchase all of the pine trees grown by Grower over the period of one growing season, this is an output contract. If, on the other hand, Builder agrees with Grower to purchase all of the trees that are needed for this site only, the parties have agreed to a requirements contract. In both cases, an enforceable contract exists despite the missing quantity.[2]

OTHER OPEN TERMS

When a contract for the sale of goods is missing certain terms—such as terms regarding the time and place of delivery, payment terms, or price—and when the parties to the sales contract have not had an established course of past conduct, the UCC provides the following gap-filling rules regarding these missing terms:

- *Delivery:* If the place of delivery is not specified in the contract, the buyer takes delivery at the seller's place of business (i.e., seller is not responsible for delivery). If no time of delivery is specified, the UCC provides for a reasonable time under the circumstances.[3]
- *Payment:* Payment is due at the time and place where the seller is to make delivery and may be made in any commercially reasonable form (such as a business check).[4]
- *Price:* The UCC requires the court to determine a reasonable price at the time of delivery, based on industry customs and market value.[5]

Acceptance

The rules provided by Article 2 for accepting an offer in a sales contract are not as rigid as the common law rules. If an offeror does not clearly provide for a method of acceptance, the UCC allows an offeree to accept the offer in any "reasonable manner."[6] Another important difference between the acceptance rules in the UCC and the common law is that acceptance may still be effective even if the acceptance does *not* match the offer exactly (recall, by contrast, the common law mirror image rule from Chapter 7). Not only does the UCC recognize that a contract may in some cases be created in which the acceptance does not match the offer, but it also fills in gaps to create certainty for the parties to the transaction.

 Quick Quiz Sales Contracts

Do the following scenarios constitute a valid agreement under Article 2 of the UCC?

1. Wholesaler delivers 1,000 iPhones to Retailer on the 15th of each month. Over a period of six months, Wholesaler has delivered the iPhones on or about the 15th of the month and Retailer has sent Wholesaler a check within 10 days. Assume that in the smartphone industry, payment is generally made within 10 days after delivery. In month seven, Wholesaler delivers the product on the 15th, but Retailer refuses to pay, arguing that it did not subjectively intend to have the iPhone contract linger into seven months. Is there an agreement?

2. Retailer agrees to purchase all its iPhones and iPhone accessories from Wholesaler during the next calendar year, but Retailer does not specify the actual number of iPhones or accessories it will purchase. Is there an agreement?

Answers to this Quick Quiz are provided at the end of the chapter.

---

[2]UCC § 2-306(1).
[3]UCC § 2-308(a).
[4]UCC § 2-310.
[5]UCC § 2-305(1).
[6]UCC § 2-206.

CONSIDERATION

Recall from Chapter 7, "Mutual Assent: Agreement and Consideration," that common law contracts must be supported by bargained-for consideration. Remember also that most contracts involving nongoods (i.e., those governed by the common law) cannot be *modified* without some additional consideration. While the UCC follows a similar rule that consideration must support a sales contract, a major difference is that the UCC allows contracts to be modified even *without* any additional consideration. The UCC recognizes that market conditions are not static and that the parties may have good faith reasons for modifying a contract without having to comply with some additional legal burden to continue its enforceability.

For example, suppose that Ernie sells 2,000 golf balls to Tiger on credit. Tiger agrees to pay Ernie $1,000 plus 6 percent interest on the principal still owed per month for a period of 24 months. After two months, Tiger's cash flow is impaired by an unexpected downturn in his business. Ernie and Tiger then agree to modify the contract to allow Tiger to pay a smaller monthly payment ($500 per month) but at the same interest rate until the balance is paid off in full. Later, Ernie runs into cash flow problems of his own and demands that Tiger honor the original credit contract terms. Despite the fact that no additional consideration was given for the modification, under the UCC the *modified* contract is fully enforceable and the original contract is deemed canceled.

LO 13-2

Compare and contrast the element of consideration under the common law and under UCC Article 2.

TAKEAWAY CONCEPT Consideration

The UCC allows contracts for the sales of goods to be modified even without any new consideration.

THE BATTLE OF THE FORMS

LO 13-3

Explain the term *battle of the forms*.

As a practical matter, businesses frequently use preprinted forms to initiate or respond to an offer to sell a good. These forms usually have some blanks for the particular negotiated terms unique to the transaction. Normally, the offer takes the form of a **purchase order** from the buyer that contains preprinted clauses (which typically favor the buyer) and blanks that a purchase manager fills in with terms such as shipment date, product information, quantity, and so forth. The seller's firm will then typically issue an **acknowledgment form**, also called an *invoice,* which also has preprinted provisions (typically favoring the seller) and blanks to accommodate the specifics of that transaction.

Figure 13.1 is a purchase order issued by the hypothetical buyer, Blue Jay Industries.

Figure 13.2 is an invoice prepared by a hypothetical seller, Cardinal LLC.

For its part, the UCC provides guidelines on how to resolve a dispute when the terms in these forms conflict. This dilemma is known as the **battle of the forms**. In a battle of the forms case, the UCC provides that (1) a document may constitute acceptance even though it states terms that are additional to or different from those offered by the offeror and (2) in certain transactions the additional terms proposed in the acceptance may become part of the sales contract.

Nonmerchant Transactions

If one of the parties to a sales contract is *not* a merchant, the contract is formed as *originally* offered. That is, the contract is considered accepted, but the additional terms are *not* part of the contract.

FIGURE 13.1   Purchase Order

Blue Jay Industries

PURCHASE ORDER
Vendor's Name and Address
Roberts' Robes, Inc.
1 First St NE
Washington, DC 20543

SHIP TO:
Blue Jay Industries
100 Alpha Drive
Carltown, PA 17022
Attn: Warehouse Manager

P.O. Date	P.O. Number	Shipping Terms/F.O.B.	Terms
27 August 2019	18-4401	Carrier/Jobsite	30 days from delivery
Buyer Contact	**Freight**	**Date of Delivery**	**Remarks**
Ed Chung	N/A	15 September 2019	Time is of the essence

Quantity Required	Units	Item #/ Description	Unit Cost	Extended Cost
1,000	Clothing piece	White, terry cloth bathrobes (Large) Catalog Item # A5400	$20	$20,000
500	Clothing piece	White, terry cloth bathrobes (Medium) Catalog Item # B5400	$20	$10,000
1,500	Accessory	Specialty bathrobe tote bags	$5	$7,500
		TOTAL		$37,500

Authorized by: _Ed Chung_ Title: Purchase Manager   Date: 8/27/2019

Terms and Conditions
1. This Purchase Order is Blue Jay Industries' (BJI) offer to the vendor named above and acceptance is expressly limited to its terms.
2. Please send an invoice/acknowledgment/confirmation to BJI's shipping address.
3. Vendor shall notify BJI as soon as possible if it is unable to fulfill this order on the terms and conditions in this Purchase Order.
4. Delivery beyond the date stated in this Purchase Order shall be subject to cancellation without penalty.

Merchant Transactions

If both parties are merchants, the rules for additional terms are more complicated. In a sales contract acceptance between merchants, additional terms *automatically* become part of the enforceable contract unless one of the following conditions exists:

- The offeror has expressly and clearly limited acceptance to the original terms through language such as "The terms of this purchase order may not be altered or changed and any alteration of the original terms are expressly rejected" (this is common language on a purchase order).

- The additional term is a *material* change that diverges significantly from those contained in the offer (i.e., one that changes the value of the contract or affects the parties' obligation to perform in a significant way).

- The offeror raises an objection to the additional terms within a reasonable time period according to industry standards.

In some cases, one merchant proposes a certain term in the offering document (e.g., the purchase order), but the other merchant's acceptance (e.g., the invoice or

FIGURE 13.2 | Invoice Form

CARDINAL LLC

5000 Anyold Drive, Suite 2500
Anyold Town, NY, 12800, USA
(514) 985-4550

info@cardinalllc.com

www.cardinalllc.com

INVOICE

INVOICE NO: 20XX-354

DATE: 11/20/20XX

TO:	FROM:
Aztec Energy Systems Attn: Raymond Parent 245-3055 Victoria St. St Laurent, QC J4S 1H1 (450) 754-1379	Robert Christenson (as per letterhead co-ordinates)

DESCRIPTION:	COST:
Conduct of a Strategic Planning Review and development of a Corporate Business Plan for Aztec Energy Systems to cover the period 20XX to 20XX as per memorandum of agreement date April 07, 20XX. Itemized cost as follows:	
1. Project initiation, research and familiarization	1,500.00
2. Meetings and preparation of documents for Strategic Planning Session	3,700.00
3. Conduct of 2-Day Strategic Planning Session	2,200.00
4. Drafting of Business Plan for management review	9,700.00
5. Revising and finalizing report as per management comments	1,400.00
6. Executive presentation and submission of final report	1,100.00
7. Travel and accommodation expenses (as per attached receipts)	2,300.12
8. Services Tax at 7%	1,533.00
9. Prov. Tax at 7.5%	1,757.48
TOTAL:	**$ 25,190.60**

TERMS:

Payment in full due within 30 days of invoice date. Interest charge thereafter at 1.25% per day.

SIGNATURE:

acknowledgment form) states a term that is *different* from the offer. In such a case, the majority of states use the **knockout rule**, under which the conflicting clauses knock each other out and neither clause becomes part of the contract. Instead, the courts look to the UCC's gap-filler provisions to supply the term.

TAKEAWAY CONCEPT Battle of the Forms

A battle of the forms occurs when the terms of a buyer's purchase order do not match the terms of a seller's invoice.

LO 13-4

Articulate when sales contracts must be in writing and specify what the writing must contain to be enforceable under the statute of frauds.

STATUTE OF FRAUDS

The statute of frauds is a legal requirement that certain contracts be in writing in order to be enforceable. The UCC contains a specific section detailing the writing requirements for sales transactions. Any sales contract for goods with a total value of *$500 or more* must be in writing.[7]

Why does the UCC require that certain sales contracts be in writing? From a strategic perspective, there are at least two reasons sales contracts over $500 should be in writing. One reason is *cautionary.* By making the parties write down their agreement, the parties will take their agreement more seriously and consider the consequences of breach before entering the agreement. The other reason is *evidentiary.* Without a written contract, one or both of the parties could come into court and lie about the existence or terms of a contract.

Unlike the common law, however, the UCC is much more flexible concerning what contract terms must be in writing. Specifically, for the statute of frauds provision in the UCC to be satisfied, the sales contract must contain in writing (1) the quantity, (2) the signature of the party against whom enforcement is sought, and (3) language that would allow a reasonable person to conclude that the parties intended to form a contract. All other terms and conditions may be proved by testimony concerning oral agreements, past practices, and industry standards.

In Case 13.1, a federal court applies the UCC's statute of fraud to a sales contract between world-famous artist Jean-Michel Basquiat and art dealer Michelle Rosenfeld.

CASE 13.1 Rosenfeld v. Basquiat, 78 F.3d 84 (2d Cir. 1996)

FACT SUMMARY Artist Jean-Michel Basquiat had agreed to sell several of his original paintings to Michelle Rosenfeld, an art dealer in New York City. Rosenfeld requested a receipt for a deposit, and Basquiat, a known eccentric, found a brown piece of wrapping paper and, with a crayon in hand, wrote the names of the paintings, the amount paid, and the names of the parties and then signed the wrapping paper. Basquiat died soon after the sale of the paintings but before the art dealer could take delivery. Basquiat's estate refused to honor the contract on the basis that the writing was not a formal enough contract because it never specified delivery terms. The art dealer sued and won damages. Basquiat's estate appealed.

SYNOPSIS OF DECISION AND OPINION The U.S. Court of Appeals for the 2nd Circuit concluded that a brown piece of wrapping paper that had in crayon the quantity, price, deposit amount, the name of the goods to be sold, and the signature of both parties (also in crayon) complied with Article 2

Michelle Rosenfeld, owner of the famed Rosenfeld Gallery in New York City
©John Roca/NY Daily News Archive via Getty Images

(continued)

---

[7]UCC § 2-201(1).

of the UCC and that the delivery terms were not required to satisfy the UCC's statute of frauds. As a result, the court affirmed the trial court's decision on the statute of frauds.

WORDS OF THE COURT: Statute of Frauds "Because the writing, allegedly scrawled in crayon by Jean-Michel Basquiat on a large piece of paper, easily satisfied the requirements of section 2-201 of the UCC, the estate is not entitled to judgment as a matter of law. It is of no real significance that the jury found Rosenfeld and Basquiat settled on a particular time for delivery and did not commit it to writing. . . ."

Case Questions

1. What if Basquiat had not included the prices of the paintings in question? Would the sales contract still have been enforced?

2. What if Basquiat's estate had produced a more recent sales contract signed by Basquiat agreeing to sell the same paintings for a higher price to another art dealer? Would this second contract have been enforceable?

3. *Focus on Critical Thinking:* Should the law require sales contracts of more than $500 to have additional authentication of a signature (e.g., notarized) to prevent fraud? Why or why not?

The statute of frauds section of the UCC also provides a relatively lenient rule for sales contracts between two merchants. For example, a merchant who receives a signed **confirmation memorandum** from the other merchant will be bound by the memorandum just as if she had signed it, unless she promptly objects. Thus, if Abel telephones Cain to order 1,000 golf balls and then Cain sends a written confirmation of the agreement with the correct quantity and price, Abel will be bound by the contract and the statute of frauds is satisfied.

It is also important to note that the UCC recognizes electronic records and signatures in a sales transaction as valid. This means that the hard copies of documents with original signatures are not always necessary. Although the UCC does not require electronic transactions, it makes clear that a sales contract cannot be held unenforceable simply because it is in electronic form.[8]

TAKEAWAY CONCEPTS Statute of Frauds

- For the statute of frauds provision in the UCC to be satisfied, a sales contract must contain the following items in writing: (1) the quantity, (2) the signature of the party against whom enforcement is sought, and (3) language that would allow a reasonable person to conclude that the parties intended to form a contract.

- All other terms and conditions may be proved by testimony concerning oral agreements, past practices, and industry standards.

 THINKING STRATEGICALLY

©valterZ/Shutterstock

The Battle of the Forms

PROBLEM: If your business receives or issues purchase orders or invoices for products on a regular basis, you may have encountered a situation where both the buyer and seller have issued forms with different terms for the same transaction. In the legal world, we call this situation a *battle of the forms*. Often, when forming a contract, one party makes the offer, whether by invoice, credit application, or otherwise, and the other party accepts or rejects the offer by signing the credit

---

[8]UCC § 2-211.

application, by paying the invoice, or by doing nothing. There usually is no battle of the forms when that happens, as both parties have agreed to identical terms for the transaction. However, in some circumstances a seller will send an invoice that contains one set of terms, while the buyer will issue a purchase order that contains additional or different terms. When a conflict exists, the question becomes, is there a contract at all, and if so, whose terms govern—the buyer's or the seller's? When these problems arise, they often end up in court. A battle of the forms can lead to delays and confusion, and, in the worst cases, to costly and protracted litigation.

STRATEGIC SOLUTION: To avoid a battle of the forms, the first step is to examine how you do business and the forms you use. For instance, if you are a seller of goods or services and you want the contractual terms in your form to control the entire sales process, your liability, or any other specific business concerns you may have, your form should have a provision that makes acceptance by the buyer "expressly conditional on the buyer's assent to only the terms set forth in the seller's contract." If, on the other hand, you are the buyer, and you want your terms to control the purchase, your liability, or any other specific business concerns you may have, you must state in your form/purchase order that your acceptance is expressly conditional on the seller's agreement to the additional or different forms set forth in the buyer's (your) form.

There are many variations of this strategic problem. Basically, if the parties cannot agree, they are letting a court decide what their contract is. The bottom line is: *The forms that your customer or supplier sends to you can change the terms you thought applied.* If you have any questions concerning whether your form says what it needs to say to avoid a battle of the forms, have your attorney take a look. Nothing you or your attorney do can completely eliminate the risk of a battle of the forms and subsequent litigation; however, close scrutiny of your forms and the way you do business can minimize that risk.

QUESTIONS

1. Why does the battle of the forms pose a strategic risk to business firms?
2. How can business firms reduce this risk?

KEY TERMS

Merchant's firm offer p. 241   An offer in writing between merchants to buy or sell goods along with a promise without consideration to keep that offer for a stated amount of time or, if unstated, no longer than three months.

Open terms p. 241   Unspecified terms in a sales contract that do not detract from the validity of the contract so long as the parties intended to make the contract and other specified terms give a basis for remedy in case of breach.

Output contract p. 241   A contract in which the buyer agrees to buy all the goods that the seller produces for a set time and at a set price and the seller may sell only to that one buyer. The quantity for the contract is the seller's output.

Requirements contract p. 241   A contract in which the buyer agrees to buy whatever he needs from the seller during a set period and the buyer may buy only from that one seller. The quantity for the contract is what the buyer requires.

Purchase order p. 243   A form commonly used in sales contracts as an offer from the buyer; contains preprinted clauses along with blanks to accommodate the specifics of the transaction.

Acknowledgment form p. 243   A form commonly used in sales contracts as an acceptance from the seller in response to a purchase order; contains preprinted provisions and has blanks to accommodate the specifics of the transaction. Also referred to as an *invoice*.

Battle of the forms p. 243   The conflict between the terms written into standardized purchase (offer) and acknowledgment (acceptance) forms, which differ in that one form favors the buyer and the other the seller. The UCC attempts to broker a truce in this battle while keeping the contract of sale intact.

Knockout rule p. 245   As applied in many states, the view that when a buyer and seller engage in a battle of the forms and different terms are exchanged, both the seller's and buyer's differing terms drop out and UCC gap fillers are substituted to complete the contract.

Confirmation memorandum p. 247   A written verification of an agreement. Under the statute of frauds section of the UCC, a merchant who receives a signed confirmation memorandum from another merchant will be bound by the memorandum just as if she had signed it, unless she promptly objects.

Battle of the Forms

Mozaffarian signed a credit agreement in which he expressly acknowledged receipt of, and agreed to be bound by, terms and conditions contained in an extrinsic (external) document, which he had neither read nor requested a copy of to read. The credit agreement identified the terms and conditions as those contained on each invoice. After the credit application was approved, he then saw, for the first time, the terms and conditions, which contained a New York forum selection clause. Movado proved by a preponderance of the evidence that the terms and conditions of the extrinsic document were incorporated into the credit agreement that the defendant acknowledged having received. The credit

agreement, which identified the terms and conditions as those contained on each invoice, was sufficient to put the defendant on notice that there was an additional document of legal import to the contract he was executing.

CASE QUESTIONS

1. Was the forum selection clause an additional term, a different term, a confirmatory writing, or a term incorporated into the document? Explain.
2. In your opinion, does the fact that Mozaffarian never requested to see the extrinsic document have any bearing on the outcome of this case? Why or why not?

Additional Terms

Hebberd-Kulow Enterprises (HKE) sold agricultural supplies to Kelomar over a period of approximately 20 years between 1987 and 2007. During that time, Kelomar routinely ordered products over the phone. In these phone calls, the parties' representatives would discuss and agree to the type of item, its quantity, and its price. Kelomar provided HKE with a purchase order number for the requested items, but it never sent a formal purchase order document. After delivery of the items to Kelomar, HKE would send Kelomar an invoice that corresponded to the applicable purchase order number. In 2003, HKE began to include a provision for late payments on its invoices: "Unpaid invoices beyond terms will be assessed a monthly service charge of 1-1/2%." According to HKE, the late penalty interest rate was standard in the industry. Although Kelomar often paid late, HKE never charged Kelomar interest on the late payments because of their long-term business relationship. HKE never informed Kelomar of the new provision and Kelomar never objected to it.

A dispute between the parties arose after HKE delivered approximately $250,000 worth of goods in 2007. These goods were shipped separately with corresponding invoices. Kelomar refused to pay the invoices

because it claimed to have incurred damages in a *different* set of contractual transactions with HKE that were unrelated to the $250,000 shipment. HKE sued for the price of the goods and also for late payment interest on the amount due based on the late payment provision included on the invoices. A jury awarded HKE damages for the unpaid 2007 invoices as well as for the late payment interest included on the invoices. Kelomar appealed, arguing, among other things, that the penalty interest was not part of the agreement under the UCC's battle of the forms provision and that failing to enforce the late payment penalty in the past barred HKE from recovering it in this case.

The California Court of Appeals affirmed the jury's award in favor of HKE. The court concluded that the jury had properly applied the battle of the forms standards in finding that the late payment penalty was part of the contract in the 2012 invoices, and the court rejected Kelomar's argument that the interest language on the invoices, even if known to it, contained an additional term that would never be enforced because of their course of past dealing. The court pointed out that HKE established that Kelomar did not raise a timely objection to the interest provision and that such provision was a standard one in the industry that was not unexpected between merchants.

CASE QUESTIONS

1. Why didn't HKE charge Kelomar the late interest charge until this dispute?

2. In your opinion, why did the court reject Kelomar's argument that it was reasonable to think that HKE had waived the late interest charge and was barred from enforcing it? Should HKE be able to choose when it does and when it doesn't enforce the clause?

CASE SUMMARY 13.3 Daitom, Inc. v. Pennwalt Corp., 741 F.2d 1569 (10th Cir. 1984)

Battle of the Forms Redux

Daitom invited bids from manufacturers of commercial vacuum dryers to supply it with machinery Daitom needed to build a chemical manufacturing plant. Pennwalt submitted a proposal specifying the equipment to be sold, the price, and delivery and payment terms. Several pages of Pennwalt's pre-printed terms and conditions were attached and incorporated into its bid, including a clause providing for a one-year statute of limitations and a clause disclaiming any and all implied warranties. Daitom accepted Pennwalt's proposal by issuing its own "purchase order" containing 17 pages of detailed terms and conditions. The purchase order language did not contain a statute of limitations, but it did include an implied warranty clause. When the machinery sold by Pennwalt failed to work properly, Daitom brought a proceeding against Pennwalt more than one year later, alleging, among other things, a breach of the implied warranty.

CASE QUESTIONS

1. Should the court apply the knockout rule to this case? (Be sure to explain how the knockout rule works.)
2. What steps could Daitom have taken to avoid a battle of the forms?

CHAPTER REVIEW QUESTIONS

1. If the parties have not agreed otherwise, what are the default delivery terms in a contract for the sale of goods?
   a. Buyer takes delivery at seller's place of business.
   b. Seller delivers to carrier.
   c. Seller delivers to buyer's place of business.
   d. Buyer takes delivery at the closest port or warehouse.
   e. The contract is void for vagueness.

2. Which of the following things do courts **not** consider when filling gaps in incomplete or slightly ambiguous contracts for the sale of goods?

   I. Past commercial conduct
   II. Industry standards or norms
   III. Judicial imputation of any terms necessary to maintain fairness
   IV. Previous correspondence or verbal exchanges between the parties

   a. I and II
   b. II and III
   c. III
   d. I, III, and IV
   e. I, II, III, and IV

3. If Continental Tires agrees to purchase all the rubber produced by a particular Brazilian rubber plantation, this agreement would be:
   a. An output contract.
   b. An input contract.
   c. A requirements contract.
   d. A purchase order.
   e. An invoice.

4. **When one merchant sends another merchant a pre-printed purchase order and the receiving merchant then issues a preprinted invoice that has additional terms, this situation is known as:**

   a. A nonmerchant transaction.

   b. An open terms form.

   c. Battle of the forms.

   d. An output contract.

   e. An additional term sheet.

5. **For a writing to satisfy statute of frauds requirements under the UCC, it must include each of the following except:**

   a. Quantity.

   b. Number of goods to be sold.

   c. The signature of the party against whom enforcement is sought.

   d. Language that a reasonable person would believe constitutes an intent to form a contract.

   e. Place of delivery.

6. **A firm offer is always revocable.**

   a. True

   b. False

7. **An offer for the sale of goods with open terms regarding quantity, delivery, or payment terms is not legally enforceable under the UCC.**

   a. True

   b. False

8. **A sales agreement with a total value under $500 need not be in writing in order to be legally enforceable.**

   a. True

   b. False

9. **The UCC allows contracts to be modified even without any additional consideration.**

   a. True

   b. False

10. **The knockout rule usually applies when there is a battle of the forms between merchants.**

    a. True

    b. False

 Quick Quiz ANSWERS
Sales Contracts

1. Most courts would hold that the transaction on the seventh month constituted an enforceable contract under Article 2 of the UCC, even though Retailer did not subjectively intend to have the iPhone contract linger into seven months. Under the UCC, the larger picture was that the parties' *conduct* indicated that they had an ongoing series of contracts with certain terms. Retailer must exercise some conduct to indicate that the contract is at an end (a simple e-mail would suffice) before the delivery date in the seventh month in order for the contract to be considered at an end.

2. Despite the missing quantity, courts will generally enforce an agreement in which the buyer agrees to purchase all or up to an agreed amount of what the buyer needs for a given period. This type of commercial transaction is known as a *requirements contract.*

CHAPTER REVIEW QUESTIONS: Answers and Explanations

1. **a.** When the parties have not agreed otherwise, UCC § 2-308 requires the buyer to take delivery at the seller's place of business. Answers *b, c,* and *d* are inconsistent with the UCC provision governing delivery terms. Answer *e* is nonsensical.

2. **c.** The UCC does not authorize courts to impute any terms necessary to maintain fairness. It does, however, allow courts to enforce a sales contract based on past commercial conduct, industry standards and norms, and correspondence or verbal exchanges between the parties.

3. **a.** An output contract occurs when the buyer agrees to purchase *all* of the known goods that a seller produces. Answer *b* is incorrect because it uses the wrong terminology. Answer *c* is incorrect because a requirements contract occurs when the buyer agrees to purchase all or up to an agreed amount of what the buyer needs for a given period. Answer *d* is incorrect because a purchase order is simply an offer from a buyer. Answer *e* is incorrect because an invoice is an acceptance from a seller in response to a purchase order.

4. **c.** *Battle of the forms* is the term used to describe the process of determining which additional terms become part of a contract and which do not. Answer *a* is incorrect because both parties are merchants. Answers *b* and *e* are nonsensical. Answer *d* is incorrect because it does not refer to conflicting terms.

5. **e.** As we saw in Case 13.1, terms of delivery are not required to be in writing under the UCC. The statute of frauds provision in the UCC is satisfied so long as the sales contract contains in writing the quantity (or number of items to be sold), the signature of the party against whom enforcement is sought, and language that would allow a reasonable person to conclude that the parties intended to form a contract. All other terms and conditions may be proved by testimony concerning oral agreements, past practices, and industry standards.

6. **b. False.** When a seller makes a firm offer (i.e., promises in a signed writing to keep an offer for the sale of goods open for a period of time), such a firm offer is deemed irrevocable under Article 2 of the UCC.

7. **b. False.** An offer with open terms is entirely acceptable under the UCC so long as there is evidence that the parties intended to enter into a contract and the other terms are sufficiently articulated to provide a basis for some appropriate remedy in case of breach.

8. **a. True.** Only sales contract for goods with a total value of $500 or more must be in writing.

9. **a. True.** Although the UCC requires consideration to support a new sales contract, the UCC allows existing contracts to be modified even without any additional consideration.

10. **a. True.** The knockout rule applies to merchant transactions involving a battle of the forms.

CHAPTER 14

Title, Allocation of Risk, and Insurable Interest

THINKING STRATEGICALLY

A critical issue in business is the appropriate management of risk. In this chapter's *Thinking Strategically* section, you will learn how companies can strategically manage risk of title, shipping, and insurance in the purchase and sale of goods.

Learning Objectives

After studying this chapter, students who have mastered the material will be able to:

14-1   Recognize the elements necessary to identify goods to a contract.

14-2   Demonstrate how title passes from the seller to the buyer.

14-3   Describe an insurable interest.

14-4   Compare the various shipment terms to determine who bears the risk of loss during shipment.

CHAPTER OVERVIEW

Title is an important legal concept that implies the ownership of property. The sale of goods (movable property) is governed by the Uniform Commercial Code (UCC) and involves the transfer of title from a seller to a buyer. Business owners and managers should have a working knowledge of the UCC provisions regarding title and risk allocation because these rules determine commercial risks at various stages of a business transaction. Every business, even those that are service-based, will need to purchase goods. However, once a contract has been entered into by the parties, there is likely to be a lapse of time before the buyer acquires title to the goods.

For example, assume Blaze Pizza Oven Co. promises to sell a new commercial pizza oven to University Pies, LLC for $12,000 to be delivered within 30 calendar days. What happens if, during the delivery process, the oven is damaged in a trucking accident? Or suppose that the oven is manufactured overseas and will be delivered to a port to be picked up by University Pies, but during the unloading process the oven is damaged. Who bears the burden of loss? In both cases, University Pies still needs a pizza oven, whereas Blaze Pizza Oven Co. made good faith efforts to deliver the goods as promised. The UCC provides answers to these types of questions with its default provisions governing title and risk of loss.

IDENTIFICATION OF GOODS

Title is the legal term for a claim of ownership to property. The UCC requires two things to occur before title to the goods can pass from the seller to the buyer. First, the goods must actually exist.[1] This is not an issue if the buyer purchases goods from the seller's existing inventory of goods for sale. In some cases, however, the goods have yet to be manufactured and do not exist at the time of contracting. Dell, for example, pioneered a made-to-order personal computer business. A buyer contracts for the purchase of computing hardware ahead of time that is made-to-order according to the buyer's specifications. The items are then shipped by Dell to the buyer after the purchase.

The second requirement is that the goods must be **identified to the contract**.[2] What this means is that the parties have specifically identified which goods will be sold to the buyer. This requirement is satisfied during the sale of an automobile when the car is identified to the contract with a description and vehicle identification number (VIN). Similarly, goods may be identified to the contract with specific lot numbers or markings. Otherwise, if goods are not identified to the contract, they become identified when the seller marks, ships, or separates the goods for sale to the buyer.[3] In their contract, the parties may agree on any method they desire to identify the goods.

TAKEAWAY CONCEPTS Identification of Goods

- Title is the legal term for a claim of ownership to property.
- For title to pass to the buyer, the goods must exist and be identified to the contract.
- The parties may agree on any method they desire to identify the goods to the contract.

ISSUES RELATED TO TITLE TRANSFERS

When the goods exist and are identified in the contract, title may pass to the buyer if the parties specify how title will be transferred. If the parties fail to specify how title will pass to the buyer, the UCC has default provisions that determine this issue. Under the UCC, a good faith buyer may, in some circumstances, acquire valid title to goods he bought from someone who improperly obtained the property, for example, through fraud. Each of these issues is discussed next.

Passing of Title

The parties may specify in their contract how and when title will pass to the buyer. The UCC states that title may pass in any manner on which the parties agree.[4] For example, the parties may agree that the title will pass when the buyer pays for the goods upon delivery, for example cash on delivery, or COD. Or they may agree that the title passes once the goods leave the seller's warehouse. In cases where the parties do not specify when title will pass, UCC Section 2-401 provides the following three default-rule possibilities.

---

[1] UCC § 2-105 (2).
[2] UCC § 2-401(1).
[3] UCC § 2-501(1).
[4] UCC § 2-401(1).

1. If the goods are to be shipped, title passes to the buyer once the seller meets its obligation to ship the goods as specified in the contract. Note that the contract may only require the seller to deliver the goods to a common freight carrier, such as the U.S. Postal Service, FedEx, or a rail company, who will then transport the goods to the buyer's location. In this case, title passes when the seller delivers the goods to the common freight carrier.

2. If the contract does not require shipment, the goods will remain stored, for example in a warehouse. In this case, the contract may require the seller to deliver documents of title, such as a warehouse receipt or a bill of lading (documents of title are discussed in Chapter 23), to the seller. Title passes to the buyer when the seller delivers these documents of title to the buyer as required in the contract.

3. If the contract does not require shipping or the delivery of documents of title, title passes to the buyer when the contract is made effective and the goods are identified to the contract.

Figure 14.1 illustrates the path to obtain title in the sale and purchase of goods.

FIGURE 14.1   UCC Title Default Rules

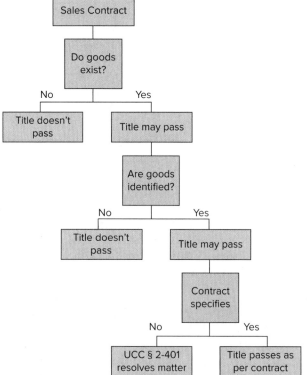

Good Faith Buyers

The UCC has a rule regarding when a good faith buyer can acquire valid title to improperly obtained goods. A **good faith buyer** is someone who acts honestly and provides reasonable value for the goods. A good faith buyer must not know or suspect that the goods were obtained improperly. The UCC rule is that a good faith buyer acquires valid title so long as the seller obtained a *voidable* title. In contrast, a good faith buyer does not acquire valid title if the seller obtained a *void* title. A **voidable title** involves a purchase of goods through fraud or deceit. A **void title** involves property obtained through theft. Therefore, the acquisition of stolen property, even by a good faith purchaser, always results in the stolen property being returned to its rightful owner. If the property was acquired through fraud or deceit, however, a purchaser may keep the property and retain valid title as long as he was a good faith buyer.

Case 14.1 involves a state appellate decision that illustrates the concept of multiple good faith buyers who purchased a used car.

CASE 14.1 Hodges Wholesale Cars and Cleveland Auto Sales v. Auto Dealer's Exchange of Birmingham and Express Drive Away, 628 So.2d 608 (1993)

FACT SUMMARY Doyle Alexander, a Georgia resident, owned a 1986 Mercury Grand Marquis automobile. He sold that car to an individual whose identity was not disclosed in the record ("the initial buyer"). Alexander endorsed the back of the certificate of title to the car and gave it to the initial buyer. In return, the initial buyer fraudulently gave Alexander a check that later proved to have insufficient funds. After he purchased the car from Alexander, the initial buyer quickly resold the car to Express Drive Away. Express then resold the car to Cleveland Auto Sales through an auction conducted by Auto Exchange. Cleveland resold the car to M & T Motors through Big H Auto Auction in Houston, Texas. The car was ultimately sold to Rosa DeLara.

When he discovered the check had insufficient funds, Alexander told Georgia law enforcement authorities that the car had been stolen. The car was located in Texas by Texas authorities and was taken from Ms. DeLara. M & T Motors voluntarily refunded the purchase price of the car to Ms. DeLara, and Cleveland voluntarily reimbursed M & T Motors. Cleveland then brought the present action against Express and Auto Exchange, alleging breach of contract, fraud, and breach of warranty of good title. The trial court entered summary judgments for Express and Auto Exchange.

SYNOPSIS OF DECISION AND OPINION The appellate court affirmed the lower trial court and held that the sale involved a voidable title, therefore a good faith buyer could acquire valid title. Since Express was a good faith buyer, it acquired and transferred valid title to Cleveland and was not liable for breach of contract, fraud, or breach of implied warranty.

WORDS OF THE COURT: UCC's Treatment of Good Faith Buyers' Ability to Acquire Valid Title "Cleveland's basis of this action is founded upon the assumption that when Cleveland purchased the car from Express at the auction conducted by Auto Exchange, it did not receive a good, unencumbered title to the car. In other words, Cleveland contends that it received a 'void' title to the car. Based on Ala.Code 1975, § 7-2-403, we find this assumption to be false. That section reads in part as follows:

1. A purchaser of goods acquires all title which his transferor had or had power to transfer. . . . A person with voidable title has power to transfer a good title to a good faith purchaser for value. When goods have been delivered under a transaction of purchase the purchaser has such power even though:
   (a) The transferor was deceived as to the identity of the purchaser, or
   (b) The delivery was in exchange for a check which is later dishonored, or
   (c) It was agreed that the transaction was to be a 'cash sale,' or
   (d) The delivery was procured through fraud punishable as larcenous under the criminal law.

"Pre-Uniform Commercial Code law generally held that a party to a transfer could convey no better title to goods than he had. However § 7-2-403 modifies this rule and establishes that a party with only voidable title can pass good title to a third-party purchaser who acts in good faith. The good faith purchaser is then sheltered from attempts by the original seller to regain the goods.

(continued)

"Therefore, the initial question is whether Alexander conveyed 'voidable title' to the initial buyer, within the meaning of Ala.Code 1975, § 7-2-403. Although the delivery of the car may have been procured through fraud, it was not a theft. 'A thief who wrongfully takes goods is not a purchaser . . . but a swindler who fraudulently induces the victim to voluntarily deliver them is a purchaser. . . .' Therefore, there was a 'transaction of purchase' within the meaning of § 7-2-403, and the buyer had 'voidable' title to the car.

"Because the initial [fraudulent] buyer had voidable title to the car, rather than void title, he had the power to transfer good title to a good faith purchaser for value. It is undisputed that Express acted in good faith when it purchased the car from the initial buyer. Express did not know, and had no reason to know, that the initial buyer's representations were false. Express received good title to the car, which it conveyed to Cleveland at the auction conducted by Auto Exchange. Therefore, the trial court properly entered the summary judgments against Cleveland. The summary judgments are affirmed."

Case Questions

1. Was the car properly taken from Ms. DeLara by the police?
2. Was M & T Motors legally or ethically obligated to refund the purchase price to Ms. De Lara?
3. *Focus on Critical Thinking:* Had Ms. DeLara been able to keep the car as a good faith buyer, who would bear the risk of loss? Why is this a good or bad policy?

Under Section 1-201 of the UCC, a good faith **buyer in ordinary course of business** may acquire valid title to goods that were entrusted to a merchant seller. For example, Rita owns a painting, which she loans to Rico, an art dealer, to display in his art gallery. While on display, Rico sells the artwork to Anthony. Since Rico is a merchant who deals in the kind of goods involved in the sale and Anthony is a good faith purchaser who assumed the artwork was purchased legitimately, the sale will be upheld. Rita's sole recourse will be against Rico, not Anthony.

TAKEAWAY CONCEPTS Issues Related to Title Transfers

- The parties may specify in their contract how and when title will pass to the buyer.
- In cases where the parties do not specify when title will pass, UCC Section 2-401 applies.
- A good faith buyer is someone who acts honestly and provides reasonable value for the goods.
- Good faith buyers can acquire valid title if the seller obtained a voidable title.

LO 14-3

Describe an insurable interest.

INSURABLE INTEREST

Parties may wish to insure goods under various scenarios after the goods have been purchased. For example, if the goods are stolen from the seller's warehouse or they are damaged in transit to the buyer, someone will bear the loss. Insurance provides a way for the parties to allocate the risk of loss through contract with an insurer. Insurance companies will not insure property, however, unless the party seeking insurance has an **insurable interest**. An insurable interest exists when loss or damage to something or someone causes a person to suffer a financial or other kind of recognizable loss. Title to property is one way to obtain an insurable interest; however, the UCC recognizes that the buyer may want to insure the goods before acquiring title.

For example, say University Pizza contracts with Blaze Pizza Oven Co. for the purchase of a commercial pizza oven, and the contract identifies a specific oven with a serial number. The contract specifies that Blaze need only deliver the oven to a common carrier; therefore, title will not pass until the common carrier takes possession of the oven for delivery. Before then, University Pizza may wish to insure the goods after signing the contract in case the common carrier lacks appropriate insurance and the goods are damaged in transit. The UCC, therefore, allows the buyer to obtain an insurable interest in the goods without title as long as the goods are identified to the contract. Under this framework, both the buyer and the seller may have overlapping insurable interests in the goods since title has not yet passed.

TAKEAWAY CONCEPTS Insurable Interest

- An insurable interest exists when loss or damage to something or someone causes a person to suffer a financial or other kind of loss.
- Title creates an insurable interest.
- A buyer acquires an insurable interest when the goods are identified to the contract.

RISK OF LOSS

LO 14-4

Compare the various shipment terms to determine who bears the risk of loss during shipment.

The UCC determines when the title passes between the seller and the buyer and allocates **risk of loss** from an accident, mishandling, or theft based on whether the agreement is categorized as a *shipment contract* or a *destination contract.*

Shipment contracts require the seller to use a carrier (a delivery company such as the U.S. Postal Service, FedEx, or UPS) to deliver the goods. As a general rule, all contracts for the sale of goods are considered shipment contracts *unless* the parties have agreed otherwise. Thus, the seller needs only to deliver the goods to the "hands" of the carrier to achieve complete performance. Once the seller has accomplished this, title is deemed to have passed to the buyer.[5] Normally, the risk of loss is allocated to the seller until such time as the seller has delivered the goods to the carrier. If the goods are destroyed after that point, the loss is ordinarily borne by the buyer. Note that the buyer may have recourse against the carrier but not against the seller. For example, Schubert Co. agrees to sell Hristo a specially designed grand piano for $50,000. Hristo instructs Schubert to deliver the piano from his factory via a specific carrier, Piano Delivery Services (PDS), within 10 business days. On day 1, Schubert delivers the piano to PDS in good condition. On day 2, the PDS truck collides with another vehicle and the piano is destroyed. Because the title and risk of loss passed to Hristo at the point when Schubert delivered the piano to the carrier, Hristo has no course of action against Schubert. However, he may have a claim against the carrier (PDS).

Destination contracts require the seller to deliver the goods to a specified destination. Typically, the destination is the buyer's place of business or home, but it also can be a third-party destination that the buyer designates, such as a warehouse. The UCC provides that complete performance occurs when the goods have been **tendered** at the specified destination. *Tendering* is the legal term for delivery of conforming goods; that is, the seller delivered what the buyer actually ordered to a destination that allows the buyer to take delivery.[6] Normally, so long as the goods are properly tendered as agreed, the risk of loss is allocated to the buyer at the time of tender. For example, in the Schubert-Hristo contract discussed

---

[5]UCC § 2-401(2)(a).
[6]UCC § 2-503.

above, suppose that the parties specifically designate their agreement as a *destination contract* and agree that Schubert must deliver the piano to Hristo's performance studio in New Orleans. Schubert selects his own carrier, Cheapo Trucks, Inc., and the truck catches fire in transit. In this case, the loss must be borne by the seller (Schubert) because the piano is destroyed before it arrives at its New Orleans destination.[7]

The International Chamber of Commerce has published a set of international shipping terms, called the International Commercial (INCO) terms, that allocate risk of loss. Table 14.1 lists the various INCO terms used by businesses worldwide.

TABLE 14.1   International Chamber of Commerce (INCO) Shipping Terms

INCO Term	Description
Free on Board (FOB)–place of shipment	Seller must put the goods in the possession of a carrier at the place identified, usually the seller's warehouse. Buyer then pays for the shipment costs and assumes the risk once the goods are in the carrier's possession. The buyer must rely on its own or a carrier's insurance to cover the risk of loss during transit.
Free on Board (FOB)–place of destination	Seller is responsible for shipping the goods to the place named and must incur all the shipping costs to that destination, usually the buyer's location. Seller also assumes the risk during transit and must rely on its own or the carrier's insurance to cover risk of loss.
Cost, Insurance, and Freight (CIF)	The buyer's purchase price includes shipment and insurance for risk of loss. Seller is responsible for delivering the goods to the carrier, who will then ship to the buyer's location. Title and risk of loss will transfer to the buyer once the carrier obtains the goods.
Cost and Freight (CF)	The buyer's purchase price includes shipment expenses. Seller is responsible for delivering the goods to the carrier, who will then ship to the buyer's location. Title and risk of loss will transfer to the buyer once the carrier obtains the goods. The buyer must ascertain whether the goods are properly insured during transit.

An important UCC provision that protects the buyer when a seller has shipped nonconforming goods relates to the risk of loss. The UCC protects a buyer when delivery of nonconforming goods creates a right of rejection. It provides that the risk of loss remains on the seller until the seller corrects the problem or the buyer accepts the goods. This protection also exists when the buyer rightfully revokes acceptance. The idea is that the law does not allow a seller to shift the risk of loss to the buyer unless the contract conforms with all the agreed-upon conditions.

 Quick Quiz   Using INCO Shipping Terms

1. Seller is located in Seattle and Buyer is located in Phoenix. The contract specifies FOB Seattle. Who bears the risk of loss if the goods are stolen halfway between Seattle and Phoenix?

2. Seller is located in Seattle and Buyer is located in Phoenix. The contract specifies FOB Phoenix. Who bears the risk of loss if the goods are damaged halfway between Seattle and Phoenix?

3. Seller is located in Seattle and Buyer is located in Phoenix. The contract specifies CIF. Who bears the risk of loss if the goods are lost halfway between Seattle and Phoenix?

Answers to this Quick Quiz are provided at the end of the chapter.

---

[7] UCC § 2-509(3).

- *Shipment contracts* require the seller to use a carrier (a delivery company such as the U.S. Postal Service, FedEx, or UPS) to deliver the goods.
- *Destination contracts* require the seller to deliver the goods to a specified destination.
- As a general rule, all contracts for the sale of goods are considered shipment contracts unless the parties have agreed otherwise.
- Normally, the risk of loss is allocated to the seller until such time as the seller has delivered the goods to the carrier.
- INCO shipping terms that allocate risk of loss are standardized internationally.

THINKING STRATEGICALLY

©valterZ/Shutterstock

Strategic Assessment of Shipping Terms

PROBLEM: Managers tasked with logistics or supply chain oversight will often authorize purchase contracts. The terms in these purchase agreements should be carefully assessed to maximize value and minimize risks during shipment.

STRATEGIC SOLUTION: In this chapter we discussed how shipment terms can minimize risks of loss in transit and ensure adequate delivery. Consider the following fact scenario to identify the potential risks and pitfalls during shipment and how these can be avoided or managed.

Peter is the general manager of High Rollers Casino in Las Vegas. Peter and his marketing team have devised a new plan to introduce an all-you-can-eat caviar buffet to reward and entice high rollers who meet certain gambling thresholds. To execute this strategy, Peter needs to have large quantities of caviar shipped to the casino on a weekly basis. Peter is ready to sign a sales contract with a company based out of Brooklyn, New York, called Premium Seafoods, Inc. Fred, the general manager of Premium Seafoods, quotes a price of $800 per pound for caviar. The purchase price for Peter's initial order of 20 pounds of caviar is $16,000. Fred sends Peter a written contract to sign with the following shipping terms:

CAVIAR PURCHASE AGREEMENT FOB (WAREHOUSE LOADING) BROOKLYN, NY

This Caviar Purchase Agreement is entered by High Rollers Casino, Inc., domiciled in Las Vegas, Nevada (hereinafter the "BUYER"), and PREMIUM SEAFOODS, INC., domiciled in Brooklyn, New York (hereinafter the "SELLER"), on June 10, 2017, under the following terms and conditions:

2. CLAUSE TWO: PURCHASE

2.1. GENERAL CONDITIONS

2.1.1. CAVIAR taken from general inventory will be sold by the SELLER to the BUYER, who will acquire it under F.O.B. Seller's Warehouse in Brooklyn, NY, to be shipped with due care by FlybyNight Trucking, LLC, properly crated/packaged/boxed suitable for cross-country motor freight transit.

2.1.1.1. PROPERTY AND RISK: By virtue of this agreement and as indicated hereof, the BUYER will assume the property and the risk for the CAVIAR upon being stowed on the trucks at SELLER'S warehouse. Upon stowing the CAVIAR onboard the trucks, the BUYER will assume all risks for losses of such CAVIAR, whether in transit to the destination markets, during unloading, or at any later point of the distribution and sale chain, with no prejudice to what is stipulated further down regarding hidden quality conditions that are impossible to detect during loading.

QUESTIONS

1. Peter would like to obtain an insurable interest upon signing the contract. Will he be able to do this? Explain.

2. Peter is concerned about the product arriving as quickly as possible due to the product's spoilage potential. What should he be concerned about? How can he mitigate this risk?

3. Peter runs a company search and learns that Flyby-Night Trucking has a history of failing to maintain adequate insurance. What should Peter do to minimize risk when dealing with FlybyNight Trucking?

4. Given the nature of the goods, is there a better shipping method than the one specified in the contract?

5. Which shipping terms would offer better security to High Rollers Casino?

KEY TERMS

Title p. 255   The legal term for ownership in property; confers on the titleholder the exclusive use of personal property and the rights to sell, lease, or prohibit another from using the property.

Identified to the contract p. 255   When the parties have specifically identified which goods will be sold to the buyer.

Good faith buyer p. 256   Someone who acts honestly and provides reasonable value for the goods.

Voidable title p. 257   An invalid title obtained through fraud or deceit.

Void title p. 257   An invalid title obtained through theft.

Buyer in ordinary course of business p. 258   A person who buys goods from a merchant in the business of selling the goods without knowledge that the sale violates the rights of another person.

Insurable interest p. 258   An interest by the insured in the value of what is being insured that arises from a financial or legal relationship.

Risk of loss p. 259   The uncertainty an event will occur that triggers liability or loss of property.

Shipment contract p. 259   Contract that requires the seller to use a third-party carrier to deliver the goods.

Destination contract p. 259   Contract that requires the seller to deliver the goods to a specified destination, usually the buyer's location.

Tendered p. 259   When the seller delivers conforming goods to a destination that allows the buyer to take delivery.

CASE SUMMARY 14.1 3L Communications v. Merola d/b/a NY Telecom Supply, No. M2012- 02163-COA-R3-CV, Court of Appeals of Tennessee (2013)

Rejected Goods and Risk of Loss

In accordance with their agreement, Merola shipped circuit boards to 3L via Federal Express, with the balance of $35,090 due on delivery in the form of a cashier's check. The circuit boards arrived at 3L's office and were paid for as agreed. However, upon inspection of the circuit boards, 3L discovered that the boards were damaged and were not as Merola had described. 3L immediately contacted Merola and notified her that the boards were unusable and that 3L was returning them. In response, Merola provided shipping instructions and an account number to be used for returning the goods. 3L followed the shipping instructions and the boards were returned to Merola's address. Two weeks later, 3L sent an e-mail message to Merola regarding the refund for the boards. Merola responded that she had not received the returned boards. After Merola stopped responding to 3L's inquiries, 3L filed suit to recover its $35,090 payment.

CASE QUESTIONS

1. Was this a shipment contract, or a destination contract? Explain.

2. Who bears the risk of loss in this case?

Insurable Interest

Frelinghuysen Morris Foundation (FMF) was established to house the unsold collection of American abstract artists L.K. Morris and Estelle "Suzy" Frelinghuysen, who died in 1975 and 1988, respectively. Since 1995, the trust had consigned with the Salander-O'Reilly Galleries to occasionally display these paintings for exhibition and/or sale. FMF filed an insurance claim for its estimated $2.1 million in losses from the gallery's sale of 41 paintings, from which it did not receive any proceeds. AXA Insurance denied the claim, stating, among other reasons, that the circumstances did not constitute a fortuitous physical loss of artwork and that, since the art was seized by the New York State Court, claims for it were excluded under the $30 million policy in question.

CASE QUESTIONS

1. Does the ownership of artwork create an insurable interest?
2. If artwork is given to an art gallery to display and sell on behalf of the owners, and then the gallery commits fraud against the art owners, does this fraud create an insurable interest?

Destination Contracts

Brawn mails clothing to customers and requires them to pay the listed price for the goods, plus a delivery fee and an insurance fee to replace items lost or damaged in transit. Brawn then hands the clothing to a carrier for delivery to the customer. Buyers sued, arguing that the contracts were destination contracts because Brawn made sure the goods were to be delivered to the buyers and that, as destination contracts, Brawn as the seller already had responsibility to insure the goods until they reached the buyer. Brawn argued that the contracts were CIF contracts and that the added insurance fee was proper due to the status of the contracts as shipment contracts.

CASE QUESTIONS

1. Are these contracts shipment or destination contracts?
2. How would buyers ensure that Brawn was responsible for insuring the goods until delivery to the buyer?

Shipment Contracts

Shared Imaging, an American corporation, entered into a contract for the purchase of an MRI scanner with Neuromed, a German corporation. According to the complaint, the MRI was loaded aboard the vessel *Atlantic Carrier* undamaged and in good working order. When it reached its destination of Calumet City, Illinois, it had been damaged and was in need of extensive repair, which led the plaintiffs to conclude that the MRI had been damaged in transit. The one-page contract of sale contains nine headings, including: "Product"; "Delivery Terms"; "Payment Terms"; "Disclaimer"; and "Applicable Law." Under "Product," the contract specifies the "system will be delivered cold and fully functional." Under "Delivery Terms" it states, "CIF New York Seaport, the buyer will arrange and pay for customs clearance as well as transport to Calumet City." In addition, under "Disclaimer" it states, "system including all accessories and options remain the property of Neuromed till complete payment has been received." The plaintiff argued that this last item negated the CIF clause and that, because Neuromed retained title, Neuromed assumed the risk of loss in transit.

1. Who bears the risk of loss if the court finds that the contract was indeed a CIF contract?
2. Who should bear the risk of loss in this case and why?

CASE SUMMARY 14.5 Windows, Inc. v. Jordan Panel Systems Corp., 177 F.3d 114 (1999)

Risk of Loss

Windows, Inc. sold windows to a subcontractor, Jordan Panel Systems. The windows were transported by a carrier called Consolidated Freightways and arrived badly damaged. Jordan refused payment. The purchase contract stated: "All windows to be shipped properly crated/packaged/boxed suitable for cross country motor freight transit and delivered to New York City." The contract did not use any of the standard INCO shipping terms.

CASE QUESTIONS

1. Is this a shipment or destination contract?
2. Who should bear the loss of these broken windows?

CHAPTER REVIEW QUESTIONS

1. **For title to pass from the seller to the buyer, the UCC requires:**
   a. That the goods exist.
   b. That the goods be worth more than $500.
   c. That the goods be identified to the contract.
   d. A and C.
   e. B and C.

2. **A good faith buyer has unknowingly purchased stolen goods. That good faith buyer has:**
   a. A voidable title.
   b. A void title.
   c. Tendered the goods.
   d. A valid title.
   e. None of the above.

3. **A good faith buyer has unknowingly purchased goods obtained through fraud. That good faith buyer has:**
   a. A voidable title.
   b. A void title.
   c. Tendered the goods.
   d. A valid title.
   e. None of the above.

4. **All of the following are examples of an insurable interest except:**
   a. Insurance on the home you own.
   b. Insurance on the car you own.
   c. Insurance on the goods you bought that are in shipment.
   d. Insurance on your neighbor's home.
   e. Insurance on your inventory.

5. **If the buyer wants the seller to be responsible for shipping the goods to the buyer and for the seller to pay all costs of shipping and insurance, the appropriate shipping term to use is:**
   a. FOB seller's location.
   b. FOB buyer's location.
   c. CIF.
   d. CF.
   e. None of the above.

6. **If the seller wants the buyer to be responsible for shipment expenses, the appropriate shipping term to use is FOB buyer's location.**
   a. True
   b. False

7. If the buyer wants the seller to be responsible for shipping the goods to the buyer and the buyer agrees to pay all costs of shipping, the appropriate shipping term to use is CF.

   a. True

   b. False

8. If the seller wants the buyer to be responsible for the payment of shipping, the appropriate shipping term is FOB seller's location.

   a. True

   b. False

9. Only a buyer can obtain an insurable interest in goods.

   a. True

   b. False

10. If the goods are nonconforming, the risk of loss is borne by the seller.

    a. True

    b. False

 Quick Quiz ANSWERS
Using INCO Shipping Terms

1. In a shipment contract, the buyer bears the risk of loss once the seller delivers the goods to the carrier.

2. In a destination contract, the seller bears the risk of loss until the goods arrive at the buyer's destination.

3. A CIF contract is a shipment contract, which means the risk of loss falls on the buyer; however, because the buyer purchased insurance, the loss is covered.

CHAPTER REVIEW QUESTIONS: Answers and Explanations

1. **d.** For title to pass from the seller to the buyer, the UCC requires that the goods exist and be identified to the contract.

2. **b.** A good faith buyer cannot acquire title to stolen goods.

3. **d.** A good faith buyer can acquire title to goods obtained by fraud.

4. **d.** An insurable interest requires a recognizable loss.

5. **c.** CIF requires the seller to pay freight and insurance.

6. **b. False.** FOB buyer's location obligates the seller to pay shipping costs.

7. **a. True.** CF requires the seller to ship the goods to buyer but passes the shipping costs on to the buyer.

8. **a. True.** FOB seller's location requires the buyer to assume shipping expenses.

9. **b. False.** A buyer, seller, and common carrier can all have an insurable interest against loss.

10. **a. True.** If the goods are nonconforming, the risk of loss is borne by the seller.

CHAPTER 15

Performance and Cure in Sales Contracts

 THINKING STRATEGICALLY

©valterZ/Shutterstock

One of the most significant risks for businesses engaged in the buying and selling of goods is when the seller has shipped goods that don't conform to the buyer's wishes (nonconforming goods). In this chapter's *Thinking Strategically,* we discuss the strategic advantage of being proactive about having a system in place to minimize the risks associated with nonconforming goods.

Learning Objectives

After studying this chapter, students who have mastered the material will be able to:

15-1 Define *good faith* and explain the duty for merchants to act in a commercially reasonable manner.

15-2 Differentiate between course of performance, course of dealing, and usage of trade.

15-3 Explain the perfect tender rule in the context of obligations of the seller under the UCC.

15-4 Determine when a seller has the right to cure after the buyer has rejected goods.

15-5 Explain the buyer's right of inspection under the UCC.

CHAPTER OVERVIEW

After our discussion in previous chapters on the formation and enforceability of sales contracts, we now turn to the obligations of the parties to perform. Because sales contracts involve goods, the UCC provides a framework for understanding how the parties must deliver, inspect, accept, or reject those goods. Remember that some UCC rules are different for performance of sales contracts compared with contracts formed under the common law. In this chapter, we discuss the general obligations owed by each party as well as the specific obligations and rights of buyers and sellers of goods.

THE UCC AND GOOD FAITH

The UCC provides the parties with maximum flexibility in how they carry out their obligations. Both industry standards and how the parties have performed in past dealings play an important role in determining the parties' obligations and rights. In all cases, the UCC has a *good faith* provision (similar to the duty of good faith in a common law contract) that imposes a duty of good faith and commercial reasonableness as the bedrock of any sales contract. Good faith is defined in the UCC as "honesty in fact in the conduct or transaction concerned."[1] Additionally, merchants also have the duty to act in a *commercially reasonable* manner. Generally, this means that merchants (and only merchants) must observe industry standards and practices that may be unique to a particular industry or field.

For example, in *Sons of Thunder v. Borden,* the New Jersey Supreme Court held that a buyer breached the duty of good faith by willfully trying to circumvent its contractual obligations to a seller that made a significant investment to carry out its obligations. The case involved a contract between a food company and a supplier of clams to purchase a certain number of clams per month. The seller purchased two specialty boats to fulfill the contract and took out a significant loan to finance the purchase. Soon thereafter, the buyer's company changed management and concluded that the contract was not profitable. As a result, the buyer began to buy only a fraction of its clams from the seller's boats, which significantly reduced the revenue produced by the boats. When the seller sued for breach of contract, the jury awarded damages to the seller, including damages for breach of good faith. The court ruled:

> The obligation to perform in good faith exists in every contract, including those contracts that contain express and unambiguous provisions permitting either party to terminate the contract without cause. . . . Accepting those facts and the reasonable inferences therefrom offered as true, we determine that the jury had sufficient evidence to find that [the buyer] was not 'honest in fact' as required by the UCC.[2]

LO 15-1

Define *good faith* and explain the duty for merchants to act in a commercially reasonable manner.

TAKEAWAY CONCEPTS The UCC and Good Faith

- The UCC provides the parties with maximum flexibility in how they carry out their obligations.
- In all cases, the UCC has a good faith provision: honesty in fact in the conduct or transaction concerned.
- Merchants also have the duty to act in a commercially reasonable manner.

PERFORMANCE, PAST DEALINGS, AND TRADE PRACTICES

Terminology used by the parties in commercial transactions may have more than one meaning that varies from industry to industry or region to region. The UCC embraces a broad approach for the parties to show that a particular term or practice is within the customary norm for that industry. The **course of performance** is a method to show what the parties intended through their own actions in performing the specific contract in question. For example, if a contract calls for "premier microchips" to be delivered in five installments over the course of a year, the quality of the first installment of microchips delivered and accepted by the buyer would establish a course of performance that will help to determine whether the microchips delivered in the later stages meet the contract's standards.[3]

Course of dealing is similar to course of performance in that both refer to patterns of performance by the parties, except that course of dealing refers to how the parties acted in

LO 15-2

Differentiate between course of performance, course of dealing, and usage of trade.

---

[1] UCC Section 1-203.

[2] *Sons of Thunder v. Borden,* 148 N.J. 396 (1997).

[3] UCC § 1-303(a).

past contracts instead of the specific contract in question.[4] These past dealings provide a reference point for what the parties reasonably expected in terms of performance on a new contract.

Usage of trade refers to any general practice of method of performance that is specific to a particular trade or industry. The parties may use these methods to help define expectations of the parties engaged in specific transactions that are common in the industry.[5]

TAKEAWAY CONCEPTS Course of Performance versus Course of Dealing versus Usage of Trade

Course of performance	Method to show what the parties intended through their own actions in performing the specific contract in question.
Course of dealing	Refers to how the parties acted in *past* contracts instead of the specific contract in question.
Usage of trade	Method of performance that is specific to a particular trade or industry used to define expectations of the parties engaged in specific transactions that are common in the industry.

LO 15-3

Explain the perfect tender rule in the context of obligations of the seller under the UCC.

OBLIGATIONS OF THE SELLER

Fundamentally, the seller's obligation is to transfer and deliver conforming goods to the buyer. *Conforming goods* simply means the goods bargained for in an agreement. Under the doctrine referred to as **tender of delivery**, the UCC obligates the seller to have or tender the goods, give the buyer appropriate notice of the tender, and take any actions necessary to allow the buyer to take delivery. Absent any specific agreement between the parties to the contrary, the UCC uses a general *reasonableness requirement* to govern the delivery process. That is, the goods must be delivered at a reasonable hour, in a reasonable manner, and in one shipment. In the case of goods that are to be picked up, the goods must be made available at a reasonable time to allow the buyer to take possession.

Perfect Tender

Under the UCC, the seller's obligation actually goes beyond just delivering conforming goods. The seller must tender the goods in a manner that matches the contract terms in every respect. This is known as the **perfect tender rule**. If the seller fails to achieve perfect tender, the buyer has three options:

1. Reject the entire shipment of goods within a reasonable time;
2. Accept the shipment of goods as is; or
3. Accept any number of commercial units and reject the rest of the goods in a reasonable time (e.g., accepting 100 nonconforming computer chips from a delivery of 500 nonconforming computer chips).

Although the perfect tender rule may sound oppressive, the UCC also gives the seller certain rights intended to promote the completion of the original contract.

---

[4]UCC § 1-303(b).
[5]UCC § 1-303(c).

TAKEAWAY CONCEPTS Perfect Tender

Perfect tender rule	The seller must tender the goods in a manner that matches the contract terms in every respect.
Buyer's Options	If the seller fails to achieve perfect tender, the buyer has three options: ■ reject entire shipment ■ accept entire shipment ■ accept any number of units and reject the remainder of a shipment

---

RIGHTS OF THE SELLER

If the seller has delivered goods and the buyer rejects them under the perfect tender rule, the seller has the right to repair or replace the rejected goods *so long as the time period for performance has not expired.* Once the time contemplated for performance has expired, the seller's right to **cure** also expires. If, however, the time for the seller's performance has not expired, the seller may cure by (1) giving notice of her intent to cure and (2) tendering conforming goods in replacement of the rejected goods. For example, on April 1, Lewis contracts with Clarke to provide Clarke with 100 Type-A compasses at $10 per unit to be delivered no later than May 1. Lewis delivers 100 Type-B compasses on April 15, and Clarke rejects the goods as nonconforming. At this point, Lewis has the option to cure because the date for performance is still two weeks away. If Lewis notifies Clarke that he intends to cure and then ships 100 Type-A compasses to Clarke on April 30, he has completed performance consistent with the UCC requirements and, assuming the new shipment of goods conforms, Clarke must accept the goods.

In some instances, the right to cure may exist even *after* the time period for performance has come due. The UCC provides that if the seller reasonably believes that the nonconforming goods will be acceptable to the buyer (perhaps because the seller has shipped a more expensive product or because of a course of past dealing between the buyer and seller) with or without a money allowance, then the seller gets additional time to cure after the time under the contract has passed. The seller must seasonably notify the buyer of her intent to cure.

In the Lewis-Clarke contract discussed above, suppose that Lewis discovers that the Type-A compasses are out of stock, so he instead ships Clarke Type-A1A compasses (a more expensive and newer model) on the last day for performance. If Clarke rejects the goods, most courts would allow Lewis, so long as he has given Clarke seasonable notice, to cure even though the time period for performance has passed. This is because Lewis has been reasonable in his assumption that a newer and more expensive model would be an acceptable substitute for the ordered model.

In Case 15.1, a federal appeals court examines a seller's right to cure after a good faith delivery of nonconforming goods.

LO 15-4

Determine when a seller has the right to cure after the buyer has rejected goods.

CASE 15.1 Car Transportation Brokerage Company v. Blue Bird Body Co., 322 Fed. Appx. 891 (11th Cir. 2009)

FACT SUMMARY Car Transportation ("the Buyer") purchased a Blue Bird luxury motor coach from Blue Bird's authorized dealer, Bleakly ("the Seller"), for $650,000. Although neither the Buyer nor the Seller performed any predelivery inspection, the Seller provided assurances to the Buyer that the coach was new

(continued)

CHAPTER FIFTEEN | Performance and Cure in Sales Contracts   269 and in working condition. On the day of the purchase, however, the Buyer's principal drove the coach from the Seller's lot and began to notice certain defects with the coach's electrical system. The next day, the Buyer returned the coach to the Seller for repairs, and the Seller's service technicians repaired several electrical problems to the Buyer's satisfaction. The Buyer retook possession of the coach and placed it into service for the Buyer's business on January 5.

Over the next two months, the coach had additional electrical system defects and several other mechanical problems. Instead of returning the coach to the Seller once again, the Buyer opted to return the coach to the manufacturer for repairs. On February 18, the manufacturer returned the coach to the Buyer, but the electrical problems were still not fully resolved. On March 22, the Buyer notified the Seller that it was revoking the acceptance of the coach due to the mechanical problems. Eventually, the Buyer sued the Seller, asserting, among other claims, revocation of the Buyer's acceptance. The Seller argued that it had not been given the opportunity to cure the second set of defects as required by Georgia's commercial law statutes. The trial court found in favor of the Seller, and the Buyer appealed.

SYNOPSIS OF DECISION AND OPINION

The U.S. Court of Appeals for the 11th Circuit affirmed the trial court's ruling in favor of the Seller. The court held that the UCC's *opportunity to cure* required the Buyer to provide the Seller with a reasonable time in which to attempt to make repairs. What constitutes a reasonable time in which to cure depends on the nature, purpose, and circumstances of the particular case. The court held that the Seller was entitled to notice of the additional problems occurring after delivery and an opportunity to repair them at some time during the three months prior to the Buyer's revocation.

WORDS OF THE COURT: Inadequate Opportunity to Cure

"[T]he Buyer gave the Seller one opportunity to cure after the defect in the electrical system first became apparent. After these initial repairs, the Buyer did not inform the Seller when the Coach continued to have additional problems; rather, it returned the Coach to the manufacturer for repairs. Nearly three months after acceptance, after the manufacturer also had made one failed attempt to correct the defect, the Buyer informed the Seller that it was revoking its acceptance of the Coach. Based upon this undisputed evidence, we agree with the district court that, as a matter of law, the Buyer provided the Seller with an insufficient opportunity to cure. Providing only one opportunity to repair—before the extent of the defect was truly apparent—is not reasonable, especially where the product in question is as complicated as a motor coach."

Case Questions

1. Shouldn't the Buyer's attempts to have the coach fixed by the manufacturer be considered an attempt to cure under the UCC? Why or why not?

2. How much time is "reasonable" to allow the Seller to fix the electrical problems? Isn't the Buyer suffering additional damages from not having the coach in service?

3. *Focus on Critical Thinking:* Is the court's decision consistent with the underlying premise of the UCC? Does it help promote fairness among merchants?

Commercial Impracticability

Recall from the previous chapter that the common law excuses the seller's performance when a contract becomes **commercially impracticable**. The UCC applies the commercial impracticability rule when the delivery or nondelivery of goods has been made impracticable by the occurrence of an unanticipated event, *and* the unanticipated event directly affects a basic assumption of the contract. Commercial impracticability is a *narrow doctrine.* For example, in *Maple Farms, Inc. v. City School District of Elmira,*[6] a state appellate court in New York ruled that an unexpected increase in prices was *not* sufficient to meet the standard of

---

[6] 76 Misc.2d 1080 (1974).

commercial impracticability for a supplier to be excused from performance because a reasonable businessperson should have been aware that the general inflation at the time (early 1970s) could affect the price of the contract.

In Case 15.2, a federal appellate court considers the commercial impracticability defense.

CASE 15.2 Hemlock Semiconductor Operations, LLC v. SolarWorld Industries, 867 F.3d 692 (6th Cir. 2017)

FACT SUMMARY Hemlock Semiconductor Operations, LLC (Hemlock) and SolarWorld Industries (Sachsen) are both involved in manufacturing components of solar-power products. They entered into a series of long-term supply agreements (LTAs), by which Hemlock in Michigan would supply Sachsen in Germany with set quantities of polysilicon (Silicon) at fixed prices between the years 2006 and 2019. The market price of Silicon was above the LTA price in the initial year of the agreement. However, the market price of Silicon plummeted several years later when the Chinese government began subsidizing its national production of polysilicon materials. As a result, Hemlock and Sachsen reached a temporary agreement to lower the LTA price in 2011. When that agreement expired in 2012, however, the price reverted to the original amount. Hemlock then demanded that Sachsen pay the original LTA price for the specified quantity of Silicon for the 2012 billing year. Sachsen refused, and Hemlock sued Sachsen for breach of contract. The trial court granted Hemlock's motion for a summary judgment and awarded the company $800 million in damages. Sachsen appealed based on, among other theories, commercial impracticability due to the Chinese government's unforeseeable and extreme actions.

SYNOPSIS OF DECISION AND OPINION The U.S. Court of Appeals for the Sixth Circuit affirmed the trial court's judgment in favor of Hemlock. The court ruled that the commercial impracticability defense applies only if an unanticipated circumstance has made performance of the promise vitally different from what should reasonably have been within the contemplation of both parties when they entered into the contract. In other words, the defense is viable only if an unforeseen event occurs and the non-occurrence of that event was a basic assumption on which both parties made the contract. Since a shift in

market prices for goods and supplies is a basic fact of doing business, it cannot be the basis of a commercial impracticability defense.

WORDS OF THE COURT: Shifts in Market Prices "The expectation that current market conditions will continue for the life of the contract is not [a] basic assumption; [Thus] shifts in market prices ordinarily do not constitute impracticability. Likewise, the simple fact that a contract has become unprofitable for one of the parties is generally insufficient to establish impracticability. This is especially true when the parties have entered into a contract for the sale of goods at fixed prices because such contracts are made for the very purpose of establishing a stable price despite a fluctuating market. . . . Neither a rise or a collapse in the market itself can be a justification for asserting the impracticability defense, for that is exactly the type of business risk which business contracts made at fixed prices are intended to cover. . . . Even relatively drastic changes in the market have been held insufficient to trigger the impracticability defense."

Case Questions

1. The court ruled that the Chinese government's subsidization of polysilicon was not the basis for a commercial impracticability defense. Is the economic turbulence caused by one of the world's largest economies an "unforeseen event"? Why or why not?

2. What does the court suggest in saying, "such contracts are made for the very purpose of establishing a stable price despite a fluctuating market"?

3. *Focus on Critical Thinking:* Is there any way of drafting a sales contract that *does* consider market conditions? Try using a sliding-scale type of price agreement to adjust the contract in this case. Would it work or not? Explain.

TAKEAWAY CONCEPTS Seller's Rights

- The perfect tender rule requires the seller to tender (deliver) the goods in a manner that matches the contract terms in every respect.
- If a seller delivers nonconforming goods, the buyer has three options: (1) Reject the entire shipment of goods within a reasonable time, (2) accept the shipment of goods as is, or (3) accept any number of commercial units and reject the rest of the goods within a reasonable time.
- If the seller has delivered goods and the buyer rejects them as nonconforming, the seller has the right to repair or replace the rejected goods *so long as the time period for performance has not expired.* Once the time contemplated for performance has expired, the seller's right to cure also expires.
- Commercial impracticability is a narrow doctrine that excuses the seller's performance when the delivery or nondelivery of goods has been made *impracticable* by the occurrence of an unanticipated event, *and* the unanticipated event directly affects a basic assumption of the contract.

OBLIGATIONS AND RIGHTS OF THE BUYER

LO 15-5

Explain the buyer's right of inspection under the UCC.

The buyer's primary obligation is triggered when the seller tenders delivery. Once the buyer has accepted the goods, the buyer must pay for them in accordance with the contract. Payments may come in a variety of forms, and frequently the parties have negotiated and agreed on the details of payments (cash versus credit, terms of payment, etc.). In the absence of agreement, the UCC provides that the buyer must make full payment at the time and place that she has received the goods. When the parties have agreed on credit for payment, the amount owed is paid out over a period of time at a certain rate of interest. Typically, interest begins accruing 30 days after shipment.

Buyer's Right of Inspection: Acceptance or Rejection

Unless the parties agree otherwise, the buyer has a reasonable time period to inspect the goods to be sure they conform to the contract. After inspection, the buyer may (1) communicate to the seller that she has accepted the goods; (2) do nothing, and thus be presumed to have accepted the goods unless she gives prompt notice of a rejection (or partial rejection); or (3) notify the seller that she is rejecting the goods (or part of the goods). If the buyer properly rejects the goods, the buyer may also cancel the balance of the contract and pursue any appropriate legal remedies against the seller (breach and remedies for sales contracts are discussed in the next chapter).

If the seller has shipped conforming goods as agreed, the buyer has the *duty to accept* them and become the owner of the goods in accordance with concepts of title.[7] If the seller has shipped nonconforming goods but the buyer is still willing to accept them, the UCC provides the buyer with the opportunity to later revoke acceptance *only* if the nonconformity substantially impairs the value of the goods. The acceptance of nonconforming goods by the buyer triggers the buyer's obligation to pay consistent with the terms of the agreement.

To take a simple example of a commercial transaction between buyer and seller, suppose that a buyer orders 1,000 tectonic widgets from seller. As we discussed earlier, the seller has the obligation of perfect tender. If the seller has provided perfect tender, the buyer's

---

[7]UCC § 2-606 and § 2-607.

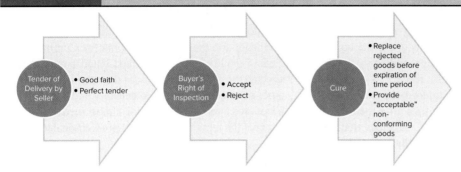

FIGURE 15.1 Commercial Transaction

obligation is to pay as agreed. The seller's delivery is always subject to the buyer's right to inspect. If the buyer discovers that the goods are nonconforming, she may accept or reject the entire shipment of nonconforming goods or may accept part of the shipment and reject the remainder. In the event the buyer rejects all or some of the shipment, the seller still has the right to cure. Figure 15.1 illustrates this transaction.

The buyer has an obligation to affirmatively notify the seller of the rejection in a timely manner so that the seller still has some opportunity to cure or a reasonable amount of time to recover the goods. In Case 15.3, a court analyzes the factors used to determine whether a rejection was timely under the UCC.

CASE 15.3 East Coast Restoration and Consulting Corp. v. SIKA Corp., 14 NY Slip Op 30361 (Supreme Court of New York 2014)

FACT SUMMARY East Coast, a roofing contractor, entered into a series of purchase order agreements with SIKA,[8] a manufacturer of roofing and waterproofing materials. The agreement called for SIKA to supply and deliver certain roofing and exterior restoration materials to East Coast for a roof restoration project in Queens, New York. Soon after, East Coast alleged the roofing material delivered by SIKA in one of their shipments was defective (Defective Materials). SIKA remedied the situation by collecting the remaining materials from the worksite, making all repairs necessitated by the use of the Defective Materials, and providing East Coast with a credit. To resolve the claim about the shipments of Defective Materials, SIKA agreed to pay East Coast $64,850 as part of a settlement agreement. However, the settlement did not address the *nondefective shipments* of the roofing and exterior restoration

materials (Nondefective Materials) delivered to East Coast before any notice of the Defective Materials.

Soon after the settlement, East Coast terminated its relationship with SIKA and declined to pay the balance of $84,397.74 for the Nondefective Materials. East Coast sent a letter to SIKA requesting that they pick up the Nondefective Materials that East Coast had stored over the seven-month period. SIKA refused to take back the materials because East Coast failed to provide any notice of rejection for the Nondefective Materials until seven months after delivery. East Coast filed suit for breach of contract, and SIKA countersued for the balance due on the Nondefective Materials.

SYNOPSIS OF DECISION AND OPINION The New York Supreme Court ruled in favor of SIKA because East Coast had failed to give timely notice

(continued)

---

[8]For the sake of accuracy, note that the original manufacturer in the agreements, Liquid Plastics, merged with SIKA prior to this lawsuit.

of any nonconformity for the remaining Nonde-fective Materials. The court explained that, under the UCC, goods are conforming when they are in accordance with the obligations under the contract. A purchaser may reject goods tendered by the seller where the goods fail in any respect to conform to the contract, and the nonconforming goods must be rejected within a reasonable time after their delivery or tender. Moreover, the UCC provides that when a purchaser timely and rightfully rejects noncon-forming goods, the purchaser is entitled to recover the purchase price, plus reasonable damages when appropriate. Here, the seven-month delay, coupled with the fact that East Coast had already rejected a part of the materials called for in the overall con-tract, constitutes an unreasonable delay for rejection.

WORDS OF THE COURT: Reasonable Time Period "[SIKA] met its burden of establishing that the delay from delivery of the non-defective roofing and exterior restoration materials to [East Coast's] purported rejection was unreasonable as a matter of law. Under the facts of this case this Court finds, as a matter of law, that plaintiff failed to make timely rejection of the goods, and is therefore liable to defendant for the sale price (Uniform Commercial Code § 2-602). . . . [East Coast] could have clearly rejected the subject materials [at the same time as] the other materials were deemed defective and the parties negotiated a resolution. Waiting almost seven months to reject the remaining materials is unreasonable."

Case Questions

1. What factors did the court consider in its analysis of whether East Coast's rejection was reasonable?

2. Since East Coast gave notice of rejection for the Nondefective Materials, does SIKA have the right to cure the defect?

3. *Focus on Critical Thinking:* How could the parties have avoided this dispute? Suggest language for the original settlement agreement that would have made the obligations of the parties more clear.

 Quick Quiz Buyer's Obligations

Does the grocer have an obligation to pay? Why or why not?

1. Grocer orders 100 Grade-A eggs per month from Farmer at market price for a period of three years. Farmer delivers Grade-A eggs every month for one year, but Grocer then begins rejecting the eggs, claiming that the market price for eggs is too high and the egg contract is commercially impracticable.

2. Grocer receives 40 bushels of corn rather than the tomatoes he ordered, but he signs a receipt for the corn anyway. The next day, Grocer changes his mind and sends back the rejected corn.

3. Grocer orders 50 gallons of whole milk from Dairy to be delivered December 23. On December 20, he receives 60 gallons of skim milk. He rejects the order but does not inform Dairy of his rejection. On January 2, Dairy demands full payment.

4. Two days before Thanksgiving, Grocer orders 100 turkeys, but the next morning he receives a delivery of 200 chickens. Afraid of losing all his customers the day before Thanksgiving, Grocer accepts 100 chickens and notifies the seller that he is rejecting part of the delivery.

Answers to this Quick Quiz are provided at the end of the chapter.

Special Rules for Installment Contracts

Delivery and billing may sometimes need to be done in two or more separate lots for cash flow or other business reasons. The UCC provides for such circumstances through use of an **installment contract**. In an installment contract, each lot must be accepted and paid for separately. This means that a buyer can accept one installment without giving up the right to reject any additional installments that are nonconforming. This is essentially an exception to the perfect tender rule because the standard for rejection is more restrictive and, thus, provides additional tender protection to the seller. In an installment contract, the buyer may reject an installment only if the nonconformity *substantially* impairs the value of that installment *and* the nonconformity cannot be cured. If a buyer subsequently accepts a nonconforming installment of the goods and does not notify the seller that she is canceling the contract, the UCC provides that the seller may assume the contract to be reinstated.

TAKEAWAY CONCEPTS Obligations and Rights of the Buyer

- Once the buyer has accepted the goods, the buyer must pay for them in accordance with the contract.
- Unless the parties agree otherwise, the buyer has a reasonable time period to inspect the goods to be sure they conform to the contract.
- In an installment contract, each lot must be accepted and paid for separately. This means that a buyer can accept one installment without giving up the right to reject any additional installments that are nonconforming.

 THINKING STRATEGICALLY

©valterZ/Shutterstock

Notice and Remediation

PROBLEM: Recall the court's decision in Case 15.3 (*East Coast Restoration and Consulting Corp. v. SIKA Corp.*) related to whether the notice given was adequate to indicate a rejection of all of the roofing materials. Courts have become increasingly strict in requiring that notice of nonconforming goods from buyer to seller must contain certain language and must be sent in a timely manner.[9]

STRATEGIC SOLUTION: Create a notice and remediation plan. By being proactive about having a system in place, managers use strategy to minimize the risks associated with nonconforming goods. The plan should include consideration of the following:

- **Beware of the battle of the forms.** In Chapter 13 we discussed the issues related to sellers and buyers using preprinted order and acknowledgement forms. The first step in a notice and remediation plan is to have a check in place to review all forms

submitted by the seller to be sure that the notice and cure provisions have not been altered.

- **Send notice early and often.** Use a systematic method to inspect goods at the earliest opportunity after receipt and to notify the seller of any nonconforming goods as soon as possible. Telephone calls or personal conversations are often the first method of notice, but they should not be the sole means of notifying the seller. Document all notification efforts, and send a follow-up letter summarizing any conversations that took place. If the seller does not respond, send follow-up notices regularly and consider contacting counsel. If you are unable to inspect the goods within a business day, notify the seller that the goods are still undergoing the inspection process. This will avoid any ambiguity as to whether your silence constitutes acceptance after a reasonable period of time.

- **Use clear language.** If you are rejecting the goods, the language should be plain and unambiguous. Courts have held that phrases such as "problematic" or "not what we were expecting" cause confusion and may not be objectively reasonable to

---

[9]*American Bumper & Manufacturing Co. v. TransTechnology Corp.,* 252 Mich. App. 340; 652 N.W.2d 252 (2002).

satisfy the UCC's notice of nonconforming goods requirement. Instead, clear, unambiguous statements should be used: "We reject Lots 1 and 2 because they are nonconforming. Lots 1 and 2 are type B parts, and we ordered type A parts."

- **If appropriate, allow the seller reasonable time to cure.** Safeguard the goods until the seller has had a chance to examine them. Do not buy replacement goods until you have given the seller the opportunity to cure or replace the goods.

KEY TERMS

Course of performance p. 267   UCC term for the method to show what the parties intended through their own actions in performing the specific contract in question.

Course of dealing p. 267   How the parties acted in *prior* contracts instead of the specific contract in question.

Usage of trade p. 268   Any general practice of method of performance that is specific to a particular trade or industry.

Tender of delivery p. 268   UCC obligates the seller to have or tender the goods, give the buyer appropriate notice of the tender, and take any actions necessary to allow the buyer to take delivery.

Perfect tender rule p. 268   Rule that requires the seller to deliver her goods exactly as the contract requires in quantity, quality, and all other respects or risk the buyer's lawful rejection of the goods.

Cure p. 269   The right of a seller to replace nonconforming goods before final contract performance is due. If nonconforming goods were delivered in good faith and were considered equal to or superior to what was ordered, the seller may cure after final contract performance is due if the buyer will not suffer injury.

Commercially impracticable p. 270   UCC rule applied when a delay in delivery or nondelivery has been made impracticable by the occurrence of an unanticipated event so long as the event directly affected a basic assumption of the contract.

Installment contract p. 274   A contract allowing delivery of goods and payments for goods at separate times, with the goods being accepted or rejected separately.

CASE SUMMARY 15.1 Ner Tamid Congregation of North Town v. Krivoruchko, 638 F. Supp. 2d 913 (N.D. Ill. 2009)

Commercial Impracticability

In 2007, real estate developer Igor Krivoruchko contracted with Ner Tamid Congregation of North Town, an Illinois not-for-profit corporation, to purchase property Ner Tamid owned on Rosemont Avenue in Chicago. After postponing the closing once, Krivoruchko refused to go forward with the deal because he said he could not obtain the kind of financing he hoped to get. The purchase contract contained no financing contingency clause because Krivoruchko believed he was "creditworthy" and had not had problems in the past with the lender with which he was dealing. Ner Tamid sued for breach of contract, and Krivoruchko defended, in part claiming commercial impracticability because he could

not obtain the financing he wanted due to an "unanticipated" and "unforeseeable" downturn in the economy.

CASE QUESTIONS

1. In its decision, the district court cited newspaper articles that discussed the volatility of the economy and specifically the real estate market. Do these articles act in any way to support or defeat Krivoruchko's claim?
2. Should a defense of commercial impracticability be effective under circumstances in which prices are affected by changes in the local or national economy? Explain.
3. How might Krivoruchko have protected himself under this contract?

Right of Rejection

Acme Refining collects, melts down, and resells scrap metal. In producing its cars, General Motors (GM) creates a massive amount of scrap metal that must be removed. Acme contracted to purchase and pick up scrap metal from GM's plant. The contract provided that the metal was to be taken "as is, where is." After removing 850,000 tons of metal from the GM plant, Acme realized the metal was corrupted by nonmetal products and waste oils, making smelting much more costly. Instead of rejecting the metal, Acme e-mailed GM over several weeks in an attempt to negotiate a lower price. Unable to bring down the price, Acme then rejected all the scrap metal.

CASE QUESTIONS

1. Was Acme's rejection lawful?
2. Did Acme give seasonable notification of rejection?

Nonconforming Goods

Furlong agreed to sell sweaters to defendant Alpha Chi Omega Sorority ("AXO") according to a specified design. AXO made a down payment ($2,000) on the purchase price and agreed to pay the balance ($1,612) upon timely delivery of the sweaters. Furlong changed the design in five particulars without notice to or consent by defendant. Immediately after timely delivery of the sweaters, defendant inspected the sweaters, found that the imprinted design did not meet the design specifications, and notified Furlong that the goods were rejected. AXO held the sweaters for Furlong, but Furlong never retrieved them. Furlong then sued AXO for the balance due.

CASE QUESTIONS

1. Were the sweaters shipped by Furlong nonconforming goods as defined by the UCC? Explain.
2. Did AXO properly reject the goods? Explain.
3. Who prevails and why?

Rejection or Revocation

Brighter Day was a retail distributor of choir robes that Murphy manufactured. Brighter Day supplied representatives from the Zion Temple with a sample robe and a "sample board" containing descriptions of various types of fabric and samples of each fabric in various colors. A disclaimer at the end of each of the descriptions stated, "All shades subject to dye lot variations." Zion ordered choir robes and overlays out of a fabric and colors selected from the sample board. After delivery, officials from Zion Temple found several problems with the robes including that the sleeves were defective and that they did not like the color or the material, which they claimed was different from the sample in the sample board. Within a week, Zion wrote a letter detailing all the problems with the robes. Murphy offered to fix the sleeves, but Zion declined this offer because of the other problems with the robes. Eventually, Murphy offered to make an additional set of robes and overlays in the style of Zion's, but Zion declined the offer. It wished to return the robes and have its purchase money refunded. When Murphy refused, Zion sued for a refund of the deposit money.

CASE QUESTIONS

1. Did Zion reject the goods or did they revoke their acceptance? Does it make a difference? Explain why or why not.
2. Did Zion have an obligation to allow Murphy to cure? Explain.
3. Who prevails and why?

1. **The UCC requires the seller to tender the goods in a manner that matches the contract terms in every respect. This requirement is called the:**
   a. Consideration doctrine.
   b. Perfect tender rule.
   c. Every respect doctrine.
   d. Mirror image rule.
   e. Matching rule

2. **Ultrawidgets agrees to purchase 1,000 Grade-B widgets from SupplyCo for $10 per part to be delivered by December 1. On November 30, SupplyCo realizes it has only 800 Grade-B widgets. SupplyCo gives Ultrawidgets seasonable notice and ships 800 Grade-B and 200 Grade-A widgets as substitute goods. Grade-A widgets are worth 20 percent more than Grade-B widgets. Ultrawidgets rejects the Grade-A widgets on December 1 and sues. Who prevails?**
   a. SupplyCo because the cure period is extended past the date of performance.
   b. Ultrawidgets because of the perfect tender rule.
   c. SupplyCo because it substantially performed.
   d. Ultrawidgets, because the time for performance has passed.
   e. SupplyCo because Ultrawidgets acted in bad faith.

3. **Which of the following are permissible options under the UCC when the seller does not tender the goods perfectly?**
   a. Reject the entire shipment of goods within a reasonable time
   b. Accept the shipment of goods as is
   c. Accept any number of commercial units and reject the rest of the goods in a reasonable time
   d. A or B
   e. A, B, or C

4. **The UCC's commercial impracticability rule excuses performance when:**
   a. One party can no longer make a profit on a contract.
   b. A delay is due to economic conditions.
   c. Delivery or nondelivery has been made impracticable by the occurrence of an unanticipated event that directly affects a basic assumption of the contract.

   d. The seller attempts to cure.
   e. None of the above

5. **Dawson Razors agrees to ship 100 Basic Brand razors to Shavers-R-Us by June 1. Instead, Dawson ships 100 Advance Brand razors (that were more expensive) on June 1 and gives Shavers-R-Us notice of the substitution. Shavers rejects the shipment as nonconforming. Which of the following is true?**
   a. Dawson's right to cure has expired.
   b. Dawson will still have a right to cure even after June 1.
   c. Shavers must accept the Advance Brand razors.
   d. Shavers may assert commercial impracticability as a defense.
   e. B and C

6. **Only merchants have a good faith obligation under the UCC.**
   a. True
   b. False

7. *Course of performance* **refers to how the parties acted in prior contracts instead of in the specific contract in question.**
   a. True
   b. False

8. **Unless the parties agree otherwise, the buyer has a reasonable time period to inspect the goods to be sure they conform to the contract.**
   a. True
   b. False

9. **In the absence of agreement, the UCC provides that the buyer must make full payment within 30 days from the time she has received the goods.**
   a. True
   b. False

10. **In an installment contract, each lot must be accepted and paid for separately.**
    a. True
    b. False

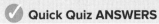
1. Grocer is obligated to buy eggs at market price from Farmer for the duration of the contract. Commercial impracticability is a narrow doctrine and generally does not apply in cases where changing economic conditions impact the contract.

2. Grocer is obligated to pay for the corn. Grocer's knowing acceptance of the nonconforming goods has triggered his obligation to pay.

3. Grocer is obligated to pay for the skim milk because he failed to affirmatively notify the seller of his rejection in a timely manner.

4. Grocer is obligated to pay the fair market value for 100 chickens (not turkeys). Because the seller didn't deliver a perfect tender, Grocer could have (1) rejected the entire shipment, (2) accepted the entire shipment, or (3) accepted part of the shipment and rejected the rest. He opted for the last choice and, thus, is obligated only for the goods he accepted.

CHAPTER REVIEW QUESTIONS: Answers and Explanations

1. b. The perfect tender rule requires a seller to go beyond delivery of conforming goods so that the tender matches the contract in every respect. Answer *a* is incorrect as consideration is unrelated to tender. Answer *c* is nonsensical. Answer *d* is incorrect because the mirror image rule does not apply in UCC transactions.

2. a. SupplyCo's right to cure is extended because it shipped more expensive substitute goods. Answers *b* and *d* are incorrect because cure is an exception to the perfect tender rule. Answer *c* is incorrect because substantial performance does not apply under the UCC.

3. e. Answers *a, b,* and *c* are all options for the buyer under the perfect tender rule (UCC § 2-601).

4. c. Impracticability is a very narrow doctrine. It only applies when the delay in delivery is caused by an unanticipated event that affects the basic assumption of a contract. Answers *a* and *b* are incorrect because economic conditions are never the basis for impracticability. Answer *d* is incorrect because impracticability is not related to cure.

5. b. The UCC provides that if the seller reasonably believes that the nonconforming goods will be acceptable to the buyer (perhaps because the seller has shipped a more expensive product) with or without a money allowance, then the seller gets additional time to cure after the time under the contract has passed.

6. b. False. All buyers and sellers covered by the UCC have an obligation of good faith. In the case of merchants, there is an additional duty to act in a commercially reasonable manner.

7. b. False. Course of performance refers to how the parties have performed in the current contract (the contract at issue). Course of past dealing refers to how the parties acted in past contracts.

8. a. True. Under the UCC and according to industry standards, the buyer has a reasonable time period to inspect the goods to be sure they conform to the contract.

9. b. False. In the absence of agreement, the UCC provides that the buyer must make full payment *at the time and place* that she has received the goods.

10. a. True. In an installment contract, each lot must be accepted and paid for separately. This means that a buyer can accept one installment without giving up the right to reject any additional installments that are nonconforming.

CHAPTER 16

Breach and Remedies in a Sales Transaction

Buyers and sellers must rely on a stable, efficient, and fair system of contract law to uphold their expectations regarding the delivery and acceptance of goods. In this chapter, you will apply the UCC law of contract breach and remedies to engage in strategic decision making that minimizes or avoids the harmful effects of a supply chain disruption.

Learning Objectives

After studying this chapter, students who have mastered the material will be able to:

16-1   Explain the nature of a breach in a contract for the sale of goods.

16-2   Categorize the various remedies available to the seller as the nonbreaching party.

16-3   Categorize the various remedies available to the buyer as the nonbreaching party.

16-4   Describe the role and limitations of liquidated damages.

CHAPTER OVERVIEW

At the time of contracting, the buyer and seller expect that the other party will perform as promised. In many instances, this is what occurs. Other times, however, one of the parties fails to perform. For example, the seller may delay shipment of the goods past the agreed-upon delivery date. Any deviation from what was agreed upon will trigger what is known as a *breach of contract*. This chapter discusses scenarios in which either the seller or the buyer has breached a UCC sales contract.

A contract breach triggers several remedies available to the nonbreaching party. This chapter will first examine the actions that trigger a breach in a sales contract and then review the remedies available to the seller or the buyer. As you read this chapter, keep in mind that the UCC provides a flexible approach

that gives the nonbreaching party several options with respect to remedies. These options are intended to put the nonbreaching party in as good a position as he would be in had the contract been properly carried out.

DEFINITION OF A BREACH

Although the UCC is grounded in the principle that the law should encourage the completion of business transactions, it also defines what constitutes nonperformance, known as a **breach**, and provides relief for parties who acted in good faith and sustained damages through no fault of their own. The opportunities to obtain relief are called **remedies**, judicial actions, which can be monetary or equitable, taken by courts that are intended to compensate an injured party in a civil lawsuit. The actions below will result in a contract breach as defined by the UCC; however, this is not an exhaustive list since a breach may occur from the deviation of anything agreed upon by the parties in their contract.

LO 16-1

Explain the nature of a breach in a contract for the sale of goods.

Seller's Breach

A seller's primary duty is to deliver **conforming goods** to the buyer as stipulated in the contract. Conforming goods are goods that match what was bargained for in the agreement. The seller may breach the contract if he delivers **nonconforming goods** or goods that are not of the type described in the contract (for example, goods of the incorrect quantity or specification). The seller may also breach if he **repudiates** his performance under the contract.

Under the common law, contracting parties have a right to cancel a contract before performance is due if it becomes clear that the other party will not perform. The UCC embraces this right by recognizing that if the seller or the buyer communicates in a way that is inconsistent with performance—whether in writing, orally, or by some action—this amounts to a repudiation of the contract. The UCC treats a repudiation as a breach even if performance is due. Lastly, the seller may breach if he fails to deliver the goods altogether.

Buyer's Breach

The buyer's primary obligation is triggered when the seller tenders delivery of conforming goods (the perfect tender rule is discussed in Chapter 15). Once the buyer has accepted the goods, the buyer must pay for them in accordance with the contract.[1] The buyer must also provide adequate facilities to receive the goods.[2] A buyer breaches if she repudiates the contract before the seller delivers the goods, fails to make payment, wrongfully rejects conforming goods, or wrongfully revokes her acceptance of conforming goods.[3]

Important Breach-Related Dates

There are four critical dates that impact the rights and duties of the buyer or seller and the availability of remedies to either of them. These dates, which will be discussed in the sections that follow, include:

$t_{contract}$	The contract's effective date.
$t_{delivery}$	The scheduled delivery date.
$t_{rejection}$	When the buyer rejects the goods.
$t_{revocation}$	When the buyer revokes his acceptance of the goods.

These dates establish four general time periods that impact the duties, rights, and remedies available to the buyer or the seller. These time periods include:

Time Period 1:	Time between the contract's effective date and the delivery date.
Time Period 2:	Time between the scheduled delivery date and when the buyer may reject the goods.
Time Period 3:	Time between when the buyer fails to reject the goods and when the buyer revokes his acceptance of the goods.
Time Period 4:	Time after the buyer is allowed to revoke his acceptance of the goods and indicates he accepts the goods.

---

[1] UCC § 2-301.
[2] UCC § 2-503(b)(1).
[3] UCC § 2-703.

- Remedies are designed to place the innocent (nonbreaching) party in the same position she would have enjoyed had the contract been performed by the parties as originally contemplated in their agreement.
- A seller's primary duty is to deliver conforming goods to the buyer as stipulated in the contract.
- A party repudiates the contract if, before performance, she says something or acts in a way that is inconsistent with her performance duties.
- The buyer's primary obligation to pay is triggered when the seller tenders delivery of conforming goods.

SELLER'S REMEDIES

LO 16-2

Categorize the various remedies available to the seller as the nonbreaching party.

Upon the buyer's breach, the seller has various options to pursue remedies that depend to some extent on whether the buyer has rejected the goods or accepted them. Keep in mind that the UCC allows the seller more than one remedy as long as each remedy is necessary to help the seller recover damages. To illustrate these remedies, a case will be used to highlight the various scenarios and outcomes.

Midwest Tools (MT) is a manufacturer and supplier of handheld tools. MT contracts to sell Great Lakes Hardware (Great Lakes), a regional hardware chain, 10,000 socket wrenches at $10 per wrench for delivery on June 1 and payment of $100,000 due upon delivery.

Time Period 1 *(Time between the contract's effective date and the delivery date.)*

During this period, MT has the obligation to deliver conforming goods to Great Lakes as stipulated in the contract. If MT suspects Great Lakes cannot pay because of accounts in the trade press that Great Lakes is delaying payments to outstanding suppliers, MT has the right to receive adequate written assurances regarding payment. Alternatively, if MT sends an incorrect shipment or defective goods before June 1, MT has the right to cure and ship conforming goods before that date. If Great Lakes repudiates before June 1 (e.g., by failing to assure MT it has the capacity to pay or by failing to pay upon delivery), Great Lakes will breach the contract. If Great Lakes breaches before accepting the goods, MT has the following options for remedies:

1. Stop or interrupt the delivery of the goods if they are already in transit.
2. Cancel the contract and be discharged of its performance obligation (delivering the wrenches). MT may also identify the goods to the contract if it hasn't already (Chapter 14 discusses identifying goods to the contract for title purposes). This will allow MT to resell the goods.
3. Resell the goods at fair market value to another party or dispose of the goods for recycling in accordance with reasonable commercial standards. Commercial standards vary depending on the nature of the goods and are subject to state law. If goods are nonperishable, commercial standards and state law may require a public auction advertised over a period of time. Perishable goods are excluded from typical advertising requirements in an effort to mitigate damages. During a resale, the seller may recover the difference

between the resale price and the contract price. If, during the resale, MT obtained only $9 per wrench, they would be able to sue Great Lakes for the $1 difference.

4. Sue for the purchase price if a resale is unsuccessful or not feasible due to the unique nature of the goods. The latter would apply, for example, if the wrenches were cast with Great Lakes's trademarked logo, preventing them from being resold to another retailer. This remedy is essentially a forced sale whereby the buyer must pay the contracted purchase price. Under this scenario, MT would obtain the $100,000 contract value.

5. Sue for damages for nonacceptance. This remedy is available if MT decided not to resell even if it was possible or if MT resold the goods in a way that was unreasonable (e.g., at an unreasonably low price or if they took too long to resell the goods). If this remedy is pursued, a seller obtains the difference between the contract price and the fair market value of the goods at the time of delivery. In this case, if the fair market value on June 1 is $9.50 per wrench, the damages awarded to MT will equal $5,000.

A seller may also incur **incidental damages** at any point due to the buyer's breach. These damages include expenses related to holding goods that were wrongfully rejected, shipping, and advertising for resale. Incidental damages are added to any additional damages incurred as a result of the buyer's breach.

Time Period 2 (*Time between the scheduled delivery date and when the buyer rejects the goods.*)

In this time period, the seller delivers conforming goods to the buyer, who then wrongfully rejects them and fails to pay the seller. At this point, the seller may elect to resell the goods in a commercially reasonable manner if it is feasible. The resale may be private or through a public auction; however, notice must be given to the buyer under both scenarios. Remedies 2 through 5 from Time Period 1 are available to the seller in these circumstances. Remedy 1 is not available because the goods were already delivered to the buyer.

Time Period 3 (*Time between when the buyer may reject the goods and when the buyer revokes his acceptance of the goods.*)

Here the buyer states acceptance of conforming goods or waits long enough to indicate acceptance but later wrongfully revokes the acceptance. For example, the goods may be accepted and stored in the buyer's warehouse but are later sent back to the seller. As in the case of Time Period 2, the seller may elect to resell the goods in a commercially reasonable manner if it is feasible, and the same restrictions apply. Likewise, remedies 2 through 5 from Time Period 1 apply. Remedy 1 is not available because the goods were already delivered to the buyer.

Time Period 4 (*Time after the buyer fails to revoke his acceptance of the goods and indicates that he will accept the goods.*)

Here, the buyer accepts the conforming goods delivered by the seller and simply does not pay for them as required in the contract. In these circumstances, the only remedy available to the seller is to sue for the purchase price. For MT, this amounts to $100,000. Resale is not available because the buyer has possession of the goods, and the seller is entitled to the price as agreed upon in the contract.

These various events involving a buyer's breach and the seller's rights and duties under the UCC are visually represented in Figure 16.1.

Case 16.1 is a trial court decision that deals with a buyer who wrongfully rejected goods involving scrap metal.

FIGURE 16.1 Seller's Duties, Rights, and Remedies

Time period:	1	2	3	4
Buyer's breach:	• Repudiates; • Fails to make payment.	• Wrongfully rejects goods.	• Wrongfully revokes acceptance.	• Accepts goods and fails to make payment.
	$t_{contract}$	$t_{delivery}$	$t_{rejection}$	$t_{revocation}$
Seller's duties:	• Deliver conforming goods to the buyer (2-301).	• If resale is private, seller must notify buyer (2-706(3)). • Resale must be conducted in a commercially reasonable manner (2-706(2)).	• If resale is private, seller must notify buyer (2-706(3)). • Resale must be conducted in a commercially reasonable manner (2-706(2)).	• Hold goods for the buyer identified to the contract (2-709(2)).
Seller's rights:	• To receive written assurances from the buyer (2-609). • To cure before delivery deadline (2-508); • Identify goods to the contract (2-704).	• To cure if seller has reasonable grounds to believe goods will be acceptable (2-508).		
Seller's remedies:	• Cancel contract (2-106(4)); • Stop delivery (2-705); • Resell (2-706); • Collect for the purchase price (2-709); • Obtain damages for nonacceptance.	• Cancel contract (2-106(4)); • Resell(2-706); • Collect for the purchase price (2-709); • Obtain damages for nonacceptance.	• Cancel contract (2-106(4)); • Resell(2-706); • Collect for the purchase price (2-709); • Obtain damages for nonacceptance.	• Collect for the purchase price (2-709).

CASE 16.1 General Motors Corp. v. Acme Refining Co., 513 F. Supp. 2d 906 (E.D. Mich. 2007)

FACT SUMMARY General Motors (GM) owns manufacturing facilities that generate scrap metal, which GM then sells to recyclers. In August 2005, GM invited Acme to bid on scrap metal generated by GM's Dynamic Manufacturing plant in Melrose Park, Illinois. Before bids were submitted, all invited

(continued)

bidders were given an opportunity to inspect the materials to be purchased from the Dynamic Manufacturing location. The invited bidders received a pre-bid sheet that stated:

> Bidders are expected to have viewed the above material prior to the submission of their bid. . . . Weights are estimated and may include nonmetallic packaging and/or contamination; the actual generation may be less than or greater than this amount. . . . Material is sold "as is, where is." No downgrades or weight adjustments will be made so please bid accordingly.

In August 2005, Acme was the successful bidder on a contract to purchase scrap metal from GM. In October 2005, Acme began pulling its first scrap loads from the Dynamic Manufacturing site. After Acme brought the scrap material back to its facility, it informed GM that it believed the scrap to be of a substandard quality since it included copper and oil, two toxic contaminants. Acme's representative wrote to GM stating that they would not pull any more loads from Dynamic and requesting a lower price adjustment. GM responded that the product was sold "as is" under the contract and that it was Acme's responsibility under the contract to inspect the material prior to bidding. GM also replied that if Acme refused to honor the terms of agreement they would be in breach. Shortly thereafter, Acme stopped picking up the material and GM terminated the contract. GM then filed an action alleging that Acme breached its contract with GM.

SYNOPSIS OF DECISION AND OPINION In October 2005, GM filed a breach of contract lawsuit seeking payment of the $112,020.71 outstanding balance on the material Acme had picked up. Acme argued that because it rejected rather than accepted the scrap materials as nonconforming, it was entitled to offset any amounts it owed under the contract with the actual fair market value of the nonconforming goods. Alternatively, Acme argued that it revoked its acceptance of the scrap materials as permitted under Michigan's version of the Uniform Commercial Code. The trial court rejected each of Acme's arguments and awarded damages to GM.

WORDS OF THE COURT: Acceptance of Goods "[T]here was no rejection of the subject scrap materials within a reasonable time

after Acme went to Dynamic Manufacturing and removed over 850,000 gross tons of scrap material from that GM manufacturing facility. In each of its October 2005 emails, Acme did not notify GM that it was rejecting the scrap materials. *See* Mich. Comp. Laws § 440.2602(1) ('Rejection of goods must be within a reasonable time after their delivery or tender. It is ineffective unless the buyer seasonably notifies the seller.'). Rather, in each email, Acme sought to modify or adjust the price quoted in its contract with GM. . . . Because there was no rejection, Acme is not entitled to a set-off as provided under Michigan's U.C.C. § 44.2604. Moreover, a buyer who accepts goods 'must pay at the contract rate for any goods accepted.' Mich. Comp. Laws § 440.2607(1).

"Second, similar to the rejection, Acme never notified GM that it was revoking its acceptance of the subject scrap materials. Section 2608 of Michigan's U.C.C. provides that:

> Revocation of acceptance must occur within a reasonable time after the buyer discovers or should have discovered the ground for it and before any substantial change in condition of goods which is not caused by their own defects. It is not effective until the buyer notifies the seller of it.

"Mich. Comp. Laws § 440.2608(2). Because Acme never notified GM that it was revoking its acceptance, it is not entitled to invoke the provisions of § 440.2608. . . .

A seller of scrap metal is afforded UCC contract rights.
©Sastra Suwanasri/Shutterstock

(continued)

"Acme breached and GM did not. Accordingly, GM's motion for summary judgment is granted as to its breach of contract claim against Acme. . . ."

Case Questions

1. How could Acme have ensured a proper rejection of the goods?

2. How could Acme have ensured a proper revocation of acceptance?

3. *Focus on Critical Thinking:* Had Acme properly rejected or revoked acceptance, would the case have been decided differently? Explain.

TAKEAWAY CONCEPTS Seller's Remedies

- A seller has the following remedies in the event of the buyer's breach:
  - The right to cancel the contract;
  - The right to stop delivery;
  - The right to resell the goods;
  - The right to collect for the purchase price; or
  - The right to obtain damages for nonacceptance.
- A seller may incur incidental damages due to the buyer's breach.

BUYER'S REMEDIES

LO 16-3

Categorize the various remedies available to the buyer as the nonbreaching party.

If a seller breaches, the buyer has various options to pursue remedies that depend to some extent on whether the buyer has rejected the goods or accepted them. The UCC allows the buyer to pursue more than one remedy as long as each remedy is necessary to help the buyer recover damages. Also, in an **installment contract** each lot must be accepted and paid for separately. This means that a buyer can accept one installment without giving up the right to reject any additional installments that are nonconforming. This is essentially an exception to the perfect tender rule because the standard for rejection is more restrictive and, thus, provides additional tender protection to the seller. In an installment contract, the buyer may reject an installment only if the nonconformity substantially impairs the value of that installment and the nonconformity cannot be cured. If a buyer subsequently accepts a nonconforming installment of the goods and does not notify the seller that she is canceling the contract, the UCC provides that the seller may assume the contract to be reinstated.

The following case will be used to highlight the various scenarios and outcomes with respect to the buyer's remedies.

Napoleon Oven Co. (Napoleon) manufactures and sells industrial-grade, high-temperature, wood-burning pizza ovens. Well-Done Pies (WDP) has contracted with Napoleon to purchase an oven for $13,000 with a delivery date of March 1. WDP paid a $3,000 deposit upon

The purchase of a pizza oven affords the buyer rights under the UCC.
©Mike Pellinni/Shutterstock

signing the contract, with the remaining $10,000 balance due when the oven is delivered. In the contract, WDP specified that "time is of the essence to ensure the timely grand opening of the pizzeria."

Time Period 1 *(Time between the contract's effective date and the delivery date.)*

During this period, WDP must provide adequate facilities to receive the oven, allow Napoleon to cure before the delivery deadline if the oven is nonconforming, and pay the remaining $10,000 balance if the oven is conforming and delivered on or before March 1. If WDP suspects Napoleon may not deliver, it has the right to request written assurances. Napoleon may repudiate and breach if it fails to provide assurances or states that it will not perform before delivery. Napoleon may also breach if it fails to deliver the oven by March 1. In either scenario, WDP has the following remedies as the nonbreaching party:

1. Cancel the contract and be discharged of its performance obligation (paying the remaining $10,000 contract balance).

2. Recover its down payment of $3,000.

3. Cover and purchase the same or a similar oven from another seller. In this case, WDP requires an oven to open the restaurant, conduct business operations, and prevent losses. The UCC provides the buyer with an option to take immediate steps by canceling the contract and purchasing substitute goods from another vendor, known as the **right to cover**, to continue business operations and minimize losses. The UCC requires the covering party to purchase the substitute goods in good faith and without unreasonable delay. The right to cover also allows the covering party to bring a lawsuit to recover from the seller the difference between the cost of covering and the original contract value. However, if the buyer actually saved expenses because of the breach by the seller, those costs are deducted. In this case, if an oven purchased from a different seller costs $15,000, WDP would be able to recover the $2,000 difference plus any incidental costs such as rushed shipping expenses.

4. Sue for nondelivery damages. In some cases, a buyer elects not to cover even though it is possible or covers in a manner that is unreasonable (e.g., by purchasing goods that are unreasonably expensive or by unreasonably delaying the purchase). In either case, the UCC offers this remedy and limits the damages to the difference between the market price at the time the buyer learns of the breach and the contract price. In this case, if WDP purchases an oven that is twice as large and made of more expensive materials at a cost of $20,000, it will not be permitted to cover. Instead WDP will obtain the difference between the market price of a similar oven and the original contract price of $13,000. If the market price of a similar oven at the time WDP learns of the breach is $14,000, then the damages WDP is entitled to will be $1,000.

5. Sue for specific performance. Sometimes it is not feasible for the buyer to cover or it is disadvantageous to file suit for money damages. This occurs, for example, when the goods in question are unique and cannot be obtained elsewhere in the market. In these circumstances, the UCC provides the buyer with the remedy of **specific performance**, an equitable remedy whereby a court orders the breaching party to render the promised performance by ordering the party to take a specific action.

A buyer may incur incidental and **consequential damages** at any point due to the seller's breach. For a buyer, incidental damages include the costs of advertising for replacements, sending agents to purchase goods for cover, and shipping the replacement or nonconforming goods. Consequential damages are foreseeable losses caused by the seller's breach and may include lost profits. In the case above, because the restaurant opening will be delayed, WDP may pursue consequential damages equaling lost profits since these damages were foreseeable. Both types of damages are added to any additional damages incurred as a result of the seller's breach.

Time Period 2 *(Time between the scheduled delivery date and when the buyer rejects the goods.)*

During this time period, nonconforming goods are delivered to the buyer. The buyer accepts the goods but then rightfully rejects them upon discovering the defect. In these cases, the buyer must notify the seller of the rejection within a reasonable time. For example, the pizza oven may be nonconforming if it does not maintain the correct temperature consistently as advertised in the product specification. At this point, WDP may rightfully reject the oven and may elect to cover. Remedies 1 through 5 discussed in Time Period 1 are available to the buyer in these circumstances.

Time Period 3 *(Time between when the buyer may reject the goods and when the buyer revokes his acceptance of the goods.)*

Here, the buyer states her acceptance of nonconforming goods or waits long enough to indicate acceptance. The buyer may do this if it is difficult to determine whether the goods are nonconforming, or if the seller provides assurances that it will cure the defect after the buyer accepts the nonconforming goods. At this point, however, the buyer rightfully revokes her acceptance because the goods are discovered to be nonconforming or because the seller fails to cure the defect. For a buyer to effectively revoke her acceptance, the UCC requires that the nonconformance **substantially impair** the value of the goods (i.e., the defects must be substantial rather than minor). Also, the buyer must notify the seller within a reasonable time after she discovers (or should have discovered) the breach. When this occurs, remedies 1 through 5 from Time Period 1 are available to the buyer. In the pizza oven case, a defect that prevents the pies from cooking properly would substantially impair the value of the oven and would allow WDP to revoke its acceptance even after the oven was installed in the restaurant's kitchen.

Time Period 4 *(Time after the buyer fails to revoke his acceptance of the goods and indicates that he will accept the goods.)*

In this scenario, the buyer notifies the seller that he will accept the nonconforming goods. The buyer may do this, for example, because alternative goods are not available through cover. In these circumstances, the buyer receives damages equal to the difference between the goods as promised and those delivered, plus any incidental or consequential damages.

These time periods with their corresponding events involving a seller's breach and the buyer's rights and duties under the UCC are visually represented in Figure 16.2.

Case 16.2 involves an appellate case that deals with a failed contract for the supply of integrated circuits and the calculation of damages awarded to the buyer for covering.

✅ Quick Quiz Buyer's Remedies

1. The seller never delivers and the buyer must purchase substitute goods from another seller. This is referred to as _____.
2. The seller breaches and never delivers a rare work of art that is one-of-a-kind. To obtain this artwork, the buyer may seek to obtain _____.
3. If the buyer accepts the goods after the scheduled delivery date and later discovers that the goods are defective, the buyer can _____.

Answers to this Quick Quiz are provided at the end of the chapter.

FIGURE 16.2 **Buyer's Duties, Rights, and Remedies**

Time period:	1	2	3	4
Seller's breach:	• Nondelivery; • Repudiates	• Nonconforming goods delivered	• Nonconforming goods delivered	• Nonconforming goods delivered
	$t_{contract}$	$t_{delivery}$	$t_{rejection}$	$t_{revocation}$
Buyer's duties:	• Accept & pay for conforming goods (2-301); • Provide adequate facilities to accept goods (2-503(1)(b)); • Allow seller to cure before delivery deadline (2-508).	• Seasonably notify seller of defects & rejection (2-601/2); • Hold goods for seller's account (2-602(2)(b)) & (2-604).	• Seasonably notify seller of revocation of acceptance (2-608(1)); • Buyer must show that defects substantially impair value in the goods (2-608(1)).	• Seasonably notify seller of defects (2-714(1)).
Buyer's rights:	• To receive written assurances from the seller (2-609)	• To inspect goods (2-513(1)); • Reject non-conforming goods in whole or units (2-601).	• To revoke acceptance (2-608); • Partially accept commercial units (2-608).	
Buyer's remedies:	• Cancel contract (2-106(4)); • Recover payments; • Cover; • Sue for non-delivery damages (2-713); • Specific performance (2-716).	• Cancel contract (2-106(4)); • Recover payments; • Cover; • Sue for non-delivery damages (2-713); • Specific performance (2-716).	• Cancel contract (2-106(4)); • Recover payments; • Cover; • Sue for non-delivery damages (2-713); • Specific performance (2-716).	• Sue for damages due to buyer's acceptance of nonconforming goods (2-714).

CASE 16.2 Micrel, Inc. v. TRW, Inc., 486 F.3d 866, 880 (6th Cir. 2007)

FACT SUMMARY TRW assembles components for airbag systems and sells them to car manufacturers. The airbag modules require application-specific integrated circuits (ASICs). On October 10, 2001, Micrel and TRW signed contracts for Micrel to design and supply ASICs for use in TRW's airbag systems. TRW hoped that these ASICs would be less expensive than the ones it was sourcing from a company called National.

The contract specified a development schedule with production in June 2002 and declared that "time was of the essence" in Micrel's performance.

(continued)

Failure of either party to complete its obligations would be cause for termination, but termination would not become effective unless the breaching party failed to correct the deficiencies within a period not to exceed three months.

Micrel informed TRW that it would not be able to meet the June 2002 delivery and asked for an extension. TRW reluctantly agreed and mentioned that any further delays would not be accepted. Micrel later asked for a second extension into January/February 2003. TRW rejected this proposal and terminated the contract after giving Micrel three months to correct the deficiencies. In December 2002, Micrel filed a complaint alleging that TRW breached the contract. TRW answered and asserted its own claims for breach of contract and damages.

After two weeks of trial, the jury found in favor of TRW and awarded the company damages of $9,282,188. The decision was then appealed.

SYNOPSIS OF DECISION AND OPINION

Micrel argued that it was a mistake to allow the jury to consider cover damages based on the difference in price TRW paid for National's ASICs and the price it would have paid Micrel under the agreement. The appellate court affirmed the trial court's jury verdict granting cover damages to TRW.

WORDS OF THE COURT: Buyer's Cover Damages

"The district court instructed the jury in connection with both parties' claims that if one party proved that the other breached the contracts, that party would be entitled to damages 'in an amount sufficient to place [the party] in the same position in which it would have been if the contracts had been fully performed by [the other].'

"The district court explained that if Micrel breached the parties' contracts, and 'TRW made reasonable purchase of substitute parts in good faith and without unreasonable delay, TRW is entitled to recover the amounts by which the cost of the substitute parts exceeded the contract price.'

"In terms of TRW's proofs, nearly all of TRW's damage award was based on the differential between what TRW paid National and what TRW would have paid Micrel for the replacement ASICs from the end of 2002 through 2004. The amount of TRW's request of more than $9.66 million took into account the agreed-upon extension of the production release dates, interest, and a reduction to present value. In denying the motion for new trial, the district court specifically found that the damage award of more than $9.28 million was 'a reasonable number within the range of proof presented by the parties'."

AFFIRMED.

Case Questions

1. Why is this case unusual with respect to covering?

2. What role did the "time is of the essence" clause play in this contract?

3. *Focus on Critical Thinking:* Termination discharges the parties' obligations under the contract. In this case TRW terminated the contract. Should TRW's termination impact the remedies available for the breach? Why or why not?

TAKEAWAY CONCEPTS Buyer's Remedies

- A buyer has the following remedies in the event of the seller's breach:
  - The right to cancel the contract;
  - The right to recover payments;
  - The right to cover;
  - The right to sue for nondelivery damages;
  - The right to sue for specific performance; or
  - The right to sue for damages due to the acceptance of nonconforming goods.
- A buyer may incur incidental and consequential damages due to the seller's breach.

LIMITATION OF REMEDIES

LO 16-4

Describe the role and limitations of liquidated damages.

The remedies discussed earlier are default rules that apply in cases where the parties have not contractually specified the remedies in advance. If the parties desire, they may craft their own remedies as express terms in the contract. These contractual remedies are deemed optional, however, unless the parties agree that they are to be the exclusive remedies available.[4] For example, the parties may agree that consequential damages will not be awarded. This express term will apply unless the term is declared unconscionable.

The parties may alternately decide to define and limit the amount of monetary damages in the event of a breach. **Liquidated damages** are damages that the parties expressly define in the contract and agree will compensate the nonbreaching party. In the pizza oven case, Napoleon may add the following liquidated damages clause: "If the Buyer fails to pay the remaining balance due upon delivery of the goods, the Buyer will forfeit its deposit as liquidated damages to the Seller." Liquidated damages clauses will not be enforced, however, if the amount is unreasonably high and works as a penalty.[5] Likewise, a liquidated damages amount that is unreasonably low will not be enforced as unconscionable.[6]

For example, Napoleon Oven Co. (Seller) and Well-Done Pies (Buyer) might add the following liquidated damages clause in their contract:

> *If Seller breaches its obligation to deliver goods in accordance with the contract, Buyer shall have the option to recover $_____ per day for each day of delay as liquidated damages.*

If the dollar amount is unreasonably high, for example, $10,000 a day, the courts will view this as a penalty and will not enforce it. Conversely, if the dollar amount is unreasonably low, for example, $100 a day, the courts will view it as unconscionable and likewise will fail to enforce the provision.

TAKEAWAY CONCEPTS Limitation of Remedies

- If the parties desire, they may craft their own remedies and add those as express terms in the contract.
- The parties may add a liquidated damages provision to define and limit the amount of monetary damages in the event of a breach.
- Liquidated damages clauses will not be enforced if the amount is unreasonably high and functions as a penalty.
- Liquidated damages that are unreasonably low will not be enforced as unconscionable.

 ## THINKING STRATEGICALLY

©valterZ/Shutterstock

Reacting to a Potential Sales Contract Breach[7]

PROBLEM: Product distributors must ensure an adequate supply of goods to honor their timely delivery obligations to retailers and other merchants in the value chain. There are times, however, when supply is disrupted.

STRATEGIC SOLUTION: Consider the following case to appreciate how UCC sales contracts can offer

---

[4]UCC § 2-719(1)(b).
[5]UCC § 2-718(1).
[6]UCC § 2-718.
[7]*See* Tonia Murphy, "Nutrisoya v. Sunrich: Anatomy of a Sales Dispute," *Journal of Leadership, Accountability, and Ethics* 9, no. 1 (2012), pp. 11–18.

Market Share

buyers adequate assurances to minimize supply shortages or remedies in the worst-case scenario involving a supply disruption.

Rice-Ready Beverages is a small, California-based company that sells rice milk as a dairy alternative. The national trend is toward greater consumption of dairy alternatives. However, rice milk is the smallest category within this market (2 percent) and has experienced little growth compared to soy milk and almond milk. According to a recent industry report, the market is broken down as follows:

Despite the sales figures above, Rice-Ready was excited because they had just signed a contract to supply their rice milk to GreenValley, a regional organic specialty-foods retailer. To meet these commitments, Rice-Ready contracted with HealthyDrinks, a very large and well-known manufacturer of packaged beverages including almond milk, soy milk, coconut milk, and rice milk. Most of HealthyDrinks's client accounts are far larger than Rice-Ready's.

In January, Rice-Ready and HealthyDrinks entered into a written contract whereby HealthyDrinks agreed to manufacture and package Rice-Ready's rice milk product subject to the terms and conditions of their agreement. Among the terms and conditions, Healthy-Drinks would incur the expense of having the product delivered to Rice-Ready's warehouse in Sacramento, California. The initial contract term was for three years, and their contract provided the following terms:

9.0 PRODUCT STORAGE AND SHIPPING

9.1 HealthyDrinks shall arrange, at its own cost, for transport of Product to Rice-Ready's designated warehouse in Sacramento, California; all shipments of Product shall be F.O.B. Rice-Ready's Sacramento warehouse.

9.2 Until delivery to Rice-Ready's warehouse, HealthyDrinks assumes full responsibility for Products and all risks of loss or damage to Products.

9.3 Delivery shall be made to Rice-Ready's warehouse within 30 days of HealthyDrink's receipt of the relevant and written purchase order submitted by Rice-Ready.

10 PRICE AND TERMS OF PAYMENT

10.1 The price of $9.00 USD per case of 12 units of 946 mL (32 oz.) each represents the price applicable as of the Effective Date, charged to Rice-Ready by HealthyDrinks for the Product and shall include transportation (the "Prices") F.O.B. Rice-Ready's Sacramento warehouse.

Each month, Rice-Ready would submit a purchase order and the product would arrive within 30 days at its warehouse. On October 15, Rice-Ready submitted Purchase Order 109 to purchase 20,000 cases of the product with a requested delivery date of December 30. Two days later, on October 17, HealthyDrinks issued the following press release:

PRESS RELEASE

For Immediate Release
For more information, contact:
HealthyDrinks, Inc.
1-800-123-4567

HEALTHYDRINKS SIGNS MULTIMILLION DOLLAR AGREEMENT WITH ABCMART, NATION'S LARGEST RETAILER

New York—Today HealthyDrinks, Inc. signed an agreement valued at $20,000,000/year with ABCMart, the nation's largest retailer. The contract is to supply ABCMart with soy milk, a milk alternative that is growing in popularity. HealthyDrinks will use its existing manufacturing capacity to expand the production of soy milk to meet increasing consumer demand for this product.

The same day the press release was issued, Healthy-Drinks's Vice President of Operations called Rice-Ready's Vice President of Sales and Marketing to advise her that HealthyDrinks was considering "getting out of the rice business." On November 1, HealthyDrinks sent Rice-Ready an e-mail stating that in relation to Purchase Order 109, "the product would be available for pickup in Sacramento sometime around the first weeks of March next year." Rice-Ready is running very low on inventory and cannot wait until March to meet its contractual obligation to ship rice milk to GreenValley.

QUESTIONS

1. What actions, legal and nonlegal, should Rice-Ready take?
2. If you were Rice-Ready, would you have added a "time is of the essence" clause and notified Healthy-Drinks of your contract with GreenValley? Explain.
3. When and how was the contract breached?
4. How would you minimize losses if you were in Rice-Ready's position?
5. What UCC remedies are available to Rice-Ready?
6. Assume that Rice-Ready has to cover with another supplier and incurs the cost of shipping with this new supplier. What UCC remedies are best for Rice-Ready? Explain.
7. HealthyDrinks argues that each purchase order under the agreement constitutes a separate "offer" requiring HealthyDrinks's acceptance to create a contract and that because HealthyDrinks never "accepted" Purchase Order 109, there was no contract. Is this argument valid?

KEY TERMS

Breach p. 280   Condition that exists when one party has failed to perform her obligation under a contract. If the breach is material, the nonbreaching party is excused from his performance and can recover monetary damages.

Remedies p. 280   Judicial actions, which can be monetary or equitable, taken by courts that are intended to compensate an injured party in a civil lawsuit.

Conforming goods p. 281   Goods bargained for in an agreement.

Nonconforming goods p. 281   Goods that fail to match what was bargained for in the contract (e.g., goods of the incorrect quantity or specification).

Repudiate p. 281   A party repudiates the contract if, before performance, he says or does something that is inconsistent with his performance duties.

Incidental damages p. 283   Damages that reimburse a buyer's reasonable expenses incurred in handling rightfully rejected goods or in effecting a cover.

Installment contract p. 286   A contract allowing delivery of goods and payments for goods at separate times, with the goods being accepted or rejected separately.

Right to cover p. 287   A remedy offered to a buyer to cancel the contract and purchase substitute goods from another vendor.

Specific performance p. 287   An equitable remedy whereby a court orders the breaching party to render the promised performance by ordering the party to take a specific action.

Consequential damages p. 287   Foreseeable losses caused by the breach; may include lost profits.

Substantial impairment p. 288   Defects in the goods that are substantial in nature.

Liquidated damages p. 291   Damages that the parties expressly define in the contract and agree will compensate the nonbreaching party.

CASE SUMMARY 16.1 Glenn Distributors Corp. v. Carlisle Plastics, Inc., 297 F.3d 294 (3d Cir. 2002)

Right to Cover

Glenn Distributors sells closeout merchandise to discount stores. The merchandise consists of goods that have been changed or discontinued, so large quantities can be bought at bargain prices. Carlisle Plastics makes "Ruffies" name-brand trash bags. Glenn contracted to buy $990,000 worth of Ruffies bags from Carlisle, but Carlisle shipped Glenn only $736,000 worth of the bags and sold the others to a different buyer. Glenn claimed it was unable to cover because the only name-brand bag for that price was Ruffies and only Carlisle made Ruffies. Unable to cover, Glenn sued for $230,000 in lost profits.

CASE QUESTIONS

1. Did Glenn make reasonable efforts to cover?
2. Should Glenn have to cover the lost profits by buying products other than trash bags? Why or why not?

CASE SUMMARY 16.2 S.W.B. New England, Inc. v. R.A.B. Food Group, LLC, 2008 WL 540091 (S.D.N.Y. 2008)

Specific Performance

S.W.B. New England ("SWB") is a distributor of kosher food products in New England. SWB's only substantial competitor is Millbrook. SWB entered a contract to buy kosher products from Rokeach. Rokeach is the dominant kosher food supplier in the region and has established a trusted brand name in New England for kosher products. After the SWB-Rokeach contract was in place, RAB Food Group (Food Group) purchased Rokeach. Food Group refused to honor the SWB-Rokeach contract and began to sell only to Millbrook. SWB brought suit, asking for specific performance from Food Group and Rokeach.

CASE QUESTIONS

1. What are the specific requirements for a court to grant specific performance to SWB?
2. Do the requirements in question 1 fit this case?

CASE SUMMARY 16.3 Swan Lake Holdings, LLC v. Yamaha Golf-Car Co., U.S. Dist. LEXIS 19684 (U.S. Dist. Ct. North. Dist. Ind., S. Bend Div., 2011)

Revocation of Acceptance

A golf resort purchased 10 golf carts from Yamaha. The carts would not charge properly, but the resort kept the carts, in part due to the promises Yamaha made to fix them. None of the repairs worked, and the resort attempted to revoke its acceptance. The court rejected the revocation since the resort had been using the carts for one year after Yamaha had stopped trying to repair the carts. The resort, the court said, waited an unreasonably long time to revoke its acceptance as required under UCC § 2-608.

CASE QUESTIONS

1. Why didn't the resort reject the goods?
2. When should the resort have revoked its acceptance?

CASE SUMMARY 16.4 Huntsville Hospital v. Mortara Instrument, 57 F.3d 1043 (11th Cir. 1995)

Rejection of Goods

Huntsville Hospital purchased electrocardiogram equipment from Mortara. When the equipment did not work properly, the hospital notified Mortara within a reasonable time to let the company know the hospital was rejecting the goods. The hospital requested that Mortara pick up the equipment and asked for a refund of the purchase price. Mortara did neither of those things. In court, Mortara argued that the hospital should have shipped the goods back to them. The court disagreed and awarded damages to the hospital.

CASE QUESTIONS

1. Why did the court rule in favor of the hospital?
2. What duties do buyers have when they rightfully reject nonconforming goods?

Liquidated Damages

Aero Consulting purchased a business jet from Cessna. The contract price was $3,995,000 and required a $125,000 deposit from Aero and another $300,000 deposit six months before delivery. A liquidated damages provision stated that Cessna would keep the deposits if Aero failed to pay the remaining balance upon delivery of the aircraft. Cessna tendered delivery of the plane; however, Aero failed to pay the balance and sued for the return of its deposits. The court ruled that the deposits amounted to a fair and reasonable amount of liquidated damages.

CASE QUESTIONS

1. Why is the liquidated damages clause in this contract not unreasonably low?
2. Why is the liquidated damages clause in this contract not unreasonably high?

CHAPTER REVIEW QUESTIONS

1. If a seller delivers goods that are defective, the goods are called:
   a. Conforming goods.
   b. Cover goods.
   c. Substitute goods.
   d. Nonconforming goods.
   e. None of the above.

2. John accepts a car he purchased. After a month he realizes the car is not working properly and sends the car back to the seller. This is called:
   a. Rejecting the goods.
   b. Revoking acceptance.
   c. Perfect tender.
   d. Covering.
   e. Reselling.

3. Which of the following remedies can a seller obtain *only* during the time period before the buyer accepts the goods?
   a. He can stop delivery of the goods.
   b. He can sue for the purchase price.
   c. He can sue for nonacceptance damages.
   d. He can resell the goods.
   e. None of the above.

4. A seller never delivers the goods and breaches. If the buyer has to pay higher shipping expenses due to the breach, these may be recovered as:
   a. Lost profits.
   b. Consequential damages.
   c. Incidental damages.
   d. Cost of cover.
   e. Specific performance.

5. The buyer of an antique and rare car is suing the seller for failing to deliver. To obtain the car, the buyer would request:
   a. Consequential damages.
   b. Lost profits.
   c. Incidental damages.
   d. Specific performance.
   e. All of the above.

6. A buyer may revoke her acceptance if the goods have a major defect. In this case, the goods are nonconforming and substantially impared.
   a. True.
   b. False.

7. If a contract calls for various periodic shipments in lots that must each be paid for separately, this is called a shipment contract.
   a. True.
   b. False.

8. Buyer and seller agree that the buyer is entitled to $1,000 in damages if the seller breaches, and they add this term to the contract. This is called a gap filler.
   a. True.
   b. False.

9. If the seller fails to deliver and the buyer purchases substitute goods from another seller, this is known as covering.
   a. True.
   b. False.

10. If the buyer discovers the goods are nonconforming and wishes to obtain damages, he must seasonably notify the seller of the defects.
    a. True.
    b. False.

 Quick Quiz ANSWERS
Buyer's Remedies

1. Covering
2. Specific performance
3. Reject the goods or revoke acceptance

CHAPTER REVIEW QUESTIONS: Answers and Explanations

1. **d.** Defective goods are nonconforming.

2. **b.** John has accepted the vehicle and is now revoking acceptance.

3. **a.** Before the goods are delivered, the seller may stop delivery.

4. **c.** Higher shipping expenses are incidental damages.

5. **d.** The remedy to obtain actual property is called specific performance.

6. **a. True.** To be able to revoke acceptance, the goods must be nonconforming and substantially impaired.

7. **b. False.** Contracts of this nature are installment contracts.

8. **b. False.** This is a liquidated damages provision.

9. **a. True.** Buying substitute goods due to a seller's breach is known as covering.

10. **a. True.** A buyer must always seasonably notify the seller of nonconforming goods to obtain a remedy.

CHAPTER 17

UCC Article 2A: Lease Contracts

©valterZ/Shutterstock

After reviewing the rules governing lease transactions under Article 2A of the Uniform Commercial Code, this chapter will then explore a strategic choice that many business firms must make: the choice between buying and leasing.

Learning Objectives

After studying this chapter, students who have mastered the material will be able to:

17-1 Articulate the advantages of leasing.

17-2 Define what a lease is and the scope of coverage in UCC Article 2A.

17-3 Distinguish between lessors and lessees.

17-4 Distinguish between a lease and a secured transaction.

17-5 Identify what types of warranties apply to leases.

17-6 Understand what a finance lease is.

17-7 Explain which leases must be in writing under Article 2A.

CHAPTER OVERVIEW

This chapter focuses on leases of goods under Article 2A of the Uniform Commercial Code (UCC). Because leasing is such an essential feature of the modern economy, it is important for business owners and managers to understand the UCC leasing rules and how they are applied by courts. In this chapter, students will learn:

- The advantages of leasing.
- The scope of Article 2A coverage regarding leases of goods.
- The definitions of *lessor* and *lessee.*
- The difference between sales and leases.

- The difference between leases and secured transactions.
- The institution of finance leases.
- Which lease agreements must be in writing to be enforceable.

INTRODUCTION TO ARTICLE 2A OF THE UCC

Contracts for the lease of goods are governed by state statutory laws that are modeled after Article 2A of the UCC, which defines what a lease is. Knowledge of

Article 2A is essential because the leasing industry now makes up a large part of the modern economy.[1] In fact, many business firms prefer to *lease* personal property, such as the machinery and heavy equipment pictured in Figure 17.1, rather than purchase it outright. From a strategic perspective, leasing is often an attractive alternative because the business can use equipment on an exclusive basis without the large up-front investment required to purchase it. There also may be tax advantages for the lessee in some situations.

LO 17-1

Articulate the advantages of leasing.

TAKEAWAY CONCEPTS Introduction to Article 2A of the UCC

- Contracts for the lease of goods are governed by Article 2A of the UCC.
- Leasing is an attractive option for many firms because it allows the firm to use equipment on an exclusive basis without having to make a large up-front investment.

FIGURE 17.1 Lease or Buy?

---

[1] See Michael Fleming, "The Leasing Industry's Impact on the Economy," *Equipment Leasing Today,* April 2004. See also William H. Lawrence, *Understanding Sales and Leases of Goods* (Newark, NJ: LexisNexis, 1996), p. 8.

LO 17-2

Define what a lease is and the scope of coverage in UCC Article 2A.

UCC ARTICLE 2A COVERAGE

Article 2A applies to the lease of goods, including machinery, equipment, and vehicles. The UCC does *not* cover real estate leases. Examples of equipment that a business may lease include information systems equipment, telephones, furniture, and even heavy machinery used for manufacturing or construction.

Article 2A "applies to any transaction, regardless of form, that creates a lease."[2] But what is a lease? Article 2A defines a **lease** as "a transfer of the right to possession and use of goods for a term in return for consideration, but a sale or retention of a security interest is not a lease."[3] So, what is a security interest? A **security interest** is a legal right granted by a debtor to a creditor over the debtor's property (usually referred to as *collateral*). A security interest enables the creditor to have recourse to the property—that is, to retake possession of the property—if the debtor defaults in making payment or in otherwise performing its obligations. We must thus distinguish between leases, sales, and secured transactions.

A sale is relatively easy to distinguish from a lease. A **sale** transfers ownership, or *title,* to the goods from the seller to the buyer. When there is a sale, the seller does not retain any ties to the goods. (As a result, if the buyer does not pay for the goods, the seller has an action for the price but does not have the right to repossess the goods themselves.)

A true lease, by contrast, does not transfer title. The lessor gives possession and the right to use the goods to the lessee for a fixed period of time in return for rent. The title to the property and a meaningful residual interest remain with the lessor. The lessee acquires only the right to the use and enjoyment of the goods for a limited period of time. Title to the goods does not pass, since the lessor retains it in the form of a *residual interest* in the goods. The goods revert back to the lessor at the end of the lease term, and the lessor generally has the right to repossess the goods sooner if the lessee breaches during the term of the lease.

Distinguishing leases from secured transactions can be more challenging, since secured transactions often look like a lease, as Case 17.1 demonstrates.

CASE 17.1 *In re* Pillowtex, Inc., 349 F.3d 711 (3d Cir. 2003)

FACT SUMMARY Pillowtex, Inc. was a textile manufacturing company with headquarters in Dallas, Texas. Duke Energy Corporation is an electric power holding company with headquarters in Charlotte, North Carolina. On June 3, 1998, the parties entered into an eight-year "Master Energy Services Agreement" in which Duke Energy agreed to install energy-saving lighting fixtures at Pillotex's factory in Columbus, Georgia. The Master Agreement provided that the cost of acquiring and installing the lighting fixtures would be paid by Duke Energy, which incurred total costs of $10.41 million. In exchange, Pillowtex agreed to pay Duke Energy on a monthly basis one-twelfth of Pillowtex's annual energy savings, in an amount the parties agreed to in advance. Specifically, the payments to be made by Pillowtex were structured to guarantee that Pillowtex would make predetermined, equal monthly payments and that Duke would recover its costs within five years.

On November 14, 2000, however, Pillowtex filed for bankruptcy and stopped making payments under the Master Agreement. Duke Energy then filed a motion to compel Pillowtex to make the lease payments on the equipment it had provided to Pillowtex under the Master Agreement. In response to Duke Energy's motion to compel, Pillowtex claimed that the Master Agreement was not a true lease. After a hearing on the matter, the United States District Court for the District of Delaware, sitting in Bankruptcy, denied Duke Energy's motion, finding that the Master Agreement was, in fact, a secured financing arrangement and not a lease. Duke Energy then appealed to the Third Circuit Court of Appeals.

(continued)

---

[2]UCC § 2A-102.
[3]UCC § 2-103(j).

SYNOPSIS OF DECISION AND OPINION The Third Circuit Court of Appeals, which hears appeals from the federal district courts located in Pennsylvania, New Jersey, and Delaware, applied the economic realities test to the transaction and held that, even though the parties intended the Master Agreement to be a lease, the transactions was, in fact, a secured financing arrangement.

WORDS OF THE COURT: Economic Realities of the Underlying Transaction "It is undisputed that Duke and Pillowtex intended to structure the [Master Agreement] to have the characteristics of a lease and that the parties were trying to create a true lease. . . . [But] the Court must subordinate the parties' intent to the economic reality that Duke would not have plausibly reclaimed the fixtures at the end of the [Master Agreement's] term. This is not mere speculation on our part. The uncontroverted evidence shows that removal of the fixtures would be prohibitively expensive, and that the fixtures' value on the market would not make it worth Duke's while to reclaim them. In short, the economic realities analysis not only permits, but *requires* us to examine the state of affairs at the end of the [Master Agreement's] term."

Case Questions

1. The Court emphasizes the fact that Duke would not have wanted the lighting fixtures at the end of the lease term. Why is this fact so relevant to the Court's conclusion?

2. Why does the Court disregard the intent of the parties in deciding whether the transaction is a lease or not?

3. *Focus on Critical Thinking:* Which party is acting "strategically" in this case, and what is the strategy it is employing?

TAKEAWAY CONCEPTS UCC Article 2A Coverage

- Article 2A applies to the lease of goods, such as machinery, equipment, and vehicles. It does not apply to the lease of real estate.
- A sale, unlike a lease, transfers ownership, or *title,* to the goods from the seller to the buyer.
- A lease does not transfer title.

SOME BASIC TERMINOLOGY: LESSORS AND LESSEES

LO 17-3

Distinguish between lessors and lessees.

Before we proceed any further, let's define two key terms. True leases always involve two parties: (1) the **lessor**, the party who owns the leased goods and is making them available for lease; and (2) the **lessee**, the party who acquires the right to the temporary possession and use of goods under a lease. For example, check out the sample *equipment lease* contract in Figure 17.2 in which the lessor (the owner of the property) gives the lessee (the party using the property) the exclusive right to possess and use the equipment for a fixed period of time. The lessee often makes a monthly payment to the lessor, but at the end of the lease term, the equipment is returned to the lessor.

TAKEAWAY CONCEPTS Some Basic Terminology: Lessors and Lessees

- The lessor is the party who owns the leased goods and who makes them available for lease for a period of time.
- The lessee is the party who acquires the right to the temporary possession and use of goods under a lease.

FIGURE 17.2 Equipment Lease Contract

ACME

EQUIPMENT LEASE CONTRACT

acmeleasingco.com

Lessor ("We" or "Us"): ☐ **ACME Leasing Corporation**   or   ☐ **ACME Business Bank**   • *Processing Office*
100 Main Street • Mt. Laurel, NJ 08054   100 Main Street • Salt Lake City, UT 84121   100 Main Street
phone: 555.555.5555   *phone:* 555.555.5555   Philadelphia, PA 19106

DESCRIPTION OF LEASED EQUIPMENT (Include quantity, make, model, serial number and accessories. Attach schedule if necessary.)   **MUST BE COMPLETED**

LEASING CUSTOMER ("YOU")

Company Name (Exact business name): _____

Address: _____
                Street   City   County   State   Zip

Phone: _____ Fax: _____ ☐ Corp. ☐ Limited Liability Corp. ☐ Partnership ☐ Prop.

Equipment Location: _____   State of Incorporation/Organization: _____

Vendor: _____ Address: _____

Lease Term (Mos.)	Total No. of Payments	Amount of Each Payment $ (plus applicable taxes)	Security Deposit $	Payment Frequency ☐ Monthly ☐ Quarterly ☐ Other:

TERMS OF LEASE

1. REQUEST FOR US TO ACQUIRE EQUIPMENT FOR YOU. You (the Leasing Customer identified above) wish to acquire certain equipment from the equipment vendor identified above. Rather than purchasing it yourself, you have come to us (one of the Lessors identified above) and asked us to purchase it and then lease it back to you. In exchange for our agreement to do this, you have agreed to the terms in this lease agreement (the "Lease"). We have given you an opportunity to discuss and negotiate these terms with us, and the following is the final version of our contract. If there is any information deleted from the above boxes, you give us permission to fill it in. This Lease is not binding on us until we sign it.

2. THE EQUIPMENT. We agree to lease to you, and you agree to lease from us, the equipment identified above and on any schedules attached to this Lease. This Lease also covers any and all replacement equipment, add-ons, substitutions or accessories (collectively referred to as the "Equipment"). The other details of the Lease such as the rental amount, the initial Lease term and other matters are set forth in the boxes above.

3. YOUR SELECTION OF THE EQUIPMENT VENDOR AND THE EQUIPMENT. You hereby acknowledge and agree that:
(a) YOU SELECTED THE EQUIPMENT VENDOR AND THE EQUIPMENT BASED ON YOUR OWN SKILL AND KNOWLEDGE.
(b) WE DID NOT SELECT OR INSPECT THE EQUIPMENT, HAVE NEVER SEEN THE EQUIPMENT AND HAVE NO EXPERT KNOWLEDGE REGARDING IT.
(c) YOU AGREE THAT THIS LEASE IS A FINANCE LEASE AS DEFINED IN ARTICLE 2A OF THE UNIFORM COMMERCIAL CODE. IT IS ALSO A "TRUE LEASE," MEANING THAT IT IS NOT A "LEASE INTENDED AS SECURITY," A CONDITIONAL SALE, A LOAN OR A SIMILAR ARRANGEMENT.

(d) PRIOR TO EXECUTING THE LEASE, YOU RECEIVED AND APPROVED THE SUPPLY CONTRACT (IF ANY) BETWEEN US AND THE EQUIPMENT VENDOR, AND YOU HAVE BEEN ADVISED IN WRITING (OR ARE NOW ADVISED HEREBY) THAT YOU MAY HAVE RIGHTS AGAINST THE VENDOR UNDER THE SUPPLY CONTRACT (IF ANY) AND THAT YOU MAY CONTACT THE VENDOR FOR INFORMATION ABOUT WHAT YOUR RIGHTS AGAINST THE VENDOR ARE (IF ANY).

4. NO RIGHT TO CANCEL; OTHER IMPORTANT TERMS OF THE LEASE. YOU AGREE AS FOLLOWS:
(a) LEASE CANNOT BE REVOKED; NO "TEST PERIOD." BECAUSE WE ARE PURCHASING THE EQUIPMENT FOR YOU AT YOUR REQUEST AND CANNOT GET A REFUND, THIS LEASE CANNOT BE CANCELLED OR REVOKED BY YOU FOR ANY REASON AT ANY TIME, INCLUDING BUT NOT LIMITED TO EQUIPMENT FAILURE OR DEFECTS, DAMAGE OR LOSS. THE LEASE CANNOT BE PREPAID EXCEPT WITH OUR PRIOR WRITTEN PERMISSION ON TERMS ACCEPTABLE TO US. THERE IS NO "TEST PERIOD" FOR THE EQUIPMENT.
(b) LESSOR IS NOT RELATED TO MANUFACTURER OR VENDOR; NO CLAIMS TO BE MADE AGAINST LESSOR. WE ARE NOT RELATED IN ANY WAY TO THE EQUIPMENT MANUFACTURER OR VENDOR. NEITHER THE VENDOR NOR ANYONE ELSE IS AN AGENT OF OURS, AND NO STATEMENT, REPRESENTATION, GUARANTEE OR WARRANTY MADE BY THE VENDOR OR OTHER PERSON IS BINDING ON US OR WILL AFFECT YOUR OBLIGATIONS TO US. ONLY AN EXECUTIVE OFFICER OF THE LESSOR IS AUTHORIZED TO WAIVE OR ALTER ANY OF THE TERMS OF THIS LEASE, AND THEN ONLY IN WRITING. IF THE EQUIPMENT FAILS TO OPERATE PROPERLY, OR THE VENDOR OR

(Agreement continues on reverse side)

ACCEPTANCE OF LEASE AGREEMENT   THIS IS A BINDING CONTRACT. IT CANNOT BE CANCELLED. READ IT CAREFULLY BEFORE SIGNING AND CALL US IF YOU HAVE ANY QUESTIONS.

X _____
Signature of Leasing Customer   Print Name of Signer   Title   Date

_____
Accepted and Signed by the Lessor identified above   Print Name of Signer   Title   Date

PERSONAL GUARANTY

IN CONSIDERATION OF MY RECEIVING BENEFIT AND VALUE FROM THE ABOVE LEASE, I (OR WE, IF THERE IS MORE THAN ONE OF US, INDIVIDUALLY, JOINTLY AND SEVERALLY) HEREBY PERSONALLY AND UNCONDITIONALLY GUARANTEE ALL PAYMENTS AND OBLIGATIONS OWED BY THE LEASING CUSTOMER UNDER THIS LEASE, AND I ALSO AGREE TO PAY THE LESSOR'S LEGAL FEES AND COSTS INCURRED IN ENFORCING THE LEASE AND THIS PERSONAL GUARANTY. I WAIVE NOTICE OF ACCELERATION, DEFAULT, RENEWALS, EXTENSIONS, TRANSFERS, AMENDMENTS AND OTHER CHANGES IN THE TERMS OF THE LEASE AND AGREE THAT I WILL BE BOUND BY ANY AND ALL SUCH CHANGES. I AGREE THE LESSOR MAY PROCEED AGAINST ME SEPARATELY FROM THE LEASING CUSTOMER. I AGREE THAT ANY SUIT RELATING TO THIS LEASE OR PERSONAL GUARANTY SHALL BE BROUGHT ONLY IN A STATE OR FEDERAL COURT IN PENNSYLVANIA AND I IRREVOCABLY CONSENT AND SUBMIT TO THE JURISDICTION OF SUCH COURTS, AND I WAIVE TRIAL BY JURY. I AGREE THAT THIS PERSONAL GUARANTY WILL BE BINDING UPON MY HEIRS AND PERSONAL REPRESENTATIVES. I HAVE AUTHORIZED THE LESSOR AND ITS AFFILIATES AND DESIGNEES TO USE MY CONSUMER CREDIT REPORTS FROM TIME TO TIME IN ITS CREDIT EVALUATION AND COLLECTION PROCESSES, AS WELL AS TO OFFER FUTURE CREDIT PRODUCTS AND SERVICES. I AGREE THAT MY FAXED SIGNATURE SHALL BE CONSIDERED AS GOOD AS MY ORIGINAL SIGNATURE AND ADMISSIBLE IN COURT AS CONCLUSIVE EVIDENCE OF THIS PERSONAL GUARANTY.

GUARANTOR #1 (Print Name) _____   GUARANTOR #2 (Print Name) _____

X _____   X _____
Signature (Individually; No Titles)   Date   Signature (Individually; No Titles)   Date

ACCEPTANCE OF DELIVERY

I AM AUTHORIZED TO SIGN THIS CERTIFICATE ON BEHALF OF THE LEASING CUSTOMER. I CERTIFY TO THE LESSOR THAT THE EQUIPMENT HAS BEEN DELIVERED AND IS FULLY INSTALLED AND WORKING PROPERLY. I HEREBY AUTHORIZE THE LESSOR TO PAY THE EQUIPMENT VENDOR AND COMMENCE THE LEASE.

X _____
Authorized Signature   Name and Title (Please Print)   Equipment Delivery Date

TRUE LEASES VERSUS SECURED TRANSACTIONS

LO 17-4

Distinguish between a lease and a secured transaction.

A secured transaction occurs when the seller retains a security interest in the goods being sold. (Secured transactions are discussed in more detail in Chapter 23, "Secured Transactions.") In essence, a **secured transaction** passes *conditional* title to the buyer. The transfer of title is conditional because the buyer can retain the goods if the payment obligations are satisfied, but the seller or secured party can repossess the goods in the event of default. Generally, in cases of default, the secured party must dispose of the goods and apply the proceeds to the outstanding indebtedness. Any surplus proceeds belong to the buyer.

A lessor may not only retake the goods following a default by the lessee; a lessor, unlike a seller, is not required to dispose of the goods and need not distribute any proceeds of disposition to the lessee. As stated in the UCC, "A true lease of goods [versus a secured transaction] involves the payment for temporary possession . . . with an expectation that the goods will be returned to the owner at the end of the lease term."[4]

In summary, an apparent lease transaction for goods will create a *security interest* in the goods if the lessee (buyer) is obligated to make payments on the goods for the entire term of the lease without a right to early termination, *and* if any of the following is true:

- The lease term is equal to or greater than the remaining useful life of the goods;
- The lessee is required either to renew the lease for the remaining useful life of the goods or to become the owner of the goods;
- The lessee has the option to renew the lease for the remaining useful life of the goods at no additional charge or for a nominal charge upon compliance with the lease agreement; or
- The lessee has the option to become the owner of the goods for no additional charge or for a nominal charge upon compliance with the lease agreement.

Transactions may thus superficially appear to be lease contracts but may in fact be disguised secured transactions. In these situations, "lessors" (actually, sellers) need to take additional steps to protect their interests in the goods. Most importantly, the seller should file a *UCC financing statement* with the appropriate government office. Otherwise, the seller will have fewer rights in the event of the buyer's bankruptcy. (The basics of bankruptcy are discussed in more detail in Chapter 26, "Bankruptcy.")

 Quick Quiz Secured Transactions

Is each of the following a true lease or a secured transaction?

1. Your business signs a three-year "lease" for a very old office machine that only has an additional two-year useful life.
2. Your business signs a two-year "lease" for the same office machine in question 1. The lease can be renewed at the end of the two years at no additional charge.
3. Your business signs a five-year "lease" for an office machine that gives you an option to become the owner of the machine at the end of the five-year period at no additional charge.

Answers to this Quick Quiz are provided at the end of the chapter.

---

[4]See UCC § 1-201.

WARRANTIES

Broadly speaking, a **warranty** is a guarantee or promise providing assurance by one contracting party to the other party that specific facts or conditions are true or will happen. The UCC applies its warranty rules for the sale of goods to leases. Thus, just as there are rules for express warranties and implied warranties when goods are sold, there are also rules for express warranties and implied warranties when goods are leased. In fact, the rules for the major types of warranties—express warranties, the implied warranty of merchantability, and the implied warranty of fitness for a particular purpose—are all nearly identical for sales and for leases. The rules regarding exclusion of warranties in lease contracts are also quite similar to the exclusion rules for sales contracts. (See Chapter 18, "Sales Warranties.") One important exception, however, applies to finance leases, which are discussed next.

FINANCE LEASES

Lessors serve a unique middleman role in some lease transactions. Rather than supplying the lessee with goods from an inventory maintained by the lessor, the lessor sometimes serves merely as a financing conduit, facilitating the lessee's acquisition of the goods from a supplier. This type of transaction is called a **finance lease**—a lease in which the lessor is not the fundamental supplier of the goods leased, but leases goods to lessees as a means of financing its acquisition from the supplier. (See an example of a finance lease ad in Figure 17.3.)

Finance leases thus involve a relationship among three separate parties: the supplier, the lessee, and the finance lessor (the party who is financing the lease). Being able to spot a finance lease is important because Article 2A relieves a finance lessor of any liability for implied warranties of quality with respect to the goods. The lack of involvement in selecting and supplying the goods provides the basis for relieving finance lessors from this warranty responsibility.

To qualify as a finance lease under Article 2A, an agreement must, in addition to qualifying as a true lease, satisfy three conditions. First, the finance lessor cannot participate in selecting, manufacturing, or supplying the goods. The essential function of the finance lessor is simply to facilitate the finance lessee's acquisition of the goods from the supplier, rather than having anything to do with supplying the goods.

FIGURE 17.3 | Finance Lease Ad Touting the Benefits of Leasing

The second requirement for a lease to qualify as a finance lease is that the finance lessor's acquisition of the goods must be "in connection with the lease." This means that the lessor cannot acquire goods from a supplier and then later decide to lease them. It thus further restricts the finance lessor to a financing function and further ensures that the finance lessee has dealt with the supplier and will look to the supplier for satisfaction of any product liability claims.

The final requirement for a finance lease is that one of four stated methods must be used to give the lessee advance notification of applicable warranties and promises by the supplier. Because a finance lessee will have to turn to the supplier, rather than the finance lessor, with respect to any dissatisfaction with the goods, this requirement is designed to apprise the finance lessee of the extent of available warranties. The requirement is logical because the supplier's contract is with the finance lessor rather than with the finance lessee, and the finance lessee might not otherwise be adequately informed about available warranties against the supplier.

TAKEAWAY CONCEPTS Finance Leases

- In a finance lease, the lessor is not the fundamental supplier of the goods leased, but leases goods to lessees as a means of financing its acquisition from the supplier.
- Article 2A relieves the finance lessor of any liability for implied warranties of quality with respect to the goods.

LEASES THAT MUST BE IN WRITING

In legal lingo, a law governing which contracts must be in writing in order to be enforceable is known as a **statute of frauds**. The UCC has a statute of frauds for leases. The general rule is that if the total payments to be made under the lease, *excluding payments for options to renew or buy,* are $1,000 or more, the lease must be in writing.

There are also certain exceptions to the $1,000 or more rule, most notably in cases involving (1) "specially manufactured" goods or (2) goods that have already been received and accepted by the lessee. In these two special cases, the parties' agreement need not be in writing to be enforceable. Also, the requirements for the enforceability of a lease are relatively flexible, allowing for omission or incorrect statement of certain terms.

TAKEAWAY CONCEPT Leases That Must Be in Writing

A lease must be in writing if the total payments to be made under the lease, excluding payments for options to renew or buy, are $1,000 or more.

THINKING STRATEGICALLY

©valterZ/Shutterstock

Lease or Own?

PROBLEM: Business firms like UPS and FedEx may require a large fleet of vehicles for their business operations. By way of example, UPS's delivery fleet includes over 100,000 motor vehicles, including vans, trucks, and tractor-trailers. So, when should a firm lease its vehicles, and when should it buy them outright?

STRATEGIC SOLUTION: The decision whether to lease or own will depend on a wide variety of factors, such as the firm's cash flow, tax considerations, and other issues specific to the business. Here are some factors to consider:

- Initial costs: Up-front costs for leasing and buying are different (down payment vs. first month/security deposit), so the firm would need to consider these up-front costs on a case-by-case basis.
- Additional costs: Leased cars may have mileage limits, so the lessee can be penalized for going over the limit. On a car you own, excessive wear and tear (all those little dings in the body) can reduce resale value. With a leased car, you may be charged if the wear and tear is considered excessive.

- Tax benefits (depreciation and mileage): Firms can deduct mileage expenses for both leased and purchased vehicles, but ownership may confer additional tax benefits. For example, a leased car typically doesn't qualify for depreciation deductions, while owning the car may allow the firm to take such depreciation deductions. To claim these depreciation or mileage tax benefits for business use, the firm must be able to prove the car is being driven at least 50 percent of the time for business purposes.
- Risk of going underwater: Buying a car means taking out a loan for a specific amount, which the firm will have to pay back even if the value of the car goes below the amount of the loan. The risk of going underwater becomes more likely if the car is involved in an accident.

QUESTIONS

1. In 2018, UPS owned 239 aircraft and leased or chartered another 297 aircraft. Why do you think UPS owns some aircraft and leases others?
2. In deciding whether to buy or lease, which of the eight reasons set forth in the chart in Figure 17.4 do you think is the most important one? Explain.

FIGURE 17.4   Eight Reasons to Lease

8 Reasons to Finance Equipment for Your Business

The vast majority (78%) of U.S. businesses of all sizes—from small entrepreneurs to Fortune 100 companies—in all industries—from construction to healthcare—lease or finance their equipment. Here are some reasons why:

100% **Finance 100%** — Arrange 100% financing of your equipment, software and service with 0% down payment.

Keep up-to-date — Keep up-to-date with technology by acquiring more and better equipment than you could without financing.

Accelerate ROI — Rather than paying one lump sum for your equipment, make smaller payments while the equipment generates revenue.

Benefit from bundling — Bundle the equipment, installation, maintenance and more into a single, easy-to-mange solution.

Save cash — Save your limited cash for other areas of your business, such as expansion, improvements, marketing or R&D

Outsource asset management — Let your equipment financing company manage your equipment from delivery to disposal.

Customize your terms — Set customized payments to match your cash flow and even seasonal income fluctuations.

Hedge against inflation — Lock in rate when you sign your lease to avoid inflation in the future.

Do you need equipment to operate and grow your business? Learn the benefits of leasing and financing your equipment today and equip your business for success at www.EquipmentFinanceAdvantage.org.

EQUIPMENT FINANCE ADVANTAGE
Equip Your Business for Success

http://www.equipmentfinanceadvantage.org/rsrcs/info/8Reasons.cfm.

Lease p. 300   A contract in which the terms of an agreement are set out for a person to use someone else's property for a specific period of time (*ch. 17*). An agreement between a landlord and a tenant for the rental of property (*ch. 48*).

Security interest p. 300   A legal right granted by a debtor to a creditor over the debtor's property (usually referred to as *collateral*); enables the creditor to have recourse to the property (i.e., retake possession of the property) if the debtor defaults in making payment or in otherwise performing its obligations.

Sale p. 300   Transaction that transfers ownership, or *title,* to the goods from the seller to the buyer.

Lessor p. 301   The party who owns the leased goods and is making them available for lease.

Lessee p. 301   The party who acquires the right to the temporary possession and use of goods under a lease.

Secured transaction p. 303   A transaction in which the buyer can retain the goods if the payment obligations are satisfied, but in the event of default, the seller or secured party can repossess the goods. Generally, the secured party must dispose of the goods and apply the proceeds to the outstanding indebtedness. Any surplus proceeds belong to the buyer (*ch. 17*). A financing agreement between a lender (creditor) and a borrower (debtor) in which the borrower pledges assets to secure the loan (*ch. 23*).

Warranty p. 304   A guarantee or promise providing assurance by one contracting party to the other party that specific facts or conditions are true or will happen (*ch. 17*). A seller's promise to a consumer concerning an important aspect of the goods (*ch. 18*).

Finance lease p. 304   A true lease in which the lessor is not the fundamental supplier of the goods leased, but leases goods to lessees as a means of financing its acquisition from the supplier.

Statute of frauds p. 306   The law governing which contracts must be in writing in order to be enforceable.

CASE SUMMARY 17.1 Cucchi v. Rollins Protective Services, 574 A.2d 565 (Pa. 1990)

Lease or Sale?

Anthony and Grace Cucchi transacted with Rollins Protective Services for the installation of a burglar alarm system in their home. Anthony Cucchi and a sales representative for Rollins signed a printed form entitled "Installation-Service Contract" in which Cucchi would pay the sum of $500.00 for installation of the burglar alarm system and a $15.00 monthly fee for service and maintenance of the system. This contract further provided that the "Rollins Protective System shall remain personal property and title thereto shall continue in Rollins" and that upon termination of the contract, the alarm system would be returned to Rollins. Additionally, the contract contained a $250.00 limitation of liability provision for all loss or damage resulting from failure of the system in operation or performance.

CASE QUESTIONS

1. In your opinion, was the transaction in this case a lease or a sale?
2. Why do Article 2 and Article 2A have different writing requirements for leases and sales?

CASE SUMMARY 17.2 Corporate Center Associates v. Total Group and Office Outfitters, 462 N.W.2d 713 (Iowa Ct. App. 1990)

Lease or Secured Transaction?

Corporate Center Associates (CCA) leased office space to Total Group Services of Iowa (Total Group) for a five-year term. After Total Group took possession of the premises, Total Group obtained office furniture from Office Outfitters. Total Group and Office Outfitters signed a payment plan agreement. Under this agreement, Total Group (the lessee) would make payments for the furniture for a period of 60 months. The agreement further provided that at the end of 60 months Total Group would have the option to purchase the furniture for the sum of $1. The following year, however, Total Group defaulted on its office lease with CCA and then abandoned the premises permanently, leaving the office furniture behind. CCA sued Total Group for unpaid rent. In addition, CCA sued Office Outfitters and requested the court to determine whether CCA or Office Outfitters had the legal right to take possession of the furniture that was left behind in CCA's office space.

CASE QUESTIONS

1. Was the transaction in this case a true lease or a secured transaction?
2. Does the answer to the previous question depend on whether CCA or Office Outfitters has the legal right to take possession of the office furniture that Total Group left behind?

CASE SUMMARY 17.3 Brankle Brokerage & Leasing, Inc. v. Volvo Financial Services, 394 B.R. 906 (2008)

Lease or Disguised Secured Transaction?

Brankle Brokerage leased six Volvo tractor trucks from Volvo Financial Services pursuant to a single "Master Lease Agreement." The base lease term for the tractor trucks was for a period of 60 months. During this time, Brankle Brokerage could not terminate the agreement for any reason whatsoever, and at the end of the 60-month lease term, Brankle Brokerage had three options:

a. it could buy the tractor trucks for a "purchase price" that was equal to 20 percent of Volvo Financial's cost for the vehicles; or
b. it could sell the tractor trucks on Volvo Financial's behalf, as long as the net sale proceeds were not less than the 20 percent purchase price due if the purchase option was exercised; or
c. it could return the tractor trucks to Volvo Financial, and upon doing so, pay an amount equal to the

20 percent-option purchase price, whereupon Volvo Financial would endeavor to sell them.

Thus, regardless of which option Brankle Brokerage chose—purchase, sell, or have Volvo Financial sell—at the end of each 60-month lease Brankle Brokerage was required to pay Volvo Financial the 20 percent purchase price of the tractor trucks. As a result, Brankle Brokerage stood to benefit only if, at the end of the 60-month lease term, the tractor trucks were worth more than the 20 percent purchase price, but Brankle Brokerage also bore the risk that the vehicles might be worth less than that amount.

CASE QUESTIONS

1. Was the transaction in this case a true lease or a secured transaction?
2. Why would the parties want to "disguise" this transaction as a lease?

CHAPTER REVIEW QUESTIONS

1. **Which of the following statements best describes what a secured transaction is?**

   a. A secured transaction is when the seller retains a security interest in the goods being sold.
   b. A secured transaction is when the seller retains title to the goods being sold.

   c. A secured transaction is when the buyer obtains a security interest in the goods being sold.
   d. A secured transaction is when the lessee obtains a security interest in the goods being sold.
   e. A secured transaction is when the lessor retains title to the goods being sold.

2. **Which party acts as a middleman in a finance lease?**

   a. The lessee.

   b. The supplier.

   c. The seller

   d. The lessor.

   e. The premise of this question is false, because there is no middleman in finance leases.

3. **A finance lease involves how many parties?**

   a. One: a lessor

   b. One: a lessee

   c. Two: a lessee and a supplier

   d. Two: a lessor and a lessee

   e. Three: a lessor, a lessee, and a supplier

4. **Acme Inc. wants to lease a crane from Crane Corp. for use in its construction business. Acme's bank agrees to purchase the equipment from Crane Corp. and then lease the equipment to Acme. In this scenario, which party is the lessor?**

   a. Acme Inc.

   b. Crane Corp.

   c. The bank

   d. The bank and Crane Corp.

   e. Crane Corp. and Acme Inc.

5. **Leasing of equipment is often an attractive option for business firms because:**

   a. The lessee acquires title to the leased goods.

   b. The lessee obtains a security interest in the leased goods.

   c. The lessee is not required to put the lease contract in writing.

   d. The lessee can transfer its title to the leased goods.

   e. The lessee can use the equipment on an exclusive basis without a large up-front investment.

6. **A lessee is one who transfers the right to the possession and use of goods under a lease.**

   a. True

   b. False

7. **A lessor is one who acquires the right to the possession and use of goods under a lease.**

   a. True

   b. False

8. **A lease of a vehicle for $2,000 with an option to renew for $200 must be in writing to be enforceable.**

   a. True

   b. False

9. **A lease of a vehicle for $600 with an option to renew for $600 must be in writing to be enforceable.**

   a. True

   b. False

10. **The main difference between a lease and a sale is that a lease transfers title to the goods being leased.**

   a. True

   b. False

 Quick Quiz ANSWERS
Secured Transactions

1. This "lease" is, in fact, a sale on an installment plan and creates a security interest.
2. This transaction is effectively a sale and creates a security interest.
3. This is effectively a sale and creates a security interest.

CHAPTER REVIEW QUESTIONS: Answers and Explanations

1. **a.** A secured transaction is when the seller retains a security interest in the goods being sold. The remaining responses are therefore incorrect.

2. **d.** It is the lessor who acts as a middleman between the supplier of the good and the lessee. The remaining responses are thus incorrect.

3. **e.** A finance lease involves three parties: a lessor, a lessee, and a supplier. The other answer choices are therefore incomplete or only partially correct.

4. **c.** The bank becomes the lessor since it purchases the crane from Crane Corp. and then leases it to Acme. Answer *a* is incorrect because Acme is the lessee. Answer *b* is wrong because Crane Corp. is the seller. Both *d* and *e* are incorrect because only one party is the lessor in this situation.

5. **e.** Leasing of equipment is often an attractive option for business firms because the lessee can use the equipment on an exclusive basis without a large up-front investment. Answers *a* and *d* are incorrect because a lessee does not acquire title to the leased goods. Answer *b* is incorrect because a lessee does not acquire a secured interest in leased goods. Answer *c* is incorrect because leases of goods over $1,000 must be in writing.

6. **b. False.** A *lessor* is the one who transfers the right to the possession and use of goods under a lease.

7. **b. False.** A *lessee* is one who acquires the right to the possession and use of goods under a lease.

8. **a. True.** Under UCC Article 2A, a lease must be in writing if the total payments to be made under the lease are $1,000 or more.

9. **b. False.** Under UCC Article 2A, a lease must be in writing only if the total payments to be made under the lease are $1,000 or more, *excluding payments for options to renew or buy.*

10. **b. False.** The main difference between a lease and a sale is that a sale transfers title (ownership) to the goods from the seller to the buyer, while a lease does not transfer title.

CHAPTER 18

Sales Warranties

Businesses naturally aim to promote their products to generate sales. Yet, how far can a business go when it makes statements regarding its offerings to consumers? At the conclusion of this chapter, you will assess a product's marketing and advertising to determine the level of risk related to any potential warranties that may have been made.

Learning Objectives

After studying this chapter, students who have mastered the material will be able to:

18-1   Describe and identify the various types of warranties.

18-2   Recognize the appropriate use of disclaimers.

18-3   Discuss the extent of third-party rights in breach of warranty cases.

18-4   Identify the applicability of the Magnuson-Moss Warranty Act.

CHAPTER OVERVIEW

Caveat emptor is the well-known Latin term meaning "buyer beware." The body of law that protects buyers has increased dramatically ever since the American industrial revolution. This chapter discusses various Uniform Commercial Code (UCC) sections that protect consumers by requiring sellers to offer *warranties,* or promises regarding important aspects of the goods. In the spirit of freedom of contract, however, sellers are allowed by the UCC to eliminate the duty to provide warranties by issuing disclaimers in their sales contracts. For example, if you purchase software and read the contract, you may notice that the seller has added something like the following disclaimer:

> THE SOFTWARE IS PROVIDED "AS IS," WITHOUT WARRANTY OF ANY KIND, EXPRESS OR IMPLIED, INCLUDING BUT

NOT LIMITED TO THE WARRANTIES OF MERCHANTABILITY, FITNESS FOR A PARTICULAR PURPOSE, AND NONINFRINGEMENT.

After reading this chapter, you will understand the various warranties imposed by the UCC to protect consumers and how sellers can use disclaimers such as the one above to waive the obligations and risks associated with these warranties.

TYPES OF WARRANTIES

A **warranty** is a seller's promise to a consumer concerning an important aspect of the goods. Warranties are recognized as legally enforceable promises under state statutory laws based on Article 2 of the UCC. Recall that in Chapter 12, "Contracts for the Sale of Goods: Overview of Article 2," Article 2 was covered in the context of formation and performance of sales contracts. This chapter focuses on the warranty provisions of Article 2 that protect consumers. When the seller makes a promise regarding the goods or a representation of fact about the goods, this is known as an **express warranty**. If the seller has not made a specific promise or representation about the product, the buyer may still be protected by a UCC-imposed **implied warranty**.

LO 18-1

Describe and identify the various types of warranties.

Express Warranties

To increase the appeal of their products, sellers often represent that their goods have certain qualities or achieve a certain level of efficiency. If a company has generated an effective marketing program, it will communicate the functional aspects of its goods to consumers through its sales and advertising channels. UCC Section 2-313, however, has a great deal to do with these marketing- and sales-related activities. For example, if the goods turn out not to have the advertised qualities, the buyer may sue for breach of an express warranty. As a practical matter, seller representations are often made through advertising. In one famous case,[1] the Washington Supreme Court held that a car manufacturer breached an express warranty when it advertised in its brochures that the car had "shatterproof glass" that would not fly or shatter even upon the "hardest impact." After a small pebble struck a driver's windshield, resulting in shattered glass and injuries to the driver, the court ruled in favor of the injured driver, stating that the buyer had reasonably relied on those representations and had no reason to suspect they were false.

Because many express warranties arise in the context of advertising, the UCC makes a distinction between factual promises and "puffery." Puffery is a nonfactual statement commonly used in advertising with such claims as, "This car gets great gas mileage" or "This sweater is made from finest wool." Of course, neither of these statements is fact-based because there is no method to verify words such as "great" or "finest." Thus, neither of these statements constitutes an express warranty. However, if the statements are changed slightly to "This car gets 35 miles per gallon when driven on the highway" or "This sweater is 100 percent Irish wool," then they may be considered factual promises to the buyer and will be considered express warranties made by the seller.

Implied Warranties

Even when the seller makes no express promises or statements of fact about the goods, the UCC imposes the following implied warranties on all sales transactions.

Implied Warranty of Title and Noninfringement
Under Section 2-312 of the UCC, every seller (merchant and nonmerchant) must guarantee to the buyer that the title to the goods is free and clear of any claims by others. This is an important guarantee that the goods were not stolen or acquired through fraud. This UCC section also requires the seller to guarantee that the goods are free of any security interests or lien. For example, through this warranty the seller implicitly promises that the goods for sale will not later be seized by someone who claims to have a collateral interest in them from an unpaid loan. Chapter 23, "Secured Transactions," discusses security interests and liens in greater detail.

Lastly, this section of the UCC requires merchants to warrant that the goods shall be delivered free of the rightful claim of any third person claiming infringement. For example, it may be that the software infringes a third party's patent. Because many separate technologies are embedded within the average software, it is very difficult to foresee all potential cases of infringement. This warranty allows the buyer to sue the merchant software seller if the buyer is found liable for patent infringement due to her use of the software.

In Case 18.1, a California appellate court considers the issue of the implied warranty of noninfringement in the context of the apparel industry.

---

[1] *Baxter v. Ford Motor Co.,* 12 P.2d 409 (Wash. 1932).

FACT SUMMARY Olaes supplied Pacific Sunwear of California (PacSun) with T-shirts imprinted with graphic designs for resale in PacSun stores. In 2004, PacSun purchased 16,000 "Hot Sauce Monkey" T-shirts from Olaes. On the front, these T-shirts depicted a monkey drinking a bottle of hot sauce; on the back the same monkey, in apparent pain, was depicted expelling fire. Centered underneath each of the images was a two-word caption: on the front, the phrase "Smile Now"; on the back, the phrase "Cry Later." PacSun was later sued by a company called Smile Now Cry Later, Inc. (SNCL) for infringing their federal trademark on that phrase.

SYNOPSIS OF DECISION AND OPINION A federal trial court judge in Hawaii had previously denied SNCL's trademark-related injunction to prevent PacSun from selling the T-shirts. In this California state appellate court case, PacSun sued its supplier, Olaes, for breaching the implied warranty of noninfringement. The California trial court judge granted Olaes's motion for summary judgment reasoning that because SNCL had not demonstrated likelihood of winning their trademark suit in the federal Hawaii litigation, they did not have a "rightful claim" against the T-shirt sellers under UCC Section 2-312. PacSun appealed that decision to this court, which reversed the lower trial court.

WORDS OF THE COURT: Rightful Claim "The phrase 'rightful claim' is not defined in the California Uniform Commercial Code, and is not a legal term of art that can be interpreted by reference to existing California statutory or case law. . . .

"As explained below, the commentary to Uniform Commercial Code section 2-312 demonstrates that, contrary to Olaes's position, the term 'rightful claim'

as used in the statute is intended to encompass any nonfrivolous claim of infringement that significantly interferes with the buyer's use of a purchased good. . . .

"Finally, if the section 2-312(3) warranty were determined by reference to the ultimate success or failure of third party infringement litigation, the buyer would be placed in an untenable position when a third party sues, contending infringement of a trademark, patent or copyright. Only by losing the lawsuit—or helping the third party claimant to maintain an appearance of success prior to settlement—would the buyer preserve the right to recover from the seller under Uniform Commercial Code section 2-312. This would create a perverse incentive that would undermine the adversary process—a public policy outcome unlikely to have been intended by California Uniform Commercial Code section 2-312's drafters. . . .

"A rightful claim under section 2-312(3) is a nonfrivolous claim of infringement that has any significant and adverse effect, through the prospect of litigation or otherwise, on the buyer's ability to make use of the purchased goods. Applying the above standard to the facts of the instant case, we conclude that the trial court erred in granting Olaes's motion for summary judgment."

Case Questions

1. How could Olaes have prevented this lawsuit?
2. What damages should PacSun try to recover against Olaes if its breach of warranty claim is successful?
3. *Focus on Critical Thinking:* Who should be liable if the goods infringe a third parties' rights, such as a patent, copyright, or trademark? Why?

Implied Warranty of Merchantability Under UCC Section 2-314, the implied warranty of merchantability applies to every sale of a product from a merchant seller to a buyer (the buyer need not be a merchant) and requires the seller to warrant that the product is fit for its ordinary use. Section 2-104(1) of the UCC defines a *merchant* as one who is regularly engaged in the sale of that product or who holds himself out as having knowledge or skill peculiar to the practices or goods involved in the transaction. Thus, if you purchase a new or used lawn mower from your neighbor who is an accountant, no implied warranty exists. Merchants must also conform to industry safety standards in packaging and labeling the goods in order for the goods to qualify as merchantable. This UCC requirement also applies to food and drink consumed either on the merchant's premises or somewhere else.

 QUICK QUIZ Merchants

Take a look at the following ad displayed by the online retailer eBay.

Source: http://pages.ebay.com/seller-center/grow-your-business/power-seller. html#how-to-qualify

1. Is a PowerSeller on eBay a merchant under the UCC? Explain.

2. If the answer is yes, what does this imply for PowerSellers?

Answers to this Quick Quiz are provided at the end of the chapter.

In Case 18.2, a federal appellate court considers whether alleged hearing loss from an iPod can be the basis of a breach of implied warranty of merchantability claim.

CASE 18.2 Birdsong v. Apple, Inc., 590 F.3d 955 (9th Cir. 2009)

FACT SUMMARY Apple's iPod media player comes with a set of earbud headphones that are detachable from the device. The iPod may be used to play music through different headphones or through various speaker systems. Apple includes the following warning with each iPod:

Avoid Hearing Damage

Warning: Permanent hearing loss may occur if earphones or headphones are used at high volume. You can adapt over time to a higher volume of sound, which may sound normal but can be damaging to your hearing. Set your iPod's volume to a safe level before that happens. If you

experience ringing in your ears, reduce the volume or discontinue use of your iPod.

Birdsong sought to bring a class action suit against Apple, alleging that the iPod is capable of producing 115 decibels, and the class members were iPod owners who had allegedly suffered hearing loss using the iPod earbuds set at the highest decibel level. Birdsong's theory of liability (among other claims) was based on Apple's breach of the implied warranty of merchantability. The trial court dismissed Birdsong's suit, and he appealed.

(continued)

The Court of Appeals for the Ninth Circuit upheld the decision in favor of Apple. The court rejected Birdsong's theory that the iPod was not merchantable because it comes with stock earbuds that are designed to be placed deep into the ear canal rather than over the ears, which increases the danger of hearing damage. The court pointed out that the ordinary use of the iPod was to listen to music and that the product was fit for that use. There was no allegation of malfunction, and Birdsong did not allege that the iPods failed to do anything they were designed to do, nor did he allege that he had suffered inevitable hearing loss or other injury directly from iPod use.

WORDS OF THE COURT: The Merchantability Standard "The plaintiffs admit that the iPod has an 'ordinary purpose of listening to music,' and nothing they allege suggests iPods are unsafe for that use or defective. The plaintiffs recognize that iPods play music, have an adjustable volume, and transmit sound through earbuds. The [complaint] includes statements that (1) the iPod is capable of playing 115 decibels of sound; (2) consumers may listen at unsafe levels; and (3) iPod batteries can last 12 to 14 hours and are rechargeable, giving users the opportunity to listen for long periods of time. Taken as true, such statements suggest only that users have the option of using an iPod in a risky manner, not that the product lacks any minimum level of quality."

Case Questions

1. If the iPod is capable of playing at a certain level of sound, isn't it foreseeable that users would assume that a high level of sound was "ordinary" use?

2. If Apple did not provide the warning, how would that impact your analysis?

3. *Focus on Critical Thinking:* Do you believe that most consumers know that earbuds cause more hearing loss than earphones? Should the court have considered the knowledge of the "average" consumer?

Implied Warranty of Fitness for a Particular Purpose Under UCC Section 2-315, an implied warranty arises when a seller (merchant or nonmerchant) promises that the product is fit for a particular purpose. For this warranty to exist, the buyer must prove that the seller knew of the buyer's desire to use the product in a specified way (not necessarily in its ordinary way) and the buyer relied on the seller's advice and recommendation. For example, suppose that Buyer consults with Salesperson and indicates that she requires a new set of boots for a hiking trip that will involve walking through small streams. Salesperson recommends that Buyer purchase Brand A boots for the hiking trip. Buyer purchases the boots, but while hiking, she discovers the boots are not waterproof and they fall apart on the first day of hiking through a small stream. Buyer's boots are destroyed, and she suffers injuries to her feet that require medical care. Because no express promise was made concerning the boots, Buyer must turn to an implied-warranty theory. In this case, Buyer will be able to recover based on a breach of implied warranty of fitness for a particular use.

TAKEAWAY CONCEPTS Types of Warranties

- UCC warranties are an important source of consumer protection.
- UCC warranties are either express or implied.
- The UCC implied warranties include the warranties of: title and noninfringement, merchantability, and fitness for particular purpose.
- The UCC makes a distinction between factual statements and puffery.
- Factual statements create express warranties, whereas puffery does not.

DISCLAIMERS AND LIMITATIONS

LO 18-2

Recognize the appropriate use of disclaimers.

The UCC allows a seller to avoid the risks associated with warranties and **disclaim** both implied and express warranties under certain conditions. The UCC requires that sellers give consumers reasonable notice; therefore, the seller must make disclaimers conspicuous in the contract by using, for example, capital letters, bold print, or a larger font that stands out from the rest of the writing. Although the UCC does not require specific language to disclaim warranties, courts have held that phrases such as "with all faults" or "as is" are sufficient to disclaim the implied warranties of fitness for a particular purpose and non-infringement. However, the UCC does require that any disclaimer of the warranty of merchantability actually use the word "merchantability" in the disclaimer. Likewise, the UCC requires that any disclaimer of the warranty of title include language that makes it clear to the buyer that the seller is not conveying free and clear title to the goods. To protect buyers, sellers may not disclaim any express warranties they have made regarding the goods. Once an express warranty has been made regarding a promise, or statement of fact regarding the goods, the seller is bound to honor that warranty.

The following language is a sample disclaimer from a sales contract:

> OTHER THAN THE EXPRESS WARRANTY ABOVE, SELLER MAKES NO OTHER WARRANTIES ABOUT THE PERFORMANCE OF THE PRODUCTS AND DISCLAIMS ALL OTHER WARRANTIES, EXPRESS OR IMPLIED, RELATING TO THE PRODUCTS, INCLUDING WITHOUT LIMITATION ANY WARRANTY OF MERCHANTABILITY, FITNESS FOR A PARTICULAR PURPOSE OR NONINFRINGEMENT.

Sellers may also, under certain circumstances, limit the remedies of a buyer who has suffered damages because of a seller's breach of warranty. This limitation of remedies is primarily used when the only harm suffered by the buyer was the loss of use of the product. In such cases, the seller may attempt to limit the remedy to replacement or repair of the product and thus avoid paying any consequential damages (as might arise, for example, if the buyer suffered loss of profit due to the defective product). However, the UCC makes clear that any attempt to limit damages when a personal injury is involved will be automatically void. It is important to note that the Magnuson-Moss Act, discussed later in this chapter, restricts certain disclaimers and limitations of remedies by sellers.

Section 2-316(3)(b) of the UCC allows a seller to disclaim defects by making the goods available to the buyer for inspection. If the seller offers the buyer the chance to inspect the goods before entering into the contract, there is no implied warranty on defects that an examination ought to have revealed. If the buyer passes on the opportunity to inspect the goods offered by the seller, there is likewise no warranty on any defects.

TAKEAWAY CONCEPTS Disclaimers and Limitations

- A seller can eliminate warranties through the use of disclaimers.
- A disclaimer must be conspicuous in the contract.
- An express warranty cannot later be disclaimed.
- Offering the goods for inspection to the buyer creates a disclaimer for any defects that the examination ought to reveal.

LO 18-3

Discuss the extent of third-party rights in breach of warranty cases.

THIRD-PARTY RIGHTS

The law has evolved to protect consumers and largely eliminate the **privity of contract** requirement. Under the privity of contract requirement, someone could only sue the party he contracted with. If the end consumer, for example, sued the manufacturer, the manufacturer would have a defense under privity of contract since they did not contract with the consumer and would be removed from the lawsuit. The consumer would only be allowed to sue the party he contracted with, typically a retailer. The privity of contract requirement prevented many suits for breach of warranty and also encouraged multiple lawsuits along the chain of distribution. For these reasons, most states have removed the privity of contract requirement.

Privity of contract dealing with the distribution chain is referred to as **vertical privity**, and most states have done away with this requirement. A few states still require privity of contract, however, in suits seeking damages for economic losses related to nonconforming goods. Section 2-318 of the UCC deals with **horizontal privity**, or the extension of a warranty to someone other than the buyer. This section of the UCC provides two options for states to adopt. It extends a warranty to anyone in the buyer's household and their guests. Alternatively, it extends a warranty to any person who may be reasonably expected to use, consume, or be injured by the goods.

Figure 18.1 illustrates the concepts of vertical and horizontal privity.

A buyer must give notice to the seller of a breach of warranty within a reasonable time after the breach is discovered. Failing to notify the seller of the breach of warranty will result in the dismissal of a case. The requirement that notice be given within a reasonable time is interpreted flexibly. For example, consumers are generally provided a longer time to give notice than businesses.

FIGURE 18.1 Concepts of Vertical and Horizontal Privity

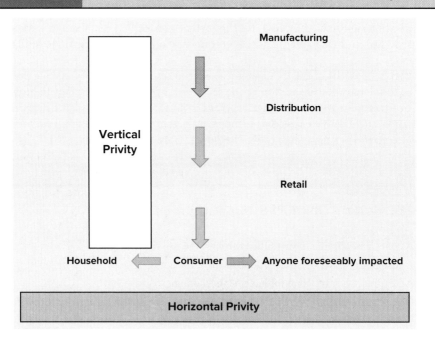

- The vertical privity of contract requirement has been largely eliminated.
- The UCC recognizes horizontal privity.
- A buyer must give notice to the seller of a breach of warranty within a reasonable time after the breach is discovered.

MAGNUSON-MOSS WARRANTY ACT

The Magnuson-Moss Warranty–Federal Trade Commission Improvement Act,[2] generally referred to as the *Magnuson-Moss Act,* regulates warranties given by a seller or lessor to a consumer. As with other consumer protection statutes, the Magnuson-Moss Act does not apply to purely merchant transactions where both the buyer and seller are regularly engaged in the sale of goods. A *consumer* is defined as one who purchases or leases a good with the intent of using it for personal reasons rather than for resale or use in a business. The Magnuson-Moss Act does not mandate that a seller offer a warranty to a buyer. However, if the seller or lessor does offer a **written express warranty**, the transaction is subject to the provisions of the statute.

It is important to note that the Magnuson-Moss Act did not create any additional implied warranties upon which consumers can base a lawsuit; rather, it created a federal cause of action for the breach of consumer warranties contained in state statutes. This is accomplished by permitting consumers to bring a lawsuit directly against a seller to recover damages. However, the statute does allow the seller to resolve disputes using an alternative dispute resolution system (such as binding arbitration) so long as the seller made appropriate disclosures about the dispute resolution requirement at the time of contracting. The Federal Trade Commission (FTC) is responsible for implementing and enforcing the Magnuson-Moss Act's requirements.

If the product being warranted costs $10 or more, the Magnuson-Moss Act requires that the warranty itself contain a label stating the conditions of the warranty. Sellers and lessors of products that carry a full-warranty label must honor a repair or replacement promise for defects. A full warranty must also include a term of duration (e.g., "full one-year warranty"). A limited-warranty label means only that the seller does not bind itself to promises of full warranty in some way (e.g., "limited warranty: engine transmission not covered by warranty").

The Magnuson-Moss Act also requires that warranties be written conspicuously and in plain and clear language. The language must be specific to the parts, products, characteristics, or functionality covered by the warranty. The Magnuson-Moss Act preempts state law and imposes a restriction on disclaimers made by sellers and lessors. The statute modifies rules on disclaimers that were previously allowed by state law with respect to the implied warranty of merchantability and the implied warranty of fitness for a particular use. If the transaction is covered by the Magnuson-Moss Act (because it involves a written express warranty), the seller may not disclaim any implied warranties. Sellers are permitted to set a time frame on the implied warranties so long as the expiration date corresponds with the expiration of any express warranties. If the seller wishes to limit certain damages, the Magnuson-Moss Act requires that such limits be conspicuously featured in the warranty. Typically,

[2]15 U.S.C. § 2301.

LO 18-4

Identify the applicability of the Magnuson-Moss Warranty Act.

the seller complies with this conspicuous-disclosure requirement by featuring the limitation language in bold type or setting it apart in some other way in the document. Figure 18.2 provides an example of a warranty disclaimer and a limitation of remedies.

TAKEAWAY CONCEPTS Magnuson-Moss Warranty Act

- The Magnuson-Moss Act regulates warranties made by a seller.
- The Magnuson-Moss Act applies when the seller offers a written express guarantee.
- When the Magnuson-Moss Act applies, sellers cannot disclaim any implied warranties.

FIGURE 18.2 | **Sample Disclaimer and Limitation of Remedies**

Disclaimer of warranties
The buyer agrees to take the product with ***all faults*** and ***as is***. The seller does not make any express warranties about the product and ***expressly disclaims the implied warranty of merchantability*** and ***disclaims*** any other ***implied warranty*** created by law including the ***implied warranty of fitness for a particular use.***

Limitation of remedies
Seller's sole obligation and Buyer's ***sole remedy*** for any damages related to the failure of the product to perform are ***limited to adjustment or replacement*** of any part causing the failure or at the ***Seller's option*** to refund the purchase amount to the Buyer.

 THINKING STRATEGICALLY

Advertising and Express Warranties

PROBLEM: The marketing, sales, and advertising functions within businesses face a dilemma. They must promote their product to make it appealing to consumers, yet, they must also be careful not to offer any unintended warranties or to make statements of fact that prove to be untrue.

STRATEGIC SOLUTION: In this chapter, we discussed how statements may become express warranties and the potential liability these can trigger. Consider the following case to decide whether the company has made any warranties.

Airborne is a popular herbal and vitamin formula. The product was created by a former second-grade teacher whose motivation to develop the product was triggered by her exposure to germs in the classroom. The company makes the following claim in its advertising:

> Helps boost the immune system with seven herbal extracts and a proprietary blend of vitamins, electrolytes, amino acids and antioxidants.

The company produced the following packaging for its product:

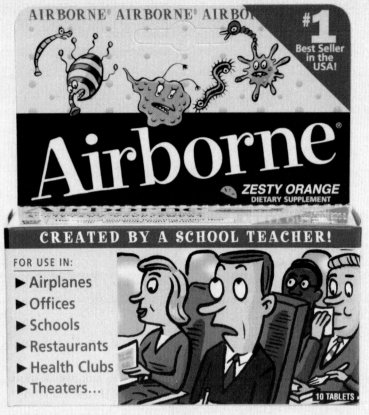

©The Photo Works/Alamy

Independent scientific studies have conclusively shown that there is no evidence that Airborne can prevent the cold or flu or protect people from germ-filled environments.

QUESTIONS

1. Did Airborne offer any warranties?
2. What types of warranties did Airbone offer?
3. Are the statements made by Airbone puffery? Explain.
4. What liability arises if Airborne breached a warranty?
5. How should Airborne avoid this liability moving forward?

KEY TERMS

Warranty p. 312   A guarantee or promise providing assurance by one contracting party to the other party that specific facts or conditions are true or will happen (*ch. 17*). A seller's promise to a consumer concerning an important aspect of the goods (*ch. 18*).

Express warranty p. 313   Warranty in which the seller makes a promise regarding the goods or a representation of fact about the goods.

Implied warranty p. 313   Warranty automatically imposed by law on the seller for every sales contract.

Disclaim p. 317   When a seller uses language in the contract to remove any of the implied warranties.

Privity of contract p. 318   The requirement that a contract with a party is necessary to bring a legal action against that party.

Vertical privity p. 318   Privity of contract issues dealing with parties in the distribution chain.

Horizontal privity p. 318   Privity of contract issues dealing with the extension of a warranty to someone other than the buyer.

Written express warranty p. 319   The type of warranty that triggers coverage under the Magnuson-Moss Warranty Act.

CASE SUMMARY 18.1 Giles v. POM Wonderful, LLC, No. 10-32192 (Cir. Ct., 17th Jud. Cir., Broward County, Fla., filed August 6, 2010)

Express Warranty

A class action lawsuit was filed against the maker of POM Wonderful pomegranate juice in a Florida state court. Plaintiffs alleged that the company misled consumers by marketing its product "as having special health benefits." Among the product claims alleged to be false are that it will prevent, mitigate, and/or treat atherosclerosis, blood flow/pressure, prostate cancer, erectile dysfunction, cardiovascular disease, LDL cholesterol, and other age-related medical conditions.

CASE QUESTIONS

1. Are the claims made by POM Wonderful express warranties?
2. How could POM Wonderful reduce this potential liability?

CASE SUMMARY 18.2 Mennonite Deaconess Home & Hospital, Inc. v. Gates Engineering Co., 219 Neb. 303, 363 N.W.2d 155 (1985)

Express and Implied Warranties

Mennonite Deaconess Home & Hospital (MDHH) experienced leaks in its roof and hired a contractor to install a new roof that was manufactured by Gates. A Gates representative made statements to MDHH and offered brochures that described the roofing system. MDHH relied on the Gates representative's skill and knowledge to select the appropriate roof. The contractor installed the roof, which started leaking shortly thereafter. MDHH sued Gates for breach of warranty. The court found in favor of MDHH.

CASE QUESTIONS

1. Was an express warranty created? Explain.
2. Were any implied warranties created? Explain.

CASE SUMMARY 18.3 City of LaCrosse v. Schubert, Schroeder & Associates, 72 Wis. 2d 38, 240 N.W.2d 124 (1976)

Privity of Contract

The City of LaCrosse, Wisconsin, hired a contractor to install a new roof for an elementary school. The roof was purchased by the contractor from Kaiser Aluminum Sales Corporation (KASC). Shortly after the new roof was installed, it began to leak. The roof then fell apart, and a new roof was needed. The City sued KASC for breach of implied warranties. The court held in favor of KASC since the City lacked privity of contract and was suing for economic damages.

CASE QUESTIONS

1. Who would the City have to sue to recover damages?
2. Does this ruling make sense? Explain.

CASE SUMMARY 18.4 Consumers Power Co. v. Mississippi Valley Structural Steel Co., 636 F. Supp. 1100 (E.D. Mich. 1986)

Privity of Contract

The owner of a nuclear power plant sued the manufacturer of anchoring bolts for breach of warranty even though there was no privity of contract between the parties. The sole damages were economic in nature. The court did not require privity of contract between the parties and allowed the case to proceed to its merits.

CASE QUESTIONS

1. Does this case involve horizontal or vertical privity of contract?
2. Does this ruling make sense? Explain.

CASE SUMMARY 18.5 Webster v. Blue Ship Tea Room, Inc., 198 N.E. 2d 309 (Supreme Judicial Court of Massachusetts, 1964)

Implied Warranty of Merchantability

The plaintiff ordered a bowl of fish chowder at the well-known Blue Ship Tea Room in Boston. After eating a few spoonfuls, the plaintiff felt a fish bone lodge in her throat. She required medical care and sued the restaurant for breach of implied warranty of merchantability. The appellate court found in favor of the restaurant stating that customers who order fish chowder should anticipate having to remove some fish bones from their meal.

CASE QUESTIONS

1. Should chefs have to ensure that a dish like fish chowder is free of any fish bones?
2. Do you agree with the court's decision? Explain.

CHAPTER REVIEW QUESTIONS

1. A car dealership lists a car for sale as "a new vehicle." This is a(n):
   a. Implied warranty.
   b. Privity of contract.
   c. Express warranty.
   d. Disclaimer.
   e. None of the above.

2. A car dealership advertises a used car as "a real gem of a car." This is a(n):
   a. Implied warranty.
   b. Privity of contract.
   c. Express warranty.
   d. Puffery statement.
   e. None of the above.

3. If the goods are of below-average quality, the following warranty may have been breached:
   a. Express warranty.
   b. Implied warranty of title.
   c. Implied warranty of merchantability.
   d. Implied warranty of fitness for a particular purpose.
   e. None of the above.

4. If the buyer relies on the seller's expertise and purchases goods that do not meet the buyer's specific criteria, the following warranty may have been breached:
   a. Express warranty.
   b. Implied warranty of title.
   c. Implied warranty of merchantability.
   d. Implied warranty of fitness for a particular purpose.
   e. None of the above.

5. If the buyer purchases goods from a seller and is later sued for patent infringement related to use of the goods by a third party, the following warranty may have been breached.

   a. Express warranty.

   b. Implied warranty of noninfringement.

   c. Implied warranty of merchantability.

   d. Implied warranty of fitness for a particular purpose.

   e. None of the above.

6. If the buyer buys goods from a seller and it later turns out that the goods were stolen, the implied warranty of title may have been breached.

   a. True

   b. False

7. A seller may avoid providing a warranty through use of a disclaimer.

   a. True

   b. False

8. Joe lives in a state where he can sue the manufacturer of goods he purchased for breach of warranty even though he never contracted with that company. The courts in this state have done away with the requirement of horizontal privity.

   a. True

   b. False

9. Joe lives in a state where his wife can sue the retailer of goods Joe purchased for breach of warranty even though she never contracted with that company. The courts in this state have done away with the requirement of horizontal privity.

   a. True

   b. False

10. Seller X states in their advertising that the electric water heaters they are selling are guaranteed to withstand power surges during electrical storms. In the sales contract, Seller X adds a disclaimer on all express or implied warranties. The disclaimer with respect to the power surge guarantee is not valid under the UCC.

   a. True

   b. False

 Quick Quiz ANSWERS
Merchants

1. Yes, PowerSellers on eBay are merchants. UCC § 2-104(1) defines a merchant as one who is regularly engaged in the sale of a product or who holds himself out as having knowledge or skill peculiar to the practices or goods involved in the transaction. The ad states that a PowerSeller maintains high sales volumes and consistently offers superior customer service to buyers.

2. This means that PowerSellers are classified as merchants under the UCC and face additional liability.

CHAPTER REVIEW QUESTIONS: Answers and Explanations

1. **c.** This is an objective statement of fact.

2. **d.** This is a subjective statement that cannot be proven to be true or false.

3. **c.** The implied warranty of merchantability guarantees goods of at least average quality.

4. **d.** The implied warranty of fitness for a particular purpose requires the buyer to rely on the seller's expertise regarding a specific use of the goods.

5. **b.** If the goods violate the rights of a third party, this breaches the implied warranty of noninfringement.

6. **a. True.** Every sale imposes a warranty of title that guarantees that the goods are not stolen.

7. **a. True.** Disclaimers allow sellers to avoid providing warranties.

8. **b. False.** The vertical privity requirement applies within the chain of distribution.

9. **a. True.** Horizontal privity relates to members in the household who may be able to sue for breach of warranty even though they never contracted with the seller.

10. **a. True.** The UCC provides that if a seller offers an express warranty they cannot later disclaim it.

UNIT THREE Commercial Paper and Secured Transactions

CHAPTER 19

Definition, Creation, and Categories of Negotiable Instruments

 THINKING STRATEGICALLY

©valterZ/Shutterstock

In this chapter you will learn about the unique characteristics of debt instruments known as negotiable instruments. Negotiable instruments offer a great deal of flexibility that allow businesses to manage their finances. For example, at the end of this chapter, you will learn how to strategically manage cash flows by negotiating a company's accounts receivable.

Learning Objectives

After studying this chapter, students who have mastered the material will be able to:

19-1   Describe the features of a negotiable instrument.

19-2   Categorize the types of negotiable instruments.

19-3   Explain the steps necessary to negotiate and indorse an instrument.

19-4   Summarize how negotiable instruments relate to securitization in debt capital markets.

CHAPTER OVERVIEW

What do checks, home mortgages, credit card debt, car loans, bank CDs, bonds issued by a corporation, and student loans have in common? They are all referred to as *negotiable instruments* and are subject to Article 3 of the Uniform Commercial Code (UCC). As will be discussed in greater detail in this chapter (and Chapters 20, 21, and 22), negotiable instruments have unique characteristics that allow them to be transferred and sold to third parties, such as investors. This introductory chapter offers an overview of the various types of negotiable instruments, the UCC law that governs them, and their application to business.

FEATURES OF A NEGOTIABLE INSTRUMENT

A negotiable instrument is:

1. An unconditional promise or order;
2. To pay a fixed amount of money;
3. That must be in writing;
4. Signed;[1]
5. Made payable "to order," "to bearer," or "to cash;" and
6. Made payable either on demand or at a definite time in the future.

---
[1]UCC § 3-104(a).

Each of these elements must be readily apparent within the "four corners" of the instrument and are worth exploring in greater detail to gain a better sense of what makes a particular legal instrument a *negotiable* instrument.

If the instrument is classified as a negotiable instrument, it can be readily exchanged or sold to third parties for value. In this capacity, negotiable instruments serve two vital commercial purposes. First, as with the example of a check or a draft, they can act as a substitute for money. Second, they facilitate financing. Selling a loan that is a negotiable instrument, such as a promissory note, offers liquidity, encourages lending, and provides an investment opportunity for the purchaser of that debt instrument.

LO 19-1

Describe the features of a negotiable instrument.

Unconditional Promise

The UCC defines a **promise** as "a written undertaking to pay money signed by the party undertaking to pay."[2] A promise to repay is usually made in exchange for receiving a loan or to pay for goods and services that have been rendered. Note that the UCC requires that the promise to repay must be unconditional. This means that the promise to repay must not be conditional on any other occurrence or event contingent on another writing, such as a separate contract. For example, if Sam issues a signed written promise that states, "I promise to pay Barbara $10,000 if she sells me her car before June 10," this would fail to be a negotiable instrument because it is a promise that is conditioned on the sale of the car. To be an unconditional promise, the promise would have to be rephrased, "I promise to pay Barbara $10,000 on June 10."

A negotiable instrument can mention another writing if it uses language only to reference the other agreement, for example, using the terms *as per contract*. If the instrument, however, references another contract with language such as *subject to contract,* this will make the instrument conditional on this other agreement and will destroy its negotiability.

Order

A negotiable instrument can be an unconditional promise to repay or it can be an **order**. An order is a written instruction to pay money signed by the person giving the instruction.[3] For example, Ben owes Francisco $50 to repay a short-term loan. Francisco owes Maggie $50 for cat-sitting services. Francisco can order Ben to pay Maggie. If the order is in the form of the paper represented in Figure 19.1, it will be considered a negotiable instrument.

FIGURE 19.1 Order to Pay

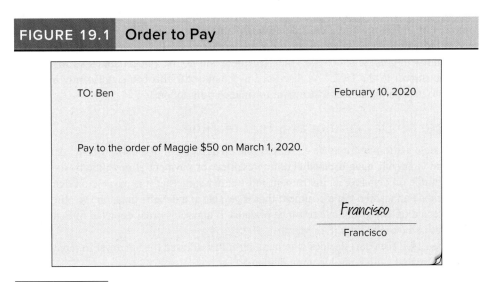

TO: Ben   February 10, 2020

Pay to the order of Maggie $50 on March 1, 2020.

Francisco
_____
Francisco

---
[2]UCC § 3-103(a).
[3]Ibid.

Fixed Amount

The UCC requires that all negotiable instruments be issued as fixed amounts of money.[4] In the case of a promise, this means that the precise amount of repayment is stated explicitly on the negotiable instrument. The use of anything other than money (e.g., gold or diamonds) to repay will result in the item not being classified as a negotiable instrument. Under the UCC, *money* is defined as a medium of exchange authorized or adopted by a domestic or foreign government. Foreign currency is, therefore, acceptable as a basis for creating a negotiable instrument.[5] A promise to repay with a variable interest rate will be a negotiable instrument as long as the principal or total loan amount is a fixed amount. The same is true of an order; it must indicate a specific dollar amount, as in the case of Francisco issuing an order to Ben to pay Maggie $50.

In Writing and Signed

The UCC requires that a promise or order be in writing and be signed by the party obligated to repay the debt or the person issuing the order to pay. Negotiable instruments, therefore, require some kind of tangible paper evidence. The writing is usually on paper, but it may be handwritten rather than typed. Any signature (other than an electronic signature) will suffice as long as it is a symbol that demonstrates the intention to authenticate a writing.

Payable to Order or to Bearer

Negotiable instruments must either identify the party to whom payment will be made or specify that the person who possesses the negotiable instrument is the party to be paid. In the first case, the negotiable instrument is **payable to order** and will require the words "pay to the order of [name]." The order issued by Francisco to Ben to pay Maggie, for example, used the words "pay to the order of Maggie" and appropriately identified Maggie as the person entitled to be paid.

In the second case, the negotiable instrument is **payable to bearer** and will require the words "pay to bearer" or "pay to cash." This indicates that whoever possesses the instrument will be entitled to payment. For example, a check that is made "pay to bearer" or "pay to cash" can be exchanged for funds by anyone in possession of that instrument. The use of the specific terms "pay to the order of," "pay to bearer," or "pay to cash" are referred to as the **magic words of negotiability** and are a strict formality required by the UCC if those promises or orders are to be considered negotiable instruments. The failure to use these specialized words of negotiability may create an agreement that is enforceable under the common law of contracts; however, the agreement will not be a negotiable instrument, nor will it be subject to the UCC. As discussed in Chapter 20, this can significantly limit the options to use that particular instrument to finance transactions.

Payable on Demand or at a Future Time

A negotiable instrument must be either payable on demand or at a definite time. An instrument that is **payable upon demand** can be presented for payment at any time by its holder. To be payable on demand, an instrument must either state that it is payable on demand or omit the date altogether. An instrument that is **payable at a definite time**, on the other hand, will be repaid on any given date or range of dates. Francisco's order depicted in Figure 19.1 is payable at a definite time (i.e., March 1, 2020).

In Case 19.1, the court decides whether a term that allowed the borrower to repay "when you can" created a note payable upon demand.

---

[4] UCC § 3-104(a).
[5] UCC § 1-201(b)(24).

FACT SUMMARY Vaughn signed a document stating that the Smiths had loaned him $9,900. As to the date of repayment, the document stated "when you [Vaughn] can." Eighteen months later, the Smiths sued Vaughn for failing to pay as promised. At the trial court, the Smiths filed a motion for summary judgment arguing that the document was a promissory note and a negotiable instrument that was payable upon demand. The trial court denied the motion, and the appellate court affirmed this decision.

SYNOPSIS OF DECISION AND OPINION The appellate court agreed with the trial court that the note was not payable upon demand because the language did not state so and omitted a date altogether.

WORDS OF THE COURT: Payable on Demand "The Smiths and Vaughn agree that the terms of the promissory note control in this case. They argue, however, over what law applies to determine the meaning of the phrase 'when you can.' The Smiths

contend that the note was payable on demand and that it was a negotiable instrument. It was neither. An instrument is payable on demand if it states that it is, or if no time is specified for repayment. Here, 'when you can' was when payment was due. This was not the equivalent of completely failing to identify a repayment date. And this conditional term of repayment destroyed negotiability. This argument has no merit."

Case Questions

1. Why is the "when you can" repayment term a condition that destroys negotiability?

2. How could the Smiths have ensured this paper was a negotiable instrument and payable upon demand?

3. *Focus on Critical Thinking:* How would you interpret a contract that stipulates "repayment when you can"? Is there a date that can apply to this statement? What are the risks of entering into a loan contract with such a term?

TAKEAWAY CONCEPTS Negotiability

- A negotiable instrument is an unconditional promise or order to pay a fixed amount of money that must be in writing and signed.
- Negotiable instruments must include the "magic words of negotiability"; be made payable "to order," "to bearer," or "to cash"; and be made payable either on demand or at a definite time in the future.
- A negotiable instrument can be readily exchanged or sold to third parties for value.
- Negotiable instruments serve two vital commercial purposes: They can act as a substitute for money and facilitate financing.

TYPES OF NEGOTIABLE INSTRUMENTS

LO 19-2

Categorize the types of negotiable instruments.

We have defined negotiable instruments as orders or promises. There are, however, different types of negotiable instruments within these categories, as indicated in Figure 19.2. An order, for example, can be classified as a draft or a check.

Draft

A **draft** is simply a written order to pay money signed by the person giving the order. The order given by Francisco to Ben in Figure 19.1 would be classified as a draft. A draft involves three parties: a drawer, a drawee, and a payee. The **drawer** is the party issuing the payment

FIGURE 19.2   Types of Negotiable Instruments

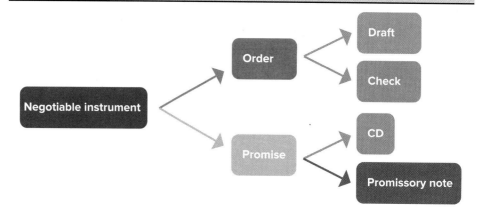

order (Francisco), and the **drawee** (Ben) is that party who must make the payment as specified to the person receiving the funds, or the **payee** (Maggie). A draft may be either a **time draft**, which is payable at a determined future date, or a **sight draft**, which is payable at any time upon demand once it is presented to the drawee.

Check

A **check** is a specialized type of order and draft payable on demand and drawn on a bank.[6] For example, Francisco as the drawer could have issued an order to his drawee bank to pay $50 to Maggie as the payee. This could have been achieved using a check instead of a draft, as shown in Figure 19.3. The law that governs checks and bank payment systems is covered in greater detail in Chapter 22.

Whereas an order can be a draft or a check, a promise to repay can be either a certificate of deposit (CD) or a promissory note.

FIGURE 19.3   Check

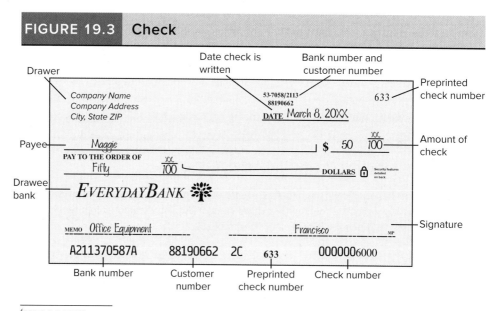

[6]UCC § 3-104(f).

Certificate of Deposit (CD)

A **certificate of deposit** is a written note that indicates a bank has received money as a loan and promises to repay the amount in the future with interest, typically at a higher rate than that offered by a savings account. As indicated in the advertisement below, bank customers often are given the opportunity to lend a bank funds through a certificate of deposit.

> **Save big with our 15-month CD special – available for a limited time!**
>
> **1.50** **%**
> **APY**
> **ON A 15-MONTH CD**
>
> $1,000 MINIMUM OPENING DEPOSIT,
> NEW MONEY ONLY
> PENALTY FOR EARLY WITHDRAWAL

Source: norstatesbank.com

Promissory Note

A **promissory note** is any type of loan (personal or commercial) whereby one party offers to lend a specific amount of money with repayment in the future. A promise to repay involves two parties, the maker and the payee. A **maker** is the party who receives the loan and promises to repay.[7] The **payee** is the party who extends credit and is entitled to repayment.[8]

A promissory note that would function as a negotiable instrument can be as simple as the written and signed promise made in Figure 19.4, or it can be a much more detailed contract, such as that evidencing an auto loan.

Time notes are payable at a definite time. In the case of Figure 19.4, payment will be made January 31, 2019. **Demand notes** are payable at any time upon the request of the payee. Omitting the date from Figure 19.4, for example, would transform this note into a demand note that is payable whenever Nick presents the note for payment to Francisco.

FIGURE 19.4	A Simple Promissory Note

I promise to pay $100 to the order of Nick Mazza on January 31, 2019.

Francisco

Francisco

---

[7] UCC § 3-103(a).
[8] Ibid.

✓ **QUICK QUIZ** Aspects of a Negotiable Instrument

TO: Chris

Pay to the order of Melanie $100 Swiss Francs.

Robinson

_____

Robinson

1. Is this a negotiable instrument? Why or why not? If so, what kind of instrument is it?

2. How would you refer to Chris, Melanie, and Robinson using the terms discussed earlier?

Answers to this Quick Quiz are provided at the end of the chapter.

TAKEAWAY CONCEPTS Categories of Negotiable Instruments

- Negotiable instruments are classified as either orders or promises to repay.
- Orders can be further classified as either a draft or a check.
- A promise to repay can be further classified as either a certificate of deposit (CD) or a promissory note.

LO 19-3

Explain the steps necessary to negotiate and indorse an instrument.

STEPS TO NEGOTIATE AND INDORSE AN INSTRUMENT

One of the major features of a negotiable instrument, as its name implies, is its negotiability. For example, if Francisco had given Maggie the $50 draft in Figure 19.1, she would be able to negotiate this paper because it is a negotiable instrument. Say Maggie owes Wendy $50. If Wendy accepts the draft as payment, Maggie can negotiate the draft to Wendy by indorsing it and handing it to Wendy.

A **negotiation** is, therefore, the various steps used to transfer a negotiable instrument from party to party through a legally defined process.[9] One can become a holder in two ways: Either the instrument can be issued to a specific person or it can be transferred to that person by negotiation. The negotiation of an instrument will depend on whether it is payable to an identified person as order paper or to the bearer as bearer paper.

---

[9]UCC § 3-201(a).

Negotiation of Order Paper

If the instrument is **order paper** and thus payable to an identified person, its negotiation requires that the identified party physically transfer the instrument *and* indorse the instrument to its new holder. An **indorsement** is a signature, other than that of a signer as maker, drawer or acceptor of the instrument, for the purpose of negotiating the instrument.[10] A drawer of an instrument can make it payable to more than one person; however, care must be taken to specify whether it is payable to *either* party or to *all* the parties. If the payment is to either party, then either of the parties can negotiate, indorse, or collect payment.[11] If the payment is to all the parties, then negotiation, indorsement, or payment will require everyone's signature.[12]

In Case 19.2, a bankruptcy court decides how to interpret a check that was ambiguously made payable to two parties using a virgule ("/") symbol.[13]

CASE 19.2 Danco, Inc. v. Commerce Bank/Shore, 675 A.2d 663 (N.J. Super. Ct. App. Div. 1996)

FACT SUMMARY   The plaintiff, Danco, Inc., sells plumbing supplies. One of its customers, San-Fran Plumbing, purchased supplies on credit and became delinquent on the account. San-Fran was in the process of completing development projects for Hovnanian and received payment directly from Hovnanian for plumbing work. Danco and San-Fran reached an agreement whereby checks made by Hovnanian to San-Fran would be made payable to both Danco and San-Fran. San-Fran sent the following message to Hovnanian:

> We would appreciate it, if all checks to San-Fran Plumbing, Inc., will be made out to two parties. First party San-Fran Plumbing, Inc., and the second party to be Danco Plumbing, Inc.

Hovnanian complied and wrote the checks out to San-Fran Plumbing, Inc./Danco Plumbing, Inc. Danco would then cash the checks from Hovnanian; if there was any money after deducting what San-Fran owed for supplies, Danco would credit that amount to San-Fran. San-Fran declared bankruptcy, and it was later discovered that there were three checks totaling $22,332 that were issued by Hovnanian but were never forwarded to Danco by San-Fran. Instead, San-Fran deposited these checks into its business account with Commerce Bank. Danco sued Commerce Bank for cashing the checks without the proper indorsement of both parties. The trial court judge granted Commerce Bank's motion for summary judgment and held that the checks were payable alternately to either Danco or San-Fran. Danco appealed that decision to the appellate court.

SYNOPSIS OF DECISION AND OPINION   The appellate court decided that the checks were made payable to either party; therefore, under UCC § 3-110, either party could indorse the checks and deposit them into its account. The key issue was the interpretation of whether the virgule ("/") symbol, meant "and" or "or."

WORDS OF THE COURT: Indorsement of Both Parties   "The Official Comment to this Revised U.C.C. section states the following as to construing ambiguities in favor of alternative payees: 'In the case of ambiguity persons dealing with the instrument should be able to rely on the indorsement of a single payee.' Official Comment, *U.C.C.* (Revised) § 3-110(d). Although this provision was not in effect at the time of this transaction, we believe there are persuasive reasons to hold in accordance with the U.C.C. revision. As we have noted, it is the objective intent of the maker that is controlling as to

(continued)

---

[10]UCC § 3-204(a).

[11]UCC § 3-110(d).

[12]Ibid.

[13]Ibid.

the indorsements required. Thus, unless the maker makes it clear that indorsement by a single payee is unacceptable, persons dealing with the instrument should be able to rely on the single indorsement without suffering the risk of incurring liability. The maker is in the best position to guard against the ambiguity and that is where the duty should be.

"Only one case in our State has dealt with the question of what the [slash symbol] means. . . . In *Kinzig,* the trial court held that 'use of a [slash] permits payment to either of the payees listed on a check, and proper payment requires the indorsement of only one of the payees.' *Ibid.* In modern writing, [a slash] means a short slanting stroke drawn between two words and indicating that *either* may be used by the reader to interpret the sense of the text. 'It denotes the *disjunctive or alternative.*' . . .

"Even though we conclude that a [slash] when placed between two names specifically indicates that alternative indorsement is acceptable, and that payment on an indorsement is proper with the signature of either, we nonetheless would reach the same result if the use of the [slash] here were deemed to have resulted in ambiguity. We base this on our acceptance of the reasoning of the Revised *U.C.C.* § 3-110(d). . . .

"In conclusion, we are satisfied that the motion judge properly granted summary judgment in favor of Commerce [Bank]. . . . The indorsements of Danco were not required on the checks in question."

Case Questions

1. Do you agree that a slash symbol indicates either party may indorse? Why or why not?

2. How would the court have decided this case if it had found that there was ambiguity with respect to payment?

3. *Focus on Critical Thinking:* How could Danco have avoided this problem altogether?

Indorsements fall into three categories: blank or special, restrictive or nonrestrictive, and qualified or unqualified.

Blank or Special Indorsements
A **blank indorsement** consists solely of the indorser's signature and nothing else. This will convert order paper into bearer paper. If Nick, for example, signs the back of the note issued by Francisco in Figure 19.4 and writes nothing else, this will convert the order paper into bearer paper, and anyone possessing it can present it to Francisco for payment.

A **special indorsement** specifically identifies the party to whom the instrument is to be payable. To use the same example, if Nick writes on the back of the promissory note: "Pay to Zhang," only Zhang will now have the ability to present the note to Francisco for payment. This also gives Zhang the ability to negotiate the draft to someone else if he wishes to do so. A special indorsement does not require the words of negotiability; therefore, any indorsement that identifies the party who is to be paid will suffice.

Restrictive or Nonrestrictive Indorsements
A **restrictive indorsement** is one that seeks to limit the negotiability of an instrument or impose a condition on the payee. Generally, the UCC disfavors restrictive indorsements because they prevent the negotiability of an instrument.[14] For example, if Nick writes on the back of the note "Pay to Zhang only" or "Payable to Zhang if Zhang edits Nick's manuscript," these restrictive indorsements would be ineffective and would not limit the negotiability of the note. Zhang would be free to negotiate the paper to someone else despite these restrictive instructions.

One restrictive indorsement that is allowed for checks is "For deposit only." If a payee wants to restrict any further negotiation of the draft, he would sign his name on the back of

---

[14]UCC § 3-206.

the draft and write or stamp "For deposit only." This would limit any further negotiation and would only allow a bank to deposit the funds in the payee's account rather than cash the proceeds. Businesses often stamp "For deposit only" on the back of checks they receive as a risk management safeguard to have stricter control of their checks and to ensure they will be deposited to the businesses' account. This eliminates the risk of someone fraudulently cashing the check. A **nonrestrictive indorsement** lacks any type of language that seeks to limit the negotiability of an instrument or conditions to its payment or transfer.

Figure 19.5 illustrates a check with a restrictive indorsement.

Qualified or Unqualified Indorsements

If Nick negotiates the note to Zhang and Francisco fails to pay as promised on the note, Nick will assume the liability for payment unless he adds a qualified indorsement. A **qualified indorsement** adds language such as "Without recourse" to limit the indorser's loss exposure due to nonpayment. Adding a qualified indorsement will still leave the indorser with some liability related to warranties, which is discussed in greater detail in Chapter 21. An **unqualified indorsement** does not include any language that limits the indorser's nonpayment liability.

FIGURE 19.5 Check with a Restrictive Indorsement

Endorse Here
X _____ *Felipe* _____
_____ *For deposit only* _____
_____
_____

Do Not Write, Stamp or Sign Below This Line
Reserved For Financial Institution Use*

Negotiation of Bearer Paper

If the instrument is payable to bearer, negotiation occurs when the holder physically transfers possession of the instrument to its new holder. In these cases, indorsement is not necessary. For example, if a note or check is made payable "To bearer" or "To cash," the person who has physical possession of this instrument is its holder and may negotiate it simply by transferring possession of the instrument to someone else. Bearer instruments should, therefore, be viewed and treated as cash.

TAKEAWAY CONCEPTS Negotiability and Indorsement

- Negotiation of an instrument is a transfer of possession, whether voluntary or involuntary, of an instrument by a person other than the issuer who then becomes its holder.
- If the instrument is order paper and thus payable to an identified person, its negotiation requires that the identified party indorse the instrument and physically transfer it to its new holder.
- Indorsements will be either blank or special, restrictive or nonrestrictive, and qualified or unqualified.
- If the instrument is payable to bearer, negotiation occurs when the holder physically transfers possession of the instrument to its new holder.

LO 19-4

Summarize
how negotiable
instruments relate
to securitization
in debt capital
markets.

NEGOTIABLE INSTRUMENTS AND SECURITIZATION IN DEBT CAPITAL MARKETS

Negotiable instruments play a major role in finance. As mentioned at the beginning of the chapter, negotiable instruments facilitate lending and provide an investment opportunity for the purchaser of debt instruments such as promissory notes. For example, many automobiles today are purchased with a bank loan or through a lease financed by an auto financing company, such as the Toyota Motor Credit Corp. When an individual finances an auto purchase and signs a vehicle purchase agreement, she also executes a promissory note with the financing company. This note contains the required elements of a negotiable instrument: an unconditional promise to repay a fixed amount that is in writing, signed, payable to order, and payable at a specific future date.

The financing company (i.e., the "issuer" or "originator") packages thousands of auto loans and sells them to a separate corporation, called a *special purpose vehicle (SPV)*, which is created specifically to own these notes. The SPV is created to avoid the risk of the financing company's bankruptcy and the claims its creditors would have on the notes. The now "bankruptcy-remote" SPV issues bonds that are secured by the notes (Chapter 23 covers secured transactions), and these bonds are then purchased by investors.

This entire process relies on the law of negotiable instruments, particularly the negotiability of promissory notes to the SPV. The process of packaging promissory notes and negotiating their sale to investors is called **securitization**. Figure 19.6 depicts the securitization process. The issuer (or the loan originator) participates in a securitization to obtain greater liquidity in the form of cash up front and can also profit from the loans it has originated.

Table 19.1 includes information on the market size of various types of debt and the percentages within each category that are securitized. In most cases, the promissory notes behind these various categories of debt are likely instruments that can be negotiated and sold to investors.

TABLE 19.1	The Securitization Market
Loan Type ($ billions)	2017
Auto loans	$ 1,119
Securitized	17%
Non-securitized	83%
Credit cards	$ 1,009
Securitized	12%
Non-securitized	88%
Student loans	$ 1,438
Securitized	13%
Non-securitized	87%
Commercial mortgages	$ 3,856
Securitized	16%
Non-securitized	84%
Residential mortgages	$10,330
Securitized	8%
Non-securitized	92%
Business loans	$899
Securitized	51%
Non-securitized	49%

FIGURE 19.6 The Securitization Process

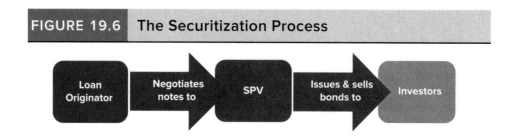

Negotiable Instruments and the Subprime Mortgage Crisis

Many believe that debt securitization played an influential role in the subprime mortgage crisis that triggered the Great Recession. The economic basis of that major financial downturn was the collapse of real estate prices that had been fueled by a speculative investment bubble. Investors bought a significant number of bonds that were securitized with risky subprime mortgages. This created the demand for the approval of home loans to borrowers with risky or poor credit (i.e., subprime borrowers). According to one source, nearly 80 percent of subprime mortgage–backed securities were securitized.[15]

Discussion Questions

1. Should securitization be curtailed or regulated more closely to avoid a future financial collapse, or should banks be left to self-regulate themselves?
2. What other solutions might exist besides regulation?
3. Do you think the banking community has a duty to use legal strategies and techniques such as securitization in a prudent or ethical way?

The securitization of home mortgages played a key role in the mortgage crisis.
©Andy Dean Photography/Alamy

TAKEAWAY CONCEPTS Negotiable Instruments and Securitization

- Negotiable instruments facilitate lending, increase liquidity, and provide an investment opportunity for purchasers of debt instruments such as promissory notes.
- The process of packaging promissory notes and negotiating their sale to investors is called securitization.
- Various types of debt undergo securitization.

---

[15]Investopedia, "What Role Did Securitization Play in the U.S. Subprime Mortgage Crisis?," May 2018.

Negotiating Accounts Receivable

Sarah Sturges owns Fabulous Leather Creations, LLC, a maker of high-end leather goods such as handbags, wallets, and laptop briefcases. Her biggest customer is a national luxury retailer called Hampton Market. Sarah currently ships the leather goods to Hampton's warehouse in California and receives payment within 30 days of sending an invoice. The typical invoice looks like this:

Fabulous Leather Creations, LLC
Where leather comes to life!™

INVOICE

123 Woodville Highway

Phoenix, AZ 85054

602-231-2222

INVOICE #100
DATE: 06/01/19

TO:
Hampton Market, Inc.

432 Rodeo Drive

Beverly Hills, CA 90210

310-123-4567

SHIP TO:
Hampton Market, Inc.

123 Warehouse Drive

Long Beach, CA 90712

562-999-0000

SALESPERSON	P.O. NUMBER	REQUISITIONER	SHIPPED VIA	F.O.B. POINT	TERMS
Sarah Sturges	100-101	Martin Kretchmer	Railway/ Semi-Trailer	Long Beach warehouse	Due in 30 days

QUANTITY	DESCRIPTION	UNIT PRICE	TOTAL
1,000	Purses – *Echo* design	$100	$100,000
500	Wallets – *Ambition* design	$50	$25,000
1,000	Laptop briefcases – *Pursuit* design	$200	$200,000
	SUBTOTAL		$325,000
	SALES TAX		8%
	SHIPPING & HANDLING		--
	TOTAL DUE		$351,000

Make all checks payable to Fabulous Leather Creations, LLC
If you have any questions concerning this invoice, contact Sarah Sturges, 1-800-631-2000x999

THANK YOU FOR YOUR BUSINESS!

PROBLEM: Sarah just got a call from Martin Kretchmer, the purchasing manager at Hampton Market. Martin informed Sarah that Hampton's new corporate policy is to pay all suppliers on 90-day terms. Moving forward, Hampton will pay all suppliers in 90 days rather than 30 days. Because it will now take longer for

Sarah to receive payment from her largest customer, her company will face a cash flow shortage that must be addressed. One option is to obtain a short-term working capital loan from her bank. That option, however, is not attractive because the interest rate on the loan will be high. She also has outstanding debt and is worried her business's credit rating will be negatively impacted. She also is concerned that her business may not be able to repay the loan, which would trigger a potential bankruptcy petition.

STRATEGIC SOLUTION: Another option for Sarah is to use the law of negotiable instruments to resolve the cash flow and liquidity concerns. Sarah can convert the invoices sent to Hampton Market into promissory notes. Sarah can then negotiate the notes for cash to an investor who will purchase them. After conducting research, Sarah has identified First Finance Factoring, Inc. as an investor that would be willing to purchase the promissory notes for 95 percent of their face value.

1. Convert the invoice presented above into a promissory note that has all the required elements of a negotiable instrument.
   a. Should this negotiable instrument specify any promises other than the promise to pay? Why or why not?
   b. Should the note be payable to order or to bearer? Explain.
   c. Should the note be payable on demand or at a specific date in the future? Explain.
   d. What other requirements are necessary for the note to be a negotiable instrument?
2. How would Fabulous Leather Creations negotiate the promissory note to First Finance Factoring?
3. Explain whether any indorsement should be:
   a. Blank or special.
   b. Restrictive or unrestrictive.
   c. Qualified or unqualified.
4. What would Fabulous Leather Creations have to do to avoid guaranteeing the payment to First Finance in case Hampton Market fails to pay for the leather goods?

KEY TERMS

Promise p. 327   A written undertaking to pay money signed by the party undertaking to pay.

Order p. 327   A written instruction to pay money signed by the person giving the instruction.

Payable to order p. 328   Designation on a negotiable instrument that identifies the party to whom payment will be made.

Payable to bearer p. 328   The specification that the person who possesses the negotiable instrument is the party to be paid.

Magic words of negotiability p. 328   The use of the specific terms "pay to the order of," "pay to bearer," or "pay to cash" that are a strict formality required by the UCC if a promise or order is to be considered a negotiable instrument.

Payable upon demand p. 328   An instrument that can be presented for payment at any time by its holder.

Payable at a definite time p. 328   An instrument that will be repaid on any given date or range of dates.

Draft p. 329   A written order to pay money signed by the person giving the order (e.g., a check).

Drawer p. 329   The party issuing the payment order.

Drawee p. 330   The party who must make a payment as specified to the person receiving the funds in a payment order.

Payee (draft) p. 330   The person who will be paid on a payment order.

Time draft p. 330   A draft that is payable at a determined future date.

Sight draft p. 330   A draft that is payable at any time upon demand once it is presented to the drawee.

Check p. 330   Negotiable instrument that is an unconditional order issued to a bank to pay a fixed amount that is in writing and signed by the party undertaking to pay.

Certificate of deposit p. 331   A written note that indicates a bank has received money as a loan and promises to repay the amount in the future with interest, typically at a higher rate than that offered by a savings account.

Promissory note p. 331   Any type of loan (personal or commercial) in which one party offers to lend a specific amount of money with repayment in the future.

Maker p. 331   A party who receives a loan and promises to repay it.

Payee (promissory note) p. 331   A party who extends credit and is entitled to repayment on the loan.

Time note p. 331   A note that is payable at a definite time.

Demand note p. 331   A note that is payable at any time upon the request of the payee.

Negotiation p. 332   Various steps used to transfer a negotiable instrument from party to party through a legally defined process.

Order paper p. 333   An instrument that is payable to an identified person.

Indorsement p. 333   The process of negotiating a check by signing the check and making it payable to someone else.

Blank indorsement p. 334   An indorsement that consists solely of the indorser's signature.

Special indorsement p. 334   An indorsement that specifically identifies the party to whom the instrument is to be payable.

Restrictive indorsement p. 334   An indorsement that seeks to limit the negotiability of an instrument or impose a condition on the payee.

Nonrestrictive indorsement p. 335   An indorsement that lacks any type of language that seeks to limit the negotiability of an instrument or conditions to its payment or transfer.

Qualified indorsement p. 335   An indorsement that adds language such as "Without recourse" to limit the indorser's loss exposure due to nonpayment.

Unqualified indorsement p. 335   An indorsement that does not include any language that limits the indorser's nonpayment liability.

Securitization p. 336   The process of packaging promissory notes and negotiating their sale to investors.

CASE SUMMARY 19.1 Cooperatieve Centrale Raiffeisen-Boerenleenbank B.A. v. William H. Bailey, 710 F. Supp. 737 (C.D. Cal. 1989)

Words of Negotiability

The plaintiff, Cooperatieve Centrale Raiffeisen-Boerenleenbank B.A. ("the Bank") sued the maker of the note, William Bailey, M.D. ("Bailey"). Bailey had executed the note in favor of "California Dreamstreet," a cattle-breeding operation seeking investment. California Dreamstreet negotiated the note to the Bank. When Bailey failed to pay on the note, the Bank sued for payment. Bailey claimed the instrument was not negotiable.

The note states in relevant part:

> DR. WILLIAM H. BAILEY . . . hereby promises to pay to the order to CALIFORNIA DREAMSTREET . . . the sum of Three Hundred Twenty Nine Thousand Eight Hundred ($329,800.00) Dollars. . . .

The sole issue for the court to decide was whether the unusual language in the note obliging Bailey to "pay to the order *to* California Dreamstreet" rendered the note nonnegotiable.

The court held that "pay to the order to" was akin to "payable to the order of," and the instrument was therefore a negotiable instrument.

CASE QUESTIONS

1. Do you agree with the court that "pay to the order to" was equivalent to "payable to the order of"? Why or why not?
2. What do you think motivated the court's decision in this case?

CASE SUMMARY 19.2 *In re* AppOnline, Inc., 321 B.R. 614; 2003 U.S. Dist. LEXIS 26258 (2003)

Unconditional Promise

Broward paid off the mortgages associated with two promissory notes ("the Amarante note" and "the Ciceron note"). These notes were negotiated to another party who claimed ownership. Broward disputed whether the

two mortgages were negotiable instruments. The promissory notes in questions stated:

> In return for a loan . . . Borrower promises to pay . . . plus interest. . . . Interest will be charged on unpaid principal, from the date of disbursement of the loan proceeds

by Lender, at the rate of nine percent (9.000%) per year until the full amount of the principal has been paid. . . . Borrower shall make payment of principal and interest to Lender on the first day of each month beginning on [specified date]. . . . Payment shall be made at . . . Melville, New York. . . . Each monthly payment of principal and interest will be in the amount of $663.01. This amount will be part of a larger monthly payment required by the Security Instrument [defined in P 3 as the mortgage], that shall be applied to principal, interest and other items in the order described in the Security Instrument. . . . If Lender has not received the full monthly payment required by the Security Instrument . . . by the end of fifteen calendar days after the payment is due, the Lender may collect a late charge in the amount of FOUR percent (4.0000%) of the overdue amount of each payment.

The court found that both the Amarante note and the Ciceron note contained unconditional promises to pay. In addition, neither note contained any language that the notes were "subject to" or "governed by" the mortgages, as required to eradicate negotiability under UCC § 3-105.

CASE QUESTIONS

1. Was the notes' reference to the existence of a separate agreement a conditional promise? Why or why not?
2. When does a separate agreement not affect the negotiability of an instrument?

CASE SUMMARY 19.3 Blasco v. Money Services Center, 352 B.R. 888 (N. Dist. Ala. 2006)

Fixed Amount of Money

Blasco provided a check to Money Services Center ("MSC"), which operated as a payday loan center, in exchange for a short-term loan that totaled $587.50. Blasco filed for bankruptcy before MSC cashed the check. The check, if it was considered a negotiable instrument, would take priority over bankruptcy creditor claims. The bankruptcy administrator claimed the check was not a negotiable instrument due to ambiguity in the amount value written on the check. Blasco

had written out the words "five eighty-seven and 50/100 dollars" on the check and "$587.50" in the box where the amount was to be placed. Recall that the UCC requires a negotiable instrument to specify a fixed amount of money.

CASE QUESTIONS

1. Who should prevail in this case? Why?
2. Should words or numbers take priority in cases where there is ambiguity? Explain.

CHAPTER REVIEW QUESTIONS

1. A negotiable instrument must:
   a. Be an unconditional promise or order.
   b. Pay a fixed amount of money.
   c. Be in writing.
   d. Be signed.
   e. All of the above.

2. The "words of negotiability" include:
   a. Pay to the order of.
   b. Pay to bearer.
   c. Pay to cash.

   d. A, B, and C.
   e. None of the above.

3. Paul is the payee on a check. Paul has indorsed the check to Ivan by signing "Paul" on the back of the check. This is known as a:
   a. Special indorsement.
   b. Blank indorsement.
   c. Restrictive indorsement.
   d. Qualified indorsement.
   e. None of the above.

4. Paul is the payee on a check. Paul has indorsed the check to Ivan by writing "Pay to Ivan" and signing "Paul" on the back of the check. This is known as a:

a. Special indorsement.

b. Blank indorsement.

c. Restrictive indorsement.

d. Qualified indorsement.

e. None of the above.

5. Premier Auto Financing has many auto loans that it would like to package and sell to investors as promissory notes. It can negotiate these notes through their sale to a special purpose vehicle that will then sell bonds backed by the notes to investors. This is known as:

a. Refinancing.

b. A leveraged buyout.

c. Securitization.

d. Restructuring.

e. Recapitalization.

6. A check is a specialized type of promissory note.

a. True

b. False

7. Bearer paper requires an indorsement for its negotiation.

a. True

b. False

8. The negotiation of an instrument will depend on whether it is payable to an identified person as order paper or to the bearer as bearer paper.

a. True

b. False

9. Very few negotiable instruments are ever securitized.

a. True

b. False

10. Omitting the date from a note results in the instrument being a demand note.

a. True

b. False

 Quick Quiz ANSWERS
Aspects of a Negotiable Instrument

1. Yes, it has all the characteristics of a negotiable instrument. It is written, signed, includes a fixed payment amount of money (in a foreign currency), and does not include any other promises. It is a sight draft made payable to order.

2. Chris is the drawee, Melanie is the payee, and Robinson is the drawer.

CHAPTER REVIEW QUESTIONS: Answers and Explanations

1. **e.** All of the above are required for an instrument to be negotiable.

2. **d.** Pay to the order of, pay to bearer, and pay to cash are all words of negotiability.

3. **b.** Simply signing a check is a blank indorsement.

4. **a.** Indorsing a check to someone is a special indorsement.

5. **c.** The process of negotiating a package of instruments for sale to investors is known as securitization.

6. **b. False.** A check is a specialized type of order.

7. **b. False.** Bearer paper only requires its physical transfer for negotiation.

8. **a. True.** Order paper will require an indorsement *and* physical delivery.

9. **b. False.** Securitization occurs across many types of debt.

10. **a. True.** Omitting the date from a note converts it into a demand note.

CHAPTER 20

Negotiation, Indorsements, and Holder in Due Course

As you read this chapter you will begin to understand the importance of having a system intended to detect fraud in certain financial transactions. This chapter's *Thinking Strategically* discusses how business owners' use of artificial intelligence systems prevents losses related to fraudulent behavior.

Learning Objectives

After studying this chapter, students who have mastered the material will be able to:

20-1 Explain the process a holder follows to negotiate a negotiable instrument.

20-2 Explain the requirements for holder in due course (HDC) status and the shelter rule.

20-3 Articulate the third-party defenses from which a holder in due course is insulated.

20-4 Apply the holder in due course rules in the context of a consumer transaction.

CHAPTER OVERVIEW

This chapter continues our discussion of negotiable instruments by focusing on the process used to transfer the instrument from one party to another. We also examine how certain holders of negotiable instruments, known as a Holder in Due Course (HDC), are protected from many of the defenses that could typically be asserted against the holder. Finally, we consider the impact of federal regulation that is intended to protect consumers from unscrupulous merchants and creditors.

NEGOTIATION

The most important part of understanding the role of negotiable instruments is realizing that they move from party to party through a legally defined process.

This process, called **negotiation**, includes various steps that determine the roles and rights of the parties.[1] In a certain sense, each negotiable instrument has a story behind it made up of a series of events beginning with the *issuance* of the instrument by the party promising to make a payment and ending with *presentment* of the instrument by the party seeking to receive payment. To take a simple example, suppose that Tectonic Industries pays an invoice from Ace Supply Company with a check for $1,000. Ace receives the check and either deposits it in its own bank or cashes the check at Tectonic's bank. This simple example is governed by Article 3 of the UCC in which Tectonic issues the negotiable instrument to Ace, which presents the check to

---

[1]UCC § 3-201(a).

the bank for payment. The process of negotiation also may involve several intermediary steps between issuance and presentment. We will discuss these intermediary steps a bit later in this chapter.

LO 20-1

Explain the process a holder follows to negotiate a negotiable instrument.

Holder

The **holder** plays a central role in the story of a negotiable instrument. One becomes a holder either because (1) she is in actual physical possession of a negotiable instrument that is *bearer* form (i.e., the instrument is payable to cash or to any party that is in possession of the instrument) or (2) the instrument was made payable to a specific party and that party is in possession of the instrument (called an *order* instrument). If the instrument is in bearer form, one needs only to be in physical possession to be considered a holder. In contrast, order instruments require both physical possession *and* an indorsement. Recall from Chapter 19, "Definition, Creation, and Categories of Negotiable Instruments," that an indorsement is simply an authentication signature and/or instruction or restrictions written on the back of a negotiable instrument, such as "For Deposit Only." The holder of an instrument has only limited rights against the possible liability to a third party, and this carries an inherent risk. The UCC recognizes a fuller complement of rights if the holder qualifies as a holder in due course (discussed later in this chapter).

Negotiation and Transfer

The transfer of a negotiable instrument to another party results in that party becoming a holder, regardless of whether the instrument was negotiated to an *original* holder or the original holder transferred the instrument to another party who became a holder. Traditionally, transfer occurred through physical delivery (i.e., handing or mailing the instrument) to the holder. Increasingly, legislatures and courts have recognized electronic transfers as meeting the delivery requirement. In any case, a negotiable instrument may only be transferred to the party the transferor intended as a holder. For example, suppose Baker is a consultant for Tectonic Industries and they issue him a $5,000 check payable to cash as payment. Baker is in a hurry, so he stuffs the check in his briefcase without indorsement. Later that day, his briefcase is stolen, and the thief then signs his own name and indorses it with "Pay to the Order of Prime Casino." The thief delivers the check to the casino to satisfy an outstanding debt. Your common sense may tell you that the thief would not prevail in this case, but what is the legal reasoning? Tectonic issued a bearer instrument (i.e., a check payable to cash) to Baker and delivered it to him. Therefore, Baker is a holder. Although it is a bearer instrument, the thief was not the intended payee; therefore, the delivery requirement cannot be met, and the thief cannot qualify as a holder.

TAKEAWAY CONCEPTS Negotiation

- Negotiation is a series of events beginning with the issuance of the instrument by the party promising to make a payment and ending with presentment of the instrument by the party seeking to receive payment.
- A holder has actual physical possession of a negotiable instrument (in bearer form) or possession of the instrument (pay to order form) if the instrument was made payable to a specific party.

LO 20-2

Explain the requirements for holder in due course (HDC) status and the shelter rule.

HOLDER IN DUE COURSE (HDC) STATUS

A holder gains a sort of super status if she meets the Article 3 requirements as a **holder in due course (HDC)**. This super status protects the HDC from certain claims by other parties related to the enforceability or validity of the negotiable instrument. Recall from earlier in this chapter that the UCC recognizes an individual who has physical possession of a complete and authentic negotiable instrument as a *holder*. However, being an ordinary holder is a risky proposition in that a holder is subject to an array of defenses by other parties that might render the instrument worthless. Understanding who qualifies as an ordinary holder versus an HDC helps business managers and owners to reduce risk. Article 3 sets out a series of conditions required to obtain HDC status. The holder of a negotiable instrument is an HDC if the holder has taken the instrument:

- for *value;*[2]
- in *good faith;*[3] and
- *without notice* of it being overdue,[4] fraudulent,[5] or subject to claim by another party.[6]

Value

The first step in an HDC analysis is to determine whether the negotiable instrument was issued or transferred for **value** or whether the holder took the instrument without providing anything in *exchange.* If it is a gift, the holder cannot meet the requirements for HDC status. Similarly, one who *finds* a negotiable instrument has not taken it for value and cannot meet the UCC's value criterion. For example, suppose Fernandez is cleaning out a storage locker and discovers a certificate of deposit (CD) payable "To Bearer" tucked inside an old book he purchased at a flea market 20 years earlier. It turns out that the CD is extremely valuable, but when the bank refuses to pay, Fernandez sues asserting his status as an HDC. A court would be likely to rule that Fernandez has *not* met Article 3's value requirement because even though Fernandez purchased the book, he did not pay any value in return for the negotiable instrument itself (i.e., the CD).[7]

You may recognize the concept of exchange of value from Unit Two: Contracts, Sales, and Leases. In that context, the value exchanged was in the context of *consideration* as an element of forming a valid contract. However, Article 3 of the UCC sets a higher bar in its value exchange rule by requiring that a negotiable instrument be taken for value by the holder for *a promise that has already been performed.* This means that generally the holder must be able to identify a specific preexisting promise and the performance of the promise prior to taking the negotiable instrument. For example, suppose that Adams gives a check to Byron as a graduation gift. Byron negotiates the check to Cornelius in exchange for Cornelius's promise to repair Byron's car next week. Adams is the drawer since he issued the check to Byron. Since the Adams check was a gift, Byron does not qualify for HDC status since he hasn't provided any services or goods in exchange for the check. Similarly, Cornelius cannot be an HDC since the promised repair of Byron's car was a promise for *future* services. Table 20.1 illustrates the status of the parties in the A-B-C transaction.

---

[2]UCC § 3-303.

[3]UCC § 3-103(a)(4).

[4]UCC § 3-304.

[5]UCC § 3-305(a).

[6]UCC § 3-306.

[7]Based on *Griffith v. Mellon Bank, N.A.,* 328 F. Supp. 2d 536 (E.D. Pa. 2002).

TABLE 20.1 Analysis of A-B-C Transaction

Party	Status	Reason
Adams	Drawer	Issued the check as a gift.
Byron	Holder	Not an HDC because the check was a gift (not for value) transfer.
Cornelius	Holder	Not an HDC because the promise (repair) had not been performed at the time of the transfer.

Good Faith

Because **good faith** is a central component to HDC status, it is important to understand the specifics of this requirement in an HDC analysis. Article 3 of the UCC provides a two-part definition that describes good faith as meaning "honesty in fact and the observance of reasonable commercial standards."[8] The first part, *honesty in fact,* means that parties did not conceal or misrepresent any aspect of the transaction. The second part, *reasonable commercial standards,* requires a court to determine whether the conduct of the holder was within the boundaries of that particular industry or commercial setting. Article 3 uses the word *reasonable* to indicate that we should use an *objective standard* when determining whether the holder was factually honest and acting in accordance with commercial standards. It is also important in this context to understand that the UCC draws a distinction between conduct that may be negligent (or even reckless) and that which is considered bad faith. In Case 20.1, a state appellate court analyzes the HDC's good faith requirement.

CASE 20.1 Banco Bilbao Vizcaya Argentaria v. Easy Luck Co., 208 So. 3d 1241 (Fla. Dist. Ct. App. 2017)

FACT SUMMARY Easy Luck is a Florida company that entered into an agreement to sell shoes to JAMS Technologies, Inc. ("JAMS"), a distributor located in the Dominican Republic. The parties agreed that JAMS would purchase $43,337 worth of shoes from Easy Luck. At the time of the transaction, JAMS owed an outstanding debt to Easy Luck in the amount of $77,000. Easy Luck told JAMS that it would ship the shoes to JAMS only if it received payment in advance.

Anxious to expedite delivery of the shoe order, a JAMS principal carried a negotiable instrument for $85,000 to Miami and personally delivered it to Easy Luck's president with instructions to apply the remaining monies in excess of JAMS's $43,337 shoe order to the unpaid debt owed by JAMS to Easy Luck. However, the instrument was not issued by JAMS but rather by a large Dominican paint company, Lanco Manufacturing Corporation, against Lanco's account at Banco Bilbao Vizcaya Argentaria ("BBVA"). JAMS's principal explained that the Lanco negotiable instrument was necessary for local tax reasons and that JAMS had an ongoing business relationship with Lanco.

Although Easy Luck first attempted to confirm the validity of the draft with BBVA, the bank declined to provide any information regarding the Lanco instrument or Lanco's BBVA account. Easy Luck deposited the instrument in its Florida bank, SunTrust, which advised them that payment for the draft would take several weeks to clear. Easy Luck then notified JAMS that the shoe order would not be shipped until the instrument cleared and the funds were credited to Easy Luck's Florida bank. After BBVA paid the

(continued)

---

[8]UCC § 3-103.

instrument against Lanco's account, the funds were credited to Easy Luck's account at SunTrust and Easy Luck shipped the shoes to JAMS and applied the leftover funds to JAMS's outstanding balance.

Soon after, BBVA discovered that the instrument was a counterfeit and forgery and that it had paid the instrument by mistake. BBVA then credited Lanco's account, notified SunTrust of the fraud, and demanded that SunTrust reverse the deposit. SunTrust refused to reverse the credit based on BBVA's having cleared the instrument as valid. Easy Luck was not notified until BBVA filed suit against it to recover the $85,000 loss it had suffered by payment of the forged instrument. The trial court ruled in favor of Easy Luck as holders in due course. BBVA appealed arguing that Easy Luck did not meet the HDC's good faith requirement.

SYNOPSIS OF DECISION AND OPINION   The Florida appellate court affirmed the trial court's holding in favor of Easy Luck. The court rejected BBVA's argument that Easy Luck did not take the draft in good faith, as required by the HDC statute. The court held that holders may be accorded HDC status if they act in accordance with good faith and reasonable commercial standards of fair dealing. As evidence of good faith and adherence to reasonable commercial standards, the court pointed to Easy Luck's attempt to verify the instrument with BBVA and the fact that Easy Luck could not reasonably have detected the forgery.

WORDS OF THE COURT: Good Faith and Commercial Standards   "In this case, Easy Luck did take precautionary measures upon delivery of the draft by [a JAMS principal] to Easy Luck's office in Miami. First, [Easy Luck's president] inquired of the local BBVA office about the funds prior to depositing the draft. Second, Easy Luck resisted pressure by [JAMS] to send the shoe shipment before the draft cleared and the funds were available in Easy Luck's account. Lastly, Easy Luck had no actual knowledge the check was forged until it was served with the complaint in this case. In retrospect, one could always do more. However, the standard of 'fairness' by which Easy Luck's actions are to be judged is not a negligence standard. Rather, we are told that the standard of 'fairness' to be applied in cases such as this should be measured by taking a global view of the underlying transaction and all of its participants. We believe these facts are sufficient to support the finding of the trial court that Easy Luck acted in good faith."

Case Questions

1. Should Easy Luck have accepted the third-party negotiable instrument as payment in the first place given that it was issued by Lanco and not JAMS? Does that arrangement strike you as having a potential for fraud? Why or why not?

2. Another issue in the case was whether the Lanco negotiable instrument was accepted for value by Easy Luck as required for HDC status. Did Easy Luck accept the instrument for value? Name the specific exchanges for value in this transaction.

3. *Focus on Critical Thinking:* While the court ruled that Easy Luck did not have any legal obligation to repay BBVA, does Easy Luck have an ethical obligation to do so? Given that its customer, JAMS, perpetrated the fraud, shouldn't Easy Luck share in the losses? Explain your answer.

Without Notice

The **without notice** requirement is particularly important to obtaining HDC status because it separates innocent holders from those who know or should know that the negotiable instrument is defective or fraudulent in some way. To obtain HDC status, Article 3 requires the holder to overcome two hurdles. First, the holder cannot have had any *actual* notice (either firsthand knowledge or notice by a third party) that the instrument was overdue, defective, fraudulent, or subject to a claim by another party. Note that constructive notice (e.g., notice published in a newspaper) is *not* sufficient notice to the holder under Article 3. Second, given all the facts and circumstances known by the holder at the time, no reasonable person would question whether the instrument was overdue, defective, fraudulent, or subject to a claim by another party.[9] Table 20.2 provides an overview of the "without notice" factors.

[9]UCC § 1-201(25).

TABLE 20.2 Without Notice Factors

Factor	Rule	Example
Overdue	Check is overdue 90 days after its date.[10] Other demand instruments overdue if the instrument has been outstanding (not paid) for an "unreasonable" period.[11]	A check dated January 1 becomes overdue March 31.
Overdue	Time instrument such as a promissory note becomes overdue after the due date fixed on the instrument.[12]	A promissory note payable on January 15 becomes overdue January 16.
Claim by another party	Actual knowledge that another party has a claim or defense to an instrument prevents a holder from obtaining HDC status.[13]	A holder discovers another party is alleging rights to be paid under the negotiable instrument before taking the instrument. The holder is barred from HDC status.

In Case 20.2, a state appellate court determines whether a holder should have known that a negotiable instrument was forged or fraudulent.

CASE 20.2 Triffin v. Pomerantz Staffing Services, 851 A.2d 100 (N.J. Super. 2004)

FACT SUMMARY Friendly Check Cashing Corp. was presented with 18 counterfeit checks, in amounts ranging between $380 and $398, purporting to have been issued by defendant Pomerantz Staffing Services on its account with Bank of New York. Each check bore Pomerantz's full name and address and a facsimile signature of "Gary Pomerantz." Also printed on the face of each check was a warning: "THE BACK OF THIS CHECK HAS HEAT-SENSITIVE INK TO CONFIRM AUTHENTICITY." Without examining the checks as suggested by this warning, Friendly cashed the checks, which the bank returned unpaid as counterfeit. Friendly assigned its rights to Triffin, who filed suit against Pomerantz. The trial court ruled in favor of Pomerantz, and Triffin appealed claiming,

among other things, that he was entitled to payment as a holder in due course.

SYNOPSIS OF DECISION AND OPINION The New Jersey Superior Court affirmed the trial court's decision in favor of Pomerantz. With respect to HDC status, the court ruled that Friendly's (and Triffin's as its assignee) failure to examine the checks to determine whether they had heat-sensitive ink prevented them from becoming a holder in due course because they failed to meet the "without notice" requirement. The court pointed to the fact that if Friendly had used the heat-sensitive test, it would have unquestionably revealed that the checks were counterfeit. A party that fails to make an inquiry, reasonably required by the circumstances of the transaction, so

(continued)

---

[10]UCC § 3-304(a)(2).

[11]UCC § 3-304(a)(3).

[12]UCC § 3-304(b-c).

[13]UCC § 3-302(a)(2)(v).

as to remain ignorant of facts that might disclose a defect cannot claim HDC status.

WORDS OF THE COURT: Commercially Unreasonable "This result is further compelled by the fact that the party claiming to be a holder in due course was in the business of cashing checks. It is reasonable, in considering whether the instruments were received in good faith and whether the holder comported with reasonable commercial standards, that the holder be expected to fully examine the front and back of the instrument and, where the instrument purports to contain a method by which its authenticity may be tested, that the holder actually utilize that method. While this failure would likely preclude any holder of these instruments from claiming holder in due course status, it particularly precludes entities in the business of cashing checks. Accordingly, we reject plaintiff's contention that this information was irrelevant. Instead, we hold that it is commercially unreasonable for a check cashing entity to fail to utilize the heat sensitive test when so cautioned on the face of the check."

Case Questions

1. Aren't Friendly/Triffin innocent parties in this transaction? If so, why should they bear the risk that the checks were counterfeit? If not, why not?

2. Why does the court consider it important that Friendly was a check-cashing business? Would the result be different if it was another type of business? Explain.

3. *Focus on Critical Thinking:* How far should one have to go to meet the "without notice" requirement? What methods could be used to ensure that a business qualifies as an HDC and does not face the same fate as Friendly/Triffin?

 Quick Quiz Holder in Due Course

In each of the following fact patterns, is Holmes an HDC? Why or why not?

1. Andrews shows Holmes a check for $7,000 made out to Andrews and signed by Jackson. Holmes notices that the "7" on the check is smudged and that the word "Seven" on the line where the amount has been written also appears smudged and in a different color ink than other parts of the check. Andrews convinces Holmes to cash the check for him. Later, Jackson's bank refuses to honor the check and Holmes asserts HDC status.

2. Andrews issues a check in the amount of $50,000 payable to O'Connor to pay a debt he owes her. O'Connor negotiates the check to her nephew Holmes as a gift to help him buy a house.

3. Andrews sells a first edition copy of *The Old Man and the Sea,* signed by Ernest Hemingway, to O'Connor for $100,000. However, the book's first edition imprint is fraudulent, and Hemingway's signature is forged—all perpetrated solely by Andrews. Andrews negotiates O'Connor's check to Holmes in payment of a debt owed by Andrews to Holmes. The check appears as follows:

Front of Check

O'Connor	50-70/220 1004
One Liberty Place	
Greentown, Pennsylvania	
	January 5, 2019
Pay to the Order of ___ *Andrews*	$ *100,000.00*
One Hundred Thousand and 00/100 _____ Dollars	
MegaBank of Greentown	
Memo: *Sale of OMTS First Edition*	*O'Connor*
:987654321: 00123456: 1004	

Back of Check

Pay to the Order of Holmes

Andrews

Do Not Write, Stamp, or Sign Below This Line. Reserved for Financial Institution Use

4. Andrews issues a $5,000 promissory note to O'Connor that is due and payable by Andrews on September 1. O'Connor negotiates this note to Holmes on October 1 for cash.

Answers to this Quick Quiz are provided at the end of the chapter.

The Shelter Rule

The shelter rule[14] provides that the transferee of an instrument acquires the same rights that the transferor had. Simply put, one who does not himself qualify as an HDC can still acquire that status *if some previous holder* was an HDC. In fact, the instrument does not even need to be transferred directly from an HDC so long as the current holder can point to *any party* having HDC status after issuance of the instrument. These previous parties are sometimes referred to as *upstream* parties, and once HDC status has attached to a negotiable instrument, any future holder may also obtain HDC status. For example, suppose that Tectonic Industries issues a check payable to Jensen for $1,000 as payment for Jensen's services. Jensen decides to negotiate the check to his daughter Ally as a graduation gift. Ally then negotiates the check to her friend Jasper as a wedding gift. Table 20.3 illustrates each party's rights under the shelter rule.

TABLE 20.3 Who's Protected under the Shelter Rule?

Party	Status	Reason
Tectonic	Drawer	Issued check.
Jensen	HDC	Took check for value, in good faith, without notice.
Ally	Holder with HDC rights	Check was a gift and thus no HDC status, but gains HDC rights under the shelter rule.
Jasper	HDC with HDC rights	Shelter rule allows HDC status because Jensen is an upstream HDC.

TAKEAWAY CONCEPTS Holder in Due Course Requirements

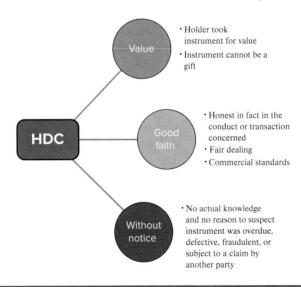

---

[14]UCC § 3-203(b).

LO 20-3

Articulate the third-party defenses from which a holder in due course is insulated.

DEFENSES AND THIRD-PARTY CLAIMS

The HDC's rights to enforce a negotiable instrument (i.e., the right to demand payment) are part of an HDC's super status, which provides insulation from certain defenses that may be asserted by the drawer/maker, acceptor, financial institution, or indorser. The UCC, however, does not confer a *complete* bar for parties asserting a defense against an HDC. In general, Article 3 of the UCC contains three sets of defenses: *real, personal,* and *claims in recoupment.* While HDC status provides immunity from personal defenses or claims in recoupment, it does *not* protect an HDC from being subjected to any real defenses. You'll recognize the language used in these defenses from your study of contract law. We recommend reviewing the relevant section of Unit Two: Contracts, Sales, and Leases before continuing your study of HDC defenses.

Real Defenses

Article 3 provides a laundry list of **real defenses** that may be asserted by a third party.[15] It includes fraud in the essence (e.g., tricking a party into signing a document), bankruptcy, forgery, material alterations of a completed instrument, and infancy (i.e., the party is a minor). For example, suppose that 16-year-old Andrews is developing smartphone apps for profit and convinces Brennan, his neighbor, to lend him $10,000 in exchange for a promissory note payable to Brennan at 6 percent interest in one lump some one year from the date of issuance. Brennan then negotiates that note to Cardozo to repay an existing debt. When the note becomes due, Andrews refuses to pay on the basis that he was a minor at the time the note was issued. In this case, although Cardozo is undoubtedly an HDC, Andrews's obligation to pay the note is subject to the real defense of infancy.

Personal Defenses

Personal defenses are any "defense of the obligor that would be available if the person entitled to enforce the instrument were enforcing a right to payment under a simple contract."[16] This includes defenses associated with formation of a contract (e.g., illegality, duress, lack or failure of consideration, or mental capacity) and defenses associated with enforceability (e.g., unauthorized completion or materially altering the instrument, fraud in the inducement, or breach of contract).

Note that *fraud* is both a real defense and a personal defense. The distinction is important because HDCs are immune from one type of fraud (personal defenses) but not from the other (real defenses). *Fraud in the essence* is a real defense applied when the fraudulent behavior is intended to obtain an individual's signature on a document without the signer's knowing or having a reasonable opportunity to discover what the document contained (e.g., the maker is tricked into signing a note believing it to be a mere receipt).[17] *Fraud in the inducement* is a personal defense and is more common. It covers fraudulent misrepresentations of material facts by one party that another party relied on when entering into a contract.

Claims in Recoupment

Although not classified as a real or personal defense, HDCs also have immunity from **claims in recoupment**. These claims center on the notion that the amount owed by the obligor should be reduced by some amount due to an offsetting claim the obligor can

---

[15]UCC § 3-305(a)(1).

[16]UCC § 3-305(a)(2).

[17]UCC § 3-305(a)(1)(iii), *Comment 1.*

assert for the same transaction. For example, Microseller sells 1,000 microchips to Retailer for $10,000 for delivery by November 1. Microseller receives a promissory note signed by Retailer for $10,000 due on December 1. The microchips arrive on time, but Retailer determines 20 percent of the chips are faulty. Because of a seasonal deadline in the microchip industry, Retailer opts to purchase the remaining microchips from a more expensive vendor. Retailer's efforts to secure the new microchips cost an extra $4,000. Must Retailer pay the $10,000 note on December 1? No, because Retailer is entitled to assert a claim of recoupment for $4,000 against Microseller, and Microseller now is only entitled to $6,000.

TAKEAWAY CONCEPTS Defenses and Third-Party Claims

Defense	Examples	Impact on HDC
Real	Bankruptcy, forgery	HDC subject to defense
Personal	Illegality, duress	HDC protection
Recoupment	Offset for breach of warranty	HDC protection

HDC AND CONSUMERS

LO 20-4

Apply the holder in due course rules in the context of a consumer transaction.

While we certainly can understand the benefits of allowing negotiable instruments to be transferred and providing reasonable protections to the holders of the instruments in the context of commercial transactions (e.g., flexibility and ease of commerce), take a step back from a commercial setting and think about the impact of an HDC's rights on ordinary consumers.

For instance, suppose that Pablo purchases a brand-new, expensive lawn tractor from Local Garden, a garden supply store in Pablo's neighborhood. He finances his purchase via a consumer loan in which Pablo issues a promissory note payable to Local Garden for $3,000 payable over two years at the prime interest rate. Local Garden then transfers Pablo's note to Mega Bank for value. Soon after, the tractor breaks down. It turns out that the tractor was not new, as Local Garden advertised, but rather reconditioned with used parts. Consider Pablo's dilemma: A broken, used tractor was sold to him with fraudulent representations by the seller, but he still must make a monthly payment to Mega Bank. To add insult to injury, Mega Bank is an HDC; therefore, if Mega Bank were to demand payment, Pablo would be barred from asserting a personal defense of fraud in the inducement or breach of warranty in the underlying tractor contract. As an HDC, Mega Bank would also be immune from any claims in recoupment that Pablo could assert as an offset. Pablo is left trying to recover damages from Local Garden but must continue to make payments to Mega Bank under the note.

Holder Rule

Recognizing that predicaments such as Pablo's were becoming increasingly common as the prevalence of consumer credit contracts increased in the 1960s and 1970s, state courts and state legislatures began to create consumer protections based on common law and state law that outlined exceptions to the HDC rules. Although some of those common law and state legislative protections still exist, they have largely faded into secondary status in favor of Federal Trade Commission (FTC) regulations known as the **Holder Rule**.[18] One court succinctly described the commercial environment that made the Holder Rule a necessity:

> The Holder Rule takes away the financers' traditional status as a holder in due course and subjects it to any potential claims and defenses the purchaser has against the seller. Based on a simple public policy determination, as between an innocent consumer and a third party financer, the latter is generally in a vastly superior position to: (1) return the cost to the seller, where it properly belongs; (2) exert an influence over the behavior of the seller in the first place; and (3) to the extent the financer cannot return the cost (as in the case of fly-by-night dealers), "internalize" the cost by spreading it among all consumers as an increase in the price of credit. Knowing that it bears the cost of seller misconduct, the creditor will simply not accept the risks generated by the truly unscrupulous merchant. The market will be policed in this fashion and all parties will benefit accordingly.[19]

The FTC's Holder Rule *preserves* a consumer's rights against an HDC when the transaction involves the consumer entering into credit contracts related to the sale of goods and services. The Holder Rule allows a consumer to assert claims and defenses against any holder of the contract, even if the original seller subsequently transfers the credit contract to a third-party creditor. A creditor or assignee of the credit contract is subject to all claims and defenses that the consumer could assert against the seller.

Requirements

The Holder Rule sets out specific requirements for consumer protection and imposes certain important limits.

- *Consumer transactions:* Only transactions between a consumer and a merchant who is *regularly engaged* in the sale/lease of the products or service at issue are covered by the Holder Rule.[20] For example, if one party purchases a used car from his neighbor, an accountant, via a promissory note, the Holder Rule does not apply.
- *Notice:* FTC regulations make it an "unfair or deceptive act or practice" under the Federal Trade Commission Act[21] for any seller to use a consumer note unless it contains a notice statement that is specified in the regulations. The following must appear in 10-point bold type:

NOTICE

ANY HOLDER OF THIS CONSUMER CREDIT CONTRACT IS SUBJECT TO ALL CLAIMS AND DEFENSES WHICH THE DEBTOR COULD ASSERT AGAINST THE SELLER OF GOODS OR SERVICES OBTAINED PURSUANT HERETO OR WITH PROCEEDS HEREOF. RECOVERY HEREUNDER BY THE DEBTOR SHALL NOT EXCEED AMOUNTS PAID BY THE DEBTOR HEREUNDER.

- *No new rights:* As central as the Holder Rule is to preserving the rights of consumers, it is also important to understand its limitations. Most significantly, it does not create any *new* claims or defenses for a consumer; it protects a consumer claim from being extinguished by an HDC of a consumer credit contract. The rule does not authorize

---

[18] 16 CFR § 433.

[19] *Duran v. Quantum Auto Sales,* No. G052968, Cal. Ct. App. (2017).

[20] 16 CFR § 433.2.

[21] 15 USC § 45.

an *independent cause* of action (i.e., the right to sue) for an aggrieved consumer; it merely restores personal defenses and any claims in recoupment as a defense by a consumer against a holder demanding payment. Most courts have held that the Holder Rule only comes into play to allow a consumer's claim/defense against the seller to be asserted against the creditor that is demanding payment under the consumer creditor contract.

In Case 20.3, a court analyzes a Holder Rule claim in the context of a lawsuit for breach of contract and breach of warranty.

CASE 20.3 Hemmings v. Camping Time RV Centers and Bank of America, No. 1:17-CV-1331-TWT (D. Ct. N.D. Georgia 2017)

FACT SUMMARY Hemmings purchased a Fuzion Fifth Wheel RV camper for over $70,000 from Camping Time RV Centers ("Camping Time"). Bank of America was the holder of a promissory note used to finance the camper, which qualifies as a consumer credit contract subject to, among other regulations, the Holder Rule. Hemmings experienced significant mechanical problems while using the RV camper including, most significantly, a defective air conditioner. Although Camping Time and the RV manufacturer attempted to repair the air conditioner, they were ultimately unsuccessful after a series of tries over a period of approximately six weeks. Finally, Hemmings's counsel sent a letter to Camping Time and Bank of America to advise them of the problems with the camper and demand that they repurchase the camper. Hemmings also demanded that Bank of America refund "all monies paid to date." After Camping Time received the letter, the RV camper's manufacturer attempted one more unsuccessful repair and returned the camper to Hemmings with the defects still in place. Hemmings filed suit against Camping Time for multiple claims related to the transaction including breach of warranty. He also filed suit against Camping Time and Bank of America for violation of the Holder Rule. Camping Time and Bank of America asked the court to dismiss all claims.

SYNOPSIS OF DECISION AND OPINION Although finding in favor of Hemmings on the claims related to the defects, the federal district court dismissed the Holder Rule claims against both Camping Time and Bank of America. The court held that Camping Time was not covered under the rule because it was not a holder of a consumer credit contract. It also reasoned that the Holder Rule did not provide a consumer with a private right of action and therefore Hemmings could not maintain a claim against Bank of America.

WORDS OF THE COURT: No Independent Cause of Action "However, no private right of action exists under the Holder Rule. Instead, it allows a debtor to assert any claim or defense against a holder of a consumer credit contract that it could assert against the seller. Thus, [Hemmings] cannot assert an independent cause of action under the Holder Rule against Bank of America. The Holder Rule only allows [Hemmings] to assert claims that he has against Camping Time as derivative claims against Bank of America, since Bank of America is the 'holder' of the consumer credit contract. [Hemmings] agrees that 'his claims against Bank of America are derivative claims.' Therefore, [Hemmings's] independent claims under the FTC Holder Rule are dismissed."

Case Questions

1. What does the court mean by "derivative claims"? How does that impact the court's analysis?

2. Should Bank of America be responsible for providing Hemmings with a full refund for the RV camper?

3. *Focus on Critical Thinking:* Should the FTC or Congress enhance the Holder Rule to provide consumers with an independent cause of action in federal courts for Holder Rule violations? What would be the impact of such a protection on sellers, creditors, and consumers? Explain.

- The FTC's Holder Rule *preserves* a consumer's rights against an HDC when the transaction involves the consumer entering into credit contracts related to the sale of goods and services.

- The Holder Rule allows a consumer to assert claims and defenses against any holder of the contract, even if the original seller subsequently transfers the credit contract to a third-party creditor.

- The Holder Rule applies to merchant-consumer transactions only and requires that a specific notice be printed on a consumer credit contract, but it does *not* authorize an independent cause of action for consumers.

 THINKING STRATEGICALLY

©valterZ/Shutterstock

Preventing Fraud through Artificial Intelligence

PROBLEM: Recall from Case 20.2, *Triffin v. Pomerantz Staffing Services,* that a court ruled that the plaintiff/holder did not have HDC status because it had not taken proper care to determine whether the checks were valid and did not meet the "without notice" qualification required by Article 3. That resulted in the plaintiff/holder bearing the brunt of the losses.

STRATEGIC SOLUTION: One way business owners can avoid losses like those in the *Triffin* case is by developing internal systems that deploy machine learning (a form of artificial intelligence) to detect fraud and to ensure HDC status. While it may be true that some (perhaps even the majority of) business owners may never need to be concerned with the status of holders of negotiable instruments, any business that accepts or issues checks, promissory notes, or other forms of commercial paper is subject to certain risks that can be reduced through an internal fraud-detection process.

Step 1: *Decide on an objective for your system.* Will it be a narrow practice intended to ensure HDC status, or will it be part of a larger system using machine learning/artificial intelligence to detect and prevent fraud? Your objective should match your business and your resources.

Step 2: *Examine your collection practices.* Are checks routinely deposited without being examined? Explore a two-part method that combines machine learning/artificial intelligence to scan for fraudulent checks or notes and refers suspicious cases for individual examination. Firms such as SAS, NEC, and Kofax offer products that use machine learning to detect existing and potentially new fraudulent payment schemes.

Large-scale machine learning technology can collect massive amounts of data relating to fraudulent activities worldwide and analyze them instantly. Thousands of traces left behind by fraudsters, which might otherwise have remained unconnected in the vast ocean of data, are now linked to produce a clear predictor of fraud threats. As artificial intelligence sorts through all data, it is able to detect irregularities and indicate potential areas of fraud. Companies like Yelp, Airbnb, and Jet.com already use these insights to protect themselves from payment fraud, fake accounts, and account takeover.

Step 3: *Examine your payment practices.* Do your checks have fraud-detection mechanisms that will alert a holder to a counterfeit check? How are checks issued and how are they tracked?

Step 4: *Review your internal controls.* If you are a holder of a consumer credit contract, what internal controls are in place to be sure that the instrument has the FTC's required Holder Rule notice printed on the instrument?

1. Use your favorite search engine to find out more about fraud-detection software marketed by SAS, NEC, and Kofax. How do they compare? Look for firms that sell fraud-detection software that caters to smaller businesses. What are the advantages and disadvantages to deploying fraud detection via artificial intelligence?

2. Based on your own experience, what would you look for when determining whether a check was authentic? Explain.

KEY TERMS

Negotiation p. 344 Various steps used to transfer a negotiable instrument from party to party through a legally defined process.

Holder p. 345 One who has actual physical possession of a negotiable instrument (in bearer form) or is in possession of the instrument (pay to order form) if the instrument was made payable to a specific party.

Holder in due course (HDC) p. 346 A statutory super status that protects the holder from certain claims by other parties related to the validity of the negotiable instrument.

Value p. 346 Requirement for HDC status that a holder take a negotiable instrument in exchange for the performance of a preexisting promise.

Good faith p. 347 Requirement for HDC status that a holder take the instrument in accordance with honesty in the transaction and reasonable commercial standards.

Without notice p. 348 Requirement for HDC status that a holder take an instrument without notice that the instrument was overdue, defective, fraudulent, or subject to a claim by another party.

Real defenses p. 352 Article 3 defenses that may be asserted against an HDC, including fraud in the essence (e.g., tricking a party into signing a document), bankruptcy, forgery, material alterations of a completed instrument, and infancy (i.e., party is a minor).

Personal defenses p. 352 Any defense of the obligor that would be available if the person entitled to enforce the instrument were enforcing a right to payment under a simple contract; includes defenses associated with formation of a contract and with enforceability. HDCs are immune from this defense.

Claims in recoupment p. 352 A defense in which the amount owed by the obligor is reduced by some amount due to an offsetting claim by the obligor.

Holder Rule p. 354 FTC-promulgated regulation that *preserves* a consumer's rights against an HDC when the transaction involves the consumer entering into credit contracts related to the sale of goods and services.

CASE SUMMARY 20.1 Carter & Grimsley v. Omni Trading, Inc., 716 N.E.2d 320 (Ill. App. Ct. 1999)

Value

On February 2, 1996, Omni issued two checks, totaling $75,000, to Country Grain for grain it had purchased. Country Grain, in turn, indorsed the checks over to Carter & Grimsley as a retainer for future legal services. Carter deposited the checks on February 5; Country Grain failed the next day. On February 8, Carter was notified that Omni had stopped payment on the checks. Carter subsequently filed a complaint against Omni alleging that it was entitled to the proceeds of the checks, plus prejudgment interest, as a holder in due course.

CASE QUESTIONS

1. Did Carter take the instrument for value as defined in Article 3? Why or why not?
2. Who prevails and why?

CASE SUMMARY 20.2 Any Kind Checks Cashed, Inc. v. Talcott (Fla. Dist. Ct. App. 2002)

HDC Status

As part of a fraudulent scheme, Rivera induced Talcott to send Rivera a check for $10,000 as an investment made out to Guarino. The following day, Rivera told Talcott that the $10,000 was unnecessary and requested that Talcott instead send $5,700. Talcott stopped payment on the $10,000 check and sent Rivera a check for $5,700 made out to Guarino. Guarino brought the $10,000 check to Any Kind Checks Cashed, Inc. ("Any Kind") and misrepresented himself as a broker, explaining that the check was intended as an investment. Any Kind's manager was unable to contact Talcott by phone. Any Kind cashed the check and deducted a 5 percent fee. Guarino returned to Any Kind to cash the $5,700

check. For the $5,700 check, Any Kind obtained Talcott's approval via phone to cash the $5,700 check, but there was no discussion of the $10,000 check. Any Kind cashed the $5,700 check and deducted a 3 percent fee. Talcott then stopped payment on the $5,700 check. Talcott's bank sent the checks back to Any Kind as unpaid due to Talcott's stop order.

CASE QUESTIONS

1. If Any Kind sues Talcott for claiming HDC status, what will the result be? Explain.
2. Does the fact that the check was part of a fraudulent scheme impact your analysis? How?

CASE SUMMARY 20.3 Zener v. Velde, 17 P.3d 296 (Idaho Ct. App. 2000)

Defenses and HDC

The Zeners purchased approximately 14 acres of forested property from Gutierrez, which resulted in the Zeners giving Gutierrez a promissory note. The Zeners then began to discover that trees were being removed from the parcel without their permission. Eventually, the Zeners filed a complaint accusing Guiterrez of hiring agents to remove the trees without the Zeners' knowledge or permission. In the meantime, Gutierrez assigned the Zener promissory note to Velde for value. The Zeners claimed that, because of the damage to

their property, they were entitled to a reduction in the amount owed on the promissory note. Velde asserted HDC status.

CASE QUESTIONS

1. Is the Zeners' claim a real defense, personal defense, or recoupment?
2. Is Velde an HDC? Why or why not?
3. How does Velde's HDC status impact the Zeners' claim?

CHAPTER REVIEW QUESTIONS

1. **Negotiation begins with the _____ of the instrument and ends with _____ of the instrument by the party seeking to receive payment.**
   a. Issuance, payable
   b. Creation, presentment
   c. Holder, termination
   d. Issuance, presentment
   e. Presentment, issuance

2. **Which of the following is *not* a requirement for HDC status on a negotiable instrument?**
   a. Taken for value
   b. Taken in good faith
   c. Taken from the original maker
   d. Taken without notice of it being overdue, fraudulent, or subject to claim by another party
   e. All of the above are required

3. Which HDC requirement separates innocent holders from holders who know or should know that the negotiable instrument is defective or fraudulent in some way?
   a. Value
   b. Negotiability
   c. Alteration
   d. Without notice
   e. A and D

4. HDCs are immune from what category(ies) of defense?
   a. Real
   b. Personal
   c. Claims in recoupment
   d. B and C
   e. A and B

5. The FTC regulation that preserves the rights of consumers to assert claims and defenses against any holder of a consumer credit contract is called the:
   a. Consumer Protection Rule.
   b. Holder Rule.
   c. Immunity Exception.
   d. Defense Preservation Rule.
   e. Unfair Trade Rule.

6. HDCs are immune from a defense of breach of the underlying contract.
   a. True
   b. False

7. An HDC analysis of good faith applies the subjective standard.
   a. True
   b. False

8. White Whale Publishing issues a check to Raleigh for $1,000 as payment for freelance writing. Raleigh negotiates that check to his alma mater as a gift donation. Raleigh's alma mater is an HDC.
   a. True
   b. False

9. One who does not himself qualify as an HDC can still acquire that status if some previous holder was an HDC under the shelter rule.
   a. True
   b. False

10. Fraud in the inducement is a personal defense that covers fraudulent misrepresentations of material facts by one party.
    a. True
    b. False

 Quick Quiz ANSWERS
Holder in Due Course

1. Holmes is not an HDC. This is an altered instrument, and the smudges and ink color are sufficient notice to Holmes that the check is not authentic in some way. The "without notice" requirement would not be met in this case.

2. Holmes is not an HDC. Holmes does not meet the "value" prong required for HDC status. Holmes received the instrument as a gift. He becomes a holder of the check, but not as an HDC because he did not take the instrument for value as required by UCC § 3-302(a).

3. Holmes is an HDC. While it may seem appropriate to focus on the "good faith" requirement, note that Holmes did not participate in the fraudulent scheme. In terms of "without notice," Holmes had no actual or constructive notice, nor any reason to believe that the instrument was a result of a fraudulent transaction. Therefore, Holmes was a holder who took the instrument for value, in good faith, and without notice or reasonable suspicion that the instrument was overdue, fraudulent, or subject to claim by a third party.

4. Holmes is not an HDC. Holmes had notice that the promissory note was overdue because the face of the note indicates it was due and payable on September 1. Because O'Connor negotiated the instrument to Holmes for cash on October 1, Holmes (although a holder) would not meet the "without notice" prong required for HDC status.

CHAPTER REVIEW QUESTIONS: Answers and Explanations

1. d. Negotiation begins with the issuance of the instrument to a holder and ends with presentment of the instrument by the party seeking to receiving payment. Answers *a, b,* and *c* are wrong because each contains an inaccurately used term.

2. c. HDC status requires that the holder take the instrument for value, in good faith, and without notice. However, there is no requirement that an HDC take the instrument from the original maker.

3. d. The "without notice" requirement separates innocent holders from holders who know or should know that the negotiable instrument is defective or fraudulent in some way. Answer *a* is wrong because the value requirement is not related to notice of fraud. Answers *b* and *c* are incorrect because they not HDC-related terms.

4. d. While HDC status provides immunity from personal defenses or claims in recoupment, the HDC status does not protect an HDC from being subjected to any real defenses.

5. b. The FTC regulation that preserves the rights of consumers to assert claims and defenses against any holder of a consumer credit contract is called the Holder Rule. The other answers are wrong because no such rules exist in the FTC context.

6. a. True. HDCs are immune from personal defenses such as breach of the underlying contract, but not from real defenses.

7. b. False. An HDC analysis of good faith applies the *objective* (not subjective) standard.

8. b. False. Raleigh's alma mater cannot be an HDC because it did not take the instrument for value and thus cannot meet the requirement in UCC § 3-302(a)(2).

9. a. True. One who does not himself qualify as an HDC can still acquire that status if some previous holder was an HDC under the shelter rule in UCC § 3-203(b).

10. a. True. Fraud in the inducement is a personal defense and is more common. It covers fraudulent misrepresentations of material facts by one party intended to induce another party to enter into an agreement.

CHAPTER 21

Liability, Defenses, and Discharge

THINKING STRATEGICALLY

After reviewing the relevant liability rules and defenses relating to negotiable instruments, this chapter's *Thinking Strategically* will explore the problem of "judgment-proof" defendants.

Learning Objectives

After studying this chapter, students who have mastered the material will be able to:

21-1   Differentiate between primary and secondary signature liability on a negotiable instrument.
21-2   Articulate the UCC's procedures for presentment and dishonoring an instrument.
21-3   Explain how agency principles operate in the context of negotiable instruments.
21-4   Articulate the basic rules of warranty liability.
21-5   Identify which defenses always apply against a holder of a negotiable instrument.
21-6   Describe the main ways in which an instrument can be discharged or terminated.

CHAPTER OVERVIEW

This chapter continues our discussion of negotiable instruments by examining a question that is especially important to business owners and managers. Namely, who is liable to pay for company notes and checks? We start by discussing signature liability on a negotiable instrument and Uniform Commercial Code (UCC) procedures for lawfully presenting the instrument. Then we look at various types of warranty liability, and we conclude the chapter by reviewing the ways in which parties may defend or be discharged from liability.

LIABILITY ON THE INSTRUMENT

The fundamental promise behind any negotiable instrument is the agreement by the maker/drawer to pay a sum of money. In most cases, this promise to pay a draft is completed without any interruption, delay, or interference. There are instances, however, when not all goes according to plan. For example, suppose that the maker does *not* keep the promise because the maker believes (rightly or wrongly) that the obligation to pay has been extinguished. Or suppose that the drawee of the draft (such as a bank) refuses to make payment. In such cases, Article 3 of the UCC provides a relatively detailed map for enforcing the instrument when the holder's efforts to be paid in the ordinary course have been unsuccessful. Two threshold questions are useful for understanding payment liability of a negotiable instrument:

LO 21-1

Differentiate between primary and secondary signature liability on a negotiable instrument.

- Who is entitled to enforce the instrument?
- Against whom may the holder enforce an instrument?

Recall from our discussion in Chapter 20, "Negotiation, Indorsements, and Holder in Due Course," that a *holder* is the party that is in actual physical possession of the instrument and who is authorized by law to enforce the terms of the instrument or to transfer it to a third party.

The UCC sets out general rules to qualify as a "person entitled to enforce"[1] by defining a holder's right to enforce as the right to be paid *at any given moment* depending on indorsements and other factors we have described in previous chapters of this section. This physical possession requirement may seem outdated in the digital age, but it remains a touchstone of enforcement under Article 3. If a holder intends to enforce the instrument through a lawsuit, the physical instrument itself must be produced in court. This means that if the instrument was stolen, destroyed, or lost, the holder cannot enforce the instrument without satisfying a strict set of criteria set out in the UCC and convincing a court that the instrument existed, what the terms of the instrument were, and the holder's right to enforce.[2]

Assuming the holder qualifies as a person entitled to enforce, the focus then turns to who is liable for paying the instrument. Article 3 of the UCC lays out a basic starting point:

> A person is not liable on an instrument unless (i) the person signed the instrument, or (ii) the person is represented by an agent who signed the instrument and the signature is binding on the represented person. . . .[3]

The first part of that section creates what is known as **signature liability**. The second part relates to signature liability when an *agent* signs on behalf of a principal. Agency-related signature issues are discussed in detail later in this chapter. Fundamentally, as you may imagine, signature liability arises from a party's (individual or corporate) authentic signature on the instrument. The UCC provides a broad definition that includes any signature that is affixed to the instrument either "manually or by means of a device or machine" and using any "name, including any trade or assumed name, or by any word, mark, or symbol" with an intention to authenticate a writing.[4] Signature liability may be either *primary* or *secondary* depending on the status of the signer (e.g., maker versus indorser).

Primary Liability

Makers and acceptors of drafts are considered to have **primary liability** for payment of an instrument. This means that both makers and acceptors are liable for the amount of the instrument as soon as it is issued and are required to pay the instrument as soon as it is presented for payment. A *maker* is the person who signs a check, draft, promissory note, or other negotiable instrument (thereby assuming the liability to pay when it becomes due) and who has the authority for doing so. The maker's promise to pay is a contractual obligation and a key part of any negotiable instrument transaction. The obligation is owed to a person entitled to enforce the note or to an indorser that has rights under the instrument.[5]

An *acceptor*, or *drawee*, is the person that accepts a negotiable instrument and agrees to be primarily responsible for its payment or performance. The acceptor or drawee's signature

---

[1]UCC § 3-301.

[2]UCC § 3-309(a).

[3]UCC § 3-401(a).

[4]UCC § 3-401(b).

[5]UCC § 3-412.

FIGURE 21.1 Certified Check

Certified Check

A check that is guaranteed by the bank that sufficient funds will be withheld from the drawer's account to pay the amount stated on the check

triggers this acceptance and, thus, the drawee as acceptor is primarily liable. The acceptance must be written on the draft by some means. The signature is usually accompanied by some wording, such as "accepted" or "I accept." A common example of signature liability of an acceptor is when a bank *certifies* a maker's check. When a bank certifies a check, the bank marks the check with its certification, which acts as notice of the drawee bank's acceptance. The bank has become an acceptor and is now liable to the holder. The drawer is no longer liable.[6]

Figure 21.1 shows a sample certified check.

For example, suppose that Andrews writes a personal check on his account at Big Bank to Cardozo Consulting Company (CCC) for $1,000 as payment for a $5,000 invoice for consulting services. Andrews also signs a promissory note for the remaining $4,000. When CCC tries to cash the check, Big Bank refuses to honor it because it reasonably suspects it is not an authentic check. CCC approaches Andrews and, having learned its lesson, now requires Andrews to provide either a *certified check* or cash for the $1,000 payment. Andrews and CCC agree to cancel the Big Bank check in lieu of a new check written on Andrews's Neighborhood Credit Union (NCU) account. Andrews takes the check to NCU and they certify the check. Andrews then delivers the NCU check to CCC. Figure 21.2 illustrates the Article 3 liability for each party in the Andrews-CCC transaction.

In Case 21.1, a court analyzes the impact of the bank's acceptance of a check.

FIGURE 21.2 Andrews-CCC Check Liability

Party	Role	Liability for Promissory Note	Liability for Big Bank Check	Liability for NCU Certified Check
Andrews	Maker/Drawer	Primary	None. Check was canceled by agreement.	None. Once NCU certified the check, Andrews was no longer liable.
CCC	Holder	N/A	N/A	N/A
Big Bank	Drawee	N/A	None. They did not accept the check.	N/A
NCU	Acceptor	N/A	N/A	Primary

---

[6]UCC § 3-414(b).

FACT SUMMARY Affiliated Health Group (AHG) is an organization owned by two physicians who provide medical services in Chicago and the surrounding area. AHG alleged that two employees from its billing department embezzled millions of dollars from the company beginning in the early 1990s and continuing through 2013. The employees perpetrated this fraud by creating sham entities with similar names to AHG and then opening accounts for these sham entities at Devon Bank. Checks intended for AHG were deposited into the sham entity's bank account and collected by the embezzlers. Healthcare Services Corp. d/b/a Blue Cross Blue Shield of Illinois ("Insurer") is a health insurance company that issued checks for the medical services provided by AHG for its customers. Although Insurer issued and delivered the checks to the correct AHG entities, many of these checks were subsequently deposited into sham entity's Devon Bank accounts. Soon thereafter, all of Insurer's checks were cleared for payment by Insurer's bank. AHG sued Insurer arguing that Insurer remained liable under Article 3 of Illinois' version of the UCC.

SYNOPSIS OF DECISION AND OPINION The Illinois court of appeals ruled in favor of Insurer. The court held that Article 3 extinguished Insurer's obligation to pay when the drafts (i.e., the checks) were accepted at the depositing banks. They pointed to UCC § 3-414(c) to explain that the drawer is discharged once a draft is accepted by a bank, regardless of when or by whom the acceptance was obtained. Based on this, whether Insurer was discharged centers on whether the draft was "accepted," regardless of when or by whom acceptance was obtained.

WORDS OF THE COURT: Acceptance "Section 3-409(a) states that '[a]cceptance' means the drawee's signed agreement to pay a draft as presented. Acceptance may be made at any time and becomes effective when notification pursuant to instructions is given or the accepted draft is delivered for the purpose of giving rights on the acceptance to any person. The UCC defines a drawee as 'a person ordered in a draft to make payment.' The drawee in this case [is Insurer's] bank who cleared the checks, not the [Insurer itself]. Based on the above, we agree with [Insurer] that because the drafts were accepted by the banks, [Insurer's] obligation to pay for the medical services performed by [AHG] was discharged pursuant to section 3-414(c)."

Case Questions

1. Who is the acceptor in this case, and why is this question important?

2. Why is the concept of "acceptance" a primary factor in the court's decision in this case?

3. *Focus on Critical Thinking:* AHG sued Insurer. Why didn't it sue the bank?

Secondary Liability

Unlike primary liability, **secondary liability** is *conditional,* arising only if the primarily liable party fails to pay. The two parties that can become liable through secondary liability are *drawers* and *indorsers.*[7] Secondarily liable parties are responsible to pay the amount of an unaccepted instrument to any subsequent holder so long as: (1) the instrument was dishonored and, in some cases, (2) notice of dishonor is given to the drawer or indorser. So long as the check was properly presented (covered in the next section) and the instrument was not honored, and the drawer/indorser had notice of the dishonor, the drawer/indorser is now liable to pay the holder. Recall from previous chapters that a *drawer* is the individual or entity who signs as a party ordering payment. An *indorser* is a party who signs an instrument to either restrict payment, negotiate payment, or incur the liability.

Recall our Andrews-CCC hypothetical. Suppose instead that Big Bank didn't honor the first check because Andrews had closed his account the week before. Nevertheless,

---

[7]UCC §§ 3-414 and 3-415.

when CCC approaches Andrews, he refuses to discuss it, calling it "a problem between you and the bank." In this case, Big Bank has no primary liability because it is not an acceptor. However, Big Bank's refusal to accept the check then triggers the secondary liability of the drawer (Andrews) for payment. CCC is entitled to recover the money owed through a lawsuit.

TAKEAWAY CONCEPTS Liability of the Instrument

LO 21-2

Articulate the UCC's procedures for presentment and dishonoring an instrument.

PRESENTMENT

Presentment is the process used by a holder to demand that the drawee pay the instrument.[8] Article 3 sets out three UCC requirements for payment of a negotiable instrument. First, the instrument must be presented to the *appropriate individual or entity.* For drafts such as a check, the holder's presentment is made to the drawer's bank because the bank is the drawee and thus is responsible for paying the check. For a negotiable instrument such as a promissory note, the holder presents the note to the maker since, in that instance, there is no drawee. The maker of the note is obligated to pay the note upon presentment (if other presentment requirements are met).

The second requirement is that the instrument must be presented in a *specific way* in accordance with the instrument's terms and conditions. This requirement can be met by the holder so long as the instrument was presented in a commercially reasonable manner, or through a check clearinghouse process, or at the place designated in the instrument itself.

Finally, the instrument must be presented in a reasonably *timely* manner. This last requirement is particularly important for secondary liability since the UCC sets a deadline of 30 days from creation of the instrument for presentment as an expiration date. That is, if the instrument is not presented within that time period, the drawer or indorser is relieved of any secondary liability to the holder.[9]

Returning to our Andrews-CCC transaction, the NCU check written by Andrews is presented correctly by depositing the check in a timely manner in CCC's account or by presenting the check to NCU for cash payment. The promissory note that Andrews signed must be presented by CCC to Andrews based on the terms and conditions in the note.

Instruments That Are Dishonored

In some cases, presentment is made to the correct party, in the correct way, and in a timely manner, but a third party (e.g., a drawee) refuses to pay the instrument. This may be because the holder cannot meet a routine requirement such as providing identification to a drawee bank to cash a check. In other cases the drawee may refuse to pay because the instrument is fraudulent or the drawer does not have sufficient funds to cover the check. In those cases, the instrument has been **dishonored**. Once a check has been dishonored, the holder must

---

[8]UCC § 3-501.
[9]UCC §§ 3-414(f) and 3-415(e).

then resort to enforcing the instrument against secondarily liable parties such as the drawer. It also is important to note that the payor bank is given some time—until the end of the day on which the presentment has been made—to determine whether to honor the check presented. It *does not* dishonor the check by simply refusing to pay it. In fact, the UCC provides some specific reasons for refusing to pay that *do not* constitute dishonoring an instrument.[10]

- Authority: A holder may be required to exhibit the instrument and provide reasonable identification and/or authorization to present the instrument.
- Banking day: Article 3 sets a daily 2:00 p.m. cutoff deadline after which a party to whom presentment is made may treat the presentment as occurring on the next business day.

In Case 21.2, a state appellate court considers the question of what is "reasonable identification" under Article 3.

CASE 21.2 Messing v. Bank of America, 821 A.2d 22 (Md. 2003)

FACT SUMMARY Messing received a check payable to him that had been written by Burruss, the drawer, in the amount of $976. Instead of depositing the check into his account at his own bank, Messing elected to present the check for payment at a branch of Burruss's bank, Bank of America (BoA), the drawee. Using a computer, the BoA teller confirmed the availability of funds on deposit and placed the check into the computer's printer slot. The computer stamped certain data on the back of the check, including the time, date, amount of the check, account number, and teller number. The computer also effected a hold on the amount of $976 in the customer's account. The teller gave the check back to Messing, who indorsed it. The teller then recorded information from Messing's identification on the back of the check as well.

Before paying the cash to Messing, the teller asked if Messing was a customer of BoA. When Messing told her that he was not, the BoA teller returned the check to Messing and requested, consistent with bank policy when cashing checks for non-customers, that Messing place his thumbprint on the check. The thumbprint identification program was designed by various banking and federal agencies to reduce check fraud. Messing refused the thumbprint request, and the teller informed him that she would be unable to complete the transaction without it. Rather than take the check to his own bank and deposit it there, or return it to Burruss, Messing sued BoA claiming that they had violated the Maryland Uniform Commercial Code (UCC) by refusing to pay the check upon proper presentment. The trial court entered summary judgment in favor of BoA. Messing appealed arguing that the thumbprint requirement is not a request for "reasonable identification" under UCC § 3-501.

SYNOPSIS OF DECISION AND OPINION The Maryland Supreme Court upheld the lower court's decision in favor of BoA. The court ruled that the BoA thumbprint requirement has been upheld, in other noncriminal circumstances, as a reasonable and necessary industry response to the growing problem of check fraud. They also agreed with the lower court's conclusion that the form of identification was not defined by the statute, but that the Code itself recognized a thumbprint as a form of signature, and that requiring thumbprint or fingerprint identification has been found to be reasonable and not to violate privacy rights in several noncriminal contexts.

WORDS OF THE COURT: Reasonable Identification "We disagree [with Messing's] conclusion that a thumbprint signature is not 'reasonable identification' for purposes of [Article 3].... Nowhere does the language of [the relevant section in Article 3] suggest that 'reasonable identification' is limited to information [BoA] can authenticate at the

(continued)

---

[10]UCC § 3-501(b).

time presentment is made. Rather, all that is required is that the 'person making presentment must . . . give reasonable identification.' While providing a thumbprint signature does not necessarily confirm identification of the check holder at presentment—unless of course the drawee bank has a duplicate thumbprint signature on file—it does assist in the identification of the check holder should the check later prove to be bad. It therefore serves as a powerful deterrent to those who might otherwise attempt to pass a bad check. That one method provides identification at the time of presentment and the other identification after the check may have been honored, does not prevent the latter from being 'reasonable identification' . . ."

Case Questions

1. Why did Messing believe that the thumbprint requirement was unreasonable?

2. What alternatives did Messing have for receiving payment on the check?

3. *Focus on Critical Thinking:* Messing argued that the BoA teller, by placing the check in the slot of her computer, and the computer then printing certain information on the back of the check, accepted the check as defined in Article 3 and could not subsequently dishonor it. Does that strike you as a compelling argument? Explain.

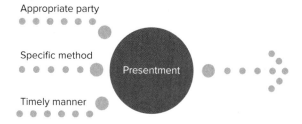

TAKEAWAY CONCEPTS Presentment

Appropriate party

Specific method

Presentment

Timely manner

AGENCY ISSUES

LO 21-3

Explain how agency principles operate in the context of negotiable instruments.

Recall the basic formula set out in Article 3 of the UCC for liability to pay an instrument: signature liability and agent signature liability.[11] While we have discussed signature liability, certain issues that surround an agent's signature on a negotiable instrument are also important since it is relatively common for business entities to designate certain agents for the purpose of signing checks, drafts, and so forth. The law of agency is important in a UCC Article 3 context, for the language used in the UCC is the functional equivalent of the terminology used to describe an agency relationship. Therefore, you should recognize that in Article 3, **represented person** means *principal,* while **representative** means *agent.*

The language in UCC § 3-401 requires not just that the representative sign the instrument, but also that the signature be binding on the represented person. Once it has been established that the representative had authority to bind the represented party, the represented party is now bound to the instrument's terms and conditions. The UCC does not replace the law of agency; in fact, it defers to agency law for determining whether the agent had authority. You will learn in future chapters that agents derive their authority to bind the principal from express authority. The same is true in a negotiable instruments context. If the represented party, for instance, tells an employee representative that she has the authority to sign checks from the represented party's account for buying inventory so long as the checks do not exceed $1,000, then the representative has no actual authority to sign checks

---

[11]UCC § 3-402.

for any other purpose nor in any greater amount. Representatives also can gain the power to bind through implied authority or through apparent authority. These slightly more complex theories are explained in Chapter 37, "Agency Formation, Categories, and Authority."

TAKEAWAY CONCEPTS Agency Issues

- The language used in the UCC is the functional equivalent of the terminology used to describe an agency relationship. Therefore, you should recognize that in Article 3, *represented person* means principal, while *representative* means agent.
- Article 3 requires not just that the representative sign the instrument, but also that the signature be binding on the represented person.
- Once it has been established that the representative had authority to bind the represented party, the represented party is now bound to the instrument's terms and conditions.

WARRANTY LIABILITY

Thus far, we have discussed the legal liability of primary and secondary parties—the liability that applies to those who sign an instrument. Liability can occur a second way, too: by warranty. In general, the legal liability of *someone who receives payment* on an instrument is referred to in the law as **warranty liability**. This special set of rules applies when someone receives payment on an instrument that has been forged, altered, or stolen.

There are two basic rules of warranty liability:

> Rule #1: *The wrongdoer is always liable.* The person who forges, alters, or steals a check is always liable for the value of the instrument and for any other expenses or lost interest resulting from the wrongdoing.
>
> Alas, forgers have a habit of skipping town, and even if the wrongdoer is caught (a big if), he may not have sufficient money to pay for his wrongdoing. This is where the second basic rule of warranty liability comes into play.
>
> Rule #2: *The drawee bank (the bank named in the forged check or instrument) is also liable if it pays a check on which the drawer's name is forged.* The bank, however, can recover from the payee (the person to whom the check or instrument is payable) if the payee himself had reason to suspect the forgery.

LO 21-4

Articulate the basic rules of warranty liability.

✅ QUICK QUIZ Warranty Liability

Who is liable?

1. Wisin signs Yandel's name on one of his checks. Who is liable: Wisin, Yandel, or both parties?
2. A bank cashes Yandel's forged check. Must the bank reimburse Yandel even if the bank is unable to recover from Wisin?
3. Suppose that Wisin forged a check to pay for a new dragon tattoo. If Enrique, the owner of the tattoo parlor, deposits the check and the bank pays it, may the bank recover from Enrique?

Answers to this Quick Quiz are provided at the end of the chapter.

In all other cases of wrongdoing, the person who first acquires an instrument from the wrongdoer is liable to anyone else who pays value for it. The liability of the first acquirer is based on two types of warranties set forth in Article 3 of the Uniform Commercial Code: transfer warranties and presentment warranties.

Transfer Warranties

By operation of law, when someone transfers an instrument for consideration (i.e., in exchange for something of value), the transferor automatically makes the following five implied **transfer warranties**:

1. The transferor is the legitimate owner of the instrument.
2. All signatures on the instrument are authentic and authorized.
3. The instrument has not been wrongfully altered in any way.
4. No defense or claim can be asserted against the holder of the instrument.
5. As far as the transferor knows, the issuer of the instrument is solvent (i.e., has the ability to pay it).

Transfer warranties generally come into play when there is no indorsement, when the indorsement is qualified, or when the holder fails to make timely presentment or notice of dishonor, thereby discharging a previous indorsee. In such cases, the transferee (the person who receives the instrument from the transferor) can sue a prior party on one or more of these five implied warranties. These warranties may be enforced by the immediate transferee or, if the transfer was by indorsement, by any subsequent holder who takes the instrument in good faith. The warranties thus run "with the instrument."[12]

Presentment Warranties

By operation of law, anyone who presents a check for payment makes the three following **presentment warranties**:

1. The presenter is the legitimate owner of the check.
2. The check has not been wrongfully altered in any way.
3. The presenter has no reason to believe that the drawer's signature is forged.

As a general rule, payment on an instrument is final, and the payer has no right to a refund. But there is an exception to this general rule. The payer does have the legal right to a refund if any one of the implied warranties described above turns out to be untrue.

---

[12]UCC § 3-416.

TAKEAWAY CONCEPTS Transfer Warranties

Transfer Warranties

The five transfer warranties made by a person who transfers a negotiable instrument to someone else for consideration are:

1. The warrantor is entitled to enforce the instrument.

2. All signatures on the instrument are authentic or authorized.

3. The instrument has not been altered.

4. The instrument is not subject to a defense or a claim in recoupment that any party can assert against the warrantor.

5. The warrantor has no knowledge of any insolvency proceedings commenced with respect to the maker or acceptor or, in the case of an unaccepted draft, the drawer.

Who	What Warranties	To Whom
Nonindorsing transferor	Makes all five transfer warranties	To his immediate transferee only
Indorsing transferor	Makes all five transfer warranties	To his immediate transferee and all subsequent transferees

In Case 21.3, the U.S. Supreme Court becomes embroiled in a check fraud case involving the Paymaster's Office of the U.S. Marine Corps. The facts in this case involve the application of a presentment warranty.

CASE 21.3 National Metropolitan Bank v. United States, 323 U.S. 454 (1945)

FACT SUMMARY Foley, a civilian clerk in the Paymaster's Office of the U.S. Marine Corps, procured the issuance of 144 government checks by forging pay and travel mileage vouchers in the names of several living Marine Corps officers. These forgeries occurred during a two-year period—between July 14, 1936, and November 16, 1938. All 144 checks were drawn on the United States Treasury payable to the order of the Marine Corps officers and delivered to Foley for distribution to them. Foley, however, forged their signatures, added his own name as a second indorser, and then deposited or cashed the checks at Anacostia Bank. That bank, without investigating the genuineness of the payees' signatures, indorsed the checks and transmitted them to National Metropolitan Bank, which collected on them from the government. The government formally demanded a refund from National Metropolitan Bank after it discovered Foley's fraud and his forgeries, but the bank refused to refund the government. As a result, the

©B Christopher/Alamy

government sued in the federal district court for the District of Columbia. The district court ruled for the government, and the court of appeals affirmed the lower court's decision. The bank then appealed to the U.S. Supreme Court.

(continued)

SYNOPSIS OF DECISION AND OPINION The U.S. Supreme Court rejected National Metropolitan Bank's defense that it was the government that breached its implied warranties when it issued the 144 checks in the first place. Instead, the Supreme Court affirmed the decision of the two lower courts, thus requiring the bank to refund the government for all 144 forged checks.

WORDS OF THE COURT: Presentation Warranty
" . . . [P]resentation of a government check to it for payment with an express guaranty of prior indorsements amounts to a warranty that the signature of the payee was not forged, but genuine. Breach of that warranty, . . . by presenting a check on which the payee's signature is a forgery, gives the government a right to recover from the guarantor when payment is made. The checks in the instant case were presented to the government by the bank bearing forged indorsements of the payee's name, and a specific [presentment warranty] by the bank. . . . [T]he government should recover, unless other principles here invoked exempt it from liability."

Case Questions

1. In your opinion, was this decision (requiring the bank to refund the government) a just one? In other words, did the courts decide this case correctly?

2. According to National Metropolitan Bank, it was the government who breached its implied warranties when it issued the 144 checks in the first place. Specifically, the bank argued that the issuance of the checks by the government was a warranty that they were not fictitious, but genuine and issued for a valuable consideration. Is the bank right?

3. *Focus on Critical Thinking:* Why didn't the government sue Foley, the actual mastermind behind this two-year fraudulent scheme?

TAKEAWAY CONCEPTS Presentment Warranties

Presentment Warranties

If an unaccepted draft (such as a check) is presented for payment or acceptance and the drawee pays or accepts the draft, then the person obtaining payment or acceptance and prior transferors warrant to the drawee:

1. The warrantor is a person entitled to enforce payment or authorized to obtain payment or acceptance on behalf of a person entitled to enforce the draft.

2. The draft has not been altered.

3. The warrantor has no knowledge that the signature of the drawer of the draft has not been authorized.

If (*a*) a dishonored draft is presented for payment to the drawer or indorser or (*b*) any other instrument (such as a note) is presented for payment to a party obligated to pay the instrument and the presenter receives payment, the presenter (as well as a prior transferor of the instrument) makes the following warranty to the person making payment in good faith:

> The person obtaining payment is a person entitled to enforce the instrument or authorized to obtain payment on behalf of a person entitled to enforce the instrument.

LO 21-5

Identify which defenses always apply against a holder of a negotiable instrument.

DEFENSES AGAINST HOLDERS OF NEGOTIABLE INSTRUMENTS

A holder is a person who legally obtains a negotiable instrument, with his name on it as payee. Holders of negotiable instruments generally have the legal right to receive payment according to the terms and conditions of the instruments they hold. But holder beware: The maker or issuer of the instrument may assert any of the following defenses against a holder at any time:

1. The signature on the instrument is forged.
2. The amount on the instrument was altered after the maker signed it, unless the maker left the instrument blank.
3. The instrument itself is not valid under the common law of contracts. An instrument would not be valid if, for example, the issuer or maker was underage when he signed the instrument; the issuer or maker signed the instrument under duress, with mental incapacity, or as part of an illegal transaction; or the issuer or maker was induced to sign the instrument under false pretenses.

In short, if any of these defenses apply, the maker or issuer of a negotiable instrument is not required to pay the holder.

TAKEAWAY CONCEPTS Defenses Against Holders of Negotiable Instruments

- A maker or issuer of a negotiable instrument may assert the following defenses against a holder of a negotiable instrument:
    - The signature on the instrument is forged.
    - The amount on the instrument was altered after the issuer or maker signed it, unless the issuer or maker left the instrument blank.
    - The instrument itself is not valid under the common law of contracts.

DISCHARGE

LO 21-6

Describe the main ways in which an instrument can be discharged or terminated.

Negotiable instruments eventually expire. The expiration or death of a negotiable instrument is called **discharge**. In general, an instrument can be discharged or terminated in the following ways:

- payment or tender of payment,
- cancellation or renunciation,
- material and fraudulent alteration,
- certification,
- acceptance varying a draft,
- and—in some cases—unexcused delay in giving notice of presentment or dishonor.

Let's review each one of these discharge or termination methods in detail.

Discharge by Payment

Payment is the most common method of discharging an obligation. Unless the payment is made in bad faith to one who unlawfully obtained the instrument, a person who is primarily liable discharges his liability on an instrument to the extent of payment—by paying or otherwise satisfying the holder—and the discharge is good even if the payor knows that another person has a claim to the instrument.

Discharge by Tender

A person who tenders full payment to a holder on or after the date due discharges any subsequent liability to pay interest, costs, and attorneys' fees. If the holder refuses to accept the tender, any party who would have had a right of recourse against the party making the tender is discharged.

Discharge by Cancellation or Renunciation

The holder may discharge any party, even without consideration, by marking the face of the instrument or the indorsement in an unequivocal way, as, for example, by intentionally canceling the instrument or the signature by destruction or mutilation or by striking out the party's signature. The holder also may renounce his rights by delivering a signed writing to that effect or by surrendering the instrument itself.[13]

Discharge by Material and Fraudulent Alteration

If a holder materially and fraudulently alters an instrument, any party who is affected by the alteration is discharged.[14]

Discharge by Certification

When a drawee certifies a draft for a holder, the drawer and all prior indorsers are discharged.

Discharge by Acceptance Varying a Draft

If the holder assents to an acceptance varying the terms of a draft, the obligation of the drawer and of any indorsers who do not expressly assent to the acceptance is discharged.[15]

 Quick Quiz Discharge

Discharge or no discharge?

1. Parents loan their daughter $6,000 to attend college, and she gives them a promissory note in return. At her graduation party, the parents ceremoniously tear up the note. Is the daughter's obligation terminated?

2. Juan signs Roberta's note to Creditor, agreeing to serve as Roberta's surety or guarantor for two years. At the end of the two-year term, Roberta has still not paid Creditor, who—without Juan's knowledge—gives Roberta an extra six months to pay. She fails to do so. Does Creditor still have recourse against Juan?

3. Marcus makes a note for $100 payable to Pauline. Pauline fraudulently raises the amount to $1,000 without Marcus's knowledge and negotiates it to Ned, who qualifies as a holder in due course (HDC). How much money does Marcus owe to Ned, $100 or $1,000?

4. Charlene writes a check payable to Lumber Yard and gives it to a contractor to buy materials for a deck replacement. The contractor fills it in for $1,200: $1,000 for the decking and $200 for his own unauthorized purposes. How much does Lumber Yard owe under this check?

Answers to this Quick Quiz are provided at the end of the chapter.

---

[13]UCC § 3-604.

[14]UCC § 3-407.

[15]UCC § 3-410.

Notice Requirement

As we have seen thus far, the UCC provides a number of ways by which an obligor on an instrument is discharged from liability. Nevertheless, no discharge of any party operates against a subsequent holder in due course unless she has notice when she takes the instrument.[16]

TAKEAWAY CONCEPTS Discharge

An obligor is discharged from liability by:

1. Payment of the instrument.
2. Tender of the instrument.
3. Cancellation of the instrument.
4. Fradulent alteration of the instrument.
5. Acceptance of a draft by a bank (e.g., if a check is certified by a bank).
6. Unexcused delay in presentment or notice of dishonor with respect to a check.

---

[16]UCC § 3-601.

THINKING STRATEGICALLY

©valterZ/Shutterstock

Judgment-Proof Defendants

PROBLEM: The general rule is that a person who forges an instrument is always legally liable for the value of the instrument and for any other expenses or lost interest resulting from the forgery. The problem, however, is that persons who commit forgery are often "judgment proof." The term *judgment proof* refers to a strategic concept in law commonly used to refer to defendants or potential defendants who are financially insolvent, or whose income and assets cannot be obtained in satisfaction of a judgment. As a result, if a plaintiff were to secure a legal judgment against an insolvent defendant, such as a forger of a negotiable instrument, the defendant's lack of funds would make the satisfaction of that judgment difficult, if not impossible, to secure. Even if the defendant wrongdoer is not insolvent, the cost of collecting a judgment may also contribute to an assessment of whether a debtor is judgment proof. If the amount that a judgment holder can collect from the debtor is insufficient to cover ongoing legal expenses and related costs of collection, collection efforts become uneconomical.

A good example of a judgment-proof defendant is Frank Abagnale, Jr., who was played by Leonardo

©RGR Collection/Alamy

DiCaprio in the movie *Catch Me If You Can,* based on Mr. Abagnale's best-selling memoir of the same name. Mr. Abagnale became one of the most famous (and youngest!) check forgers and con men in the world. He assumed no fewer than eight identities, including an airline pilot, a physician, and a lawyer, all before the age of 21. And, as dramatically depicted in the movie, Mr. Abagnale developed different ways of defrauding banks, such as printing out his own almost-perfect copies of checks such as payroll checks, depositing them, and encouraging banks to advance him cash based on his account balances.[17]

STRATEGIC SOLUTION: The law provides a strategic solution to this judgment-proof problem by allocating the risk of loss due to forgery. In general, a drawee bank (the bank named in a forged check or instrument) is liable to the payee or issuer if it pays a check on which the drawer's name is forged. At the same time, the bank can recover from the payee (the person to whom the check or instrument is payable) if the payee himself had reason to suspect the forgery.

[17]Jim Hammerand, "Q & A: 'Catch Me If You Can' Conman Abagnale Tells How to Prevent Fraud," *Minneapolis Business Journal,* December 11, 2012.

QUESTIONS

Check out this memorable scene from the award-winning movie, *Catch Me If You Can:* https://www .youtube.com/watch?v=njgbmeiGi4E. In this scene Frank Abagnale, Jr., who is played by Leonardo DiCaprio, asks a hotel clerk if he can cash a personal check. The hotel clerk replies: "For airline personnel we cash personal checks up to $100; payroll checks we cash up $300."

1. Based on what you have learned in this chapter, aside from Mr. Abagnale, which other parties could incur liability for Mr. Abagnale's fake checks?
2. What steps, if any, could these parties have taken to avoid liability on Mr. Abagnale's forged checks?

KEY TERMS

Signature liability p. 363   Liability that arises by a party's (individual or corporate) authentic signature on the instrument, which may be either primary or secondary depending on the status of the signer.

Primary liability p. 363   Liability for the amount of the instrument as soon as it is issued; required to be paid as soon as the instrument is presented for payment.

Secondary liability p. 365   Conditional liability that arises only if the primarily liable party fails to pay.

Presentment p. 366   Process used by a holder to demand that the drawee pay the instrument.

Dishonored p. 366   Status of an instrument in which the drawee refuses to pay for any reason other than those defined in the UCC related to identification authority and cutoff time.

Represented person p. 368   UCC Article 3 equivalent for *principal.*

Representative p. 368   UCC Article 3 equivalent for *agent.*

Warranty liability p. 369   The legal liability of someone who receives payment on an instrument.

Transfer warranties p. 370   Warranties made by operation of law when someone transfers an instrument for consideration.

Presentment warranties p. 370   Warranties made by operation of law by anyone who presents a check for payment.

Discharge p. 373   In contract law, the removal of all legal obligations under the agreement.

CASE SUMMARY 21.1 Bank of Nichols Hills v. Bank of Oklahoma, 196 P.3d 984 (Okla. Civ. App. 2008)

Presentment

In payment of a claim for a loss due to a fire that destroyed the mobile home belonging to Russell, the Oklahoma Farm Bureau Mutual Insurance Company (Farm Bureau) negotiated a $69,000 settlement and issued a joint check in this amount payable to Russell *and* Conseco Financial. Conseco Financial was the mortgagee of the property and was entitled to payment under the policy. The check was drawn on Farm Bureau's account at Bank of Nichols Hills (BNH), and Russell deposited the check into his personal account at Bank of Oklahoma (BOK). The check contained an authentic indorsement by Russell and a forged indorsement for Conseco. Upon receipt, BOK presented the check to BNH. BNH paid the $69,000 check and notified Farm Bureau that the check had been paid from its account. When Conseco Financial learned of the check, it demanded that Farm Bureau pay off the balance of the mortgage. Farm Bureau paid Conseco Financial and notified BNH of the forgery. BNH reimbursed Farm Bureau the amount paid to Conseco. BNH then sued BOK on a theory of breach of presentment warranty.

CASE QUESTIONS

1. Which presentment warranty is at issue?
2. Who prevails and why?

CASE SUMMARY 21.2 Flatiron Linen v. First American State Bank, 23 P.3d 1209, Supreme Court of Colorado (2001)

Primary Liability

Flatiron Linen received a personal check for $4,100, drawn on an account at First American Bank. Flatiron attempted to deposit the check the same day, but First American returned the check to Flatiron due to insufficient funds in the issuer's account. The next day, the issuer of the check contacted First American and requested a stop payment order on the dishonored check. Five months later, without knowledge of the stop payment order, Flatiron took the check to a First American branch and presented it for payment once again. The teller verified that the account had sufficient funds to cover the check but failed to notice the stop payment order on the check. In exchange for the personal check, First American issued Flatiron a cashier's check for $4,100. Flatiron deposited the cashier's check in its account at Colorado National Bank (CNB) and withdrew the $4,100 in cash. Meanwhile, First American discovered the stop payment order on the original check and informed Flatiron that it intended to dishonor the cashier's check upon presentment.

CASE QUESTIONS

1. What is Flatiron's best theory as to why it should prevail under Article 3?
2. Is the cashier's check an indication that First American is an acceptor? Explain.

CASE SUMMARY 21.3 Cooper v. Union Bank, 507 P.2d 609, Supreme Court of California (1973)

Warranties

Joseph Stell, an attorney, employed Bernice Ruff as a secretary and bookkeeper for his law firm. During a period of approximately a year and one-half, Ruff stole some 29 checks intended for Stell and forged the necessary indorsements thereon. She cashed some of these checks at Union Bank and deposited the rest in her personal account at Crocker Bank. After depositing the checks in her account, Ruff withdrew the entire amount of these deposits. After Stell discovered the fraud, he sued Union Bank and Crocker Bank (the payor banks). The banks, however, refused to issue any refund to Stell.

CASE QUESTIONS

1. In your opinion, who should win this case, and why?
2. Did Ruff breach any transfer or presentment warranties in this case? If so, why wasn't she sued?

CASE SUMMARY 21.4 Cooper v. Union Bank, 507 P.2d 609, Supreme Court of California (1973)

Forgery

Joseph Stell, an attorney, employed Bernice Ruff as a secretary and bookkeeper. Over a one-year period, Ruff purloined 29 checks intended for attorney Stell by forging the necessary indorsements on those checks. Ruff then cashed some of the checks at two banks, Union Bank and Crocker Citizens National Bank, and deposited the remainder to her personal account at the latter bank (Crocker Citizens National Bank). The entire amount of such deposits was subsequently withdrawn by Ruff prior to discovery of the forgeries. Certain of the checks were forwarded to and paid by defendants Crocker Citizens National Bank, Security First National Bank, and First Western Bank and Trust Company. Stell sued both the collecting banks as well as the payor banks to recover the amounts of the instruments handled by them on the forged indorsements.

1. Are the defenses available to the collector banks and to the payor banks the same or different? What are these defenses?
2. Who will prevail in this case? Stell or the banks?

CHAPTER REVIEW QUESTIONS

1. **Which of the following are required for a holder to enforce a negotiable instrument?**
   a. The holder has held the instrument for at least 30 days.
   b. The holder has physical possession of the instrument.
   c. The holder had a bank certify the instrument.
   d. The holder signed the instrument.

2. **Which of the following parties have primary signature liability?**
   I. Maker
   II. Drawer
   III. Acceptor
   IV. Indorser

      a. I, II, and III
      b. I and III
      c. II and IV
      d. III and IV

3. **Which of the following is *not* a transfer warranty?**
   a. The instrument has not been altered.
   b. The transferor may not enforce the instrument.
   c. All signatures are authentic and authorized.
   d. The instrument is not subject to a defense or claim of any party that can be asserted against the transferor.

4. **What are the two kinds of liability associated with negotiable instruments?**
   a. Withholding and reverse
   b. Warranty and signature
   c. Essential and nonessential
   d. Dispatch and relief

5. **Which of the following is *not* a universal defense available to a holder in due course (HDC)?**
   a. Minority or duress
   b. Forgery
   c. Discharge by payment
   d. Material alteration

6. **Secondary signature liability is conditional in that it is triggered only when an instrument is dishonored.**
   a. True
   b. False

7. **Dishonoring an instrument is the refusal by a drawee to pay an instrument because the holder did not have proper identification.**
   a. True
   b. False

8. **In Article 3 of the UCC, the term for agent is represented person.**
   a. True
   b. False

9. **A person who transfers a negotiable instrument or presents it for payment may incur liability from implied warranties.**
   a. True
   b. False

10. **Payment is the most common way that obligations represented by commercial paper are discharged.**
    a. True
    b. False

Quick Quiz ANSWERS

Warranty Liability

1. Wisin is liable, not Yandel, since Wisin is the one who forged Yandel's signature.
2. If the bank cashes Yandel's forged check, it must reimburse Yandel regardless of whether the bank ever recovers from Wisin.
3. The bank can only recover from Enrique, the owner of the tattoo parlor, if Enrique had reason to suspect the forgery.

Discharge

1. Yes, the daughter's obligation is terminated because a holder may discharge any party, even without consideration, by marking the face of the instrument or the indorsement in a clear and unequivocal way. For example, the holder may intentionally cancel the instrument or the signature by destruction or mutilation or by striking out the party's signature.
2. If the holder assents to an acceptance varying the terms of a draft, the obligation of the drawer and any indorsers who do not expressly assent to the acceptance is discharged, so the creditor does not have recourse against Juan.
3. If a holder materially and fraudulently alters an instrument, any party whose contract is affected by the change is discharged, so Marcus only owes Ned $100.
4. A payor bank or drawee paying a fraudulently altered instrument or a person taking it for value, in good faith, and without notice of the alteration, may enforce rights with respect to the instrument according to its original terms or, if the incomplete instrument was altered by unauthorized completion, according to its terms as completed. Therefore, Lumber Yard, if innocent of any wrongdoing, could enforce the check for $1,200, and Charlene must go after the contractor for the unauthorized $200.

CHAPTER REVIEW QUESTIONS: Answers and Explanations

1. b. The holder must have possession to enforce a negotiable instrument. The other answers are not part of Article 3.

2. b. Only makers and acceptors have primary liability. Drawers and indorsers have secondary liability.

3. b. Transfer warranties include the right of the transferor to enforce the instrument. The remaining choices are all transfer warranties.

4. b. Warranty and signature liability are the two kinds of liability associated with negotiable instruments. Answer *a* is incorrect because withholding and reverse are not the two kinds of liability associated with negotiable instruments. Similarly, answer *c* is incorrect because there is no such thing as essential and nonessential liability for negotiable instruments, while answer *d* is incorrect because there is no dispatch and relief liability for negotiable instruments.

5. c. Discharge by payment is not a universal defense but a form of discharge. The remaining choices are all universal defenses against holders.

6. a. True. Unlike primary liability, secondary liability is conditional.

7. b. False. The refusal to pay a draft because of lack of identification is not a dishonoring under the UCC.

8. b. False. In Article 3, the term for agent is representative, *not* represented person.

9. a. True. Transfer warranties and presentment warranties automatically apply when instruments are transferred or presented for payment.

10. a. True. Payment is the most common way that instruments are discharged or terminated.

CHAPTER 22

Checks, Deposits, and Financial Institutions

Payment systems offer great efficiency, and scale and support a well-functioning marketplace. They can also trigger liability concerns related to fraud. In this chapter, you will strategically assess the risks of using checks in the event a check is stolen.

Learning Objectives

After studying this chapter, students who have mastered the material will be able to:

22-1 Explain how checks are used in commercial transactions.

22-2 Summarize the various methods of electronic payment and the laws that apply to each one.

22-3 Identify the various types of mobile payment apps and the laws that apply to each one.

22-4 Apply UCC state law to determine who faces liability when a check is forged, stolen, or altered.

CHAPTER OVERVIEW

How often do you pay for goods or services with cash? The costs and risks associated with carrying substantial amounts of cash rise significantly as the frequency and dollar amounts increase. This is the reason checks and electronic payment systems, such as debit and credit cards, have become an important daily aspect of our financial system.

This chapter concerns the law that applies to checks and other types of electronic payment. Checks, originally called *bank notes,* are fairly old financial instruments that date back to use by ancient Asian traders. More recent payment systems, such as automated teller machines (ATMs), bank debit cards, cash apps such as PayPal, and cryptocurrencies that rely on the blockchain, are in some ways modern extensions of the more familiar check-based payment system. Even today, checks remain a vital

component of the financial system, as nearly 20 billion checks are cashed every year in the United States.

CHECKS IN COMMERCIAL TRANSACTIONS

Checks are negotiable instruments as defined in Chapter 19. Recall that Article 3 of the UCC defines a negotiable instrument as "an unconditional promise or order to pay a fixed amount."[1] The promise must be in writing and signed by the party undertaking to pay.[2] If you take a look at the check in Figure 22.1, you will see that the

---

[1] UCC § 3-104.

[2] UCC § 3-103(a).

FIGURE 22.1 Image of a Check

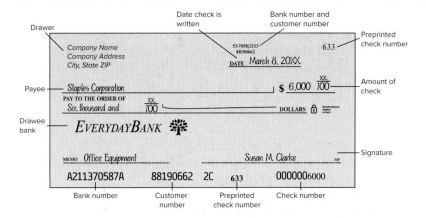

check is preprinted with the words "Pay to the order of," followed by a blank line that lets the check writer indicate to whom the check should be made payable. A check is an unconditional order to a bank to pay a certain fixed amount that will be drawn from the check writer's account. It is *unconditional* because there is no annotation to the check that stipulates any conditions. The bearer simply needs to present the check for payment and need not satisfy any promises, such as those included in a contract. Checks are payable on demand, which means that they can be cashed at any time, regardless of the date on the check.[3]

Recall that negotiable instruments must be in writing and signed by the person promising to pay; therefore, every valid check must be physically retained and signed if it is to be honored.[4] Because checks are orders rather than promises (notes), they are also referred to as **drafts**. The strict language of negotiability discussed in Chapter 19 applies to checks; therefore, a check must indicate whether it is payable "to the order of," "to the bearer," or "to cash." In the first case, the check is made out to a specific party. In the second two cases, anyone who physically possesses the check may cash it. Making a check out "to cash" transforms the check into a bearer negotiable instrument. That means anyone who finds it by accident or steals it can negotiate the instrument, or cash it. This makes instruments that are payable to the bearer or to cash fairly risky. A **cashier's check** is a check issued by a bank with funds drawn from the bank's own account. A **certified check** is a check drawn from a personal account that the bank guarantees will clear with sufficient funds.

Checks are issued and ultimately paid by a **drawee bank**. The relationship between a customer who opens a checking account, known as the **drawer**, and the drawee bank is governed by the common law of service contracts. As with any negotiable instrument, a check can be negotiated and transferred to another party. This is achieved through a process known as **indorsement**, which must be accompanied by the physical transfer of the check. The **payee**, the person to whom the check was originally made out (or given in the case of a "pay to the bearer" check), has the right to negotiate the check to someone else, usually for value.

An indorsement requires the signature of the indorser on the back of the check, and the signature must be done for the purpose of negotiating the check.[5] The indorsement also

LO 22-1

Explain how checks are used in commercial transactions.

---

[3]Sometimes a payor "postdates" a future date on the check. This will have no effect unless the payor contacts their bank to let them know. This will alert the payee bank to dishonor the check if it is presented before the postdated date. The payor must alert the payee bank of this because the date is not included in the magnetic-ink character recognition (MICR) code on the bottom of the check. MICR codes are used by banks to transmit information regarding payment processing and will be discussed in greater detail later in the chapter.

[4]UCC § 2-103a.

[5]UCC § 3-204(a).

should specify to whom the check is being indorsed, for example, by writing on the back of the check "pay to Jane Doe." If the check is made payable to the bearer or "to cash," all it requires for negotiation is the physical transfer to another party. A transferee, as the holder of the check, may likewise negotiate the check to someone else, and so on, until someone demands payment from the drawee bank. The key is to obtain the proper indorsement and to retain the physical check; otherwise the check will be dishonored by the drawee bank.

The process through which a check is paid and honored by the drawee bank is governed by Article 4 of the UCC and involves a series of interbank transactions. Article 4 applies to "any instrument or a promise or order to pay money handled by a bank for collection or payment."[6] The process involves several banks because the **depositor**, the person seeking to cash the check, often deposits the check into her own account and authorizes her bank, known as the **depository bank**, to collect the proceeds from the drawee bank. The depository bank may be located in a place that is remote from the drawee bank and may request another intermediary bank to present the check to the nearby drawee bank. This process was all done manually by bank employees prior to the advent of high-speed computers and scanning equipment. Today, the process is almost completely automated, which allows checks to be processed for collection much more quickly and efficiently.

Figure 22.2 depicts the parties involved in the check collection process.

Computers today take an image of a check and scan the line of digits at the bottom known as the **magnetic-ink character recognition (MICR) code** to decode valuable information such as the drawee bank's routing number and the drawer's checking account number. This information is then relayed from one bank to another until one intermediary bank presents the image of the check and its MICR information to the drawee bank for payment. The drawee bank has two business days to decide whether to **rightfully dishonor** the check due to an inactive account, insufficient funds, or a stop payment order placed on the check. If the drawee bank fails to dishonor the check after two business days, the amount ordered to be paid is credited to each intermediary bank until the funds reach the depository bank, and then the amount is credited to the depositor's checking account. Ninety-nine percent of all checks are honored by the drawee bank.

In some cases, a bank may **wrongfully dishonor** a check that is properly payable.[7] The liability to the bank in this case is only to its banking customer (the drawer) for all damages proximately caused, not to the party who received the "bounced" check.[8] If multiple checks are presented to the bank for payment and the funds are insufficient, a bank may develop its own internal rules for deciding which checks to honor if funds are sufficient to pay some but not all of the checks.[9]

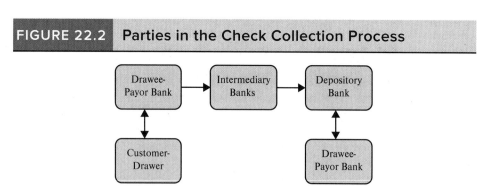

FIGURE 22.2   **Parties in the Check Collection Process**

---

[6]UCC § 4-104(a)(9).
[7]UCC § 4-402(a).
[8]UCC § 4-402(b).
[9]UCC § 4-303(b).

In Case 22.1, a state appellate court decides whether Wells Fargo Bank lawfully implemented its check-honoring policy.

CASE 22.1 Fetter v. Wells Fargo Bank Texas, N.A., 110 S.W.3d 683, 51 U.C.C. 2d 201 (Tex. App. 2003)

FACT SUMMARY Fetter sued Wells Fargo claiming that the bank's practice of posting (paying) checks from the highest dollar amount to the lowest dollar amount was done solely to increases the fees Wells Fargo could collect for checks returned for nonsufficient funds (NSF fees). According to Fetter, this violated the bank's checking account agreement and a general duty of good faith toward its checking account customers

Wells Fargo's Account Agreement stated:

Your account may be debited on the day an Item is presented by any means, including without limitation electronically, or at an earlier time based on notification received by the Bank that an Item drawn on your account will be presented for payment or collection. The Bank may pay Items presented against your account in any order it chooses, unless a particular order is either required or prohibited by law. In particular, the Bank may, if it chooses, pay Items in the order of highest dollar amount to lowest dollar amount (unless such a practice is specifically prohibited by an applicable state or federal law, rule, or regulation). The Bank may change the order of posting Items to your account at any time without notice to you.

SYNOPSIS OF DECISION AND OPINION The trial court dismissed Fetter's lawsuit by granting Wells Fargo's motion to dismiss and held that the express language of the checking account agreement and UCC Section 4-303(b) precluded Fetter's claims as a matter of law. The state appellate court in this decision affirmed the trial court's judgment.

WORDS OF THE COURT: The UCC and a Bank's Check-Posting Policies "With these principles in mind, we turn now to the statutory and contractual provisions at issue in the present case. . . .

"UCC section 4.303(b) provides:

Subject to Subsection (a), items may be accepted, paid, certified, or charged to the indicated account of a bank's customer in any order and before or after the bank's regular banking hours. A bank is under no obligation to determine the time of day an item is received and without liability may withhold the amount thereof pending a determination of the effect, consequence or priority of any knowledge, notice, stop-payment order, or legal process concerning the same, or interplead such amount and the claimants thereto.

"Under the plain language of this section, the legislature has authorized Wells Fargo's practice of posting from high to low.

. . .

"Finally, the relationship between Fetter and Wells Fargo is governed by an Account Agreement. Under that Agreement Wells Fargo 'may, if it chooses, pay Items in the order of highest dollar amount to lowest dollar amount (unless such a practice is specifically prohibited by an applicable state or federal law, rule, or regulation).'

"Fetter, in essence, is asking this court to write this provision out of the Agreement, and authorization for the provision out of the UCC.

. . .

"Fetter has cited no reported case in which a court has held a bank violates the UCC duty of good faith when it implements, performs, or enforces a high to low method of posting checks. We have found none.

. . .

"We affirm the judgment of the trial court."

Case Questions

1. Why will banks benefit from the internal rule of paying checks from highest amount to lowest amount?

2. What arguments can Wells Fargo make that paying checks from highest to lowest is actually best for customers?

3. *Focus on Critical Thinking:* What policy arguments do you think the drafters of the UCC had in mind when they drafted Section 4-303(b)? Would you have drafted a different rule? Why or why not?

QUICK QUIZ Negotiating a Check

Chuan has received a check payable to him and now wants to use that check to pay off his debt to Felipe.

1. What does Chuan have to do to negotiate the check to Felipe as repayment of his debt?

2. Can Felipe then negotiate the check to Melanie to repay his debt toward her? If so, what would he have to do?

Answers to this Quick Quiz are provided at the end of the chapter.

TAKEAWAY CONCEPTS Checks in Commercial Transactions

- A check is a negotiable instrument that is an unconditional order issued to a bank to pay a fixed amount that is in writing and signed by the party undertaking to pay.
- A check must say whether it is payable "to the order of," "to the bearer," or "to cash."
- A check can be negotiated and transferred to another party. This is achieved through a process known as *indorsement* and accompanied by the physical transfer of the check.
- The process through which a check is paid and honored by the drawee bank is governed by Article 4 of the UCC and involves a series of interbank transactions.
- Checks are processed through an automated system that scans the check's magnetic-ink character recognition (MICR) code.
- The drawee bank has two business days to decide whether to rightfully dishonor the check due to an inactive account, insufficient funds, or a stop payment order placed on the check.
- A bank wrongfully dishonors a check when it fails to disburse funds on a check that is properly payable.

ELECTRONIC PAYMENT SYSTEMS

LO 22-2

Summarize the various methods of electronic payment and the laws that apply to each one.

Information technology has facilitated payment-related innovations such as debit cards, credit cards, automated clearing house (ACH) transactions, and electronic funds transfers (EFT's, also known as *wire transfers*). Figure 22.3 demonstrates the growing use and popularity of electronic payments in an increasingly cashless society.

Debit Cards

A **debit card** is a card linked to the cardholder's checking account that is used at the point of sale with a merchant. Once the card is read by a terminal, the information is sent to the cardholder's bank, which then debits the amount from the cardholder's checking account and authorizes nearly instantaneous payment. The use of a debit card is not governed by Article 3 of the UCC because no signed written instrument, or order to pay, is created.

FIGURE 22.3 Growing Use of Electronic Payments

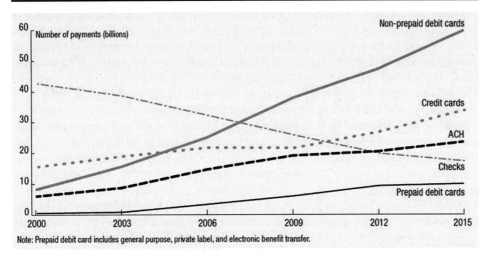

Note: Prepaid debit card includes general purpose, private label, and electronic benefit transfer.

Source: The Federal Reserve Payments Study 2016.

Instead, the use of debit cards is governed by the Electronic Funds Transfer Act (EFTA)[10] and the Federal Reserve Board's Regulation E.[11] Much of the EFTA and Regulation E deal with disclosure requirements that apply to any bank that agrees to process debit card transactions. Some of the disclosure requirements involve providing periodic statements and notifications of any fees associated with debit card transactions.

Credit Cards

A **credit card** allows a cardholder to make purchases through an electronic network on pre-negotiated credit terms with the card-issuing bank. To be accepted as a type of payment, the card must participate in a technology platform called an **interbank network**, of which Visa and Mastercard are the largest participants. This technology platform connects the bank that issued the credit card, such as Citibank, with the merchants who accept the charge and their respective banks. Note that interbank network service providers such as Visa or Mastercard are not banks; instead, they provide the technology infrastructure that allows banks to communicate and process payments. The merchant's bank and the interbank network service provider each take a fee from the transaction, and the merchant usually is paid within a few days of the transaction. At the end of a credit cardholder's billing cycle, the cardholder can opt to pay the balance charged on the card or to pay only a portion and pay interest on the outstanding balance. The bank that issues the credit card earns a profit from yearly fees and interest rates on the unpaid balances associated with credit card purchases.

The law that governs credit cards is largely the common law of contracts because a credit card is not linked to a bank account. The card-issuing bank enters into a loan and service contract with the cardholder and the interbank network provider. The interbank network provider enters into a contract with the merchant's bank, and the merchant's bank has its own contractual arrangement with merchants.

---

[10] 15 U.S.C. § 1601, et seq.

[11] 12 C.F.R. Part 205.

Automated Clearing House (ACH) Transactions

An **ACH transaction** uses an electronic interbank network to process large batches of direct payments and deposits. Unlike credit cards, these networks allow banks to communicate and settle large bulk orders with each other through a different communications network, such as the Federal Reserve Bank's FedACH system, which accounts for nearly 60 percent of commercial interbank ACH transactions. These transactions are governed by the Electronic Funds Transfer Act (EFTA),[12] the Federal Reserve Board's Regulation E, and trade association rules passed by the National Automated Clearing House Association (NACHA).

The ACH network facilitates the use of online banking by consumers. For example, individuals can authorize their bank to make recurring mortgage or utility payments with funds taken from their bank accounts. ACH transactions also facilitate the direct deposit of paychecks into individuals' accounts. Note that although this process references a *paycheck,* a physical check ("a writing") is never created. Article 3 of the UCC, therefore, does not regulate direct deposits.

A business that chooses to meet its employee payroll with direct deposit versus checks may realize cost savings. Establishing a direct deposit payment system with a bank costs anywhere from $50 to $150. After that initial expense, a fee is calculated for each employee who receives a direct deposit, and that amount usually does not exceed $2 per employee. Thus, direct deposit reduces the expense of purchasing physical checks and maintaining a manual bookkeeping system to account for the checks that have been written. It also minimizes the risk of lost or stolen checks and the time that employees must take to physically visit a bank branch to deposit their checks.

Electronic Funds Transfers (Wires)

Commercial wires are used among businesses and typically involve large sums of money. In a commercial wire, the **originator** sends a payment order instruction to his or her bank (the originating bank) to send funds to a beneficiary's bank account. Banks often use a commercial wire service offered by the Federal Reserve called *FedWire.* In this case, the originating bank sends a payment order (the wire transfer) and its instructions to the Federal Reserve Bank with which it has an account. The Federal Reserve debits this amount from the bank's account and sends the payment order to the beneficiary's bank, which then credits the amount to the beneficiary's account. Commercial wires are regulated by Article 4A of the UCC, which governs funds transfers between commercial entities. Consumer wires offered by banks and services such as Western Union, on the other hand, are governed by the Electronic Funds Transfer Act (EFTA).

Walmart has entered the money transfer business.
©tupungato/123RF

Consumer wire services are a thriving business that have attracted the attention of various parties. Walmart, the nation's largest retailer, has entered the money transfer business through its Walmart Money Centers. A customer at one store can use cash or a debit card to transfer money to any Walmart store located within the state where the money transfer recipient resides. The transaction uses an electronic payment system and takes a few minutes to complete. Through the introduction of this relatively low-cost service, Walmart hopes to tap into the 28 percent of Americans who lack a bank account or have poor access to financial services.

Table 22.1 provides a summary outline of the various electronic payment systems and the laws that apply to them.

---

[12]15 U.S.C. § 1601 et seq.

TABLE 22.1	Regulation of Electronic Payments Systems

Payment System	Governing Law
Debit card	Electronic Funds Transfer Act (EFTA) and Federal Reserve Board's Regulation E
Credit card	Common law of service contracts
ACH transaction	Electronic Funds Transfer Act (EFTA), Federal Reserve Board's Regulation E, and National Automated Clearing House Association (NACHA) trade association rules
Commercial wire	Article 4A of the UCC
Consumer wire	Electronic Funds Transfer Act (EFTA)

TAKEAWAY CONCEPTS Electronic Payment Systems

- Information technology has facilitated payment-related innovations such as debit cards, credit cards, automated clearing house (ACH) transactions, and electronic funds transfers (EFTs, also known as *wire transfers*).
- Debit cards are regulated by the Electronic Funds Transfer Act (EFTA) and the Federal Reserve Board's Regulation E.
- A credit card relies on merchants and banks to participate in a technology platform called an interbank network, of which Visa and Mastercard are the largest participants.
- Credit cards are regulated by the common law of contracts.
- ACH transactions are governed by the Electronic Funds Transfer Act (EFTA), the Federal Reserve Board's Regulation E, and trade association rules passed by the National Automated Clearing House Association (NACHA).
- Commercial wires are regulated by Article 4A of the UCC.
- Consumer wires are governed by the Electronic Funds Transfer Act (EFTA).

MOBILE PAYMENT APPS AND THE BLOCKCHAIN

Mobile Payment Apps

Some envision a future in which a smartphone will replace a wallet. Mobile payment apps are expected to grow significantly and already amount to a multibillion-dollar-per-year business that is experiencing rapid growth. A **mobile payment app** is software that is loaded on a mobile device that allows users to track expenses, pay bills, and send money to or receive money from businesses or personal accounts. For example, if Jonathan owes Delia money for landscaping services, each may prefer to process the payment using an online mobile phone app to bypass traditional banking services. Financial services that allow individuals to transact directly with one another are referred to as *peer-to-peer (P2P) transactions.*

Many mobile payment apps, such as PayPal, are linked to existing bank accounts and credit cards and allow users to create an account with the mobile payment company. The app then allows users to make payments or transfer money to other app users. Other apps known as **digital wallets**, such as Google Pay, allow users to pay using a contactless

LO 22-3

Identify the various types of mobile payment apps and the laws that apply to each one.

point-of-sale system. Large retailers such as Target and Starbucks have introduced their own mobile apps to facilitate payments and reduce bank transaction fees. As an inducement to use these mobile payment apps, many retailers offer customers loyalty points or discounts.

Mobile payment apps may face regulatory scrutiny, particularly if they begin to engage in traditional banking services such as maintaining customer funds as deposits or money lending. If that is the case, the Office of the Comptroller of Currency (OCC), a federal banking regulatory agency, may require the mobile payment app company to apply for a national bank charter. The OCC requires chartered banks to meet minimum capital requirements and to comply with a host of risk management procedures. In other cases, mobile payment apps that solely process debit and credit transactions (e.g., those that are linked to a debit card) must comply with the Federal Reserve Bank's Regulation E because a smartphone is considered an access device under that regulation. Also, recall that Regulation E imposes various disclosure requirements.

Even if a mobile payment app company is not considered a bank because it does not provide deposits or make loans, it still may be subject to federal and state regulation as a "money transmitting" business. One federal statute criminalizes the operation of an unlicensed money transmitting business.[13] A money transmitter is required to register and is defined as "a person who transmits 'currency, funds, or other value that substitutes for currency' between persons or locations 'by any means;' or '[a]ny other person engaged in the transfer of funds.'"[14]

Blockchain

Bitcoin is a type of **cryptocurrency**. A cryptocurrency is a software-based currency that is created using encryption techniques and accounted for through an online peer-to-peer ledger system known as the **blockchain**. Bitcoin typically is purchased on an exchange using a traditional payment system such as a credit card. Bitcoins can be kept on the exchange or transferred to a personal digital wallet on a mobile phone device. Although Bitcoin is viewed by many as a speculative investment, its original purpose was to serve as an online, decentralized, and unregulated currency and payment system. Although not currently regulated by the Federal Reserve or any other regulatory institutions, Bitcoin has been declared property by the Internal Revenue Service.

In Case 22.2, a federal trial court decides whether Bitcoin falls within the definition of "money" with respect to the federal licensing requirements imposed on money transmitting businesses. The defendant was an active Bitcoin trader who went by the online alias *BTCKing* and who conducted business on the infamous and now-defunct Silk Road website.

CASE 22.2 United States v. Robert M. Faiella, a.k.a "BTCKing," and Charlie Shrem, 39 F. Supp. 3d 544 (S.D.N.Y. 2014)

FACT SUMMARY From 2011 to 2013, Faiella operated a Bitcoin exchange on the Silk Road website, an anonymous online black market where illegal drugs were bought and sold by the site's users. Under his online username "BTCKing," Faiella sold bitcoins to users to facilitate the purchase of illegal goods and services. Faiella was charged by federal prosecutors with one count of operating an unlicensed money transmitting business in violation of 18 U.S.C. § 1960. This case was litigated in the federal trial court in the Southern District of New York.

(continued)

---

[13] 18 U.S.C. § 1960.

[14] 31 C.F.R. § 1010.100(ff)(5).

SYNOPSIS OF DECISION AND OPINION Following the indictment, Faiella moved to dismiss the case against him on three grounds: (1) that bitcoin does not qualify as "money" under Section 1960; (2) that operating a Bitcoin exchange does not constitute "transmitting" money under Section 1960; and (3) that Faiella was not a "money transmitter" under Section 1960. In this opinion, federal trial court Judge Jed Rakoff denied Faiella's motion.

WORDS OF THE COURT: Liability for Operating a Bitcoin Exchange "Bitcoin clearly qualifies as 'money' or 'funds' under . . . plain meaning definitions. Bitcoin can be easily purchased in exchange for ordinary currency, acts as a denominator of value, and is used to conduct financial transactions.

. . .

"Second, Faiella's activities on Silk Road constitute 'transmitting' money under Section 1960. Defendant argues that while Section 1960 requires that the defendant sell money transmitting services to others for a profit. . . . Faiella merely sold Bitcoin as a product in and of itself. But, as set forth in the Criminal Complaint that initiated this case, the Government alleges that Faiella received cash deposits from his customers and then, after exchanging them for Bitcoins, transferred those funds to the customers' accounts on Silk Road. . . . Thus, the Court finds that in sending his customers' funds to Silk Road, Faiella 'transferred' them to others for a profit.

"Third, Faiella clearly qualifies as a 'money transmitter' for purposes of Section 1960. The Financial Crimes Enforcement Network ('FinCEN') [a bureau of the U.S. Department of the Treasury that collects and analyzes information about financial transactions to combat domestic and international money laundering, terrorist financing, and other financial crimes] has issued guidance specifically clarifying that virtual currency exchangers constitute 'money transmitters' under its regulations. See FinCEN Guidance at 1 ('[A]n administrator or exchanger [of virtual currency] *is* an MSB [money services business] under FinCEN's regulations, specifically, a money transmitter, unless a limitation to or exemption from the definition applies to the person.') FinCEN has further clarified that the exception on which defendant relies for its argument that Faiella is not a 'money transmitter' . . . is inapplicable. See FinCEN Guidance at 4 ('It might be argued that the exchanger is entitled to the exemption from the definition of "money transmitter" for persons involved in the sale of goods or the provision of services. . . . However, this exemption does not apply when the only services being provided are money transmission services')."

Case Questions

1. Was Faiella a money transmitter in the traditional sense? Why or why not?

2. If an online merchant such as Amazon accepts Bitcoin for payment, is the merchant a money transmitter and therefore subject to Section 1960 regulation? Why or why not?

3. *Focus on Critical Thinking:* Should Bitcoin be considered money? What arguments exist that it should not?

TAKEAWAY CONCEPTS Mobile Payment Apps and the Blockchain

- A mobile payment app is software loaded on a mobile device that allows users to track expenses, pay bills, and send money to or receive money from businesses or personal accounts.
- Many mobile payment apps, such as PayPal, are linked to existing bank accounts and credit cards and allow users to create an account with the mobile payment company.
- Mobile payment apps allow users to make payments with merchants under a contactless point-of-sale system.
- Cryptocurrencies such as Bitcoin are encrypted and unregulated digital currencies that rely on blockchain technology.

LO 22-4

Apply UCC state law to determine who faces liability when a check is forged, stolen, or altered.

FRAUD RULES RELATED TO CHECKS AND ELECTRONIC PAYMENT SYSTEMS

Banks must comply with UCC state law to determine who faces liability when a check is forged, stolen, or altered. The general rule is that a drawee bank that pays on a forged or stolen check must assume liability. If a fraudster alters the name on a check or the dollar amount, the rule is that the depositor bank incurs the liability. If a fraudster indorses a forged or stolen check and a party negotiates the forged or stolen check to someone else, the party who negotiated it must assume liability. Additional regulations are in place to ensure that bank customers have access to financial statements that convey important information related to issued checks, such as the check number, amount, and the date it was cashed. Although not mandated, banks often maintain scanned images of cashed checks that are available to its account holders.

With respect to debit cards, the Federal Reserve Bank's Regulation E limits the losses associated with the theft or loss of a debit card.[15] When a cardholder provides the bank with "timely notice" within two business days of learning of the loss or theft of her card, the cardholder's liability is capped at the lesser of $50 or the amount of unauthorized transfers before notice was provided. For example, if Maria leaves her credit card at a café Friday night and realizes her mistake on Saturday, she has until midnight on Tuesday to notify her bank.

On October 1, 2015, the major credit card networks (Visa, Mastercard, American Express, and others) implemented the Europay, Mastercard and Visa (EMV) chip card liability standard rule ("shift"). To combat credit and debit card theft, these large payment processors adopted the more secure EMV standard, which requires a card user to insert his chip-enabled card into the merchant's card reader terminal. This process is considered to be more secure than swiping the card's magnetic strip at a terminal. Prior to the use of these chip-based cards, the banks issuing the cards would almost always shoulder the cost of fraud, which totals nearly $8 billion per year. The EMV liability shift allows banks and card issuers to shift the liability of fraud onto merchants who fail to implement this more secure electronic payment system. The result has been increased, albeit not universal, use and acceptance of this more secure technology.

TAKEAWAY CONCEPTS Fraud Rules Related to Checks and Electronic Payment Systems

- Banks must comply with UCC state law to determine who faces liability when a check is forged or stolen.
- Generally, a drawee bank that pays on a forged or stolen check must assume liability.
- If a thief indorses a forged or stolen check, the party who negotiates the check must assume liability.
- The Federal Reserve Bank's Regulation E limits the losses associated with the theft or loss of a debit card.
- The EMV standard requires a card user to insert a chip-enabled card into the merchant's card reader terminal and shifts any theft or fraud liability onto merchants who fail to adopt this technology.

---

[15]Reg. E., § 1005.6(b).

Stolen and Forged Business Checks

PROBLEM: Peggy Rolando owns a hair salon called Hair on Earth that caters to a wealthy clientele. Peggy employs Sarah and Brian, two full-time hairstylists, and pays them each $3,500 at the end of the month with checks drawn from Peggy's personal checking account at BankUSA. On August 15, Peggy hosted a large party at her house. During the party, Tristam Shandy, a friend of an acquaintance, was casing her house. He slipped unnoticed into a room and saw Peggy's personal checkbook on a table. He quickly removed check number 159, placed the check in his jacket's inner pocket, and rejoined the festivities. The next day, Mr. Shandy wrote a check payable "To cash" in the amount of $7,500, forged Peggy's signature, and cashed it at BankUSA.

On August 31, Peggy issued checks numbered 157 and 158 to pay Sarah and Brian, respectively, their monthly wages. Peggy was unaware that the funds in her personal checking account totaled only $5,000 due to the forgery. When presented with both checks for payment on the same day, BankUSA decided to honor Brian's check but

dishonored Sarah's check. Sarah uses ACH transactions that debit her account the first week of every month to pay her mortgage, credit card bills, and utilities. Because her paycheck bounced, her ACH transactions were declined due to insufficient funds. Sarah now faces losses related to penalties and late payment fees.

QUESTIONS

1. Who is liable for the forged check? What is the relevant law?
2. Was Peggy careless in failing to secure her checks? Should that matter in the liability determination?
3. Did BankUSA rightfully or wrongfully dishonor check number 157? Explain your answer.
4. Does Sarah have recourse against anyone? Who and why? What damages would she be able to claim, if any?
5. If you were Peggy, how would you address this scenario? What safety procedures would you advise her to take to minimize her risk in the future?

KEY TERMS

Check p. 380   Negotiable instrument that is an unconditional order issued to a bank to pay a fixed amount that is in writing and signed by the party undertaking to pay.

Draft p. 381   A written order to pay money signed by the person giving the order (e.g., a check).

Cashier's check p. 381   A check issued by a bank with funds drawn from the bank's own account.

Certified check p. 381   A check drawn from a personal account that the bank ensures will clear with sufficient funds.

Drawee bank p. 381   Bank that issues and ultimately pays a check.

Drawer p. 381   The party issuing the payment order.

Indorsement p. 381   The process of negotiating a check by signing the check and making it payable to someone else.

Payee p. 381   The person who will be paid on a payment order.

Depositor p. 382   The person seeking to cash a check.

Depository bank p. 382   Bank authorized by a depositor to present a check for payment against the drawee bank.

Magnetic-ink character recognition (MICR) code p. 382   The line of digits at the bottom of a check that includes the drawee bank's routing number and the drawer's checking account number.

Rightfully dishonor p. 382   When a drawee bank fails to pay a check due to an inactive account, insufficient funds, or a stop payment order placed on the check.

Wrongfully dishonor p. 382   When a drawee bank fails to cash a check that is properly payable.

Debit card p. 384   A card linked to a cardholder's checking account and used at a merchant's point of sale.

Credit card p. 385   A card that allows a cardholder to make purchases through an electronic network on credit terms that have been pre-negotiated with the card-issuing bank.

Interbank network p. 385   A technology platform used by credit cardholders, merchants, and banks, of which Visa and Mastercard are the largest participants.

ACH transaction p. 386   An electronic interbank network used to process large batches of direct payments and deposits that are associated with bank accounts.

Commercial wires p. 386   Electronic transfers between businesses that typically involve large sums of money.

Originator p. 386   In a commercial wire, party that sends a payment order to its bank with instructions to send funds to a beneficiary's bank account.

Mobile payment app p. 387   Software loaded on a mobile device that allows users to track expenses, pay bills, and send money to or receive money from businesses or personal accounts.

Digital wallet p. 387   Mobile payment app that allows a user to make payments to merchants using a contactless point-of-sale system.

Cryptocurrency p. 388   A deregulated, decentralized software-based currency that is created using encryption techniques

Blockchain p. 388   An online peer-to-peer ledger system to account for cryptocurrency transactions.

CASE SUMMARY 22.1 Wachovia Bank, N.A. v. Foster Bankshares, Inc., 457 F.3d 619, 60 U.C.C. 2d 1126 (7th Cir. 2006)

Check Liability

A company called Media Edge made a check out to CMP Media for $133,026 to be drawn from its Wachovia Bank account. A woman named Choi somehow came into possession of this check and deposited it in her account at Foster Bank. Wachovia cashed the check and later realized either the name had been "chemically washed" (scraped away) or the entire check had been forged. An original copy of the check was destroyed, and all that remained was a digital copy. Being unable to decide whether the check was altered or forged, the court had to decide whether the liability should fall on Wachovia Bank or Foster Bank.

CASE QUESTIONS

1. If the court had found that the check was altered through a chemical wash, which bank would face liability?
2. If the court had found that the check was forged, which bank would face liability?

CASE SUMMARY 22.2 Halifax Corp. v. First Union National Bank, 26 Va. 91, 546 S.E.2d 696, 44 U.C.C. 2d 661 (2001)

One-Year Preclusion Rule

The plaintiff, Halifax, had to bear liability after its comptroller embezzled in excess of $1 million through the issuance of more than 80 fraudulent checks written between 1995 and 1997. The company discovered the fraud in 1999. The court ruled in First Union's favor because it had paid the checks, largely in reliance of UCC § 4-406, which states:

> Without regard to care or lack of care of either the customer or the bank, a customer who does not within one year after the statement or items are made available to the customer (subsection (a)) discover and report the customer's unauthorized signature on or any alteration on the item is precluded from asserting against the bank the unauthorized signature or alteration.

CASE QUESTIONS

1. What duty does Section 4-406 impose on the bank customer?
2. What kind of controls should a company have in order to avoid this kind of liability?

Commercial Wire Execution Error

Appellant TME made a wire transfer for $1 million through its bank, Pacific Business Bank, to an account Vieri Gaines Guadagni (Gaines) maintained at Norwest Bank. Although the appellant believed the account specified in its wire transfer was a trust account for the benefit of appellant James McDaniel and designated in the wire transfer "Vieri Gaines Guadagni, Trustee fbo [for the benefit of] McDaniel" as the named beneficiary, the account was in fact the joint personal checking account of Gaines and his wife, Janet Guadagni. Norwest Bank's wire transfer system would not reject an incoming wire transfer if there was a discrepancy between the designated beneficiary's name and account number and would process the transaction so long as the account number was valid.

UCC § 4A-207(b), provides a "safe harbor" for a beneficiary's bank that relies on the account number specified in a wire transfer order to identify the beneficiary of the order. The safe-harbor provision applies so long as the bank does not know that the beneficiary's name and account number refer to different persons. To "know" means to have actual knowledge, and the beneficiary's bank has no duty to determine whether the name and account number specified in the wire transfer refer to the same person.

CASE QUESTIONS

1. Who faces liability in this scenario?
2. Do you agree with the effects of UCC § 4A-207? Why or why not?

CHAPTER REVIEW QUESTIONS

1. A check is:
   a. A negotiable instrument.
   b. An unconditional order issued to a bank.
   c. An order to pay a fixed amount.
   d. Signed by the party undertaking to pay.
   e. All of the above.

2. Someone who signs a check and delivers it to someone else for the purposes of transferring the check is a(n):
   a. Depositor.
   b. Payee.
   c. Indorser.
   d. Drawee.
   e. None of the above.

3. A direct deposit paycheck would be achieved through:
   a. A debit card.
   b. An ACH transaction.
   c. A commercial wire.
   d. A consumer wire.
   e. A credit card.

4. Article 4A of the UCC regulates:
   a. Consumer wires.
   b. Direct deposits.
   c. ACH transactions.
   d. Commercial wires.
   e. Credit cards.

5. The machine-readable code on the bottom of a check is called the:
   a. ACH code.
   b. FedWire code.
   c. Magnetic-ink character recognition (MICR) code.
   d. CHIPS code.
   e. Visa code.

6. Checks are negotiable instruments.
   a. True
   b. False

7. Bitcoin is not legally classified as money.
   a. True
   b. False

8. A digital wallet is a type of mobile app payment system.
   a. True
   b. False

9. The Federal Reserve Bank's Regulation E limits the losses associated with the theft or loss of a debit card.
   a. True
   b. False

10. If a check is properly payable, a bank should wrongfully dishonor it.
    a. True
    b. False

✅ Quick Quiz ANSWERS

Negotiating a Check

1. Because the check is made "payable to Chuan," Chuan must indorse the check to Felipe. He would need to write "payable to Felipe" on the back of the check and sign it. He then would have to physically transfer the check to Felipe.

2. Felipe is allowed to negotiate the check to Melanie. He would have to write "payable to Melanie" on the back of the check and sign it. Likewise, he would have to physically transfer the check to Melanie.

CHAPTER REVIEW QUESTIONS: Answers and Explanations

1. **e.** A check has all of these properties.

2. **c.** An indorser signs a check and transfers it to someone else through the process of negotiation.

3. **b.** Direct deposits rely on ACH transactions.

4. **d.** Article 4A of the UCC regulates commercial wires.

5. **c.** The MIRC code is located on the bottom of a check.

6. **a. True.** Checks have all the qualities of a negotiable instrument as discussed in Chapter 19.

7. **b. False.** Federal courts have declared that bitcoin is legally considered money.

8. **a. True.** Digital wallets are a type of mobile app payment system.

9. **a. True.** Regulation E limits these types of losses.

10. **b. False.** If a check is properly payable, a bank should rightfully honor it.

CHAPTER 23

Secured Transactions

Lenders must be aware of the various risks associated with different types of collateral used to secure a loan. At the end of this chapter, you will take actions as a savvy lender to strategically assess various types of collateral offered by a prospective borrower.

Learning Objectives

After studying this chapter, students who have mastered the material will be able to:

23-1   Identify the classifications of collateral in a secured transaction.

23-2   Describe the steps necessary to create a security interest.

23-3   Compare the ways a security interest can be perfected.

23-4   Apply the priority rules to a scenario in which several parties have competing claims to collateral.

23-5   Explain the consequences of a borrower's default.

CHAPTER OVERVIEW

If you plan to finance the purchase of equipment for your business or a vehicle for your own personal use, odds are you will enter into a secured, transaction-based financial arrangement with a merchant lender or bank. In these common contractual arrangements, the buyer puts up collateral to secure a loan. This chapter will give you an overview of the various legal requirements to create a secured transaction and discusses some of the critical issues that arise during these important financial dealings.

CLASSIFICATIONS OF COLLATERAL IN SECURED TRANSACTIONS

Secured transactions involve a financing agreement between a lender (creditor) and a borrower (debtor) in which the borrower pledges its assets as **collateral** to secure the loan. These transactions, as they relate to personal property, are governed by state law under Article 9 of the UCC and serve a variety of important functions in the financial world. First, the lender may not offer credit unless the borrower provides additional security in the form of collateral. A lender, for example, may view the borrower's financial position as too risky in the alternate. In these cases, the law of contractual remedies (see Chapters 11 and 16) may not be enough to induce the lender to offer credit because the buyer's default on a loan will only lead to repayment after a lengthy and expensive litigation process. Without security in the form of collateral, lenders become **unsecured creditors** who have a relatively low priority during bankruptcy if the business fails and are entitled to repayment only after secured creditors are reimbursed. Lastly, it is very likely that borrowers will benefit from better credit terms, such as a lower interest rate, if they offer collateral to secure their loan. Secured transactions, therefore, facilitate deal making among lenders and borrowers by reducing risk and expense.

LO 23-1

Identify the classifications of collateral in a secured transaction.

Secured transactions are not only reserved for big-ticket items such as a home, business equipment, or a vehicle. They exist when someone pawns something of value at a pawn shop or when an appliance retailer sells a refrigerator on installment and issues **chattel paper**, a document issued by a seller that indicates financing terms for the sale of goods and a repayment schedule. Companies make widespread use of secured transactions. For example, a manufacturer might obtain a loan and back that up by offering its accounts receivable (future customer payments) to the bank as security. Or a car dealership might finance its auto inventory through a loan with the financing company that takes a security interest in each car on the dealership's lot.

The collateral used by an individual or business to secure a loan must fit within one of the 11 categories specified under Article 9. These categories are mutually exclusive, so the collateral can only fit within one category. If the collateral is used in more than one manner, however, the legal test to determine its classification is the principal use of the property.[1] The various categories of collateral, with examples, are presented in Table 23.1.

A secured transaction may lead to a financial process known as **securitization**. In these cases, a secured loan such as a car or home loan is stripped of its payment obligation to

| TABLE 23.1 | Categories of Collateral |

Type of Items	Categories of Collateral	Examples
Goods	Consumer goods	Items used for personal, family, or household use, such as appliances, jewelry, artwork, and automobiles
	Farm products	Seeds and crops
	Inventory	Items manufactured by a business intended for sale
	Equipment	Machinery used to produce goods, or devices that support business operations, such as computers
Financial products	Document	A document of title, such as a bill of lading or warehouse receipt
	Instrument	A check or other negotiable instrument, such as a promissory note
	Chattel paper	A document indicating an obligation to pay through installments
	Investment property	Any type of security such as stocks, bonds, or shares in a mutual fund
	Deposit account	A checking account
Intangibles	Account	An invoice or account receivable
	General intangibles	Intellectual property, such as a patent, copyright, or trademark

[1]UCC § 9-102, Comment 4(a).

create a negotiable instrument (see Chapter 19). These repayment obligations are bundled into large packages that are then sold to investors as financial products with certain yield and risk characteristics.

 QUICK QUIZ Identify the Secured Transaction

Classify the collateral described in the following scenarios.

1. A farmer purchases a pickup truck. The farmer uses the truck in the following manner: 50 percent for farming, 30 percent for family use, and 20 percent for community charity work. How will the truck be classified as collateral?

2. In 1997, rock star and recording artist David Bowie sold $55 million of bonds to Prudential Insurance Co. These 10-year "Bowie bonds" had a security interest to back up the loan that included Bowie's copyright royalties on more than 20 albums that included classic hits like "Heroes." How would these copyright royalties be classified under the UCC?

Answers to this Quick Quiz are provided at the end of the chapter.

Recording artist David Bowie issued bonds secured with copyright royalties from various albums.
©Georges De Keerle/Getty Images

TAKEAWAY CONCEPTS Classifications of Collateral in Secured Transactions

- Secured transactions involve a financing agreement between a lender (creditor) and a borrower (debtor) in which the borrower pledges its assets as collateral to secure the loan.
- Secured transactions are governed by state law under Article 9 of the UCC.
- Without security in the form of collateral, lenders become unsecured creditors who have a relatively low priority during bankruptcy if the business fails and are entitled to repayment only after secured creditors are reimbursed.
- The collateral used by an individual or business to secure a loan must fit within 1 of the 11 categories specified under Article 9.

THE STEPS TO CREATE A SECURITY INTEREST

Enter into Contract with Lender That Defines and Creates Security Interest

LO 23-2

Describe the steps necessary to create a security interest.

The first step to create a secured transaction is to enter into a contract with the lender that defines and creates a **security interest**. As defined by the UCC, a security interest is an interest in personal property or **fixtures** (i.e., items that can be detached from real estate, such as cabinetry) that is used to secure the payment of an obligation.[2] Note that because the definition is limited to personal property and fixtures, real estate is excluded from Article 9 and this chapter.

A security interest can be narrowly defined as a particular item. For example, Cynthia might offer as collateral her beloved blue 1999 Chevy Metro. Alternatively, collateral can be broadly defined as a **floating lien** to include future acquisitions of property. For example, Giant Corporation can offer as collateral "all equipment currently owned and hereafter acquired." This broad language creates a security interest with respect to any future equipment acquired by Giant Corporation, including equipment bought after the security interest is created. It is important to carefully consider the description of the collateral in the security agreement because anything that falls outside of this description will likely lead to an unsecured claim.

Article 9 of the UCC concerns itself with contracts that generate a security interest as defined above. It is not, however, concerned with leases because those common law contracts do not require security interests. In a **true lease**, the title to the property is never transferred; rather, the contract involves granting another party limited-life usage rights to the property. Because title is never exchanged, as with a purchase/sale under Article 9, there is no need under the law to obtain a security interest. When the title to goods is exchanged through a sale, however, and the sale or its financing creates a security interest, then Article 9 will apply to that transaction.

Attach a Security Interest to Property

For a security interest to be enforceable, the parties must ensure that it has attached to the property.[3] The UCC requires that three criteria must be met if a security interest is going to **attach to the property** used as collateral. These requirements are that (1) value has been given, (2) the debtor has rights in the collateral (the power to transfer rights in the collateral to a secured party), and (3) the debtor has authenticated a security agreement that describes the collateral.[4]

In terms of *value,* this simply means that the lender has offered the approval of a loan or the actual funds to finance a purchase. A seller may also act as a lender and sell the goods to the buyer under credit or installment terms, essentially offering financing to the buyer. Both of these scenarios would satisfy the first required value element.

The second criterion refers to the fact that the borrower (debtor) has the *right* to offer the property as collateral. This is a basic assumption that the lender makes when offering a loan under these terms. This criterion usually is satisfied by demonstrating that the borrower has ownership or some other rightful legal claim to the property being offered as collateral.

The last requirement relates to a **security agreement**, which is an agreement between the borrower and the lender that stipulates the creation of a security interest in the particular property offered as security. The most prudent way to establish this attachment criterion is

---

[2]UCC § 1-207(37).

[3]UCC § 9-203(a).

[4]UCC § 9-203(b).

to execute a signed written security agreement between the parties that describes the property with sufficient detail. This is what is commonly done in a commercial context. If there is no evidence of a signed written agreement, possession of the collateral may be enough to satisfy this requirement if the parties enter into an oral security agreement.

The general default rule is that unless a secured party agrees otherwise, a valid security interest travels with the collateral in the event the collateral is sold to a third party.[5] For example, if MegaBank has a security interest in High-Tek Corp.'s used servers and High-Tek sells these servers to Netsoft Corp., the IT equipment will be subject to the secured interest held by MegaBank. This means that if High-Tek does not repay its loan to MegaBank, the bank can go after Netsoft to repossess and liquidate the servers. The major exception to this rule involves a **buyer in ordinary course of business (BOCB)**. A BOCB can purchase goods free of a preexisting security interest. According to the UCC, a BOCB is:

> . . . a person that buys goods in good faith, without knowledge that the sale violates the rights of another person in the goods, and in the ordinary course from a person, other than a pawnbroker, in the business of selling goods of that kind. A person buys goods in the ordinary course if the sale to the person comports with the usual or customary practices in the kind of business in which the seller is engaged or with the seller's own usual or customary practices. . . .[6]

The BOCB exception often arises in the context of goods classified as inventory. The secured interest may be inventory held by the borrower. However, if the borrower sells off its inventory to good faith buyers who do not know of the security interest, these goods will not have a security interest attached to them. The buyer will have clear unencumbered title to the goods purchased in the ordinary course of business. When goods are purchased outside the usual course of business, as in the case of High-Tek selling its used servers, the buyer lacks the BOCB exception and has purchased goods that remain subject to a secured interest.

In Case 23.1, a purchaser of cattle sues to assert his status as a BOCB.

CASE 23.1 Morgan County Feeders, Inc. v. McCormick, 836 P.2d 1051 (Colo. Ct. App. 1992)

FACT SUMMARY Morgan County Feeders (Morgan) signed and perfected a security agreement against Neil Allen. The security interest included a floating lien "after acquired property clause" that included any equipment purchased by Allen. Allen operated a dude ranch and purchased 45 longhorn cattle and one bull. He later sold the cattle to McCormick. When Allen defaulted on his loan to Morgan, Morgan sued to take possession of the cattle. The trial court held that the cattle were equipment under the UCC and that, because they were classified in this manner, McCormick could not be classified as a buyer in ordinary course of business (BOCB). McCormick appealed.

SYNOPSIS OF DECISION AND OPINION The appellate court decided that because the cattle were used to support the business operations of the dude ranch, the trial court correctly held that they were equipment instead of inventory. Under this classification, McCormick could not be considered a BOCB and Morgan would be entitled to claim its security interest in the cattle.

WORDS OF THE COURT: Equipment vs. Inventory "Under the Uniform Commercial Code, 'goods' are defined as, 'all things which are moveable at the time the security interest attaches.' . . . Here, the parties agree that the cattle constitute

(continued)

---

[5]UCC § 9-201(a).
[6]UCC § 1-201(9).

'goods' under the Uniform Commercial Code. They further agree that the cattle are not 'farm products.' Thus, the remaining issue surrounding the cattle is whether they should be designated as inventory or equipment. The distinction is important because buyers of inventory in the ordinary course of business take free of perfected security interests.

"In ascertaining whether goods are inventory or equipment, the principal use of the property is determinative. . . . The factors to be considered in determining principal use include whether the goods are for immediate or ultimate sale and whether they have a relatively long or short period of use in the business. . . .

"At trial, the court determined that the longhorn cattle were 'equipment' and not 'inventory' because:

> Allen did not acquire or hold them for the principal purpose of immediate or ultimate sale or lease. . . . Instead, the cattle were to be used principally for recreational cattle drives. . . . While Allen might have occasionally leased the cattle to other entrepreneurs, it was his intention to utilize the cattle principally in his own recreational business. . . .

"Thus, the court concluded that McCormick bought the cattle subject to Morgan County Feeders' security interest. . . . Allen testified that his purpose for purchasing the longhorn cows was to use them on cattle drives and that these cows have a relatively long period of use in comparison to rodeo calves and feeder cattle. Several other witnesses also testified

that Allen had stated his intent to use the longhorn cows for recreational cattle drives. Thus, the trial court was justified in rejecting McCormick's contention that the cattle were purchased only for rodeos. And, it did not err in finding that, under these unique circumstances, the cattle should be classified as 'equipment.'

"The judgment is affirmed."

Cattle may be classified as equipment and used as a security interest.
©Carson Ganci/Design Pics

Case Questions

1. Do you agree that cattle are equipment in this case? Why or why not?

2. How could McCormick have avoided this problem?

3. *Focus on Critical Thinking:* Why does the law allow buyers in ordinary course of business to purchase goods free of a security interest?

TAKEAWAY CONCEPTS The Steps to Create a Security Interest

- As defined by the UCC, a security interest is an interest in personal property or fixtures.
- For a security interest to be enforceable, the parties must ensure that it has attached to the property.
- The requirements for attachment are that value has been given, the debtor has rights in the collateral, and the debtor has authenticated a security agreement.
- The general default rule is that unless a secured party agrees otherwise, a valid security interest travels with the collateral in the event the collateral is sold to a third party.
- A buyer in ordinary course of business (BOCB) can purchase goods free of a pre-existing security interest.

PERFECTING A SECURITY INTEREST

Attachment may not be enough, however, for a secured lender to obtain a claim to a borrower's collateral. For example, Ace Manufacturing may use its inventory of finished goods to obtain several secured loans, all of which may have gone through the attachment process with respect to the same collateral. To reduce the risk of obtaining a subordinate position with respect to the collateral, lenders often will try to **perfect a security interest**. The term *perfecting a security interest* describes how a secured lender can protect its security interest from other creditors who might assert claims against the same collateral. Creditors who might have competing claims against the secured lender include a bankruptcy trustee if the borrower becomes insolvent; lien holders, such as those who have won a legal judgment against the borrower (e.g., taxing authorities); and other secured creditors who have a claim on the same collateral.[7]

If the secured lender simply relies on attachment without perfecting its security interest, any of these creditors might have priority rights and defeat the secured lender's claim to the collateral. For example, a bankruptcy trustee will have priority over the collateral if she files a bankruptcy petition before the collateral is perfected. Perfecting a security interest is, therefore, an important step to ensure that the borrower's collateral is not subject to overriding claims by other creditors. In practice, a secured creditor's claim that is behind another creditor's claim is unlikely to yield the funds necessary to repay the loan if the borrower is insolvent.

Under Article 9 of the UCC, there are four main ways to perfect a security interest. These include perfection by filing, perfection by possession, automatic perfection, and perfection by control.

Perfection by Filing

Creditors can perfect their security interest if they file a **UCC-1 financing statement** with the secretary of state where the borrower resides. For a natural person, this is where the person lives or primarily does business. For a legal person, such as a corporation or other business entity, the statement is filed in the state where it is registered. The financing statement itself is fairly basic, inexpensive to procure, and lasts for five years unless it is renewed. The essential information that must be included in a UCC-1 financing statement includes the names of the borrower and the secured party and a description of the collateral. A sample UCC-1 financing statement is provided in Figure 23.1.

Certain types of collateral, such as patents or trademarks (intangibles), must be perfected with a financing statement. Other types of collateral, such as goods, equipment, inventory, and financial products (except deposit accounts), *may* be perfected with a filing but can also be perfected through other means, such as possession or automatic perfection. Lastly, deposit accounts *cannot* be perfected with a UCC-1 filing and instead require control.

A legal strategy among astute lenders is to **pre-file** a UCC-1 statement as soon as possible. This can be done even before the security agreement is created and before attachment. For example, if ReliableBank is considering whether to extend a secured loan to HappyPrinters, LLC, the bank might ask the borrower for permission to file a UCC-1 financing statement before the loan is approved. A secured lender should always search the UCC financing statement database in the state where the borrower resides to find out if the collateral it is going to accept has any preexisting claims. If it does, there is a strong likelihood the lender's security interest will be subordinate to those who filed earlier under the first-to-file priority rules discussed below.

---

[7]UCC § 9-317.

FIGURE 23.1   Sample UCC-1 Financing Statement

UCC FINANCING STATEMENT
FOLLOW INSTRUCTIONS (front and back) CAREFULLY

A. NAME & PHONE OF CONTACT AT FILER [optional]
Phone: (800) 331-3282   Fax: (818) 662-4141

B. SEND ACKNOWLEDGEMENT TO: (Name and Address)

117756 TRUE VALUE CO

UCC Direct Services
P.O. Box 29071
Glendale, CA 91209-9071

14589735

AZAZ

SECRETARY OF STATE
FILED

2008 JUN -6   AM 11:40

200815427059

THE ABOVE SPACE IS FOR FILING OFFICE USE ONLY

1. DEBTOR'S EXACT FULL LEGAL NAME - insert only one debtor name (1a or 1b) - do not abbreviate or combine names

1a. ORGANIZATION'S NAME			
Hardware. Inc.			
1b. INDIVIDUAL'S LAST NAME	FIRST NAME	MIDDLE NAME	SUFFIX

1c. MAILING ADDRESS	CITY	STATE	POSTAL CODE	COUNTRY
6016 N 16th St	PHOENIX	AZ	93514	USA

1d SEE INSTRUCTIONS	ADD'L INFO RE ORGANIZATION DEBTOR	1e TYPE OF ORGANIZATION CORPORATION	1f. JURISDICTION OF ORGANIZATION AZ	1g. ORGANIZATIONAL ID #. if any 1449552-4	☐ NONE

2. ADDITIONAL DEBTOR'S EXACT FULL LEGAL NAME- insert only one debtor (2e or 2b) - do not abbreviate or combine names

2a. ORGANIZATIONS NAME			
2b. INDIVIDUAL'S LAST NAME	FIRST NAME	MIDDLE NAME	SUFFIX

2c. MAILING ADDRESS	CITY	STATE	POSTAL CODE	COUNTRY

2d. SEE INSTRUCTIONS	ADD'L INFO REORGANIZATION DEBTOR	2e. TYPE OF ORGANIZATION	2f. JURISDICTION OF ORGANIZATION	2g. ORGANIZATIONL ID #. if any	☐ NONE

3. SECURED PARTY'S NAME (or NAME of TOTAL ASSIGNEE of ASSIGNOR S/P - insert only one secured party name (3a or 3b)

3a. ORGANZATIONS NAME			
True Value Company			
3b. INDIVIDUAL'S LAST NAME	FIRST NAME	MIDDLE NAME	SUFFIX

3a. MAILING ADDRESS	CITY	STATE	POSTAL CODE	COUNTRY
8600 W Bryn Mawr Ave	Chicago	IL	60631	USA

4. This FINANCING STATEMENT covers the following collateral:

DEBTOR hereby grants to SECURED PARTY a continuing Security Interest in: All goods, inventory, merchandise and supplied including, but not limited to, all provate branded equipment and their accessories and components or replacement parts now owned or hereafter acquired by debtor wherever located. All furniture, fixtures, equipment, supplies and other personal property now owned or hereafter acquired by debtor wherever located. All cash accounts, contract rights, chattel paper, instruments, security agreements, goods and notes receivable now or hereafter acquired by debtor arising from the dale or lease of inventory; all proceeds now owned or hereafter acquired by debtor from the sale or lease of inventory; all insurance proceeds now owned or hereafter acquired by debtor relating to inventory, furniture, fixtures, equipment and supplies.

5. ALTERNATIVE DESIGNATION (if applicable)	☐ LESSEE/LESSOR	☐ CONSIGNEE/CONSIGNOR	☐ BAILEE/BAILOR	☐ SELLER/BUYER	☐ AG. LIEN	☐ NON-UCC FILING

6. ☐ This FINANCING STATEMENT is to be filed (for record) (or recorded) in the REAL ESTATE RECORDS. Attach Addendum (if applicable)	7. Check REQUEST SEARCH REPORT(S) on Debtor(s) (ADDITIONAL FEE) (optional)	☐ All Debtors	☐ Debtor 1	☐ Debtor 2

8. OPTIONAL FILER REFERENCE DATA
14589735   08 18428-6

FILING OFFICE COPY - NATIONAL UCC FINANCING STATEMENT (FORM UCC1) (REV. 05/22/02)

Prepared by UCC Direct Services, P.O. Box 29071, Glendale, CA 91209-9071 Tel (BOO) 331-3282

Source: Arizona Secretary of State

Perfection by Possession

Collateral may be perfected if the borrower physically transfers it to the lender. Goods such as jewelry, artwork, precious metals, or financial products that have a tangible feature (e.g., a bond or stock certificate) may be perfected through possession. Whereas financial products evidenced with tangible certificates can be perfected by possession, deposit accounts require perfection through control. For security interests that are perfected by possession, the priority date occurs when the lender has physical control over the items.

Automatic Perfection

If a merchant or a lender offers financing to a borrower to purchase goods, these parties may take a security interest in the purchased goods and issue chattel paper to memorialize the financing and secured interest. These transactions will then generate a **purchase-money security interest (PMSI)**. A unique feature of a PMSI is that it achieves perfection automatically when it is executed within the context of consumer goods. If the PMSI involves financing to purchase business equipment, the secured lender must take two additional steps to perfect the security interest. In these cases, lenders must ensure that the equipment is in the borrower's possession within 20 days of the security agreement and must file a UCC-1 financing statement within that time period.

Perfection by Control

The UCC allows investment products such as stocks, bonds, mutual fund shares, and deposit accounts to be perfected through control. This is particularly important if the investments are **uncertificated securities**, which are simply recorded as an account with a financial institution. In these cases, the secured lender acquires control when it is in the position to have the securities sold.[8] For example, if you have purchased stocks with a brokerage firm and would like to borrow money to make additional investments, you can offer your stocks to the brokerage firm as collateral and make additional stock purchases on **margin**. These secured transactions require the borrower to cede control of the stocks he is providing as collateral to the brokerage firm, which will now have the ability to sell the stocks if necessary to repay the loan without the borrower's permission. In most cases, investments are held by a separate company called a **transfer agent**. In these cases, a separate loan collateral account may be created with the transfer agent to house the pledged investments, and a stop order will be placed on this account to prevent the investments from being sold or transferred without the secured lender's approval.

TAKEAWAY CONCEPTS Perfecting a Security Interest

- Perfecting a security interest describes how a secured lender can protect its security interest from other creditors who might assert claims against the same collateral.
- Under Article 9 of the UCC, there are four main ways to perfect a security interest: perfection by filing, perfection by possession, automatic perfection, and perfection by control.

---

[8]UCC § 8-106.

- Creditors can perfect their security interest if they file a UCC-1 financing statement with the secretary of state where the borrower resides.
- A purchase-money security interest (PMSI) achieves perfection automatically when it is executed within the context of consumer goods.

PRIORITY AMONG CREDITORS' CLAIMS TO COLLATERAL

LO 23-4

Apply the priority rules to a scenario in which several parties have competing claims to collateral.

Recall that the purpose of creating a security interest is to be able to claim collateral in case a loan is not repaid. This becomes a critical issue when multiple parties claim that they have a security interest with respect to the same collateral. If this occurs, the general rule is that a perfected security interest has priority over an unperfected security interest. Also, secured creditors generally have priority over unsecured lien holders, such as a trustee who is overseeing a bankruptcy.

The UCC also has rules regarding who has priority when multiple creditors have perfected a security interest on the same collateral. The general rule is that priority goes to the party who first perfected the interest *or* filed a UCC-1 financing statement.[9] For example, say John offers his valuable artwork to his brokerage firm as collateral, and the firm perfects the security interest through possession in January. John later uses the same artwork as collateral for a personal loan with his bank, and the bank files a UCC-1 form in March of that year. In this case, because the brokerage firm is the first lender to perfect (through possession in this instance), it will have priority over the artwork if John fails to repay his loan. His bank will still be a secured creditor, but it will only get repaid if there are funds left after the loan to the brokerage firm is paid.

Another general rule concerns parties who have exclusively used UCC-1 financing forms to perfect their security interests. In these cases, the first party to file has priority. For example, BioCorp may have an expensive electron microscope that it offers as collateral to ReliaBank and FirstBanc. ReliaBank files its UCC-1 financing statement in January, and FirstBanc files its statement in June. Because both lenders filed their UCC-1 financing statements, they both perfected their security interests against BioCorp's electron microscope. In this case, however, the general rule regarding the timing of UCC-1 filings is **first-in-time is first-in-right**. Under this scenario, ReliaBank has priority over BioCorp's microscope because it was the first to file.

Another priority rule involves investment property (e.g., stocks) that is offered as collateral. In these cases, the only way to attain priority over other creditors is to have custody or control over the investment property. A secured lender obtains control over investment property when it legally obtains the right to sell or dispose of the investment property without having to consult with the borrower.[10]

Lastly, there is a priority rule that concerns PMSIs. A PMSI will override a prior perfected security interest, for example, a security interest that was obtained through an earlier UCC-1 filing. Suppose Johnny's Auto Repair obtained a loan from FirstBank to purchase new equipment for the garage. FirstBank took a floating lien security interest in "any equipment at Johnny's Auto Repair currently owned or hereinafter acquired." If Johnny's Auto Repair obtains financing from SecondBank to purchase a new hydraulic car lift system, SecondBank can take out a PMSI on the hydraulic lift system. SecondBank's security interest would have priority over FirstBank's security interest, even though FirstBank was the first to file.

Figure 23.2 summarizes the general priority ranking among creditors.

---

[9]UCC § 9-322.

[10]UCC § 9-328, Comment 3.

FIGURE 23.2 Priority among Creditors' Claims to Collateral

Priority	Creditor Type	Security Interest	Method of Perfecting
1	Secured	Perfected	PMSI; first-to-file UCC-1 financing statement; possession or control
2			Second-to-file UCC-1 financing statement
3		Not perfected	None
4	Unsecured	None	None

TAKEAWAY CONCEPTS Priority among Creditors' Claims to Collateral

- The general rule is that a perfected security interest has priority over an unperfected security interest.
- Secured creditors generally have priority over unsecured lien holders, such as a trustee who is overseeing a bankruptcy.
- Generally, priority goes to the party who first perfected the interest *or* filed a UCC-1 financing statement.
- The general rule regarding the timing of UCC-1 filings is "first-in-time is first-in-right."
- A PMSI will override a prior perfected security interest.

LO 23-5

Explain the consequences of a borrower's default.

THE CONSEQUENCES OF A BORROWER'S DEFAULT

A borrower who fails to perform under the contract with the lender is said to be in **default**. Often, a security agreement will define the various occurrences that will trigger a default. For example, any of the following might trigger a default:

- The borrower fails to make a payment.
- The borrower provides false or misleading information.
- The collateral is lost or destroyed.
- The borrower declares bankruptcy.
- The borrower's business is dissolved.

Although it might seem like the creditor would act promptly to seize and liquidate the collateral in the event of default, this is usually not the case. This is because the lender is often in an unsuitable position to sell or liquidate the collateral in a way that will make them whole. A bank that has business equipment or real estate as collateral, for example, will not be in a good position with respect to personnel or knowledge of the market to suitably liquidate the collateral at the best price. It is also likely that seizing the collateral will further weaken the borrower, who is already experiencing financial difficulties. Instead, lenders often try to work with the borrower to refinance the terms of the loan and maximize the possibility of full repayment. In practice, creditors typically seize collateral only as a last resort.

There are instances, however, when the secured lender may decide to take actions to seize the collateral. This can be done through a judicial action that is later enforced with a sheriff's warrant or by contracting with a repo agent service to physically repossess the collateral. If a creditor contracts with a repo agent service, however, the repossession must be done in a way that does not "breach the peace."[11]

In Case 23.2, a car was repossessed from the plaintiff, who argued that a breach of the peace had occurred, making the repossession unlawful.

CASE 23.2 Stephanie Ann James and Roland James v. Ford Motor Credit Co. et al., 842 F. Supp. 1202 (U.S. Dist. Minn. 1994)

FACT SUMMARY   The plaintiffs purchased a Ford vehicle that was financed and secured by Ford. When the plaintiffs fell behind on their car payments, Ford sent them a notice of repossession. The plaintiffs contacted Ford and objected to any repossession efforts. On June 29, 1992, Ford's "repo man," Robert Klave, took possession of the car from a public parking lot. Approximately one hour later, Stephanie James noticed the vehicle parked with Klave in it. She entered the vehicle, and an altercation ensued whereby James took control of the vehicle and drove away. Klave reported the vehicle stolen, and when the authorities apprehended James on July 8, 1992, Klave regained possession of the vehicle. James sued, claiming that her objection to the repossession and the manner in which it was conducted resulted in an unlawful repossession because it had breached the peace.

SYNOPSIS OF DECISION AND OPINION   Ford and Klave argued that because the auto was repossessed without incident in a public parking lot and because Klave had possession of the car for approximately one hour on June 29, 1992, the repossession was not wrongful or in breach of the peace. The trial court agreed with the defendants and granted them the motion to dismiss the case.

WORDS OF THE COURT: Dominion Over Collateral   "When debtors specifically object to repossession, they revoke any implied right previously granted to the creditors to enter the debtor's property without consent. Entering the debtor's property after consent is revoked constitutes a breach of the peace. . . . The basis for favoring debtors over creditors in these circumstances appears to be 'the

law's historical . . . aversion to trespass.' Creditors are not without recourse when a debtor revokes the implied right of repossession. But they must secure those rights through judicial means rather than through self-help repossession. . . .

"In this case, however, defendants did not repossess the car from plaintiffs' property. On June 29, 1992, the car was removed from a public parking lot. On July 8, 1992, the car was repossessed from a public street. The court has found no case which holds that repossession of an automobile from a public street in itself constitutes a breach of the peace. . . .

"It is evident that a breach of the peace occurred on June 29, 1992. Defendants contend that the altercation cannot be considered a breach of the peace during the repossession, which would have violated the self-help repossession statute, because Klave was already in control of the car thereby making the repossession complete before he was attacked by James. Once a repossession agent has gained sufficient dominion over collateral to control it, the repossession has been completed. . . . There is no dispute that Klave was in control of the car for approximately one hour after he removed it from the parking lot. He drove the car away from the lot, informed Ford that he had the car and was proceeding to deliver it to a location specified by Ford when he was attacked by James. The court finds that, once Klave had control of the car the repossession was complete and James' protest was to no avail. It would be unjust to hold that the violence caused by James in a public place after the repossession was complete could somehow dispossess defendants of their present right to possession. . . .

(continued)

---
[11]UCC § 9-609(b).

"Therefore, the court finds that Klave's repossession of the car was properly executed under Minnesota law. . . . Accordingly, this court has no subject matter jurisdiction to consider the complaint and must dismiss the complaint."

Case Questions

1. At what point does a repo agent obtain control over a car? Once the agent obtains control and a breach of the peace occurs, who is likely to win a case of wrongful repossession?

2. Why did it matter to the court that the repossession occurred in a public parking lot?

3. *Focus on Critical Thinking:* Under Minnesota law, if a borrower does not object to a repossession notice, when is the secured lender allowed to enter the borrower's property to repossess the property?

TAKEAWAY CONCEPTS The Consequences of a Borrower's Default

- A borrower who fails to perform under the contract with the lender is said to be in default.
- Often, a security agreement will define the various occurrences that will trigger a default.
- In practice, creditors typically seize collateral only as a last resort.
- A secured lender may decide to seize the collateral through a judicial action or by contracting with a repo agent service.
- If a creditor contracts with a repo agent service, the repossession must be done in a way that does not breach the peace.

 THINKING STRATEGICALLY

©valterZ/Shutterstock

Assessing and Perfecting a Security Interest

PROBLEM: Lenders must be aware of the various risks associated with different types of collateral used to secure a loan.

STRATEGIC SOLUTION: To minimize risk, savvy lenders will assess various types of collateral, as illustrated in the following case.

Erin O'Connor is a senior loan officer at First Arizona Bank & Trust. Erin was recently approached by the chief financial officer (CFO) at Kitchell—a large, privately held Arizona real estate development and construction company—to discuss a loan made to the company in the amount of $1,000,000. Erin has asked Kitchell's CFO to provide a list of assets that can secure the loan, and the CFO replies that the company can offer as security "all of our information technology equipment."

QUESTIONS

1. Should Erin approve the loan based on this collateral? Why or why not?

2. Before offering the loan, what should Erin do to ensure that First Arizona Bank & Trust will have priority with respect to this collateral?

3. Visit the Arizona Secretary of State website and conduct a UCC lien search of the state's publicly accessible database. Search for UCC-1 filings under the organization name "Kitchell." What did you find? How will this impact whether First Arizona Bank & Trust will offer the secured loan? What should Erin do now?

4. Erin contacts the Kitchell CFO and mentions that her bank will require another type of collateral. The CFO mentions that Kitchell has "valuable artwork in the office and $750,000 sitting in a low-interest-bearing money market account at Sun Valley National Bank." How can First Arizona Bank & Trust perfect these assets if they are used as collateral to obtain priority over any other creditors?

Secured transaction p. 396   A transaction in which the buyer can retain the goods if the payment obligations are satisfied, but in the event of default, the seller or secured party can repossess the goods. Generally, the secured party must dispose of the goods and apply the proceeds to the outstanding indebtedness. Any surplus proceeds belong to the buyer *(ch 17)*. A financing agreement between a lender (creditor) and a borrower (debtor) in which the borrower pledges assets to secure the loan *(ch 23)*.

Collateral p. 396   The assets a borrower has pledged to secure a loan.

Unsecured creditor p. 397   A lender who lacks a security interest in collateral to secure the loan.

Chattel paper p. 397   A document issued by a seller that indicates financing terms for the sale of goods and a repayment schedule.

Securitization p. 397   The process of packaging promissory notes and negotiating their sale to investors.

Security interest p. 399   A legal right granted by a debtor to a creditor over the debtor's property (usually referred to as *collateral*); enables the creditor to have recourse to the property (i.e., retake possession of the property) if the debtor defaults in making payment or in otherwise performing its obligations.

Fixtures p. 399   Items that can be detached from real estate, such as cabinetry.

Floating lien p. 399   A security interest that includes future acquisitions of property (e.g., "all equipment currently owned and hereafter acquired").

True lease p. 399   A contract in which title is never transferred and instead involves granting another party limited-life usage rights to the property.

Attachment to the property p. 399   The requirement that, for a security interest to be enforceable, value must be given, the debtor must have rights in the collateral, and the

debtor must authenticate a security agreement that describes the collateral.

Security agreement p. 399   An agreement between the borrower and the lender that stipulates the creation of a security interest in the particular property offered as security.

Buyer in ordinary course of business (BOCB) p. 400   A person who buys goods in good faith, without knowledge that the sale violates the rights of another person in the goods, and in the ordinary course from a person, other than a pawnbroker, in the business of selling goods of that kind.

Perfect a security interest p. 402   Actions taken by a secured lender to protect its security interest from other creditors who might assert claims against the same collateral.

UCC-1 financing statement p. 402   A legal document filed in the state where the borrower resides that indicates a security interest.

Pre-file p. 402   A legal strategy among lenders that involves filing a UCC-1 financing statement before the security agreement is created and before attachment.

Purchase-money security interest (PMSI) p. 404   An automatically perfected security interest in consumer goods when a merchant or lender offers financing to a borrower to purchase goods.

Uncertificated securities p. 404   Securities that are simply recorded as an account with a financial institution.

Margin p. 404   When a client of a brokerage firm borrows money to make additional investments and offers securities as collateral.

Transfer agent p. 404   A separate company that has custody and record of any investment products.

First-in-time is first-in-right p. 405   The general rule regarding the timing of UCC-1 filings where the first to file obtains priority.

Default p. 406   When a borrower fails to perform under the contract with the lender.

CASE SUMMARY 23.1 *In re* Estate of Joseph M. Silver, 2003 Mich. App. LEXIS 1389

Classification of Collateral

Kathleen Wilson signed a security agreement with Mark S. Conti and filed a UCC-1 financing statement in 1996 for collateral described as equipment. In 1998, Conti offered 11 paintings as security to the Silver Trust. The

trust took possession of the paintings that year. The appellate court held that the trial court had incorrectly classified 4 of the paintings as consumer goods. The appellate court held that all 11 paintings were used for business purposes in offices and model homes. Because the paintings were for business use, they were classi-fied as equipment, which meant that Wilson's security interest was perfected before that of the Silver Trust and all of the paintings would be transferred to Wilson to secure her loan.

CASE QUESTIONS

1. What would Conti have to do for the law to consider these paintings consumer goods?
2. How could the Silver Trust have avoided this outcome?

CASE SUMMARY 23.2 *In re* Pfautz, 264 B.R. 551 (W.D. Miss. 2001)

Perfecting a Security Interest

Debtor Pfautz offered as security to Liberty Bank mutual fund shares that were uncertificated. Liberty Bank signed a loan collateral account with Pfautz that required the transfer agent and custodian of shares to release the securities only upon Liberty Bank's instruc-tions. A stop transfer was placed on the account to ensure the shares would not be sold or transferred to any other party, essentially freezing the assets. When Pfautz filed for bankruptcy a few years later, the bankruptcy trustee attempted to collect the shares, arguing that the loan collateral account did not give Liberty Bank con-trol of the investments.

CASE QUESTIONS

1. How can an investment product be perfected?
2. Did Liberty Bank perfect its security interest in the mutual fund shares? Who should get the proceeds from the collateral and why?

CASE SUMMARY 23.3 *In re* Piknik Products Co., 346 B.R. 863 (Bankr. M.D. Ala. 2006)

Purchase-Money Security Interest

In 2005, Piknik purchased equipment from Crouch for $369,865 that was delivered and installed in Piknik's fac-tory. Piknik offered 35 percent as a down payment and financed the rest from Crouch. Crouch failed to file a UCC-1 financing statement within 20 days of when Piknik took possession of the goods. Although the equip-ment was fully installed in the factory, it was not opera-tional when Piknik filed for bankruptcy a few months later. Wachovia Bank had filed a UCC-1 financing statement on all equipment owned by Piknik and claimed ownership of the equipment to secure its loan to Piknik.

CASE QUESTIONS

1. Was Piknik in possession of the goods even though the equipment was not operational? Why or why not?
2. Had Crouch filed a UCC-1 financing statement within 20 days, would it have priority over Wacho-via's security interest? Why or why not?

CHAPTER REVIEW QUESTIONS

1. **Secured transactions with respect to personal prop-erty are governed by:**
   a. UCC Article 2A.
   b. UCC Article 9.
   c. The common law.
   d. Federal law.
   e. UCC Article 3.

2. **All of the following fit within the "goods" category of collateral, except:**
   a. Equipment.
   b. Inventory.
   c. Stocks.
   d. Consumer goods.
   e. Farm products.

3. The only way to perfect a security interest in an uncertificated stock is through:

   a. Filing a UCC-1 financing statement.

   b. A PMSI.

   c. Possession.

   d. Control.

   e. None of the above.

4. A secured lender files a UCC-1 financing statement and describes the borrower's collateral as "all equipment, inventory or accounts, now existing or hereafter acquired." This is known as a:

   a. PMSI.

   b. Chattel paper.

   c. Floating lien.

   d. Securitization.

   e. True lease.

5. Value has been given to the debtor; the debtor has rights in the collateral; and the debtor has authenticated a security agreement. These are the requirements for:

   a. Perfection.

   b. Attachment.

   c. Securitization.

   d. A security agreement.

   e. A floating lien.

6. A UCC-1 financing statement should be filed where the corporate borrower is incorporated.

   a. True

   b. False

7. ABC Bank filed a UCC-1 financing statement for all equipment owned by X Corp in 2017. In 2018, FinanceCorp financed the sale of new equipment to X Corp and properly perfected a PMSI on the equipment. FinanceCorp's security interest has priority over ABC Bank's.

   a. True

   b. False

8. If a borrower fails to perform under the contract with the lender, they are said to be in bankruptcy.

   a. True

   b. False

9. If two parties perfected their security interests to the same collateral by filing UCC-1 financing statements, the party who filed first has priority.

   a. True

   b. False

10. A BOCB can purchase goods free of a preexisting security interest.

   a. True

   b. False

 Quick Quiz ANSWERS
Identify the Secured Transaction

1. The truck is predominantly used for farming. The collateral would be classified as a good and, more specifically, as equipment because it is mainly used as a long-term asset to support the business.

2. The Bowie bonds rely on copyrights as a security to repay the loan in the event of default. Copyrights are classified as general intangibles.

CHAPTER REVIEW QUESTIONS: Answers and Explanations

1. **b.** The only UCC article to govern secured transactions for personal property is Article 9.

2. **c.** Stocks are classified as financial products.

3. **d.** Control is the only means to perfect a security interest in uncertificated securities.

4. **c.** A floating lien involves a group of assets that might change over time.

5. **b.** These are the three required elements of attachment.

6. **a. True.**

7. **a. True.** Perfected PMSIs have priority.

8. **b. False.** A borrower who fails to perform under the contract with a lender is is said to be in default.

9. **a. True.** This reflects the first-in-time is first-in-right rule.

10. **a. True.**

CHAPTER 24

Creditors' Rights

©valterZ/Shutterstock

The *Thinking Strategically* feature at the end of this chapter explains the use of statutory liens as a method for business owners to reduce the risk of nonpayment by a customer.

Learning Objectives

After studying this chapter, students who have mastered the material will be able to:

24-1 Explain the role of a personal guaranty in the context of a debtor-creditor relationship.

24-2 Provide examples of the rights that creditors have against sureties and guarantors.

24-3 Differentiate between various types of liens.

24-4 Explain methods available to creditors to collect unsecured debt.

CHAPTER OVERVIEW

This chapter continues our discussion of commercial law by providing a creditor's perspective on sales transactions. Although many business transactions involve debt secured by collateral, it's important to realize that in some cases creditors are faced with collecting debts that are unsecured as well. Specifically, we discuss what rights creditors have against third parties who provide payment assurances on behalf of the debtor, the role of liens in business transactions, and options available to creditors for collecting unsecured debt.

PERSONAL GUARANTIES

You may recall that certain business entities provide comprehensive insulation of the personal assets of principals from liabilities of the business entity. In an unsecured transaction such as a business loan or line of credit, a creditor may agree to allow the principals of

the business to substitute a personal guaranty instead of collateral to assure that the loan will be paid back if the business entity defaults on payment. For example, suppose Mid-Size Corporation is planning to expand operations by launching a new interactive website. In order to finance the development of the website, Mid-Size approaches Neighborhood Bank for a loan. Because the creditor cannot take a security interest in a website, Neighborhood Bank allows Mid-Size's principals to give their personal guaranty to back up the business loan. This means that in the event of a default by Mid-Size, the principals have pledged their personal assets (such as individual bank accounts, equity in a property, or other assets) should the assets of the business be insufficient to repay the loan. Creditors realize that without this guaranty, the principals of a debtor corporation can simply walk away from the debt without any personal liability for the loan.

Even in cases where the loan is secured by collateral, creditors often wish to make the principals more accountable by securing a business loan with both a security interest in certain collateral *and* the personal guaranties of the principals. For example, suppose that Caulfield is the principal of Rye Inc., a manufacturing firm specializing in the production of high-quality baseball catcher's mitts, with annual revenues of $25 million. Rye has been successful over the past 10 years. Now Caulfield wishes to expand his operations and manufacture other baseball equipment, and he plans to fund the expansion with a loan from Big Bank. Although Rye has been profitable in the past and will likely have no problem repaying the loan from existing revenues, Big Bank not only will require a security interest in any collateral owned by Rye but also will likely require Caulfield to provide a personal guaranty as an additional measure of security. From Big Bank's perspective, the personal guaranty gives the bank maximum leverage over Caulfield in the event of a default by Rye.

The issue of personal guaranties also occurs in a commercial lease context. In essence, the landlord is a creditor who allows a tenant to enter into a lease agreement on the promise that the tenant will make all payments as they become due. In a commercial lease, the tenant may be a corporate entity that insulates its principals' personal assets from liability under the lease agreement and the landlord may require a personal guaranty as part of the lease. The personal guaranty serves the same function as it does for a creditor such as a bank. In Case 24.1, an appellate court considers the enforceability of a landlord-tenant personal guaranty.

LO 24-1

Explain the role of a personal guaranty in the context of a debtor-creditor relationship.

CASE 24.1 Triple T-Bar, LLC v. DDR Southeast Springfield, LLC, 769 S.E.2d 586 (Ga. Ct. App. 2015)

FACT SUMMARY In November 2006, Triple T-Bar, LLC entered into a six-year agreement to lease a commercial property in Lawrenceville, Georgia, until February 2012. The lease was signed by both Todd and Barbara Blackwell (Blackwells) as officers of Triple T-Bar, and the Blackwells were identified in the lease as the guarantors. The Blackwells' personal guaranty was attached to the lease and incorporated into the lease in accordance with the lease agreement. The personal guaranty cross-referenced the lease agreement, again identified the Blackwells as the guarantors, and also identified the landlord and listed Triple T-Bar as the tenant. In April 2007, Triple T-Bar's rent payment check was returned for insufficient funds. Triple T-Bar then failed to pay rent for the months of April 2008 and September 2008, and it made its last rent payment in October 2008.

In February 2009, Triple T-Bar closed its business operations and vacated the premises without the landlord's consent, in violation of the lease agreement. When Triple T-Bar failed to reopen for business and pay past-due rent as the landlord requested, the landlord filed suit against the Blackwells and Triple T-Bar. The trial court awarded summary judgment to

the landlord against Triple T-Bar and the Blackwells individually. The Blackwells appealed arguing, among other things, that the guaranty was incomplete (no date appeared on the guaranty itself) and the Blackwells did not intend to be personally liable for the lease.

SYNOPSIS OF DECISION AND OPINION The Court of Appeals of Georgia affirmed the ruling of the trial court against the Blackwells. The court found that (1) the lease and guaranty both identified the Blackwells as the guarantors and the guaranty was incorporated into the lease, and (2) the guaranty served as an inducement for the landlord to enter into the lease given that Triple T-Bar, LLC, had no assets at the time of the lease.

WORDS OF THE COURT: Enforceable Guaranty "The Blackwells' argument that the guaranty is unenforceable because it was not dated is meritless because the guaranty provided that it was executed contemporaneously with the lease, which was signed on November 8, 2006. The Blackwells further argue that the guaranty is not enforceable because they did not initial every page and the document was not

(continued)

notarized, but they point to no authority holding that these omissions render the guaranty unenforceable. The Blackwells' signatures are plainly on the guaranty and the signatures are not alleged to be forged. Therefore, the Blackwells are charged with knowledge of and are bound by the terms of the guaranty."

Case Questions

1. The court points out that the guaranty served as an inducement for the landlord to enter into the agreement. What does the court mean by that and why is it important?

2. Why did the court reject the Blackwells' argument that the lack of a date on the guaranty made it invalid?

3. *Focus on Critical Thinking:* Could the Blackwells have strategically negotiated terms of the lease that could have either prevented or limited any liability? What language would you suggest that may accomplish that?

TAKEAWAY CONCEPTS Personal Guaranties

- In an unsecured loan, a personal guaranty means that in the event of a default by the business entity debtor, the principals have pledged their personal assets (such as individual bank accounts, equity in a property, or other assets) in the event that the assets of the business are insufficient to repay the loan.

- Even in cases where the loan is secured by collateral, creditors often wish to make the principals more accountable by securing a business loan with both a security interest in certain collateral and the personal guaranties of the principals.

- The issue of personal guaranties also occurs in a commercial lease context in which the landlord is a creditor who allows a business entity/tenant to enter into a lease agreement on the promise that the principals will guaranty lease payments.

LO 24-2

Provide examples of the rights that creditors have against sureties and guarantors.

RIGHTS AGAINST THIRD PARTIES

Another common method for helping to secure a loan is to require a third party to back up the promises made by the debtor regarding repayment of the loan. In some cases, a creditor may be willing to extend a loan to a borrower, but the borrower's creditworthiness may be either questionable or too brief to qualify for the credit required. In such a case, the creditor usually will require a third party with sufficient creditworthiness and assets to also sign the loan agreement and become jointly liable with the debtor for his promise to repay the loan (thus the commonly used term *cosigning*). When a party agrees to be primarily liable to pay the loan, she is known as a **surety**. When a party agrees to be liable only if the debtor actually defaults, she is known as a **guarantor**.

For example, in order to secure a loan for the purchase of a new car, Bank requires Cook to have a cosigner because Cook's credit is insufficient to qualify for the loan. Cook convinces Abel to be his cosigner, and Bank requires Abel to cosign as a surety. In the first year of the loan, Abel is late in making payments and eventually becomes 60 days' past due. Bank now has the option of pursuing remedies against either Cook or Abel to pay the debt. Because Abel has more assets, he is most likely the best party to pursue. However, suppose that Abel signed as a guarantor instead of as a surety. In that case, Bank would have to pursue full remedies against Cook by obtaining a court judgment and attempting to collect as much as possible (such as repossessing the car for resale) before pursuing Abel. Only in the event that Bank cannot recover the full amount from remedies against Cook is Abel then liable for the balance owed.

Defenses

Although a surety or guarantor may be subject to liability for a debt that is not paid by the original debtor, sureties/guarantors are also entitled to assert defenses that would relieve them of payment liability. Remember that surety/guarantor agreements are simply a form of contract. In addition to defenses that the surety/guarantor would have against the creditor directly, if the debtor has defenses to liability for the underlying contract, the surety/guarantor also may assert those defenses. For example, suppose that Andrews guarantees the debt of Cardozo's promissory note to Frankel, but the guarantee is not in writing. Recall that certain contracts must be in writing to be enforceable under the statute of frauds. Under the common law, any promise to pay the debt of another is a contract that must be in writing; thus, Andrews would have a direct defense against Frankel's attempt to enforce the guarantee against Andrews. On the other hand, suppose a contract exists between Cardozo and Frankel, and the Andrews guarantee was in writing. If Frankel fails to fulfill a contractual obligation to Cardozo, and eventually tries to sue Andrews to collect on the promissory note, Andrews could assert a defense related to breach of the Cardozo-Frankel agreement.

TAKEAWAY CONCEPTS Rights Against Third Parties

- Parties that agree to be primarily liable to payback a loan are known as sureties.
- Parties that agree to be liable only if the debtor actually defaults are known as guarantors.
- Sureties and guarantors are entitled to assert defenses that would relieve them of payment liability.

LIENS

Recall from Chapter 23, "Secured Transactions," that a **lien** is an interest in property that gives the holder of the lien the right to possession of some of a debtor's property if the debtor fails to perform its obligations (e.g., fails to pay back a loan). We have discussed liens in the context of Article 9 of the UCC, called a *judicial lien,*[1] but a lien may exist in other contexts as well. In addition to judicial liens, creditors may use *statutory liens* or *consensual liens* to protect their interests in assuring payment.

Judicial Liens

A **judicial lien**, as you may expect, is one that arises from a judicial proceeding, most commonly a lawsuit filed by a creditor. As in any lawsuit, the aggrieved party (creditor) files a complaint and, unless the debtor files an answer to the complaint, the creditor is the

LO 24-3

Differentiate between various types of liens.

---

[1] UCC § 9-102(a)(52).

beneficiary of a *default judgment*. Cases in which liability is in dispute are resolved through a trial as with any other judicial dispute. In any case, note that a judgment in favor of the creditor is *not* a lien in and of itself. A judgment by a court is a judicial recognition that the creditor is owed a certain sum of money by the debtor. The judgment must then be executed in order to obtain the lien. In some cases (e.g., when real property is offered as collateral), this is simply a matter of the judgment creditor recording the judgment with a county recorder of deeds.

Statutory Liens

Certain creditors may obtain a **statutory lien** on a debtor's property authorized by a state statute or, less often, state common law. Because these liens are created by the state legislature and state courts, the actual procedures, terminology, and lien interest vary from state to state, and sometimes these variances are considerable. Perhaps the most common statutory liens are state statutes that provide contractors and subcontractors who work on real estate (e.g., constructing a new addition onto a home) an interest in the labor and materials used to improve the property. Also, state statutes typically provide parties that provide service and materials to repair equipment with a statutory lien on the repaired real/personal property. For example, most states provide an auto mechanic with a statutory lien on cars that have been repaired in order to assure payment for those repairs. Other examples include hotels that have a statutory lien on any personal property brought into a hotel room by a guest and landlords that have a lien on any personal property brought on to the leased premises. In each of these instances, the policy goal is to provide a creditor with some measure of security intended to assure payment. In Texas, for instance, the state statute defines who is entitled to a lien for labor and materials for improving properties like homes, buildings, fixtures, improvements, and certain other lands. These people include laborers, materials fabricators, suppliers, architects, engineers, surveyors, landscapers, and demolition services.[2]

Traditionally, most statutory liens were labeled as either (1) a mechanic's lien, which covered real estate, or (2) an artisan's lien, which covered real/personal property. However, states have adopted a variety of different names and there is a significant lack of conformity from state to state. Some states use the term *contractor's lien* for construction projects only and *mechanic's lien* for other types of providers of labor or materials. (See Figure 24.1 for a sample mechanic's lien.) Some states have eliminated the term *artisan's lien* altogether, yet others define liens based on the nature of the provider (e.g., innkeeper's lien). In the Thinking Strategically feature at the end of this chapter, we discuss the steps used by providers to preserve their rights through a lien.

Fraudulent Liens Although statutory lien statutes are primarily aimed at protecting creditors, many states also include a penalty for creditors that file fraudulent liens. These typically fall into two categories: The creditor files a lien (1) for an amount that exceeds what the property owner actually owes or (2) for work that was not actually performed on the property. When either event occurs, a court may find that the lien is fraudulent, declare the lien unenforceable, and award actual and punitive damages to any person who was damaged by the fraudulent lien. For example, in Florida, the statutes define fraudulent claim by a contractor if:

- the amount of the claim was willfully exaggerated;
- a claim was made for work not performed upon the property upon which the lienor seeks to impress its lien;

---

[2]*Texas Code Ann.* Chapter 53 (a).

FIGURE 24.1 Sample Mechanic's Lien

Recording requested by (name):
Alpha General Contractors, LLC

When recorded, mail to (name and address):
Jill Alpha % Alpha General Contractors, LLC

1000 E. College Avenue

San Diego, CA 92008

Recorder's Use Only

CLAIM OF
MECHANICS LIEN

(Cal. Civ. Code § 8416)

Declaration of Exemption From Gov't Code § 27388.1 Fee
☐ Transfer is exempt from fee per GC § 27388.1(a)(2):
 ☐ recorded concurrently "in connection with" transfer subject to DTT
 ☐ recorded concurrently "in connection with" a transfer of
   residential dwelling to an owner-occupier
☐ Transfer is exempt from fee per GC 27388.1(a)(1):
 ☐ Fee cap of $225.00 reached ☐ Not related to real property

1. **Alpha General Contractors, LLC** ("claimant") claims a mechanics lien for the labor or services or equipment or materials described in paragraph 2, furnished for a work of improvement on that certain real property located in the County of **San Diego**, State of California, and more particularly described as (address and/or sufficient description): **2000 Sea View Road, San Diego, CA 92008**

2. After deducting all just credits and offsets, the sum of **$10,000**, together with interest at the rate of **5%** per annum from **Jan 2, 2020** (date when balance became due), is due claimant for the following labor, materials, services, or equipment: **improvements and materials on addition to existing house.**

3. Claimant furnished the labor or services or equipment or materials, at the request of **Joseph Coronado** (employer, person, or entity to whom labor, materials, services, or equipment were furnished).

4. The name and address of the owner or reputed owner of the real property is/are: **Joseph Coronado 2000 Sea View Road, San Diego, CA 92008**

5. Claimant's address is: **1000 E. College Avenue, San Diego, CA 92008**

Dated **1/30/20**

_____
(Signature)

VERIFICATION

I, **Jill Alpha**, am the: **Owner** ("Owner," "president," "authorized agent," "partner," etc.) of claimant on the foregoing claim of mechanics lien, and am authorized to make this verification for and on its behalf. I have read the foregoing claim of mechanics lien and know the contents of the claim of mechanics lien to be true of my own knowledge.

I declare under penalty of perjury under the laws of the State of California that the foregoing is true and correct.

Dated **1/30/20**

_____
(Signature)

- a claim was made for materials not furnished for the property upon which the lienor seeks to impress its lien; or

- a claim was compiled with such willful and gross negligence as to amount to a willful exaggeration.[3]

---

[3]Fla. Stat. § 713.31(2)(a) (2012).

In Case 24.2, a state appellate court analyzes a fraudulent lien claim.

CASE 24.2 Father & Sons Home Improvement II, Inc. v. Stuart, 2016 IL App 143666 (Ill. App. Ct. 2016)

FACT SUMMARY In April 2009, Stuart entered into a written construction agreement with Father & Sons for the construction of a deck, garage, and basement in his home. As the construction progressed, Father & Sons had Stuart sign documents titled "Final Completion Certificate for Property Improvements." These certificates purported to report Stuart's satisfaction with the construction work on the house at various stages of the project. Stuart signed certificates in November 2009, January 2010, February 2010, March 2010, and May 2010. Construction on the house was ultimately completed sometime in June 2010.

However, eight months before construction was completed, Father & Sons recorded a "Contractor's Claim for a Lien" (construction lien) with the Cook County (Illinois) Recorder of Deeds. This lien included an affidavit, signed by the president of Father & Sons, which stated that (1) the project was complete and (2) Stuart owed an additional $2,700 for "extra and additional work" completed "at the special instance and request" of Stuart. In total, the balance of the lien was $46,200.

Father & Sons filed a lawsuit to enforce the lien. During the discovery phase of the litigation, Father & Sons admitted that it actually completed work at the subject property in June 2010 and not on September 12, 2009, as the sworn and signed affidavit attached to the lien attested. Stuart asked the trial court to dismiss the case arguing that Father & Sons committed constructive fraud by misrepresenting in its mechanic's lien, and in the affidavit attached to the lien, the work performed and the amount owed at the time the lien was recorded. Father & Sons counterargued that the erroneous overcharges and overstatements in the lien did not rise to the level of constructive fraud as Stuart alleged. The trial court ruled in favor of Stuart and dismissed the case. Father & Sons appealed.

SYNOPSIS OF DECISION AND OPINION The Court of Appeals for Illinois affirmed the lower court's holding in favor of Stuart. The court explained that although overstatement in and of itself is not sufficient with regard to constructive fraud, in this particular situation there was an officer on behalf of Father & Sons who filed a sworn affidavit with the lien that contained intentionally false information in at least two instances. First, the completion date was untrue. Second, the affidavit listed unsubstantiated charges in relation to agreed-upon payment terms and the balance owed.

WORDS OF THE COURT: Fraudulent Lien "First, [Father & Sons's lien] recorded on September 17, 2009, falsely stated that all the work required under the construction agreement, including the construction of the garage, basement, and deck, was completed by September 12, 2009. This statement was proven false by [Father & Sons's] own admission that 'it completed work at the subject property on or about June 2010.' . . . Beyond providing a fabricated completion date, [Father & Sons's] lien also stated falsely that they were owed $46,200 as of September 12, 2009. This statement was proven false by the clear and unambiguous terms of the parties' contract, under which [Stuart was] not required to make the first installment payment until November 1, 2009. . . . Indeed, even construing the pleadings, admissions, exhibits, and affidavits strictly against [Stuart] and liberally in favor of [Father & Sons], the [lower] courts here had no choice but to conclude that [Father & Sons's] lien, based on patently false statements, constituted constructive fraud."

Case Questions

1. What conduct did the court consider to be evidence of constructive fraud?

2. What role did the "Final Completion Certificate for Property Improvements" play in this case?

3. *Focus on Critical Thinking:* Should Stuart be entitled to damages from Father & Sons as a result of the fraudulent lien? Should he be awarded attorney fees? Explain.

Consensual Liens

A **consensual lien** is created when the owner of property voluntarily grants a lien to a creditor. If the lien is attached to *personal property,* this is called a security interest and is governed by Article 9. However, when real estate is being used to collateralize a loan, the creditor takes an interest in the collateral through use of a **mortgage**. A mortgage is a written document that specifies the parties and the real estate and is filed with a state and/or local government agency, thereby becoming a public record that others can look up. This filing is intended to give notice to the public and other creditors of the secured party's interest in the real estate collateral. The creditor is known as the *mortgagee,* and the borrower is the *mortgagor.* A mortgage typically is accompanied by a promissory note. The promissory note is a contract in which the borrower promises to pay back the creditor at a certain rate of interest over a specified period of years (usually 15, 20, or 30 years).

State statutes primarily govern the relationship between mortgagor and mortgagee. These statutes define the procedures that the creditor must follow in order to pursue certain remedies against the debtor. In the most extreme measure, a creditor declares the loan in default and institutes a mortgage foreclosure in an effort to take title and possession of the real estate in hopes of selling the property to pay off the debt owed. In the wake of the mortgage foreclosure crisis that began in 2007, Congress passed the Mortgage Forgiveness Debt Relief Act. The intent of this law is to assist homeowners in avoiding foreclosure by offering them certain guarantees and tax breaks from the government when they refinance a mortgage loan. Properties owned by business entities, or by individuals for business purposes (such as a vacation rental property), are not eligible for relief under this law.

 Quick Quiz Types of Liens

Is the lien judicial, statutory, or consensual?

1. Major is an auto mechanic who repairs a delivery truck for Snowball Company. Snowball's corporate credit card is declined when paying for the repairs. Major does not release the truck until payment is made.

2. Boxer purchases supplies to build a windmill with funds borrowed from Farmer's Bank. In order to ensure repayment, Farmer's takes a security interest in the windmill supplies. Boxer defaults on payments and Farmer's exercises its rights over the collateral by filing a lawsuit. The court awards Farmer's a judgment against Boxer for the debt owed plus interest and penalties.

3. On March 1, Jones hires General Contractor to renovate and expand his warehouse. On July 1, General Contractor files a construction lien in the appropriate state government office on which she falsely claims that Jones owes her $10,000 for "extra work not contemplated by the original agreement."

4. Mollie purchases a house that is secured by a 30-year mortgage from Farmer's Bank.

Answers to this Quick Quiz are provided at the end of the chapter.

TAKEAWAY CONCEPTS Liens

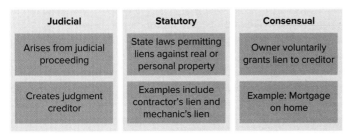

Judicial	Statutory	Consensual
Arises from judicial proceeding	State laws permitting liens against real or personal property	Owner voluntarily grants lien to creditor
Creates judgment creditor	Examples include contractor's lien and mechanic's lien	Example: Mortgage on home

COLLECTING UNSECURED DEBTS

LO 24-4

Explain methods available to creditors to collect unsecured debt.

Recall our discussion of the process used by creditors to collect a debt that is the subject of a security agreement from Chapter 23. Because unsecured debt is not tied to any collateral, creditors do not have the powerful tools provided them by Article 9. Still, this does not mean that unsecured creditors are entirely without options. The most significant obstacle to collecting an unsecured debt is the time and expense required to take the debtor to court and then enforcing any judgment issued by the court, especially if the debtor is without any business or personal assets.

For example, suppose that Big Box Retailer (BBR) agrees to sell 10 laptop computers to New Venture, Inc. in exchange for an unsecured promissory note for $5,000 whereby New Venture agrees to pay a monthly payment of principal and interest over two years. One year after the purchase, New Venture begins to miss payments and then stops payments entirely. Although BBR is a creditor of New Venture, BBR has no lien on the equipment and cannot repossess the laptops. Moreover, even if BBR obtains a court judgment against New Venture, there is no guarantee that BBR will ever recover the sum owed to it. Nor does BBR have any special rights to the laptops simply because they were the products connected to the promissory note.

Obtaining and Enforcing a Judgment

The process for collecting an unsecured debt begins in the courthouse. As in any other lawsuit, the creditor, now as plaintiff, files a complaint to start the judicial process. Obtaining a judgment may not be as easy as it sounds. Unfortunately for the creditor, the debtor may use delay tactics to extend the creditor's recovery efforts further into the future than expected, which will also increase legal fees. Or the debtor may not answer at all. In any case, obtaining a judgment is merely the first step in what could be a long and fruitless process, particularly if the debtor is "judgment proof." A judgment proof defendant is one that is without any assets or, depending on state law, one whose assets are statutorily outside the reach of the creditor (called an *exemption*, which is discussed later in this section).

Garnishment

Once the creditor has obtained a judgment against the debtor, she becomes a **judgment creditor** and is now entitled to enforce the judgment. The reality is that the creditor faces an uphill battle in enforcing a judgment where no collateral exists. The most obvious place for a judgment creditor to look for assets of the debtor are in the debtor's bank accounts. Intangible property (e.g., cash) is normally reached through the process of *garnishment*. Garnishment involves serving a legal document on a third party that is holding funds belonging to the debtor, such as a bank. Supported by a court order, the document directs the bank to pay the judgment creditor rather than the debtor that owns the account. A judgment creditor can garnish the wages of the debtor through the debtor's employer, but many states have either limited wage garnishment or eliminated it entirely as an option for judgment creditors.[4]

Levy

In cases where the judgment creditor is attempting to execute the judgment on real property or real estate, the judgment creditor must rely on a **levy**. A levy is a court order that authorizes the sheriff to take possession of the defendant's personal property on behalf of the judgment creditor in order to preserve the property from being transferred or sold by the debtor. In cases where the property is too large or cumbersome to move, the sheriff will typically tag the property to give notice to any third party that the property is subject to levy and cannot be moved, transferred, or sold. Even property that is locked in a structure (e.g., a warehouse) can be levied

---

[4]For example, Pennsylvania prohibits garnishment of wages for all judgment creditors except landlords. See 42 Pa Code 8147.

by the sheriff posting a levy notice at the entrance of the structure. If the property is real estate, the sheriff files a notice with the county recorder of deeds stating that the sheriff has levied the property. Some states do not require a sheriff's notice for real estate; instead, the notice is filed directly by the judgment creditor. However, note that many states exempt real estate (up to a certain dollar value) used by the debtor as a primary residence from levy and sale.

Discovery

While this process may seem fairly routine, as a practical matter it can be an exercise in futility. The creditor must be able to instruct the sheriff precisely *where* the property is located and must provide a specific description. To assist the judgment creditor in her efforts to collect the judgment, she is entitled to conduct discovery similar to the discovery stage of litigation. This involves having the debtor testify under oath to discover (1) what assets the debtor owns and (2) the location of the assets.

Sale of Property

If the sheriff is successful in locating and levying the debtor's assets, the sheriff is then responsible for selling the property at a *sheriff sale.* Again, the procedure varies widely from sheriff's office to sheriff's office, but typically notice of the sheriff sale is published in local newspapers and online and is held as an auction. If the auction does not produce enough revenue to satisfy the debt, the creditor continues to search (or wait) for assets and must levy any real property or real estate as they become known to the judgment creditor. In the unlikely event that the auction brings in more money than required to pay the judgment, the surplus is given back to the debtor.

State laws permit the sheriff to sell the debtor's property in order to satisfy a judgment against the debtor.
©stone18/Gettty Images

State Exemption Laws

State statutes on garnishment and levy provide certain exemptions that place assets outside the reach of an unsecured judgment creditor. The fundamental policy behind exemption is that there are certain untouchable assets that should be protected because they are related to the safety and well-being of the debtor. The most common full exemption is the debtor's primary residence. State statutes also provide partial exemption for other items: cars, furniture, clothing, and designated retirement funds. This means that these items are exempt only up to a *certain dollar amount.* Because these items are often described in very general terms in the exemption statute, courts are sometimes faced with deciding what does and does not fit into the exemption. In Case 24.3, the Colorado Supreme Court considers an exemption question.

CASE 24.3 Roup v. Commercial Research, LLC, 349 P.3d 273 (Colo. 2015)

FACT SUMMARY Commercial Research, LLC (Commercial) obtained a default judgment that had been entered against Roup in a Texas court. Based on information that Commercial obtained about Roup's assets, it then filed the judgment in a Colorado court and began collection proceedings against

(continued)

Roup's assets. Among other assets, Commercial discovered that Roup had $3,729.24 held in a health savings account (HSA). Roup asserted these funds were exempt from attachment or garnishment because an HSA is a retirement plan under a Colorado statute that exempts certain types of property, including funds held in any retirement plan, from levy and sale. The trial court ruled in favor of Commercial and held that an HSA is not a retirement plan, reasoning that an HSA merely permits individuals to defer income on a tax-exempt basis to pay medical expenses. Roup appealed arguing that the exemption statute should include HSAs as retirement plans because they could potentially provide benefits in retirement in the form of reimbursement for health care costs.

SYNOPSIS OF DECISION AND OPINION   The Colorado Supreme Court upheld the trial court's decision that an HSA was not an exempt asset as a retirement plan. The court held that under prior decisions and common dictionary definitions, a retirement plan is a systematic arrangement established by an employer for guaranteeing an income to employees upon retirement according to definitely established rules with or without employee contributions. Since HSAs do not fit within that definition, they are not exempt as retirement assets.

WORDS OF THE COURT: Meaning of Retirement Plan   "Because Colorado's exemption statute does not define the term 'retirement plan,' we apply the principles of statutory construction to determine and give effect to the legislature's intended meaning. We conclude that the meaning of 'retirement plan' in [the exemption statutes] is unambiguous and can be resolved with reasonable certainty. Drawing from relevant case law, common dictionary definitions, and the statutory context, we determine that the plain and ordinary meaning of 'retirement plan' excludes HSAs."

Case Questions

1. According to the court, what is the difference between an HSA and a retirement plan?

2. How did the court "apply the principles of statutory construction" in this case?

3. *Focus on Critical Thinking:* If the underlying policy goal for exemptions is a protection of the debtor's safety and welfare, how does this decision square with that goal? Aside from the retirement plan exemption, should HSAs be exempt? Why or why not?

TAKEAWAY CONCEPTS Collecting Unsecured Debts

Creditor obtains judgment → Judicial process → Enforcement • Garnishment • Levy • Discovery → Sale • Sheriff sells property • Some assets exempt from levy and sale

---

THINKING STRATEGICALLY

Using Statutory Liens

PROBLEM: In certain industries, those who provide services and materials (providers) face a dilemma. While it is standard practice for consumers to pay some of the costs up front, the bulk of the risk and liability for payment remains with the provider until the work is completed.

STRATEGIC SOLUTION: Use a statutory lien to spread the risk for nonpayment. As we discussed, a statutory lien is a state statute that allows a provider to file a lien that restricts the owner from selling, refinancing, or transferring the property without accommodating the lien. Remember, too, the impact of a fraudulent lien from Case 24.2, *Father & Sons Home Improvement v. Stuart*. The following steps can help ensure successful use of statutory liens:

1. *Learn the lingo.* The process for filing a lien can vary greatly from state to state. Some states use the words "mechanic's lien" as a generic phrase for all types of statutory liens including construction liens. While some businesses use an attorney for liens, as a practical matter many liens are filed by the principals of the provider. This means that the provider's principals must become familiar with statutory liens in any state where they provide services. Some states call these statutes "lien laws."

2. *Know your lien rights.* Determine whether your state specifically authorizes you to file a lien. Each state allows some types of construction participants to file liens but prohibits others from doing so. For example, some states prohibit "suppliers to material suppliers" from filing mechanic's liens (i.e., supply wholesalers who sell to contractors or subcontractors). Typically, prime/general contractors, subcontractors, and material suppliers are given lien rights.

3. *Note the notice requirement.* Is preliminary notice required, and if so, did you give notice? If you were required to send preliminary notice, and you didn't, you may have forfeited your lien rights. Also, every state sets out a deadline to file a lien. This deadline is usually tied to the completion of the project, or the last day that labor or materials are provided to the owner.

4. *Realize that details matter.* Because of the nature of a lien, state laws are very strict in terms of what must be included in the lien. For example, a lien statute typically requires the provider to identify any real estate with a legal property description as opposed to a simple address. County recording offices also have strict font, margin, and paper size requirements. Failure to follow these standards results in additional fees or in having the lien rejected.

5. *Complete post-filing notification.* After the lien is filed, state statutes typically require post-filing notification of appropriate parties. All states require the provider to give notice of the lien to the owner. Some states require that you also serve the prime/general contractor and construction lender (e.g., a bank involved with the project).

6. *Keep an eye on expiration.* A statutory lien is only enforceable for a defined period of time (which varies), and some states allow providers to extend this period with permission from the property owner. If the lien is close to expiration, the provider has three options: (1) extend the lien date, (2) contact an attorney to enforce the lien through a lawsuit, or (3) release the lien, assuming the provider has been paid.

QUESTIONS

1. Try to find the lien statute in your state. It may be as simple as using your favorite search engine to locate a "lien law." Who is covered by that statute? What terminology do they use (i.e, mechanic's lien, construction lien, or artisan's lien)?

2. Statutory liens often center on construction projects, but many states have lien laws for a broader range of providers. Besides contractors, what types of providers might also have the right to file a lien?

3. Suppose that you're a provider and the owner objects to you filing a lien. Are there any alternatives that may help assure payment?

KEY TERMS

Surety p. 414   A third party that agrees to be primarily liable to pay a loan.

Guarantor p. 414   A third party that agrees to be liable to pay a loan only if the debtor actually defaults.

Lien p. 415   An interest in property that gives the holder of the lien the right to possession of some of a debtor's property if the debtor fails to perform its obligations.

Judicial lien p. 415   A lien that arises from a judicial proceeding, most commonly a lawsuit filed by a creditor.

Statutory (common law) liens p. 416   A lien on a debtor's property by virtue of a state statute or state common law.

Consensual lien p. 419   A lien that a property owner voluntarily grants to a creditor (e.g., a mortgage for real estate).

Mortgage p. 419   A written document that specifies the parties and the real estate, is filed with a state and/or local government agency, and is intended to give notice to the public and other creditors of the secured party's interest in the real estate collateral.

Judgment creditor p. 420   Creditor party that has obtained a court judgment against the debtor.

Levy p. 420   A court order that authorizes the local sheriff to take possession of the defendant's personal property on behalf of the judgment creditor in order to preserve the property from being transferred or sold by the debtor.

CASE SUMMARY 24.1 Anthony DeMarco & Sons Nursery, LLC v. Maxim Construction Service Corp., 130 A.D.3d 1409 (N.Y. Sup. Ct. App. Div. 2015)

Fraudulent Lien

LeChase Construction contracted with the State University of New York at Binghamton to build a campus dormitory. LeChase, as the general contractor for the project, hired Maxim Construction Service Corporation (Maxim) to be the site contractor responsible for coordinating various subcontractors. Maxim entered into a subcontract with DeMarco & Sons Nursery (DeMarco) to provide certain landscaping services for the project. Although Maxim paid DeMarco a total of $192,126.40 for its work on the project, DeMarco claimed that it was owed an additional $106,994.27 for labor and materials provided in connection with the landscaping project. DeMarco filed a construction lien in this amount in May 2012. In response, LeChase withheld $160,491.41—a sum representing one and a half times the value of DeMarco's lien, from Maxim's payment.

CASE QUESTIONS

1. Is this a case of a fraudulent lien? Explain.
2. What options did LeChase have once DeMarco filed the lien?

CASE SUMMARY 24.2 On the Level Enterprises, Inc. v. 49 East Houston LLC, 2013 NY Slip Op. 01614 [104 A.D.3d 500]

Statutory Lien

On the Level LLC (LLC) owned property upon which it planned to erect a new residential condominium. LLC contracted with McGrath for McGrath to act as general contractor on the project. Due to market changes, the project was abandoned soon after foundation work commenced. Shortly thereafter, McGrath filed a mechanic's lien against the property. LLC challenged the lien because McGrath was unable to support many of the charges appearing on the lien's breakdown list.

CASE QUESTIONS

1. Does the fact that McGrath could not support many of the charges render the lien invalid automatically? Why or why not?
2. What kind of evidence would McGrath need to supply in order to support his lien claim?

CASE SUMMARY 24.3 Assevero v. Rihan, 144 A.D.3d 1061 (App. Div. Sup. Ct. of NY 2016)

Personal Guaranties

Home Pros Realty Corp. (Home Pros) is owned by Rihan. In order for Home Pros to make a purchase from Assevero, Rihan was required to sign a personal guarantee. Eventually, Home Pros defaulted on the debt, and Assevero sued Rihan to enforce the note pursuant to the personal guarantee. Assevero submitted proof of the underlying note, a personal guarantee bearing

Rihan's signature, the failure of Home Pros to make payment in accordance with the terms of the note, and Rihan's failure to make payment in accordance with his personal guarantee. Rihan defended on the basis that he erroneously signed the promissory note that should have been signed only in the name of Home Pros.

CASE QUESTIONS

1. Who prevails and why?
2. Is Assevero a secured creditor? Explain.

CASE SUMMARY 24.4 Barrie-Chivian v. Lepler, 87 Mass. App. Ct. 683 (2015)

Guaranties and the Statute of Frauds

Lepler approached Barrie-Chivian about the possibility of loaning money to his real estate company, Russell Development, LLC. Barrie-Chivian agreed and lent the company a total of $150,000 in capital. At trial, Barrie-Chivian testified that he would not have agreed to the loans if Lepler had not promised to provide written personal guaranties. Lepler agreed to do so, but never did. Lepler/Russell Development never repaid the $150,000

loan, and Barrie-Chivian sued to recover the loss. At trial, Lepler admitted that he had promised to provide personal guaranties of the loans, but asserted that the statute of frauds barred recovery on the personal guaranties absent a writing.

CASE QUESTIONS

1. Who prevails and why?
2. Why is the statute of frauds so important in resolving this dispute?

CHAPTER REVIEW QUESTIONS

1. A provision in a debtor-creditor agreement (or attachment) that provides assurances of payment by the principals of a business entity in the event of a default is called a:
   a. Demand agreement.
   b. Principals pledge.
   c. Pledge guaranty.
   d. Personal guaranty.
   e. None of the above.

2. In *Father & Sons Home Improvement v. Stuart,* the court held that Father & Sons:
   a. Filed a fraudulent lien.
   b. Could not garnish an HSA.
   c. Had made an error that did not impact the lien.
   d. A and B.
   e. B and C.

3. Big Time Construction (BTC) failed to pay Cary Carpenter for services rendered by Cary as a subcontractor on one of BTC's construction projects. What category would Cary's lien fall into?
   a. Judicial
   b. Statutory
   c. Consensual

   d. Payment
   e. Extraordinary

4. A judgment creditor who attempts to satisfy a debt using the debtor's intangible assets (such as cash) initiates what process?
   a. Levy
   b. Asset allocation
   c. Lawsuit
   d. Garnishment
   e. Cash Out

5. A creditor who obtains a court order against a debtor is known as a _____ creditor.
   a. Judgment
   b. Primary
   c. Secondary
   d. Common law
   e. Super

6. When a party agrees to be liable only if the debtor actually defaults, she is known as a surety.
   a. True
   b. False

7. Once a creditor obtains a judgment against a debtor, a judicial lien is automatic.

a. True

b. False

8. A mortgage is an example of a consensual lien.

a. True

b. False

9. A judgment creditor uses a local sheriff's office to execute a levy.

a. True

b. False

10. Assets that are exempt from garnishment or levy include the debtor's primary residence and jewelry.

a. True

b. False

 Quick Quiz ANSWERS

Types of Liens

1. Statutory lien. Most states provide an auto mechanic with a statutory lien on cars that have been repaired in order to assure payment for those repairs.

2. Judicial. Farmer's Bank's lien arises from a judicial proceeding, most commonly a lawsuit filed by a creditor.

3. Statutory. The most common statutory liens are state statutes that provide contractors and subcontractors who work on real estate (e.g., constructing a new addition onto a home) an interest in the work and materials used to improve the property. However, recall the court's holding in Case 24.2 as to what constitutes a *fraudulent lien*. General Contractor's lien would not be enforceable.

4. Consensual. It is a real estate mortgage for a residence.

CHAPTER REVIEW QUESTIONS: Answers and Explanations

1. d. A provision in a debtor-creditor agreement that provides assurances of payment by the principals of a business entity in the event of a default is called a personal guaranty. The other answers are wrong because they are not related to creditors' rights.

2. a. In *Father & Sons Home Improvement v. Stuart,* the court held that Father & Sons filed a fraudulent lien.

3. b. This is a typical construction/contractor lien created by statute. Answers *a* and *c* are wrong because the lien is neither the result of a judicial proceeding nor consensual. Answer *d* is wrong because no such lien exists.

4. d. A judgment creditor who attempts to satisfy a debt using the debtor's intangible assets (such as cash) initiates garnishment. Answer *a* is wrong because levy is used for real property or real estate. Answers *b* and *c* are wrong because they are not related to garnishment.

5. a. A creditor who obtains a court order against a debtor is obtaining a *judgment* and is known as a judgment creditor.

6. b. False. When a party agrees to be liable only if the debtor defaults, she is known as a guarantor, not a surety.

7. b. False. Once a creditor obtains a judgment against a debtor, the lien is *not* automatic; the creditor must take further steps (executing the judgment) for a lien to attach.

8. a. True. A mortgage is an example of a consensual lien because the debtor consents to a lien on real estate as a condition of a loan to purchase the real estate.

9. a. True. A judgment creditor uses a local sheriff's office to execute a levy after obtaining a judgment.

10. b. False. Assets that are exempt from garnishment or levy include the debtor's primary residence, but *not* jewelry.

CHAPTER 25

Alternatives for Insolvent Borrowers

 THINKING STRATEGICALLY

©valterZ/Shutterstock

One reason to study business law from a strategic perspective is to understand the importance of strategic partnerships. When business owners face an abrupt financial liability, its principals may consider partnering with professionals who specialize in guiding financially troubled companies toward financial stability. The *Thinking Strategically* feature at the end of this chapter focuses on the process of partnering with a turnaround firm.

Learning Objectives

After studying this chapter, students who have mastered the material will be able to:

25-1 Describe the process of a workout.
25-2 Identify the role of a turnaround advisor.
25-3 Explain how an assignment for the benefit of creditors can be an alternative to bankruptcy.
25-4 Define the term *lights out* in the context of insolvency.

CHAPTER OVERVIEW

When a business venture no longer has adequate assets to maintain its operations and can no longer pay its bills as they become due in the usual course of trade and business, it is considered **insolvent**. A company's specific response to insolvency is largely dependent on the type of financial crisis. For example, if the insolvency is a result of temporary poor cash flow but the receivables will likely provide enough cash to continue operations in the future, then a bankruptcy filing may not be the best option (or even an option at all, depending on the debt-to-assets ratio of the struggling venture). On the other hand, if the venture is cash-starved because of, for example, a particularly burdensome contract or the loss of a primary customer and has no realistic way to recover from the financial crisis without some statutory protection from creditors, then the law provides the venture with the ability to hold off creditors while the business reorganizes and drafts a plan for continuing its operations in the future. This plan could include a reformation of the problematic contract.

When a business becomes insolvent, its principals have several choices in dealing with the venture's debt. Some of these options do not involve any statutory protections and, therefore, may have legal ramifications for the business and its principals. In this chapter, we discuss the alternatives insolvent organizations have. Bankruptcy is covered in the next chapter.

WORKOUTS

LO 25-1

Describe the process of a workout.

Most businesses have secured creditors (e.g., a bank) whose loans are collateralized by substantially all assets of the business and unsecured creditors. As we've discussed earlier in this unit, when a business defaults on a secured loan, the bank has options related to foreclosing on its collateral or filing a lawsuit against the business to collect the amount owed. As a practical matter, a bank representative will be in touch with the business's management to review and monitor the financial affairs of the business. If the business fails to be responsive to the bank, it is much more likely that the bank will take legal action to enforce its rights. Communicating with a creditor makes it more likely that the creditor will accept a plan designed to repay the creditor in full without any need for judicial action.

In this context, such a plan is called a *workout*. A **workout** is an attempt by a debtor to solve a financial problem through a consensual agreement with creditors outside of a court proceeding. The form of the workout is limited only by the creativity of the business and the willingness of the creditors to work with the business. From the debtor's perspective, an out-of-court workout of a financial problem should always be preferred over a bankruptcy filing. However, by definition, a workout requires the consent of creditors. One or two holdouts among the creditors may prevent a workout from being successful, in which case, bankruptcy may be necessary to force the holdouts to the table.

Prior to approaching a bank or a group of creditors with a proposed workout plan, management must first determine whether there is any way to turn the business around. In a workout, creditors are normally repaid through one or more of the following sources: (1) future cash flow, (2) new financing, or (3) equity infusion. Of these three methods, payment from a future cash flow is preferable for both the creditor and the business, but to offer a realistic repayment plan, a business must have sufficient cash to sustain its normal operations *and* generate additional cash flow for the repayment plan. New financing is often problematic because, whether it be through a new creditor or through an equity infusion (i.e., through a private outside investor), the terms and conditions may defeat the purpose of new financing by draining more cash from the business. For example, if new financing requires payment of a higher interest rate, the business must generate additional cash flow just to cover the higher interest.

Turnaround Advisors

LO 25-2

Identify the role of a turnaround advisor.

A **turnaround advisor (TA)** (also called a *turnaround manager* or *turnaround professional*) is an individual or group of individuals who assist management in the workout process. In some cases, a creditor will require that the business hire a TA as a condition of negotiating a new loan or line of credit. In other cases, businesses arrange a payment schedule directly with the TA. Not only will the business have an experienced professional who has knowledge of the workout process, a TA assists management in preparing the financial projections of the business; communicating with creditors; and formulating, negotiating, and implementing the workout plan.

A TA can also act as an interim executive who only stays as long as it takes to achieve the turnaround. Assignments can take anywhere from 3 to 24 months depending on the size of the organization and the complexity of the job. Although TA firms are most often associated with companies that are insolvent, they also work with organizations in any situation where direction, strategy, or a general operational change is needed. A TA firm also provides resources associated with turnaround such as close ties with lenders and private investor groups. TA firms typically use a five-stage process to define the problem and pursue a solution:

1. *Evaluating and assessing* the organization through management and financial analysis of strengths, weaknesses, opportunities, and threats (SWOT).
2. *Resolving acute needs* such as negotiating with key creditors or suppliers that are necessary to any workout.

3. *Restructuring internal and external causes of insolvency,* which may include redefining priorities, analyzing sales and services, and revising executive compensation structures.

4. *Stabilizing financial and human resources* by obtaining long-term financing and implementing a retention plan for key employees.

5. *Revitalizing the organization* by implementing new strategies and adhering to sound financial practices.

Workout Models

Professionals involved in a workout use one or more workout models that are meant to cater to a specific type of workout. Perhaps the most common for businesses that are insolvent is the *retrenchment model.* This involves a wide range of short-term actions intended to stabilize the company as quickly as possible. Retrenchment centers on strategically reducing the scope and size of the business's operations. This includes selling assets; focusing its efforts on smaller, profitable markets; shrinking the labor force; and developing outsourcing processes. If a company's assets include intellectual property (e.g., a patent) or a trade secret that may yield revenue if it is deployed correctly, a TA will use a *repositioning model* to generate revenue with new innovations, changing product lines, and modifying the company's image or mission. In more extreme cases, a TA firm may recommend a *replacement model* in which top-level management is replaced with an interim team while a search for new top-level managers is conducted. If the TA concludes that the established leaders do not recognize that a change in the business strategy is necessary to keep the company viable, she may recommend the replacement model to the company's creditors or board of directors as part of a larger workout plan. The *renewal model* involves significant restructuring of the business's organizational chart and a specific focus on removal of inefficient practices and using resources for innovation.

Workouts versus Bankruptcy

A workout is often an effective tool in preventing creditors from taking legal action against the business in exchange for a partial or complete repayment of the delinquent debt. If an agreement can be reached with all creditors, it will accomplish many of the same goals and objectives of a bankruptcy/reorganization filing without the expenses and burdens that are associated with a bankruptcy. Using the funds that would otherwise be used to pay the costs and expenses of a bankruptcy reorganization to repay creditors is often a good incentive for creditors to consider accepting the workout plan.

A significant disadvantage to a workout, however, is that the business has no ability to involuntarily *bind* any unwilling creditor that may refuse to consent to the workout plan. A bankruptcy court has the statutory authority to compel creditors to accept a plan. Another consideration is that when faced with a workout plan, creditors may become nervous about the business's ability to repay its debts and attempt to force the business into an involuntary bankruptcy.

TAKEAWAY CONCEPTS Workouts

- The term *workout* is an attempt by a debtor to solve a financial problem through a consensual agreement with creditors outside of a court proceeding.

- A turnaround advisor assists management in the workout process. In some cases, a creditor requires that a TA be hired as a condition of negotiating a new loan or line of credit.

- A workout accomplishes many of the same objectives of a bankruptcy/reorganization filing without the expenses and burdens that are associated with a bankruptcy.
- The primary disadvantage of a workout versus a bankruptcy is the inability to involuntarily bind an unwilling creditor.

ASSIGNMENT FOR THE BENEFIT OF CREDITORS (ABC)

LO 25-3

Explain how an assignment for the benefit of creditors can be an alternative to bankruptcy.

Either as part of a workout plan or as a stand-alone transaction, another alternative to a bankruptcy filing is an **assignment for the benefit of creditors** (often called an *ABC*). An ABC is a form of liquidation that serves as an alternative to bankruptcy and is provided either by state statute, state common law, or a combination of both. For example, in Delaware, state laws permit a debtor to make "a voluntary assignment of his or her estate, real or personal, or of any part thereof to any other person in trust for his or her creditors."[1]

An ABC can be an alternative in certain cases to overcome a short-term cash crunch when a business may still be viable in the long term. For example, suppose StartUpCo. is a privately held venture. After a number of rounds of investment, the investors have lost confidence in the business's ability to succeed and decide to halt their investments. StartUpCo.'s management is faced with a lack of cash to support its operations and has no options for commercial or private funding. It is also likely that creditors will soon demand payment. Meanwhile, StartUpCo.'s principals have been in discussions with a potential buyer but have not yet agreed to terms of the sale. Also, StartUpCo.'s commercial property lease will expire in nine months, but it's possible that the buyer might want to take over the lease. StartUpCo.'s options are:

- *Reorganization under the bankruptcy code.* While this would hold off creditors temporarily, a bankruptcy reorganization filing is problematic because it would severely impact StartUpCo.'s bargaining position with a potential buyer.
- *Liquidation bankruptcy.* This would immediately scuttle any discussion between StartUpCo. and the potential buyer.
- *ABC.* In many states, another option for companies in financial trouble is an assignment for the benefit of creditors that would provide more flexibility to StartUpCo.'s principals and allow discussion with the new buyer to continue.

Assignment Agreement

Although the procedures may vary from state to state, typically the first step in ABC involves the business and the creditor (as assignee) entering into a formal *assignment agreement.* The company provides the assignee with a list of creditors, shareholders, and other interested parties. The assignee then gives *notice* to any creditors of the assignment, setting a bar date for filing claims with the assignee that is between five and six months later. As a practical matter, most businesses work with a professional liquidation firm that takes possession of the assets and arranges the sale for the largest possible amount, then pays creditors. The liquidator has a fiduciary duty to the creditors and is usually compensated based on a percentage of the sale. Recall from our earlier discussion that a fiduciary duty is the duty to carry out the best interest of another party (i.e., creditors). After the administration of assets and the expiration of the deadline to file claims, the assignee reviews the claims that are filed. If a claim is not filed before the bar date, the claim normally will be disallowed. A creditor with a lien in the assets of the business will retain the lien, even after the assignment. If a claim is in dispute, the assignee will usually file objections with the state court for a decision.

---

[1]10 Del. C. § 7381 et seq.

In Case 25.1, a state appellate court considers whether an assignee is bound by certain terms in an agreement between the business owners and its financial advisers.

CASE 25.1 Akin Bay Company, LLC v. Von Kahle, 180 So.3d 1180 (Fla. Ct. App. 2015)

FACT SUMMARY In 2012, a group of Miami-based businesses (collectively ItalKitchen) hired Akin Bay Company, LLC (Akin Bay) as their financial adviser for the purposes of providing advice related to ItalKitchen's financial restructuring, including advice on a potential business workout and the various options such as an assignment for the benefit of creditors. ItalKitchen eventually executed an assignment for the benefit of creditors ("ABC") pursuant to Florida state statutes in favor of Von Kahle as assignee. Pursuant to the assignment, Von Kahle took possession of all the assets of ItalKitchen, which included all claims and demands that ItalKitchen had against third parties. In 2014, Von Kahle filed a lawsuit against Akin Bay alleging that it had breached its fiduciary duty to ItalKitchen and that Akin Bay had been the recipient of fraudulent transfers by ItalKitchen prior to the date of the ABC. Akin Bay asked the court to dismiss the lawsuit on the grounds that the agreement by which it supplied its services to Ital-Kitchen stipulated that any dispute between Akin Bay and ItalKitchen was to be resolved by compulsory mediation, followed, if necessary, by mandatory arbitration. Von Kahle argued that the clause was not enforceable against him in his position as assignee for the benefit of creditors because (1) he was not a party to the Akin Bay-ItalKitchen agreement and (2) the claims alleged in the complaint did not "arise out of or relate to" the agreement executed by Akin Bay and ItalKitchen. The trial court held in favor of Von Kahle, and Akin Bay appealed.

SYNOPSIS OF DECISION AND OPINION The Florida Court of Appeals reversed the trial court's decision and ruled in favor of Akin Bay. The court analyzed Florida's ABC statute and concluded that the assignee was bound by any agreement between assignors and a third party such as Akin Bay. The court also rejected Von Kahle's argument that the claims did not arise from the Akin Bay-ItalKitchen agreement. Instead, the court held that a claim arises out of or relates to an agreement if it at a minimum raises some issue the resolution of which requires reference to or construction of some portion of the contract itself.

WORDS OF THE COURT: Assignee's Rights and Obligations "The assignee stands in the shoes of the assignor for this purpose. For this reason, with minor exceptions prescribed by the statute, the assignee cannot stand in any better position than his assignor. Under [state law] an assignee is subject to all the equities and burdens which attach to the property. An assignee is in no better or worse position than his assignor. While it could have done so . . . the [Florida state legislature] did not limit the ability of third parties to assert their contractual right to enforce arbitration clauses during the assignment for benefit of creditors' liquidation process. Accordingly, the mediation and arbitration clause in the agreement in this case is enforceable against Von Kahle despite the fact that he was not a signatory to the agreement."

Case Questions

1. What was the basis for Von Kahle's lawsuit in the first place?

2. What does the court mean that Von Kahle "is in no better or worse position than his assignor"? Why is that important to the case?

3. *Focus on Critical Thinking:* The court points out that the state legislature could have limited the ability of third parties to assert their contractual right to enforce arbitration clauses during the assignment for benefit of creditors' liquidation process but did not. As a matter of fairness, should the state legislature limit the rights of the parties in connection to arbitration? Should the legislature reform any other part of the ABC process? Explain.

FIGURE 25.1   StartUpCo.'s ABC Process

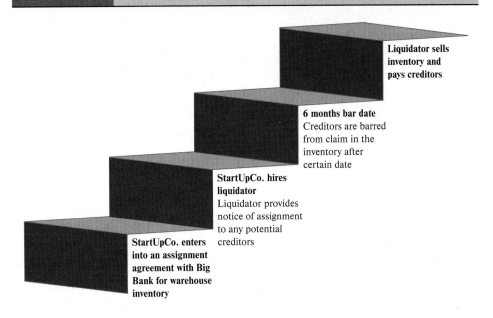

- **StartUpCo. enters into an assignment agreement with Big Bank for warehouse inventory**
- **StartUpCo. hires liquidator** Liquidator provides notice of assignment to any potential creditors
- **6 months bar date** Creditors are barred from claim in the inventory after certain date
- **Liquidator sells inventory and pays creditors**

Distribution

Upon resolving all claim disputes, the assignee distributes the funds first to any creditor that has a valid lien on assets, second to pay the fees and costs associated with administering the transaction, and third to pay priority unsecured creditors. Any cash remaining is distributed back to pay the owners of the business. If the funds are not sufficient to pay a particular class of creditors in full, the creditors in that class receive pro rata payments, and the classes junior to that class (e.g., unsecured creditors) do not receive payment. Figure 25.1 illustrates this timeline using our StartUpCo. example.

ABC Statutory Requirements

Although some states, such as California and Florida, do not require a public court filing for the parties to enter into an ABC, other states require a filing with a state court or state agency to either initiate or complete an ABC. This means that a nonjudicial ABC can be a much faster method for resolving creditor claims provided that the assignee has had time to perform due diligence on the sale and any alternatives. Given the speed at which it can be done, in the right situation an ABC can permit a going concern (i.e., a business still operating) sale to be achieved. Other states use a system of judicial oversight to be sure that no favored creditor is paid at the expense of other creditors. For example, New Jersey's ABC statute sets out the ABC proceeding as a state court–administered liquidation proceeding similar to a Chapter 7 bankruptcy proceeding whereby an individual, partnership, or corporation in financial distress can liquidate its assets in an orderly fashion to equitably pay its creditors.[2] Case 25.2 provides some insight into the process of a court-supervised ABC system.

---

[2] 44 New Jersey Practice, Debtor-Creditor Law and Practice § 3.1, at 109.

FACT SUMMARY Bierman was the principal owner, officer, and director of Export Transport Co., Inc. (Export), a New Jersey corporation that provided warehousing and refrigerated ocean container services to its clients. Export leased vehicles from Penske Truck Leasing Co. (Penske). After Export failed to make the required lease payments, Penske filed an action seeking to recover the amount due and obtained a $548,028.51 default judgment against Export. Penske was not Export's only creditor. According to documents related to an assignment for the benefit of creditors (ABC agreement), Export had dozens of other creditors and was over $2.5 million in debt. In November 2013, Bierman formed Cool Trans NJ, a single-member limited liability company. Cool Trans provided trucking and warehousing services to many of Export's clients. Export discontinued its business operations in February 2014.

Pursuant to New Jersey's ABC law, Export entered into an ABC agreement with Bruck, an attorney specializing in such matters, as the assignee. As part of the agreement, Bierman prepared a "verified inventory and list of creditors," which listed Penske's judgment against Export as a debt of the corporation. Bruck, as assignee, provided notice of the filing to Penske. Once Bruck had completed the statutory requirements of an assignee, he submitted a proposed settlement agreement to the appropriate state court, which approved it in 2015. Penske then filed a complaint against Bierman and Cool Trans arguing that the settlement agreement should not have been approved and seeking to hold Bierman and Cool Trans liable to Penske for the judgment it held against Export. Penske alleged that Bierman and Cool Trans were the successors in interest to Export and, therefore, Penske should be entitled to reach Bierman's and Cool Trans's assets. Penske also asserted breach of fiduciary duty and fraudulent conveyance claims against Bierman and Cool Trans. Bierman and Cool Trans countered that Penske's claim was barred because the settlement agreement was the product of Bruck as assignee, who had statutory authority to decide which creditors are paid which amounts.

SYNOPSIS OF DECISION AND OPINION The New Jersey Superior Court's Appellate Division affirmed the trial's court decision to approve the

settlement agreement and ruled in favor of Bierman and Cool Trans NJ. The court pointed out that under the state ABC statute, the assignee has a dual capacity. First, the assignee stands in the shoes of the assignor with general powers to act in his stead as successor. Second, the assignee also represents the assignor's entire creditor constituency. Bruck, the assignee, followed the statutory procedure and made a reasonable calculation about the best method for preserving and distributing the assets. Thus, Penske's complaint was barred by the assignment for the benefit of creditors statute.

WORDS OF THE COURT: Best Interest of All Creditors "[In concluding] that the settlement of all claims against Bierman and Cool Trans NJ for $50,000 was in the best interest of all creditors, and that the settlement was fair and reasonable under the circumstances, [the trial court] found that Bruck [as assignee] fully explained his rationale for the settlement. Although the $50,000 was only a fraction of the possible claims against Bierman and Cool Trans, the [trial court] noted that Bierman and his business entities had little or no assets and that a settlement, subject to the default provisions built into it, would 'ensure that there'll be some money paid.' The settlement would also save the cost of litigating its possible claims and defending against Bierman's claims, thereby preserving more funds for the creditors. Finally, the [trial court] found that the settlement would deter Bierman and the business entities from initiating a bankruptcy proceeding, which would jeopardize the ability of the creditors to recover anything from Export's [assets]."

Case Questions

1. Why did Penske object to the settlement that was proposed by the assignee?

2. What were some of the reasons that Bruck as assignee chose to settle with "only a fraction of the possible claims against Bierman and Cool Trans"?

3. *Focus on Critical Thinking:* Why do you think that Bierman formed Cool Trans when he did? Was Bierman's conduct ethical? Is he using the ABC law as a shield against his own misconduct? Explain.

Shareholder and Director Approval

As a matter of corporate law, businesses require both board and shareholder approval for an ABC because it involves the transfer to the assignee of substantially all of the corporation's assets. This makes ABCs impractical for publicly held corporations and for privately held corporations with a large number of shareholders. Although states provide some protection for the business, there is no automatic stay in an ABC as one has in bankruptcy. That means there is nothing that blocks a creditor from attempting to collect the debt irrespective of any ABC agreement. For creditors, an ABC process generally involves the submission to the assignee of a proof of claim by a stated deadline or bar date. Employee and other claim priorities are governed by state law and may involve different amounts than apply under the Bankruptcy Code. Other potentially important ABC statutory provisions include:

- *Landlord claims.* Unlike bankruptcy, there generally is no cap imposed on a landlord's claim for breach of a real property lease in an ABC.
- *Private sales.* In many states, sales by the assignee of the company's assets are completed as a private transaction without approval of a court.

Recall our hypothetical StartUpCo.'s dilemma. The realistic prospect of a buyer in the near term may influence whether our hypothetical company should choose an ABC or another approach. Unlike bankruptcy, where the publicity for the company and its officers and directors will be negative, in an assignment, the transaction can be fashioned as "assets of StartUpCo. acquired by Newco," instead of "StartUpCo. files bankruptcy." Moreover, the assignment process removes from the board of directors and management of the troubled company the responsibility for and burden of winding down the business and disposing of the assets. Depending on the value to be generated by a sale, these considerations may lead the company to select one approach over the other available options. Also, if the buyer decides to take the real property lease, the landlord will need to consent to the lease assignment because the ABC process generally cannot force a landlord or other third party to accept assignment of a lease.

TAKEAWAY CONCEPTS Assignment for the Benefit of Creditors

- An assignment for the benefit of creditors (ABC) is a form of liquidation that serves as an alternative to bankruptcy and is provided either by state statute, state common law, or a combination of both.
- Although the procedures may vary from state to state, ABC typically begins when the business and the creditor (as assignee) enter into a formal assignment agreement, which sets the process in motion.
- The business assigning assets typically hires a professional liquidation firm that provides notice to all creditors, sells the assets and distributes the proceeds to creditors, and returns excess cash to business owners.

OUT OF EXISTENCE

Out of existence (also known as the "lights-out option") is a nonstatutory option in which a venture simply ceases operations without paying creditors. Usually the debtor company files an out-of-existence certificate or articles of dissolution with the state corporation bureau and simply ceases doing business. However, the company's debts are still valid obligations, and a creditor may pursue a debt collection lawsuit to collect any available cash or assets to satisfy the debt. In fact, some states require that all creditors be notified before the business

LO 25-4

Define the term
lights out in
the context of
insolvency.

is recognized as legally dissolved. Out of existence is a particularly dangerous option if the debt has been secured through a personal guaranty by principals of the business (discussed earlier). However, if the debtor has no assets, no personal guaranties exist, and the debt is not substantial enough to make legal methods to collect economically viable for creditors, the lights-out option is the quickest and least expensive option. Figure 25.2 is a sample of an out-of-existence certificate required by state authorities.

FIGURE 25.2   Sample Out-of-Existence Certificate

REV-238 CM (04-13)

pennsylvania
DEPARTMENT OF REVENUE
BUREAU OF COMPLIANCE
OUT OF EXISTENCE/MERGER SECTION
PO BOX 280947
HARRISBURG PA 17128-0947

717-783-6052
TT# 800-447-3020 (Services for taxpayers
with special hearing and/or speaking needs only)

**OUT OF EXISTENCE/WITHDRAWAL
AFFIDAVIT**

PLEASE PRINT OR TYPE INFORMATION

DEPARTMENT USE ONLY

Revenue ID _____

THIS FORM MUST BE PROPERLY SIGNED AND NOTARIZED

NOTE:

- If filing a final RCT-101 corporate report for 2002 and forward, complete the "corporate status change" section in the RCT-101 in lieu of filing this form.
- The reverse side of this form must be completed. Section A pertains to a PA corporation or a foreign corporation that operated wholly within Pennsylvania. Section B pertains to all other foreign corporations.
- If you wish to be notified by email that the corporation is out of business, please provide email address on reverse side.

Date of Incorporation or
Certificate of Authority _____   Account ID/Revenue ID _____

State of Incorporation _____   Entity ID (EIN) _____

Name of Corporation/Taxpayer _____

I, the "Affiant," was connected with the above corporation and have knowledge of its affairs. Said corporation ceased to transact business in

Pennsylvania on or about* _____ , and all assets were sold, assigned or
                            Month   Day   Year

distributed on _____ , and since that time, the corporation has not owned
                Month   Day   Year

any property located in Pennsylvania, nor maintained an office therein, nor has performed any sales activity and does not intend to transact further business in the commonwealth.

*If corporation never transacted business or held assets in Pennsylvania, please use the words "NEVER TRANSACTED BUSINESS" in place of a cessation date.

The filing of this affidavit does not affect the status of the Certificate of Incorporation/Authority of this corporation but does permit the Department of State to relinquish the use of the present name of the corporation to another corporation.

This affidavit is not to be filed by a PA corporation utilizing its PA charter to conduct business in another state. Out-of-state corporations soliciting business in Pennsylvania are subject to tax and should file this document only upon ceasing activity in Pennsylvania.

Sworn to and subscribed before me this

_____ day of _____ , year _____

(Notary Public, District Justice or Authorized Agent,
Department of Revenue)

My commission expires _____ , year _____

Please Sign After Printing.
_____
(Notary Signature and Seal)

Please Sign After Printing.
_____
(Signature of Affiant)

TITLE

_____
(Present address of Affiant)

Telephone Number _____

PLEASE PRINT OR TYPE INFORMATION
NO FILING FEE

THIS SCHEDULE MUST BE COMPLETED. ENTER "NONE" ONLY IF THE CORPORATION HAS NO ASSETS AND/OR LIABILITIES.

DISTRIBUTION OF ASSETS

Please Print or Type

Name of Corporation	Revenue ID/ Corp. Box #
Business Address	Date of Final Distribution
City State ZIP Code	MM/DD/YYYY

A. CORPORATION OPERATING 100% WITHIN PA MUST COMPLETE THIS SECTION (Provide copies of Federal Form 1099-DIV)	SHARES OF STOCK OF EACH STOCKHOLDER		MONEY RECEIVED BY EACH STOCKHOLDER		AMOUNT AND NATURE OF OTHER ASSETS RECEIVED BY EACH STOCKHOLDER		
	NUMBER	PAR VALUE	DATE	AMOUNT	DATE	DESCRIPTION	AMOUNT
Stockholder Name Social Security Number			MM/DD/YYYY		MM/DD/YYYY		
Street Address City State ZIP Code							
Stockholder Name Social Security Number							
Street Address City State ZIP Code							
Stockholder Name Social Security Number							
Street Address City State ZIP Code							
Stockholder Name Social Security Number							
Street Address City State ZIP Code							
Stockholder Name Social Security Number							
Street Address City State ZIP Code							

B. CORPORATIONS WITHDRAWING FROM PA BUT CONTINUING OPERATIONS OUTSIDE OF PA MUST PROVIDE THE FOLLOWING INFORMATION AND/OR DOCUMENT(S).
1. FULL DETAILS OF DISPOSITION OF PA PROPERTY. ATTACH COPIES OF FEDERAL SCHEDULE D AND/OR FEDERAL FORM 4797, IF APPLICABLE.
2. PLEASE INDICATE IF SALES IN PA WILL CONTINUE AFTER DATE OF CESSATION. IF SO, HOW WILL THEY BE NEGOTIATED AND BY WHOM?

ATTACH STATEMENT CONTAINING THE REQUIRED INFORMATION IF ADDITIONAL SPACE IS NEEDED.
IF ANY INDIVIDUAL OR CORPORATION OTHER THAN STOCKHOLDERS AND CREDITORS RECEIVED ASSETS, LIST NAMES AND ADDRESSES OF EACH AND AMOUNT OR VALUE RECEIVED BY EACH.

- IF ANY CONSIDERATION WAS PAID FOR ANY OF THE ASSETS, STATE NAME AND ADDRESS OF INDIVIDUAL OR CORPORATION MAKING SUCH PAYMENT AND EXACT AMOUNT PAID BY EACH. (ATTACH A SEPARATE SHEET TO THIS FORM.)
- IF ANY MONEY OR PROPERTY REMAINS UNDISTRIBUTED, STATE AMOUNT, NATURE AND VALUE OF SAME, AND STATE WHY IT HAS NOT BEEN DISTRIBUTED. (ATTACH A SEPARATE SHEET TO THIS FORM.)
- IF ANY REAL ESTATE HAS BEEN DISTRIBUTED OR SOLD WITHIN THE FINAL TAX PERIOD, GIVE THE DATE OF RECORDING TITLE TRANSFER WITH LOCAL RECORDER OF DEEDS. DATE: _____
- EMAIL: _____

Name of Person Making this Report	Signature Please Sign After Printing.	Title	Date
Current Street Address	City	State	ZIP Code

Source: Pennsylvania Department of Revenue

TAKEAWAY CONCEPTS   Out of Existence

- Out of existence is a nonstatutory option in which a business ceases its operations. It is sometimes called the "lights-out option."

THINKING STRATEGICALLY

©valterZ/Shutterstock

Turning It Around

PROBLEM: As we explored earlier in this chapter, some liabilities and problems in business occur abruptly (e.g., loss of a major customer) and may blindside management, who must act quickly to pivot their strategy toward financial recovery. While some turnaround advisors are hired by banks to work with insolvent debtors, experts recommend that business owners bring in a turnaround advisor before financial distress turns into financial disaster. How do we find a qualified firm to help us?

STRATEGIC SOLUTION: Use the resources of the Turnaround Management Association (TMA), a business association established in 1988 that administers a certification process to become a Certified Turnaround Professional (CTP) or a Certified Turnaround Analyst (CTA). The TMA is a global nonprofit comprised of corporate renewal professionals with more than 8,300 members in 55 chapters, including 32 in North America.[3]

GOLD STANDARD

The TMA oversees a rigorous certification process that is seen as the gold standard in the turnaround world. Prospective CTPs must have five years of consulting work under their belt, with a minimum of three years focused on corporate renewal. They must provide three client case studies, supply names of individuals who can verify their work, and submit to a background check. Further, they must pass a three-part examination on management, law, finance, and accounting. Lastly,

[3]https://turnaround.org/certification.

assuming all of these hurdles are passed, the applicants' names are posted in the *Journal of Corporate Renewal* for 60 days to solicit objections. Each person who achieves certification must complete at least 125 hours of continuing education over a five-year period.[4]

POINT OF DEPARTURE

Before engaging a CTP, experts recommend that business owners interview the prospective CTP/CTA by raising important questions:[5]

- What kind of experience does the prospective CTP have in our industry?
- How long will the initial engagement last? What is a typical time frame?

- What is the fee structure? Is it a flat fee, hourly, or based on performance?
- What types of measurable goals are typically set when starting an engagement?

QUESTIONS

1. What are some scenarios where a CTP or CTA might be brought in to assist a company?
2. Use your favorite search engine to find the Turnaround Management Association's website. What specific services do CTPs provide? What is the difference between a CTP and a CTA?
3. Look up a turnaround firm using the TMA's database. What types of services do they provide? What kinds of backgrounds, education, and certifications do their CTP/CTAs have (e.g., accounting, law, financial)?

[4]"Hiring a Turnaround Specialist," *All Business,* January 2015.
[5]Marc Kramer, "A Turnaround Specialist's 15 Skills," *The Street,* Feb. 13, 2009.

KEY TERMS

Insolvent p. 428 Condition in which a business venture no longer has adequate assets to maintain its operations and can no longer pay its bills as they become due in the usual course of trade and business.

Workout p. 429 An attempt by a debtor to solve a financial problem through a consensual agreement with creditors outside of a court proceeding.

Turnaround advisor (TA) p. 429 Individual or group of individual professionals who assist management in the

workout process; also called a *turnaround manager* or *turnaround professional.*

Assignment for the benefit of creditors (ABC) p. 431 Form of liquidation that serves as an alternative to bankruptcy and is provided either by state statute, state common law, or a combination of both.

Out of existence p. 435 Nonstatutory option in which a venture simply ceases operations without paying creditors.

CASE SUMMARY 25.1 Sherwood Partners as ABC Assignee of Thinklink v. Lycos, 394 F.3d 1198 (9th Cir. 2005)

State Statutes and Bankruptcy

Thinklink Corp., a unified messaging service provider, entered into an agreement with Lycos, which operates a network of websites. Lycos agreed to promote Thinklink's messaging service on Lycos websites exclusively for two years. Thinklink eventually defaulted on one of its payments; Lycos nevertheless continued to display

links to Thinklink's messaging service. Lycos and Thinklink renegotiated their agreement, shortening the exclusivity period to 90 days and reducing Thinklink's remaining payments from over $17 million to $1 million plus stock. Thinklink delivered the $1 million but not the stock, and about two months later made a voluntary general assignment for the benefit of creditors to Sherwood Partners. Sherwood shut down Thinklink's business and sued Lycos in state court to recover the $1 million payment as a preferential transfer. Lycos argued that the ABC statute was preempted by the Bankruptcy Code and could not be enforced.

CASE QUESTIONS

1. Who prevails and why?
2. Why did Thinklink agree to an ABC agreement with Sherwood?

CASE SUMMARY 25.2 Moecker v. Antoine et al., 845 So.2d 904 (Fla. Ct. App. 2003)

Status of Claims

Thomas Antoine and James Matthews were employees of First Street, which lent money to residential property buyers who did not generally qualify for bank or government-sponsored lending programs. In July 1998, jointly with their respective wives, they purchased shares of common stock in First Street in response to a solicitation made to First Street employees by the management of First Street. Mr. and Mrs. Antoine purchased 0.1718 share of common stock for a price of $125,000, while the Matthews purchased 0.0687 share of common stock for a price of $50,000. In December 1998, First Street and Michael Moecker & Associates, Inc. executed an assignment

for the benefit of creditors. First Street was thereafter declared an insolvent corporation, and on December 15, 1998, Moecker filed a petition in the circuit court commencing an ABC proceeding under Florida statutes. The Antoines filed a claim in the amount of $125,000 expressly representing that the basis of the claim was as shareholders. Moecker objected to the claims, asserting that because the appellees made equity contributions to First Street, not loans, they were not creditors.

CASE QUESTIONS

1. Are the Antoines creditors? Explain.
2. What is Moecker's objection to the claim?

CHAPTER REVIEW QUESTIONS

1. **A business that cannot pay its bills as they become due in the usual course of trade and business is:**
   a. Inadequate.
   b. Insolvent.
   c. Inert.
   d. Insecure.
   e. Insincere.

2. **In a workout, creditors are typically paid from which future source(s)?**
   a. Cash flow
   b. New financing
   c. Equity infusion
   d. All of the above
   e. None of the above

3. **In most states, the process of assignment for the benefit of creditors starts with a(n):**
   a. Court order.
   b. Lawsuit.
   c. Assignment agreement.

   d. Bankruptcy filing.
   e. Decree.

4. **As a matter of corporate law, who must consent to an ABC assignment?**
   a. Shareholders
   b. Board of directors
   c. Officers
   d. A and B
   e. B and C

5. **The out-of-existence option is also known as the _____ option.**
   a. Lights-out
   b. Insolvent
   c. Bankruptcy
   d. Assignment-of-assets
   e. Cash flow

6. **A turnaround advisor typically is a permanent part of the management team.**
   a. True
   b. False

7. The primary advantage of a workout is the business's ability to bind unwilling creditors.

   a. True

   b. False

8. In most states, there is no cap imposed on a landlord's claim for breach of a real property lease in an ABC.

   a. True

   b. False

9. An assignment for the benefit of creditors (ABC) is a form of liquidation.

   a. True

   b. False

10. When a business owner files an out-of-existence certificate, it extinguishes all business debts.

    a. True

    b. False

CHAPTER REVIEW QUESTIONS: Answers and Explanations

1. **b.** A business that cannot pay its bills as they become due in the usual course of trade and business is insolvent.

2. **d.** All are sources used to pay creditors in a workout.

3. **c.** In most states, the process of assignment for the benefit of creditors is outside the judicial system.

4. **d.** As a matter of corporate law, businesses require both board and shareholder approval for an ABC because it involves the transfer to the assignee of substantially all of the corporation's assets.

5. **a.**

6. **b. False.** A TA only works with a company during the turnaround.

7. **b. False.** A business does *not* have the ability to bind unwilling creditors.

8. **a. True.**

9. **a. True.**

10. **b. False.** Debts are not extinguished.

CHAPTER 26

Bankruptcy

©valterZ/Shutterstock

What happens when a business fails or when a person is otherwise unable to pay his creditors? This chapter explores the law of bankruptcy, an essential aspect of our market system. In addition, this chapter's *Thinking Strategically* will discuss the practice of strategic bankruptcy: when a business or individual uses bankruptcy law strategically to avoid paying their creditors on time.

Learning Objectives

After studying this chapter, students who have mastered the material will be able to:

26-1   Explain how the Bankruptcy Code is organized and the effect of the automatic stay.
26-2   Articulate the steps in a Chapter 7 liquidation bankruptcy.
26-3   Differentiate between a Chapter 7 bankruptcy and a Chapter 11 reorganization filing.
26-4   Describe the process of a Chapter 13 filing and the impact of the means test on the debtor.

CHAPTER OVERVIEW

There are circumstances when a debtor's best alternative is protection from creditors via **bankruptcy** protection laws. The concept of forgiveness of debt and protection of borrowers from creditors has deep historical roots that some scholars have traced back to the Old Testament. The underlying concept and public policy objectives behind bankruptcy protection are to give debtors a "fresh start" and to prevent creditors from gaining unfair advantage over each other in being paid. For the most part, bankruptcy proceedings are a matter of federal law. State courts can have some limited involvement in issues that involve the borrower (usually called the *debtor* in a bankruptcy context) in one way or another, but they generally do not have any jurisdiction over bankruptcy proceedings.

BANKRUPTCY CODE

The law of bankruptcy is found within federal statutes called the Bankruptcy Code. The starting place for all bankruptcy matters is the federal bankruptcy court. The Bankruptcy Code is divided into chapters, and often the reference to someone filing for bankruptcy protection is known as "filing for Chapter 11." The most common forms of bankruptcy are Chapter 7 (liquidation of the debtor's assets and discharge of debts), Chapter 11 (business reorganization), and Chapter 13 (debt adjustment and repayment of consumer debt).

In summary, Chapter 7 is what most people think of when they think of bankruptcy, and an individual Chapter 7 usually results in a discharge of debts. Chapter 11, by contrast, is typically used to reorganize a business, while Chapter 13 bankruptcy, which is often called a wage earner's plan, enables individuals with regular income to develop a plan to repay all or part of their debts.

One of the primary purposes of bankruptcy is to discharge certain debts to give an individual debtor a "fresh start." Other chapters of the Bankruptcy Code contain definitions, describe procedural aspects of bankruptcy proceedings, and contain special provisions for bankruptcies by municipalities, stockbrokers, and railroads. Congress amended the Bankruptcy Code in 2005 with the Bankruptcy Abuse Prevention and Consumer Protection Act, which imposed additional requirements on those seeking protection under the Bankruptcy Code. The specific provisions of the 2005 amendment are covered later in this chapter.

LO 26-1

Explain how the Bankruptcy Code is organized and the effect of the automatic stay.

 QUICK QUIZ Petitions under Chapter 7, Chapter 11, or Chapter 13 of the Bankruptcy Code

Which chapter of the Bankruptcy Code applies?

1. An individual debtor or wage earner with regular income who wishes to develop a payment plan to repay all or part of her debts.
2. An individual debtor whose primary purpose is to discharge his debts.
3. A business debtor who prefers to remain in business and avoid liquidation.

Answers to this Quick Quiz are provided at the end of the chapter.

Automatic Stay

Filing for bankruptcy protects the debtor through an immediate **automatic stay**, which legally prohibits creditors from either initiating or continuing any debt collection action against the debtor or her property. The stay is a powerful legal tool because it stops all collection efforts, all harassment, and all foreclosure actions. It permits the debtor to attempt a repayment or reorganization plan or simply to be relieved of the financial pressures resulting from a financial crisis. The stay also allows the bankruptcy court to deal with the debtor's assets and creditors in a single forum where the rights of all concerned may be heard at once.

Bankruptcy Trustee

The Bankruptcy Code provides for the appointment of a **bankruptcy trustee** in certain cases. A trustee is appointed in cases where the debtor seeks liquidation and discharge of debts (Chapter 7) or in cases where the debtor is a consumer attempting to repay much of the debt over a period of time (Chapter 13). The trustee, often an attorney highly skilled in bankruptcy law, is charged with the duty of collecting the debtor's available assets, known as the **bankruptcy estate**, and reducing those assets to cash for distribution, preserving the interests of both the debtor and the creditors. Federal law gives the trustee extensive authority and power to accomplish this objective. For example, the bankruptcy trustee may void certain transfers that are considered to be an unfair advantage of one creditor over another. These are known as **voidable transfers**.

The most common voidable transfer is a *preferential transfer*. A preferential transfer occurs when the debtor makes a payment to satisfy a prebankruptcy petition debt to a creditor within 90 days of the petition. If the creditor receives more than it would have under the liquidation proceedings, the trustee may void the transfer. In this event, the assets are taken back from the creditor and replaced in the bankruptcy estate. The transfer is not considered preferential if the debtor simply pays a bill from a creditor in the ordinary course of business. Preferential transfers to insiders (including relatives, partners, officers, and directors of an individual or corporate debtor) are also voidable. Under certain circumstances, any insider transfers made within one year of the petition filing can be voided and placed back into the bankruptcy estate. Additionally, a transfer is voidable as a fraudulent transfer if it occurs when a debtor transfers property to a third person within one year of the petition filing with intent to delay, hinder, or defraud creditors.

For example, suppose that Eyre is the sole owner of Jane's Pretzel Company (JPC). After several years of reasonable success in business, JPC experiences financial difficulty and owes its creditors $100,000. With only $5,000 in assets, JPC files for Chapter 7 liquidation and discharge. After JPC files the petition, a trustee is appointed and discovers several transfers out of the ordinary course of business. First, two weeks before JPC's petition for bankruptcy, Eyre paid off the entire balance owed to an important vendor on a loan secured by Eyre's personal guaranty. If the trustee determines that the vendor obtained more than it would have from the distribution of JPC's assets under the Bankruptcy Code (which is likely in this situation, given the company's assets versus its debts), the payment can be voided and the money put back into the bankruptcy estate. Second, Eyre borrowed $20,000 from her brother-in-law and, despite the fact that the loan was to be paid over five years, Eyre paid back the entire amount one month before filing for bankruptcy. That transaction would be classified as an *insider preferential transfer,* and the trustee would void the transfer and recover the payment from Eyre's brother-in-law on behalf of the bankruptcy estate.

TAKEAWAY CONCEPTS Bankruptcy Code

- Upon filing for bankruptcy, a trustee is appointed by the bankruptcy court to protect the remaining bankruptcy assets, known as the bankruptcy estate, under Chapter 7 (liquidation) or Chapter 13 (individual repayment).
- A trustee has the legal power to void fraudulent or preferential transfers that the debtor made to certain creditors before filing for bankruptcy.

LO 26-2

Articulate the steps in a Chapter 7 liquidation bankruptcy.

CHAPTER 7: LIQUIDATION

Chapter 7 bankruptcy is perhaps the most extreme measure a business or individual can take. In essence, the debtor agrees to have most of his property liquidated and the cash distributed to creditors. In exchange, the bankruptcy court gives legal protection to the debtor by discharging any remaining debts. For example, suppose WidgetCo has $50,000 in debts and only $10,000 in nonexempt assets. The bankruptcy court will distribute the $10,000 to creditors, and the remaining debt ($40,000) will be discharged. WidgetCo will be out of business, but its principals will get a fresh start and will not have to pay any of the debts incurred. Chapter 7 outlines a very specific procedure for discharge of debt.

Bankruptcy Petition and Stay

The proceedings are started in the bankruptcy court when a bankruptcy petition is filed. The petition can be either voluntary or involuntary. A **voluntary bankruptcy petition** is filed by the debtor and includes the names of creditors; a list of debts; and a list of the debtor's assets, income, and expenses. In order to qualify for protection under Chapter 7, the debtor's income must be less than the average income in her home state (this requirement is known as the *means test*). An **involuntary bankruptcy petition** is one that is filed against a debtor by a group of three or more creditors with an unsecured aggregate claim of at least $15,775 who claim that the debtor is failing to pay the debt as it comes due. This is an extreme measure, and involuntary petitions are relatively rare. This option poses some risk for the creditors because the Bankruptcy Code allows a company to recover damages against creditors who attempt to drive a debtor into bankruptcy but are unsuccessful.

As discussed earlier, the filing of a petition gives immediate protection to the debtor. This means that creditors must suspend all collection activity as of the day the petition is filed. Note that the suspension is temporary and designed to give the bankruptcy court the time necessary to decide the validity of the petition.

Order for Relief and Trustee Appointment

Once the court determines the validity of the petition, an order for relief is granted, the automatic stay effectively becomes *permanent,* and a bankruptcy estate is created consisting of all the debtor's assets. Once the order of relief is granted, the court appoints an interim bankruptcy trustee to oversee the case. A *permanent trustee* is elected at the first meeting of creditors. Once appointed, the trustee creates a bankruptcy estate. Note that the trustee is a representative of the court and *not* a representative of either the debtor or the creditors. The trustee has the responsibility of administering the bankruptcy proceedings in accordance with the law. The trustee's primary responsibility is to preserve the bankruptcy estate and ensure that the assets are distributed in accordance with the Bankruptcy Code.

In Case 26.1, a federal court considers the motion of a bankruptcy trustee suing for recovery of funds used in a Ponzi scheme.

CASE 26.1 Kelley v. Cypress Financial Trading Co., L.P., 518 B.R. 373 (N.D. Tex. 2014)

FACT SUMMARY In 2009, Thomas Petters ("Petters") was convicted of operating a $3.6 billion Ponzi scheme[1] and sentenced to 50 years in jail. Using Petters Company Inc. ("PCI") as a vehicle for accepting investors' money, Petters fraudulently convinced investors that he was purchasing electronic goods and selling them to large retailers. One of those investors was Cypress Financial Trading Company, L.P. ("Cypress"). During the Ponzi scheme, Cypress was paid more than $11.4 million. After the Ponzi scheme was uncovered, PCI filed for bankruptcy and attorney Douglas Kelley ("Kelley") was appointed as bankruptcy trustee. In an attempt to recover as much as possible for the bankruptcy estate, Kelley sued Cypress and its individual partners, alleging that the funds paid to Cypress were fraudulent transfers. Cypress then filed a petition for bankruptcy, reporting that it had no assets. In response, Kelley filed a motion

to have Cypress's bankruptcy petition dismissed on the basis that it was filed as a litigation delay tactic and therefore constituted a bad faith filing. The bankruptcy court denied the motion and Kelley appealed.

SYNOPSIS OF DECISION AND OPINION The U.S. District Court for the Northern District of Texas reversed the bankruptcy court's decision and ruled in favor of Kelley. The court noted that the twin pillars of bankruptcy are: (1) the discharge of the debtor and (2) the satisfaction of valid claims against the estate. Since Cypress was a corporation, it could not obtain discharge from a Chapter 7 filing. Therefore, the first pillar of bankruptcy could not be achieved through this bankruptcy filing. Additionally, since Cypress had no assets for the trustee to liquidate to pay claims, it could not achieve the second pillar of bankruptcy. The court

(continued)

---

[1] A Ponzi scheme, also called a *pyramid scheme,* is a fraudulent investment arrangement whereby the wrongdoer uses proceeds from new investors to pay existing investors higher-than-market returns, thereby creating the illusion that the profits have been generated through legitimate methods.

reasoned that since neither pillar of bankruptcy could be achieved, none of the parties to this bankruptcy proceeding would be prejudiced by dismissal of the bankruptcy petition.

WORDS OF THE COURT: Bad Faith "A finding of bad faith can be cause for dismissal of a Chapter 7 proceeding. [E]very bankruptcy statute since 1898 has incorporated literally, or by judicial interpretation, a standard of good faith for the commencement, prosecution, and confirmation of bankruptcy proceedings. . . . Resort[ing] to the protection of bankruptcy laws is not proper when 'there is no going concern to preserve, there are no employees to protect, and there is no hope of rehabilitation.' . . .

No legitimate end will be served by keeping this case on the docket."

Case Questions

1. Why did Kelley believe that Cypress acted in bad faith?

2. Why did Kelley sue Cypress in the first place?

3. *Focus on Critical Thinking:* Isn't Cypress a victim here? If there was no indication that Cypress knew that Petters was running a Ponzi scheme, should it be held responsible for paying back any money it received? Is it fair to the other investors who lost all of their money in the scheme if Cypress is allowed to keep the money it received?

Creditors' Meeting and the Bankruptcy Estate

Within 30 days of the order of relief, the bankruptcy court must schedule a meeting of creditors. The debtor (usually along with an attorney) must appear and submit to questioning by the creditors regarding the debtor's assets, financial affairs, and any attempt to conceal assets or income. After the meeting of creditors and election of the trustee, the trustee takes possession of the bankruptcy estate. The estate consists of the debtor's interests in real, personal, tangible, and intangible property—no matter where that property is located at the time the petition is filed. Property acquired after the petition does not become part of the bankruptcy estate. The trustee's responsibility is to collect all assets that are legally required to be liquidated for the benefit of the creditors. Trustees separate exempt and nonexempt property, recover any improper transfers of funds before or during the filing of the petition, sell or otherwise dispose of the property, and finally distribute the proceeds to creditors.

When a debtor is an individual, not all property is subject to liquidation. The debtor is entitled to hold on to certain assets. These assets are known as *exempt assets*. Note that in a Chapter 7 bankruptcy of a business entity, there are no exempt assets. All assets must be liquidated. For individuals, some examples of exemptions are:

- Up to $23,675 in equity in the debtor's primary residence (homestead exemption).
- Interest in a motor vehicle up to $3,775.
- Interest up to $600 for a particular item, household goods, and furnishings (aggregate total limited to $12,625).
- Interest in jewelry up to $1,600.
- Right to receive Social Security and certain welfare benefits; alimony and child support; education savings accounts; and certain pension benefits.
- Right to receive certain personal injury and other awards up to $23,675.

Distribution and Discharge

Once the trustee has administered the bankruptcy estate, the trustee then distributes the proceeds to creditors in an order of priority set by the Bankruptcy Code. Secured creditors are paid first and in full so long as the value of the collateral equals or exceeds the amount of their security interests. Unsecured creditors are paid from the remaining proceeds of the

TABLE 26.1 Order of Priority for Unsecured Creditors

1. Administration expenses—court costs and trustee and attorney fees.
2. Involuntary bankruptcy expenses incurred from date of filing to order of relief.
3. Unpaid wages and commissions earned within 90 days.
4. Unsecured claims for contributions for employee benefits within 180 days prior to filing.
5. Claims by farmers or fishermen.
6. Consumer deposits before the petition in connection with the purchase, lease, or rental of property.
7. Paternity, alimony, maintenance, and support debts.
8. Certain taxes and penalties due to government units, such as income and property taxes.
9. Claims of general creditors.

bankruptcy estate (if any). The order of payment for unsecured debtors is specified in the Bankruptcy Code. Table 26.1 lists the order of priority for unsecured creditors. Note that some claims also have dollar amount limits and therefore some unsecured creditors will be only partially paid for the debt.

Some debts are *nondischargeable*. These include:

- Claims for federal, state, and local taxes (including fines and penalties related to the taxes) within two years of the petition filing.
- Debts incurred within 90 days of the petition for luxury goods of more than $650 from a single creditor or cash advances in excess of $925 obtained by a debtor using credit cards or revolving lines of credit within 70 days of the petition.
- Alimony, maintenance, and child support.
- Debts related to willful or malicious injury to a person or property.
- Debts related to court-ordered punitive damages against the debtor.
- Student loan debts, unless the debtor can prove "undue hardship."

TAKEAWAY CONCEPTS Chapter 7: Liquidation

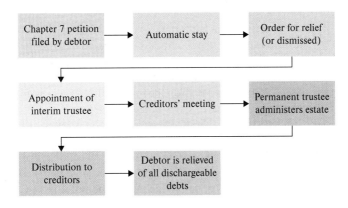

CHAPTER 11: REORGANIZATION

Although located in the Bankruptcy Code, Chapter 11 differs greatly from a liquidation bankruptcy. Chapter 11 is best thought of as *temporary* protection for a corporation from creditors while the corporation goes through a planning process to pay creditors and continue business without the need to terminate the entity completely. Chapter 11 is an acknowledgment that, as a matter of public policy, it is better to allow a business entity the opportunity to revise its business practices without the pressure of creditors who could halt the business operations and shut down the company—actions that could result in job losses and in some creditors not getting paid anything at all.

Debtor in Possession

The fundamental proceedings of a Chapter 11 case are very similar to those of a Chapter 7 case, discussed earlier. A petition is filed either voluntarily or involuntarily; the automatic stay provision is triggered; and, if the petition is proper, the order of relief then sets the reorganization process in motion. A creditor committee is appointed, and the committee can consult with the debtor and/or the trustee to formulate the repayment plan. The major difference, however, is that unlike in a Chapter 7 proceeding, the debtor generally continues to operate the business in a Chapter 11 case. The bankruptcy court may also opt to appoint a trustee to oversee the basic management of the business entity and report back to the court. This process, known as **debtor in possession (DIP)**, gives great power to the debtor to rehabilitate the business entity.

Strong-Arm Clause

In many ways, the executives in a DIP business entity have an ideal situation from a workout perspective. While the stigma of Chapter 11 may cause difficulty in raising new capital, the Bankruptcy Code gives the DIP power to void pre-petition preferential payments and to cancel or assume pre-petition contracts (including leases, supplier contracts, and service contracts). The so-called **strong-arm clause** of the Bankruptcy Code allows the DIP to avoid any obligation or transfer of property that the debtor would otherwise be obligated to perform. For larger companies, a DIP's power is most important in the context of union contracts known as *collective bargaining agreements*. The Bankruptcy Code sets forth standards and procedures under which a collective bargaining contract can be rejected if the debtor has first proposed necessary contractual modifications to the union and the union has rejected them without good cause.

Reorganization Plan

The centerpiece of a Chapter 11 case is the **reorganization plan**. It is a plan, generally filed by the debtor, that articulates a specific strategy and financial plan for emerging from financial distress. The DIP has the exclusive right to draft the plan within 120 days after the Chapter 11 petition. The court must approve the plan before it becomes binding on the creditors. The plan must be submitted to the creditors for a vote and generally must designate "classes" of claims and interests (such as secured versus unsecured) and provide an adequate means for partial payment to creditors. Creditors are given the opportunity to accept or reject the plan, but if they reject the plan, the Bankruptcy Code allows the debtor to request that the court force the creditors to accept the plan (the wording in the code is known as the **cram-down provision**). So long as the plan is fair, equitable, and feasible from the court's perspective, the court will require creditors to accept the plan even over their objections. The plan is binding on all parties upon its approval by the court. It is important to note that a Chapter 11 filing may be converted during any stage (even before the plan is submitted) to a Chapter 7 filing. Most financially distressed business entities will attempt a recovery using the generous provisions of Chapter 11 before deciding to liquidate. On the other hand, some companies do, in fact, turn around and emerge very strong from a Chapter 11 filing.

LO 26-4

Describe the process of a Chapter 13 filing and the impact of the means test on the debtor.

CHAPTER 13: INDIVIDUAL REPAYMENT

Also known as the "wage-earner plan," the Chapter 13 form of bankruptcy is limited to individuals who have substantial debt, and it cannot be used to cover any business debt (even as a sole proprietor). Chapter 13 allows debtors with a regular source of income to catch up on mortgage, car, tax, and domestic support payments; repay an adjusted debt to certain creditors over time (typically five years); and still keep all of their assets. It is less expensive and less complicated than reorganization or liquidation proceedings and can be accomplished only by filing a voluntary bankruptcy petition. Payments typically are made to the bankruptcy trustee, who distributes them to creditors. Unsecured creditors frequently are paid less than they are owed, depending on the circumstances of the case.

The Fraud Exception

The Bankruptcy Code was crafted to strike a balance between providing debtors with a fresh start by discharging debts and preventing abuses of the system by debtors. To accomplish this balance, the Code exempts from discharge any money obtained through debt "for money . . . to the extent obtained by . . . false pretenses, a false representation, or actual fraud . . ."

In Case 26.2, a federal appellate court analyzes the scope of the fraud exception.

CASE 26.2 Sauer Inc. v. Lawson (*In re* Lawson), 791 F.3d 214 (1st Cir. 2015)

FACT SUMMARY Sauer, Inc. ("Sauer") sued James Lawson ("James") in state court to recover damages related to previous business transactions between the parties and won a judgment against James for $168,351. Just before the judgment was entered, James's daughter, Carrie Lawson ("Ms. Lawson") had formed a shell entity, Commercial Construction M & C, LLC ("Commercial Construction"). Once the judgment was entered against James by the court, he transferred $100,150 to Commercial Construction, allegedly to impede Sauer's collection.

Commercial Construction was owned by Ms. Lawson but controlled by James. Ms. Lawson then transferred $80,000 of the $100,150 from Commercial Construction to herself from February 2010 through early 2011. In March 2011, James filed for bankruptcy. In 2013, Sauer successfully sued Ms. Lawson in a state court and obtained a judgment against Commercial Construction and Ms. Lawson after the court ruled that the transfers from James and Ms. Lawson were invalid under Rhode Island's fraud recovery statute. Ms. Lawson filed a petition for bankruptcy the same month that the state court issued the judgment against her. Sauer initiated an adversary proceeding with the bankruptcy court objecting to any discharge of the Sauer debt due to the fraud provisions of the Bankruptcy Code related to money "obtained by . . . actual fraud."

The bankruptcy court dismissed Sauer's adversary proceeding, reasoning that misrepresentation is a required element of actual fraud and that there was no allegation that Ms. Lawson had made a misrepresentation in the course of the transfers. Sauer appealed, arguing that because Ms. Lawson knowingly received the fraudulent transfer and acted in a willful and malicious manner toward Sauer, her acceptance of the fraudulent conveyance constituted actual fraud.

SYNOPSIS OF DECISION AND OPINION The Court of Appeals for the First Circuit reversed the decision of the bankruptcy court and ruled in favor of Sauer. The court ruled that the bankruptcy court erred in concluding that a misrepresentation by a debtor to a creditor is an essential element of establishing a basis for the nondischarge of a debt under the fraud exception to the Bankruptcy Code. It held that fraud is not limited to misrepresentations and misleading omissions. Rather, actual fraud, by definition, consists of any deceit, artifice, trick, or design involving direct and active operation of the mind, used to circumvent and cheat another. In this case, Ms. Lawson's actions were intended to circumvent the court's judgments and cheat Sauer.

WORDS OF THE COURT: Broad Definition of Fraud "We . . . hold that actual fraud under [the Bankruptcy Code] is not limited to fraud effected by misrepresentation. Rather, we hold that actual fraud includes fraudulent conveyances that are 'intended

(continued)

... to hinder [the relevant] creditors.' . . . That is, the debtor-transferee must herself be guilty of intent to defraud and not merely be the passive recipient of a fraudulent conveyance. Such intent may be inferred from her acceptance of a transfer that she knew was made with the purpose of hindering the transferor's creditor(s). . . . Our reading is confirmed by the structure of the text and the legislative history. [Congress amended the Bankruptcy Code] so that the fraud provision now explicitly lists both actual fraud and false representations as grounds for denying a discharge."

Case Questions

1. Why did the trial court dismiss Sauer's adversary proceeding that objected to the discharge of Ms. Lawson's debt?

2. How did the legislative history of the Bankruptcy Code affect the court's decision?

3. *Focus on Critical Thinking:* Could there be any legitimate and ethical reason for the transfers? Why or why not? If the appellate court had agreed with the trial court that fraud cannot exist without misrepresentation, what ethical considerations might be triggered?

Bankruptcy Abuse Prevention and Consumer Protection Act

In 2005, Congress passed legislation intended to curb perceived abuses of statutory bankruptcy protection by enacting the Bankruptcy Abuse Prevention and Consumer Protection Act (BAPCPA). While the congressional sponsors of the bill touted its public policy benefits of making the consuming public more responsible with debt, the law was widely criticized by bankruptcy attorneys and judges as unnecessarily burdening the debtor, the trustee, and the court with more paperwork and expenses while not curbing abuse. The law overhauled the Bankruptcy Code for the first time since 1994 and, fundamentally, made it more difficult for debtors to seek protection under Chapter 7. The major provision of the law centers on establishing a baseline income for which debtors are eligible for Chapter 7 discharge versus being required to repay debts under Chapter 13.

Means Test The most important change was to increase the statutory requirements for eligibility under Chapter 7 liquidation by adding a "means test" that is determined by comparing the applicant's current monthly income to the median income for the applicant's state. If the applicant's income is more than the median, the applicant is not eligible for Chapter 7. Thus, a substantial number of bankruptcy applicants who previously would have been eligible for a discharge of substantially all debts must now repay them under a Chapter 13 filing. For example, the state of Florida's annual median family income for a family of one and a family of three are $43,136 and $57,080, respectively. Therefore, if the debtor applies for a Chapter 7 bankruptcy seeking to discharge debts but her income is above the median, the petition will be denied and the debtor will have only Chapter 13 (debt repayment) as an option.

In Case 26.3, the U.S. Supreme Court analyzes the BAPCPA's provisions related to the means test.

CASE 26.3 Ransom v. FIA Card Services, 562 U.S 61 (2011)

FACT SUMMARY Ransom filed for Chapter 13 bankruptcy relief in 2006. His filings included $82,500 worth of unsecured credit card debt owed to FIA Card Services. In his repayment plan, Ransom proposed repayment of 25 percent of his outstanding debt to FIA over a five-year period. Despite the fact that he owned his car outright (no debt), Ransom listed his reasonably necessary living expenses and claimed a standard amount provided for in the Bankruptcy Code for a car: $471 per month and $210.55 for maintenance costs. FIA objected to the plan based on the fact that Ransom owned his car outright and was not required to make payments. Allowing the car deduction, FIA argued, amounted to allowing Ransom to avoid paying at least $28,000 of his FIA debt. The bankruptcy court denied confirmation of Ransom's plan, and the appellate court affirmed the decision.

SYNOPSIS OF DECISION AND OPINION The U.S. Supreme Court ruled in favor of FIA and held that Ransom could not take the car-ownership deduction. The Court ruled that the Bankruptcy Abuse Prevention and Consumer Protection Act of 2005 requires courts to apply a means test to help ensure that debtors who can pay back their creditors actually do so with the help of the Bankruptcy Code. The means test depends on accurate reporting of reasonably necessary living expenses. Since Ransom had no actual loan or lease payment due, he was not entitled to claim a car-ownership deduction. The Court rejected Ransom's argument that the language in the statute regarding applicability of the car-ownership deduction was ambiguous. The Court also explained that Ransom was entitled to "ownership costs," but that the car-ownership deduction was limited to debtors who were required to make loan or lease payments for their car.

WORDS OF THE COURT: Purpose of the Means Test "Ransom next contends that denying the ownership allowance to debtors in his position 'sends entirely the wrong message, namely, that it is advantageous to be deeply in debt on motor vehicle loans, rather than to pay them off.' But the choice here is not between thrifty savers and profligate borrowers, as Ransom would have it. Money is fungible: The $14,000 that Ransom spent to purchase his Camry outright was money he did not devote to paying down his credit card debt, and Congress did not express a preference for one use of these funds over the other. Further, Ransom's argument mistakes what the deductions in the means test are meant to accomplish. Rather than effecting any broad federal policy as to saving or borrowing, the deductions serve merely to ensure that debtors in bankruptcy can afford essential items. The car-ownership allowance thus safeguards a debtor's ability to retain a car throughout the plan period. If the debtor already owns a car outright, he has no need for this protection."

Case Questions

1. Does the Court's decision encourage responsible actions by the debtor? Does this encourage debtors to take on new debt instead of driving an old car, as Ransom suggested?

2. How did the Bankruptcy Abuse Prevention and Consumer Protection Act of 2005 affect this case?

3. *Focus on Critical Thinking:* Soon after the BAPCPA was enacted, one bankruptcy court judge wrote that "the legislation's adoption in its title of the words 'consumer protection' is the grossest of misnomers."[2] What do you suppose the judge meant by that? Does the law "protect consumers" as its name implies? Whom *does* it protect?

Other BAPCPA Requirements

BAPCPA also increased reporting requirements to include proof of the debtor's income and gave higher priority for alimony and support payments by the debtor. It also mandated credit counseling for all debtors. Prior to filing for bankruptcy, the debtor must complete a short (approximately one-hour) credit-counseling seminar and must also complete a longer course, known as Credit Education, prior to actually receiving a discharge of debts.

TAKEAWAY CONCEPTS Chapter 13: Individual Repayment

- In a Chapter 13 bankruptcy, an individual can develop a repayment plan to use his income to slowly pay back debts without having to liquidate assets.
- The BAPCPA imposed a "means test" that is determined by comparing the applicant's current monthly income to the median income for the applicant's state. If the applicant's income is more than the median, the applicant is not eligible to file for Chapter 7 bankruptcy.

---

[2]See, for example, *In re Sousa,* 336 B.R. 113 (Bankr. W.D. Texas 2005).

Strategic Bankruptcy

PROBLEM: Businesses and individuals may be faced with a short-term threat to their assets even if their long-term financial outlook is relatively bright.

STRATEGIC SOLUTION: Some individuals and businesses use bankruptcy laws strategically, a phenomenon known as *strategic bankruptcy*.[3] A strategic bankruptcy occurs when an otherwise solvent company makes use of the bankruptcy laws for some specific business purpose.

Consider various dimensions (e.g., legal, ethical) of one high-profile example of a strategic bankruptcy involving the famous recording artist 50 Cent. The artist, whose legal name is Curtis James Jackson III, filed for bankruptcy protection a few days after a jury ordered him to pay a private plaintiff $5 million in a "revenge porn" lawsuit.[4] In fact, 50 Cent is one of the most successful recording artists in the music industry and a successful entrepreneur in his own right. He reportedly made as much as $100 million from his investment in Vitaminwater after it was purchased by Coca-Cola, has produced many successful music records, and has appeared in nearly two dozen films. By all accounts, 50 Cent is not "broke," so why did he file for bankruptcy?

One clue is the type of bankruptcy 50 Cent filed for. Specifically, he filed for Chapter 11 bankruptcy, a type of bankruptcy filing usually reserved for corporations that need to be restructured while they remain open for business. Firms and individuals looking to reorganize

their debts might use Chapter 11 to buy more time to pay their debts and give them a chance to come up with a payment plan, an option such firms and individuals might not have without Chapter 11. In other words, 50 Cent's Chapter 11 filing might have been a strategic effort to stay in control of his assets.

At the same time, 50 Cent's bankruptcy filing may make it more difficult for the plaintiff in the revenge porn lawsuit to collect the $5 million judgment against 50 Cent, because the plaintiff in that lawsuit will now be one of many creditors trying to get their share of his fortune. According to Hunter Shkolnik, the plaintiff's lawyer in the revenge porn lawsuit, "We think this [50 Cent's filing for Chapter 11] is a failed attempt to avoid paying this woman who has been hurt so badly by his actions."

But filing for Chapter 11 bankruptcy also has a potential downside for 50 Cent. By filing for bankruptcy, 50 Cent will incur substantial additional legal fees, and he could potentially have his assets and personal finances scrutinized in court.[5] A bankruptcy judge would have the authority to review his spending, his earnings, and his estate. Ultimately, whether these additional legal costs and public scrutiny are worth the strategic benefits is a close call. What do you think?

QUESTIONS

1. Is the decision to engage in a strategic bankruptcy an ethical one? Is it ever unethical to exercise a legal right?

2. Is there a principled way of distinguishing between strategic and nonstrategic bankruptcies? Explain.

[3]See generally Kevin J. Delaney, *Strategic Bankruptcy* (University of California Press, 1998).

[4]Andrea Peterson, "50 Cent Filed for Bankruptcy Days after Losing a Revenge Porn Lawsuit," *Washington Post*, July 14, 2015.

[5]Katy Stech, "50 Cent Bankruptcy: By the Numbers," *The Wall Street Journal, Aug. 4, 2015.*

KEY TERMS

Bankruptcy p. 442   A procedure by which a debtor's assets are reorganized and liquidated by a court order to pay off creditors and free the debtor from obligations under existing contracts.

Automatic stay p. 443   A legal prohibition whereby creditors may neither initiate nor continue any debt collection action against the debtor or her property.

Bankruptcy trustee p. 443   An individual, often an attorney highly skilled in bankruptcy law, appointed in Chapter 7 or Chapter 13 cases and charged with the duty of taking control of the bankruptcy estate and reducing it to cash for distribution, preserving the interests of both the debtor and the creditors.

Bankruptcy estate p. 443   The debtor's available assets in a bankruptcy proceeding.

Voidable transfers p. 443   In bankruptcy proceedings, certain transfers that are considered an unfair advantage of one creditor over another.

Voluntary bankruptcy petition p. 444   A petition filed in the bankruptcy court by the debtor that includes the names of creditors; a list of debts; and a list of the debtor's assets, income, and expenses.

Involuntary bankruptcy petition p. 445   A petition filed in the bankruptcy court against a debtor by a group of three or more creditors with an unsecured aggregate claim of at least $15,775 who claim that the debtor is failing to pay the debt as it comes due.

Debtor in possession (DIP) p. 448   A Chapter 11 bankruptcy process in which the debtor generally remains in control of assets and business operations in an attempt to rehabilitate the business entity.

Strong-arm clause p. 448   Provision of the Bankruptcy Code that allows the debtor in possession to avoid any obligation or transfer of property that the debtor would otherwise be obligated to perform.

Reorganization plan p. 448   A plan, generally filed by the debtor, that articulates a specific strategy and financial plan for emerging from financial distress; serves as the keystone of a Chapter 11 case.

Cram-down provision p. 448   A term used in reference to the Chapter 11 provision that allows the debtor to request that the court force the creditors to accept a plan that is fair, equitable, and feasible.

CASE SUMMARY 26.1 *In re* Fehrs, 391 B.R. 53 (Bankr. D. Idaho, 2008)

Voidable Transfers

In 2002, Fehrs met and began living with her boyfriend, Murrietta. They also lived with her teenage son from a former marriage, Jae. Fehrs bought a housing lot at 464 Second Street and another at 117 Terrill Loop, both in the city of Mullan, Idaho. Fehrs and Murrietta contracted with Peter Axtman to build a house at 464 Second Street. As construction began, problems arose. Soon Murrietta and Fehrs broke up, and Axtman filed a lawsuit against Fehrs for what he was owed for his services. Two months after the suit was filed, Fehrs transferred her property at 117 Terrill Loop to her son Jae in exchange for $1. Fehrs said she made the transfer because Jae was always drinking and partying with friends at 117 Terrill Loop and she did not want to be liable if anything should happen. Two months later Fehrs filed for bankruptcy.

CASE QUESTIONS

1. Why do you think Fehrs sold the lot to her son?
2. What can the trustee do to make sure Axtman gets all he is owed?

CASE SUMMARY 26.2 Ellison v. Commissioner of Internal Revenue Service, 385 B.R. 158 (S.D. W. Va. 2008)

Automatic Stay

Ellison ran a small company, and both he and his company filed for bankruptcy in 1994. The court issued an automatic stay to creditors. A month later the IRS contacted Ellison about unpaid taxes from 1993. Although Ellison consented to the tax being assessed, the IRS continued to pursue payment of the back taxes even after the bankruptcy petition was filed. Ellison filed suit against the IRS for the violation of her automatic stay rights under the Bankruptcy Code.

CASE QUESTIONS

1. Will Ellison have to pay these taxes, or can they be discharged?
2. Does the IRS have any defense to pursuing the debt during the automatic stay period?
3. If Ellison wins, what does that say about the power of an automatic stay?

CASE SUMMARY 26.3 *In re* Richie, 353 B.R. 569 (Bankr. E.D. Wis. 2006)

Means Test

When Charmaine Richie filed for Chapter 7 bankruptcy, she had been making a living through odd jobs over the past year yielding an income of $22,608. The median income is $37,873 for her home state of Wisconsin. Just prior to her bankruptcy petition filing, Richie completed a master's degree in outdoor therapeutic recreation administration, which qualified her to work as a therapist for the handicapped in a camp or outdoor clinical setting. A job in this field would likely have brought Richie well above the median income and disqualified her for protection under Chapter 7 bankruptcy. Additionally, Richie had been looking for jobs in her field but only in the Racine-Kenosha area of Wisconsin, where there were very few opportunities. She was qualified to work at many other jobs that would have brought her above the median, but she wanted employment only in her chosen field and in her home geographic area. After her petition was filed, the bankruptcy trustee requested that the court reject the Chapter 7 petition and convert the case to a Chapter 13 petition, whereby Richie would have to pay all or much of her debt. The trustee alleged that Richie was abusing the Chapter 7 bankruptcy means test because she was capable of earning more money but did not. Moreover, Richie filed bankruptcy immediately after graduate school, when her future earning potential was relatively high. Richie argued that moving elsewhere to work would be a burden and having a different full-time job would hurt her future prospects for getting a job in her chosen field.

CASE QUESTIONS

1. Should Richie be forced to relocate or work in another field in order to use bankruptcy laws?
2. Richie lacked the ability to pay because she had not engaged in a broad employment search, did not wish to work outside her chosen field, and did not wish to work within her chosen field outside her geographic area. Should her creditors bear the burden of her choices?

CASE SUMMARY 26.4 *In re* Jones, 392 B.R. 116 (E.D. Pa. 2008)

Undue Hardship

Jones earned a college degree in history with a minor in economics in the 1980s. Although Jones was supposed to enter the U.S. Army upon graduation, he gained admission to law school and earned his law degree. However, Jones could not pass the bar examination after several attempts. He spent the next 14 years in various positions including the army, substitute teaching, writing, and social work. Jones then returned to school to get a master's degree in teaching the visual arts. Jones continued his education with yet another master's degree in divinity in 2005. He borrowed heavily for his education and, at the time of the bankruptcy petition, had defaulted on 18 student loans worth $140,000 of debt. Note that Jones's undergraduate and law school debts were discharged in a previous bankruptcy hearing. Jones argued that the debt was so high that to pay it would cause "undue hardship," and he asked the court to discharge the loan. His creditors maintained that Jones did not meet the undue hardship standard.

CASE QUESTIONS

1. Who prevails and why?
2. If Jones had been unable to work due to illness or injury, would that be sufficient to meet the undue hardship standard set out by the court?
3. Note that one court did not find undue hardship enough to discharge student loans for a "46-year-old part-time legal secretary, raising her 14-year-old child and living with her sister, and who had psychiatric problems and had twice attempted suicide" [*In re Brightful,* 267 F.3d 324 (3d Cir. 2001)]. Why would Congress and the courts be reluctant to allow the discharge of student loans without meeting this difficult test?

1. A bankruptcy _____ is appointed by the court and has extensive authority in handling the bankruptcy estate.
   a. Judge
   b. Jurist
   c. Trustee
   d. Director

2. The bankruptcy code shields debtors from creditor actions through what legal tool?
   a. Shield rule
   b. Automatic stay
   c. Immediate protection doctrine
   d. Creditor's bar

3. Chapter 7 bankruptcy is also commonly called:
   a. Liquidation.
   b. Elimination.
   c. Reorganization.
   d. Voidable.

4. Donald is the sole shareholder of Donald Corporation. The week before the corporation files for bankruptcy, Donald paid back a loan to his father that he used to help start the business last year. Although the loan was not due for another year, Donald paid off the balance entirely. Which of the following is true?
   a. Paying back the loan was a preferential transfer.
   b. Paying back the loan was a portable transfer.
   c. Paying back the loan was in the ordinary course of business.
   d. Both A and B are correct.

5. Which form of bankruptcy allows the business debtor to continue its operations as a debtor in possession?
   a. Chapter 7
   b. Chapter 11
   c. Chapter 13
   d. Chapter 15

6. Bankruptcy is primarily an area of federal law.
   a. True
   b. False

7. The Bankruptcy Code allows the court to force a Chapter 11 reorganization plan over the objections of its creditors.
   a. True
   b. False

8. The Bankruptcy Abuse Prevention and Consumer Protection Act does not apply to business debtors.
   a. True
   b. False

9. A means test is used to determine a debtor's eligibility for Chapter 7 relief.
   a. True
   b. False

10. A bankruptcy trustee is automatically appointed in all bankruptcy cases.
    a. True
    b. False

 Quick Quiz ANSWERS

Petitions under Chapters 7, 11, and 13 of the Bankruptcy Code

1. **Chapter 13.** A Chapter 13 bankruptcy is also called a wage earner's plan. It enables individuals with regular income to develop a plan to repay all or part of their debts.
2. **Chapter 7.** An individual Chapter 7 case usually results in a discharge of debts.
3. **Chapter 11.** Chapter 11 is typically used to reorganize a business.

CHAPTER REVIEW QUESTIONS: Answers and Explanations

1. c. The bankruptcy trustee is given extensive powers to collect the debtor's assets and void transfers.

2. b. The automatic stay is a powerful legal tool that stops all collection efforts immediately upon the filing of a bankruptcy petition. The other answers are fictitious.

3. a. Chapter 7 is known as liquidation because the debtor gives up all rights to property in exchange for legal protection and a fresh start. Answer *c* is wrong because Chapter 11 involves reorganization. Answers *b* and *d* are fictitious.

4. a. Paying back the loan is a classic preferential transfer because it occurs within 90 days before the bankruptcy filing and because the creditor (Donald's father) is an insider. Because the loan is preferential, it is also voidable. Answer *c* is incorrect because the payment is not in the ordinary course of business since the loan was paid back early. Answer choices *b* and *d* are incorrect because portable transfers do not exist in the Bankruptcy Code.

5. b. Chapter 11 allows the business to continue to operate with bankruptcy protection from creditors as the debtor reorganizes. Answer *a* is incorrect because Chapter 7 involves liquidation. Answer *c* is wrong because Chapter 13 is limited to individuals. Answer *d* is incorrect because Chapter 15 does not exist as a filing option in the Bankruptcy Code.

6. a. True. Although state courts have some involvement with bankruptcy proceedings, it is primarily federal statutory law.

7. a. True. The so-called cram-down provision gives courts this power.

8. b. False. The Bankruptcy Abuse Prevention and Consumer Protection Act applies to all debtors, including businesses.

9. a. True. A means test determines the debtor's eligibility by comparing the income of the debtor to his home state's median income. Chapter 7 relief is only available for those below the median.

10. b. False. A bankruptcy trustee is automatically appointed in Chapter 7 or Chapter 13 cases, but rarely in Chapter 11 bankruptcy cases.

UNIT FOUR   Business Entities

CHAPTER 27

Choice of Business Entity and Sole Proprietorships

As you study this chapter you'll learn of the potential risks associated with a sole proprietorship. In the *Thinking Strategically* feature at the end of this chapter, we examine how use of certain types of insurance policies are used to strategically reduce risk.

Learning Objectives

After studying this chapter, students who have mastered the material will be able to:

27-1 Articulate the factors that business owners should consider when selecting a business entity.

27-2 Identify the advantages and drawbacks to the sole proprietor form of entity.

27-3 List the choices available to capitalize a sole proprietorship.

27-4 Explain how proprietorships are managed and taxed.

27-5 Describe the impact of terminating a sole proprietorship.

27-6 Recognize the role of franchises in business.

CHAPTER OVERVIEW

All business ventures operate as a legally recognized form of business entity. Business owners and managers who have a fundamental knowledge of the structure, advantages, and risks associated with each form of business entity are more effective at focusing on business opportunities while limiting potential liability. Most states recognize at least six forms of business entities. In addition to providing an overview of the forms of business entities and factors used to determine the best choice of entity for a given business, this chapter focuses on the law governing the most basic form of entity: the sole proprietorship. We discuss other forms of entity in detail in future chapters of this section.

CHOOSING A BUSINESS ENTITY

The best choice of business entity is driven primarily by the risk, tax, and operational objectives of the owner(s) and the type of business operations contemplated. Choosing a business entity is an important part of business planning for start-up entrepreneurs and for managers who are supervising the launch of an additional venture that supplements their existing business. Each form of entity has its attendant advantages, drawbacks, and legal consequences for the *owners,* known as **principals**, of the business. In the context of business entities, *principal* is a generic word for individuals who are entitled to the profits of a business based on their percentage of ownership. In choosing a business entity, principals should consider at least the following factors:

LO 27-1

Articulate the factors that business owners should consider when selecting a business entity.

- *Formation:* How easy is the entity to form and maintain? Must there be more than one principal? What annual filings or fees are required, and what formalities need to be followed?
- *Liability:* To what extent are the principals *personally* liable for debts and other contract or tort liabilities of the business entity itself? To take a simple example, suppose Gardner owns a consulting business and rents office space from Landlord under a five-year lease agreement. After one year, Gardner loses a large client and can no longer afford the office space. He cancels his lease and moves his office to the basement of his home. If the assets of the consulting business are insufficient to pay a court judgment in favor of the damaged party (Landlord), does Landlord, as the injured party, have a claim for the balance against Gardner's personal assets (such as a personal bank account or stock portfolio)?
- *Capitalization:* How will the business entity fund its operations? May the principal(s) sell ownership rights in the business to raise capital?
- *Taxation of income:* How will tax authorities treat the entity? Will the entity itself pay taxes, or are the taxes passed through to the principals?
- *Management and operation:* How, and by whom, will the business venture be operated? Will the principals be involved in the day-to-day operations of the business? What duties do the principals owe to the business and to each other? How will the profits and losses be split? If a principal decides to leave the business entity, may the remaining principals continue to operate?

Table 27.1 sets out the most common forms of business entities.

Evolution of the Entity

The appropriate choice of business entity varies widely depending on the type of business and the nature of the liabilities associated with its businesses activities. Those engaged in business activities that are largely self-funded and have a relatively low potential for liability (e.g., marketing consultant) do not require the protection and flexibility offered by more

TABLE 27.1	Most Common Forms of Business Entities	
Name of Entity	**Brief Description**	**Coverage in Text**
Sole proprietorship	One-person entity in which the debts and liabilities of the business are also personal debts and liabilities of the principal.	Chapter 27
Partnerships: General limited	Two or more principals that agree to share profits and losses in an ongoing business venture. Debts and liabilities of the business are also personal debts and liabilities of the general partners. Limited partners have limited liability.	Chapter 28
Limited liability partnership	Two or more principals that agree to share profits and losses in an ongoing business venture. The principals have heightened liability protection from debts and liabilities of the partnership.	Chapter 28
Limited liability company	Two or more principals in an ongoing business venture with potentially favorable tax treatment and limited liability for the principals.	Chapter 29
Corporation	One or more principals that invest money in exchange for ownership (stock). The principals generally have no personal liability for debts and liabilities of the business.	Chapters 30 and 31

complex forms of entity. On the other hand, a retail business that enters into long-term contracts (e.g., a lease agreement) and is subject to liability based on negligence (e.g., a customer slips and falls) would likely require a different analysis.

Most importantly, the initial choice of entity is not set in stone. It may be changed by the principal(s) as the business evolves or as necessity demands. For example, if Zhang, a college student, runs a business doing laundry for others in his dormitory, he will not need liability protection and has only one principal. To avoid spending a lot of money on start-up costs, Zhang could form a sole proprietorship. If Zhang starts to get too busy to handle the work by himself, he will need to consider whether the entity should be turned into a partnership or whether he will simply hire an employee to help. Perhaps Zhang will also branch out and start offering a delivery service of authentic Cantonese cuisine to his customer base. In this case, Zhang will need to consider entities that limit his personal liability and allow more flexibility for raising capital. Now his choices have grown to include forming a corporation or a limited liability company.

TAKEAWAY CONCEPTS Choosing a Business Entity

- The best choice of business entity is driven primarily by the risk, tax, and operational objectives of the owner(s) and the type of business operations contemplated.
- Each form of entity has its attendant advantages, drawbacks, and legal consequences for the owners of the business (known as *principals*).
- Entities are not set in stone. Principals may decide to change the entity as the business evolves.

SOLE PROPRIETORSHIPS

LO 27-2

Identify the advantages and drawbacks to the sole proprietor form of entity.

The easiest single-person ownership entity to form and maintain is a **sole proprietorship**. A sole proprietorship requires only a minimal fee, involves a straightforward filing requirement with the appropriate state or county government authority, and typically requires no annual filings. Its ease of formation and maintenance are its primary advantages. The simplicity of a sole proprietorship makes this entity a top choice for start-up businesses with relatively low annual revenues and expenses. An individual planning to conduct a sole proprietorship under a **trade name**, rather than her individual name (e.g., "Gates IT Consulting" rather than "Joan Gates") will also file a "doing business as," or DBA, certificate (a DBA name is sometimes known as a *fictitious name*) with a local or state office. There may be additional licenses required by the state and city where the business operates (sales tax licenses, etc.). These requirements vary by jurisdiction. Figure 27.1 is a sample of a sole proprietor filing required in Florida.

In the following sections we examine the features of a sole proprietorship.

Liability of Proprietor

The chief drawback to the sole proprietorship as a form of entity is a complete lack of protection of the principal's personal assets for unpaid debts and liabilities of the business. All debts and liabilities of the business are also personal debts and liabilities of the principal. For example, suppose Redfern is the principal of Redfern Catering, a sole proprietorship. Redfern Catering has approximately $5,000 in assets. One of Redfern's employees negligently uses spoiled ingredients in a soup that is served to customers. Marshall is a customer who develops food poisoning and obtains a court judgment against Redfern Catering to compensate him for damages that resulted from medical bills in the amount of $50,000.

APPLICATION FOR REGISTRATION OF FICTITIOUS NAME

Note: Acknowledgments/certificates will be sent to the address in Section 1 only.

Section 1

1. Richard's Beach Chairs

   Fictitious Name to be Registered (see instructions for certain prohibited words, abbreviations and designations)

2. 1000 Dania Beach Boulevard

   Mailing Address of Business

   Dania Beach   FL   33004

   City   State   Zip

3. Florida County of principal place of business:

   Broward

   (see instructions if more than one county)

4. FEI Number of Business: 12-34567

   This space for office use only

Section 2

A. **Registrant if individual(s): (Use an attachment if necessary):**

1. Raleigh   Joseph   R   2. N/A

   Last   First   M.I.   Last   First   M.I.

   1000 Dania Beach Blvd

   Address   Address

   Dania Beach   FL   33004

   City   State   Zip   City   State   Zip

B. **Registrant if other than an individual(s): (Use an attachment if necessary):**

N/A   2.

Entity Name   Entity Name

Address   Address

City   State   Zip   City   State   Zip

Florida Document Number: _____   Florida Document Number: _____

FEI Number: _____   FEI Number: _____

○ Applied for   ○ Not Applicable   ○ Applied for   ○ Not Applicable

Section 3

I the undersigned, being a registrant for the above fictitious name, certify that the information indicated on this form is true and accurate. In accordance with Section 865.09, F.S., I further certify that the intention to register the fictitious name to be registered has been advertised at least once in a newspaper as defined in chapter 50, Florida Statutes, in the county in which the principal place of business of the registrant is or will be located. I understand that the signature below shall have the same legal effect as if made under oath and I am aware that false information submitted in a document to the Department of State constitutes a third degree felony as provided for in s.817.155, F.S.

Joseph R. Raleigh   1/5/2019   richard@beachchairs.com

Signature of Registrant in Section 2   Date   Email address: (to be used for future renewal notifications)

Section 4

FOR CANCELLATIONS, COMPLETE THIS SECTION 4 ONLY:

FOR FICTITIOUS NAME REGISTRATION CHANGE, COMPLETE SECTIONS 1 THROUGH 4:

I (we) the undersigned, hereby cancel the fictitious name _____, which was

registered on _____ and assigned registration number _____.

Signature of Registrant Whose Registration is Being Cancelled   Date   Signature of Registrant Whose Registration is Being Cancelled   Date

Mark the applicable boxes   ☐ Certificate of Status - $10   ☐ Certified Copy - $30

NON-REFUNDABLE PROCESSING FEE: $50

CR4E001 (11/17)

Assuming that Redfern Catering had no insurance coverage for this event, Marshall would have $45,000 of judgment unpaid after exhausting the business of its assets ($50,000 judgment minus $5,000 assets). Thus, Redfern would be personally liable to Marshall for the remaining unpaid judgment. This means that Marshall could execute the judgment against Redfern by using a judicially sanctioned process for seizing funds from Redfern's personal bank account, stock portfolio, and other assets. As a result of this lack of protection, sole proprietors often purchase comprehensive liability insurance for the business in amounts sufficient to cover potential tort liabilities such as the one described in the Redfern-Marshall example.

In Case 27.1, a state appellate court considers the impact of the sole proprietorship form of business on a contract transaction.

CASE 27.1 Lewis v. Moore (Tenn. Ct. App. 2017)

FACT SUMMARY Moore obtained a construction loan to build a home on Monroe Lane in Brentwood, Tennessee (Monroe Lane Property). As final payment for the construction loan approached, Moore was unsuccessful in seeking to refinance the loan unless she agreed to sell a vacant lot she owned on Hillsboro Road (Hillsboro Road Property). Rather than sell the property on the open market, Moore approached Lewis, a longtime friend and former business colleague, and convinced him to purchase the Hillsboro Road Property so that Moore could avoid defaulting on the construction loan. Moore promised that she would repurchase the Hillsboro Road Property from Lewis within one year. Lewis agreed but also wanted a percentage of Moore's business operation as part of the transaction.

In 2012, Lewis and Moore entered into a contract concerning both the Hillsboro Road Property and Moore's marketing and advertising business, Moore Media. Moore had owned and operated Moore Media as a sole proprietorship since 2002. The contract provided for Lewis to purchase the Hillsboro Road Property and "10 percent of Moore Media" from Moore for $300,000. The contract also included a clause providing that if Moore Media was dissolved or closed for any reason and Moore was a majority owner in a *new* company, Lewis would receive 10 percent of profits received by Moore in the new company. Six months later, Moore repurchased the Hillsboro Road Property from Lewis and continued to make payments to Lewis from Moore Media for 10 percent of the business's monthly profit.

In 2013, Moore asked Lewis to conclude their arrangement and allow her to repurchase his interest in Moore Media, but Lewis declined. In April 2014, Moore sent Lewis a letter informing him that she had closed Moore Media and formed Sandcliffs Media, LLC. According to the operating agreement for Sandcliffs Media, Moore had a 49 percent interest and another principal had a 51 percent interest in the new LLC. The letter also informed Lewis that because Moore had formed a new company of which she was not a majority owner, Lewis was no longer entitled to 10 percent of the profits.

Lewis filed suit against Moore claiming, among other things, that the 2012 agreement formed an implied partnership between Moore and Lewis and thus he was entitled to ongoing payments. The trial court held for Moore and Lewis appealed.

SYNOPSIS OF DECISION AND OPINION The Tennessee Court of Appeals affirmed the trial court's decision in favor of Moore. The court ruled that because Moore was a sole proprietor, no other individual could have had an ownership interest in Moore Media and Moore was free to dissolve the entity at any time. The court pointed out that Sandcliffs was not a sham company and that any transfer of assets was proper since, by definition, Moore had a 100 percent ownership interest in her sole proprietorship business.

WORDS OF THE COURT: No Separate Legal Existence "Addressing Mr. Lewis's first argument, we agree with the trial court that Ms. Moore had the authority to unilaterally close Moore Media. Mr. Lewis did not, as he claims, have an ownership interest in Moore Media. The parties agreed that, at least prior to the events of 2012, Moore Media was operated by Ms. Moore as a sole proprietorship. A sole proprietorship is nothing more than an

(continued)

individual conducting a business for profit, which in turn becomes his income. It has no separate legal existence or identity apart from the sole proprietor. Indeed, this court has noted that a sole proprietorship and its owner are one in the same.... Therefore, Mr. Lewis did not purchase an ownership interest in Moore Media because he could not purchase a 10% interest in Moore Media any more than he could purchase a 10% interest in Ms. Moore. Accordingly, Ms. Moore, as the sole proprietor, had the authority to close her business without Mr. Lewis's consent."

Case Questions

1. Why did the court reject Lewis's theory that an implied partnership existed between Lewis and Moore?

2. Why does the court point out that a sole proprietorship doesn't have a "separate legal existence"?

3. *Focus on Critical Thinking:* Was this a good strategy by Moore? Why or why not? Was it ethical? Was the court's decision fair, or did Moore use the law to shield her from a bad business deal?

CAPITALIZATION

LO 27-3

List the choices available to capitalize a sole proprietorship.

Sole proprietorships are limited in their options for raising money. They cannot sell ownership in their business venture and are typically left with capitalizing their operations in other ways. First, the proprietor's personal resources may provide at least a portion of operating capital. Proprietors may also finance their business through debt. **Private loans** are typically through individuals who negotiate such items as interest rate directly with the proprietor. These loans come from family members and friends and are paid back according to their individual agreement.

Sole proprietors may also raise money through **commercial loans**. A commercial loan is a more formal transaction involving a commercial lender (e.g., a bank) that lends money to the proprietor for business purposes at the market rate of interest over a fixed, relatively short period (5–10 years). This interest rate usually is not negotiable, but commercial loans often carry favorable interest rates. In exchange for the favorable interest rate, lenders typically require **collateral** for the loan. This means that the loan must be secured by an asset of equivalent value typically consisting of the proprietor's personal assets (such as a retirement account).

A close cousin to a commercial loan is a commercial **line of credit**. A line of credit allows the proprietor to draw against a predetermined credit limit, as needed, instead of receiving the full loan amount at one time like a commercial loan. The biggest advantage of a line of credit is that the borrower only pays interest on the funds actually drawn instead of the full amount of a loan. A commercial line of credit is typically secured by collateral. Sole proprietors also use unsecured credit, such as a credit card, to finance operations. Most business owners prefer lower interest rate commercial loans or lines of credit to high-interest credit cards. Table 27.2 summarizes a sole proprietor's options for raising capital.

TABLE 27.2	Capital Options for Sole Proprietors

Form of Capital	Features
Private loan	Loans from family or friends negotiated directly with the sole proprietor and paid back over a certain term at an agreed-upon rate of interest.
Commercial loan	Loan from a commercial lender with interest tied to market rates and secured with collateral.
Commercial line of credit	Allows the proprietor to draw against a predetermined credit limit as needed, instead of receiving the full loan amount at one time.
Unsecured credit	Credit account with high interest rates (e.g., credit card) that does not require collateral and is paid back in accordance with a nonnegotiable creditor agreement.

Winston is a sole proprietor seeking capital to expand his landscaping business. Identify the option Winston is using in the following fact patterns.

1. Winston uses his personal credit card to buy a new piece of machinery.
2. Winston borrows $1,000 from his wealthy aunt and promises to pay her back with interest at the end of the busy season.
3. Winston meets with a loan officer from his local bank and asks for a $30,000 secured loan to finance a new truck for his business.
4. Winston meets with a loan officer from his local bank and asks for a $30,000 loan that he can draw on to cover operating costs during the slow season. He will only need to draw on some of the loan amount during the slow season and will pay it back after the busy season.

Answers to this Quick Quiz are provided at the end of the chapter.

LO 27-4

Explain how proprietorships are managed and taxed.

TAXATION

A sole proprietorship is not subject to corporate income taxation, and no tax return is filed on behalf of the business. Rather, the principal reports business income and expenses on her own individual tax return and pays taxes on business income (or deducts business losses) based on her own individual tax rate. Figure 27.2 illustrates how a sole proprietor in the 12 percent bracket is taxed on business income.

Management and Organization

It is important to note that although most sole proprietorships are relatively small in terms of assets and revenues, they are not restricted in terms of the number of employees and can operate in as many locations as the principal desires. The proprietor has sole discretion and authority to bind the business or make any business decisions. Of course, sole proprietorships have no oversight committees (such as a board of directors) and do not require any agreements among principals. Sole proprietorships may also be converted to another form of entity at the proprietor's will.

LO 27-5

Describe the impact of terminating a sole proprietorship.

TERMINATION

A sole proprietorship is terminated either by an express act of the principal or by operation of law in the case of the death or personal bankruptcy of the proprietor. Although a sole proprietor may sell the assets of her business to another party, the proprietor's

FIGURE 27.2   How a Sole Proprietorship Is Taxed

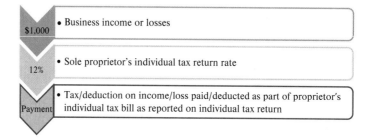

ownership interest in a sole proprietorship cannot pass to her heirs through a gift or an estate. In Case 27.2, an appellate court analyzes the termination of a sole proprietorship in the context of **successor liability**.

CASE 27.2 Biller v. Snug Harbor Jazz Bistro of Louisiana, LLC, 99 So.3d 730 (4th Cir. 2012)

FACT SUMMARY Brumat was the sole proprietor of Snug Harbor Jazz Bistro of New Orleans (Snug Harbor), a restaurant, bar, and music club. Brumat had leased a building on Frenchmen Street in New Orleans. In July 2007, Brumat died; pursuant to his last will and testament, all of his property, except a piano, was left to his niece, Luana Brumat (Luana). In September 2007, Luana and Brumat's former bookkeeper properly registered Snug Harbor, LLC, a Louisiana limited liability company. The filing listed themselves as its officers and used the Frenchmen Street address as its domicile and mailing address.

In 2009, Biller obtained an $80,000 judgment against Snug Harbor as a result of an accident that occurred at the Snug Harbor restaurant in April 2007. Seeking to enforce the judgment, Biller filed a petition alleging that the business entity Snug Harbor had operated continuously before and after the death of Brumat and that Snug Harbor, LLC, was a successor in interest to the Brumat sole proprietorship. On that basis, Biller argued that the LLC was liable for Brumat's debts in connection with the operation of the Snug Harbor restaurant.

Snug Harbor, LLC, denied liability for the judgment arguing that the original Snug Harbor was a sole proprietorship that terminated upon the death of Brumat, and Snug Harbor, LLC, was a limited liability company that was formed after Biller's injury and after Brumat's death and was a separate and distinct entity. The trial court ruled that Snug Harbor, LLC, was a not a successor in interest to Snug Harbor because at the time of the accident, Brumat owned and operated Snug Harbor as a sole proprietorship. Biller appealed.

SYNOPSIS OF DECISION AND OPINION The Court of Appeals for the Fourth Circuit affirmed the trial court's decision in favor of Snug Harbor, LLC. The court rejected Biller's argument that Snug Harbor, LLC, continued operating Snug Harbor as usual following Brumat's death because Snug Harbor's former bookkeeper was engaging in the same business at the same address. The court ruled that the business entity owned by Brumat terminated upon his death because it was a sole proprietorship. The parties (an heir and a former employee of Brumat) then properly and promptly formed a new entity that was a separate and distinct business entity (an LLC) from the sole proprietorship. The court pointed to the fact that the new entity entered into a new commercial lease agreement for the Frenchmen Street building and other necessary contracts as evidence that a new entity existed after Brumat's death.

WORDS OF THE COURT: No Successor Liability "After reviewing the record, we find no error in the trial court's conclusion that Snug Harbor, L.L.C., is a separate, distinct entity from the late Mr. Brumat and his estate, and therefore, not liable for the debts of the succession. The evidence supports the trial court's finding that Snug Harbor, L.L.C., did not exist at the time of Mr. Biller's accident and was formed after Mr. Brumat's death. . . . We also note that plaintiffs neither asserted nor offered evidence that Ms. Brumat and Mr. Schmidt formed Snug Harbor, L.L.C., with the intent to defraud any creditor(s) of the succession. Absent any evidence of fraud and considering the evidence before us, we find the trial court properly dismissed plaintiffs' claims against Snug Harbor, L.L.C."

Case Questions

1. What evidence did Biller claim indicates that the LLC was a continuing entity and not a separate entity? Why did the court reject his theory?

2. The court pointed out that there was no evidence of fraud in the formation of the new entity. Why is that important? What kind of fraud could be committed in this context?

3. *Focus on Critical Thinking:* Is this a case of business owners using the law as a shield against a legitimate claim? Is it ethical to use the LLC as a way to escape liability? Is this fair to Biller?

TAKEAWAY CONCEPTS Sole Proprietorships

Formation	Low start-up costs and minimal filing. One-person entity.
Liability of principal	All debts and liabilities of the business are the personal liabilities of the sole proprietor. All of the proprietor's assets are at risk to satisfy business debts and liabilities.
Capital	Proprietor uses personal assets, private loans, or a commercial loan.
Taxes	All income taxes of the business are paid at the proprietor's individual tax rate and reported on the proprietor's individual income tax return. Miscellaneous state and local taxes to operate business.
Management and control	One-person entity.
Designation	John Doe d/b/a Doe Consulting Services

FRANCHISES: A METHOD RATHER THAN AN ENTITY

LO 27-6

Recognize the role of franchises in business.

An existing entity that wishes to distribute its products to a broader market without the overhead costs of retail space, equipment, and employees can do so through the use of a franchise. A franchise should be thought of as a method of conducting business that centers on a contractual relationship rather than as a business entity. Federal statutes define a franchise as an arrangement of a continuing commercial relationship for the right to operate a business pursuant to the franchisor's trade name or to sell the seller's branded goods. A franchise involves the *franchisor,* a business entity that has a proven track record of success, selling to a *franchisee* the right to operate the business and use the business's trade secrets, trademarks, products, and so on. The franchisor assists the franchisee with financing, supplies, training, and other aspects of running a successful operation.

Franchise Agreements

The parties in a franchise are typically bound to each other via a franchise agreement. The franchise agreement covers some of the following terms that govern the relationship between franchisee and franchisor: (1) the term (time limit) of the agreement; (2) franchise fees, payment terms, and ongoing investment or buying requirements; (3) territory rights that usually provide the franchisee with an exclusive geographic area; (4) commitments from the franchisor for training, ongoing management support, and advertising; (5) commitments from the franchisee to follow operating protocol; (6) royalties and other fees that the franchisee must pay; and (7) franchisee termination and/or cancellation policies.

FTC Regulation

The Federal Trade Commission (FTC) is the federal regulatory authority that oversees the regulation of franchisors. The FTC regulations are primarily designed to ensure full disclosure of all information relating to a franchise company prior to a franchisee investment. The FTC regulations are very detailed, but almost all focus on mandatory disclosures about the financial condition of the franchise, success rates, and other important information used by potential franchisees faced with making the decision to invest in the franchise. The disclosure process is lengthy, complex, and almost always requires the counsel of an attorney skilled in franchise law.

State Regulation

Most states have implemented their own individual franchise rules and minimum disclosure requirements to supplement the federal legislation. These additional requirements usually entail filing a registration statement with a state regulatory agency (the state-level equivalent of the FTC). The registration statements are public documents and often require detailed disclosures and biographical information on the principals of the franchise.

Dunkin' Donuts is one of the mostly widely recognized franchises in the United States.
©Jonathan Weiss/Alamy

 THINKING STRATEGICALLY

Umbrella Insurance

PROBLEM: The most significant risk for a sole proprietor is the threat that business liabilities will become personal liabilities. To guard against that threat, sole proprietors often pay for *commercial insurance* (called a commercial general liability [CGL] policy) that would cover any liabilities related to business operations. However, much to the surprise of many business owners, commercial policies are full of *exclusions.* Exclusions are specific events that are not covered by the policy. For example, a CGL policy does not cover most contract disputes or any actions by governmental agencies charging that a business has failed to abide by regulations or statutes. Moreover, in some cases the amount of the liability may exceed the amount of the insurance policy. If a customer trips in a small retail store owned by a sole proprietor and suffers $150,000 in medical damages—exceeding the limit of the proprietor's $100,000 commercial insurance policy—the sole proprietor's personal assets are at risk for the remaining $50,000.

STRATEGIC SOLUTION: Use commercial umbrella insurance to cover gaps in coverage. The umbrella policy is intended to cover any losses in the event that the primary insurance isn't sufficient to pay the full loss. This typically occurs in two situations. First, when the CGL policy is exhausted by payment of the loss, the umbrella policy "drops down" to replace the exhausted underlying protection. Drop-down coverage also may become effective when the primary insurer is in bankruptcy. Second, umbrella coverage applies when the primary CGL policy contains an exclusion that is not excluded under the umbrella policy.

QUESTIONS

1. One of the reasons that umbrella coverage is a good choice is that it is relatively inexpensive. Do some Internet research and try to determine what the approximate cost of a $1 million policy would be.

2. Although CGL policies and umbrella coverage reduce some risks, they do not cover cases in which losses are due to an alleged breach of contract. What are some legal or business strategies for avoiding that specific risk?

3. Based on the legal strategies you learned in Chapter 1, what category of legal strategy does umbrella coverage fall into? Why?

Principals p. 458   Owners of a business entity.

Sole proprietorship p. 460   One-person business entity with minimal filing requirements.

Trade name p. 460   Name used by a sole proprietor for a business instead of the proprietor's actual name.

Private loan p. 463   Money loaned by a private source (e.g., an individual) whereby the debtor agrees to pay back the loan over a certain period of time at a certain rate.

Commercial loan p. 463   Money loaned by a commercial source (e.g., a bank) whereby the debtor agrees to pay back the loan over a certain period of time at a certain rate.

Collateral p. 463   The assets a borrower has pledged to secure a loan.

Line of credit p. 463   Form of commercial loan that allows the borrower to draw against a predetermined credit limit, as needed, instead of receiving the full loan amount at one time.

Successor liability p. 465   Doctrine that allows a creditor to seek recovery from the purchaser of assets even when the purchaser did not expressly assume such liabilities as part of the purchase.

CASE SUMMARY 27.1 Vernon v. Schuster, 688 N.E.2d 1172 (Ill. 1997)

Termination of Sole Proprietorship

James Schuster, a sole proprietor doing business as Diversey Heating and Plumbing, contracted with Vernon to install and maintain a boiler in his building. Schuster also promised Vernon a 10-year warranty, and the parties agreed to a long-term service agreement whereby Schuster was to perform an annual pre-winter inspection of the boiler and render any service needed for upkeep. Schuster performed the services for a period of three years, but he died in October 1993 before performing the pre-winter inspection on Vernon's boiler. After Schuster died, his son Jerry Schuster began to operate Diversey and serve Diversey customers. In February 1994, Vernon discovered that the boiler was broken beyond repair and needed to be replaced. Vernon brought a breach-of-warranty lawsuit against Jerry Schuster on the basis that he had continued the sole proprietorship that his father had started and therefore Jerry Schuster should honor the warranty given by James Schuster. Jerry Schuster maintained that he had no responsibility to honor a warranty provided by a predecessor business. The trial court dismissed most of the lawsuit, holding that Jerry Schuster could not be held liable for the obligations of his father's sole proprietorship interest.

CASE QUESTIONS

1. Who prevails and why? Name a case from this chapter that supports your answer.
2. If Jerry Schuster changed the name of the business but still used the tools he inherited, how would that impact your analysis?
3. As an ethical matter, should a son honor the commitments of his father in these circumstances?

CASE SUMMARY 27.2 Nazi v. Jerry's Oil Co. (Tenn. Ct. App. 2014)

Proprietor Liability

In 2007, John Nazi executed a security agreement on behalf of the Handy Peddler in favor of Jerry's Oil. On the security agreement, John Nazi signed his name, but thereunder indicated that his title was "Manager." A few days later, on April 2, 2007, John Nazi executed a fuel supply agreement. The alleged breach of this agreement is the central issue in this case. The fuel supply agreement required the "Retailer" to pay Jerry's Oil for various obligations under the contract. The Retailer was defined by the contract as the Handy Peddler. On the signature block at the conclusion of the document, John Nazi executed the agreement by only signing "John Nazi." Although the fuel supply agreement included a space for the signatory to designate his or her title, this space was left blank by John Nazi. Further, on April

20, 2007, John Nazi also executed a promissory note in favor of Jerry's Oil. The promissory note specifically identified John Nazi "doing business as" the Handy Peddler, without any designation or title.

1. Is Nazi a sole proprietor or a manager?
2. Is Nazi personally liable for the amounts under the promissory note? Why or why not?

CASE SUMMARY 27.3 Clayton v. Planet Travel Holdings, Inc., 988 N.E.2d 1110 (Ill. App. Ct. 2013)

Proprietor Liability

Clayton is a customer who brought an action against Planet Travel for violation of the state consumer protection law and breach of contract. Fuener was operating Planet Travel as a sole proprietorship during the time of the violations, and Clayton sued Fuener d/b/a Planet Travel under the state law. Fuener delayed the matter from proceeding to trial for nearly three years and eventually incorporated a new entity for Planet Travel.

CASE QUESTIONS

1. Is Fuener liable under the consumer protection law as a sole proprietor? Why or why not?
2. Does the fact that Fuener incorporated his business after the violations have any impact on your analysis?

CASE SUMMARY 27.4 England v. Simmons, 757 S.E.2d 111 (Ga. 2014)

Proprietor Interest

Haege died in December 2006. Three months earlier, Haege had made a will in which he left his "personal assets" to his brother and sister, and in which he left his "business interests, both tangible and intangible, real or personal, connected to the business known as Traditional Fine Art, Ltd." to his brother, sister, and two longtime employees. After Haege died, questions arose about the disposition of property associated with Traditional Fine Art, Ltd., insofar as Traditional Fine Art was a sole proprietorship and, therefore, had no legal existence separate and apart from Haege himself. The will was admitted to probate, and Sharon Haege

England—Haege's sister—was appointed as executrix of his estate. England failed to distribute any property to James S. Simmons and Elery Stinson—the two longtime employees—and they filed this lawsuit against England, seeking a declaratory judgment as to the meaning of the will with respect to the property associated with Traditional Fine Art.

CASE QUESTIONS

1. Who prevails and why?
2. Can Haege pass the assets of Traditional Fine Art through his will? Why or why not?

CHAPTER REVIEW QUESTIONS

1. Which of the following factors in choosing an entity refers to the business's option for funding its operations?
   a. Personal liability
   b. Capitalization
   c. Management
   d. Taxation
   e. Formation

2. All of the following are true about a sole proprietorship entity except:
   a. It does not protect the personal assets of the principal.
   b. It is formed by filing a set of forms with the federal and state government.
   c. It provides pass-through taxation for the principal.
   d. It is a single-person entity.
   e. It may be capitalized through a loan.

CHAPTER TWENTY-SEVEN | Choice of Business Entity and Sole Proprietorships 469

3. Franco is a sole proprietor who does business as Franco's Computer Consulting. After starting up the business out of his basement, he lands a big client and begins to lease office space at a local office complex. He loses the big client in one month and can no longer generate enough business revenue to sustain the lease payments. He ends up owing his landlord $5,000. Assuming no business assets exist, which is true?

a. Franco is personally liable for the lease payments.

b. Franco is not personally liable for the lease payments.

c. Franco is not personally liable for the debt if he vacates the property.

d. Franco is only liable for 50 percent of the lease payments.

e. Franco is liable only if he signed a personal guarantee.

4. Which of the following methods is/are available to capitalize a sole proprietorship?

a. Sale of equity (ownership)

b. Self-funded by the proprietor

c. Loan from a bank (private debt)

d. B and C

e. A, B, and C

5. Which of the following is/are an event(s) of termination for a sole proprietorship?

a. Death of the proprietor

b. Failing to renew the entity with state officials

c. Filing a personal tax return

d. A and B

e. A, B, and C

6. Sole proprietorships are limited in their options for raising money.

a. True

b. False

7. One advantage to being a sole proprietor is protection of the proprietor's personal assets for business debts.

a. True

b. False

8. Sole proprietorships are taxed as pass-through entities.

a. True

b. False

9. A principal is one who has ownership in a business entity.

a. True

b. False

10. A sole proprietorship can be passed on to heirs through gifts or an estate.

a. True

b. False

 Quick Quiz ANSWERS
Capitalization

1. Unsecured loan. A credit card is the most common example of an unsecured loan.

2. Private. Loans from family and friends fall into this category.

3. Commercial loan. A loan from a bank that is used for a specific purpose (e.g., purchase a vehicle) falls into this category.

4. Line of credit. Because Winston only needs to draw money as necessary during the slow season, this option is considered a commercial line of credit.

CHAPTER REVIEW QUESTIONS: Answers and Explanations

1. b. Capitalization is the factor that is used to consider options for the best way to fund a business's start-up and/or operations. All other answers are factors in the choice of entity but are unrelated to funding.

2. b. In many states, no formal filing is required to launch a sole proprietorship unless the principal is using a fictitious or trade name. In any case, no federal filing is necessary since business formation is typically a state statutory matter.

3. a. A sole proprietor has no liability protection for business debts. The lease payments are a business liability, and therefore they are also Franco's personal liability.

4. d. Sole proprietors have limited options for capitalization including private debt or commercial debt. Answer *a* is wrong because sole proprietors cannot sell equity.

5. a. Sole proprietorships end upon the death of the principal. Answers *b, c,* and *d* are incorrect because no renewal process is required and filing a personal tax return is simply a reporting of business profits and losses to taxing authorities.

6. a. True. Sole proprietors have limited options for capitalization, including private debt or commercial debt.

7. b. False. A sole proprietor has no personal liability protection for business debts.

8. a. True. Sole proprietors pay taxes on profits at their individual rates and report profits on their individual tax returns.

9. a. True. Each form of entity has owners, known as principals, of the business.

10. b. False. Sole proprietorships end upon the death of the principal, and ownership cannot be transferred.

CHAPTER 28

Partnerships

THINKING STRATEGICALLY

Some types of partnerships, such as a general partnership, can be easy to create. This can be beneficial, yet, in some cases it may generate considerable risks for the partners involved. At the end of this chapter, you will determine whether the actions of a development team create a partnership and how this may strategically impact all of the parties involved.

Learning Objectives

After studying this chapter, students who have mastered the material will be able to:

28-1	Identify the necessary elements of partnership formation.
28-2	Summarize the main differences between the RUPA and the UPA and explain their role as legal default rules.
28-3	Describe how partnership law governs the internal and external aspects of a partnership.
28-4	Recognize several important rights of partners.
28-5	Recognize several important duties of partners.
28-6	List several important partnership agreement provisions.
28-7	Explain the distinguishing attributes of limited partnerships and family limited partnerships.
28-8	Articulate the legal protections from personal liability afforded to the principals in an LLP.
28-9	Describe the various methods for partnership dissolution.

CHAPTER OVERVIEW

This chapter will examine the law of general and limited partnerships. General partnerships are among the oldest types of business associations. For example, the famed Medici Bank of Renaissance Italy thrived in part because it established bank branches throughout Europe that were locally organized as separate partnerships. General partnerships are still used today because they are easy to establish and, unlike other business associations, they do not require registration with the state. General and limited partnerships also provide a high degree of flexibility with respect to the allocation of management roles, profits and losses, and voting rights.

GENERAL PARTNERSHIP FORMATION

LO 28-1

Identify the necessary elements of partnership formation.

A general partnership is legally defined as: (1) an association of two or more people (2) who are co-owners and co-managers of the business and (3) who share in the profits of their ongoing business. General partnerships typically use the designation "GP" at the end of their business name to signify the general partnership as their chosen form of entity. In a **term partnership**, partners may set a specific future date or event for when the partnership will be dissolved and may agree to extend this date if necessary. In a **partnership at will**, on the other hand, the partners agree to continue their association indefinitely.

No formal document or government filing is necessary to form a general partnership. Most partnerships are **express partnerships**, in which the principals agree orally or in writing to form an ongoing business relationship. It is important, however, to note that the parties may not actually intend to be partners or even call themselves partners. Nonetheless, the law will recognize their relationship as an **implied partnership** as long as the three required elements are present.

For example, suppose Billy, James, D'arcy, and Jimmy are friends who used to play in the college marching band together. Billy sings, James plays guitar, D'arcy plays bass, and Jimmy is a drummer. They started a band called the Smashing Tomatoes and have enjoyed success composing music and playing at local venues. They agree that they will play as many gigs as possible and will contribute musical equipment and talent to that effort. They also agree to share profits after all expenses are paid. At this point, even if they do not speak of forming a partnership or intend to be partners, they are legally bound to each other in an implied general partnership.

In Case 28.1, a state appellate court analyzes whether a romantic relationship created an implied partnership in business.

CASE 28.1 Waddell v. Rustin, No. E2010-02342-COA-R3-CV (Tenn. Ct. App. 2011)

FACT SUMMARY Waddell and Rustin entered into a romantic relationship soon after meeting in 1999. Waddell maintained that their association started as personal and also grew into a business partnership. Rustin denied that they were ever express or implied business partners. At the time the two met, Rustin and his brother owned and operated a store called "Lots of Christmas" ("the Store"), and Waddell began working at the store in 2000. One year later, Rustin started a construction and excavation business. Both at the Store and at the construction company, Waddell claimed that she had management and oversight over business projects, had access to the company checkbook, paid company bills, helped Rustin choose construction projects, and even changed the store's name from "Lots of Christmas" to "Aluminum Decor and More" to improve sales. Waddell testified that she did not receive any paychecks for her work, but that the couple ran the businesses as partners. When the personal relationship ended, Waddell brought suit claiming that she was entitled to a percentage of the profits because the relationship had been an implied partnership. The trial court ruled that no implied partnership was created.

SYNOPSIS OF DECISION AND OPINION The Court of Appeals of Tennessee affirmed the trial court and held in favor of Rustin. The court ruled that because there was no written partnership agreement between Waddell and Rustin, Waddell bore the burden of proving the existence of a partnership by clear and convincing evidence. Given that Waddell had no experience in construction or excavation when they met and that Rustin had engaged in construction work for years, it was clear that his efforts had made the business viable. Waddell did not contribute equipment, experience, or capital. Therefore, the court held that one cannot reasonably conclude

(continued)

that Waddell's relationship with Rustin rose to the level of an implied partnership.

WORDS OF THE COURT: Partner Contributions
"Rustin acknowledges, as do we, that Waddell performed certain work related to Rustin's business enterprises. However, it cannot be said of this case that the parties' prosperity was due in equal part to Waddell's efforts. Rustin and his brother ran the store prior to Waddell's relationship with Rustin. Waddell's work at the Store is better characterized as helping out rather than the contribution of an equal partner. Notwithstanding Waddell's activities related to certain houses or cabins, the record shows that Rustin, with his experience in construction and excavation, clearly was the primary driver of the construction enterprise. Waddell testified that she contributed no real property; personal property; money; formal training in interior design; excavation experience; or construction experience to any partnership."

Case Questions

1. What was Waddell's theory of the case as to why an implied partnership existed?

2. Could a personal relationship ever be considered a partnership? At what point does a personal relationship create an implied partnership?

3. *Focus on Critical Thinking:* Given the court's ruling, what could Waddell have done differently to ensure that she would have had partner status?

TAKEAWAY CONCEPTS General Partnership Formation

- A general partnership is legally defined as: (1) an association of two or more people (2) who are co-owners and co-managers of the business and (3) who share in the profits of their ongoing business.
- No formal document or government filing is necessary to form a general partnership.

LO 28-2

Summarize the main differences between the RUPA and the UPA and explain their role as legal default rules.

OVERVIEW OF THE REVISED UNIFORM PARTNERSHIP ACT (RUPA) AND THE UNIFORM PARTNERSHIP ACT (UPA)

Unlike most business entities, general partnerships are not created by filing a form with the state. Instead, the law recognizes that two or more individuals form a general partnership if they have demonstrated an intent to carry on as co-owners of a business for profit. While some general partnerships have written agreements detailing the internal operations of the business and the rights and responsibilities of the partners, others operate without any written agreement at all. In the absence of an agreement, the **Revised Uniform Partnership Act (RUPA)** is likely to govern a general partnership.

Just like the Uniform Commercial Code (UCC), the RUPA is a model statute drafted and occasionally revised by the National Conference of Commissioners on Uniform State Laws. To date, approximately 40 states have adopted all or substantial portions of the RUPA. States that have not yet adopted the RUPA operate under the RUPA's predecessor, the **Uniform Partnership Act (UPA)**.[1] One of the major differences between the two acts relates to their treatment of the partnership as a separate legal person distinct from its partners. Under the RUPA "a partnership is an entity distinct from its partners,"[2] whereas under the UPA it is not. In contrast to the UPA, the RUPA's "entity" approach allows a

---

[1]Louisiana is the only state not to adopt the UPA or the RUPA.
[2]RUPA § 201(a).

partnership to survive if one partner withdraws and allows partnership creditors to collect from the partnership rather than from individual partners.

It is helpful to think of the RUPA and the UPA as **default rules** that apply when the partners have not expressly agreed how to regulate their internal relations with each other through a contract called a **partnership agreement**. The RUPA also outlines certain agency principles, including fiduciary duties that the partners owe each other and the partnership. In addition to the RUPA, the judge-made common law plays an important role in general partnership law in cases where principles of general fairness must be applied and the RUPA doesn't apply to a particular situation.[3]

TAKEAWAY CONCEPTS Overview of the RUPA and UPA

- In the absence of an agreement, the Revised Uniform Partnership Act (RUPA) is likely to govern a general partnership.
- States that have not yet adopted the RUPA operate under the RUPA's predecessor, the Uniform Partnership Act (UPA).
- Under the RUPA "a partnership is an entity distinct from its partners," whereas under the UPA it is not.
- The RUPA outlines certain agency principles, including fiduciary duties that the partners owe each other and the partnership.

GENERAL PARTNERSHIPS IN THE CONTEXT OF BUSINESS

LO 28-3

Describe how partnership law governs the internal and external aspects of a partnership.

For the tax year 2014–2015, approximately 574,000 U.S. general partnerships filed tax information returns with the Internal Revenue Service (IRS). Many businesses such as coffee shops, real estate investment companies, or mobile app start-ups start out as general partnerships because the business founders enter into an informal business agreement with one another. Well-known businesses have started as informal ventures among friends on little more than a handshake deal. For example, Ben and Jerry's and Apple Inc. both got their start this way. Some small companies choose to continue to operate as partnerships, whereas others morph into a business association such as a corporation to reduce liability or attract investment.

Partnership law governs the internal aspects of the business by regulating interactions among partners. These internal rules are spelled out by state statutes based on either the RUPA or the UPA. The partners at any time may decide to opt out of these default rules by entering into a contract called a *partnership agreement.* As discussed below, the statutory default rules cover important items such as how profits will be split among partners or who will have the authority to enter into contracts.

Partnership and agency law also governs the relationship between the partnership, partners, and outside third parties. The rules that govern relationships with third parties, in contrast to the rules that govern the relationship between partners, cannot be altered by a partnership agreement. For example, an important rule under the RUPA that distinguishes general partnerships from other types of business associations is that all partners face **joint-and-several liability** for contract and tort-related obligations. This means that general

---

[3]RUPA § 104(a) refers to this, stating, "Unless displaced by particular provisions of this [act], the principles of law and equity supplement this act."

partners' personal assets are at risk both together (jointly) and separately (severally) for all debts and liabilities of the partnership, regardless of the source of the debt or liability. This liability rule with respect to third parties cannot be altered by the partnership agreement. For example, if Billy from the Smashing Tomatoes band discussed earlier drives the van on partnership business and negligently injures someone, all the other band members will be liable as partners. All partners will share this liability equally; however, if only one band member has funds to pay the claim, he or she will shoulder the entire financial burden.

Partnership law also binds the partners to one another. According to Section 301 of the RUPA, "each partner is an agent of the partnership for the purpose of its business. An act of a partner . . . for apparently carrying on in the ordinary course the partnership business . . . binds the partnership, unless the partner had no authority to act . . . and the person with whom the partner was dealing knew or had received a notification that the partner lacked authority."

Just as in the case of a sole proprietorship, a partnership is a **pass-through entity**. This means that the partnership entity pays no level of corporate tax. Rather, profits are taxed after they pass through the business and are distributed to the individual partners. The income is reported on the individual general partner's personal tax return (Form 1040) and taxed based on the general partner's individual rate. In fact, the partnership entity itself does not file a tax return, but it does file an information return with the IRS for purposes of providing the government with documentation regarding how much, when, and to whom profits were paid. Partners also report business partnership losses on their individual tax returns and are permitted to deduct those losses to offset certain types of income.

TAKEAWAY CONCEPTS General Partnerships in the Context of Business

- Many well-known companies started informally as partnerships.
- Partnership and agency law also governs the relationship between the partnership, partners, and outside third parties.
- An important rule under the RUPA that distinguishes general partnerships from other types of business associations is that all partners face joint-and-several liability for contract and tort-related obligations.
- A partnership is a pass-through entity, which means that the partnership entity pays no level of corporate tax.

<table>
<tr><td>

LO 28-4

Recognize several important rights of partners.

</td><td>

THE RIGHTS OF PARTNERS

In the absence of a partnership agreement, the RUPA or UPA spell out the rights among the partners. Several important partnership rights guaranteed under these default rules are illustrated in Figure 28.1. Each of the rights is further discussed below.

Right to Share Profits and Losses Equally

Each partner is entitled to receive an equal share of the partnership's profits regardless of the partner's degree of involvement in the success of the business. It doesn't matter, for example, if one partner is responsible for 90 percent of the work that generates profits. The profits under the default rule must be split equally among all partners. The same rule applies to losses.

</td></tr>
</table>

FIGURE 28.1 Important Partnership Rights

Right to share profits and losses equally
Right to partnership property
Right to co-manage the business
Right to indemnity
Right to vote
Right to be informed

Right to Partnership Property

Under the RUPA, partners do not have rights to specific partnership property.[4] Instead, partners have an interest in the general partnership's profits. Partnership property is any property that is

- held in the name of the partnership;
- acquired in the name of a partner with their title listed as "partner";
- purchased with partnership funds; or
- used for partnership business.

Partners have equal rights to use any partnership property to conduct partnership business. Partners cannot, however, use partnership property for individual purposes. For example, a partner may not sell partnership property and use the proceeds for her personal benefit, nor can she guarantee a personal loan with partnership property.

Right to Co-manage the Business

Each partner has an equal right to co-manage the business. This important right has several components. First, it implies that partners have the right to be involved in conducting business operations, that is, to get their hands dirty and operate the business. Keep in mind, however, that under the default rules, partners who provide labor to the partnership are not entitled to a salary and their compensation is limited to an equal share of the profits. Second, this right implies the ability to sign contracts on behalf of the partnership. The right to enter into contracts with third parties is an important right.

Absent a partnership agreement that stipulates authority in a different manner, under the default rules a partner is authorized to enter into agreements that are reasonably necessary to accomplish the tasks within "the ordinary course of business of the partnership."[5] A contract that is outside the ordinary course of business, on the other hand, requires the unanimous consent of all the partners. Although it is difficult to specify what is ordinary versus what is extraordinary, courts have held that any act that substantially changes the nature of the partnership is extraordinary and requires unanimous consent of all the partners.

Right to Indemnity

If a partner within the ordinary course of business incurs a payment or liability made on behalf of the partnership, the partnership must reimburse that partner for the expense. A partnership agreement may define limits to this reimbursement, for example, by placing a dollar limit or specifying what authority a partner has to act within the ordinary course of business.

---

[4]RUPA § 501.

[5]RUPA § 401(c).

Right to Vote

Under the default rules, each partner has an equal voice when disagreements arise regarding the management of the business. A disagreement among partners is resolved through a vote. Each partner is entitled to one vote regardless of how much he or she contributed, and the majority generally wins. Situations that require a unanimous vote under the RUPA include the admission of a new partner, acts outside the ordinary course of business, and amending the partnership agreement. In cases where an equal number of partners leads to a standstill related to a substantial matter, the default rules provide that a dissolution of the partnership will occur.

Right to Be Informed

Under both the UPA and RUPA, each partner has the right to be informed of the partnership's business. This involves being able to request and review partnership records of all kinds, including contracts, minutes taken during meetings, and financial information.

 QUICK QUIZ Rights to Partnership Property

For the following questions, assume that the members of the Smashing Tomatoes (discussed above) do not create a partnership agreement and begin to earn profits by creating their own music and playing gigs.

1. Can Billy use the copyrights from the songs created by the band as collateral for his personal auto loan?
2. Can Billy sell the copyrights to the band's music to a record label?

Answers to this Quick Quiz are provided at the end of the chapter.

TAKEAWAY CONCEPTS The Rights of Partners

- In the absence of a partnership agreement, the RUPA or UPA spell out the rights among the partners.
- Important default partnership rights include the right to
  - share profits and losses equally;
  - partnership property;
  - co-manage the business;
  - indemnity;
  - vote; and
  - be informed.

THE DUTIES OF PARTNERS

LO 28-5

Recognize several important duties of partners.

Partners owe each other and the partnership several important duties as illustrated in Figure 28.2.

Together, these are known as **fiduciary duties**, and they ensure that each partner is acting in the partnership's best interests. Each of these duties will be further discussed below. It is

FIGURE 28.2   Partner Duties

| Duty of loyalty |
| Duty of care |
| Duty of good faith |

important to point out that under the RUPA, a partnership agreement may not completely eliminate the fiduciary duties.[6] There are a few situations, however, in which partners may agree to authorize or ratify a specific act or transaction that otherwise would violate the duty of loyalty.[7] Also, the courts have traditionally applied broad equitable principles to achieve flexible results with respect to defining the scope of fiduciary duties.

Duty of Loyalty

The loyalty standard prohibits a general partner from engaging in competition with the interests of the partnership and also prohibits other conflicts of interest such as using partnership property for personal gain. A partner likewise violates his duty of loyalty if he personally takes advantage of a business opportunity that would have benefited the partnership.

Case 28.2 is a landmark New York appellate court case authored by Judge Cardozo that defines the scope of duty of loyalty that is owed between partners.

LANDMARK CASE 28.2 Meinhard v. Salmon et al., 164 N.E. 545 (N.Y. 1928)

FACT SUMMARY   Meinhard and Salmon formed a general partnership to lease the Bristol Hotel located on the northwest corner of Fifth Avenue and 42nd Street in New York City for 20 years. Their agreement was to split the renovation costs to repurpose the building for commercial tenants and retail. Under the terms of their partnership, they would split the profits and losses evenly and Salmon would have sole authority to manage the business affairs of the partnership and lease. This partnership proved to be very profitable for both individuals, and the lease was set to expire on April 20, 1922.

In January 1922, the Bristol property owner offered Salmon a plan to lease the Bristol property and several adjoining lots. Under a new long-term lease, Salmon would demolish all the structures and finance the construction of a new larger building for commercial tenants. Without telling Meinhard, Salmon signed the new lease on January 25, 1922, a few months before their partnership was set to expire. The following month, Meinhard found out about the lease and sued to have the new lease transferred to

their existing partnership. The trial court ruled in favor of Meinhard, and Salmon appealed.

SYNOPSIS OF DECISION AND OPINION   Justice Cardozo, writing for the court, held that Salmon breached the duty of loyalty he owed Meinhard by usurping the business opportunity for himself. The court required Salmon to transfer half of the interest of the new lease to Meinhard.

WORDS OF THE COURT: Duty of Loyalty "Joint adventurers, like copartners, owe to one another, while the enterprise continues, the duty of the finest loyalty. Many forms of conduct permissible in a workaday world for those acting at arm's length, are forbidden to those bound by fiduciary ties. A trustee is held to something stricter than the morals of the market place. Not honesty alone, but the punctilio of an honor the most sensitive, is then the standard of behavior. As to this there has developed a tradition that is unbending and inveterate. Uncompromising rigidity has been the attitude

(continued)

---

[6]RUPA § 103(b).

[7]RUPA § 103(b)(3)(ii).

of courts of equity when petitioned to undermine the rule of undivided loyalty by the 'disintegrating erosion' of particular exceptions. . . . Only thus has the level of conduct for fiduciaries been kept at a level higher than that trodden by the crowd. It will not consciously be lowered by any judgment of this court.

. . .

"The very fact that Salmon was in control with exclusive powers of direction charged him the more obviously with the duty of disclosure, since only through disclosure could opportunity be equalized. If he might cut off renewal by a purchase for his own benefit when four months were to pass before the lease would have an end, he might do so with equal right while there remained as many years. . . . He might steal a march on his comrade under cover of the darkness, and then hold the captured ground. Loyalty and comradeship are not so easily abjured.

. . .

"We have no thought to hold that Salmon was guilty of a conscious purpose to defraud. Very likely he assumed in all good faith that with the approaching end of the venture he might ignore his coadventurer and take the extension for himself. He had given to the enterprise time and labor as well as money. He had made it a success. Meinhard, who had given money, but neither time nor labor, had already been richly paid. There might seem to be something grasping in his insistence upon more. Such recriminations are not unusual when coadventurers fall out. They are not without their force if conduct is to be judged by the common standards of competitors. That is not to say that they have pertinency here. Salmon had put himself in a position in which thought of self was to be renounced, however hard the abnegation. He was much more than a coadventurer. He was a

The Bristol Hotel (left) on the northwest corner of Fifth Avenue and 42nd Street in New York City.
©Pictorial Press Ltd/Alamy

managing coadventurer. . . . For him and for those like him, the rule of undivided loyalty is relentless and supreme. . . .

. . .

"Subject to this adjustment, we agree with the Appellate Division that the plaintiff's equitable interest is to be measured by the value of half of the entire lease, and not merely by half of some undivided part."

Case Questions

1. Did it matter to the court that Meinhard and Salmon's partnership was near its end? Explain.

2. Was Salmon justified in his view that the new lease was a different business opportunity altogether? Explain.

3. *Focus on Critical Thinking:* How could Salmon have avoided the liability and still taken advantage of the lease?

Duty of Care

Partners must also exercise due care in handling the affairs of the partnership and treat business affairs with diligence. Specifically, Section 404(c) of the RUPA states that a partner must "refrain from engaging in grossly negligent or reckless conduct, intentional misconduct, or a knowing violation of the law." Under this standard, partners are not liable if they make a business decision that results in harm due to an ordinary mistake of judgment.

Duty of Good Faith

The good faith standard requires that partners exercise appropriate discretion in dealing with other partners and third parties concerning the partnership's business. In partner-to-partner transactions, partners owe each other full disclosure. For example, imagine that Billy from the Smashing Tomatoes receives notification that a large music label wants to purchase the copyrights to the songs the band has jointly created. Billy may want to buy out his partners and own the copyrights individually; however, under the duty of good faith, he would have to inform the other band members about the interest expressed by the music label. If Billy failed to inform the other band members, they would be able to sue in court to undo the sale of the copyrights and have them returned to the partnership.

TAKEAWAY CONCEPTS The Duties of Partners

- Partnership duties include the duty of loyalty, care, and good faith.
- Together, these duties are referred to as *fiduciary duties.*
- Under the RUPA, a partnership agreement may not completely eliminate the fiduciary duties.

THE PARTNERSHIP AGREEMENT

LO 28-6

List several important partnership agreement provisions.

To avoid the default rules, partners may agree to enter into a partnership agreement that will govern their relations with one another. Figure 28.3 lists several important items that are defined in a partnership agreement. The case of Billy, James, D'arcy, and Jimmy signing a partnership agreement to launch their band, the Smashing Tomatoes, will be used in this section to highlight these various provisions.

Capital Contributions

The capital contribution lists how much value each partner has contributed to their individual capital accounts. This amount represents the initial equity investment into the partnership made by each partner. By law this amount must be returned to each partner when the partnership assets are liquidated. Services or knowledge that will be offered to the partnership cannot be recognized as a capital contribution.

For example, if Billy has written several songs, he may decide to have the copyrights to his music counted as part of his capital contribution. Likewise, if any of the band members own musical equipment, they can also have these recorded and valued as their capital contribution.

Property Provision

The default rule is that any property used for the partnership business may become subject to either partnership ownership or to the partnership's claim to its use. Therefore, partners must decide whether the property they owned individually prior to starting the

---

FIGURE 28.3 | **Important Partnership Agreement Items**

Capital contributions
Property provision
Profits and losses
Salary
Management rights
Buy-sell agreement

business will become partnership property in the event it is used by the partnership and was not identified as a capital contribution. For example, suppose James owns a van and he decides he does not want to include that in his capital contribution to the partnership. If he lets the band use his van, however, and the band uses partnership funds to repair the vehicle or pay the auto insurance, the partnership may assert an ownership claim to the van. To avoid this scenario, James would want to specify in the partnership agreement that his van is his sole and exclusive individual property during the term of the partnership.

Profits and Losses

Partners may wish to structure profits and losses to reflect their capital contributions or the level of work that will be required by each person. A partnership agreement gives the partners wide latitude to structure these terms any way they see fit. For example, if all the partners agree that Billy's capital contribution should be greater because he has provided the lyrics and melodies for the band's songs, he may be entitled to a higher proportion of the profits.

Salary

As mentioned earlier, partners are only entitled to an equal share of profits under the default rules. This provision in a partnership agreement allows partners to receive a guaranteed salary for the work they will perform on behalf of the partnership. For example, D'arcy may spend a considerable amount of time booking shows for the band and working with venues, outdoor music festivals, and promoters to schedule performances and their yearly live music tour. To compensate her for this extra level of work, D'arcy may require a guaranteed salary that is detailed in the partnership agreement.

Management Rights

Unless the agreement specifies otherwise, all partners have equal management rights and may sign contracts on behalf of the partnership that are within the ordinary course of the partnership's business. This can be dangerous if partners who lack the requisite skill make bad business decisions that are binding on the other partners. This can also lead to a frustrating situation if one partner enters into a binding agreement without consulting the other partners.

Imagine a scenario where each band member has equal management rights. This means each band member can purchase musical equipment and then seek reimbursement from the other band members. Likewise, someone may decide to contract with a venue to perform in a different state without informing the other band members. To get around this risky default scenario, the band members should create a written partnership agreement that stipulates the management authority and role of each band member. If the band members wish to transfer all management authority to one partner or someone they hire to manage their business affairs, they may do so. If they decide they all want to preserve the right to participate in business decisions, they might stipulate that certain important management decisions require a majority or unanimous approval from the other partners. The following management authority may be limited by requiring a unanimous or majority approval from the other partners:

- Signing a contract that is longer than one year in length.
- Signing a contract that exceeds a certain dollar amount.
- Borrowing money on behalf of the partnership.
- Selling partnership property.

With such a safeguard in place, any partner who fails to obtain authorization from the other partners would act without authority and the transaction could be declared void.

Buy-Sell Agreement

A buy-sell agreement allows the remaining partners to purchase the partnership interest of a withdrawing partner. This provision helps ensure the continuity of the partnership business and can avoid legal disputes if a valuation methodology is provided.

TAKEAWAY CONCEPTS The Partnership Agreement

- To avoid the default rules, partners may agree to enter into a partnership agreement that will govern their relations with one another.
- Important partnership agreement provisions include:
  - Capital contributions
  - Property provision
  - Profits and losses
  - Salary
  - Management rights
  - Buy-sell agreement

LIMITED PARTNERSHIPS AND FAMILY LIMITED PARTNERSHIPS

LO 28-7

Explain the distinguishing attributes of limited partnerships and family limited partnerships.

A **limited partnership** is an entity that exists by virtue of a state statute that recognizes one or more partners as managing the business while other partners participate only in terms of contributing capital or property. A limited partnership has at least one general partner (managing principal) and at least one limited partner (investing principal). In the absence of an agreement, the **Revised Uniform Limited Partnership Act (RULPA)** governs a limited partnership. However, the RULPA actually works in tandem with the RUPA. That is, when an issue of liability or operation arises, the written partnership agreement governs. If there is no agreement or the agreement is silent on the issue, then the RULPA resolves the issue. If the RULPA does not provide rules on a particular issue, courts may sometimes look to the RUPA for guidance.

Formation

To form a limited partnership, the general partner files a **certificate of limited partnership** with the state government authority[8] (usually the secretary of state's office). Generally, the certificate is fairly straightforward and requires routine information such as the name, address, and capital contribution of each partner. Although the RULPA does not formally require a partnership agreement, the vast majority of limited partnerships have one. The agreement details the rights, obligations, and relationships between partners. These partnerships typically use the designation "LP" at the end of their business name to signify the limited partnership as their form of entity. Figure 28.4 presents a sample certificate of limited partnership.

---

[8]RULPA § 201.

FIGURE 28.4 Sample Certificate of Limited Partnership

D The Commonwealth of Massachusetts
William Francis Galvin
Secretary of the Commonwealth
One Ashburton Place - Room 1717, Boston, Massachusetts 02108-1512

Limited Partnership Certificate
(General Laws Chapter 109, Section 8)

(1) The exact name of the limited partnership:

Redfern Catering, LP

(2) The general character of the business of the limited partnership:

Catering services

(3) The street address of the limited partnership in the commonwealth at which its records will be maintained:

1000 Restaurant Avenue
Boston, MA 02108

> Basic information including name, purpose, and address of the partnership. Note that Redfern Catering is using the LP (limited partnership) designation.

(4) The name and street address of the resident agent:

Francis Redfern   1000 Restaurant Avenue
                                   Boston, MA 02108

(5) The name and business address of each general partner:

Francis Redfern
1000 Restaurant Avenue
Boston, MA 02108

> State statutes require that all business entities have a physical address within the state jurisdiction. Out-of-state entities use a resident agent to satisfy this requirement. Some commercial services offer resident agent services for a fee. Attorneys sometimes serve as resident agents for their business clients. A resident agent typically provides services such as accepting legal documents (such as a complaint in a lawsuit) for the partnership. In-state partnerships simply use a partner as their resident agent (as in the case of Redfern Catering, LP).

(6) The latest date on which the limited partnership is to dissolve: October 10, 2030

(7) Additional matters:

Alexandra Macduff

> Most states require the partners to select an ending date for the partnership but allow the partners to continue the partnership after the ending date by simply filing an additional form extending the date.

Signed (by all general partners): _____

Consent of resident agent:

I **Francis Redfern** ,
resident agent of the above limited partnership, consent to my appointment as resident agent pursuant to G.L. c109
Section 8 (a) (3)*

*or attach registered agents consent hereto.

> The resident agent consents to serve in compliance with responsibilities set out by the state statute.

Personal Liability of Principals

Each general partner in a limited partnership is personally liable for all of the partnership's debts and liabilities, just as if the general partners were in a general partnership. However, limited partners do not have the same automatic personal liability of a general partner.[9] Rather, the limited partner's liability is limited to whatever the partner contributed to the partnership. For example, suppose that Francis Redfern initially operates Redfern Catering as a sole proprietor but decides to expand his business operations. He raises capital by selling some ownership interest in his business. Redfern convinces Alexandra Macduff to invest $20,000 in Redfern Catering. However, Macduff has substantial personal assets she wishes to protect and has no interest in running the day-to-day operations of the business. The two form Redfern Catering, LP, with Redfern as the general partner and Macduff as the limited partner. In an effort to cut food costs, Redfern negligently uses spoiled ingredients, and a customer, Marshall, is sickened. Marshall obtains a judgment against Redfern Catering, LP, but after the assets of the partnership are exhausted, Marshall is still owed a balance from the judgment. Because Redfern is a general partner, Marshall may recover the balance from Redfern's personal assets but not from Macduff as a limited partner. There are some exceptions to the liability rule spelled out in the RULPA. The primary exception occurs when a limited partner acts illegally or negligently within the scope of his partnership duties. When a limited partner engages in wrongful conduct on behalf of the limited partnership and causes an injury resulting in damages, the limited partner is personally liable to pay damages to the injured party.

Capitalization

Limited partnerships are generally funded either through debt (e.g., by borrowing money from the principals or a commercial lender) or through a sale of equity (e.g., by selling a percentage of ownership rights in the partnership and any profits of the business). Limited partnerships may not, however, sell ownership rights through the public markets such as the New York Stock Exchange (NYSE). Although not considered publicly traded equity, when limited partnership interests are sold to the public (usually through a broker-dealer with contacts in the investment community), they are subject to strict federal and state securities laws commonly known as *blue-sky laws*. Securities law is discussed extensively in Chapters 32 through 34.

Taxation of Partners and Partnership

Limited partnerships are pass-through entities just like general partnerships. The same rules apply for taxation as in a general partnership. That is, profits or losses are reported in the principal's personal tax return, and tax is paid in accordance with each partner's individual tax rate. The general partner is responsible for filing an information return with taxing authorities, but limited partnerships do not pay corporate taxes. As in the case of general partnerships, the information return informs tax authorities of profits or losses of the partnership entity.

Management and Operation of the Partnership

One of the primary differences between general partners and limited partners is the extent to which they are permitted to be involved in day-to-day operations of the business. General partners manage the business and are permitted to bind the partnership. Limited partners may not participate in daily management of the business, do not have authority to bind the partnership, and remain primarily investors. Limited partners who do engage in daily

---

[9]RULPA § 403(b).

management and operations jeopardize their limited partnership status. Under the RULPA, limited partners may engage in consulting and contribute expertise but may not engage in management activities such as supervision of employees.[10]

Although sometimes limited partners are referred to colloquially as *silent partners,* limited partners have the right to access partnership information such as business or financial records. The partnership agreement may expand the limited partner's role in management (though not to the point where the limited partner's role constitutes day-to-day involvement in running the business) and may also expand her rights and prerogatives, such as the right to remove a general partner or the right to block admission of new partners. These provisions in a partnership agreement are relatively common because they allow the limited partner to better protect her investment. Certain types of ventures, such as private investment funds, prefer to do business as limited partnerships to benefit from pass-through taxation and to limit the liability of the limited partners, who are typically passive and wealthy investors.

Limited partnerships also differ from general partnerships in terms of the default rule for sharing profits and losses. Recall from our earlier discussion that the RUPA mandates that partners, absent agreement to the contrary, share equally in profits and losses. However, in a limited partnership, the partners share in profits and losses in proportion to "the value of contributions made by each partner to the extent they have been received by the partnership and have not been returned."[11] For example, suppose Pablo, Vincent, and Frida form a limited partnership for the purpose of starting an art auction house. The partnership is initially structured as seen in Figure 28.5.

The partnership agreement provides for a salary for Pablo but is silent on distribution of profits and losses. Frida has an immediate need for cash, so the parties agree to return $10,000 of her investment. Under the RULPA, profits and losses are now allocated with 20 percent to Pablo, 35 percent to Frida, and 45 percent to Vincent.

In some cases, the principals in a partnership make specific agreements and label themselves as limited partners. This labeling is not sufficient to maintain limited partner status (and, thus, protection from certain liabilities). The focus of the inquiry is the principals' conduct. The question is not how they labeled themselves or how they signed certain documents or what they called themselves. Rather, the question is: Did the principals operate as a limited partnership?

Family Limited Partnerships

Another type of partnership is a **family limited partnership**. A family limited partnership is simply a limited partnership that is used for estate planning for families of considerable wealth. The actual process and legal procedures governing family limited partnership transactions are a very complex area of tax and estate law. The fundamental purpose of a family limited partnership is to enable wealthy members of one generation to distribute assets (in the form of an IRS-recognized gift) to heirs using a method that allows the distributing

| FIGURE 28.5 | Partners' Role and Capital Contribution |

Partner	Initial Capital Contribution	Role
Pablo	$20,000	General partner; salaried employee
Vincent	$45,000	Limited partner
Frida	$45,000	Limited partner

---

[10]RULPA § 303(b), (c).

[11]RULPA § 403(c).

generation to claim a much lower market value than the actual market value of the gift. It also allows the distributing generation to transfer assets out of their large estate into the smaller estates of their heirs and avoid estate taxes upon their death.

TAKEAWAY CONCEPTS Limited Partnerships and Family Limited Partnerships

- A limited partnership has at least one general partner (managing principal) and at least one limited partner (investing principal).
- In the absence of an agreement, the Revised Uniform Limited Partnership Act (RULPA) governs a limited partnership.
- To form a limited partnership, the general partner files a certificate of limited partnership with the state government authority.
- Limited partners enjoy limited liability, whereas general partners face unlimited liability.
- General partners manage the business and are permitted to bind the partnership.
- Limited partners may not participate in daily management of the business, do not have authority to bind the partnership, and remain primarily investors.

LIMITED LIABILITY PARTNERSHIPS (LLPs)

LO 28-8

Articulate the legal protections from personal liability afforded to the principals in an LLP.

Most states recognize limited liability partnerships through their partnership statutes. Recall that the chief danger of being a general partner is the amount of potential liability for acts of other general partners or the debts and liabilities of the partnership itself. LLP statutes provide general partnerships with the right to convert their entity and gain the protective shield ordinarily afforded only to limited partners or corporate shareholders. Although the origins of LLP laws are rooted in the protection of professional service firm partnerships (law, accounting, etc.), the use of LLPs is much more widespread now as some family businesses have also used the LLP form as a way to handle issues unique to the transition from one generation to another.

Formation

Limited liability partnerships are formed when a general partnership files a **statement of qualification** with the appropriate public official. The conversion of the partnership must be approved by a majority of the ownership. The statement includes the name and street address, an affirmative statement electing to become an LLP, an effective date, and the signatures of at least two of the partners. Some states also require a filing to inform tax authorities of the existence of the entity. Once approved, the filing becomes part of the public record.

Liability

Of all of the business entities that we have discussed thus far, the LLP has the greatest variance of liability protection under state law. While the general idea

Members of an LLP can prevent disputes from occurring by planning for events, such as death or dissociation of a member, in their operating agreement.
©Hero Images/Getty Images

behind being an LLP is that all partners have liability protection for debts and liabilities of the partnership, some states impose conditions on these limits. In cases where a partner has engaged in some misconduct or tortious conduct (such as negligence), the LLP acts to shield only the personal assets of *other* partners—never the partner who committed the misconduct or negligence.

In Case 28.3, a federal appeals court analyzes the potential personal liability of partners after an LLP has been dissolved.

CASE 28.3 Dillard Department Stores, Inc. v. Damon J. Chargois and Cletus P. Ernster, 602 F.3d 610 (5th Cir. 2010)[12]

FACT SUMMARY Chargois and Ernster (C&E) were individuals who formed and registered a limited liability partnership to operate their law practice in 2002. In an attempt to solicit business, C&E developed a website in June 2003 that included a link using Dillard Department Stores's (Dillard's) corporate name and trademarked logo. C&E had represented several Dillard's customers, and the website gave potential clients access to content created by C&E that allegedly documented acts of illegal profiling by Dillard's. Dillard's sued C&E for trademark infringement, cyber piracy, and various business torts.

In 2004, while the litigation continued, Chargois and Ernster executed a separation agreement that provided for dissolution of the partnership. C&E's registration as an LLP was not renewed with state authorities, and the registration expired later that same year. However, the defunct LLP entity remained a party to the Dillard's litigation, and no party was substituted on its behalf. On November 2, 2004, the court entered a final judgment ordering "Chargois & Ernster, L.L.P." to pay Dillard's $143,500.

Dillard's could not collect on the judgment because the entity had been dissolved and had no assets. Dillard's sought a declaration that the two principals were personally liable, jointly and severally, for the 2004 final judgment entered against C&E. Chargois and Ernster argued that they were shielded from any partnership liability or debt by the state LLP statute. The trial court granted judgment for Dillard's in the amount of $143,500 against Chargois and Ernster, jointly and severally, and each appealed.

SYNOPSIS OF DECISION AND OPINION The U.S. Court of Appeals for the Fifth Circuit ruled in favor of Dillard's and held Chargois and Ernster personally liable for the judgment owed to Dillard's. The court rejected arguments that the partners were insulated from liability because C&E's debt was incurred when the infringing website was created in June 2003, at which time C&E was still a registered limited liability partnership. Instead, the court found that the debt was incurred when the judgment was entered on November 2, 2004, at which time the LLP had lost its liability-limiting attributes and no longer protected Chargois and Ernster.

WORDS OF THE COURT: Timing of a Liability "Although the terms 'debt' and 'incurred' are not defined by the [statute], a plain reading of the statute's text supports Dillard's proffered interpretation. Neither partner was necessarily aware in June 2003 that displaying the Dillard's mark on the law firm website would ultimately lead to a partnership debt. The underlying conduct gave rise to the possibility of a future debt, but to say that a debt was 'incurred' at that time unrealistically distorts the meaning of the word. After all, [C&E's] conduct may have gone undetected, it may have been adjudged perfectly innocent, or Dillard's may have opted not to sue. Under any of those scenarios, no debt would ever have been incurred, let alone incurred in June 2003. It was only when the district court entered judgment against [C&E] in November 2004 that a payable debt came into existence. It was then that [C&E] incurred the debt within the meaning of the provision."

(continued)

---

[12]The reported citation of this case includes Evanston Insurance Company as a party for procedural reasons. For the sake of clarity, the case citation has been abbreviated.

Some states provide liability shields for LLP partners *only* when the liability arises from some *negligence* by another partner but not for other types of liabilities, such as those resulting from a breach of contract. For example, suppose that the LLP state statutes of New Chipperville provide for liability protection for partners when one partner acts negligently. Two accountants, Milton and Cowley, form a limited liability partnership called MC Tax Services LLP in New Chipperville. On behalf of the LLP, the partners sign a lease for space with Landlord and invest several thousand dollars from their own assets for start-up capital. One year later, Milton commits a serious error on a client's tax return, and the client sues the firm for malpractice and obtains a $50,000 judgment against the LLP. Because of the negative attention of this case, MC Tax Services loses several large clients and can no longer make its lease payments to Landlord, and the partnership dissolves. Assume that the judgment is not covered by insurance and exceeds the assets of the LLP. Under the law of New Chipperville, the client may pursue Milton's individual assets to pay the $50,000 judgment but not Cowley's. The liability shield protects Cowley for any acts of his partner when the liability results from a *tort* (in this case professional malpractice, a form of negligence). However, Cowley is still liable to Landlord for defaulting on the lease because the liability resulted from a *contractual* obligation.

Consider the plight of someone who has suffered damages due to another's negligence but cannot recover compensation because of the protection of an LLP. In the Milton-Cowley example, suppose that the client who was damaged by Milton's error cannot actually recover the judgment awarded to him because Milton is without assets. Because Cowley is not liable, the client is left with a court order that is worthless. In order to be sure that parties have at least some ability to recover, an increasing number of states require that the LLP and individual partners carry and maintain a certain amount of *liability insurance* as a condition of LLP formation.

Taxation

LLPs are treated as pass-through entities. They are not subject to tax; any income is taxed only when it is distributed to its partners. Because it is not a taxable entity, an LLP files an information return that informs federal and state tax authorities of the profits and losses of the LLP. All income or losses are reported on the partners' individual tax returns. Any losses are deductible and may sometimes help to reduce taxes on other sources of revenue on the individual's tax return.

Capitalization

LLPs are capitalized in the same way as a partnership: through debt via private or commercial lenders or by a sale of partnership equity for ownership in the LLP itself. The partnership agreement of the LLP often controls the amount and methods of capitalizing the business and the procedures for collecting additional contributions from partners as necessary (a process known as a *capital call*). Additional capital contribution requirements are frequently the subject of a partnership agreement. There are some cases in which the partnership has the right to "call" for more money contributions from each partner in order to keep the partnership afloat. Although terms vary, partners that are not in a position to make a call contribution may be forced to sell their interest in the partnership.

Although not required by statute, limited liability partnerships will frequently have a partnership agreement that sets out the management and operational structure. LLPs are sometimes governed by one or more managing partners and/or some type of executive committee elected by the other partners. The day-to-day operations and powers of the partners and board of partners are spelled out in the partnership agreement as well. The election procedures, qualifications, compensation, meeting times, and other organizational matters are typically addressed in the partnership agreement. In most states, the default agreement is the governing RUPA or UPA provision.

TAKEAWAY CONCEPTS Limited Liability Partnerships (LLPs)

- Most states recognize limited liability partnerships through their partnership statutes.
- The general idea behind an LLP is that all partners have liability protection for debts and liabilities of the partnership; however, some states impose conditions on these limits.
- When a partner has engaged in some misconduct or tortious conduct (such as negligence), the LLP acts to shield only the personal assets of other partners.
- Some states provide liability shields for LLP partners only when the liability arises from some negligence by another partner but not for other types of liabilities, such as those resulting from a breach of contract.
- LLPs are treated as pass-through entities. They are not subject to tax; any income is taxed only when it is distributed to its partners.
- LLPs are capitalized in the same way as a partnership: through debt via private or commercial lenders or by a sale of partnership equity for ownership in the LLP itself. Personal financial contributions of partners may be required in partnership agreement.

LO 28-9

Describe the various methods for partnership dissolution.

PARTNER DISSOCIATION AND PARTNERSHIP DISSOLUTION

When a partner no longer wishes to be a principal in the partnership, she may choose to leave the partnership. The RUPA[13] uses the term **dissociation** to describe this act of separation, while the RULPA uses the term **withdrawal**. Both the RUPA and RULPA give the partners substantial rights that govern withdrawal under the partnership agreement, but they differ significantly if the partners have not agreed to displace the RUPA and RULPA provisions.

---

[13]The rules governing dissociation and dissolution are perhaps the biggest difference between the UPA and RUPA. Under the UPA, such events cause an automatic dissolution of the partnership. The RUPA allows the partnership to continue under certain circumstances.

Dissociation under the RUPA

The RUPA lists 10 specific events of dissociation, but the majority of dissociations are the result of one of the following 3 events:

1. voluntary separation from the partnership, whereby one partner gives specific notice to withdraw from the partnership;
2. expulsion by the *unanimous* vote of the other partners; or
3. the partner's inability to carry out her duties to the partnership (as in the case of incapacity or death) or inability to have an economic stake in the business (as in the case of an individual partner filing for bankruptcy protection).

The RUPA makes a distinction between *rightful* and *wrongful* dissociation. When a partner exercises a rightful dissociation, she is no longer liable for the debts and liabilities incurred by the partnership. Although the partner is still liable for predissociation liability, she no longer owes any fiduciary duty to the partnership or the remaining principals. A wrongful dissociation occurs if a partner's withdrawal violates the partnership agreement or if a partner withdraws from a partnership before the expiration of a previously agreed-upon term or before completion of the partnership's undertaking.

In the event of a wrongful dissociation, the wrongfully dissociated partner "is liable to the partnership and to the other partners for damages caused by the dissociation."[14] For example, suppose that Abel, Baker, and Cain are general partners in ABC Landscape Design and have a written agreement about the partnership that sets the initial expiration at five years. Abel is knowledgeable in the operation of specific equipment crucial to the success of the business. ABC enters into a contract to provide services to several large office centers. After a few months, Abel withdraws from the partnership to pursue another career. As a result, the partnership cannot perform the services on time and breaches several agreements while attempting to locate a replacement to operate the equipment. In this case, Abel would be liable for damages suffered by the partnership.

In Case 28.4, a federal trial court considers one partner's allegation that another partner wrongfully dissociated.

CASE 28.4 Robertson v. Mauro et al., No. 2:13-CV-00027-CWD (D. Idaho 2013)

FACT SUMMARY Mauro operated a business conducting seminars to teach people how to trade in foreign currency. Robertson became acquainted with Mauro after attending a seminar Mauro taught in October 2009. Robertson alleges that in January 2010, he and Mauro orally agreed to form a partnership, which included an agreement to evenly divide profits among the partners. The purpose of the partnership was to facilitate Robertson's business plan to establish a series of seminars, taught by Mauro, which would instruct students on foreign currency trading. Robertson was to manage all financial and operating aspects of the partnership, which included promoting the seminars as well as other duties. Robertson began to schedule seminars in various locations, which Mauro taught. Robertson collected the fees for the seminars and distributed the profits according to the parties' agreement. This arrangement continued throughout the remainder of 2010, into the first quarter of 2011.

In early 2011, Mauro allegedly stated to Robertson that he "needed a break" temporarily from teaching the seminars but would resume the partnership later that year. Robertson alleged this

(continued)

---
[14]RUPA § 602(c).

statement was false, and that instead of taking a break, Mauro continued with the business without him. Robertson filed suit against Mauro for, among other things, wrongful dissociation because neither party expressed the intent to dissolve or wind up the partnership, yet Mauro's actions essentially accomplished a disintegration of the partnership without Robertson's consent.

SYNOPSIS OF DECISION AND OPINION The U.S. District Court in Idaho ruled in favor of Mauro on the dissociation claim. The court held that in order for a partner to wrongfully dissociate, the partner must fit into one of the categories listed in the state statutes based on the RUPA. The court ruled that since there was no partnership agreement and the entity was an at-will (implied) partnership, Mauro's action could not constitute a wrongful dissociation.

WORDS OF THE COURT: Wrongful Dissociation
"Based upon the allegations in the Complaint and Robertson's concession that the partnership was at will, Robertson's claim that Mauro's dissociation was wrongful does not meet [the partnership statute's] requirements. First, Robertson has not alleged breach of an express provision of the partnership agreement other than that the particular undertaking for which the partnership was organized had not been completed. Robertson does not identify the 'particular undertaking' at issue. And Robertson's concession in his response brief that the partnership was 'at will' is at odds with that assertion. By definition, [state partnership law] does not apply to an at-will partnership. The two provisions are mutually exclusive."

Case Questions

1. What was Robertson's theory of the case?

2. Why is it important that the partnership was "at will"?

3. *Focus on Critical Thinking:* In addition to the wrongful dissociation claim, Robertson alleged Mauro committed other wrongs related to their business relationship. Can you guess what they are? What other areas of law could be implicated in this case?

When a partner dissociates herself (rightfully or wrongfully) from the partnership, the partnership does *not* automatically dissolve. In fact, the RUPA leans toward the notion that the partnership can continue.[15] If the remaining principals wish to continue operating the business partnership, they must purchase the partnership interest of the dissociating partner based on a formula contained in the RUPA. Again, it is important to note that these are RUPA default rules and that a partnership agreement often fixes the method or formula for determining the buyout price.

There may be certain cases where the remaining principals wish to dissolve the partnership after dissociation. The dissolution does not actually end the partnership but rather triggers the process of **winding up**. Only after windup is complete is the partnership officially considered terminated. Windup is the period of time necessary to settle the affairs of the partnership and includes activities such as discharging the partnership's liabilities, settling and closing the partnership's business, marshaling the assets of the partnership, and distributing any net proceeds to the partners.

Withdrawal under the RULPA

Because the overwhelming majority of limited partnerships operate under a partnership agreement that spells out detailed rules for withdrawal of a general or limited partner, the RULPA does not play as significant a role as does the RUPA for general partnerships.

---

[15]RUPA § 606(a).

However, the RULPA does set down default rules for withdrawal of partners in the event that the written agreement does not cover withdrawal or its consequences sufficiently.

A *general partner* may withdraw at any time without causing dissolution of the partnership. The withdrawal does not result in automatic dissolution provided that (1) the partnership still has at least one remaining *general partner* and (2) all of the partners (both general and limited) agree in writing to continue the partnership. If the partner's withdrawal does not result in dissolution of the partnership, the partnership must pay the departing partner the fair market value of her interest in the limited partnership within a reasonable time after withdrawal.[16]

In contrast, *limited partners* are subject to restrictions on withdrawal. Absent an agreement in writing to the contrary, the general rule is that limited partners may *not* withdraw from a partnership before the partnership termination time agreed on by the partners. If the limited partnership agreement does not provide for a certain time before termination, limited partners must give at least six months' prior written notice to the other partners before withdrawing. Some states have passed additional restrictions, including an absolute prohibition of withdrawal, intended to address special circumstances in family limited partnerships.

Other Events of Dissolution

Dissociation is not the only way that a partnership may be dissolved. A partnership may also be dissolved when the partnership has reached its agreed-upon term (a specific date set out in the filings and/or partnership agreement); when dissolution is mandated by court order; or, in the case of a general partnership, when agreed to by unanimous consent of the partners. Note that dissolving a limited partnership does not require unanimous consent of all partners. Rather, unanimous consent of each general partner and consent of any limited partner that owns a majority of the rights to receive a distribution as a limited partner is sufficient to dissolve the partnership.

TAKEAWAY CONCEPTS Partner Dissociation and Partnership Dissolution

- The RUPA lists a variety of events of dissociation that are termed *rightful dissociations,* including voluntary separation, expulsion, incapacity, and death.
- In a rightful dissociation, the withdrawing partner is no longer liable for postdissociation liabilities of the partnership. In a wrongful dissociation (i.e., one that violates the partnership agreement), the withdrawing partner is liable for any damages the withdrawal caused.
- The RULPA plays a less significant role in a limited partnership context because so many limited partnerships operate under detailed agreements.
- Under the RULPA, a general partner may withdraw at any time without causing dissolution.
- Limited partners are subject to restrictions on withdrawal.
- Partnerships may also be dissolved upon reaching the agreed-upon term, by court order, or by unanimous consent of the parties.

---

[16]RULPA § 604.

Partnership Formation

PROBLEM: In December 2002, while they were undergraduate students at Harvard, brothers Cameron and Tyler Winklevoss and Divya Narendra developed a business plan for a new type of website called ConnectU.com that would allow students and alumni of a college to create a social network. To help them with the technical aspects of the website, they employed their friend and fellow classmate Victor Gao. Gao was unable to complete the coding for the site due to personal obligations and recommended that ConnectU contact another Harvard student named Mark Zuckerberg.

STRATEGIC SOLUTION: Gao met Zuckerberg in his dorm room sometime around November 9, 2003. According to Gao:

> During this meeting with Zuckerberg, I explained to him the compensation structures offered by the Founders [the Winklevossess and Narendra]. As requested by the Founders, I told him that they would either pay him on a rolling basis or take him on . . . with the possibility of taking an equal stake as each member of the Founders in the project. He became visibly excited. He told me that he wanted the latter option, and wanted to become a member of the Harvard Connection team because he thought the Harvard Connection website had the potential to reach out to a very large user base.[17]

Narendra later recalled a meeting where he and the Winklevosses met Zuckerberg in his dorm room sometime in December 2003. According to Narendra, "the four of us discussed ideas for the site's development as well as what was needed to be done in order to complete the site by our proposed launch deadline, the end of 2003." Narenda stated that Zuckerberg appeared enthusiastic at this meeting and continually referred to the team as "we" and suggested ideas on how "we" should develop the website."[18]

According to the Winkelvosses, Zuckerberg e-mailed on various occasions detailing how he was working on the ConnectU software code and website. Zuckerberg, however, never produced the code. When the Winklevosses inquired about the delays, Zuckerberg replied via e-mail: "I'm completely swamped with work this week. I have three

Mark Zuckerberg.
©Kristoffer Tripplaar/Alamy

programming projects and a final paper due by Monday, as well as a couple of problem sets due Friday."[19] The group met again in mid-January 2004. As Narendra recalled:

> At this meeting, Zuckerberg was noticeably less enthusiastic about the enterprise and stated that he had many personal projects which required his time. When pressed about completing the [ConnectU] website, he told us that he would be able to do so, but only after completing these other projects.[20]

On January 11, 2004, Zuckerberg registered the domain name TheFaceBook.com, and on February 4 of that year he launched thefacebook.com independently with a different group of collaborators. The ConnectU team found out about this after the *Harvard Crimson* student newspaper ran a story about the rapid growth and popularity of thefacebook.com among the student body.[21]

QUESTIONS

1. How would you respond to Zuckerberg's actions if you were a partner in the ConnectU team?

2. Given these facts, was Zuckerberg a partner of ConnectU? Explain how the three elements of partnership relate to your answer.

---

[17]Declaration of Victor Gao, ConnectU, Inc. et al. v. Facebook, Inc. et al., Civil Action No. 1:07-CV-10593-DPW (U.S. Dist. Ct. Mass) (Sept. 21, 2007).

[18]Declaration of Divya Narendra, ConnectU, Inc. et al. v. Facebook, Inc. et al., Civil Action No. 1:07-CV-10593-DPW (D. Mass., Sept. 21, 2007).

[19]J. Cassidy, "How Hanging Out in the Internet Became Big Business," *The New Yorker,* May 15, 2006.

[20]Declaration of Divya Narendra, ConnectU, Inc. et al. v. Facebook, Inc. et al., Civil Action No. 1:07-CV-10593-DPW (U.S Dist. Ct. Mass) (Sept. 21, 2007).

[21]Alan J. Tabak, "Hundreds Register for New Facebook Website: Facemash Creator Seeks New Reputation with Latest Online Project," *Harvard Crimson,* February 9, 2004, http://www.thecrimson.com/article/2004/2/9/hundreds-register-for-new-facebook-website/.

3. If a partnership was created, would it be classified as an express or an implied partnership?

4. Which of the fiduciary duties would ConnectU claim that Zuckerberg violated? Explain whether you think this duty was violated.

5. Who benefited from the fact that a partnership agreement was never created between the parties?

6. The ConnectU founders eventually sued Zuckerberg and Facebook. The case then settled. If you were Facebook, why would you settle? How much would you pay to settle this case? Would your settlement offer change if Facebook were contemplating a public stock offering? Explain.

KEY TERMS

Term partnership p. 473   A partnership in which the partners set a specific future date or event for when the partnership will be disolved.

Partnership at will p. 473   A partnership in which the partners agree to continue their association indefinitely.

Express partnership p. 473   A partnership in which the principals agree orally or in writing to form an ongoing business relationship.

Implied partnership p. 473   A partnership in which the partners are silent about their partnership status, yet the law considers them partners by virtue of their actions.

Revised Uniform Partnership Act (RUPA) p. 474   A model partnership statute drafted and occasionally revised by the National Conference of Commissioners on Uniform State Laws. Approximately 40 states have adopted all or substantial portions of the RUPA.

Uniform Partnership Act (UPA) p. 474   A model partnership statute that is the RUPA's predecessor.

Default rules p. 475   Rules that apply when partners have not expressly agreed how to regulate their internal relations with each other.

Partnership agreement p. 475   Contract between partners that is meant to supercede the default partnership rules.

Joint-and-several liability p. 475   When general partners' personal assets are at risk both together (jointly) and separately (severally) for all debts and liabilities of the partnership, regardless of the source of the debt or liability.

Pass-through entity p. 476   An entity such as a partnership that pays no level of corporate tax.

Fiduciary duties p. 478   The duties of loyalty, care, and good faith imposed on partners to ensure they are acting in the partnership's best interests.

Limited partnership p. 483   Entity that exists by virtue of a state statute that recognizes one or more partners as managing the business while other partners participate only in terms of contributing capital or property.

Revised Uniform Limited Partnership Act (RULPA) p. 483   A model partnership statute that governs limited partnerships.

Certificate of limited partnership p. 483   A form filed with the state by a general partner to create a limited partnership.

Family limited partnership p. 486   A limited partnership that is used for estate planning for families of considerable wealth.

Statement of qualification p. 487   Document filed to convert a general partnership to a limited liability partnership.

Dissociation p. 490   The term used in the RUPA when a partner no longer wishes to be a principal and chooses to leave the partnership.

Withdrawal p. 490   The term used in the RULPA when a partner no longer wishes to be a principal and chooses to leave the partnership.

Winding up p. 492   After dissolution, the process of paying the debts of the partnership and liquidating and/or distributing the remaining assets.

CASE SUMMARY 28.1 Conklin v. Holland, 138 S.W.3d 215 (Tenn. Ct. App. 2003)

Partnership Liability

Lewis and Holland bought a run-down home in Memphis, Tennessee, to renovate and then sell for a profit. The two agreed that Lewis would live in the house during the renovations. In this time period, 20-year-old Amanda Conklin visited the house, where Lewis provided her with alcohol and illicit drugs. As a result of the use of this combination, Conklin died. Lewis attempted to conceal the death by placing Conklin's body in the car in the garage of the home under construction. Police discovered Conklin's body a month and a half later and arrested Lewis. Conklin's estate sued Holland for civil damages related to Conklin's death under the theory that Holland and Lewis were partners in the co-ownership of the property and, as Lewis's partner, Holland was liable for whatever Lewis did on the land they co-owned as general partners.

CASE QUESTIONS

1. Was there a partnership?
2. What was the partnership formed to do?
3. As a practical matter, why would Conklin's estate sue Holland instead of Lewis for partnership liability?

CASE SUMMARY 28.2 Rahemtulla v. Hassam, 539 F. Supp. 2d 755 (M.D. Pa. 2008)

Good Faith

Rahemtulla met Hassam at his religious congregation. Hassam visited Rahemtulla and his wife many times at their home before he pitched his idea to open a steak house restaurant in the Howard Johnson's Inn. Hassam owned the inn along with several other partners. Hassam told the Rahemtullas that revenues from the steak house could be over $2 million per year. Hassam knew that Rahemtulla had absolutely no experience in the food and beverage industry but offered to help him. Rahemtulla quit his job in the corporate sector and borrowed $100,000 using his house as collateral. The $100,000 was Rahemtulla's capital contribution in the partnership. The two entered into a partnership and signed a lease with the Howard Johnson's Inn partnership for the restaurant space. The restaurant opened, and Rahemtulla began to jointly operate it with Hassam. From the beginning, the restaurant lost money, and Hassam began to make unilateral decisions that would help cut expenses. The restaurant was dealt a serious financial setback when authorities refused to approve a liquor license for the restaurant, thus lowering revenue potential. After several months, Rahemtulla complained that he had been cheated by Hassam, whose financial reward came from the lease without any concern about the restaurant operations. Hassam blamed Rahemtulla for incompetence in managing the venture. Rahemtulla sued Hassam for breach of fiduciary duty and dealing in bad faith.

CASE QUESTIONS

1. What duties did Hassam owe Rahemtulla?
2. Does it matter that Rahemtulla made foolish decisions when he trusted his friend?
3. What potential conflict arose when Hassam created a partnership to lease from another partnership he was part of?

CASE SUMMARY 28.3 *In re* Spree.com Corp., 2001 WL 1518242 (Bankr. E.D. Pa. 2001)

Duty of Loyalty

Technology Crosser Ventures (TCV), LP, is a venture capital fund that invests as a limited partner in technology companies that require an infusion of capital. Among the partners are Testler, Hoag, and Kimball. One of the companies they invested in was Spree.com. The partnership was structured to allow Spree, a corporation, to be the general partner with TCV as the limited partner. As part of the partnership agreement, Testler would represent TCV as a member of the board of directors of Spree.com. On August 24, 2000, the *Wall Street Journal* reported a story about TCV and its partners that depicted Testler, Hoag, and Kimball discussing their investments at Testler's office. The paper quoted Testler saying, "What do we want to do with this puppy? The cash runs out soon." Hoag then asked, "They're going to be looking at us for more capital, aren't they?" Kimball added, "I don't want to be supporting them until who knows when." The three men were talking about Spree.com. Spree became insolvent (unable to pay bills as they became due) not long after the article appeared. Spree sued TCV, arguing that the article made it impossible for the company to get more investors. Spree sued Testler for breach of loyalty and due care.

CASE QUESTIONS

1. Who prevails and why?
2. Does this case show potential problems with venture capital firms as limited partners?
3. Was TCV in "control" of Spree.com because it held the purse strings?

CHAPTER REVIEW QUESTIONS

1. **Abel and Baker formed AB Partners, LP. Abel contributed $1,000 and became the managing general partner, and Baker contributed $50,000 as a limited partner. AB Partners, LP, was successfully sued for an injury they caused to a third party. What is the potential personal liability for Abel and Baker, respectively?**
   a. $1,000/$50,000
   b. Unlimited/$50,000
   c. $0/$50,000
   d. $0/$0
   e. Unlimited/$0

2. **Whiteside is a partner in High Flyer Partners, a general partnership. The partnership agreement for High Flyer restricts the parties from leaving the partnership for one full year. Six months after Whiteside signs the agreement, he notifies his partners that he is dissociating. Under the RUPA, what is the impact of Whiteside's dissociation on High Flyer Partners?**
   a. The partnership is dissolved via operation of law.
   b. The partnership may be dissolved by express agreement of the remaining partners.
   c. There is no impact on continuation of the partnership.
   d. The remaining partners are now jointly and severally liable.
   e. Whiteside is now classified as a limited partner.

3. **John and Linda agree to form a partnership and sign a partnership agreement indicating that the partnership will last for three years. They have created a(n):**
   a. Express partnership.
   b. At-will partnership.
   c. Implicit partnership.
   d. Term partnership.
   e. A and D.

4. **Joe and Tom form a general partnership. If Joe commits a tort while acting on behalf of the business and the liability exceeds the partnership assets, Joe and Tom will assume the liability equally. This is known as:**
   a. Respondeat superior.
   b. Waiver of liability.
   c. Joint-and-several liability.
   d. An ultra vires act.
   e. None of the above.

5. **Susan and Mark form a general partnership. Susan contributes $9,000 as her capital contribution, and Mark contributes $1,000. They do not create a partnership agreement. If the partnership earns $100,000 in profits the first year, Mark will be legally entitled to:**
   a. $50,000.
   b. $10,000.
   c. $90,000.
   d. $1,000 plus interest.
   e. $100,000.

6. **Susan and Mark form a general partnership to operate a coffee shop. They do not create a partnership agreement. Susan can legally hire employees.**
   a. True
   b. False

7. **Mark and Cameron form a general partnership to operate a social media business. Mark hears of an app company that is for sale related to the partnership with Cameron. Mark may legally purchase the app company individually.**
   a. True
   b. False

8. John and Marcos agree to start a technology-based general partnership. John will provide his patents to launch the venture, and Marcos will provide financing. These items should be expressed in the partnership agreement.

a. True

b. False

9. A nonprofit motive is necessary to create a general partnership.

a. True

b. False

10. Susan and Mark form a general partnership to operate a coffee shop. Susan uses her personal funds to purchase coffee beans for the business inventory. The partnership is legally required to compensate her for this expense.

a. True

b. False

 Quick Quiz ANSWERS
Rights to Partnership Property

1. Billy cannot use the copyrights from the songs created by the band as collateral for his personal auto loan. Under the default rules of partnership property, partnership property is any property held in the partnership's name or used by the partnership to conduct its business. The copyrights are legally held in joint tenancy by the partnership, and no single partner can use the property for personal purposes.

2. Billy cannot sell the copyrights to the band's music to a record label. This would amount to an extraordinary act outside the ordinary course of business. In the absence of a partnership agreement, any substantial transaction requires unanimous consent among all the partners. The sale of the band's copyrighted music may prevent the band from exercising control over the music it plays, and this may prevent the band from continuing its business. Further, the copyrights to the music are a substantial asset held by the partnership.

CHAPTER REVIEW QUESTIONS: Answers and Explanations

1. **e.** Abel, as a general partner, has unlimited personal liability for tort liabilities of the partnership. Baker is a limited partner, so his personal assets are not at risk if the business has no assets.

2. **b.** Under the RUPA, the partners may choose to continue the venture or dissolve the partnership. Answer *a* is incorrect because the RUPA does not require the partnership to dissolve upon a disassociating partner's exit. Answer *c* is incorrect because the partners must now decide whether to continue or dissolve. Answers *d* and *e* are incorrect statements of law.

3. **e.** The agreement creates an explicit agreement, and the three-year limit indicates a term partnership.

4. **c.** When a partner faces unlimited personal liability due to the acts of another partner, this is known as joint-and-several liability.

5. **a.** Absent a partnership agreement, all partners share equally in profits.

6. a. True. Absent a partnership agreement, Susan can hire staff because this is within the ordinary course of business and she has coequal management rights.

7. b. False. Taking personal advantage of a business opportunity is a breach of the duty of loyalty.

8. a. True. The assets brought in to capitalize a partnership are recorded in the capital contribution portion of the partnership agreement.

9. b. False. A general partnership is legally required to pursue profits.

10. a. True. If a partner suffers liability or an expense from conducting partnership business, she is legally entitled to reimbursement, which is known as the right to indemnity.

CHAPTER 29

Limited Liability Companies

©valterZ/Shutterstock

A limited liability company is a business entity that combines elements of a partnership, a sole proprietorship, and a corporation. In this chapter's *Thinking Strategically,* we revisit the history of Facebook's founding to explore the choice of business entity from a strategic perspective.

Learning Objectives

After studying this chapter, students who have mastered the material will be able to:

29-1	Define what a limited liability company (LLC) is.
29-2	Identify the sources of laws that govern LLCs.
29-3	Explain the steps required to form an LLC.
29-4	Identify the primary methods for capitalizing LLCs.
29-5	Explain the function of an operating agreement.
29-6	Articulate the legal protections from personal liability afforded to the principals in an LLC.
29-7	Identify the tax treatment alternatives available to an LLC.
29-8	Compare and contrast dissolution and dissociation.

CHAPTER OVERVIEW

In this chapter, we explore the ins and outs of the limited liability company (LLC), a common business entity within the contemporary business environment. The LLC offers many strategic advantages to business firms, including easy formation, flexible operation, limited legal liability of the principals, and pass-through taxation. In this chapter, students will learn:

- What an LLC is.
- The laws that govern LLCs.

- The formation and capitalization of an LLC.
- The management and operation of LLCs.
- The limited legal liability of the members (owners) of an LLC.
- The tax treatment alternatives available to an LLC.
- The difference between dissolution and dissociation.

FIGURE 29.1 | Pros and Cons of an LLC

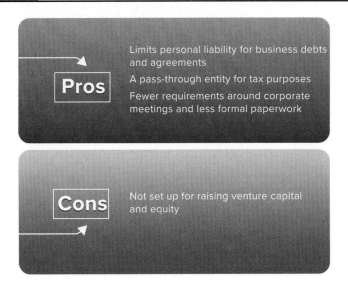

Pros

- Limits personal liability for business debts and agreements
- A pass-through entity for tax purposes
- Fewer requirements around corporate meetings and less formal paperwork

Cons

- Not set up for raising venture capital and equity

OVERVIEW OF THE LLC

A **limited liability company (LLC)** is a flexible type of business entity that offers its owners many advantages, including easy formation, flexible operation, limited legal liability of the owners, and pass-through taxation. The owners or principals of an LLC are called *members.* Figure 29.1 shows some pros and cons of an LLC.

LO 29-1

Define what a limited liability company (LLC) is.

TAKEAWAY CONCEPTS Overview of the LLC

- A limited liability company, or LLC, is a form of business entity that offers liability protection for its principals, flexible operation, and pass-through taxation.
- The owners of an LLC are called *members.*

LAWS GOVERNING LLCs

Prior to the development of the LLC, business owners who wished to avoid the double taxation of a corporation but still desired legal liability protection for their personal assets had few choices. In 1977, however, Wyoming became the first state to recognize a new hybrid business entity, one that had characteristics of a partnership but also provided limited legal liability to its owners. This hybrid entity was called a *limited liability company.*

After the Internal Revenue Service (IRS) decided to classify LLCs as a partnership for tax purposes in 1988, many states followed Wyoming's lead and enacted their own limited liability statutes.[1] Today, all states recognize LLCs and provide both procedural (formation) and internal default rules (in the event the parties are unable to agree otherwise) for the operation of LLCs.

LO 29-2

Identify the sources of laws that govern LLCs.

---

[1] A subsequent IRS ruling in 1997 made LLCs an even more attractive choice because the IRS eliminated strict operating requirements that previously had to be met for an entity to qualify as a partnership for tax purposes.

The **Uniform Limited Liability Company Act (ULLCA)** is a model statute designed to promote uniformity among various state LLC laws; however, in practice LLC statutes can vary considerably from state to state. Some states have begun to adopt statutes based on the **Revised Uniform Limited Liability Company Act (RULLCA)**, which was published in an amended form in 2013 by the Uniform Law Commission. The revised version modifies the original act in the areas of formation, organizational matters, and the operating agreement, and it attempts to clarify some of the more technical aspects of LLC governance, such as the handling of deadlocks and the rights of members who depart the LLC. Eighteen states and the District of Columbia have adopted a version of the revised act as of 2019. In areas where the RULLCA differs substantially from the original ULLCA, this chapter covers both acts.

TAKEAWAY CONCEPTS Laws Governing LLCs

- Today, all 50 states recognize LLCs.
- The Uniform Limited Liability Company Act (ULLCA) and the Revised Uniform Limited Liability Company Act (RULLCA) are model statutes designed to promote uniformity among various state LLC laws.

LO 29-3

Explain the steps required to form an LLC.

FORMATION OF THE LLC

Forming an LLC is relatively easy and inexpensive. In every state, an LLC is formed by filing the **articles of organization** (also called the *certificate of organization*) with the designated public official in that state, such as the secretary of state or the state's corporation bureau. Most states require the articles of organization to contain only basic information, such as the name of the entity, the location of its principal place of business, and the names of its owners (called *members*). Some states also require a contemporaneous filing with tax authorities to notify them of the existence of the LLC.

The owners of an LLC need only file in one state, even if the LLC will do business across state lines.

The original articles of organization of Facebook (back when it was an LLC) are presented in Figure 29.2.

TAKEAWAY CONCEPTS Formation of the LLC

- An LLC is formed by filing the articles of organization with the designated public official in that state.
- The articles of organization must contain such information as the name of the entity, the location of its principal place of business, and the names of its owners.

LO 29-4

Identify the primary methods for capitalizing LLCs.

CAPITALIZATION OF THE LLC

Unlike a corporation, an LLC does not issue shares. Instead, LLCs are capitalized primarily through debt via private lenders or commercial lenders or through the sale of equity ownership in the LLC itself. In most cases, the operating agreement of the LLC (discussed next) controls the amount and methods of capitalizing the business.

FIGURE 29.2 Facebook's Articles of Organization

ARTICLES OF ORGANIZATION
OF
the facebook LLC

ARTICLE I   NAME

The name of the limited liability company shall be: the facebook LLC

ARTICLE II   PRINCIPAL OFFICE

The principal place of business and mailing address of this Limited Liability Company shall be: ▒▒▒▒▒▒ Coral Gables, Florida 33158.

ARTICLE III   INITIAL REGISTERED AGENT & STREET ADDRESS

The name and address of the initial registered agent is: Business Filings Incorporated ▒▒▒▒▒▒ Tallahassee, Florida 32301. Located in the County of Leon

ARTICLE IV   DURATION

The duration for the limited liability company shall be: 12/31/2044.

ARTICLE V   MANAGERS/MEMBERS

The management of the limited liability company is reserved for the Members and the **names and addresses of the members of the Limited Liability Company are:**

Mark Zuckerberg, ▒▒▒▒ Dobbs Ferry, Massachusetts 10522
Eduardo Saverin, ▒▒▒▒ Coral Gables, Florida 33158
Dustin Moskovitz, ▒▒▒▒ Ocala, Florida 34474

FILED
2004 APR 13 A 4:57
SECRETARY OF STATE
TALLASSEE, FLORIDA

TAKEAWAY CONCEPT Capitalization of the LLC

- LLCs are capitalized primarily through debt via private lenders or commercial lenders or through the sale of equity ownership in the LLC itself.

THE OPERATING AGREEMENT

LLCs frequently are governed by an agreement of its members in the form of an **operating agreement**. Operating agreements, similar to partnership agreements, cover many of the internal rules for the actual operation of the business. One of the primary benefits of an LLC is that it affords its members a great deal of flexibility in terms of the rights and responsibilities of each member. This flexibility includes the following aspects of the LLC:

- *Structure of governance and voting rights:* The operating agreement typically sets forth a structure for managing the entity through a single member or a board of "managing members" (akin to a board of directors), and it defines their responsibilities in terms of

LO 29-5

Explain the function of an operating agreement.

the day-to-day operations of the entity. In addition, the operating agreement also spells out voting rights of members, procedures for voting, transactions that require a vote of the members (such as the sale of the LLC assets to another company), and procedures for the admission of any new members.

- *Death, incapacity, and dissolution:* Members often use operating agreements to spell out the preferred procedures in the event certain contingencies or what-if scenarios occur. The operating agreement may establish a procedure ahead of time for handling the circumstance of a member's death or incapacity. The procedure typically is different for members versus managing members, but in most cases the operating agreement allows the venture's remaining members to choose whether or not to continue. In the event the members choose not to continue, the procedure for dissolution (including preferences of members in terms of who gets paid first after liquidation) is typically outlined in the operating agreement.

- *RULLCA:* The revised model LLC statute addresses several issues related to the operating agreement. First, it establishes the primacy of the operating agreement in evidencing the relationship among the limited liability company and its members, the rights and duties of any managers, and the activities and affairs of the company. Second, it lists those matters that are not subject to change by the operating agreement by setting forth 17 nonwaivable statutory provisions related to liability of the entity and its members. (These nonwaivable provisions are discussed in more detail later in this chapter.) Third, it confirms that an operating agreement may include specific penalties or other consequences if a member fails to comply with its terms or upon certain events specified in the operating agreement.

> If the parties do not execute an operating agreement, then the LLC statute of the state in which the LLC is organized will govern the management and operation of the LLC through default rules.

Most state LLC statutes distinguish between a **member-managed LLC** and a **manager-managed LLC**. In a *member-managed* LLC, the management structure of the entity is similar to that of a general partnership, with all the members having the authority to bind the business. In a *manager-managed* LLC, a named manager (or managers) generally has the day-to-day operational responsibilities, while the nonmanaging members typically are investors with little input on the course of business taken by the entity except for major decisions (such as a merger). In a manager-managed LLC, nonmanaging members generally do not have the authority to act on behalf of the business venture.

Generally, an LLC's members decide whether the LLC will be manager-managed or member-managed before the initial public filing of the articles of organization, which are available to third parties for purposes of checking the authority of an individual to bind the LLC. While the new RULLCA eliminates the term *managing member* in favor of *authorized representative,* the revised act still requires an LLC to choose between being member-managed or manager-managed.

Furthermore, as in many business relationships, the managers of an LLC owe *fiduciary duties* of care and loyalty to the other members of the LLC, as shown in Figure 29.3. Controlling members (those with veto power or the ownership stake to block decisions by other members) also owe a duty of loyalty to the other members. LLC statutes regarding fiduciary duties vary by state and can be strengthened or pared back by the operating agreement. In fact, the modern trend is to specifically eliminate any liability for a breach of the duty of care through the operating agreement. This trend has been a source of controversy, and courts have been strict about requiring unambiguous language in the operating agreement that limits any fiduciary duty. In any case, managers and controlling members (i.e., members with ownership sufficient to decide or veto internal operational matters) must adhere to the duty of loyalty, are prohibited from self-dealing, and must act in good faith when dealing with the LLC's business matters.

FIGURE 29.3   Fiduciary Duties of LLC Managers and Members

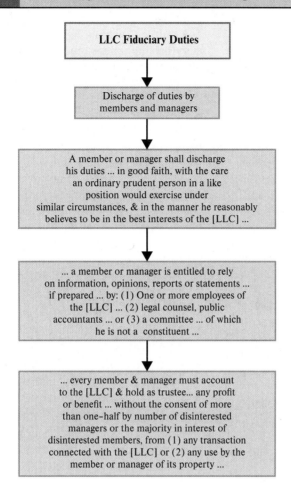

In response to this controversy, the RULLCA does not allow any manager or member to avoid personal liability under any circumstances in which the liability was the result of the member's bad faith or willful misconduct. In Case 29.1, a court in Delaware addresses the issue of limiting fiduciary liability through the operating agreement under the ULLCA.

CASE 29.1 AK-Feel, LLC v. NHAOCG, LLC, 62 A.3d 649 (Del. Ch. 2012)

FACT SUMMARY Feeley was the managing member of AK-Feel, LLC, and formed a new entity with several investors, all of whom organized a separate entity called NHAOCG, LLC ("NHA"). After a series of business discussions among the parties, the principals of the two LLCs formed a new entity, called Oculus, for the purpose of finding and developing real estate parcels and profiting from their sale. AK-Feel and NHA each held a 50 percent member interest in Oculus, but AK-Feel served as the managing member. Because Feeley served as the managing member of AK-Feel, he also controlled the activities of Oculus.

(continued)

Approximately one year later, the parties' relationship deteriorated. NHA accused Feeley of gross negligence in the handling of several real estate deals. In one case, NHA alleged that Feeley's incompetence resulted in a significant loss in an aborted real estate transaction. Dissatisfied with Feeley, the principals of NHA decided to end their business relationship with Feeley and attempted to take over Oculus themselves. Feeley and AK-Feel filed suit in which they sought to block NHA's attempt and establish their continuing control. NHA filed a countersuit for, among other things, breach of fiduciary duty and sought damages that it suffered as a result of Feeley's gross negligence. The parties resolved the control issue, but NHA did not drop its countersuit. Feeley filed a motion to dismiss NHA's countersuit, arguing that any fiduciary duty was limited or eliminated through Oculus's operating agreement.

SYNOPSIS OF DECISION AND OPINION   On the claim of breach of fiduciary duty, the Chancery Court of Delaware ruled in favor of NHA and denied Feeley's motion to dismiss. The court ruled that the operating agreement did not unambiguously limit any fiduciary duties of the managing member. The court pointed to a section of the Operating Agreement that specifically recognizes certain fiduciary duties. While some of NHA's claims were dismissed, the breach of fiduciary duty claim survived the motion to dismiss.

WORDS OF THE COURT: Limiting Fiduciary Duties   "Drafters of an LLC agreement must make their intent to eliminate fiduciary duties plain and unambiguous. . . . The plain language of this portion of [the Operating Agreement] eliminates monetary liability unless, among other things, 'the act or omission is attributed to gross negligence [or] willful misconduct or fraud. . . .' [This] [s]ection . . . does not limit or eliminate fiduciary duties . . . Rather than eliminating fiduciary duties, the [Operating Agreement's] language recognizes their continuing existence . . . If [the Operating Agreement] had eliminated fiduciary duties . . . , then it would be counter-intuitive for the same provision to recognize exceptions [for] gross negligence and willful misconduct and to authorize the managing member to obtain insurance against actual or alleged breaches of fiduciary duty and require Oculus to pay the premiums."

Case Questions

1. Why does the court state that the language in the operating agreement actually recognizes the "continued existence" of the fiduciary duties?

2. Should NHA have agreed to the structure of the Oculus entity? How could it have been more proactive during the structuring of the entity?

3. *Focus on Critical Thinking:* As explained in the text, the RULLCA limits the right of managing members to eliminate their fiduciary duty to the other members. Which approach do you agree with and why? Is the operating agreement a contract or a set of rules? If it is a contract, shouldn't the parties be able to negotiate whatever terms they wish?

TAKEAWAY CONCEPTS The Operating Agreement

- An LLC frequently is governed by an agreement of its members in the form of an operating agreement, which establishes via contract many of the internal rules for the actual operation of the business.

- In a *member-managed* LLC, the management structure of the entity is similar to that of a general partnership, with all the members having the authority to bind the business.

- In a *manager-managed* LLC, a named manager (or managers) generally has the day-to-day operational responsibilities, while the nonmanaging members are typically investors with little input on the course of business taken by the entity except for major decisions.

LIMITED LIABILITY OF THE OWNERS

Perhaps the most important feature of an LLC is the limited liability of its members. LLC members are insulated from personal liability for any business debt or liability (contract or tort) if the venture fails.

For example, suppose that Gotti is the managing member of Active Wear, LLC, and signs a five-year lease agreement with his landlord on behalf of Active Wear. One year into the lease, Active Wear has a downturn in business, is forced to breach the lease, and moves out hoping to convert to an online business model. Because the landlord's rights are against the LLC entity only, the landlord may not obtain a judgment against Gotti or collect back rent or other damages from Gotti's personal assets.

However, two important factors moderate this limited liability. First, landlords and other creditors often require a **personal guarantee** from the members whereby the members pledge personal assets to guarantee payment of the business venture's obligations. Second, a court may discard the protection in a case where the court finds that fairness demands that the LLC members should compensate any damaged party when the entity is without resources to cover the full amount owed, such as a case where the members engaged in fraud. Also note that the RULLCA imposes personal liability in cases where authorized members consent to an improper distribution. An *improper distribution* is defined as any distribution of money made when the LLC is insolvent.

 Quick Quiz Limited Liability

Is the principal personally liable?

1. Carlos is the sole member of a single-member LLC. After one year, despite his best efforts, the business fails and the bank that extended the LLC a loan sues for repayment. Is Carlos personally liable for the loan?

2. Carlos is a member of an LLC, along with three other members. After one year, despite their best efforts, the business fails and the bank that extended the LLC a loan sues for repayment. Is Carlos liable for all or part of the loan?

Answers to this Quick Quiz are provided at the end of the chapter.

TAKEAWAY CONCEPTS Limited Liability of the Owners

- LLC members are insulated from personal liability for any business debt or liability.
- Limited liability does not apply when the suing party has obtained a personal guarantee from the member or members of the LLC.
- A court may impose personal liability if it finds that fairness demands that the LLC members should compensate any damaged party when the entity is without resources to cover the full amount owed.

TAXATION OF THE LLC

Another attractive advantage of the LLC model is the various tax treatment alternatives available to the members of the LLC. Although many LLCs are treated as pass-through entities, LLC members instead may elect to be taxed as a corporation if they consider the corporate tax structure to be more favorable.

LO 29-6

Articulate the legal protections from personal liability afforded to the principals in an LLC.

By way of example, suppose that Developer Inc. wants to start a land use project to build a commercial office building. It wishes to partner with Garrett, the owner of several pieces of property in the area under consideration. Both the principals of Developer Inc. and Garrett wish to have pass-through tax treatment, but they also wish to have as much protection as possible from liability of personal assets. Because Developer Inc. is a corporate principal, the parties cannot choose a pass-through corporate entity. They can, however, achieve these objectives by forming an LLC.

Recall from the discussion in previous chapters the two main advantages of pass-through taxation. One major advantage is the ability of investors to assume the tax deductions and losses that are typically generated by an emerging company or a company with significant up-front debt. The other huge advantage is the ability of the business to distribute earnings to its owners without incurring double-level taxation—without having a tax imposed on both the entity and its members.

TAKEAWAY CONCEPT Taxation of the LLC

LLCs enjoy flexible tax treatment; specifically, they can be treated as pass-through entities, or in the alternative, the members of an LLC may elect to be taxed as a corporation.

LO 29-8

Compare and contrast dissolution and dissociation.

DISSOLUTION VERSUS DISSOCIATION

LLC laws define **dissolution** of an LLC as a liquidation process triggered by an event that is specified in the operating agreement (such as the death of a key member) or by the decision of the majority of members (or the percentage called for in the operating agreement) to dissolve the company. The members of an LLC also may have agreed to a maximum term for conducting business in the operating agreement. If the term expires but the members want the LLC to continue, they must have a unanimous vote to fix an additional term *or* the majority of LLC member interests may vote to continue the LLC at will (with no fixed term and subject to dissolution at any time).

By contrast, **dissociation** occurs when an individual member decides to exercise the right to withdraw from the partnership. Upon a dissociation, the remaining members may decide either to continue the LLC or to trigger dissolution. Of course, the parties may agree to their own unique set of rules through the operating agreement. Agreeing ahead of time on what will happen if one member decides to withdraw and documenting the agreement in writing is a strategic way of avoiding future disputes.

In Case 29.2, the Supreme Court of South Dakota considers whether to order a *judicial dissolution* of an LLC.

CASE 29.2 Kirksey v. Grohmann, 754 N.W.2d 825 (S.D. 2008)

FACT SUMMARY   Four sisters inherited an equal ownership interest in their family's land in Butte County, South Dakota. They then formed the Kirksey Family Ranch, LLC, conveying their property interests in the land to the company in exchange for equal ownership in the newly created LLC. One sister lived on the land and managed the LLC, while another sister leased the land for livestock grazing. The other two sisters, however, lived in the city a great distance away. The two "city sisters" wanted to dissolve the LLC and receive their share of the proceeds, but the two "farm sisters" were opposed to such a move. A majority vote is generally required for dissolution, but not only were the sisters evenly divided; they also refused to speak to

(continued)

each other directly. (All of their communications were through their lawyers.) The operating agreement did not contain a provision in case of deadlocks, so the city sisters petitioned a court for a judicial dissolution of the LLC. The court denied their request, so the city sisters appealed to the Supreme Court of South Dakota.

SYNOPSIS OF DECISION AND OPINION
Reversing the lower court, the Supreme Court of South Dakota ordered a judicial dissolution of the LLC on the grounds that the economic purpose of the Kirksey Family Ranch, LLC, was being unreasonably frustrated and that it was not reasonably practicable to carry on the LLC's business in conformity with its articles of organization and operating agreement.

WORDS OF THE COURT: Judicial Dissolution
"Here, we have two members of an LLC that hold all the power, with the other two having no power to influence the company's direction. We recognize that forced dissolution is a drastic remedy and may produce financial repercussions for the sisters, but how can one reasonably conclude that the economic

purpose of this company is not reasonably frustrated? The members cannot communicate regarding the LLC except through legal counsel. The company remains static, serving the interests of only half its owners. They neither trust nor cooperate with each other. The sisters formed their company contemplating equal ownership and management, yet only an impenetrable deadlock prevails."

Case Questions
1. Should the court grant the request of the city sisters? Why or why not?
2. The tracts of land owned by the LLC had been in the Kirksey family for over 100 years. Should that fact be relevant to the court's resolution of the dissolution issue?
3. *Focus on Critical Thinking:* The court emphasized the fact that the sisters refused to communicate with each other directly, except through their attorneys. Is this fact relevant to the outcome of this case? If so, should this fact work in favor of the city sisters or the farm sisters?

TAKEAWAY CONCEPTS Dissolution versus Dissociation

- Dissolution of an LLC is a liquidation process triggered by an event that is specified in the operating agreement (such as the death of a key member) or by the decision of the majority of members to dissolve the company.
- Dissociation from an LLC occurs when an individual member exercises the right to withdraw from the business.

 THINKING STRATEGICALLY

©valterZ/Shutterstock

Choice of Business Entity

PROBLEM: When entrepreneurs launch a new venture—like Harvard sophomore Mark Zuckerberg did when he invented "thefacebook" during the 2003-2004 academic year—they must figure out what type of legal structure the business will have. Specifically, will the new business be run as a sole proprietorship, a general or limited partnership, a limited liability company, or a corporation?

As it happens, Facebook provides a textbook illustration of the strategic nature of choice of business entity. Today, Facebook is a publicly held corporation with its shares listed and traded on the NASDAQ stock exchange. But years before Facebook became a multibillion-dollar corporation, it started as a humble sole proprietorship in Mark Zuckerberg's college dorm room. Moreover, Mark Zuckerberg wasn't the only founder of Facebook. Early in the company's history,

Zuckerberg decided to team up with his best friend, Harvard junior Eduardo Saverin.

Facebook evolved into a general partnership when Zuckerberg and Saverin became business partners. In exchange for Saverin's financial support, the two partners agreed to split their respective ownership interests 70/30—with Zuckerberg receiving a 70 percent stake in the new company and Saverin receiving a 30 percent interest.[2]

Zuckerberg launched The Facebook (as it was then called) from his dorm room on February 4, 2004, and his website became an instant success among Harvard students. With the help of a third Facebook co-founder, Dustin Moskovitz, Facebook soon spread to other elite college campuses, starting with Columbia (February 25), Stanford (February 26), and then Yale (February 29).[3]

Around the same time, fellow Harvard classmates Tyler and Cameron Winklevoss, along with their partner Divya Narendra—who were developing a competing

[2]See Ben Mezrich, *The Accidental Billionaires: The Founding of Facebook: A Tale of Sex, Money, Genius, and Betrayal* (Anchor Books, 2010).

[3]See David Kirkpatrick, *The Facebook Effect: The Inside Story of the Company That Is Connecting the World* (Simon & Schuster, 2011).

social network—alleged that Zuckerberg had stolen their idea and sent Zuckerberg an informal demand letter threatening to sue him if he did not take down his website. Given the company's rapid growth and the looming threat of a lawsuit, what should the original co-founders do to limit their personal liability?

STRATEGIC SOLUTION: To limit personal liability, the co-founders should register the new business as an LLC, which is exactly what the original co-founders of Facebook did. In April 2004, Zuckerberg, Saverin, and Moskovitz (who grew up in Ocala, Florida) formally registered Facebook as an LLC in Florida.

QUESTION

1. Facebook was launched in February 2004. From a legal perspective, the company began as a sole proprietorship, then morphed into a general partnership before becoming a limited liability company in April 2004. Why do you think the founders of Facebook decided to structure their company as an LLC so early in the company's history?

KEY TERMS

Limited liability company (LLC) p. 501   A form of business entity that offers liability protection for its principals, flexible operation, and pass-through taxation.

Uniform Limited Liability Company Act (ULLCA) p. 502 Early version of a model law adopted by most states related to the formation and organization of Limited Liability Companies.

Revised Uniform Limited Liability Company Act (RULLCA) p. 502   Model law adopted by 19 states and the District of Columbia related to the formation and organization of Limited Liability Companies.

Articles of organization p. 502   The document filed to create an LLC; in most states, requires only basic information such as the name of the entity, the location of its principal place of business, and the names of its members. Also called *certificate of organization.*

Operating agreement p. 503   Document that governs an LLC; sets out the structure and internal rules for operation of the entity.

Member-managed LLC p. 504   LLC management structure similar to that of a general partnership, with all the members having the authority to bind the business.

Manager-managed LLC p. 504   LLC management structure in which the members name a designated manager (or authorized representative) who generally has the day-to-day operational responsibilities, while the nonmanaging members are typically investors with little input on the course of business taken by the entity except for major decisions.

Personal guarantee p. 507   Pledge from LLC members of personal assets to guarantee payment obligations of the business venture.

Dissolution of LLC p. 508   In the context of an LLC, a liquidation process triggered by an event that is specified in the operating agreement (such as the death of a key member) or by the decision of the majority of membership interests (or the percentage called for in the operating agreement) to dissolve the company.

Dissociation from LLC p. 508   Process in which an individual member of an LLC exercises the right to withdraw from the partnership.

CASE SUMMARY 29.1 Kaycee Land and Livestock v. Flahive, 46 P.3d 323, Supreme Court of Wyoming (2002)

Liability of Single-Member LLC

Roger Flahive was the managing member of a limited liability company called Flahive Oil and Gas, LLC. He entered into an agreement with Kaycee to mine oil and gas from Kaycee's property, signing the contract on behalf of Flahive Oil and Gas, LLC. Flahive's mining work, however, was negligent and resulted in the contamination of Kaycee's property. After discovering that Flahive's LLC did not have any financial assets, Kaycee sued Flahive in his personal capacity. Flahive argued that he had no personal liability because the mining contract was between the LLC and Kaycee.

CASE QUESTIONS

1. Can the court disregard the LLC entity in this situation to hold Flahive personally liable?
2. Should it matter that Flahive's LLC was a single-member LLC?

CASE SUMMARY 29.2 Emprise v. Rumisek, 26 Kan. App. 2d. 760, Court of Appeals of Kansas (2009)

Personal Guarantees of LLC Members

Four physicians formed an LLC to operate a medical practice. They capitalized the venture with a bank loan to the LLC. Each physician signed a personal guarantee to secure a proportionate part of the loan (25 percent each). After a dispute developed, two of the physicians left and started a new practice. The bank became concerned that the loan was in jeopardy, so it brought suit against the remaining two physicians to recover the full amount due under the loan. At the same time, the two departing physicians were engaged in litigation with the remaining two physicians over mismanagement of their former practice. The remaining physicians contended that the bank could not enforce the personal guarantees until the original dispute among the four physicians was resolved, because the LLC still might have assets depending on the outcome of the litigation.

CASE QUESTIONS

1. Does the bank have to wait until the litigation is complete to enforce the personal guarantees against the remaining physicians? Why or why not?
2. What is the impact of the departing physicians' dissociation from the LLC?

CASE SUMMARY 29.3 Lamprecht v. Jordan, LLC, 75 P.3d 743, Supreme Court of Idaho (2003)

Involuntary Withdrawal

Philip D. Lamprecht was one of the founding members of an accounting firm called Jordan & Company. He and the other members of the firm formed an LLC in 1998 for the purpose of acquiring an office building in the picturesque mountain town of Pocatello, Idaho. The LLC members signed an operating agreement and then purchased the office building in the name of the LLC. Among other things, their operating agreement required an automatic withdrawal from the LLC upon termination from Jordan & Company and specified that the terminated member would be entitled only to the balance in his capital account. Two years later, Lamprecht physically attacked a colleague in the office. The police were summoned and Lamprecht was cited for battery. Jordan & Company then terminated Lamprecht and offered him the remaining balance in his capital account, which totaled a mere $3,864. Lamprecht refused to accept the payment and disputed that he was required to withdraw from the LLC, claiming that the operating agreement covered only voluntary cessation of employment. Lamprecht also claimed that any payment for his withdrawal from the LLC should be based on the fair market value of his ownership interest in the LLC (namely, the value of the office building owned by the LLC), which was $273,016.

CASE QUESTIONS

1. May the other LLC members force Lamprecht to withdraw from the LLC?
2. Is it fair to base the payment on the capital account balance (typically very small) rather than the fair market value of the LLC (typically a larger amount) when the withdrawal is forced?

CASE SUMMARY 29.4 Lieberman v. Wyoming.com, LLC, 82 P.3d 274, Supreme Court of Wyoming (2004)

Dissociation

Michael Lieberman, Steven Mossbrook, and Sandra Mossbrook formed Wyoming.com, LLC in 1994. After a dispute with the Mossbrooks in 1998, Lieberman served the LLC with a "notice of withdrawal" and demanded that the LLC pay for Lieberman's "share of the company" in the amount of $400,000 based on the LLC's current valuation. The Mossbrooks voted to accept Lieberman's withdrawal, but they offered him only $20,000 because that was his initial ownership stake. Lieberman rejected the $20,000 offer. The operating agreement was silent on the issue of dissociation.

CASE QUESTIONS

1. How should the court rule?
2. Could the Mossbrooks have avoided having to pay any money to Lieberman had they simply voted to reject his "notice of withdrawal"?

CHAPTER REVIEW QUESTIONS

1. **Under the ULLCA, which of the following is true about limited liability companies?**
   a. Its principals are called members.
   b. Principals do not have personal liability for liabilities of the LLC.
   c. Principals have joint-and-several liability for the debts resulting from an LLC contract.
   d. Principals are called partners.
   e. A and B.

2. **Which of the following typically is found in an LLC operating agreement?**
   a. Procedures to follow in the event of the death of a key member.
   b. Business advertising materials.
   c. Financial statements.
   d. Disclosures of risk.
   e. Tax returns.

3. **Principals who manage an LLC owe their members a _____ duty.**
   a. Joint-and-several
   b. Liability
   c. Manager's

   d. Fiduciary
   e. Moral

4. **José, Curt, and Drew are all principals in JCD Associates, LLC. In the operating agreement, they agree that any principal is permitted to bind the LLC. JCD Associates is:**
   a. Member-managed.
   b. Manager-managed.
   c. Principal-managed.
   d. President-managed.
   e. Legally-managed.

5. **Which of the following is not true about an LLC?**
   a. It allows pass-through taxation for the members/owners.
   b. There is no personal liability for negligent acts of other members/owners.
   c. Members are authorized to bind the LLC in contract.
   d. There is no personal liability for a member's own negligence.
   e. There is limited liability for members as well as for managers.

6. An LLC is permitted to capitalize by selling equity ownership in the LLC itself.

a. True

b. False

7. LLCs may choose to be taxed like a corporation or choose pass-through taxation treatment.

a. True

b. False

8. A corporation may be a principal of an LLC.

a. True

b. False

9. The articles of organization may restrict membership in an LLC to those possessing a professional license in a named field.

a. True

b. False

10. When a member of an LLC dies, the business entity automatically ceases to exist.

a. True

b. False

 Quick Quiz ANSWERS

Limited Liability

In either scenario (single-member or multi-member LLC), unless Carlos signed a personal guarantee, he will not be personally liable for the loan.

CHAPTER REVIEW QUESTIONS: Answers and Explanations

1. e. An LLC's principals, called members, are shielded from liabilities of the LLC's business operations. Answer *c* is incorrect because the whole point of an LLC is to avoid the joint-and-several liability associated with other entities such as partnerships.

2. a. Operating agreements typically cover events such as death, disability, or bankruptcy of a key principal. Advertisements, financial statements, disclosures, and tax returns are not typically part of an operating agreement.

3. d. Fiduciary duties are owed by managers to members to act in the best interest of the LLC, and managers are prohibited from self-dealing. The remaining answers are incorrect statements of law.

4. a. If all members may bind the LLC, this is a member-managed LLC. Answer *b* is incorrect because if one or more members is designated to manage the LLC, the entity is considered manager-managed. Answers *c* and *d* are incorrect statements of law.

5. d. In an LLC (as in any other business entity), an owner cannot escape liability for his own acts of negligence. The remaining answers are all true statements about LLCs.

6. b. False. An LLC is not permitted to capitalize by selling equity ownership in the LLC itself. This limitation is one of the main differences between LLCs and corporations.

7. a. True. LLCs may choose to be taxed like a corporation or choose pass-through taxation treatment of its individual members. This flexibility is one of the major advantages of the LLC model.

8. a. True. Both natural persons and artificial persons (e.g., a corporation) may have an ownership interest in an LLC. Again, this flexibility is another advantage of the LLC model.

9. a. True. The certificate of organization of an LLC may restrict membership in an LLC to only those who possess a professional license in a named field, such as law or medicine.

10. b. False. When a member of an LLC dies, the business entity does not cease to exist because the entity has a separate existence from its owners.

CHAPTER 30

Corporations: Formation and Organization

Principals choosing a form of business entity use legal strategy to minimize their liability and add value to the firm. For businesses organized as corporations, its principals enjoy legal protection of their personal assets for debts and liabilities associated with the business. Still, business owners and managers must be vigilant in preserving that protection or they may lose it. In this chapter's *Thinking Strategically,* we discuss strategic steps that help maintain those legal protections.

Learning Objectives

After studying this chapter, students who have mastered the material will be able to:

30-1 Articulate the concept of the corporation as a legally independent entity and identify the sources and level of law governing formation and internal corporate matters.

30-2 Categorize a corporate entity based on its operating objectives.

30-3 Explain the process of corporate formation and liability of promoters.

30-4 Explain the primary methods for financing a corporation.

30-5 Identify circumstances under which a court will pierce the veil of a corporation to access the personal assets of its principals.

30-6 List the three major groups that form the structure of a corporation and describe the roles of each group.

30-7 Define the term *fiduciary duty* and apply the various fiduciary duties in the context of a corporate transaction.

CHAPTER OVERVIEW

This chapter continues our discussion of business entities that provide liability protection for their principals. The principals of some business ventures form a *corporation* to achieve their objectives because corporations provide flexibility not found in other entities. Although the corporate form is sometimes associated with large multinational corporations, in reality many corporations are relatively small with a limited number of principals (sometimes just a single owner). In this chapter, we cover the formation, liability, and capitalization of corporations. We then turn to the roles, rights, and duties of shareholders, officer, and directors.

CORPORATION AS AN ENTITY

A **corporation** is a fictitious legal entity that exists as an independent *individual* separate from its principals. Although this corporate "person" is a legally created fiction, it is a well-established and deep-seated principal of American law. Recall from Chapter 3, "Business and the Constitution," that the U.S. Supreme Court has ruled that corporations are entitled to full First Amendment protection for political speech. In a business context, it is also important to note that a corporation, like an individual person, may file suit or be sued, or may form a contract or breach a contract. In contrast to sole proprietorships and partnerships, the obligations of corporations are separate and distinct from the personal obligations of their principals.

Corporations are created through a state law filing, and formation is governed through *state statutes.* State statutes vary in their corporate formation and governance rules, but each state has a specific law, often called the **business corporation law** or something similar, that covers such matters as the structure of the corporation, oversight of the activity of the corporation's managers, rights of the principals in the case of the sale of assets or ownership interests, annual reporting requirements, and other issues that affect the internal rules of the business venture. Over half of the states have adopted all or substantial portions of a model act known as the **Revised Model Business Corporation Act (RMBCA)**[1] drafted by the American Law Institute. While state statutes regulate the internal governance of a corporation, federal laws regulate the offering or trading of ownership interests to the public and set certain standards for internal governance for some companies.

LO 30-1

Articulate the concept of the corporation as a legally independent entity and identify the sources and level of law governing formation and internal corporate matters.

TAKEAWAY CONCEPTS Corporation as an Entity

- A corporation is a fictitious legal entity that exists as an independent *individual* separate from its principals.
- Corporations are created through a state law filing, and formation is governed through *state statutes* often modeled on the Revised Model Business Corporation Act (RMBCA).

CLASSIFICATIONS OF CORPORATIONS

Corporations are classified into one or more categories that reflect their overall purpose, capitalization (how they are funded), location, and structure. The two major categories are corporations that are owned exclusively by a group of private individuals (known as *privately held*) and corporations that sell their ownership interest via public stock exchanges (known as *publicly held*).

LO 30-2

Categorize a corporate entity based on its operating objectives.

Privately Held versus Publicly Held

The most common type of corporation is a **privately held corporation**. Privately held corporations do not sell ownership interests through sales via a broker to the general public or to financial institutions or public investors. Privately held corporations have substantial flexibility in terms of their internal operating procedures and do not generally have to comply with rigorous corporate structures or formalities. For example, in lieu of an actual meeting,

---

[1] The American Law Institute also issued *Principles of Corporate Governance* in 1994.

privately held corporations often use a single document signed by each principal to dispose of necessary tasks such as elections of directors or issuing stock. This document is known as a *unanimous consent resolution.* Many states also give privately held corporations the option of electing to become a *closely held* or *family held* entity. This option further restricts the number or type of owners that a corporation may have, but it gives even more flexibility on how the business venture may be organized and managed.

Note that even though many privately held corporations have a relatively small number of shareholders, there is no limit in terms of revenue. It is not uncommon for corporations with revenues in the eight-figure range to be privately held. Often, the flexibility of a privately held corporation outweighs any desire of the principals to be able to capitalize the business through a sale to the general public.

When a privately held corporation wishes to fund capitalization through the sale of ownership interest to the general public and commercial investors, the principals pursue an initial public offering (IPO) and then continue their corporate existence as a publicly held corporation. After the IPO, the corporation trades (buys and sells) stocks through a public stock exchange. The New York Stock Exchange (NYSE) is perhaps the most famous and influential, but many more exist. A publicly held corporation is subject to a substantial amount of federal and state regulation, primarily through securities laws and corporate governance statutes such as the Sarbanes-Oxley Act. A publicly held corporation is subject to close scrutiny by a variety of regulatory agencies because investors across the globe depend on regulation to ensure integrity among the insiders managing the corporation. Regulation of publicly held corporations is discussed extensively in Unit Five, "Regulation of Securities, Corporate Governance, and Financial Markets."

Other Categories

Besides being classified as publicly held or privately held, corporations may fall into one of the following categories:

- *Domestic.* In the state of its incorporation, a corporation is referred to as a *domestic* corporation.
- *Foreign.* A corporation that transacts business in a state other than its state of incorporation is known as a *foreign* corporation in the other state. For example, WidgetCo is incorporated in Florida and sells its widgets in Florida and Georgia. In Florida, WidgetCo is referred to as a domestic corporation. In Georgia, it is referred to as a foreign corporation.
- *Alien.* A corporation formed outside the United States that transacts business in the United States is referred to as an *alien* corporation.
- *Nonprofit and Benefit. Nonprofit* corporations are those with no profit-seeking owners; they exist to perform some service to the public at large (e.g., charities, educational institutions, and certain hospitals). *Benefit* corporations are for-profit corporate entities that align business objectives with societal objectives such as improving the community or enhancing the environment.
- *Public. Public* corporations are formed by a government body to serve the public at large, such as public mass transit companies. Public corporations have a similar structure to a corporation, but they have no owners. Be sure not to confuse *publicly held* corporations (discussed earlier) with public corporations.
- *Professional.* In *professional* corporations, ownership is restricted to a particular profession licensed in that field. These corporations have a corporate structure but are only open to members in good standing of a particular profession. For example, law firms that are organized as professional corporations may only be owned by attorneys admitted to the practice of law who are currently active and in good standing.

- Corporations are classified into one or more categories that reflect their overall purpose, capitalization (how they are funded), location, and structure.
- The two major categories of corporations are those that are owned exclusively by a group of private individuals (known as *privately held*) and those that sell their ownership interest via public stock exchanges (known as *publicly held*).

FORMATION AND START-UP ISSUES

LO 30-3

Explain the process of corporate formation and liability of promoters.

Compared to other entities, a corporation has perhaps the most formal filing and reporting requirements. Principals that wish to form a corporation do so by filing a document with a state authority, usually the corporation bureau of the secretary of state's office, that sets out the corporation's name, purpose, number of shares issued, and address of the corporation's headquarters. This document, known as the **articles of incorporation**,[2] sets in motion the incorporation process. In addition to the articles of incorporation, state statutes often require additional filings with tax authorities to notify them of a corporation's existence. Figure 30.1 is an example of articles of incorporation from California.

State authorities then review the articles. If the articles are in satisfactory form, the authorities register them in public archives and the venture is considered formed. In most states, the date of incorporation is actually made retroactive to the date of filing with the state authorities.

Pre-incorporation Activity: Liability of Promoters

In most cases, an individual or group of individuals begins to carry out a business venture's activities before actually filing the articles of incorporation. These activities may include arranging for necessary capital through a loan, recruiting personnel, leasing property, and arranging to have the business incorporated. The individual who performs these activities is known as a *promoter*. If the promoter makes a contract on behalf of a not-yet-formed corporation, she may have some degree of *personal liability* to perform under the contract. Generally, the promoter is personally liable when she knows (and the other party has *no reason* to know) that the corporation is not in existence on the day of the signing. The RMBCA provides that anyone purporting to act on behalf of a corporation, knowing incorporation has not yet occurred, is jointly and severally liable for all liabilities created by the acts. For example, suppose Edgar anticipates opening a private detective agency and enters into a one-year lease agreement for office space with Landlord signing on behalf of the yet-to-be-formed Edgar Detective Agency Inc. One month later, Edgar's financing falls through and he abandons the idea. Edgar would be a promoter and personally liable for the lease payments (or any penalty for breaching the lease contract) to Landlord.

However, a promoter's personal liability *ceases* at the moment that the corporation is formed and has adopted the contract. In the Edgar-Landlord contract above, suppose that Edgar signs on behalf of the corporation, incorporates the business venture the next day, and opens a bank account. For the first month's rent, Edgar pays the rent via company check. Because the corporation has been formed and, by virtue of using a company check, Edgar Detective Agency, Inc. (the corporate entity) has adopted the contract, Edgar's personal liability has been extinguished. If Edgar abandons the business after six months, his personal assets are not subject to Landlord's reach.

Case 30.1 is a cautionary tale in which a court analyzes the potential liability of promoters to an early-stage investor.

---

[2]In a minority of states, this is known as the *corporate charter.*

FIGURE 30.1 Articles of Incorporation from California

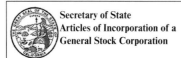

**Secretary of State
Articles of Incorporation of a
General Stock Corporation**

ARTS-GS

IMPORTANT – Read Instructions before completing this form.

Filing Fee – $100.00

Copy Fees – First page $1.00; each attachment page $0.50;
Certification Fee - $5.00

Note: Corporations may have to pay minimum $800 tax to the California Franchise
Tax Board each year. For more information, go to *https://www.ftb.ca.gov.*

This Space For Office Use Only

1. Corporate Name (Go to *www.sos.ca.gov/business/be/name-availability* for general corporate name requirements and restrictions.)

The name of the corporation is Silicon Valley Ventures Corporation

2. Business Addresses (Enter the **complete** business addresses.)

a. Initial Street Address of Corporation - **Do not list a P.O. Box**	City (no abbreviations)	State	Zip Code
1000 Hacker Avenue	Menlo Park	CA	94205
b. Initial Mailing Address of Corporation, **if different than item 2a**	City (no abbreviations)	State	Zip Code
Same as 2a			

3. Service of Process (Must provide either Individual **OR** Corporation.)

INDIVIDUAL – Complete items 3a and 3b only. Must include agent's full name and California street address.

a. California Agent's First Name (if agent is **not** a corporation)	Middle Name	Last Name		Suffix
Steven	Lee	Berners		
b. Street Address (if agent is **not** a corporation) - **Do not enter a P.O. Box**	City (no abbreviations)		State	Zip Code
1000 Hacker Avenue	Menlo Park		CA	94205

CORPORATION – Complete item 3c. Only include the name of the registered agent Corporation.

c. California Registered Corporate Agent's Name (if agent is a corporation) – Do not complete item 3a or 3b
N/A

4. Shares (Enter the **number of shares** the corporation is authorized to issue. **Do not** leave blank or enter zero (0).)

This corporation is authorized to issue only one class of shares of stock.
The total number of shares which this corporation is authorized to issue is _____ **10,000** _____ .

5. Purpose Statement (Do not alter the Purpose Statement.)

The purpose of the corporation is to engage in any lawful act or activity for which a corporation may be organized under the General Corporation Law of California other than the banking business, the trust company business or the practice of a profession permitted to be incorporated by the California Corporations Code.

6. Read and Sign Below (This form must be signed by each incorporator. **See instructions for signature requirements.**)

Signature

Steven L. Berners
Type or Print Name

CASE 30.1 Branch v. Mullineaux et al., 2010 N.Y. slip op. 31850(U), Supreme Court of New York County

FACT SUMMARY Branch agreed to provide $75,000 in short-term financing to three individuals— Mullineaux, Gefter, and Satsky (MGS)—for purposes of starting up a venture called "Stereo House" in which the principals would profit by arranging parties in a luxury beach house in the Hamptons (Long Island, New York) and charging guests to attend these events. Branch entered into an agreement with MGS

(continued)

whereby it was agreed that the yet-to-be-formed venture would pay back the money to Branch at an interest rate of 10 percent over four months. After Branch provided the funding and entered into the agreement, MGS allegedly formed the Stereo House entity but did not open a bank account, did not execute the proper legal documents, and did not ratify any of the Branch transactions. The venture was ultimately unsuccessful, and Stereo House was unable to pay back the majority of the loan. Branch sued MGS as individuals under a theory of promoter liability. MGS defended by claiming that the $75,000 was an investment and therefore the entire amount was at risk without any liability on MGS's part.

SYNOPSIS OF DECISION AND OPINION   The New York court held in favor of Branch. The court ruled that because the agreement was executed prior to formation of the entity, MGS created individual liability to Branch. MGS were liable as individuals because promoters who execute pre-incorporation contracts in the name of a proposed corporation are personally liable on the contract unless the parties have agreed otherwise. In this case, it was undisputed that the corporate entity did not exist at the time that the agreement was entered into. Thus, as pre-incorporation promoters, MGS were personally liable for the agreement executed prior to the incorporation of an entity, even if the entity would otherwise be considered the contracting party.

WORDS OF THE COURT: Liability of Promoters
"Indeed, a corporation which did not exist at the time the contract was entered into, cannot be bound by the terms thereof unless the obligation is assumed in some manner by the corporation after it comes into existence by adopting, ratifying, or accepting it. [W]hen a promoter executes a contract on behalf of a nonexistent corporation, the promoter is presumed to be personally liable under that contract absent proof of the parties' contrary intent or until there has been a novation between the corporation and the other contracting party. Here, defendants have proffered no evidence that the Stereo House entity adopted, ratified or accepted the agreement they made with plaintiff. Thus, there is no basis for the court to overcome this presumption and shift the individual [MGS's] liability for repayment to [the Stereo House entity]."

Case Questions

1. What steps should Mullineaux, Gefter, and Satsky have taken to help limit their promoter liability?

2. What steps could Branch have taken to limit his losses?

3. *Focus on Critical Thinking:* Isn't Branch's loss a risk of doing business? Why should Mullineaux, Gefter, and Satsky be individually liable?

Choice of State of Incorporation

One of the first considerations for principals forming a corporation is choosing the state in which to incorporate the business venture. Most corporations with a relatively small number of principals choose to incorporate in the state in which they will locate their principal office and operate the business venture.

Some corporations choose Delaware as the state of incorporation because of that state's permissive rules, which allow flexibility in terms of how its managers (in the form of officers and directors, discussed later) operate the business. For the most part, publicly held corporations choose to incorporate in Delaware because the Delaware statutes give their officers and directors wide latitude in decision making that does not require shareholder consent. Delaware has also adopted statutes that offer officers and directors strong protections from shareholder lawsuits alleging that managerial negligence has resulted in damages to shareholder interest. This protection, known as the *business judgment rule,* is discussed in more detail later in this chapter. Moreover, Delaware has a well-established body of case law that allows more reliability in corporate planning.

Note that despite some myths to the contrary, Delaware's tax structure is *not* favorable to out-of-state corporations that incorporate in Delaware. Although Delaware has no sales tax on retail merchandise, this rule only applies to in-state sales. Thus, an out-of-state business that uses Delaware to incorporate, but does not sell any products or services in Delaware, has no tax advantage at all. In fact, corporations with a relatively small number of principals will typically end up paying more in taxes considering the assessment of business franchise taxes or fees in both Delaware and in the state where most of the business venture's activity takes place.

Tax Matters

For multiperson ventures, it is not uncommon for the tax-related needs of the individuals to differ. For example, Abel and Baker wish to form NewCo.com. Abel may favor the corporate form, whereas Baker's interests may be better served by a partnership. Before selecting an appropriate form of entity, the parties try to anticipate the best way to minimize taxes while maintaining an appropriate degree of liability protection.

C Corporations
Every C corporation is considered a legal, taxable entity that is separate from the owners for income tax purposes. Therefore, corporations pay tax on their earnings, and then shareholders pay tax on any corporate earnings distributed to them in the form of dividends. This system is known as *double taxation.* Taxation occurs at the corporate level, when the corporation earns income, and at the individual level, when it is distributed as a dividend (profit) to the shareholder.

S Corporations
Corporations that qualify for and elect Subchapter S treatment offer *pass-through* (also known as *flow-through*) tax treatment. The term *Subchapter S* is simply a designation named after the section of the Internal Revenue Code that details requirements to qualify for pass-through tax treatment as a corporation. Subject to certain exceptions under the tax laws, Subchapter S corporations are not subject to taxation at the entity level. The taxable income or loss of the business operated by the entity flows through to the entity's shareholders. As a result, Subchapter S corporations can offer investors numerous tax benefits. It is important to note that all shareholders must consent to S corporation status.

Figure 30.2 illustrates the difference between the taxation of C corporations and S corporations.

Initial Organizational Meeting

After filing the articles of incorporation, the principals typically hold an organizational meeting. This allows the principals to resolve any pending issues and to amend the articles

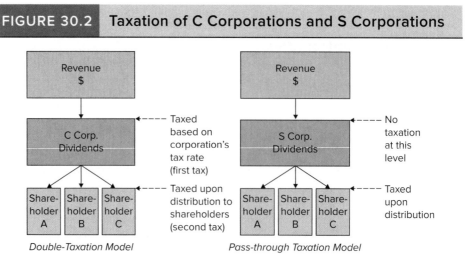

FIGURE 30.2 Taxation of C Corporations and S Corporations

Double-Taxation Model

Pass-through Taxation Model

of incorporation to reflect any changes in the principals' strategy since the time of formation. Specifically, the principals will address such issues as:

- *Bylaws.* Although state statutes govern some of the internal rules of a corporation, there are still some issues left to the principals. These rules are generally articulated in the corporation's bylaws. The bylaws typically specify the date, time, and place for the annual shareholders meetings; the number of officers and directors of the corporation; the process for electing the board of directors; and a listing of each officer along with a description of that officer's duties (responsibilities and liability of officers and directors are discussed later in this chapter). Note that the bylaws are not filed with the state filing official, and thus are not public, but are kept in the corporate records.

- *Board of directors and officers.* In some cases, the board of directors is reported in the articles of incorporation. If they are, the principals may make changes at this organizational meeting by holding another election for the board by the owners of the corporation. Officers are also identified at this meeting and, depending on the bylaws, the officers are appointed by the board or, in some special cases, elected by the board.

- *Issuance of shares.* The organizational meeting also often involves the official issuance of ownership interest consistent with the articles of incorporation filing. The ownership interests are referred to as *shares* and are evidenced by a stock certificate that indicates the owner's name and the number of shares issued. Therefore, owners of a corporation are referred to as *shareholders.* The issuance of shares is usually recorded in a stock register and kept by the secretary of the corporation along with other corporate records of the business (such as meeting minutes, resolutions, etc.). In a privately held corporation, the stock certificates and register are not public documents and are kept with the corporate records in the corporation's registered place of business.

Corporate Formalities

Once the corporation has been properly formed and postformation organizational matters have been attended to, the corporation's officers commence business operations. As a practical matter, the business entity may have already commenced operations under the promoter and, thus, the business operations are simply continued by the newly formed corporate entity. Even after commencement of business operations, officers and directors have a responsibility to comply with state statutory requirements regarding shareholders/ directors meetings, filing annual reports, and disclosures to shareholders, and they must use their best efforts to keep corporate records and bylaws up to date. These responsibilities are examples of corporate formalities. Failing to attend to corporate formalities may have serious liability consequences (discussed in detail later in this chapter).

TAKEAWAY CONCEPTS Formation of a Corporation

Articles of Incorporation
- Promoter drafts articles of incorporation and files with state agency.

→

Initial Organizational Meeting
- Principals ratify actions taken by promoter, adopt bylaws, elect directors, and issue shares.

→

Corporate Formalities
- Principals may enter into shareholder agreement and attend to corporate formalities (e.g., minutes of shareholder meetings).

SOURCES OF FINANCING

Corporations have perhaps the widest range of options when considering how to finance their operations. They may be funded through debt or through the selling of equity (ownership interests) in a variety of forms.

Debt

Corporations often borrow money from either commercial lenders (such as banks) or private investors to fund day-to-day operations, usually evidenced by loan agreements and promissory notes. For larger projects, corporations may also use more sophisticated forms of debt such as issuing bonds or debentures. Bonds are debt money issued by a corporation to the general public with promises to pay the bondholders back at a specified rate of interest for a specified length of time and to repay the entire loan upon the expiration of the bond (known as the *maturity date*). Note that bondholders are not shareholders but, rather, become creditors of the corporation. Bonds are secured through the corporation pledging certain assets. Debentures function essentially the same as bonds, but instead of pledging some specific piece of property, debentures are issued on the strength of the general credit of the corporation. Both privately held and publicly held corporations may issue bonds. Even relatively small corporations use bonds to finance expansion or the building of a new facility, and bonds can range in amount from several hundred million dollars to as little as $500,000 (referred to as *micro bonds*). The primary advantage of bonds and debentures is that the rate of interest is usually lower than that for a commercial bank loan. However, the process can be lengthy and is a more complex legal transaction than a conventional bank loan or a loan through a private individual.

Equity

Corporations also sell equity to capitalize their operations. For modest amounts of funding, corporations may turn to private investors or groups of investors. Sometimes a corporation will hire a registered broker-dealer to draft a document describing the company and the intended use of the funds and to distribute the document to qualified individuals who are seeking investment opportunities that have relatively high risk in hopes of higher returns. Because this process constitutes the issuance of a security, it is highly regulated. Securities law is discussed more extensively in Unit Five.

Venture Capital Firms

When a corporation seeks a more significant amount of capital, the corporation may turn to a *venture capital firm*. Venture capital is funding provided by a group of professional investors for use in a developing business. These firms are frequently focused on one industry (e.g., health care or high-tech). The major advantage of venture capital is that these firms often have substantial resources and are also a source of expertise in operations and expansion of the corporation. However, in exchange for this, principals usually insist on substantial control over the corporation via its board of directors and even its officers. Venture capitalists are not thought of as long-term investors. They usually require an "exit strategy" whereby the venture capital firm exits the corporation with a substantial return. This exit strategy may be to take the company public through an initial public offering or to get the company to grow to a point where a competitor would be willing to pay a substantial premium to purchase the corporation.

Public Offerings

Privately held corporations may also find that their expansion plans require even more capital than can be raised using private investors. In that case, some companies opt to proceed down a very complex and time-consuming process of converting the corporation from privately held to publicly held by engaging in an initial public offering (IPO). At that point, the corporation may raise equity by selling its shares to the general public and to financial institutions.

CORPORATE VEIL PROTECTION

LO 30-5

Identify circumstances under which a court will pierce the veil of a corporation to access the personal assets of its principals.

Perhaps the most attractive feature of a corporation is its limited liability for the personal assets of its owners and, with certain exceptions, for its officers and directors. In general, shareholders, directors, and officers of a corporation are insulated from personal liability in case the corporation runs up large debts or suffers some liability. This liability protection is often referred to as the **corporate veil**. For example, Roscoe and Pound are shareholders of Roscoe Corporation and obtain a credit card from Express Credit. They use it in good faith to make purchases to operate the business. For several years, Roscoe Corporation conducts business and pays its debts regularly. However, industry conditions worsen and Roscoe Corporation defaults on payment to Express Credit. Assuming that Roscoe Corporation has no assets, any attempt to collect the credit card debt from Roscoe or Pound individually will be thwarted by the protection of the corporate veil.

Piercing the Corporate Veil

A court will sometimes **pierce the corporate veil** when it believes that fairness demands it. In these cases, which are relatively rare, courts may sometimes hold some or all of the shareholders personally liable. Most courts have used four factors to consider whether to pierce a corporation's protective veil. If at least two of these factors are present, a court is more likely to hold shareholders personally liable for corporate debts.

- *Inadequate capitalization.* One important factor courts examine is whether a corporation has been adequately capitalized. When a corporation is merely a shell with nothing invested, courts are inclined to pierce the corporate veil as a matter of fairness. Similarly, if the corporation had initial capitalization, but the shareholders siphoned the profits and assets, a court will view this as an inadequately capitalized corporation.

- *Nature of the claim.* When the claim involves a voluntary creditor, such as a trade creditor who provides inventory for a corporation based on credit, courts generally are not inclined to pierce the corporate veil because these creditors had an opportunity to mitigate the risk of loss (such as requiring a personal guarantee). On the other hand, courts are more likely to pierce the corporate veil when the claim involves some sort of tort such as negligence by the corporation's employees or even by the principals themselves. This is essentially because the victims of negligence (such as a pedestrian struck by a delivery truck operated by a corporate employee) have become *involuntary* creditors and never had the opportunity to mitigate the risk of loss.

- *Evidence of fraud or wrongdoing.* If the shareholders, officers, or directors have committed fraud or have engaged in some type of serious and willful wrongdoing, this is an important factor in a court's decision to pierce the corporate veil. Misrepresentations to creditors regarding important facts about the financial condition of the company or lying to investors about potential liabilities of the corporation are both examples of fraud that could lead to a piercing of the veil.

- *Failing to follow corporate formalities.* Another important factor used by the courts is to examine the corporation's adherence to the statutes, rules, and practices governing a corporation. For example, corporations that file articles of incorporation but never bother to follow up with required or standard practices are in danger of losing their corporate veil protection. Specifically, courts may look at whether there is a proper separation between the corporation and the individual shareholder(s), whether stock certificates were ever issued, if shareholders meetings were ever held, and if proper corporate records (such as minutes of the meetings, resolutions, or stock register) were maintained. For example, suppose that two brothers, Abel and Carter, form AC Inc. by filing articles of incorporation. They decide to split the profits 50–50 and, wishing to save the expense of hiring an attorney, do not keep up with corporate formalities after the articles are filed. In the event that a claim is made against AC Inc., Abel and Carter have potentially exposed their personal assets to claimants if AC Inc. does not have sufficient assets to pay the claim.

Still, courts are reluctant to discard the corporate entity. In Case 30.2, a federal district court considers a plaintiff's attempt to pierce the corporate veil of an entity that breached a lease agreement.

CASE 30.2 Trefoil Park v. Key Holdings et al., Civil Action: 3:14-CV-00364 (Dist. Ct., Conn. 2016)

FACT SUMMARY Trefoil Park (Trefoil) is a corporate entity that owns and manages a parcel of commercial real estate. Trefoil entered into a 10-year lease agreement with Key Holdings (Key), a corporate entity, for commercial premises that Key intended to use for operating a fitness center. According to Trefoil's leasing agents, as the parties negotiated the lease terms, two of Key's principals, Hamlin and Levine, provided them with verbal assurances concerning their substantial personal assets and commitment to the project. They also shared the details of a business transaction between Key and a local hospital that Key claimed would guarantee significant revenue for the fitness center. Hamlin and Levine deny making such representations, and Trefoil conceded there were no written assurances or lease provisions related to personal guarantees or any pledge of personal assets of Hamlin or Levine to guarantee the lease payment obligations of Key.

After paying rent for 45 days, Key notified Trefoil that it was immediately terminating its business operations and abandoning the leased premises. Trefoil sued Key claiming that Trefoil had expended $437,000 to improve the premises as well as $67,694.90 for its broker fees and $60,723 for six months of free rent. Because both parties acknowledged Key was without any assets, Trefoil asked the court to pierce the corporate veil and allow them to reach into the personal assets of Hamlin and Levine alleging that, as Key's principals, they committed fraud by misrepresenting their commitment to financing the Key fitness center venture.

SYNOPSIS OF DECISION AND OPINION The U.S. District Court granted summary judgment in favor of Key. The court ruled that piercing the corporate veil was an extreme remedy to be used only when an entity was an instrumentality used to perpetrate injustice or fraud. In this case, there was no evidence that Hamlin or Levine had complete control over Key or that the entity was merely an undercapitalized shell. The court rejected Trefoil's theory that any verbal representations about the financial viability of a privately held entity, such as Key, were sufficient to prove that the entity was created to defraud an investor or creditor. The court pointed out that (1) Hamlin and Levine invested and lost nearly $450,000 in Key in total, (2) Key adhered to all corporate formalities, and (3) neither Hamlin nor Levine removed funds for personal use or intermingled Key funds with their personal funds.

WORDS OF THE COURT: Legitimate Business Enterprise "Although it is true that Key signed and then quickly broke a ten year lease with [Trefoil], that fact alone does not lead to the conclusion that Key was formed for the purpose of defrauding [Trefoil], or that its sole or primary function was to defraud [Trefoil]. . . . Here, the Record establishes that Key was a legitimate business enterprise that, like many start-up enterprises, failed fairly soon after it opened its doors. [Trefoil], a sophisticated landlord, was fully aware of the type of business with which they were dealing. While the result in this case, as in any case in which a court must decline to pierce the corporate veil, may seem harsh, the Court will not and cannot rescue a party from its own unfavorable or unwise business dealings. Or, in other words, a hard bargain is not enough to energize the equitable power to disregard the corporate form."

(continued)

Case Questions

1. Why is it significant that Key's principals never removed funds for personal use or intermingled Key funds with their personal funds?

2. What is your interpretation of the court's language that the decision "may seem harsh"? Harsh on whom? Why?

3. *Focus on Critical Thinking:* Are Key's principals hiding behind the law? If the corporate veil did not exist, how would that impact entrepreneurs interested in starting up new ventures? Is it ethical to sign a 10-year lease and then breach it in one month? How could Trefoil avoid this type of catastrophe in the future?

Personal Guarantees

As one would imagine, banks, landlords, and other creditors are fully aware of the limited liability provided by the corporate veil. Thus, if a corporation is a start-up or has limited assets, creditors will almost always require that the shareholders provide a personal guarantee. A personal guarantee allows the creditor to obtain a judgment against the personal assets of one or more shareholders in the event of a default by the corporation. These personal guarantees are frequently *in addition* to any collateral that is pledged by shareholders or the corporation itself. For example, suppose that Chef Perrier wishes to start up his own restaurant and forms Le Chef Inc. as the sole shareholder. In order to obtain a lease, his landlord will require a contract with Le Chef Inc. and *also* with Perrier personally. In order to obtain a loan from the local bank to purchase equipment, inventory, and furniture, the bank will require that (1) Le Chef Inc. agree to a loan repayment schedule; (2) Le Chef Inc. give the bank a right to claim the equipment and inventory as collateral; and (3) Chef Perrier provide a personal guarantee of the loan.

In Case 30.3, a creditor files a lawsuit in order to recover a business debt from the personal assets of the business owner.

CASE 30.3 De Lage Landen Financial Services v. Picasso Aesthetic and Cosmetic Dental Spa, Civil Action No. 14-2240 (E.D. Pa. 2015)

FACT SUMMARY Rubin is the sole principal of Picasso Aesthetic and Cosmetic Dental Spa (Picasso), a professional corporation with its principal place of business in Naples, Florida. In 2010, Picasso executed a loan agreement under which De Lage Landen Financial Services (De Lage) agreed to lend Picasso $25,000 for working capital; in return, Picasso agreed to repay De Lage with interest over a period of five years. In connection with the loan agreement, Rubin executed a personal guarantee "absolutely and unconditionally guarantee[ing]" all payments under the loan agreement. Soon after, Picasso entered into a finance agreement under which De Lage leased Picasso office equipment and Picasso agreed to make monthly payments over five years. The finance agreement contained a personal guarantee signed by Rubin:

> To induce [De Lage] to enter this Finance Agreement, the undersigned unconditionally guarantees the prompt payment of [Picasso's] obligations under the Agreement.

In 2013, Picasso stopped making payments on both the loan agreement and the finance agreement. After claiming that some payments were mishandled by De Lage employees and that De Lage had not given him the opportunity to renegotiate the terms, Rubin ultimately agreed to repossession of the leased equipment. Rubin and Picasso ignored De Lage's further attempts to collect the amounts

(continued)

due under the loan and finance agreements, so De Lage filed a lawsuit seeking judgment for the amounts owed against both Picasso's business assets and Rubin's personal assets under the guarantees. Rubin argued that De Lage had never given an accounting of the repossessed equipment and his personal assets should not be at risk until such an accounting had been issued.

SYNOPSIS OF DECISION AND OPINION   The U.S. District Court ordered summary judgment in favor of De Lage. In its decision, the court rejected Rubin's attempts to connect the repossession and sale of the equipment with De Lage's contractual right to seek funds from Rubin's personal assets if Picasso failed to pay. Once Picasso failed to make payments and failed to cure its default, De Lage had the contractual right to a judgment for all sums owed under the loan agreement and the finance agreement against both Picasso's business assets and Rubin's personal assets.

WORDS OF THE COURT: Picasso's Default   "Rubin does not deny in any of his filings that Picasso defaulted on both the Loan and Finance Agreements and that he is personally liable for the amounts due pursuant to the Personal Guarantees

he executed. Rather, Rubin admits that Picasso fell behind on its payments, which constitutes a default under the Agreements. Thus, even construing all facts in the light most favorable to Rubin, no material issue of fact remains on the question of Picasso's default on the Loan and Finance Agreements and Rubin's personal liability to [De Lage] by virtue of his Personal Guarantees. . . ."

Case Questions

1. Why do you suppose De Lage required Rubin to sign a personal guarantee for the loans and lease?

2. Read over the language of the guarantee that Rubin signed. How could the language be modified to make it more favorable for Rubin?

3. *Focus on Critical Thinking:* Is it possible that Rubin may not have realized the impact of a personal guarantee? He was a trained dentist and testified that he did not have an attorney review the documents. Should state legislatures pass disclosure and protection laws for small-business owners that are modeled on consumer protection laws for home mortgage loans? Could such regulation result in a decreased number of loans offered to small-business owners?

TAKEAWAY CONCEPTS Corporate Form of Entity

Personal liability of principals	A corporation exists as a separate legal "person." Officers, directors, and shareholders are not personally liable for any debts or liabilities of the corporation (absent fraud). Principals receive corporate veil protection.
Organization/start-up expenses	Formation procedures are relatively easy if the entity is privately held and has limited shareholders. Bylaws, shareholders' agreement, and resolutions are drafted by an attorney, resulting in higher costs. Publicly held companies or "private offerings" involve extensive legal documentation and higher fees.
Capital	Capital may be raised by the sale of shares (equity) or through commercial or private loans (debt). Some corporations may also raise money by issuing bonds and through other debt instruments.
Designations	Doe, Inc. Doe Corporation Doe Company

SHAREHOLDERS, DIRECTORS, AND OFFICERS

Fundamentally, corporations are structured around an allocation of power based on three categories: *shareholders, directors,* and *officers.* **Shareholders** are the owners of the corporation and act principally through electing and removing directors and approving or withholding approval of major corporate decisions. **Directors** are responsible for oversight and management of the corporation's course of direction. **Officers** carry out the directors' set course of direction through management of the day-to-day operations of the business. Although this allocation of power is based on the RMBCA, many states allow a corporation to alter the structure as necessary to meet the needs of the entity. Very large corporations and very small corporations often manage their operations using a modified form of this structure. For example, in some cases a corporation has only one or two shareholders, each of whom acts as director and an officer. The structure is essentially useless, so they may opt to adopt a slightly different structure through the bylaws and/or an agreement among the shareholders as to the rights and responsibilities of each shareholder.

LO 30-6

List the three major groups that form the structure of a corporation and describe the roles of each group.

Shareholders

Shareholders are the owners of the corporation. While shareholders do not directly manage the corporation, most states give shareholders certain rights to protect their ownership interests. Most importantly, shareholders, assuming a majority of ownership consent, have the power to elect and remove directors at the annual shareholders meetings. State statutes also give rights to shareholders to veto any fundamental changes to the corporation that are proposed by the directors and officers. Examples of fundamental changes are the sale of substantial assets, mergers, issuing more capital stock, pursuing venture capital financing, and issuing bonds. Shareholders also must approve any changes in the structure of the corporation by amending the articles of incorporation or bylaws. For example, Widget Manufacturing Inc. is structured as follows:

Name	Percentage of Total Stock Owned	Role
Abel	10%	Officer, director, shareholder
Baker	10	Officer, director, shareholder
Carter	20	Director, shareholder
David	20	Shareholder
Edward	40	Shareholder

Suppose that Abel and Baker locate what they believe to be an excellent opportunity to merge with a larger competitor. They will need to convince either Carter and David or Edward to approve the transaction in order to move ahead. If they are only able to convince Carter or David, but Edward resists the transaction, Edward and the remaining shareholder will have the ability to block the merger from taking place.

Note also that some corporations, particularly closely held corporations, issue *voting stock* to some shareholders and *nonvoting stock* to other shareholders. This is done to ensure that a certain shareholder or group of shareholders can control the corporation but still allows other shareholders to receive payments from the corporation's profit (called *dividends*) and other benefits of ownership. For example, in the Widget Manufacturing example above, suppose that Edward is the father of Abel, Baker, Carter, and David. He wishes to be sure that his heirs receive dividends in certain proportions, but he does not yet wish to cede control of the corporation to them. Edward could issue nonvoting stock to Abel,

Baker, Carter, and David but still retain the power to elect/remove them as directors or to void any transaction. However, it is important to note that shareholders cannot bind the corporation, nor can shareholders demand that the directors take a certain action or adopt a certain policy.

Board of Directors

While shareholders have the power to veto transactions, it is the board of directors that actually sets the strategy and policies of the corporation. The board of directors also has an important oversight function, and state statutes require that the body be *independent* from the shareholders and officers. Most planning initiatives that result in a change to the corporation, such as an acquisition of another corporation's assets or stock, are overseen by the board prior to submitting the plan to shareholders for approval.

Election of Directors

Shareholders elect directors. In most corporations directors hold that office for one year, but the bylaws can set any term. The bylaws also set the procedures and requirements for an election in terms of time and date, notification to shareholders, and how many shareholders must be present to hold a vote (known as the *quorum requirement*). Some states require at least three directors, except in the case of a closely held corporation where the number of directors is equal to the number of shareholders. Therefore, a one-person corporation requires only one director. Other states (such as Delaware) have abolished any minimum number of directors. The number of directors is typically set out in the corporation's bylaws.

Removal of Directors

Directors may be removed by a shareholder vote or, less frequently, by a court order. Absent a contrary provision in the articles of incorporation, shareholders may remove a director with or without cause.[3] The removal process is usually set out in the bylaws, but in almost all cases the shareholder vote must take place at a properly called shareholders meeting. Most states also allow a *court* to order a director to be removed, but only for *cause* (such as fraud). This is a rare event, but it would be necessary in the event that the director at issue is also a shareholder with sufficient voting power to defeat removal votes by minority shareholders.

Meetings

Acts of the board of directors take place only at official meetings that occur at a regular annual or semiannual time as specified in the corporation's bylaws or by a statute. Special meetings to handle pressing matters may also be called so long as a notification procedure is followed in accordance with the bylaws. The votes of a majority of directors present at a meeting are required to take action. Most states allow board action to take place without a meeting if the directors act through unanimous written consent (all directors agree in writing to the action) or they agree to meet using a means of communication that allows all directors to hear and speak with one another at the same time (e.g., through videoconferencing or webcam). For routine matters such as approving the choice of the corporation's auditing firm or legal counsel, corporations often choose these alternate routes to board action.

Committees

Much of the board's work is done through *committees,* small groups of board members who are charged with oversight or to perform a given task and make a recommendation to the full board. For example, a compensation committee investigates

---

[3]RMBCA § 8.08(a).

appropriate compensation for its officers, etc., and makes recommendations; an audit committee oversees the proper reporting of earnings and other audit functions; and an election committee supervises the procedures for director elections.

Officers

The corporation's officers are appointed by, and may be removed by, the board of directors. The officers carry out the day-to-day operations of the corporation and execute the strategy and mandates set out by the board of directors. As a practical matter, officers work closely with the directors in setting the course of a corporation's path, but major changes in the corporation may not be taken through officer action alone. Although some states still require the traditional officer roles to be filled (president, vice president, secretary, and treasurer), the current trend is to allow the names and responsibilities of the officers to be set by the bylaws or through action of the board of directors.[4]

Officers have both express and implied authority. *Express authority* comes from the bylaws or by a board of directors' resolution, which gives specific authority to a particular officer. For example, the board of directors may pass a resolution authorizing the treasurer of a corporation to open a bank account or to start a money market account for surplus cash on hand. Officers may also have inherent authority, based on their position, to act on behalf of the corporation. As discussed in Chapter 37, "Agency Formation, Categories, and Authority," certain corporate officers have *implied authority* to be agents of the corporation. This is an important concept in corporate law because it helps define the powers of corporate officers.

President Traditionally, the president of a corporation has the implied power to bind the corporation in ordinary business operation transactions and has oversight of nonofficer employees. Therefore, the president of a manufacturing corporation has the authority to enter into a distribution contract with wholesalers and to hire and fire company employees.

Vice President Depending on the size and scope of the corporation, the vice president may have some limited implied authority. For example, a vice president for marketing would likely have implied authority to bind the corporation to a vendor of advertising. A vice president might also have the implied authority to bind the corporation in ordinary business transactions if such authority is a routine practice in a certain industry.

Treasurer Aside from the routine tasks of collecting the accounts receivable and paying the accounts payable, the treasurer has little or no other implied authority.

Secretary The secretary has the implied authority to certify the records and resolutions of the company. When the board of directors passes a resolution, it is the secretary who affixes his signature to it, which confirms that the document is genuine. Third parties in a particular transaction may rely on this certification. For example, suppose that Antonin, the secretary of MusicCo, delivers a forged resolution to a bank that authorizes MusicCo to borrow $50,000. The resolution has Antonin's signature affixed to it with a statement that the resolution was duly passed at a board of directors meeting. Bank loans the money to MusicCo based on the resolution. MusicCo then becomes financially insolvent and attempts to avoid repaying the loan on the basis that MusicCo's directors did not in fact authorize the loan. The bank would prevail, because, by virtue of Antonin's implied authority, it had the right to rely on Antonin's certification as secretary.[5]

---

[4]See *Delaware General Corporate Law* § 142(a).

[5]Based on *In re Drive-In Development Corporation,* 371 F.2d 217 (7th Cir. 1966).

LO 30-7

Define the term *fiduciary duty* and apply the various fiduciary duties in the context of a corporate transaction.

FIDUCIARY DUTIES OF OFFICERS, DIRECTORS, AND CONTROLLING SHAREHOLDERS

Officers, directors, and controlling shareholders of a corporation (known as *insiders*) are in a unique position of trust to guide the corporation in a certain direction. Officers and directors owe the corporation's shareholders several well-defined fiduciary duties: the **duty of care** and the **duty of loyalty**. Breaching these duties may result in *personal liability* for the officer or director. Officers and directors must act carefully when they act on behalf of the corporation and must also not put their *own* interests ahead of the corporation's interests. The duty of loyalty also applies to *controlling* shareholders in relation to other shareholders. The duty of care is tempered by a protection for officers and directors when they have acted in good faith but still made an unwise decision that resulted in some loss to the corporation. This protection is known as the *business judgment rule*.

Duty of Care

Fundamentally, officers and directors must exercise the degree of skill, diligence, and care that a reasonably prudent person would exercise under the same circumstances. Most states define the duty of care through a three-part test. First, officers and directors must always act in good faith. Second, they must also act with the care that an objectively prudent person in a like position would exercise under similar circumstances. Third, they must carry out their duties in a manner that is reasonably calculated to advance the best interests of the corporation. This duty applies to all directors and officers without regard to the size of the corporation or whether the directors are paid or unpaid. Courts have held that a director breaches her duty of care when she has failed to fulfill her role in oversight. This may occur in several ways:

- *Negligence.* When a director doesn't read reports, financial records, or other information provided by the corporation, or doesn't attend meetings, this weighs heavily in favor of a finding of breach of duty.

- *Failure to act with diligence.* Directors have an obligation to question any suspicious activity by the corporation or its officers. If the issue is outside of their field, they must investigate it by consulting outside experts (such as a CPA or an attorney). They must attempt to have more than just a cursory understanding of the inner workings of the corporation and must monitor the corporation and the business practices of its officers.

- *Rubber stamp.* Directors have the duty to be sure that any transaction proposed by the officers (or other directors for that matter) is, from the *best information* available to them at the time, in the best interest of the corporation and is not imprudent. They have a duty to determine if the proposed action will impact the corporation in a negative way and, thus, cannot act as a "rubber stamp." If they disagree with a decision being made by the other directors, they must register their dissent in the record of the meeting.

This is not to say that the directors cannot rely on the expertise and assurances of others. Under the RMBCA, directors still fulfill their duty of care even if they do not personally verify the records or other information provided to them by officers or outside experts. Directors may rely on opinions, reports, statements, and financial records that are presented by the officers of a corporation, whom the director "reasonably believes to be reliable and competent in these matters."[6] Directors may also rely on professionals such as attorneys and auditors or on board committees, so long as that reliance is reasonable in terms of the director's belief in their competence.

---

[6]RMBCA § 8.30(b).

Business Judgment Rule

At first glance, the duty of care looks onerous. When a corporation engages in a certain transaction or in a certain course of conduct that generates losses, some shareholders may inevitably believe it was due to the directors' lack of care. The **business judgment rule** protects officers and directors from liability for decisions that may have been unwise but did not breach the duty of care. This rule insulates directors from liability when, based on reasonable information at the time, the transaction or course of action turns out badly from the standpoint of the corporation. Directors and officers often seek the protection of this rule when an individual shareholder or group of shareholders files a lawsuit against them.

Although the RMBCA does not include a business judgment rule, every state has adopted the rule (either by including it in their statutes or recognizing its applicability in common law) as a defense to a breach of the duty of care claim against a director. Fundamentally, directors must have acted in good faith to insulate themselves from liability for breach of care. Most courts define *good faith* by requiring directors and officers to clear three hurdles in order to obtain the protection of the business judgment rule:

- *No private interest.* In order to claim protection under the business judgment rule, the director must have had no financial self-interest in the disputed transactions or decision. Being a shareholder of a merging company or supplier to a corporation may be dangerous territory for a director because a transaction with the merger partner or supplier may have some degree of self-dealing contamination that will deprive the director of any business judgment rule protection.

- *Best information.* An important prerequisite to protection by the business judgment rule is the requirement that directors be active in keeping themselves informed on all material aspects of the decision or transaction at issue. Directors and officers have a duty to be diligent in investigating any proposal, decision, or transaction; this includes consulting outside experts when appropriate.

- *Rational belief.* The third requirement that directors and officers must meet to be protected under the rule is that the decision or approval of the transaction must have been the product of some reasoned decision making based on rational beliefs. This rational belief requirement means that courts focus on the process of the decision making. Directors' and officers' decision-making procedures must be set up in a way that allows careful decisions to be made regarding the best interests of the corporation. Boards often form committees to carry out their work, and this committee structure itself is a significant step in establishing a procedure that helps preserve the business judgment rule protection.

Although Delaware is generally considered to have fairly broad business judgment rule protection, the landmark case of *Smith v. Van Gorkom,* which sent shockwaves through corporate boardrooms nationwide, illustrates the importance of the duty to investigate all *material* facts of a proposed transaction before approving it.

LANDMARK CASE 30.4 Smith v. Van Gorkom, 488 A.2d 858 (Del. 1985)

FACT SUMMARY Van Gorkom was an officer, director, and shareholder of Trans Union Corporation. Trans Union's stock was traded on the New York Stock Exchange (NYSE) and had never sold for higher than $39 per share. Prior to announcing his retirement, Van Gorkom sought to sell his shares to Pritzker, an individual investor, for $55 per share. Because Van Gorkhom's holdings in Trans Union

(continued)

were substantial, he was required to get the approval of Trans Union's board of directors for the sale to Pritzker. Van Gorkom proposed the sale to the board in an oral presentation. Most of the other officers opposed the sale on the basis that the price was too low given the value of the company. Indeed, the chief financial officer advised the directors that the price was in the "low range." The directors did not review the terms of the Van Gorkom-Pritzker agreement, did not perform any valuation analysis on the company, and did not consult any of the company's investment bankers.

After Van Gorkom pressured the directors by informing them that Pritzker would withdraw the offer within three days, the board deliberated for several hours and approved the transaction. A group of shareholders brought a lawsuit against the directors of Trans Union based on breach of the duty of care that resulted in the stock being sold at a value well under its actual worth. The directors sought protection under the business judgment rule, claiming they relied on Van Gorkom's representations and the NYSE stock price.

SYNOPSIS OF DECISION AND OPINION The Delaware Supreme Court ruled against the directors, holding that they could not be afforded the protection of the business judgment rule. The court's decision was primarily based on its conclusion that the directors had failed to obtain all material information and had neglected to investigate the transaction. The court pointed to the fact that the board never even reviewed the Van Gorkom-Pritzker agreement, nor had they undertaken anything more than a cursory inquiry into the actual value of the corporation.

WORDS OF THE COURT: Duty to Be Informed
"We do not say that the Board of Directors was not entitled to give some credence to Van Gorkom's representation that $55 was an adequate or fair price.

[T]he directors were entitled to rely upon their chairman's opinion of value and adequacy, provided that such opinion was reached on a sound basis. Here, the issue is whether the directors informed themselves as to all information that was reasonably available to them. Had they done so, they would have learned of the source and derivation of the $55 price and could not reasonably have relied thereupon in good faith.

"None of the directors, management or outside, were investment bankers or financial analysts. Yet the Board did not consider recessing the meeting until a later hour that day (or requesting an extension of Pritzker's deadline) to give it time to elicit more information as to the sufficiency of the offer, either from inside management or from Trans Union's own investment banker, Salomon Brothers, whose Chicago specialist in merger and acquisitions was known to the Board and familiar with Trans Union's affairs. Thus, the record compels the conclusion that the Board lacked valuation information adequate to reach an informed business judgment as to the fairness of $55 per share for sale of the Company."

Case Questions

1. Assume that the directors were highly sophisticated business executives. Should they have been required to consult others about issues where they already have sufficient knowledge (such as a company's valuation)?

2. What else should the directors have done to satisfy their fiduciary duties?

3. *Focus on Critical Thinking:* In response to *Smith v. Van Gorkom,* many states (including Delaware) passed statutes that extended the scope of the business judgment defense. Should the business judgment rule protect directors even when they fail to verify the statements of internal management concerning a corporate transaction that is being touted to officers as advantageous to the corporation?

Duty of Loyalty

An additional fiduciary duty owed to shareholders by officers, directors, and controlling shareholders is the *duty of loyalty.* Shareholders that have some degree of control over corporate decisions also owe this duty, which is principally intended to prevent oppression of minority shareholders. The duty of loyalty is primarily focused on providing protection to shareholders when a transaction occurs in which there is a possibility of self-dealing.

Prohibition against Certain Self-Dealing   *Self-dealing* in this context occurs when an officer, director, or controlling shareholder has some personal financial stake in a transaction that the corporation is engaged in and the officer, director, or shareholder helps to influence the advancement of the transaction. For example, recall our working hypothetical structure for Widget Manufacturing Inc.

Name	Percentage of Total Stock Owned	Role
Abel	10%	Officer, director, shareholder
Baker	10	Officer, director, shareholder
Carter	20	Director, shareholder
David	20	Shareholder
Edward	40	Shareholder

Suppose that Carter owns port properties and leases warehouse space to industries using the port. Abel, as president of the corporation, searches for a warehouse for Widget Manufacturing's storage needs and identifies several potential properties. Abel writes a report for the board of directors describing the advantages and disadvantages of each property. Because Carter is an officer and director, this transaction has at least the *potential* to conflict with the best financial interests of the corporation. This potential for conflict, however, is not automatically a breach of the duty of loyalty. The RMBCA provides that a self-dealing transaction is not a breach of the duty of loyalty so long as a majority of disinterested parties (those with no self-interest conflicts) approve it after *disclosure* of the conflict.[7] In the Widget Manufacturing example, Carter would simply need to disclose his interest in the property and abstain from influencing other directors about the vote. After disclosure, Abel's and Baker's votes to approve the transaction insulate Carter from a charge of breaching his duty of loyalty to Widget's other shareholders.

Even if the transaction is not formally approved as provided in RMBCA, the modern trend has been for courts to allow such transactions so long as they are, under the circumstances, fair to the corporation and performed in good faith.

 QUICK QUIZ Business Judgment Rule

Will these directors be protected by the business judgment rule?

1. Directors of a bank consult with legal, banking, and industry experts concerning a proposed merger. They set up a directors' subcommittee to investigate the merger and ultimately approve moving ahead after two months of deliberation. The day after the merger, the bank's stock price drops substantially and shareholders lose nearly 30 percent of the value of their investment.

2. The company president recommends to the board that NewCo hire Dewey, Cheatham, and Howe as its auditing firm. In the same meeting, the directors approve the firm. One year later, it is revealed that the audits were fraudulent and that the president had been looting the company, resulting in several million dollars in losses.

(continued)

---

[7]RMBCA § 8.60.

3. Shareholders of a Major League Baseball franchise sue the directors because the team refuses to schedule night games. The shareholders argue that the revenue lost from night games is responsible for the poor financial performance of the company. The directors refuse to schedule night games because they believe it would have a deteriorating effect on the neighborhood.

4. The company vice president recommends that the directors of the corporation purchase a parcel of prime real estate on which to build a new office building for the company. Four of the six directors are members of a real estate partnership that owns that property. Without any disclosures, and on the same day as the vice president's recommendation, the directors vote unanimously to approve the purchase. One month later, it is revealed that the price paid by the corporation was 20 percent above fair market value for the property.

Answers to this Quick Quiz are provided at the end of the chapter.

Corporate Opportunity Doctrine   The duty of loyalty also requires disclosure and good faith when an insider (i.e., director, officer, or controlling shareholder) learns of a potentially lucrative business opportunity that could enrich her individually but is related to the corporation's business. That is, an insider may not *usurp* for herself a business opportunity that belongs to the corporation or would benefit the corporation in some direct way.

Courts use several factors to determine when an opportunity belongs to a corporation and is therefore off-limits to insiders who are officers, directors, or controlling shareholders unless they have followed specific disclosure steps:

1. Did the corporation have a current interest or expected interest in the opportunity (such as an existing contract to purchase a piece of property)?
2. Is it fair to the corporation's shareholders to allow another to usurp a certain interest?
3. Is the opportunity closely related to the corporation's existing or prospective business activities?

In answering these questions, courts will take into consideration whether the officer, director, or controlling shareholder learned of the opportunity because of his role in the corporation and whether a party used corporate resources to take advantage of the opportunity. In Case 30.5, a state appellate court analyzes a corporate opportunity claim.

CASE 30.5 Ebenezer United Methodist Church v. Riverwalk Development Phase II et al., 42 A.3d 883 (Md. Ct. App. 2012)

FACT SUMMARY   Green, a real estate developer, was president and part owner of Synvest Real Estate Trust (Synvest). Synvest's practice was to hold undeveloped property in its own name while it arranged construction financing, then transfer the property to a newly created entity once the funds had been secured and development could begin. In the course of this business, Synvest came to own certain properties that it prepared for construction and conveyed

to a new entity known as River Walk Development (Riverwalk I). In 2002, Ebenezer United Methodist Church (EUMC) purchased a 50 percent interest in Riverwalk I for $250,000, and construction commenced soon afterwards.

At some point before EUMC completed its investment in Riverwalk I, it learned that Synvest had come to own a new 32-acre parcel and six additional lots in the same county as Riverwalk I.

(continued)

In 2003, Synvest formed River Walk Development Phase Two (Riverwalk II), which purchased the 32-acre parcel later that month. In 2004, Green arranged for Riverwalk I, Riverwalk II, and a third entity to enter into a line-of-credit agreement for $2.1 million for the three entities, collectively. Riverwalk I developed and sold several units and conveyed the proceeds to EUMC. Eventually Synvest repurchased EUMC's interest, which yielded EUMC a profit of $30,000 on its $250,000 investment. Only after this business had concluded did EUMC learn of the line-of-credit agreement that had been tied to the Riverwalk I assets.

EUMC filed suit against Green, Synvest, and Riverwalk II, alleging that they violated the corporate opportunity doctrine by failing to disclose the additional real estate transaction involving the new 32-acre parcel, transferring it secretly to Riverwalk II, a new entity solely owned by Green. EUMC claimed that it should share in any profits of Riverwalk II. The trial court ruled in favor of Green/Riverwalk II, and EUMC appealed.

SYNOPSIS OF DECISION AND OPINION   The Maryland Court of Special Appeals upheld the trial court's judgment in favor of Green/Riverwalk II. While the court acknowledged that Green owed fiduciary duties to Riverwalk I and the other members, including the duty not to exclude principals from corporate opportunities, the court used the reasonable expectations test to determine if the corporate opportunity was usurped. It held that a reasonable expectation or interest in a corporate opportunity requires something more than mere proximity of geography, management, or finance.

WORDS OF THE COURT: Reasonable Expectations Test   "This test focuses on whether the corporation could realistically expect to seize and develop the opportunity. If so, the director or officer may not appropriate it and thereby frustrate the corporate purpose. If the opportunity is a corporate one, then the director or officer to whom it is presented or who becomes aware of it must first present it to the corporation, before pursuing it himself. Only if the corporation rejects the opportunity may a director or officer exploit it for his own benefit. . . . [P]rojects related by management are not automatic mutual corporate opportunities. Joint financial risk is simply too common to give rise to any particularized interest or expectancy."

Case Questions

1. Why did EUMC believe that it was entitled to become a partner in Riverwalk II?

2. EUMC reaped a substantial profit from its Riverwalk I investment. Should that be a factor in the court's analysis? Why or why not?

3. *Focus on Critical Thinking:* What other fiduciary duties may Green have breached given these facts? Explain. Could Green assert the business judgment rule as a defense?

Duty to Disclose   Officers, directors, and controlling shareholders who become aware of an opportunity belonging to the corporation must disclose the opportunity to the corporation in total. That is, all plans and relevant information on the opportunity must be presented to the board of directors. If the board, for whatever reasons, rejects the opportunity, the insider is then free to pursue the opportunity with no fear of liability.

In our Widget Manufacturing example, suppose that the directors all discuss the need for a new warehouse facility and authorize Abel to find a suitable lot on which to build. While Abel pursues this objective, Carter's neighbor makes him aware of a parcel of land that would fit Widget's needs in terms of space, zoning, workforce population, access, and price. Carter purchases the property for himself at a price of $100,000. He then tells a commercial real estate broker to contact Abel and advise him that the property is on the market for $200,000. In this case, because Carter was an insider who knew of a corporate opportunity that would benefit Widget Manufacturing, and knew that the corporation was in the market for a new warehouse, he had an obligation to disclose the opportunity to the corporation first rather than buying it.

However, suppose that, instead of buying the lot, Carter discloses the opportunity to the corporation's board of directors. If the directors reject that opportunity to purchase, then Carter is free to make the purchase and even to sell or lease the land to Widget Manufacturing at a profit. Failing to follow the disclosure rules is a breach of the duty of loyalty.

TAKEAWAY CONCEPTS Fiduciary Duties

- Officers, directors, and controlling shareholders (sometimes called *insiders*) owe corporate shareholders the fiduciary duties of care (use of skill, diligence, and care to advance the best interests of the corporation) and loyalty (prohibition against self-dealing or conflicts of interest).
- The business judgment rule protects insiders from liability for breach of the duty of care so long as the insider acted in good faith, was diligent about making a well-informed decision, and had no financial self-interest in the decision.

 THINKING STRATEGICALLY

©valterZ/Shutterstock

Strengthening Your Corporate Veil

PROBLEM: While principals of a corporation or a limited liability corporation enjoy legal protection of their personal assets from the debts and liabilities of their business entity, as we discussed in this chapter, the law permits a court to disregard the corporate veil protections in certain circumstances. One empirical study concluded that piercing the corporate veil is the most litigated issue in corporate law.[8] The overwhelming majority of cases where a litigant seeks to pierce the veil involve closely held businesses.[9]

STRATEGIC SOLUTION: Recall our discussion from Chapter 1 on how business owners and managers employ a prevention strategy to minimize their liability and add value to the firm. Use your knowledge of the law related to the corporate veil to design policies and procedures that lower your liability risk by strengthening your corporate veil protection. Generally, if principals want to maintain their veil protection, they must *act* as a corporation, not as a partnership or proprietorship. Nearly all cases in which a litigant attempts to pierce the corporate veil fall into one of two general categories: *corporate formalities* or *arm's-length transactions/operations*.

---

[8]Robert B. Thompson, "Piercing the Corporate Veil: An Empirical Study," *Cornell Law Review* 76, Issue 5 (July 1991), pp. 1036, 1037.
[9]*Id.* at 1039.

CORPORATE FORMALITIES

Observing corporate formalities is perhaps the most cost-efficient method for strengthening your corporate veil, but in the sometimes frenzied world of business, a company's books and records can easily be forgotten in a file cabinet drawer. The first step is to designate an individual in the company who is specifically responsible for maintaining corporate records and complying with filing requirements. Specifically, observing corporate formalities involves:

- *Maintaining a corporate record file and updating the organizational documents of the company.* Your corporate record file should include the articles of incorporation, bylaws, amendments, corporate resolutions (e.g., banking), shareholders' agreements, and the stock or ownership ledger. Minutes of required annual meetings (depending on your state of incorporation) for shareholders or directors should be included in your corporate record file. The meetings need not be elaborate or overly formal; they simply document events in your corporate history.

- *Filing annual reports and tax returns.* Some states require an annual filing typically used to report any changes in the structure of the corporation or additional shares issued. All tax filings should be included in your corporate file.

Some companies leave these relatively simple tasks to their attorney. Others find that an efficient principal or employee can handle the maintenance and compliance necessary to adhere to corporate formalities. Still others use a web-based legal service, such as Legal-Zoom, that offers a compliance calendar and templates for corporate minutes and other records.

ARM'S-LENGTH TRANSACTIONS AND OPERATIONS

If any of the principals use the entity in a fraudulent scheme, courts are inclined to pierce the corporate veil automatically as an equitable matter. However, in a closely held corporation, the principals may be conducting business very informally without realizing the hazards associated with day-to-day transactions that are not fraudulent, but not necessarily at arm's-length. An *arm's-length transaction* is one that is conducted between two parties who are not related or on close terms and who are presumed to have roughly equal bargaining power.[10] Services and equipment should be bought and sold at market value and documented through a contract or receipt. Loans, employment terms, and agreements among shareholders should all be documented and reviewed by an attorney.

In addition to being aware of arm's-length transactions, the principals must *operate* the corporation as an entity separate and apart from its principals. First, the corporation must maintain its own corporate bank and credit accounts. Anything paid out of the corporation's account must be for a business-related expense that should be supported with a receipt or other documentation. Business income and expenses should be tracked on a separate ledger as part of your corporate records file.

---

[10]*Black's Law Dictionary,* 10th ed.

Second, consider using your corporate designator (e.g., *Inc.* or *Corp.*) as part of your brand or trademark. This gives notice to any customer, creditor, merchant, or landlord that your business entity is separate from its principals and refutes any notion that the principals misrepresented the existence or status of the corporation. Business cards, stationery, invoices, advertising, and all corporate records should always contain the full corporate name and designator. All contracts related to the corporation should have the full corporate name and designator. For example, see the signature block on the sample lease below:

Landlord	**Tenant**
Long Island Realty, LLC	Palsgraf's Pianos, Inc.
Bill Andrews	*Ben Cardozo*
_____	_____
William S. Andrews, Managing Member	Benjamin S. Cardozo, President

Finally, be aware that courts may look at the *capitalization* of a corporation when deciding whether the principals were operating the entity as a corporation. This means that principals should in good faith put funds into the business that are reasonably adequate for its prospective liabilities. There is no formula or magic number. Rather, the law requires only what a reasonable business owner would anticipate is necessary to fund operations.

QUESTIONS

1. Why is it important to take steps to preserve the corporate veil?
2. What kinds of methods and systems could be put into place to ensure that these corporate veil protection steps take place on a systematic basis? Who should be responsible?

KEY TERMS

Corporation p. 515   A fictitious legal entity that exists as an independent "person" separate from its principals.

Business corporation law p. 515   Often the title for a specific state law that covers such matters as the structure of the corporation, oversight of the activity of the corporation's managers, rights of the principals in the case of the sale of assets or ownership interests, annual reporting requirements, and other issues that affect the internal rules of the business venture.

Revised Model Business Corporation Act (RMBCA) p. 515   Model act drafted by the American Law Institute and adopted by over half of the states as a template for compiling their own statutes governing corporations.

Privately held corporation p. 515   A corporation that does not sell ownership interests through sales via a broker to the general public or to financial institutions or investors.

Articles of incorporation p. 517   The document filed with a state authority that sets in motion the incorporation process; includes the corporation's name and purpose, number of shares issued, and address of the corporation's headquarters.

Corporate veil p. 523   The liability protection shareholders, directors, and officers of a corporation have from personal liability in case the corporation runs up large debts or suffers some liability.

Piercing the corporate veil p. 523   When the court discards the corporate veil and holds some or all of the shareholders personally liable because fairness demands doing so in certain cases of inadequate capitalization, fraud, and failure to follow corporate formalities.

Shareholders p. 527   The owners of a corporation; act principally through electing and removing directors and approving or withholding approval of major corporate decisions.

Directors p. 527   Individuals responsible for oversight and management of the corporation's course of direction.

Officers p. 527   Individuals appointed by the board of directors to carry out the directors' set course of direction through management of the day-to-day operations of the business.

Duty of care p. 530   A fiduciary duty owed to shareholders by officers and directors; requires that the fiduciaries exercise the degree of skill, diligence, and care that a reasonably prudent person would exercise under the same circumstances, acting in good faith, and in a manner that is reasonably calculated to advance the best interests of the corporations.

Duty of loyalty p. 530   A fiduciary duty owed to shareholders by officers, directors, and controlling shareholders; requires that the fiduciaries put the corporation's interests ahead of their own and do not engage in self-dealing or conflicts of interest.

Business judgment rule p. 531   A principle that protects corporate officers and directors from liability when they have made an unwise decision that results in a loss to the corporation but they have acted in good faith, had no private financial self-interest, and used diligence to acquire the best information related to the decision.

CASE SUMMARY 30.1 Miner v. Fashion Enterprises, Inc., 794 N.E.2d 902 (Ill. App. Ct. 1999)

Piercing the Corporate Veil

Karen Lynn, Inc. (Lynn Corporation) was a wholly owned subsidiary of Fashion Enterprises, Inc. This meant that the sole shareholder of Lynn Corporation was the corporate entity of Fashion Enterprises, Inc. Lynn Corporation entered into a 10-year lease for retail space in Chicago with Miner with no personal guarantees or guarantee by Fashion Enterprises. The company defaulted on the lease by not making rental payments, and Miner obtained a court judgment against Lynn Corporation. The corporation was without assets, and Miner asked the court to pierce the corporate veil and allow the judgment to be enforced against its sole shareholder, Fashion Enterprises. The trial court dismissed the suit, holding that Miner was entitled only to the assets of Lynn Corporation. Miner appealed.

CASE QUESTIONS

1. Who prevails and why?
2. What factors would the court weigh in deciding whether to pierce the veil?

CASE SUMMARY 30.2 Village at Camelback Property Owners Association v. Carr, 538 A.2d 528 (Pa. Super. 1988)

Corporate Veil

Carr was a real estate developer who formed several corporations to develop and sell residential real estate parcels called Village at Camelback. The owners of the real estate parcels formed a homeowners' association, and a dispute developed between Carr and the property owners. Eventually the association sued Carr's development corporations. However, since the development corporations were at the end of their existence, the corporations had little or no assets. The homeowners' association asked the court to hold Carr liable individually alleging that he was the alter ego of the development corporation. They pointed to intermingling of Carr's personal funds with corporate funds, that Carr was a sole shareholder with a nonfunctioning board of directors, and that he failed to follow corporate formalities. Carr moved to be dismissed from the suit as an individual asserting that each

development entity was properly incorporated and all agreements of sale were in the name of the corporation.

CASE QUESTIONS

1. Which factors weigh in favor of the court piercing the corporate veil?
2. Should Carr be able to avoid liability even if he was the sole shareholder?

CASE SUMMARY 30.3 Goodman v. Darden, Doman & Stafford Associates 670 P.2d 648 (Wa. 1983)

Promoter Liability

Goodman entered into a contract with Darden, Doman & Stafford (DDS) for extensive renovation of an apartment building. Goodman signed the contract "Building Design and Development Inc. (In formation) John A. Goodman," but Goodman had not filed articles of incorporation or taken any other steps toward incorporation. Goodman also informed DDS that all payments should be made to his corporate entity. DDS was unhappy with the quality of the renovations and demanded that the problems be remedied. Goodman then filed articles of incorporation for Building

and Design Development Inc. and attempted to remedy the problems raised by DDS. The parties were unable to agree, and DDS took action to bring the dispute to arbitration pursuant to the original contract and named both the corporation and Goodman as an individual for promoter's liability.

CASE QUESTIONS

1. Was Goodman acting as a promoter when he negotiated the contract?
2. When, if ever, does Goodman's liability as a promoter end?

CASE SUMMARY 30.4 *In re* the Dow Chemical Company Derivative Litigation, Cons. Civil Action No. 4349-CC. (De. Ct. Chancery 2010)

Business Judgment Rule

Dow Chemical entered into a multibillion-dollar acquisition agreement with Rohm & Haas that required Dow to pay for certain Rohm & Haas assets on an agreed-upon closing date. Due to unforeseen circumstances, Dow was unable to generate the money needed to close the Rohm & Haas deal when the appointed time arrived. The original agreement included a "ticking fee" to accrue daily if the deal was not closed on time. Eventually, the parties reached a settlement in which the acquisition was completed in accordance with its initial terms, but the entire

transaction ended up costing Dow significantly more than originally planned. A group of Dow's shareholders filed suit against the directors for breach of fiduciary duty in approving and carrying out the transaction. The directors countered that that the transaction was the product of the board's good faith and informed business judgment.

CASE QUESTIONS

1. Who prevails and why?
2. Are the directors seeking protection by the law for their own negligence? Explain.

1. The formation of a corporation is governed by:
   a. Federal statutes.
   b. State statutes.
   c. Federal regulations.
   d. State common law.
   e. Federal common law.

2. Fresh Farm Corporation (FFC) operates 50 produce stands across Georgia and 100 stands in its home state of Florida. The company is incorporated in Florida. In Florida, what category of corporation is FFC?
   a. Domestic
   b. Foreign
   c. Offshore
   d. Nonprofit
   e. Alien

3. Corporations that do not sell ownership interests through a broker to the general public or financial institutions are categorized as:
   a. Privately held firms.
   b. Publicly held firms.
   c. Public interest firms.
   d. Equity firms.
   e. Nonprofit firms.

4. Which of the following are typically handled at the initial organizational meeting?
   I. Officers and directors are appointed/elected.
   II. Shares of stock are issued.
   III. Personal guarantees are given for all corporate debt.
   IV. Articles of incorporation are filed.
      a. I and II
      b. I, II, and III
      c. II, III, and IV
      d. I, III, and IV
      e. I, II, III, and IV

5. Which of the following is not considered a factor by a court when judging whether fairness demands that the corporate veil be pierced?
   a. Inadequate capitalization
   b. Fraudulent transactions by the principals
   c. Personal wealth of the principals
   d. Failure to follow corporate formalities
   e. The nature of the claim

6. A corporation's directors are responsible for oversight and management of the corporation's general course of direction.
   a. True
   b. False

7. Self-dealing by failing to disclose a corporate opportunity is a breach of a director's duty of loyalty.
   a. True
   b. False

8. NewCo's officers and directors made a good faith and well-informed decision to acquire OldCo, but because the transaction resulted in a loss they are not protected by the business judgment rule.
   a. True
   b. False

9. A disgruntled shareholder files a breach of duty lawsuit against the directors of WidgetCo alleging that they do not read relevant reports. The shareholder's likely breach of fiduciary duty theory is that the directors breached their duty of care.
   a. True
   b. False

10. Under the Revised Model Business Corporation Act (RMBCA), approval from the board of directors is required for an asset purchase acquisition.
    a. True
    b. False

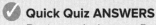

Quick Quiz ANSWERS
Business Judgment Rule

1. Yes. The directors fulfilled their duties by consulting outside experts and appointing an oversight subcommittee. They acted in good faith and had a rational belief that the merger was in the interests of the company.

2. No. The directors have an obligation to investigate the auditing firm and not to rubber stamp the decision of the president. This is either gross negligence or willful ignorance. Either way, the directors violated their duty of care and were not acting with best information and, thus, cannot be shielded by the business judgment rule.

3. Yes. Even if the directors' explanation is a result of poor business judgment, it is not an act of bad faith and is done with a rational belief. Thus, the directors are protected by the business judgment rule.

4. No. The four directors violated the corporate opportunity doctrine by failing to disclose their financial interest in the real estate. This is an act of bad faith and, therefore, those four directors are not shielded by the business judgment rule.

CHAPTER REVIEW QUESTIONS: Answers and Explanations

1. b. The formation of a corporation is exclusively a matter of state statutory law. While other aspects of corporate law may involve federal statutes, formation (such as filing the articles of incorporation) is accomplished at the state level. Therefore, answers *a, c, d,* and *e* are incorrect.

2. a. The category of this corporation in its state of incorporation is domestic. Answer *b* is wrong because *foreign* refers to an out-of-state business. Answers *c* and *d* are not indicated in the question, and answer *e* is wrong because it refers to a corporation from outside the United States.

3. a. Privately held corporations, those that do not sell ownership interests through sales via a broker to the general public and financial institutions, are the most common category of corporation. Answer *b* is wrong because it refers to publicly issued stock. Answers *c, d,* and *e* are incorrect statements of law.

4. a. Elections and issuance of stock certificates are typically handled at the initial organizational meeting. Answers *b, c, d,* and *e* are wrong because articles

are filed before the initial meeting and personal guarantees are not an initial organizational matter.

5. c. When considering whether or not to pierce the corporate veil, courts do *not* consider the personal wealth or business judgment of the principals. Answers *a, b, d,* and *e* are all factors used by courts, so they are incorrect.

6. a. True. The key words are "oversight" and "general course of direction," which indicate that the answer is directors.

7. a. True. The duty of loyalty prohibits self-dealing and imposes a duty prohibiting a director from usurping a corporate opportunity.

8. b. False. The business judgment rule insulates directors from liability so long as they acted in good faith and followed reasoned decision making.

9. a. True. Failing to read reports is a classic breach of the duty of care.

10. a. True. This question focuses on the issue of board approval for certain business transactions. Asset acquisitions require board approval.

CHAPTER 31

Corporate Transactions: Acquisitions and Mergers

 THINKING STRATEGICALLY

©valterZ/Shutterstock

Mergers and acquisitions are often motivated by a wide array of business and strategic considerations. In this chapter's *Thinking Strategically,* we will focus on one strategic aspect of acquisitions: how to reduce the risk of successor liability.

Learning Objectives

After studying this chapter, students who have mastered the material will be able to:

31-1   Distinguish between mergers and acquisitions.

31-2   Identify some strategic aspects of mergers and acquisitions.

31-3   Articulate the successor liability doctrine.

31-4   Understand the fiduciary duties of board members in corporate transactions.

31-5   Define a hostile takeover.

31-6   Summarize the nuts and bolts of corporate transactions.

CHAPTER OVERVIEW

This chapter focuses on mergers and acquisitions (M&A), strategic business transactions in which the ownership of companies is transferred or combined. From a legal point of view, a *merger* is the legal consolidation of two or more separate business firms into a single company, while an *acquisition* occurs when one business firm takes ownership of the stock or assets of another business. Either way, both types of transactions result in the consolidation of assets and liabilities under a single business firm. Specifically, we cover differences between mergers and acquisitions, consider recent examples, and examine the role of strategy in the M&A context. Finally, we'll focus on specific fiduciary duties related to M&A and walk through various corporate transactions including hostile takeovers.

TYPES OF CORPORATE TRANSACTIONS

A **merger** occurs when two or more companies combine to form a new entity altogether, and neither of the previous companies remains in existence. By contrast, an **acquisition** (or takeover) is the purchase of one company by another company: The acquiring corporation takes over the target corporation by stepping into the shoes of the target, while the target company disappears by operation of law. Such purchase may be of the stock or the assets of the acquired entity. In addition, acquisitions can be either private or public, depending on whether the target company is or is not listed on a public stock exchange.

FIGURE 31.1 Largest Deals in History*

Date Announced	Acquiror Name	Acquiror Industry	Acquiror Nation	Target Name	Target Industry	Target Nation	Value of Transaction ($mil)
11/14/1999	Vodafone AirTouch PLC	Wireless	United Kingdom	Mannesmann AG	Wireless	Germany	202,785.13
01/10/2000	America Online Inc	Internet Software & Services	United States	Time Warner	Motion Pictures/ Audio Visual	United States	164,746.86
06/26/2015	Altice Sa	Cable	Luxembourg	Altice Sa	Cable	Luxembourg	145,709.25
09/02/2013	Verizon Communications Inc	Telecommunications Services	United States	Verizon Wireless Inc	Wireless	United States	130,298.32
08/29/2007	Shareholders	Other Financials	Switzerland	Philip Morris Intl Inc	Tobacco	Switzerland	107,649.95
09/16/2015	Anheuser-Busch Inbev SA/NV	Food and Beverage	Belgium	SABMiller PLC	Food and Beverage	United Kingdom	101,475.79
04/25/2007	RFS Holdings BV	Other Financials	Netherlands	ABN-AMRO Holding NV	Banks	Netherlands	98,189.19
11/04/1999	Pfizer Inc	Pharmaceuticals	United States	Warner-Lambert Co	Pharmaceuticals	United States	89,167.72
12/01/1998	Exxon Corp	Oil & Gas	United States	Mobil Corp	Oil & Gas	United States	78,945.79
01/17/2000	Glaxo Wellcome PLC	Pharmaceuticals	United Kingdom	SmithKline Beecham PLC	Pharmaceuticals	United Kingdom	75,960.85

*The top 10 largest deals in M&A history cumulate to a total value of 1,118.963 mil. USD (1,118 tril. USD).

Source: Institute for Mergers, Acquisitions and Alliances (IMAA), "M&A Statistics—Worldwide, Regions, Industries & Countries," available at https://imaa-institute.org/mergers-and-acquisitions-statistics/.

Many public companies rely on mergers and acquisitions as an important value creation strategy (see Figure 31.1). Recent examples include Google's acquisition of YouTube in 2006, Facebook's acquisition of Instagram in 2012, and AT&T's proposed merger with Time Warner. Here is a closer look at some of the strategic aspects of these corporate deals:

LO 31-1

Distinguish between mergers and acquisitions.

- In 2006, Google acquired YouTube, the popular video-sharing website, for stock that it valued at $1.65 billion. (See Figure 31.2.) During this process, Google had to outbid many other YouTube suitors, including Microsoft, Yahoo!, and Viacom. But once it completed this acquisition, Google established itself as the Internet's dominant player.

- Facebook made one of the riskiest acquisitions in the history of Silicon Valley when it negotiated a $1 billion stock purchase of Instagram in April of 2012. (See Figure 31.3.) At the time of the acquisition, Instagram had only 30 million users and zero revenue. Today, however, Instagram has more than one billion users (!) and has become even more popular among young users than Facebook.

FIGURE 31.2 Google and YouTube

©tanuha2001/Shutterstock; ©rvlsoft/Shutterstock

FIGURE 31.3 Facebook and Instagram

©fyv6561/Shutterstock

FIGURE 31.4 Time Warner and AT&T

©360b/Shutterstock; ©Joan Cros Garcia/Corbis via Getty Images

■ When AT&T proposed an $85 billion merger with Time Warner in 2017 (see Figure 31.4), the U.S. Department of Justice (DOJ) challenged this deal in court. During the trial, AT&T's CEO Randall Stephenson testified that a key goal of the merger was to generate new streams of advertising revenue by targeting Time Warner's media programming—including HBO, CNN, and Warner Bros., all of which are owned by Time Warner—to AT&T's 141 million U.S. wireless subscribers. Although the DOJ won at the trial court level, AT&T won on appeal.

 QUICK QUIZ Mergers and Acquisitions

Is each of the following a merger or an acquisition (see Figure 31.5)?

1. NorthStar Asset Management Group, its former parent NorthStar Realty Finance, and Colony Capital agreed to combine into a single real estate investment company. The combined company, with roughly $58 billion in assets, would be named Colony NorthStar. "We are confident that Colony NorthStar, with its lower leverage, larger balance sheet, and improved liquidity profile, is poised for meaningful multiple expansion and substantially enhanced long-term returns for shareholders," said David Hamamoto, executive chairman of NorthStar Asset Management.

(continued)

2. Microsoft announced it would buy social networking company LinkedIn for a smooth $26.2 billion in an all-cash deal. That took LinkedIn's stock up 47 percent in trading. The deal, Microsoft's largest ever by a $20 billion long shot, would "accelerate the growth of LinkedIn, as well as Microsoft Office 365 and Dynamics," according to Microsoft CEO Satya Nadella. The deal was the sixth-largest tech merger and acquisition on record.

Answers to this Quick Quiz are provided at the end of the chapter.

FIGURE 31.5 | **Acquisitions versus Mergers**

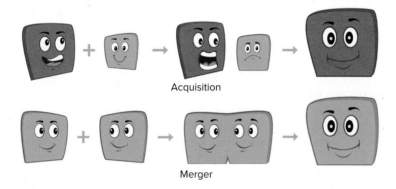

Acquisition

Merger

TAKEAWAY CONCEPTS Types of Corporate Transactions

- A merger occurs when two companies combine to form a new entity altogether, and neither of the previous companies remains in existence.
- An acquisition is the purchase of one company by another company. The acquiring corporation steps into the shoes of the target corporation, while the target company disappears by operation of law.

SOME STRATEGIC ASPECTS OF MERGERS AND ACQUISITIONS

LO 31-2

Identify some strategic aspects of mergers and acquisitions.

Corporate acquisitions can be characterized for legal purposes as either **stock purchases**, in which the buyer purchases equity interests in a target company from one or more selling shareholders, or **asset purchases**, in which the seller sells business assets to the buyer.

- *In a stock purchase, a buyer buys the* shares, *and therefore control, of the target company being purchased.* Ownership of the company in turn conveys effective control over the assets of the company. However, because the company is acquired intact as a going concern, this form of transaction carries with it all the legal liabilities accrued by that business over its past and all of the risks that company faces in its commercial environment.
- *In an asset purchase, a buyer buys the* assets *of the target company.* This type of transaction leaves the target company as an empty shell if the buyer buys out all of its assets. Moreover, a buyer may structure a transaction as an asset purchase in order to

cherry-pick the assets that it wants and leave out the assets and liabilities that it does not. This strategy can be particularly important when foreseeable liabilities may include future damage awards, such as those that could arise from litigation over defective products, employee benefits or terminations, or environmental harms.

Asset purchases are common in technology transactions in which the buyer is interested in particular intellectual property rights but does not want to acquire the target's legal liabilities or other preexisting contractual relationships. An asset purchase structure also may be used when the buyer wishes to buy a particular division or unit of a company that is not a separate legal entity.

The term *acquisition* usually refers to a purchase of a smaller firm by a larger one. Sometimes, however, a smaller firm will acquire control of a larger or longer-established company and retain the name of the latter for the post-acquisition combined entity. This type of transaction is called a **reverse takeover**. Another type of acquisition is the **reverse merger**, a form of transaction that enables a private company to be publicly listed in a relatively short time frame. A reverse merger occurs when a privately held company (often one that has strong prospects and is eager to raise financing) buys a publicly listed shell company, usually one with no business and limited assets.

There are also a variety of structures used in securing control over the assets of a company, which have different tax and regulatory implications. The terms *demerger, spin-off,* and *spin-out* are sometimes used to indicate a situation where one company splits into two, generating a second company that may or may not be listed separately on a stock exchange.

Regardless of how a transaction is characterized, special legal considerations come into play when the companies involved in a merger or acquisition have shareholders. Generally speaking, whether a deal is structured as a merger or an acquisition, shareholder approval of both companies is required.[1] Shareholder approval is not required, however, if the transaction does not involve "all or substantially all" of the target's company's business. In Case 31.1, a court applies the "all or substantially all" test to a corporate transaction.

CASE 31.1 Gimbel v. Signal Companies, Inc., 316 A.2d 599 (Del. Ch. 1974)

FACT SUMMARY Signal was a large business conglomerate that started out as an oil company. At a special meeting, the board of directors approved the sale of stock of its oil subsidiary to another company. The oil subsidiary accounted for 41 percent of its net worth, 26 percent of Signal's total assets, and 15 percent of its total revenues and earnings. Louis Gimbel III, a stockholder of Signal, sued Signal in a Delaware court to stop the sale and require shareholder approval of the sale under Delaware General Corporation Law § 271(a).

SYNOPSIS OF DECISION AND OPINION The Delaware Court of Chancery denied Mr. Gimbel's petition, holding that the sale of the oil subsidiary was not a sale of "all or substantially all" in the ordinary course of business of Signal.

WORDS OF THE COURT: All or Substantially All "It is important to note in the first instance that the statute does not speak of a requirement of shareholder approval simply because an independent, important branch of a corporate business is being sold. [Mr. Gimbel] cites several non-Delaware cases for the proposition that shareholder approval of such a sale is required. But that is not the language of our statute. Similarly, it is not our law that shareholder approval is required

(continued)

---

[1] See, e.g., Del. Gen. Corp. L. § 251(c).

upon every 'major' restructuring of the corporation. Again, it is not necessary to go beyond the statute. The statute requires shareholder approval upon the sale of 'all or substantially all' of the corporation's assets. That is the sole test to be applied. While it is true that test does not lend itself to a strict mathematical standard to be applied in every case, the qualitative factor can be defined to some degree notwithstanding the limited Delaware authority. But the definition must begin with and ultimately necessarily relate to our statutory language."

Case Questions

1. In your opinion, was the sale of the oil subsidiary a sale of "all or substantially all" of Signal's business? Why or why not?

2. Why doesn't the law require shareholder approval every time a board decides to sell or transfer a part of the company's business?

3. *Focus on Critical Thinking:* Why doesn't the court just adopt a fixed numerical cutoff or simple quantitative rule to determine whether a sale constitutes "all or substantially all" of a company's assets?

TAKEAWAY CONCEPTS Some Strategic Aspects of Mergers and Acquisitions

- A stock purchase occurs when the buyer buys the shares, and therefore control, of the target company being purchased.
- An asset purchase occurs when the buyer purchases some or all of the assets of the target company.

SUCCESSOR LIABILITY

Firms that buy and sell businesses often look to structure the deal as an asset purchase in order to avoid getting stuck with the liabilities of the seller. The general rule is that a company that acquires a seller's assets is not responsible for the seller's liabilities simply due to the ownership of those assets. By contrast, in a merger or consolidation the liabilities of the acquired corporation are assumed by the buyer.

However, there is no guarantee that a buyer in an asset-only deal will be completely insulated from successor liability. For example, taxes are a well-established exception to the general rule that the buyer does not automatically assume the seller's debts in an asset purchase. The buyer corporation (and even its shareholders, in their personal capacity) can be liable, by operation of law, for the target corporation's tax obligations.

In addition, courts have carved out several exceptions to the general rule against successor liability in asset transactions. There are four well-recognized exceptions. The first exception applies to situations where there is an *express or implied agreement* on the part of the buyer to assume the liabilities of the seller.

The second exception is the *de facto merger doctrine,* which applies to a transaction that is essentially a merger or consolidation between the buyer and seller. In order to determine whether a de facto merger has occurred, courts will consider the following four factors:

1. Continuity of management, personnel, physical location, and general business operations.
2. Continuity of ownership.
3. Dissolution of the seller as soon as possible after the transaction.
4. Assumption by the buyer of the seller's obligations necessary for uninterrupted operation of the business.

The third exception is the *mere continuation exception,* which applies when the asset buyer is a "mere continuation" of the seller. Courts will look for common ownership between the buyer and seller as well as the common identity of officers or directors. Factors like a continued use of the seller's name, facilities, and employees might trigger the "mere continuation" exception.

The fourth exception occurs when there has been a *fraudulent transaction* used to evade liability for debts. Generally, however, if a transaction is conducted at arm's length and is reasonable it will not be considered fraudulent. But if the seller was insolvent at the time of the transfer, if inadequate consideration was paid, or if the seller was undercapitalized, courts might consider the transaction as fraudulent.

TAKEAWAY CONCEPT Successor Liability

Courts have carved out several exceptions to the general rule against successor liability in asset transactions.

LO 31-4

Understand the fiduciary duties of board members in corporate transactions.

FIDUCIARY DUTIES

We have already discussed fiduciary duties in Chapter 30, "Corporations: Formation and Organization." In general, members of the board of directors have a fiduciary relationship to the shareholders of the corporation, so board members have a legal duty to always act in the best interest of the corporation, as opposed to their own personal interests. Specifically, directors owe shareholders a special duty of care as well as a duty of loyalty. These fiduciary duties are especially relevant when a board is considering whether to approve or reject a proposed merger or acquisition. As a result of these duties, board members should seek the advice and counsel of third parties such as attorneys, investment bankers, and valuation experts before deciding whether to approve or reject a proposed merger or acquisition.

Case 31.2 shows why it is generally a good practice for a board to obtain an independent third-party fairness opinion on a transaction.

CASE 31.2 Paramount v. QVC Network, Inc., 637 A.2d 34 (Del. 1994)

FACT SUMMARY Viacom proposed a tender offer acquisition of Paramount, followed by a second-step merger in a Merger Agreement that prohibited Paramount from soliciting competing offers. The Merger Agreement also imposed extremely high penalties on Paramount if it accepted a competing offer. Subsequently, QVC made a significantly higher per share tender offer, to which Viacom counteroffered in an Amended Merger Agreement. The Amended Merger Agreement increased the purchase price but did not eliminate the penalty provisions. QVC then made a significantly higher final offer and sued Paramount in the Delaware Court of Chancery, alleging that Paramount's board acted improperly by refusing to negotiate with QVC even though its offer was much more valuable on its face. The lower court ruled in favor of QVC and issued an order stopping the Viacom-Paramount merger. Paramount appealed to the Delaware Supreme Court.

SYNOPSIS OF DECISION AND OPINION The Delaware Supreme Court affirmed the decision of the lower court, applying an "enhanced scrutiny test" to the facts of the case and holding that the

(continued)

conduct of Paramount's board was not reasonable as to process or result.

WORDS OF THE COURT: Enhanced Scrutiny Test "The key features of an enhanced scrutiny test are: (a) a judicial determination regarding the adequacy of the decision-making process employed by the directors, including the information on which the directors based their decision; and (b) a judicial examination of the reasonableness of the directors' action in light of the circumstances then existing. The directors have the burden of proving that they were adequately informed and acted reasonably.

"Although an enhanced scrutiny test involves a review of the reasonableness of the substantive merits of a board's actions [footnote omitted], a court should not ignore the complexity of the directors' task in a sale of control. There are many business and financial considerations implicated in investigating and selecting the best value reasonably available. The board of directors is the corporate decision-making body best equipped to make these judgments. Accordingly, a court applying enhanced judicial scrutiny should be deciding whether the directors made a reasonable decision, not a perfect decision. If a board selected one of several reasonable alternatives, a court should not second-guess that choice even though it might have decided otherwise or subsequent events may have cast doubt on the board's determination. Thus, courts will not substitute their business judgment for that of the directors, but will determine if the directors' decision was, on balance, within a range of reasonableness."

Case Questions

1. Did the Paramount board of directors breach its fiduciary duty to Paramount's shareholders by refusing to pursue the better offer from QVC? Why or why not?

2. Paramount argued that it had a contractual duty not to consider competing offers, but at the same time, Paramount's directors have a fiduciary duty to act in the best interests of Paramount's shareholders. In your opinion, which of these two duties should prevail when they are in conflict with each other?

3. *Focus on Critical Thinking:* Should all merger or acquisition decisions by a board be subjected to the "enhanced scrutiny test"? If so, is there any possible way a board's decision can pass this judicial test? If not, why does the court apply this test to the facts of this case?

TAKEAWAY CONCEPTS Fiduciary Duties

- Members of the board of directors have a fiduciary relationship to the corporation, so they must act in the best interest of the corporation, as opposed to their own.
- Specifically, directors owe shareholders a special duty of care as well as a duty of loyalty.
- These fiduciary duties are especially relevant when a board is considering whether to approve or reject a proposed merger or acquisition.

HOSTILE TAKEOVERS

A dramatic type of acquisition is the so-called **hostile takeover**, when the board of a target company has no prior knowledge of an acquirer's purchase offer. Despite its name, there is no law against hostile takeovers! Whether a purchase is perceived as friendly or hostile depends significantly on how the proposed acquisition is communicated to and perceived by the target company's board of directors, employees, and shareholders.

LO 31-5

Define a hostile takeover.

FIGURE 31.6 Hostile Takeover Defense Strategies

M&A Hostile Defense Strategies
• Shareholder rights plan (poison pill)
• White knight bidder
• Management buyout (MBO)
• Stagger board
• Delay annual shareholder's meeting
• Trigger acceleration of debt repayment
• Litigation

Ordinarily, most corporate transactions occur in a so-called "confidentiality bubble" in which the flow of information is restricted pursuant to confidentiality agreements. In the case of a friendly transaction, the companies cooperate in negotiations. But in the case of a hostile deal, the board or the management of the target company is unwilling to be bought or the target's board has no prior knowledge of the offer. Hostile acquisitions can, and often do, ultimately become "friendly" if the acquirer is able to obtain endorsement for the transaction from the board of the target company by improving the terms of the takeover offer.

Broadly speaking, a business deal may be called a *merger of equals* if the CEOs of both firms agree that joining together is in the best interest of both of their companies. By contrast, when the deal is unfriendly (that is, when the management of the target company opposes the deal), the acquisition may be regarded as a hostile takeover. In such cases, the board of the target company may adopt a wide variety defensive measures to prevent the acquirer's takeover attempt from succeeding (see Figure 31.6).

As Case 31.3 shows, however, the use of defensive measures may raise serious legal issues because board members have a fiduciary duty to act in the best interest of the corporation, not in their own best interests.

CASE 31.3 Unitrin, Inc. v. American General Corp., 651 A.2d 1361 (Del. 1995)

FACT SUMMARY American General wanted to initiate a tender offer for a sufficient proportion of Unitrin's stock in order to initiate a merger with Unitrin. The board of directors of Unitrin, however, felt that the tender offer price was too low. Deeming American General's tender offer a "hostile takeover," Unitrin's board initiated two proactive defensive measures to prevent the takeover: a poison pill shareholder's rights program and an open-market stock repurchase program. American General and some of Unitrin's stockholders sued Unitrin to stop it from instituting these defensive measures, alleging that the measures were an unreasonable and disproportionate response to the takeover threat posed by

American General. The lower court ruled for the shareholders, so American General appealed the case to the Supreme Court of Delaware.

SYNOPSIS OF DECISION AND OPINION The Delaware Supreme Court reversed the decision of the lower court, ruling that Unitrin's poison pill and stock repurchase programs were reasonable and proportionate responses to the takeover bid by American General. Here, the court concluded that the board had reasonably perceived two real dangers resulting from the proposed takeover—inadequate price and antitrust complications—and that the board's response was proportional to the danger.

(continued)

Case Questions

1. How should the court determine whether the defensive measures approved by the board were reasonable?

2. In general, board members owe a fiduciary duty to the shareholders of the corporation. That means board members must act in the shareholders' best interests. As such, when there are divergent views between shareholders and the board over a tender offer, whose views should prevail?

3. *Focus on Critical Thinking:* Why doesn't the court apply the enhanced scrutiny test in this case? Doesn't the decision in this case totally contradict the decision in the *Paramount* case (Case 31.2)?

TAKEAWAY CONCEPTS The Law of Hostile Takeovers

- A hostile takeover occurs when the board of a target company has no prior knowledge of an acquirer's purchase offer.
- There is no law against hostile takeovers.

NUTS AND BOLTS OF CORPORATE TRANSACTIONS

LO 31-6

Summarize the nuts and bolts of corporate transactions.

Legally speaking, a corporate transaction usually begins with a **letter of intent** followed by a process of **due diligence** in which the acquirer reviews the financial state of the target company and identifies any potential or actual legal liabilities of the target. An intent letter is a special kind of contract. Although it generally does not legally bind the parties to commit to a transaction, it may bind the parties to confidentiality and exclusivity obligations so that the transaction can be considered through a due diligence process.

After due diligence is completed, the parties may proceed to draw up a definitive agreement, known as a *merger agreement, share purchase agreement,* or *asset purchase agreement,* depending on the structure of the transaction. Such contracts are typically 80–100 pages long and focus on six key types of terms.

- *Conditions,* which must be satisfied before there is an obligation to complete the transaction. Conditions typically include matters such as regulatory approvals and the lack of any material adverse change in the target's business.
- *Representations and warranties* by the seller with regard to the company, which are claimed to be true at both the time of signing and the time of closing. Sellers often attempt to craft their representations and warranties with knowledge qualifiers, dictating the level of knowledge applicable and which seller parties' knowledge is relevant. Some agreements provide that if the representations and warranties by the seller prove to be false, the buyer may claim a refund of part of the purchase price, as is common

in transactions involving privately held companies (although in most acquisition agreements involving public company targets, the representations and warranties of the seller do not survive the closing). Representations regarding a target company's net working capital are a common source of post-closing disputes.

- *Covenants,* which govern the conduct of the parties both before the closing (e.g., covenants that restrict the operations of the business between signing and closing) and after the closing (e.g., covenants regarding future income tax filings and tax liability or post-closing restrictions agreed to by the buyer and seller).

- *Termination rights,* which may be triggered by a breach of contract, by a failure to satisfy certain conditions, or by the passage of a certain period of time without consummating the transaction. Termination rights may include fees and the payment of damages for termination caused by certain events (also known as *breakup fees*).

- *A legal approval clause* or provisions related to obtaining required shareholder approvals under state law and related SEC filings required under federal law, if applicable, and terms related to the mechanics of the legal transactions to be consummated at closing (such as the determination and allocation of the purchase price) and post-closing adjustments (such as adjustments after the final determination of working capital at closing or earnout payments payable to the sellers, repayment of outstanding debt, and the treatment of outstanding shares, options, and other equity interests).

- *An indemnification clause,* which provides that an indemnitor will indemnify, defend, and hold harmless the indemnitee(s) for losses incurred by the indemnitees as a result of the indemnitor's breach of its contractual obligations in the purchase agreement.

TAKEAWAY CONCEPTS Nuts and Bolts of Corporate Transactions

- A letter of intent is a special kind of contract that binds the parties to confidentiality and exclusivity obligations during the due diligence phase of a corporate transaction.
- Due diligence is the pre-closing process in which the acquirer reviews the financial state of the target company and identifies potential or actual legal liabilities of the target.

 THINKING STRATEGICALLY

©valterZ/Shutterstock

Successor Liability

PROBLEM: Buying a business could subject the buyer to potential legal liability. As a result, a buyer will often look to structure the deal as an asset purchase to avoid getting stuck with the liabilities of the seller. The general rule is that a company that acquires a seller's assets is not responsible for the seller's legal liabilities simply due to the ownership of those assets. But there is no guarantee that a buyer in an asset-only deal will be completely insulated from successor liability, as courts have carved out several exceptions to the general rule against successor liability. What can the buyer do to minimize the risk of successor liability?

STRATEGIC SOLUTION: Nothing beats a well-drafted asset purchase agreement and thorough due diligence before committing to an asset purchase. Contracts and due diligence are the keys to minimizing the risk of successor liability.

- **Draft a carefully worded asset purchase agreement.** It's very important that the asset purchase agreement contain "representations and warranties" by the seller, indicating the current liabilities of the seller and the disposition of those liabilities. The agreement also should include an indemnification clause in which the seller commits to indemnify and hold the purchaser harmless for any outstanding liabilities. Also, beware of offering stock in the purchasing company as part of the consideration.
- **Create an escrow account for outstanding liabilities.** During the due diligence phase of the transaction, if the buyer learns of any potential legal liabilities, the buyer could demand that the seller take care of those liabilities before the closing date or, in the alternative, execute an escrow agreement in which the seller places sale funds in escrow subject to the seller taking care of the liabilities before being paid.

- **Conduct a title and lien search for titled assets.** As part of the due diligence process, if the buyer is purchasing assets that have a title (e.g., vehicles, real estate, and leaseholds), the buyer should be sure to conduct a title search to ensure it is acquiring perfected and clean title to those assets.

QUESTION

1. From the perspective of reducing the risk of successor liability, how could you improve the sample asset purchase agreement in Figure 31.7? In particular, what if the asset to be purchased consists of intellectual property, such as the rights to a trademark or a patent? What specific steps could the buyer of such an intangible asset take to protect its interests in the event a third party were to challenge the trademark or the patent?

FIGURE 31.7 Asset Purchase Agreement

In consideration of the payment by the Buyer to the Seller of an amount equal to $[INSERT FIGURE]("**Consideration**"), the Seller hereby sells and assigns with full title guarantee and the Buyer hereby purchases with effect from and as at the Transfer Date the following Assets of the Seller:

2.1.1   the Moveable Assets;

2.1.2   the Fixed Assets;

2.1.3   the right to use the Business Name;

2.1.5   the Business Intellectual Property Rights;

2.1.6   the Stock; and

2.1.7   the Goodwill.

As soon as is reasonably practicable after the Transfer Date, the Seller shall:

2.2.1   deliver to the Buyer physical possession of all Assets which are capable of transfer by delivery and which are in the Seller's possession including all discs, materials, documents and source code in whatever medium that embody the Business intellectual Property Rights and the IT system; and

2.2.2   deliver to the Buyer the assignments of ownership of the Domain Names.

Risk in the Assets shall pass to the Buyer upon the Transfer Date.

Merger p. 542   When two companies combine to form a new enterprise altogether; neither of the previous companies remains independently.

Acquisition (takeover) p. 542   The purchase of one company by another company; such purchase may be of the stock or assets of the acquired entity.

Stock purchase p. 545   When a buyer purchases equity interests in a target company from one or more selling shareholders.

Asset purchase p. 545   When a buyer purchases some or all of the target company's assets.

Reverse takeover p. 546   When a smaller firm acquires control of a larger or longer-established company and

retains the name of the latter for the post-acquisition combined entity.

Reverse merger p. 546   A transaction in which a privately held company buys a publicly listed shell company.

Hostile takeover p. 549   A transaction in which the board of a target company has no prior knowledge of an acquirer's purchase offer.

Letter of intent p. 551   A special kind of contract that binds the parties to confidentiality and exclusivity obligations during the due diligence phase of a corporate transaction.

Due diligence p. 551   The pre-closing process in which the acquirer reviews the financial state of the target company and identifies potential or actual legal liabilities of the target.

CASE SUMMARY 31.1 Bernard v. Kee Manufacturing Co., Inc., 409 So. 2d 1047 (Fla. 1982)

Successor Liability

James Bernard was injured by a lawn mower manufactured and sold in 1967 by the Kee Manufacturing Company ("Old Kee"). In 1972, a new company called Kee Manufacturing Company, Inc. ("New Kee") purchased the assets of Old Kee. These assets included the factory, inventory, goodwill, and the right to use the trade name "Key Mowers" and the business name "Kee Manufacturing Company." Nevertheless, New Kee, by the terms of its acquisition, did *not* agree to assume the legal liabilities or obligations of its predecessor, Old Kee. Moreover, the former owner of Old Kee had no interest in the new company. Under its new owner, New Kee used Old Kee's assets to continue the manufacture of lawn

mowers, maintaining the same factory and employees and using the same trade name, but at the same time, New Kee discontinued the manufacture of the particular model that injured Mr. Bernard. Although New Kee's brochure states that it has been manufacturing lawn mowers since 1948, New Kee is operated under a new management team.

CASE QUESTIONS

1. In your opinion, should the court impose successor liability based on the facts of this case? Why or why not?
2. Would your answer to question 1 change if New Kee had chosen a different name for its business?

CASE SUMMARY 31.2 Smith v. Van Gorkom, 488 A.2d 858 (Del. 1985)

Fiduciary Duties

The CEO of Trans Union, a Delaware corporation, negotiated a leveraged buyout with an investor. The deal was made outside of the knowledge of the other

members of the board of directors and was proposed to them in a summary fashion in a relatively short board meeting with no supporting data or figures. The buyout plan was approved by the board without significant investigation, and the price was approved at $55 per share, which was far above the stock market price. The majority of the shareholders approved the merger, but a group of shareholders opposed to the deal sued the board in the Delaware Court of Chancery, demanding the fair market value of their shares.

CASE QUESTIONS

1. Is the board's decision to approve the buyout protected by the business judgment rule (i.e., made in good faith) under these facts? Why or why not?
2. How likely is it that a court will apply the enhanced scrutiny test to these facts?

CASE SUMMARY 31.3 *In re* Riverstone National, Inc. Shareholder Litigation, C.A. No. 9796-VCG (Del. Ch. 2016)

Enhanced Scrutiny?

In 2008, Riverstone became interested in the single-family home rental business. At the time of the transaction at issue, Riverstone's majority stockholder was CAS Capital Limited ("CAS"). CAS, in turn, was controlled by two of Riverstone's five directors, Nicholas and Peter Gould. In March 2012, Riverstone formed an investment fund, which it pitched to institutional investors, including Blackstone Group LP ("Blackstone"). Blackstone, in turn, agreed to "help execute" Riverstone's business plan, which included forming a limited partnership known as Invitation Homes. Although Riverstone never received an ownership interest in Invitation Homes, all but one of its directors were given the opportunity to, and did, acquire a stake in Invitation Homes. On May 20, 2014, two of Riverstone's stockholders informed Riverstone that its directors and officers breached their fiduciary duties by usurping Riverstone's corporate opportunity to invest in Invitation Homes and demanded that all their individual equity interests in Invitation Homes be transferred to Riverstone.

CASE QUESTIONS

1. Did the directors of Riverstone breach their fiduciary duties to the corporation when they acquired an ownership interest in Investment Homes? Why or why not?
2. How likely is it that a court will apply the enhanced scrutiny test to these facts?

CASE SUMMARY 31.4 Terry v. Penn Central Corp., 668 F.2d 188 (3d Cir. 1981)

Triangular Merger

Penn Central Corp. created a wholly owned subsidiary called PCC Holdings. The parent company, Penn Central, then sought to carry out a triangular merger by merging Colt Industries, Inc. (the target company) with PCC Holdings, thereby bypassing the right of Penn Central shareholders to vote on, or dissent from, the proposed merger. Some shareholders of Penn Central then sued Penn, claiming that the merger between PCC Holdings and Colt was a de facto merger between Penn Central and Colt.

CASE QUESTIONS

1. Should the court apply the de facto merger doctrine to the facts of this case? Why or why not?
2. Should the law permit triangular mergers?

1. **What is the main difference between a merger and an acquisition?**
   a. There is no real difference—the terms are synonymous.
   b. An acquisition is a merger involving a hostile takeover.
   c. In a merger, there is never an acquirer or a target—two companies simply fuse together.
   d. A merger is a type of acquisition in which the acquirer and the target combine to become one legal entity.
   e. Whether a transaction is a merger or an acquisition depends on the common law of the state in which the transaction occurs.

2. **The absorption of one firm by another such that the acquired firm no longer exists as a separate entity is called a:**
   a. Merger.
   b. Stock sale.
   c. Asset sale.
   d. Tender offer.
   e. Consolidation.

3. **When is shareholder approval of an asset sale required?**
   a. When the transaction involves a merger
   b. When the transaction involves a consolidation
   c. When the transaction involves a tender offer
   d. When the transaction involves a hostile takeover
   e. When the transaction involves "all or substantially all" of the target's business

4. **Which of the following is not an exception to the general rule against successor liability in asset sales?**
   a. The de facto merger doctrine
   b. When the buyer makes an *express or implied agreement* to assume the liabilities of the seller
   c. When the buyer is a "mere continuation" of the seller
   d. The de jure merger doctrine
   e. When there has been a *fraudulent transaction* in order to evade liability for debts

5. **What are the main features of stock purchase and asset purchase agreements?**
   I. In a stock purchase, the buyer purchases equity interests in a target company from one or more selling shareholders. In an asset purchase, the seller sells business assets to the buyer.
   II. In a stock purchase, a buyer buys the assets of the target company, while in an asset purchase, a buyer buys a controlling interest of shares of the target company being purchased.
   III. Stock purchase and asset purchase agreements are generally used to complete acquisitions, not mergers.
   a. I and III.
   b. II.
   c. III.
   d. I, II, and III.
   e. II and III.

6. **The key difference between a merger and an acquisition is that a merger creates an entirely new firm whereas an acquisition does not.**
   a. True
   b. False

7. **With an acquisition, the acquiring firm maintains its legal existence but the acquired firm does not.**
   a. True
   b. False

8. **A tender offer is a public offer to purchase the assets of a target firm.**
   a. True
   b. False

9. **In an acquisition of stock, it is board approval rather than shareholder approval that is required.**
   a. True
   b. False

10. **A hostile takeover occurs when the acquiring company makes a secret offer to the board of a target company.**
    a. True
    b. False

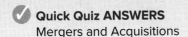
1. The first real-world fact pattern describes a merger because NorthStar Asset Management Group, NorthStar Realty Finance, and Colony Capital agreed to combine into a single real estate investment company.

2. The second real-world fact pattern describes an acquisition because Microsoft is buying a controlling interest in LinkedIn's stock in an all-cash deal.

CHAPTER REVIEW QUESTIONS: Answers and Explanations

1. d. A merger occurs when the acquirer and the target combine to become one legal entity. The remaining responses are incorrect because an acquisition occurs when one business firm takes ownership of the stock or assets of another business.

2. a. In a merger, two or more companies combine to form a new entity altogether, and neither of the previous companies remains in existence.

3. e. Shareholder approval of an asset sale is required when the transaction involves "all or substantially all" of the target's business. Answer choices *a* and *b* are incorrect because the sale of assets does not produce a merger or consolidation. Answer choices *c* and *d* are incorrect because hostile takeovers and tender offers refer to stock purchases.

4. d. Answer choices *a, b, c,* and *e* are all exceptions to the general rule against successor liability in asset sales.

5. a. In a stock purchase, the buyer purchases equity interests in a target company from one or more selling shareholders; in an asset purchase, by contrast, the seller sells business assets to the buyer. Both methods are generally used to complete acquisitions.

6. a. True. A merger is the legal consolidation of two or more separate business firms into a single company and thus creates an entirely new firm.

7. a. True. Unlike a merger, in an acquisition the acquiring corporation takes over the target corporation by stepping into the shoes of the target, while the target company disappears by operation of law.

8. b. False. A tender offer is a public offer to purchase the *shares* of a target firm.

9. b. False. Whether a deal is structured as a merger or an acquisition, shareholder approval of both companies is required.

10. b. False. A hostile takeover occurs when the board of a target company has no prior knowledge of an acquirer's purchase offer.

UNIT FIVE   Regulation of Securities, Corporate Governance, and Financial Markets

CHAPTER 32

Overview of the Securities Market: Definition, Categories, and Regulation

Financing is an integral part of business operations. In this chapter's *Thinking Strategically,* we apply some of the concepts learned in this chapter to produce a table of financing alternatives from a legal perspective, which helps us understand how to decrease risk while adding value to the firm.

Learning Objectives

After studying this chapter, students who have mastered the material will be able to:

32-1   Explain the factors that differentiate the primary and secondary securities markets.

32-2   Identify the parties that participate in securities transactions and their specific roles.

32-3   Apply the legal test for what constitutes a security.

32-4   Distinguish between classifications of equity and debt instruments and give an example of each.

32-5   Recognize the fundamental reason behind securities regulation and demonstrate a working knowledge of federal securities law.

32-6   Describe the role of the Securities and Exchange Commission (SEC) in securities law.

32-7   Explain the impact of state securities regulations relative to issuers, compliance, and enforcement.

CHAPTER OVERVIEW

When the principals of a business venture wish to raise capital for its operations or expansion, one option is to turn to the securities market. This chapter focuses on business entities that raise capital from investors via the public markets by either: (1) selling a percentage of ownership of the venture, known as **equity**, to investors who are interested in receiving a return on their investment based on the success of the business; or (2) issuing **debt** instruments to public investors who wish to receive a fixed rate of return regardless of the profitability of the business entity.

The issuance and trading of equity and debt instruments to public investors is highly regulated by federal and state **securities law**. The actions of business owners and managers who are engaged in raising capital or operate in the financial markets, as well as corporate governance of publicly held entities, are subject to the scrutiny of regulatory authorities. The consequences of noncompliance may include civil and/or criminal liability. In this chapter, we provide an overview of the securities market by examining the role of the securities regulatory agency, defining a security, discussing classifications of various forms of securities, and introducing the major federal statutes that regulate securities.

FUNDAMENTALS OF SECURITIES TRANSACTIONS

LO 32-1

Explain the factors that differentiate the primary and secondary securities markets.

Securities transactions occur in two settings: (1) original and reissuance of securities by a business to raise capital (known as the *primary market*), and (2) the purchase and sale of issued securities between investors (known as the *secondary market*). Both of these markets are governed by federal and state *securities law* and regulations. Various securities regulations require registration and disclosures and prescribe certain procedures intended to give investors confidence in the value of a particular security and to prevent fraud.

In the primary market, issuers raise capital by selling securities in public markets (to the general investment community) or in private placements (to limited groups of investors, such as venture capitalists or institutional investors). Issuing securities to the public markets for the first time is known as an *initial public offering (IPO)*. A company is said to "go public" when it sells its voting common shares for the first time to outside investors through use of public markets such as the New York Stock Exchange (NYSE). The sale is made through the use of a mandatory registration statement that discloses important facts about the offering to potential investors.

Not all securities offerings and transactions are subject to the full burden of the federal and state regulatory schemes. Some securities transactions are exempt from full registration, and the law allows a fast-track system for securities that fall into the category of relatively small offerings or private placements. These exemptions are not automatic. The issuer or trader of a security must structure the security transaction in such a way that it qualifies for an exemption according to federal and state laws. The federal laws, regulations, and exemptions governing the primary market are found in the Securities Act of 1933. We discuss the laws governing the issuance of securities in detail in Chapter 33.

In the secondary market, the trading of previously issued securities does not raise capital for the issuing business. Rather, investors sell to other investors in hopes of making a profit or preventing a loss. Once a company has sold shares to the public, it becomes subject to extensive reporting requirements to federal regulators. In theory, this secondary market provides cash flow for investors to continue their investments in primary markets. The secondary market is largely regulated through the Securities Exchange Act of 1934 (Exchange Act). We discuss the Exchange Act in detail in Chapter 34.

TAKEAWAY CONCEPTS Primary and Secondary Markets

Primary market	Original and reissuance of securities by a business to raise capital	Regulated by the Securities Act of 1933
Secondary market	Purchase and sale of previously issued securities between investors	Regulated by the Securities Exchange Act of 1934

LO 32-2

Identify the parties
that participate
in securities
transactions and
their specific roles.

ROLE OF THE PARTIES IN A SECURITIES TRANSACTION

The securities market functions through the interaction of three parties: investors, issuers, and intermediaries. **Investors** seek a return from their investment based on the value of the security. They include individual investors, who hold securities directly or through a brokerage firm, and institutional investors such as pension funds and mutual funds. **Issuers** are those institutions and entities that sell securities to investors. They include business corporations, state and local governments, and other entities that are seeking to raise capital through investors. **Intermediaries** are financial institutions that provide services for investors and issuers related to securities transactions. Most commonly, intermediaries are brokerage firms, referred to as *broker-dealers,* that buy and sell securities on behalf of a client. Intermediaries also include mutual funds, investment banks, and some commercial banks.

For example, suppose Williams calls her stockbroker at Mega Brokers and finds out that NewCo is raising capital by selling its stock to the public. She believes the stock is priced low and that she will make a profit in the future, so she orders her broker to purchase 1,000 shares. In that case, Williams is the investor, NewCo is the issuer, and Mega Brokers is the intermediary.

TAKEAWAY CONCEPTS Roles of the Parties in Securities Transaction

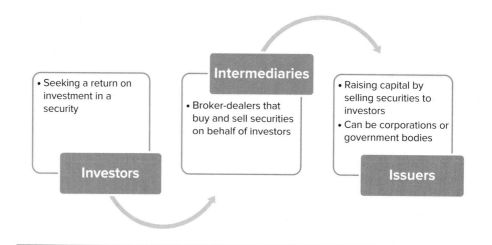

- Seeking a return on investment in a security

Investors

Intermediaries

- Broker-dealers that buy and sell securities on behalf of investors

- Raising capital by selling securities to investors
- Can be corporations or government bodies

Issuers

LO 32-3

Apply the legal test
for what constitutes
a security.

DEFINING A SECURITY

Given the regulatory requirements that are triggered by a securities transaction, business owners and managers need a working knowledge of the instruments and transactions that federal and state laws define as securities and securities offerings. The regulations include registration and disclosure requirements, specific requirements to exempt a securities offering from the federal securities scheme, liability for misrepresentation or omissions in the offering materials, anti-fraud protections for buyers of securities, and criminal sanctions under certain circumstances for those engaged in fraud while selling or trading securities.

Federal Securities Law

Stocks and bonds are perhaps the best-known types of securities that are regulated by federal and state law. In addition, partnership interests, stock options, warrants, agreements to invest, participation in a pool of assets, use of crowdfunding resources, certain types of promissory notes, and many other arrangements that might commonly be considered investments are also regulated by securities laws.

Federal securities statutes define securities very broadly using a two-prong approach. First, the law recognizes specific forms of securities, such as notes, stocks, treasury stocks, transferable shares, bonds, and debentures. Second, securities statutes use a catchall definition of other investment transactions in a more generic sense, including participation in profit-sharing agreements; collateral trust certificates; preorganization certificates or subscriptions; investment contracts; and a fractional, undivided interest in gas, oil, or other mineral rights. In some cases even a business plan, depending on the language and circumstances, may constitute a securities offering. Note that certain types of debt instruments, such as a promissory note secured by a home mortgage or by accounts receivable or other business assets, are *not* securities.

Based on these definitions, the general standard for determining whether an arrangement or offering qualifies as a security is quite broad: A security is any *investment* that involves a person giving something with an *expectation of profit* through the efforts of a *third party*.

The U.S. Supreme Court articulated a four-part test that helped to give lower courts a framework for defining a security and securities offering in the landmark case of *SEC v. W. J. Howey Co.*[1] In *Howey*, the defendant offered investment opportunities in its citrus operations through a contractual arrangement that combined a real estate purchase with an option to share in the profits from citrus grown on that parcel of land. The SEC alleged that these opportunities constituted a securities offering. The Court agreed:

> [A]n investment contract for the purposes of the Securities Act means a contract, transaction or scheme whereby a person invests his money in a common enterprise and is led to expect profits solely from the efforts of the promoter of a third party, it being immaterial whether the shares in the enterprise are evidenced by formal certificates or by nominal interests in the physical assets employed in that enterprise.

The Court's opinion is the basis for what is now called the *Howey* test. Although the *Howey* test remains largely intact, federal courts have added further clarification that has expanded the definition of what constitutes a securities offering.

Modern Application of the *Howey* Test

The Supreme Court clarified the *Howey* test in the more recent case of *United Housing Foundation v. Forman*.[2] The *United Housing* case gave courts further guidance and expanded the definition of what constitutes a securities offering. Courts now apply a more sweeping standard including the investment itself, commonality, profit expectations, and the efforts of others.

- *Investment.* The investment may be cash or a noncash instrument where the investing party receives only the speculative promise of a return and not any tangible commodity or assets.
- *Commonality.* Courts have ruled that an investment scheme satisfies this requirement either through *horizontal commonality* (multiple investors have a common expectation of profit in the investment) or via *vertical commonality* (a single investor has a common expectation of profit with the *promoter* of the investment).
- *Profit expectations.* The expectation of a return on investment (profitability) must be the primary reason for the investment.
- *Efforts of others.* The efforts of the promoter(s) or agents of the promoter(s) must be the primary sources of revenue that resulted in profits. Note that *Howey* actually required that the investor not be involved in any way with generating the profits. However, the modern trend is for courts to allow some *limited passive involvement* by the investor so long as the promoter/agent has been the primary source of the efforts.

---

[1]328 U.S. 293 (1946).

[2]421 U.S. 837 (1975).

Family Resemblance Test

In 1990, the U.S. Supreme Court took up the specific issue of whether a promissory note (a legal document in which the borrower promises to pay back the lender the principal amount plus a stated rate of interest on a certain date) should be classified as a security. In *Reves v. Ernst & Young*,[3] the Court adopted the *family resemblance test* in order to determine whether a promissory note fell under the jurisdiction of securities laws. The Court made clear that there is a presumption that promissory notes *are* securities. However, this presumption may be challenged if the issuer shows that the promissory note has a strong resemblance to a category of instrument that is not classified as a security (e.g., a note that is secured by a mortgage on a home). Courts now compare any investment instrument with the securities categories recognized by law in order to determine whether the offering resembles an investment or a non-investment. In Case 32.1, a federal appeals court applies the family resemblance test.

CASE 32.1 SEC v. Thompson et al. 732 F.3d 1151 (10th Cir. 2013)

FACT SUMMARY Thompson was among a group of principals who founded Novus as a vehicle for his business ventures in China and elsewhere. By 2005, Novus's connections in China had yielded some lucrative business opportunities. The most promising prospect involved selling a quantity of biodiesel reactors to a Chinese company at a substantial profit. However, the group needed to raise $12 million to facilitate that transaction. In fact, each prospect in China required significant capital.

In order to capitalize Novus to the point where it could take advantage of the opportunities in China, its principals issued a series of instruments that they labeled as "unsecured promissory notes" (Notes). The Notes promised that Novus would repay the principal amount after a term of six months, plus monthly interest of between three and five percent. However, the Note also contained a provision that gave Novus the option to extend the term of the Note for a period of six months as long as the monthly interest payments on the unpaid principal were being paid to the investor (Note holder). Finally, the Note stated on its face that it was not a security, and it had features such as acceleration conditions, a waiver-of-presentment clause, a nonassignment clause, and an attorney-fee-collection clause.

After Novus had raised in excess of $1.3 million from 60 different investors, the Securities and Exchange Commission (SEC) launched an investigation that resulted in the SEC filing a complaint against Novus for selling unregistered securities and obtaining a temporary restraining order against

Novus. The trial court granted the SEC's motion for summary judgment against Novus and its principals. Novus appealed on the basis that the trial court erred in classifying the Notes as securities because they were private loan transactions not under the ambit of securities laws.

SYNOPSIS OF DECISION AND OPINION The Court of Appeals for the 10th Circuit ruled in favor of the SEC. The court applied the family resemblance test to the Notes and concluded they were securities because (1) the Note holders/investors were clearly motivated by profit; (2) Novus intended to make, and did make, its Notes available to any member of the public who could afford them; (3) Novus principals talked about the Notes as though they were an investment, characterizing them as less risky than putting money in the bank; and (4) no other regulatory scheme significantly reduced the risk of the instrument.

WORDS OF THE COURT: Family Resemblance Test "We conclude that Novus's [Notes] are securities under the family-resemblance test. . . . Our analysis of the test's four factors confirms that the [Notes] bear little resemblance to the categories of non-securities instruments on the [Court's] judicially crafted list. In sum, even construing all of the facts and reasonable inferences to be drawn therefrom in [Novus's] favor, we hold that [they] cannot rebut the presumption that the Novus Instruments were securities."

(continued)

---

[3]494 U.S. 56 (1990).

Case Questions

1. Should the court have given more weight to the fact that the Notes were plainly marked with a disclaimer?

2. The SEC intervened in this transaction even though no investors had lost money. Did the SEC overstep its bounds?

3. *Focus on Critical Thinking:* The SEC claimed that the Notes could be considered investment contracts under *Howey,* but the court did not reach that issue. Do you agree with the SEC's position that the Notes were investment contracts similar to that in *Howey?* Why or why not?

Defining a Seller of Securities

While in some cases the offering of an investment opportunity clearly falls within the definition of a security, some are more difficult to discern. For example, suppose an entrepreneur e-mails a document to a group of friends and family members that provides an overview of an idea for a new venture but does not specifically solicit money for the venture. Suppose that one friend writes a check and sends it to the entrepreneur with a note indicating that the funds are for a 20 percent interest in the new venture. If the entrepreneur then deposits the check with the intention of providing his friend with a 20 percent split of any profits, is the document part of a securities offering? In Case 32.2, a trial court analyzes a real estate development opportunity in the context of defining a security and who qualifies as a seller of securities.

CASE 32.2 San Francisco Residence Club, Inc. v. Amado, 773 F. Supp. 2d 822 (N.D. Cal. 2011)

FACT SUMMARY   Broda, the founder and CEO of Aspire Real Estate and Aspire Investments, was an investment advisor for Donahue and his family for a number of years. Donahue formed San Francisco Residence Club (SFRC) as a California corporation for purposes of managing real estate investments, which were typically arranged by Broda. In 2007, Broda contacted Donahue about a new real estate investment opportunity in White Sands Estates (White Sands). The opportunity involved the development of an unimproved 42-acre parcel of real estate in Kailua-Kona, Hawaii, by Amado, a real estate developer. According to Broda, he simply acted as a referral for White Sands but had no other involvement. However, Donahue contended that Broda advised him to invest in White Sands and represented that: (1) the project would be profitable during the development stage and would provide a return on investment of 12 percent

annually; (2) at the end of two years, Donahue would yield a full return on the investment as well as a constant percentage share in any profits generated by the sale of completed residential units; and (3) Amado had the expertise and skill to make the venture profitable.

Broda then sent Donahue two documents titled "Executive Summary" and "Operating Agreement." The documents described the project and represented that the most recent appraisal projected a value of approximately $19 million and that White Sands had the property under contract for $9,950,000. Subsequently, the parties discussed the opportunity in a conference call with Broda and Amado. Shortly thereafter, Donahue used SFRC to purchase an interest in White Sands for $2 million. White Sands purchased the acreage with the SFRC investment and through funds obtained from a series of loans from other entities. Amado paid

(continued)

Broda a fee for arranging the SFRC-White Sands transaction. For a variety of reasons, White Sands quickly became insolvent. The entity defaulted on the loan, failed to pay any property taxes or vendors, and sunk to $11 million in debt. The lenders foreclosed on the property and any investment in White Sands became worthless.

SFRC brought suit against Broda, Amado, and others alleging, among other theories, that Broda's solicitation of Donahue constituted an unregistered and nonexempt offering under the Securities Act of 1933. Broda filed a motion for summary judgment on the basis that his conversations and the documents presented to Donahue were merely advice, the fee he collected from Amado was a thank-you gift and not a commission, and Broda did not fall into the statutory definition of seller because he acted only as a referral agent.

SYNOPSIS OF DECISION AND OPINION The U.S. District Court ruled in favor of SFRC and denied summary judgment for Broda and the other defendants. The court held that a reasonable fact-finder could conclude that the SFRC transaction could be classified as an "investment contract" under the *Howey* standard. The court reasoned that the *Howey* factors were a fact-based inquiry and therefore summary judgment should not be granted. The court also found that Broda and Amado could also fit the definition of statutory sellers because SFRC had credibly alleged that Broda solicited many other investors for the White Sands project and that the definition of seller in the law was very broad.

WORDS OF THE COURT: Solicitation by Promoter "As an initial matter, the money Broda received (and the money he stood to gain) indicates that his advice could have been motivated by his own potential profit. Next, while [SFRC] views the Executive Summary Broda transmitted as promoting something more than an unformed investment scheme, they argue that even if it were nothing grander, the result would be no different. [The court agrees.] This is because . . . Broda's involvement in the [White Sands] project did not end with the referral in August. They insist he was deeply involved in the negotiations in the fall of 2007 leading up to [SFRC]'s investment. . . . Beyond this, [SFRC alleges that] Broda solicited every other [White Sands] investor, and made an unknown number of offers. . . . Determining which version is more credible, however, is a task reserved for the finder of fact."

Case Questions

1. Compare the SFRC-Broda transaction to the standards used in the modern *Howey* test. Was this an investment contract? Why or why not?

2. How does the fact that Broda received a fee from Amado impact your analysis under the *Howey* test? Could it have been a thank-you gift from Amado as Broda contends?

3. *Focus on Critical Thinking:* In hindsight, is this a case of fraud? The investors had experience in real estate investing and access to all of White Sands's financial information. If they had made money on White Sands, the investors never would have brought this lawsuit. Does that strike you as fair? Would the required disclosures under securities law have made any difference in the investors' decision?

TAKEAWAY CONCEPTS Modern *Howey* Test

Investment	Commonality	Promoter
Cash or noncash instrument.	Multiple investors in single transaction (horizontal).	Uses investor money to generate profits primarily by promoter's efforts.
Investor's primary motive is expectation of profit.	Single investor in single transaction (vertical).	Modern rule: Limited passive action by the investor is acceptable.

✅ **QUICK QUIZ** Definition of a Security

Do these opportunities constitute a securities offering under the *Howey* test?

1. Smith offered to sell earthworms to third-party investors. The investors entered into a contract whereby, after the purchase, Smith would raise the worms in a way that would promote massive reproduction, and he guaranteed to repurchase the worms from the investor at a certain rate based on the actual sale price to third-party farmers. Thus, an investor could purchase a certain dollar amount of worms, have Smith raise the worms and locate a farmer buyer, then have Smith repurchase the worms from the investor at a higher price than the investor's original price based on the sale price to the farmer.

2. Utley offered to sell one-half acre beachfront lots to the public at $50,000 per lot. After the completion of a sale, Utley offered to perform services as a general contractor for purposes of building a shore house on the lot. Twenty percent of the owners hired Utley to build the houses, but the other 80 percent either hired their own contractors or left the land undeveloped. Once the houses were built, Utley offered to find a buyer for a 10 percent commission on a complete sale.

3. Alliance was a leasing company that devised an opportunity for third-party investors in which the investors paid money to Alliance for the purchase of commercial or kitchen equipment. Alliance then acted as an agent to arrange an equipment lease with the business/lessee that needed the equipment. Alliance entered into a joint venture agreement with the investors to sell them the equipment and to broker a lease between the investor and a lessee. The lease agreement provided for lease payments to be paid by the lessees directly to the investor on a monthly basis over a two-year period, at the end of which a balloon payment (the entire principal) would be due. Alliance represented that the investors would earn a 14 percent rate of return on their investment and that risk was low.

Answers to this Quick Quiz are provided at the end of the chapter.

Stock Market Games

Potential investors who are interested in learning more about the market or wish to try a particular trading strategy without risking their money have several Internet-based stock market simulators at their disposal. These simulators, often referred to as *stock market games, virtual stock exchanges,* or *investment games,* are programs/applications that reproduce some features of a live stock market so that a player can simulate a particular strategy or method and compare the performance of several different models. Participation in stock market games has increased markedly since major financial firms began to develop their own versions for their clients and potential clients.

The transactions in a stock market game are similar to the fantasy sports model in that the buying and selling are imaginary. However, government regulators have kept a close eye on websites that blur the line between simulation and reality by offering some type of reward or prize for successful trading. For example, in *SEC v. SG Ltd.,*[4] the government alleged that a company that operated a stock market gaming website called StockGeneration (SG) was violating securities laws. SG offered users the opportunity to purchase shares in fantasy companies listed on the website's virtual stock exchange. Although the website was clearly marked as a game, the court ruled against the company because SG had gone beyond personal entertainment in representing that investors could expect a 10 percent profit monthly.

---

[4]265 F.3d 42 (1st Cir. 2001).

Crowdfunding

The media attention generated by crowdfunding investments has made it a permanent part of the fundraising lexicon. One industry analyst quoted in *Forbes* magazine estimated that more than 1 million campaigns globally raised more than $5 billion in one year. Fundamentally, crowdfunding is asking a large number of people to invest or donate a defined amount of money for a specific cause. From an entrepreneurial standpoint, crowdfunding is a way to raise money by asking individuals who are interested in investing to fund a certain business venture. Because the investments can be very small, crowdfunding has the potential to tap into a larger investor community and generate significant sums of money for business ventures in relatively short order.

This type of fundraising is done via the Internet through crowdfunding firms such as Kickstarter or Peerbackers. Crowdfunding may be used to raise money either through debt or equity, and the crowdfunding firm typically charges a percentage fee for its services. Crowdfunding sites range from those that work only for charitable donations to those that focus on funding entrepreneurs and innovation. Although the SEC and state agencies have struggled with applying an appropriate amount of regulation, they have recently settled on rules to govern crowdfunding. These rules are discussed in more detail in Chapter 33. Figure 32.1 lists the top 10 crowdfunding companies based on Internet traffic.

Blue-Sky Laws: State Securities Law

State securities laws are commonly known as **blue-sky laws**, named after the original state statutory protection of investors from unsavory issuers selling nothing more than blue sky. Blue-sky laws are frequently constructed to match federal securities statutes. In theory, these state statutes are intended to cover purely intrastate securities offerings (when the issuers and all potential investors are within one state's borders), but as a practical matter state securities regulators are an additional safeguard for investors when the federal government declines to exercise its jurisdiction over a particular securities offering. Regulation of securities issuance and trading by states are discussed in detail later in this chapter.

| FIGURE 32.1 | Top 10 Crowdfunding Sites Based on Traffic |

Name	Campaigns	Fee
1. Kickstarter	Creative projects such as design, film, publishing, music, gaming, and technology.	3–5%
2. Indiegogo	Originally focused on film; now accepts all types of campaigns.	9%
3. YouCaring	Personal and charitable.	5%
4. Causes	Nonprofits and charities.	4.75%
5. GiveForward	Personal fundraising only.	5%
6. RocketHub	Projects related to science, education, business, and social good projects. Also partnered with A&E cable network.	5%
7. Peerbackers	Entrepreneurs and innovators.	5%
8. SoMoLend	Peer-to-peer platform to facilitate business or personal loans.	Variable
9. Crowdrise	Personal and creative fundraising.	5–6%
10. Fundly	Personal or charitable fundraising.	4.9%

Source: Assembled by the authors based on Crowdfunding.com and Entreprenuer.com.

CATEGORIES OF SECURITIES

Securities fall into one of two general categories: equity or debt. Each category includes an inventory of *instruments* that are tangible representations of the security and that define the rights of the owner of the security. Some securities have restrictions on the ownership rights (such as the right to sell the security to another party).

LO 32-4

Distinguish between classifications of equity and debt instruments and give an example of each.

Equity Instruments

Equity instruments represent ownership interests whereby financial return on the investment is based primarily on the performance of the venture that issued the securities. However, equity holders have no specific right or guarantee on the investment. Therefore, investors with equity interests may profit considerably from a company that is consistently profitable. However, if the company fails, the equity interest becomes worthless and the investor is without any legal recourse (assuming that no fraud or malfeasance occurred that led to the company's demise) to recover her original investment. Two prevalent forms of equity instruments issued by corporations are *common stock* and *preferred stock.*

Common Stock   The most frequently used form of equity instrument is **common stock** (also called *common shares*), which entitles the equity owner to payments based on the current profitability of the company. The payments are known as *dividends,* and the decision to pay and how much to pay in dividends to equity owners rests with the company's board of directors. Common stock owners also have the right to payment if the corporation is sold for a profit or if the company is dissolved (assuming any value is left in the company). In certain companies, common stock may be *voting* or *nonvoting.* A nonvoting common stockholder is entitled to all benefits of ownership except the right to vote for directors or in major corporate decisions. In any case, most common stockholders are typically entitled to full voting rights. Recall that we discussed the rights and duties of shareholders, directors, and officers in detail in Chapter 30, "Corporations: Formation and Organization."

While common stockholders share in a company's profits, they also bear the greatest risk of loss because they are typically *subordinate* to all creditors and preferred stockholders if the corporation files for bankruptcy protection or simply dissolves with limited assets. In the context of stock ownership rights, a subordinate position is a lower or secondary position in terms of being entitled to profits or assets. For example, common stockholders are subordinate to preferred stockholders.

Preferred Stock   An alternative form of equity that has less risk than common stock because it has certain quasi-debt features is **preferred stock**. Perhaps the biggest advantage of preferred stock is that preferred stockholders have preference rights over common stockholders in receiving dividends from the corporation. In the event that the corporation fails or files for bankruptcy, preferred stockholders are ahead of common stockholders when trying to recover their losses from the liquidation proceeds. Preferred stock may be voting or nonvoting. When a business must liquidate assets because a venture fails and either dissolves or files for bankruptcy protection, payments to creditors and shareholders are made according to priority. Those that qualify as senior in priority get paid first.

Debt Instruments

Companies also raise capital by issuing debt instruments (e.g., promissory notes) to holders who expect a fixed rate of return through payback of principal and interest. Bank loans and family loans fall into this category. This may be attractive for some investors because debt holders typically are entitled to payments that are senior in priority to investors holding stock. *Senior in priority* means that those investors are paid first if the business must liquidate its assets. Of course, the downside of a debt investment is that the investor does not share in the success of a venture. The rate of return for a debt instrument is the same for business ventures that are highly profitable and those that are not profitable.

Bonds and Debentures   Some corporations issue debt to public investment markets in the form of bonds (secured by a specific asset) or debentures (secured by a corporation's general credit). In the past decade, even smaller companies have taken advantage of low rates on bond debt through issuance of micro bonds that are typically between $500,000 and $1 million.

Larger corporations prefer bonds as a method of splitting up their long-term debt, and they blend the use of bonds with conventional borrower-lender (bank) loans for short-term debt. Because bonds are debt instruments, investors expect fixed payments at regular intervals until the bond *matures,* at which time the principal amount of the bond, known as its *face amount,* is paid to the investor.

Peer-to-Peer Lending

One impact of the global recession that began in 2008 was the extreme tightening of available capital and credit to businesses, especially to entrepreneurs who did not have the traditional track record of success that is important to lenders. *FinTech,* a term coined by the financial media to describe a new financial sector model, has become an increasingly popular alternative to traditional lending. FinTech firms leverage innovative technology in order to lower overhead costs and provide higher levels of service to users.

One of the most successful FinTech models centers on peer-to-peer lending (abbreviated as P2PL) in which a firm offers a web-based platform to match borrowers with investors. Most of these loans are fundamentally unsecured personal loans from investors to one or more principals of a business venture. While interest rates are set based on the borrower's creditworthiness, these rates and fees are often lower than those offered by traditional lenders. Prosper and Lending Club, early pioneers in peer-to-peer lending, have collectively serviced over 180,000 borrowers with over $2 billion in loans. Loans by peer-to-peer lenders are considered by regulatory authorities to be securities offerings and therefore must comply with all securities laws and regulations. Market conditions have also been a significant challenge to the FinTech industry. Figure 32.2 shows one example of a peer-to-peer lender.

| FIGURE 32.2 | A Peer-to-Peer Lender |

©Louisa Svensson/Alamy

TAKEAWAY CONCEPTS Categories of Securities

- Securities fall into one of two categories: equity (selling ownership) or debt (fixed rate of return for the investor).
- Equity is commonly offered as *common stock* or *preferred stock*.
- Debt may be offered in various forms such as promissory notes or bonds.
- Peer-to-peer lending is treated by the SEC as a security.

SECURITIES REGULATION

The federal securities laws are rooted in the stock market crash of 1929 and represent one of the major reforms offered in the New Deal era. The **Securities Act of 1933** regulates the issuance of securities to public investors by requiring that companies file certain information intended to inform investors who are considering entering into a securities transaction. The **Securities Exchange Act of 1934** created the SEC and regulates the trading of previously issued securities primarily by setting out ground rules for the buying and selling of securities. Fundamentally, all securities regulation has the same rationale: protection of investors and assuring public confidence in the integrity of the securities market. Note that securities laws are not meant to provide insurance for losses or to punish a venture's principals simply because the business does not earn a profit. The underlying premise of all securities regulation is **disclosure**. Much of the regulation concerning fraud or securities sales boils down to whether the seller or issuer has made truthful and sufficiently full disclosures about the security itself. Securities law is primarily a matter of federal statutes and regulations, but all states have similar disclosure and fraud laws within state borders.

The issuance and trading of securities are also regulated through laws that have been passed in response to various historical events in the financial markets that have undermined public confidence in its institutions, such as the corporate and accounting scandals in 2001[5] and the global recession of 2008.[6] This includes the Sarbanes-Oxley Act of 2002,[7] the Dodd-Frank Wall Street Reform and Consumer Protection Act of 2010,[8] and the Jumpstart Our Business Startups (JOBS) Act of 2012. Regulation of securities issuance, transactions, trading, and the financial markets in general are covered in detail in Chapters 33 through 35.

LO 32-5

Recognize the fundamental reason behind securities regulation and demonstrate a working knowledge of federal securities law.

TAKEAWAY CONCEPTS Securities Regulation

- The fundamental underpinning of all securities regulation is disclosure to inform investors and prevent fraud.
- The issuance of securities is regulated by the Securities Act of 1933.
- Trading of previously issued securities is regulated by the Securities Exchange Act of 1934.

---

[5]The most notorious of these scandals occurred between 2001 and 2003 at publicly held companies that included Enron, WorldCom, Tyco International, Adelphia, Health South, Nortel, Vivendi Universal, Global Crossing, and Peregrine Systems.

[6]The U.S. Bureau of Economic Research concluded that the recession began in December 2007 as a result of the global financial crisis and the subprime mortgage crisis and lasted until June 2009.

[7]15 U.S.C. § 7201 et seq.

[8]12 U.S.C. § 5300.

LO 32-6

Describe the role
of the Securities
and Exchange
Commission (SEC) in
securities law.

THE SECURITIES AND EXCHANGE COMMISSION

As part of the Exchange Act, Congress created the **Securities and Exchange Commission (SEC)** to be the federal administrative agency charged with rulemaking, enforcement, and adjudication of federal securities laws. Unlike many administrative agencies, the SEC is an *independent agency* that does not have a seat in the president's cabinet and is not subject to direct control by the president. Five commissioners, appointed by the president and subject to advice and consent approval by the Senate, compose the SEC. Commissioners may be removed for misconduct, but no commissioner has been removed since the SEC was formed by Congress in 1934. In addition to being a source of expert information on securities laws, the SEC has wide-ranging executive, legislative, and judicial powers.

The SEC's executive powers include the power to investigate potential violations of securities laws and regulations. They also have a variety of administrative enforcement mechanisms such as issuing a cease and desist order.[9] In egregious cases, the SEC initiates criminal charges against an individual and/or company that has allegedly violated securities law. The SEC's legislative authority is granted by Congress and allows the SEC to draft and publish securities regulations and interpretations of statutes, rules, and court decisions. Pursuant to its legislative powers, the SEC also issues interpretative letters and no-action letters to advise the securities investment and trading community on how the SEC will treat a proposed transaction. These letters are not binding on the SEC, but they do carry significant weight with courts and are crucial to the day-to-day operations of publicly held companies. The SEC's judicial powers are primarily rooted in its role as a hearing tribunal for enforcing certain securities violations, including alleged indiscretions of brokers in their business dealings. The SEC has the power to suspend or revoke the professional licenses of brokers and others regulated by securities laws.

Though the SEC is the primary regulatory authority of the securities markets, it works closely with many other institutions, including Congress, other federal agencies, self-regulatory organizations (such as stock exchanges), state securities regulators, and various private sector organizations. The chair of the SEC is one of four members[10] of the President's Working Group on Financial Markets.

The SEC is composed of several divisions and departments. The highest-profile divisions are Enforcement and Corporation Finance because they are primarily responsible for investigation and enforcement action against violators. Much of the SEC's day-to-day work is done through 11 regional offices that are spread throughout the United States.

Figure 32.3 shows the SEC's organizational structure.

EDGAR

An important function of the SEC is to maintain a national clearinghouse for public corporation disclosures and filings required by federal securities laws. This clearinghouse is made available to the public through the SEC's computer database known as *EDGAR*. In addition to EDGAR, the SEC's website also serves as a source of information to educate investors on risks and SEC procedures. EDGAR provides the most recent filings and disclosures for all publicly held companies.

---

[9]An administrative order requiring a certain party to halt unlawful activity.

[10]The other members are the chair of the Federal Reserve, the chair of the Commodity Futures Trading Commission, and the Secretary of the Treasury.

FIGURE 32.3 Structure of the Securities and Exchange Commission

SECURITIES AND EXCHANGE COMMISSION

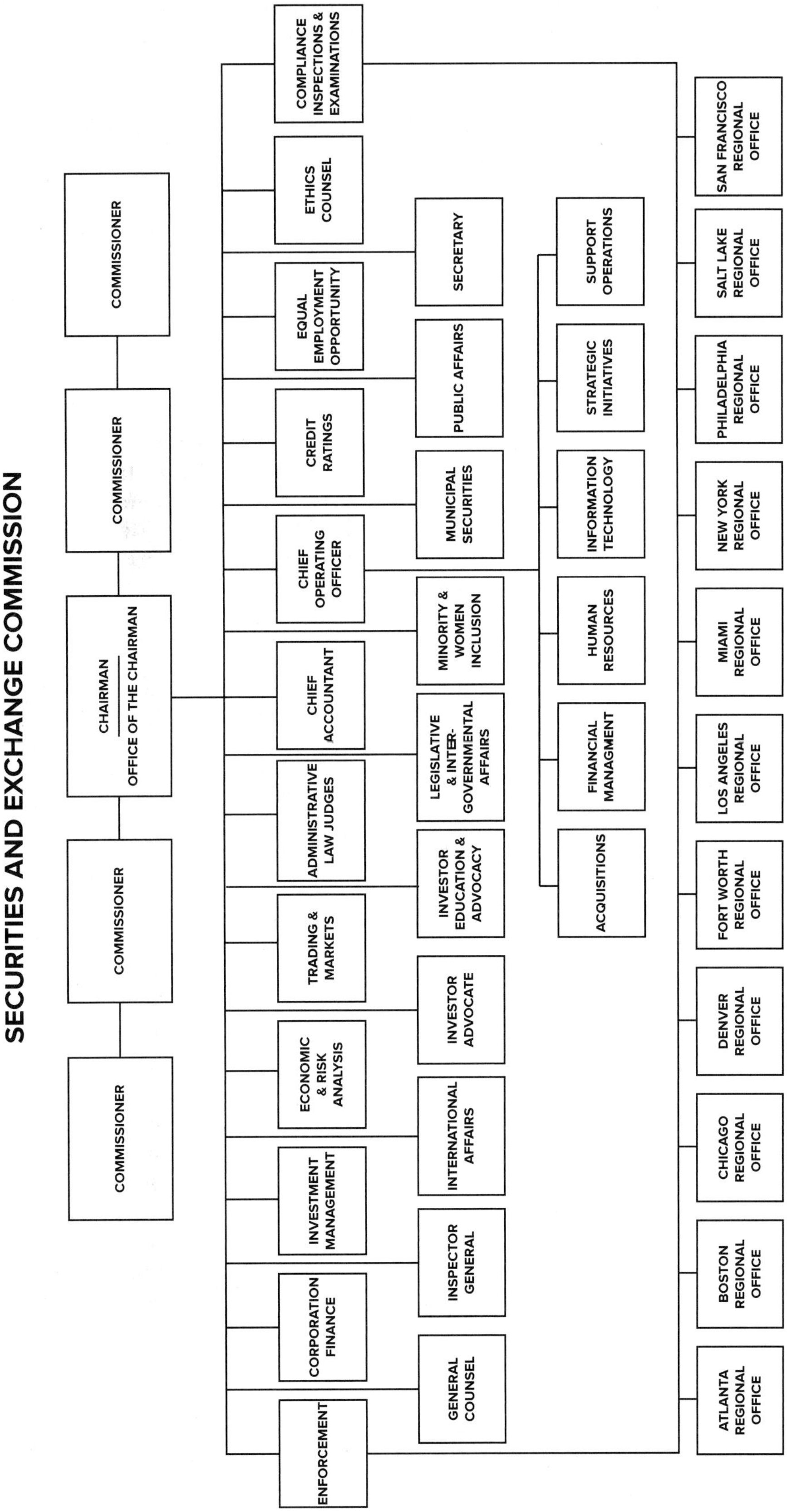

Source: www.sec.gov/about/secorg.pdf.

What is Facebook worth these days? Check on EDGAR:

1. Go to sec.gov/edgar/quickedgar.htm and take the Quick EDGAR Tutorial.
2. Look up "Facebook" in the main search engine.
3. Click on the most recent **10-Q filing** that is marked **"Interactive Data"** and click on the link to see Facebook's quarterly balance sheets and financial statements.

TAKEAWAY CONCEPTS The SEC

- The Securities and Exchange Commission (SEC) is the federal administrative agency charged with rulemaking, enforcement, and adjudication of federal securities laws.
- The SEC is an independent agency that does not have a seat in the president's cabinet and is not subject to direct control by the president.

LO 32-7

Explain the impact of state securities regulations relative to issuers, compliance, and enforcement.

STATE REGULATION OF SECURITIES

Recall from earlier in this chapter that blue-sky laws (state securities statutes) and state regulatory agencies play an important part in securities law. Both the Securities Act of 1933 and the Securities Exchange Act of 1934 work in tandem with similarly structured state securities law. However, in 1996 Congress limited the types of transactions that may be regulated by the states by passing the National Securities Markets Improvement Act. The law generally allows states to regulate securities only when the security is intrastate. States are restricted from regulating any security listed on a stock exchange, mutual funds, or certain offerings that are exempt under federal securities law.

Although a majority of states have adopted all or substantially all of the Uniform Securities Act, some differences between state regulatory requirements still exist. Typical provisions include prohibition against fraud in the sale of securities, registration requirements for brokers and dealers, exemptions, civil liability for issuers that fail to comply, and state court remedies for defrauded investors.

Risk Capital Test

Although the SEC and the majority of states recognize the *Howey* test, some state courts, including California, Georgia, and Kansas, have adopted an even broader definition of security to analyze whether an opportunity falls under the purview of their state's blue-sky laws. The risk capital test addresses whether: (1) an investor's funds are subject to the risk of the business venture as a whole and (2) the investor has no control over the risks of the venture. The risk capital test is a much easier standard to meet than the *Howey* test because it requires neither commonality nor that the profit be derived from the efforts of others. For example, in *Bender v. Wind River Mining Project*,[11] a California appellate court held that "gold delivery certificates" were securities under the risk capital test. The court ruled that agreements for an opportunity to invest in Wind River's gold production and delivery operations did not involve any participation by the investors and were subject to inherent risks of the business.

---

[11]219 Cal. App. 3d 1390 (1980).

©valterZ/Shutterstock

Considering Legal Issues in Financing

PROBLEM: Businesses have a variety of options to finance their operations and strategies. While many compare these options from a financial perspective, little weight is given to the legal impact of each of these options.

STRATEGIC SOLUTION: Prepare a table of financing alternatives that includes each one's legal effect.

Option	Description	Legal Impact
Common stock	Form of equity issued in exchange for investment in a business venture.	Common stockholders share in the profits but also bear the greatest risk of loss because they are typically *subordinate* to all creditors and preferred stockholders if the corporation files for bankruptcy protection or simply dissolves with limited assets.
Preferred stock	Form of equity issued in exchange for investment in a business venture.	In the event that the corporation fails or files for bankruptcy, preferred stockholders are ahead of common stockholders when trying to recover their losses from the liquidation proceeds.
Bonds/debentures	Form of debt issued by a business venture that is either collateralized with specific assets (bond) or with general credit of the company (debentures).	Attractive for some investors because debt holders typically are entitled to payments that are *senior in priority* to investors holding stock in the event of bankruptcy.
Promissory note	Borrowing business promises to pay back the lender the principal amount plus a stated rate of interest on a certain date.	May be considered a security under the family resemblance test and therefore must be registered before offering.
Crowdfunding	Internet-based fundraising through firms such as Kickstarter or Peerbackers through either debt or equity with the crowdfunding firm typically charging a percentage fee for its services.	The small investments used in crowdfunding campaigns are typically not large enough to make recovering the investment a viable option. Thus, the potential for losses due to fraud or negligence increase substantially.

QUESTIONS

1. If you were considering investing in a start-up venture and wanted to limit your personal risk, what option(s) would fit best?

2. If you were the owner of a business that had substantial assets, which options would you consider for financing the research and development of a new product line? Why?

KEY TERMS

Equity p. 560   Ownership interest in a corporation whereby financial return on the investment is based primarily on the performance of the venture.

Debt p. 560   A common tool for raising capital that includes promissory notes, bonds, and debentures that offer investors a fixed rate of return, regardless of the profitability of the corporation, with repayment expected after a certain period of years.

Securities law p. 560   The body of federal and state laws governing the issuance and trading of equity and debt instruments to public investors.

Investors p. 562   Individuals or entities seeking a return from their investment based on the perceived value of the security.

Issuers p. 562   Institutions and entities that sell issued securities to investors.

Intermediaries p. 562   Financial institutions that provide services for investors and issuers related to securities transactions.

Blue-sky laws p. 568   State securities laws designed to protect investors from unsavory issuers selling nothing more than blue sky.

Common stock (common shares) p. 569   A form of equity instrument that entitles the equity owner to payments based on the current profitability of the company.

Preferred stock p. 569   A form of equity instrument that has less risk than common stock because it has certain quasi-debt features. Preferred stockholders have preference rights over common stockholders in receiving dividends from the corporation.

Securities Act of 1933 p. 571   Federal legislation that covers the processes of issuing and reissuing securities to the public; requires registration and certain disclosures and authorizes the Securities and Exchange Commission to oversee the transactions.

Securities Exchange Act of 1934 p. 571   Federal legislation that regulates the sale of securities between investors after an investor has purchased them from a business entity issuer.

Disclosure p. 571   The underlying premise of all securities regulation in which companies are to release all information, positive or negative, that might bear on an investment decision.

Securities and Exchange Commission (SEC) p. 572 The independent federal administrative agency charged with rulemaking, enforcement, and adjudication of federal securities laws.

CASE SUMMARY 32.1 Mark v. FSC Securities Corporation, 870 F.2d 331 (6th Cir. 1989)

Securities

FSC was a securities brokerage firm that sold limited partnership interests to Mark and 27 other investors. All investors executed a *subscription agreement* in which they revealed their income and represented that they had had the opportunity to review relevant information, including risk factors, and were sufficiently knowledgeable and savvy to understand the implications of the investment. However, FSC managers never actually reviewed the completed subscription agreements, and

all who applied to be investors were admitted. When the interests dropped in value, Mark sued to rescind the contract on the basis that the limited partnerships were securities and were not registered. FSC defended that the offering was not a security.

CASE QUESTIONS

1. Should Mark prevail?
2. Is it relevant that FSC never reviewed the subscription agreements?

CASE SUMMARY 32.2 SEC v. ETS Payphones, Inc., 408 F.3d 727 (11th Cir. 2005)

Definition of a Security

Edwards was the primary principal in ETS Payphones and sold investment contracts whereby an investor would purchase a pay telephone from an ETS affiliate, then would lease the phone back to ETS for management services in exchange for a fixed monthly fee. Investors

always had the option of selling the phone back to ETS at a prearranged price (the buyback guarantee) or canceling the ETS lease entirely and taking possession of the telephone. As the financial position of ETS deteriorated, Edwards sought even more investors to cover losses with earlier investors. Edwards did not register these investment contracts with the SEC. When ETS filed a voluntary petition for bankruptcy, it ceased making payments to investors and would not honor its buyback guarantee. The SEC took enforcement action alleging a violation of the Securities Act of 1933, and Edwards defended on the basis that the investment contracts could not be considered securities because the opportunity did not meet the requirements of the *Howey* test.

CASE QUESTIONS

1. Analyze the ETS investment contracts in terms of the *Howey* test. What factors favor Edwards's position?
2. Is the fact that Edwards continued to seek investors to cover losses enough to satisfy the "commonality" requirement that the investors' fortunes be tied together in some way?

CASE SUMMARY 32.3 Eberhardt v. Waters, 901 F.2d 1578 (11th Cir. 1990)

Howey Test

Eberhardt invested in an unregistered opportunity with International Cattle Embryo (ICE), which was owned by Waters and involved the production and sale of cattle embryos. In exchange for an investment, ICE provided a variety of services to investors, including storing the embryos in liquid nitrogen freezers, transfer of embryos, care of any resulting calves, registering the calves, and maintaining appropriate records. Investors had the opportunity to choose to have either ICE or another facility perform the maintenance services. When ICE began to encounter financial difficulty, Eberhardt requested that his embryos be transferred to another facility, but the transfer never took place because the records needed to consummate the transfer were not kept as ICE promised. Eberhardt sued ICE under the Securities Act of 1933 claiming that the opportunity was an unregistered security. ICE argued that the opportunities were not securities because they lacked commonality and that the success of the investment was not dependent on ICE but rather on how well the investor exercised the option of transferring the embryo to another facility.

CASE QUESTIONS

1. Who prevails and why?
2. If the court finds in favor of Eberhardt, what remedies are appropriate?

CASE SUMMARY 32.4 Foltz v. U.S. News and World Report, Inc., 627 F. Supp. 1143 (D.D.C. 1986)

Profit-Sharing Plans as Securities

U.S. News and World Report, Inc. offered a profit-sharing plan to its employees that, among other features, distributed stock to its employees based on years of service with the goal of making the company entirely employee-owned. Although the employee stock had equal voting rights, the stock was restricted and employees could not sell, pledge, or transfer their stock during their employment. Upon termination of employment or retirement, the stock had to be sold back to the company using a predetermined procedure that valued the stock annually through an outside appraiser. In 1984, U.S. News was purchased for $176 million, and Foltz brought a class action suit for employees who had sold their stock back to U.S. News alleging their stock had been grossly undervalued. One of their claims centered on whether the employees' interest in the profit-sharing claim constituted unregistered securities.

CASE QUESTIONS

1. Can a noncontributory profit-sharing plan be a security under the *Howey* test? Why or why not?
2. If employees were required to purchase the interests, would that change your answer in Question 1? Why or why not?

1. In the _____ _____, issuers raise capital by selling securities in the public markets or in private placements.
   a. Stock exchange
   b. Primary market
   c. Secondary market
   d. Debt exchange
   e. Bond market

2. Federal securities statutes define "security" by recognizing specific forms of securities such as:
   I. Stocks
   II. Bonds
   III. Bank accounts
   IV. Certificates of deposit (CDs)
   a. I and II
   b. I and III
   c. II, III, and IV
   d. III and IV
   e. II and III

3. Which of the following is not a part of the *Howey* test used to define a security?
   a. Investment of money
   b. Common enterprise
   c. Nominal interest of investor
   d. Expectation of profit
   e. All of the above are part of the test

4. A security that represents an investor's ownership interests whereby the financial return on the investment is based primarily on the performance of that venture is called a(n) _____ instrument.
   a. Equity
   b. Debt

   c. Common
   d. Subordinate
   e. Private

5. The Securities and Exchange Commission (SEC) has broad authority over:
   a. Securities issuance
   b. Transactions
   c. Brokers
   d. All of the above
   e. None of the above

6. The issuance and trading of securities is regulated by Securities Act of 1933.
   a. True
   b. False

7. The securities market typically functions through the effort of three parties: an investor, the issuer, and the intermediary.
   a. True
   b. False

8. Peer-to-peer lending (P2PL) is an example of equity financing.
   a. True
   b. False

9. State statutes that regulate securities are known as gray-sky laws.
   a. True
   b. False

10. State authorities typically regulate intrastate securities offerings.
   a. True
   b. False

✅ **Quick Quiz ANSWERS**
Howey Test

1. This question is based on *Smith v. Gross*,[12] where the court decided that the earthworm scheme did constitute a securities offering. It fit all elements of the *Howey* test and had vertical commonality where the investor profited from the work of the promoter.

(continued)

---

[12]604 F.2d 639 (9th Cir. 1979).

2. Careful! This question first appears to be a replica of the *Howey* case's facts, but there are substantial differences in the investment opportunities. Utley's plan would likely *not* constitute offering a security. He offered development and real estate services, but those were not a requirement for purchasing the property. Owners of the property might simply be purchasing it for their own vacation use and not as an investment with expectations of return. Utley's services did not have the required commonality, nor did investors necessarily benefit from Utley's efforts.

3. This question is based on *SEC v. Alliance Leasing Corp.,*[13] in which the court held that Alliance's leasing plan was a securities offering under the *Howey* standards. The investment opportunity had both vertical and horizontal commonality, and the investors profited primarily due to the efforts of Alliance in arranging the leases.

CHAPTER REVIEW QUESTIONS: Answers and Explanations

1. b. *Primary market* is the term used to refer to the original issuance (or reissuance) by a business entity that sells its securities to the public markets (the general investment community) or in private placements (limited groups of investors). Answer *c* is wrong because the trading of previously issued securities, which does not raise capital for the issuing business, is referred to as the *secondary market.*

2. a. Federal securities statutes define a security in two ways: (1) by recognizing specific forms of securities (e.g., stocks, bonds, and debentures) and (2) by providing a broadly defined category of other investment transactions in a more generic sense under *Howey.* However, bank accounts and certificates of deposit are not considered securities under either definition.

3. c. The *Howey* test is used by courts to examine whether the investment opportunity at issue is a security. The opportunity must be: (1) an investment of money, (2) in a common enterprise, (3) undertaken by the investor with expectations of profits, and (4) having profits generated primarily by the efforts of persons other than the investor.

4. a. Equity instruments promise a return based on a venture performance where the investors have no specific right or guarantee on the investment

(e.g., stock). Answer *b* is wrong because a debt instrument involves an investor lending money to the business entity with expectation of a fixed return and repayment of the money.

5. d. The SEC is an independent regulatory agency with broad executive, legislative, and judicial authority over securities issuance, transactions, investors, and brokers.

6. a. True. Securities are regulated through the Securities Act of 1933 and the Securities Exchange Act of 1934.

7. a. True. The parties are an investor (seeking return on investment), an issuer (raising capital through equity or debt), and an intermediary (typically a financial institution).

8. b. False. P2PL involves matching investors with borrowers who expect funds to be paid back at a set rate of interest.

9. b. False. Blue-sky laws, not gray-sky laws, refer to state regulation of securities offerings to prevent swindlers from selling nothing more than blue sky to investors.

10. a. True. States are permitted to regulate intrastate offerings.

---

[13]2000 U.S. Dist. LEXIS 5227 (S.D. Cal. 2000).

CHAPTER 33

Regulation of Issuance:
The Securities Act of 1933

While there are significant advantages for a company that is raising money to list their stock on public stock exchanges (e.g., the NYSE), there is also a considerable regulatory burden. In this chapter's *Thinking Strategically,* we'll examine how Facebook used a Special Purpose Vehicle to strategically limit their liability and achieve their funding objectives.

Learning Objectives

After studying this chapter, students who have mastered the material will be able to:

33-1   Recognize the fundamental underpinnings of securities issuance regulation.

33-2   Exhibit a working knowledge of the legal process leading to issuance of original securities under the Securities Act of 1933.

33-3   Compare the requirements for various exemptions from the statutory registration requirements and apply the exemptions within fact scenarios.

33-4   Describe special rules for raising capital through crowdfunding.

33-5   List and discuss remedies and penalties for violation of the Securities Act of 1933.

33-6   Explain the impact the Private Securities Litigation Reform Act of 1995 and the Securities Litigation Uniform Standards Act of 1998 have on issuers and investors.

33-7   Identify when and how issuers assert defenses of materiality and the bespeaks caution doctrine.

CHAPTER OVERVIEW

Once an opportunity has been determined to be a securities offering, the focus of the inquiry then shifts to registration and disclosure requirements for that specific offering. The underlying principle of the regulation of securities issuance is transparency by the issuer and disclosure of relevant facts to the investor. This chapter examines the requirements related to registration of securities, disclosures mandated by federal and state securities law, and registration exemptions for certain offerings. The chapter also discusses statutory anti-fraud protections for investors and covers defenses and safe harbors that are available to issuers that are alleged to have made misrepresentations in their statements and disclosures.

THE SECURITIES ACT OF 1933

The primary scope of the **Securities Act of 1933**[1] (the '33 Act) is the regulation of original issuance (and reissuance) of securities to investors by business venture issuers. The '33 Act mandates: (1) a registration filing for any venture selling securities to the public, (2) certain *disclosures* concerning the issuer's governance and financial condition, and (3) regulatory oversight over the registration and issuance of securities. The system is designed to give potential investors a transparent view of the business entity's financial information, potential liabilities, management practices, and other pertinent information that a business venture is required to disclose in its registration materials. The '33 Act also provides defrauded investors with remedies against issuers that violate the statutory requirements. Congress has also provided *special exemptions* for issuance of securities to relatively small groups of qualified investors.

The '33 Act was the first of several pieces of legislation enacted after the financial collapse in 1929, which resulted in stocks losing more than half their value by 1933. The law was designed to protect investors by requiring a procedure that would test the soundness of securities to be sold to the general public. Subsequent laws, notably the Securities Exchange Act of 1934, focused on other aspects of securities regulation such as the trading of existing securities and oversight of stock exchanges and securities firms. We discuss the Securities Exchange Act of 1934 in detail in Chapter 34.

TAKEAWAY CONCEPTS The Securities Act of 1933

- The '33 Act covers the process of issuing or reissuing securities to the public. The law requires registration and certain disclosures and mandates government registration, regulation, and oversight of the offerings of securities to the public.
- The '33 Act also provides special exemptions for issuance of securities to relatively small groups of qualified investors.

THE PROCESS OF A PUBLIC OFFERING

The centerpiece of the '33 Act is Section 5, which makes it illegal to sell any security by use of mail or facilities of interstate commerce unless the security has been registered or unless the security fits into one of the statutory exemptions. Section 5 also requires that the registration statement become "effective" prior to the actual sale of a security. What is commonly referred to as a *public offering* is actually a process of registration and disclosure mandated by the '33 Act. The '33 Act separates the registration process into three stages related to the issuance of a security—the prefiling period, the waiting period, and the posteffective period—and sets out statutory requirements for each. In addition to mandates set out in the '33 Act, the SEC has added significant requirements pursuant to its authority as an independent regulatory agency. It is also important to understand that, as a practical matter, the '33 Act requirements for registration only apply to a limited number of issuers. This is because the law exempts a significant number of nonpublic offerings known as *private placements*. Private placements are discussed in more detail later in this chapter.

---

[1] 15 U.S.C. § 77a et seq.

Preregistration Documentation

The '33 Act and the SEC regulations require extensive documentation even before the registration statement is filed. This documentation requires the expertise of a variety of professionals, but ultimately it includes legal documents that are drafted by highly specialized attorneys skilled in securities law. Required documentation before registration includes:

- a *letter of intent* in which the issuer indicates management and board approval of the issuing of shares;

- *comfort letters,* including an opinion of the issuer's corporate counsel verifying the business venture's adherence to corporate formalities and compliance and an opinion from the business venture's accounting firm verifying the accuracy of the business's financial records; and

- an *underwriting agreement* in which the issuer enters into an agreement with a syndicate of underwriters[2] specifying the amount of securities offered, the compensation for the underwriters, and terms related to representations and warranties of the issuer and underwriters.

Registration

Section 5's registration requirement is at the very heart of the public offering process. Registering a security is a relatively complex process that is divided into four phases. First, as discussed above, the issuer assembles preregistration documents. Second, the issuer begins the prefiling period while the registration statement is being prepared. The form of the registration statement is prescribed by SEC regulations and is broken down into two parts. The first part is the **prospectus**, which is intended to give investors a realistic view of the issuer's business, risk factors, financial position, financial statements, and disclosures concerning directors, officers, and controlling shareholders. The second part of the registration statement is *supplemental information* that documents and supports the prospectus.

Filing the Registration Statement and Waiting Period

Once the prospectus is drafted, the next phase requires the issuer to file the registration for review by the SEC. During these preliminary phases of the registration process, the securities may *not* be marketed or sold to the public. Once submitted, the SEC reviews the registration notice for incomplete or misleading disclosures and may notify the issuer through one or more "letters of comment" (also known as a *deficiency letter*). During this waiting period, the SEC may issue a *refusal order* that prevents the registration from taking effect. If the SEC does not act, the registration statement becomes effective 20 days after it was filed. Even after the SEC's review period has expired, the SEC may issue a *stop order* if it determines there was a defect in the disclosures. The effect of the stop order is a suspension of the effectiveness of an already effective registration statement.

During the SEC review phase, the security may not be sold, but it may be *marketed* to the public subject to strict SEC regulations. Oral offers, for example, are permitted during the waiting period so long as the offer doesn't contain a material misstatement. Written offers are more tightly regulated. Issuers may not send "free writings," such as a brokerage firm's research report, but may use newspaper or other media advertising that contains limited information about the offering (called a "tombstone ad" because it is typically enclosed in a black border). Although issuers are permitted to make these offers during the waiting period, offers to buy or accept the securities at a certain price are not binding.

---

[2]In this context, an underwriter is a professional in the securities market that agrees to facilitate the sale of stock to the public for a fee.

Materiality One of the most important concepts to understand in the context of disclosures and statements made by issuers and sellers of a securities offering is the definition of *material* facts. The **materiality** requirement uses an objective standard to test whether misinformation is likely to have induced the investor to purchase the securities. It also protects the issuer by distinguishing between misinformation that is important and misinformation that lacks significance. The U.S. Supreme Court has defined a fact as material under federal securities laws if "there is a substantial likelihood a reasonable investor would consider it important" in making a securities-related decision.[3] Materiality is typically raised as a defense by the issuer when the investor (or the SEC) alleges that statements in the prospectus or other offering materials were misleading. Materiality as a defense is discussed in more detail later in this chapter.

Postregistration

The final phase begins when the offering's contemplated registration statement expires and the securities' registration becomes effective. Once the registration statement has become effective, the securities are permitted to be sold to the public, but the prospectus and marketing materials are still subject to the SEC's oversight. The final prospectus with all price adjustments and underwriting information must be sent to any purchaser either before or at the time she purchases the securities.

TAKEAWAY CONCEPTS Phases of Securities Registration

Phase 1: Preregistration	Phase 2: Registration Statement	Phase 3: SEC Review	Phase 4: SEC Response
Proposed issuer assembles preregistration documents such as letters of intent, comfort letters, and an underwriting agreement.	Proposed issuer drafts prospectus with disclosures and financial information and submits the statement to the SEC.	The SEC reviews the registration statement and may issue deficiency letters to the issuer.	The SEC may: (1) Issue a refusal order during the review period or issue a stop order after the review period. Proposed issuer must revise and resubmit; or (2) Take no action and the registration becomes effective 20 days after the original SEC filing. The security may now be sold to the public.

EXEMPTIONS FROM REGISTRATION

While the SEC regulations for registering securities are intended to protect investors, the process itself is extremely onerous and expensive for issuers who are engaged in a relatively small offering. To assist business ventures seeking smaller amounts of capital from the public investment community, the securities laws allow a number of **exemptions** from registration for smaller issuers. For a number of economic, legal, and other practical reasons, *most businesses offer their securities on an exempt basis.* Section 3 of the '33 Act exempts certain *securities,* whereas Section 4 exempts certain *transactions.*

LO 33-3

Compare the requirements for various exemptions from the statutory registration requirements and apply the exemptions within fact scenarios.

---

[3]*TSC Industries, Inc. v. Northway, Inc.,* 426 U.S. 438 (1976).

From a federal standpoint, the most common exemption is for *nonpublic* offerings to a limited number of sophisticated investors who have prior business relationships with the issuer or who privately negotiate their securities purchases. Another common exemption, known as a regulatory *safe harbor*, involves offerings with specified dollar limitations and/or limitations on the number of *nonaccredited investors*. While a security may be exempt from the burdensome regulations of the '33 Act, a seller of securities is still required to make available or prepare and deliver certain *disclosures* to prospective investors as a condition to establishing an exemption. The breadth and content of these disclosures varies depending upon the particular requirements for registration or exemption imposed by law.

The following are common examples of securities that are exempt from full registration requirements:

- Commercial paper (such as promissory notes that are purchased by sophisticated investors and investment banks) with a maturity date of less than nine months.
- Securities of charitable organizations.
- Annuities and other issues of insurance companies.
- Government-issued securities such as municipal bonds.
- Securities issued by banks and other institutions subject to government supervision.
- Securities that qualify as exempt under SEC Regulation D, Regulation A, and Regulation Crowdfunding (explained next).

Regulation D: Private and Small Transactions

In addition to the exemption for some *types* of securities, the securities laws also exempt certain *transactions* that an issuer may use to sell the security. Some of the more common transaction exemptions fall under the securities law provision **Regulation D**. Regulation D exemptions are for limited offers of a relatively small amount of money or offers made in a limited manner. The exemption is grounded in an assumption that certain investors are sophisticated enough that they do not need the level of protection afforded by the '33 Act's full disclosure requirements. This allows issuers to keep transaction costs significantly lower than required for nonexempt offerings. Offerings under Regulation D are often called *private placements*.[4]

Accredited Investors

A crucial component of the exemption rules depends on categorizing investors as *accredited* versus *nonaccredited*. Rule 501 of Regulation D sets out various ways in which investors may be categorized as accredited. Institutional investors (e.g., banks, mutual funds), corporations with assets exceeding $5 million, venture capital firms, and key insiders of the issuers (e.g., officers, directors, partners) are automatically considered accredited investors. In order for individual investors to be accredited, they must have (1) a net worth of over $1 million or (2) income in excess of $200,000 (or joint income with a spouse of $300,000) in each of the two most recent years and a reasonable expectation of reaching the same income level in the current year to meet the accredited investor criteria.[5]

Rule 504: Smaller Offerings

Rule 504 exemptions are for relatively small offerings through which privately held, noninvestment companies seek to raise capital for a specific purpose. The exemption covers offerings up to $5 million in any 12-month period. There are no disclosure requirements, the prospectus is not required to be registered, there is no

---

[4]Strictly speaking, *private placement* refers only to Rule 506 offerings. However, many investor publications refer to any Regulation D offering as a private placement.

[5]Rule 501 also includes sophisticated trusts and accredited-owned entities as accredited investors.

limit on the number of investors, and there is no requirement that the investor be accredited. However, most issuers will nonetheless include important disclosures in their offering materials because it helps the issuer defend against later allegations that the issuer violated anti-fraud laws. As a general matter, the offering cannot be publicly advertised or accomplished through widespread solicitation. The issuer is required to take steps to be sure that there are no resales of the securities to the public.

Rule 506: Larger Private Placements Regulation D provides an important exemption for a larger offering through Rule 506 that is typically referred to as a **private placement**. Rule 506 exempts private, noninvestment company offerings in unlimited amounts that are not generally advertised or available to the general public. However, Rule 506 offers two alternatives for private placement based on restrictions in terms of the type and sophistication of investors who may purchase the securities. Rule 506(b) placements may be offered to an unlimited number of investors who qualify as accredited under SEC rules. Rule 506(b) offerings may *also* have up to 35 nonaccredited investors who qualify as "sophisticated." This means that the issuers must reasonably believe that the investors have sufficient experience, business savvy, and knowledge of the market that the law imputes a certain cognizance of investment risk and the ability to protect their own interests. Additionally, Rule 506(b) requires issuers to give any nonaccredited investors disclosure documents that generally contain the same type of information that is provided in a registered offering. Rule 506(c) provides issuers with the right to broad general solicitation and advertisement of a security to an unlimited number of *accredited investors only*. The SEC requires the issuer to take reasonable steps in order to ensure that investors are accredited. Note that while the offering amount is limited by the rule, issuers may (and often do[6]) use Rule 506 for smaller offerings. For example, if an issuer plans on a $5 million offering, it may choose its exemption category from either Rule 504 or Rule 506.

Regulation A: Large Exempt Offerings

Regulation A allows large offerings to be exempt from registration, although these offerings are more closely regulated than either Rule 504 or Rule 506 exemptions. Regulation A is split into two tiers: Tier 1, for securities offerings of up to $20 million in a 12-month period; and Tier 2, for securities offerings of up to $50 million in a 12-month period. Regulation A sets out special requirements for issuer eligibility, offering circular contents, advertising, disclosures, and disqualification for some individuals. Tier 2 issuers are required to include audited financial statements in their offering documents and to file annual, semiannual, and current reports with the SEC on an ongoing basis. Securities offered under Tier 1 have no qualifications regarding who may invest, whereas purchasers of Tier 2 offerings must either be accredited investors or be subject to certain limitations on their investment.

 QUICK QUIZ Exemptions

Which exempt category/categories, if any, do these offerings fall into?

1. NewCo intends to issue a $10 million offering and offer it privately to 100 nonaccredited investors.
2. Bison Brothers intends to issue a $4 million offering without general solicitation. It plans to sell the securities to three investors. Investor A is an investment bank

(continued)

---

[6]See Rutherford B. Campbell, Jr., "The Wreck of Regulation D," *The Business Lawyer* 66, no. 4 (August 2011), pp. 919, 928.

and has a net worth of $2 million and $100,000 in annual income. Investor B is a partner in Bison Brothers, has a net worth of $250,000, and has an annual income of $150,000. Investor C is the high school–aged son of Investor B and has a negative net worth with $15,000 in annual income.

3. Dorm Shirts Inc. intends to issue a $1 million offering over 12 months. Its principals plan to offer it exclusively to 50 friends who all attend the same college, have net worth under $50,000, and have annual incomes below $25,000.

4. Mega-Company will use general solicitations to attract investors to a $19 million offering over 12 months. The company anticipates that investors will not have the income or net worth to become accredited.

Answers to this Quick Quiz are provided at the end of the chapter.

Disclosures Required

It is important to emphasize that exempt private placement offers under Rules 504 and 506 are still required to make important anti-fraud-related disclosures to potential investors about the business and its principals. These disclosures are made through a *private placement memorandum.*

TAKEAWAY CONCEPTS Exemptions from Registration

- For a number of economic, legal, and other practical reasons, most businesses offer their securities on an exempt basis.
- Exemption from registration does not exempt issuers from anti-fraud laws, disclosures to nonaccredited investors, and financial transparency for all investors.

	Rule 504	Rule 506(b)	Rule 506(c)	Regulation A
Maximum issue in 12 months	$5 million	Unlimited	Unlimited	*Tier 1:* $20 million *Tier 2:* $50 million
Investor requirements	Unlimited investors (no accreditation requirements)	Thirty-five sophisticated/ nonaccredited; unlimited accredited	Unlimited; all investors must be accredited	*Tier 1:* None *Tier 2:* Unlimited accredited; nonaccredited subject to investment limits
Solicitation regulations	Limited solicitation	No requirements	General solicitation permitted	General solicitation permitted

---

REGULATION OF CROWDFUNDING

Crowdfunding gained a significant boost after the passage of the Jumpstart Our Business Startups (JOBS) Act of 2012. The law required the SEC to carve out a niche in securities laws that permitted crowdfunding as a fundraising tool for small business. In 2015, the SEC adopted rules that attempt to balance concerns about protecting relatively unsophisticated investors from fraud with helping to grow the economy by making more capital available from the investing public. Known as *Regulation Crowdfunding,* the SEC's rules are similar to the Regulation D exemptions discussed earlier in that the SEC imposes less onerous disclosure rules on the issuer than are required by the '33 Act. Regulation Crowdfunding also sets out investment limits for individuals based on net worth and income.

Rules for Issuers

A company issuing securities in reliance on Regulation Crowdfunding (the issuer) may raise a maximum aggregate amount of $1,070,000 during a 12-month period. Additionally, the issuer must electronically file its offering statement on SEC Form C, which discloses:

- biographical information about officers, directors, and owners of 20 percent or more of the issuer;
- a description of the issuer's business and the use of proceeds from the offering;
- the price to the public of the securities or the method for determining the price;
- the target offering amount and the deadline to reach the target offering amount;
- whether the issuer will accept investments in excess of the target offering amount; and
- the issuer's financial condition and financial statements.

Once the crowdfunding campaign has started, the issuer must provide an update on its progress toward meeting the target offering amount within five business days after reaching 50 percent and 100 percent of its target offering amount. The issuer is also required to provide an annual report no later than 120 days after the end of its fiscal year. The annual report requires updated information similar to what is required in the offering statement.

Rules for Investors

In addition to the requirements for issuers, the SEC rule also sets limits on how much individuals may invest through crowdfunding. The rule focuses on an investor's annual income and her net worth.[7] Table 33.1 provides an illustration of how investor limits are calculated under Regulation Crowdfunding.

- If either of an investor's annual income or net worth is less than $107,000, then the investor's investment limit is the *greater* of (a) $2,200 or (b) 5% of the *lesser* of the investor's annual income or net worth.
- If both annual income and net worth are equal to or more than $107,000, then the investor's limit is 10% of the *lesser* of (a) the investor's annual income or (b) the investor's net worth.
- During the 12-month period, the aggregate amount of securities sold to an investor through all Regulation Crowdfunding offerings may not exceed $107,000, regardless of the investor's annual income or net worth.

TABLE 33.1	Crowdfunding Investor Qualifications and Limits		
Investor Annual Income	**Investor Net Worth**	**Calculation**	**Investment Limit**
$30,000	$105,000	Greater of $2,200 or 5% of $30,000 ($1,500)	$2,200
$150,000	$80,000	Greater of $2,200 or 5% of $80,000 ($4,000)	$4,000
$150,000	$107,000	10% of $107,000 ($10,700)	$10,700
$200,000	$900,000	10% of $200,000 ($20,000)	$20,000
$1,200,000	$2,000,000	10% of $1,200,000 ($120,000), subject to $107,000 cap	$107,000

Source: Composed by the authors based on SEC's "Regulation Crowdfunding: A Small Entity Compliance Guide for Issuers."

---

[7]In this context, an individual's net worth is calculated by subtracting liabilities (e.g., credit card debts, loans, etc.) from assets (e.g., cash in the bank, stock investments, etc.). The amount of assets that exceed liabilities determines net worth. If liabilities exceed assets, an individual's net worth is zero.

Investor Status	Maximum Investment over 12-Month Period
Either annual income or net worth less than $107,000	Greater of (a) $2,200 or (b) 5% of investor's annual income/net worth (whichever is less)
Both annual income/net worth equal to or exceeding $107,000	10% of investor's annual income/net worth (whichever is less)
All investors	$107,000 of investment

LIABILITY FOR VIOLATIONS

LO 33-5

List and discuss remedies and penalties for violation of the Securities Act of 1933.

The '33 Act and its subsequent amendments impose both civil and criminal penalties on issuers and sellers of securities who violate the Act's provisions. Investors who purchased unregistered securities are entitled to rescind the investment and to be paid back in full. In cases of misrepresentations or omissions, investors have an automatic right of action to sue the issuer for damages. Penalties also include civil penalties, fines, and incarceration for egregious cases. The SEC has broad authority to pursue civil and criminal sanctions when an offering is accomplished by false or misleading means.

Section 11: Misrepresentations in the Registration Statement

Section 11 is the primary anti-fraud provision of the '33 Act. This section creates a civil remedy for purchasers of a registered offering if the investor can prove that the issuer made a material misrepresentation or omission in the registration statement. Typically courts require preliminary proof of false (i.e., factually untrue) statements or omissions of material facts which ultimately misled the investor. Allegations of a Section 11 violation are subject to an array of defenses by the issuer. We discuss these defenses later in this chapter.

False Statements The most important determination in a case alleging false statements under Section 11 is whether the statement is actually one of fact or one of opinion. A statement of fact expresses certainty about a thing, whereas a statement of opinion does not. An opinion does not imply definiteness or certainty. Congress incorporated that distinction in the first part of Section 11 by exposing issuers to liability only for untrue statements *of fact,* not for untrue statements.

For example, suppose a company's CEO states: "The smartphones we manufacture have the highest-resolution screen available on the market." Then suppose the CEO transforms that factual statement into one of opinion: "I *believe* the smartphones we manufacture have the highest-resolution screen available on the market." The first version would be an untrue statement of fact if a competitor had introduced a smartphone with a higher-resolution screen a month before—even assuming the CEO had not yet learned of the new product. The CEO's assertion is not mere puffery, but a verifiable statement about her company's smartphone and the CEO, however innocently, got the facts wrong. But in the same set of circumstances, the second version would remain true. Just as she said, the CEO really did believe, when she made the statement, that her company's smartphones had the sharpest picture around. And although a plaintiff could later prove that opinion erroneous, the words "I believe" cannot give rise to liability for an untrue statement of fact under Section 11.

Omissions Clause If a registration statement omits material facts about the issuer's inquiry into or knowledge concerning a statement of opinion, and if those facts conflict with what a reasonable investor would take from the statement itself, then the statement violates Section 11's omissions clause. However, an opinion statement is not necessarily misleading when an issuer knows, but fails to disclose, some fact cutting the other way. Reasonable investors understand that opinions sometimes rest on a weighing of competing fact, but a reasonable investor cannot expect that *every* fact known to an issuer supports its opinion statement.

In Case 33.1, the U.S. Supreme Court analyzes an issuer's statements under the false statements provision and omissions clause of Section 11.

CASE 33.1 Omnicare, Inc. v. Laborers District Council Construction Industry Pension Fund et al., 135 S.Ct. 1318 (2015)

FACT SUMMARY Omnicare, the nation's largest provider of pharmacy services for residents of nursing homes, filed a registration statement with the SEC in connection with a public offering of its common stock. The registration statement contained all disclosures mandated by the '33 Act as well as an analysis of the effects of various federal and state laws on its business model. One analysis included Omnicare's acceptance of rebates from pharmaceutical manufacturers. Most significantly, two sentences in the registration statement expressed Omnicare's view of its compliance with legal requirements:

> [Statement 1] We believe our contract arrangements with other healthcare providers, our pharmaceutical suppliers, and our pharmacy practices are in compliance with applicable federal and state laws.

> [Statement 2] We believe that our contracts with pharmaceutical manufacturers are legally and economically valid arrangements that bring value to the healthcare system and the patients that we serve.

Several caveats accompanied those two opinion statements. On the same page as the first statement, Omnicare mentioned several state-initiated "enforcement actions against pharmaceutical manufacturers" for offering payments to pharmacies that dispensed their products. The caveat also cautioned that the

laws relating to that practice might "be interpreted in the future in a manner inconsistent with our interpretation and application." Adjacent to the second statement, Omnicare noted that federal regulators had expressed "significant concerns" about some manufacturers' rebates to pharmacies, and Omnicare warned that revenue might suffer "if these price concessions were no longer provided."

Several pension funds (Funds) that purchased Omnicare stock in the public offering brought suit alleging that the company's two opinion statements about legal compliance give rise to liability under Section 11 of the '33 Act. Citing lawsuits that federal agencies later pressed against Omnicare, the Funds argued that the company's receipt of payments from drug manufacturers violated anti-kickback laws. On that basis, the Funds alleged that Omnicare made materially false representations about legal compliance.

The Funds also accused Omnicare of omitting material facts necessary to render its representations to be classified as "not misleading." The Funds claimed that none of Omnicare's officers and directors possessed reasonable grounds for thinking that the opinions offered were truthful and complete. The Funds cited proof that one of Omnicare's attorneys had warned that a particular contract carried a heightened risk of liability under

(continued)

anti-kickback laws. At the same time, the Funds made clear that in light of Section 11's strict liability standard, they chose to exclude any allegation that could be construed as alleging fraud or intentional or reckless misconduct.

The federal trial court granted Omnicare's motion to dismiss holding that the statements regarding a company's belief as to its legal compliance are considered "soft" information and are actionable only if those who made them knew they were untrue at the time. The Court of Appeals for the Sixth Circuit reversed and ruled that, although the two statements expressed Omnicare's opinion of legal compliance rather than hard facts, the Funds had to allege only that the stated belief was "objectively false." The court also held that it was not necessary for the Funds to contend that anyone at Omnicare disbelieved the opinion at the time it was expressed.

SYNOPSIS OF DECISION AND OPINION The U.S. Supreme Court reversed the appellate court's decision and remanded the case back to the trial court because neither the trial court nor the appellate court applied the correct standard under Section 11. The Court held that statements of opinion do not constitute an untrue statement of fact simply because the stated opinion ultimately proved to be incorrect. Because a statement of opinion admits the possibility of error, such a statement remains true even if the opinion turns out to be wrong. The only time that an issuer can be liable for misrepresentation in a statement of opinion is when the issuer does not subjectively believe the stated opinion or if supporting facts of the opinion were untrue. However, the Court also held that an issuer *could* be held liable for opinion statements under Section 11's omissions clause if an objectively reasonable investor would be misled by the statement.

WORDS OF THE COURT: Section 11 Liability
"Section 11 thus creates two ways to hold issuers liable for the contents of a registration statement—one focusing on what the statement says and the other on what it leaves out. Either way, the buyer need not prove (as he must to establish certain other securities offenses) that the defendant acted with any intent to deceive or defraud. . . .

"[L]iability under Section 11's false-statement provision would follow (once again, assuming materiality)

not only if the speaker did not hold the belief she professed but also if the supporting fact she supplied were untrue."

WORDS OF THE COURT: Omissions Clause
". . . [A] reasonable investor may, depending on the circumstances, understand an opinion statement to convey facts about how the speaker has formed the opinion—or, otherwise put, about the speaker's basis for holding that view. And if the real facts are otherwise, but not provided, the opinion statement will mislead its audience. Consider an unadorned statement of opinion about legal compliance: 'We believe our conduct is lawful.' If the issuer makes that statement without having consulted a lawyer, it could be misleadingly incomplete. In the context of the securities market, an investor, though recognizing that legal opinions can prove wrong in the end, still likely expects such an assertion to rest on some meaningful legal inquiry—rather than, say, on mere intuition, however sincere. Similarly, if the issuer made the statement in the face of its lawyers' contrary advice, or with knowledge that the Federal Government was taking the opposite view, the investor again has cause to complain: He expects not just that the issuer believes the opinion (however irrationally), but that it fairly aligns with the information in the issuer's possession at the time. Thus, if a registration statement omits material facts about the issuer's inquiry into or knowledge concerning a statement of opinion, and if those facts conflict with what a reasonable investor would take from the statement itself, then Section 11's omissions clause creates liability."

Case Questions

1. What is the difference between the objective standard and the subjective standard in this case? Why is it important to the outcome of this case?

2. Since one of Omnicare's attorneys had concern about the company's business model, should Omnicare have disclosed that in its registration statement? Is failing to include that single legal opinion an omission?

3. *Focus on Critical Thinking:* Could Omnicare's statements constitute a breach of contract? Is this good or bad for the investment community? Explain.

Section 12(a)(2): Misrepresentations in Public Offerings

Section 12(a)(2) is a provision of the '33 Act that complements Section 11 by providing for **rescissionary liability** of issuers that are engaged in *public* securities transactions. Rescissionary liability is liability of a wrongdoer to an innocent party whereby the proper legal remedy is to rescind the transaction and set the parties back to their pretransaction position. This is typically accomplished through a court order requiring the wrongdoer to pay back any money it received from the innocent party in relation to the transaction. Section 12(a)(2) does not apply to private transactions or aftermarket transactions (i.e., trading). The focus of Section 12(a)(2) is typically on whether statements made in the prospectus and/or any oral statements by the issuers were materially false or misleading.

Scope   In 1995, the U.S. Supreme Court clarified the scope of Section 12(a)(2) in the landmark case *Gustafson v. Alloyd Co.*[8] The case involved a privately held company with three shareholders who sold all of their shares of the company to a group of investors. Although there was no prospectus and no registration statement filed, the parties executed the transaction through an agreement of sale for the stock. The investors sued the sellers claiming that the sellers had misrepresented the company's financial position in the agreement of sale. They sought rescission of the transaction under Section 12(a)(2). The Court held that the agreement of sale was not a "prospectus" as defined in the Act and therefore no Section 12(a)(2) attached. Indeed, the Court's decision narrowed the scope of what could be considered a prospectus by defining it as a written communication that offers a security for sale, is widely distributed to the public, and "must include information contained in a registration statement."[9] In a registered public offering, sellers covered by Section 12(a)(2) are typically retail broker-dealers or selling shareholders.

False Statements and Omissions   As is the case with many securities law protections, investors must show either a material untruth or the omission of a material fact necessary to make what is said not misleading. The investor must also overcome the seller's defense that she did not know and could not have known (exercising reasonable care) that the statements were false. Section 12(a)(2) also covers omissions of material facts that a reasonable investor would find necessary to make an informed purchase decision. Liability under Section 12(a)(2) attaches only when the misinformation was instrumental in the sale. That is, the investor must prove a connection between the misinformation and the transaction.

Section 17(a): Liability for Negligent Misrepresentation

One of the SEC's most powerful weapons in enforcing anti-fraud provisions is the broad coverage provided by Section 17(a), which applies to public, private, and exempt offerings of securities. Section 17(a) was the primary enforcement mechanism used by the SEC in pursuing issuers after the financial crisis that began in 2008. Similar in purpose and structure to its more famous cousin, Rule 10b-5 under the Securities Exchange Act (discussed in the next chapter), Section 17(a) is a broad-based prohibition of the sale of securities that obtain money through fraud, material misstatements, or misleading omissions. This also includes liability for sellers whose misstatements or omissions are a result of *negligent* misrepresentation and does not require proof of intent by the seller to mislead. It is also important to note that Section 17(a) does not create any right of private lawsuit for the misled investor.

---

[8]513 U.S. 561 (1995).

[9]*Id.* at 571.

TABLE 33.2 '33 Act Penalties and Remedies

Violation	Penalty/Remedy
Noncompliance with registration requirements	Investors who purchased unregistered securities are entitled to rescind the investment and are entitled to be paid back in full.
Fraud in registration statement or offering	Investors may recover damages from the issuer if they relied on the statements in considering the purchase.
Fraud in any transaction or offering	Issuers are subject to criminal penalties, including substantial fines and incarceration.

Penalties and Remedies

The '33 Act provides for an array of penalties and remedies for violation of its provisions. Penalties range from a civil fine to incarceration. The primary remedy for defrauded or misled investors is rescinding the sale transaction and requiring the seller to pay back the investor the transactional amount. Table 33.2 sets out a basic structure of penalties and remedies under the '33 Act.

TAKEAWAY CONCEPTS Liability for Violations of the '33 Act

- **Section 11:** Primary anti-fraud provision of the '33 Act. This section creates a civil remedy for purchasers of a registered offering if the investor can prove that the issuer made a material misrepresentation or omission in the registration statement.
- **Section 12(a)(2):** Anti-fraud provision that triggers rescissionary liability that is limited to sellers of public offerings and typically focuses on whether a prospectus was used to make material misstatements or omissions.
- **Section 17(a):** Primary enforcement mechanism used by the SEC to pursue sellers who made material misstatements or omissions. Requires only negligent misrepresentation.

LO 33-6

Explain the impact the Private Securities Litigation Reform Act of 1995 and the Securities Litigation Uniform Standards Act of 1998 have on issuers and investors.

SAFE HARBORS AND OTHER DEFENSES

Businesses that have issued stock in a public or private sale (both exempt and nonexempt) and are alleged to have violated the anti-fraud provisions of the '33 Act have two categories of defenses at their disposal. First, the issuer may avoid liability or penalties by successfully asserting that both the transaction and issuer are immune from liability through a **statutory safe harbor**. Second, the issuer may avoid liability through the common law defenses of materiality or the bespeaks caution doctrine. If the violator is not actually the issuer of the stock but a third party involved in the transaction (such as an underwriter), that party may avoid liability by proving she acted with *due diligence* in verifying the veracity and completeness of the required disclosures.

Safe Harbors: The Private Securities Litigation Reform Act of 1995

In the early 1990s, the securities regulation community and publicly held companies became concerned about what they believed to be an increasingly unwarranted number of lawsuits that they characterized as abusive or frivolous. Indeed, a number of law firms specialized in the initiation of class action litigation on behalf of allegedly defrauded shareholders. In many class action cases, the shareholders recovered minimal amounts, but sizable legal fees were awarded to law firms. The lawsuits were frequently based on optimistic predictions of future growth and other such public comments by company executives. Congress, in an attempt to curtail this type of litigation, passed the **Private Securities Litigation Reform Act of 1995 (PSLRA)**.[10] The PSLRA imposed significant procedural rules and substantive standards that made it more difficult to pursue litigation under the securities laws based solely on written or oral statements by the company's officers and directors. The PSLRA defines suits as frivolous if the "shareholder derivative actions [are] begun with [the] hope of winning large attorney fees or private settlements, and not with intention of benefiting [the] corporation on behalf of which [the] suit is theoretically brought."

The centerpiece of the PSLRA is its *safe-harbor* provision, which shields the issuer from liability based on statements and forecasts contained in the prospectus or made by executive management and authorized spokespersons of the issuer. The law provides the issuer with an automatic defense to any private lawsuit arising out of federal securities laws. In the context of the '33 Act, the safe-harbor provision is typically used to halt a claim of misrepresentation under Section 11 and/or Section 12(a)(2). The PSLRA also covers the anti-fraud provisions of the Securities Exchange Act of 1934, discussed in the next chapter.

PSLRA safe harbors offer substantial protection for issuers because there is no "state of mind" requirement in order for the company to be insulated from liability for violations of the '33 Act. The safe harbors protect issuers from private investor lawsuits by shielding the issuer from liability related to forward-looking statements in its prospectus or made orally by its officers or directors. The law defines forward-looking statements broadly and includes:

- projections of total revenues, income, or income losses;
- projections of earnings/losses per share, capital expenditures, or capital structure; and
- statements of the plans or objectives of management for future operations.

The safe harbor is most easily understood as a two-pronged liability protection shield for forward-looking statements. First, the statements must be identified as "looking ahead" and must be accompanied by *meaningful cautionary language* identifying important factors that could cause actual results to be materially different from those predicted by the statement. Second, if the investor's claim does not establish that the statement was made with actual knowledge that the statement was false or misleading, the statement falls under safe-harbor protection.[11]

It is also important to understand that some issuers and transactions are not covered by the PSLRA. Companies who have entered into an agreement with the SEC to settle fraud-related charges are not eligible for safe-harbor protections for a period of three years. Other exclusions include initial public offerings, partnership offerings, and transactions that bring a public company back to privately held status.

Securities Litigation Uniform Standards Act of 1998
After the passage of the PSLRA, corporate concerns about shareholder litigation continued after plaintiffs' lawyers began to bring similar class action lawsuits against corporations for inadequate or overly optimistic statements in state courts under *state* securities statutes. Congress responded by enacting the **Securities Litigation Uniform Standards Act of 1998**.[12] The law requires that class actions involving allegations of securities fraud by a publicly traded company under any securities statute be litigated exclusively in federal courts.

---

[10] 15 U.S.C. § 78u.

[11] There is some disagreement among federal courts in applying the "actual knowledge standard."

[12] 15 U.S.C. § 77z et seq.

LO 33-7

Identify when and how issuers assert defenses of materiality and the bespeaks caution doctrine.

MATERIALITY AS A DEFENSE

Recall from our earlier discussion of the PSLRA that not every issuer or transaction is covered by the safe-harbor provision. However, even non-PSLRA issuers may still assert several defenses to allegations of misrepresentation. First, an issuer is not liable to a private investor if the alleged misrepresentations are not *material*. The definition of materiality is significant because the import and truthfulness of information that is disclosed in a prospectus is at the very heart of statutory requirements. As discussed earlier in the chapter, materiality is rooted in whether an objectively reasonable investor would require that fact to make a decision in purchasing a security. However, because disclosure is a concept that depends on context, courts use a "total mix" test to determine whether or not an omission or representation is material. That is, even when the most important information is omitted from the prospectus, an omission cannot be considered material if the *total mix* of information was already reasonably available to the investing public. If an investor should have known about a particular fact that was available in the total mix of information, she cannot later claim that the undisclosed fact was a material omission. In Case 33.2, a federal appellate court applies the total mix standard.

CASE 33.2 Lowinger v. Pzena Investment Mgmt., 341 F. App'x 717 (2d Cir. 2009)

FACT SUMMARY Esther Lowinger and Chaoxu Zhao (Lowinger) were investors who purchased stock in Pzena Investment Management, Inc. (Pzena), an investment firm, during Pzena's initial public offering (IPO) in 2007. Pzena's prospectus included statements related to their assets under management (AUM) holdings, which are an important indicator of an investment firm's profitability. Specifically, the prospectus articulated Pzena's strategy for and ability to increase its AUM in the future. The prospectus also contained warnings and cautionary statements about the risk of the impact of market depreciation and fluctuation on its AUM and Pzena's potential revenue. Although Lowinger conceded that the challenged statements in the prospectus were literally true, they alleged that the statements were misleading with respect to the extent to which Pzena actually remained attractive to investors and, in turn, its capability for increasing its AUM holdings in the future. Lowinger alleged that these statements created an inaccurately positive image of Pzena's operations. In support of their misleading statements theory, Lowinger cited news reports from November 2007 that the performance of Pzena's largest client, the John Hancock Classic Value Fund, had been substandard and resulted in Pzena's AUM falling by $2.1 billion in the quarter ending approximately three weeks prior to the date of Pzena's IPO. Although the loss in AUM was disclosed in subsequent filings, Lowinger alleged that Pzena had failed to disclose any information related to the Hancock fund and its impact on Pzena's potential future revenue.

Lowinger filed suit against Pzena under Sections 11 and 12(a)(2) of the Securities Act of 1933 alleging that Pzena was liable for misleading statements in its prospectus and seeking to recover their investment. The trial court dismissed the complaint ruling that the statements were not materially misleading and that the warnings were sufficient to cause a reasonable investor to take note of the risk.[13] Lowinger appealed.

SYNOPSIS OF DECISION AND OPINION The U.S. Court of Appeals for the Second Circuit ruled in favor of Pzena. The court held that liability for misrepresentation under Sections 11 and 12(a)(2) accrues if either the registration statement or prospectus includes: (1) any untrue statement of a material fact or (2) an omission of a material fact that is necessary to make the statements found therein not misleading. An omission is material only if there is a substantial likelihood that the disclosure of the omitted fact would

(continued)

---

[13]The court also dismissed Lowinger's complaint against Goldman Sachs & Co. and UBS Securities, who were also named as defendants in the case against Pzena.

have been viewed by the reasonable investor as having significantly altered the total mix of information made available. In this case, Lowinger's contentions were based on a selective reading of the prospectus as a whole. The court also pointed out that the prospectus contained numerous direct warnings about the impact of market depreciation on Pzena's AUM, including that market depreciation would "tend to result in" and "would be expected to" negatively impact Pzena's revenue. Taken together, the disclosure of a significant decline in Pzena's AUM and the warnings would have made a reasonable investor aware of the risks faced by Pzena current and potential investors.

WORDS OF THE COURT: Total Mix and Materiality "When considering whether a complaint states a claim under the Securities Act, we examine the prospectus together with the allegations contained on the face of the complaint. . . .

"Whether a statement is materially misleading is a fact-specific inquiry. For example, when examining a prospectus, even if particular statements, 'taken separately, were literally true,' they are actionable if 'taken together and in context, [they] would have misled a reasonable investor about the nature of the [securities].' . . . As a general matter, '[c]ertain alleged misrepresentations in a stock offering are immaterial as a matter of law because it cannot be said that any reasonable investor could consider them important in light of adequate cautionary language set out in the same offering.' . . .

"[Lowinger's] contention that Pzena failed to disclose a materially adverse trend in its business operations . . . is similarly unpersuasive. . . . The prospectus fulfilled [statutory obligations] by disclosing the market-depreciation-driven decline in Pzena's AUM for the quarter prior to the IPO and warning that this development could be expected to result in withdrawals from Pzena's investment strategies and lower revenues and income."

Case Questions

1. What was Lowinger's theory as to why the statements in the prospectus were misleading? Since Lowinger conceded that the statements were true, how could they prove that the statements were misleading?

2. What standard did the court use to determine whether the statements were materially misleading? In your view, did the court apply the standard correctly? Why or why not?

3. *Focus on Critical Thinking:* The court attempts to draw a legal line for materiality by using the "average investor" as the standard for considering what is important enough to disclose. Who is the average investor? Should the same standard apply to weekend investors (i.e., nonprofessional investors who buy and sell stocks based on their own research) that applies to large institutional investors (such as mutual funds)? If "average investor" is not a fair one-size-fits-all standard, what would be fair?

Buried Facts Doctrine Although omission of material facts is the most frequent allegation in an anti-fraud case against an issuer, too much information may also trigger liability under the *buried facts doctrine*. This doctrine recognizes that disclosures can be misleading if they contain material information that is inaccessible or difficult to assemble for an objectively reasonable investor.

Bespeaks Caution Doctrine

One of the most powerful defenses of an issuer is the judicially created *bespeaks caution doctrine*. The doctrine was a precursor to and provided the structure for the PSLRA's safe-harbor provision, but the doctrine still applies and it may be asserted by any issuer in any transaction (i.e., it is not limited by the scope of the PSLRA). This defense allows an issuer who included specific and narrowly tailored cautionary disclosures in their prospectus to negate any allegedly misleading or overly optimistic prediction. However, an issuer cannot be protected through the bespeaks caution doctrine if the cautionary statements were overly broad or too general. Rather, courts require that the cautionary language be specifically tailored to the prediction. As a practical matter, the doctrine allows a court to look at the prospectus materials as a whole to analyze whether a particularly optimistic statement by the issuer was rendered immaterial by extensive cautionary statements in other parts of the prospectus. The key consideration is whether the cautionary statements are directly tied to the overly optimistic statement.

In Case 33.3, an appellate court applies the bespeaks caution doctrine in the context of an investment in the Trump Taj Mahal hotel and casino in Atlantic City, New Jersey.

CASE 33.3 *In re* Donald J. Trump Casino Securities Litigation—Taj Mahal Litigation, 7 F.3d 357 (3d Cir. 1993)

FACT SUMMARY Trump and his co-defendants offered securities to the public in order to finance the purchase, construction, and operation of the Trump Taj Mahal, which was billed as the most lavish casino resort in Atlantic City. The prospectus accompanying the bonds estimated the costs for completion and disclosed the plan for securing the entire financing package, which included bond proceeds, capital from Trump, and various loans and lines of credit. The prospectus stated: "The Partnership believes that the funds generated from the operation of the Taj Mahal will be sufficient to cover all of its debt service (interest and principal)." The prospectus also contained numerous cautionary statements including the intense competition in the casino industry, the absence of an operating history for the Taj Mahal, and the possibility that the enterprise might become unable to repay the interest on the bonds in the event of a mortgage default and subsequent liquidation of the Taj Mahal. When investors discovered that Trump and his co-defendants planned to file for reorganization under Chapter 11 of the Bankruptcy Code, they filed a suit alleging that the Taj Mahal offering prospectus contained material misstatements and omissions and constituted fraud. The trial court ruled in favor of Trump and held that the cautionary statements that surrounded each representation barred any misrepresentation claim. The investors appealed.

SYNOPSIS OF DECISION AND OPINION The U.S. Court of Appeals for the Third Circuit affirmed the trial court's ruling in favor of Trump. The court applied the bespeaks caution doctrine whereby cautionary language in a prospectus negates the materiality of an alleged misrepresentation. The court held that the defendants had included substantive statements that were tailored to address specific future projections and estimates or opinions in the prospectus. The bespeaks caution doctrine means that cautionary statements included in a prospectus may render the challenged predictive statements or opinions immaterial as a matter of law.

WORDS OF THE COURT: Bespeaks Caution Doctrine "Because of the abundant and meaningful cautionary language contained in the prospectus, we hold that [the investors have] failed to state an actionable claim regarding the statements that the Partnership believed it could repay the bonds. We can say that the prospectus here truly bespeaks caution because, not only does the prospectus generally convey the riskiness of the investment, but its warning and cautionary language directly address the substance of the statement of [the investors'] challenge. That is to say, the cautionary statements were tailored precisely to address the uncertainty concerning the partnership's ability to repay the bondholders."

Case Questions

1. Do issuers have a duty to disclose all negative information in the prospectus? How does the definition of materiality apply to statements by issuers that may be considered negative disclosures?

2. What specific material fact did the investors claim that the prospectus failed to disclose? What specific cautionary statements did the court find to be tailored to that material fact?

3. *Focus on Critical Thinking:* Is the bespeaks caution doctrine consistent with the '33 Act's public policy goal of transparency and disclosure in a securities issuance? Why or why not? How could the doctrine be modified to be more favorable to the public investor community?

Facebook's Special Purpose Vehicle

PROBLEM: A year before Facebook went through its initial public offering in 2012, it hired Goldman Sachs, a well-known Wall Street investment firm, to raise $1.5 billion to expand its operations and fund new research until it was ready to raise more money by going public. At this point, Facebook's executives and owners wanted to maintain control and avoid the onerous securities regulations that come with a public offering, so they chose the private placement route.

STRATEGIC SOLUTION: While normally Goldman Sachs could accomplish a nonpublic offering to accredited investors through a quiet private placement, the popularity of Facebook led to information being leaked about the offering.[14] Even though the disclosure of information was unintended, the offer's public disclosure threatened to violate SEC regulations prohibiting *general solicitation* of investors sought in private placements. Faced with potential liability from the public disclosures, Goldman created a special purpose vehicle. The purpose of the vehicle was to exploit a loophole in securities law that requires full SEC registration once an issuer has 500 investors "of record." However, Goldman

created a vehicle that acted as a sort of mini-mutual fund that owned only Facebook shares. Although hundreds of investors were buying shares of the mini-mutual fund, in reality they were investing in Facebook. Because the mini-mutual fund was the only shareholder of record, the special purpose vehicle allowed Facebook to avoid registration or reporting. At the same time, it allowed Goldman to offer an investment in Facebook to its most valued clients.

QUESTIONS

1. What type of legal strategy did Goldman Sachs employ? Is it avoidance or value creation? Could it be a combination of both? Why?
2. Although experts agreed that the special purpose vehicle did adhere to securities regulations,[15] some commentators criticized Goldman Sachs's approach as undercutting the transparency requirements that make U.S. securities markets appealing to investors.[16] Is that criticism fair? Is it possible that the special vehicle arrangement follows the letter of the law but not the spirit of the law? If the plan is legal, does that mean it is ethical as well?

---

[14]Steven D. Solomon, "Facebook and the 500-Person Threshold," *The New York Times,* January 3, 2011.

[15]"The Goldman Sachs Facebook Deal: Is This Business as Usual?" *Knowledge@Wharton,* January 19, 2011.

[16]Liz Rappaport, "Goldman Limits Facebook Offering," *The Wall Street Journal,* January 18, 2011.

KEY TERMS

Securities Act of 1933 p. 581　Federal legislation that covers the processes of issuing and reissuing securities to the public; requires registration and certain disclosures and authorizes the Securities and Exchange Commission to oversee the transactions.

Prospectus p. 582　The first part of the security registration statement prescribed by Securities and Exchange Commission regulations; intended to give investors a realistic view of the issuer's business, risk factors, financial position, financial statements, and disclosures concerning directors, officers, and controlling shareholders.

Materiality p. 583　Element in a securities fraud case requiring that a misleading fact be one that an objectively reasonable investor would require in order to make a decision in purchasing a security.

Exemptions p. 583　Types of securities or transactions that an issuer may use to sell a security that are not subject to certain Securities and Exchange Commission regulations pertaining to registering securities; intended to assist business ventures seeking smaller amounts of capital from the public investment community.

Regulation D p. 584　A securities law provision that exempts an issuer from registration when the issuer is selling the security for limited offers of a relatively small amount of money or offers made in a limited manner.

Private placement p. 585　A securities law provision exempting an issuer from registration where the issuer only accepts investments from those who meet the standards for accredited investors.

Rescissionary liability p. 591   Liability of a wrongdoer to an innocent party whereby the proper legal remedy is to rescind the transaction and restore the parties to their pre-transaction positions.

Statutory safe harbor p. 592   Statute providing immunity for certain transactions and issuers who meet a good faith criteria.

Private Securities Litigation Reform Act of 1995 (PSLRA) p. 593   Federal legislation making it more difficult to pursue litigation under the securities laws that is based solely on commentary by company executives; intended to protect publicly held companies from frivolous litigation.

Securities Litigation Uniform Standards Act of 1998 p. 593   An amendment to the Securities Act of 1934, intended to prevent a private party from instituting certain lawsuits in federal or state court based on the statutory or common law of any state that punishes "a misrepresentation or omission of a material fact" or the use of "any manipulative device or contrivance" concerning the purchase or sale of a covered security.

CASE SUMMARY 33.1 *In re* The Vantive Corporation Securities Litigation, 110 F. Supp. 2d 1209 (N.D. Cal. 2000)

Material Misstatements

Vantive is a manufacturer of client management software designed for use by sales representatives from various industries. Vantive is also a retailer and provides support services for the software. After a successful public offering in 1995, the company's stock sold for $6 per share and soon rose to as high as $35 per share. When the tech sector slumped in 1998, the stock dropped to less than $15 per share over an eight-month period. During this eight-month period, management forecasted strong gains in income by using a model that recognized millions of dollars in revenue based on software licenses that would *not* actually be realized unless the licensees were successful in selling *sublicenses* for the software.

CASE QUESTIONS

1. Were the forecasts sufficient to constitute a material misstatement of fact and an omission that violated securities laws? Explain.
2. Is Vantive protected by the PSLRA?

CASE SUMMARY 33.2 Mark v. FSC Securities Corporation, 870 F.2d 331 (6th Cir. 1989)

Exempt Securities

FSC was a securities brokerage firm that sold limited partnership interests to Mark and 27 other investors. All investors executed *subscription agreements* in which they revealed their income, represented that they had had the opportunity to review relevant information including risk factors, and affirming that they were sufficiently knowledgeable and savvy to understand the implications of the investment. However, FSC managers never actually reviewed the completed subscription agreements, and all who applied to be investors were admitted. When the interests dropped in value, Mark sued to rescind the contract on the basis that the securities were not registered and that he was not a qualified investor. FSC defended that the offering qualified under the '33 Act safe-harbor provision of Regulation D.

CASE QUESTIONS

1. Should Mark prevail?
2. Is it relevant that FSC never reviewed the subscription agreements?

CASE SUMMARY 33.3 P. Stolz Family Partnership L.P. v. Daum, 355 F.3d 92 (2d Cir. 2004)

Bespeaks Caution

Smart World Technologies was a technology company that generated revenue through advertising to users of their free Internet access points. In 1997, Smart World began to use a prospectus to offer "membership interests" in the company to the public which were not registered under the '33 Act. Based on the prospectus, Stolz, an investor, purchased $250,000 worth of the unregistered securities, which became effective on April 28, 2000. Smart World, unable to survive the bursting of the tech bubble, filed for bankruptcy in June of 2000. Stolz filed suit against Smart World and three of its officers alleging that Smart World's prospectus contained material misrepresentations in violation of the '33 Act. Smart World argued that there was a sufficient balance with the alleged misrepresentation such that no reasonable investor would be misled about the nature and risk of the offered security. Smart World provided cautions about the need for additional capital, risks in obtaining financing, market value, and other important investor risks.

CASE QUESTIONS

1. Were Smart World's disclosures sufficient to bar the investor's claim under the bespeaks caution doctrine? Why or why not?
2. Give an example of specific language that Smart World could have used to increase the likelihood that the statements would negate any alleged misrepresentations.

CASE SUMMARY 33.4 Panther Partners v. Ikanos, 681 F.3d 114 (2d Cir. 2012)

Omissions

Ikanos is a publicly traded company that develops and markets programmable semiconductors. The semiconductors enable fiber-fast broadband services over telephone companies' existing copper lines. All of Ikanos's revenues derive from the sale of semiconductor chip sets. Several months prior to its offering of stock to the public, Ikanos learned that there were quality issues with the chips. In the weeks leading up to the offering, the defect issues became more pronounced. The registration statement simply cautioned in generalized terms that "[h]ighly complex products such as those that [Ikanos] offer[s] frequently contain defects and bugs . . . " After the offering, Ikanos was forced to recall the chip sets and suffered substantial losses. Panther was an investor in Ikanos and filed suit alleging that Ikanos's failure to disclose the magnitude of the defect issue in either the registration statement or the prospectus violated Sections 11 and 12(a)(2).

CASE QUESTIONS

1. Should Ikanos have disclosed the chip defect more specifically in its registration statement and prospectus? Why do you think it did not?
2. What is Panther's likely theory of the case?
3. Is Ikanos's language related to a caution about defects and bugs sufficient to assert the bespeaks caution doctrine?

CHAPTER REVIEW QUESTIONS

1. **The primary scope of the '33 Act is the regulation of:**
   a. Trading of securities.
   b. Original issuance (and reissuance) of securities.
   c. Brokerage houses selling existing securities.
   d. Corporate insiders.
   e. None of the above

2. **All of the following statements concerning the prospectus required by the '33 Act are true except:**
   a. It is part of the registration statement.
   b. It is intended to give investors a realistic view of the issuer's business.

   c. It includes risk factors and financial statements.
   d. It must be included as part of the preregistration materials.
   e. None are true.

3. **Which safe harbor immunizes an issuer from civil liability for "forward-looking" statements?**
   a. Bespeaks caution doctrine
   b. Private Securities Litigation Reform Act (PSLRA)
   c. Forward-Looking Accountability Act
   d. Safe-harbor doctrine
   e. Reform in Industry Act

Facts for questions 4 and 5: NewCo is planning to expand its global operations and is considering financing the operations as follows:

I. Issuance of $500,000 of securities in a 12-month period to 145 investors

II. Borrowing $1,000,000 from a bank through a secured promissory note

III. Issuance of $2,000,000 securities over three years to 10 investors

4. Which transaction(s) would require registration under the '33 Act?

a. I and II

b. II and III

c. I only

d. III only

e. I, II, and III

5. Which transaction(s) would be exempt from registration under Regulation D?

a. I and II

b. II and III

c. I only

d. III only

e. I, II, and III

6. Investment through crowdfunding is not regulated by securities laws.

a. True

b. False

7. If an offer is exempt from registration, anti-fraud-related disclosures must still be made to potential investors.

a. True

b. False

8. Although omission of material facts is the most frequent allegation in an anti-fraud case against an issuer, too much information may also trigger liability under the buried total mix test.

a. True

b. False

9. Investors who purchased unregistered securities (non-exempt) are entitled to rescind the investment and are entitled to be paid back in full.

a. True

b. False

10. The bespeaks caution doctrine allows an issuer who included specific and narrowly tailored cautionary disclosures in its prospectus to negate an overly optimistic prediction.

a. True

b. False

 Quick Quiz ANSWERS
Exemptions

1. Not exempt. Because of the size of the offering and without general solicitation, it must fall under 506(b) or (c). In both cases, the number of nonaccredited investors is limited to 35.

2. Exempt under Rule 504 only. Although the size of the offering fits under 504 or 506, the requirement for nonaccredited investors to be sophisticated excludes 506 as a choice. 504 has no investor qualifications.

3. Exempt under Rule 504 only. The lack of accredited and/or sophisticated investors limits the offering to Rule 504.

4. Exempt under Regulation A, Tier 1. The size of the offering fits under Regulation A, Tier 1 or Tier 2, and Rule 506(b) or (c). However, general solicitation rights only exist on Regulation A (Tier 1 and 2) and 506(c). The lack of accredited investors rules out 506(c) and Tier 2. Investors have no requirements under Tier 1.

CHAPTER REVIEW QUESTIONS: Answers and Explanations

1. b. The '33 Act covers the issuance of securities through registration and disclosure requirements. Answers *a* and *c* are incorrect because they are covered under the Securities Exchange Act of 1934. Answer *d* does not apply.

2. d. The prospectus is required to contain *a, b,* and *c,* which means all three are incorrect.

3. b. The PSLRA is the only safe harbor that refers specifically to "forward-looking" statements.

4. d. Because the offer spans a period of three years, it does not qualify for exemption. Answers *a, b, c,* and *e* are incorrect because the $500,000 offering is exempt under Rule 504 and a bank's promissory note is not considered a security under the '33 Act.

5. c. The amount of the offering and limited time period bring this transaction squarely under the exemption in Rule 504 under Regulation D. Answers *a, b, d,* and *e* are incorrect because the $2,000,000 offering is not exempt due to the three-year time period, and a bank's promissory

note is not considered a security (therefore does not require an exemption) under the '33 Act.

6. b. False. Investment through crowdfunding is regulated by the SEC's Regulation Crowdfunding rule.

7. a. True. Anti-fraud-related disclosures must be made to potential investors regardless of whether the security is exempt from registration.

8. b. False. There is no buried total mix doctrine. The *buried facts doctrine* recognizes that disclosures can be misleading if they contain material information that is inaccessible or difficult to assemble for an objectively reasonable investor. The *total mix test* determines whether or not an omission or representation made in a prospectus is material.

9. a. True. Rescission is a remedy available to investors who have purchased unregistered securities that are not exempt.

10. a. True. The bespeaks caution doctrine protects issuers from liability if they used narrow cautionary language to disclose risks.

CHAPTER 34

Regulation of Trading: The Securities Exchange Act of 1934

The trading of securities involves risk and an understanding of the structure of a complex legal and regulatory framework. In this chapter's *Thinking Strategically,* we use a consequences-based strategic lense to examine practices used by some investors.

Learning Objectives

After studying this chapter, students who have mastered the material will be able to:

34-1 Explain the primary scope and objectives of the Securities Exchange Act of 1934.

34-2 Identify factors that trigger SEC reporting requirements.

34-3 Articulate the fundamental anti-fraud provisions of Section 10(b) and Rule 10b-5.

34-4 Differentiate and apply the legal tests for traditional insider trading, the misappropriation theory, and tipper-tippee liability.

34-5 Explain how Section 16 restrictions work in tandem with Rule 10b-5 liability.

34-6 Identify defenses to fraud allegations.

CHAPTER OVERVIEW

Recall from our earlier discussions that federal securities laws regulate both the primary market (issuance of securities) and the secondary market (trading securities that have already been issued). This chapter focuses on the secondary market and examines disclosure, transparency, and anti-fraud rules for securities offered to the public *after* their issuance. This chapter also covers the Exchange Act's broad-based anti-fraud provisions with particular attention to trading restrictions on parties who have an insider relationship with the company. In addition to regulating corporate officers and directors, securities laws impose liability on third parties who trade stock based on access to nonpublic information; these individuals face stiff civil and criminal penalties under federal statutes. In this chapter, we concentrate on the regulation of securities trading. We discuss regulation of corporate governance in Chapter 35.

THE SECURITIES EXCHANGE ACT OF 1934

LO 34-1

Explain the primary scope and objectives of the Securities Exchange Act of 1934.

The centerpiece of the regulation of trading of securities is the **Securities Exchange Act of 1934** (Exchange Act).[1] The Exchange Act's focus is twofold. First, the law establishes a system of oversight over the self-regulation of the securities exchanges and trading industry practices. Second, the Exchange Act mandates extensive disclosures for publicly traded companies. Whereas the '33 Act regulates the *issuance* of securities to the public by a corporation, the Exchange Act regulates the sale of securities between investors *after* an investor has purchased them from a business entity issuer. Therefore, the Exchange Act's authority is over brokers, dealers, securities associations, brokerage firms, and other business entities that are engaged in the sale of securities between investors.

Similar to the structure of the '33 Act, this statute requires registration with the SEC for issuers who wish to have their securities offered on a *national exchange,* such as the New York Stock Exchange (NYSE), and compels all sellers of securities to fully disclose all pertinent details to potential investors. The Exchange Act also regulates the relationship between existing stockholders and the corporation by requiring disclosure of information concerning (1) the financial performance of the company, (2) corporate governance procedures, and (3) any changes that increase or decrease risk that have occurred since the last report (such as the company being named as a defendant in a lawsuit).

TAKEAWAY CONCEPT The Securities Exchange Act of 1934

The Exchange Act (1) establishes a system of oversight over securities exchanges and trading industry practices and (2) mandates extensive disclosures for publicly traded companies.

REPORTING COMPANIES

LO 34-2

Identify factors that trigger SEC reporting requirements.

The Exchange Act's purpose of ensuring integrity of trading securities in the public markets is also accomplished through regulation of companies whose shares are publicly traded. Companies whose securities (equity or debt) are listed on a national stock exchange are subject to extensive regulatory requirements. There are two other statutory provisions that trigger reporting under the Exchange Act. The first trigger is based on the size of the issuer in terms of the number of shareholders and total assets of the company. A company becomes a reporting company subject to the Exchange Act if: (1) a class of its equity securities (other than exempted securities) is held by either 2,000 investors or 500 investors who are not accredited investors, and (2) on the last day of the issuer's fiscal year, its total assets exceed $10 million.[2] The second trigger is when a public offering occurs *without* a securities exchange listing. A company that files a registration statement under the Securities Act of 1933 becomes a reporting company subject to the Exchange Act once the registration company becomes effective.[3]

---

[1] 15 U.S.C. § 78a et seq.

[2] § 12(g).

[3] § 15(d).

MANDATORY DISCLOSURES AND RECORDS

The Exchange Act's broad array of mandates on public companies includes: (1) regular disclosure reports; (2) record-keeping requirements; (3) restrictions on proxy voting; (4) disclosure of tender offers; and (5) disclosure requirements and trading restrictions for officers, directors, and shareholders owning more than 10 percent of the stock. As mentioned earlier, the Sarbanes-Oxley Act of 2002 imposed new requirements on both reporting requirements and corporate governance. The reporting requirements are discussed in this chapter. The impact of Sarbanes-Oxley on corporate governance is discussed in detail in Chapter 35.

Section 13: Periodic Disclosure

Section 13 of the Exchange Act requires public companies to file regular reports with the SEC in order to maintain their registration and to provide the public with ongoing disclosures via *annual, quarterly,* and *special* reports. The SEC is required to perform regular and systematic reviews of the filing of each company at least every three years. However, the sheer number of reports is such that most reports rarely receive much regulatory scrutiny upon filing. Nonetheless, the reporting requirements are at the very core of the Exchange Act's purposes of integrity, disclosure, and transparency to the investing community. Although these reports are not delivered directly to investors, the reports are available through EDGAR (the SEC's online public database) and from the websites of the reporting companies.

Annual reports are filed using Form 10-K and contain extensive disclosure requirements similar to the disclosures required under the '33 Act when a company goes public. *Quarterly reports* are filed using Form 10-Q within 45 days of the close of the company's financial quarter and serve as an interim report with updates on any important items previously disclosed as well as being an original source of any new disclosures and risks. *Special reports* are filed using Form 8-K and are required when a material event occurs. Examples of material events that trigger a special report requirement include: loss of a significant customer, financial restructuring or report revision, insider trading, changes in corporate control, and compensation agreements.

To understand how these reporting requirements work in tandem, suppose that Ahab, the CEO of White Whale Corp., announces his retirement in February and the board of directors undertakes a search for a new president immediately thereafter. In November, the board announces it has selected Ishmael as the new president. Ahab's retirement, the search announcement, and the hiring of Ishmael are all material events that would trigger a responsibility for White Whale to file a special report (a Form 8-K) after each event. Ahab's retirement would also be reported in the next quarterly report which, given the timing, would typically be the first quarter's Form 10-Q. The retirement, search, and hiring of Ishmael in November would also be included in White Whale's annual report.

Section 14: Proxies

A proxy is a device used by a shareholder to grant another shareholder the right to vote on his or her behalf. Congress sought to stop abuses by public companies that routinely obtained open-ended proxies from shareholders without fully disclosing the issues surrounding the vote. Section 14 of the Exchange Act was intended to prevent proxies from being used by company management as a "rubber stamp" on corporate matters that required shareholder approval including, most alarmingly, the election of directors. The Exchange Act requires that anyone who solicits a proxy from a shareholder must file a proxy statement with the SEC and distribute that proxy statement to shareholders. The statement must contain disclosures and relevant information about the issues being voted on. If used in director elections, the proxy statement must contain background information on the candidates as well as conflict of interest and compensation details. The Exchange Act also expressly prohibits ongoing proxies and requires that a proxy relate to only one specific meeting. Any misrepresentation on the proxy statement may be the basis for civil liability for proxy fraud.

Tender Offers

A tender offer is an offer in which the investor is attempting to purchase enough stock in a single transaction to establish a controlling interest in the company. Because of the impact of a tender offer on investors and potentially on the wider securities market, the Exchange Act imposes disclosure and regulatory requirements on any person (or group) that acquires more than 5 percent of a public company's equity securities. This means that anyone who reaches the 5 percent threshold must file a disclosure document with the SEC that includes the fundamentals of investor identity, source of funds, structure of the transaction, purposes of the acquisition, and any relevant arrangements with third parties. The idea behind these disclosures is to make tender offers transparent to the investment community so that transactions are not secret. The Exchange Act also imposes certain restrictions on the terms of a tender offer, such as requiring that the tender offer be kept open for a certain time period, rules for when investors may revoke their shares, and other protections for existing investors.

Delisting

In some cases, a company subject to the Exchange Act wants to **delist**, which results in the termination of the statutory mandates. This may be because the company's board of directors wishes to voluntarily delist from an exchange, or perhaps the company has begun the dissolution and wind-down process. In general, reporting companies are entitled to delist their securities voluntarily and to deregister them by filing a Form 25 with the SEC. The company must give notice of its intention to file Form 25 and issue a press release announcing that intention 10 days prior to filing the form.[4] The reporting company's duty to file reports is suspended 10 days after filing, but the actual termination of registration does not occur until 90 days after the delisting.

TAKEAWAY CONCEPTS Regulation and Disclosures

- The Exchange Act contains prohibitions against market manipulation and regulates short selling.
- Reporting companies have a broad array of reporting and disclosure requirements including ongoing disclosures.

(continued)

---

[4] § 12(b).

10-K	Annual report	Extensive disclosure requirements.
10-Q	Quarterly	Interim report (updates on important items previously disclosed). New disclosures (any new disclosures and risks since the last report).
8-K	Special report	Material events that trigger a special report requirement include loss of a significant customer or financial restructuring.

ANTI-FRAUD PROVISIONS

LO 34-3

Articulate the fundamental anti-fraud provisions of Section 10(b) and Rule 10b-5.

Section 10(b) of the Exchange Act is the primary *anti-fraud* provision covering the trading of securities. The section makes it a criminal offense to engage in any fraud, directly or indirectly, in connection with the purchase and sale of any security. The SEC instituted a more specific rule called *Rule 10b-5*. Although the term "10b-5" is perhaps best known for its use by the SEC in prosecuting insider trading cases, in reality this section is a very expansive anti-fraud provision covering *all* types of securities fraud. Specifically, 10b-5 prohibits:

- employing any device, scheme, or artifice to defraud;
- making any untrue statement of a material fact or omitting to state a material fact necessary in order to make the statements made, in the light of the circumstances under which they were made, not misleading; and
- engaging in any act, practice, or course of business that operates or would operate as a fraud or deceit upon any person in connection with the purchase or sale of any security.

Material Fact

In the context of securities law, a material fact is one that, if known to an investor, would impact her decision as to whether or not to invest in the security. Material facts can be related to financial disclosures, risks, threatened litigation, or any other event that may increase the investor's risk.

Right of Private Suit

In addition to the SEC's enforcement rights, private citizens also have the right to file lawsuits against companies and individuals for violations of Rule 10b-5. The most common 10b-5 lawsuits involve market manipulation, fraud in connection with public offerings and takeovers, fraud in connection with the purchase or sale of securities, or insider trading.

INSIDER TRADING

LO 34-4

Differentiate and apply the legal tests for traditional insider trading, the misappropriation theory, and tipper-tippee liability.

The SEC has continued to be aggressive in enforcing Rule 10b-5 with respect to **insider trading**. Essentially, when a corporate *insider* has access to certain information not available to the general investing public, the insider may not trade in the company's stock. In 1988, Congress passed the **Insider Trading and Securities Fraud Enforcement Act**, which raised the criminal and civil penalties for insider trading, increased the liability of brokerage firms for wrongful acts of their employees, and gave the SEC more power to pursue violations of Rule 10b-5. In order to trigger liability under 10b-5 for insider trading, the investor must have: (1) bought or sold stock in a publicly traded company, (2) possessed nonpublic information that was material and was significant to the decision of the investor, and (3) had a special relationship with the source of information as an insider or as a "tippee" if he received information from an insider. Insiders include executives, managers, corporate or outside counsel, consultants, managers, brokers, internal or external accountants, vendors, partners, and even majority shareholders. Moreover, even lower-level employees such as secretaries who learn inside information as part of their employment are considered insiders.

The SEC's Broken Windows Approach

Recall that although insider trading laws prohibit investors in public markets from profiting by using nonpublic information to guide their investments, the rule does not *explicitly* define insider trading. The result is that courts have struggled to apply uniform standards to insider transactions. Headlines filled with stories of insider trading involving celebrities, professional athletes, and entertainers have become almost commonplace. In several cases that have garnered substantial media attention, appellate courts have overturned the convictions of investors who profited from insider knowledge. The lack of uniformity in enforcement and interpretation has spawned significant uncertainty in the investment community and created both legal and ethical conundrums.

As you learn more about the government's efforts to enforce insider trading laws, consider the following questions. First, does the murkiness that surrounds insider trading laws contradict the very purpose of federal securities regulation: promoting investor confidence in the markets? Second, is it fair to impose substantial prison sentences on those convicted of such a vaguely defined crime? Third, if the legal rules are not clear, how can an investor understand what the ethical boundaries are? Finally, are government prosecutors who pursue questionable insider trading cases driven more by politics than by the public good?

The SEC Unleashed

Beginning in 2013, the SEC stepped up its enforcement activity by pursuing record numbers of insider trading cases. Consider the comments of SEC Chair Mary Jo White from a speech at the Securities Enforcement Forum, where she made clear the SEC's "broken windows" approach to enforcing securities laws:

> One of our goals is to see that the SEC's enforcement program is—and is perceived to be—everywhere, pursuing all types of violations of our federal securities laws,

big and small. . . . I believe the SEC should strive to be that kind of cop—to be the agency that covers the entire neighborhood and pursues every level of violation. An agency that also makes you feel like we are everywhere. And we will do our best not to disappoint. . . . Over the last four years, we have filed an unprecedented number of insider trading actions—some 200 actions—against more than 450 individuals and firms charging illicit trading gains of nearly $1 billion. In these types of cases, one of the most challenging issues is establishing the relationship between tippee and tipper.[5]

After a number of high-profile losses, the SEC's aggressive enforcement actions became the subject of criticism by securities lawyers, commentators, and even courts. Still, the SEC continued to expand its enforcement division and set a record of 755 enforcement actions in 2014, approximately 10 percent higher than the previous year. Critics argued that the SEC had shifted its assets away from other important responsibilities to avoid political criticism that Wall Street bankers were not being held accountable for the financial crisis in 2008.

A Shift in Strategy

Despite aggressive enforcement and increased use of technology to detect insider trading, the SEC began to lose a string of enforcement actions (including insider trading cases) in federal courts. The SEC then shifted to a different tactic: It increased its use of in-house courts called *administrative law courts* (ALCs). As part of the Dodd-Frank Act, the SEC's enforcement powers were expanded to allow the agency to pursue securities enforcement through administrative hearings rather than in federal courts. ALCs operate much differently than federal courts. There is no independent jury, no discovery, no rules of evidence, and only limited opportunity for appeals. ALCs are staffed by administrative law judges (ALJs). ALJs are government attorneys who are selected, maintained, and funded by the SEC. Although they are

(continued)

---

[5]www.sec.gov/news/speech/detail/speech/1370539872100.

theoretically impartial, some commentators have alleged that ALJs have a pro-SEC bias. For example, federal judge Jed S. Rakoff warned about the loss of the securities laws' neutral character and pointed out the trend in which the SEC would essentially directly make, enforce, and adjudicate these laws. Despite these warnings, however, the SEC looks to continue its reliance on administrative proceedings unless prevented from doing so by the courts. One can understand Judge Rakoff's concern, especially in light of the statistics, which provide a stunning commentary on the SEC's home-court advantage. According to a recent *Washington Post* article, the SEC's preference for home-court advantage in insider trading cases resulted in a 100 percent conviction rate, compared to a 66 percent conviction rate in federal courts.

A jury acquitted investor Mark Cuban of insider trading.
©Mike Fuentes/Bloomberg via Getty Images

Discussion Questions

1. The SEC responded to criticism of its ALCs with the rationale that ALJs are experts in securities law and therefore better at applying the law to various circumstances. It also cited the efficiency of ALCs in comparison with federal courts. Does that strike you as compelling? Why or why not? Should securities cases be decided by untrained jurors who may not fully understand the issues?

2. Does the SEC's shift toward ALCs comport with the ethical conduct that is expected of those who hold power?

3. Analyze the SEC's decision to shift toward ALCs under both a principles-based approach and a consequences-based approach to ethical decision making (see Chapter 2, "Business, Societal, and Ethical Contexts of Law," for a review of the approaches). What are the results?

4. According to the SEC's website, the mission of the U.S. Securities and Exchange Commission is to "protect investors, maintain fair, orderly, and efficient markets, and facilitate capital formation." Do the actions of the SEC comport with its mission?

Cuban the Critic

One of the SEC's most vocal critics is billionaire entrepreneur Mark Cuban, who battled the SEC over a period of eight years. In 2008, the SEC alleged that Cuban violated insider trading laws by selling shares of stock in Mamma.com Inc. after learning material, nonpublic information concerning a planned private investment offering by the company. The SEC's case centered on an eight-minute telephone conversation between Mamma.com's CEO and Cuban in which the CEO reported to Cuban that an investment transaction was to take place in the near future. According to the CEO, Cuban reacted angrily to the news and agreed not to disclose or trade on the information, and Cuban ended the conversation with the comment, "Now I'm screwed, I can't sell." Cuban denied that he ever agreed to keep the information confidential or that he ever agreed not to trade on that information. Although the trial court dismissed the case against Cuban, the SEC was successful in convincing an appellate court that the case had enough to merit sending it to a jury trial. After a two-week trial in October 2013, the jury acquitted Cuban of all counts.

Discussion Questions

1. An important underlying objective of federal securities laws is to provide the public with confidence in the securities market. Did the SEC achieve that objective by bringing this case against Cuban?

2. Do the SEC and other government regulators target high-profile celebrities for enforcement under the theory that it deters lower-profile illegal activity? Does the deterrent effect work? Is it ethical? Why or why not?

3. After the trial, Cuban was highly critical of the government's conduct in the case and accused the prosecutor of lying. The government's case took five years to get to trial at an enormous cost to taxpayers. Was it worth it even if Cuban had been found guilty? Should an entire case hinge on an eight-minute telephone call?

The U.S. Supreme Court has recognized three complementary theories of insider trading: (1) *traditional insider trading* (sometimes called the "classic" insider trading theory), (2) *misappropriation,* and (3) *tipper-tippee liability.*

Traditional Insider Trading

Under the traditional insider trading theory, an insider trades in securities based on material, nonpublic information learned as an insider who owes a duty either to abstain from trading or to disclose the inside information. Under the abstain/disclose rule, those who have a fiduciary duty of trust/confidence and encounter information that is nonpublic and material have a duty to *abstain* from trading or to *disclose* the information publicly. In Case 34.1, a federal appeals court applies a traditional insider trading theory to an insider who bought stock in Microsoft based on information he had obtained from his own company's work on the Xbox.

CASE 34.1 United States v. Bhagat, 436 F.3d 1140 (9th Cir. 2006)

FACT SUMMARY NVIDIA, a publicly traded corporation that manufactured graphics processors and media communication devices located in Silicon Valley, employed Bhagat as an engineer. On Sunday, March 5, 2000, the chief executive officer of NVIDIA sent an e-mail to all company employees announcing that NVIDIA had entered into a contract with Microsoft to develop and manufacture 3-D graphics for Microsoft's Xbox. The e-mail contained a prediction that the deal would result in nearly $2 billion in revenue over the next five years. On Monday, March 6, NVIDIA's management sent out several follow-up e-mails, including one from the Vice President of Marketing entitled "Xbox shhhh," which gave specific instructions to keep the information confidential. NVIDIA's management also imposed a trading blackout (i.e., employees were not permitted to purchase or sell any NVIDIA stock) for several days. Employees were also required to cancel any open or outstanding orders for NVIDIA stock.

Bhagat arrived at his office on that same Monday morning. Approximately 20 minutes after the trading blackout e-mail was sent, he purchased a large quantity of NVIDIA stock—his largest purchase in three years. After the news about NVIDIA's contract with Microsoft was released, NVIDIA's stock rose sharply and Bhagat reaped a substantial profit. On the same day he purchased his stock, Bhagat also contacted two friends who also purchased unusually large quantities of NVIDIA. The Securities and Exchange Commission (SEC) investigated the trade, and Bhagat claimed he had read his e-mail only after he had already bought the

stock, and that by the time he tried to cancel the transaction, he was told it was too late. Bhagat was convicted by a jury of insider trading, securities tipping, and lying to SEC investigators. Bhagat appealed on the grounds that the government presented no direct evidence that Bhagat read his e-mail prior to executing the trade.

SYNOPSIS OF DECISION AND OPINION The U.S. Court of Appeals for the Ninth Circuit upheld Bhagat's convictions. The court held that even without direct evidence that Bhagat read any of the e-mails prior to purchasing the stock, the jury was allowed to infer Bhagat's insider knowledge by virtue of the fact that he had probably read his company e-mail upon entering the office as a normal, reasonable person would. The court rejected Bhagat's contention that his trades were made on "general strength of the stock" and questioned his credibility based on his testimony at trial that he had tried to cancel the transaction once he read the trading blackout e-mail, but he could not recall the branch of the brokerage house he called, nor the name, or even the gender, of the representative he spoke with.

WORDS OF THE COURT: Insider Knowledge "The government offered significant evidence to support the jury's conclusion that Bhagat was aware of the confidential X-Box information before he executed his trades. The X-Box e-mails were sent prior to his purchase. The e-mails were found on his computer. Bhagat was at his office for several hours prior to executing his trade, which provided him the

(continued)

---

opportunity to read the e-mails. Finally, Bhagat took virtually no action to divest himself of the stock, or to inform his company that he had violated the company's trading blackout. The fact that this evidence was all circumstantial does not lessen its sufficiency to support a guilty verdict."

Case Questions

1. Is Bhagat liable as an insider even though he was just an employee? Why?

2. What role did Bhagat's credibility play in this case?

3. *Focus on Critical Thinking:* Given that NVIDIA had access to this confidential information, should the company have taken more precautions than simply sending out an e-mail and imposing a trading blackout on employees? Is it possible that Bhagat did not know at the time that his conduct was illegal? Does that matter? Were his actions ethical? Why or why not?

Misappropriation Theory

Under the misappropriation theory, deceptive trading is performed by an *outsider* who owes no duty to shareholders but does owe some type of duty to the *source* of the information. The insider trading occurs when a person misappropriates confidential information for securities trading purposes, uses the information for trading, and breaches a duty to disclose that is owed to the *source* of the information. Such conduct violates Rule 10b-5 because the misappropriator engages in deception by pretending loyalty to the principal while secretly converting the principal's information for personal gain. For example, suppose that O'Hagan is an attorney who buys stock in Tectonic Corporation after learning that Mega Inc., a client of O'Hagan's law firm, is planning a takeover of Tectonic. Because O'Hagan is an outsider to Tectonic, he cannot be held liable under a traditional insider trading theory. However, O'Hagan still violated 10b-5 under the misappropriation theory because he violated a duty to disclose the source of his information to Mega and to his law firm.[6]

It is also important to note that courts do not require that the breach of duty required to trigger liability be a breach of *fiduciary* duty. In Case 34.2 , a federal appeals court analyzes whether the misappropriation theory applies absent any fiduciary duty owed to the source.

CASE 34.2 United States v. McGee, 763 F.3d 304 (3d Cir. 2014)

FACT SUMMARY Timothy McGee, a financial advisor with more than 20 years of experience, first met Christopher Maguire while attending Alcoholics Anonymous ("AA") meetings. As a newcomer to AA, Maguire sought support from McGee, who shared similar interests and had successfully achieved sobriety for many years. For the better part of a decade, McGee informally mentored Maguire in AA. They shared intimate details about their lives to alleviate stress and prevent relapses. Given the sensitive nature of their communications, McGee

assured Maguire that their conversations would remain private. Likewise, Maguire never repeated information that McGee entrusted to him. This conformed to the general practice in AA, where a "newcomer can turn . . . with the assurance that no newfound friends will violate confidences relating to his or her drinking problem."

During this same time, Maguire was a member of executive management at Philadelphia Consolidated Holding Corporation ("PHLY"), a publicly traded company. In early 2008, Maguire was closely

(continued)

---

[6]*United States v. O'Hagan,* 521 U.S. 642, 651–652.

involved in negotiations to sell PHLY and experienced sporadic alcohol relapses. During a conversation in which McGee was trying to convince Maguire to return to AA, Maguire blurted out inside information about PHLY's imminent sale, telling McGee that he was under extraordinary pressure and that "we're selling the company . . . for three times book [value]." McGee agreed that he would keep the information that Maguire had told him confidential as he had in all previous conversations.

After this conversation, McGee purchased a substantial amount of PHLY stock on borrowed funds without disclosing to Maguire his intent to use the inside information. Before the conversation, PHLY stock represented one-tenth of McGee's stock portfolio. Less than a month later, it constituted 60 percent of his holdings. Before this information became public, McGee borrowed approximately $226,000 to help finance the purchase of PHLY shares. Shortly after the public announcement of PHLY's sale, McGee sold his shares, resulting in a $292,128 profit. On November 15, 2012, a jury found McGee guilty of violating the insider trading laws under Rule 10b-5. McGee appealed arguing that he could not be liable under the misappropriation theory absent a fiduciary relationship between a misappropriator (McGee) and his source (Maguire).

SYNOPSIS OF DECISION AND OPINION   The U.S. Court of Appeals for the Third Circuit ruled against McGee and upheld his conviction for insider trading. The court rejected McGee's defense that the misappropriation theory required a fiduciary duty between McGee and Maguire in order to trigger insider trading liability. The court held that the U.S. Supreme Court's precedent cases did not define the relationship so narrowly. Rather, any duty of loyalty, confidentiality, trust, or confidence would suffice for "recognized duties" to establish misappropriation liability.

WORDS OF THE COURT: Meaning of "Recognized Duties"   "Contrary to McGee's contention, Supreme Court precedent does not unequivocally require a fiduciary duty for all § 10(b) nondisclosure liability. In [the precedent case], though the defendant's duty to disclose undoubtedly arose from his position as a fiduciary, the Court stressed that misappropriation liability extends to those who breach a recognized duty. The Court did not unambiguously define recognized duties or cabin such duties to fiduciary relationships. The Court painted with a broader brush, referring to the requisite relationship as a fiduciary or other similar relationship, an 'agency or other fiduciary relationship,' a 'duty of loyalty and confidentiality,' and a 'duty of trust and confidence.' We will not assign a meaning to 'recognized dut[ies]' that the Court did not acknowledge.

"The Supreme Court's traditional insider trading precedent does not change this result. [The seminal cases on insider trading] call for a 'specific relationship between two parties.' Although these cases often referred to fiduciaries, they spoke also in broader terms. [For example], for traditional insider trading, there is no duty to disclose if the trader is not an agent, a fiduciary, or 'a person in whom the sellers [of the securities] had placed their trust and confidence' . . ."

Case Questions

1. Why was this considered a misappropriation theory case rather than a traditional insider case?

2. If McGee had disclosed his trading to Maguire, would that have relieved him from liability? Why or why not?

3. *Focus on Critical Thinking:* Was McGee's conduct what Congress intended to prohibit, or has Rule 10b-5 been applied too broadly? Isn't the underpinning of the Exchange Act's Section 10(b) to prevent insiders from using confidential information to profit? Why should that apply to outsiders such as McGee? If McGee had overheard the information while Maguire told someone else, would that change your analysis? Was McGee's conduct ethical? Why or why not?

Tipper-Tippee Liability

Insider trading liability is not confined to insiders or misappropriators who trade for their own account. Rule 10b-5 also applies to situations where the insider or misappropriator *tips* another who trades on the information. This is known as *tipper-tippee liability* and is

Martin Shkreli, who became a hedge-fund manager at age 32, was convicted of multiple counts of securities fraud in 2018.
©Louis Lanzano/Bloomberg/Getty Images

a criminal offense under the Exchange Act. Tippee liability can also be extended to other parties that the tippee told about the internal information who used the information to trade for their personal benefit. The tipper and tippees are all part of a tipping chain, and each may have liability under Rule 10b-5. *Tipper* liability under Rule 10b-5 is triggered if: (1) the tipper had a fiduciary duty or other type of duty to keep material nonpublic information confidential, (2) the tipper breached that duty by intentionally or recklessly relaying the information to a tippee, and (3) the tipper received a personal benefit from the tip. *Tippee* liability requires that (1) the tipper breached a duty by tipping confidential information, (2) the tippee knew or had reason to know that the tippee improperly obtained the information, and (3) the tippee, while in knowing possession of the material, nonpublic information, used the information by trading or by tipping someone else for her own benefit.

For example, suppose that Charles, the executive assistant to the chief financial officer at a public company, discovers information that is likely to adversely impact the price of the stock of the company. Because Charles owns no stock in the company, there is no possibility of direct 10b-5 liability for insider trading. However, suppose that Charles knows that his *neighbor* owns stock in the company and offers his neighbor the information in exchange for a fee. When the neighbor hears the insider information, he sells all of his stock in the company. The next day, the stock price falls by 50 percent. Both Charles (as tipper) and the neighbor (as tippee) are liable for violating Rule 10b-5 under the tipper-tippee theory. Charles benefited by earning the fee, and the neighbor benefited by selling the stock on the basis of the inside information.

Personal Benefit Test

There has been some disagreement among courts as to how valuable a personal benefit must be to trigger tipper-tippee liability. Courts define personal benefit to the tipper to include not only financial gain (e.g., a cut of the profits or payment of a fee by the tippee), but also a *nonfinancial benefit* obtained from making the tip *a gift or favor* to a relative or friend who trades based on the tip. Recent case law has divided personal benefits into two categories: (1) when the tipper makes the gift to a *nonrelative acquaintance,* or (2) when the tipper makes the tip a gift to a *relative* who later trades on the information (trading relative). When the information is a gift to nonrelated parties, the burden is on the government to show that potential gain is an objective benefit:

> If the benefit to the tipper is not financial, the government must prove that the tip generated an exchange that is objective, consequential, and represents at least a potential gain of a pecuniary or similarly valuable nature. When an unlawful tip occurs, the tippee is also liable if he knows (or should know) that the information is from a tipper who breached a fiduciary duty (such as an insider or a misappropriator) and the tippee trades or tips for personal benefit. If the tippee reveals the inside information to yet another third-party tippee, a tipper/ tippee liability chain may be established.[7]

More recently, the U.S. Supreme Court has made clear that if the tip was a gift to a trading relative, then proof "of at least a potential gain of a pecuniary or similarly valuable nature" is not required. In Case 34.3, the U.S. Supreme Court distinguishes between trading relatives and nonrelative acquaintances.

---

[7] *U.S. v. Newman,* 773 F.3 438 (2d Cir. 2014).

FACT SUMMARY Maher Kara (Maher) was an investment banker in Citigroup's health care investment banking group. He dealt with highly confidential information about mergers and acquisitions involving Citigroup's clients. Soon after Maher started at Citigroup, he began discussing aspects of his job with his older brother Michael Kara (Michael). At first he relied on Michael's chemistry background to help him grasp scientific concepts relevant to his new job. Then, while their father was battling cancer, the brothers discussed companies that dealt with innovative cancer treatment and pain management techniques. Michael began to trade on the information Maher shared with him.

Eventually, Maher began to assist Michael's trading by sharing inside information about pending mergers and acquisitions. Maher sometimes used code words to communicate corporate information to his brother. Other times, he shared inside information about deals he was not working on in order to avoid detection. Without his younger brother's knowledge, Michael fed the information to others—including Salman, Michael's friend and Maher's brother-in-law. However, neither Maher nor Michael received any payments or gifts from Salman in exchange for the information. By the time the authorities caught on, Salman had made over $1.5 million in profits that he split with another relative who executed trades via a brokerage account on Salman's behalf.

Salman was convicted and sentenced to 36 months and over $730,000 in restitution. He appealed his conviction arguing that a close family relationship is not sufficient to satisfy the personal benefit test required in a tipper-tippee insider trading theory. The Court of Appeals for the Ninth Circuit rejected Salman's appeal and Salman appealed to the U.S. Supreme Court.

SYNOPISIS OF DECISION AND OPINION The U.S. Supreme Court upheld Salman's conviction for insider trading. The Court specifically rejected any requirements that there be a concrete or tangible pecuniary or other financial benefit to the tipper in order to be convicted of trading on inside information given to a trading relative or friend. The Court explained that in such situations, the tipper benefits personally because giving a gift of trading information is the same thing as trading by the tipper followed by a gift of proceeds—a violation of insider trading laws.

WORDS OF THE COURT: Personal Benefit Test "[In our previous tipper-tippee cases], we explained that a tippee is exposed to liability for trading on inside information only if the tippee participates in a breach of the tipper's fiduciary duty. Whether the tipper breached that duty depends in large part on the purpose of the disclosure to the tippee. [T]he test . . . is whether the insider personally will benefit, directly or indirectly, from his disclosure. Thus, the disclosure of confidential information without personal benefit is not enough. In determining whether a tipper derived a personal benefit, we instructed courts to focus on objective criteria, i.e., whether the insider receives a direct or indirect personal benefit from the disclosure, such as a pecuniary gain or a reputational benefit that will translate into future earnings. This personal benefit can often be inferred from objective facts and circumstances, [including] a relationship between the insider and the recipient that suggests a *quid pro quo* from the latter, or an intention to benefit the particular recipient."

WORDS OF THE COURT: Trading Relatives "[W]hen a tipper gives inside information to a trading relative or friend, the jury can infer that the tipper meant to provide the equivalent of a cash gift. Here, by disclosing confidential information as a gift to his brother with the expectation that he would trade on it, Maher breached his duty of trust and confidence to Citigroup and its clients—a duty Salman acquired, and breached himself, by trading on the information with full knowledge that it had been improperly disclosed."

Case Questions

1. Identify the tipper and all tippees in this case.
2. What duty was breached by the tipper in this case?
3. *Focus on Critical Thinking:* If Maher had no knowledge of his brother's use of the information, would that mean he did not engage in insider trading? Why or why not?

TAKEAWAY CONCEPTS Insider Trading

- Section 10(b) and Rule 10b-5 are the primary anti-fraud provisions of the Exchange Act.
- Insiders must have possessed material, nonpublic information and must have traded on the basis of the information.

Theory of Insider Trading	Basic Requirements	Case
Traditional (classic)	Insider obtains confidential information and trades based on the information.	*United States v. Bhagat*
Misappropriation	Outsider obtains confidential information from an insider and trades without disclosure to the source of information.	*United States v. McGee*
Tipper-tippee	Insider (tipper) obtains confidential information, breaches a duty by revealing the information to an outsider (tippee), and both benefit from the tippee's trade.	*Salman v. United States*

 QUICK QUIZ Theory of Insider Trading

Which theory of insider trading is at issue?

1. Aaron is a psychologist who overhears his patient discussing a confidential corporate acquisition with a business associate on his smartphone while in the waiting room. Aaron knows that the patient is the CEO of publicly held Moors, Inc., so he acquires 50,000 shares of Moors the next day. One week later, Moors announces the acquisition and Aaron nets a $100,000 profit.

2. Edmund works in the mailroom at publicly held Gloucester Company. While he is delivering mail, he notices a document marked "Confidential" addressed to the company CFO. Before delivering it, Edmund ducks into a break room and reads the document. Based on that information, Edmund sells all of his stock in Gloucester. The next day, a federal regulatory agency reveals that Gloucester is being investigated for fraud. Gloucester's stock price drops 20 percent.

3. Cornwall is an internal accountant at publicly held Lear Corp. After discovering that Lear Corp. has just landed a multimillion-dollar contract with a new client, he conspires with his sister, Regan, to purchase 50,000 shares of Lear stock in Regan's name. The next week, Lear announces the new deal and its stock price rises by 25 percent. Cornwall and Regan split the profits.

Answers to this Quick Quiz are provided at the end of the chapter.

LO 34-5

Explain how Section 16 restrictions work in tandem with Rule 10b-5 liability.

SECTION 16 RESTRICTIONS

While Rule 10b-5 prohibits insider trading using information based on insider or tipper-tippee knowledge, **Section 16** of the Exchange Act imposes restrictions and reporting requirements on ownership positions and stock trades made by certain corporate insiders named in the statute. It was most recently amended in 1991 to clarify certain provisions and extend its reporting requirements, but fundamentally Section 16 provides transparency of all stock trades by insiders and prohibits insiders from earning short-swing profits.

Section 16(a) classifies any person who is an executive officer, a director, or a shareholder with 10 percent or more of ownership of the total stock as an *insider* and requires these insiders to file regular reports with the SEC disclosing stock ownership and trading of their company's stock. This reporting requirement allows the SEC and the investment community to monitor unusual stock activity such as whether a company's chief executive officer sells substantial portions of his stock in the company during a short time frame. Although an insider's stock sale could be the result of outside influences unrelated to the company, many investors would see it as a sign of trouble. The SEC regularly investigates such activity as it may be indicative of stock manipulation.

Section 16(b) includes a clawback provision that allows a corporation to recapture any profits earned by an insider on the purchase and sale of the company's stock that occurred within a six-month period. These earnings are called *short-swing profits,* and the prohibition against them is intended to deter insiders from profiting by manipulating the stock's short-term performance. Section 16(b) is a strict liability statute because it applies even if the insider did not use any insider information or intend any stock manipulation in realizing a short-swing profit.

Rule 10b-5 and Section 16 in Tandem

To understand how the two primary regulations of insiders work in tandem, consider the following example. Suppose that RocketCo is a publicly held corporation subject to the provisions of the Exchange Act. Armstrong is the company's chief financial officer, and Shepard is on the board of directors. The company has invested several million dollars on a 10-year research project to produce an alternate fuel product that will result in substantially lower pollution. As of the end of the last year, Armstrong and Shepard each owned 10,000 shares of RocketCo's stock. This year, they traded as follows:

January 1	Armstrong purchases 1,000 shares at $10/share. Shepard purchases 5,000 shares at $10/share.
March 1	Shepard purchases 5,000 additional shares at $10/share.
May 1	Shepard purchases 1,000 additional shares at $20/share. Armstrong sells 1,000 shares at $20/share.
November 1	Shepard sells all of his shares of RocketCo at $25/share.
December 1	RocketCo stock drops to $2/share.

Assume further that on October 30, both Armstrong and Shepard learned in advance of public knowledge that the Environmental Protection Agency (EPA) failed to give regulatory approval to RocketCo's new alternative fuel and that improvements to the formula would likely take many more years of research and testing. After the public disclosure by the EPA of the adverse decision on November 30, RocketCo's stock price dropped precipitously. These events can be analyzed in terms of Section 16 and Rule 10b-5 as follows:

■ *10b-5 liability.* Because Armstrong and Shepard are both unquestionably insiders, the information about the EPA's adverse decision cannot be used as the basis for selling RocketCo stock. The timing of Shepard's sale of a substantial portion of

RocketCo's stock gives rise to an inference that the insider information precipitated the sale of the stock. If Shepard engaged in insider trading, he faces potential civil liability to injured shareholders as well as possible criminal liability and SEC enforcement action under the Exchange Act. Because there is no indication that Armstrong's May sale of stock was related to the EPA's adverse decision, she does not face 10b-5 liability.

- *Section 16(a) coverage.* Armstrong and Shepard are both statutory insiders of RocketCo and, therefore, are required to report each and every trade to the SEC. Indeed, Section 16(a) is designed to alert investors and the SEC to potential wrongdoing when an insider takes abrupt action in trading as in the case of Shepard's selling of all of his stock.

- *Section 16(b) liability.* Because Shepard did not profit from a short-swing (his last purchase was in May and he did not sell until November), he does not have Section 16(b) liability. Armstrong's sale of 1,000 shares in May would trigger liability under Section 16(b) because she reaped profits of $10 per share when selling within six months of her purchase. Therefore, the corporation would be entitled to recapture the $10,000 profit realized by Armstrong's short-swing. Note that it is irrelevant that Armstrong did not use insider information to make the profit. Section 16(b) short-swing liability is a *strict liability* provision.

SCIENTER

LO 34-6

Identify defenses to fraud allegations.

Recall our discussion from Chapter 33 related to the statutory safe harbors afforded to issuers under the Private Securities Litigation Reform Act (PSLRA). The PSLRA safe harbors also protect those alleged to have misrepresented material facts to investors in a securities trading context (purchase or sale) that resulted in a private action brought by investors under Section 10(b) and Rule 10b-5. However, under the Exchange Act, investors face an additional hurdle of proving **scienter** as an essential element of a fraud case. The element of scienter in the context of a securities fraud case means that the seller of securities either knew or believed the represented facts to be untrue. Scienter may also be established if the seller lacked a reasonable basis for the representation. Based on the scienter requirement, courts require investor plaintiffs to *itemize* particular facts that give rise to a strong inference that the defendant acted with the required deceptive state of mind.

♟ THINKING STRATEGICALLY

©valterZ/Shutterstock

Noncompliance

We have thus far shown a wide variety of legal and business strategies in the Thinking Strategically sections of this textbook. Yet there is one particular legal strategy we have barely mentioned: noncompliance.

PROBLEM: Simply put, we can't always assume that people and firms will comply with the law because noncompliance is always an option.

STRATEGIC SOLUTION: Understand the consequences of noncompliance as a strategy. One of the most egregious examples of the legal noncompliance strategy is Wall Street investor Bernie Madoff's massive, multibillion-dollar fraudulent investment scheme.

Before his ultimate downfall, Madoff was a respected member of the Wall Street elite and the founder and chairman of a successful investment firm, Bernard L. Madoff Investment Securities LLC. But unbeknownst to his unsuspecting and innocent investors, Madoff was actually operating one of the most elaborate and enormous fraudulent investment firms in the history of Wall Street! The essence of Madoff's

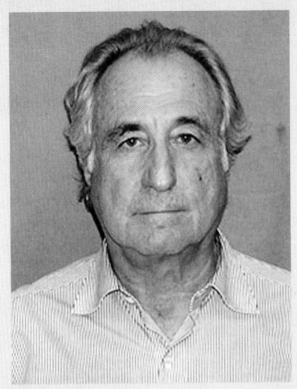

Bernard Madoff.
©Bureau of Prisons/Getty Images

subsequent investors, rather than from profits earned by the operator. In other words, instead of investing his clients' monies in legitimate investments and generating steady returns as his clients had believed, Madoff would simply deposit his clients' money into his own bank account. When clients wanted their money, Madoff "used the money in the Chase Manhattan bank account that belonged to them or other clients to pay the requested funds." Noncompliance on such a massive scale is no doubt a dangerous and reckless strategy with catastrophic legal consequences. For example, after Madoff confessed to operating the largest private Ponzi scheme in history and pleaded guilty to 11 federal crimes, the financier was sentenced to 150 years in prison and ordered to pay restitution of $170 billion to his victims.

QUESTIONS

1. In response to cases of severe domestic loss (e.g., the 9/11 attacks or the BP-*Deepwater Horizon* oil spill), Congress and other parties have created special victim compensation funds. Should a special fund be set up for victims of financial crimes (such as Madoff's scam)? Why or why not?

2. Madoff was effectively given a life sentence for his crimes. Should financial crimes be treated the same as crimes against persons (assault) or property (theft)? Why or why not?

3. Have you ever used noncompliance as a strategy in your daily life? What was the result?

fraudulent operation was a so-called Ponzi scheme.[8] In brief, a Ponzi scheme is a fraudulent investment operation in which the operator pays returns to his or her initial investors from funds paid to the operator by

---

[8]See generally, "Ponzi Schemes—Frequently Asked Questions," U.S. Securities and Exchange Commission; Jonathan Stempel, "Madoff Trustee Sues JPMorgan for $6.4 Billion," *Reuters*, Dec. 2, 2010.

KEY TERMS

Securities Exchange Act of 1934 p. 603   Federal legislation that regulates the sale of securities between investors after an investor has purchased them from a business entity issuer.

Delist p. 605   Process by which a reporting company voluntarily changes its status, thereby eliminating reporting and disclosure mandates under the Exchange Act.

Insider trading p. 606   When a corporate insider has access to certain information not available to the general investor public and uses that information as the basis for trades in the company's stock.

Insider Trading and Securities Fraud Enforcement Act p. 606   Legislation passed by Congress in 1988 that

raised the criminal and civil penalties for insider trading, increased the liability of brokerage firms for wrongful acts of their employees, and gave the Securities and Exchange Commission more power to pursue violations of insider trading.

Section 16 p. 614   Provision of the Securities Act of 1934 that imposes restrictions and reporting requirements on ownership positions and stock trades made by certain corporate insiders named in the statute.

Scienter p. 616   Specific intent to deceive, manipulate, or defraud.

CASE SUMMARY 34.1 Dirks v. SEC, 463 U.S. 646 (1983)

Liability of a Tippee

Dirks was an analyst who specialized in analyzing securities issued by insurance companies. While analyzing an insurance company, Equity Funding Co., Dirks learned from one of Equity's former officers, Secrist, and from several employees that Equity's assets had been vastly overstated through various fraudulent practices. Although the information could not be verified, Dirks told some of his investor customers about his

suspicions, and they sold their stock in Equity. Sometime later, the fraud was exposed and Equity's stock plummeted. The SEC charged Dirks with a violation of Rule 10b-5.

CASE QUESTIONS

1. Under tipper-tippee liability, could Dirks be liable as a tipper or as a tippee? Why or why not?
2. Is Dirks considered an insider?

CASE SUMMARY 34.2 United States v. Nacchio, 519 F.3d 1140 (10th Cir. 2008)

Materiality

Nacchio was the CEO of Qwest, a publicly held telecommunications company, when it completed a merger with U.S. West. After the merger, Nacchio made public statements concerning the future of the company and predicted that earnings would increase steadily. During the time of the statements, Nacchio was being told by his financial analysts that the revenue targets were too high and that it was likely that Qwest would have a significant shortfall in meeting the publicly announced targets. Other officers of the company informed Nacchio that the market for their main product was "drying up." Despite this information and urging from his executive team to disclose the problems, Nacchio

held conference calls with investors and claimed the company was "still confirming" the original predictions. While Nacchio was giving assurances to investors touting the success of Qwest, he was disposing of over 1 million shares of his own stock. When conditions at Qwest worsened, the stock collapsed. The SEC charged Nacchio with insider trading. Nacchio defended on the basis that the information he received was not material but information he received in the normal course of operations.

CASE QUESTIONS

1. Who prevails in this case and why?
2. Are all of the elements of insider trading met here?

CASE SUMMARY 34.3 United States v. Chestman, 947 F.2d 551 (2d Cir. 2008)

Insider Trading among Family Members

The president of a publicly held supermarket chain negotiated the sale of the company to a larger competitor at a substantial premium. The president told his spouse and cautioned her against revealing the information to the public. The information was passed through several family members and eventually to Loeb, who was the husband of the president's niece. Loeb informed his stockbroker, Chestman, that he had information about a certain stock that would be profitable for his company's

investors. Chestman purchased the stock for himself and for several clients who had given him general authorization to trade on their behalf. When the SEC charged Chestman with insider trading, he defended on the basis that Loeb had not breached any fiduciary duty and thus no violation of 10b-5 had occurred.

CASE QUESTIONS

1. Who prevails and why?
2. Should the rules for insider trading among family members be different? Why or why not?

CASE SUMMARY 34.4 SEC v. Switzer et al., 503 F. Supp. 756 (W.D. Okla. 1984)

Tipper-Tippee Liability

Although Barry Switzer is best known for his success as a professional and college football coach, he also had significant involvement in various business ventures in Oklahoma and Texas. While attending his son's track meet in 1982, Switzer was filling time between events and lay down in the bleachers to sunbathe. Sitting in the bleachers in front of Switzer was Platt, an executive at Texas International Corporation (TIC). Switzer and Platt knew each other and had greeted one another earlier in the track meet, but Platt was unaware of Switzer's presence in the bleachers at that time. Within earshot of Switzer, Platt discussed some of the challenges and troubles of TIC with his wife who was sitting next to him in the bleachers. The 20-minute conversation included highly confidential information about Phoenix, one of TIC's subsidiary companies.

The next day, Switzer, without expressly mentioning what he had overheard, convinced several investors to form a partnership for purposes of buying Phoenix stock. Switzer, both as an individual and as a partner with other investors, purchased large amounts of Phoenix stock. Before overhearing Platt's conversation, neither Switzer nor his partners had ever heard of Phoenix. Ultimately, Switzer and his partners earned a substantial profit from the purchase and sale of the Phoenix stock. After an investigation of Phoenix, the SEC filed a complaint alleging that Switzer was a tippee and tipped others on insider information. They charged that Switzer and his partners violated Rule 10b-5 of the Exchange Act by engaging in insider trading because Switzer had used the information that he overheard from Platt while lying in the bleachers.

CASE QUESTIONS

1. Who prevails and why? Do you believe that the SEC prosecuted Switzer because of his high profile?
2. Although Platt did not intend to disclose the information to Switzer, could Platt's choice to discuss confidential corporate matters with his spouse in a public place where one could easily overhear him constitute the requisite breach of duty required for a tipper-tippee case?
3. Did Switzer's partners have a legal and/or ethical duty to inquire about the source of Switzer's information? Why or why not? Did their actions affect the overall market? Other investors?

CASE SUMMARY 34.5 SEC v. Obus et al., 693 F.3d 276 (2d Cir. 2012)

Tipping Chain

Thomas Strickland was an assistant vice president and underwriter at General Electric Capital Corporation ("GE Capital"). In 2001, Allied Capital Corporation ("Allied") began negotiations with GE Capital concerning financing of Allied's planned acquisition of SunSource, Inc. ("SunSource"), a publicly traded company that distributed industrial products. Strickland was assigned to perform due diligence on SunSource as part of the GE Capital team working on the SunSource-Allied financing proposal. His tasks included analyzing SunSource's financial performance and other due diligence tasks. In the course of his work, Strickland learned nonpublic information about SunSource, including the basic fact that SunSource was about to be acquired by Allied. Each page of the transaction's deal book, which Strickland received, was marked "Extremely Confidential." Strickland was also bound to GE Capital's employee code of conduct, which required employees to "safeguard company property [including] confidential information about an upcoming deal." GE Capital also maintained a transaction-restricted list, containing the companies about which GE Capital and its employees possessed material, nonpublic information and which were, therefore, off-limits for securities trading.

Peter Black, a friend of Strickland's from college, worked as an analyst at Wynnefield Capital, Inc. ("Wynnefield"), which managed a group of hedge funds. In the course of his due diligence research, Strickland learned from publicly available sources that Wynnefield was a large holder of SunSource stock. After Strickland completed the Allied-SunSource acquisition due diligence, he and Black had a conversation about SunSource and, according to the SEC, Strickland revealed material, nonpublic information by telling Black that Allied was about to acquire SunSource. Immediately after Black's conversation with Strickland,

Black relayed the information he had learned to his boss at Wynnefield, Nelson Obus.

On June 8, 2001, two weeks after the conversation between Strickland and Black, Wynnefield purchased a total block of 287,200 shares, about 5 percent of SunSource's outstanding common stock. On June 11, 2001, Wynnefield sold 6,000 shares of SunSource. As a result, Wynnefield's June 8, 2001, purchase of SunSource stock nearly doubled in value, producing a paper profit to Wynnefield of over $1.3 million.

CASE QUESTIONS

1. What kind of insider trading occurred here?
2. Did Strickland violate a duty? If yes, to whom? Why or why not?

CHAPTER REVIEW QUESTIONS

1. **A primary scope of the Securities Exchange Act of 1934 is the regulation of:**
   a. Trading of securities.
   b. Original issuance (and reissuance) of securities.
   c. Exemptions.
   d. A and C.
   e. A, B, and C.

2. **Which of the following corporate actions would trigger reporting requirements under the Exchange Act?**
   a. Hiring over 500 employees
   b. Sale of 5 percent of the company's assets
   c. Listing shares on a national exchange
   d. Issuing nonvoting stock
   e. Surpassing revenue estimates by 1 percent

3. **Carla is an accountant for WidgetCo. In the course of her employment, she discovers that WidgetCo's application for a patent has been approved. Before the news is announced publicly, she calls her neighbor Sam, tells him about the patent, and instructs him to buy as much WidgetCo stock as possible. The two agree to split any profit. After the patent news is announced, WidgetCo's stock price doubles. Which of the following is true?**
   a. Carla's tip violated Rule 10b-5, but Sam has no liability.
   b. Sam is not liable because he did not benefit from the tip.
   c. Carla and Sam both violated Rule 10b-5.
   d. Sam violated Section 16 because of a short-swing.
   e. Sam and Carla have no liability under the Exchange Act.

4. **Which of the following individual(s) are considered a corporate insider for purposes of the registration and reporting under the Exchange Act?**

   I. Member of the board of directors
   II. Vice president/general counsel
   III. Stockholder owning 25 percent of the company's outstanding stock
   IV. Owner of 25 percent of the company's outstanding bonds
   a. I and II
   b. II only
   c. I, II, and III
   d. I, II, III, and IV
   e. I and IV

5. **Which of the following events must be reported to the SEC under the reporting provisions of the Exchange Act?**
   a. Tender offers
   b. Insider trading
   c. Director resolutions
   d. A and B
   e. A, B, and C

6. **Under the misappropriation theory, the investor acting on the nonpublic information need not be an insider.**
   a. True
   b. False

7. **The Securities Exchange Act of 1934 regulates the issuance of securities to investors.**
   a. True
   b. False

8. **A "reporting company" is exempt from the Exchange Act.**
   a. True
   b. False

9. Section 16 of the Exchange Act imposes restrictions and reporting requirements on ownership positions and stock trades made by certain corporate insiders named in the statute.
   a. True
   b. False

10. Rule 10b-5 applies to situations where the insider or misappropriator tips another individual who trades on the information.
    a. True
    b. False

Quick Quiz ANSWERS
Theory of Insider Trading

1. *Misappropriation.* Aaron is an outsider, but he learned of nonpublic, material information from an insider. He breached his duty of confidentiality with his patient and never disclosed the transaction to the source of information while he traded based on the information.

2. *Traditional insider trading.* Edmund, despite his position, is considered an insider. He used nonpublic, material information to avoid losses in connection with Goucester's stock price.

3. *Tipper-tippee liability.* Cornwall was the insider who gave Regan nonpublic, material information that Regan acted on. Both profited.

CHAPTER REVIEW QUESTIONS: Answers and Explanations

1. **a.** The Exchange Act covers the trading of securities. Answers *b* and *c* are incorrect because issuance and exemptions are covered by the '33 Act.

2. **c.** Only the listing of stock on a national exchange would trigger coverage. Answers *b, c,* and *d* are incorrect because the Exchange Act is not triggered based on number of employees, sale of assets, or the issuance of nonvoting stock.

3. **c.** Under Rule 10b-5, both have liability. Carla has liability as a tipper (an insider who breached a duty by revealing inside information to a third party), and Sam has liability as a tippee (one who benefited from the tip from an insider and knew the information was not public). Answer *d* is incorrect because Sam is not an insider and cannot have Section 16 liability.

4. **c.** Directors, officers, and shareholders who own more than 10 percent of the company are all insiders under the Exchange Act. Answer *d* is incorrect because debt (bond) holders are not considered insiders.

5. **d.** Directors' resolutions need not be reported to the SEC, but tender offers, insider trading, and solicitation of proxies require the company to notify the SEC.

6. **a. True.** The misappropriation theory occurs when a person misappropriates confidential information from an insider.

7. **b. False.** The Securities Exchange Act of 1934 regulates the sale of securities *after* their issuance to investors. Issuance is regulated under the '33 Act.

8. **b. False.** A company is subject to the Exchange Act's reporting requirements if: (1) its securities are listed on a public stock exchange, or (2) the number of shareholders and assets of the company reach the threshold requirement, or (3) the company filed a registration statement under the '33 Act.

9. **a. True.** Section 16(a) classifies any person who is an executive officer, a director, or a shareholder with 10 percent or more of ownership of the total stock as an *insider* and requires these insiders to file regular reports with the SEC disclosing stock ownership and trading of their company's stock.

10. **a. True.** Insider trading liability is not confined to insiders or misappropriators who trade for their own account. This is known as tipper-tippee liability and is a criminal offense.

CHAPTER 35

Regulation of Corporate Governance

©valterZ/Shutterstock

Data breaches and malicious attacks on computer systems have become almost commonplace in today's business world. Yet a recent study reveals that only 24 percent of directors at public companies rated their cybersecurity plans as above average or excellent. In this chapter's *Thinking Strategically,* we discuss specific best practices recommended by experts for developing a cybersecurity action plan.

Learning Objectives

After studying this chapter, students who have mastered the material will be able to:

35-1   Describe the impact of corporate scandals on corporate governance rules for public companies.

35-2   Articulate the major provisions of the Sarbanes-Oxley Act of 2002 and explain how they apply to public corporations.

35-3   Identify and explain the corporate governance provisions of the Dodd-Frank Act.

35-4   Differentiate between whistleblower provisions of the SOX and Dodd-Frank Acts.

CHAPTER OVERVIEW

As we have seen in the previous two chapters, the issuance and trading of a public company's securities are regulated by state and federal laws. In addition to this external regulation, public companies also are subject to certain internal constraints on **corporate governance** and to statutory safeguards intended to help ensure integrity in their securities disclosures and transactions. These internal controls and safeguards are part of a larger statutory backdrop that regulates securities, corporate governance, and financial markets.

In this chapter, we focus on two of the most prominent laws related to corporate governance. First, we discuss the Sarbanes-Oxley Act, which was passed in 2002 in reaction to well-publicized corporate wrongdoing. Second, we focus on the corporate governance provisions of the Wall Street Reform and Consumer Protection Act of 2010. More commonly known as the *Dodd-Frank Act,* this law reflects congressional efforts to stem the global financial crisis that began in late 2008 through a variety of government programs. Dodd-Frank also had a significant impact on the regulation of financial markets, which is covered in the next chapter.

GOVERNANCE OF PUBLIC COMPANIES

Public companies have been subject to regulatory safeguard requirements since the Exchange Act of 1934 was enacted. However, in the wake of multiple corporate fraud and malfeasance scandals that began to emerge in 2000—most memorably those involving Enron, MCI WorldCom, Global Crossing, HealthSouth, and Tyco—a public outcry and a growing lack of investor confidence in corporate financial disclosures caused Congress to overhaul the entire corporate governance regulatory structure by passing the **Sarbanes-Oxley Act of 2002 (SOX Act).**[1] Because so much of the SOX Act is a direct reaction to corporate fraud, it is important to have a fundamental understanding of what led to its creation.

The Enron Scandal

Of the high-profile corporate scandals that erupted at major public companies in 2000 and 2001, the one at Enron is perhaps the most notorious. The systematic looting of a corporation by its executives and the massive fraud and subsequent cover-ups that culminated in a public crash made Enron a symbol of corporate greed and arrogance. After a meteoric rise to the top, Enron's shareholders lost about $62 billion over a two-year period. Employees, believing in Enron's vision and leadership, had filled their retirement portfolios with Enron stock, only to have their savings wiped out when the company sank into bankruptcy.

Public and Regulatory Response   After an intensive investigation, federal prosecutors brought charges of wire fraud, securities fraud, conspiracy, insider trading, falsifying financial reports and tax returns, and obstruction of justice against Enron's most notorious executives. In all, 34 people either pled guilty or were convicted on charges stemming from the Enron scandal. Enron's CEO, Kenneth Lay, was convicted of fraud but died of a heart attack before he could be sentenced. Jeffrey Skilling, Enron's high-profile CFO, was sentenced to 24 years in prison. Other Enron-related defendants received sentences ranging from probation to six years of incarceration.

The public outcry over the scandal and waning public confidence in the oversight of financial frauds in the market led Congress to pass several laws to improve the quality of financial disclosure by public corporations. The Sarbanes-Oxley Act was a direct response to the Enron scandal, and it dramatically increased the responsibilities of people in charge of managing the finances of public companies, including officers, directors, and outsiders such as attorneys and accountants.[2]

The government also indicted the entire firm of Arthur Andersen on charges of obstruction of justice. The charges stemmed from the government's allegations that Andersen insiders, led by Andersen partner David Duncan, engaged in a pattern of cover-up by ordering widespread shredding of documents once they suspected that the Securities and Exchange Commission would investigate Enron. In June 2002, the firm was convicted of the obstruction charges, sentenced to pay a $500,000 fine, and banned from performing audits for publicly traded companies. The firm that had once employed 28,000 people worldwide was nearly defunct.

However, in a stunning reversal that could be described as too little too late, the U.S. Supreme Court reversed Andersen's conviction in 2005 and ordered a retrial. The decision is featured in Case 35.1. Shortly after the Court's decision, the government announced that the case would not be retried.

---

[1]15 U.S.C. § 7241.

[2]15 U.S.C. § 7241(a)(4).

CASE 35.1 Arthur Andersen LLP v. United States, 544 U.S. 696 (2005)

FACT SUMMARY As Enron Corporation's financial difficulties became public, Arthur Andersen ("Andersen"), Enron's auditor, instructed its employees to destroy documents pursuant to its established document retention policy. Andersen was indicted under a federal statute that makes it a crime to "knowingly . . . corruptly persuad[e] another person . . . with intent to . . . cause" that person to "withhold" documents from or "alter" documents for use in an "official proceeding." The jury returned a guilty verdict, and the Fifth Circuit Court of Appeals affirmed, holding that the district court's jury instructions properly conveyed the meaning of "corruptly persuades" and that the jury need not find any consciousness of wrongdoing in order to convict.

SYNOPSIS OF DECISION AND OPINION In a unanimous decision by the Supreme Court, Andersen's conviction was overturned. The Court reasoned that the instructions allowed the jury to convict Andersen without proving that the firm knew it had broken the law or that there had been a link to any official proceeding that prohibited the destruction of documents.

The Court specifically held that the jury's instruction—which stated that, even if Andersen honestly and sincerely believed its conduct was lawful, the jury could still convict them—was a serious error. The statute under which Andersen was charged used the language "knowingly . . . corruptly persuade." Andersen managers did instruct their employees to

delete Enron-related files, but those actions were within the firm's document retention policy. If the document retention policy was constructed to keep certain information private, even from the government, Andersen still was not corruptly persuading its employees to keep the information private.

WORDS OF THE COURT: Improper Jury Instruction "The jury instructions failed to convey properly the elements of a 'corrup[t] persuas[ion]' conviction. [. . .] The jury instructions failed to convey the requisite consciousness of wrongdoing. Indeed, it is striking how little culpability the instructions required. For example, the jury was told that, even if petitioner honestly and sincerely believed its conduct was lawful, the jury could convict. The instructions also diluted the meaning of 'corruptly' such that it covered innocent conduct."

Case Questions

1. Why is corrupt persuasion an important issue in this case?

2. According to the Court, does the government need to prove consciousness of wrongdoing for a conviction?

3. *Focus on Critical Thinking:* The government's action in this case was in essence a death sentence, as it caused the firm's clients and key employees to defect to competitors. Should the government have that much power before a final court hearing?

LO 35-2

Articulate the major provisions of the Sarbanes-Oxley Act of 2002 and explain how they apply to public corporations.

THE SARBANES-OXLEY ACT OF 2002 (SOX ACT)

The SOX Act provided a sweeping and comprehensive amendment to the '33 and '34 Acts to address the corporate misdeeds that became public in 2000. While substantial portions of the SOX Act are aimed at solving specific mechanism failures in auditing and other accounting procedures, the law also imposes higher levels of fiduciary responsibility for those involved in corporate governance. It was widely believed that a lack of oversight by gatekeepers, such as auditors and federal regulators, was a leading factor in the fraud and malfeasance that caused the high-profile demise of a number of large, publicly held corporations.

The SOX Act was intended to impose stricter regulation and controls on how corporations do business through regulation of three broad areas: *auditing, financial reporting,* and internal *corporate governance.* The SOX Act also provided for additional enforcement apparatus and increased penalties for violation of existing securities laws.

Reforms in the Accounting Industry

As various corporate fraud and mismanagement scandals came to the public's attention, incidents of public corporations misreporting important financial information had spiked,[3] and Congress replaced the accounting industry's self-regulation of auditing with a new federal agency called the Public Company Accounting Oversight Board (PCAOB). The PCAOB implements, administers, and enforces the SOX Act mandates. Accounting firms that audit public companies accessing U.S. capital markets are required to register with the PCAOB and are subject to its oversight and enforcement authority. The PCAOB also establishes regulations that standardize certain auditing procedures and ethical parameters.

Recall from our earlier discussion of Enron that one major contributing factor to the company's collapse was the lack of independence of the Andersen auditing partner assigned to Enron. The SOX Act seeks to increase auditor independence through setting mandatory rotation of auditing partners, banning accounting firms from providing nonauditing consulting services for public companies for which they provide auditing, and restricting accounting firm employees involved in auditing from leaving the auditing firm to go to work for an audit client.

Financial Reporting

The SOX Act makes key corporate officers more accountable for financial reporting by requiring that chief executive officers and chief financial officers personally certify the accuracy of all required SEC filings. Corporate officers must ensure that this certification is based on reliable and accurate information by maintaining internal financial fraud-detection controls that are subject to review by outside auditors. SOX Act regulations set standardized financial reporting formats and restrict certain types of accounting methods that are not transparent to auditors, such as using special offshore tax entities to hold corporate assets.

Corporate Governance

The SOX Act requires that public companies maintain audit committees composed entirely of independent directors. Each committee must contain at least one director with sufficient financial acumen to probe audits in depth. Audit committees have substantial regulatory obligations under the SOX Act. These obligations include (1) having the authority to engage, monitor, and terminate the company's outside auditing firm; (2) implementing a system of controls that involves a comprehensive examination of the audit reports and methods used by the company and outside auditors to properly report information that truly reflects the financial condition of the company; and (3) establishing a structure that facilitates communication directly between the audit committee and the auditors (not using corporate officers as a go-between).

Code of Ethics Required   The SOX Act requires public companies to establish a code of ethics and conduct for its top financial officers and prohibits certain practices such as a public corporation lending money to its officers and directors (with some narrow exceptions). In addition, officers and directors are obligated to disclose their own buying and selling of company stock within a certain time frame. To prevent the secret looting of a company by its officers, executive performance bonuses are required to be retroactively forfeited back (known as a *clawback provision*) to the company if the bonuses were tied to any financial reports that later were deemed to be false or to have been issued without appropriate controls.

---

[3]From 1990 to 1997, the number of publicly held corporations that misreported their revenue and had to restate earnings averaged 49 per year. In 2002, 330 corporations restated earnings.

SOX Act Enforcement The SOX Act also greatly expanded the scope and methods of enforcing securities law. The SEC's jurisdiction, enforcement alternatives, and enforcement budget were substantially increased by the SOX Act.

Emergency Escrow

Recognizing that many of the remedies in the SOX Act are largely useless if the corporation's assets have been looted by insiders engaged in fraud, the law specifically gives the SEC the authority to intervene in any extraordinary payments made by a company that may be the subject of an SEC investigation. Upon approval by a federal court, the SOX Act allows the SEC to force any extraordinary corporate payouts into a government-controlled emergency escrow fund that is held pending further investigation by authorities. This is a powerful weapon in the SEC's enforcement arsenal because the SOX Act does not require any formal allegation of wrongdoing as a prerequisite for intervening in an extraordinary payment.

The term *extraordinary payment* has generated some legal controversy as to what evidence is sufficient for the SEC's deployment of the escrow. In Case 35.2, now considered a landmark case in SOX law, a federal appeals court reviews the SEC's use of emergency escrow.

CASE 35.2 SEC v. Gemstar-TV Guide International, Inc., 401 F.3d 1031 (9th Cir. 2005)

FACT SUMMARY In April 2002, Gemstar-TV Guide International, Inc. ("Gemstar"), a public corporation, filed the required annual disclosures with the SEC for 2001. Gemstar's chief executive officer, Dr. Henry Yuen (Yuen), and its chief financial officer, Elsie Leung (Leung) signed the filings as required by SOX. The filing reported that the $107.6 million Gemstar previously had claimed as revenue had not actually been realized. Gemstar also revealed that it had claimed as substantial revenue receipts from a single "nonmonetary transaction" that was not properly booked.

The next day, Gemstar's stock price declined by 37 percent. Four days before these revelations, Yuen, whose compensation was tied to the performance of Gemstar's financial results, disposed of 7 million Gemstar shares, receiving an initial payment of $59 million. Simultaneous with the internal and external unraveling of these false claims, both Yuen and Leung were negotiating with Gemstar's board to resign from their respective executive positions but to remain as employees. As part of the deal, they would receive payments in cash from Gemstar—$29.48 million to Yuen and $8.16 million to Leung—plus large shares of stock and stock options.

The SEC commenced a formal investigation to determine whether Gemstar and its former and present officers and directors had engaged in actionable securities fraud by making materially false and misleading public statements regarding revenue, earnings and losses, etc., for the relevant years. In response to a formal application by the SEC, a federal court entered an order placing in escrow in excess of $37 million, representing contemplated one-time payments by Gemstar to Yuen and Leung. The parties appealed the order on the basis that the payments were negotiated and therefore not extraordinary as required under the SOX statute.

SYNOPSIS OF DECISION AND OPINION The Court of Appeals for the Fifth Circuit ruled in favor of the SEC and held that the agency was reasonable in intervening in the company's governance and finances based on the board of directors' authorization of multimillion-dollar payments to its executives, who were resigning under fire after the company had to revise its past earnings statements sharply downward. The court held that the payments to two executives constituted an extraordinary payment and triggered the SEC's right to intervene and the court's right to approve the SEC's request for an emergency escrow. The court pointed out that, although the SEC had not concluded its formal investigation, the substantial revision of earnings statements coupled

(continued)

---

with the fact that insiders were departing the company in wake of the scandal was sufficient to give the SEC intervention rights for any authorized payments by the board of directors because they were out of the ordinary in every sense of the word.

WORDS OF THE COURT: Extraordinary Payments "'Extraordinary' means, in plain language, out of the ordinary. In the context of a statute aimed at preventing the raiding of corporate assets, 'out of the ordinary' means a payment that would not typically be made by a company in its customary course of business. The standard of comparison is the company's common or regular behavior. Thus, the determination of whether a payment is extraordinary will be a fact-based and flexible inquiry. Context-specific factors such as the circumstances under which the payment is contemplated or made, the purpose of the payment, and the size of the payment may inform whether a payment is extraordinary, as the district court properly noted in this case. For example, a payment made by a company that would otherwise be unremarkable may be rendered extraordinary by unusual circumstances. . . .

"A nexus between the suspected wrongdoing and the payment itself may further demonstrate that the payment is extraordinary, although such a connection is not required. Evidence of the company's deviation from an 'industry standard'—or the practice of similarly situated businesses—also might reveal whether a payment is extraordinary."

Case Questions

1. According to the court, what was "extraordinary" about these payments?

2. Why did the SEC take action before its formal investigation was concluded?

3. *Focus on Critical Thinking:* Is the SEC's power to create an emergency escrow too overreaching? Why or why not? Could the law contain a "safety valve" that provides a hearing prior to escrow?

Substantial Penalties Violators of the SOX Act are subject to both civil penalties and criminal prosecution. For example, an officer who certifies a required financial report filing knowing that the report either is inaccurate or was not subject to required controls before the certification will be subject to criminal penalties of up to $1 million in fines and 10 years of incarceration. For cases in which certification is used as part of a larger fraudulent scheme, the penalties increase to $5 million in fines and 20 years of incarceration. The SOX Act also specifically directs the U.S. Sentencing Commission to amend sentencing guidelines to provide for harsher penalties for those convicted of securities fraud statutes.

Whistleblowers Parties that communicate information relating to illegal conduct in financial reporting or corporate governance are protected against retaliation by the company. Audit committees must have a structure in place to process and investigate any whistleblower complaints, and any party that engages in retaliation is subject to civil action and federal criminal prosecution.

Document Destruction Rules The SOX Act creates new provisions to punish individuals who destroy evidence that might be relevant to the investigation of a violation of federal securities laws. Anyone who alters, destroys, or conceals relevant documents is subject to up to 20 years of incarceration. The law applies universally to any party who has control over the documents and covers any actions performed either before, during, or after a formal investigation is commenced.

Conspiracy to Commit Fraud The definition of securities fraud was expanded by the SOX Act, and the creation of a new federal criminal law outlawing *conspiracy* to commit fraud has made it substantially easier for government prosecutors to pursue criminal fraud charges against officers and directors. The law also extended the statute of limitations for civil lawsuits to be filed by defrauded investors attempting to recover lost money.

LO 35-3

Identify and explain the corporate governance provisions of the Dodd-Frank Act.

THE DODD-FRANK ACT

As the financial crisis that began in 2008 unfolded, increasing fears of a disastrous global financial meltdown and substantial public pressure caused Congress to act on two fronts. First, the government would prevent massive business failures by providing loans to key industries to help them through the crisis. Second, through the **Dodd-Frank Wall Street Reform and Consumer Protection Act**, also known simply as *Dodd-Frank,* Congress imposed tighter restrictions on public corporations, financial markets, and the extent to which firms engaged in risky investment transactions.

Troubled Assets Relief Program (TARP)

Once it was apparent that several key industries were in financial jeopardy, Congress authorized direct government loans to corporations that were most acutely impacted by the crisis. These loans were intended primarily for large corporations in the financial services and insurance sectors (such as Citigroup and AIG), but federal loans were also extended to companies in other troubled industries such as auto manufacturers.[4] However, as a condition of the loan, recipients were required to abide by corporate governance and executive compensation mandates. The loan program and its mandates were created by the **American Recovery and Reinvestment Act of 2009,**[5] which established the **Troubled Assets Relief Program (TARP)** to administer the loans. In general, TARP loan recipients agreed to (1) impose restrictions on compensation (including bonuses) of officers; (2) form an independent compensation committee; and (3) give shareholders more say regarding the compensation of officers and directors. The TARP provisions empowered the Department of the Treasury to recover any bonuses paid that were inconsistent with the law's requirements.

TARP Today The restrictions imposed on recipients of TARP funds have led several recipients to repay the funds as soon as possible. TARP recipients are required to apply for

---

[4]These loans were dubbed "bailouts" by the media.
[5]Pub. L. No. 111-5, 123 Stat. 115 (2009).

release from the program after showing that their assets are sufficient to continue operations and lending programs. Within five months of the TARP law executive compensation mandates, approximately 34 banks were approved to pay back the TARP funds. By May 2009, investment banking firm JPMorgan Chase had paid back $25 billion, while Capital One Financial had repaid a $3.6 billion TARP loan. Interestingly, the government actually *profited* from the TARP loans. According to the U.S. Treasury Department, while $632 billion was distributed to TARP recipients, the inflows (money returned and paid to Treasury as interest, dividends, fees, or to repurchase their stock) was $740 billion within 10 years of the creation of the program.[6]

Financial Stability Oversight Council

The financial crisis of 2008 made clear how important oversight was to financial stability. The creation of a Financial Stability Oversight Council (FSOC) as a new independent body with a board of regulators was intended to provide that stability. Because the FSOC is primarily concerned with financial markets, we discuss its structure and authority in detail in Chapter 36, "Regulation of Financial Markets."

Expansion of SEC Jurisdiction and Enforcement

Dodd-Frank expanded the SEC's jurisdiction and provided it with more money and mechanisms for investigation and enforcement of securities law violations. Additionally, the SEC is not required to disclose records or information related to its investigations or inquiries. This includes surveillance, risk assessments, or other regulatory and oversight activities (except for judicial or congressional inquiry). The effective result of this change is that the federal Freedom of Information Act no longer applies to the SEC; the SEC can refuse to supply documents it deems to be part of its regulatory and oversight activities.

Corporate Governance

Although much of Dodd-Frank is related to financial regulation, some of its provisions impose new corporate governance regulations not just on Wall Street banks but also on all Main Street public corporations. However, Dodd-Frank also includes some limited regulatory relief from Sarbanes-Oxley for the smallest public corporations. Dodd-Frank's corporate governance provisions center on transparency for the investment community and disclosures to the SEC, primarily in the areas of compensation and board structure.

Executive Compensation   Dodd-Frank requires companies to adopt a "say-on-pay" policy through a nonbinding resolution in their proxy statements asking shareholders whether they approve the compensation or any severance agreement provision (i.e., golden parachute) for their executive management. Dodd-Frank also requires that each reporting company's annual statement contain a clear exposition of the relationship between executive compensation and the issuer's financial performance. The disclosure must give investors an easy way to compare executive compensation and firm performance over time.

Compensation Clawbacks   Recall that under Sarbanes-Oxley, in the event a corporation is obliged to restate its financial statements due to "misconduct," the CEO and CFO must return to the corporation any bonus, incentive, or equity-based compensation they received during the 12 months following the original issuance of the restated financials, along with any profits they realized from the sale of corporate stock during that period. Dodd-Frank significantly expands this provision.

---

[6]U.S. Department of the Treasury, *Monthly Report to Congress, Troubled Asset Relief Program* (June 2019).

Employee-CEO Pay Ratio Disclosure Requirement   In 2015, the SEC issued a rule required by the Dodd-Frank Act that requires a company to disclose (1) the median of the annual total compensation of all its employees except the CEO, (2) the annual total compensation of its CEO, and (3) the ratio of those two amounts. A company is permitted to use its total employee population or a statistical sampling of that population and/or other reasonable methods. For example, a company chooses between using the median of its employee population or using a sample of annual total compensation as determined under existing executive compensation rules as reported in its payroll or tax records. Because the rule did not require disclosures until 2017, we are only now seeing the disparities the rule was intended to make transparent. The *Wall Street Journal* recently reported that food giant Kraft Heinz Company's CEO made $4.2 million in 2016. That is 91 times its median worker's compensation of $46,000. Whirlpool Corporation's median workers earned $19,906, while the company's CEO was paid about 356 times as much ($7.08 million).[7]

Board Structure Disclosure   Rules mandated by Dodd-Frank require companies to disclose their board leadership structure in their SEC filings. Specifically, the law requires transparency in disclosing whether the company uses a split structure (i.e., two different persons holding CEO and board chair positions) or a combined structure (i.e., same person for the CEO and chair positions). The law does not endorse or prohibit either method. Instead, Dodd-Frank opted for disclosure rather than a substantive mandate that the two positions be separated. In any case, a company must also disclose the reasoning behind the structure.

LO 35-4

Differentiate between whistleblower provisions of the SOX and Dodd-Frank Acts.

Dodd-Frank Whistleblower Provisions

An important part of the new regulatory scheme is the protection of whistleblowers who report illegal conduct committed by employees, directors, and executives of the company. In this chapter, we cover the structure of the Dodd-Frank whistleblower provision and the statutory definition of a whistleblower. In the next chapter, we discuss whistleblower provisions related to financial markets in more detail.

Fundamentally, the Dodd-Frank whistleblower provisions are based on a bounty plan. That is, money is awarded to individuals who provide information that leads to an SEC enforcement action in which certain sanctions are levied. Whistleblower rewards range from 10 to 30 percent of the recovery. The law also has a strong anti-retaliation provision that protects the job status of SEC whistleblowers and promises confidentiality for them. In the event an employee is terminated for whistleblowing, the Dodd-Frank anti-retaliation provision allows the whistleblower to sue for up to double back pay.

Whistleblower Controversy   One significant legal controversy surrounding the whistleblower provision was created when the SEC defined a whistleblower as anyone who reported the illegal conduct to the SEC, to another federal agency, *or to the company's internal management.* One appellate court found that the SEC's interpretations were entitled to deference.[8] However, a conflict arose among the circuit courts when another appellate court found that the express words of Dodd-Frank indicate that a whistleblower only qualifies for anti-retaliation protection if he or she reported the violations *to the SEC* before the retaliation.[9] In Case 35.3, the U.S. Supreme Court resolves the conflict as it analyzes the statutory definition versus the SEC's interpretation of Dodd-Frank's whistleblower provision.

---

[7]T. Francis, "In a First, U.S. Firms Reveal Workers' Pay Gap with CEO," *The Wall Street Journal,* Feb. 28, 2018.

[8]*Berman v. Neo@Ogilvy LLC,* 801 F.3d 145, 155 (2nd Cir. 2013).

[9]*Asadi v. G.E. Energy (USA), L.L.C.,* 720 F.3d 620, 630 (5th Cir. 2013).

FACT SUMMARY Somers worked as vice president of Digital Realty Trust ("Digital Realty") from 2010 to 2014. In the course of his duties, Somers discovered possible violations of securities laws by Digital Realty, which caused him to file several reports to senior management. Soon after these reports were filed, he was terminated by Digital Realty's executive management. Somers did not report his concerns to the Securities and Exchange Commission (SEC) before he was terminated. Somers then sued Digital Realty alleging violations of state and federal laws, including the anti-retaliation protections created by the Dodd-Frank Act. Digital Realty argued that because Somers did not report the possible violations to the SEC, he was not a whistleblower as defined in Dodd-Frank and thus not entitled to protection under its provisions. Somers argued that the SEC was entitled to enforce its interpretation of the statute and that the SEC's interpretation was more consistent with Dodd-Frank's intent and purpose. The trial court ruled in favor of Somers stating that the provision extends to all who make disclosures of suspected violations, regardless of whether the disclosures are made internally or to the SEC. The court of appeals upheld the trial court's decision, and Digital Realty appealed to the U.S. Supreme Court.

SYNOPSIS OF DECISION AND OPINION The U.S. Supreme Court reversed the lower court's decision and ruled in favor of Digital Realty. The Court held that the anti-retaliation provision for whistleblowers in the Dodd-Frank Act protects only individuals who report alleged misconduct to the SEC. The Court reasoned that Dodd-Frank explicitly defines a whistleblower as any individual who provides information on possible securities violations *to the Commission,* and this definition is corroborated by Dodd-Frank's purpose to aid the SEC's enforcement efforts by incentivizing people to tell the SEC about violations. Whistleblowers who report violations to other federal agencies or an internal supervisor are not within the scope of this express definition of whistleblower in the Dodd-Frank Act. Because the language of the statute is clear, the SEC is not permitted its own interpretation.

WORDS OF THE COURT: Statutory Definition of Whistleblower "When a statute includes an explicit definition, we must follow that definition, even if it varies from a term's ordinary meaning. . . . Our charge in this review proceeding is to determine the meaning of 'whistleblower' in Dodd-Frank's anti-retaliation provision. The definition section of the statute supplies an unequivocal answer: A 'whistleblower' is 'any individual who provides . . . information relating to a violation of the securities laws *to the Commission*' (emphasis added). Leaving no doubt as to the definition's reach, the statute instructs that the 'definition shall apply in this section,' that is, throughout the [Dodd-Frank statute]."

WORDS OF THE COURT: Statute's Design and Purpose "Dodd-Frank's purpose and design corroborate our comprehension of [the] reporting requirement. [According to its legislative history] the 'core objective' of Dodd-Frank's robust whistleblower program, as Somers acknowledges, is to motivate people who know of securities law violations to tell the SEC. By enlisting whistleblowers to assist the Government in identifying and prosecuting persons who have violated securities laws, Congress undertook to improve SEC enforcement and facilitate the Commission's recovery of money for victims of financial fraud. To that end, [the statute] provides substantial monetary rewards to whistleblowers who furnish actionable information to the SEC."

Case Questions

1. Why didn't the Court defer to the SEC's interpretation?

2. Why does the Court examine Dodd-Frank's "core objective"?

3. *Focus on Critical Thinking:* Somers argued that the Court's interpretation creates "an incredibly unusual statutory scheme in that identical misconduct—i.e., retaliating against an employee for internal reporting—will go punished or not based on the happenstance of a separate report to the SEC, of which the wrongdoer may not even be aware." Is that a compelling argument? Is the Court going too far in enforcing the letter of the law rather than the public policy behind the whistleblower provisions?

Cybersecurity and Disclosures

PROBLEM: According to research by the Poneman Institute,[10] the global average cost of a data breach is $3.62 million. The average cost for each lost or stolen record containing sensitive and confidential information is $141. Although most boards have robust processes for addressing their most pressing responsibilities, such as financial planning and compliance, processes related to cybersecurity issues such as regular discussions about cyber risks were lacking or nonexistent. In a study published in *Harvard Business Review,* researchers found that only 24 percent of directors at public companies rated cybersecurity as above average or excellent.[11]

STRATEGIC SOLUTION: Corporate governance experts suggest a two-prong approach involving *planning* and *disclosures.* First, the board of directors should take specific planning steps to examine and plan for risk in the same way that they plan for other risks—through a specialized subcommittee. Second, the board should closely examine the SEC's recent Interpretation Action[12] for guidance on preparing disclosures about cybersecurity risks and incidents.

BOARD PLANNING

A board of directors can take the following steps to minimize cybersecurity risks:

- Prioritize cybersecurity issues by forming a subcommittee (similar to an audit committee) to ask questions and determine whether appropriate processes are in place.
- Hold executive management accountable for evaluating cybersecurity risks and maintaining prevention and response plans.

- Include cybersecurity debriefings as a regular agenda item at full board meetings. The subcommittee may report on (1) authorizing investments in data security and infrastructure and (2) consulting with external experts on prevention and response plans.
- Use a risk calculator to assess the potential cost of a cyber attack; one may be found at https://databreachcalculator.mybluemix.net/

DISCLOSURES

A board of directors should consider the following guidelines regarding disclosure of cybersecurity risks and incidents:

- Public companies should disclose the role of boards of directors in cyber risk management, at least when cyber risks are material to a company's business.
- Companies should have identifiable controls that ensure important cyber risk and incident information is a significant factor in disclosure decisions.
- Cyber risks and incidents may constitute material nonpublic information implicating insider-trading laws. This means that the SEC expects companies to examine their controls and procedures, not only in regard to their securities law disclosure obligations but also in terms of their reputation regarding sales of securities by executives.
- The SEC also advises companies to carefully consider how disclosures of cyber incidents to affected individuals or transaction partners as part of due diligence aligns with disclosures made publicly to investors.

QUESTIONS

1. Have you ever been the victim of fraud because of a data breach? How did the business notify you of the breach and what did they do to remedy the situation?
2. Should every business have a cybersecurity strategy? In what ways could small business owners tailor the above strategy to fit their own needs?

---

[10]Poneman Institute, "2017Annual Cost of Data Breach Study," available at https://www.ibm.com/security/data-breach.

[11]J. Cheng and B. Groysberg, "Why Boards Aren't Dealing with Cyberthreats," *Harvard Business Review,* Feb. 22, 2017.

[12]SEC Release Nos. 33-10459; 34-82746, "Commission Statement and Guidance on Public Company Cybersecurity Disclosures," Feb. 26, 2018.

KEY TERMS

Corporate governance p. 622   The process used by corporate officers and directors to establish lines of responsibility, approval, and oversight among key stakeholders and set out rules for making corporate decisions.

Sarbanes-Oxley Act of 2002 (SOX Act) p. 623
Amendments to the 1933 and 1934 Securities Acts that impose stricter regulation and controls on how corporations do business, through regulation of auditing, financial reporting, and internal corporate governance.

Dodd-Frank Wall Street Reform and Consumer Protection Act p. 628   Federal legislation designed to overhaul the regulation of public companies and U.S. financial services and markets *(ch. 35)*. A law enacted in 2010, commonly referred to as *Dodd-Frank*, that made sweeping reforms to the financial regulatory system, including expanded SEC enforcement powers, the creation of a new Financial Stability Oversight Council, and a new bounty plan for whistleblowers *(ch. 36)*.

American Recovery and Reinvestment Act of 2009 p. 628   Federal legislation that created a loan program and underlying mandates for corporations most acutely impacted by the financial crisis that began in 2008; also established the Troubled Assets Relief Program (TARP) to administer the loans.

Troubled Assets Relief Program (TARP) p. 628 A program established by the American Recovery and Reinvestment Act of 2009 to purchase assets and equity from financial institutions and thereby strengthen the U.S. financial sector.

CASE SUMMARY 35.1 SEC v. Platforms Wireless, 617 F.3d 1072 (9th Cir. 2010)

Extraordinary Payments

Platforms was a publicly traded company that developed new technology to provide cellular service to large geographic territories. Martin was the chairman and CEO of Platforms, but he also was an officer in another company called Intermedia that provided consulting services. In two transactions, Platforms transferred 17.45 million shares to Intermedia as payment for Intermedia consulting fees. At least two of Intermedia's officers were also officers in Platforms. The SEC filed an enforcement action alleging that Platforms had misrepresented material facts about the company in a press release. When the SEC discovered the stock transfer, it claimed that the proceeds of $1.7 million constituted an extraordinary payment.

CASE QUESTIONS

1. Was the stock transfer an extraordinary payment under the SOX Act?
2. If it were shown that the stock transfer was a legitimate transaction, how would that affect your analysis?

CASE SUMMARY 35.2 Leon v. IDX Systems Corporation, 464 F.3d 951 (9th Cir. 2006)

Whistleblower Protection

Leon was the director of medical information at IDX systems. After IDX began an investigation of Leon's activities, it required him to turn over his company-issued laptop computer. When Leon refused, IDX terminated his employment and required him to return his laptop computer. After initial resistance, Leon turned over his laptop. A forensic examination of the laptop showed that files had been deleted and that a user had deployed special software in an attempt to "write over" and hide documents. Leon eventually filed suit claiming that IDX terminated his employment in violation of the whistleblower provision of the SOX Act and that his termination was based on the fact that he had evidence on his laptop about IDX improprieties.

CASE QUESTIONS

1. Is Leon protected under the SOX Act even if there is no evidence that he actually had information about unlawful IDX activities?
2. Could Leon be in violation of the SOX Act document destruction rules for deleting files?

CASE SUMMARY 35.3 *In re* Huffy Corp. Securities Litigation, 577 F. Supp. 2d 968 (D.C. S.D. Ohio 2008)

PSLRA

Huffy is a public company that engaged in negotiations in 2002 with Gen-X, a Canadian manufacturer of snowboards, inline skates, and other sporting goods. Huffy reported the acquisition in a press release and made several forward-looking statements concerning the extensive due diligence used by Huffy's executive team in evaluating the purchase. Huffy discovered soon after purchasing Gen-X that Gen-X's costs were not controlled, its inventory was in a state of disrepair, its invoices had not been collected, and its bills were unpaid. Investors sued Huffy alleging that its officers had engaged in materially false and misleading statements through their reports and press releases.

1. Analyze the investors' claim under Section 10b-5. Are Huffy's statements about due diligence considered "material"?
2. What facts would help the investors prove scienter under the PSLRA?

CASE SUMMARY 35.4 Asadi v. GE Energy, 720 F.3d 620 (5th Cir. 2013)

Whistleblowers

In 2006, Asadi accepted GE Energy's offer to serve as its Iraq Country Executive and relocated to Amman, Jordan. At a meeting in 2010, while serving in this capacity, Iraqi officials informed Asadi of their concern that GE Energy hired a woman closely associated with a senior Iraqi official to curry favor with that official in negotiating a lucrative joint venture agreement. Asadi, concerned that this alleged conduct violated the Foreign Corrupt Practices Act, reported the issue to his supervisor and to the GE Energy ombudsperson for the region. Shortly following these internal reports, Asadi received a "surprisingly negative" performance review. GE Energy pressured him to step down from his role as Iraq Country Executive and accept a reduced role in the region with minimal responsibility. Asadi did not comply and, approximately one year after he made the internal reports, GE Energy fired him.

Asadi filed a lawsuit alleging that GE Energy violated Dodd-Frank's whistleblower protection provision by terminating his employment following his internal reports of the possible violation of federal law. GE Energy filed a motion for summary judgment on the basis that Asadi's whistleblowing did not fit the definition of a whistleblower under Dodd-Frank because the statute requires the wrongdoing to be reported to the SEC in order to be eligible for anti-retaliation protections. The trial court ruled in favor of GE Energy and dismissed Asadi's lawsuit. On appeal, Asadi argued that the SEC's published regulations interpreted the definition of a Dodd-Frank whistleblower broadly enough to cover Asadi.

CASE QUESTIONS

1. Who prevails and why?
2. What U.S. Supreme Court case helps you answer this question?

CHAPTER REVIEW QUESTIONS

1. **The Sarbanes-Oxley Act of 2002:**
   a. Established an emergency escrow procedure.
   b. Was a response to corporate scandals, including the one at Enron.
   c. Invalidated the U.S. Supreme Court's ruling in favor of the Arthur Andersen firm.
   d. A and B.
   e. A, B, and C.

2. **The SOX Act sought to increase auditor independence through:**
   a. Setting mandatory rotation of auditing partners.
   b. Banning accounting firms from providing non-auditing consulting services for public companies for which they provide auditing.

   c. Restricting accounting firm employees involved in auditing from leaving the auditing firm to go to work for an audit client.
   d. All of the above.
   e. None of the above.

3. **High Flyer Inc., a public company, made an extraordinary corporate payout of a bonus to its CEO while the company was under investigation by the SEC for fraud. Under SOX, the SEC may:**
   a. Claw back the bonus into an emergency escrow fund.
   b. Require High Flyer to register the payment.
   c. Terminate the auditing company.
   d. Assess civil penalties against directors who authorized the bonus.
   e. Not take any enforcement action.

4. Accounting firms that audit public companies accessing U.S. capital markets are required to register with the:
   a. SEC.
   b. Public Company Accounting Oversight Board.
   c. American Institute of Certified Public Accountants.
   d. Public Accountability Commission.
   e. U.S. Department of the Treasury.

5. Drake, the chief financial officer of a public company called BigCo, becomes aware of a potential fraud. Instead of reporting it, he destroys the relevant documents. One year later, the SEC launches an investigation into insider trading at BigCo and the document destruction is uncovered. If Drake is charged with destroying the documents, who prevails?
   a. Drake, because the documents were destroyed prior to the SEC investigation.
   b. Drake, because he is an insider and had the right to destroy the documents.
   c. The government, because Drake would have to have certified the financial statements.
   d. The government, because under the SOX Act destroying documents, even prior to the investigation, triggers culpability.
   e. A and B

6. The SOX Act was a congressional response to the financial crisis of 2008.
   a. True
   b. False

7. The SOX Act requires that public companies maintain audit committees composed entirely of independent directors.
   a. True
   b. False

8. The SOX Act emergency escrow provisions are intended to prevent looting by corporate insiders.
   a. True
   b. False

9. The Dodd-Frank Act was the first law to criminalize destruction of documents by insiders.
   a. True
   b. False

10. The U.S. Supreme Court has ruled that the language of Dodd-Frank requires one to report unlawful conduct to the SEC in order to be protected under the whistleblower provisions.
    a. True
    b. False

CHAPTER REVIEW QUESTIONS: Answers and Explanations

1. d. The SOX Act established an emergency escrow fund and was a direct response to the Enron scandal.

2. d. The SOX Act requires rotation, bans consulting by auditing firms, and restricts accountants from job jumping from a firm to a client.

3. a. The SOX Act gives the SEC the power to preserve corporate assets and prevent looting of the corporation by creating an emergency escrow fund for extraordinary payments, such as bonuses.

4. b. The SOX Act created the PCAOB to register and regulate auditing firms that work for public companies.

5. d. Individuals may be criminally and civilly liable for any destruction of documents of a publicly held corporation even if it is done without any current threat of investigation.

6. b. False. The SOX Act was a congressional response to the Enron, MCI, HealthSouth, and Tyco scandals from 2002, not to the financial crisis of 2008.

7. a. True. Under the SOX Act, company audit committees are made up of independent directors.

8. a. True. Any extraordinary payment qualifies for the SOX Act emergency escrow provisions.

9. b. False. The SOX Act was the first law to criminalize destruction of documents by insiders.

10. a. True. In *Digital Realty,* the U.S. Supreme Court ruled that reporting unlawful conduct to the SEC was a prerequisite for protection as a whistleblower.

CHAPTER 36

Regulation of Financial Markets

♟ THINKING STRATEGICALLY

©valterZ/Shutterstock

In this chapter we shall survey financial markets and the legal regulation of systemic financial risks—large-scale risks that could wipe out or destroy an entire industry, not just a single firm. This chapter's *Thinking Strategically* will explore a real-world example of strategic behavior called moral hazard.

Learning Objectives

After studying this chapter, students who have mastered the material will be able to:

36-1 Define what a financial market is.

36-2 Distinguish between primary and secondary capital markets.

36-3 Identify the main parties in capital markets and the role played by each one.

36-4 Articulate the problem of systemic risk.

36-5 Summarize the key provisions of Dodd-Frank relating to the problem of systemic risk and the regulation of financial markets.

36-6 Explain how Dodd-Frank protects whistleblowers.

CHAPTER OVERVIEW

This chapter focuses on the strategic problem of systemic risk. In today's modern economy, many business firms are so large and interconnected that a collapse in one part of the financial market could threaten the entire financial system. Therefore, in addition to the landmark federal laws we have already studied in previous chapters, such as the Securities Act of 1933 (Chapter 33), the Securities Exchange Act of 1934 (Chapter 34), and the SOX Act of 2002 (Chapter 35), in this chapter we will focus on the Dodd-Frank Act of

Wall Street is the capital of U.S. financial markets.
©Marcio Jose Bastos Silva/Shutterstock

2010, a law enacted by Congress to solve the problem of systemic risk. In this chapter, students will learn:

- What a financial market is.

- The domain of primary and secondary markets and the main parties in capital markets.

- What the problem of systemic risk entails.

- The main provisions of the Dodd-Frank Act.

- How Dodd-Frank is designed to address the problem of systemic risk.

TYPES OF FINANCIAL MARKETS

LO 36-1

Define what a financial market is.

In daily parlance, the term "market" is often used to refer to *exchanges* (e.g., a stock exchange or a commodity exchange), which are organizations that facilitate trade in securities or commodities. Two of the best-known exchanges are the New York Stock Exchange (NYSE), located on Wall Street in lower Manhattan, and the Chicago Mercantile Exchange (CME), located at 20 South Wacker Drive in downtown Chicago. However, an exchange need not have a physical location. Some exchanges, like the NASDAQ, are run entirely using electronic systems.

This chapter, however, will focus on *financial markets* and the problem of systemic risk. A **financial market** is a highly regulated institution in which people and firms trade such things as securities (such as stocks and bonds), commodities (such as precious metals and agricultural goods), and domestic and foreign currencies (such as the U.S. dollar and the British pound) at prices that reflect supply and demand as well as publicly and privately available information. Regardless of whether the items being traded are securities, commodities, or currencies, financial markets are regulated by a wide variety of federal laws.

Although there are many types of financial markets, the term "financial markets" is most often used to refer to *capital markets,* that is, highly regulated markets that specialize in long-term debt or equity financing of business ventures. Capital markets, in turn, consist of *stock markets,* which provide financing through the issuance and subsequent trading of shares or stock, as well as *bond markets,* which provide financing through the issuance and subsequent trading of bonds.

In addition to capital markets, there are many other types of financial markets. Consider some of the examples below:

- *Commodity markets,* which are designed to facilitate the trading of such physical commodities as precious metals (e.g., silver and gold) and agricultural products (e.g., wheat and pork bellies).

- *Futures markets,* which provide standardized "forward contracts" for trading commodities at some future date.

- *Money markets,* which are designed to provide short-term debt financing and investment.

- *Derivative markets,* which provide instruments for the management of various financial risks.

- *Foreign exchange markets,* which facilitate the trading of foreign currencies like the British pound, the Canadian dollar, or the Mexican peso, just to name a few.

Figure 36.1 shows various types of financial markets.

FIGURE 36.1 Taxonomy of Financial Markets

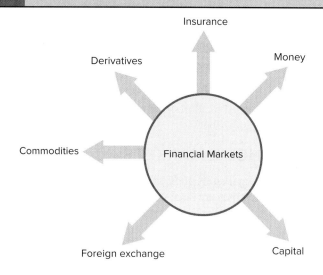

TAKEAWAY CONCEPT Types of Financial Markets

A financial market is a highly regulated institution in which people and firms trade securities, commodities, currencies, and other things of value at prices that reflect supply and demand as well as publicly and privately available information.

PRIMARY AND SECONDARY CAPITAL MARKETS

LO 36-2

Distinguish between primary and secondary capital markets.

Capital markets consist of *primary markets* and *secondary markets.* In the **primary market**, firms (called *issuers*) raise capital by selling securities in public markets (to the general investment community) or in private placements (to limited groups of investors, such as venture capitalists or institutional investors). Issuing securities to the public for the first time is known as an *initial public offering,* or *IPO.* A firm is said to "go public" when it sells its voting common shares for the first time to outside investors through a public market such as the New York Stock Exchange (NYSE). As part of the IPO process, a firm must prepare a mandatory registration statement that discloses important facts about the offering to potential investors. Once a firm sells shares to the public, it becomes subject to extensive and periodic disclosure and reporting requirements imposed by various federal and state securities laws. (These laws are discussed in detail in Chapters 33, 34, and 35.)

In the **secondary market**, the trading of already issued securities, does not raise capital for the issuing business. Instead, investors sell to other investors with the goal of making a profit or preventing a loss. Liquidity is a crucial aspect of securities that are traded in secondary markets. *Liquidity* refers to the ability to convert a security into cash. Securities with an active secondary market mean that there are many buyers and sellers at a given point in time, so such securities are highly liquid. Investors in secondary markets benefit from such liquid securities because they can sell their assets whenever they want; an illiquid security, by contrast, may force the seller to get rid of an asset at a large discount.

Firms that do business in financial markets such as the primary and secondary markets described above are regulated by a wide variety of federal laws and regulations that are enforced through a complex network of federal administrative agencies and regulatory bodies, including the Securities and Exchange Commission (SEC), the Federal Reserve, the Office of the Comptroller of the Currency, and the Federal Trade Commission (FTC). All of these agencies have some degree of jurisdiction over various aspects of global financial markets. The regulated financial transactions include not only the sale of securities but also such things as commercial and consumer loans, investment schemes, credit and insurance markets, and commodities exchanges.

TAKEAWAY CONCEPTS Primary and Secondary Capital Markets

■ Capital markets consist of primary markets and secondary markets. In the *primary market,* firms (called issuers) raise capital by selling securities to investors.

■ In the *secondary market,* investors sell to other investors with the goal of making a profit or preventing a loss.

THE MAIN PARTIES IN CAPITAL MARKETS

Both primary and secondary capital markets function through the interaction of three parties: *investors, issuers,* and *intermediaries.*

Investors seek a return from their investment based on the perceived value of the securities in which they invest. Investors come in all shapes and sizes, so to speak, including *individual investors,* who hold securities directly or through a brokerage firm, and *institutional investors,* such as pension funds and mutual funds.

Issuers are those institutions and entities that sell securities to investors. They include business corporations, state and local governments, and other entities that are seeking to raise capital through the sale of securities or bonds.

Intermediaries are financial institutions that provide services for investors and issuers related to securities transactions. Most commonly, intermediaries are brokerage firms (referred to as *broker-dealers*) that buy and sell securities on behalf of a client. Intermediaries also include mutual funds, investment banks, and some commercial banks.

The complex interaction between investors, issuers, and intermediaries is shown in Figure 36.2.

LO 36-3

Identify the main parties in capital markets and the role played by each one.

FIGURE 36.2 | The Main Parties in Private Capital Markets

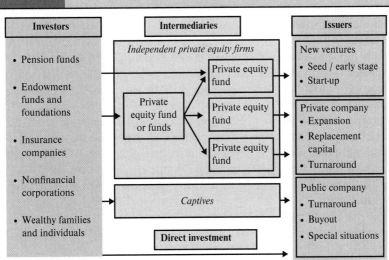

TAKEAWAY CONCEPT The Main Parties in Capital Markets

Primary and secondary capital markets function through the interaction of three parties: investors, issuers, and intermediaries.

 Quick Quiz Main Parties in the Securities Market

Cardi B calls her stockbroker at Bodak Brokers and finds out that Offset, Inc. is raising capital by selling its stock to the public. She believes the stock is priced low and she will make a profit in the future, so she orders her broker to purchase 1,000 shares of Offset, Inc. stock. Which party is the investor, which is the issuer, and which is the intermediary?

Answers to this Quick Quiz are provided at the end of the chapter.

Cardi B.
©Jstone/Shutterstock

LO 36-4

Articulate the problem of systemic risk.

THE STRATEGIC PROBLEM OF SYSTEMIC RISK

Thus far, we have focused on the individual parts of financial markets. Now let's take a step back and try to see the financial system as a whole. Today's modern financial markets are composed of business firms and financial institutions that are highly interconnected. A large firm that is interconnected with others can be a source of **systemic risk**, which is the possibility that an event at the firm could trigger severe instability in financial markets or the collapse of an entire industry or economy.

The classic example of a systemic risk is a bank run that has a cascading effect on other banks that are owed money by the first bank in trouble. As depositors sense the ripple effects of default, a panic can spread through a market and lead to a sudden "flight to quality," which in turn creates many sellers (but few buyers) for illiquid assets.

Governments and monitoring institutions, such as the U.S. Securities and Exchange Commission and central banks, often put policies and rules in place with the justification of safeguarding the interests of the market as a whole. In plain English, this means that some companies are viewed as "too big to fail." These are companies that are large relative to their respective industries or that make up a significant part of the overall economy.

Systemic risk should not be confused with market, or price, risk, which is specific to the item being bought or sold. Unlike a systemic risk, the effects of a market risk are isolated to the entities dealing in that specific item. This kind of risk can be mitigated with various hedging strategies.

Systemic risk was a major contributor to the financial crisis of 2008 and led to the passage of Dodd-Frank Act (Figure 36.3).

FIGURE 36.3 **The Dodd-Frank Wall Street Reform and Consumer Protection Act**

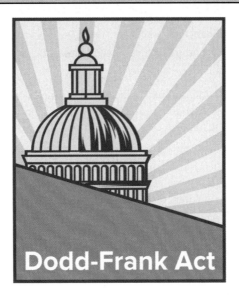

Dodd-Frank Act

TAKEAWAY CONCEPTS The Strategic Problem of Systemic Risk

Systemic risk is the risk of collapse of the entire financial market as opposed to the risk associated with any one part of the financial system.

DODD-FRANK

In response to the 2008 financial crisis and the problem of systemic risk, Congress enacted, and President Obama signed into law, the **Dodd-Frank Wall Street Reform and Consumer Protection Act**, named after its principal sponsors in Congress, Senator Chris Dodd and Representative Barney Frank. This law, commonly referred to as *Dodd-Frank,* made sweeping reforms to the financial regulatory system. We will highlight some of the major provisions of the Dodd-Frank Act below, including expanded SEC enforcement powers, the creation of a new (and controversial) Financial Stability Oversight Council, and a new bounty plan for whistleblowers.

Expanded SEC Jurisdiction and Enforcement

The **Securities and Exchange Commission (SEC)** is an independent agency consisting of five commissioners appointed by the president. The SEC conducts most of its work in 11 regional offices located across the United States. It not only has the power to enforce federal securities laws; it also has the authority to regulate all aspects of U.S. capital markets, including the issuance and trading of securities in primary and secondary markets. In particular, companies that issue publicly traded shares must submit quarterly and annual reports to the SEC. These mandatory disclosures are essential to many investors, who use the information in these reports to make crucial decisions before investing in capital

LO 36-5

Summarize the key provisions of Dodd-Frank relating to the problem of systemic risk and the regulation of financial markets.

markets. Moreover, a firm that makes material misstatements on its reports or is involved in other fraudulent activities could be subject to an SEC enforcement action and to lawsuits by investors.

Broadly speaking, the objectives of these disclosure requirements are usually as follows:

- Creating *confidence* in financial markets;
- Maintaining the integrity and *stability* of financial markets; and
- Securing the appropriate degree of *protection* for investors.

Among other things, Dodd-Frank expanded the SEC's jurisdiction and provided it with a powerful set of new tools for the investigation and enforcement of securities law violations. These new tools include the following:

- *Secret investigations.* Under Dodd-Frank, the SEC is no longer required to disclose its records or any other information related to its ongoing investigations or inquiries, including surveillance, risk assessments, or other regulatory and oversight activities (except for judicial or congressional inquiry). Effectively, this means that the federal Freedom of Information Act (FOIA) no longer applies to the SEC, so the SEC can refuse to supply documents it deems as being part of its regulatory and oversight activities.
- *Fiduciary duty of broker-dealers.* Dodd-Frank authorizes the SEC to impose a fiduciary duty on brokers and dealers when providing personalized investment advice to retail customers—the same standard that is applicable to investment advisers.
- *Hedge funds.* Advisers to hedge funds and private equity funds must register with the SEC as investment advisers and provide information about their trades and portfolios necessary to assess systemic risk.

Financial Stability Oversight Council

In addition to expanding the SEC's investigation and enforcement powers, Dodd-Frank also created the **Financial Stability Oversight Council (FSOC)**, a new and independent body with a board of regulators to address dangerous risks to global financial markets posed by risky investments or the actions of large, interconnected financial institutions. The FSOC monitors the stability of the U.S. financial system and responds to emerging threats to that system.

President Obama signs the Dodd-Frank Act into law with Senator Dodd (center) and Representative Frank (right) looking on.
©SAUL LOEB/AFP/Getty Images

The FSOC is chaired by the Secretary of the Treasury and consists of 10 voting members who are the heads of various agencies involved in the financial system. The FSOC's voting members include, among others, the Secretary of the Treasury, the Chairman of the Federal Reserve, the Comptroller of the Currency, the Director of the Consumer Financial Protection Bureau, the Chairman of the Securities and Exchange Commission, and the Chairman of the Federal Deposit Insurance Corporation (see Figure 36.4). The FSOC possesses statutory authority to designate certain "too big to fail" (as they are colloquially known) financial companies for additional regulation in order to minimize the systemic risk that such a company's financial distress will threaten the stability of the American economy. The FSOC also has 5 nonvoting members, representing the FSOC's research arm and state-level financial and insurance regulators.

FIGURE 36.4 **The United States Financial Stability Oversight Council**

Secretary of The Treasury, Chair of FSOC	Chair, Federal Deposit Insurance Corporation
Chair, Federal Reserve Board of Governors	Director, Federal Housing Finance Agency
Comptroller of the Currency	Chair, National Credit Union Administration
Director, Consumer Financial Protection Bureau	Independent Member with Insurance Expertise
Chair, Securities and Exchange Commission	Chair, Commodity Futures Trading Commission

In summary, the FSOC exercises its oversight function over financial markets in three ways:

1. *Risk analysis:* The FSOC assesses systemic risks to financial markets and prepares annual reports to Congress.
2. *Early warning:* The FSOC identifies emerging threats to the overall stability of financial markets and sounds the alarm when such threats emerge.
3. *Identification of financial risk in firms:* The FSOC is charged with identifying nonbanking financial institutions that pose a risk to the stability of the U.S. economy and designating them as *systemically important financial institutions.*

In 2013, the FSOC designated four firms—MetLife, American International Group (AIG), GE Capital Corporation (GECC), and Prudential Financial—as *systemically important financial institutions* or SIFIs. Since then, the FSOC has voted to rescind the designation of AIG, GECC, and Prudential Financial as SIFIs, leaving MetLife as the only FSOC-designated SIFI. Being classified as a SIFI subjects the firm to heightened scrutiny by the Federal Reserve and other regulators. The FSOC also has a significant role in identifying financial firms that pose a grave threat to financial stability and determining what action should be taken to break up such firms. These institutions have been dubbed by commentators as "too big to fail" and were a central issue in the financial crisis of 2008.

Once the FSOC has designated a nonbank financial institution as a SIFI, Dodd-Frank empowers the Federal Reserve to assume oversight and impose heightened standards on the institution. In addition, banks with over $50 billion in assets are subject to the Federal Reserve's tougher capital requirements and must undergo annual *stress tests* that are designed to test the bank's ability to withstand financial market volatility. Dodd-Frank also requires that all financial institutions follow certain prudent practices that discourage speculative investing practices and encourage maintaining sufficient reserves to protect consumers.

The FSOC has been the subject of legal controversy. Some have even argued that the FSOC is unconstitutional because its SIFI designation powers are too broad and essentially unchecked. In Case 36.1, a federal appeals court determines whether a West Texas bank has standing to challenge the constitutionality of the FSOC.

FACT SUMMARY State National Bank ("the Bank") is a regional bank located in West Texas. After the passage of the Dodd-Frank Act, State National Bank decided to challenge the constitutionality of various provisions of the Act, including the constitutionality of the new Financial Stability Oversight Council (FSOC). Among other things, the Act gives the FSOC the authority to impose on certain financial companies that are "too big to fail" additional regulations in order to minimize the risk that such a company's financial distress will threaten the stability of the American economy. The Bank argued that the FSOC is unconstitutional because the FSOC has broad and unchecked power to decide which companies should face additional regulation. The Bank filed suit in the U.S. District Court for the District of Columbia. The district court concluded that the Bank did not yet have standing to challenge the constitutionality of the Dodd-Frank Act. The Bank then appealed to the U.S. Court of Appeals for the District of Columbia.

SYNOPSIS OF DECISION AND OPINION The court of appeals affirmed the decision of the lower court, holding that State National Bank did not have standing because its claims were not ripe. In other words, the court of appeals did not rule on the merits of the Bank's challenge; instead, it dismissed the case on procedural grounds.

WORDS OF THE COURT: Ripeness "The Dodd-Frank Act created a new Financial Stability Oversight Council 'to identify risks to the financial stability of the United States that could arise from the material financial distress or failure, or ongoing activities, of large, interconnected bank holding companies or nonbank financial companies.' 12 U.S.C. § 5322(a)(1)(A).

"To meet that objective, the [FSOC] has the authority to designate certain 'too big to fail'

financial institutions for additional regulation, including supervision by the Federal Reserve. *See* 12 U.S.C. §§ 5323(a)(1), 5365. So far, the [FSOC] has designated American International Group, GE Capital Corporation, MetLife, and Prudential Financial for additional regulation and supervision. . . .

"The Bank argues that the [FSOC's] designation of GE Capital for additional regulation has indirectly harmed State National Bank. According to the Bank, 'GE Capital receives a reputational subsidy as a result of' its designation by the [FSOC] for additional regulation, 'which allows GE Capital to raise money at lower costs than it otherwise could, negatively impacting the Bank's ability to compete for the same finite funds.'

"As we have noted, if a party is the 'object' of a government action, 'there is ordinarily little question' that the party has standing to challenge the action. [Citation omitted.] A bank adversely affected because it was designated 'too big to fail' would presumably have standing to challenge such a designation. This is not such a case. To begin with, at the time of the complaint, GE Capital had not yet been designated for additional regulation. In any event, the Bank here is complaining about the 'too big to fail' designation of someone else."

Case Questions

1. According to State National Bank, how was it harmed when the FSOC designated GE Capital as "too big to fail"?

2. Why didn't the court allow State National Bank to challenge the constitutionality of the FSOC?

3. *Focus on Critical Thinking:* If this case had been ripe for judicial review and not moot, would State National Bank have won on the merits? In other words, do you agree with the Bank that the FSOC's powers are too broad?

CEO Pay Ratio Disclosure Rule

Dodd-Frank requires publicly traded corporations to disclose the pay ratio between the company's median employee and the company's chief executive officer or other principal executive officer. Dodd-Frank also directs the SEC to issue regulations enforcing this rule. The SEC issued a final rule exempting certain types of companies from this pay disclosure rule, including emerging-growth companies, smaller reporting companies, and foreign private issuers. Below is the SEC's official press release dated August 5, 2015, announcing the SEC's final pay disclosure rules.

Press Release

SEC Adopts Rule for Pay Ratio Disclosure

Rule Implements Dodd-Frank Mandate While Providing Companies with Flexibility to Calculate Pay Ratio

FOR IMMEDIATE RELEASE
2015-160

Washington D.C., Aug. 5, 2015 —

The Securities and Exchange Commission today adopted a final rule that requires a public company to disclose the ratio of the compensation of its chief executive officer (CEO) to the median compensation of its employees. The new rule, mandated by the Dodd-Frank Wall Street Reform and Consumer Protection Act, provides companies with flexibility in calculating this pay ratio, and helps inform shareholders when voting on "say on pay."

"The Commission adopted a carefully calibrated pay ratio disclosure rule that carries out a statutory mandate," said SEC Chair Mary Jo White. "The rule provides companies with substantial flexibility in determining the pay ratio, while remaining true to the statutory requirements."

The new rule will provide shareholders with information they can use to evaluate a CEO's compensation, and will require disclosure of the pay ratio in registration statements, proxy and information statements, and annual reports that call for executive compensation disclosure. Companies will be required to provide disclosure of their pay ratios for their first fiscal year beginning on or after Jan. 1, 2017.

The rule addresses concerns about the costs of compliance by providing companies with flexibility in meeting the rule's requirements. For example, a company will be permitted to select its methodology for identifying its median employee and that employee's compensation, including through statistical sampling of its employee population or other reasonable methods. The rule also permits companies to make the median employee determination only once every three years and to choose a determination date within the last three months of a company's fiscal year. In addition, the rule allows companies to exclude non-U.S. employees from countries in which data privacy laws or regulations make companies unable to comply with the rule and provides a *de minimis* exemption for non-U.S. employees.

The rule does not apply to smaller reporting companies, emerging growth companies, foreign private issuers, MJDS filers, or registered investment companies. The rule does provide transition periods for new companies, companies engaging in business combinations or acquisitions, and companies that cease to be smaller reporting companies or emerging growth companies.

The rules will be effective 60 days after publication in the Federal Register.

Source: https://www.sec.gov/news/pressrelease/2015-160.html.

Say-on-Pay on Executive Compensation

Say-on-pay refers to a vote by shareholders of a company approving or rejecting the compensation of executives at that company. Dodd-Frank requires that, at least once every three years, public companies (firms that issue securities on financial markets) must conduct a shareholder vote "to approve the compensation of executives."[1] These shareholder say-on-pay votes, however, are not binding either on the issuer or on the issuer's board of directors.[2]

This say-on-pay provision was the subject of some legal controversy in Case 36.2. In particular, when shareholders of a public company are unhappy with the level of executive compensation, which type of court—state or federal—should adjudicate a shareholder lawsuit involving a board's compensation policies?

CASE 36.2 Dennis v. Hart, 724 F.3d 1249 (9th Cir. 2013)

FACT SUMMARY PICO Holdings, Inc., a California holding company, reported negative net income and negative cash flow in 2010. Despite these disappointing financial results, PICO's board of directors increased executive compensation that same year, a move that upset many shareholders. In a May 2011 advisory vote mandated by Dodd-Frank, 61 percent of shareholders voted against the board's compensation package, but PICO's board took no action in response to the vote. After the vote, the plaintiff shareholders filed a shareholder derivative action in a California state court against PICO and the members of the board. Among other things, the shareholders claimed that the board's compensation practices and its utter failure to respond to the say-on-pay vote by the shareholders constituted a breach of fiduciary duty under state law. The defendant board members removed the case from state court to federal court and then moved the federal court to dismiss the case altogether because "say-on-pay" votes are not binding under Dodd-Frank. The federal district court issued an order sending the case back to state court; the defendant board members appealed this order to the Ninth Circuit Court of Appeals.

SYNOPSIS OF DECISION AND OPINION The court of appeals affirmed the decision of the lower court, sending the case back to state court on the grounds that the breach of fiduciary duty claims of the shareholders did not raise an issue of federal law. In addition, the court of appeals awarded attorney fees to the plaintiff shareholders. In short, the shareholders of PICO won the first battle of this case because they were able to pursue their claims in state court.

WORDS OF THE COURT: Jurisdiction "The defendants argue that . . . Section 27 of the Exchange Act [as amended by the Dodd-Frank Act] vests federal courts with exclusive jurisdiction over actions 'brought to enforce any liability or duty created by [the Exchange Act] or the rules and regulations thereunder.' 15 U.S.C. § 78aa(a). Section 27 is inapplicable because the plaintiffs' suits do not seek to enforce any liability or duty created by the Exchange Act [as amended by Dodd Frank]. . . . Nothing in [the] complaint alleges any implicit or explicit violation of the say-on-pay provision or any other provision of the Exchange Act. On the contrary, the parties agree that PICO did what the Act requires: it held a vote. The suits allege violations of state law and seek to enforce liabilities created by state law."

Case Questions

1. Who won this case and why?

2. Why did the defendant board members want to argue this case before a federal court instead of a state court? By the same token, why did the plaintiff shareholders want to argue this case before a state court instead of a federal court?

3. *Focus on Critical Thinking:* Under Dodd-Frank, shareholder say-on-pay votes are not binding. Should they be?

---

[1] 15 U.S.C. § 78n-1(a)(1).

[2] *Id.* § 78n-1(c).

Consumer Financial Protection Bureau

Last but not least, Dodd-Frank also created a new federal administrative agency called the Consumer Financial Protection Bureau (CFPB) in order "to provide a single point of accountability for enforcing federal consumer finance laws and protecting consumers in the financial marketplace."[3] In particular, Dodd-Frank delegates to the CFPB direct oversight authority over companies that provide mortgages, credit cards, savings accounts, and annuities directly to consumers. The CFPB also has the authority to impose new regulations regarding mandatory disclosures, fees, and restrictions on certain consumer lending practices.

Among other things, the CFPB has the following core functions:

- Rooting out unfair, deceptive, or abusive acts or practices by writing rules, supervising companies, and enforcing the law.
- Enforcing laws that outlaw discrimination in consumer finance.
- Taking consumer complaints.
- Enhancing financial education.
- Researching the consumer experience of using financial products.
- Monitoring financial markets for new risks to consumers.

Before the enactment of Dodd-Frank, these multifarious responsibilities were divided across several different agencies. The CFPB is discussed in greater detail in Chapter 44, "Consumer Protection."

TAKEAWAY CONCEPTS Dodd-Frank

- Congress enacted the Dodd-Frank Wall Street Reform and Consumer Protection Act in 2010.
- Dodd-Frank made sweeping reforms to the financial regulatory system, including expanded SEC enforcement powers, the creation of a new Financial Stability Oversight Council, and mandated (but nonbinding) say-on-pay votes by shareholders.

WHISTLEBLOWER PROTECTIONS

LO 36-6

Explain how Dodd-Frank protects whistleblowers.

One of the most original and innovative aspects of Dodd-Frank is the way this law creates substantial financial incentives for **whistleblowers**. A whistleblower is a person who reports illegal conduct committed by employees, directors, and executives of a company.

In brief, Dodd-Frank's whistleblower provision is modeled after a bounty plan in which money is awarded directly to individuals who disclose information about securities fraud leading to a successful SEC enforcement action. To this end, Dodd-Frank created a $300 billion fund to reward whistleblowers. In addition, employees of publicly held entities may collect a bounty of 10 to 30 percent of any monetary sanctions collected in an SEC enforcement action if the information they provide to government agencies results in a penalty exceeding $1 million. The SEC has broad discretion to base the amount of the whistleblower award on the significance of the information provided, the level of assistance provided by the whistleblower, and the government's interest in deterring securities fraud. Figure 36.5 describes how the process works in sequential fashion.

Dodd-Frank also has a strong anti-retaliation provision that protects the job status of whistleblowers and promises them confidentiality. In the event an employee is terminated

---

[3]See "About Us," CFPB website, available at www.consumerfinance.gov/about-us/the-bureau/.

FIGURE 36.5   The Whistleblower Process under Dodd-Frank

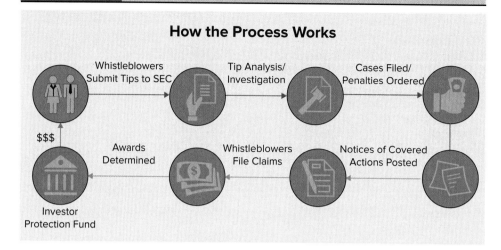

How the Process Works

for whistleblowing, the Dodd-Frank anti-retaliation provision allows the whistleblower to collect double his back pay as well as litigation costs, expert witness fees, and attorneys' fees.

TAKEAWAY CONCEPT Whistleblower Protections

Dodd-Frank creates a bounty plan to incentivize whistleblowing.

 THINKING STRATEGICALLY

Dodd-Frank and the Moral Hazard Problem

PROBLEM: A "moral hazard" is a strategic situation that can occur when one is protected from the consequences of one's risky actions. For example, if you are a loan officer at a bank and you know that the government will bail out your bank if it is unable to collect on its loans, then you might be tempted to invest the bank's money in risky investments. If the investments pay off, you will have made a fortune. But if the investments go south, you will get repaid by the government.

Let's consider one aspect of the Dodd-Frank Act in light of the moral hazard problem. Although this historic law was supposed to reduce systemic risks, address concerns about companies being "too big to fail," and protect the American taxpayer by ending bailouts, some have argued that the law does just the opposite!

How? Some commentators have contended that Dodd-Frank increases systemic risks by creating a

strategic moral hazard problem for certain financial institutions. For example, according to Gretchen Morgenson, a respected business reporter for *The New York Times,* the Dodd-Frank Act granted eight financial clearinghouses the right to tap the Federal Reserve for funding in the event of a future crisis.[4] Among these clearinghouses are the Chicago Mercantile Exchange (CME), the Intercontinental Exchange (ICE), and the Options Clearing Corporation (OCC), all of which handle billions of dollars' worth of transactions a day. In the words of Morgenson, these clearinghouses are "large, powerful institutions that clear or settle options, bond, and derivatives trades."

So, where is the moral hazard problem here? As Morgenson notes, Dodd-Frank exempts those same eight clearinghouses from the FSOC orderly liquidation rules that apply to institutions that get into financial trouble. In other words, these lucky eight firms obtain

---

[4]Gretchen Morgenson, "One Safety Net That Needs to Shrink," *The New York Times,* Nov. 3, 2012.

the best of both worlds: access to the Fed's money if they get into trouble and no penalty for failure!

STRATEGIC SOLUTION: From a strategic perspective, one could argue that Dodd-Frank should apply the same FSOC liquidation rules to all financial institutions, including the eight clearinghouses, and that financial regulators should precommit to not authorizing bailouts in a future crisis. This solution, however, poses a new strategic dilemma. After all, how can regulators make a credible commitment ahead of time not to bail out a firm that is "too large to fail" if that firm's failure could threaten the entire financial system?

QUESTIONS

1. Generally speaking, how do government bailouts generate a moral hazard problem?
2. Do you buy Morgenson's argument against Dodd-Frank?

KEY TERMS

Financial market p. 637   A highly regulated institution in which people and firms trade securities, commodities, and currencies at prices that reflect supply and demand as well as publicly and privately available information.

Primary market p. 638   A financial market in which firms (called *issuers*) raise capital by selling securities to investors.

Secondary market p. 638   A financial market in which investors sell to other investors with the goal of making a profit or preventing a loss.

Investors p. 639   Individuals or entities seeking a return from their investment based on the perceived value of the security.

Issuers p. 639   Institutions and entities that sell issued securities to investors.

Intermediaries p. 639   Financial institutions that provide services for investors and issuers related to securities transactions.

Systemic risk p. 640   The possibility that an event at a single firm could trigger severe instability in the entire financial market or the collapse of an entire industry or economy.

Dodd-Frank Wall Street Reform and Consumer Protection Act p. 641   Federal legislation designed to overhaul the regulation of public companies and U.S. financial services and markets (*ch. 35*). A law enacted in 2010, commonly referred to as *Dodd-Frank*, that made sweeping reforms to the financial regulatory system, including expanded SEC enforcement powers, the creation of a new Financial Stability Oversight Council, and a new bounty plan for whistleblowers (*ch. 36*).

Securities and Exchange Commission (SEC) p. 641   The independent federal administrative agency charged with rulemaking, enforcement, and adjudication of federal securities laws.

Financial Stability Oversight Council (FSOC) p. 642   An independent body with a board of regulators to address dangerous risks to global financial markets posed by risky investments or the actions of large, interconnected financial institutions.

Say-on-pay p. 646   A vote by shareholders of a company approving or rejecting the compensation of the company's executives.

Whistleblower p. 647   An employee or agent who reports illegal misconduct or a statutory violation by his or her employer to the authorities.

CASE SUMMARY 36.1 MetLife, Inc. v. Financial Stability Oversight Council, 177 F. Supp. 3d 219 (2016) (sealed opinion)

Material Financial Distress

The Financial Stability Oversight Council (FSOC) determined that "material financial distress" at MetLife, Inc., could "pose a threat to the financial stability of the United States." The quoted phrases appear in the Dodd-Frank Act, 12 U.S.C. § 5323(a)(1), and were formally defined by the FSOC years before MetLife's designation. During the MetLife designation process, however, officials at the FSOC ignored or abandoned two of its definitions of "material financial distress."

CASE QUESTIONS

1. Should Congress itself define key terms in the laws it enacts, or should Congress have the discretion to delegate the definition of key terms to administrative agencies?
2. In your opinion, were the actions of the FSOC in this case consistent with the concept of rule of law?

CASE SUMMARY 36.2 PHH Corporation v. Consumer Financial Protection Board, 839 F.3d 1 (D.C. Cir. 2016)

Constitutionality of the CFPB

A provision in the Dodd-Frank Act creates a single director to lead the CFPB and limits the president's ability to remove the CFPB director during his five-year term. PHH Corporation, a New Jersey company, challenged this provision in federal court, arguing that it was an unconstitutional interference with the president's powers as chief executive of the federal government.

CASE QUESTIONS

1. In your opinion, should the president have the ability to fire the director of the CFPB? Why or why not?
2. Other federal agencies created by Congress, like the FCC and FTC, have multiple directors. Why do you think Congress created a single-director structure for the CFPB when it enacted Dodd-Frank?

CASE SUMMARY 36.3 Digital Realty Trust, Inc. v. Somers, 583 U.S. ___ (2018)

Definition of Whistleblower

Digital Realty Trust, Inc. fired one of its employees, Paul Somers, shortly after he reported to senior management suspected securities-law violations by the company. Somers, however, did not report the suspected securities-law violations to the Securities and Exchange Commission (SEC), so instead of applying for a bounty, he filed a lawsuit alleging a claim of "whistleblower retaliation" under Dodd-Frank. In reply,

Digital Realty moved to dismiss the lawsuit on the ground that Somers was not a "whistleblower" under Dodd-Frank, since he did not report the misconduct to the SEC.

CASE QUESTIONS

1. How does Dodd-Frank define who a whistleblower is?
2. Why did this case go all the way to the U.S. Supreme Court?

CHAPTER REVIEW QUESTIONS

1. **Which of the following markets is *not* an example of a financial market?**
   a. Commodity market
   b. Futures market
   c. Capital market
   d. Foreign exchange market
   e. Prediction market

2. **What is the main purpose of the Dodd-Frank Wall Street Reform and Consumer Protection Act of 2010?**
   a. To protect consumers
   b. To reform Wall Street
   c. To protect whistleblowers

   d. To identify and reduce systemic risks to the financial system
   e. To replace the SEC with the Financial Stability Oversight Council

3. **The SEC is composed of how many commissioners and maintains how many regional offices throughout the United States?**
   a. 5 commissioners and 11 regional offices
   b. 5 commissioners and 9 regional offices
   c. 7 commissioners and 7 regional offices
   d. 9 commissioners and 5 regional offices
   e. 11 commissioners and 3 regional offices

4. What does the term *systemic risk* refer to?

a. Systemwide or global environmental risks

b. Investments that are structured like a Ponzi scheme

c. Risky investment strategies across multiple financial markets.

d. The integrity of financial exchanges like the New York Stock Exchange or the Chicago Mercantile Exchange

e. The possibility that an event at a single firm could trigger severe instability in the entire financial market

5. The Financial Stability Oversight Council (FSOC), created by the Dodd-Frank Wall Street Reform and Consumer Protection Act of 2010, has the power to:

a. Break up companies deemed to pose a threat to the nation's financial markets even if the company is not insolvent.

b. Compel the SEC to assume an oversight position over institutions that pose a global risk to financial markets.

c. Approve or reject executive compensation packages, including bonuses, regarding companies deemed "too big to fail."

d. Criminally prosecute officers and board members of companies that are found to have committed fraud and that have harmed the public or the national economy.

e. Impose more demanding disclosure requirements on firms engaged in IPOs.

6. Financial markets include the sale of securities but not the sale of commodities.

a. True

b. False

7. Issuing securities to the public markets for the first time is called an initial public offering.

a. True

b. False

8. The sale of securities in the secondary market raises capital for the business whose stock is sold.

a. True

b. False

9. Systemic risks occur when large firms in financial markets are interconnected with many other firms.

a. True

b. False

10. The SEC is an independent agency that is under the direct control of the president.

a. True

b. False

 Quick Quiz ANSWERS
Main Parties in the Securities Market

Cardi B is the investor, Offset, Inc. is the issuer, and Bodak Brokers is the intermediary.

CHAPTER REVIEW QUESTIONS: Answers and Explanations

1. e. Answers *a, b, c,* and *d* are all examples of financial markets. Prediction markets, by contrast, are currently considered a form of illegal gambling in the United States.

2. d. Although the title of Dodd-Frank refers to "Wall Street Reform" and "Consumer Protection," the main purpose of Dodd-Frank is to address and reduce systemic risks to the financial system. The remaining responses are therefore incorrect.

3. a. The SEC is composed of five commissioners who are appointed by the president. Much of the day-to-day work of the SEC is conducted by its 11 regional offices located throughout the United States.

4. e. Although answers *a, b, c,* and *d* may sound plausible, they do not describe situations involving systemic risk, which refers to the possibility that an event at a single firm could trigger severe instability in the entire financial market.

5. a. The Financial Stability Oversight Council (FSOC) may break up, when necessary, companies deemed to be a threat to the stability of our financial markets. Answer *b* is incorrect because Dodd-Frank confers on the FSOC, not the SEC, the ability to assume an oversight position over institutions that pose a global risk to financial markets. Answers *c, d,* and *e* refer to powers of the SEC.

6. b. False. All kinds of things are bought and sold on financial markets, including securities, commodities, and currencies.

7. a. True. An IPO, by definition, is the issuance of securities to the public for the first time.

8. b. False. The sale of securities in secondary markets does not raise capital for the issuer. Instead, investors sell to other investors with the goal of making a profit or preventing a loss.

9. a. True. A large financial firm that is highly interconnected with others can be a source of systemic risk, which is the possibility that an event at the firm could trigger severe instability in financial markets or the collapse of an entire industry or economy.

10. b. False. The president appoints the commissioners that comprise the SEC, but the SEC is not directly controlled by the president.

UNIT SIX   Agency and Employment Law

CHAPTER 37

Agency Formation, Categories, and Authority

THINKING STRATEGICALLY

Business carry out their strategic initiatives through the use of agents. The evolution of technology in the global economy has created new opportunities but has given rise to new dilemmas as to how those agents are to be classified for purposes of taxes, benefits, and liability of the business for acts of the agent. In this chapter's *Thinking Strategically,* we discuss strategic methods for limiting liability for agent misclassification.

Learning Objectives

After studying this chapter, students who have mastered the material will be able to:

37-1 Recognize, define, and give examples of an agency relationship and transaction.

37-2 Explain the process for creating an agency relationship.

37-3 Classify agents as either employees or independent contractors by applying the direction and control tests.

37-4 Articulate the ABC test factors used by state courts.

37-5 Explain how agency relationships are terminated.

CHAPTER OVERVIEW

Agency relationships are fundamental to the business environment because they set out rules and standards for situations in which one party hires another party to act on the hiring party's behalf. When business owners and managers understand the obligations and liabilities of such a relationship, they are better able to limit their company's liability to both the hired party and third parties. Understanding **agency law** is also a crucial first step to understanding laws that govern rights, duties, and obligations between employers and employees. In this chapter, we examine the definitions, categories, and sources of law that govern agency relationships. We discuss the liabilities, duties, and obligations that are created by an agency relationship in the next chapter.

DEFINITIONS AND SOURCES OF AGENCY LAW

Agency is a legal relationship in which the parties agree that one party will act as an **agent** for another party, called the **principal**, subject to the control of the principal. Agency relationships are common and essential in the business environment and exist in a variety of forms. A common form of agency is an employer-employee relationship, but there are other important forms of agency as well.

In all agency relationships, the principal authorizes the agent to provide services or accomplish some task on behalf of the principal and under the principal's charge. Understanding agency law also requires one to be aware of (1) legal requirements for *creating* an agency, (2) *liability* of a principal for the agent's conduct, and (3) *duties* and obligations of the parties. Creation of an agency and agent classification are discussed in this chapter. Duties and obligations of the parties are covered in the next chapter. The principal and agent may be either individuals or entities (such as a corporation). Much of agency law exists on the state statutory level and is based on the ***Restatement (Third) of Agency***. Some states (and some federal courts) also have retained some common law doctrines of agency that operate in tandem with statutes.

LO 37-1

Recognize, define, and give examples of an agency relationship and transaction.

Agency Transactions

It may facilitate your understanding of agency law if you think of agency in terms of a transaction (or set of transactions). Fundamentally, an agency transaction involves one party hiring another party to transact business on behalf of (or perform a task for) the hiring party. In a business context, this relationship is crucial because business owners and managers depend on agents to carry out the daily operations of a business.

Businesses use agents to enter into contracts, perform necessary services, and advance their objectives in various ways. First, an agency relationship typically is created expressly by the parties, and the duties of the agent are defined by the principal. Second, the parties perform their respective duties in accordance with their agreement and agency law. Finally, an agency transaction ends when the agency is terminated by the parties. In some cases, the agency is terminated by operation of law (e.g., the principal hires the agent to paint a building, but the building is destroyed by fire before the agent begins to paint). Table 37.1 provides an overview of an agency transaction.

TABLE 37.1	Agency Transaction Overview	
Creation of Agency	**Performance of Obligations and Duties**	**Termination of Agency**
Principal wishes to form agency and agent consents.	Agent performs as agreed and in accordance with fiduciary obligations. Principal's primary obligation is payment of the agent.	Express act of parties or operation of law.

TAKEAWAY CONCEPTS Definitions and Sources of Agency Law

- Agency is a legal relationship in which the parties agree that one party will act as an agent for another party, called the *principal.*
- Agency transactions are common and essential in the business environment and exist in a variety of forms (e.g., an employer-employee relationship).

CREATION OF AN AGENCY RELATIONSHIP

The *Restatements* define the creation of an agency relationship in terms of *consent* and *control*. Specifically, agency is described as a *fiduciary* relationship that results when a principal manifests consent to an agent to act on the principal's behalf subject to the principal's control. A fiduciary relationship requires the parties to act with a high level of integrity and good faith in carrying out the best interests of the principal. Fiduciary duties are covered extensively in the next chapter. The agent also must give consent to perform the act.

Manifestation and Consent

To create an agency relationship, a principal first must **manifest** some offer to form an agency. **Consent** occurs when an agent agrees to act for the principal. To determine whether the parties have in fact manifested an offer of agency and acceptance by the agent, courts apply an objective standard. That is, given the parties' *outward expressions,* actions, and words, would a reasonable person believe that the principal intended for an agency to be created and that the agent did in fact consent to the agency relationship? Courts do not look to the subjective intent of the parties as definitive. Rather, courts use the *objective* standard of what a reasonable person would have concluded about the manifestations and consent in the context of the relationship between the parties.

Control

In addition to consent, the parties must have an understanding that the principal is in control of the agency relationship. The control need not be total or continuous and need not extend to the way the agent performs, but there must be some sense that the principal is defining the tasks and objectives of the agency relationship.

Formalities

The law does not require any formal expression of an agency relationship between the parties. Most states do not require that the parties consent to the agency in writing. In fact, conduct alone can be sufficient basis for formation of the agency relationship and can create rights and obligations of the principal and agent. However, a minority of states have a statutory equal dignity rule that sets out formalities for certain principal-agent transactions.

In Case 37.1, an appellate court considers whether the conduct of parties gave rise to an agency relationship.

CASE 37.1 Bosse v. Brinker Restaurant Corporation d/b/a Chili's Grill and Bar, 2005 Mass. Super. LEXIS 372

FACT SUMMARY Bosse was part of a group of four teenagers who ordered and ate a meal at the Chili's restaurant in Dedham, Massachusetts. The tab for the meal came to $56, but the group left the restaurant without paying and drove off. A regular patron of the restaurant saw the group leave without paying and followed them in his own car. The teenagers saw the patron following them, so they stopped their car and confronted him in a parking lot at a nearby retail center. The pursuing patron yelled that he had seen them skip out on their bill at Chili's and that they would not get away with it. The patron's car was unmarked; it bore no Chili's insignia. He wore civilian clothing and no uniform or other insignia of employment at Chili's.

The teenagers then fled the lot, and a high-speed chase ensued through residential side streets. During the chase, the patron used his cell phone to call a

(continued)

Chili's employee and provided him with a description of the teenagers' car and the path of the chase. The Chili's employee then related this information to a 911 dispatcher. In the course of the high-speed chase, the teenagers collided with a cement wall and were injured. The pursuing patron left the crash scene and was never identified.

Bosse sued the restaurant owner, Brinker Restaurant Corp. doing business as Chili's Grill and Bar, for damages related to the crash. Bosse argued that the actions of the parties resulted in the Chili's patron being converted to an agent of Chili's, that he conducted his chase as an agent of the restaurant, and that the restaurant should be liable for the consequences of his negligent or reckless pursuit. Brinker filed a motion for summary judgment on the grounds that no genuine issue of fact existed regarding the lack of an agency relationship through express acts or implication.

SYNOPSIS OF DECISION AND OPINION The Massachusetts Superior Court granted Brinker's motion for a summary judgment. The court held that an agency relationship requires three elements: (1) the principal must give consent, (2) the principal must maintain the right of control, and (3) the agent's conduct must benefit the principal in some way. In this case, the court ruled that the evidence was insufficient to create a genuine issue whether Chili's authorized the patron to conduct a chase. There did not appear to be any preliminary communication between the patron and restaurant employees. The events were spontaneous and occurred quickly. No member of Chili's house staff joined in the pursuit and, in fact, Chili's had an unwritten but express policy forbidding staff to pursue a nonpaying customer out of the building. The court concluded that Chili's had no chance or desire to control the patron and that any benefit Chili's received was minimal at best.

WORDS OF THE COURT: Elements of an Agency Relationship "For these reasons no genuine issue of material fact emerges upon a claim of an agency relationship. The information generated by discovery does not permit an inference that Chili's consented to such a relationship; that it had the right of control necessary for such a relationship; or that it possessed a genuine interest or benefit in such a relationship. The burden of the plaintiffs is to establish at least a genuine question of the presence of all three elements. If the evidence had failed to materialize upon any one of those elements, the deficiency would be fatal to the lawsuit. The evidence appears to have failed to materialize upon all three of the elements. Consequently, the plaintiffs enjoy no reasonable expectation of proving an agency relationship. Full summary judgment is appropriate."

Case Questions

1. If the pursuing patron had been an off-duty employee of Chili's, how would that impact your agency analysis?

2. When the pursuing patron called the Chili's employee with a description of the pursuit, and that employee in turn called the police, isn't that an act of consent by Chili's?

3. *Focus on Critical Thinking:* What facts would you change in this case that might change the court's ruling?

CLASSIFICATION OF AGENTS

LO 37-3

Classify agents as either employees or independent contractors by applying the direction and control tests.

Agents are classified into one of three broad categories: (1) employee agents, (2) independent contractors, or (3) gratuitous agents. Understanding these categories is important for business owners and managers primarily because the liability of the principal for acts of the agent depends on the agency relationship between the principal, the agent, and any relevant third parties.

Employee Agents

Individual employees who are authorized to transact business on behalf of the employer/principal are called **employee agents**. Principals are liable for the actions or omissions (such as negligence) of employee agents. However, it is important to understand that not every employee is an agent. To be classified as an employee agent, the employee must have some source of authority to represent the employer. The nonagent employee relationship is sometimes referred to as the *master-servant relationship* in order to distinguish it from an employer-employee agent relationship. For example, at the local branch of Mega Bank, the teller is an employee agent of Mega Bank who is authorized to conduct certain limited transactions (such as cashing a check) on Mega Bank's behalf. The branch manager at Mega Bank is also an employee agent, and her agency is likely wider in scope to include approval of small-business loans and similar transactions. The maintenance worker who cleans the bank branch is also an employee, but he is *not* an employee agent because he does not have authority to transact business on Mega Bank's behalf. Therefore, the worker would be classified as the nonagent employee (servant) in a master-servant relationship.

Independent Contractors

By contrast, an agent classified as an **independent contractor** is not considered an employee and has no legal protections of employees such as minimum wage and overtime compensation laws. An equally important factor is that the principal generally has no liability for actions and omissions of an independent contractor. In the business environment, professional service providers, such as attorneys, accountants, and financial advisers, who provide services to several different clients are examples of independent contractors.

Gratuitous Agents

Agents who act on behalf of a principal without receiving any compensation are called **gratuitous agents**. For example, if you ask your roommate to pick up your laundry as a favor, he is your gratuitous agent. In most respects, the rights and duties of gratuitous agents are the same as those of paid agents *except* that the duty of care applicable to the gratuitous agent is not as great (an agent's duty of care is discussed in the next chapter).

Employee Agents versus Independent Contractors: Direction and Control

Although the parties themselves may agree to a certain classification, the status of an agent is based not on what the parties agreed to but on the *actual* working relationship between principal and agent. Courts apply the *substance over form* analysis to determine the classification of an agent. Fundamentally, the agent is classified based on the amount of *direction and control* the principal has over the agent in terms of setting the agent's work schedule, pay rate, and the level of day-to-day supervision required. In an employer–employee agent relationship, the employer/principal typically sets work hours, decides what salary to pay, and exercises control over the employee agent's working conditions and responsibilities. Independent contractors usually work based on a deadline, but they typically choose their own schedule to achieve that deadline. In terms of payment, independent contractors usually send an invoice on a monthly basis (sometimes longer) for services rendered rather than drawing a weekly or biweekly paycheck.

Courts may use other criteria that focus on the nature of the agent's duties to determine the agent's status. For example, an *independent occupation/profession* in which the agent has more than one customer/client (e.g., accountants, attorneys, financial advisers) indicates the agent is an independent contractor. On the other hand, if the principal provides tools or heavy equipment to the agent at the workplace, this generally indicates that the agent is an employee. In Case 37.2, a federal court analyzes the agency status of a telemarketer.

FACT SUMMARY Royal Administration Services, Inc. ("Royal") sells vehicle service contracts (VSCs). A VSC is a type of extended warranty that promises to perform (or pay for) certain repairs or services on an automobile after the warranty expires. Royal sells its VSCs through automobile dealers and through about 20 different marketing vendors. These marketing vendors sell Royal's VSCs through direct mail or telemarketing. One of these marketing vendors, All American Auto Protection ("AAAP"), used telemarketing to contact Charles Jones (Jones). Jones claimed that AAAP's telemarketers violated a federal law that prohibits telemarketers from calling consumers who have signed up with the National Do Not Call Registry. Jones brought suit against Royal seeking to hold the company responsible for the telemarketing violations by AAAP under the theory that AAAP was acting as Royal's agent. The trial court dismissed the case after finding that AAAP was not an agent of Royal. Jones appealed.

SYNOPSIS OF DECISION AND OPINION The U.S. Court of Appeals for the Ninth Circuit upheld the trial court's decision in favor of Royal. The court applied the federal common law test for agency and concluded that AAAP was an independent contractor and therefore Royal had no liability. Although the court acknowledged that Royal exercised *some* amount of control over AAAP (e.g., AAAP was required to keep records of its interactions with consumers who purchased Royal VSCs), Royal did not have the right to control the hours the telemarketers worked, nor did it set quotas for the number of calls or sales the telemarketers had to make. Thus, Royal had only limited control of AAAP's telemarketers.

WORDS OF THE COURT: Limited Control "Significantly, Royal did not have any control of a telemarketer's call until the telemarketer decided to pitch a Royal VSC to the consumer. AAAP sold VSCs for multiple companies (all of whom, presumably, had their own standards and procedures AAAP telemarketers were required to comply with). When an AAAP telemarketer reached a consumer, they first had to sell the consumer on the idea of a VSC. Royal did not have control over this sales pitch. Only after the consumer was sold on the idea of a VSC, would an AAAP telemarketer pitch a specific VSC. If this specific VSC was a Royal VSC, [AAAP followed] then Royal controlled the 'scripts and materials' the telemarketer was permitted to use in the sale."

Case Questions

1. Why did the court hold that AAAP was not an agent of Royal?

2. Although Royal provided AAAP with scripts, the court ruled that these scripts were not enough to transform an independent contractor into an agent. Do you agree? Why or why not?

3. *Focus on Critical Thinking:* Why do you suppose that Jones chose to bring suit against Royal rather than directly against AAAP? Was the decision to name Royal in the lawsuit strategic? Why or why not?

ABC TEST

Courts look to state common law and statutes for guidance in determining independent contractor status. Many states have adopted the **ABC test** in their agency law as a standard for determining agency status.[1] Statutes that set out the ABC factors typically create a presumption that the agent is an employee unless three tests are satisfied: (*A*) the individual is free from direction and control, applicable both under contract for the performance of service and in fact; (*B*) the service is performed outside the usual course of business of the employer; and (*C*) the individual is customarily engaged in an independently established trade, occupation, profession, or business of the same nature as that involved in the service performed. In Case 37.3, a state appellate court uses the ABC test to analyze the agency status of a sales representative.

LO 37-4

Articulate the ABC test factors used by state courts.

---

[1]See, e.g., Mass. Gen. Laws Ann., Ch. 149, § 14B(a)(1)-(3).

FACT SUMMARY Waiau was an employee of One Coast, a company that represented various businesses, including Avanti. In early 2009, One Coast dissolved. Waiau, who had nearly 30 years of experience as a product sales representative in the greeting card and gift industries, entered into a written service agreement (Agreement) with Avanti to sell the company's greeting cards, journals, and calendars. The Agreement provided, among other things, that:

1. Waiau would be Avanti's exclusive sales representative for retail outlets in southwestern Oregon and would personally visit Avanti customers at their retail outlets at least once every 12 weeks for purposes of soliciting orders in accordance with the Agreement and Avanti's policies, catalogs, supplements, and price information furnished to Waiau by Avanti.

2. Waiau had no authority to bind Avanti to any sales and had no authority to accept orders or receive payments on Avanti's behalf.

3. Avanti reserved the right to establish and change prices, products, ways, methods, or terms of payment or shipment, and any other conditions or terms of sale.

4. Waiau had the authority to hire, fire, and train her own sales associates. Waiau would pay all employee taxes and all her own expenses.

In exchange for Waiau's services, Avanti would pay her a commission based on a percentage of the product invoice price less cash discounts, taxes, shipping, insurance, and other deductions. The Agreement would automatically renew for one-year terms unless earlier terminated by 30 days' written notice from either party.

During the relevant time, Waiau maintained a home office with a desk, chair, fax machine, scanner, printer, telephone, computer, travel case, and sample bags. She used the office equipment almost exclusively for business and deducted home office expenses on her personal income tax return. She also used her personal vehicle for business travel. Avanti did not reimburse Waiau for postage, travel, meals, or lodging expenses. Waiau set her own work schedule and decided how frequently to visit customers. Her commissions were based entirely on her sales and not on the number of hours that she worked.

However, Waiau did not register a business name, nor did she carry liability insurance or performance bonds, and she did not advertise or market her services as a product sales representative. During that period, she passed out business cards that stated, "Andrea Waiau, Avanti Greeting Cards."

After Waiau sought unemployment insurance benefits claiming that she was an employee rather than an independent contractor, the state's labor agency determined that Waiau was, in fact, an employee of Avanti, thereby making Avanti liable for unemployment taxes. An administrative law judge (ALJ) ruled that Waiau was an employee, and Avanti appealed.

SYNOPSIS OF DECISION AND OPINION The Oregon Court of Appeals reversed the findings of the ALJ and ruled in favor of Avanti. The court reasoned that Avanti did not have a sufficient amount of direction and control over Waiau and that she should be classified as an independent contractor. The court concluded that Waiau controlled when and how often she worked. Specifically, the court pointed to the fact that Waiau set her own schedule and that Waiau could decide how frequently to visit customers. The court also found that Waiau worked strictly as a commissioned salesperson; worked as frequently or infrequently as she liked; and that a commissioned sales representative who works on a part-time basis, selling only at her convenience or when the opportunity presents itself, is typically an independent contractor. The court rejected the assertion that managerial control existed because the company expected her to make a certain amount of sales per month because such an expectation has to do solely with end results rather than with method.

WORDS OF THE COURT: Direction and Control "Waiau had her own home office and vehicle; set her own hours and visited customers as frequently

(continued)

or infrequently as she desired; was compensated solely based on commission; communicated with Avanti concerning only the results of her efforts; and could simultaneously perform the same services for other greeting card companies. Those facts, too, must be considered in the context of the agreement itself. As noted, Waiau had been performing the same services for Avanti while she was employed by another company, One Coast; after One Coast dissolved, Waiau and Avanti entered into an agreement by which she agreed to provide the same services directly to Avanti as an independent contractor. The terms of that agreement and the parties' conduct are consistent with their express understanding that Waiau would be working as an independent contractor, not an employee subject to the company's direction and control."

Case Questions

1. If Waiau had been paid a salary in addition to her commission, how might that impact the court's analysis?

2. Although the Agreement did not prohibit Waiau from working for another company, as a practical matter she was working full-time for Avanti. Shouldn't that be a factor in the court's analysis? Why or why not?

3. *Focus on Critical Thinking:* Is there a danger that employers will opt to create independent contractor positions rather than employee positions in order to avoid liability and taxes? Is it ethical to generate revenue based on the efforts of sales representatives but not provide them with benefits available to employees such as managers and clerical workers?

California's Independent Contractor Law

California has been an epicenter of the independent contractor classification battles since 2013 when its state labor board began to classify gig-economy workers as employees rather than independent contractors. Most famously, Uber resisted employee-classification efforts, arguing that its drivers have so much flexibility that they are not under any direction or control as in a traditional employer-employee relationship. In 2018, the California Supreme Court decided *Dynamex Operations West, Inc. v. Superior Court,*[2] which discarded a previously used multifactor test and adopted the ABC test for determining an agent's category. The practical impact was that agents were to be classified as employees by default unless the employer established each of the three prongs of the test. The court decision not only expanded the definition of employee under the California labor law, it also imposed an affirmative burden on businesses to prove that independent contractors are being properly classified.

Although the court's adoption of the ABC test was clear, other issues of jurisdiction and coverage were left unanswered until 2019 when the California state legislature stepped in by passing Assembly Bill 5 which codified (i.e., legislative body adopting principles from a court decision by incorporating into their statutory code) and expanded the *Dynamex* decision by amending the California labor code. Beginning in January 2020, workers classified under the new state law will be eligible for wage and overtime protections, workers' compensation coverage, unemployment insurance, various benefits, paid sick days, and state family leave. They will also be protected by state anti-discrimination laws and have the right to unionize. The new law does limit the protections via *exempting* certain workers from the ABC test:

- doctors, dentists, and veterinarians;
- lawyers, architects, engineers, private investigators, and accountants;
- securities broker-dealers and investment advisers;

---

[2]4 Cal.5th 903 (2018).

- travel agents;

- marketers, graphic designers, grant writers, fine artists, certain photographers or photojournalists, and certain freelance writers and editors.

IRS Three-Prong Test

Because so many questions regarding agency status occur in an employment tax context (e.g., determining whether the employer is liable to pay legally mandated employment taxes on a certain worker), the Internal Revenue Service (IRS) has devised a three-prong test to determine an agent's status. While this test is not binding on courts, some appellate courts cite it as a useful tool in determining an agent's classification.[3] The IRS considers the following:

1. The *behavioral* aspects of the agency. (Does the company control what the worker does and how the worker does the job assigned?)
2. The *financial arrangements* between principal and agent. (Are the business aspects of the worker's job controlled by the payer?)
3. The type of *working relationship* the parties have in terms of benefits and promises of continuing employment.

Liability for Misclassification

The consequences of a business owner or manager misclassifying an employee can be severe. For example, suppose that Computer Warehouse Corporation (CWC) classifies five computer programmers as independent contractors even though CWC sets the programmers' schedule and supervises the work product. This continues for one year until the IRS audits CWC and determines that the programmers are actually employees. The IRS will then assess CWC back employment taxes, plus a penalty for the wrongful classification, plus interest owed to the government for the one-year period. Depending on the salaries and the length of time the employees were misclassified, the amount due could exceed several hundred thousand dollars of unplanned tax liability. A Department of Labor audit would likely follow to determine compliance with federal labor and wage statutes. In *Thinking Strategically,* featured at the end of this chapter, we provide a strategic solution for limiting liability for misclassification.

 Quick Quiz Agency Classification

What is More's agency classification?

1. More, an author, is hired by Henry VIII Publications to write a book tentatively titled *Utopia.* The parties agree that More will be paid a lump sum of $50,000 when the book is complete and that the manuscript will be due in six months.

2. More is hired by Henry to work as a computer consultant. The parties agree that More will be on-site at Henry's office on Mondays from 9 a.m. to 5 p.m. for eight consecutive weeks and will be paid each week upon receipt of an invoice by Henry's bookkeeper. More has eight other clients.

(continued)

---

[3]This three-prong approach replaced the IRS's notorious 20-point test in 1997. The IRS specifically disclaims the 20-point test and takes the position that there is "no magic or set number of factors that makes the worker an employee or an independent contractor."

3. More is hired by Henry to work as a sales associate for his retail clothing store. The parties agree that More will work at the store Monday through Friday from 10 a.m. to 6 p.m. at a rate of $9 per hour plus a 15 percent commission on merchandise sold by More.

4. More is Henry's neighbor and agrees to do him a favor by transporting Henry's valuable rare coin collection to a local trade show.

5. More is hired by Henry to make telemarketing calls for Henry's media company. The parties enter into a written agreement titled "Independent Contractor Agreement" in which both parties agree that More will be an independent agent. Henry sets More's schedule and pays him $1,000 every other week plus a $500 bonus every year during the holiday season. More uses equipment owned by the media company.

6. More, a professional athlete, is hired by Henry, the owner of a major-league baseball franchise, to play baseball at an annual salary of $1 million. More's contract requires that he show up for all off-season camps, practices, and games for the entire length of the event. If he fails to show up, he agrees to a reduction in pay via a fine. More is paid every other week, and Henry pays for More's health and retirement benefits.

Answers to this Quick Quiz are provided at the end of the chapter.

TAKEAWAY CONCEPTS Agent Classification

	Direction	Control	Financial	Example
Employee agent	Principal prescribes job tasks, duties, and procedures. Agent typically has authority to act on behalf of principal.	Principal/employer sets work schedules and supervises agent's work. Typically an ongoing arrangement.	Payment at regular intervals such as weekly or biweekly. Principal sometimes provides other benefits (e.g., health care insurance).	Manager of a retail store.
Master/ servant (employee nonagents)	Principal prescribes job tasks, duties, and procedures, but employee does not have authority to act on behalf of principal.	Principal/employer sets work schedules and supervises agent's work. Typically an ongoing arrangement.	Payment at regular intervals such as weekly or biweekly. Principal sometimes provides other benefits (e.g., health care insurance).	Line worker in an industrial manufacturing company.
Independent contractor (IC)	Principal assigns task to IC but does not prescribe particular methods or procedures.	IC sets own work schedule and is not directly supervised by principal. Typically a single transaction or a series of separate engagements.	IC keeps track of work hours and sends principal an invoice for payment. Principal does not provide benefits.	Attorney
Gratuitous agent	Principal and agent agree to a certain task.	N/A	None	Neighbor agrees to cut the lawn of vacationing neighbor.

TERMINATION OF AN AGENCY RELATIONSHIP

An agency relationship may be terminated in a variety of ways. Termination is an important issue for business owners and managers because termination of the agency relationship also terminates the principal's duties and obligations to the agent and to third parties. It is equally important to understand the circumstances under which a third party must be notified of the termination in order to cut off the liability of the principal at a definite point. Failing to properly notify appropriate parties may result in continued liability of the principal for acts of the agent despite the termination. In general, an agency relationship is terminated either through **express acts** or through **operation of law**.

Express Acts

In a typical agency relationship, both the principal and the agent have the power to dissolve the agency at any time. Either party may end the agency through **termination** simply by communicating the desire to terminate the relationship. Termination by the principal is known as *revocation*. When the agent initiates the termination, it is known as *renunciation*. It is important to understand that the legal power of termination is not synonymous with the legal right of termination. Therefore, the principal may terminate the agreement (thereby revoking her authority for the agent to act in her place), but the termination still may be unlawful because the law did not give the principal the right to end the agreement before mutual performance. Thus, the agent may be entitled to damages as a result of the principal's conduct of wrongful termination. For example, suppose that Foley hires Paul to paint the lobby of Foley's office building. The parties agree that Paul will paint the lobby over a period of two weeks and that Foley will pay him $1,000 upon completion. Halfway through the work, Foley learns that a major tenant has filed for bankruptcy, so he calls Paul and tells him to stop work because he can no longer afford the costs of painting. In this case, Foley, as the principal, has the power to terminate the agency relationship by revocation. However, because Foley's actions are a breach of the Foley-Paul contract, Foley's termination is unlawful and Paul may recover any damages that he suffered as a result of the breach of contract.

More often than not, the parties in an agency relationship will have agreed to a fixed term for the representation. In that case, the agency relationship may be terminated by **expiration**. The expiration may be tied to a time period (e.g., the principal hires the agent for a one-year period) or an event (e.g., the principal hires the agent as a substitute worker only until an injured worker returns). Instead of setting a fixed time or event, the parties may agree to end the agency once the agency's purpose has been accomplished. For example, in the Foley-Paul agency relationship, suppose that Foley did not attempt to terminate the agency and the painting services were finished on time. In this case, the agency ends automatically because the purpose of the agency, as originally contemplated by the parties, has been accomplished.

Operation of Law

Agency may also be terminated as provided for by statute or through certain common law doctrines. First, an agency relationship is terminated by the *destruction* of essential subject matter of the relationship. If the agent's role is predicated on some particular property being at the disposal of the principal and the property is no longer practically or legally available, agency is automatically terminated. For example, Foley hires Paul to paint the lobby of Foley's office building. The day after the two agree, Foley's building burns down. The Foley-Paul agency relationship is thus terminated.

An agency relationship also is terminated automatically if either the principal or the agent *dies*, files for *bankruptcy*, or does not have the requisite *mental capacity* to continue the relationship. However, it is important to note that exceptions exist to these common law doctrines. Increasingly, various jurisdictions have prescribed statutory exceptions to certain events of termination. For example, in the case of the death of a principal, some state statutes permit the agent to continue to have actual authority until the agent learns of the death. Therefore, if the agent is acting in good faith, the agent may continue his duties until he actually receives notice of the death of the principal.

TAKEAWAY CONCEPT Termination of an Agency Relationship

An agency relationship is terminated either through express acts (termination or expiration) or through operation of law (destruction of subject matter, death, bankruptcy, or mental capacity).

 THINKING STRATEGICALLY

Limiting Liability for Misclassification

PROBLEM: While some agent classifications are clear, as the global economy evolves and new positions and types of occupations are created, managers may face difficulties in classification. Misclassification can result in significant tax, benefit, and tort liability.

STRATEGIC SOLUTION: Limit liability through (1) screening, (2) agreements, (3) operational controls, and (4) verification.

SCREENING

A strategic step in limiting liability for misclassification is to hire independent contractors who have incorporated their own businesses rather than those who operate as sole proprietors or partners in a partnership. When a principal hires an incorporated independent contractor, the law treats that transaction as a contract between the principal and the *corporation* rather than as an arrangement between the principal and the individual independent contractor. The principal pays the worker's corporation, which pays the worker, who is an employee of the corporation. The corporation is a legal "person" that stands between the principal and the independent contractor. Therefore, the corporation is responsible for state and federal payroll taxes, benefits, and workers' compensation insurance.

Managers also should consider hiring an employee leasing company (sometimes called a temp agency), which provides many of the benefits of hiring independent contractors directly. The benefit of leasing workers is that the leased workers are the leasing firm's employees, not the principal's. The leasing company pays all wages, taxes, and benefits required by law.

AGREEMENT

Although a written agreement with an independent contractor is not required for classification purposes, it can help to document the working relationship. The agreement need not be lengthy or complicated, but it should be clear that no employment relationship exists and should describe the work assignment or project the independent contractor is to perform. After the original assignment is complete, any new work assignments should be articulated in a new agreement. The agreement also should detail the terms of payment and require the independent contractor to submit monthly invoices, which are to be paid at the same time other outside vendors' invoices are paid. Independent contractors should not be paid on a weekly or biweekly basis or be given benefits or bonuses, because these are all indicators of an employer-employee relationship.

The agreement also should make clear that independent contractors are not required to work set days or hours and that any deadlines for work assignments are met through the independent contractor's judgment as to when, how, and where the work is completed.

OPERATIONAL CONTROLS

Even when independent contractors are incorporated or provided by employee leasing companies, it is important to continue to limit liability through operational methods related to *direction and control.* Most importantly, the principal should not supervise the independent contractor or his or her assistants. The independent contractor should perform services without direction of the principal. In order to monitor quality control, the independent contractor should submit progress reports as part of the monthly invoices. Other operational methods to consider are listed below:

- An independent contractor should not work at the business's offices or locations unless the nature of the services absolutely requires it.
- An independent contractor should not receive employee handbooks or company policy manuals.
- An independent contractor should not be given ongoing instructions or training.
- Independent contractors should use their own equipment or materials if possible.
- Use of company business cards or stationery by an independent contractor should be restricted.
- An independent contractor should not be given a title or any supervisory authority.
- An independent contractor should not attend employee meetings or functions.

VERIFICATION

Form SS-8 was created by the IRS to assist business owners and managers in complying with tax regulations regarding independent contractor status. Filing the form gives the principal/employer assurances that either (1) the classification by the employer is correct or (2) the classification needs to be changed and similar positions should be classified in the same way in the future. The other benefit to filing the form is that it may be evidence of good faith efforts to comply with the tax law. If the IRS determines that the principal/employer made a good faith mistake in classifying the agent, no penalty is imposed. If the IRS regards the principal/employer's classification as reckless or made without requisite good faith compliance efforts, penalties and interest are added to the assessment of back taxes.

QUESTIONS

1. If you went to work for a business and believed you were misclassified as an independent contractor rather than as an employee, how would you handle that situation?

2. What are some of the ethical dimensions to agent classification? Do some employers try to use an avoidance strategy by classifying workers as independent contractors so they don't have to pay employment taxes? Is that ethical? Explain.

KEY TERMS

Agency law p. 654   The body of laws that govern the relationships created when one party hires another party to act on the hiring party's behalf.

Agent p. 655   One who agrees to act and is authorized to act on behalf of another, a *principal,* to legally bind the principal in particular business transactions with third parties pursuant to an agency relationship.

Principal p. 655   An agent's master; the person from whom an agent has received instruction and authorization and to whose benefit the agent is expected to perform and make decisions pursuant to an agency relationship.

Restatement (Third) of Agency p. 655   A set of principles, issued by the American Law Institute, intended to clarify the prevailing opinion of how the law of agency stands.

Manifest p. 656   Apparent and evident to the senses. In the context of agency law, courts apply an objective standard to determine whether the principal intended that an agency be created.

Consent p. 656   An agent's agreeing to act for the principal. In the context of agency law, courts apply an objective standard to determine whether the agent did in fact agree to the agency relationship.

Employee agents p. 657   One of three broad categories of agents; generally, anyone who performs services for a principal if the principal controls what will be done and how it will be done.

Independent contractor p. 658   One of three broad categories of agents; generally, anyone who performs services for a principal if the principal has the right to control or direct only the result of the work and not the means and methods of accomplishing the result.

Gratuitous agents p. 658   One of three broad categories of agents; generally, anyone who acts on behalf of a principal without receiving any compensation.

ABC test p. 659   Statutory standard used by many states to determine agency status.

Express acts p. 664   Acts by which an agency relationship is terminated; can be either simple communication of the desire to terminate the relationship, the expiration of a fixed term, or satisfaction of purpose.

Operation of law p. 664   Method whereby an agency relationship is terminated as provided for in a statute or through certain common law doctrines covering the destruction of essential subject matter, death, bankruptcy, or lack of requisite mental capacity.

Termination p. 664   Method of ending an agency relationship whereby either the principal (revocation) or the agent (renunciation) simply communicates the desire to dissolve the relationship.

Expiration p. 664   Method of ending an agency relationship whereby the parties agree to a fixed term for the relationship.

CASE SUMMARY 37.1 Futrell v. Payday California, Inc. et al., 190 Cal. App. 4th 1419 (8th Div. 2010)

Classification of Agents

Futrell was hired by Reactor Films for traffic control on the site of a television commercial shoot. Rather than maintain a staff of full-time employees, Reactor hired freelance crew members as needed for each commercial. Reactor outsourced its payroll functions to Payday California, a payroll processing company. Over a period of four years, Futrell worked on several commercial productions; the number of hours varied per commercial depending on the circumstances of the production. Futrell filed suit against Reactor and Payday claiming that they were joint employers and that he was an employee, which entitled him to overtime benefits. Futrell claimed that Payday was an employer because

he submitted all time cards and employee information sheets to Payday and his W-2 tax form identified Payday as his employer. Reactor and Payday claimed that Futrell was an independent contractor and not entitled to employee benefits.

CASE QUESTIONS

1. How compelling is the evidence that Futrell supplied (i.e., time cards, W-2 forms, etc.) that Payday was his employer and he was not an independent contractor? Does tax status help determine agency status?
2. How much direction and control did Reactor have over Futrell? Was it sufficient to indicate an agency status?

CASE SUMMARY 37.2 Harris v. Vector Marketing Corp., 753 F. Supp. 2d 996 (D.C. N.D. Cal. 2009)

Sales Representatives

Vector is a direct sales company that markets a line of high-quality kitchen cutlery through the use of sales representatives, many of whom are college students. Harris was hired as a sales representative and attended a three-day training program for which she was not paid. Vector does not provide sales representatives with prospective leads, help with scheduling customers, or supply vehicles, office space, computers, or any other equipment to assist with sales efforts. Therefore, Vector claimed that the agency relationship with sales representatives was as an independent contractor. Harris argued that she should have been classified as an employee because Vector's control

included price setting, approval for advertising, mandatory use of Vector's prospectus and in-home sales demonstration kits, and a requirement that the sales representatives call their managers to report each day's activities.

CASE QUESTIONS

1. Using the direction and control analysis, determine whether Harris was an employee or independent contractor.
2. If Vector had a written agreement with each sales representative that made clear that the agency relationship was an independent contractor relationship, how would that impact your analysis?

Consent

Warren operated a grain processing company in which Cargill, Inc. was his main source of financing operations. As the lender, Cargill exercised significant control over Warren's operations, including approving any expenditure over $500, approving any sale of Warren's stock, and requiring mandatory disclosures from Warren for any withdrawals from the bank account. Warren also sold Cargill the majority of the grain produced. Jensen Farms was a creditor to Warren and became concerned about Warren's ability to survive financially, but Cargill gave Jensen Farms assurances that Warren was financially stable. Warren's financial condition continued to worsen, and the company owed Jensen Farms nearly $2 million when it ceased business operations. Jensen brought suit against Cargill claiming that Cargill's manifestation of an offer to be a principal in an agency relationship with Warren made Cargill liable for Warren's debt. Cargill argued that it never manifested an offer and that Warren never expressly consented to the agency.

CASE QUESTIONS

1. Is it possible for Warren to consent to an agency without doing so expressly?
2. Compare this case to *Bosse v. Brinker* (Case 37.1). Should the Bosse court reasoning apply here, or are there different circumstances?

Agent Classification

All employees who were hired by Federal Express (FedEx) as long-haul delivery drivers were required to sign an operating agreement that identified them as independent contractors. Under the terms of the agreement, each driver would provide his own truck, mark the truck with the FedEx logo, pay all costs of operating and maintaining the truck, and use the truck exclusively in the service of FedEx along with other specific obligations. The drivers brought a class action suit contending that, for the purpose of their entitlement to reimbursement for work-related expenses, they were employees, not independent contractors.

CASE QUESTIONS

1. Should the drivers be classified as independent contractors?
2. What tests should the court apply to determine the status of the drivers?

CHAPTER REVIEW QUESTIONS

1. A principal and agent relationship requires a(n):
   a. Formal written agreement.
   b. Definite time period.
   c. Express oral agreement.
   d. Agreement of consent and control.
   e. Attorney.

2. Which of the following are agent classifications?
   I. Employee agents
   II. Independent contractors
   III. Sports agents
   IV. Gratuitous agent
   a. I and II
   b. I, II, and III
   c. I, II, and IV
   d. I, III, and IV
   e. II and III

3. A manager hires Ernest to supervise all shipments made from the company's central delivery center. Ernest's

workweek is set by the manager, he is paid a salary, and he gets benefits. What is Ernest's agency classification?

a. Employee agent

b. Independent contractor agent

c. Nonagent employee (master-servant)

d. Gratuitous agent

e. Supervisory agent

4. George has been called away by his employer in Europe, so he hires Bartram to take care of his prize garden for the summer months until he returns. George agrees to send Bartram $1,000 per month, and Bartram agrees to use his own equipment. Which of the following is true about the relationship between George and Bartram?

a. George is a gratuitous agent.

b. Bartram is an employee agent of George.

c. No agency agreement exists.

d. Bartram is an independent contractor.

e. A written agreement is required.

5. Which of the following are included in determining the status of an agent?

I. Frequency of payments to the agent

II. A written agreement between the parties

III. Type of working relationship between principal and agent

IV. Whether the agency was created or implied

a. I and III

b. I and IV

c. I, II, and III

d. I, III, and IV

e. II and IV

6. A bank manager is an employee agent of the bank.

a. True

b. False

7. An independent contractor is not controlled directly by the principal.

a. True

b. False

8. Jay is a landscaper with 10 clients. One of his clients is responsible for 45 percent of his business and requires Jay to perform landscaping work only on Saturdays and Sundays so that it doesn't interfere with customer traffic. He pays Jay once every three months. Jay is an employee.

a. True

b. False

9. Ernest is a supervisor at an office supply store where he supervises a staff of three. He is an employee agent.

a. True

b. False

10. An agency relationship may only be terminated by an express act of the parties.

a. True

b. False

 Quick Quiz ANSWERS

Agency Classification

1. Independent contractor. Factors: (a) A publisher has very little direction and control of an author in terms of time and schedule, (b) lump sum payment; and (c) no ongoing relationship.

2. Independent contractor. While More may appear at first glance to be an employee due to the schedule, consider that (a) More has eight such clients (he doesn't work exclusively for Henry); (b) More is paid through invoice; and (c) a short-term agreement exists with no promise of continuing employment.

3. Employee. Factors: (a) full direction and control over More's schedule; and (b) hourly wages (in addition to the commission).

4. Gratuitous agent.

(continued)

5. Employee. While this may appear at first glance to be an independent contractor relationship because of the agreement, remember that courts apply a substance-over-form analysis in determining agency status. Consider that (a) More's schedule is set by Henry; (b) More is paid the same amount on a biweekly basis; (c) the annual holiday bonus may be evidence of a continuing employment; and (d) More uses Henry's equipment to do his job.

6. Employee. Level of salary is not determinative in an agency classification analysis. More's schedule is set, Henry provides his pay and benefits, and More predominantly uses Henry's equipment to perform his work.

CHAPTER REVIEW QUESTIONS: Answers and Explanations

1. d. An agency is fundamentally about the elements of consent (by words or actions) and control of the agent by the principal. Answers *a* and *b* are wrong because no formal agreement is required and no definite time period need exist. Answer *c* is wrong because parties may form an agency relationship not only expressly but also implicitly.

2. c. Although sports agents may be a type of agent, only three classifications are recognized by the *Restatements*: employee agents, independent contractors, and gratuitous agents.

3. a. Because the manager sets Ernest's workweek (direction and control) and Ernest is paid a regular salary and benefits rather than being paid upon invoice, he must be an employee agent; thus, answer *a* is correct and answers *b* and *d* are wrong. Answer *c* is wrong because Ernest was hired to "supervise."

4. d. Given his work schedule, conditions, and method of payment, Bartram is an independent contractor. He is paid, but there are no signs that he is a regular employee, so answers *a* and *b* cannot be correct. Answer *c* is wrong because the parties manifested consent and control through express agreement.

5. c. The classification of an agent is unrelated to whether the agent is an express agent. The other factors (I, II, and III) roughly track the ABC test.

6. a. A bank manager is an employee agent of the bank because he is authorized to act on behalf of the principal/employer.

7. a. Independent contractors set their own schedules and are not controlled directly by the principal.

8. b. Because Jay has multiple clients and is only paid once every three months, Jay is *not* an employee.

9. a. Because Ernest is a supervisor, he cannot be a master/servant agent.

10. b. An agency relationship may be terminated by an express act of the parties *or* by operation of law.

CHAPTER 38

Duties and Liabilities of Principals and Agents

A well-functioning organization carefully and clearly defines the scope of authority granted to its employees. Otherwise, businesses may be liable for the decisions made by employees that were never fully assessed. At the end of this chapter, you will strategically assess the risk of liability in a contract as it applies to principals, agents, and third parties.

Learning Objectives

After studying this chapter, students who have mastered the material will be able to:

38-1   Identify the relationship between principals, agents, and third parties.

38-2   Analyze scenarios in which an agent may create contract liability for a principal.

38-3   Demonstrate cases in which an agent is liable to a third party in a contract.

38-4   Analyze scenarios in which an agent may create tort liability for a principal.

CHAPTER OVERVIEW

Organizations could not function without being able to delegate tasks to individuals called *agents* who are authorized to act on the organization's behalf. Corporations, for example, need employees who are authorized to carry out the company's business activities. Legally astute managers, however, understand that an agent's behavior can create liability for the principal organization. Liability can arise either through a contract obligation or through vicarious liability (liability for another) in tort. For example, when a third party claims that the principal is liable for an agent's act, the third party is claiming that the principal is responsible for the legal consequences of that act. Legally astute business owners and managers who understand the obligations and liabilities that arise from agency relationships are better positioned to limit their own and their company's liability.

©TriStar/Getty Images

In the 1996 film *Jerry Maguire,* Tom Cruise stars as a sports agent who negotiates athletes' employment contracts with professional sports teams.

PRINCIPALS, AGENTS, AND THIRD PARTIES

This chapter will focus on how the law of agency impacts three parties: principals, agents, and third parties. Chapter 37 focused on how principals and agents form a legal relationship known as *agency*. This chapter examines how obligations and liabilities arise when the principal and agent interact with a separate individual or business known as a *third party*. The principal–agent–third party relationship depicted in Figure 38.1 will be referenced throughout this chapter.

One of the reasons agency is such a useful legal concept is because it allows businesses as principals to grow and transfer authority to agents within the organization's chain of command. Think of a start-up corporation as the principal that delegates general day-to-day management responsibilities to its chief executive officer (CEO). As an agent with broad authority, the CEO may decide that as the start-up grows, it is best to hire and supervise other agents who can carry out more specialized responsibilities. For example, the CEO may need to hire a chief financial officer (CFO) to handle finances, a chief operations officer (COO) to handle logistics and manufacturing, and a chief legal officer (CLO) to handle the company's legal affairs. In turn, the CEO may authorize these "C-level" executives to hire additional agents within their respective departments. The CEO is referred to as a **superior agent**, and the C-level executives are **subordinate agents**. The C-level executives may also be superior agents if they hire and oversee employees within their departments. In this manner, agency allows responsibility and authority to be delegated throughout the organization. All of these individuals are co-agents of the principal, which in this case is the business. As agents, they may under certain circumstances create liability to the principal in contract and tort.

LO 38-1

Identify the relationship between principals, agents, and third parties.

TAKEAWAY CONCEPTS Principals, Agents, and Third Parties

- Agency is a useful legal concept because it allows businesses as principals to grow and transfer authority to agents within the organization's chain of command.
- Agents with authority over other agents are referred to as superior agents.
- Agents who report to other agents are called subordinate agents.
- Agents may under certain circumstances create liability to the principal in contract and tort.

A PRINCIPAL'S LIABILITY FOR THE AGENT'S CONTRACTS

Principals often create agency relationships to give agents the power to enter into contracts with third parties that are legally binding on the principal. Take the case of a property owner who owns an apartment building.[1] As the principal, the property owner may decide

LO 38-2

Analyze scenarios in which an agent may create contract liability for a principal.

FIGURE 38.1	Principal–Agent–Third Party Relationship

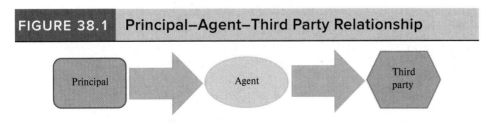

---

[1]As with all principals, the property owner may be a real person (referred to as a *natural person* in the law) or a legal person such as a corporation or some other type of business association.

to devote her time and skill to investing in properties. To achieve this goal, she decides it is best to transfer the authority to manage the apartment building to a separate real estate management company. The real estate management company will interact with third parties such as tenants and maintenance companies and will oversee activities such as leasing, collecting rent, and maintaining the property. As part of the agency relationship, the property owner (principal) will transfer authority to the real estate management company (agent) to execute contracts, such as leases, that bind the property owner with third parties such as tenants. The following language from a college apartment lease agreement indicates that Sunshine Properties (the principal property owner) has authorized DiPaolo Properties to act as its leasing and management agent:

> THIS LEASE AGREEMENT ("Agreement") made and entered into this 1st day of July, 2018 (the "Effective Date"), by and between DiPaolo Properties and Investments, LLC, a Florida limited liability company, as the authorized leasing and management agent of Sunshine Properties ("Landlord"), which owns that certain real property being, lying and situated in Leon County, Florida, and having a street address of 123 Call Street Tallahassee, Florida ("The Premises") and the undersigned individuals below collectively the ("Tenant") . . .

An agent's power to bind a principal in contract is derived from the agent's authority. This authority arises from (1) actual authority, (2) apparent authority, and (3) ratification.

Actual Authority

Typically, an agent's power to bind the principal in contract is through **actual authority** which arises in one of two ways. First, the principal may grant **express authority** through a written or oral statement that describes the authority granted to an agent. This can be done informally, such as when a principal verbally authorizes an agent to act, or formally, such as when a contract describes the agent's authority. Second, the law attaches **implied authority** in every instance where there is actual authority. Implied authority is the authority that is reasonably necessary to further the principal's objectives. Implied authority can also be based on custom, or the course of past dealings.

For example, Sunshine Properties gave express authority for DiPaolo to sign lease contracts with tenants on its behalf. Sunshine, however, never mentioned its position with respect to renters who own pets. DiPaolo would nonetheless have the implied authority to decide whether pets are forbidden on the premises and include this policy in leases that are binding on Sunshine.

Apparent Authority

Sometimes an agent acts in an unauthorized manner (without express or implied authority), yet she still binds the principal in contract. This occurs when a third party relies on a statement or action of the principal that creates a false appearance of an agent possessing authority. This scenario is referred to as **apparent authority**. Determining whether an agent has apparent authority can be difficult because it is a source of power that is not expressly authorized by the principal. The key to understanding this power is to determine whether a third party was objectively reasonable in his belief that the apparent agent is in fact authorized to act for the principal.[2] Apparent authority arises from the actions of a principal that lead a third party to believe that an agent has the authority to act on the principal's behalf.

For example, providing an agent with a title can create the impression of authority when that is not the case. When Sunshine grants DiPaolo the title "Authorized Leasing and Management Agent," this can create the appearance of authority even in cases where there

---

[2] *Restatement (Third) of Agency,* § 27.

is none. It may be that Sunshine expressly told DiPaolo not to sign leases that are longer than one year. If DiPaolo signs a two-year lease, however, Sunshine will be bound by this agreement because granting DiPaolo the Leasing and Management Agent title creates the reasonable impression on third parties that DiPaolo is authorized to sign longer-term leases.

In Case 38.1, a state appellate court analyzes the doctrine of apparent authority in the context of a wrongful death lawsuit.

CASE 38.1 GGNSC Batesville, LLC d/b/a Golden Living Center v. Johnson, 109 So. 3d 562 (Miss. 2013)

FACT SUMMARY Johnson was the court-appointed representative of her brother's estate and filed a wrongful death lawsuit against GGNSC Batesville, LLC d/b/a Golden Living Center ("Golden Living") alleging that Golden Living's negligence caused the death of her brother, Mose Cooper, who was a former resident of the Golden Living nursing home. Golden Living moved to compel arbitration based on an arbitration clause in its standard admission agreement. The trial court denied the motion and ruled that no valid contract existed because Johnson, not Cooper, signed the agreement during the nursing home's admissions process and Johnson had no legal authority to act as Cooper's agent.

SYNOPSIS OF DECISION AND OPINION The Mississippi Supreme Court affirmed the decision of the trial court and ruled in favor of Johnson. The court held that Golden Living had failed to provide any evidence that Johnson had any actual authority for health care or other decisions on Cooper's behalf. The court rejected Golden Living's argument that the relationship between Johnson and Cooper, coupled with Johnson's presence during the admissions process, was sufficient to establish apparent authority.

WORDS OF THE COURT: Apparent Authority "To prove that Johnson had apparent authority over Cooper, Golden Living must put forth sufficient

evidence of (1) acts or conduct of the principal indicating the agent's authority, (2) reasonable reliance upon those acts by a third party, and (3) a detrimental change in position by the third person as a result of that reliance. The record is utterly devoid of any acts or conduct of Cooper indicating that Johnson was his agent for the purpose of making health care decisions. Because Golden Living failed to put forth sufficient evidence, or indeed any evidence at all, of prong one, we need not address prongs two and three. Thus, Johnson did not have the apparent authority to bind Cooper to the contract, and consequently, a valid contract does not exist."

Case Questions

1. As a practical matter, what was the impact of the court's ruling on Johnson and Golden Living?

2. Was it reasonable for Golden Living to assume that Johnson had authority for Cooper's health care decisions? Why or why not? Could Cooper's conversation with the nursing home staff during admissions be sufficient to satisfy the first prong of the test? What words would indicate authority?

3. *Focus on Critical Thinking:* What other areas of the law are important to this analysis? Is it consistent with good public policy for courts to invalidate an agreement even when there was no question that the party (e.g., Cooper) gained a benefit as a result of the agreement? Why or why not?

Ratification

An agent can also obtain retroactive (after-the-fact) power to bind a principal through **ratification**. Ratification occurs when the principal affirms a previously unauthorized act. In these cases, even though an agent behaved in an unauthorized manner, the principal may provide after-the-fact authority by either (1) expressly ratifying the transaction or (2) not repudiating the act (e.g., by remaining silent or retaining the benefits while knowing that they resulted from an agent's unauthorized act).

To illustrate, suppose DiPaolo hires Greenpanels to install an expensive solar energy paneling system on Sunshine's apartment properties to reduce power consumption. The two parties had never done business before, and DiPaolo incorrectly tells Greenpanels that DiPaolo has authority to enter into the contract on behalf of Sunshine. During the monthlong installation, Sunshine notices Greenpanels's workers on the site and asks DiPaolo for an explanation. It is at this point that the authority is either ratified or repudiated. Sunshine never expressly gave DiPaolo the authority to contract with Greenpanels, and given the expense and nature of the contract and lack of past dealing, it is unlikely that any implied or apparent authority exists. Nonetheless, Sunshine may be pleased with DiPaolo's decision and may ratify the transaction through affirmation or silence. Thus, if Sunshine learns of the transaction, says nothing, and receives the benefits, it may not refuse to honor the contract on the basis that DiPaolo lacked the agency power to bind Sunshine in contract with Greenpanels.

In Case 38.2, the Delaware Supreme Court analyzes the issue of ratification in the context of the company's CEO terminating the employment of another top executive.

CASE 38.2 *In re* The Walt Disney Company Derivative Litigation, 907 A.2d 693 (Del. 2005)

FACT SUMMARY Michael Eisner, the CEO of The Walt Disney Company, fired the company's president, Michael Ovitz, after a bitter internal struggle. The firing triggered a multimillion-dollar severance payment to Ovitz. Walt Disney Company shareholders brought suit against the board to prevent the firing and the large severance payment to Ovitz, claiming that Eisner lacked the authority to fire Ovitz without first obtaining the board's approval.

SYNOPSIS OF DECISION AND OPINION The Delaware Chancery Court found that the board had granted this authority to Eisner due to his exercise of this authority in the past, and the Delaware Supreme Court affirmed the trial court's decision.

WORDS OF THE COURT: Authority to Remove an Officer "If the certificate of incorporation vested the power of removal exclusively in the board, then absent an express delegation of authority from the board, the presiding officer would have not have a concurrent removal power. If, on the other hand, the governing instruments expressly placed the power of removal in both the board and specified officers, then there would be concurrent removal power. This case does not fall within either hypothetical fact pattern, because Disney's governing instruments do not vest the removal power exclusively in the board, nor do they expressly give the Board Chairman/CEO a concurrent power to remove officers. Read together, the governing instruments do not yield a single,

indisputably clear answer, and could reasonably be interpreted either way.

. . .

"[T]he extrinsic evidence clearly supports the conclusion that the board and Eisner understood that Eisner, as Board Chairman/CEO had concurrent power with the board to terminate Ovitz as President. In that regard, the Chancellor credited the testimony of new board members that Eisner, as Chairman and CEO, was empowered to terminate Ovitz without board approval or intervention; and also Litvack's testimony that during his tenure as general counsel, many Company officers were terminated and the board never once took action in connection with their terminations. Because Eisner possessed, and exercised, the power to terminate Ovitz unilaterally, we find that the Chancellor correctly concluded that the new board was not required to act in connection with that termination . . ."

Case Questions

1. Was Eisner's authority grounded in actual authority, implied authority, or ratification? Explain.

2. Would granting Eisner the express authority to hire the president give him the implied authority to fire this individual? Explain.

3. *Focus on Critical Thinking:* How could the board have retained the exclusive power to terminate the company's president?

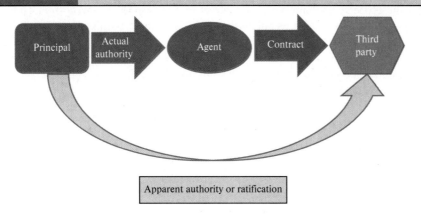

Figure 38.2 illustrates the concepts of actual authority, apparent authority, and ratification in relation to the principal, agent, and third party.

An agent may be liable to a third party if he acts without actual or apparent authority and the principal does not ratify the behavior. The following section will discuss how this liability is impacted by the status of the principal in the agency relationship.

TAKEAWAY CONCEPTS A Principal's Liability for the Agent's Contracts

- An agent's power to bind a principal in contract is derived from the agent's authority. This authority arises from (1) actual authority, (2) apparent authority, and (3) ratification.
- Actual authority is comprised of express and implied authority.
- Apparent authority requires the principal to create the impression authority exists, and the third party must have an objectively reasonable belief that the apparent agent is authorized to act for the principal.
- Ratification occurs when the principal affirms a previously unauthorized act.

AGENT'S CONTRACT LIABILITY TO THIRD PARTIES

LO 38-3

Demonstrate cases in which an agent is liable to a third party in a contract.

An authorized agent who enters into a contract with a third party binds the principal because the third party may legally enforce the contract against the principal. There are circumstances, however, where the agent may be held liable to perform the contract in the event the principal fails to perform. An agent's liability to third parties in a contract hinges on whether the agency relationship is fully disclosed, partially disclosed, or undisclosed.

Fully Disclosed Agency

When the third party entering into the contract is aware of the principal's identity and knows that the agent is acting on behalf of the principal in the transaction, then the agency relationship is a **fully disclosed agency**. In a fully disclosed agency relationship, only the principal is contractually obligated to the third party for authorized acts. Because the agent has no liability, third parties have no legal recourse against the agent if the principal fails to meet her obligations under the contract. For example, suppose that Abel is hired by Peters to locate and purchase a suitable piece of real estate for Peters's new warehouse. Abel locates the property and enters into a contract to purchase the property from Thompson. Abel signs the contract "Abel, as purchasing agent for Peters." In this case, if Peters changes his mind and decides not to complete the transaction, Abel has no liability because his agency was fully disclosed. Thompson's sole remedy is to pursue a breach of contract lawsuit against Peters. Abel will have sole liability to Thompson, however, if he exceeds his authority in the transaction.

Partially Disclosed Agency

If the third party knows that the agent is representing a principal but does not know the actual identity of the principal, the agency relationship is a **partially disclosed agency**. In some cases, the agent may identify the principal only as an "interested real estate buyer" or by some other terminology. In a partially disclosed agency relationship, both the principal and the agent may be liable for the obligations under the contract.[3] Because the principal is not identified, the third party must rely on the agent's good faith dealings and credit. Therefore, the law imposes liability on the agent in the event that the principal does not perform her contractual obligations. For example, in the Abel-Peters-Thompson transaction, suppose that Peters is a high-profile real estate developer who hires Abel to purchase Thompson's land on Peters's behalf. Peters believes that Thompson may hold out for a higher price if he knows that the buyer is a wealthy land developer, so he instructs Abel not to make his identity known when entering into the real estate contract with Thompson. Although Thompson is aware that Abel is an agent, he is not aware of the principal's identity. Abel signs the contract without any indication that Peters is the principal. If Peters later changes his mind and refuses to perform under the contract, Thompson may pursue remedies against Abel and/or Peters. If Thompson is successful in his case against Abel, Abel has the right of indemnification from Peters. Abel will have sole liability to Thompson if he exceeds his authority in the transaction.

Undisclosed Agency

When a third party is completely unaware of an agency relationship and believes that the agent is acting on her own behalf when contracting, this is called an **undisclosed agency**. In an undisclosed agency relationship, the agent is fully liable to perform the contract. Because the third party has no reason to know that an agency exists, he relies on the agent's good faith dealings and credit. Therefore, the law imposes liability on the agent in the event that the principal does not perform the contractual obligations. For example, in the Abel-Peters-Thompson transaction, suppose that Peters is a high-profile real estate developer and he hires Abel to purchase Thompson's land on Peters's behalf. Peters believes that Thompson may hold out for a higher price if he knows that the buyer is a wealthy land developer. Moreover, Peters is sufficiently confident in his belief that his identity will drive up the price that he takes extraordinary efforts to keep his interest in the property confidential. He instructs Abel not to inform Thompson of his status as an agent and to enter into the real estate purchase contract with Thompson in Abel's individual name. Since Thompson is not aware that Abel is an agent, nor is he aware of the principal's identity, this is an undisclosed agency relationship. Therefore, if Peters later changes his mind and refuses to perform under the contract, Thompson may pursue remedies against Abel. In some states, if Thompson subsequently finds out that Peters is the actual principal, he may pursue legal remedies against Peters as well. In any case, if Abel is made to pay, he has the right to indemnification from Peters if he acts in an authorized manner.

---

[3]*Restatement (Third) of Agency,* § 321.

- An agent's liability to third parties in a contract hinges on whether the agency relationship is fully disclosed, partially disclosed, or undisclosed.
- In a fully disclosed agency relationship, only the principal is contractually obligated to the third party for authorized acts of the agent.
- In a partially disclosed agency relationship, the law imposes liability on the agent in the event that the principal does not perform her contractual obligations.
- In an undisclosed agency relationship, the agent is fully liable to perform the contract.

A PRINCIPAL'S LIABILITY FOR THE AGENT'S TORTS

A principal may face **joint-and-several liability** for an agent's tort, most commonly the tort of negligence, even though the principal has not engaged in any wrongful conduct. This is particularly true when the agent is an employee. For example, suppose Pep's Pizza Parlor employs a driver to deliver its products. On the way to a delivery, the driver is negligent and injures a pedestrian. Pep's is held jointly liable with the driver for damages suffered by the pedestrian even though it exercised all due care by checking the driver's record and training the driver. Since it is likely that Pep's will be the party with assets or insurance to satisfy the claim, Pep's will pay the total outstanding liability under joint-and-several liability.

Liability for agents who are classified as employees is derived from the doctrine of **respondeat superior**.[4] Under respondeat superior, employers are liable for the negligent acts of employee agents. This is a form of vicarious liability because it involves one party's liability for the act of another party. Principals are generally not liable, however, for the negligent acts of independent contractors. Respondeat superior liability is yet another reason the correct classification of agents by business owners and managers is crucial to managing risk.

Physical Injury Requirement

Parties who suffer purely economic losses as a result of another's negligence may only recover if those losses were a result of injury to person or property. This is also important in the context of respondeat superior. As a general rule, if the employee's misconduct causes physical harm to a third party's person or property, the employer is liable for both the injury and any related economic losses. However, if the employee's negligent misconduct results in harm only to emotional state, reputation, or a purely economic loss, respondeat superior does not apply.

Scope of Employment

The doctrine of respondeat superior is also limited by a requirement that in order for a principal (employer) to be liable for the employee's tort, the act must have occurred within the employee's *scope of employment*. Respondeat superior is a powerful tool for an injured third party because under a "deep pocket" scenario, it allows the injured party to recover damages from the employer under the assumption that the employer's resources and insurance coverage are more abundant than those of the employee agent who committed the negligence. The scope of employment rule is an attempt to place some limitations on the

LO 38-4

Analyze scenarios in which an agent may create tort liability for a principal.

---

[4]Literal Latin translation: "Let the master answer"; *Collins Latin* (2008).

principal's vicarious liability. For the principal to be liable, the agent's tortious conduct must have (1) been related to her duties as an employee of the principal, (2) occurred substantially within the reasonable time and space limits, and (3) been motivated, in part, by a purpose to serve the principal.

Frolics and Detours
Another kind of exception to the respondeat superior doctrine occurs when an agent, during a normal workday, does something purely for her own reasons that are unrelated to employment. During this time, the employee's conduct is thought of as being outside the zone that is governed by respondeat superior. The law recognizes this activity, called a **frolic**, as a protection for the principal against any harm suffered as a result of an agent's negligence while on the frolic. The frolic exception is sometimes thorny to apply because determining the precise times that the frolic began and ended can be difficult. Moreover, if the conduct is a small-scale deviation that is normally expected in the workday, it is not considered a frolic but rather a simple **detour**. Detours are still within the ambit of respondeat superior. Courts use a case-by-case approach to applying the frolic doctrine because the conduct is judged based on the degree to which it is or is not within the scope of employment.

To understand the difference between frolic and detour, consider the following two hypothetical cases. Flash is employed by Apollo Messenger Service as the driver of its delivery van. During his workday, he is speeding in the delivery van and negligently injures a pedestrian. Suppose that at the time of the accident Flash is on his lunch break and driving the van to the local stadium to purchase tickets for his family to a ball game to be played that night. In this case, a court will likely rule that Apollo is not liable under respondeat superior because of the frolic exception. Alternatively, suppose that Flash was on his way to pick up a cup of coffee at the local coffee shop and he struck the pedestrian in the parking lot. The coffee stop would likely be considered a detour. Although he was not acting for his employer, the negligence would likely be imputed to Apollo because Flash made only a short stop that constituted a small-scale deviation from his employment duties. Because it can reasonably be expected that delivery van drivers will take short breaks during the workday, a court may find that Apollo is liable for Flash's conduct under respondeat superior.

Case 38.3 is a landmark case dealing with a driver's potential frolic.

LANDMARK CASE 38.3 Riley v. Standard Oil Co. of New York, 231 N.Y. 301 (N.Y. 1921)

FACT SUMMARY Standard Oil employed a driver named Million and directed him to travel from the company-owned mill to the freight yard 2.5 miles away. There, he was supposed to load some barrels of paint onto his truck and immediately bring them back to the mill. Million arrived at the freight yard and picked up the paint. He then noticed some scrap wood, however, and loaded that onto his truck. Instead of returning to the mill as he was instructed, Million decided to drop off the scrap wood at his sister's house four blocks away from the freight yard in the direction opposite from the mill. Million dropped off the wood at his sister's house and approached the freight yard as he was making his way back to the mill. As he was nearing the freight yard, he struck and injured a child named Riley.

SYNOPSIS OF DECISION AND OPINION The trial court had entered a verdict in favor of the plaintiff, and the appellate court reversed and dismissed the complaint. The high court in this opinion reversed the appellate court and ordered that a new trial be scheduled on the basis that a jury should decide whether Million was acting on behalf of his employer at the time of the accident.

(continued)

WORDS OF THE COURT: No Fixed Formula to Determine a Frolic   "No formula can be stated that will enable us to solve the problem whether at a particular moment a particular employee is engaged in his employer's business. We recognize that the precise facts before the court will vary the result. We realize that differences of degree may produce unlike effects. However, whatever the facts, the answer depends upon a consideration of what the employee was doing, and why, when, where and how he was doing it.

. . .

"We are not called upon to decide whether the defendant might not have been responsible had this accident occurred while Million was on his way to his sister's house. That would depend on whether this trip is to be regarded as a new and independent journey on his own business, distinct from that of his employer or as a mere deviation from the general route from the mill and back. Considering the short distance and the little time involved, considering that the truck when it left the yards was loaded with the defendant's goods for delivery to the mill and that it was the general purpose of Million to return there, it is quite possible a question of fact would be presented to be decided by a jury."

Case Questions

Refer to Figure 38.3 below representing Million's travel route to answer the questions.

1. Should the court have decided differently if the accident had occurred when Million was on his way to his sister's house to drop off the wood? Explain.

2. What can Standard Oil, or any other company, do to reduce their respondeat superior liability in cases like these?

3. *Focus on Critical Thinking:* Did Million engage in a detour or a frolic? At what point should Million be considered back "on the job"? Explain.

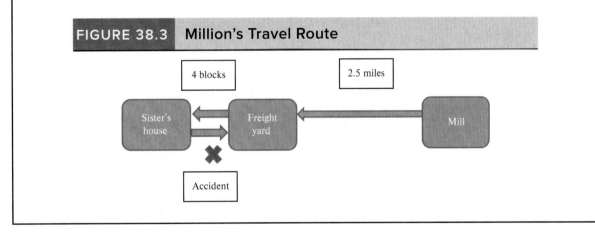

FIGURE 38.3   Million's Travel Route

Traveling to and from Work   One case that arises in the context of respondeat superior liability is when an employee causes an injury while traveling to or from the workplace. Many courts have adopted the **going-and-coming rule** whereby employers are generally not liable for tortious acts committed by employees while on their way to and from work. The law shields the employer from liability because employees are said to be outside of the course and scope of employment during their daily commute. Rather, the employment relationship is said to be suspended from the time the employee leaves or returns to the workplace.

An important exception to the going-and-coming rule is when the employee's use of her own car gives some incidental benefit to the employer. This is known as the *required-vehicle exception,* and it applies if the use of a personally owned vehicle is either an express or an implied condition of employment. It also applies if the employee has agreed, expressly or implicitly, to make the vehicle available as an accommodation to the employer.

Intentional Torts

Generally, intentional torts by an agent (such as committing assault and battery in the workplace) are thought to be outside the scope of employment, and, therefore, employers are not liable for such conduct unless the tort has a close connection to serving the principal. In a well-known decision on this topic, however, a state supreme court ruled that a sales associate employed by Nabisco who had physically assaulted the manager of a store in his territory was acting within his scope of employment because the original dispute involved shelf space at the store where the assault took place. The court held that because the employee agent was in the store pursuant to Nabisco's business and the injury stemmed from his job as a sales associate, even an intentional tort such as battery could be covered by respondeat superior.[5] As this case illustrates, even unauthorized intentional acts by an agent do not necessarily exempt the principal from liability that arises from the agent's wrongful behavior.

Negligent Hiring Doctrine

A majority of states recognize a tort-based theory of employer liability when the employer had reason to know that the employee might cause intentional harm within the scope of employment. This liability theory is called the **negligent hiring doctrine**, and it requires employers to take reasonable steps (such as criminal background investigation and reference checks) to protect third parties, particularly customers and other employees, from harm at the hands of an employee. Courts are especially inclined to hold employers liable under this doctrine in cases where (1) the employees are required to have a high level of public contact, as occurs with service and maintenance personnel, real estate agents, or delivery persons; or (2) the employees are entrusted with caring for the sick, elderly, or other particularly vulnerable populations.

Negligent hiring occurs when, prior to the time the employee is actually hired, the employer knew or should have known of the employee's unfitness.[6] Liability generally focuses on the employer's methods of determining suitability for the position. For example, in *Abbott v. Payne*[7] a state appellate court in Florida held the owners of a pest control company liable for negligent hiring when the company's management failed to run a criminal background check on an employee who subsequently sexually assaulted a customer during a home service call. The employee had a record of multiple arrests for sexually related crimes, and the court found that the employer had a duty to screen the employee for any information that indicated that the employee should not have been placed in a position of trust with regular access to customer information and regular contact with the public on the employer's behalf. The doctrine also includes *negligent retention* if circumstances arose after the hiring process that should have given notice to the employer of the potential for an employee to cause harm.

Independent Contractors

Recall from earlier in this chapter that, as a general rule, principals are not liable for the negligent acts or omissions of an independent contractor. One important exception to this rule occurs when the principal has been negligent in hiring, and it is based on the *peculiar*

---

[5]*Lange v. National Biscuit Company,* 211 N.W.2d 783 (Minn. 1973).

[6]*Restatement (Third) of Agency,* §§ 401–411.

[7]457 So. 2d 435 (Fla. App. 1984).

FIGURE 38.4 Independent Contractor Factors

The degree to which the employer controls or directs the manner in which work is performed
Whether the worker's opportunity for profit or loss depends on his or her managerial skills
Whether the worker's duties are performed for the employer on an ongoing or permanent basis
Whether the service performed by the worker is an integral part of the employer's business
The extent of the worker's investment in equipment or materials needed to perform the job
The degree to which the worker is engaged primarily for the benefit of the employer

risk doctrine that is rooted in the Restatements. The doctrine requires a principal to take reasonable steps to determine the fitness of an independent contractor to perform an inherently dangerous task. For example, a land developer that hires a demolition company to take down a large old building with dynamite has a legal obligation to ensure that the demolition company has reasonable safety measures in place, experienced personnel, and proper safety licensing and permitting.

Figure 38.4 includes some of the factors courts use to determine whether an agent is an independent contractor.

Ride-sharing app company Uber has pioneered an innovative business model that connects drivers with people seeking rides. The company, however, has been the subject of multiple agency-related lawsuits. For example, drivers have sued Uber in various states claiming that they are employees, not independent contractors as Uber insists. This important agency question will have significant financial and legal ramifications for the company. If the drivers are considered employees, then respondeat superior will apply as discussed previously and Uber may be legally responsible for the torts committed by its drivers.

In its contract with drivers, Uber added the following language:

13. Relationship of the Parties

13.1 Except as otherwise expressly provided herein with respect to Company acting as the limited payment collection agent solely for the purpose of collecting payment from Users on your behalf, the relationship between the parties under this Agreement is solely that of independent contractors. The parties expressly agree that: (a) this Agreement is not an employment agreement, nor does it create an employment relationship, between Company and you; and (b) no joint venture, partnership, or agency relationship exists between Company and you.

Uber logo.
©TY Lim/Shutterstock

QUICK QUIZ Agency Law at Uber

Consider the case of Uber and its drivers in the feature above.

1. If a driver injures a pedestrian and the court finds that Uber drivers are independent contractors, what liability will Uber face? What liability will Uber face if the court finds find its drivers are agents?

2. Review the factors in Figure 38.4. Are Uber drivers independent contractors? Explain your answer.

Answers to this Quick Quiz are provided at the end of the chapter.

TAKEAWAY CONCEPTS A Principal's Liability for the Agent's Torts

- A principal may face joint-and-several liability for an agent's tort, most commonly the tort of negligence, even though the principal has not engaged in any wrongful conduct.
- Liability for agents who are classified as employees is derived from the doctrine of respondeat superior.
- The doctrine of respondeat superior is also limited by a requirement that in order for a principal (employer) to be liable for an employee's tort, the act must have occurred within the employee's scope of employment.
- A frolic is an exception to the respondeat superior doctrine that occurs when an agent, during a normal workday, does something purely for her own reasons that is unrelated to employment.
- Generally, intentional torts by an agent are considered outside the scope of employment, and, therefore, employers are not liable for such conduct unless the tort has a close connection to serving the principal.
- As a general rule, principals are not liable for the negligent acts or omissions of an independent contractor.

 ## THINKING STRATEGICALLY

Employee Authority and Supplier Liability

PROBLEM: Businesses face liability if employees are authorized to hold third parties (such as suppliers) harmless for any liability.

STRATEGIC SOLUTION: Consider the following case and how agency law and managerial oversight can reduce the risk of incurring liability due to another party's behavior.

Pam started her first day as the Vice President of Finance at Kirkland Gas, Inc. Kirkland owns and operates several hundred gas stations across the United States.

©Robyn Beck/AFP/Getty Images

On her first day at work, Pam decides to review the gas hauling agreements with suppliers to approve the payments of outstanding invoices. As Pam reviews the agreements to begin processing payment, she notices the following language at the top of various gas hauling agreements with Gulf Oil Co., one of Kirkland's largest gas suppliers:

> **LEGAL TERMS:** Customer hereby acknowledges and agrees to the terms and conditions on the reverse side hereof which include, but are not limited to, **PAYMENT, RELEASE, INDEMNITY, and LIMITED WARRANTY** provisions.

Pam turns the page and sees the following:

> CUSTOMER ALSO AGREES TO DEFEND, INDEMNIFY AND HOLD GULF OIL CO. HARMLESS FROM AND AGAINST ALL LIABILITY, CLAIMS, COSTS, EXPENSES, ATTORNEY'S FEES AND DAMAGES WHATSOEVER FOR PROPERTY DAMAGE AND LOSS RESULTING FROM IMPROPER GAS TRANSPORTATION, STORAGE AND DELIVERY TO THE CUSTOMER'S FILLING STATIONS. CUSTOMER'S RELEASE, DEFENSE AND INDEMNITY AND HOLD HARMLESS OBLIGATIONS WILL APPLY EVEN IF THE LIABILITY AND CLAIMS ARE CAUSED BY THE NEGLIGENCE OF GULF OIL CO. AND ITS EMPLOYEES.

Pam is taken aback because earlier that week she read a story in a trade magazine about how a gasoline delivery truck had exploded at a competitor's gas station, causing great personal injury and property damage.

As she reviews the various Gulf Oil Co. gas delivery agreements, she notices that they are all signed upon delivery by Kirkland gas station employees. One of the agreements was signed by Al Hennipin, a Kirkland gas station cashier. Pam reaches out to Al to inquire about the delivery agreement and Al replies: "I knew about the legal stuff, but I never bothered to look into it. I've always been told by Fred [the district manager] that I have authority to sign the paperwork. And really I have to otherwise the Gulf driver won't unload the gas. So I just go ahead and sign the papers." After she hangs up with Al, Pam notices that in a folder marked "To Do" her predecessor wrote in a memo: *Met with John Mack [Kirkland's CEO] yesterday. He gave me the authority to negotiate liability release agreements with our gas suppliers. Need to schedule a meeting with legal ASAP!*

QUESTIONS

1. Do Al or any of the gas station employees have authority to sign the delivery agreements? If so, what is the nature of that authority?

2. What arguments can Kirkland make to claim that Al lacked authority and therefore hold Gulf Oil responsible for liability in the event their negligence causes injury?

3. How would you proceed if you were in Pam's situation? What steps can she take to protect her company?

KEY TERMS

Superior agent p. 673   An agent who oversees other agents within an organization.

Subordinate agent p. 673   An agent who is overseen by another agent within an organization.

Actual authority p. 674   Authority granted by a principal to an agent.

Express authority p. 674   When a principal makes an affirmative statement that authorizes an agent to act.

Implied authority p. 674   Authority that is reasonably necessary to carry out the principal's instructions.

Apparent authority p. 674   When the principal creates a false appearance of an agent possessing authority.

Ratification p. 675   When a principal affirms a previously unauthorized act of an agent.

Fully disclosed agency p. 677   When a third party knows the principal's identity.

Partially disclosed agency p. 678   When a third party knows a principal exists but does not know the principal's identity.

Undisclosed agency p. 678   When a third party does not know that a principal exists.

Joint-and-several liability p. 679   When general partners' personal assets are at risk both together (jointly) and separately (severally) for all debts and liabilities of the partnership, regardless of the source of the debt or liability.

Respondeat superior p. 679   When an employer is liable for the torts committed by an employee acting within the scope of employment.

Frolic p. 680   When an employee does something purely for her own reasons that are unrelated to employment, which releases the employer from respondeat superior liability.

Detour p. 680   When an employee engages in a minor deviation from employment that creates liability for the employer under respondeat superior.

Going-and-coming rule p. 681   A rule adopted by some courts whereby employers are generally not liable for tortious acts committed by employees while on their way to and from work.

Negligent hiring doctrine p. 682   A tort-based theory of employer liability when the employer had reason to know that the employee might cause intentional harm within the scope of employment.

CASE SUMMARY 38.1 Hannington v. University of Pennsylvania, 809 A.2d 406 (Pa. Super. Ct. 2002)

Apparent Authority

Hannington, a graduate student at the University of Pennsylvania (Penn), brought suit against the university for breach of contract. Attorneys for both sides appeared to have reached a settlement when, just prior to trial, Hannington's attorney notified the court that a settlement had been reached and sent Penn a final draft of the settlement agreement. Penn agreed to the settlement terms and sent the settlement agreement back to Hannington's attorney with Penn's authorized signatures. However, Hannington refused to sign the settlement agreement, hired a new attorney, and opted to proceed to trial. The trial court refused to allow

Hannington's case to go forward and held that Penn had reasonably relied on Hannington's attorney as being an agent with apparent authority to settle the case.

CASE QUESTIONS

1. Who prevails and why? Did Hannington's attorney have apparent authority? What is the standard?
2. Since Hannington never actually signed the agreement, was it reasonable for Penn to assume that Hannington's attorney had obtained his express consent to the terms? Has the court effectively deprived Hannington of his right to proceed to trial? Explain your answers.

CASE SUMMARY 38.2 Estrada v. FedEx Ground Package System, Inc., 64 Cal. Rptr. 3d 327 (2007)

Independent Contractor Status

All employees who were hired by Federal Express (FedEx) as long-haul delivery drivers were required to sign an operating agreement that identified the driver as an independent contractor. Under the terms of the agreement, the driver would provide his own truck, mark the truck with the FedEx logo, pay all costs of operating and maintaining the truck, and use the truck exclusively in the service of FedEx, along with other specific obligations. The drivers brought a class action

suit contending that for the purpose of their entitlement to reimbursement for work-related expenses, they were employees, not independent contractors.

CASE QUESTIONS

1. Should the drivers be classified as independent contractors? Why or why not?
2. What tests should the court apply to determine the status of the drivers?

CASE SUMMARY 38.3 Edgewater Motels, Inc. v. A. J. Gatzke and Walgreen Company, 277 N.W.2d 11 (Minn. 1979)

Scope of Employment

Gatzke was employed as a district manager for Walgreen Company (Walgreen), which owned a chain of restaurants. He was assigned to supervise the opening and

preliminary operations of a new Walgreen-owned restaurant in Duluth, Minnesota. This assignment required Walgreen to pay for Gatzke's temporary housing at the Edgewater Motel, which was located near the Duluth site, for several weeks. He used his motel room as a makeshift office and used the desk in the room for routine paperwork, including expense reports. Gatzke was a management-level, salaried employee and, therefore, had no set work hours. On one workday, Gatzke and several employees had spent the entire day on-site at the new restaurant and then had a business dinner and after-dinner drinks until approximately midnight. Gatzke then returned to his motel room and was filling out his expense report when he accidentally dropped a lit cigarette in the trash can next to the desk in his room. A fire started, and although Gatzke escaped unharmed, the motel was severely damaged. Among other defendants, Edgewater sued Walgreen claiming that it was vicariously liable for the acts of Gatzke as its employee agent.

CASE QUESTIONS

1. Was Gatzke's negligent smoking outside the scope of his employment? Why or why not?
2. If the evidence showed that Gatzke had intentionally tried to commit arson, how would that impact the court's analysis?
3. Suppose that Gatzke had been writing out personal postcards rather than filling out an expense report when he started the fire. Would Walgreen be liable? Why or why not?

CHAPTER REVIEW QUESTIONS

1. **Paul tells Sally to mail a payment. This is:**
   a. Express authority.
   b. Implied authority.
   c. Ratification.
   d. A frolic.
   e. A detour.

2. **Paul tells Sally to mail a payment. The letter is not stamped. Sally goes ahead and buys a stamp for the letter. This is:**
   a. Express authority.
   b. Implied authority.
   c. Ratification.
   d. A frolic.
   e. A detour.

3. **Paul tells Sally to mail a letter using regular mail delivery. Sally sends the mail using overnight rushed shipping with delivery confirmation. Paul approves of the mailing. This is:**
   a. Express authority.
   b. Implied authority.
   c. Ratification.
   d. A frolic.
   e. A detour.

4. **Paul tells Sally, an employee, to mail a letter. Before mailing the letter, Sally visits her uncle the next town** over and on her way she crashes her car and injures another driver. This is:
   a. Express authority.
   b. Implied authority.
   c. Ratification.
   d. A frolic.
   e. A detour.

5. **A wealthy real estate investor tells his agent to sign the real estate purchase contract in the agent's name and never mention they are working for the principal. This is:**
   a. Fully disclosed agency.
   b. Partially disclosed agency.
   c. Undisclosed agency.
   d. Respondeat superior.
   e. Apparent authority.

6. **One of the reasons why agency is such a useful legal concept is because it allows businesses as principals to grow and transfer authority to agents within the organization's chain of command.**
   a. True
   b. False

7. **Apparent authority is a type of actual authority.**
   a. True
   b. False

8. Respondeat superior describes the situation in which an employer is liable for the torts committed by an employee acting beyond the scope of employment.

a. True

b. False

9. Generally, a hiring party is liable for the torts committed by an independent contractor.

a. True

b. False

10. An agent acting with actual authority to sign a contract is a party to the contract and shares contract liability with the principal.

a. True

b. False

 QUICK QUIZ ANSWERS

Agency Law at Uber

1. If the court finds the drivers to be independent contractors, Uber will face no liability. If the court finds them to be agents, Uber will have joint-and-several liability under respondeat superior.

2. There is no clear answer. Several of the factors can go either way.

CHAPTER REVIEW QUESTIONS: Answers and Explanations

1. **a.** Paul has given express instructions.

2. **b.** For Sally to carry out her instructions, buying a stamp is reasonably necessary.

3. **c.** Paul has approved an unauthorized act.

4. **d.** Sally engaged in an act unrelated to her employment.

5. **c.** The principal's identity is hidden from the third party.

6. **a. True.** Agency provides the flexibility for superior agents to delegate authority to subordinate agents.

7. **b. False.** Apparent authority is not actual authority but instead is an act of the principal that reasonably leads a third party to believe the authority exists.

8. **b. False.** Respondeat superior is when an employer is liable for the torts committed by an employee acting *within* the scope of employment.

9. **b. False.** Generally, the hiring party is *not* liable for the torts committed by an independent contractor.

10. **b. False.** Agents with authority are not parties to a contract.

CHAPTER 39

Employment at Will

©valterZ/Shutterstock

Nearly every employer provides its employees with some type of manual or handbook that details employer policies in their workplace. In this chapter's *Thinking Strategically,* we'll discuss the potential for legal danger zones associated with employee handbooks and strategies for avoiding unintended liability.

Learning Objectives

After studying this chapter, students who have mastered the material will be able to:

39-1 Explain the fundamentals of the employment-at-will doctrine and the impact of an express or implied contract on an employee's status.

39-2 List and apply common law exceptions to the employment-at-will doctrine.

39-3 Articulate federal and state statutory protections for at-will employees.

39-4 Discuss the requirements for protection under federal and state whistleblower laws.

39-5 Explain the "separate and independent" defense to a whistleblower claim.

CHAPTER OVERVIEW

Perhaps the most common agency relationships in the business environment are those between employers and employees. In this chapter, we outline the touchstones of the employer-employee relationship by focusing on the combination of state common law and statutory law at the federal, state, and local levels that affects employers and employees. Traditionally, common law doctrines governed employer-employee relationships. However, lawmakers increasingly have displaced common law doctrines in favor of modern statutes designed to protect workers through laws aimed at preventing workplace discrimination and achieving other important public policy objectives.

EMPLOYMENT-AT-WILL DOCTRINE

The starting point for analyzing the legal relationships between employers and employees is the **employment-at-will doctrine**, a deep-seated common law rule that exists in some form in every U.S. jurisdiction.[1] Fundamentally, the doctrine permits an employer to terminate an employee with or without advance notice and with or without just cause, subject to certain exceptions. So long as it does not fall under one of the exceptions, the employer is insulated from a wrongful-termination lawsuit. The employment-at-will doctrine reflects the

---

[1]One state, Montana, does not use the term *employment-at-will.* Instead, courts apply a common law doctrine that insulates employers from wrongful-termination claims under certain circumstances.

principal's wide latitude in decision making when exercising the power and right to terminate an employee. However, several important exceptions limit the applicability of the rule. The employment-at-will doctrine does not apply in cases where (1) the employee has an express contract, (2) courts have fashioned a common law exception that protects the employee, or (3) some specific statutory protection against job termination (such as antidiscrimination laws) protects the employee.

LO 39-1

Explain the fundamentals of the employment-at-will doctrine and the impact of an express or implied contract on an employee's status.

Express Contracts

One major exception to the employment-at-will rule is when an employee has an express contractual relationship with the employer that is intended to displace the employment-at-will rule. When the parties enter into a contract, the employee's rights in the case of termination are spelled out in the contract. Typically, an employment contract will provide that employers may terminate the employee only for "good cause," such as a violation of a workplace rule or committing a criminal act in the course of his employment. The contract ordinarily lists the events of cause for termination, and the parties agree as to any post-termination obligations. The parties also may formally agree to some type of severance pay in the event that the employer terminates the employee for any reason other than those listed in the contract.

Labor Contracts

While some employment agreements are contracts between managers and a business entity, some contracts give rights to nonmanagement employees as well. These contracts, called *collective bargaining agreements (CBAs)*, are negotiated by a labor union on behalf of a group of employees. CBAs often provide protection by prescribing a process the employer must follow before terminating an employee. The process is designed to ensure that treatment of employees is consistent with the standards in the CBA. Collective bargaining agreements and labor unions are covered in detail in Chapter 40, "Employment Regulation and Labor Law."

TAKEAWAY CONCEPTS Employment-at-Will Doctrine

- Agency-based legal doctrines that apply to the interaction between employer and employee are governed by a combination of state common law and statutory law at the federal, state, and local level.
- The employment-at-will doctrine mandates that an employer has the right to terminate an employee with or without advance notice and with or without just cause, subject to certain exceptions.
- An important exception to the employment-at-will rule is when an employee has an express contractual relationship or a collective bargaining agreement with the employer.

COMMON LAW EXCEPTIONS

LO 39-2

List and apply common law exceptions to the employment-at-will doctrine.

The employment-at-will rule is decidedly biased toward protecting the interests of the employer, and courts have recognized that a strict application of the rule sometimes results in unjust treatment of the employee and is a detriment to the public at large. Courts have fashioned three common law exceptions that help to limit the harshness of the rule on employees. They

FIGURE 39.1   Employment-at-Will Exceptions by State

are (1) the **public policy exception**, (2) **implied contract** protection, and (3) the **covenant of good faith and fair dealing**. It is important to note that not every state recognizes every exception, and some states, such as Georgia, Florida, and Rhode Island, do not recognize any common law exceptions to the rule. Figure 39.1 shows the employment-at-will exceptions by state.

Public Policy Exception

The most widely used exception that displaces the employment-at-will rule recognizes that allowing employers to terminate an employee for certain reasons may contradict *public policy* (i.e., the welfare of the general public). The public policy exception is a narrowly applied common law rule that places the public welfare ahead of the rights of an employer. This provision is best thought of as a backstop provision for situations in which no specific statute is applicable but the termination is inconsistent with the public's well-being. The exception protects employees from job termination if they are exercising some legal right. The public policy objective being claimed by the employee must be explicit and well established. Typically, courts will consider the public policy objective to be explicit and well established if it is related to an existing statute, the state constitution, or previously established policy. For example, suppose that Rogers, an at-will employee in NewCo's warehouse, injures her back on the job. NewCo's manager tells Rogers that the company frowns on employees who file claims under the workers' compensation law. Rogers files the claim and is fired one week later without being given a reason. Rogers fits the common law public policy exception because she is exercising a statutory right that is explicit and well established.

In Case 39.1, an appellate court analyzes an employee's claim under the state common law public policy exception.

Narrow Doctrine   Many courts have been reluctant to expand the public policy exception. For example, in *Bammert v. Don's Super Valu, Inc.,*[2] the Wisconsin Supreme Court

---

[2]646 N.W.2d 365 (Wis. 2002).

CASE 39.1 Jasper v. H. Nizam, Inc., 764 N.W.2d 751 (Iowa 2009)

FACT SUMMARY Jasper was hired as the director of Kid University ("KU"), a child care facility in Johnston, Iowa. She was paid an hourly wage, and there were no specific terms of employment. Within a short time after Jasper started her employment, the husband and wife owners of KU announced that the facility would need to cut staff to reduce overhead. Jasper complained that any staff cuts would place KU in jeopardy of violating state administrative regulations related to the minimum ratios between staff and children. The staff-to-child ratio was a source of considerable tension between Jasper and KU's owners. The owners insisted that Jasper find a way to cut staff expenses, and Jasper continued to assert that current staffing was necessary for compliance with state regulations. The owners eventually proposed that Jasper and her assistant director begin to work in the classroom to help reduce staffing costs. However, Jasper protested any job responsibility change and asserted that the staffing ratios still would not be compliant with state regulations. Soon thereafter, KU terminated Jasper from her employment.

Jasper brought a wrongful-discharge suit against KU and its owners claiming that her firing was based on her refusal to violate the staff-to-child ratios and that such a termination was a violation of public policy. The trial court found in favor of KU because Jasper was an employee at will and had not demonstrated that KU violated "well-recognized and clearly defined public policy." The trial court held that the public policy exception could not apply because the staff-to-child ratio was an administrative rule and not mandated by statute. The court of appeals reversed and found in Jasper's favor, holding that, even absent a statute, a clear public policy existed that child care centers be adequately staffed.

SYNOPSIS OF DECISION AND OPINION The Iowa Supreme Court ruled in favor of Jasper and held that administrative regulations are a reliable source of public policy because of the strong similarities between statutes and administrative regulations. The court noted that administrative regulations are a means for the legislature to deal with the array of complex and technical problems it faces. The administrative regulations in this case were a direction by legislature to the Department of Human Services to establish rules concerning proper staff-to-child ratios as a means to ensure the health, safety, and welfare of children in child care facilities. Any termination that resulted from Jasper's insistence that the ratios be maintained was a violation of public policy and an exception to the employment-at-will rule.

WORDS OF THE COURT: Public Policy Exception "We adhere to the common-law employment-at-will doctrine in Iowa. However, we joined the parade of other states twenty years ago in adopting the public-policy exception to the employment-at-will doctrine. In doing so, we recognized a cause of action in Iowa for wrongful discharge from employment when the reasons contravene public policy. . . . Without question, the protection of children is a matter of fundamental public interest. These factors satisfy the goal that the [child-staff ratio] regulation affects the public interest. . . . We conclude that the particular administrative rule at issue in this case supports a clear and well-defined public policy that gives rise for [a lawsuit based on] wrongful discharge."

Case Questions

1. KU pointed out that there was no evidence that it actually violated the regulation during Jasper's period of employment. Should an employer have to "act" before any public policy concerns justify an exception to the employment-at-will rule? Why or why not?

2. Does the court's ruling mean that all state administrative regulations are now the source of public policy considerations? Explain.

3. *Focus on Critical Thinking:* Is the court overreaching in establishing that administrative regulations can be the basis for a public policy exception? Where should the ultimate responsibility for establishing public policy lie? Are there any disadvantages to tying administrative regulations to the public policy exception?

refused to apply the public policy exception when the wife of a police officer alleged that she was fired in retaliation after her husband arrested her employer's wife. The court, while acknowledging the outrageous conduct of the employer, held that the public policy exception was too narrow to include specific retaliatory conduct where the connection to any public policy objective was not rooted in a statute, the state constitution, or existing state public policy. The *Bammert* decision illustrates an important point regarding the public policy exception to the employment-at-will doctrine: its limited scope. Absent a specific statutory protection (such as a whistleblower law), the threshold for relief using a public policy justification is very high. Some examples include refusing to commit an illegal act (such as filing a false tax return), exercising a legal right (such as refusing to take a polygraph test), or performing an important act (such as the protection of children as discussed in the *Jasper* case).

Implied Contracts

In addition to express contracts as discussed earlier, an employment-at-will relationship may be converted to a contract relationship if the employer acted in a manner that would lead a reasonable person to believe that the employer intended to offer an employee protection from termination without cause. This protection, called an *implied contract,* arises in two circumstances. First, a manual or bulletin (such as an employee handbook) that is drafted and distributed by the employer may give rise to an implied contract theory if the manual extends some protections or process to the employee that she would not have under the employment-at-will doctrine. For example, if an employer designs a process whereby supervisors use a system of progressive discipline before a termination may occur (e.g., warning for the first violation of a workplace rule, suspension for the second violation, and termination for the third violation), this may be the basis for an implied contract that displaces the employment-at-will rule. Second, an oral promise made by an employer that a reasonable person would believe extends protection against termination without cause may constitute an implied contract. Suppose, for example, that Rousseau has worked for 20 years at World Industries. At a luncheon honoring Rousseau, the president of World Industries says, "In honor of your excellent service, you have a job at this company until you wish to retire!" The next week, Rousseau is terminated. If a court determines that the language used by the president would lead a reasonable person to believe that Rousseau was more than just an employee at will, World Industries may be liable for a wrongful-termination claim.

In Case 39.2, an appellate court analyzes a claim based on an implied contract created by a handbook.

CASE 39.2 Smothers v. Solvay Chemicals, 740 F.3d 530 (10th Cir. 2014)

FACT SUMMARY Smothers was employed for approximately 18 years as a surface maintenance mechanic at a mine owned by Solvay Chemicals ("Solvay"). During his career with Solvay, Smothers generally had received positive reviews for his work. However, in 2005 Smothers began a pattern of absenteeism that he claimed was related to a medical condition. Smothers began to receive negative reviews on his performance evaluations and was denied a promotion because of his absenteeism.

In 2008, Smothers was assigned to perform a routine acid wash on mining equipment. The process involves the use of hydrochloric acid, which is a dangerous but widely used commercial chemical. Because the acid may harm humans if it is inhaled or ingested or touches the skin or the eyes, Solvay had specific safety standards in place to prevent injury. During the process, Smothers violated one of the safety standards. When a co-worker confronted Smothers about the violation, he reacted angrily and

(continued)

engaged in a heated exchange with the co-worker. The next day, Solvay managers learned of the safety violation and the subsequent confrontation. After they investigated the incident, the management team terminated Smothers. Smothers sued Solvay for, among other claims, breach of an implied contract allegedly created by Solvay's employee handbook. The trial court awarded summary judgment to Solvay on all claims, and Smothers appealed.

SYNOPSIS OF DECISION AND OPINION The U.S. Court of Appeals for the Tenth Circuit ruled that Solvay had not breached an implied contract created by the employee handbook. The court reasoned that under Wyoming law, breach of an implied employment contract arises if an employer fails to follow its own required procedures or fires an employee without cause. The court ruled that an employee handbook may provide the basis for the terms of an implied employment contract. However, Wyoming law allows immediate termination for serious offenses when expressly permitted by the employee handbook. In this case, the Solvay employee handbook contained a provision allowing Solvay to terminate an employee immediately for a serious offense, including a safety violation.[3]

WORDS OF THE COURT: Handbook as an Implied Contract "When Mr. Smothers began employment with Solvay's predecessor in 1990, the company provided him with an employee handbook outlining workplace policies and disciplinary procedures ("the Handbook"). The district court concluded that the Handbook was an implied employment contract, and Solvay does not challenge this holding. The Handbook contained a four-step progressive disciplinary process, with termination as a last resort. But it also contained a provision allowing Solvay to terminate an employee immediately for a serious offense, including a safety violation.

"When determining whether an employer followed its own procedures, a court should ask whether the factual basis on which the employer concluded [the employee committed an offense] was reached honestly, after an appropriate investigation and for reasons that are not arbitrary or pretextual. . . .

"The Handbook provision at issue does not prohibit any particular motive. Nor does it require Solvay to exercise its discretion consistently when responding to different employees' violations. It sets out the disciplinary policy Solvay will follow for its employees.

"Thus, to prove Solvay violated his implied employment contract, Mr. Smothers must show that it failed to comply with the disciplinary policy as defined in the Handbook. But the Handbook provision unambiguously gives [Solvay] the discretion to discharge employees who violate safety rules. And Mr. Smothers concedes that he violated a safety rule. He has not shown how Solvay's decision to discharge him violated the terms of the Handbook."

Case Questions

1. Could Smothers claim that the real reason he was fired was his absenteeism rather than the safety violation? Was his termination arbitrary in your view? Why or why not?

2. Is it fair to leave sanctions for safety violations entirely to the employer? Should employers be able to decide how they administer sanctions on a case-by-case basis? Explain.

3. *Focus on Critical Thinking:* What public policy implications are presented in this case? Should the law support a sanction as harsh as termination for any safety violation? What other types of violations would call for such a sanction? How should society balance safety versus fairness to an employee?

Covenant of Good Faith and Fair Dealing

The covenant of good faith and fair dealing, adopted by a minority of states, represents a significantly different approach to the traditional notions of an employment-at-will relationship. States that recognize this exception protect employees from job termination (1) without just cause or (2) in bad faith or with malicious intent. The covenant is very broad in coverage. California courts, for example, have held under their common law that an airline

---

[3]It should be noted that the court actually did find in favor of Smothers on other claims. For purposes of clarity, only the court's implied contract analysis is excerpted here.

employee with 18 years on the job could not be fired without just cause even though he had no express or implied contract.[4] For example, suppose that Whiteside is a sales representative who is the primary contact for a large sale for his company. Two weeks before the sale is set to close, Whiteside's company terminates him without cause and denies he is owed any commission on the sale. It is this type of employee termination that fits into the covenant of good faith and fair dealing.

✓ Quick Quiz Common Law Exceptions

Which common law exception best fits the employee's circumstances?

1. Baker's employer provides her with an employee handbook that sets out rules and sanctions related to employees who are late for work. The handbook provides for termination if the employee is late more than two times in any given work month. The first time Baker is late, she is fired.

2. Andrews complains to his manager that working conditions in certain areas of the warehouse are not safe because of toxic fumes. He tells his manager that unless the conditions are corrected, he cannot work in the warehouse. The next day, Andrews is fired.

3. During an employee recognition dinner, the company's CEO awards Andrews a plaque and bonus check for being the highest-grossing sales representative. During the ceremony, the CEO states, "As long as I am CEO of this company, Andrews has a job—guaranteed." Two weeks later, Andrews is terminated as part of a workforce reduction plan, even though the CEO is the same one who gave Andrews the award.

4. Holmes has been employed for 29 years as a manager of a retail store chain. His employer provides retirement benefits for any employee with 30 or more years of service. Ten months before his 30th anniversary date, Holmes is terminated as part of a cost-cutting plan.

Answers to this Quick Quiz are provided at the end of the chapter.

Common Law Tort-Based Exceptions

Some states recognize tort-based exceptions to the employment-at-will rule. For example, if an employer terminates an employee on the basis of a supervisor or co-worker's reports or actions, and the supervisor or co-worker acted maliciously, the employee may have a claim against an individual based on intentional interference with a contract and against the employer for wrongful termination. At-will employees who are subject to tortious acts by their employer, such as defamation, also may have a tort-based claim against their employer in the context of a termination. Torts are discussed in more detail in Chapter 42, "Torts and Products Liability."

TAKEAWAY CONCEPTS Common Law Exceptions

- Courts have fashioned three common law exceptions that help to limit the harshness of the rule on employees. They are (1) the public policy exception, (2) implied contract protection, and (3) the covenant of good faith and fair dealing.

(continued)

---

[4]*Cleary v. American Airlines, Inc.,* 111 Cal. App. 3d 443 (1980).

- The public policy exception is a narrow common law rule that places the public welfare ahead of the rights of an employer and recognizes that allowing employers to terminate an employee for certain reasons may contradict public policy.
- Some courts have used an implied contract theory exception where the employer extends protections or processes (e.g., progressive discipline) via a handbook or oral promise.
- A minority of states allow exceptions based on a covenant of good faith and fair dealing or tort-based theories.

STATUTORY PROTECTIONS FOR AT-WILL EMPLOYEES

LO 39-3

Articulate federal and state statutory protections for at-will employees.

Certain federal and state statutes displace common law employment-at-will rules. Perhaps the best examples are the antidiscrimination laws that prohibit termination (and many other workplace actions) based on certain discriminatory motivations such as race or gender. Other statutes prevent employers from terminating employees for specific reasons such as absence due to jury duty[5] or for attempting to form a union. These statutes are discussed in more detail in future chapters in this unit (labor law in Chapter 40 and employment discrimination in Chapter 41).

False Claims Act

The False Claims Act[6] is a federal statute that contains an anti-retaliation provision that protects employees who disclose that their firm has committed fraud in dealing with contracts with the federal government. In addition to providing the government with a powerful tool to combat fraudulent practices and recover taxpayer money, the law also allows the reporting party to file a lawsuit against the organization that is accused of the fraud. The reporting party stands to receive a portion of any monetary recovery that is tied to the fraud (typically 15 to 25 percent of the judgment). Generally, a whistleblower begins by notifying the government of her intention to file a False Claims Act suit. The Department of Justice then has the right to pursue the case on behalf of the government or may decline to intervene in the case. If the Department of Justice declines, the whistleblower then may pursue the case on her own. According to the National Whistleblower Center, approximately 70 percent of the money recovered under the False Claims Act over the past decade was from cases brought by employees of contractor firms.[7]

State Laws

Many state legislatures have enacted their own versions of the False Claims Act under state law. Thirty states and the District of Columbia have created statutes that provide an incentive to report fraud involving state-funded programs. While some states have modeled their law on the federal statute, others have limited recovery to fraud involving Medicaid.[8]

Some states have extended protection of at-will employees beyond the traditional statutory protection provided by antidiscrimination and false claims laws. For example, Montana has established protections for at-will employees through its Wrongful Discharge from

---

[5]For example, a statute in Pennsylvania prohibits employers from terminating, demoting, or depriving employees of seniority or other benefits because they have responded to a jury summons or have served as a juror. *See* 42 Pa. Cons. Stat. Ann. § 4563.

[6]31 U.S.C. § 3729–3733.

[7]https://www.whistleblowers.org/faq/false-claims-act-qui-tam/.

[8]See https://taf.org/states-false-claims-acts.

Employment Act. The law prohibits termination of an employee without cause once the employee has completed a probationary period, and it allows employees to challenge their termination through an arbitration system.[9] While these rights do not currently exist in most states, a growing number of state legislatures are extending more protection to at-will employees who are terminated without cause.

TAKEAWAY CONCEPTS Statutory Protections for At-Will Employees

- Certain federal and state statutes displace common law employment-at-will rules.
- The False Claims Act is a federal law that contains an anti-retaliation provision that protects employees who disclose that their firm has committed fraud in dealing with contracts with the federal government.
- Some states have extended protection of at-will employees beyond the traditional statutory protection provided by antidiscrimination and false claims laws.

LO 39-4

Discuss the requirements for protection under federal and state whistleblower laws.

WHISTLEBLOWER STATUTES

Perhaps the most important statutory prohibition of employer termination is provided by federal and state statutory protection of **whistleblowers**. *Whistleblower* is a colloquial term used to describe an employee or agent who reports an employer's unlawful conduct or a statutory violation to the authorities. In general, employers may not terminate an employee as retaliation for reporting the employer to the authorities (i.e., blowing the whistle). Federal employees are protected from retaliation for whistleblowing by the *Whistleblower Protection Act of 1989*.[10] The law also covers employees of companies that contract with the government to provide goods or services (e.g., a construction company building a federal highway). Additionally, some federal statutes give specific anti-retaliation protections for employees who disclose conduct that violates that law. For example, the Fair Labor Standards Act (regulation of wages and hours) and the Sarbanes-Oxley Act (regulation of corporations) both provide whistleblowers with specific statutory protections for reporting or testifying against their employer in an investigation, hearing, or trial.

State Whistleblower Laws

State whistleblower laws are more complex because each state has its own whistleblowing statute, and they vary from state to state. Most commonly, whistleblowers are protected when they report the violation of a law or standard by their employer to the authorities. Some states only cover whistleblowing by government employees or employees of government contractors. Although certain jurisdictions limit whistleblower protection to employees whose disclosures involve conduct that could result in some harm to the employees or the public at large, a minority of states have extended that same protection to disclosures that involve *any* illegal or improper conduct. Some jurisdictions, such as the state of New York, have set a relatively high threshold for whistleblowers to gain statutory protection. New York statutes require that disclosures be related to conduct that is "dangerous" to the public.

Most states also require that the whistleblower must suffer an adverse employment action to be covered under the statute. In Case 39.3, a state supreme court analyzes a state

---

[9]Mont. Code Ann. § 39-2-901.

[10]5 U.S.C. § 1201.

FACT SUMMARY The Beecher Metropolitan District ("the District") manages water and sewage for a municipality in Michigan. The District has five elected board members and also employs a part-time district administrator who manages District operations on a day-to-day basis. Wurtz was hired as the district administrator for a 10-year period, as spelled out in a contract between the District and Wurtz. There was no language in the contract concerning any future extension. By 2009, the working relationship between Wurtz and the board members had deteriorated significantly. Wurtz accused members of the board of violating public meeting laws and reported the conduct to the local prosecutor, who ultimately declined to prosecute. Despite the tension between Wurtz and the board members, he proposed an extension to his contract, which was rejected by the District's board.

Relations between Wurtz and the board became even more contentious after he leveled criminal allegations against several board members related to improper reimbursement for expenses submitted by the board for costs of attending a professional conference. The board members were criminally charged in connection with the reimbursements, but all were acquitted of wrongdoing or had the charges against them dismissed.

At a November 2009 meeting of the District, Wurtz warned the board that he would consider the board's failure to extend his contract to be retaliation for the criminal investigation. The board, however, refused to heed Wurtz's warning and voted 3 to 2 not to renew Wurtz's contract citing legitimate reasons for its decision. The board countered that the tumultuous relationship between Wurtz and the board members preceded any alleged whistleblowing activities. Wurtz sued the District under the Michigan Whistleblower Protection Act (WPA). The trial court dismissed the claim reasoning that Wurtz had not suffered any "adverse employment action" as required for recovery under the WPA. The appellate court partially reversed, and the parties appealed to the Michigan Supreme Court.

SYNOPSIS OF DECISION AND OPINION The Michigan Supreme Court ruled in favor of the District. The court reasoned that Wurtz was not entitled to relief under the WPA because he alleged that the District violated the WPA by deciding not to *renew* his contract. In other words, Wurtz only alleges that the District took some action against him in his capacity as an applicant for *future* employment. But the court held that the WPA does not apply to job applicants, nor does it apply to contract employees seeking renewal of their contracts. The court focused exclusively on the language in the WPA that required that the whistleblower be subject to an adverse employment action. In this case, the District paid all money and other benefits owed to Wurtz by virtue of his 10-year contract. Therefore, he did not suffer any of the consequences that are required for relief under the WPA.

WORDS OF THE COURT: Limited Protections "Significantly, as gleaned from the WPA's express language, the statute only applies to individuals who currently have the status of an employee. The Legislature defined an employee in the WPA as 'a person who performs a service for wages or other remuneration under a contract of hire, written or oral, express or implied.' Noticeably absent from the WPA's definition of 'employee' is any reference to prospective employees or job applicants. And indeed, the actions prohibited under the WPA could only be taken against a current employee. Only an employee could be discharged and only an employee could be threatened or discriminated against regarding his or her compensation, terms, conditions, location, or privileges of employment. . . .

"During Wurtz's ten years as an employee—when he enjoyed the protections of the WPA—he endured no action prohibited by the WPA. He was not discharged, threatened, or discriminated against regarding his compensation, terms, conditions, location, or privileges of employment. He served the District for the entire duration of his contract and received every cent and every benefit to which he was entitled. Thus, the District did not engage in any action prohibited by the WPA."

Case Questions

1. If the District had terminated Wurtz's contract before it expired, how would that change the court's analysis?

(continued)

law whistleblower claim in which a whistleblower's contract had expired and the employer refused to renew it.

Separate and Independent Defense

LO 39-5

Explain the "separate and independent" defense to a whistleblower claim.

Employers may terminate employees who are whistleblowers if they can show that the termination was for reasons that are *separate* from and *independent* of any whistleblowing. For example, suppose that Padraig is an employee of Celtic Crystal Company (CCC). Over the past year, Padraig has been suspended twice for poor work and lateness. His manager warned him that any additional instances of lateness would result in termination. On Monday, Padraig discovers that CCC has failed to take appropriate measures to remove a hazardous substance from the CCC warehouse. Padraig notifies the authorities that CCC is out of compliance. CCC learns of the complaint and its source on Tuesday. On Friday, Padraig is late for work and is terminated. Padraig clearly is protected as a whistleblower in most jurisdictions. However, if CCC provides evidence that it intended to terminate Padraig prior to the whistleblowing or that the decision, in light of Padraig's disciplinary record at CCC, was made independent of the whistleblowing, CCC most likely will avoid liability for wrongful termination in violation of the whistleblower statute.

In Case 39.4, a trial court analyzes whether an employer's reasons for termination of an employee were sufficiently separate and independent to avoid liability under a state whistleblower law.

CASE 39.4 McQueary v. The Pennsylvania State University, Pa. Ct. of Common Pleas, No. 2012-1804 (2016)

FACT SUMMARY After the results of a grand jury investigation related to the sexual abuse of children by a Pennsylvania State University ("Penn State") employee and a subsequent cover-up by Penn State administrators were released in November 2011, Penn State's interim athletic director summoned Mike McQueary, an assistant football coach at Penn State, to a meeting. At the meeting, the interim athletic director read a script prepared by a Penn State attorney that informed McQueary that he was being placed on administrative leave and was banned from

all Penn State facilities and activities, including his own office. He also was required to turn in his keys, cell phone, and any university-owned property. Subsequently, McQueary learned during a July 2012 press conference called by Penn State administrators that he had been officially terminated.

McQueary filed a claim under the Pennsylvania Whistleblower Act alleging that Penn State administrators had fired him when they discovered that McQueary had provided testimony to the grand jury about having witnessed the sexual abuse of a minor

(continued)

by Penn State football coach Jerry Sandusky in a Penn State locker room in 2001. McQueary testified that he told head football coach Joe Paterno, Penn State athletic director Tim Curley, and vice president Gary Schultz about the incident. Based on McQueary's and other witnesses' testimony, the grand jury charged Sandusky, Curley, and Schultz with various criminal offenses related to sexual abuse of minors and failing to report the abuse to authorities. Penn State defended the whistleblower claim by asserting that McQueary was an employee at will whose appointment was not renewed after the new incoming head football coach determined there was no room for McQueary to continue as part of the team's new coaching staff.

SYNOPSIS OF DECISION AND OPINION The court ruled in favor of McQueary and awarded him $5 million in damages plus $1.7 million in legal fees under the Pennsylvania Whistleblower Act. The court held that McQueary's good faith reporting of the sexual abuse to his supervisors qualified under the statute as a protected act of whistleblowing. Under the Pennsylvania Whistleblower Act, the burden shifted from McQueary to Penn State to prove that the termination was for "separate and legitimate reasons" from any whistleblowing activity. The court rejected Penn State's contention that McQueary's termination was unrelated to his grand jury testimony and was the result of routine personnel changes of an incoming head coach. The court pointed to evidence that the new head coach had never interviewed McQueary and had never looked at his personnel file and that the decision to fire McQueary was contemporaneous with the administrators finding out about his grand jury testimony.

WORDS OF THE COURT: Separate and Legitimate Reason "Penn State's asserted defenses must be analyzed in the context of its conduct both pre- and post-Grand Jury presentment as this is a case where actions speak louder than words. . . . But for the Grand Jury presentment, no Penn State

Former assistant coach Mike McQueary successfully sued Penn State University under a state whistleblower statute.
© Gene J. Puskar/AP Images

coach would have lost their job and [the new head coach] would not have been hired. Accordingly, [the new head coach's] decision not to interview or hire Mr. McQueary does not constitute a separate and legitimate reason for his firing."

Case Questions

1. What does the court mean when it calls this "a case where actions speak louder than words"?

2. If the new head football coach had interviewed McQueary, reviewed his personnel file, and then concluded that he was not qualified for the job, would that have affected McQueary's whistleblower claim? Why or why not?

3. *Focus on Critical Thinking:* In addition to his whistleblower claim, McQueary also filed suit against Penn State for intentional torts. What other claims might McQueary have against Penn State? McQueary reported the sexual abuse to his supervisors but not to any law enforcement agency. Did he have an ethical obligation beyond reporting it to Penn State administrators? Should he have reported it directly to law enforcement authorities? Should he have intervened when he witnessed the abuse? Explain.

TAKEAWAY CONCEPTS Whistleblower Statutes

■ *Whistleblower* is a colloquial term used to describe an employee or agent who reports an employer's unlawful conduct or a statutory violation to the authorities.

(continued)

- Federal employees are protected from retaliation for whistleblowing by the Whistle-blower Protection Act of 1989.

- State whistleblower statutes vary from state to state. Most commonly, whistleblowers are protected when they report the violation of a law or standard by their employer to the authorities.

- Employers may terminate employees who are whistleblowers if they can show that the termination was for reasons that are separate from and independent of any whistleblowing.

 THINKING STRATEGICALLY

Avoiding Implied Contracts

PROBLEM: As we learned in this chapter, courts have recognized employee handbooks as implied contracts even when an employer does not intend to convert an employee from at-will status. One state's highest court has gone so far as to rule that disclosure language in an employee handbook, which specifically stated that the terms and procedures contained in an employee handbook "are not contractual and are subject to change and interpretation at the sole discretion of the Company, and without prior notice or consideration to any employee," was defective and did not defeat the employee's claim of an implied contract.[11] At the same time, employee handbooks are an important part of business operations because they set employee standards and provide employees with guidelines and procedures for carrying out their job responsibilities.

STRATEGIC SOLUTION: Deploy best practices for avoiding implied contracts on two fronts. First, recognize possible danger zones by understanding how courts have recognized implied contracts in the past. Second, take specific steps that protect against any claim of employer liability based on an implied contract via the employee handbook.

DANGER ZONES

- **Disciplinary policies:** When employers use a system that disciplines employees for certain violations based on the severity and frequency of the violation (e.g., written warning for the first time reporting late to work and termination after three times late to work), this is called a "progressive discipline" system. This is a danger zone because the employer has displaced the at-will status with

its own system. Although systems of progressive discipline are relatively common in the workplace, employers must strictly adhere to the systems in place. If an employee is terminated for a violation that is not listed in the manual or the termination is inconsistent with the manual, the employer may face a breach of implied contract claim.

- **Good cause language:** Any reference in the employee handbook to "good cause" can be problematic because it displaces the employers' common law right to terminate at-will employees for good cause *or* no cause at all. Therefore, any assurances in the employee handbook of continued employment based on positive performance can signal a danger zone if an employee could reasonably understand that language as a promise of continued employment. Any reference to an employee being terminated only for good cause may convert an at-will employee into an employee with an implied contract.

PROACTIVE STEPS

- **At-will disclaimer and employee acknowledgment:** The most common way to guard against converting an at-will employee into an employee with an implied contract via employee handbook is to use a specific, plain-language disclaimer that is clearly demarcated from the rest of the handbook and is repeated in several places within the handbook itself. Moreover, it is a good practice to have employees sign an *employee acknowledgment* stating that their employment is at will and specifying that at-will employment can only be altered by a written contract signed by the president of the company. Because different states have various requirements for at-will disclaimers,

---

[11]*Nicosia v. Wakefern Food Corp.,* 136 N.J. 401 (1994).

it is important to seek the counsel of an attorney when determining exactly what language will appear and how that language will appear in the employee handbook (e.g., bold capital letters on the title page of the handbook).

■ **Policy review and manager training:** Executive and midlevel management should engage in regular reviews of company policies to be sure there are no indications of promises for continuing employment in terms of awards, employee evaluations, bonuses, layoffs, or other personnel policies that may be tied to an employee's reasonable expectation of continued job security. Managers also should have regular training on the impact any *oral* assurances (formal or informal) by a manager will have on converting an at-will employee to an employee with an implied contract.

QUESTIONS

1. Have you ever had a job or internship where an employee handbook or manual was used? Was there any language related to implied contracts? If so, did you understand what it meant at the time? Explain.
2. Are there other methods to communicate policies and procedures to employees that do not involve the distribution of a handbook? Could these other communication methods give rise to an implied contract theory?

KEY TERMS

Employment-at-will doctrine p. 690   Deep-seated common law principle that an employer has the right to terminate an employee with or without advance notice and with or without just cause, subject to certain exceptions.

Public policy exception p. 692   Most widely accepted exception to the employment-at-will principle; protects an employee from being terminated if the action violates established public policy.

Implied contract p. 692   Common law exception to at-will employment whereby employees are protected if their at-will status is altered by promises of continued employment that form an implied contract between employer and employee.

Covenant of good faith and fair dealing p. 692   Common law exception adopted by a minority of states that imposes a duty on every employer to act in good faith and protects employees from terminations without cause that result in unjust treatment.

Whistleblower p. 698   An employee or agent who reports illegal misconduct or a statutory violation by his or her employer to the authorities.

CASE SUMMARY 39.1 Brundridge v. Fluor Federal Services, Inc., 164 Wash. 2d 432 (2008)

Public Policy

A crew of five pipe fitters was employed by a contractor and was ordered to install a valve on a transfer pipe to a high-level nuclear waste tank. However, the crew had sufficient experience to realize that the wrong valve had been ordered. The valve to be installed was rated at 1,975 pounds per square inch (psi) in a system of pipes that was to be tested at 2,235 psi. The crew was concerned that the underrated valve could cause nuclear contamination and injury to workers. They refused their supervisor's orders to install the underrated valve and stopped work at the site until management relented and ordered the sturdier valve to be installed. One month later, the company terminated the whole crew citing financial cutbacks in the company.

CASE QUESTIONS

1. What exceptions could the pipe fitters assert to displace the employment-at-will doctrine?
2. What theory would be best advanced by the pipe fitters? Explain.

Whistleblower Protection

Haynes, an animal keeper at the Zoological Society of Cincinnati ("the Zoo"), was assigned to the bear and walrus area with responsibilities for feeding and general care of the animals. Haynes lodged several complaints with her supervisors about the unsafe conditions in her assigned areas, but the Zoo failed to address her concerns. One afternoon, Stober, a co-worker, stopped in front of a male polar bear's den and offered the bear a grape through the bars of the bear's cage. The bear pulled Stober's hand through the bars and bit off a portion of her arm. Haynes, who was with Stober when the attack occurred, gave a statement to authorities about the incident and blamed lack of personnel training and poor conditions inside the bear den as contributing factors to Stober's injuries. The next day, Haynes was demoted to an entry-level position at the birdhouse; a few days later, she was suspended without pay for insubordination. Haynes sued the Zoo asserting that the Zoo had demoted and suspended her in retaliation for reporting alleged unsafe working conditions to authorities. The Zoo countered that Haynes was a member of a union and therefore could not avail herself of whistleblower protections that were available only to at-will employees.

CASE QUESTIONS

1. Should Haynes be prevented from asserting a whistleblower claim because she is a member of a union?
2. Could Haynes be protected from termination by a common law exception?

Public Policy

Gardner was an armored car guard employed at will by Loomis. The company had a strict rule that required guards to stay with the armored car under any circumstances and that a violation of this rule would result in immediate termination. During a routine armored car delivery, Loomis witnessed an armed robbery taking place nearby and left his armored car to foil the robbery. The robbery was prevented, but Gardner was terminated for violating workplace rules.

CASE QUESTIONS

1. Should the law prevent Loomis from terminating the guard in this case? Why or why not?
2. Was there a well-defined and clear public policy in this case? If so, what was it?

CHAPTER REVIEW QUESTIONS

1. The employment-at-will rule does <u>not</u> apply when:
   a. An employee has an express contract.
   b. An employee is covered by a collective bargaining agreement (CBA).
   c. The employee has worked for more than one year for an employer.
   d. A and B.
   e. A, B, and C.

2. Sven is employed at will by BigCo. One day at work, Sven reports to his supervisor that he hurt his lower back on a delivery and wants to make a claim under the workers' compensation system. BigCo believes that Sven is faking the injury, so the supervisor warns him not to file a claim. Sven files the claim and is fired by BigCo. If Sven sues for wrongful discharge, what is his likely theory of exception to the employment-at-will doctrine?

a. Discrimination

b. Public policy

c. Labor standards

d. Implied contract

e. Good faith and fair dealing

3. **Which of the following may be the basis for the implied contract exception to the employment-at-will rule?**

   a. Labor union contract

   b. An employee handbook with a disciplinary system

   c. Reasonable reliance on oral promises of continued employment by the employer

   d. A and B

   e. B and C

4. **In the hypothetical state of Freedonia, the legislature passes a statute that prohibits an employer from retaliating against an employee who notifies authorities of employer actions that may harm the public. The Freedonia law is an example of what exception to the employee-at-will rule?**

   a. Public policy

   b. Whistleblower statute

   c. Federal antidiscrimination

   d. Implied contract

   e. Good faith and fair dealing

5. **When considering whether to apply the good faith and fair dealing exception to the employment-at-will doctrine, courts typically:**

a. Apply the exception very broadly.

b. Consider whether the exception is based on a statute.

c. Require that the employee handbook contain a statement of fair dealing.

d. Examine any labor union contracts at issue.

e. Apply the exception vary narrowly.

6. **The employment-at-will doctrine is based on a federal statute.**

   a. True

   b. False

7. **The public policy exception may be asserted on the basis of an employee handbook.**

   a. True

   b. False

8. **Whistleblower laws exist at both the state and federal levels.**

   a. True

   b. False

9. **Most states require that a whistleblower must suffer an adverse employment action to be covered by the statute.**

   a. True

   b. False

10. **The "separate and independent" defense may be asserted by a whistleblower who has been terminated.**

    a. True

    b. False

 Quick Quiz ANSWERS
Common Law Exceptions

1. *Implied contract.* A manual or bulletin (such as an employee handbook) that is drafted and distributed by the employer may give rise to an implied contract theory if the manual extends some protections or process to the employee that she would not have under the employment-at-will doctrine.

2. *Public policy.* Typically, courts will consider the public policy objective to be explicit and well established if it is related to an existing statute, the state constitution, or previously established policy.

3. *Implied contract.* An oral promise made by an employer that a reasonable person would believe extends protection against termination without cause may constitute an implied contract.

4. *Covenant of good faith.* In some states, the covenant of good faith and fair dealing protects employees from being terminated in bad faith or with malicious intent.

CHAPTER REVIEW QUESTIONS: Answers and Explanations

1. d. Express contracts between the parties, including collective bargaining agreements (labor contracts), are outside the realm of the employment-at-will doctrine because it is assumed that the terms of employment were negotiated rather than at will. Answer *c* is incorrect because the length of employment is not related to the scope of the employment-at-will doctrine.

2. b. The public policy exception applies when an employer retaliates against an employee for taking an action that the employee is legally entitled to take under a statute or administrative regulation. Answer *a* is wrong because the retaliation is not discriminatory. Answer *c* is wrong because no labor contract is involved. Answers *d* and *e* are wrong because there aren't any implied contract or fair dealing elements in the question.

3. e. Any promise made to an employee that a reasonable person would believe displaces the employment-at-will doctrine either by employee handbook or oral promise fits the implied contract exception. Answer *a* is incorrect because a labor contract is a form of express contract.

4. b. A whistleblower statute is one where the legislature carves out an exception to the employment-at-will rule in cases where the employee has reported illegal or improper conduct by his employer. Answers *a, d,* and *e* are wrong because they are common law exceptions and are not applicable when a statute exists. Answer *c* is wrong because there are no elements of antidiscrimination statutes in the question.

5. e. Courts apply all common law exceptions to the employment-at-will doctrine very narrowly—thus answer *a* is wrong. Answer *b* is wrong because a statute is not necessary in a fair dealing claim. Answer *c* is wrong because it is related to implied contracts. Answer *d* is wrong because labor contracts are express contracts and not related to fair dealing.

6. b. False. The employment-at-will doctrine is a common law doctrine that can be displaced by federal or state statutes.

7. b. False. The public policy exception is not related to an employee handbook. Rather, employee handbooks may give rise to an *implied contract exception.*

8. a. True. Federal whistleblower statutes include the Whistleblower Protection Act. States also have their own whistleblower statutes.

9. a. True. State statutes typically require that a whistleblower must suffer an adverse employment action (such as termination) in order to be covered by the statute. See Case 39.3, *Wurtz v. Beecher Metro District.*

10. b. False. The "separate and independent" defense is an *employer* defense to a whistleblower claim.

CHAPTER 40

Employment Regulation and Labor Law

THINKING STRATEGICALLY

Companies constantly face the pressure to reduce costs to remain profitable. Sometimes, the law may be strategically used to contain costs in a lawful and ethical manner. The opposite may also be true, however. For example, companies may wish to lower labor costs. At the end of this chapter, you will review an employer's practices to determine if it has strategically violated employment laws to decrease costs.

Learning Objectives

After studying this chapter, students who have mastered the material will be able to:

40-1 Explain the principal aspects of the Fair Labor Standards Act and state laws that protect workers.

40-2 Identify the laws that regulate retirement and health benefits.

40-3 Demonstrate how a worker becomes entitled to workers' compensation.

40-4 Describe how a worker becomes entitled to benefits under the Family and Medical Leave Act (FMLA).

40-5 Discuss the circumstances under which an employer is liable for invading an employee's privacy.

40-6 Summarize the process for forming a collective bargaining unit.

40-7 Identify the role of professional licensing in the workplace.

CHAPTER OVERVIEW

Federal and state legislatures have passed important laws that protect employees from oppressive or unfair workplace practices. These employment protection laws are intended to safeguard the welfare of individual workers who have little or no bargaining power in the employer-employee relationship. Federal law often works in tandem with state law to regulate employers in the areas of minimum wages, overtime pay, use of child labor, sudden job loss, workplace injuries, workplace safety, and medical leaves. Employment regulation and labor laws are intimately tied to the well-being of the workforce and, therefore, are critical aspects of running a business. Supervisors and human resource managers in particular should take care to ensure their business is in compliance with these laws and regulations.

THE FAIR LABOR STANDARDS ACT AND STATE LAWS

LO 40-1

Explain the principal aspects of the Fair Labor Standards Act and state laws that protect workers.

The **Fair Labor Standards Act (FLSA)**[1] is a major piece of federal legislation enacted in 1938 that regulates several important employment matters. The FLSA, however, cannot be properly understood without reference to two major historical events that occurred during the earlier parts of the 20th century. The first was the Industrial Revolution, and the second was the Great Depression. These major events brought to light several issues that will be discussed in this chapter.

The Industrial Revolution is described as the time period during the 19th and 20th centuries that saw great advances in science and technology. During this time, societies transitioned from being primarily agrarian to primarily industrial economies. Factories and large-scale manufacturing became prominent, and captains of industry such as Henry Ford, Andrew Carnegie, and John D. Rockefeller amassed enormous wealth as leaders of vast businesses.

During this time, working conditions in factories were often dangerous and harsh. Before the enactment of the FLSA, factory workers enjoyed few protections. After the Great Depression, greater pro-labor sentiment among the population and organized labor represented by unions led to New Deal legislation put forth by President Franklin D. Roosevelt.[2] One of the most important aspects of New Deal legislation was the enactment of various employment laws, one of which was the FLSA. When President Roosevelt signed the FLSA into law, he stated, "I do think that next to the Social Security Act it is the most important Act that has been passed in the last two years."[3]

The FLSA applies to all employees of enterprises that employ workers engaged in interstate commerce; produce goods for interstate commerce; or handle, sell, or otherwise work on goods or materials that have been moved in or produced for such commerce. The act, therefore, covers all employers broadly defined that engage in interstate commerce.

Although the FLSA is expansive, its primary provisions mandate (1) payment of a minimum wage, (2) a maximum 40-hour workweek, (3) overtime pay, and (4) restrictions on children who work in certain occupations and during certain hours. The FLSA and its regulations are administered and enforced by the federal administrative agency known as the *U.S. Department of Labor.*

Minimum Wage

The FLSA establishes a minimum wage to be paid to every employee covered under the act. Over the years, Congress has raised the minimum wage to its current level of $7.25. However, states are permitted to set a higher minimum wage level for employees working within their jurisdiction. Many legal issues that surround the wage and hour provisions of the FLSA involve whether employees are entitled to be paid for time in the workplace that is not directly related to the employee's job duties. Congress provided clarification by amending the FLSA with the

Before the passage of the FLSA and similar state statutes, children were allowed to work in harsh and dangerous factory environments.

© Everett Historical/Shutterstock

---

[1] 29 U.S.C. § 201.

[2] The New Deal was a series of federal programs, public works projects, financial reforms, and regulations enacted in the United States during the 1930s in response to the Great Depression.

[3] *The Public Papers and Addresses of Franklin D. Roosevelt, 1938 volume* (New York: Macmillan, 1941), p. 404.

Portal-to-Portal Act[4] to provide guidelines regarding what constitutes compensable work. The Portal-to-Portal Act provides two broad exceptions to FLSA wage and hour requirements. Unless the activity is integral and indispensable to their principal job, employees are not entitled to compensation for (1) time spent traveling to and from the actual place of employment or (2) time spent performing activities before or after the principal activities in a workday.

Courts have interpreted *principal activity* to include all activities that are an integral and indispensable part of the business. For example, the U.S. Supreme Court ruled that the time battery-plant employees spent showering and changing clothes was compensable[5] because the chemicals in the plant are toxic to human beings. The Court also held that the time meatpackers spent sharpening their knives was compensable because dull knives would slow down production on the assembly line and affect the appearance of the meat, cause waste, and lead to accidents.[6] In contrast, courts rejected a claim by poultry-plant employees that time spent waiting to don protective gear was compensable because such waiting was two steps removed from the production activity on the assembly line.[7]

In Case 40.1, the U.S. Supreme Court considers whether employees' time spent undergoing routine security screenings is compensable under the FLSA.

Maximum Workweek and Overtime Compensation

In addition to setting the minimum wage, the FLSA sets a standard workweek at 40 hours in a seven-day period. An employee is entitled to **overtime compensation** for any hours worked in excess of the standard workweek. Overtime compensation is calculated by multiplying the hourly base rate of the employee times one and one-half. For example, an employee making $10 per hour in her normal base pay is entitled to $15 per hour for overtime compensation. Note that all wage and hour laws under the FLSA assume a base unit of time of one week. For example, suppose that Mikhail has morning child care responsibilities and requests a schedule for seven hours a day on Monday through Friday and five hours on Saturday. Although Mikhail works six days per week, he is not entitled to overtime pay under the FLSA because his total hours do not exceed 40 in a one-week period. Employees are not entitled to overtime pay based on an eight-hour workday. If Mikhail were to work four days a week for 10 hours a day, no overtime would be earned.

An important concept that business owners and managers should understand about the FLSA is that the act does not cover all employees. Employers are not bound by the FLSA for employees classified as **exempt employees**. The underlying concept behind the FLSA is to level the playing field for employees who are in an untenable bargaining position with employers. Consistent with that concept, the law assumes a certain level of bargaining power for professional and management-level employees and, therefore, exempts them from FLSA protections. Workers without significant managerial or supervisory roles and who perform repetitive tasks or manual labor are considered **nonexempt employees** and are legally entitled to overtime pay.

When the FLSA was first enacted, the division between management and labor was relatively clear and classification was based on salary thresholds. However, the lines between labor and management blurred during the rise of the information age and the general rise in the skill, education, and wages of workers, and classification became increasingly problematic. In 2016, the U.S. Department of Labor issued a rule to update the annual salary threshold below which workers qualify for FLSA protection (including overtime pay). To be

---

[4]29 U.S.C. § 251.

[5]*Steiner v. Mitchell*, 350 U.S. 247 (1956).

[6]*Mitchell v. King Packing Co.*, 350 U.S. 260 (1956).

[7]*IBP, Inc. v. Alvarez*, 546 U.S. 21 (2005).

FACT SUMMARY Integrity Staffing Solutions, Inc. ("Integrity") provides warehouse staffing to Amazon throughout the United States. Jesse Busk (Busk) worked as an hourly employee at Integrity's warehouses in Nevada. As a warehouse employee, Busk retrieved products from the shelves and packaged them for delivery to Amazon customers. Integrity required its employees to undergo a security screening before leaving the warehouse at the end of each day. During this screening, employees removed items such as wallets, keys, and belts from their persons and passed through metal detectors.

In 2010, Busk and another employee filed suit against Integrity for alleged violations of the FLSA and Nevada labor laws, alleging that they were entitled to compensation under the FLSA for time spent waiting to undergo and actually undergoing the security screenings. They alleged that such time amounted to roughly 25 minutes each day and that the screenings were conducted to prevent employee theft and thus occurred solely for the benefit of the employers and their customers. The trial court ruled in favor of Integrity, but the court of appeals reversed. The court of appeals held that the screenings were compensable because they were required by the employer, necessary to the employees' primary work as warehouse employees, and done for Integrity's benefit. Integrity appealed.

SYNOPSIS OF DECISION AND OPINION The U.S. Supreme Court reversed the court of appeals's decision and found in favor of Integrity. The Court ruled that the lower court erred by focusing on whether the activity was required by the employer. Instead, the appropriate test was based on whether the activities were the principal activity or activities that the employee was employed to perform. Because Integrity did not employ its workers to undergo security screenings but to retrieve products from warehouse shelves and package them for shipment to Amazon customers, the activities did not qualify as compensable under the FLSA. Moreover, the activity did not meet the "integral and indispensable" standard.

WORDS OF THE COURT: Intrinsic Element Requirement "The security screenings also were not 'integral and indispensable' to the employees' duties as warehouse workers. [A]n activity is not integral and indispensable to an employee's principal activities unless it is an intrinsic element of those activities and one with which the employee cannot dispense if he is to perform those activities. The screenings were not an intrinsic element of retrieving products from warehouse shelves or packaging them for shipment. And Integrity Staffing could have eliminated the screenings altogether without impairing the employees' ability to complete their work."

Case Questions

1. The employees in this case pointed to the fact that Integrity could have reduced the amount of time for screening to just a few minutes by employing more personnel and metal detectors. Should the Court have given more weight to that fact? Why or why not?

2. What did the Court identify as the error made by the court of appeals? Why was it important?

3. *Focus on Critical Thinking:* Is this decision consistent with the objectives of the FLSA? Does it protect workers from unfair and harsh treatment by an employer? Should Congress or the Department of Labor define *work hours* more carefully? How would you craft a definition?

considered exempt, an employee must make a minimum salary of $47,476 per year, or $913 per week. Those earning more than $134,004 are classified as highly compensated employees and are always presumed to be exempt.

Typically, workers paid by the hour are not exempt and thus are entitled to overtime pay. However, being paid a salary does not automatically make an employee exempt. Exempt duties can be classified as executive, administrative, or professional. In the context of FLSA law, white-collar employees generally engage in employment that does not require physical labor or involve repetitive tasks, and they typically are paid an annual salary rather than an hourly wage. In classifying an employee as covered or exempt, employers must take into account the following factors, known as the *duties* test:

- Education, skill level, or certifications required for the position; salary level; and compensation method (commission versus hourly).
- Amount of physical labor required.
- Amount of repetitive tasks (e.g., performing an unskilled task over and over again, as does a clerk in a company mailroom).
- Degree of supervision required by the employer.

Examples of employees who are not covered by the FLSA include (1) professionals who require specialized study and certifications, such as attorneys, physicians, teachers, and accountants; (2) management or supervisory employees; (3) computer programmers and engineers; and (4) employees subject to certain certification and regulatory requirements, such as insurance adjusters or dental hygienists.

A good human resources compliance practice is to document exempt versus nonexempt positions in a company handbook.

Figure 40.1 demonstrates how a manufacturing company could categorize its employees based on job titles and responsibilities to comply with the FLSA.

In Case 40.2, a federal appeals court analyzes the FLSA's executive exemption.

The consequences of employee misclassification may be severe. Unless an employee is clearly exempt from FLSA coverage, she should be classified as a covered (nonexempt) employee under the FLSA provisions to avoid liability.

To understand the consequences of employee misclassification, suppose that Fernanda hires Alden as a customer service agent to handle complaints over the phone. Alden has a significant amount of practical experience and a diploma from a technical school. Fernanda agrees to pay Alden an annual base salary of $26,000. Because the work does not involve physical labor, Fernanda classifies Alden as exempt from the FLSA. Over the course of the next six months, due to an increase in customer complaints, Alden works an average of 50 hours per week on the phones trying to resolve complaints. Because Fernanda classified Alden as an employee with an annual salary and exempt from the FLSA, he does not pay Alden any overtime compensation. If the Department of Labor audits Fernanda's business, it may reclassify Alden as being covered by the FLSA because of his relatively low salary level, the minimal educational requirements for the position, and the repetitive task of answering customer calls. In addition to fines levied against Fernanda for violating the FLSA, the Department of Labor will order Fernanda to pay Alden back pay for any time worked by Alden over the 40-hour workweek.

Figure 40.2 represents a sample calculation of Fernanda's potential liability.

FIGURE 40.1 Exempt and Nonexempt Employees

Exempt Employees
Director of Administration & Finance
Director of Human Resources
Director of Marketing & Sales
Director of Manufacturing
Die Supervisor
Plant Manager
Sales Representative

Nonexempt Employees	
Accounts Clerk	Pack & Ship Lead
CAD Technician/In-House Sales	Packer/Shipper
Clerk/Typist	Press Operator/Assistant Press Operator
Die Repairman	Production Scheduler/Controller
Die Repairman Helper	Saw Operator
Fabrication Lead	Saw Operator Helper
Fabrication Worker	Secretary/Receptionist
Maintenance Supervisor	Shift Supervisor
Maintenance Worker, Buildings & Grounds	Stretch Operator
Maintenance Worker, Equipment	Stretch Operator Helper

FACT SUMMARY Madden, O'Bar, and Wortman were hired by Lumber One Home Center ("Lumber One") to serve as supervisors and managers in a newly established Lumber One store. The employees were salaried, labeled as executives, and classified by Lumber One as exempt from overtime pay under the FLSA provision that exempted "any employee employed in a bona fide executive, administrative, or professional capacity" from overtime pay requirements.

In anticipation of the new store opening, Madden and O'Bar assembled shelves and received merchandise. Once the store opened, Madden and O'Bar completed data entry tasks and helped out in the lumberyard by assisting customers, unloading trucks, and collecting trash when needed. Wortman worked in the lumberyard and waited on customers, helped load trucks, and on occasion directed the truck drivers regarding where to make deliveries. The parties agreed that the plaintiffs worked overtime throughout their employment at Lumber One. However, because Lumber One classified Madden, O'Bar, and Wortman as executives, the employees were not paid overtime.

Madden, O'Bar, and Wortman filed suit against Lumber One claiming they were improperly classified as executives rather than as employees and therefore were entitled to overtime pay under the FLSA. The jury found in favor of Lumber One, but the trial court overturned the jury's verdict and ruled in favor of the employees. Lumber One appealed the court's ruling.

SYNOPSIS OF DECISION AND OPINION The U.S. Court of Appeals for the Eighth Circuit ruled in favor of Madden and O'Bar, but it reversed the trial court's ruling relating to Wortman. The court reasoned that in order to qualify for an executive exemption, Lumber One must show, among other things, that the exempt employees had the authority to hire or fire employees or that their recommendations regarding personnel decisions were given particular weight by the decision maker. Because Lumber One's owner made all of the hiring and firing decisions at the store and did not consult Madden or O'Bar, the court reasoned that Lumber One did not satisfy the "authority" test or the "particular weight" required to exempt an employee from FLSA coverage. The court rejected Lumber One's argument that the owner's informal solicitation of input from existing employees about an applicant was sufficient to meet the exemption requirements.

In the case of Wortman, the court ruled that Lumber One had made a sufficient showing that Wortman had been involved in recommending at least one driver to Lumber One's owner. Therefore, the court held that Wortman reasonably could be classified as a supervisor who was exempt from overtime under the FLSA.

WORDS OF THE COURT: Personnel Decisions Requirement "[Lumber One's owner] testified that none of the plaintiffs hired or fired other employees. Therefore, in order to satisfy the fourth element, Lumber One needed to present evidence at trial that the plaintiffs were consulted about personnel decisions and that [the owner] gave each of their opinions particular weight regarding specific hiring decisions. Prior to hiring a new employee, [the owner] generally asked all of the [store] employees if they knew the applicant and could provide information about that person, and Lumber One believes this is sufficient to support the jury's verdict.

"At trial, [the owner] generically described how he elicited input from employees about applicants and how he used the information he received. For example, when asked if the plaintiffs were ever consulted during the screening process for new applicants, [he] responded: '[W]e would always ask all of our people if they knew someone before we hired them. When we would be interviewing them, we would ask for input from them because these guys were from the local area and we'd always ask if they knew the people or could recommend or knew anything at all about them.' [The owner] also said he took this information seriously, adding that 'it was good information. We're hiring blind here, so any input we could have or reference, it was used in making that determination.' Lumber One did not present any evidence that the plaintiffs were involved in, for instance, screening applicants, conducting interviews, checking references, or anything else related to its hiring process. . . .

"The material point, however, is that in order to meet the fourth element of the executive exemption,

(continued)

Lumber One must present some proof that the purported executives' input into personnel decisions was given particular weight. For example, one way they could have done this is to show that the purported executives' input had more influence than hourly employees' input. This is especially true if that recommendation is the only evidence relied on for the exemption, which is what happened in this case."

Case Questions

1. What was Lumber One's primary argument as to why these employees were exempt from FLSA protection?

2. What distinction did the court make between Madden and O'Bar's role at Lumber One versus Wortman's role?

3. *Focus on Critical Thinking:* Recall from Chapter 5 that a court can sometimes disregard a jury's verdict and substitute its own ruling, which is what happened in this case. Is that fair? A jury of the employees' peers found that the employees were exempt under the FLSA, but a single judge disagreed. Should a judge have that power? What impact does such a ruling have on the community's confidence in the justice system?

FIGURE 40.2 FLSA Liability

1. Calculate Alden's approximate hourly base rate:	$26,000/52 wks = $500 per week $500/40 hrs = $12.50 per hour
2. Calculate Alden's overtime rate:	$12.50 × 1.5 = $18.75 10 hrs/wk × 24 wks (6 mos.) = 240 hrs
3. Calculate overtime pay owed:	$18.75 × 240 = $4,500

Because Alden was misclassified as exempt for six months, Fernanda owes Alden $4,500 in back pay, plus interest, as set out by FLSA regulations.

 Quick Quiz Employment Law in the Gig Economy

The "gig economy" has helped to reshape the employment landscape and is characterized by jobs that involve short-term work and independent contractors (discussed in Chapter 37). TaskRabbit (www.taskrabbit.com) is an online marketplace that matches freelance labor with local demand. It helps online users find "taskers," who will help with everyday tasks such as cleaning, moving, delivery, and handyman work.

1. Can a tasker ever be covered by the FLSA? Explain.
2. Did the FLSA envision the gig economy when it was drafted? What implications does this have on employment regulation?

Answers to this Quick Quiz are provided at the end of the chapter.

Child Labor

The FLSA outlaws the once-common practice of sending school-age children to work instead of to school by imposing restrictions on hiring workers under 18 years of age. Table 40.1

TABLE 40.1	Child Labor Restrictions	

Age (years)	Restriction
Under 14	No employment except newspaper sale and delivery
14–15	Limited hours during school days in nonhazardous jobs (such as a busser or dishwasher in a restaurant)
16–17	No limits on hours, but cannot work in dangerous jobs such as mining or heavy industry and other hazardous jobs as defined in FLSA regulations

sets out restrictions for the age requirements that have been issued by the Department of Labor pursuant to its FLSA authority. It is important to note that children in family agricultural jobs and child actors are not subject to FLSA restrictions, but state statutes often require appropriate educational standards to be met through the use of tutors and homeschooling.

Every state has passed a child labor statute to supplement the federal law. For example, while the FLSA sets no limits on the hours a 16- or 17-year-old may work, most states have implemented their own hour limits for this age group. The FLSA is silent regarding employment certificates, commonly called *working papers,* yet most states have mandated some sort of documentation policy. It is imperative that a manager be aware of both federal and state requirements.

All employers subject to the FLSA are required to post a notice explaining the act where employees can readily read it (e.g., in the workplace kitchen or mailroom). The poster in Figure 40.3, issued by the Department of Labor, is used by businesses to meet this requirement.

State Laws

States also have enacted laws that provide employee guarantees. These protections fit into one of four general categories:[8]

- *Minimum paid rest periods.* Some states require a minimum rest period for workers that typically is based on the ratio of rest period versus hours worked. For example, in Kentucky, employers are required to provide a 10-minute break for every four hours worked. These rest periods must be in addition to the regularly scheduled meal break.

- *Minimum paid meal periods.* Twenty-one states require employers to provide a certain period of time, typically 30 minutes, for a meal break during a normal workday. For example, in Nebraska, employers are required to pay employees for a 30-minute meal break for each eight-hour shift.

- *Payday requirements.* Many states regulate the frequency of paydays for employees. For example, in Maine, employers are required to pay employees twice per month with no more than a 16-day interval between pay periods.

- *Prevailing wage requirements.* The majority of states require that whenever taxpayer money is involved in a construction project above a certain threshold, the contractor must pay the prevailing wage. The prevailing wage refers to the hourly wage, usual benefits, and overtime paid in the largest city in each county to the majority of workers, laborers, and mechanics. For example, in Montana, prevailing wages must be paid for any publicly funded construction project costing more than $25,000.

---

[8]See "State Labor Laws," U.S. Department of Labor.

FIGURE 40.3 | Department of Labor Poster

EMPLOYEE RIGHTS
UNDER THE FAIR LABOR STANDARDS ACT

FEDERAL MINIMUM WAGE
$7.25 PER HOUR
BEGINNING JULY 24, 2009

The law requires employers to display this poster where employees can readily see it.

OVERTIME PAY
At least 1½ times the regular rate of pay for all hours worked over 40 in a workweek.

CHILD LABOR
An employee must be at least 16 years old to work in most non-farm jobs and at least 18 to work in non-farm jobs declared hazardous by the Secretary of Labor. Youths 14 and 15 years old may work outside school hours in various non-manufacturing, non-mining, non-hazardous jobs with certain work hours restrictions. Different rules apply in agricultural employment.

TIP CREDIT
Employers of "tipped employees" who meet certain conditions may claim a partial wage credit based on tips received by their employees. Employers must pay tipped employees a cash wage of at least $2.13 per hour if they claim a tip credit against their minimum wage obligation. If an employee's tips combined with the employer's cash wage of at least $2.13 per hour do not equal the minimum hourly wage, the employer must make up the difference.

NURSING MOTHERS
The FLSA requires employers to provide reasonable break time for a nursing mother employee who is subject to the FLSA's overtime requirements in order for the employee to express breast milk for her nursing child for one year after the child's birth each time such employee has a need to express breast milk. Employers are also required to provide a place, other than a bathroom, that is shielded from view and free from intrusion from coworkers and the public, which may be used by the employee to express breast milk.

ENFORCEMENT
The Department has authority to recover back wages and an equal amount in liquidated damages in instances of minimum wage, overtime, and other violations. The Department may litigate and/or recommend criminal prosecution. Employers may be assessed civil money penalties for each willful or repeated violation of the minimum wage or overtime pay provisions of the law. Civil money penalties may also be assessed for violations of the FLSA's child labor provisions. Heightened civil money penalties may be assessed for each child labor violation that results in the death or serious injury of any minor employee, and such assessments may be doubled when the violations are determined to be willful or repeated. The law also prohibits retaliating against or discharging workers who file a complaint or participate in any proceeding under the FLSA.

ADDITIONAL INFORMATION
- Certain occupations and establishments are exempt from the minimum wage, and/or overtime pay provisions.
- Special provisions apply to workers in American Samoa, the Commonwealth of the Northern Mariana Islands, and the Commonwealth of Puerto Rico.
- Some state laws provide greater employee protections; employers must comply with both.
- Some employers incorrectly classify workers as "independent contractors" when they are actually employees under the FLSA. It is important to know the difference between the two because employees (unless exempt) are entitled to the FLSA's minimum wage and overtime pay protections and correctly classified independent contractors are not.
- Certain full-time students, student learners, apprentices, and workers with disabilities may be paid less than the minimum wage under special certificates issued by the Department of Labor.

WAGE AND HOUR DIVISION
UNITED STATES DEPARTMENT OF LABOR

1-866-487-9243
TTY: 1-877-889-5627
www.dol.gov/whd

WH1088   REV 07/16

Source: U.S. Department of Labor.

- The Fair Labor Standards Act (FLSA) is a major piece of federal legislation enacted in 1938 that regulates several important employment matters.
- The FLSA establishes a minimum wage to be paid to every employee covered under the act.
- An employee may be entitled to overtime compensation for any hours worked over the standard workweek.
- Overtime compensation is calculated by multiplying the hourly base rate of the employee times one and one-half.
- The law assumes a certain level of bargaining power for professional and management-level employees and, therefore, exempts them from FLSA protections.
- Workers without significant managerial or supervisory roles and who perform repetitive tasks or manual labor are considered nonexempt employees and are legally entitled to overtime pay.
- The FLSA outlaws the once-common practice of sending school-age children to work instead of to school by imposing restrictions on hiring workers under 18 years of age.
- States also have enacted laws that provide employee guarantees. These protections include minimum paid rest periods, minimum paid meal periods, payday requirements, and prevailing wage requirements.

RETIREMENT AND HEALTH CARE BENEFITS

LO 40-2

Identify the laws that regulate retirement and health benefits.

Employers are not required to establish retirement plans for their employees, although many do so to attract and retain high-quality employees. If an employer does offer retirement benefits, they are typically offered in the form of a **pension** or through a **tax-deferred retirement savings account** such as a 401(k)[9] plan. In a pension plan, the employer promises to pay a monthly sum to employees who retire from the company after a certain number of years of service. The amount ordinarily is based on the length of service and the employee's salary rate as of the date of retirement. In a retirement savings account, the employee commits to saving a certain percentage of base pay in an account that is controlled directly by the employee, not the employer. The employee then has the ability to allocate her savings via various investment vehicles that range from very safe to high risk. Some employers match the employee's contribution by paying an extra amount into the account based on a certain percentage of the employee's base salary. The major benefit for the employee is that retirement savings grow without triggering any tax liability until the employee is ready to make retirement withdrawals from the account.

Regulation of Pensions and Retirement Accounts

If employers establish either a pension fund or a retirement savings plan, the employer is subject to the requirements of a federal statute called the **Employee Retirement Income Security Act (ERISA)**[10] of 1974. ERISA is a comprehensive set of laws and regulations that requires employers to make certain disclosures related to investment risk, thus providing

---

[9]The term *401(k)* is a shorthand reference to the Internal Revenue Code that regulates tax-deferred savings plans.
[10]29 U.S.C. § 1001 et seq.

transparency for plan beneficiaries. ERISA establishes rules for conflict of interest (such as how much of a company's own stock can be held in a pension plan) and imposes certain fiduciary standards for investing and managing pension plans or administering retirement savings plans. Employers must adhere to record-keeping regulations and must treat all employees in accordance with a set of standardized vesting rules. ERISA authorizes the Department of Labor to monitor pension and retirement savings plan administration. The department oversees the Labor Management Services Administration, in part to implement, administer, and enforce ERISA.

Social Security Act

In addition to any pension or retirement plans offered by employers, workers are entitled to a retirement income from the federal government by virtue of the **Social Security Act (SSA) of 1935**. The SSA provides workers a broad set of benefits that are funded by mandatory employment taxes paid by both employer and employee into a trust fund administered by the federal government. These employment taxes are mandated by the Federal Insurance Contributions Act (FICA).[11] Employees are entitled to retirement benefits based on how many credits they have earned during their working life. Credits are accrued as a worker progresses through his career regardless of how many different employers the worker has over a lifetime. The SSA also provides for payments to be made when a worker becomes disabled, and it provides survivor benefits for spouses and children upon the death of a worker.

Health Care Benefits

On March 23, 2010, the Patient Protection and Affordable Care Act (PPACA or commonly referred to as the ACA) was signed into law. One week later, on March 30, 2010, the Health Care and Education Reconciliation Act (HCERA)[12] of 2010 was enacted, adding to and amending parts of the PPACA. Together, these acts overhauled the U.S. health care system. Although the legislation was the subject of intense debate and extended media coverage when it was first passed, from a business manager's perspective, much of the law's mandate was not triggered until 2015.

The law requires employers with 50 or more full-time employees to purchase health care insurance for their employees or face a penalty. It also offers small-business owners (those employing fewer than 25 full-time workers) immediate tax incentives if they offer health care coverage to their employees and pay at least 50 percent of the total costs for their employees' coverage. Individuals not covered through their employer's policy are legally required to purchase health care insurance from a health care exchange that is set up by individual states (or groups of states). Starting in 2022, employers that offer high-end health care plans (plans that cost more than $27,500 per year) to their employees will be required to pay an additional tax based on the total cost of the plan.

If an employer provides a health care plan, two federal statutes regulate certain aspects of administering the plan. First, the Health Insurance Portability and Accountability Act (HIPAA)[13] sets administrative rules and standards designed to protect employee medical information and records from disclosure to a third party. Second, the Consolidated Omnibus Budget Reconciliation Act (COBRA)[14] mandates that employers provide continuous coverage to any employee who has been terminated, even if the worker was terminated for cause.[15]

---

[11] 26 U.S.C. § 3111 et seq.

[12] Pub.L. 111-152 (2010).

[13] Pub.L. 104-191 (1996).

[14] 29 U.S.C. § 1161.

[15] In egregious cases, such as that of an employee who is terminated for theft from the company, COBRA benefits may not apply.

COBRA requires that the employer provide a terminated employee the exact same health coverage for up to 18 months. It is important to note that COBRA does not require employers to *pay* for the health plan premiums of a former employee. The employee has full responsibility for payment of all insurance premiums and administrative fees.

TAKEAWAY CONCEPTS Retirement and Health Care Benefits

- If an employer offers retirement benefits, they are typically offered in the form of a pension or through a tax-deferred retirement savings account such as a 401(k) plan.
- If an employer establishes either a pension fund or a retirement savings plan, the employer is subject to the requirements of a federal statute called the Employee Retirement Income Security Act (ERISA).
- In addition to any pension or retirement plans offered by employers, workers are entitled to retirement income from the federal government by virtue of the Social Security Act (SSA) of 1935.
- The Patient Protection and Affordable Care Act (PPACA) requires employers with 50 or more full-time employees to purchase health care insurance for their employees or face a penalty.

WORKERS' COMPENSATION AND UNEMPLOYMENT BENEFITS

LO 40-3

Demonstrate how a worker becomes entitled to workers' compensation.

While historically tort law was the only mechanism for compensating an employee who suffered an injury on the job or a job-related illness, all states now have **workers' compensation** statutes. These statutes establish a structure for an injured employee to be compensated through a statutorily mandated insurance program as the *exclusive* remedy for workplace injuries or illnesses. Employees with job-related injuries or illnesses are paid based on a percentage of the employee's salary at the time of the occurrence. Workers' compensation statutes typically require the establishment of a system for processing claims through the state workers' compensation board (or a similarly named agency), and the compensation is funded through employer-paid insurance policies. Companies also may be self-insured if they meet their individual state's requirements for establishing a fund that is sufficient to make payments to injured employees.

The most important aspect of the workers' compensation system is that the employee generally is paid regardless of any issues related to fault or negligence of the employee, the employer, or any third party; however, certain defenses to a workers' compensation claim may be asserted by the employer. This plan ensures an injured worker a continuous income for an injury that requires him or her to stop working. In exchange for this compensation, the employee is barred from pursuing a negligence lawsuit related to the injury against the employer. The state statutes often are broad in terms of coverage, but most states exempt domestic workers and temporary or seasonal employees from protection.

Defenses to Workers' Compensation Claims

In many states, an injured worker is not entitled to workers' compensation if the injury was intentionally self-inflicted or resulted from (1) a knowing violation of safety rules by the employee, (2) the employee's willful misconduct or horseplay not condoned by the employer, or (3) the employee's intoxication or illegal drug use. Should the employee fail to give the employer timely notice of the injury as determined by state statute, the claim is lost, and a failure to bring a claim within the state's statute of limitations will bar a claim. An employer should defend against unjustified workers' compensation claims to avoid paying higher premiums as a result of its claims history.

Intentional Actions or Recklessness of the Employer

Two important exceptions to the workers' compensation laws are cases in which (1) an employer has engaged in actions that intentionally create conditions that result in harm or (2) an employer acts with reckless disregard for the safety of its employees. In these cases, the injured or ill party may bypass the workers' compensation system and sue the employer for a full recovery including punitive damages. As a practical matter, however, although an injured employee may recover a higher amount through litigation, the prospect of immediate compensation and the uncertainties and delays inherent in litigation lead many people to file a workers' compensation claim rather than pursue litigation. In any case, once an injured party files a workers' compensation claim, he is barred from suing his employer in any suit related to the injury.

Course of Employment

To trigger protection under workers' compensation laws, the injury must meet two main criteria: (1) The injury was accidental and (2) the injury occurred within the course of employment. Accidental injuries are injuries that occur without any intent to cause harm or injure. The course of employment requirement varies by jurisdiction, but most state courts have interpreted the scope of employment requirement broadly and in favor of coverage for the injured worker. While cases where the employee is injured on the job at the worksite during regular business hours clearly are covered, off-premises activity also is covered as long as it is sufficiently related to the worker's employment. Even when the injury is indirectly related to the employee's job responsibilities, courts have been willing to extend workers' compensation coverage to the injured employee.

Regulation of Workplace Safety

While workers' compensation laws are designed to protect workers who are injured, the federal statute intended to prevent workplace injuries is the **Occupational Safety and Health Act (OSHA)**,[16] passed in 1970. The objective of OSHA statutes and regulation is to make the workplace as safe as possible for workers engaged in business operations by (1) setting national safety standards, (2) mandating information disclosure and warnings of hazardous working areas and assignments, (3) establishing record-keeping and reporting requirements, and (4) imposing a general duty on employers to keep a workplace reasonably safe. The OSHA law has broad coverage that encompasses virtually every private employer. Federal, state, and local government units are exempt.

The OSHA statute created an agency called the Occupational Safety and Health Administration, under the jurisdiction of the Department of Labor, to administer and enforce the statute. This administrative agency has expansive enforcement authority to carry out the provisions of the law, which includes routine or unscheduled worksite inspections. Industries that are ultrahazardous (such as mining) are highly regulated by OSHA administrative rules. The administration also investigates complaints made by employees alleging that an employer violated safety standards. Employees who make a complaint to the administration are protected from retaliation by the employer via OSHA's whistleblowing provisions.

---

[16]29 U.S.C. § 553.

OSHA regulations have evolved into a complex and lengthy set of rules and standards because so many of the regulations are industry specific. However, there are some provisions that apply to all employers. For example, employers with 11 or more employees are required to maintain company safety records and to document the investigation of any accidents. These reports must be kept current and available for inspection by the administration without need for a subpoena or advance notice. If an employee is killed in a work-related accident or if three or more employees are hospitalized in one event, the employer is required to notify the administration as soon as possible and no later than eight business hours after the accident. Once notification is made, the administration dispatches an inspector to investigate the accident. If the employer is found to have been in violation of a specific or general safety standard, then the administration takes appropriate enforcement action, including levying fines, issuing cease and desist orders, and, in egregious cases, pursuing criminal charges against the company and its officers. In the event of a workplace death, the administration cooperates with local authorities that also may have jurisdiction, especially in criminal cases.

Under OSHA rules, employees have a limited right to walk off the job when faced with a hazardous workplace condition. In *Whirlpool v. Marshall*,[17] the U.S. Supreme Court held that the OSHA statute permits employees this right under the narrow circumstances in which (1) the employee faces a condition that he reasonably believes will result in serious injury or death and (2) the context makes it impractical for the employee to contact administration inspectors.

Unemployment Compensation

After the Great Depression of the 1930s sent unemployment rates soaring to 20 percent and higher, Congress responded by enacting the **Federal Unemployment Tax Act (FUTA)**[18] of 1935, which provides limited payments to workers who have been temporarily or permanently terminated from employment through no fault of their own. The FUTA established a state-administered fund to provide payments to workers who have suffered sudden job loss. Only the employer pays FUTA taxes. To obtain unemployment benefits, the worker must actively seek new employment and, if necessary, retrain in a different field. Unemployment compensation is intended to cover workers who lose their jobs because of economic difficulties; it is not intended to reward an employee who was terminated for cause. However, because states set their own standards and procedures, the exact eligibility requirements and the amount available vary between jurisdictions. The amount paid to those who qualify for assistance generally is nowhere near the gross or even the net salary the displaced worker was earning.

TAKEAWAY CONCEPTS Worker's Compensation and Unemployment Benefits

- Workers' compensation statutes establish a structure for an injured employee to be compensated through a statutorily mandated insurance program as the *exclusive* remedy for workplace injuries or illnesses.
- In many states, an injured worker is not entitled to workers' compensation if the injury was intentionally self-inflicted or resulted from (1) a knowing violation of safety rules by the employee, (2) the employee's willful misconduct or horseplay not condoned by the employer, or (3) the employee's intoxication or illegal drug use.

(continued)

---

[17]445 U.S. 1 (1980).

[18]26 U.S.C. § 3301 et seq.

- Two important exceptions to the workers' compensation laws are cases in which (1) an employer has engaged in actions that intentionally create conditions that result in harm or (2) an employer acts with a reckless disregard for the safety of its employees.
- To trigger protection under workers' compensation laws, the injury must meet two main criteria: (1) The injury was accidental and (2) the injury occurred within the course of employment.
- The Occupational Safety and Health Act (OSHA) was passed in 1970. The objective of OSHA statutes and regulation is to make the workplace as safe as possible for workers engaged in business operations.
- The Federal Unemployment Tax Act (FUTA) of 1935 provides limited payments to workers who have been temporarily or permanently terminated from employment through no fault of their own.

THE FAMILY AND MEDICAL LEAVE ACT (FMLA)

LO 40-4

Describe how a worker becomes entitled to benefits under the Family and Medical Leave Act (FMLA).

As American society has changed since the Industrial Revolution, so has society's need to provide for employees who are faced with choosing between caring for a loved one and losing a job, seniority, or a promotion. In response to pressures on the workforce to care for a family member, in 1993 Congress passed the **Family and Medical Leave Act (FMLA)**,[19] which sets out basic protections for workers who need a brief leave from work to care for themselves or an immediate family member. Some states have similar leave statutes that allow for additional time periods or provide additional medical leave protections to employees within the state's jurisdiction.

FMLA Scope and Coverage

The FMLA is administered by the Department of Labor and applies to employers that have 50 or more employees within 75 miles. For example, if JavaHouse operates three coffeehouses in Kansas City with 20 employees at each location, the company would be considered to have 60 employees within a 75-mile radius. An employee, to be eligible for FMLA benefits, must have worked for the company for at least 12 months and have worked 1,250 hours during the past 12 months. The law mandates that employers provide up to 12 weeks of unpaid leave to employees for purposes related to family medical matters during any 12-month period. An FMLA leave may be taken when an eligible employee needs to care for a newborn or newly adopted child or when a serious health condition affects the employee or the employee's spouse, child, or parent. For an employee to be eligible for an FMLA leave, the serious health condition must require continued treatments by a health care provider and must be severe enough to render the person unable to care for herself for three consecutive days. The employee must give 30 days' notice of his intent to take a leave unless an emergency arises, which allows reduced notice. All conditions that are covered under the FMLA must be properly documented by a physician and are subject to periodic reevaluation at the employer's request.

Some states have enacted laws reducing the size of the companies covered, and some have expanded coverage to include organ donations and bone marrow transplants. Certain states also have extended coverage to include the care of grandparents, domestic partners, and others.

FMLA Protections

Although the FMLA does not require employers to pay employees on leave, it does require that the employer maintain the employee's health care benefits uninterrupted throughout

---

[19]29 U.S.C. § 2601 et seq.

the leave period. The FMLA also affords employees certain protections related to job security: (1) Employers are restricted from taking or threatening any adverse job action against the employee because of an FMLA leave; (2) employees are guaranteed employment in the same or a similar job at the same rate of pay upon returning from leave; and (3) employers must reinstate an FMLA-leave employee immediately upon the employee's notification that the leave is over. The FMLA does not require, however, that returning employees be credited with seniority that was accrued while on leave.

There are two distinct theories of recovery under the FMLA. The *interference/entitlement theory* applies when an employee alleges that the employer denied him the right to use FMLA provisions. The *retaliation/discrimination theory* applies when an employee alleges that the employer took an adverse employment action against him (e.g., termination) that was connected to an FMLA claim made by the employee. An employee may use either or both theories in pursuing an FMLA claim.[20]

In Case 40.3, a federal appeals court considers an FMLA retaliation claim.

CASE 40.3 Jaszczyszyn v. Advantage Health Physician Network, 2012 WL 5416616 (6th Cir. 2012)

FACT SUMMARY Advantage hired Jaszczyszyn as a part-time employee in 2008, and she eventually was promoted to a full-time position in Advantage's billing department. After a period of time in which Jaszczyszyn failed to report for work due to back pain, Advantage's human resources department informed Jaszczyszyn that she did not have enough paid time off to cover her absences and recommended that she submit FMLA forms to formalize the request. One form was a Certification of Health Care Provider ("Certification") to show that she suffered from a serious medical condition. Although the Certification submitted to Advantage reflected a need for intermittent FMLA leave (to be taken whenever she was having a back pain flare-up) Jaszczyszyn treated the leave as continuous, open-ended, and effective immediately upon Advantage's receipt of the Certification, never returning (or attempting to return) to work.

One month after submitting the Certification, Jaszczyszyn attended Pulaski Days, a local Polish heritage festival. Over a period of at least eight hours, she visited three Polish Halls with a group of her friends. One friend shared approximately 127 pictures from that day with Jaszczyszyn, who posted pictures featuring herself dancing and laughing on her Facebook page. Because Jaszczyszyn was Facebook friends with several of her co-workers,

the pictures were visible to them. One of those co-workers, upset about Jaszczyszyn's behavior, brought the photographs to the attention of Advantage's management. At a meeting with Advantage management, Jaszczyszyn could not explain the discrepancy between her claim of complete incapacitation and her activity in the photos. Advantage gave Jaszczyszyn her notice of termination at the conclusion of the meeting.

Jaszczyszyn sued Advantage, alleging that she was terminated in retaliation for exercising her rights pursuant to the FMLA. The trial court granted Advantage's motion for summary judgment, and Jaszczyszyn appealed.

SYNOPSIS OF DECISION AND OPINION The U.S. Court of Appeals for the Sixth Circuit affirmed the trial court's decision in favor of Advantage. The court held that for a retaliation claim, a plaintiff must establish that: (1) she was engaged in an activity protected by the FMLA; (2) the employer knew that she was exercising her rights under the FMLA; (3) after learning of the employee's exercise of FMLA rights, the employer took an employment action adverse to her; and (4) there was a causal connection between the protected FMLA activity and the adverse employment action. In this case, the court ruled that Jaszczyszyn failed to prove any causal connection.

(continued)

---

[20]*Seeger v. Cincinnati Bell Telephone Company, LLC,* 681 F.3d 274, 281 (6th Cir. 2012).

The evidence of fraud, in and of itself, was sufficient justification for the termination and was not related to her legitimate rights under the FMLA.

WORDS OF THE COURT: Retaliation and Fraud "As in [precedent cases], Advantage 'rightfully considered workplace [FMLA] fraud to be a serious issue,' and its termination of Jaszczyszyn because of her alleged dishonesty constituted a non-retaliatory basis for her discharge. While Jaszczyszyn relies heavily upon a significant amount of after-the-fact medical evidence (such as the deposition of her treating physician) in trying to cast Advantage's justification as [not the actual reason for the termination], Advantage's investigation was adequate and turned in large part on Jaszczyszyn's own behavior at the termination interview, which she does not address at all. She did not refute Advantage's honest belief that her behavior in the photos was inconsistent with her claims of total disability. Thus, as a result of her fraudulent behavior, her claim of FMLA retaliation fails. We therefore conclude that the district court did not err in granting summary judgment to Advantage."

Case Questions

1. If the photos of Jaszczyszyn had not been not posted on Facebook, would Advantage still have been justified in terminating her? Why or why not?

2. What steps should Advantage take to be sure this doesn't happen again?

3. *Focus on Critical Thinking:* What type of employee privacy issues may be involved in this case? Is it ethical for employers to monitor social media to police their employees? Should employers be permitted to monitor all of their employees' nonwork activities? Explain your answers.

Key Employees

If an employee's salary is in the top 10 percent of all salaries in the company, the FMLA classifies that person as a key employee. Although key employees are entitled to FMLA protections, employers have a right not to reinstate an employee if reinstatement would cause a "substantial and grievous economic injury." However, courts apply this exception narrowly, and employers must comply with required notifications and procedures set out by the statute, including the duty to notify an employee who is taking the leave of her key employee status and the limits of the FMLA protections. Table 40.2 lists some employment regulation laws.

TAKEAWAY CONCEPTS The Family and Medical Leave Act

- The Family and Medical Leave Act (FMLA) sets out basic protections for workers who need a brief leave from work to care for themselves or an immediate family member.

- To be eligible for FMLA benefits, an employee must have worked for the company for at least 12 months and have worked 1,250 hours during the past 12 months.

- The law mandates that employers provide up to 12 weeks of unpaid leave to employees for purposes related to family medical matters during any 12-month period.

- Although the FMLA does not require employers to pay employees on leave, it does require that the employer maintain the employee's health care benefits uninterrupted throughout the leave period.

- The FMLA affords employees certain protections related to job security.

TABLE 40.2 | Employment Regulation Laws

Federal Statute	General Provisions	Coverage
Fair Labor Standards Act (FLSA)	Wages and hours; child labor	Mandates (1) payment of minimum wage, (2) maximum 40-hour workweek, (3) overtime pay rate, and (4) restriction on children working in certain occupations and during certain hours.
Employee Retirement Income Security Act (ERISA)	Pensions and retirement funds	Subjects employers that establish retirement benefits to the requirements of ERISA laws and regulations, which primarily require employers to (1) make certain disclosures related to investment risk and (2) provide transparency to plan beneficiaries.
Social Security Act	Retirement income	Provides a broad set of benefits for workers, including a retirement income from the federal government; funded by mandatory employment taxes paid into a trust fund by both employer and employee and administered by the federal government.
Federal Unemployment Tax Act (FUTA)	Temporary and permanent unemployment	Provides limited payments to workers who have been temporarily or permanently terminated from employment through no fault of their own; funded by the employer only.
Workers' compensation statutes (state level)	Workplace injuries	Serves as a mandatory alternative to negligence lawsuits by offering compensation to an employee who suffers an accidental injury (in the course of employment) as the exclusive remedy for the injury; funded through employer-paid insurance policies.
Occupational Safety and Health Act (OSHA)	Workplace safety	Sets workplace rules and regulations, administered and enforced by the Occupational Safety and Health Administration, to promote the safety of workers and prevent workplace injuries.
Family and Medical Leave Act (FMLA)	Medical leaves	Requires that an employee returning from a medical leave, whether taken to care for herself or an immediate family member, be reinstated at the same rate of pay.

EMPLOYEE PRIVACY

The privacy of employees while they are at the workplace or off-site performing work-related tasks is an issue of growing concern because many employers regularly monitor employee behavior in some form. In a study coauthored by the American Management Association and the ePolicy Institute, 73 percent of employers reported that they monitored employee e-mail messages, and 48 percent regularly employed video surveillance. Ten percent even monitored social networking sites.[21] Other issues related to employee privacy include telephone and voicemail monitoring and drug and alcohol testing in various employment contexts. As a general matter, an employee's right to privacy in the workplace is very limited. However, employees may have some limited rights that typically are afforded by statute.

LO 40-5

Discuss the circumstances under which an employer is liable for invading an employee's privacy.

Monitoring of E-mail, Internet Usage, and Social Media

An employee's activities while using an employer's computer system are not protected by any privacy laws. All computer use ordinarily is subject to employer monitoring, including the right to:

- Track websites visited by employees.
- Count keystrokes and mouse clicks.
- Block employees from visiting specific Internet sites.
- Limit the amount of time an employee may spend at a specific website.

[21]See *The 2007 Electronic Monitoring & Surveillance Survey* (New York: American Management Association, 2007).

Social Media Passwords

Some employers require employees and job applicants to provide the usernames and passwords to their social media accounts. A proposed federal bill to forbid this practice, called the Password Protection Act, was introduced in 2015. However, the bill died in committee and was never enacted. Nearly half of the states have passed legislation to prevent this type of monitoring activity in the workplace.

Social media passwords are now being surrendered to employers as part of the employment relationship.
©Richard Atrero de Guzman/NurPhoto via Getty Images

Discussion Questions

1. Is an employer ever justified in requesting a social media password from an employee or a prospective hire? Why or why not?
2. Assume the proposed federal legislation was defeated due to the strategic lobbying efforts of business trade associations. Is this type of behavior ethical?

A company's information technology services may use filters, keystroke-recording software, and other detection devices to determine whether an employee's use of e-mail is inconsistent with company policy. At large companies, part of the management team may include compliance officers assigned to coordinate monitoring and ensure that employees are following all company e-mail and Internet policies.

It is becoming increasingly common for employers to use elaborate employee-monitoring measures, primarily to limit their risk of vicarious liability (liability for the act of an employee) in areas such as defamation and employment discrimination. For example, in the AMA/ePolicy survey cited earlier, 15 percent of the companies surveyed had faced a lawsuit triggered by employee e-mail use. Companies typically adopt specific guidelines and policies for e-mail and Internet use and inform employees that all Internet, e-mail, and social media usage is subject to monitoring.

Telephone and Voicemail

While the right of an employer to monitor e-mail and Internet usage of workplace computers for business reasons is very expansive, employees are afforded certain protections for telephone calls and voicemail by the **Electronic Communications Privacy Act (ECPA).**[22] The ECPA updated existing wiretap laws and restricts an employer from monitoring an employee's personal calls (even those from the workplace) without the employee's consent. Employers may monitor business calls but must disconnect the moment they recognize that a call is personal. Employers also are restricted from accessing an employee's office voicemail without the employee's consent. However, the ECPA has two exceptions that severely limit its protections for employees. First, the business-extension exception permits an employer to monitor employee electronic communications on company-owned devices so long as this is done in the ordinary course of business. Second, the ECPA allows an employer to avoid liability if the employee consents to the monitoring. Some employers now routinely require employees to consent to monitoring as a condition of employment.

---

[22] 18 U.S.C. § 2510 et seq.

Drug and Alcohol Testing

Employee privacy protection from use of regular or random drug or alcohol tests in the workplace is governed primarily by state statutes, which vary considerably. Some states permit employee testing so long as the employer follows certain procedural safeguards intended to ensure confidentiality, safety, and accuracy. Other states permit testing only when the employee's job carries a great deal of risk to the employee or the public or when a worker has been involved in a work-related accident in which drug use is suspected.

Drug and alcohol testing raises important issues regarding the rights of an employee under the Americans with Disabilities Act (ADA). The ADA, which is discussed in detail in Chapter 41, "Employment Discrimination," prohibits discrimination based on a physical disability. If the testing uncovers a former drug addiction (or current alcoholism), under certain circumstances the employee is protected from discipline or termination under the ADA.

The ADA also places restrictions on medical examinations and tests. Employers may require a medical examination only after a job offer has been made. The job offer may be made contingent upon passing the medical test, so the test must be administered after all other hiring information is obtained and found satisfactory. If an employer requires medical testing, the tests must be administered to all prospective employees and may not be used to target those with disabilities or to determine whether women are pregnant. Data obtained through medical testing must be kept in a separate file and be available only to those with a demonstrable "need to know."

In Case 40.4, a company requires a medical test and is sued by two prospective employees.

CASE 40.4 Leonel v. American Airlines, 400 F.3d 702 (9th Cir. 2005)

FACT SUMMARY Leonel and two other applicants were given conditional offers of employment by American Airlines. The offers of employment were contingent upon passing background checks and medical examinations. Prior to the background checks being completed, American sent Leonel and the other applicants to its on-site facility for the required medical exams, and each applicant filled out a medical questionnaire. Although Leonel and the other applicants were HIV positive, they did not disclose their condition or related medications on the questionnaire. After blood tests revealed that the applicants were HIV positive, American rescinded the employment offers, citing each applicant's failure to disclose relevant information on the medical questionnaires. Leonel and the other applicants filed suit under the Americans with Disabilities Act (and similar state statutes), arguing that the medical exams were premature. The trial court ruled in favor of American Airlines.

SYNOPSIS OF DECISION AND OPINION The Court of Appeals for the Ninth Circuit reversed the trial court and ruled in favor of Leonel and the other

two applicants. The court held that the ADA and California state statutes prohibit the use of medical testing prior to completion of the application process. The court rejected American's argument that the expedited medical examinations were necessary to remain competitive for the best candidates.

WORDS OF THE COURT: Premature Medical Testing "Here, it is undisputed that American's offers were subject to both medical and non-medical conditions when they were made to the appellants and the appellants were required to undergo immediate medical examinations. Thus the offers were not real, the medical examination process was premature and American cannot penalize the appellants for failing to disclose their HIV-positive status—unless the company can establish that it could not reasonably have completed the background checks before subjecting the appellants to medical examinations and questioning. It has not done so. As justification for accelerating the medical examinations, American's Manager of Flight Service Procedures,

(continued)

Julie Bourk-Suchman, explained that the company found it important to minimize the length of time that elapsed during the hiring process in order to compete for applicants. But competition in hiring is not in itself a reason to contravene the ADA's and FEHA's (California's Fair Employment and Housing Act) mandates to defer the medical component of the hiring process until the non-medical component is completed."

Case Questions

1. Why should medical tests only be given after all nonmedical tests are completed satisfactorily?

2. Why did the court determine that American had not truly tendered a conditional offer of employment?

3. *Focus on Critical Thinking:* At what point would a true conditional offer of employment have been appropriate?

Polygraph Testing

In 1988, Congress passed the **Employee Polygraph Protection Act**,[23] which prohibits most private sector employers from requiring a polygraph (lie detector) test as a condition of employment. Additionally, employers are prohibited from taking or threatening action against current employees who refuse to take the test. However, the act permits employers to use polygraph tests when investigating losses attributable to theft or other economic loss or when the employee is in the security or pharmaceutical industry. The law does not apply if the employer is a federal, state, or local government entity.

TAKEAWAY CONCEPTS Employee Privacy

- An employee's activities while using an employer's computer system are not protected by any privacy laws.
- Nearly half of the states have passed legislation to prevent employers from requiring employees and job applicants to provide the usernames and passwords to their social media accounts.
- While the right of an employer to monitor e-mail and Internet usage on workplace computers for business reasons is very expansive, employees are afforded certain protections for telephone calls and voicemail by the Electronic Communications Privacy Act (ECPA).
- In 1988, Congress passed the Employee Polygraph Protection Act, which prohibits most private sector employers from requiring a polygraph (lie detector) test as a condition of employment.

LABOR LAWS AND UNION MEMBERSHIP

LO 40-6

Summarize the process for forming a collective bargaining unit.

Another source of legal protections for workers are labor unions. Union membership peaked in the early 1950s, when nearly one-third of American workers were unionized. By 2012, the percentage of wage and salary workers who were members of a union was 11.3 percent, down from 11.8 percent in 2011.[24] Today, most labor unions in America are members of one

---

[23]29 U.S.C. § 2001 et seq.

[24]U.S. Department of Labor, Bureau of Labor Statistics, *Economic News Release, Union Members Summary,* January 23, 2013.

of the two larger umbrella organizations: the American Federation of Labor and Congress of Industrial Organizations (AFL-CIO) and the Change to Win Federation, which split from the AFL-CIO in 2005.

Labor Law

The **National Labor Relations Act (NLRA)**[25] of 1935 is the centerpiece of labor-management regulation statutes. It provides general protections for the rights of workers to organize, engage in **collective bargaining**, and use economic weapons (such as a strike) in the collective bargaining process. Collective bargaining is the process of negotiating an agreement on behalf of an entire workforce as opposed to individuals negotiating privately on their own behalf (or not negotiating at all). The statute also contained an enabling provision that formed the **National Labor Relations Board (NLRB)** to administer, implement, and enforce the law's wide-sweeping provisions. In addition to the traditional administrative agency duties of implementation and enforcement, the NLRB monitors union elections for fraud and sets guidelines for employers and unions in regard to fair labor practices.

In general, the NLRA covers all employers whose business activity involves some aspect of interstate commerce. As a practical matter, under modern interpretation by the courts, this means that NLRA coverage is practically universal. Some workers are specifically exempted by statute, including railroad and airline employees.[26] To be eligible for protection under the NLRA, the worker must be a current employee rather than an applicant or a retiree.

Through amendments to the NLRA since its enactment, Congress has clarified and reformed the legal standards applicable to employers and unions to ensure fairness to both labor and management in resolving differences. These laws deemed certain labor practices illegal, thus making them *unfair* labor practices under the NLRA.

Labor Management Relations Act

Passage of the NLRA brought about a wave of industrial strikes that impacted daily commercial activity across the United States. This created a backlash sufficient to cause Congress to limit certain union practices and rights by amending the NLRA with the **Labor Management Relations Act**[27] in 1947. The amendment prohibited employers and employees from agreeing that union membership is required as a condition for employment. The law also authorizes states to enact **right-to-work laws**, which make it illegal for employers to agree with unions that union membership is required for continued employment. Under the right-to-work statutes, employees who are not union members also do not have to contribute a portion of their salary to union membership dues. In sum, this permitted states to outlaw what had become a common part of labor-management agreements: forcing employees to join or continue membership in a union as a condition of employment. The law also made clear that employers had the right to voice their reasons for opposition to formation of a union and gave specific authorization for the president of the United States to suspend a strike for up to 80 days in times of national emergency.[28]

---

[25]29 U.S.C. § 151 et seq. This law, also called the *Wagner Act,* displaced an earlier attempt at labor regulation, the Norris-LaGuardia Act, which proved ineffective.

[26]Separate statutes govern railroad and airline labor-management regulations.

[27]29 U.S.C. § 141 (also known as the *Taft-Hartley Act*).

[28]Labor unions waged an extensive lobbying campaign to oppose the bill, but the provision related to the right to suspend a strike in the event of a national emergency was popular with the citizenry—many of whom still had vivid memories of World War II. President Truman vetoed the law, but Congress overrode the veto.

Labor-Management Reporting and Disclosure Act

In response to increasing allegations of corruption in major trade unions, Congress enacted the **Labor-Management Reporting and Disclosure Act** in 1959,[29] which established a system of reporting and checks intended to uncover and prevent fraud and corruption among union officials. The law (1) regulates the internal operating procedures of a union, including election processes, procedures, and rights of members at membership and officer meetings; (2) requires extensive financial disclosures by unions; and (3) gives the NLRB additional oversight jurisdiction for internal union governance.

Union Formation

While major labor unions such as the AFL-CIO are a well-known part of the American landscape, regional unions—or even unions that have only one employer—are recognized by the NLRA as well. If an employer has not already recognized a union, and a group of employees decides that it wants to form a **collective bargaining unit** to deal with labor-management matters such as negotiating a contract, the NLRA sets out a procedure for forming a union.

Authorization Cards
Typically, a group of employees organizes an effort to have other workers sign **authorization cards** indicating that they wish to form a local union or join an existing union. At least 30 percent of the authorization cards must be signed by employees in a certain bargaining unit. Employees may bargain collectively only if they have a mutuality of interests (e.g., similar nonmanagement jobs, worksites, and conditions). Bargaining units may be recognized as employees of a single employer or those of an entire region or industry.

Election
Once the union organizers obtain authorization cards from at least 30 percent of the members of a bargaining unit, the authorization cards are filed with the NLRB. The formal union certification process begins when the NLRB sets a date for an **election** (a vote to accept or reject unionization) by the entire bargaining unit. Prior to the election, union organizers are permitted to campaign, for example by distributing flyers and leaflets to employees. However, employers still have a right to limit any union campaign activities that take place on the employer's property or during the regular workday so long as they can justify that the limits are based on business reasons (such as safety or interference with business operations) and are not simply an effort to stop unionization. One appellate court has held, for example, that employer restrictions on distribution of pro-union literature during an unpaid lunch hour in an employee cafeteria were overly restrictive and not sufficiently related to legitimate business objectives.[30] Although employers may not impose overly burdensome restrictions on employees engaging in pro-union campaigns, employees cannot use threats or coercion in their efforts to convince other bargaining-unit employees to unionize. In a 1992 case, the Supreme Court ruled that nonemployee union organizers may not distribute pro-union flyers in a company-owned parking lot without permission from the company.[31]

Misconduct during a campaign constitutes an unfair labor practice and results in the NLRB or a court setting aside any election results as well as taking other enforcement action (and sometimes levying criminal charges).[32] Employers also have a right to campaign

---

[29]29 U.S.C. Section 401 et seq. (also known as the *Landrum-Griffin Act*).

[30]*International Transportation Service v. NLRB,* 449 F.3d 160 (D.C. Cir. 2006).

[31]*Lechmere, Inc. v. NLRB,* 502 U.S. 527 (1992).

[32]*Associated Rubber Co. v. NLRB,* 296 F.3d 1055 (11th Cir. 2002).

against unionization, but they are subject to regulatory restrictions designed to prevent employers from using economic pressure to influence employee voting. The NLRA regulations prohibit employers from using threats of termination or demotion or using incentives (such as a bonus or additional vacation time) in exchange for a nonunion vote.

Certification   After a legally sound election is held, a simple majority of pro-union votes is required for the NLRB to **certify** the collective bargaining unit as a union. The employer must then recognize the union as the exclusive bargaining representative of the workers and is required to bargain in good faith with the union thereafter. Table 40.3 summarizes the union formation process.

Collective Bargaining

Collective bargaining is the process of negotiating terms and conditions of employment for employees in the collective bargaining unit. These terms typically are negotiated and, if a collective bargaining agreement is reached, the parties enter into a binding contract. The NLRA regulations set out certain guidelines regarding which terms must be negotiated and which terms are not subject to the bargaining requirements. Union contracts typically include terms related to wages, benefits (such as health care insurance and pension accounts), work hours, overtime procedures, and promotion systems, as well as procedures for handling disciplinary violations, suspensions, terminations, and layoffs.

The NLRA requires that both parties engage in good faith negotiations. This is not a requirement that one side or the other concede a particular term. Rather, the parties are obligated to demonstrate that they are engaged in moving toward an agreement. Tactics by either side that are intended to delay, stall, or hinder the process or to undermine the union through economic pressure on workers constitute unfair labor practices, and the NLRB may opt to intervene and conduct labor negotiations or pursue enforcement action if appropriate.

Grievances

Union contracts normally specify the means of arbitrating union **grievances** against an employer action or practice. Enforcement is initiated when an affected union member files

TABLE 40.3	Forming a Union			
Authorization Cards	**Filing with NLRB**	**Campaign**	**Election**	**Certification or Rejection**
A group of employees, with a mutuality of interests, organizes an effort to have other workers sign authorization cards; 30 percent of the collective bargaining unit must sign in order to proceed to the next step.	Authorization cards are filed with the NLRB, and a formal union certification process begins when the NLRB sets a date for an election.	Union organizers campaign according to fair labor practices. Management also is permitted to engage in certain practices to campaign against unionization.	The entire bargaining unit votes to either elect or reject unionization. A simple majority is required to certify the union.	If a simple majority voted *for* unionization, the union is certified. The employer must recognize the union as the exclusive bargaining representative of the workers and is required to bargain in good faith with the union thereafter. If a simple majority voted *against* unionization, the union is rejected.

an employee grievance. The union is given the exclusive authority to invoke the arbitration provisions of the agreement, and it conducts the proceedings before the arbitrator on behalf of the employee. The arbitrator's decision is always subject to review by courts that apply federal standards related to fairness and good faith. However, a court will not set aside an arbitrator's decision simply because the court disagrees with it. Courts give great deference to arbitrators and will intervene only in cases of fundamental unfairness in some procedural or substantive way.

If the union chooses not to bring a grievance to arbitration, the individual union member normally is not authorized to pursue a lawsuit against the employer to enforce contract provisions. The union has broad discretion in deciding when to seek arbitration on the basis of a union member's grievance.

Strikes and Other Work Stoppages

The NLRA specifically provides that union employees can commence a **strike** to induce the employer to concede certain contract terms during collective bargaining. However, certain occupations may be restricted from striking by statute if allowing a strike would significantly jeopardize public health or safety (such as air traffic controllers, law enforcement, or emergency services). Although the right to strike is protected, the NLRA also provides guidelines on when, where, and how a strike may be carried out. Most strikes are commenced when the employer-union negotiations have reached an impasse and the union membership has determined that extreme action is necessary to continue the bargaining process. During an impasse, union leadership will call for the members to vote for "strike authorization" to be given to leadership if the employer refuses to continue the bargaining process. Although most strikes occur in a collective bargaining context, unions also may commence a strike against an employer that is engaging in unfair labor practices.

While a strike is a potent economic weapon of a union, its impact on striking union members can be harsh. Workers are cut off from any pay, medical benefits, and other compensation until the strike is over. Moreover, employers have no legal obligation to rehire striking workers or to provide retroactive pay in cases of a strike for economic reasons. Although, as a practical matter, the rehiring of striking workers and partial or full retroactive pay frequently are guaranteed by the poststrike contract agreement, it is still a risk for some workers. However, if a strike is commenced due to an unfair labor practice rather than for economic reasons, the striking employees are entitled to immediate reinstatement with back pay once they unconditionally return to work. Economic strikes typically arise in the context of union members' failing to agree with the employer on wages or benefits.

In Case 40.5, a federal appeals court distinguishes between economic strikes and unfair labor practice strikes.

From the perspective of the union, a strike has the potential to result in significant economic harm to the employer. Because the NLRA also gives other employees the right to refuse to cross a picket line, a strike can be devastating to the revenue of the employer if the strike requires a full or partial shutdown of business operations.

Strikers have the right to engage in **picketing** at the employer's facilities, although there is no right to picket at the actual property site owned by the company. Picketing must be peaceful and not interfere with the operations of the employer. Picketing cannot be used to prevent or harass customers or nonstriking employees.

Unions also may call for union member and public boycotts of the employer's product or services as a method of pressuring management to engage in negotiations or concede a disputed point in a collective bargaining contract. If other unions recognize the boycotts, the economic impact on the employer may be significant.

FACT SUMMARY Midwestern Personnel Services ("MPS") provided cement and transport truck drivers to River City Holdings ("River City"), a construction materials company that serviced a variety of locations in different states. MPS contracted to supply drivers to River City for a project at a union job site. The contract for the project guaranteed that MPS would supply River City with unionized drivers. MPS obtained driver-employee signatures on union authorization cards by advising drivers that membership in an out-of-state union, which MPS had selected, was required to keep their jobs at MPS. Eventually, the drivers became dissatisfied with the out-of-state union and formed a local union for collective bargaining purposes. When MPS refused to recognize the local union on the basis that the agreement with the out-of-state union remained in effect, the drivers went on strike. MPS subsequently refused the employees' unconditional offer to return to work and hired replacement workers. The National Labor Relations Board (NLRB) concluded that the employees' strike at MPS was based on MPS's unfair labor practices rather than an economic dispute and ordered the drivers reinstated with back pay. MPS appealed.

SYNOPSIS OF DECISION AND OPINION The U.S. Court of Appeals for the Seventh Circuit ruled in favor of the employees and affirmed the NLRB's findings. The court held that the strike was clearly based on MPS's unfair labor practices and, thus, the employees were entitled to reinstatement with back pay. The court noted that MPS unlawfully assisted the out-of-state union by negotiating with and recognizing it without any indication of uncoerced majority support by the employees. Further, the union authorization cards were unlawfully obtained by threats of termination, and the refusal to reinstate the employees was itself an unfair labor practice.

WORDS OF THE COURT: Unfair Labor Practice Strikes "Under [the NLRA], unfair labor practices strikers are entitled to immediate reinstatement with back pay once they unconditionally offer to return to work, whereas economic strikers may be permanently replaced. An unfair labor

practices strike does not lose its character as such if economic motives contribute to its cause, however; it remains an unfair labor practices strike so long as the employees are motivated in part by unfair labor practices. . . .

"In determining whether management-labor cooperation has crossed over from permissible cooperation to unlawful coercion, courts consider a confluence of factors, with no one factor being dispositive. This nonexclusive list of factors includes whether the employer solicited contact with the union; the rank and position of the company's solicitor; whether the employer silently acquiesced in the union's drive for membership; whether the employer shepherded its employees to meetings with a prospective union; whether management was present at meetings between its employees and a prospective union; whether the signing of union authorization cards was coerced; and whether the employer quickly recognized the assisted union after the employees signed authorization cards yet exhibited prejudice against another union selected by the employees. . . .

"Normally a court defers to the credibility determinations of the NLRB unless there is some extraordinary reason why the court should ignore them, for instance if those findings are inherently incredible or patently unreasonable. . . .

"We conclude that substantial evidence in the record as a whole supports the Board's conclusions that the strike was an unfair labor practices strike."

Case Questions

1. Why does the court criticize MPS for recognizing the out-of-state union as the exclusive bargaining representative of the workers?

2. Suppose that MPS did recognize the local union and, subsequently, MPS and the local union negotiations reached an impasse over wages. Does MPS have any legal obligations to rehire the striking workers? Explain.

3. *Focus on Critical Thinking:* What are the public policy justifications for differentiating the type of strike (unfair labor practice versus economic)? Isn't an economic issue strike a legitimate reason for a work stoppage? Why or why not?

The NLRA provides unionized workers with the right to strike and picket in a peaceful manner in front of the employer's facilities.
©Christopher Kerrigan/McGraw-Hill Education

TAKEAWAY CONCEPTS Labor Laws and Union Membership

- The National Labor Relations Act (NLRA) of 1935 is the centerpiece of labor-management regulation statutes. It provides general protections for the rights of workers to organize, engage in collective bargaining, and use economic weapons (such as strikes) in the collective bargaining process.
- Collective bargaining is the process of negotiating an agreement on behalf of an entire workforce as opposed to individuals negotiating privately on their own behalf (or not negotiating at all).
- The NLRA contained an enabling provision that formed the National Labor Relations Board (NLRB) to administer, implement, and enforce the law's wide-sweeping provisions.
- Right-to-work laws make it illegal for employers to agree with unions that union membership is required for continued employment. Also, employees who are not union members do not have to contribute a portion of their salary to union membership dues.
- After a legally sound election is held, a simple majority of pro-union votes is required for the NLRB to certify the collective bargaining unit as a union.
- The NLRA specifically provides that union employees can commence a strike to induce the employer to concede certain contract terms during collective bargaining.
- Strikers have the right to engage in picketing at the employer's facilities, although there is no right to picket at the actual property site owned by the company.

EMPLOYMENT LICENSING REQUIREMENTS

An increasing number of professions are subject to various state licensing regulations. Some economists estimate that as many as 29 percent of American workers are licensed.[33] These state licensing statutes and regulations typically compel workers to complete a training program, pass an exam, and pay a fee to legally work in a licensed profession. Therefore, an employee must be licensed to perform the work legally, and businesses must comply with these requirements before allowing the worker to engage in certain areas of employment. The licensing requirements for professions vary from state to state. Some professions that commonly are subject to regulation and licensure include stockbrokers, taxi drivers, cosmetologists, barbers, social workers, massage therapists, dental hygienists, lawyers, architects, funeral directors, and plumbers. To obtain a license, one typically must apply in the office of business regulation of any state in which the work will be performed.

LO 40-7

Identify the role of professional licensing in the workplace.

TAKEAWAY CONCEPTS Employment Licensing Requirements

- An increasing number of professions are subject to various state licensing regulations.
- To obtain a license, one typically must apply in the office of business regulation of any state in which the work will be performed.

---

[33]Morris M. Kleiner and Alan B. Krueger, 2013. "Analyzing the Extent and Influence of Occupational Licensing on the Labor Market," *Journal of Labor Economics,* University of Chicago Press, Vol. 31(S1), pp. 173–202.

 THINKING STRATEGICALLY

©valterZ/Shutterstock

Employee Classification

PROBLEM: Businesses face pressure to contain costs to remain profitable and competitive. This pressure, however, may result in a legal avoidance scenario as discussed in Chapter 1. One area where managers may seek to reduce expense involves labor costs.

STRATEGIC SOLUTION: The following case highlights some strategic decisions to reduce labor costs, yet, trigger penalties due to the potential violation of labor laws.

Gladys is the human resources manager at the U.S. subsidiary of Banco Libertad, a Latin American bank with a subsidiary branch in New York City. Many of the loans on the books of the New York office of Banco Libertad originated in Latin America and are in Spanish. Banking regulators, however, require that all loan documentation be in English. To help with this translation task, Gladys hired Miguel, a sophomore undergraduate business student fluent in both languages who had taken a leave of absence from school. Gladys hired Miguel on October 1 on an hourly basis at $11/hour without benefits. His job duties were "[t]o translate loan documentation from Spanish to English." With respect to the FLSA, he was classified as nonexempt and, therefore, was entitled to overtime pay.

Soon after hiring Miguel, Gladys receives notification from a New York bank regulator stating that a full review of all the bank's loan files will be initiated in November. Gladys realizes that this will require Miguel to work considerably more hours and at a faster pace to meet the bank regulator's deadline. To reduce expenses, Gladys is considering whether to hire Miguel as a full-time, salaried employee at $21,120, which is what he would earn working full-time on an hourly basis. She would do this to categorize his work as exempt from overtime. She also would expand his job description to "[t]o translate loan documentation from Spanish to English and organize files for compliance with bank regulatory inspections." This also would be done to make his work exempt from overtime. Once Miguel agrees to this reassignment, Gladys plans to strongly urge Miguel to volunteer to work on weekends and thus work seven days a week. This would be necessary, as she would explain, to meet the tight deadline imposed by the regulators. Glady is aware of Section 161 of the New York Labor Law, which requires a day of rest for employees. However, she believes the bank is excluded from the law's requirements. That New York law states:

> Section 161. One day rest in seven. 1. Every employer operating a factory, mercantile establishment, hotel, restaurant, or freight or passenger elevator in any building or place shall, except as herein otherwise provided, allow every person employed in such establishment or in the care, custody or operation of any such elevator, at least twenty-four consecutive hours of rest in any calendar week. Every employer operating a place in which motion pictures are shown shall allow the projectionist or operator of the motion picture machine and engineers and firemen therein at least twenty-four consecutive hours of rest in any calendar week. Every employer operating a place in which legitimate theatre productions such as dramatic and musical productions are shown or exhibited shall allow all employees, including the performers in the cast therein and engineers and firemen, at least twenty-four consecutive hours of rest in each and every calendar week, but this shall not apply to any place wherein motion pictures, vaudeville or incidental stage presentations or a combination thereof are regularly

given throughout the week as the established policy of such place; except that engineers and firemen employed in such place shall be allowed at least twenty-four consecutive hours of rest in any calendar week. No employer shall operate such establishment, place or elevator on Sunday unless he shall comply with subdivision three. This section does not authorize any work on Sunday not permitted now or hereafter by law. . . .

Source: https://www.labor.ny.gov/formsdocs/wp/LS611.pdf.

QUESTIONS

1. Is Miguel's job exempt from overtime? Why or why not?
2. Would reclassifying Miguel as an employee make his work exempt from overtime? Why or why not?
3. Would adding the administrative duties to his job description make Miguel's work exempt? Why or why not?
4. Is Banco Libertad exempt from the New York law? Why or why not?
5. What actions should Gladys take to ensure compliance with the FLSA and the New York statute?
6. What is a good business solution that complies with the law and allows Banco Libertad to meet its deadline with the regulators?

KEY TERMS

Fair Labor Standards Act (FLSA) p. 709   A federal law enacted in 1938 and intended to cover all employers engaged in interstate commerce; mandates payment of a minimum wage, a maximum 40-hour workweek, overtime pay, and restrictions on children working in certain occupations and during certain hours.

Portal-to-Portal Act p. 710   Legislation that provides guidelines for what constitutes compensable work under the FLSA's wage and hour requirements.

Overtime compensation p. 710   A higher rate of pay for the hours that nonexempt employees work in excess of 40 hours in one seven-day workweek; calculated at one and one-half times the employee's hourly base rate.

Exempt employees p. 710   Classification of employees who are not covered by FLSA protections; generally consists of employees whose responsibilities are primarily executive, administrative, or professional.

Nonexempt employees p. 710   Employees who are protected by the FLSA and other statutes.

Pension p. 717   A retirement benefit in which the employer promises to pay a monthly sum to employees who retire from the company after a certain number of years of service. The amount is ordinarily based on the length of service and the employee's final salary rate.

Tax-deferred retirement savings account p. 717   A retirement savings plan in which the employee commits to saving a certain percentage of base pay in an account that is controlled directly by the employee. The funds grow tax-free until they are withdrawn.

Employee Retirement Income Security Act (ERISA) p. 717   A federal law enacted in 1974 consisting of a comprehensive set of laws and regulations that requires employers to make certain disclosures related to investment risk, thus providing transparency for plan beneficiaries.

Social Security Act (SSA) of 1935 p. 718   A federal law providing a broad set of benefits for workers, including a retirement income; funded by mandatory employment taxes paid into a trust fund by both employer and employee and administered by the federal government.

Workers' compensation p. 719   State statutes that provide an employee who is injured in the course of employment with a partial payment in exchange for mandatory relinquishment of the employee's right to sue the employer for the tort of negligence; funded through employer-paid insurance policies.

Occupational Safety and Health Act (OSHA) p. 720   A federal law enacted in 1970 that sets forth workplace rules and regulations to promote the safety of workers and prevent workplace injuries.

Federal Unemployment Tax Act (FUTA) p. 721   A federal law enacted in 1935 that established a state-administered fund to provide payments to workers who have suffered sudden job loss; funded through employment taxes shared by employer and employee.

Family and Medical Leave Act (FMLA) p. 722   A federal law enacted in 1993 that requires certain employers to give time off to employees to take care of their own or a family member's illness or to care for a newborn or adopted child.

Electronic Communications Privacy Act (ECPA) p. 726   A federal law enacted in 1986 that extends legal protection against wiretapping and other forms of unauthorized interception and explicitly allows employers to monitor employee communications on company equipment as long as this is done in the ordinary course of business or the employee consents to the monitoring.

Employee Polygraph Protection Act p. 728   A federal law that prohibits most private sector employers from requiring a polygraph test as a condition of employment.

National Labor Relations Act (NLRA) p. 729   A federal law enacted in 1935 that provides general protections for the rights of workers to organize, engage in collective bargaining, and take part in strikes and other forms of concerted activity in support of their demands. Also known as the *Wagner Act*.

Collective bargaining p. 729   The process of negotiating terms and conditions of employment for employees in the collective bargaining unit.

National Labor Relations Board (NLRB) p. 729   An independent federal agency created by the NLRA and charged with administering, implementing, and enforcing NLRA provisions, as well as monitoring union elections

for fraud and setting guidelines for employers and unions in regard to fair labor practices.

Labor Management Relations Act p. 729   A federal law, enacted in 1947 as an amendment to the NLRA, that prohibits requiring employees to join or continue membership in a union as a condition of employment. Also known as the *Taft-Hartley Act*.

Right-to-work laws p. 729   A state law prohibiting employers from requiring that employees join a union to continue working and that nonunion employees contribute to certain union costs such as the cost related to collective bargaining.

Labor-Management Reporting and Disclosure Act p. 730   A federal law enacted in 1959 that established a system of reporting and checks intended to uncover and prevent fraud and corruption among union officials by regulating internal operating procedures and union matters. Also known as the *Landrum-Griffin Act*.

Collective bargaining unit p. 730   An employee group that, on the basis of a mutuality of interests, is an appropriate unit for collective bargaining.

Authorization cards p. 730   Signed statements by employees indicating that they wish to unionize and/or are electing to be represented by an existing union.

Election p. 730   A vote by the entire bargaining unit to accept or reject unionization.

Certify p. 731   In labor law, to recognize a collective bargaining unit as a union. The NLRB's certification process occurs when a legally sound election reveals a simple majority of pro-union votes.

Grievance p. 731   In labor law, a complaint filed with or by a union to challenge an employer's treatment of one or more union members.

Strike p. 732   A concerted and sustained refusal by workers to perform some or all of the services for which they were hired in order to induce the employer to concede certain contract terms during collective bargaining or to engage in fair labor practices.

Picketing p. 732   A union's patrolling alongside the premises of a business to organize the workers, to gain recognition as a bargaining agent, or to publicize a labor dispute with the owner or whomever the owner deals with.

CASE SUMMARY 40.1 Sisco v. Quicker Recovery, Inc., 180 P.3d 46 (Or. Ct. App. 2008)

Workers' Compensation

Sisco worked as a tow truck driver for Quicker Recovery, a towing company in Oregon that had a contract to provide towing services for a municipal police department.

The contract required Quicker to provide a tow truck within 30 minutes of receiving a request for services. Sisco was dispatched to tow an impounded truck and was en route to the location when the police stopped him for speeding in the tow truck. Sisco refused to produce his driver's license or any other identification and was arrested pursuant to a state statute allowing the police to arrest any traffic violator who cannot be identified sufficiently for purposes of issuing a citation. Sisco physically resisted arrest, but eventually he was subdued by officers who used an electronic stun gun to take him into custody. The day after the arrest, Sisco complained of neck pain and recurring spasms caused by the altercation with the officers. He claimed that the pain prevented him from carrying out his job

responsibilities as a tow truck driver and submitted a workers' compensation claim.

CASE QUESTIONS

1. Suppose Sisco's altercation had occurred while he was en route to his house during an unpaid one-hour lunch break. Would he still be eligible for compensation? Why or why not?
2. Would Sisco have been better served trying to articulate a negligence claim? Explain.

CASE SUMMARY 40.2 Sullivan v. U.S. Postal Service, 2011-3220 (Fed. Cir. 2012)

Family and Medical Leave Act

Sullivan was employed by the U.S. Postal Service (USPS). In January 2009, he requested leave under the Family and Medical Leave Act (FMLA). In support of his request, he submitted a physician's certification that he suffered from frequent and painful attacks of gout in his feet and ankles that would require his absence from work for 5–10 days every month in 2009. A USPS committee, including the FMLA coordinator, reviewed the certification and decided to exercise the agency's right to obtain a second medical opinion. Sullivan was sent a letter notifying him that he was required to obtain the second medical evaluation. He was told when and where to report for the examination and advised that failure to appear could result in the denial of his FMLA request. Sullivan did not report for the examination. USPS informed Sullivan that his failure to appear was considered a failure to act in good faith but gave him an opportunity to explain his absence. Sullivan claimed

that he hadn't received the notification letter. This reason was deemed not credible because the FMLA director had confirmed delivery of the letter. Sullivan was told that his application was denied and no leave would be approved in 2009. Sullivan still submitted 6–7 additional FMLA leave requests in 2009 and approximately 14 FMLA leave requests in 2010. All were denied for failure to show entitlement. He was disciplined twice for noncompliance with rules, and after 45 unscheduled absences for which he did not follow agency leave-requesting procedures, he was terminated for failure to comply with the agency's leave regulations.

CASE QUESTIONS

1. Even though Sullivan supplied a physician's certification, did the agency have the right to require a second medical evaluation? Explain.
2. How could Sullivan have avoided this conflict and qualified for leave?

CASE SUMMARY 40.3 Bonilla v. Baker Concrete Construction, 487 F.3d 1340 (2007)

Compensation for Commuting

Bonilla was one of several workers hired by Baker Concrete to work on construction at the Miami airport. During construction, airport security required the

workers to pass through a security gate and ride in an airport-authorized bus to the site. Baker Concrete paid the workers for being at the site from 7:30 a.m. until 4 p.m. Because of the security requirements, the workers had to arrive at the airport an hour early in order to get to the site on time, and their commute home was extended 15 additional minutes. The workers sued, contending that under the Fair Labor Standards Act they should have been compensated for time spent being transported to and from the employee parking area to the construction site.

CASE QUESTIONS

1. Who prevails and why?
2. Explain your analysis and construct a hypothetical situation in which the losing party might have prevailed.

CHAPTER REVIEW QUESTIONS

1. The Fair Labor Standards Act (FLSA) does not include:
   a. Setting the minimum wage.
   b. Restrictions on child labor.
   c. Workplace safety standards.
   d. A standard pay rate for overtime.
   e. Setting a maximum 40-hour workweek.

2. All computer use is ordinarily subject to employer monitoring, including the right to:
   a. Track websites visited by employees.
   b. Count keystrokes and mouse clicks.
   c. Block employees from visiting specific Internet sites.
   d. Limit the amount of time an employee may spend at a specific website.
   e. All of the above.

3. Ahab is covered by the FLSA and works four consecutive weeks as follows: week 1, 45 hours; week 2, 41 hours; week 3, 38 hours; and week 4, 36 hours. How many hours of overtime must Ahab's employer pay for this time period?
   a. 0
   b. 6
   c. 8
   d. 16
   e. 24

4. The Family Medical Leave Act (FMLA) provides for:
   a. Paid leave for caring for a sick spouse or child; unpaid leave for all other relatives.
   b. Paid leave for childbirth; unpaid leave to care for family members.
   c. Unpaid leave for non-key employees; paid leave for key employees.
   d. Unpaid leave to care for a newborn baby.
   e. Unpaid leave to attend parenting and childbirth classes.

5. The _____ sets out basic protections for workers who need a brief leave from work to care for themselves or an immediate family member.
   a. Family Medical Leave Act
   b. Social Security Act
   c. Fair Labor Standards Act
   d. Employee Retirement Income Security Act
   e. Employee Polygraph Protection Act

6. Just a handful of professions are subject to various state licensing regulations.
   a. True
   b. False

7. Collective bargaining is the process of negotiating terms and conditions of employment for employees in the collective bargaining unit.
   a. True
   b. False

8. To trigger protection under workers' compensation laws, the injury must meet two main criteria: (1) The injury was accidental and (2) the injury occurred outside the course of employment.
   a. True
   b. False

9. All employers subject to the FLSA are required to post a notice explaining the act where employees can readily read it.
   a. True
   b. False

10. Workers' compensation statutes establish a structure for an injured employee to be compensated through a statutorily mandated insurance program as the exclusive remedy for workplace injuries or illnesses.
    a. True
    b. False

1. It is possible that a tasker could fall within the FLSA's coverage. The FLSA applies to all employees of enterprises that employ workers engaged in interstate commerce; produce goods for interstate commerce; or handle, sell, or otherwise work on goods or materials that have been moved in or produced for such commerce. If a tasker is hired by a business, for example, and the law considers this employment, then the tasker will fall within the FLSA's coverage.

2. The FLSA did not envision the gig economy when it was drafted in the 1930s. This means that one of the most important employment regulation statutes does not fully encompass or apply to the gig economy and many workers are not protected by the act.

CHAPTER REVIEW QUESTIONS: Answers and Explanations

1. c. Workplace safety standards are set out in laws such as the Occupational Safety and Health Act and are not part of the FLSA. All other answers are provisions of the FLSA.

2. e. All of the above are subject to monitoring.

3. b. Employees covered under the FLSA have a maximum 40-hour workweek as calculated weekly. Anything over 40 hours in any one workweek must be paid at an overtime rate. In week 1, Ahab worked five extra hours. In week 2, he worked one extra hour. It is not relevant that he did not work 40 hours in weeks 3 and 4.

4. d. The FMLA allows employees to take an unpaid leave of absence for family-related care (such as caring for a newborn baby). Answers *a, b,* and *c* are all incorrect because the FMLA has no paid leave provisions. Answer *e* is incorrect because the law only covers caregiving.

5. a. None of the other statutes set out basic protections for workers who need a brief leave from work to care for themselves or an immediate family member.

6. b. False A significant number of professions are subject to various state licensing regulations.

7. a. True. Collective bargaining is the process of negotiating terms and conditions of employment for employees in the collective bargaining unit.

8. b. False To trigger protection under workers' compensation laws, the injury must meet two main criteria: (1) The injury was accidental and (2) the injury occurred *within* the course of employment.

9. a. True. All employers subject to the FLSA are required to post a notice explaining the act where employees can readily read it.

10. a. True. Workers' compensation statutes establish a structure for an injured employee to be compensated through a statutorily mandated insurance program as the exclusive remedy for workplace injuries or illnesses.

CHAPTER 41

Employment Discrimination

Sexual harassment is a form of discrimination that creates a toxic environment in the workplace that results in low morale, severe stress, illness, and high turnover among the workforce. In this chapter's *Thinking Strategically* we use legal strategy to create a harassment prevention framework that is intended to prevent, investigate, and remediate harassment in the workplace.

Learning Objectives

After studying this chapter, students who have mastered the material will be able to:

41-1 Define the term *employment discrimination,* articulate the origins of antidiscrimination law, and explain the role of the Equal Employment Opportunity Commission (EEOC).

41-2 Describe the protections afforded under the major federal antidiscrimination statutes and identify the protected classes and theories of discrimination under Title VII.

41-3 Identify two theories of discrimination in the context of sexual harassment.

41-4 List remedies available under Title VII.

41-5 Explain antidiscrimination laws that apply to age, disabilities, and equal pay.

41-6 Apply the major defenses available to employers in a discrimination claim and explain the role of affirmative action in the context of employment discrimination.

41-7 Explain the role of state law in employment discrimination cases.

CHAPTER OVERVIEW

Some of the most frequent legal challenges in business involve laws that prohibit discrimination in the workplace. Lawsuits related to employment discrimination have increased dramatically in the past two decades, and managers frequently find themselves involved in employment discrimination claims as witnesses, supervisors, defendants, or plaintiffs/victims. This area of law has developed very rapidly over the past 50 years, and the assortment of statutes—along with standards and tests developed by courts to apply the rules—all combine to form a relatively complex body of law from a variety of sources. In this chapter, we discuss the definition, sources, and statutory framework of discrimination law. We also discuss the role of affirmative action in the workplace and additional workplace antidiscrimination protections in state statutes.

DEFINITIONS AND SOURCES OF LAW

LO 41-1

Define the term *employment discrimination*, articulate the origins of antidiscrimination law, and explain the role of the Equal Employment Opportunity Commission (EEOC).

Recall from previous chapters that one of the major exceptions to the employment-at-will doctrine, whereby employers may discharge employees with or without cause without triggering liability, is when a statute prohibits the employer's action. One of the major categories of statutes that prohibit employers from terminating employees is antidiscrimination statutes that bar any job action (such as termination) based on certain discriminatory motives. The term **employment discrimination** has a broad-based definition encompassing workplace-related discrimination that includes (1) the hiring process; (2) treatment of employees in terms of promotions and demotions, work schedules, working conditions, or assignments; and (3) disciplinary action such as reprimands, suspension, or termination. Historically, U.S. common law had recognized virtually no protections for employees from discrimination based on race, color, gender, religion, national origin, age, disabilities, and other characteristics. In fact, until the Equal Pay Act of 1963, employers were not prohibited from making job decisions that adversely affected women in terms of pay disparity. One year later, Congress passed the most sweeping antidiscrimination protections for workers in U.S. history as part of the Civil Rights Act of 1964. In addition to federal statutes, some states have statutes that provide additional antidiscrimination protections in the workplace.

Equal Employment Opportunity Commission (EEOC)

An important part of the Civil Rights Act of 1964 was the creation of an agency to monitor employer compliance with the statute. The **Equal Employment Opportunity Commission (EEOC)** is the administrative agency[1] charged with carrying out federal workplace antidiscrimination laws. The EEOC is a five-member commission whose members are appointed by the president with approval of the Senate. The EEOC uses its rulemaking authority, investigatory powers, and enforcement action to administer the statutory mandates established by Congress. The EEOC plays two important roles in ensuring protection for victims of discrimination under various statutes. Filing a complaint with the EEOC is the first step for a party claiming unlawful employment discrimination (procedures for asserting a discrimination claim are discussed later in this chapter). Second, in certain cases the EEOC will sue on *behalf* of an aggrieved employee. This is a powerful method of enforcing antidiscrimination laws because it gives aggrieved employees the full resources of the federal government, which can be particularly crucial when bringing an individual claim of employment discrimination against a large employer.

As a practical matter, the EEOC can pursue only a fraction of claims that are made by employees. The agency often focuses on cases that have some important legal significance or where the employer's conduct was particularly egregious or in bad faith (e.g., attempting to prevent an employee's claim with a threat of termination or demotion).

Asserting a Discrimination Claim

Federal antidiscrimination statutes prescribe a specific procedure for employees alleging employment discrimination. First, an aggrieved employee must file a **complaint** against the employer with the local office of the EEOC (generally within 180 days of the adverse job action). The EEOC then notifies the employer and commences a preliminary investigation. As an administrative agency, the EEOC may use its authority to obtain documents, statements from witnesses, and other evidence that will aid in the investigation. Courts

---

[1] An administrative agency is a statutorily created body with responsibilities related to the formation, implementation, and enforcement of regulations intended to administer a federal law. Administrative agencies and law are covered in detail in Chapter 43, "Administrative Law."

have granted the EEOC wide latitude in investigating discrimination claims, including the authority to access confidential employer files.

During and immediately after the investigation, the EEOC is required by statute to engage in **conciliation negotiations**. This means that the EEOC has an affirmative statutory duty to make good faith efforts in favor of settlement of the case instead of filing a lawsuit. If efforts at conciliation fail, the EEOC may choose to file suit against the employer on the employee's behalf or may decide not to take any action at all. After 180 days have passed from the time of the complaint, the employee may demand that the EEOC issue a right-to-sue letter. This letter entitles the employee to file a lawsuit in a federal court. Note that even though all employment discrimination claims must begin with the EEOC, ultimately the employee will have an opportunity to present his case in court. This is true even if the EEOC decides that the case has no merit and declines to investigate.

TAKEAWAY CONCEPT Employment Discrimination Defined

The term *employment discrimination* has a broad-based definition encompassing workplace-related discrimination that includes (1) the hiring process; (2) treatment of employees in terms of promotions and demotions, work schedules, working conditions, or assignments; and (3) disciplinary action such as reprimands, suspension, or termination.

<table>
<tr><td>

LO 41-2

Describe the protections afforded under the major federal antidiscrimination statutes and identify the protected classes and theories of discrimination under Title VII.

</td><td>

PRIMARY FEDERAL WORKPLACE ANTIDISCRIMINATION STATUTES

The primary federal antidiscrimination statutes are (1) **Title VII** of the Civil Rights Act of 1964[2] and its subsequent amendments, especially the Civil Rights Act of 1991;[3] (2) the **Age Discrimination in Employment Act (ADEA) of 1967**;[4] and (3) the **Americans with Disabilities Act (ADA) of 1990**,[5] which was last amended in 2009. The **Equal Pay Act of 1963** is part of the Fair Labor Standards Act, but it contains some antidiscrimination provisions as well.

These statutes may be categorized into two classes that aid in understanding their purpose. The first are laws that require the person in the protected class to receive *equal treatment* as nonclass members. The second are laws that require the person in the protected class to receive *special treatment*. For example, Title VII of the Civil Rights Act of 1964 requires men and women to be treated equally. However, the Americans with Disabilities Act (discussed later in this chapter) requires that persons with certain disabilities be given special treatment via reasonable accommodations by their employer.

Prescott v. WidgetCo

To illustrate the contours of the federal antidiscrimination statutes, suppose that Prescott is seeking employment as an internal accountant and provides a résumé and supporting application materials to WidgetCo, a manufacturing firm with 50 employees. This hypothetical is used throughout the chapter to discuss possible scenarios involving various employment discrimination theories and defenses.

</td></tr>
</table>

---

[2]42 U.S.C. § 2000e et seq.

[3]42 U.S.C. § 1981a et seq.

[4]29 U.S.C. § 620 et seq.

[5]42 U.S.C. § 12002 et seq.

Title VII

Title VII of the Civil Rights Act of 1964 and its amendments make up the centerpiece of anti-discrimination statutes. Even when interpreting antidiscrimination statutes that are not part of Title VII, courts often apply the antidiscrimination law using the Title VII statutory model and application procedures. Title VII applies to any private sector employer with 15 or more full-time employees as well as to labor unions, employment agencies, state and local governments, and most federal government employees. The law covers a comprehensive set of job-related transactions, including hiring and firing, promotion and demotion, disciplinary actions, work schedule, pay rate, job assignment, and other employer actions. Referred to simply as *Title VII*, the law prohibits discrimination in the workplace on the basis of an employee's race, color, national origin, gender, or religion. These classifications are called **protected classes**. In 1978, Congress amended Title VII to specifically add pregnancy as a protected class.[6]

Protected Classes

One fundamental tenet of federal antidiscrimination laws is that not all discrimination is illegal. Under Title VII or any other antidiscrimination laws, statutory protection is extended only to those who have been discriminated against based on their membership in a protected class. For example, in our Prescott hypothetical, discussed earlier, suppose that Prescott has been hired by WidgetCo as an accountant. Prescott shows up on the first day wearing a T-shirt and blue jeans. Her manager points out that her attire is not consistent with company dress policy and requests that she leave and return in more formal business attire. Prescott refuses to comply with her manager's request, so she is terminated. For purposes of understanding employment discrimination statutes, there are two important questions. First, was Prescott discriminated against? The answer is clearly yes. Prescott was terminated not for her poor performance but for wearing certain attire. Thus, it can be said that Prescott was the victim of anti–blue jeans discrimination. However, the second question is more important: Was Prescott discriminated against based on her membership in a protected class? In other words, did WidgetCo terminate Prescott based on her color, race, national origin, religion, or gender? The answer is clearly no. Because this particular case of discrimination was not based on Prescott's association with a protected class, WidgetCo's discriminatory action (her termination) is not prohibited by Title VII.

It is also important to note that a plaintiff need not be in a minority within the protected classes in order to be covered by Title VII. While the majority of discrimination cases filed are based on discrimination related to a minority within a protected class, the statute protects against any discrimination based on association with a protected class and does not require that the plaintiff be a member of a certain ethnic category. For example, in *McDonald v. Santa Fe Train*,[7] the U.S. Supreme Court held that racial discrimination against white employees violates Title VII if the employer was motivated by race. However, there are certain instances in which an employer's preference for certain minority class members in an employment decision is permitted by an affirmative action plan (discussed later in this chapter).

Sexual Orientation

One area of Title VII law that has developed significantly in a relatively short period of time is whether sexual orientation may be a protected class. Proponents of the theory of recognizing sexual orientation as a protected class argue that if an employer discriminates against

---

[6]Pregnancy Discrimination Act of 1978, 42 U.S.C. § 2000e(k).

[7]427 U.S. 273 (1976). The case involved a lawsuit brought by a white employee who was terminated for allegedly stealing from the company. The same incident involved a black employee who also was alleged to have stolen from the company but was given only a reprimand.

an employee based on sexual orientation, it amounts to discrimination based on sex and is thus illegal under federal discrimination statutes. Until recently, no court of authority has ruled that sexual orientation is covered under Title VII. However, in 2015, the EEOC issued a ruling that *recognized* discrimination based on sexual orientation as a form of sex discrimination.[8] The EEOC reasoned that sexual orientation is inherently a sex-based consideration and, accordingly, an allegation of discrimination based on sexual orientation is necessarily an allegation of sex discrimination under Title VII. Although the rulings in federal courts have been mixed since the EEOC's decision,[9] both the U.S. Court of Appeals for the Seventh Circuit[10] and the U.S. Court of Appeals for the First Circuit[11] recently ruled that Title VII *does* cover sexual orientation claims. Because of this split in the circuit courts, this issue will have to be decided by the U.S. Supreme Court.

Most recently, another federal appellate court reversed its previous position on the issue of sexual orientation in the context of Title VII. In Case 41.1, the court explains the reasoning behind its reversal. It is important to note that this decision is under review by the U.S. Supreme Court.

CASE 41.1 Zarda v. Altitude Express, 883 F. 3d 100 (2nd Cir. 2018)

FACT SUMMARY In 2010, Donald Zarda, a gay man, worked as a skydiving instructor at Altitude Express. As part of his job, he regularly participated in tandem skydives, strapped hip-to-hip and shoulder-to-shoulder with customers. In an environment where close physical proximity was common, Zarda's co-workers routinely referenced sexual orientation, and Zarda sometimes told female customers about his sexual orientation to alleviate any concerns they might have about being strapped to a man for a tandem skydive. During preparation for a tandem jump, Zarda told a female client that he was gay "and ha[d] an ex-husband to prove it." According to Zarda, this disclosure was intended simply to preempt any discomfort the client may have felt in being strapped to the body of an unfamiliar man. However, the customer alleged that Zarda inappropriately touched her and disclosed his sexual orientation to excuse his behavior. After the customer complained to Altitude management, Zarda was fired. Zarda denied inappropriately touching the client and insisted he was fired solely because of his reference to his sexual orientation.

Zarda filed a discrimination charge with the EEOC concerning his termination and later brought a lawsuit against Altitude claiming that, in addition to being discriminated against because of his sexual orientation, he also was discriminated against because of his gender. The trial court dismissed Zarda's complaint, ruling that Zarda had failed to establish a gender discrimination case because previous case law had never recognized sexual orientation as a protected class.

SYNOPSIS OF DECISION AND OPINION The U.S. Court of Appeals for the Second Circuit reversed the trial court's decision and ruled in favor of Zarda. The court considered the EEOC's position on the matter of sexual orientation being a protected class under Title VII and agreed that there was an inescapable link between allegations of sexual orientation discrimination and sex discrimination. The court reasoned that if sexual orientation is a function of sex and sex is protected under Title VII, then sexual orientation must also enjoy that same protection because sex is necessarily a factor in sexual orientation. The court pointed out that the Zarda case was an example of associational discrimination because an employee alleging discrimination on the basis of sexual orientation is alleging that his or her

(continued)

---

[8]*Baldwin v. Department of Transportation,* EEOC Appeal No. 0120133080 (July 15, 2015).

[9]For example, the U.S. Court of Appeals for the Eleventh Circuit declined to adopt the EEOC's position in *Evans v. Georgia Regional Hospital,* 850 F.3d 1248 (11th Cir. 2017).

[10]*Hively v. Ivy Tech Community College,* 853 F.3d 339 (7th Cir. 2017).

[11]*Franchina v. City of Providence,* No. 16-2401 (1st Cir. 2018).

employer took his or her sex into account by treating him or her differently for associating with a person of the same sex.

WORDS OF THE COURT: Sex as a Motivating Factor "Title VII's prohibition on sex discrimination applies to any practice in which sex is a motivating factor. . . . Sexual orientation discrimination is a subset of sex discrimination because sexual orientation is defined by one's sex in relation to the sex of those to whom one is attracted, making it impossible for an employer to discriminate on the basis of sexual orientation without taking sex into account. Sexual orientation discrimination is also based on assumptions of stereotypes about how members of a particular gender should be, including to whom they should be attracted. Finally, sexual orientation discrimination is associational discrimination because an adverse employment action that is motivated by

the employer's opposition to association between members of particular sexes discriminates against an employee on the basis of sex."

Case Questions

1. Why was Zarda's case an example of "associational discrimination"?

2. Should the fact that a customer complained about Zarda impact a Title VII analysis? Why or why not?

3. *Focus on Critical Thinking:* The dissent in this case pointed out that Congress had ample opportunity to add sexual orientation into the statute but did not. The dissent accused the majority of filling in a portion of Title VII that the court found lacking, but the legislature has not changed the law in decades. Is that a compelling argument? Why or why not? Did the court "legislate from the bench"?

TAKEAWAY CONCEPTS Federal Statutes

- The primary federal antidiscrimination statutes are (1) Title VII of the Civil Rights Act of 1964 and its subsequent amendments; (2) the Age Discrimination in Employment Act (ADEA) of 1967; and (3) the Americans with Disabilities Act (ADA), which was last amended in 2009.

- Title VII prohibits discrimination in the workplace on the basis of membership in a protected class. The protected classes are race, color, national origin, gender, religion, and pregnancy.

Theories of Discrimination

For several years following the passage of the Civil Rights Act of 1964, courts struggled with having to apply such a massive statutory scheme in the workplace with virtually no comparable protections in the history of labor law to use as precedent. The result was that federal courts applied the statutes unevenly and variously, which resulted in overly broad or overly narrow interpretations of the law. Beginning in 1971, the Supreme Court began to develop guidance for the courts on how to apply Title VII. In a number of landmark cases, the Court developed several theories of discrimination that plaintiffs may pursue based on the type of discrimination alleged. These cases also provided the lower courts with a system of tests that are used to apply the various theories of discrimination. Thus, the three most common theories and attendant tests are sometimes referred to by their case names. The theories are **disparate treatment** (the *McDonnell Douglas*[12] standard); **mixed motives** (the *Hopkins*[13]

---

[12]*McDonnell Douglas Corp. v. Green,* 411 U.S. 792 (1973).

[13]*Price Waterhouse v. Hopkins,* 490 U.S. 228 (1989).

standard); and **disparate impact** (the *Griggs*[14] standard). Note that subsequent amendments to Title VII have added statutory language consistent with the case law on disparate treatment and disparate impact. Nonetheless, the theories are still commonly referred to by their case names.

Disparate Treatment   Disparate treatment is overt and intentional discrimination. Simply put, when an employer treats an employee (or potential employee) differently based on her membership in a protected class, this constitutes discrimination under Title VII. Specially, the statute makes it unlawful for an employer:

> (1) To fail or refuse to hire or to discharge any individual, or to otherwise discriminate against any individual with respect to his compensation, terms, conditions, or privileges of employment, because of such individual's race, color, religion, sex, or national origin; or

> (2) To limit, segregate, or classify employees or applicants for employment in any way which would deprive or tend to deprive any individual of employment opportunities or otherwise adversely affect his status as an employee, because of such individual's race, color, religion, sex, or national origin.[15]

Disparate treatment may be proved through the use of either *direct* or *indirect* evidence. Direct evidence is evidence that proves a fact without any further inference or presumption. For example, suppose in our working hypothetical that Prescott is a woman who has applied for the position at WidgetCo. After the interview, the manager informs her that she will not get the position and states: "I think you are the most qualified applicant, but we prefer a man in that role, because this job may involve night work and I would be concerned about a woman's safety." Here, WidgetCo is treating Prescott differently based on a protected class—gender. Even though the manager's decision seems to be based on a true concern for Prescott's well-being, the fact that Prescott is being deprived of an employment opportunity solely because she is a woman violates Title VII. The manager's statement is direct evidence.

Overt discrimination does not have to be done with *discriminatory intent* in order to trigger liability for the employer.[16] In fact, in some cases, the employee does not need to prove that his employer had actual knowledge that the employee required a Title VII accommodation that was in conflict with the employer's policy. In Case 41.2, the U.S. Supreme Court analyzes Title VII's provisions relating to religious discrimination and whether the employer had actual knowledge of the discrimination.

CASE 41.2 Equal Employment Opportunity Commission v. Abercrombie & Fitch Stores, Inc., 135 S. Ct. 2028 (2015)

FACT SUMMARY   Abercrombie & Fitch Stores ("Abercrombie") operates several lines of clothing stores and maintains policies consistent with the image Abercrombie seeks to project. One such policy, known as the Look Policy, governs its employees' dress. The policy prohibits "caps" as too informal for Abercrombie's desired image. Samantha Elauf is a practicing Muslim who, consistent with her understanding of her religion's requirements, wears a headscarf. She applied for a position in an Abercrombie store, and the interviewer gave Elauf a rating that qualified her to be hired using Abercrombie's ordinary system for evaluating applicants. However, the interviewer was concerned that Elauf's headscarf, known as a *hijab,* would conflict with the store's Look Policy and consulted Abercrombie's

(continued)

---

[14]*Griggs v. Duke Power Co., 401 U.S. 424 (1971).*
[15]42 U.S.C. § 2000e–2(a).
[16]See *Vaughn v. Edel, 918 F.2d 517 (5th Cir. 1990).*

district manager. The manager concluded that the headscarf would violate the Look Policy, as would all other headwear, religious or otherwise, and Elauf was not hired. The EEOC sued Abercrombie on Elauf's behalf, claiming that its refusal to hire Elauf violated Title VII. The trial court granted EEOC summary judgment on the issue of liability and awarded $20,000 in damages. The U.S. Court of Appeals for the Tenth Circuit reversed and awarded Abercrombie summary judgment based on its conclusion that ordinarily an employer cannot be liable under Title VII for failing to accommodate a religious practice until the applicant (or employee) provides the employer with actual knowledge of his need for an accommodation. The EEOC appealed to the U.S. Supreme Court.

SYNOPSIS OF DECISION AND OPINION The U.S. Supreme Court reversed the decision of the lower court and ruled in favor of the EEOC. The Court focused on the text of Title VII that gives religion favored status and provided a straightforward rule for disparate treatment claims based on a failure to accommodate a religious practice: An employer may not make an applicant's religious practice, confirmed or otherwise, a factor in employment decisions. The Court rejected Abercrombie's argument that the employer must have actual knowledge of the employee's need for religious accommodation because there was no language in the statute that required such knowledge in order to trigger liability. Instead, an applicant need only show that his need for an accommodation was a motivating factor in the employer's decision.

WORDS OF THE COURT: Actual Knowledge Not Required "Abercrombie urges this Court to adopt the Tenth Circuit's rule 'allocat[ing] the burden of raising a religious conflict.' This would require the employer to have actual knowledge of a conflict between an applicant's religious practice and a work rule. The problem with this approach is the one that inheres in most incorrect interpretations of statutes: It asks us to add words to the law to produce what is thought to be a desirable result. That is Congress's

province. We construe Title VII's silence as exactly that: silence."

WORDS OF THE COURT: Religious Accommodation "A request for accommodation, or the employer's certainty that the practice exists, may make it easier to infer motive, but is not a necessary condition of liability. . . . Nor does the statute limit disparate-treatment claims to only those employer policies that treat religious practices less favorably than similar secular practices. Abercrombie's argument that a neutral policy cannot constitute 'intentional discrimination' may make sense in other contexts. But Title VII does not demand mere neutrality with regard to religious practices. . . . Rather, it gives them favored treatment, affirmatively obligating employers not 'to fail or refuse to hire or discharge any individual . . . because of such individual's religious observance and practice.' An employer is surely entitled to have, for example, a no headwear policy as an ordinary matter. But when an applicant requires an accommodation as an 'aspec[t] of religious . . . practice,' it is no response that the subsequent failure to hire was due to an otherwise neutral policy. Title VII requires otherwise-neutral policies to give way to the need for an accommodation."

Case Questions

1. Why does the Court conclude that "actual knowledge" is not necessary?

2. What strategies should employers deploy to reduce their liability for violating the religious accommodations requirement in Title VII?

3. *Focus on Critical Thinking:* Just before the decision in this case was announced, Abercrombie changed its policies relating to how employees look and dress. This was a significant change to its business model. To what extent should business owners and managers consider legal doctrines when designing or redesigning their business models? Are there any other areas of law that should be taken into consideration by businesses when designing polices related to their business models?

McDonnell Douglas **Test** In *McDonnell Douglas Corp. v. Green,* the U.S. Supreme Court crafted a template for disparate treatment proof that plaintiffs could use to obtain relief under Title VII. This method of proof usually is referred to as the *McDonnell Douglas* standard, and it contemplates a burden-shifting analysis (explained below). The *McDonnell Douglas* standard has three stages. In the first stage, the plaintiff must establish a *prima facie*[17] case of discrimination. A plaintiff establishes a *prima facie* case by producing certain evidence that is sufficient to prevail in a discrimination claim without proving additional facts unless disproved or rebutted by the opposing party.

To establish a claim of discrimination that satisfies the *prima facie* requirement under the *McDonnell Douglas* standard, the Supreme Court created a four-prong disparate treatment test that lower courts adapt to fit the type of discrimination at issue. The plaintiff must establish that:

1. She is a member of a protected class.
2. She applied for and was qualified for the job (or promotion, etc., depending on the factual circumstances of the controversy) and met the employer's legitimate expectations.
3. She was rejected by the employer.
4. The employer continued to seek applicants or filled the position with a person outside the protected class.

In cases involving types of discriminatory action unrelated to hiring or promotion, the appropriate prong is adjusted accordingly. For example, in a wrongful-termination claim, the plaintiff would have to satisfy prongs 2 and 3 (the candidate was qualified and rejected despite the qualification) by proving that she was terminated by her employer despite qualifications and performance and that, following the discharge, she was replaced by someone with comparable qualifications who was not in the same protected class.

Once the plaintiff makes out a *prima facie* case, the second stage of the *McDonnell Douglas* standard requires the **burden of proof** to *shift* to the employer, who then must articulate a legitimate, nondiscriminatory reason for the discriminatory action. If the employer does provide a legitimate, nondiscriminatory reason for firing the plaintiff, the third stage of the standard contemplates that the burden then shifts back to the employee to show that the reason given by the employer is not the actual reason for the employment action. A false reason under these circumstances is called a **pretext**. It should be noted that issues related to proving discrimination and pretext are fact questions for the jury to decide. In a disparate treatment case, the plaintiff is alleging intentional discrimination and the employer is asserting a legitimate reason for its action. It is up to the jury as the finder of fact to decide which version of facts is more compelling and believable. Figure 41.1 illustrates how the *McDonnell Douglas* burden-shifting system operates.

FIGURE 41.1   Disparate Treatment Burden-Shifting System

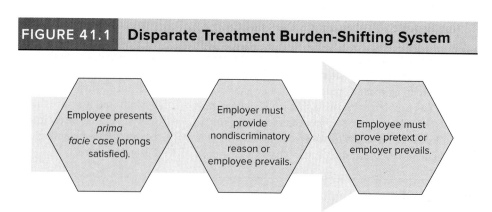

---

[17]A Latin phrase meaning "at a first view," which, according to the authoritative *Collins Latin Gem,* is sometimes mistakenly translated as "on its face."

Prescott v. WidgetCo Suppose that in our hypothetical case Prescott is African-American and was hired by WidgetCo as a junior accountant. After three years, she was promoted to senior accountant and given a pay raise. When a managerial position was posted a year later, Prescott applied and was hopeful that with her four years of experience and other qualifications she would get the promotion. However, she was passed over for this position and for several subsequent openings for management positions. Eventually, she learned that two managers who had been promoted ahead of her each had only one year of experience and that all of the managers promoted ahead of her were either white or male. Prescott's disparate treatment claim under the *McDonnell Douglas* standard's four-prong test likely would be sufficient to establish a *prima facie* case because (1) Prescott was in a protected class; (2) she had applied for and was qualified for the promotion; (3) she was not promoted; and (4) WidgetCo promoted less experienced individuals. At this point, the burden of proof shifts to WidgetCo to provide a legitimate, nondiscriminatory reason for not promoting Prescott. Suppose that WidgetCo submits employee records that indicate that Prescott was late for work three times in the past two years, which the company cites as its legitimate reason. The burden of proof then shifts back to the employee/plaintiff to provide evidence that WidgetCo's reason is merely a pretext for discriminatory action. For example, Prescott could provide evidence of pretext by citing attendance records of others in the company to prove that a record of only three incidents of lateness did not disqualify other employees from being promoted.

Mixed Motives
Although the U.S. Supreme Court made it easier for plaintiffs to assert their Title VII rights under a disparate treatment theory, employers were being consistently insulated from liability from Title VII by asserting legitimate, subjective-based reasons (such as inability to work as a member of a team) to defeat a Title VII claim. Even when these cases involved unlawful discriminatory reasons for the employment action, so long as the employer could cite even one legitimate reason, the employee could not recover under a disparate treatment theory. To alleviate this problem, the U.S. Supreme Court articulated an alternative theory of protection under Title VII when the cause of the employment action was motivated by both legitimate and discriminatory motives. The mixed motives theory was articulated in *Price Waterhouse v. Hopkins.*[18]

The case involved Hopkins, a woman employed as an associate at the global accounting and consulting firm of Price Waterhouse (now PricewaterhouseCoopers). As in many professional service firms, associates are proposed for partnership in the firm after a certain length of time. Hopkins was proposed for partnership, and, as part of the process, the firm's partners were asked to write evaluations of Hopkins and make a recommendation as to whether the firm should offer her partnership. In general, associates who are not voted in as partners either are terminated or are held over for reconsideration in the next year. Hopkins's evaluations were mostly positive, with partners praising her role in securing a large government client. They also evaluated her as extremely competent, bright, and hardworking. However, a significant number of partners were concerned about her interpersonal skills. She was abrasive, shouted at the staff, and used foul language in public. Several partners, though, went further and criticized her using gender-stereotypical, demeaning comments, such as advising Hopkins to "act more like a lady" or to "take a course in charm school." One partner even made a suggestion that Hopkins should "walk more femininely, talk more femininely, dress more femininely, and wear makeup" if she wanted to improve her chances for partnership. As a result of these negative comments, the firm initially opted to hold Hopkins over for one more year but eventually notified her that she would not be placed for a partnership vote again. Hopkins sued under Title VII using a theory of disparate treatment, but the firm pointed to the documented, legitimate reasons relating to Hopkins's inability to work as a team member.

---

[18]490 U.S. 228 (1989).

In essence, the case involved legitimate reasons for the job action that were mixed with illegitimate discriminatory motives as evidenced by the evaluations written by the partners. Ultimately, the Supreme Court adopted a new theory and framework for certain intentional discrimination: *mixed motives.* Under this theory, an employee is protected under Title VII in a case where legitimate motives are mixed with illegitimate motives if the employee proves the protected class membership was a *substantial factor* in the decision-making process. Once established, the burden then shifts to the employer to offer evidence that it would have made the same employment decision regardless of the protected characteristics. In the *Hopkins* case, the Court held that Hopkins had met her burden of proving that gender was a substantial factor in the firm's decision-making process because the language of the evaluations was so closely tied to gender discrimination.[19]

Disparate Impact

First announced in *Griggs v. Duke Power Co.,*[20] the Supreme Court recognized that *intent* was *not* always a necessary element to prove discrimination and that certain evaluation techniques for employee selection, promotion, and assignment, such as written tests, height and weight requirements, educational requirements, or oral candidate interviews, could be administered uniformly to all candidates yet still *impact* certain protected class members adversely. In other words, even facially neutral policies and procedures could be discriminatory in their impact on certain applicants or employees. The Court ruled that some testing mechanisms operate as "built-in headwinds" for minority groups and are unrelated to measuring job capability.

The disparate impact framework is similar to that of intentional discrimination cases in that the plaintiff must first prove a *prima facie* case by showing that certain methods resulted in statistically significant differences that adversely impacted members of a protected class. To satisfy this requirement, the plaintiff frequently provides statistical data related to a testing measure. The EEOC's Uniform Guidelines on Employee Selection Criteria define adverse impact as occurring when members of a protected class are selected at a rate less than 80 percent of that of the highest-scoring group.[21]

For example, suppose that Prescott's mother is Cuban and, therefore, Prescott can be considered Latino in the national-origin class under Title VII. Prescott was required to take a test for the accounting position at WidgetCo. Of all candidates taking the exam, Asian candidates fared best, with 10 of 20 candidates passing the test. Among Latino candidates as a group, only 3 out of 20 candidates passed. Because the number of Latino candidates who passed was less than 80 percent of the number who passed among the highest-scoring group (Asians), this would be important evidence in Prescott's disparate impact claim of discrimination.

Once the *prima facie* elements are established, the burden of proof then shifts to the employer to provide evidence that the challenged practice is *job related* for the position in question and is a **business necessity**. However, even if the employer shows a valid business necessity, the plaintiff may still prevail if he proves that the employer refused to adopt an alternative practice that would satisfy the employer's interests without having the adverse impact.

Avoiding Disparate Impact Liability

Despite the EEOC guidelines and federal court decisions, disparate impact is still a very thorny area of discrimination law. In *Ricci v. DeStefano,*[22] the U.S. Supreme Court ruled that the City of New Haven's decision to discard

---

[19]In the majority opinion, Justice Brennan opined that "if an employee's flawed 'interpersonal skills' can be corrected by a soft-hued suit or a new shade of lipstick, perhaps it is the employee's sex and not her interpersonal skills that has drawn the criticism."

[20]401 U.S. 424 (1971).

[21]29 CFR § 1607.4(D).

[22]557 U.S. 557 (2009).

results of a promotional exam for firefighters was a violation of Title VII, even if the discriminatory treatment was based on the employer's concern that promotion examination results would possibly lead to a disparate impact lawsuit. The Court ruled:

> [Employers] may not take the . . . step of discarding the test altogether to achieve a more desirable racial distribution of promotion-eligible candidates—absent a strong basis in evidence that the test was deficient and that discarding the results is necessary to avoid violating the disparate impact provision.

TAKEAWAY CONCEPTS Theories of Discrimination

- Disparate treatment is overt and intentional discrimination and occurs when an employer treats an employee differently based on membership in a protected class. Under the *McDonnell Douglas* test, a plaintiff must make out a *prima facie* case showing (1) membership in a protected class, (2) that the plaintiff was qualified for and applied for a job, (3) that the plaintiff was rejected, and (4) that the position was filled by a nonclass member.

- The mixed motives theory articulated in *Hopkins* protects employees when legitimate motives are mixed with illegitimate motives and an employee is discriminated against. Under this theory, the employee must prove that membership in a protected class was a substantial factor in the decision-making process. The burden then shifts to the employer to offer evidence that it would have made the same employment decision regardless of membership in a protected class.

- The disparate impact test articulated in *Griggs* prohibits an employer from using a facially neutral practice that has an adverse impact on members of a protected class. Under the disparate impact theory, a plaintiff must prove that the evaluation methods resulted in statistically significant differences that adversely impacted members of a protected class.

SEXUAL HARASSMENT

Because Title VII includes gender as a protected class, federal law extends protection to employees who are being sexually harassed. Unwelcome sexual advances, requests for sexual favors, and other verbal or physical conduct of a sexual nature are considered violations of Title VII if the conduct is (1) in the context of explicit or implicit conditions of an individual's employment or as a basis for any employment decisions or (2) unreasonably interfering with an individual's work performance or creating an offensive work environment. Courts have also held that if the behavior was sufficiently abusive and the abuse led the employee to quit, the employee is still permitted to bring an action against the harasser.[23] Note that this is different from a typical discrimination case in which the employer must have actually taken some adverse action for a violation to occur.

LO 41-3

Identify two theories of discrimination in the context of sexual harassment.

Theories of Sexual Harassment

Generally, a victim of sexual harassment alleges one of two theories. In the **quid pro quo theory** (derived from the Latin phrase meaning "something for something else"), for example, the harasser demands sexual favors as a condition of continued employment or as a prerequisite for a promotion or pay raise. More commonly, sexual harassment takes the

---

[23]*Harris v. Forklift Systems, Inc.,* 510 U.S. 17 (1993).

form of a **hostile work environment**. Under this theory, a violation of Title VII occurs when the conduct of the harasser (or group of harassers) is of such a severe and crude nature, or is so pervasive in the workplace, that it interferes with the victim's ability to perform her job responsibilities. It is important to understand, however, that the standards for proving hostile work environment are relatively burdensome and require a discriminatory activity that is beyond teasing, offhand comments, or isolated incidents. In *Faragher v. City of Boca Raton*, the U.S. Supreme Court gave guidance on the hostile work environment theory:

> Workplaces are not always harmonious locales, and even incidents that would objectively give rise to bruised or wounded feelings will not on that account satisfy the severe or pervasive standard. Some rolling with the punches is a fact of workplace life.[24]

However, if the behavior is sufficiently abusive and the abuse led the employee to quit, the employee is still permitted to file a complaint. This rule is different from a typical discrimination case in which the employer must have actually taken some adverse action for a violation to occur. While there is no formula for determining a hostile work environment, courts have deemed certain behaviors as a violation of Title VII. These include (1) initiating a discussion of sexual acts, activities, or physical attributes in workplace areas (such as the employee cafeteria); (2) engaging in unnecessary or excessive physical contact; (3) crude, demeaning, or vulgar language; or (4) display of pornographic pictures or movies.

In Case 41.3, an appellate court considers whether certain conduct in a workplace is sufficiently "severe" or "pervasive" enough to constitute a hostile work environment.

CASE 41.3 Morris v. City of Colorado Springs d/b/a Memorial Health System, 666 F.3d 654 (10th Cir. 2012)

FACT SUMMARY Morris was a registered nurse at Memorial Health System ("Memorial") beginning in 2000. In 2007, she joined a group of Memorial employees assigned to perform all heart surgeries done at the hospital known as the "Heart Team." Dr. Bryan Mahan (Mahan) was a surgeon on Memorial's Heart Team. During the time Morris was on the Heart Team with Mahan, she contends that he harassed her on multiple occasions. Specifically, she alleges that he made a number of demeaning comments to her and treated her differently than male employees.

The primary incident at the crux of this case occurred later that year as Morris was assisting Mahan with a surgical procedure. After Mahan surgically removed heart tissue from the patient on the operating table, he threw it in Morris's direction. Although Mahan claimed that he intended only to throw the tissue on the floor behind him, the tissue hit Ms. Morris's leg and Mahan joked about it afterwards. Morris reported the incident to her supervisor, Memorial's director of surgery, and Memorial's

director of human resources. In response, Memorial's chief of staff temporarily suspended Mahan from the operating room and required members of the Heart Team to attend a team-building exercise. Both Morris and Mahan attended the training and worked together for three months afterwards.

Still, Morris filed a Notice of [Discrimination] Claim alleging that she had suffered damages as a result of the heart tissue incident and stated she would pursue claims against Memorial and Mahan. Memorial's human resources office sent Morris an acknowledgment of the claim and notified her that she would be removed from the Heart Team and assigned to the main operating room because of Memorial's obligation to place her in a work environment that was comfortable.

In 2009, Morris filed suit against Memorial in federal district court. Among other claims, Morris asserted a claim under Title VII alleging that Mahan engaged in unlawful gender-based harassment and created an abusive and hostile working environment. The trial dismissed the case on summary judgment,

(continued)

---

[24]524 U.S. 775, 788 (1998).

ruling that Morris could not establish that the alleged harassment was based on her gender or that it was sufficiently "severe" or "pervasive" to affect her working environment.

SYNOPSIS OF DECISION AND OPINION The Court of Appeals for the Tenth Circuit ruled in favor of Memorial and affirmed the trial court's dismissal of the case. The court held that Mahan's conduct did not rise to the level of a hostile work environment. The court explained that the comments made by Mahan to Morris and the tissue-throwing incident were not sufficient to meet the "severe or pervasive" standard. The court pointed to past cases that were based on sexual discrimination where there was evidence that the plaintiffs had been subjected both to a number of gender-based incidents occurring over a long period of time, including sexual propositions, and multiple incidents of hostile and physically threatening conduct. Because Mahan's conduct did not fit that legal standard, the court concluded that summary judgment at the trial court level was appropriate.

WORDS OF THE COURT: Severe or Pervasive Standard "Title VII does not establish a general civility code for the workplace. Accordingly, the run-of-the-mill boorish, juvenile, or annoying behavior that is not uncommon in American workplaces is not the stuff of a Title VII hostile work environment claim. . . . Not all offensive conduct is actionable as harassment; trivial offenses do not suffice. An employer creates a hostile work environment when the workplace is permeated with discriminatory intimidation, ridicule, and insult, that is sufficiently severe or pervasive to alter the conditions of the victim's employment and create an abusive working environment. . . .

"While Dr. Mahan's conduct (construing the facts in the light most favorable to Ms. Morris) was unquestionably juvenile, unprofessional, and perhaps independently tortious, viewed in context, we cannot conclude from this record that it objectively altered the terms and conditions of Ms. Morris's employment."

Case Questions

1. Why did the court find that Mahan's conduct did not rise to the level necessary to create a hostile work environment? Do you agree?

2. What type of conduct is required for harassment to be considered severe or pervasive? Give an example of hypothetical conduct by Mahan that may have led the court to believe that Morris had met her burden of proof.

3. *Focus on Critical Thinking:* Could Morris pursue other legal avenues against Mahan for his conduct? Is there any civil liability in tort? Could Morris pursue a breach of contract claim against the hospital for reassigning her from the Heart Team?

Same-Sex Harassment

In *Oncale v. Sundowner Offshore Services, Inc.,*[25] the U.S. Supreme Court held that an employee on an oil rig who was subjected to homosexual advances by his co-workers was protected under Title VII. The Court made clear that Title VII was gender-neutral and recognized sexual harassment as a form of discrimination regardless of the gender of the victim or the harasser.

Vicarious Liability of Employers

Recall from Chapter 38, "Duties and Liabilities of Principals and Agents," that employers typically are liable for the tortious actions of their employees when they are acting within their scope of employment. In 1998, the U.S. Supreme Court decided two companion cases that extended vicarious liability to employers for sexual harassment under certain circumstances. The Court held in the *Faragher*[26] and *Ellerth*[27] cases that an employer could be held vicariously

---

[25]523 U.S. 75 (1998).

[26]*Faragher v. City of Boca Raton,* 524 U.S. 775 (1998).

[27]*Burlington Industries v. Ellerth,* 524 U.S. 742 (1998).

liable for sexual harassment by an employee when a nonsupervisory co-worker is the harasser if the employee can prove that the employer was negligent in either (1) discovering the conduct or (2) failing to respond to a sexual harassment complaint made to a supervisor.

Strict Liability for Harassment by Supervisor

If the harassing employee is a supervisor, then the employer is strictly liable for any sexual harassment claim if the harassment culminates in a tangible employment action such as termination or transfer to a less desirable job. If the harassment does not result in a tangible employment action (e.g., demotion), employers may avoid liability via the *Faragher/Ellerth* defense by proving that a system was in place that was intended to deter, prevent, report, and correct any harassment. The employer also must prove that the employee failed to take advantage of the preventive or corrective opportunities that the employer provided.

One important issue in a vicarious liability case centers on the definition of a *supervisor.* In *Vance v. Ball State,*[28] the U.S. Supreme Court clarified the definition of a supervisor for purposes of liability for harassment by co-workers. In that case, Vance was employed as a catering assistant at Ball State University (BSU) and was allegedly subject to harassment primarily by a BSU employee whose job title was "Catering Specialist." Although the alleged harasser was responsible for oversight of catering occasions where Vance was working, the alleged harasser did not have the power to hire, fire, demote, promote, transfer, or discipline Vance. The Court ruled that the alleged harasser did not qualify as a supervisor and thus BSU could not be held vicariously liable unless Vance could prove that BSU was negligent either in discovering the conduct or in failing to respond to a harassment complaint made to a supervisor.

Impact of #MeToo Movement

In response to high-profile celebrities who began to accuse Hollywood mogul Harvey Weinstein of covering up a long pattern of sexual assault and sexual harassment, the #MeToo movement used social media to bring to the forefront of the world's consciousness the magnitude and severity of sexual harassment in all aspects of society. The hashtag went viral after actress Alyssa Milano tweeted, "If all the women who have been sexually harassed or assaulted wrote 'Me too' as a status, we might give people a sense of the magnitude of the problem."

Although the #MeToo movement broadly encompasses sexual assault and harassment, it has helped to educate society on the hurdles that litigants face when accusing employers of sexual harassment in the workplace. Moreover, because sexual harassment can be the result of one party feeling that he or she has the power to abuse a subordinate without consequences, this type of social movement helps to curb abuses before they begin.

TAKEAWAY CONCEPTS Sexual Harassment

- Employers have vicarious liability for sexual harassment by their employees if they are negligent in either discovering the conduct or in failing to respond to a sexual harassment complaint made to a supervisor.
- If the harasser is a supervisor who has the power to hire, fire, demote, promote, transfer, or discipline the employee, and the harassment culminates in a tangible employment action, the employer is strictly liable.
- If no employment action was taken, an employer may avoid liability by proving that a deterrent and correction system was in place and that the employee did not take advantage of benefits provided by the system.

---

[28] 133 S. Ct. 2434 (2013).

Quick Quiz Theories of Discrimination

What is the best potential theory of discrimination for the plaintiff to pursue?

1. Lian, an American of Chinese descent, is employed as an architect in a large regional firm. His evaluations by his superiors have been mostly positive for two years, with the consistent exception that he frequently arrived late for client meetings. On one evaluation, his superior wrote, "I thought Asians were supposed to be efficient. What happened here?" One month later, Lian is denied a promotion based on his record of "tardiness and other general considerations."

2. Dothard applies for a position as a firefighter. She is excluded because she cannot lift the free-weight requirement mandated in the job description. Over the past five years, men have passed the test 50 percent of the time and women have passed 20 percent of the time.

3. Pettigrew is an insurance adjuster for a company that has a rule that no adjusters are allowed to enroll in law school because the employer perceives it as a conflict of interest. The company was aware of several male adjusters who were enrolled in law school, but no actions were taken against them. Pettigrew enrolled in law school, and when the company found out about it, she was terminated.

4. Bronte is employed as a bookkeeper at the nation's largest toy store, where she works with Barnes. Barnes has a reputation as the office comedian and, over the course of several months, has made various jokes related to Bronte's figure and recommended that she come on casual day dressed in sexy lingerie. Bronte tried to laugh at the jokes, but she was in fact very upset about the remarks. When she confronted Barnes about the behavior, he advised her to "lighten up" and told her that he was equally sarcastic toward male employees. Bronte quit one day later.

Answers to this Quick Quiz are provided at the end of the chapter.

REMEDIES

LO 41-4

List remedies available under Title VII.

Title VII provides aggrieved employees with a broad range of remedies to compensate for unlawful discrimination. These remedies include an *injunction* (a court order to cease engaging in a particular unlawful practice or an order compelling a party to act), *reinstatement, compensatory damages* in the form of back pay, *retroactive promotions,* and requirements that the employer take certain actions in order to remedy patterns or practices resulting in discrimination. *Punitive* damages (intended to deter future conduct of employers) are available only when a plaintiff proves that a private employer acted with malice, in retaliation, or with reckless disregard for the employment discrimination laws.

AGE DISCRIMINATION

LO 41-5

Explain antidiscrimination laws that apply to age, disabilities, and equal pay.

One of the fastest-growing varieties of employment discrimination claims are those based on age. Under the Age Discrimination in Employment Act (ADEA), employers are prohibited from discriminating against employees on the basis of their age once an employee has reached age 40. The ADEA is similar to Title VII in that protected employees are not entitled to *special* treatment, but they are included as members of a protected class when employers discriminate against them in favor of a *substantially younger* employee.

Courts use a Title VII–based analysis for evaluating age claims. For example, disparate treatment under the ADEA requires that the employer's intentional discrimination against the employee based on the employee's age be proved using a modified *McDonnell Douglas* standard for establishing a *prima facie* case. Therefore, plaintiffs may only make ADEA claims based on (1) protected class membership (40 or over), (2) satisfactory job performance (based on an employer's legitimate expectations), (3) adverse job action such as termination or demotion, (4) replacement with someone substantially younger (or more favorable treatment toward someone substantially younger), or (5) other evidence that indicates that it is more likely than not that the employee's age was the reason for the adverse employment action.[29] If the employee makes a *prima facie* case, then the employer must present a nondiscriminatory reason for the adverse employment action. Once the employer presents the nondiscriminatory reason, it is up to the employee to convince the fact finder that the reason the employer gave is false (pretextual) and the real reason is age discrimination. The ADEA also acts to prohibit mandatory retirement policies. Exceptions are made for certain executives and those with high policymaking positions,[30] federal law enforcement officers, pilots, air traffic controllers, and firefighters.[31] States also are permitted to set defensible police and firefighter retirement ages.[32] If an employer can prove a bona fide occupational qualification (BFOQ), discussed later in this chapter, age may be taken into consideration regarding mandatory retirement.[33]

Substantially Younger Requirement

If a plaintiff is attempting to prove age discrimination based on the fact that younger employees are treated more favorably, then the plaintiff must prove that the younger employees are substantially younger. The federal courts vary greatly in their interpretation of what constitutes *substantially younger,* but many courts follow the general rule that the age difference must be at least 10 years in order to qualify as substantially younger.[34]

One important distinction of an ADEA claim is that it is irrelevant whether the younger employee is a member of the protected class or not. For example, let's assume Prescott is hired at WidgetCo and is 50 years old. He is terminated and replaced by another employee who is 40 years old. Both employees are members of the protected class (40 years old and older), but because someone substantially younger has replaced Prescott, he may still pursue his claim by proving that the reason he was replaced was based on age discrimination. However, if Prescott, a 69-year-old employee, is replaced by a 67-year-old employee, that age difference is not sufficient to make a claim of age discrimination.

The ADEA protects only older employees. In fact, the U.S. Supreme Court has said that the ADEA does not prohibit employers from discriminating against employees under 40 years old in favor of those in the intended protected class.[35] Disparate impact claims under the ADEA, which do not require proof of an intent to discriminate, are rare; however, disparate impact (similar to a *Griggs*-type standard based on statistical evidence of exclusion) was specifically recognized as an ADEA discrimination theory by the U.S. Supreme Court in *Smith v. City of Jackson, Miss.*[36] In that case, the Court held that the ADEA authorizes disparate impact claims, but the employer's burden to show the reasonableness of the business practice at issue is minimal. That is, the employer does not have to meet the higher standard of proof required in Title VII disparate impact cases: that the practice at issue was a *business necessity.* Thus, it is easier for employers to prevail in an ADEA disparate impact action than in a disparate impact action alleging, for example, race discrimination under Title VII.

---

[29]*Robin v. Espo Engineering Corp.,* 210 F.3d 1081 (7th Cir. 2000).

[30]29 U.S.C. § 631(c)(1).

[31]29 U.S.C. § 8335.

[32]29 U.S.C. § 623(j).

[33]29 U.S.C. § 623(f)(1).

[34]*Pitasi v. Gartner Group, Inc.,* 184 F.3d 709 (7th Cir. 1999).

[35]*General Dynamics Land Systems v. Cline,* 540 U.S. 581 (2004).

[36]125 S. Ct. 1536 (2005).

AMERICANS WITH DISABILITIES ACT

One of the most significant federal antidiscrimination laws that impacts business owners and managers is the Americans with Disabilities Act (ADA).[37] The ADA was originally passed in 1990, but it was amended in 2008 in order to settle some of the more controversial interpretations by courts related to the *definition* of a disability. Fundamentally, the ADA seeks to eliminate discriminatory employment practices against disabled persons that would prevent otherwise qualified employees from obtaining or continuing employment, being promoted, or obtaining benefits available to nondisabled employees. The ADA requires an employer with 15 or more employees to make **reasonable accommodations** for a disabled employee in the workplace so long as the accommodation does not cause the employer to suffer an undue hardship.

Documented-Disability Requirement

To qualify for an accommodation, the employee must have a documented **disability**. The ADA defines *disability* as a physical or mental impairment that substantially limits a person's ability to participate in major life activities. Courts have ruled that certain disabilities, such as blindness, cancer, heart disease, paraplegia, and acquired immune deficiency syndrome (AIDS), all fit squarely into the disability category. However, the definition and interpretation of the disability requirement have been the subjects of considerable uncertainty since the passage of the original version of the ADA. Because Congress did not specify examples of major life activities in the original ADA statute, courts and the EEOC have struggled to establish appropriate limits. In a series of cases beginning in 1999, the Supreme Court narrowed the definition of which disabilities were covered under the ADA and ruled that any condition that could be corrected, such as severe myopia causing poor vision,[38] was not a disability covered by the act. In subsequent years, the Court ruled that carpal tunnel syndrome also was not covered because it could not be considered so debilitating as to interfere with any major life activity.[39]

ADA Amendments Act of 2008

As the narrow interpretation of ADA solidified in federal courts, Congress passed an amendment to the ADA that effectively reversed the Supreme Court's efforts to read the disabilities category as a narrow class of ailments. The ADA Amendments Act of 2008 (ADAAA) became effective for any ADA discrimination occurring on or after January 1, 2009. The ADAAA expanded the definition of disability with specific statutory definitions intended to urge courts to interpret the definition of disability "in favor of broad coverage of the individuals under this Act, to the maximum extent permitted by terms of the Act."[40] Although the basic definition of disability under the original ADA was left in place, the ADAAA expanded the statutory protections to specifically cover disabilities that had been excluded from coverage by virtue of the Supreme Court's ADA case law. The ADAAA includes a requirement that courts make a determination of one's disability without regard for the ability to correct the condition with "medication, artificial aids," and other "assistive technology." However, for an individual to be protected under the ADAAA, the plaintiff still must have a physical or mental impairment that substantially limits one or more major life activities.[41]

---

[37] 42 U.S.C. § 12101.

[38] *Sutton v. United Airlines,* 527 U.S. 471 (1999).

[39] *Toyota Motor Manufacturing v. Williams,* 534 U.S. 185 (2002).

[40] 42 U.S.C. § 12002(4)(a).

[41] The statute also requires that there be "a record of" the disability. As one commentator has pointed out, this requirement is nearly obsolete and unaffected by the ADAAA. See A. Long, "Introducing the New and Improved Americans with Disabilities Act: Assessing the ADA Amendments Act of 2008," *Northwestern University Law Review Colloquy,* Vol. 103 (2008).

"Regarded-as" Test

Even if an individual does not meet the definitional requirements of disability under the ADA, employees still may be protected by the ADA under an alternative theory of the act known as the *regarded-as test.* Like the definitional scope of the disability requirement in the ADAAA, the regarded-as standard has been substantially broadened by Congress as well. The standard applies when an employee is regarded as having impairment by her employer (even if the impairment is not actually a disability). For example, Babak is diagnosed with a chronic medical condition, but the condition doesn't require any accommodation in the workplace. Babak applies for a promotion to supervisor but is denied because his manager is fearful that Babak's condition will limit his energy level and impact his ability to fulfill his role. Under the ADAAA, Babak would be protected by the statute even though his condition is not a disability as defined in the ADA because Babak's employer regarded him as disabled by virtue of his condition.[42]

Qualified Individual

The ADA defines a *qualified individual* as someone who, with or without reasonable accommodation, can perform the "essential functions" of the employment position that such individual holds or desires.[43] Essential functions are the fundamental job duties of the employment position, but they do not include the marginal functions of the position.[44] In Case 41.4, a federal appellate court interprets the essential functions requirement.

CASE 41.4 Samson v. Federal Express Corporation, 746 F.3d 1196 (11th Cir. 2014)

FACT SUMMARY In 2009, Richard Samson (Samson) applied for a position as a technician with Federal Express (FedEx) at its facility in Fort Myers, Florida. According to FedEx's online job description, a successful candidate would provide timely, quality maintenance for FedEx vehicle fleet and ground support equipment, including preventive maintenance, troubleshooting, repairs, modifications, and documentation. After an interview, FedEx sent Samson, who it acknowledged was the best candidate to apply, a letter offering him the position. The letter stated that the job offer was contingent upon successful completion of a DOT medical examination because technicians were occasionally required to test-drive FedEx fleet vehicles.

During the medical examination, Samson disclosed to the medical examiner that he is a type 1 insulin-dependent diabetic. Because insulin-dependent diabetics are automatically disqualified from being medically certified as physically qualified to operate

a commercial motor vehicle in interstate commerce, absent an exemption, Samson failed his medical examination. Two days later, FedEx sent Samson a letter withdrawing his job offer solely because he had failed his DOT medical examination.

Samson filed suit alleging FedEx violated the ADA by failing to hire him because of his diabetes. He argued that test-driving was not an essential function of the technician position and cited evidence of another technician who had test-driven FedEx trucks only three times in three years and never across state lines. The trial court granted FedEx's motion for summary judgment, ruling that the job description and FedEx safety policies both satisfied the requirement that test-driving was an essential element of the job.

SYNOPSIS OF DECISION AND OPINION The Court of Appeals for the Sixth Circuit reversed the trial court's ruling and held in favor of Samson. The court reasoned that there was a genuine issue of

(continued)

---

[42]There is an ongoing debate as to the coverage of the regarded-as test in light of the passage of the ADAAA. This explanation and example are based on EEOC public guidance.

[43]42 U.S.C. § 12111(8).

[44]29 C.F.R. § 1630.2(n)(1).

fact as to whether the test-driving requirement was truly "essential" to the job. The court considered several factors that could lead a reasonable jury to differ on whether test-driving FedEx trucks is an essential function of the technician position. The court cited evidence from other FedEx technicians that the amount of time test-driving FedEx vehicles was insignificant.

WORDS OF THE COURT: Essential Function
"[Many] factors, however, weigh in favor of finding that test-driving is not an essential function of the [technician] position. First, although FedEx employs only one [technician] at its airport facility in Fort Myers, there are nine other licensed truck drivers at that facility among whom the test-driving could be distributed. In fact, Rotundo—the technician hired instead of Samson—testified that, at least on one occasion, another employee test-drove while he sat in the passenger seat diagnosing the reported mechanical problem. Second, the amount of time that the incumbent [technician] at the Fort Myers facility actually spends test-driving is miniscule. Indeed, Rotundo further testified that in the approximately three years he has been on the job, he has only test-driven FedEx trucks three times. If test-driving were such an essential function, as FedEx contends, one would expect it to be performed with regularity. Third, with respect to the current work experience of employees in similar jobs, the record shows that other FedEx [technicians] throughout Florida generally test-drive an average of about 3.71 hours per year—an insignificant portion of their total time on the job. . . . This issue, therefore, should not have been taken away from the jury and resolved as a matter of law."

Case Questions

1. Is it reasonable to conclude that the online job description implies that test-driving is part of the job? Why or why not?

2. What steps could FedEx take to avoid liability for a similar incident in the future?

3. *Focus on Critical Thinking:* Is the court interfering with FedEx's legitimate safety concerns in its own business operations? Is this a concern for public safety? Why or why not?

EQUAL PAY ACT

In 1963, the Equal Pay Act (EPA) became law, making it illegal for employers to pay unequal wages to men and women who perform substantially equal work. Technically, the EPA is an amendment to the Fair Labor Standards Act[45] and is, therefore, not always categorized as an antidiscrimination statute. Nonetheless, the EPA does prevent discrimination by requiring an employer to provide equal pay for men and women who perform equal work, unless the difference is based on a factor other than gender.[46]

To establish a *prima facie* case, a plaintiff must demonstrate that (1) the employer pays different wages to employees of the opposite sex; (2) the employees perform equal work on jobs requiring equal skill, effort, and responsibility; and (3) the jobs are performed under similar working conditions.[47] If a *prima facie* case is established, the burden shifts to the employer to prove that the wage differential is justified by a preponderance of the evidence under one of four affirmative defenses: (1) a seniority system, (2) a merit system, (3) a system pegging earnings to quality or quantity of production, or (4) any factor other than sex. Equal Pay Act claims are often combined with Title VII claims of sex discrimination in compensation. Courts, however, have found separate essential elements and standards of proof for the two statutory claims.

---

[45]29 U.S.C. § 206(d).

[46]At the time of the EPA's passage in 1963, women earned only 59 cents for every dollar earned by men.
Although enforcement of the EPA as well as other civil rights laws has helped to narrow the wage gap, disparities remain.

[47]*Corning Glass Works v. Brennan,* 417 U.S. 188 (1974).

Lilly Ledbetter Fair Pay Act of 2009

The Lilly Ledbetter Fair Pay Act (Ledbetter Act) effectively reversed the U.S. Supreme Court's decision in *Ledbetter v. Goodyear Tire & Rubber Co.*[48] In the *Ledbetter* case, a 19-year veteran of Goodyear Tire & Rubber Co. sued the company when she learned that, for much of her career, male counterparts had been paid more for doing the same work that she did. Although the Supreme Court did not deny that Ledbetter had been discriminated against, it ruled that she should have filed suit within 180 days of receiving her first unfair pay-check, not 180 days from the time she learned of the difference in pay. The ruling upended the long-standing practice in courts across the country that had held that the 180-day period begins when an employee becomes aware of his or her plight. Under the Supreme Court's framework, any employer that could hide pay discrimination for six months could effectively avoid liability under the law and leave workers with no recourse. Because pay information is often confidential, pay discrimination is difficult to detect. Thus, if employers are insulated from liability after 180 days, they have little incentive to correct pay discrimination.

The Ledbetter Act declared that each discriminatory paycheck, not simply the employee's first check, resets the period of time during which a worker may file a pay discrimination claim. The Ledbetter Act therefore ensures that employees subject to wage discrimination on the basis of race, color, national origin, gender, religion, age, or disability have the opportunity to challenge every discriminatory paycheck that they receive.

TAKEAWAY CONCEPTS Age, Disability, and Pay Discrimination Statutes

- The Age Discrimination in Employment Act (ADEA) prohibits employers from discriminating against employees on the basis of their age if (1) the employee is 40 years old or over, (2) the employee's job performance is satisfactory, (3) the employee is adversely affected by the job action, and (4) better treatment is given to someone substantially younger.
- The Americans with Disabilities Act (ADA) seeks to eliminate discriminatory employment practices against disabled persons by requiring that an employer with 15 or more employees make reasonable accommodations to allow the disabled employee to perform essential job functions, so long as the accommodation does not cause the employer to suffer an undue hardship.
- The Equal Pay Act (EPA) makes it illegal for employers to pay unequal wages to men and women who perform substantially equal work unless the difference is based on a factor other than sex.

LO 41-6

Apply the major defenses available to employers in a discrimination claim and explain the role of affirmative action in the context of employment discrimination.

EMPLOYER DEFENSES

Earlier in the chapter, we saw that the burden-shifting scheme in a discrimination case is subject to the employer offering either a nondiscriminatory motive for the action in question or asserting a legally recognized *defense.* Each antidiscrimination statute has its own set of defenses, but there is some level of commonality among employer defenses.

---

[48]550 U.S. 618 (2007).

Faragher/Ellerth Defense

The *Faragher/Ellerth* defense is a judicially created affirmative defense whereby an employer may avoid vicarious liability by proving that a system was in place that was intended to deter, prevent, report, and correct any harassment. The employer also must prove that the employee failed to take advantage of the preventive or corrective opportunities that the employer provided. Although the defense initially was created in the context of sexual harassment claims, courts have allowed employers to use the defense in other types of harassment cases such as racial harassment.[49] An employer's strategic use of the *Faragher/Ellerth* defense as part of a harassment prevention practice is the subject of Thinking Strategically: Proactive Harassment Prevention Framework at the end of this chapter.

Business Necessity Defense

Perhaps the broadest defense to employment discrimination is when a business can justify discrimination on the basis that it is *legitimately necessary* to the business operations of the company. This defense is used to rebut a *disparate impact* claim when a certain practice or procedure has impacted a particular protected class. For example, suppose MovingCo requires all of its workers to be able to lift 100 pounds. During the job application process, applicants are required to pick up a 100-pound piece of furniture. After one year, the test resulted in more women than men being eliminated from job consideration. If sued under a disparate impact theory, MovingCo has a strong business necessity defense as long as the standard was applied neutrally to all candidates. Another common business necessity is a particular level of education, such as a requirement by an accounting firm that all of its professionals have at least a bachelor of science degree in accounting.

Bona Fide Occupation Qualification

Federal antidiscrimination statutes allow employers to hire and employ on the basis of religion, gender, or national origin when the classification is a **bona fide occupational qualification (BFOQ)** that is reasonably necessary to the normal operation of that particular business or enterprise.[50] Note that the statutes *do not* allow race to be used as a BFOQ. The ADEA has a similar BFOQ defense. Although the ADA does not have an express BFOQ provision, the statutory scheme allows exclusion of persons with disabilities if the person, with or without reasonable accommodation, cannot perform essential job functions (a concept similar to BFOQ).

Classic examples of BFOQ classifications are religion for the employment of clergy and the use of gender to hire a movie actor. In cases that are not as clear, the employer must prove that members of the excluded class cannot safely and effectively perform essential job duties. Courts have held that BFOQ cannot be based on paternalism (protecting women from work in potentially dangerous positions such as mining, construction, or law enforcement). In the landmark case of *Diaz v. Pan Am World Airways, Inc.,*[51] a U.S. court of appeals made clear that customer preference could not be used as a BFOQ, rejecting the airline's justification for employing only women as flight attendants based on passenger surveys. Similarly, when an oil company refused to promote a woman because many foreign companies will not do business with women, a federal appellate court ruled, "No foreign nation can compel the non-enforcement of Title VII here."[52]

---

[49]*Vance v. Ball State University,* 133 S. Ct. 2434 (2013).

[50]42 U.S.C. § 2000e-2(e).

[51]442 F.2d 385 (5th Cir. 1971).

[52]*Fernandez v. Wynn Oil Co.,* 653 F.2d 1273 (9th Cir. 1981).

This rule is subject to qualification. When a business is protecting the modesty of its employees or customers, as in female locker rooms, or when the privacy of medical patients is involved, gender may be a valid BFOQ.

Seniority

Federal antidiscrimination statutes also provide a defense for employers using a seniority system as the basis for certain job decisions. In order to assert this defense, the seniority system must be based on objective elements of seniority (actual number of years on the job), and the employment decisions must have been made in good faith and pursuant to that established objective system. The employee/plaintiff has the burden of proving improper motivation behind the employer's adoption or use of the system.

Employee Misconduct

Employers are not required to overlook misconduct when complying with antidiscrimination statutes. When an employee commits an act of misconduct, so long as that act has been identified to the employee as misconduct, employers may discipline the employee in accordance with the company's general practices without liability for discrimination. If the employer's practices and procedures are set forth in a workplace publication (usually in the employee handbook or a similar company document), misconduct is a powerful defense. The U.S. Supreme Court has even extended that protection to employers when the employer discovered the misconduct *after* the adverse employment action.[53] So long as the employer shows that the misconduct was sufficiently grave as to warrant the adverse employment action (such as termination for theft of a petty cash account), after-acquired evidence of misconduct may be used as a defense.

TAKEAWAY CONCEPTS Employer Defenses

Each antidiscrimination statute has its own set of defenses, but there is some level of commonality among the following employer defenses:

- *Faragher/Ellerth* defense (employer antidiscrimination systems to avoid liability).
- Business necessity (discrimination legitimately necessary to the business operations of the company).
- BFOQ.
- Seniority.
- Misconduct.

AFFIRMATIVE ACTION PROGRAMS

Affirmative action as it is understood today includes, but goes beyond, outreach attempts to recruit minority applicants, special training programs, and the reevaluation of the effect of selection criteria. Affirmative action in employment began during World War II when President Franklin D. Roosevelt issued an executive order banning racial, religious, and gender discrimination in the defense industry. Executive Order 11246, issued by President Lyndon B. Johnson in 1965, extended affirmative action's reach by requiring that employers who have a contract with the federal government for services and supplies initiate good faith

---

[53]*McKennon v. Nashville Banner Publishing Co.,* 513 U.S. 352 (1995).

efforts to implement an affirmative action plan in their companies. Although most employers are not subject to the executive order, social pressures and/or threat of litigation have induced many employers to adopt voluntary affirmative action plans. Affirmative action also may be imposed on an employer by courts as a judicial remedy when they find that the employer acted in a pattern of egregious discrimination against employees.

Legality

Although federal antidiscrimination statutes do not require employers to give preferential treatment to minority employees, the Supreme Court has upheld the constitutionality of Executive Order 11246 and has allowed certain affirmative action plans to apply to private employers as a condition to contracts with the federal government. State and local governments soon followed suit with affirmative action plans aimed at addressing inequalities in the workplace and in education.[54]

Affirmative action does not require absolute equality. Companies must work to ensure that their employee workforce reflects the available qualified workforce with respect to race and gender. Therefore, a local company in a city whose population is 75 percent white and 25 percent black (assuming all are qualified) may have an employee workforce that is 75 percent white and 25 percent black. As long as the company advertises openings properly and conducts legal and appropriate hiring policies, the company is in compliance.

Should a discrepancy exist, a company may be approved, through a plan, to allow preferences in hiring until the proper goal is met. In *Adarand Constructors, Inc. v. Peña,*[55] the Supreme Court ruled that state and local government affirmative action plans in race- or gender-based preferences for hiring contractors would be subject to the strict scrutiny standard. Recall from Chapter 3, "Business and the Constitution," that the strict scrutiny standard is the highest level of scrutiny; more often than not, it results in a finding of unconstitutionality. However, the Court's ruling made clear that a state or local government affirmative action program is constitutional so long as it (1) attempts to remedy an actual past practice of discrimination and (2) does not employ a system of quotas (e.g., hiring according to a mathematical formula based on race). One of the most misunderstood issues under affirmative action involves quotas. Many businesses and organizations wrongly adopted mathematical quotas as a simplistic means of compliance; however, the U.S. Supreme Court has ruled that the strict use of quotas not only is prohibited under affirmative action but is unconstitutional.[56]

STATE ANTIDISCRIMINATION STATUTES

In addition to complying with federal antidiscrimination statutes, certain employers are also subject to regulation under a state antidiscrimination statutory scheme. Each state has its own statutes that are often modeled after the federal statutes (although they have different titles, such as the Human Relations Act). In addition, states also have their own administrative agencies (modeled after the EEOC) charged with enforcing and adjudicating discrimination cases. State antidiscrimination statutes sometimes differ substantially from federal laws in two ways that impact business owners and managers. First, state statutes tend to cover more employers, with some states imposing antidiscrimination statutes

LO 41-7

Explain the role of state law in employment discrimination cases.

---

[54]The Supreme Court decided several cases specifically related to admissions by state-sponsored universities beginning in 1978. Most recently, in *Gruttinger v. Bollinger,* 539 U.S. 306 (2003), the Court held that affirmative action in admissions is constitutional so long as the minority status of the applicant is used as a plus factor and not in accordance with a rigid formula reserving certain seats for minority applicants.

[55]15 U.S. 200 (1995).

[56]*Wygant v. Jackson Board of Education,* 106 S. Ct. 1842 (1986): Laying off white employees to hire minorities to achieve the goal violates the Equal Protection Clause; and *Regents of the University of California v. Bakke,* 438 U.S. 265 (1978): A medical school's strict racial admission quota violated the Fourteenth Amendment.

on small businesses with just one employee. Many federal statutes cover only employers (unions, etc.) with 15 or more employees. Second, while federal statutes are relatively conservative in exactly what constitutes a protected class, some states have expanded protected class membership, most notably to discrimination based on sexual orientation or gender transformation. In Case 41.5, a state appellate court compares New Jersey's state statutory antidiscrimination protections with the protections under Title VII.

CASE 41.5 Enriquez v. West Jersey Health Systems, 777 A.2d 365 (N.J. Super. Ct. App. Div. 2001)

FACT SUMMARY Enriquez, a biological male, was hired as a medical director for an outpatient treatment center operated by West Jersey Health Systems ("Health Systems"). Soon after his employment began, Enriquez began an external transformation from male to female. This transformation was a result of Enriquez's gender identity disorder. During the transformation, Enriquez was approached by co-workers and managers who voiced discomfort with her transformation. A Health Systems manager, citing Enriquez's obligation to contribute to a productive work atmosphere, requested that Enriquez halt the transformation process and go back to her prior appearance. When her contract came up for renewal, Enriquez was told that her contract would not be renewed unless she ceased the transformation. After Enriquez refused, her contract was not renewed and she was informed that the termination was permanent. After the termination, Enriquez completed the surgical portion of her transformation.

SYNOPSIS OF DECISION AND OPINION The New Jersey Superior Court held that while Title VII does not bar discrimination based on sexual orientation or gender identity disorders, New Jersey's Law Against Discrimination (LAD) does. The court reasoned that because the LAD makes it unlawful to discriminate against someone based on sex or sexual orientation, individuals who are transsexual or affected by a gender identity disorder are also considered to be members of a protected class and are protected from discrimination.

WORDS OF THE COURT: Coverage under LAD "Title VII of the Civil Rights Act of 1964 does not contain language barring discrimination based on one's affectional or sexual orientation. Moreover, the federal courts construing Title VII have unanimously concluded that discrimination on the basis of gender dysphoria is not sex discrimination. Basically, the federal courts conclude that discrimination on the basis of sex

outlaws discrimination against women because they are women, and against men because they are men.
. . .
"We disagree with [this] rationale [. . .]. A person who is discriminated against because he changes his gender from male to female is being discriminated against because he or she is a member of a very small minority whose condition remains incomprehensible to most individuals.
. . .
"It is incomprehensible to us that our Legislature would ban discrimination against heterosexual men and women; against homosexual men and women; against bisexual men and women; against men and women who are perceived, presumed or identified by others as not conforming to the stereotypical notions of how men and women behave, but would condone discrimination against men or women who seek to change their anatomical sex because they suffer from a gender identity disorder. We conclude that sex discrimination under the LAD includes gender discrimination so as to protect plaintiff from gender stereotyping and discrimination for transforming herself from a man to a woman."

Case Questions

1. Why couldn't this case have been covered by Title VII on the basis of gender?

2. If Enriquez's employment with Health Systems had not been terminated, would she still have a claim for discrimination? Would the conduct of her co-workers and managers have been sufficient to prevail in a discrimination suit? Why or why not?

3. *Focus on Critical Thinking:* Should Congress consider amending federal discrimination laws to include sexual orientation, or should it be left to individual states? Why? What cultural, political, or societal interests are at the heart of this question? Should culture, political, and societal concerns factor into creating public policy? Why or why not?

©valterZ/Shutterstock

Proactive Harassment Prevention Framework

PROBLEM: Sexual harassment in the workplace creates a toxic environment for employees that results in low morale, severe stress, illness, and high turnover among the workforce, which translates into significant lost revenue for both the business and employee.[57] Vicarious liability for harassment may result in multimillion-dollar jury verdicts against businesses.[58]

STRATEGIC SOLUTION: Create a harassment prevention framework that is intended to prevent, investigate, and remediate harassment in the employer's workplace. By incorporating elements of the *Faragher/Ellerth* defense into the framework, the employer also limits vicarious liability for harassment.

STEP 1—PREVENTION: *DEFINE, DISTRIBUTE, AND DETER*

The primary goal of a harassment prevention framework is to prevent incidents of sexual harassment in the first place. The strongest deterrent to harassment is the knowledge by employees as to what constitutes sexual harassment and how to report it, assurances that reports will be investigated thoroughly, and a commitment by the employer to discipline those found responsible.

Review all job descriptions and revise them if necessary to be sure they clearly identify which employees are considered supervisors (i.e., those with the authority to hire, fire, demote, promote, transfer, or discipline a subordinate). Work with counsel to develop a specific anti-harassment policy that addresses sexual harassment as well as other forms of workplace harassment (e.g., racial). The policy should define harassment, provide specific examples, and set out sanctions for violators. Employers also should consider incorporating an anti-bullying policy into their harassment prevention framework.

---

[57]L. Fitzgerald and S. Schulman, "Sexual Harassment: A Research Analysis and Agenda," *Journal of Vocational Behavior* 42, no. 5 (2003).

[58]For example, according to *Business Insider,* juries have awarded the following for sexual harassment claims: $10.6 million to a UBS sales assistant (2011), $11.6 million to an executive of the New York Knicks (2007), $30 million to clerks of Ralph's Fresh Fare grocery chain (2002), $95 million to a salesperson at Aaron's Rent-to-Own (2011), $168 million to a physician's assistant at Mercy General Hospital (2012), and $250 million to female staffers at Novartis (2010).

- Incorporate the anti-harassment policy into all employee handbooks within the organization and distribute the policy as a separate document to all employees. Place "Anti-Harassment Policy" posters that summarize the policy in all employee common areas, such as cafeterias, locker rooms, lounges, etc.
- Have the chief executive officer or another high-profile leader personally speak to groups of employees about the policy and explain how the policy aligns with the company's values and ethics.
- Dedicate in-service training periods to the subject of sexual harassment in order to have a frank discussion of specific examples of inappropriate behavior that constitutes sexual harassment and a legal primer on personal and vicarious liability under Title VII. If possible, have an outside expert conduct a seminar on recognizing and preventing sexual harassment. For new employees, ensure that the anti-harassment policy is distributed and discussed during their orientation. Supervisors should have special training in detecting, identifying, and reporting harassment.

STEP 2—REPORTING AND INVESTIGATION

A crucial part of your anti-harassment policy should be the reporting procedure and a defined investigative path. The policy cannot be effective if employees are not assured of a safe, confidential method for reporting harassment and do not have a degree of assurance that their claims will be taken seriously.

- Designate multiple "intake supervisors" from various departments throughout the business who are trained to take detailed information for use in a harassment investigation. These supervisors should be identified as intake supervisors in company publications, websites, and at in-service training.
- Create alternatives for employees to report harassment such as a designated voice mailbox. Consider establishing a link on the company website that helps employees find more information about the anti-harassment policy and provides a mechanism for reporting violations of the policy.
- Appoint one senior corporate official (typically from executive management) to investigate all claims received by intake supervisors and

the website. This includes the investigation of anonymous complaints. This official must have sufficient training, authority, and experience to investigate and properly document the review, investigation, and conclusions related to the complaint.

■ Begin the investigation of the complaint no later than one business day if possible. Conclude the investigation as soon as possible without sacrificing thoroughness or accuracy. Counsel may be alerted at this stage, but it typically is not necessary to hire counsel to conduct the investigation.

■ Ensure that confidentiality and fairness are the two guiding principles of the investigation and that reporting employees are informed about the progress of the investigation and protected from retaliation.

STEP 3—ENFORCEMENT AND REMEDIATION

If the investigation reveals that an employee was subject to harassment, employers are required to take immediate disciplinary and remedial action in order to avoid liability through the *Faragher/Ellerth* defense. It is important to realize that employers should also examine potential changes to operational practices and workplace rules that may have contributed to the harassment.

■ Discipline any employee who has violated the anti-harassment policy by applying sanctions as set out in the policy (or which may be set out in other parts of the employee handbook). Many companies have adopted a zero tolerance policy for harassment that includes termination of harassers.

■ Incidents that do not rise to the level of harassment should still be considered serious, and appropriate sanctions should be applied.

■ As in any employee-related discipline matter, documentation is pivotal to reducing the liability of the employer and establishing a record that will be helpful if litigation or other legal proceedings become necessary.

■ Remediate any workplace condition, operation, policy, or procedure that may have contributed to the harassment.

QUESTIONS

1. Have you ever had a job or internship where the employer distributed a handbook or manual? Did the handbook have a sexual harassment provision? If so, how does it compare to the steps outlined in *Thinking Strategically* (above)? Explain.

2. Why is the *Faragher/Ellerth* defense important to this strategy for limiting employer liability?

3. Do you have a sexual harassment policy on your campus? How is the policy distributed? How does it compare to the steps outlined in *Thinking Strategically* (above)? Explain.

KEY TERMS

Employment discrimination p. 743   Workplace-related discrimination in the hiring process and treatment of employees; encompasses everything from promotions and demotions to work schedules, working conditions, and disciplinary measures.

Equal Employment Opportunity Commission (EEOC) p. 743   A five-member federal administrative agency that administers congressional mandates that ensure adequate protection for victims of discrimination; accepts and investigates worker complaints; and, in certain cases, will sue on behalf of employees.

Complaint (discrimination) p. 743   A form that an aggrieved employee files against his employer with the EEOC that details how the employee was discriminated against.

Conciliation negotiations p. 744   The required attempts by the EEOC to settle a discrimination case instead of filing a lawsuit.

Title VII p. 744   The section of the Civil Rights Act of 1964 that serves as the centerpiece of antidiscrimination law; covers a comprehensive set of job-related transactions and prohibits discrimination in the workplace on the basis of an employee's race, color, national origin, gender, religion, or pregnancy. The law applies to any private sector employer with 15 or more full-time employees and to unions, employment agencies, state and local governments, and most of the federal government.

Age Discrimination in Employment Act (ADEA) of 1967 p. 744   A federal statute that prohibits employers from discriminating against employees on the basis of their age once employees have reached age 40.

Americans with Disabilities Act (ADA) of 1990 p. 744 A federal statute that seeks to eliminate discriminatory employment practices against disabled persons; requires that employers with 15 or more employees make reasonable accommodations for a disabled employee in the workplace as long as the accommodations do not cause the employer to suffer an undue hardship.

Equal Pay Act of 1963 p. 744 A federal statute that makes it illegal for employers to pay unequal wages to men and women who perform substantially equal work.

Protected classes p. 745 The classifications of individuals that are specified in Title VII, including color, race, national origin, religion, gender, and pregnancy.

Disparate treatment p. 747 Theory of employment discrimination predicated on overt and intentional discrimination; includes being treated differently because of one's membership in a protected class.

Mixed motives p. 747 Theory of employment discrimination in which the cause of an adverse employment action was motivated by both legitimate and discriminatory motives.

Disparate impact p. 748 Theory of employment discrimination in which employee evaluation techniques that are not themselves discriminatory have a different and adverse impact on members of a protected class.

Burden of proof p. 750 The responsibility of producing sufficient evidence in support of a fact or issue and favorably convincing the fact finder of that fact or issue.

Pretext p. 750 A false reason offered to justify an action.

Business necessity test p. 752 A defense used to rebut disparate impact claims when a business can prove that a certain skill, ability, or procedure is absolutely necessary to the operation of the business. Discrimination is permitted even if a protected class is adversely affected.

Quid pro quo theory p. 753 Theory of sexual harassment whereby harasser demands sexual favors as a condition of continued employment or as a prerequisite for a promotion or pay raise.

Hostile work environment p. 754 Theory of liability under Title VII for sexual harassment that is of such a severe and crude nature or is so pervasive in the workplace that it interferes with the victim's ability to do the job.

Reasonable accommodations p. 759 Accommodations, required under the Americans with Disabilities Act, that allow disabled individuals to adequately perform essential job functions.

Disability p. 759 A physical or mental impairment that substantially limits a person's ability to participate in major life activities.

Bona fide occupational qualification (BFOQ) p. 763 A provision in certain federal antidiscrimination statutes that allows discrimination based on religion, gender, or national origin when it can be shown that such discrimination is reasonably necessary to the business operation.

Affirmative action p. 764 An action plan designed to maintain equal employment opportunities and to remedy past employment discrimination against women, persons of color, persons with disabilities, and other underutilized protected classes.

CASE SUMMARY 41.1 Dumas v. Union Pacific Railroad Co., 294 Fed. App. 822 (5th Cir. 2008)

Misconduct

Dumas was an African-American employee of Union Pacific Railroad Company (UPRC), which employed him as a regional manager. UPRC, a rail freight company, was named in a discrimination claim by a co-worker of Dumas. During the EEOC investigation, Dumas supported his co-worker's claims by offering statements verifying discriminatory practices at UPRC. After the co-worker's claim was settled, UPRC conducted a routine audit that found that Dumas had falsified his track inspection records over a period of time in the past. UPRC immediately terminated Dumas.

CASE QUESTIONS

1. Does Dumas have a valid employment discrimination claim?
2. If so, what theories would best be advanced by Dumas?

ADEA

Harding was the CEO of Head Hunters International (HHI). After HHI was bought by MonsterCareers.com (MCC), the two firms were integrated. Soon after the merger, MCC informed Harding that his performance was lacking and he was terminated from his position. Harding later found out that Carey, a relative newcomer to MCC, was being promoted to his position. Harding, who was 51, alleged discrimination on the basis of his age because Carey was 42.

CASE QUESTIONS

1. Does Harding have a claim for employment discrimination under ADEA? Why or why not?
2. Would your answer change if Carey was 24, 39, or 41? Explain.

ADA

Barnett, a baggage loader for U.S. Airways (USA), injured his back while loading an inordinately heavy suitcase. His doctor diagnosed him with a permanently slipped disk and recurring back spasms. Barnett's condition is permanent and he is considered to be disabled under the ADA. Upon returning to work, USA offered to reassign him from baggage loader to luggage deliverer, where he would drive the baggage carts from plane to plane. However, Barnett wanted a position in the mailroom sorting mail. USA denied Barnett's request because the company operated on a strict seniority system for filling vacancies.

CASE QUESTIONS

1. Does Barnett have a cause of action under the ADA? Why or why not?
2. Has USA fulfilled its duty of reasonable accommodation?

Pretext

Aquino, a man of Chinese-Filipino origin, worked on a Honda assembly line. His time at Honda was tumultuous, and he had been suspended on numerous occasions for disciplinary violations. Upon returning from a suspension in 2001, Aquino was assigned to an engine installation station. Concurrent with Aquino's assignment, Honda experienced a number of cases of vehicle tampering and vandalism. A Honda manager conducted an investigation and concluded that Aquino was the only person with access to the tools necessary to conduct the vandalism. Upon Honda's complaint, Aquino was arrested, but the charges were eventually dropped due to insufficient evidence. Nonetheless, Honda terminated Aquino's employment after an internal investigation confirmed its initial conclusions on the matter. Aquino filed suit, claiming his termination was based on the fact that he was the only nonwhite employee assigned to the unit. At trial, Honda asserted that its investigation and conclusion that Aquino had committed the vandalism were legitimate reasons for firing Aquino. When the burden shifted back to Aquino, he asserted, but did not provide any evidence, that Honda manipulated the evidence of the incidents.

CASE QUESTIONS

1. Who prevails and why?
2. Why did Aquino have the burden of proving that Honda's reason for discharging him was a pretext? Didn't he already prove a *prima facie* case?
3. Considering the criminal charges against him were dropped, what would Aquino need to have shown in order to meet his burden of proof that Honda's reasons for dismissing him were pretextual?

1. **Reilly is a waiter at an exclusive hotel that requires male waiters to have short hair. After he refuses to cut his hair in accordance with the standards, he is fired. Which of the following is true?**

   a. Reilly has a claim under Title VII based on disparate impact.

   b. Reilly has a claim under the Age Discrimination in Employment Act if they replace him with someone younger.

   c. Reilly has no claim under Title VII because of the protected class requirement.

   d. Reilly has no claim under Title VII because he is an exempt employee.

   e. Reilly has a claim unless the employer has a legitimate seniority system.

2. **Which of the following theories of discrimination typically is based on statistical data that show that some method or measure resulted in discrimination?**

   a. Disparate impact

   b. Disparate treatment

   c. Mixed motives

   d. Disparate motives

   e. Statistical systems

3. **Dawson is a 50-year-old sales representative who was terminated by High Flyer Corporation due to poor performance. Dawson finds out that he was replaced by a 41-year-old employee, so he files suit under the Age Discrimination in Employment Act. Dawson will:**

   a. Prevail because he was replaced by a younger employee.

   b. Prevail under the mixed motives theory.

   c. Prevail only if High Flyer's reason is pretextual.

   d. Not prevail because the replacement employee is not substantially younger than Dawson.

   e. Not prevail so long as High Flyer had a legitimate seniority system.

4. **The Americans with Disabilities Act (ADA) requires:**

   a. Employers to accommodate disabled employees regardless of costs.

   b. A documented disability of an employee in order to trigger coverage.

   c. Employers who "regard employees as" having disabilities to reasonably accommodate them.

   d. B and C.

   e. A and B.

5. **Blackwell works in Shipping Supplies, Inc.'s warehouse. Although no employees have ever made sex-based comments, the male employees regularly watched pornographic videos in the company cafeteria during their lunch hour and passed around publications with lewd sexual content among employees. If Blackwell brings a claim for sexual harassment, what is her likely theory of the case?**

   a. Disparate impact

   b. Quid pro quo

   c. Hostile work environment

   d. Protected class membership

   e. Bona fide occupational qualification

6. **State antidiscrimination statutes sometimes will expand protected class membership beyond the protections of federal law.**

   a. True

   b. False

7. **Affirmative action programs have their genesis in an executive order issued to World War II contractors.**

   a. True

   b. False

8. **The Age Discrimination in Employment Act prohibits discrimination on the basis of age once the employee has reached age 21.**

   a. True

   b. False

9. **One example of reasonable accommodations would be for an employer to install wheelchair ramps for a disabled employee in the workplace.**

   a. True

   b. False

10. **The Lilly Ledbetter Fair Pay Act reversed a U.S. Supreme Court interpretation of the Americans with Disabilities Act.**

    a. True

    b. False

1. Mixed motives. This is similar to the *Price Waterhouse* case. There are legitimate reasons for the denial of promotion (tardiness) mixed with potentially illegitimate reasons (based on national origin stereotyping).

2. Disparate impact. Based on the EEOC guidelines, a disparate impact claim could be made because women are impacted in a disparate manner. The fire department must show that the free-weight requirement is a business necessity in order for it to be valid.

3. Disparate treatment. A neutral workplace rule (prohibition) was applied (or not applied) differently to men than to women. The *McDonnell Douglas* framework applies here.

4. Sexual harassment via hostile work environment theory so long as there is evidence that the behavior was so crude as to interfere with the plaintiff's job function and led her to resign.

CHAPTER REVIEW QUESTIONS: Answers and Explanations

1. c. Any Title VII claim must be based on discrimination because of an employee's membership in a protected class. Hair length is not a protected class, so Reilly is not eligible to bring a claim and therefore answers *a* and *b* are wrong. Answers *d* and *e* are wrong because they are incorrect statements of law.

2. a. Whenever the plaintiff in a Title VII claim is alleging discrimination based on statistical data, the theory is disparate impact. Answers *b* and *c* are theories of discrimination, but they do not involve statistical data. Answers *d* and *e* are incorrect statements of law.

3. d. In order to bring a claim under the ADEA, the plaintiff must demonstrate that the replacement employee was substantially younger (10 years or more age difference), which means answer *a* is wrong. Answers *b, c,* and *e* are incorrect statements of law.

4. d. The ADA requires that an employee have a documented disability to be covered under the act. Also covered are employees the employer believes are not able to work because of a disability ("regarded as"). Answers *a* and *e* are wrong because employers are not required to make accommodations regardless of costs.

5. c. Hostile work environments are created when employees engage in behavior that is of such a severe and crude nature that it interferes with the victim's ability to perform the job (e.g., displaying pornographic movies or photographs in the workplace). Answer *b* is wrong because a quid pro quo theory requires a promise in exchange for sexual favors. Answers *a, d,* and *e* are incorrect statements of law.

6. a. True. State antidiscrimination statutes will sometimes expand protected class membership beyond the protections of federal law as seen in the *Enriquez* case for New Jersey's antidiscrimination statute.

7. a. True. Affirmative action programs have their genesis in an executive order issued to World War II contractors who were required to make a good faith effort to diversify their labor force.

8. b. False. The Age Discrimination in Employment Act prohibits discrimination on the basis of age once the employee has reached age 40, not 21.

9. a. True. An example of reasonable accommodations is for an employer to install wheelchair ramps for a disabled employee in the workplace because it is not too onerous on the employer.

10. b. False. The Lilly Ledbetter Fair Pay Act reversed a U.S. Supreme Court interpretation of the Equal Pay Act, not the Americans with Disabilities Act.

UNIT SEVEN   Regulatory Environment of Business

CHAPTER 42

Torts and Products Liability

Limiting liability for injuries to customers is often a primary strategic goal of any business. In fact, some business ventures have a certain degree of risk as part of their business model. In this chapter's *Thinking Strategically,* we consider how businesses make strategic use of liability waivers as a method for reducing the risk of liability exposure inherent in many business operations.

Learning Objectives

After studying this chapter, students who have mastered the material will be able to:

42-1   Articulate a basic definition of a tort and identify the source of law governing various types of torts.

42-2   Determine the classification of tort based on the conduct of the wrongdoer.

42-3   Explain defamation, trade libel, and product disparagement in the context of the business environment.

42-4   Distinguish business competition torts from other intentional torts and understand their applicability in commercial relationships.

42-5   Explain the elements of negligence.

42-6   Identify potential defenses to a negligence claim.

42-7   Reach a conclusion based on a strict products liability analysis and applicable defenses.

CHAPTER OVERVIEW

Learning to recognize situations in which a business venture may have potential liability to another party is an important part of limiting risk in business operations. Tort law and products liability law set out certain conduct and standards of reasonableness and provide legal recourse when a violation of those standards results in an injury causing losses. Because business owners ordinarily are responsible for the intentional or accidental conduct of their employees who cause another party harm, it is essential for managers to understand ways to control risk and reduce liability. In this chapter, we discuss the fundamental principles of tort law, types of torts, and how each applies in a business context. The latter part of the chapter covers special rules governing products liability.

OVERVIEW OF TORT LAW

A **tort**[1] is a civil wrong in which one party has acted, or in some cases failed to act, and that action or inaction causes a loss to be suffered by another party. The law provides a remedy for one who has suffered an injury by compelling the wrongdoer to pay compensation to the injured party. Tort law is intended to compensate injured parties for losses resulting in harm from some unreasonable conduct by another.[2] One who commits a tort is known as the **tortfeasor**. The tortfeasor's wrongful conduct is described as **tortious conduct**. Recall from Chapter 1 that an individual may commit a criminal offense and a civil wrong in the very *same* act. While criminal statutes are intended to punish and deter the wrongdoer, the common law of torts is primarily intended to provide *compensation* for the victim. In some cases, tort law also may be used to deter wrongful conduct in the future.

LO 42-1

Articulate a basic definition of a tort and identify the source of law governing various types of torts.

Sources of Law

For the most part, tort law is governed by state common law principles. Recall from Chapter 1 that courts look to rules articulated by the American Law Institute (ALI) for guidance on applying common law legal principles. Known as the ***Restatement of Torts***, the ALI has amended the Restatements twice and, therefore, these sources of law are called the *Restatement (Second) of Torts* and the *Restatement (Third) of Torts*. Remember that courts are not bound by any of the Restatements, but they do recognize them as widely applied principles of law. The Second Restatements have the benefit of volumes of case law and wide acceptance; therefore, references to the Restatements in this chapter refer to the Second Restatements unless otherwise noted.

Products Liability

Laws that cover individuals who are injured by a product, known as *products liability laws,* may take the form of state common law or state statutes that expressly impose liability for injuries that result from products. These statutes are based primarily on the Restatements and are relatively uniform from state to state.

TAKEAWAY CONCEPTS Overview of Tort Law

- A tort is a civil wrong in which one party has acted, or in some cases failed to act, and that action or inaction causes a loss to be suffered by another party.
- Most tort law is governed by state common law based on the *Restatement of Torts.*
- Products liability laws are typically a blend of state common law and state statutory law.

TORT CLASSIFICATION

Torts fall into one of three general classes: *intentional torts, negligence,* and *strict liability.* An **intentional tort** is one in which the tortfeasor is *willful* in bringing about a particular event that causes harm to another party. Willful conduct is intentional behavior directed by an

LO 42-2

Determine the classification of tort based on the conduct of the wrongdoer.

---

[1] The term *tort* originally derives from the Latin root *tortus,* meaning "twisted" or "wrested aside." As with many legal terms, Latin words were given a French twist in English common law via the Norman kings. Thus, the shortened term *tort* is a French root meaning "wrong."

[2] *Black's Law Dictionary.*

individual's free will. **Negligence** is an accidental (without willful intent) event that causes harm to another party. The difference between the two is the mind-set and intent of the tortfeasor. For example, suppose that Pangloss is the delivery van driver for Cultivate Your Garden Flowers, Inc. While making a delivery, he spots his archenemy crossing the street, so he accelerates his truck and hits him. In this case, Pangloss has committed an intentional tort (battery). If, on the other hand, Pangloss is late for his delivery, carelessly speeds around a turn, and accidentally hits a pedestrian crossing the street, he has committed the tort of negligence. **Strict liability** torts, in which a tortfeasor may be held liable for an act regardless of intent or willfulness, apply primarily in cases of defective products and abnormally dangerous activities (such as major construction demolition).

TAKEAWAY CONCEPTS Tort Classification

Tort	Definition	Example
Intentional	Tortfeasor willfully intended to cause harm.	Tortfeasor intentionally assaults the victim, which requires the victim to seek medical care.
Negligence	Tortfeasor's action (or failure to act) accidentally caused injury to another.	Tortfeasor accidentally drives his car in a pedestrian zone and injures a pedestrian who is crossing the street.
Strict liability	Tortfeasor's mind-set is not relevant.	Defective product causes injury to a consumer.

INTENTIONAL BUSINESS-RELATED TORTS

LO 42-3

Explain defamation, trade libel, and product disparagement in the context of the business environment.

While the law provides relief for injured parties in a variety of circumstances, there are some intentional torts that are more important to business owners and managers because they have the potential to impact business relationships and operations.

Defamation

The law recognizes an individual's or a company's reputation as a valuable asset by imposing liability on any party that makes false and defamatory statements affecting another party's reputation. In this context, the term *party* means an individual, business, or product. As in all civil lawsuits, the *untrue statements* must have caused the victim to suffer *damages*. Generally, we think of written defamation as **libel** and oral (spoken) defamation as **slander**. In order to recover for a defamation action, the plaintiff must prove four elements:

1. *Defamatory statement.* A *false* statement concerning a party's reputation for honesty or a statement that subjects a party to hate, contempt, or ridicule. In order to qualify as defamatory, the statement must have a tendency to harm the reputation of the plaintiff.[3] Because many statements can be interpreted in more than one way, the law provides that the statement is defamatory so long as a defamatory interpretation is an objectively

---

[3]*Restatement (Second) of Torts*, § 559.

reasonable one and the plaintiff shows that at least one of the recipients did in fact make that interpretation. Note that the statement must be false, not merely unkind. Moreover, if a statement is *pure opinion,* that statement is not defamatory. That is, a defamatory statement is one that must be *provable as false.*

2. *Dissemination to a third party.* In the Restatements, this requirement is referred to as *publication,* but in this context it does not literally require the statement to be published. Rather, this element requires that the statement must somehow reach the ears or eyes of someone other than the tortfeasor and the victim. For example, suppose a manager telephones one of his employees and says, "You are the one who stole $100 in petty cash, so you're fired." Even if the accusatory statement is false, the manager has not defamed the employee based on that action alone. No third party heard the statement and, thus, the dissemination element is missing.

3. *Specificity.* The statement must be about a particular party, business, or product. Thus, any general statement about a profession as a whole cannot constitute defamation, but a false statement about a specific company can be the basis of a reputation claim.

4. *Damages.* The aggrieved party must be able to prove that he or she suffered some pecuniary harm (i.e., lost revenue or profits, both actual and potential). Examples of damages in a defamation suit include situations in which the victim has lost a valuable client due to the tortfeasor's defamatory comment or the victim has been unable to secure employment because of a tortfeasor's defamatory comment during a reference check.

Public Figure Standard

If the victim is a public figure, such as a candidate for political office, the defamation must have been committed with *malice* or reckless disregard for the truth. Malice typically is defined as intentional doing of a wrongful act with intent to harm. However, in the context of defamation, evidence of ill will is not required for the plaintiff to prevail. This "public figure" rule is based on the U.S. Supreme Court's landmark ruling in *New York Times v. Sullivan.*[4] The case involved a public official, a police commander, who sued *The New York Times* for defamation based on allegations printed in the newspaper that accused him of complicity in criminal activity. In announcing the public figure standard, the Court ruled that, in order for a public figure to prevail in a defamation case, the plaintiff must provide evidence that the defamer either had "actual knowledge" that the statement was false or had "reckless disregard for the truth."

Privilege Defenses to Defamation

If the injured party meets all of the requirements of a defamation claim, the defendant still may avoid liability if the defamatory statement falls into a category of *privileged statements.* Privilege is a defense that recognizes either a legal or public policy–based immunity from a defamation claim. It is divided into two categories: **absolute privilege**, whereby the defendant need not offer any further evidence to assert the defense, and **qualified privilege**, whereby the defendant must offer evidence of good faith and be absent of malice to be shielded from liability.

Absolute Privilege   Courts generally recognize three categories of absolute privilege:

■ *Government officials.* The framers of the Constitution recognized the need for free debate among members of Congress and gave immunity via the Speech or Debate Clause, which shields members of Congress from liability for any statement made during a congressional debate, hearing, and so on, while in office. The U.S. Supreme Court later extended that protection to all federal officials.[5]

---

[4]376 U.S. 254 (1964).

[5]*Barr v. Matteo,* 360 U.S. 564 (1959).

- *Judicial officers/proceedings.* All states now recognize some protection of participants of a judicial proceeding for statements made during the proceeding. This includes judges, lawyers, and, in some cases, witnesses.
- *State legislators.* Similar immunity has been extended by the states to protect state legislators for statements made in the course of carrying out their duties.

Qualified Privilege Courts also recognize certain qualified privileges that are grounded in public policy:

- *Media.* Employees of media organizations (e.g., television, radio, periodicals) are afforded a qualified protection from defamation liability. So long as the media has acted in good faith, *absent of malice,* and without a reckless disregard for the truth, the media is protected from liability through privilege as a defense for unintentional mistakes of fact in its reporting.
- *Employers.* An increasing number of states have extended some liability protection for employers who are providing a reference for an ex-employee. Under these employer privilege statutes, employers do not have liability if the employee's defamation claim is connected to a reference check *so long as the information is factual* and the employer has not acted with malice.

In Case 42.1, a state appellate court considers an employer reference privilege defense to a defamation claim in the context of a reference check.

CASE 42.1 Nelson v. Tradewind Aviation, 111 A.3d 887, Appellate Court of Connecticut (2015)

FACT SUMMARY Tradewind Aviation (TA) employed Nelson as a pilot for a small commercial airline that primarily flew from New York and New Jersey to Martha's Vineyard and Nantucket. Over the course of the summer of 2007, Nelson co-piloted 137 flights without incident or complaint from passengers. Nelson was never removed from flying status for a performance-based or disciplinary reason. Although some senior pilots did complain about Nelson, he was never given a written warning, disciplined, or suspended. As the summer ended, TA announced that some pilots would be laid off due to a decrease in demand during the off-season. Nelson committed to working during the first part of the off-season; however, TA informed Nelson it would be unable to continue his employment. TA's human resources office completed necessary paperwork indicating that Nelson was laid off due to "lack of work."

In December 2007, Nelson was offered a job by Republic Airways (Republic). As part of his initial interview, Nelson signed authorizations that gave TA permission to verify his employment with TA and to release all of his employment records to Republic.

This authorization also required TA to send copies of these records to Nelson so that he had an opportunity to submit written comments to correct any inaccuracies. TA completed the reference forms and indicated that (1) Nelson had been involuntarily terminated from TA and (2) Nelson had been involuntarily removed from flying status based on poor performance. Responding to Republic's request for more details, TA faxed Republic a letter stating that Nelson was terminated "after he failed to perform to company standards" and that, prior to that date, "he was given several opportunities to discuss the need for improvement as well as additional training to help him perform at the levels we needed." TA never sent the records or letter to Nelson. Republic subsequently revoked its job offer. Nelson sued TA for, among other claims, defamation. The jury awarded the plaintiff a total of $307,332.94 in damages. TA appealed, asserting the employer reference privilege.

SYNOPSIS OF DECISION AND OPINION The Appellate Court of Connecticut affirmed the jury's

(continued)

---

verdict in favor of Nelson. The court reasoned that it was well settled that defamation is actionable if it charges improper conduct or lack of skill or integrity in one's profession or business and is of such a nature that it is calculated to cause injury to one in his profession or business. The court rejected TA's argument that Nelson had not proven that TA's statements rose to the level of malicious. The court held that a qualified privilege in a defamation case may be defeated if it can be established that the holder of the privilege acted with malice in publishing the defamatory material. Based on the facts in this case, the jury's conclusion that the statements were made with malice was reasonable.

WORDS OF THE COURT: Malice "A review of the evidence reveals that the jury reasonably could have concluded that the defendant's defamatory statements were made with knowledge that they were false and with an improper motive. The jury reasonably could have found that [Nelson] was laid off due to lack of work, that [TA supervisors] never removed the plaintiff from a flight for performance or professional competency reasons, that [Nelson] was never offered or sent for any additional training . . . Additionally, the jury reasonably could have found that the statements were made with an improper motive in light of the timing and manner in which the statements were made."

Case Questions

1. What statements by TA, specifically, do you consider to be malicious? Why?

2. How could TA's management have prevented the defamation from occurring?

3. *Focus on Critical Thinking:* What is the public policy behind the employer reference privilege? Is it fair to the employee, who may have a different perspective on the circumstances of his or her termination? Have you ever heard an employer defaming an ex-employee?

Trade Libel and Product Disparagement Laws

In cases where a competitor has made a false statement that disparaged a competing product, an injured party may sue for **trade libel**. This tort requires that the statement (1) be a clear and *specific* reference to the disparaged party or product (e.g., using the actual brand name of the product), (2) be made with either knowledge that the statement is false or shows reckless disregard for the truth, and (3) be communicated to a third party (similar to defamation).

Some states have passed **product disparagement statutes** intended to protect the interest of a state's major industries, such as agriculture, dairy, or beef.[6] In perhaps the most famous product disparagement case, the Texas Cattle Ranchers Association sued Oprah Winfrey under a Texas law allowing recovery for any rancher who suffers damages as a result of false disparagement. On her television show, Winfrey agreed with statements made by one of her guests that alleged certain U.S. market hamburger meat could cause mad cow disease, which is fatal to humans. At the end of the segment, Winfrey took the position that she would cease eating hamburgers. The ranchers showed evidence that beef sales dropped precipitously immediately after the broadcast and alleged that Winfrey's statements were false and caused the ranchers lost revenue. The jury rejected the cattle ranchers' claim as too broad and without sufficient evidence that the remarks alone were the cause of the losses.[7]

Fraudulent Misrepresentation

Recall the discussion of misrepresentation and fraudulent misrepresentation in the context of contracts from Chapter 9, "Enforceability." There are some important overlapping

---

[6]For example, disparagement of Idaho potatoes is covered in Idaho Code § 6-2003. For a list of many such laws, see David J. Bederman, Scott M. Christensen, and Scott Dean Quesenberry, "Of Banana Bills and Veggie Hate Crimes: The Constitutionality of Agricultural Disparagement Statutes,"*Harvard Journal on Legislation* 34 (1997), p. 135.

[7]Affirmed in *Texas Beef Group v. Winfrey,* 201 F.3d 680 (5th Cir. 2000).

legal principles between tort law and contract law. For example, in some cases, contract law allows a contract to be canceled if one party makes false representations concerning a *material fact.* This means that the misrepresented fact must involve an important aspect of the basis of the contract, such as a change in the value of the contract or an increase in one party's risk. Fraudulent misrepresentation (sometimes referred to simply as *fraud*) is *also* recognized as a tort in cases where the law provides a remedy to recover damages when the innocent party suffers a pecuniary loss as a result of the false representation. In cases of fraudulent misrepresentation, the law allows the innocent party to recover if (1) the misrepresentation was a material fact known to be false by the tortfeasor (or a reckless disregard for the truth); (2) the tortfeasor intended to persuade the innocent party to rely on the statement and the innocent party did, in fact, rely on it; and (3) damages were suffered by the innocent party.

For example, suppose Buyer asks Seller about whether Seller's property is properly zoned for a manufacturing facility. In an effort to induce Buyer to purchase the property, Seller misrepresents that the property is zoned for manufacturing. Buyer then enters into a purchase agreement for the property with a 10 percent down payment, balance due in 30 days. Buyer proceeds to spend money by hiring an architect to visit the site and draw plans for the new facility. The day after the agreement is signed, Seller applies to the zoning board for a change in zoning, hoping that it will be changed before the Buyer completes the agreement by paying the balance owed. The zoning board does not change the status. In a case against Seller for fraud, Buyer would be entitled to cancel the contract *and* recover any losses in tort suffered as a result of Seller's fraudulent misrepresentations (such as the money spent hiring the architect).

Negligent Misrepresentation

Courts also allow recovery for misrepresentations that are not intentional but are *negligent* misrepresentations. In most cases, the parties have to have some type of business relationship for the innocent party to recover. Any statement made by a party that turns out not to be accurate may still allow the innocent party to recover if the tortfeasor's statement was negligent. In the Buyer-Seller case above, suppose that Seller had no actual knowledge of the zoning status for the property but made a statement that it was zoned for manufacturing. Buyer still would be able to recover despite the fact that Seller did not know that the statement was false. Seller is still liable because he was negligent in his duty to know such an important fact (negligence is discussed in detail later in this chapter).

False Imprisonment

The tort of false imprisonment is defined by the Restatements as the "intentional infliction of a confinement upon another party." In the business context, a merchant most commonly encounters these circumstances in cases of suspected retail theft. While the merchant has the right to briefly detain a suspected shoplifter, she must be cautious about giving rise to a false imprisonment claim when detaining an individual or attempting to recover the merchandise. The Restatements provide for a **merchant's privilege**[8] to shield a merchant from liability for temporarily detaining a party who is *reasonably* suspected of stealing merchandise. This privilege, however, is very narrow. In order to gain protection under the merchant's privilege, the merchant must follow certain guidelines:

■ *Limited detention.* The privilege only applies for a short period of time under the circumstances. Some courts have limited this time period to as few as 15 minutes. However, most courts follow a case-by-case analysis with the general framework that the

---

[8]Also known as "shopkeeper's privilege." See *Restatements (Second) of Torts,* § 120A.

TABLE 42.1 Other Intentional Torts

Tort	Definition	Example
Battery	Intentional infliction of harmful or offensive bodily contact.	One party strikes another, causing injury. The injury requires payment for medical treatment.
Intentional infliction of emotional distress	Extreme, outrageous, or reckless conduct that is intended to inflict emotional or mental distress (physical harm is not necessary).	A bill collector contacts a debtor's mother and threatens physical harm and imprisonment for the son and to put a lien on the mother's house. The mother suffers two heart attacks after the threats persist.*
Trespass (land)	Trespass occurs when a party enters another's land or causes another person or object to enter land owned by a private party.	A survey crew mistakenly surveys the wrong property. While working, the crew damages landscaping. The landowner is entitled to compensation as a result of the crew's trespass.
Trespass (chattel†)	Trespass occurs when a party interferes with another's use or possession of chattel (such as personal property).	An employee takes home his employer's drill for personal use without the employer's permission and with the intent to return it the next morning. The drill is broken while under the employee's control. The employee is liable for costs of repair/replacement and any lost profits resulting from the downtime.
Conversion	The civil counterpart to theft intended to reimburse a party who suffers damages as a result of theft or any other substantial interference with a party's ownership, where fairness requires that the tortfeasor reimburse the injured party for the full value of the property.	The controller of a corporation embezzles corporate funds and covers up discrepancies on the financial statements. In addition to criminal charges, the controller's employer may also sue her for conversion in an attempt to recover the embezzled funds.

*Based on *George v. Jordan Marsh Co.,* 268 N.E.2d 915 (Mass. 1971).
†*Chattel* is the English common law term for personal property or equipment that is movable.

detention may last the amount of time necessary to confront the accused party, recover any goods stolen, and wait for the authorities to arrive (if necessary).

- *Limited to premises.* Generally, the privilege only applies if the suspected party is confronted on the merchant's premises or an immediately adjacent area (such as a parking lot).
- *Coercion.* The merchant or merchant's agent (such as a store security guard) may not attempt to coerce payment, purport to officially arrest the detained party, or attempt to obtain a confession.

Table 42.1 provides an overview of other types of intentional torts and examples of each.

BUSINESS COMPETITION TORTS

Tort law also provides for the promotion of fairness in business dealings and for the reimbursement of a party that has suffered some damages as a result of a competitor's tortious acts. These common law torts arise when a tortfeasor (typically a competitor to the harmed party) interferes with an existing contract or hinders a prospective contract between two parties.

LO 42-4

Distinguish business competition torts from other intentional torts and understand their applicability in commercial relationships.

Tortious Interference with Existing Contractual Relationship

When one party *induces* another party to break an existing contract with another party, the inducing party may be liable for any damages suffered by the innocent party as a result of breaking the contract. In order for the injured party to recover damages, the tortfeasor must have (1) had *specific knowledge* of the contract, (2) actively *interfered* with the contract, and (3) caused some identifiable damages (losses) to the injured party. Business owners and managers may encounter contract interference torts in the context of restrictions against working for competitors in an employment contract (known as a *restrictive covenant*[9]) or in defending an allegation of interference in the process of hiring a new employee away from a competitor.

For example, suppose Lee, a talented software programmer, signs a contract with Computer Researchers Inc. (CRI) for three years. The contract stipulates that Lee will not work for any of CRI's competitors during that time, even if he is terminated or voluntarily resigns from CRI. After one year, one of CRI's competitors, MultiCom, contacts Lee and attempts to convince him to leave CRI and work for MultiCom. During the negotiations, Lee shows MultiCom his contract with CRI, and MultiCom's manager then offers a higher salary and a $1,000 signing bonus to Lee. Lee resigns from CRI with two years left on his contract and goes to work for MultiCom. As a result, CRI must spend several thousand dollars recruiting and training a new programmer to finish Lee's projects. In this case, many courts would consider holding MultiCom liable for CRI's damages because CRI was injured as a result of MultiCom's tortious interference with the CRI-Lee contract. Of course, CRI also would be entitled to recover damages from Lee for breaking the contract.

Note that interference does *not* occur when a competitor merely offers a better price to a competitor's customer. For example, suppose that Chung, the owner of several self-service car washes, signs a two-year agreement with Mega Distributor to supply snack vending machines in the lobby of each of his car washes. Under the contract, Chung will receive 30 percent of the sales from the machines. Shortly thereafter, Chung is contacted by a sales rep from Start-Up Snacks, who offers the same terms as the Mega contract, except that Chung will receive 60 percent of the sales from the machines. Chung crunches the numbers and concludes that the increase in revenue will more than make up for any penalties incurred for breaching the Chung-Mega contract, so he breaks his contract with Mega and enters into a new contract with Start-Up. Despite the fact that Start-Up knew of the Mega contract, the level of interference is *not* sufficient to constitute a tort. In this case, Chung decided on his own to break the contract with Mega and was not *induced* to do so by Start-Up. To induce another party means to "bring about" or "give rise to." In the context of tortious interference, liability is triggered if inducement causes the harm. It is important to note, however, that Mega could still sue Chung for failing to perform his obligations as agreed in the contract.[10]

Tortious Interference with Prospective Advantage

In addition to providing protection against interference from third parties in existing contracts, the law also protects against interference with *potential* contract (prospects) or other business relationships. The protections and definition of interference are similar to the existing contractual interference rules discussed above. However, because no contract actually exists, courts only allow recovery for this tort under limited circumstances where the tortfeasor's conduct was highly anticompetitive. For example, assume that OldCo intends to sabotage NewCo's efforts to obtain a new customer through a competitive bidding process. An OldCo employee hacks into NewCo's computer and destroys the proposal forms. NewCo cannot submit the bid before the deadline and, thus, doesn't get the contract. Assuming that NewCo can prove it suffered damages, OldCo could be held liable for interference with prospective advantage.

---

[9]Restrictive covenants are covered in detail in Chapter 6 "Contracts: Overview, Definition, Categories, and Source of Law."

[10]Based on *Restatements (Second) of Torts,* § 766, Illustration 3.

Quick Quiz Intentional Torts

Which tort, if any, fits each of the following fact patterns?

1. Jason and Elaine are both being considered for a promotion to VP of Sales. Jason starts a false rumor that Elaine doctored the books to make her accounts look better than they actually are. Because of the investigation and the need to fill the position, Elaine is dropped from consideration and Jason gets the promotion.

2. MOT Corporation does all of its banking with Second National Bank. MOT receives a 1 percent interest rate on its savings account and pays a fee of $.02 per check written. A representative of Third National Bank visits MOT's offices and tells the company that Third National pays 1.25 percent interest and has free corporate checking. MOT closes its accounts with Second National and moves all of its banking business to Third National.

3. Wayne gets into his car after work, but it won't start. He returns to his office, and everyone has gone home. He takes the keys to a company vehicle and drives home, intending to drive it back to the office in the morning. That night, a violent storm causes a tree branch to fall on the car, causing extensive damage.

4. Nancy has triplets who are attending eighth grade. Every once in a while, she takes small quantities of paper, pens, paper clips, and other stationery supplies home from work and gives them to her kids for school use.

5. Frank is a used-car salesman. He is working with a customer who decides to buy a car. The price is agreed to, and the customer tells Frank that he will go to the bank to get a certified check. They shake hands. Frank then says, "You should know that this car used to be owned by Bill Gates!" The customer returns with the certified check, all paperwork is signed, and the customer drives the car home. The next day, the customer discovers that Bill Gates never owned the car.

Answers to this Quick Quiz are provided at the end of the chapter.

TAKEAWAY CONCEPTS Business-Related Intentional and Competition Torts

- Defamation is a false statement that is directed specifically at a party, company, or product; is aired to a third party; and results in pecuniary harm to the victim.

- A victim of fraud must show intentional misrepresentation by the tortfeasor of a material fact, reliance on that fact, and damages resulting from that reliance.

- False imprisonment is an intentional tort unless the tortfeasor is a merchant who temporarily and reasonably detains a suspected thief.

- When a business competitor's actions exceed standard competitive practices, a company may be liable for intentional interference with a contract by a third party if the company had specific knowledge of a contract and intentionally disrupted its proper execution.

NEGLIGENCE

Tort law also applies when one party fails to act reasonably and harm occurs, even though that party did not intend for harm to occur. The negligent party is liable for any injuries or damages suffered by another party as a result of the unreasonable conduct. This category of tort is called *negligence.* Recall from the first section of this chapter that the primary difference between intentional torts and negligence is the mind-set of the tortfeasor. When a tortfeasor causes harm to an injured party by creating an *unreasonable risk of harm,* the law provides the injured party a remedy regardless of the tortfeasor's intent. The Restatements also recognize certain defenses that may be asserted in a negligence case.

Elements of Negligence

The law requires that specific elements be proven in order to recover in a lawsuit against a tortfeasor for negligence. The injured party must prove five fundamental elements by answering certain questions about the conduct in question:

- *Duty:* Did the tortfeasor owe a duty of care to the injured party?
- *Breach of duty:* Did the tortfeasor fail to exercise reasonable care?
- *Cause in fact:* Except for the breach of duty by the tortfeasor, would the injured party have suffered damages?
- *Proximate (legal) cause:* Was there a legally recognized and close-in-proximity link between the breach of duty and the damages suffered by the injured party?
- *Actual damages:* Did the injured party suffer some physical harm that resulted in identifiable losses?

Duty   The initial consideration in a negligence analysis is whether the tortfeasor owed the injured party a *legal* **duty.** The law imposes a general duty on all parties to act reasonably and not to impart unreasonable risk to others. In addition to this general duty, some parties owe a special (heightened) duty of conduct to avoid liability for negligence.

General Duty of Reasonable Conduct   The law imposes a general duty on every party to act as a *reasonably prudent person* would under the circumstances. That is, everyone owes a duty to everyone else to act in a manner that does not impose unreasonable risk. The reasonably prudent person standard emphasizes that the conduct must be *objectively* reasonable. This means that a fact finder (such as the jury) at trial could conclude that a reasonably prudent person in the same circumstances should have realized that certain conduct would be risky or harmful to another person. In general, the scope of that duty is defined by *foreseeability.* In tort law, the term *person* in the reasonably prudent person standard is meant to be a generic term. The scope of duty frequently is defined by a particular industry or occupation. For example, the level of duty for a physician is defined by what a reasonably prudent *physician* would have done under the circumstances.

It is important to understand that duty is an element that *expands* and *contracts* based on whether or not it was foreseeable that the conduct in question would cause an unreasonable risk of harm. For example, suppose Cain is a guest on a shock-host television show. The owners of the show arrange to have Abel surprise Cain on the show with an embarrassing secret. When the secret is revealed during the show, Cain is embarrassed and runs off the stage; no further incident ensues. Three days later, Abel persists in calling Cain and harassing him about this secret. Later that afternoon, Cain shoots and kills Abel. Cain is sentenced to a life term, and Abel's heirs sue the owners of the shock-host television show for negligence, claiming they owed Abel a duty to protect him from Cain. In this case, a court will likely rule that due to the time period between the show and the shooting (three days) and the fact that no incident occurred on the show or immediately thereafter, the duty owed to Abel ended when the show ended and did not extend to the time of the incident. This is primarily because it was not reasonably foreseeable under the factual circumstances of this case that Cain would act in such a rash manner then or thereafter.[11]

---

[11]Based on *Graves v. Warner Brothers,* 656 N.W.2d 195 (Mich. App. 2002).

No General Duty to Act The duty of care discussed above does *not* include a general duty to act or to rescue another. Tort law allocates liability based on a fundamental difference between some *act* by one party that harms or endangers another party, known as **misfeasance**, and the failure to act or intervene in a certain situation, known as **nonfeasance**. While injured parties generally may recover for misfeasance, they may not hold a defendant liable for failing to act *unless* the parties had a **special relationship** to each other. Special relationships that are set out in the Restatements include a common carrier (such as a bus company) to its passengers, innkeepers to guests, employers to employees, a school to students, and a landlord to tenants.[12] One important special relationship of interest to business owners and managers is a business's duty to *warn* and *assist* any business visitors or patrons in terms of potential danger or harm (such as a slippery floor) on business premises. Therefore, businesses have a special relationship with visitors and patrons that would allow recovery even in cases of nonfeasance.

In Case 42.2, an appellate court focuses on foreseeability as it analyzes a negligence claim made against a manufacturer of violent video games.

CASE 42.2 James v. Meow Media, Inc., 300 F.3d 683 (6th Cir. 2002)

FACT SUMMARY After a rampage shooting by 14-year-old Michael Carneal at his Kentucky high school resulted in the deaths of three of his classmates, the parents and estate administrators of the victims (collectively "James") filed a negligence lawsuit against several companies that produced or maintained certain movie, video game, and Internet websites (collectively "Meow Media"), claiming that these movies, games, and websites had contributed to Carneal's homicidal state of mind. The lawsuit relied on a post-shooting investigation that revealed that Carneal had regularly played violent video games that depicted a player shooting at video characters, watched movies that glamorized violence, and viewed pornographic Internet sites produced by Meow Media. James argued that these activities "desensitized" Carneal to violence and caused a lethal state of mind that led to the shooting spree. The lawsuit contended that Meow Media's production and distribution of this material to high school–aged students constituted negligence and also triggered strict liability under Kentucky's products liability law. The U.S. district court dismissed the negligence claim and ruled that Carneal's actions were not sufficiently foreseeable to impose a duty of reasonable care on the defendants with respect to the

victims. The district court also ruled that the movies, video games, and Internet sites were not "products" as defined in state strict liability statutes.

SYNOPSIS OF DECISION AND OPINION The U.S. Court of Appeals for the Sixth Circuit upheld the trial court's ruling in favor of Meow Media. The court used a negligence analysis in which the duty of care is defined by whether the harm to the injured party resulting from the defendant's negligence was *foreseeable*. Specifically, the court held that, except under extraordinary circumstances or where the parties had a "special relationship," individuals generally are entitled to assume that third parties will not commit intentional criminal acts. Therefore, it was not objectively reasonable for Meow Media to foresee that Carneal would commit any criminal act and, thus, no duty was owed to James. Moreover, the court held that even if a duty did exist, James could not meet the requirements for proximate causation because Carneal's intentional, violent actions constitute a superseding cause of James's damages and severed Meow Media's liability for the death of Carneal's victims. The court also upheld the dismissal of the products liability claims against Meow Media because Kentucky law does not recognize video

(continued)

---

[12]*Restatements (Second) of Torts,* § 314A.

game cartridges, movie cassettes, and Internet transmission as sufficiently tangible to constitute products in the sense of their communicative content.

WORDS OF THE COURT: Foreseeability "This court has encountered this foreseeability inquiry under Kentucky law before in a situation similar to this case. [In that case], the mother of a suicide victim sued [the video game manufacturer] for manufacturing 'Dungeons and Dragons.' . . . We held that the boy's suicide was simply not a reasonably foreseeable result of producing the game, notwithstanding its violent content. To have held otherwise would have been 'to stretch the concepts of foreseeability and ordinary care to lengths that would deprive them of all normal meaning.'"

WORDS OF THE COURT: Liability for Intentional Criminal Actions "Arguably, the defendants' games, movie, and internet sites gave Carneal the ideas and emotions, the 'psychological tools,' to commit three murders. However, this case lacks such crucial features of our jurisprudence in this area. First, the defendants in this case had no idea Carneal even existed, much less the particular idiosyncrasies of Carneal that made their products particularly dangerous in his hands. [. . .] Second, no court has ever held that ideas and images can constitute the tools for a criminal act under this narrow exception."

Case Questions

1. Why did the court hold that Meow Media could not have foreseen the damages caused by Carneal?

2. Was there a special relationship duty in this case? Why or why not?

3. *Focus on Critical Thinking:* What type of evidence might bolster the plaintiffs' theory of the case? If they could prove that scientific evidence existed that there was a correlation between the video games, the desensitization, and violence, would that be enough? Why or why not?

Landowners Landowners owe a general duty to parties off the land from any unreasonable risks to them caused by something on the land. Courts use a reasonableness standard to determine the point at which the landowner should have acted. For example, suppose the owner of GreenAcre plants several trees on the edge of his property, which is adjacent to a busy suburban street. One month later, one tree is dead with no green vegetation and with evidence of decaying bark and cracks in the roots. Eventually, the tree falls onto the road and injures a passerby. In this instance, a court may find that the landowner had a duty to inspect and remove the tree because it was foreseeable that the dead tree would be a risk to passersby if it fell.[13]

Landowners also owe a special duty to certain parties based on categories spelled out in the Restatements. It is important to understand that in a situation where a tenant is in possession of *leased space,* the tenant has the same special duties and level of liability that is imposed on landowners. Once a landlord/owner has given possession of the property to the tenant, the landlord generally is not held liable except for certain common areas (e.g., common stairwells, restrooms, or lobby).[14] The expected level of care varies by category.

Table 42.2 sets out the categories of special relationship duties owed by landowners to licensees, invitees, and trespassers.

Assumption of Duty Another exception to the no general duty to act/rescue doctrine is when one party voluntarily begins to render assistance even when there is no legal obligation to do so. This is known as *assumption of duty,* and it requires that the party rendering assistance must proceed with reasonable care. This includes the duty to continue rendering

---

[13]Although the Restatements do except "natural" conditions from the general duty, if a landowner planted the shrubs or excavated the land, this falls under the category of *artificial* and is not an exception to the landowner's general duty to persons off the property.

[14]There are exceptions to this rule, such as when the landlord transferred possession knowing of a certain defect but failed to warn the tenant about it.

TABLE 42.2 Special Relationship Duties Owed by Landowners

Special Relationship to	Definition	Example	Duties Owed
Licensee	Party has owner's consent to be on property for a nonbusiness purpose.	Social guest	Warn licensee of any known dangerous conditions on or about the premises. *No* duty owed to licensee to inspect for hidden dangers.
Invitee	Party is invited by owner for business purposes or when landowner holds the premises open to the public.	Customer in a retail store	Warn invitee of any known dangerous conditions on or about the premises. Duty to inspect the premises for hidden dangers and take reasonable efforts to fix any defects.
Trespasser	Party enters premises without owner's consent.	Landscaping crew accidentally mows wrong property	No duty to warn, inspect, or repair. Exceptions are a general duty of care when (1) the owner has reason to know of regular trespass (such as a worn pathway) or (2) owner has reason to anticipate that young children might trespass on the property.

aid and to take care not to leave the injured party in a worse position. For example, suppose that Davis, a delivery truck driver, hears a call for help during one of his deliveries. He discovers that the call is coming from a nearby apartment that is on fire. Davis enters the building and rescues the caller. Although Davis has no legal duty to rescue, he undertakes the rescue and therefore assumes the duty to keep the caller safe. For example, if the caller is unconscious, Davis must use reasonable care to secure medical help and cannot abandon the caller.

In Case 42.3, a state appellate court considers a claim by a college student, injured as part of a fraternity prank that went awry, that he was owed a duty under both a landowner theory and an assumption of duty theory.

CASE 42.3 Yost v. Wabash College, Phi Kappa Psi Fraternity et al., 3 N.E.3d 509 (Ind. 2014)

FACT SUMMARY Brian Yost was an 18-year-old first-year student at Wabash College ("Wabash") and a pledge at the local Phi Kappa Psi fraternity ("Local Fraternity"). Part of the Local Fraternity's traditions involve "creeking," meaning that a fraternity brother is thrown into a nearby creek. In September 2007, Yost and his pledge brothers confronted some of the Local Fraternity's member brothers in an attempt to toss one of these members, Yost's Pledge Father, into a nearby creek. Later that night, several Local Fraternity brothers retaliated by attempting to forcibly place Yost in the shower. This action was also a tradition of the Local Fraternity, and one in which Yost and his pledge brothers had previously participated two other times the evening of his injury. During this attempt, several Local Fraternity member brothers were carrying Yost to the shower when one of the fraternity members put him into a headlock that rendered Yost unconscious. The other member brothers panicked and dropped Yost to the ground.

Yost suffered significant physical and psychological injuries from the incident that caused him to withdraw from college. Yost filed suit alleging his injuries were a result of negligence and seeking damages

(continued)

Phi Kappa Psi Fraternity House at Wabash College.
© B.O'Kane/Alamy

from, among others: (1) Wabash College (the owner and landlord of the fraternity house), contending that a special relationship existed; and (2) the Local Fraternity on an assumption of duty theory. The trial court granted summary judgment to both Wabash and the Local Fraternity, and Yost appealed.

SYNOPSIS OF DECISION AND OPINION The Indiana Supreme Court affirmed the summary judgment for Wabash but reversed the summary judgment for the Local Fraternity. In the case of Wabash, the court reasoned that a landlord has no liability to tenants or others for injuries on the property when the tenant is in full control of the leased premises. In the case of the Local Fraternity, the court held that there was sufficient evidence to reasonably conclude that Yost may be able to show that the Local Fraternity assumed a duty and that the actions of its members increased the risk of harm to him. This was especially true because the activity that led to the incident was a fraternity tradition.

WORDS OF THE COURT: Wabash College's Duty as Property Owner "Within the contours of this duty, we have held that landowners have a duty to take reasonable precautions to prevent foreseeable criminal acts against invitees. However, when the landowner is a lessor and the lessee is in operational control of the premises, such duty rarely exists. . . .

In the absence of statute, covenant, fraud or concealment, a landlord who gives a tenant full control and possession of the leased property will not be liable for personal injuries sustained by the tenant or other persons lawfully upon the leased property."

WORDS OF THE COURT: Local Fraternity's Assumed Duty "Here, Yost's argument is not that a conventionally recognized duty (such as a landowner's duty to an invitee or common carrier's duty to a passenger) existed, but rather that the local fraternity assumed a duty requiring the local fraternity to act with reasonable care. As the above facts show, Yost was living at the local fraternity, subject to the mentorship of a Pledge Father from the local fraternity, participating in traditions maintained at the local fraternity, was involved in the pledgeship program being run by local fraternity members, and, therefore, at least partially under the control and direction of the local fraternity. . . . The undisputed designated evidence does not preclude the possibility that Yost may show at trial that the local fraternity undertook to render supervisory services intended to reduce the risk of harm to members like Yost, that upon which supervision Yost relied, and further that by failing to exercise reasonable care the local fraternity increased the risk of harm to Yost."

Case Questions

1. What factors did the court use to determine that the Local Fraternity may have assumed a duty here? Do you agree? Why or why not?

2. Why did the court find that Wabash College had no liability for this incident?

3. *Focus on Critical Thinking:* One of Yost's unsuccessful arguments against Wabash centered on a doctrine called *in loco parentis* (i.e., in place of the parent). The doctrine has largely disappeared from higher education since 1961. Yost claimed that the college had a duty to protect him and should have had a system in place to prevent fraternity pranks from becoming dangerous. Do you agree? Should an 18-year-old college student have full responsibility for his own safety while in a college-owned facility? Should colleges and universities have *in loco parentis* liability?

Breach of Duty   Once it has been established that one party owes another party a general or special duty, the next factor is to assess whether or not that party has fulfilled her obligations. Failing to meet these obligations is known as a **breach of duty**. As discussed above, duties include (1) general obligations to act in a reasonable manner so as not to put another in harm's way; (2) special duties to certain parties, including the duty to inspect or duty to warn of defects; and (3) assumption of duty. While the Restatements don't actually list events of breach, courts traditionally have looked to certain guideposts to determine whether a breach of duty has occurred.

Violation of Safety Statute   If the legislature has passed a statute intended to promote safety and one party violates the statute, there is a strong presumption that the party violating the statute has also breached her general duty to those who are protected by the law. Violations of these safety statutes are sometimes referred to as *negligence per se.* For example, suppose the state legislature passes a law requiring that construction companies provide hard hats for all workers and visitors on a construction site. One day, a prospective tenant visits an office building construction site to check on its progress, but there are not enough hard hats available. The site manager allows the visitor on the site without a hard hat. The visitor is then injured by falling debris. In this case, the construction company has violated the state safety statute, and a court may find a breach of duty occurred without delving into a reasonably prudent person analysis.

States also pass statutes intended to establish specific liability standards in certain circumstances. For example, *dram shop laws* impose liability on the owners and employees of a public establishment where alcohol is being served. These laws allow a third party who has been injured or harmed by an intoxicated tortfeasor to recover damages against an owner or employee who served an obviously intoxicated patron.[15]

Common Law Standards of Behavior   When the state legislature has been silent, appellate courts in individual states usually have developed a fairly extensive body of cases in their common law so that certain standards of behavior may be used in judging whether a breach has occurred. Standards related to maintenance of property (such as when ice must be cleared) and safety measures (such as keeping one's car in good repair if driving on public roads) are examples of nonstatutory standards for reasonable behavior.

Res Ipsa Loquitur   The doctrine of *res ipsa loquitur* (a Latin phrase meaning "the thing or matter speaks for itself ") is deep-seated in American tort law. This doctrine allows an injured party to create a presumption that the tortfeasor was negligent by pointing to certain facts that infer negligent conduct without showing exactly how the tortfeasor behaved.[16] An English judge first used this Latin phrase over a century ago in a case in which a pedestrian was struck by a flour barrel that fell from a warehouse owned by the defendant. Although the injured party could not actually show how or why the barrel fell, the court held that the facts themselves were sufficient to impute a presumption of negligence.[17]

For example, assume that Ginsberg notices smoke coming from under the hood of her car. She has the car towed to a mechanic, who determines that a valve cover gasket is leaking. She instructs him to make the necessary repairs. When she picks up the car, she pays the bill and drives off. One mile later, while stopped at a light, Ginsberg sees smoke coming

---

[15]Note that an increasing number of state legislatures have imposed similar liability for all social hosts, including the serving of alcohol in a private home.

[16]*Restatement (Second) of Torts,* § 328(D).

[17]*Byrne v. Boadle,* 159 Eng. Rep. 299 (Eng. 1863). The court wrote, "A barrel could not roll out of a warehouse without some negligence, and to say the plaintiff who is injured by it must call witnesses . . . is preposterous."

from the hood again and gets out of the car just before it catches fire. The fire consumes the car, causing the engine to melt, and thus no specific cause for the fire can be determined. Ginsberg cannot prove exactly what the mechanic did wrong, but the car should not have caught fire if the mechanic had repaired the car properly. She can use *res ipsa loquitur* to infer negligence.

Cause in Fact

After establishing that a breach of duty has occurred, the injured party also must prove that the tortfeasor's conduct was the **cause in fact** of the damages suffered by the injured party. In other words, there must be a *link* between breach of duty and damages. The overwhelming majority of courts use a simple test, known as the *but-for test*, to establish a link. Thus, the question that must be answered is: "But for (except for) the breach of duty by the tortfeasor, would the injured party have suffered damages?" If the answer is no, then there is a link between the tortfeasor's conduct and the harm suffered by the injured party. Another way to ask this question is: "If the tortfeasor had complied with her legal duty, would the injured party have suffered damages?" Again, a no answer indicates a link and, thus, cause in fact. For example, suppose that Donald checks into Hotel's 20th-floor luxury suite. He watches a beautiful sunset while leaning on the balcony railing, but the railing snaps and Donald falls 20 stories. In a negligence analysis, one can reasonably conclude that Hotel owes Donald both a general duty and a special duty (innkeeper) and that the duty was breached because the rail presumably was defective in some way. To establish cause in fact, one would ask: But for the breach of duty by Hotel, would Donald have suffered damages? The answer is clearly no because if Hotel hadn't breached its duty (e.g., had inspected and kept the railing in good repair), Donald would not have suffered damages. Thus, the breach of duty by Hotel was the *cause in fact* of Donald's injuries.

Scope of But-For Test

One problem in applying the but-for test is its overreaching broadness. Its application may result in holding a tortfeasor liable for injuries that occurred well beyond the foreseeable scope of the wrongdoing. For example, in the Donald-Hotel case, suppose that after Hotel's balcony rail snaps, Donald falls, but the broken balcony rail also falls and penetrates the windshield of a car on the street below, injuring the driver. The injury causes the driver of the car to swerve, hit a pedestrian, and crash into an adjacent canal. A witness to the accident then attempts to rescue the driver of the car from the canal, but he drowns doing so. Five blocks away, a shopkeeper is so startled by the noise from the accident that she drops a priceless vase on her foot. In this set of accidental chain reactions, using the but-for test would impose liability on Hotel for each injury/damage, including those sustained by Donald, the driver of the car, the struck pedestrian, the drowned rescuer, and the shopkeeper. Yet, a sense of fairness demands that the law cannot reasonably impose *all* of this liability on Hotel. At what point, if any, is the tortfeasor relieved from liability? The broad sweep of the but-for test requires a further step to establish liability. This step, known as **proximate (legal) cause**, is discussed next.

Proximate (Legal) Cause

In addition to showing that the tortfeasor's breach of duty was the cause in fact of the damages, the injured party also must prove that (1) the tortfeasor's conduct was also the closest-in-proximity cause of the damages and (2) the tortfeasor's liability wasn't canceled due to a superseding cause. These *proximate cause* concepts protect tortfeasors from liability for far-reaching and out-of-the-ordinary injuries resulting in damages from the tortious act.

Closest-in-Proximity

The majority of courts favor using *foreseeability* to define the scope of the risk. In the Donald-Hotel example above, the jury would be charged with determining the scope of Hotel's liability. Liability would hinge on whether or not it was foreseeable that a faulty balcony railing would result in damages to be suffered by Donald (probable liability), the driver of the car (possible liability), the pedestrian (possible liability), the drowned rescuer (improbable liability), and the owner of the vase (very improbable liability). The Restatements define proximate cause as that which helps draw the line that determines when a tortfeasor is "not liable for harm different from harms whose risk made the [tortfeasor's] conduct tortious."

This proximate cause concept was first enunciated in Landmark Case 42.4, perhaps the most famous case in American tort law.

LANDMARK CASE 42.4 Palsgraf v. Long Island Railroad Co., 162 N.E. 99 (Ct. App. N.Y. 1928)

FACT SUMMARY Palsgraf bought a railroad ticket for Rockaway Beach, New York, and was waiting on the platform for her train. A different train arrived on a platform 100 yards away, allowed passengers to board, and began to depart from the station. Running to catch the departing train, two commuters grabbed onto the side and tried to hoist themselves up and into the moving car. To aid one of the men, the conductor on the train pulled him onto the train but dislodged a package covered in newspaper that the passenger was carrying. The package, which turned out to be fireworks, fell to the platform and exploded. The blast shook the station with sufficient force that large iron scales (used to weigh freight on various trains) hanging over Palsgraf fell on her, resulting in a severe injury. Palsgraf sued the Long Island Railroad for the conductor's negligent conduct of pulling the commuter onto the train, which caused the explosion and her injury from the falling scales.

SYNOPSIS OF DECISION AND OPINION In a famous opinion written by Judge Benjamin Cardozo (who would later serve on the U.S. Supreme Court), the New York Court of Appeals ruled in favor of the Long Island Railroad. Cardozo reasoned that because the conductor *could not have known* the man he was helping onto the train was carrying a package full of fireworks, the action of the conductor was not a proximate enough cause to incur liability for Palsgraf's injuries.

WORDS OF THE COURT: Proximate Cause "[T]he orbit of the danger as disclosed to the eye of reasonable vigilance would be the orbit of the duty. One who jostles one's neighbor in a crowd does not invade the rights of others standing at the outer fringe when the unintended contact casts a bomb upon the ground. The wrongdoer as to them is the man who carries the bomb, not the one who explodes it without suspicion of the danger. Life will have to be made over, and human nature transformed, before prevision so extravagant can be accepted as the norm of conduct, the customary standard to which behavior must conform. [. . .] The risk reasonably to be perceived defines the duty to be obeyed, and risk imports relation; it is risk to another or to others within the range of apprehension."

Case Questions

1. Are all the other elements of a negligence tort satisfied in this case?

2. Who else might Palsgraf have sued? For what?

3. *Focus on Critical Thinking:* Context is always important. This case was decided before any federal or state benefits for health care or lost time from work. The dissenting opinion in this case argued that public policy demanded that the railroad pay for the injury because it was in the best position to pay and that some correlation existed between conduct and injury. In the 1928 context, does that strike you as a convincing argument? Why or why not?

Superseding Cause Sometimes an *intervening* event takes place after the tortfeasor's negligent act. This intervening act may also contribute to that negligence in causing additional damages to the injured party. Some (but not all) of these intervening acts may be the basis for limiting a tortfeasor's liability. These acts, called *superseding causes* (i.e., they supersede the tortfeasor's liability), are also defined by *foreseeability*. For example, in the Donald-Hotel case, suppose that Donald only fell one story and sustained a broken wrist.

While being driven to the hospital, a freak tornado hits the car that Donald is in and the wrist injury is made worse. In a case for damages related to the injury, even though the but-for test would impose liability on Hotel even for the aggravated broken wrist, Hotel's liability is discontinued (though not eliminated for the original injury) once the tornado hits as a superseding cause, and Hotel is not liable for the aggravated injury. This limit applies because it was not reasonably foreseeable by Hotel that Donald would be injured by a tornado en route to the hospital.

✅ Quick Quiz Proximate Cause

Is proximate cause met in these situations?

1. A truck driver crashes into a guardrail. During the accident, a defective steering wheel rapidly spins around, breaking the driver's arm. The driver sues the maker of the steering mechanism.

2. A tenant hurts herself falling down defective steps. The tenant sues the landlord's insurance company, alleging that it knew the steps were defective but insured the landlord anyway, thus discouraging the landlord from fixing them.

3. An employer burns down his warehouse for the insurance money. An employee is arrested and falsely imprisoned by the police for the crime. The employee sues the employer for negligence.

4. A passenger is injured in an automobile accident. The passenger sues the liquor store that sold alcohol to the driver of the car, who was already visibly intoxicated.

Answers to this Quick Quiz are provided at the end of the chapter.

Actual Damages   In order to recover in a negligence case, the tortfeasor must have caused another party **actual damages**. This means that the party alleging injury must prove that she suffered some type of *physical harm* derived from an injury caused by the tortfeasor. An injured party may not prevail if the injuries were limited to mental/emotional harm alone. However, once a party has proved some physical harm, she is eligible for a variety of other types of damages, including out-of-pocket economic losses (such as medical bills), pain and suffering, lost time from employment, and similar categories. Punitive damages may be awarded, but they are rare because they can only be awarded when the tortfeasor's conduct was extremely reckless or willful and wanton.[18]

Many states also allow a spouse or children of an injured party to recover damages related to the negligence. This includes loss of companionship or marital relations (known as *loss of consortium*). Moreover, if the injured party dies, her estate may sue for any damages that the injured party would have recovered had she survived. A person's estate includes not only land, assets, and personal property, but it also includes legal rights and entitlements after death. This includes the right to sue for the tortious conduct that caused the death. Spouses and children may also recover damages for losses sustained by virtue of the death of an injured party.

---

[18]Punitive damages were sought in 12 percent of the estimated 25,000 tort and contract trials concluded in state courts in 2005. Punitive damages were awarded in 700 (5 percent) of the 14,359 trials in which the plaintiff prevailed. Among the trials in which punitive damages were requested by plaintiff winners, 30 percent received these damages. The median punitive-damage award among the 700 trials that resulted in punitive damages was $64,000 in 2005, and 13 percent of these cases had punitive awards of $1 million or more. (*Punitive Damage Awards in State Courts, 2005,* Special Report, U.S. Department of Justice, Office of Justice Programs, 2011.)

DEFENSES TO NEGLIGENCE CLAIMS

Once the elements of negligence are met, the analysis then shifts to potential defenses available to the tortfeasor. The two primary defenses to claims of negligence are *comparative negligence* and *assumption of the risk.*

Comparative Negligence

In cases in which the injured party's conduct has played a factor in the harm suffered, the Restatements allow the tortfeasor to assert the defense of **comparative negligence**. This defense requires a jury to divide up the proportion of negligence committed by the parties in terms of percentage (see Figure 42.1). Ultimately, successfully asserting comparative negligence reduces (but does not eliminate) the final award to the plaintiff.

Comparative negligence is a cousin to the common law doctrine of *contributory negligence,* whereby even *1 percent* of negligence on the part of the plaintiff is a complete bar to any plaintiff recovery. The overwhelming majority of states do not follow this standard because of its harshness on the injured party. Four states—Alabama, Maryland, North Carolina, and Virginia—along with the District of Columbia continue to recognize the contributory negligence defense. Indiana follows the contributory negligence rule in medical malpractice cases only.

Assumption of the Risk

When an injured party knows that a substantial and apparent risk is associated with certain conduct, and the party goes ahead with the dangerous activity anyway, the Restatements allow the tortfeasor to assert the defense of **assumption of the risk** so long as (1) the injured party/plaintiff knew or should have known (by virtue of the circumstances or warning signs, etc.) that a risk of harm was inherent in the activity and (2) the injured party/plaintiff voluntarily participated in the activity. Certain activities are considered to be "inherently dangerous" (such as bungee jumping or parachuting), and companies that provide these activities may have limited protection from liability if they acted reasonably in minimizing the dangers and made full disclosures of the risks to participants.

In Case 42.5, a state appellate court considers the assumption of the risk defense in the context of leisure sports.

FIGURE 42.1	Comparative Negligence Formula

Suppose Abel is injured by Baker's conduct and suffers damages totaling $100,000. A jury finds that Baker was 80 percent responsible for the injury but that Abel also contributed to his own injury and was 20 percent responsible for the harm. How much does Abel ultimately recover?

Damages suffered	×	Percentage of Baker's negligence	=	Recovery amount
$100,000	×	80%	=	$80,000

CASE 42.5 Zeidman v. Fisher, 980 A.2d 637 (Pa. Super. Ct. 2009)

FACT SUMMARY Zeidman and Fisher were participants in a golf foursome at a charity tournament. On one hole where the view of the fairway was partially blocked, the foursome became concerned that they might inadvertently hit any players that might be hidden by the blind spots on the fairway ahead of them. The group agreed that Zeidman would take a golf cart and ride ahead to see if the course was clear

(continued)

for the group to hit. Zeidman made his observation and returned to his foursome in the cart. Because he intended to return to his foursome to report that the group ahead was out of harm's way and because he never signaled to his group that it was safe to hit, Zeidman never entertained the possibility that one of his group would hit a shot. Before Zeidman returned, Fisher, becoming impatient, hit his shot while Zeidman was driving his cart back to the foursome. Fisher's shot was errant and the ball struck Zeidman in the face, causing serious and permanent injuries. The trial court dismissed Zeidman's negligence lawsuit against Fisher on summary judgment, ruling that Zeidman had assumed the risk of participating in the golf match, which barred any recovery. Zeidman appealed.

SYNOPSIS OF DECISION AND OPINION   The Pennsylvania Superior Court reversed the trial court's decision and ruled in favor of Zeidman. The court reasoned that the assumption of the risk doctrine requires that the evidence show that the injured party (1) fully understood the specific risk, (2) voluntarily chose to encounter it, and (3) manifested a willingness to accept the known risk. In this case, an objectively reasonable person may have assumed that no risk existed because Zeidman's agreed-upon task was to check whether the fairway was clear and then report his findings to his own foursome. Because he had not yet completed this task, Zeidman did not manifest a willingness to accept a known risk.

WORDS OF THE COURT: Assumption of the Risk Doctrine   "In the circumstances of the present case, it is obvious that Zeidman, on returning from his forward observer mission, did not consciously assume the risk of friendly fire when, to the contrary, he had every right to anticipate none of his playing partners would attempt a tee shot until his return to the tee box. To grant summary judgment on the basis of assumption of the risk it must first be concluded, as a matter of law, that the party consciously appreciated the risk that attended a certain endeavor. . . . Accordingly, whether Zeidman is able to convince a jury that his version of events is true remains to be seen, he, in any event, is entitled to his day in court."

Case Questions

1. If Zeidman had signaled to his partners that all was clear from the fairway and was then hit while returning in the cart, would Fisher be entitled to a summary judgment based on assumption of the risk?

2. What duty did Fisher owe Zeidman in the first place? Was it a special relationship duty?

3. *Focus on Critical Thinking:* What other leisure sports or activities might be covered under the assumption of the risk doctrine? Is it good public policy to shield negligent parties with the doctrine?

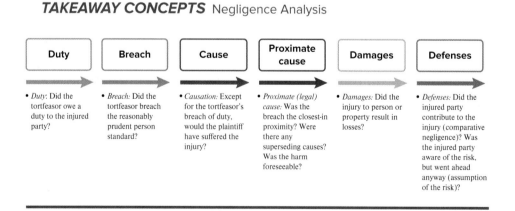

TAKEAWAY CONCEPTS Negligence Analysis

Duty	Breach	Cause	Proximate cause	Damages	Defenses
• *Duty:* Did the tortfeasor owe a duty to the injured party?	• *Breach:* Did the tortfeasor breach the reasonably prudent person standard?	• *Causation:* Except for the tortfeasor's breach of duty, would the plaintiff have suffered the injury?	• *Proximate (legal) cause:* Was the breach the closest-in proximity? Were there any superseding causes? Was the harm foreseeable?	• *Damages:* Did the injury to person or property result in losses?	• *Defenses:* Did the injured party contribute to the injury (comparative negligence)? Was the injured party aware of the risk, but went ahead anyway (assumption of the risk)?

STRICT LIABILITY TORTS

LO 42-7

Reach a conclusion based on a strict products liability analysis and applicable defenses.

The tort liability theories covered so far in this chapter have been based on either intent or negligence. The Restatements also provide for liability in certain cases where neither intent nor negligence need be proved. This category of tort is known as *strict liability* and is recognized in the Restatements primarily for abnormally dangerous activities and for defective products (discussed in the next section).[19] Strict liability is rooted in the notion that the general public benefits when liability is imposed on those who engage in certain activities that result in harm to another party, even if the activities are undertaken in the most careful manner possible (without negligence).

Abnormally Dangerous Activities

The Restatements set out a six-factor test to determine whether abnormally dangerous activities trigger strict liability for any harm caused by the activity.

1. Does the activity involve a high degree of risk of some harm?
2. Is there a likelihood that the harm that results will be great?
3. Is it possible to eliminate the risk by exercising reasonable care?
4. Is the activity relatively common?
5. Is the location of the activity appropriate to the risk?
6. Is there any community value that outweighs the dangerous attributes?

For example, suppose that ChemicalCo produces 100 pounds of plastic explosives for use in the demolition of a building. The company leases a railroad car and ships the explosives to its storage warehouse until the buyer can pick them up. Before the buyer picks up the shipment, thieves break in and inadvertently ignite the car. The explosion causes damage to several buildings and an injury to a party standing in the surrounding area. Using the six-factor test, a court will likely impose strict liability on ChemicalCo due to the nature of the abnormally dangerous activity of the storage of explosives. Other strict liability cases involve storage and use of toxic chemicals, flammable liquids, nuclear power, and blasting for demolition or construction.

PRODUCTS LIABILITY

Products liability refers to the liability of any seller (including the manufacturer, retailer, and any intermediary seller such as a wholesaler) of a product that, because of a defect, causes harm to a consumer. Note that modern products liability law protects not only the actual purchaser, but also any ultimate users that are harmed by the product's defect. In a products liability case, the injured party may pursue a legal remedy against the seller under one of three theories: (1) negligence, (2) warranty, or (3) strict liability.

Negligence

The negligence analysis covered earlier in this chapter may also be applied to the seller of a product. Although historically negligence was severely limited as a remedy because the law protected only the actual purchaser, a revised rule announced in the landmark case of *MacPherson v. Buick*[20] has been adopted in every state. Under the *MacPherson* rule, one

---

[19]Strict liability is also imposed under the common law for the keepers of wild or dangerous animals.

[20]111 N.E. 1050 (N.Y. 1916). The historical requirement that negligence suits could only be brought by the direct purchaser was known as *privity of contract.*

who negligently manufacturers a product is liable for *any injuries to persons* (and, in some limited cases, property) proximately caused by the negligence. For example, suppose that Holmes purchases a motorcycle from a dealer and gives it to his son Wendell. Wendell is injured on the motorcycle and sues the manufacturer for negligence. So long as Wendell can prove negligence, the manufacturer will be liable for Wendell's injuries despite the fact that Wendell was not the one who entered into the purchase agreement with the dealer or the manufacturer.

Courts have found that manufacturers have the duty of care regarding proper design, manufacturing, testing, inspection, and shipping. Retailers do not have as comprehensive a duty as the manufacturer, but they still have a duty to warn consumers of any product they know or suspect to be unreasonably dangerous.

Warranty

Historically, warranty laws were important protection for purchasers because they imposed liability even in the absence of negligence. Recall from Chapter 18, "Sales Warranties," that a warranty is a particular representation and guarantee to the user about a product. When the seller makes a representation of fact about a product, this is known as an *express* warranty. If the seller has not made a specific representation about the product, the buyer still may be protected by a Uniform Commercial Code–imposed *implied* warranty. Because warranties are set out in Article 2 (Sales) of the UCC, they are discussed in detail in Chapter 18.

Strict Liability

The most appealing option for pursuing a products liability case is the doctrine of strict liability, because the injured party need not prove the elements of negligence. In *Greenman v. Yuba Power Products, Inc.,*[21] the California Supreme Court decided a groundbreaking case that paved the way for adoption of a strict liability standard for product defects by ruling that "a manufacturer is strictly liable in tort when an article he places on the market, knowing that it is to be used without inspection for defects, proves to have a defect which causes injury to a human being." Two years after the *Greenman* case was decided, a similar doctrine of strict liability tort for the sellers of products was included in the *Restatements (Second) of Torts* in § 402A. The Restatements specifically indicate that liability still exists even if the seller used all possible care. Note that the term *seller* means not only the product's manufacturer, but also all the parties through the chain of commerce, including the retailer.

Section 402A is a bedrock for strict products liability because a substantial majority of states have adopted the section that imposes special liability on the seller of a product that could harm the user. Specifically, § 402A imposes strict liability on the seller so long as the injured party can show that the product was in a *defective* condition and that the defect rendered the product *unreasonably dangerous.* Section 402A liability is triggered only when:

- the seller is engaged in the business of selling such a product; and
- the product is expected to and does reach the user or consumer without a substantial change in the condition in which it is sold.

Section 402A's strict liability is imposed on the seller even though:

- the seller has exercised all possible care in the preparation and sale of the product; and
- the user or consumer has not bought the product from or entered into any contractual relationship with the seller.

---

[21]377 P.2d 897 (Cal. 1963).

Defining "Defect" In order to recover for an injury caused by a product, the product must have been defective and must have created a danger that is outside the reasonable consumer's expectations. Courts have recognized several theories of unreasonably dangerous defects.

Design or Manufacturing Defect A product may become dangerous if it is *designed* improperly in that foreseeable risks of harm posed by the product could have been reduced or avoided by some *alternative* design. Even products that are designed properly may still be rendered dangerously defective by some mistake made during the *manufacturing* process. For example, suppose CarCo designs a new car intended to have higher than average gas mileage. They achieve this by moving the gas tank to a different position on the car. The design, however, results in the gas tank rupturing during a rear-end crash. This is a classic design defect. However, if CarCo designs the new car properly but one of the factory workers improperly installs the brakes, which eventually results in an injury, the product has been rendered unreasonably dangerous via a manufacturing defect.

Inadequate Warning Products that are ostensibly safe may also carry risks unknown to a reasonable consumer. In such cases, the law requires the product to carry sufficient warnings and instructions. Most courts have held that the manufacturer of a product has a duty to warn unless the danger is "open and obvious." Failure to warn may render the product unreasonably dangerous even absent any manufacturing or design defect. One common category of inadequate warning cases involves prescription drugs, but the theory of unreasonable danger applies to all products that carry some danger in use (such as a lawn mower or snow thrower). In Case 42.6, an appellate court in California considers a failure to warn claim against the manufacturer of an aboveground pool.

CASE 42.6 Bunch v. Hoffinger Industries, 20 Cal. Rptr. 3d 780 (Cal. App. 2004)

FACT SUMMARY Bunch, an 11-year-old girl, dove into an aboveground pool that was only four feet deep. As a result, Bunch suffered a severe injury to her spine that rendered her a quadriplegic. Bunch filed suit against Hoffinger as the manufacturer of the pool liner alleging, among other theories, that Hoffinger was liable for failing to provide adequate warnings that could have prevented the tragedy. Hoffinger argued that it did not owe any duty to warn consumers because the danger was "open and obvious." At trial, Bunch testified that she saw only a sticker that depicted a man doing a "pike" dive (knees straight and body bent at the waist) with the word "caution" and she thought that the caution referred only to pike diving. Bunch also called expert witnesses to testify that warnings to children between the ages of 7 and 12 must be concrete and spell out any consequences of diving into shallow

water. Another of Bunch's experts testified that the risk of spinal paraplegia was not readily apparent to an 11-year-old and that it was difficult for someone in that age group to judge the depth of a pool. Hoffinger countered that (1) warning labels on pools were not feasible before it left the factory because the label would become distorted by the stretching of the liner and (2) Bunch had assumed the risk because she had swum at that same pool prior to that occasion and ignored an adult present at the pool who warned against diving. The jury returned a verdict in Bunch's favor and awarded her $16,112,306. Hoffinger appealed.

SYNOPSIS OF DECISION AND OPINION The California Court of Appeals affirmed the judgment and verdict in favor of Bunch. The court rejected Hoffinger's contention that it owed no duty to warn

(continued)

Bunch of possible head injury from the open and obvious danger of diving headfirst into a shallow aboveground pool. Although the court acknowledged that some previous cases have held that no recovery was available for those who made a shallow dive into an aboveground pool because the danger was obvious, they distinguished those cases from the facts in this case because Bunch was only 11 years old. Age was one of the important factors in determining an awareness of open or obvious danger. It also rejected Hoffinger's assumption of the risk argument and ruled that any assumed risk by an injured party does not insulate equipment suppliers from liability for injury from providing defective equipment.

With respect to the failure-to-warn issue, the court held that the jury's conclusions were sound and in accord with expert testimony that pool industry standards require manufacturers to prominently display permanent warnings on their pools and that Hoffinger's sticker was below industry standards. Thus, the court concluded that the record supported the jury's determination that Hoffinger's warnings were inadequate.

WORDS OF THE COURT: Lack of Effective Warning "Given the testimony of Bunch and her two expert witnesses, we find sufficient evidence to support the conclusion that the lack of an adequate warning label was neither a negligible nor theoretical contribution to Bunch's injury. The evidence presented at trial revealed that the lack of a persuasive label outlining the consequences of diving into the pool was a substantial factor in causing the injury. As the [California] Supreme Court points out 'a very minor force that does cause harm is a substantial factor.' Here, at the very least, the lack of an effective warning was a minor force in bringing about the fateful dive."

Case Questions

1. Why is the injured party's age one of the most important factors in considering a failure-to-warn claim?

2. Do you agree with Hoffinger's contention that the injured party assumed the risk? Why or why not?

3. *Focus on Critical Thinking:* What other products can you think of that may require a more effective warning given the age of the average user? Should bicycles, skateboards, and snowboards fall into the same category? Why or why not?

Improper Packaging   A product can be rendered unreasonably dangerous by a defect in the packaging. Cases that have recognized this theory of defect are primarily asserted against manufacturers of products that require safety-proof containers as well as food or beverage packages that clearly indicate whether the product has been tampered with (such as a seal on a bottle of juice). Perhaps the most famous improper packaging case involved the well-publicized Tylenol scare in 1986. In *Elsroth v. Johnson & Johnson,*[22] a federal court in New York held that Johnson & Johnson, the manufacturer of Tylenol, was not liable for the death of a consumer who was the victim of tampering by an unknown third party. The estate of the consumer brought suit, claiming that improper packaging had led to the tampering when an unknown third party removed a package of Tylenol from a supermarket shelf, laced it with cyanide, and then resealed the container and box so the tampering was not readily detectable. However, the court pointed to the fact that the Tylenol bottle featured a foil seal glued to the mouth of the container, a shrink-wrap seal around the neck and cap of the bottle, and a box sealed with glue in which the bottle was placed. Because Johnson & Johnson went above and beyond existing standards by using three different methods to prevent consumption of a tampered product, the company could not be held liable under § 402A.

Unavoidably Unsafe   Some products are inherently dangerous. That is, some products are designed and manufactured correctly, and adequate warning has been given, but the product is still dangerous. Courts have struggled to adjudicate strict liability standards in

---

[22]700 F. Supp. 151 (1988).

Products Liability and Guns

The prevalence of gun violence in America has led some victims to use products liability theories in an attempt to halt sales of certain guns used in mass shootings and to hold gun manufacturers liable for damages suffered by the victims. The families of the victims in the 2012 Sandy Hook Elementary School massacre in Newtown, Connecticut, filed a products liability lawsuit against Remington Firearms International for, among other claims, wrongful death and pain and suffering. Remington is the parent company that manufactures and markets the Bushmaster XM-15, a version of the notorious AR-15 semiautomatic rifle. The AR-15 has a bloody pedigree. In addition to the Sandy Hook murders, killers used an AR-15 style rifle in mass shootings at a high school in Parkland, Florida (2018), a concert in Las Vegas, Nevada (2017), a nightclub in Orlando, Florida (2016), a workplace in San Bernardino, California (2015), community college campuses in Roseburg, Oregon (2015), and Santa Monica, California (2013), and a movie theater in Aurora, Colorado (2012).

Sandy Hook Lawsuit

The Sandy Hook lawsuit is a products liability claim based on both negligence and strict liability for unsafe products. The suit alleged that the AR-15 is the "weapon of choice for shooters looking to inflict maximum casualties," and "American schools are on the forefront of such violence."[23] The Sandy Hook plaintiffs drew on similar legal strategies used in the past to hold cigarette manufacturers liable for smoking-related deaths. As more than 40 states brought lawsuits against the tobacco industry by 1998, manufacturers agreed to an array of marketing and product use restrictions such as a ban on billboards, transit advertisements, and tobacco brand logos on clothing and merchandise. The tobacco settlement also required cigarette makers to pay $1.45 billion to finance advertisements deterring underage tobacco

use. Despite the settlement, tobacco companies still faced increasingly successful lawsuits from individuals and were stung recently by a $51 million award of a California jury to a heavy smoker with inoperable lung cancer. The jury rejected big tobacco's standard defense, assumption of the risk, after finding substantial evidence that tobacco manufacturers had conspired to cover up the known dangers and addictions of cigarette smoking for decades.[24] Tobacco companies continue to suffer heavy losses in courtrooms across America.

Statutory Barriers

The Sandy Hook plaintiffs had to overcome a significant barrier that tobacco plaintiffs did not. The Protection of Lawful Commerce in Arms Act (PLCAA)[25] exempts gun manufacturers from products liability lawsuits brought by parties suffering damages as a result of a third party's criminal act. The law was a response to a wave of products liability lawsuits filed against gun manufacturers starting in 2002. Nonetheless, the law does contain important exceptions related to negligent entrustment and improper marketing. Therefore, the Sandy Hook plaintiffs strategically decided to focus primarily on Remington's marketing and sales strategies as reckless:

> Remington knowingly sold the AR-15 with no conceivable use . . . other than the mass killing of other human beings and unscrupulously marketed and promoted the assaultive qualities and military uses of AR-15s to a demographic of young civilians. . . . Invoking the unparalleled destructive power of the weapon, [Remington's] advertising copy read: "Forces of opposition, bow down. You are single-handedly outnumbered."[26]

Remington filed a motion to dismiss the lawsuit asserting immunity under the PLCAA. The trial court refused to dismiss the claims ruling that the Sandy Hook plaintiffs had asserted a legally cognizable theory that Remington's conduct fell into a

(continued)

---

[23]*Soto v. Bushmaster Firearms,* Conn. Super. Ct., Plaintiff's First Amended Complaint (Oct. 29, 2015).

[24]*Williams v. Phillip Morris, Inc.,* 2002 WL 1677722 (N.D. Cal. 2002).

[25]15 U.S.C. §§ 7901 et seq.

[26]*Soto v. Bushmaster Firearms,* Conn. Super. Ct., Plaintiff's First Amended Complaint 72–74 (Oct. 29, 2015).

PLCAA exception. The court ruled that the issue of whether the PLCAA exception applied was one for a jury and therefore the lawsuit could not be dismissed.[27]

State Consumer Protection Law

Facing the prospect of overcoming the PLCAA, the Sandy Hook plaintiffs pursued a claim against Bushmaster under the Connecticut Unfair Trade Practices Act (CUTPA). Their claim centered on a statutory prohibition of "unethical, oppressive, immoral and unscrupulous" advertising within the meaning of CUTPA because Bushmaster's marketing campaign promoted the illegal offensive use of the rifle used in the killings. In a victory that some legal scholars called "stunning" the Connecticut Supreme Court agreed that the Sandy Hook case could proceed to trial under CUTPA and that the PLCAA did not bar the CUTPA claim.[28]

Discussion Questions

1. Should gun manufacturers be held strictly liable for harm caused by their products? Why or why not? Is it good public policy?

2. Compare and contrast the theories used by tobacco plaintiffs versus gun manufacturing plaintiffs. How are they similar and how are they distinguishable?

3. Why did Congress opt to pass legislation to protect gun manufacturers when no other industry has similar protection? Was it pure politics, or is there a policy justification? Was it ethical?

4. *The Wall Street Journal* reported that the sale of guns increased after the Sandy Hook and Orlando massacres. How do you account for that phenomenon?

5. According to CNBC, over 5 million Americans own an AR-15 style weapon.[29] As a practical matter, would an outright ban on the weapon be effective? What would be the commercial, social, and political impacts of a government-imposed ban on semiautomatic rifles?

6. Use your favorite search engine to find "Sandy Hook Hoax," which reveals a dark side of social media. Should the First Amendment cover such speech? What remedies are available to the families of the victims against the hoax theorists? Is the theory of Sandy Hook as a hoax proper subject matter to debate? Should Facebook or other social media sites take action against the hoax theorists?

cases relating to prescription drugs, cigarettes, and guns. In each case, the product was properly manufactured and designed. The evolving view of products liability theories for cigarettes and guns is explored in more detail in the nearby Law, Ethics, and Society feature.

Causation and Damages

Once it has been established that the product was unreasonably dangerous, the injured party need now prove only that the defective product was the cause of the injuries and that the product caused an actual injury that resulted in damages.

Seller's Defenses

Although strict liability imposes a relatively onerous burden on the seller, the law recognizes several defenses for a seller even if the injured party has established all of the required elements for liability.

---

[27] *Soto v. Bushmaster Firearms,* Conn. Super. Ct., Memorandum of Decision, Docket FBT-CV-15-6048103-S (April 14, 2016).

[28] *Soto v. Bushmaster Firearms,* 202 A.3d 262 (Conn. 2019).

[29] www.cnbc.com/2016/06/13/owned-by-5-million-americans-ar-15-under-renewed-fire-after-orlandomassacre.html.

Substantial Change   The Restatements draw a line of liability based on the condition of the product at the time it leaves the seller's control. In order for strict liability to apply, the product must reach the end user without substantial change. Thus, if a product leaves the manufacturing plant in a reasonable condition (not dangerous) and then is contaminated or damaged in the next stage of the commercial chain of delivery, any resulting harm is outside the strict liability model. Depending on the circumstances, of course, the manufacturer may still be liable for negligence, but not under strict liability.

Assumption of the Risk   Although courts apply the assumption of the risk defense narrowly,[30] it is still recognized as a defense for sellers in a strict products liability case. An injured party has assumed the risk if the party knew or should have known about the risk and disregarded this risk by continuing with the activity at issue for her own benefit. For example, suppose that WidgetCo owns a high-speed machine for producing widgets and a foreign object lodges in the machine while it is operating. The instructions warn to shut down the machine before removing the object, but the plant manager decides against a shutdown, fearing it will cost money from lost production time. If the plant manager is injured while removing the object from the operating machinery and sues the machine's manufacturer under a strict product liability theory, the manufacturer may successfully assert the assumption of the risk defense.[31]

Misuse of Product   When the injured party may *not* have known of a certain risk but fails to use the product in a manner in which an ordinarily prudent person would, then the seller may use product misuse as a defense. Courts have been reluctant to allow this defense unless that particular use of the product was so far from its ordinary use that it was not reasonably foreseeable by the seller.

---

[30]See "Assumption of Risk and Strict Products Liability," 95 *Harvard Law Review* 95, no. 4 (Feb. 1982), p. 872.

[31]Based on *Micallef v. Miehle Co.,* 348 N.E.2d 571 (N.Y. Ct. App. 1976).

 THINKING STRATEGICALLY

Managing Risk through Liability Waivers

PROBLEM: As we've discussed in this chapter, business ventures may have some degree of risk as part of their business model. Although amateur sports and recreation facilities are one example, consider the broad-based risks to which other businesses may be exposed. For instance, a 2018 article from the *Journal of Emergency Medicine* recounts the case of a patient who suffered a tear in his esophagus after participating in a local restaurant's pepper eating contest.[32]

STRATEGIC SOLUTION: Limit liability through an effective voluntary waiver (sometimes called a *release*).

---

[32]A. Arens, et al. "Esophageal Rupture after Ghost Pepper Ingestion," *Journal of Emergency Medicine* 51, no. 6 (Dec. 2016).

This can be an effective way to transfer risk at no cost. Although state statutes vary considerably as to the effectiveness of these waivers, there are some commonalities that help to limit a business's liability when a customer is injured while engaging in an activity that is part of the business model.

■ Courts generally are hostile to waivers of liability, so it is imperative that you work with an attorney to use precise waiver language in the document. The waiver must clearly state that the customer is waiving legal rights related to any possible negligence or strict liability by the business that results in an injury. The more specific the risk, the more likely that a customer cannot claim that he did not know, understand, or accept the risk. The waiver should be a stand-alone document and should not be incorporated with other customer documents, such as membership or billing agreements. Note that in cases of gross negligence or reckless conduct, courts typically will not enforce a waiver.

- Make the waiver part of your standard operating procedures. If waivers are used sporadically or inconsistently (e.g., only some customers sign it) or if customers are made to believe the waiver is a funny part of a marketing campaign, a court may find that the waiver was not signed knowingly and is therefore invalid. Customers at Mikey's Late Night Slice in Columbus, Ohio, are required to sign a waiver before eating their "Fiery Death with Hate Sausage," a pizza loaded with a mix of spicy peppers. According to the owner of Mikey's, "We do everything we can within reason to let them know this is not a joke."[33]

---

[33]B. Parkin, "Want to Try Our Insanely Spicy Pizza with 'Hate Sausage'? First, Sign the Waiver," *The Wall Street Journal,* Jan. 17, 2018.

- Don't depend on signs or general notices posted in the business. Obtain a signed waiver from each individual. This helps to make the case that each individual knew and voluntarily accepted the risk.

QUESTIONS

1. Have you ever signed a liability waiver? Was it related to amateur sports, such as skiing, golf, racquetball, or the like? Did you understand what you were waiving?

2. Is it ethical for a business to ask for a waiver? Isn't the idea behind the tort system to spread risk among parties? In theory, a waiver eliminates all the risk on one side and allocates it to the other side. Is that fair?

3. Should minors be able to sign a waiver without parental consent? Why or why not?

KEY TERMS

Tort p. 775   A civil wrong in which one party's action or inaction causes a loss to be suffered by another party.

Tortfeasor p. 775   One who commits a civil wrong against another that results in injury to person or property.

Tortious conduct p. 775   The wrongful action or inaction of a tortfeasor.

Restatement of Torts p. 775   An influential document issued by the American Law Institute (ALI) that summarizes the general principles of U.S. tort law and is recognized by the courts as a source of widely applied principles of law. The ALI has amended the Restatements twice, resulting in the *Restatement (Second) of Torts* and the *Restatement (Third) of Torts.*

Intentional torts p. 775   A category of torts in which the tortfeasor was willful in bringing about a particular event that caused harm to another party.

Negligence p. 776   A category of torts in which the tortfeasor was without willful intent in bringing about a particular event that caused harm to another party.

Strict liability p. 776   A category of torts in which a tortfeasor may be held liable for an act regardless of intent or willfulness; applies primarily to cases of defective products and abnormally dangerous activities.

Libel p. 776   Written defamation in which someone publishes in print (words or pictures), writes, or broadcasts

through radio, television, or film an untruth about another that will do harm to that person's reputation for honesty or subject a party to hate, contempt, or ridicule.

Slander p. 776   Oral defamation in which someone tells one or more persons an untruth about another that will harm the reputation for honesty of the person defamed or subject a party to hate, contempt, or ridicule.

Absolute privilege p. 777   A defense to a defamation claim whereby the defendant need not proffer any further evidence to assert the defense; provided to government officials, judicial officers and proceedings, and state legislatures.

Qualified privilege p. 777   A defense to a defamation claim whereby the defendant must offer evidence of good faith and be absent of malice to be shielded from liability; provided for the media and employers.

Trade libel p. 779   A tort in which a competitor has made a false statement that disparaged a competing product.

Product disparagement statutes p. 779   Statutes intended to protect the interest of a state's major industries, such as agriculture, dairy, or beef.

Merchant's privilege p. 780   A narrow privilege, provided for in the Restatements, that shields a merchant from liability for temporarily detaining a party who is reasonably suspected of stealing merchandise.

Duty p. 784   A fundamental element that must be proved to recover in a negligence lawsuit against a tortfeasor: The injured party must prove that the tortfeasor owed him a duty of care.

Misfeasance p. 785   An act by one party that harms or endangers another party.

Nonfeasance p. 785   The failure to act or intervene in a certain situation.

Special relationship p. 785   In tort law, a heightened duty created between certain parties, such as that of a common carrier to its passengers, innkeepers to guests, employers to employees, businesses to patrons, a school to students, and a landlord to tenants and landowners.

Breach of duty p. 789   A fundamental element that must be proved to recover a negligence lawsuit against a tortfeasor: The injured party must prove that the tortfeasor failed to exercise reasonable care in fulfilling her obligations.

Cause in fact p. 790   A fundamental element that must be proved to recover in a negligence lawsuit against a tortfeasor:

The injured party must prove that, if not for the breach of duty by the tortfeasor, he would not have suffered damages.

Proximate (legal) cause p. 790   A fundamental element that must be proved to recover a negligence lawsuit against a tortfeasor: The injured party must prove a legally recognized and close-in-proximity link between the breach of duty and the damages suffered.

Actual damages p. 792   A fundamental element that must be proved to recover in a negligence lawsuit against a tortfeasor: The injured party must prove that she suffered some physical harm that resulted in identifiable losses.

Comparative negligence p. 793   A defense to claims of negligence in which the injured party's conduct has played a factor in the harm suffered and, thus, the proportion of negligence should be divided.

Assumption of the risk p. 793   A defense to claims of negligence in which the injured party knew that a substantial and apparent risk was associated with certain conduct and the party went ahead with the dangerous activity anyway.

CASE SUMMARY 42.1 Mattison v. Johnston, 730 P.2d 286 (Ariz. App. 1986)

Tortious Interference

Mattison owned Hidden Hills Beauty Salon and hired Drowne as a hair stylist in 1982. In 1984, Drowne signed a contract agreeing not to work at any competing hair salon within one year of termination from Hidden Hills (known as a *restrictive covenant contract*). Over the next 10 months, Johnston, the owner of a competing beauty salon located one-half mile from Hidden Hills, actively solicited Drowne to leave Hidden Hills and work for his salon. Eventually, Drowne quit Hidden Hills and began working for Johnston. Mattison sued

Johnston for intentional interference with the restrictive covenant contract. Johnston claimed he was simply engaging in standard business competition and that it was Drowne's individual choice to break her contract with Hidden Hills.

CASE QUESTIONS

1. Who prevails and why? Are there conflicting public policy concerns in this case?
2. Why would Mattison sue Johnston for interference rather than suing Drowne for breach?

CASE SUMMARY 42.2 Maher v. Best Western Inn, 717 So. 2d 97 (Fla. App. 5th Dist. 1998)

Special Relationships

Maher was a blind woman who checked into a Best Western Inn that welcomed pets like her Seeing Eye dog, Ina. Shortly after Maher checked in with her parents, another motel patron walked by with two unleashed dogs—a German shepherd and a pit bull. The two unleashed dogs attacked Ina, Maher, and her parents. Maher sued Best Western for negligence.

CASE QUESTIONS

1. What duty did Best Western owe Maher?
2. Was it *reasonable* for Best Western to do more to prevent the attack?
3. Would a bystander have had a duty to prevent the attack had it occurred on the street?

CASE SUMMARY 42.3 Wurtzel v. Starbucks Coffee Co., 257 F. Supp. 2d 520 (E.D.N.Y. 2003)

Res Ipsa Loquitur

Wurtzel bought a cup of coffee in her local Starbucks and placed it in her car's cup holder. While making a turn shortly after leaving the store, the lid came off the coffee and the liquid spilled over Wurtzel's right leg, burning her severely. Wurtzel never looked to see if the lid was on correctly and did not see the coffee spill or the clerk secure the lid to the cup. She sued Starbucks for negligence, invoking the doctrine of *res ipsa loquitur*.

CASE QUESTIONS

1. Was Starbucks clearly negligent without any need for witnesses?
2. Who else may have been negligent?

CASE SUMMARY 42.4 Coker v. Wal-Mart Stores, Inc., 642 So. 2d 774 (Fla. App. 1st Dist. 1994)

Negligence Per Se

Bonifay and Fordham bought a box of .32 caliber bullets from a Walmart store in Florida. Four hours later, the two men robbed an auto-parts store and killed Coker with those same bullets. When they bought the ammunition, Bonifay and Fordham were both under 21 years of age. The federal Gun Control Act makes it illegal to sell ammunition to anyone under 21. Coker's wife sued Walmart for the wrongful death of her husband.

CASE QUESTIONS

1. Is Walmart liable?
2. What if it was reasonable to assume that the two men were over 21?
3. Could Walmart have foreseen the robbery any more than the train conductor could have foreseen the package full of fireworks in *Palsgraf*?

CASE SUMMARY 42.5 Burton v. MDC PGA Plaza Corp., 78 So. 3d 732 (Fla. App. 4th Dist. 2012)

Dangerous Condition and Comparative Negligence

Burton worked for a marketing and merchandising company that helped new retail businesses prepare for openings. She was brought in to work at a new CVS Pharmacy getting ready for its grand opening. While unloading trucks, Burton noticed a pothole about 10 or 15 feet from the store's back door. The pothole was approximately 1 foot wide and 2 inches deep. Burton informed her co-workers and CVS's management of the pothole and urged everyone to exercise caution. One week later, Burton was seriously injured when, while loading a vehicle, she stepped into the pothole, tripped, and fell to the ground. Burton filed suit against both CVS and its landlord, MDC.

CASE QUESTIONS

1. Can a property owner be liable for injuries when a dangerous condition is open and obvious? Does the owner have a duty to warn when the dangerous condition is open and obvious?
2. Can a property owner be liable for injuries when a dangerous condition is open and obvious and the injured party was well aware of the dangerous condition?
3. Does Burton's knowledge of the dangerous condition merely raise an issue of fact as to her own comparative negligence?

1. **Which of the following is not an element of defamation?**
   a. Specificity
   b. Damages
   c. Dissemination to a third party
   d. Malice
   e. None of the above

2. **A breach of duty may be established by showing:**
   a. Violation of a safety statute.
   b. Breach of common law standards of behavior.
   c. *Res ipsa loquitur* ("the thing/matter speaks for itself").
   d. A, B, and C
   e. A and B

3. **Ginger uses the wrong type of cleaner fluid to clean out the deep fryer in her café and causes an explosion. The explosion causes the café's front window to shatter, and a pedestrian walking on the public sidewalk in front of the café at the time of the explosion is injured. In a suit against Ginger for negligence:**
   a. Ginger wins because she owed no duty to the pedestrian.
   b. Ginger wins because there is not sufficient proximate cause.
   c. The pedestrian wins because Ginger owes him a special duty.
   d. The pedestrian wins because Ginger's actions were the cause and proximate cause of the injury.
   e. The pedestrian wins due to strict liability.

4. **Stuart attends a baseball game and, on his way to his seat, he is struck by a foul ball. He sues the stadium owner for negligence. What will be the owner's best defense?**
   a. Contributory negligence
   b. Comparative negligence

   c. Assumption of the risk
   d. Products liability
   e. Misuse of the product

5. **A product may be unreasonably dangerous due to a _____ or _____ defect.**
   a. risk, reward
   b. risk, design
   c. design, manufacturing
   d. manufacturing, assumption
   e. strict, negligence

6. **A defendant asserting absolute privilege as a defense to defamation need not offer any further evidence to assert the defense.**
   a. True
   b. False

7. **Tortious interference with an existing contractual relationship is a strict liability tort.**
   a. True
   b. False

8. **The law imposes a general duty to rescue another who is in peril.**
   a. True
   b. False

9. **Landowners owe both a general duty to the public and a special duty to a licensee (e.g., a social guest).**
   a. True
   b. False

10. **Comparative negligence is a defense whereby the injured party knows about a substantial risk associated with certain conduct and accepts that risk.**
    a. True
    b. False

 Quick Quiz ANSWERS
Intentional Torts

1. Defamation. Specifically, it is slander because the statements Jason made were oral.
2. No tort has been committed. This is not a tortious interference with a contract because Third Bank merely offered a better price for its services and MOT made the decision to switch.

3. Trespass to chattel. Wayne has interfered with his company's ability to use the car and will be responsible for the repairs and any damages suffered by the company because the car is unavailable.

4. Conversion. Nancy is stealing the stationery supplies and is civilly responsible for paying the company back for the full value of the supplies she has taken.

5. No tort has been committed. This is not a fraud because the deal had already been agreed to and the intentionally false statement was not material to the deal.

Proximate Cause

1. Yes. The injury (broken arm) was sufficiently proximate to the negligence (defective steering column). See *McCown v. International Harvester Co.,* 342 A.2d 381.

2. No. There were too many acts of intervening negligence on the part of the landlord. See *Matthias v. United Pacific Ins. Co.,* 67 Cal. Rptr. 511, 514.

3. Yes. It was reasonably foreseeable that the employee would have been falsely arrested for the fire. The jury found that the employer had framed the employee. See *Seidel v. Greenberg,* 260 A.2d 863, 871.

4. Yes. It was reasonably foreseeable and violated state dram shop laws. See *Gonzales v. Krueger,* 799 P.2d 1318, 1321.

CHAPTER REVIEW QUESTIONS: Answers and Explanations

1. d. Malice is only required when the defamed party is a public figure or to disqualify a qualified privilege (e.g., media). Answers *a, b,* and *c* are incorrect because they are all elements of a defamation claim.

2. d. Each of the listed responses in answers *a, b,* and *c* is a breach of duty.

3. d. Ginger owes a general duty not to cause harm to the pedestrian. This duty was breached (*res ipsa*) and the explosion was the cause and proximate cause of the injuries. Answer *a* is incorrect because she owes him a general duty. Answer *b* is nonsensical. Answer *c* is incorrect because there is no special duty owed, only a general duty.

4. c. The fan knew of the risk, understood the risk, and went ahead with the activity. Answers *a* and *b* are incorrect because the fan did not contribute to his own injury. Answer *d* is unrelated to a negligence analysis.

5. c. Products can be made unreasonably dangerous by either a design (improperly engineered) or a manufacturing (improperly made) defect. Answers *a,*

b, and *c* are wrong because each contains a term unrelated to products liability.

6. a. True. Defendants asserting absolute privilege as a defense to defamation need not offer any further evidence to assert the defense. Only defendants asserting qualified privilege need to offer evidence of good faith.

7. b. False. Tortious interference with an existing contractual relationship is an intentional tort, not a strict liability tort.

8. b. False. The law imposes a general duty only to act as a reasonably prudent person would, and there is no general duty to act/rescue.

9. a. True. Landowners owe both a general duty (to parties off their land) and a special duty (to certain parties on their land).

10. b. False. Comparative negligence is a defense whereby the injured party contributes to his own damages. When a party knows about a substantial risk associated with certain conduct, this is called assumption of the risk.

CHAPTER 43

Administrative Law

THINKING STRATEGICALLY

©valterZ/Shutterstock

Businesses will inevitably face regulations and the regulators tasked with overseeing the enforcement and compliance of applicable laws. Legally astute managers understand the importance of engaging regulators to ensure compliance with the law. At the end of this chapter, you will consider a situation where a business owner must respond to an administrative enforcement action.

Learning Objectives

After studying this chapter, students who have mastered the material will be able to:

43-1 Explain how administrative agencies derive authority from statutes to regulate business.

43-2 Describe the sources of administrative law.

43-3 Categorize the functions of administrative agencies.

43-4 Distinguish the types of limits on administrative agency authority.

43-5 Demonstrate how state and federal administrative laws relate to one another.

CHAPTER OVERVIEW

Administrative law is, to put it plainly, where the law and its implementation meet. Many of the legal issues that businesses encounter will be decided by administrative agencies applying administrative law. For example, if a restaurateur wishes to open an establishment, she will likely need to obtain financing or counseling from the Small Business Administration, obtain a building and signage permit and a liquor license, establish procedures to operate a kitchen that passes a health inspection, register a trademark, and resolve employment-related disputes. Each of these real-world legal issues will be primarily addressed by a state or federal agency applying administrative law. This chapter offers a guide to administrative law and its processes as an important aspect of business regulation.

©Alija/Getty Imageas

ADMINISTRATIVE LAW IN A BUSINESS CONTEXT

The restaurant example provided in the chapter opener is not a unique setting. Businesses of all sizes and across different sectors interact with administrative agencies. Some federal agencies such as the Internal Revenue Service have sweeping authority over millions of individuals and businesses. Other agencies such as the California Department of Resources Recycling and Recovery, which administers mandatory recycling programs, are more specialized and operate at the state level.

Business regulation has generally increased, and as a result administrative law's reach over business has greatly expanded and increased in complexity. This has occurred because many competing stakeholders demand that the government regulate business activities to protect society's diverse interests. For example, consumers in the financial sector may seek protection against the unequal bargaining power large banks have relative to consumers. Labor groups advocate for expanded worker protections. Environmentalists advocate for laws that penalize companies that pollute the environment. Businesses also have a powerful voice and seek laws and regulations that promote their interests. For example, pharmaceutical companies seek strong patent laws to protect their investments in research and development. Manufacturers seek limits on product liability tort claims. High-tech firms prefer flexible immigration laws that provide them with access to an educated migrant workforce.

Legislators must respond to these various stakeholders and enact legislation that promotes the betterment of society as the by-product of legislative compromise. Legislation, however, is just a starting point; there must also be a government actor to ensure that the law is being faithfully implemented as intended by the legislature. This important task falls within the executive branch of government headed by the president. Every time the legislature enacts legislation, either an existing administrative agency must oversee the new law or a new agency must be created to oversee it. The statutes that create an agency or give the agency explicit authority to implement a statute are called **enabling statutes**.

For example, in 2011 the U.S. Congress updated the patent laws when it enacted the America Invents Act (AIA). A key aspect of this legislation was the creation of a new tribunal called the Patent Trial and Appeal Board (PTAB) within the U.S. Patent and Trademark Office (USPTO) to review patent application denials and oversee challenges to existing patents. The USPTO is the administrative agency within the president's administration that

LO 43-1

Explain how administrative agencies derive authority from statutes to regulate business.

FIGURE 43.1	Statutory Enabling Language Authorizing the PTAB's Creation

"**§ 6. Patent Trial and Appeal Board**

"(a) In General.—There shall be in the Office a Patent Trial and Appeal Board. The Director, the Deputy Director, the Commissioner for Patents, the Commissioner for Trademarks, and the administrative patent judges shall constitute the Patent Trial and Appeal Board. The administrative patent judges shall be persons of competent legal knowledge and scientific ability who are appointed by the Secretary, in consultation with the Director. Any reference in any Federal law, Executive order, rule, regulation, or delegation of authority, or any document of or pertaining to the Board of Patent Appeals and Interferences is deemed to refer to the Patent Trial and Appeal Board.

"(b) Duties.—The Patent Trial and Appeal Board shall—

"(1) on written appeal of an applicant, review adverse decisions of examiners upon applications for patents pursuant to section 134(a);

"(2) review appeals of reexaminations pursuant to section 134(b);

"(3) conduct derivation proceedings pursuant to section 135; and

"(4) conduct inter partes reviews and post-grant reviews pursuant to chapters 31 and 32.

approves or denies patent applications and oversees the execution of the Patent Act. The AIA's enabling legislation language, which authorizes the USPTO to create the PTAB and to decide patent challenges (called *reexaminations* and *reviews*), is reproduced in Figure 43.1.

The PTAB has an active docket now that businesses have a faster and less expensive administrative option to challenge the validity of competitors' patents compared to the more expensive and lengthy patent invalidity litigation process available in the federal trial courts. The Law, Ethics, and Society feature below discusses an ethical and strategic issue that emerged as an unintended consequence of the PTAB's creation.

Federal regulatory agencies include bodies that function within a particular executive branch department (e.g., the Internal Revenue Service functioning within the Department of the Treasury) as well as nondepartment agencies (e.g., the Environmental Protection Agency). The federal government also has independent agencies (e.g., the Securities and Exchange Commission) that have been designated by Congress as independent of the executive branch and do not exist by virtue of the authority of the president or a department. Departments are headed by a cabinet secretary who reports directly to the president. Department agencies, nondepartment agencies, and independent agencies are either headed by administrators or composed of commissioners and headed by the commission chair. These department, nondepartment, and independent agencies are collectively referred to as **administrative agencies**.

Figure 43.2 is an organizational chart that shows the major federal administrative agencies.

LAW, ETHICS, AND SOCIETY

State Sovereignty for Sale?

Some patent owners believe that the administrative courts within the PTAB benefit those who favor a weaker patent system, such as large firms in the financial or high-tech industries, because the odds of invalidating a patent at the PTAB are higher than those in trial court. Some have gone so far as to describe the PTAB's administrative courts as "patent death squads."

Enterprising attorneys from the Dallas law firm Shore, Chan, DePumpo may have found a strategically ingenious and controversial method for removing patent invalidity suits at the PTAB. This firm advises patent owners, such as branded pharmaceutical companies, to sell their patents to state universities and Native American tribes and then sign exclusive license

agreements with the universities and tribes to practice the patents. This transaction transfers patent ownership to the universities and tribes, who then assert constitutionally derived sovereign immunity against the PTAB and file motions to withdraw the patent challenges.

Some members of Congress view this as "state sovereignty for sale" and have threatened to sponsor legislation to withdraw sovereign immunity for these purposes. The courts have yet to decide on the legality of this patent transfer strategy.

Discussion Questions

1. What do you think of this legal strategy to remove cases from the PTAB?

2. When is it desirable or ethical to weaken patent rights?

TAKEAWAY CONCEPTS Administrative Law in a Business Context

- Business regulation has generally increased, and as a result administrative law's reach over business has greatly expanded and increased in complexity.
- Every time the legislature enacts legislation, an existing administrative agency must oversee the new law or a new agency must be created to oversee it.
- The statutes that create an agency or give the agency explicit authority to implement a statute are called enabling statutes.
- Department, nondepartment, and independent agencies are collectively referred to as administrative agencies.

FIGURE 43.2

Administrative Agencies in the Context of the U.S. Government Organization Chart

The Government of the United States

The Constitution

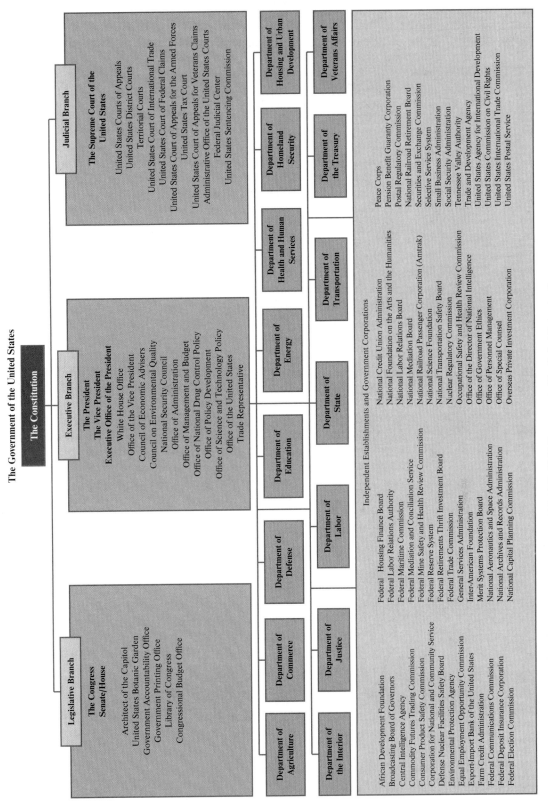

Legislative Branch

The Congress
Senate/House

Architect of the Capitol
United States Botanic Garden
Government Accountability Office
Government Printing Office
Library of Congress
Congressional Budget Office

Executive Branch

The President
The Vice President
Executive Office of the President
White House Office
Office of the Vice President
Council of Economic Advisers
Council on Environmental Quality
National Security Council
Office of Administration
Office of Management and Budget
Office of National Drug Control Policy
Office of Policy Development
Office of Science and Technology Policy
Office of the United States
Trade Representative

Judicial Branch

The Supreme Court of the United States

United States Courts of Appeals
United States District Courts
Territorial Courts
United States Court of International Trade
United States Court of Federal Claims
United States Tax Court
United States Court of Appeals for the Armed Forces
United States Court of Appeals for Veterans Claims
Administrative Office of the United States Courts
Federal Judicial Center
United States Sentencing Commission

Department of Agriculture

Department of Commerce

Department of Defense

Department of Education

Department of Energy

Department of Health and Human Services

Department of Homeland Security

Department of Housing and Urban Development

Department of the Interior

Department of Justice

Department of Labor

Department of State

Department of Transportation

Department of the Treasury

Department of Veterans Affairs

Independent Establishments and Government Corporations

African Development Foundation
Broadcasting Board of Governors
Central Intelligence Agency
Commodity Futures Trading Commission
Consumer Product Safety Commission
Corporation for National and Community Service
Defense Nuclear Facilities Safety Board
Environmental Protection Agency
Equal Employment Opportunity Commission
Export-Import Bank of the United States
Farm Credit Administration
Federal Communications Commission
Federal Deposit Insurance Corporation
Federal Election Commission

Federal Housing Finance Board
Federal Labor Relations Authority
Federal Maritime Commission
Federal Mediation and Conciliation Service
Federal Mine Safety and Health Review Commission
Federal Reserve System
Federal Retirements Thrift Investment Board
Federal Trade Commission
General Services Administration
Inter-American Foundation
Merit Systems Protection Board
National Aeronautics and Space Administration
National Archives and Records Administration
National Capital Planning Commission

National Credit Union Administration
National Foundation on the Arts and the Humanities
National Labor Relations Board
National Mediation Board
National Railroad Passenger Corporation (Amtrak)
National Science Foundation
National Transportation Safety Board
Nuclear Regulatory Commission
Occupational Safety and Health Review Commission
Office of the Director of National Intelligence
Office of Government Ethics
Office of Personnel Management
Office of Special Counsel
Overseas Private Investment Corporation

Peace Corps
Pension Benefit Guaranty Corporation
Postal Regulatory Commission
National Railroad Retirement Board
Securities and Exchange Commission
Selective Service System
Small Business Administration
Social Security Administration
Tennessee Valley Authority
Trade and Development Agency
United States Agency for International Development
United States Commission on Civil Rights
United States International Trade Commission
United States Postal Service

Source: https://www.gpo.gov/fdsys/pkg/GOVMAN-2015-07-01/pdf/GOVMAN-2015-07-01-Government-of-the-United-States-4.pdf.

SOURCES OF ADMINISTRATIVE LAW

Administrative law integrates four distinct sources of law that operate in conjunction: the U.S. Constitution, enabling statutes, the Administrative Procedure Act (APA), and the common law.

The U.S. Constitution

As discussed in Chapter 3, the U.S. Constitution establishes a national government of three coordinating branches. Article I vests legislative power in the Congress; Article II vests executive power in the president; and Article III vests judicial power in the federal court system. This separation of powers was designed to prevent any branch of government from obtaining too much power. James Madison said, "The accumulation of all powers, legislative, executive, and judiciary in the same hands, whether of one, a few, or many, and whether hereditary, self appointed, or elective, may justly be pronounced the very definition of tyranny."[1]

Administrative agencies, however, can occupy an uncomfortable position within a constitutional system of separation of powers. The constitutional authority of administrative agencies fits within the president's Article II power to implement, or carry out, legislation. However, as discussed in the next section, agencies often have broad authority to enact rules that have the effect of legislation and to conduct trials and hearings in ways that are similar to how the courts operate. Some have consequently said that federal agencies make up a "fourth branch of government," because large agencies can combine extensive powers that resemble those of the legislative, executive, and judicial branches.

In light of the broad authority some agencies possess, the Constitution places limits on the type of powers that agencies may exercise and how agencies go about executing their functions. For example, the Constitution may limit agency actions that violate the Fourth Amendment against unreasonable searches or seizures or the Due Process Clause, which protects fundamental expectations of fairness. Courts can also review the scope of an agency's authority and may determine that the agency action violates the constitutional principle of separation of powers, or more specifically the **nondelegation doctrine**. The nondelegation doctrine stands for the proposition that Congress may not give an agency so much rulemaking discretion that Congress abdicates its responsibility to exercise "[a]ll legislative Powers" granted in the Constitution."[2] The U.S. Supreme Court nonetheless recognizes that in a complex society such as ours, Congress is unable to do its job unless it delegates substantial rulemaking authority under broad directives to administrative agencies.

Enabling Statutes

When agencies make decisions that impact the rights of individuals or businesses, they must act pursuant to legal authority granted by a statute. As previously mentioned, when Congress authorizes an existing agency or creates a new administrative agency, it passes a federal law called an enabling statute. Enabling statutes are important because they are the source of an agency's authority and establish the agency's scope and jurisdiction over certain matters. For example, in 1970 Congress passed the Occupational Safety and Health Act,[3] which established the Occupational Safety and Health Administration (OSHA). OSHA's mission is the prevention of workplace injuries and the assurance of safe working conditions

---

[1]The Federalist No. 47 (1788).

[2]U.S. Constitution, Article I, § 1.

[3]29 U.S.C, §§ 651–678.

FIGURE 43.3	The Flow of Administrative Authority to Regulate Business

Congress authorizes agency with an enabling statute → Agency creates rules pursuant to delegated statutory authority → Businesses are subject to administrative agency's rules and authority

for employees. The enabling portion of the law placed OSHA under the authority of the Department of Labor, provided for the jurisdiction necessary to study and develop workplace safety regulations, and established the agency's authority to investigate, enforce, and adjudicate matters involving those regulations.

Figure 43.3 provides an overview of how administrative agencies derive authority to regulate businesses.

The Administrative Procedure Act (APA)

The Administrative Procedure Act (APA)[4] of 1946 is a federal statute that imposes specific procedural requirements on administrative agencies' various functions and is discussed in greater detail below. The APA also provides for the judicial review of agency actions and determinations.

Common Law

Prior to the establishment of the APA, a body of common law existed that regulated administrative agencies. While much of the common law has been codified through the APA, courts sometimes still refer to the common law when they apply or interpret the APA.

TAKEAWAY CONCEPTS Sources of Administrative Law

- Administrative law combines four distinct sources of law that operate in tandem: the U.S. Constitution, enabling statutes, the Administrative Procedure Act (APA), and the common law.
- The constitutional authority of administrative agencies fits within the president's Article II power to implement, or carry out, legislation.
- Courts can review the scope of an agency's authority and may determine that the agency action violates the constitutional principle of separation of powers, or more specifically, the nondelegation doctrine.
- When agencies make decisions that impact the rights of individuals or businesses, they must act pursuant to legal authority granted by a statute.

---

[4]5 U.S.C. §§ 551–706.

PRIMARY FUNCTIONS OF ADMINISTRATIVE AGENCIES

Agencies primarily engage in the following activities:

Rulemaking
Licensing
Investigation and enforcement
Adjudications
Administering public benefits

These activities as they relate to business will be discussed in the following sections.

Rulemaking

Rulemaking is the agency process for making rules, which can have a similar effect as legislation. Agency rules that have legal effect and impact the rights of parties are known as **legislative rules**. An agency can create legislative rules only if it is authorized to do so by statute. For example, in 1970 Congress enacted the Highway Safety Act, which created the National Highway Traffic Safety Administration (NHTSA). The enabling language of this statute authorized the NHTSA to administer safety standards for motor vehicles. Because it was authorized to further this legislative objective, the NHTSA developed a rule, called Standard 111–Rear Visibility, which states that "[e]ach passenger car shall have an inside rearview mirror . . . " The rules issued by the NHTSA and all other federal administrative agencies are published in the **Code of Federal Regulations**, or CFR.

Other rules express an agency's interpretation of a statute or describe the agency's policy views. These **nonlegislative rules** are not legally binding on parties. Under the APA, many of an agency's rulemaking duties are carried out through **informal rulemaking**, procedures that are permitted under the basic structure of the APA.[5] Despite its name, informal rulemaking actually involves a detailed procedure set down in the APA that centers on the concepts of notice, public comment, publication of a final rule, and the opportunity to challenge a rule in court. **Formal rulemaking** is used only when Congress has specifically indicated in the enabling statute that the agency rules must be made "on the record after a hearing." In the case of formal rulemaking, the agency is required to engage in an extensive hearing process, outlined in the APA, to develop the rules.[6] Formal rulemaking is a fairly cumbersome process and is seldom used. Instead, the vast majority of administrative rules are adopted through the informal rulemaking process comprised of the following steps:

1. The agency conducts a study and research.
2. The agency gives public notice and publication of the proposed rule.
3. The agency solicits public comments.
4. The agency revises and publishes the final rule.

The informal rulemaking process yields legislative and nonlegislative rules that can substantially impact businesses. Each of the informal rulemaking steps is discussed below.

---

[5]APA § 553.
[6]APA §§ 556 and 557.

Agency Study and Research   Depending on any specific mandates in the enabling statute, the agency begins to study and research the various alternatives for achieving the goals set by Congress. In some cases, such as in environmental regulation, much of the study and research function is performed by government scientists or outside experts who provide data and conclusions to regulatory policymakers in the agency. In addition to working with scientists, outside experts, and policymakers, regulatory agencies also typically employ a significant number of attorneys who ensure that the rulemaking process is compliant with various sources of administrative law.

Notice: Publication of the Proposed Rule   After research and study, the agency drafts a proposed rule that seeks to achieve one or more objectives set out in the enabling statute. The APA requires that notice of proposed rulemaking be published in the *Federal Register* and that the notice must include "actual terms, substance and description" of the proposed rule.[7] In theory, this requirement puts parties that have some stake in the rule on notice that the rule will become law unless the regulatory agency is persuaded otherwise or a court challenge is initiated. Agencies are also required to publicly disclose any studies, reports, data, or other pertinent material that the agency relied upon to create the proposed rule.

Figure 43.4 is an excerpt from the *Federal Register.* It sets out a proposed rule by the Environmental Protection Agency pursuant to its authority under the Clean Air Act.

Public Comment   Once the proposed rule has been published in the *Federal Register,* the agency must then give time for the public to comment. In fact, the APA requires that the affected parties be allowed to participate in the rulemaking through submission of their own research and findings and that the agency make a good faith effort to study anything submitted. In cases that impact a particular region of the country, agencies sometimes choose to hold public hearings at strategic times and locations during the comment period. In practice, many of the comments and much of the evidence submitted on proposed rules are generally delivered by representatives from, among others, (1) various representatives from business and industry (such as the National Manufacturers Association); (2) professional associations that represent large blocks of constituents (such as the National Association of Realtors); and (3) public advocacy groups (such as the Natural Resources Defense Council).

For example, suppose the Securities and Exchange Commission (SEC) (the federal administrative agency created to execute the Securities Exchange Acts of 1933 and 1934) proposes new rules relating to corporate reporting disclosure requirements for publicly held companies. The SEC would likely expect various groups representing publicly held companies, as well as the executives of the affected companies, to submit comments urging the SEC to avoid making the requirements too burdensome on these companies. On the other hand, the SEC is also likely to receive comments from consumer advocacy and shareholder watchdog groups urging the agency to adopt even stricter disclosure requirements.

Revision or Final Publication   After the comment period has ended, the agency may either revise the rule or simply publish the final rule in the *Federal Register.* If the agency revises the rule between the time that it was originally proposed and the time it is published as final, there is generally no legal obligation to provide an additional comment period. As a practical matter, agencies publishing controversial proposed rules may opt for a second comment period, but there is generally no legal requirement to do so. One exception to this rule occurs when the agency's revised rule is a substantial or material alteration of the originally proposed rule. Courts have given agencies broad latitude to publish a revised final rule without an additional comment period so long as the revisions are a logical outgrowth of the

---

[7]APA § 553.

Federal Register / Vol. 75, No. 13 / Thursday, January 21, 2010 / Proposed Rules   3423

ENVIRONMENTAL PROTECTION AGENCY

40 CFR Part 55

[EPA–R10–OAR–2009–0799; FRL–9095–7]

Outer Continental Shelf Air Regulations Consistency Update for Alaska

AGENCY: Environmental Protection Agency (EPA).

ACTION: Proposed rule.

SUMMARY: EPA is proposing to include in the regulations the revised applicability dates in the emissions user fees provision in 18 AAC 50.410. Requirements applying to Outer Continental Shelf ("OCS") sources located within 25 miles of States' seaward boundaries must be updated periodically to remain consistent with the requirements of the corresponding onshore area ("COA"), as mandated by section 328(a)(1) of the Clean Air Act ("the Act"). The portion of the OCS air regulations that is being updated pertains to the emission user fee requirements for OCS sources operating off of the State of Alaska. The intended effect of approving the OCS requirements for the State of Alaska is to regulate emissions from OCS sources in a manner consistent with the requirements onshore. The change to the existing requirements discussed below is incorporated by reference into the regulations and is listed in the appendix to the OCS air regulations.

DATES: Written comments must be received on or before *February 22, 2010.*

ADDRESSES: Submit your comments, identified by Docket ID Number EPA– R10–OAR–2009–0799, by one of the following methods:

A. *Federal eRulemaking Portal: http://www.regulations.gov:* Follow the on-line instructions for submitting comments;

B. *E-Mail: greaves.natasha@epa.gov;*

C. *Mail:* Natasha Greaves, Federal and Delegated Air Programs Unit, U.S. Environmental Protection Agency, Region 10, 1200 Sixth Avenue, Suite 900, Mail Stop: AWT–107, Seattle, WA 98101;

D. *Hand Delivery:* U.S. Environmental Protection Agency Region 10. Attn: Natasha Greaves (AWT–107), 1200 Sixth Avenue, Seattle, Washington 98101, 9th Floor. Such deliveries are only accepted during normal hours of operation, and special arrangements should be made for deliveries of boxed information.

Please see the direct final rule which is located in the Rules section of this **Federal Register** for detailed instructions on how to submit comments.

FOR FURTHER INFORMATION CONTACT: Natasha Greaves, Federal and Delegated Air Programs Unit, Office of Air, Waste, and Toxics, U.S. Environmental Protection Agency, Region 10,

1200 Sixth Avenue, Suite 900, Mail Stop: AWT–107, Seattle, WA 98101; telephone number: (206) 553–7079; e- mail address: *greaves.natasha@epa.gov.*

SUPPLEMENTARY INFORMATION: Forfurther information, please see the direct final action, of the same title, which is located in the Rules section of this**Federal Register.** EPA is incorporating 18 AAC 50.410 as amended through June 18, 2009 as a direct final rule without prior proposal because EPA views this as noncontroversial and anticipates no adverse comments. A detailed rationale for the approval is set forth in the preamble to the direct final rule. If EPA receives no adverse comments, EPA will not take further action on this proposed rule.If EPA receives adverse comments, EPA will withdraw the direct final rule and it will not take effect. EPA will address all public comments in a subsequent final rule based on this proposed rule. EPA will not institute a second comment period on this action. Any parties interested in commenting on this action should do so at this time. Please note that if we receive adverse comments on an amendment, paragraph, or section of this rule and if that provision may be severed from the remainder of the rule, EPA may adopt as final those provisions of the rule that are not the subject of an adverse comment.

Administrative Requirements

Under the Clean Air Act, the Administrator is required to establish requirements to control air pollution from OCS sources located within 25 miles of States' seaward boundaries that are the same as onshore air control requirements. To comply with this statutory mandate, EPA must incorporate applicable onshore rules into part 55 as they exist onshore. 42 U.S.C. 7627(a)(1); 40 CFR 55.12. Thus, in promulgating OCS consistency updates, EPA's role is to maintain consistency between OCS regulations and the regulations of onshore areas, provided that they meet the criteria of the Clean Air Act. Accordingly, this action simply updates the existing OCS requirements to make them consistent with requirements onshore, without the exercise of policy discretion by EPA. For that reason, this action:

• Is not a "significant regulatory action" subject to review by the Office of Management and Budget under Executive Order 12866 (58 FR 51735, October 4, 1993);

• Is certified as not having a significant economic impact on a substantial number of small entities under the Regulatory Flexibility Act (5 U.S.C. 601 *et seq.*);

• Does not contain any unfunded mandate or significantly or uniquely affect small governments, as described in the Unfunded Mandates Reform Act of 1995 (Pub. L. 104–4);

• Does not have Federalism implications as specified in Executive Order 13132 (64 FR 43255, August 10, 1999);

• Is not an economically significant regulatory action based on health or safety risks subject to Executive Order 13045 (62 FR 19885, April 23, 1997);

• Is not a significant regulatory action subject to Executive Order 13211 (66 FR 28355, May 22, 2001);

• Is not subject to requirements of Section 12(d) of the National Technology Transfer and Advancement Act of 1995 (15 U.S.C. 272 note) because application of those requirements would be inconsistent with the Clean Air Act; and

• Does not provide EPA with the discretionary authority to address, as appropriate, disproportionate human health or environmental effects, using practicable and legally permissible methods, under Executive Order 12898 (59 FR 7629, February 16, 1994).

In addition, this rule does not have tribal implications as specified by Executive Order 13175 (65 FR 67249, November 9, 2000), because it does not have a substantial direct effect on one or more Indian tribes, on the relationship between the Federal Government and Indian tribes, or on the distribution of power and responsibilities between the Federal Government and Indian tribes, nor does it impose substantial direct compliance costs on tribal governments, nor preempt tribal law.

Under the provisions of the Paperwork Reduction Act, 44 U.S.C. 3501*et seq.*, an agency may not conduct or sponsor, and a person is not required to respond to, a collection of information unless it displays a currently valid OMB control number. OMB has approved the information collection requirements contained in 40 CFR part 55 and, by extension, this update to the rules, and has assigned OMB control number 2060–0249. Notice of OMB's approval of EPA Information Collection Request ("ICR") No. 1601.07 was published in the **Federal Register** on February 17, 2009 (74 FR 7432). The approval expires January 31, 2012. As EPA previously indicated (70 FR 65897– 65898 [November 1, 2005]), the annual public reporting and recordkeeping burden for collection of information under 40 CFR part 55 is estimated to average 549 hours per response, using the definition of burden provided in 44 U.S.C. 3502(2).

List of Subjects in 40 CFR Part 55

Environmental protection, Administrative practice and procedures, Air pollution control, Hydrocarbons, Incorporation by reference, Intergovernmental relations, Nitrogen dioxide, Nitrogen oxides, Outer Continental Shelf, Ozone, Particulate matter, Permits, Reporting and recordkeeping requirements, Sulfur oxides.

Dated: December 14, 2009.

Michelle L. Pirzadeh,
Acting Regional Administrator, Region 10.
[FR Doc. 2010–1108 Filed 1–20–10; 8:45 am]
BILLING CODE 6560-50-P

originally proposed rule. Revisions that stay within the original scope of the proposed rule do not trigger the requirement of a second comment period.

In the feature below, a federal administrative agency announced a rule change that will impact millions of Internet users and perhaps the fate of the Internet itself.

In Case 43.1, a federal court of appeals applies the logical outgrowth test of the APA to the U.S. Department of Education's decision to revise a proposed rule and publish it in final form.

CASE 43.1 Association of Private Sector Colleges and Universities v. Duncan and the U.S. Department of Education, 681 F.3d 427 (D.C. Cir. 2012)

FACT SUMMARY Congress passed the Higher Education Act (HEA) to foster access to higher education and provides more than $150 billion in new federal aid to approximately 14 million postsecondary students and their families. Students receiving this aid attend private for-profit institutions, public institutions, and private nonprofit institutions. The U.S. Department of Education ("Department") is charged with the oversight and administration of the HEA. After several investigations into for-profit universities (such as the University of Phoenix) revealed systematic attempts to mislead and engage in fraud, the Department promulgated a set of new rules because it determined that the existing regulations were too lax. The proposed rules impacted institutions of higher education in several operational ways and were intended to deter fraud and improve accountability. After a public comment period, the Department published the final rules as originally proposed, but it also included an additional final rule with new regulatory requirements for colleges offering distance learning.

The final rules were challenged by the Association of Private Sector Colleges and Universities (APSCU), which represents for-profit institutions of higher education. APSCU alleged a violation of the APA on the basis that the Department had failed to provide adequate notice of the distance learning rule to regulated parties. The trial court agreed and ruled in favor of APSCU on the issue of the distance learning rule. The Department appealed arguing that the new distance learning rule was simply a logical outgrowth of the existing rule and that the other proposed regulations gave fair notice that the Department was considering changing the rule related to distance education programs.

SYNOPSIS OF DECISION AND OPINION The Court of Appeals for the D.C. Circuit upheld the trial

court's ruling on the distance learning regulations in favor of APSCU. The court ruled that the Department had not provided interested parties with a sufficient opportunity to comment on the proposed rule and therefore violated the APA. The court rejected the Department's argument that the new rule was a logical outgrowth of the original rule because the new rule was a significant regulatory shift for providers of distance education programs. As such, the Department was required to publish the proposed rule and provide interested parties with an opportunity to comment.

WORDS OF THE COURT: Logical Outgrowth "[The proposed rule] and the final rule need not be identical: '[a]n agency's final rule need only be a logical outgrowth of its notice.' A final rule qualifies as a logical outgrowth 'if interested parties should have anticipated that the change was possible, and thus reasonably should have filed their comments on the subject during the notice-and-comment period.' By contrast, a final rule fails the logical outgrowth test and thus violates the APA's notice requirement where 'interested parties would have had to divine [the agency's] unspoken thoughts, because the final rule was surprisingly distant from the proposed rule' [quoting from *CSX Transportation, Inc. v. Surface Transportation Board*].

"The Department does not point to anything in its Notice of Proposed Rulemaking that specifically addressed distance education. Nor did the Department solicit comments about the adoption of such a rule. These failures cut against the Department's claim that the distance education regulation is a logical outgrowth of the proposed rules. More importantly, we find the Department's claims that parties should have anticipated the regulation [without merit]."

(continued)

Licensing

Administrative agencies regulate and administer laws through **licensing**. Agencies are frequently delegated the statutory power to issue, renew, suspend, or revoke a license to conduct a certain business operation. Once a company is licensed, the agency may impose fines or restrictions upon the licensee for any violation of agency regulations. One of the more high-profile examples of an agency that regulates through licensing is the Federal Communications Commission (FCC), which issues licenses for use of broadcast frequencies. Administrative agencies at the state level often issue occupational licenses and regulate professionals such as attorneys and physicians, as well as occupations such as those of hairstylists and contractors. State administrative agencies are discussed further below.

Investigation and Enforcement

Some agencies also monitor compliance with administrative regulations by conducting **inspections** of businesses and individuals within their jurisdiction. Recall from Chapter 3 that government agents are restricted from engaging in unreasonable searches without a search warrant. Administrative agencies are, of course, covered by the same restriction, and ordinarily an agency must secure an administrative warrant before government agents may enter and inspect a business to monitor compliance with an administrative regulation. Certain businesses are classified as being pervasively regulated and, therefore, the Supreme Court has fashioned an exception to the warrant requirement that covers situations in which the agency conducts regularly scheduled inspections pursuant to a rule. For example, suppose MillCo operates several mills that are subject to a hypothetical enabling statute called the Mill Control Act (MCA). The MCA provides that all mills must be maintained in a certain way and that the administrative agency with jurisdiction over the MCA should enact rules that include monthly inspections to ensure compliance. Any inspections of MillCo's facilities pursuant to the rule would generally not require a warrant because MillCo qualifies as a pervasively regulated business as defined in the MCA.

Even in cases where courts have held that administrative agencies are required to obtain an administrative warrant to conduct an inspection of a business, the Supreme Court has held that agencies are subject to a lower standard of probable cause to obtain a warrant than the standard that must be met by the government to obtain a criminal warrant.

In Case 43.2, a federal appeals court considers the difference between an administrative warrant and a criminal warrant.

In terms of enforcement, the U.S. Supreme Court has ruled that agencies have broad discretion as to when and whom to regulate. This authority, known as the agency's **prosecutorial discretion**, has been held as practically unreviewable by the judiciary. While enabling statutes can sometimes narrow the agency's authority, courts are still highly deferential to an agency's decision on when and how to enforce its regulations. Absent a showing that the

FACT SUMMARY Compliance officers from the Occupational Safety and Health Administration (OSHA)[8] arrived at the facilities of Trinity Marine Products to conduct an inspection pursuant to their authority under the Occupational Safety and Health Act. Trinity's managers turned the OSHA inspectors away, so OSHA obtained an administrative warrant and returned with federal marshals. After the threat of arrest by the marshals, Trinity officials allowed the search under protest. Trinity later brought an action against OSHA, contending that the warrant had been issued without probable cause and that administrative warrants could not be legally executed by using force against nonconsenting parties. Trinity argued that refusal by a party to honor an administrative warrant should trigger a contempt-of-court proceeding to determine the validity of the warrant and that the government may not use force or arrest to enforce an administrative warrant.

SYNOPSIS OF DECISION AND OPINION The Fifth Circuit Court of Appeals ruled in favor of OSHA, reasoning that the standards for probable cause were lower for administrative warrants than for criminal warrants and that federal statutes and case law allowed administrative warrants to be executed using a reasonable degree of force. In this case, the government had shown that it had sufficient information to justify an inspection and, because Trinity would not honor the warrant, that use of the marshals to gain entry was appropriate and consistent with the statutory intent that allows OSHA to "investigate and inspect without delay."

WORDS OF THE COURT: Probable Cause for Administrative Warrants "[A]dministrative warrants are distinguishable from traditional criminal warrants in a number of ways. They have, for instance, a different—linguistically idiosyncratic—'probable' cause standard: Probable cause may be based either on specific evidence of an existing violation, as in the traditional criminal context, or on a lesser showing that 'reasonable legislative or administrative standards for conducting an inspection are satisfied with respect to a particular establishment.'"

Case Questions

1. Would Trinity's case against OSHA have been stronger if the inspectors had shown up with the marshals and forcibly searched the premises without first attempting to inspect without a warrant? Why or why not?

2. What are some examples of situations in which the probable cause standard for administrative warrants would not be met?

3. *Focus on Critical Thinking:* Should the standards for warrants be different for different companies? Does that raise any constitutional concerns? Explain your answers.

agency abused its enforcement discretion, parties challenging administrative agency actions face a substantial hurdle to justify judicial interference. Agencies have a separate division (apart from rulemaking) that carries out enforcement responsibilities through the use of investigators and the agency's Office of General Counsel.

Also within the agencies' enforcement powers is the right to require businesses subject to the agency's jurisdiction to (1) keep certain records for inspection, (2) turn over relevant documents that may be useful to determine compliance with a particular rule, and (3) request statements or other information from the business's principals or managers.

Adjudications

Many, but not all, administrative agencies have authority to adjudicate matters under their jurisdiction. Adjudication is a hearing in which the government and the private party each present evidence in a quasi-judicial setting. In most agencies, the presiding officer is an

---

[8]OSHA is an administrative agency within the Department of Labor.

administrative law judge (ALJ) who is typically an attorney employed by the agency to adjudicate disputes. The judges who resolve patent reviews at the PTAB discussed earlier in this chapter are administrative law judges.

Recall from Chapter 3 that federal adjudicatory powers are constitutionally vested exclusively in federal courts. The federal courts, however, have permitted agency adjudication when it occurs in the context of public rights disputes (a private party dispute with an agency over the agency's action or inaction) or when two private parties are disputing rights that arise within an area of the agency's jurisdiction.[9]

Administering Public Benefits

When Congress confers a benefit to the citizenry at large, administrative agencies are the intermediary parties that distribute those benefits. Agencies are involved in the application process and distribute benefits according to law. These benefits include loan guarantees for students, medical care for the poor and elderly, compensation for workers laid off by their employers, and many other federal programs. For example, the Social Security Administration is responsible for distributing retirement and medical benefits to eligible citizens.

TAKEAWAY CONCEPTS Primary Functions of Administrative Agencies

- Agencies primarily engage in rulemaking; licensing; investigation and enforcement; adjudications; and administering public benefits.

- Rulemaking is the agency process for making rules, which can have a similar effect as legislation.

- Agency rules that have legal effect and impact the rights of parties are known as legislative rules.

- The rules promulgated by the NHTSA and all other federal administrative agencies are published in the Code of Federal Regulations (CFR).

- Other rules called nonlegislative rules express an agency's interpretation of a statute or describe the agency's policy views and are not legally binding on parties.

- Under the APA, many of an agency's rulemaking duties are carried out through informal rulemaking procedures that are permitted under the basic structure of the APA.

- The rulemaking process involves the following: an agency study and research; notice and publication of the proposed rule; public comment; and revision or final publication.

LO 43-4

Distinguish the types of limits on administrative agency authority.

LIMITS ON ADMINISTRATIVE AGENCIES

Although the powers delegated to administrative agencies are broad, it is important to remember that all administrative agencies, including independent agencies, are limited in their authority by the three-part system of the federal government. The legislative, executive, and judicial branches all have various tools to limit the power and authority of administrative agencies. Public oversight also ensures a degree of transparency and accountability.

---

[9]Some agencies use their adjudication power to actually set policy as an alternative method to their traditional rulemaking authority when they wish to take a particular course of action in a given case. This is a controversial method of making policy, but the U.S. Supreme Court has allowed agencies to use adjudication instead of rulemaking in instances where the adjudication promotes a fundamental fairness. However, the Court made clear that this was a relatively narrow power that may be exercised only when fundamental fairness to the parties requires it.

Legislative Oversight

Congress retains significant power to influence, amend, or void the actions of an administrative agency. For example, Congress may exercise its constitutionally granted power of the purse and delay or restrict funding to particular agencies. Congress may also enact legislation that restricts an agency's authority or may pass a law to overrule an administrative regulation. In 1996, Congress amended the APA to restore its own authority to cancel an agency's final rule if (1) both houses agree, (2) the houses pass a resolution to overrule within 60 days, and (3) the overruling resolution is presented to the president.

Congress also has oversight over administrative agencies through the Senate's power of *advice and consent*[10] in the appointment of high-ranking agency administrators. Congress also has the power to remove an administrative agency head via impeachment by the House of Representatives and removal by the Senate. An additional means for Congress to exert influence over agencies is by sponsoring legislative hearings related to administrative actions or policy. These hearings are organized by congressional subcommittees that have direct oversight over administrative agencies.

Executive Control

Administrative agencies are extensions of the executive branch's authority to carry out legislative mandates, and the Supreme Court has acknowledged that the president of the United States has some inherent general right to exercise power over administrative agencies in a variety of ways. Although this inherent power is notoriously vague, from an administrative law perspective, the president's power is derived from the Appointments Clause,[11] executive orders, and to a lesser degree through budgetary control.

The Appointments Clause   The Constitution gives the president the power to appoint "officers of the United States" consistent with the Appointments Clause in Article II. Although subject to confirmation by the Senate, the president has the exclusive right to nominate principal officers such as cabinet members or commissioners of independent agencies that report directly to the president. Although not specifically articulated in the Constitution, the Supreme Court has held that the president also has the power to remove any principal officers at any time with or without cause and without any congressional approval. However, Congress sometimes passes an enablement act with a restriction on the president's power to remove a particular officer of the government. Federal courts have held that this limiting type of statutory restriction is constitutional so long as the restrictions do not impair the president's ability to carry out his constitutional duty. In fact, Congress has designated certain agencies, such as the Securities and Exchange Commission (SEC) and the Federal Trade Commission (FTC), as independent of the president's direct powers, and the heads and commissioners of independent agencies may be removed only for good cause (such as corruption) and not for mere differences in policy views between the agency and the president.

Executive Orders   For the past several decades, presidents have exercised direct power over administrative agencies to accomplish the president's public policy objectives. For example, in 1982 President Reagan, in response to what he perceived as an overly burdensome regulatory system, issued an executive order requiring that all federal administrative agencies submit a cost-benefit analysis along with any proposed regulation as part of a mandatory review process by the Office of Management and Budget (OMB). The OMB was assigned to encourage agencies to be as cost-conscious as possible when imposing regulatory schemes on certain industries. This executive order is thought of as direct power over the agencies because the OMB reports directly to the president.

---

[10]U.S. Constitution Article II, § 2, cl. 2 (the Appointments Clause).

[11]Ibid.

Judicial Review

The APA sets various standards of review for cases where administrative agency actions are challenged in a federal court. Of course, courts will set aside any agency action that is inconsistent with the Constitution. But the APA also authorizes courts to void agency actions if the agency has exceeded its statutory authority or if agency actions have been taken without adhering to the statutorily established procedure.

Statutory Interpretation by Agencies   Because Congress uses very broad objectives when it passes enabling acts and other laws, administrative agencies must sometimes interpret ambiguous statutes to carry out their duties. In 1984, the Supreme Court adopted the *Chevron* test[12] as the framework to analyze the validity of administrative agency statutory interpretation and action. First, courts look to the language of the statutory authority given to the agency by Congress. If the agency's interpretations or actions conflict with the plain-language meaning of the statute, then a court may hold that the agency's interpretation or actions were unlawful. If, however, the statute is silent or ambiguous on the agency's authority, the court applies the **arbitrary and capricious standard** to determine whether the agency's actions were lawful. A heightened standard, known as the *substantial evidence test,* applies only in a relatively small number of cases where the formal rulemaking process has been required by the enabling act.

Applying the Arbitrary and Capricious Standard   To meet the judicial review requirements, agencies must provide evidence that a reasoned decision-making process was used rather than an action that was arbitrary and capricious. This standard applies to all agency actions, including rulemaking, adjudication, enforcement, inspection, and licensing. Arbitrariness and capriciousness is found when the agency has taken action that is not based on a consideration of relevant factors, including viable alternatives available to the regulatory agency, or is a result of a clear error of judgment. The APA specifically requires that courts review only the information that the agency had available to it at the time it took the action in question. Although the power of courts to set aside an administrative agency's action is clear, courts have traditionally been sparing in the use of this power. The U.S. Supreme Court has consistently held that judicial deference to administrative agencies is an important part of administrative law and that a court should not substitute its judgment for that of the agency.[13]

The Supreme Court provided guidance for lower courts in applying the arbitrary and capricious standard in *Motor Vehicle Manufacturing Association v. State Farm Mutual Automobile Association.*[14] In that case, the Court ruled that agency action was arbitrary and capricious if the agency (1) relied on factors that Congress had not intended it to consider, (2) failed to consider an important aspect of the problem, (3) offered an explanation for its decision that ran counter to the evidence before the agency, or (4) offered an explanation that was so implausible that it could not be ascribed to a difference in view or the product of agency expertise.

The arbitrary and capricious standard received significant media attention when it was the central issue in a case challenging the Department of the Interior's six-month ban on deepwater drilling in the wake of the *Deepwater Horizon* (BP) oil spill disaster. The government's drilling moratorium suspended drilling on 33 exploratory wells and halted the issuing of any new permits. In a June 2010 ruling by the U.S. District Court in Louisiana, the government's drilling moratorium was found to be arbitrary and capricious, and the court issued an injunction against the government's action. Judge Martin Feldman wrote that "[t]he court is unable to divine or fathom a relationship between the findings [of the

---

[12]*Chevron USA, Inc. v. NRDC,* 104 S. Ct. 2778 (1984).

[13]*Citizens to Preserve Overton Park, Inc. v. Volpe,* 401 U.S. 402 (1971).

[14]463 U.S. 29 (1983).

government agency] and the immense scope of the moratorium." The court invalidated the agency's actions based on its conclusion that the government failed to "cogently reflect the decision to issue a blanket, generic, indeed punitive, moratorium."[15] Ultimately, the U.S. Secretary of the Interior withdrew the moratorium.

In Case 43.3, a federal appellate court applies the *Motor Vehicle Manufacturing Association* reasoning to a decision by the Federal Election Commission.

Public Accountability

Because administrative agencies are granted broad powers and discretion, Congress has developed several safeguards to make agencies accountable to the public and to make their work as transparent as possible. This is accomplished through statutorily authorized citizen suits as well as mandatory-disclosure laws.

CASE 43.3 Van Hollen v. Federal Election Commission, No. 15-5016 (D.C. Cir. 2016)

FACT SUMMARY In 2002, Congress passed the Bipartisan Campaign Reform Act (BCRA) to regulate electioneering communications, which the law defines as communications that refer to a clearly identified candidate made within 60 days of a general election or 30 days of a primary election. Among other provisions, the BCRA banned corporations and unions from using their general treasuries to fund electioneering communications. In BCRA's wake, the Federal Election Commission (FEC) promulgated several rules to enforce the various statutory reforms. Christopher Van Hollen, Jr. (Van Hollen), a member of the United States House of Representatives, challenged this rule as arbitrary and capricious. The trial court ruled in favor of Van Hollen that the new rules represented an arbitrary and capricious use of the FEC's regulatory authority.

SYNOPSIS OF DECISION AND OPINION The Court of Appeals for the D.C. Circuit reversed the trial court's decision and ruled in favor of the FEC. The court rejected Van Hollen's argument that the FEC failed to adequately explain its decision to adopt the new rules. The court held that, while an agency is required to adequately explain its decision, this does not mean that its explanation must be a model of analytical precision. Rather, so long as the reviewing court can reasonably discern the agency's analytical path, that is sufficient to satisfy the reasoned decision-making standard. The court concluded that

the FEC cleared that low hurdle because it examined the relevant data and articulated a satisfactory explanation for its action, including a rational connection between the facts found and the choice made.

WORDS OF THE COURT: Arbitrary and Capricious Standard "Here, we acknowledge the FEC's explanation was not one of 'ideal clarity,' but, again, ideal clarity is not the standard. The FEC advanced three explanations for its [rule], which we refer to as the 'support,' 'burden,' and 'privacy' rationales. Because we can reasonably discern the FEC's analytical path from these three rationales, we uphold its purpose requirement against Van Hollen's challenge. . . . Granted, as Van Hollen is quick to point out, the FEC's assertions here were not corroborated with any hard evidence [to support its decision]. But these assertions are, at the very least, speculation based firmly in common sense and economic reality."

Case Questions

1. The court ruled that the FEC's rationale was not of "ideal clarity." What is the best way for an agency to avoid a finding of arbitrariness?

2. Why do you think Van Hollen objected to these rules?

3. *Focus on Critical Thinking:* Does the BCRA violate the rights of corporations and unions by banning electioneering completely? Why or why not?

---

[15]*Hornbeck Offshore Services, LLC v. Salazar,* U.S.D.C. Civil Action 10-1663 (E.D. La.).

Private Citizen Suits   In addition to limits imposed on federal administrative agencies by the executive, legislative, and judicial branches, many enabling statutes contain provisions authorizing any member of the public at large who is directly affected by a particular agency action (or inaction) to bring a lawsuit against violators of a particular regulation and/or the administrative agency itself for failing to fulfill a duty imposed by a statute. These suits are called **citizen suits** and are particularly prevalent in statutes related to protection of the environment.

For example, asbestos is a human-made material that was commonly used to make ceiling and floor tiles until the 1980s, when governmental health agencies determined that asbestos dust was linked to cancer. Activist groups such as the Sierra Club and the Natural Resources Defense Council (NRDC) often file citizen suits. In terms of suits against the government, it is important to realize that citizen suits cannot be used to attack the substance of a regulation that has been properly promulgated. Citizen suit provisions may be used only to compel the agency to act in a manner consistent with the enabling act or another federal statute. For example, suppose that Congress passed an enabling statute that required the Occupational Health and Safety Administration (OSHA) to promulgate regulations that provide a safe procedure for the removal of asbestos-laden ceiling tiles within one year of the date of the law's passage. OSHA properly promulgates a regulation pursuant to the statute, but an activist group, Friends of Workers (FOW), believes that the regulations do not do enough to protect employees in workplaces with asbestos. If FOW files a citizen suit against OSHA claiming that OSHA failed to carry out the enabling act's objectives, most courts would dismiss the suit because FOW is challenging the substance of the regulation. However, suppose that OSHA fails to provide any regulations within the statutorily prescribed one-year period. In that case, FOW would be able to bring a citizen suit against OSHA to compel it to promulgate the regulation.

Federal Disclosure Statutes   Another way that administrative agencies are accountable to the public is through transparency, which requires public access to informational records held by the government and disclosures concerning open hearings and other business conducted by federal agencies. Congress provides two primary mechanisms to achieve these transparency objectives: the **Freedom of Information Act (FOIA)**, which gives the public the right to examine a great many government documents, and the Government in the Sunshine Act, which requires that certain agency meetings be open to the public.

The Freedom of Information Act (FOIA—frequently pronounced *foy-a*) was passed by Congress in 1966 (and expanded by amendments in 1974) to open up certain agency records for public inspection. Fundamentally, the FOIA requires agencies to publish certain matters and, upon the request of an individual or agency (such as a media outlet), to allow public inspection of all other records created or obtained by the agency in the course of doing its work. In order to ensure agency cooperation in complying with the FOIA, the law allows private parties to sue the agency if the records are wrongfully withheld.

However, the FOIA also contains nine separate categories of exceptions designed to protect legitimate interests. The most commonly excluded records are documents that contain (1) sensitive national defense or foreign policy information; (2) agency personnel matters or agency policies on purely administrative issues, such as schedules, performance reviews, records related to personnel, medical files, and other private matters; and (3) trade secrets and privileged commercial information, such as a secret process or device submitted by a business to the agency. For example, assume that ProductCo applies to the Environmental Protection Agency for a permit to discharge waste products into a stream after they are treated for pollution using a secret cleaning process designed by ProductCo's scientists. This process would likely need to be identified in ProductCo's permit application and, thus, would be within the ambit of the FOIA. However, it would fall into the trade secret exception and would be protected from disclosure to the public at large.

In Case 43.4, an appellate court considers whether daily calendars of government officials that contain personal entries are records subject to FOIA disclosure.

CASE 43.4 Consumer Federation of America v. Department of Agriculture, 455 F.3d 283 (D.C. Cir. 2006)

FACT SUMMARY In February 2001, the U.S. Department of Agriculture (USDA) published notice of a proposed rule regulating exposure to *Listeria,* a dangerous, food-borne bacterium that can be found in ready-to-eat meat and poultry. The USDA later issued an interim final rule that the Consumer Federation of America (CFA) regarded as significantly weaker than the originally proposed rule. CFA suspected that the interim final rule was the result of pressure applied by industry representatives during lobbying meetings with agency officials.

Seeking to learn whether USDA officials had met exclusively, or nearly exclusively, with industry representatives who favored the weakening of the original proposed rule, CFA filed a Freedom of Information Act (FOIA) request for access to the public calendars of five senior USDA officials and one USDA administrative assistant. When the USDA failed to provide a substantive response within the statutory time period, CFA filed suit in district court to compel production of the calendars.

Ultimately the USDA took the position that the calendars were not "agency records" as defined in the FOIA and therefore CFA had no right to access. The trial court agreed and ruled that the officials' appointment calendars were not agency records. CFA appealed.

SYNOPSIS OF DECISION AND OPINION The D.C. Circuit Court of Appeals ruled in favor of CFA and held that the calendars were agency records under the FOIA and were subject to public access. The court ruled that since the USDA calendars were continually updated, distributed to employees, and used to conduct agency business, the calendars were included under the FOIA. The court pointed out that unlike a personal diary containing an individual's private reflections on his or her work—but which the individual does not rely upon to perform his or her duties—the USDA calendars were in fact relied upon by both their authors and their authors'

colleagues to facilitate the day-to-day operations of the department's work. The court also ruled that the administrative assistant's calendar was *not* an agency record covered by the FOIA because it was not distributed among senior officials and was more of a personal time schedule.

WORDS OF THE COURT: Personal Information and Agency Records "USDA protests that, because the calendars contain personal as well as business entries, they cannot be considered 'agency records.' There is no doubt that the presence of such information may be relevant in determining the use of a document. But as we said in [previous cases], the inclusion of personal information does not, by itself, take material outside the ambit of FOIA. Were that not true, an official could avoid disclosure of the only documentation of a meeting held with industry officials during the pendency of a rulemaking—the very information that CFA seeks in this case—simply by adorning the document with personal entries. In [a previous case], we held that [a government official's] daily agendas were agency records, notwithstanding that the personal information contained in the agendas [was] identical to that found in [his] appointment calendars, which we found to be personal records. The distinguishing factor was that the agendas were distributed to staff for their use in determining [his] availability for meetings."

Case Questions

1. What did CFA expect to uncover through the use of the FOIA?

2. What were the key factors in the court's determination that calendars fell under FOIA?

3. *Focus on Critical Thinking:* If government officials know they will have to reveal their personal calendars, how if at all might this affect necessary debate within or outside the agency?

LO 43-5

Demonstrate how state and federal administrative laws relate to one another.

STATE ADMINISTRATIVE LAW

In addition to federal agencies, business owners and managers should expect to encounter various state administrative agencies. Although our discussion has focused primarily on federal administrative law, state agencies also have significant executive, legislative, and adjudication discretion in matters of state administrative law. Indeed, many state agencies exist to accomplish substantially the same objectives as those of federal agencies, but they operate at a comparatively micro level, with state administrative law more tailored to the needs of a particular state. California, for example, supplements existing federal air pollution regulations with additional state regulations designed to reduce smog problems in its major cities.

States often have their own versions of federal agencies. For example, all states have a department of revenue (or some similarly named agency) that is the state's version of the Internal Revenue Service. States frequently have agencies devoted to the regulation of parties within the state's borders involved in the sale of securities (selling a business entity's stock to the public), environmental protection, business and professional licensing, regulation of banking and insurance companies, workplace safety, consumer protection, and labor and employee antidiscrimination regulations. Federal and state agencies also share information and work together on joint operations. State administrative law often mirrors the federal system in terms of how regulations are developed, implemented, and enforced.

 Quick Quiz State Administrative Regulation

The state legislature is planning to regulate the size of beer growlers that customers can purchase at microbreweries. If you are a microbrewery owner, how will the various functions of the state agency that oversees alcoholic beverages impact your business?

Answers to this Quick Quiz are provided at the end of the chapter.

THINKING STRATEGICALLY

©valterZ/Shutterstock

Responding to an Administrative Investigation

PROBLEM: Companies must be alert to administrative regulations and enforcement actions that relate to a wide variety of business activities.

STRATEGIC SOLUTION: In this case, a business must decide how to best respond to an administrative enforcement action.

Sarah launched a successful start-up company that manufactures and distributes a mayonnaise substitute made from peas called "Fair Mayo." Fair Mayo is touted as being a more environmentally friendly, humane, and healthier option than traditional mayonnaise, which uses eggs as a key ingredient. A few days ago, however, Sarah received a warning letter from the U.S. Food and Drug Administration (FDA), a federal administrative agency. The letter stated:

> The U.S. Food and Drug Administration (FDA) reviewed the labels for your "Fair Mayo" products. Based on our review, we have concluded that your product is in violation of Section 403(g) of the Federal Food, Drug and Cosmetic Act (the Act) [21 U.S.C § 343(g)] and its implementing regulations found in Title 21, Code of Federal Regulations, Part 169.140©.
>
> The significant violation is as follows:
>
> Your Fair Mayo product is misbranded within the meaning of Section 403(g) of the Act [21 U.S.C. § 43(g)] in that it purports to be a food for which a definition and standard of identity has been prescribed by regulation; however, it fails to conform to

such definition and standard. Specifically, the product purports to be mayonnaise by prominently featuring on its labels the word "Mayo," which has long been used to refer to mayonnaise. Mayonnaise is a food for which a definition and standard of identity has been prescribed by regulation [See 21 CFR 169.140(c)]; however, based on the ingredient information on the label, your product does not contain eggs. Therefore, your product does not conform to the standards for mayonnaise.

> It is your responsibility to ensure that your products comply with the Act and its implementing regulations. You should take prompt action to correct the violations cited in this letter. Failure to promptly correct these violations may result in regulatory action without further notice such as seizure and/or injunction. . . .

Sarah looked up the section of the Federal Food, Drug and Cosmetic Act cited in the letter [21 U.S.C § 343(g)] and found that it states:

> A food shall be deemed to be misbranded–
>
> If it purports to be or is represented as a food for which a definition and standard of identity has been prescribed by regulations as provided by Section 341 of this title, unless (1) it conforms to such definition and standard, and (2) its label bears the name of the food specified in the definition and standard, and, insofar as may be required by such regulations, the common names of optional ingredients (other than spices, flavoring, and coloring) present in such food.

The FDA regulation cited in the letter [21 CFR 169.140(c)] states:

TITLE 21--FOOD AND DRUGS
CHAPTER I--FOOD AND DRUG ADMINISTRATION
DEPARTMENT OF HEALTH AND HUMAN SERVICES
SUBCHAPTER B--FOOD FOR HUMAN CONSUMPTION

PART 169 -- FOOD DRESSINGS AND FLAVORINGS

Subpart B--Requirements for Specific Standardized Food Dressings and Flavorings

Sec. 169.140 Mayonnaise.

(a) *Description.* Mayonnaise is the emulsified semisolid food prepared from vegetable oil(s), one or both of the acidifying ingredients specified in paragraph (b) of this section, and one or more of the egg yolk-containing ingredients specified in paragraph (c) of this section. One or more of the ingredients specified in paragraph (d) of this section may also be used. The vegetable oil(s) used may contain an optional crystallization inhibitor as specified in paragraph (d)(7) of this section. All the ingredients from which the food is fabricated shall be safe and suitable. Mayonnaise contains not less than 65 percent by weight of vegetable oil. Mayonnaise may be mixed and packed in an atmosphere in which air is replaced in whole or in part by carbon dioxide or nitrogen.

(b) *Acidifying ingredients.* (1) Any vinegar or any vinegar diluted with water to an acidity, calculated as acetic acid, of not less than 2 1/2 percent by weight, or any such vinegar or diluted vinegar mixed with an optional acidifying ingredient as specified in paragraph (d)(6) of this section. For the purpose of this paragraph, any blend of two or more vinegars is considered to be a vinegar.

(2) Lemon juice and/or lime juice in any appropriate form, which may be diluted with water to an acidity, calculated as citric acid, of not less than 2 1/2 percent by weight.

(c) *Egg yolk-containing ingredients.* Liquid egg yolks, frozen egg yolks, dried egg yolks, liquid whole eggs, frozen whole eggs, dried whole eggs, or any one or more of the foregoing ingredients listed in this paragraph with liquid egg white or frozen egg white.

(d) *Other optional ingredients.* The following optional ingredients may also be used:

(1) Salt.

(2) Nutritive carbohydrate sweeteners.

(3) Any spice (except saffron or turmeric) or natural flavoring, provided it does not impart to the mayonnaise a color simulating the color imparted by egg yolk.

(4) Monosodium glutamate.

(5) Sequestrant(s), including but not limited to calcium disodium EDTA (calcium disodium ethylenediamine- tetraacetate) and/or disodium EDTA (disodium ethylenediaminetetraacetate), may be used to preserve color and/or flavor.

(6) Citric and/or malic acid in an amount not greater than 25 percent of the weight of the acids of the vinegar or diluted vinegar, calculated as acetic acid.

(7) Crystallization inhibitors, including but not limited to oxystearin, lecithin, or polyglycerol esters of fatty acids.

(e) *Nomenclature.* The name of the food is "Mayonnaise".

(f) *Label declaration.* Each of the ingredients used in the food shall be declared on the label as required by the applicable sections of parts 101 and 130 of this chapter.

[42 FR 14481, Mar. 15, 1977, as amended at 57 FR 34246, Aug. 4, 1992; 58 FR 2886, Jan. 6, 1993]

The product packaging and labeling for Fair Mayo is captured below.

1. Does the Fair Mayo packaging misbrand the product and violate the statute and the FDA regulation? Why or why not?

2. Should Sarah challenge the FDA warning letter? How can she go about doing this?

3. What else can Sarah do to reach a compromise with the FDA and ensure compliance? Should Sarah change her labeling? How?

4. How would you respond to the FDA's letter? Would you seek professional legal advice? Why or why not?

KEY TERMS

Enabling statutes p. 809   The statutes that create an agency or give the agency explicit authority to implement a statute.

Administrative agencies p. 810   Department, nondepartment, and independent agencies.

Nondelegation doctrine p. 812   The doctrine that Congress may not give an agency so much rulemaking discretion that Congress abdicates its responsibility to exercise "[a]ll legislative Powers" granted in the Constitution.

Legislative rules p. 814   Agency rules that have legal effect and impact the rights of parties.

Code of Federal Regulations p. 814   Publication containing the rules promulgated by federal administrative agencies.

Nonlegislative rules p. 814   Rules that are not legally binding on parties and express an agency's interpretation of a statute or describe the agency's policy views.

Informal rulemaking p. 814   Under the APA, many of an agency's rulemaking duties are carried out through procedures that center on the concepts of notice, public comment, publication of a final rule, and the opportunity to challenge a rule in court.

Formal rulemaking p. 814   Procedures for rulemaking that are used only when Congress has specifically indicated in the enabling statute that the agency rules must be made "on the record after a hearing."

Licensing p. 818   A process through which administrative agencies regulate and administer laws.

Inspection p 818   The process through which some agencies monitor compliance with administrative regulations.

Prosecutorial discretion p. 818   Agencies have broad discretion as to when and whom to regulate.

Administrative law judge (ALJ) p. 820   The presiding officer in a quasi-judicial administrative hearing.

Arbitrary and capricious standard p. 822   Arbitrariness and capriciousness is found when an agency has taken action that is not based on a consideration of relevant factors, including viable alternatives available to the regulatory agency, or is a result of a clear error of judgment.

Citizen suit p. 824   Lawsuit brought by any member of the public who is directly affected by a particular agency action (or inaction) against violators of a particular regulation and/or the administrative agency itself for failing to fulfill a duty imposed by a statute.

Freedom of Information Act (FOIA) p. 824   A statute that gives the public the right to examine a great many government documents.

CASE SUMMARY 43.1 American Medical Association v. United States Internal Revenue Service, 887 F.2d 760 (7th Cir. 1989)

Rulemaking under the APA

The Internal Revenue Service (IRS) proposed a rule concerning the allocation of membership dues paid to nonprofit organizations under which certain nondues revenue was to be treated as taxable revenue. According to the proposed rule, the IRS intended to determine tax liability from this revenue using a seven-factor test. After the comment period, the IRS replaced the seven-factor test with a new allocation method that the IRS considered to be more fair and consistent. The new method carved down the factors used in the original rule, and a new *three-factor test* was published as a final rule without any additional comment period.

The American Medical Association (AMA) is a non-profit corporation that charges its members dues that cover a variety of services. The AMA also publishes several journals from which the AMA derives revenue. Under the IRS's three-factor test for allocation, the AMA's tax liability increased significantly. After the IRS assessed the AMA's tax liability under the three-factor test, the AMA brought a lawsuit claiming that the new three-factor allocation regulation was invalid because the IRS had never given the proper public notice required by the APA when the agency departed from its original seven-factor test.

CASE QUESTIONS

1. Is the new test a logical outgrowth of the original test? Why or why not?
2. How could the IRS have avoided a successful challenge to this new rule?

CASE SUMMARY 43.2 Federal Express Corporation v. Holowecki, 128 S. Ct. 1147 (2008)

Judicial Review

Paul Holowecki was employed by Federal Express Corporation (FedEx) when FedEx implemented two new performance programs that tie employee compensation and continued employment to certain performance measures. Holowecki, along with other FedEx employees over the age of 40, claimed that the incentive programs unlawfully discriminated against older employees. Under the Age Discrimination in Employment Act (ADEA), claimants must file a *charge* with the Equal Employment Opportunity Commission (EEOC) and then wait a statutorily defined period of time before filing suit in federal court. However, the ADEA does not define what constitutes a charge. The EEOC, using its authority to implement procedures necessary to carry out its objectives, promulgated a rule that states a "charge shall mean a statement filed with the Commission by or on behalf of an aggrieved person which alleges that the named prospective defendant has engaged in or is about to engage in actions in violation of the Act." Before filing suit, Holowecki submitted an intake questionnaire with the EEOC and filed a six-page affidavit. FedEx claimed that the questionnaire and affidavit did not constitute a formal charge against the company because they were only one step in a formal complaint procedure. FedEx argued that the EEOC's interpretation of the definition of "charge" was outside the agency's statutory authority.

CASE QUESTIONS

1. Who prevails and why?
2. Will the court defer to the EEOC's interpretation? Why or why not?

CASE SUMMARY 43.3 Ranchers Cattlemen Action Legal Fund United Stockgrowers of America v. U.S. Department of Agriculture, 499 F.3d 1108 (9th Cir. 2007)

Arbitrary and Capricious

In response to outbreaks of mad cow disease, the Food and Drug Administration and the U.S. Department of Agriculture (USDA) implemented a number of regulations to protect American consumers and cattle herds. Chief among them was a regulation banning cattle imports from countries in which mad cow disease was known to exist. Shortly after the ban went into effect, the USDA partially reversed course and published a proposed rule allowing certain low-risk products into the United States. During the comment period, some groups objected to the proposed rule due to evidence of potential contamination even in low-risk products. The agency then published its final rule, which modified existing regulations to allow the import of low-risk products. The Ranchers Cattlemen Action Legal Fund United Stockgrowers of America challenged the agency's decision to allow low-risk products as arbitrary and capricious even though the agency had held several comment periods.

CASE QUESTIONS

1. Is the decision arbitrary and capricious? Why or why not?
2. Does the fact that the agency held several comment periods impact your analysis? Why or why not?

CHAPTER REVIEW QUESTIONS

1. Statutes that create an agency or give the agency explicit authority to implement a statute are called:
   a. Enabling statutes.
   b. Due process statutes.
   c. Informal statutes.
   d. Formal statutes.
   e. None of the above.

2. Each of the following is a source of administrative law except:
   a. The Constitution.
   b. Statutes.
   c. The APA.
   d. The common law.
   e. International treaties.

3. Congress exercises oversight over administrative agencies through:
   a. Oversight hearings.
   b. The power of the purse.
   c. Advice and consent.
   d. A, B, and C.
   e. None of the above.

4. If an agency action violates the constitutional principle of separation of powers, the agency has violated the:
   a. Nondelegation doctrine.
   b. Commerce clause.
   c. First amendment.
   d. Fourth amendment.
   e. None of the above.

5. Agencies primarily engage in:
   a. Rulemaking.
   b. Licensing.
   c. Investigation and enforcement.
   d. Adjudications.
   e. All of the above.

6. Federal administrative agencies are published in the Code of Federal Regulations.
   a. True
   b. False

7. In most agencies, the presiding officer at an administrative hearing is an administrative law judge (ALJ).
   a. True
   b. False

8. Most rules implemented by administrative agencies undergo the formal rulemaking process.
   a. True
   b. False

9. State administrative law should not be of great concern to businesses.
   a. True
   b. False

10. The informal rulemaking process is a very quick and simple process.
    a. True
    b. False

 QUICK QUIZ ANSWERS
State Administrative Regulation

The department that regulates alcoholic beverages will engage in rulemaking, licensing, investigation and enforcement, adjudications, and administering public benefits.

CHAPTER REVIEW QUESTIONS: Answers and Explanations

1. a. Enabling statutes create an agency or give the agency explicit authority to implement a statute.

2. e. International treaties are not a source of administrative law.

3. d. Congress exercises oversight over administrative agencies through all of these methods.

4. a. If an agency action violates the constitutional principle of separation of powers, the agency has violated the nondelegation doctrine.

5. e. Agencies primarily engage in all of the above.

6. a. True. Federal administrative agencies are published in the Code of Federal Regulations.

7. a. True. In most agencies, the presiding officer at an administrative hearing is an administrative law judge (ALJ).

8. b. False. Most rules implemented by administrative agencies undergo the informal rulemaking process.

9. b. False. State administrative law should be of great concern to businesses.

10. b. False. The informal rulemaking process is not a very quick and simple process.

CHAPTER 44

Consumer Protection

©valterZ/Shutterstock

Consumer protection laws continue to grow and expand, both at the state and federal levels. But what protections do business firms have against consumers who write fake online reviews? In this chapter's *Thinking Strategically*, we'll explore the problem of fake online reviews.

Learning Objectives

After studying this chapter, students who have mastered the material will be able to:

44-1 Summarize the role played by state lemon laws in business transactions with consumers.

44-2 Articulate the standards used by the U.S. Federal Trade Commission to define false advertising and other deceptive practices.

44-3 Explain the role of the U.S. Food and Drug Administration in protecting consumers with respect to food and drugs.

44-4 Summarize the role of the U.S. Department of Transportation with respect to automobile safety and odometer settings.

44-5 Explain the role of the Consumer Financial Protection Bureau with respect to consumer loans, credit transactions, and the collection of consumer debt.

CHAPTER OVERVIEW

Since the height of the American Industrial Revolution, the body of law that protects consumers in transactions with merchants and creditors has grown dramatically. Today, an extensive number of state and federal laws, as well as many administrative regulations, are on the books. This massive corpus of laws and regulations, commonly referred to as *consumer protection law,* applies to practically all individuals and firms in a wide variety of business transactions. In this chapter, we discuss:

- The scope and role of state lemon laws in protecting consumers who purchase new and used vehicles.
- The role of the Federal Trade Commission (FTC) in protecting consumers against unfair advertising practices.
- The role of the Food and Drug Administration (FDA) in protecting consumers with respect to food and drugs.

- The role of the Department of Transportation (DOT) with respect to automobile safety and odometer settings.
- The role of the Consumer Financial Protection Bureau (CFPB) with respect to loans to consumers and the collection of consumer debt.

STATE LEMON LAWS

Lemon law protection arises under state law, for every U.S. state, as well as the District of Columbia, has enacted its own lemon laws. In general, a *lemon* refers to a new or used vehicle that turns out to have serious manufacturing defects affecting its safety, value, or utility. Although the exact criteria vary from state to state, new-vehicle lemon laws require that an auto manufacturer repurchase a vehicle that has a significant defect that the manufacturer is unable to repair within a reasonable amount of time. Contrary to popular belief, it is not the dealership that has the obligation to buy back the vehicle; it is the manufacturer.

Broadly speaking, lemon laws consider the nature of the problem with the vehicle, the number of days that the vehicle is unavailable to the consumer for service of the same mechanical issue, and the number of repair attempts made. If repairs cannot be completed within the total number of days described in the state statute, the manufacturer becomes obligated to buy back the defective vehicle.

Some state lemon laws cover only certain classes of vehicles, such as vehicles purchased for individual use but not for business use, or vehicles under a certain gross weight. A small number of states also have enacted lemon laws that cover used vehicles as well.

LO 44-1

Summarize the role played by state lemon laws in business transactions with consumers.

✓ Quick Quiz Lemon Law 101

Answer the following basic questions about lemon laws.

1. What is a lemon?
2. What remedy do state lemon laws provide?
3. Who is required to provide this remedy, the dealership or the manufacturer of the automobile?

Answers to this Quick Quiz are provided at the end of the chapter.

DECEPTIVE TRADE PRACTICES

Over a century ago, Congress established the **Federal Trade Commission (FTC)** as an independent agency of the United States government. The principal mission of the FTC is to protect consumers against anticompetitive, deceptive, and unfair business practices. (The FTC's logo is depicted in Figure 44.1.)

False Advertising

Until the creation of the FTC, the only legal protection that most consumers had against unscrupulous sellers who engaged in deceit during a sale was a tort action for fraud. But in 1914, Congress passed the **Federal Trade Commission Act (FTCA)**, one of the very first federal laws enacted to protect consumers. The act not only established the FTC; it also charged the FTC with the broad mandate of preventing unfair and deceptive acts or trade practices in commercial transactions. Under this legal authority, the FTC has issued regulations that

LO 44-2

Articulate the standards used by the U.S. Federal Trade Commission to define false advertising and other deceptive practices.

FIGURE 44.1 | Federal Trade Commission Logo

define a deceptive practice as one that is likely to *mislead* a reasonably prudent consumer and that results in some sort of *detriment* to the consumer.

Today, deceptive advertising is a significant source of consumer complaints. FTC regulations and memoranda provide several specific examples of prohibited deceptive advertising, such as making *expressly false statements* in an advertisement about a product's quality, ingredients, or effectiveness. Note that in addition to violating the FTC's regulations, expressly false advertisements also may give rise to a breach of warranty. The FTC rule also prohibits the use of fake testimonials or endorsements and the use of fake pictures of the product performing in a manner that is inaccurate.

The FTC also investigates complaints by consumers of bait-and-switch ploys. In a **bait-and-switch scheme**, a seller advertises an item for sale at a particularly good price (say, 30 percent off retail) or on favorable terms (zero down, zero interest), but the seller has no intention of actually selling that product at that price or on those terms. When a consumer comes to the business after seeing the advertisement, the seller discourages the purchase of the advertised item and instead tries to convince the buyer to purchase a different item for a higher price or on less favorable terms. Although the seller's techniques for discouraging the purchase of the product may vary (e.g., telling the consumer that the product has been sold out or perhaps advertising a product that was never actually available), the end result is the same: The buyer walks out of the store with a more expensive product than the one that was advertised.

In addition, pricing practices are also subject to FTC consumer protection regulations. Some of the more common forms of deceptive advertising via pricing are:

- Misrepresenting the prices of a competitor.
- Artificially inflating the original retail price of a product when featuring it as a sale item in order to make it appear that the original price was higher than it actually was.
- Using phrases such as "clearance priced" or "marked down for sale" when the items are not being sold at reduced rates.

Telemarketing and the Do Not Call Registry

Congress has also enacted several laws regulating telemarketing firms and practices and gave the FTC the power to enforce these laws. The main telemarketing statutes are the **Telephone Consumer Protection Act** and the **Telemarketing and Consumer Fraud and Abuse Prevention Act**. Combined, these laws (1) allow consumers to *opt out* of receiving unwanted calls from telemarketers, (2) ban the use of unsolicited recorded calls and faxes, (3) regulate 900-number calls to prevent consumers from unknowingly generating charges, (4) prohibit telemarketers from making false representations, and (5) require disclosure of all material terms of a proposed transaction. The laws prescribe *how* and *when* a telemarketer may obtain permission to receive payment from the consumer's checking, savings, or credit accounts. It also prohibits any harassment, threats, or deceit by the telemarketer.

As part of its enforcement authority under these laws, the FTC established a national **Do Not Call Registry** whereby consumers may sign up to be on a list that protects them from certain unsolicited calls by telemarketers. Some organizations, however, are exempt from the Do Not Call list prohibitions. They include (1) charitable organizations, (2) certain political organizations, and (3) business firms with whom the consumer has had past commercial contacts.

CAN-SPAM Act

With the growth of the Internet in the 1990s, the problem of *spam*—unsolicited e-mails advertising products or services—became more and more serious. Although many states enacted anti-spam legislation, there was no *federal* law on the books until Congress passed the **Controlling the Assault of Non-Solicited Pornography and Marketing Act of 2003**, better known as the CAN-SPAM Act. This federal law preempted state anti-spam laws, outlawed most of the dubious methods used by certain spam suppliers, and imposed criminal sanctions in severe cases.

The CAN-SPAM Act also prohibits online marketing providers from falsifying the "from" name and information in the subject line designed to fool consumers into opening an unsolicited e-mail message. It requires the sender to provide a physical address of the producer of the e-mail and to specifically label any pornographic links with adult-content warnings. The law also imposes an affirmative obligation on the sender to notify the recipient of procedures to opt out of receiving any future e-mail from the sender. One controversial provision of the law required the FTC to start a "do-not-spam" list modeled on the Do Not Call list. However, the FTC resisted the notion of creating such a list based on technology and privacy grounds, and the list was never implemented.

The FTC has been aggressively enforcing the law against the most serious offenders and pursuing criminal charges where appropriate. For example, in June 2007, two spammers were convicted under the CAN-SPAM Act for sending out millions of e-mail messages with highly offensive pornographic images. The defendants were sentenced to five years in prison and ordered to pay $1.3 million from the profits of their front company. The FTC has also used its enforcement authority to file civil complaints against companies that are engaged in spamming as part of their marketing strategy. The FTC is particularly strict in its enforcement of the CAN-SPAM Act when pursuing companies whose primary market is Internet pornography.

In addition to FTC enforcement, the CAN-SPAM Act also allows e-mail recipients the right to bring a private lawsuit directly against the spammer as a compliance mechanism in egregious cases and in cases where the plaintiff can prove that the spam caused actual damages, such as a shutdown of a retail store's computer server that caused loss of profits or repair charges.

Critics of the CAN-SPAM Act, however, have argued that the act is ineffective and difficult to enforce and that the decrease in spam in recent years has been due primarily to enhanced technology improvements in e-mail filtering. One report featured in *PC* magazine concluded that less than 1 percent of spam complied with the CAN-SPAM Act. Responding to some industry criticism of the effectiveness of the law, the FTC revised its regulations in 2008 to widen its jurisdiction and specifically prohibit spam distributors from charging a consumer a fee in order to process an opt-out request.

Consumer Review Fairness Act of 2016

In December 2016, Congress enacted the **Consumer Review Fairness Act (CRFA)**, which protects people's ability to share their honest opinions about a business's products, services, or conduct in any forum, including social media. The CRFA was passed in response to reports that some businesses tried to prevent people from giving honest reviews about products or services they received. Some companies put contract provisions in place, including in their online terms and conditions, that allowed them to sue or penalize consumers for posting negative reviews. Contracts that prohibit honest reviews, or threaten legal action over them, harm people who rely on reviews when making their purchase decisions.

To discourage these practices, Congress delegated enforcement authority to the Federal Trade Commission and to state attorneys general. The law specifies that a violation of the CRFA will be treated the same as violating an FTC rule defining an unfair or deceptive act or practice.

TAKEAWAY CONCEPTS Deceptive Trade Practices

- The Federal Trade Commission (FTC) is charged with preventing unfair and deceptive acts or practices in commercial transactions. In doing so, the FTC has wide-ranging authority over advertising, price disclosures, and representations made during the sales process of consumer goods.

- In bait-and-switch schemes, a seller advertises an item for sale at a very good price or on favorable terms but in reality has no intention of actually selling that product at that price or on those terms. Instead, when the consumer comes to the business after seeing the advertisement, the seller discourages the purchase of the advertised item and tries to convince the buyer to purchase a different item for a higher price or on less favorable terms.

- Pricing is also subject to consumer protection regulations, including a ban on misrepresenting the prices of a competitor, artificially inflating the original retail price of a product when featuring it as a sale item, and using phrases such as "clearance priced" or "marked down for sale" when the items are not being sold at reduced prices.

- The FTC established the Do Not Call Registry whereby consumers sign up to be on a list that protects them from certain unsolicited calls by telemarketers.

- The Controlling the Assault of Non-Solicited Pornography and Marketing (CAN-SPAM) Act of 2003 regulates the sending of unsolicited e-mail (spam) by prohibiting certain online marketing practices, including falsifying the "from" name and information in the subject line, and mandating that senders provide a physical address of the producer of the e-mail.

LO 44-3

Explain the role of the U.S. Food and Drug Administration in protecting consumers with respect to food and drugs.

FOOD AND DRUG SAFETY

The **Food and Drug Administration (FDA)** is a federal agency of the United States Department of Health and Human Services, one of the many cabinet-level executive departments of the federal government. (The FDA's logo is depicted in Figure 44.2 below.)

In summary, the FDA was empowered by Congress to enforce the **Food, Drug, and Cosmetic Act (FDCA)** to regulate the testing, manufacture, and distribution of foods, medications (including over-the-counter medications and prescription drugs), medical devices, and cosmetics. A major component of the act is the requirement that makers of certain food ingredients, additives, drugs, or medical devices obtain formal FDA approval prior to selling the product to the general public. When the FDA has approved a drug for public use, any advertising for the drug is subject to FDA regulation in terms of what representations may be made and what disclosures must be included.

FDA regulations also govern the *labeling* of food packages. FDA regulations define specific *food safety* processes, procedures, and standards, such as the requirement that employees handling food wear rubber gloves and hair netting. The statute also sets out a broader catchall standard by outlawing any generally *adulterated* food that has potential for public harm. The FDA defines adulterated food as that which contains a "filthy, putrid, or decomposed substance" or any food "unfit for consumption."

The FDA also investigates any public outbreaks of illness related to food contamination. During its investigation of such outbreaks, the FDA uses its broad enforcement powers to detect and prevent any further contamination. These powers include seizure of contaminated products, mandatory recalls, civil enforcement lawsuits, fines, and criminal prosecution for egregious cases. One of the largest fines ever levied by the FDA was against Odwalla Juice Company in the 1990s, when Odwalla was accused of producing a bad batch of apple juice using blemished fruit contaminated with the infectious *E. coli* bacterium. Odwalla's contaminated batch killed a 16-month-old girl and sickened 66 people. (In addition to food safety, the FDA enforces other laws relating to consumer safety, including Section 361 of the Public Health Service Act and associated regulations, many of which are not directly related to food or drugs. These include regulating lasers, cellular phones, condoms, and control of disease on products ranging from certain household pets to sperm donation for assisted reproduction.)

The FDA is led by the Commissioner of Food and Drugs, who is appointed by the president with the advice and consent of the Senate. The Commissioner reports to the Secretary of Health and Human Services. (Dr. Scott Gottlieb, the current commissioner, took over in May 2017.) The FDA has its headquarters in White Oak, Maryland. The agency also has 223 field offices and 13 laboratories located throughout the 50 states, the U.S. Virgin Islands, and Puerto Rico. In 2008, the FDA began to post employees to foreign countries, including China, India, Costa Rica, Chile, Belgium, and the United Kingdom.

FIGURE 44.2 | U.S. Food and Drug Administration Logo

©grzegorz knec/Alamy

TAKEAWAY CONCEPTS Food and Drug Safety

- The Federal Food, Drug, and Cosmetic Act empowers the FDA to regulate the testing, manufacture, and distribution of foods, medications (including over-the-counter medications and prescription drugs), medical devices, and cosmetics.

- The FDA also regulates the labeling of food packages and investigates any public outbreaks of illness related to food contamination.

- The FDA defines adulterated food as that which contains a "filthy, putrid, or decomposed substance" or any food "unfit for consumption."

AUTOMOBILES

The United States Department of Transportation (DOT), a cabinet-level department of the U.S. government, is concerned with transportation and public safety. It was established by an act of Congress on October 15, 1966, and began operation on April 1, 1967.

In addition, Congress also enacted the Highway Safety Act of 1970, which created the National Highway Traffic Safety Administration (NHTSA, typically pronounced "NITS-uh"), an agency of the U.S. Department of Transportation. Among other things,

LO 44-4

Summarize the role of the U.S. Department of Transportation with respect to automobile safety and odometer settings.

NHTSA is charged with writing and enforcing motor vehicle safety standards as well as regulations for motor vehicle theft resistance and fuel economy under its Corporate Average Fuel Economy (CAFE) system. NHTSA also licenses vehicle manufacturers and importers, allows or blocks the import of vehicles and safety-regulated vehicle parts, administers the vehicle ID number (VIN) system, develops the dummies used in safety testing as well as the test protocols themselves, and provides automobile insurance cost information.

Another of NHTSA's major activities is the creation and maintenance of the data files maintained by the National Center for Statistics and Analysis. In particular, the Fatality Analysis Reporting System (FARS), has become a resource for traffic safety research not only in the United States, but throughout the world. Research contributions using FARS by researchers from many countries appear in many non-U.S. technical publications and provide a significant database and knowledge bank on the subject.

Odometers

The U.S. Department of Transportation estimates that odometer rollback, the process of physically altering a vehicle's odometer in order to make it appear as if the vehicle has traveled fewer miles than it actually has, is a $3-billion-a-year enterprise. Odometer fraud is perpetrated both easily and surreptitiously, and it is often impossible for a consumer to detect.

The **Federal Odometer Act** makes it a crime to change vehicle odometers and requires that any faulty odometer be plainly disclosed in writing to potential buyers. This law (1) defines and prohibits odometer tampering, (2) prohibits buying or installing any device used for tampering, (3) prescribes procedures for odometer repair, (4) requires certain disclosures related to the actual mileage of the vehicle when it is sold to a new owner, (5) gives jurisdiction for the implementation and enforcement of the law to the Secretary of Transportation, and (6) imposes a record-keeping requirement on vehicle dealers and distributors. In addition to giving the Secretary of Transportation the authority to enforce the statute, the law also provides victims of odometer tampering with a remedy of *triple* the actual damages suffered. Any such private lawsuit, however, must take place within two years of the date of purchase.

LO 44-5

Explain the role of the Consumer Financial Protection Bureau with respect to consumer loans, credit transactions, and the collection of consumer debt.

CONSUMER DEBT

The **Consumer Financial Protection Bureau (CFPB)**, one of the newest federal regulatory agencies to be created by Congress, is empowered to monitor and regulate consumer financial markets, including consumer loans and credit cards. (The logo of the CFPB is pictured in Figure 44.3 below.)

As part of its sweeping overhaul of U.S. financial markets, Congress created the CFPB when it enacted the Dodd-Frank Wall Street Reform and Consumer Protection Act in 2010. The Dodd-Frank Act consolidates into the CFPB previously existing agencies that had oversight over consumer lending practices.

In brief, the main mission of the CFPB is to provide consumer protection by offering education programs and information, by performing research and providing data to lawmakers and the public, and by creating policy and enforcing rules to protect consumers from fraud or unfair practices. The CFPB also plays a significant role in the enforcement of consumer protection laws even outside of loans and credit cards. For example, the Dodd-Frank law authorizes the CFPB to take action against any company or individual, including online lenders and debt collectors, that engages in unfair and deceptive acts or practices in the consumer financial marketplace.

Credit Transactions

Credit is one of the most important components of a stable economy. The use of credit by consumers in the business environment is widespread and primarily exists in the form of loans and credit cards. A consumer credit transaction takes place between a **creditor** (typically a financial institution, but any party regularly extending credit to consumers is considered a creditor) and a **borrower** (sometimes referred to as a *debtor*). Merchants are considered creditors when they regularly engage in extending credit terms to a patron. It is important for business owners and managers to be aware that establishing a credit relationship with a consumer borrower triggers protections for the borrower via federal and state statutes. There is a large body of administrative law that regulates credit transactions as well.

FIGURE 44.3 Consumer Financial Protection Bureau Logo

©B Christopher/Alamy

Under the **Fair and Accurate Credit Transactions Act (FACTA)**, consumers are entitled to request a free copy of their credit reports once every 12 months. Financial institutions use the information contained in this report to determine risk in lending to consumers. In general, consumers usually find out about this report only after there has been negative information reported (mishandled accounts, erroneous data, and so on).

A credit report can be obtained annually for free from credit reporting agencies that contains accounts opened and checks ordered in your name. However, it is not the same as the free full consumer credit report. This report is a completely separate report that the majority of consumers only find out about after they have been declined by a financial institution to open a checking or savings account. The majority of banks and credit unions use the information contained in the report to approve, decline, or determine what type of account if any can be opened at their financial institution. Consumers who have a negative report may not be able to open a checking or savings account for five years.

The centerpiece of federal statutory regulation of credit transactions is the **Consumer Credit Protection Act (CCPA)**. The CCPA has been amended several times and now has six components that regulate credit transactions between a creditor and a borrower. These components include consumer protections in the areas of disclosure of credit terms, credit reporting, antidiscrimination laws for credit applicants, and collection of debts from consumers. The CCPA was enhanced by the Dodd-Frank Wall Street Reform and Consumer Protection Act in 2010. Congress also centralized enforcement responsibilities of all consumer credit regulation through creation of the Consumer Financial Protection Bureau.

The **Truth in Lending Act (TILA)** is the part of the CCPA that requires lenders to disclose to borrower applicants certain information about the loan or terms of credit. It also mandates uniform methods of computation and explanation of the terms of the loan or credit arrangements. The primary objective behind TILA is to allow consumers access to reliable information related to interest rates and other important terms and to provide a standardized reporting system for consumers to compare loan offers. TILA's scope is limited to credit extensions made to consumers and is used primarily for personal, family, or household purposes.

TILA covers only creditors that are *regularly* engaged in extending credit for goods and services (such as banks, department stores, suppliers, wholesalers, and retailers) plus those that are regularly engaged in *arranging* credit that is for personal, family, or household goods (such as a mortgage broker). For example, suppose Armstrong wishes to renovate the kitchen in his home and plans to finance the renovation through a loan. If Armstrong applies for a home improvement loan from his local bank, the transaction is covered under the TILA and the bank will be required to strictly comply with the act's requirements.

In Case 44.1, an appellate court considers a consumer's claim that she was entitled to cancel a loan contract because the required cancellation notice was inadequate.

CASE 44.1 Palmer v. Champion Mortgage, 465 F.3d 24 (1st Cir. 2006)

FACT SUMMARY In March 2003, Palmer obtained a debt-consolidation loan from Champion that was secured by a second mortgage on her home. (This type of loan is also known as a *home equity loan*.) On the day the loan closing took place (March 28, 2003), she signed several loan documents as well as the required TILA disclosures. Several days later, Palmer received copies of these documents by mail along with the "notice of her right to cancel" disclosure required by the TILA. The notice of her right to cancel provided that Palmer could "cancel the transaction for any reason within three business days of (1) the date of the transaction, (2) the date she received her TILA disclosures, or (3) the date she received the notice of right to cancel." The notice also provided that if she were to cancel the transaction by mail or telegraph, the cancellation had to be postmarked no later than April 1, 2003. Palmer did not cancel the transaction within the allotted time period. In August 2004, however, she filed for cancellation of the transaction under the extended three-year statute of limitations under the TILA, claiming that Champion failed to make TILA disclosures because the time frames in the cancellation notice were too confusing.

SYNOPSIS OF DECISION AND OPINION The U.S. Court of Appeals for the First Circuit affirmed the trial court's decision and dismissed Palmer's claim. The court reasoned that the notice of right to cancel provided by Champion complied with the TILA disclosure requirements and that an objectively reasonable consumer would not find the notice confusing. Therefore, Palmer's right to rescind was not extended based on her failure to follow TILA procedures.

WORDS OF THE COURT: Objectively Reasonable Notice "[I]n the TILA context . . . we, like other courts, have focused the lens of our inquiry on the text of the disclosures themselves rather than on plaintiffs' descriptions of their subjective understandings. . . . This emphasis on objective reasonableness, rather than subjective understanding, is also appropriate in light of the sound tenet that courts must evaluate the adequacy of TILA disclosures from the vantage point of a hypothetical average consumer—a consumer who is neither particularly sophisticated nor particularly dense. . . .

Thus, we turn to the question of whether the average consumer, looking at the Notice objectively, would find it confusing. We conclude that she would not. . . . It clearly and conspicuously indicates that the debtor can rescind 'within three (3) business days from whichever of [three enumerated] events occurs last.' . . . We fail to see how any reasonably alert person—that is, the average consumer—reading the Notice would be drawn to the April 1 deadline without also grasping the twice-repeated alternative deadlines. . . . Because we find the Notice clear and adequate, and because the plaintiff otherwise concedes receiving all the required disclosures, her right of rescission under the TILA had long expired by the time she commenced this action."

Case Questions

1. Given the language of the time frame notice, do you agree with the court's statements that it was clear and that objectively reasonable consumers would not be confused by it? Why or why not?

2. The court says that any "reasonably alert" person is the average consumer. Do you agree that the average consumer is reasonably alert? What standard should be used to judge the "average consumer"?

3. *Focus on Critical Thinking:* Examine Figure 44.4. This is a notice that is similar to the notice Palmer received. Does it affect your analysis?

(continued)

FIGURE 44.4   Sample Home Equity Loan Notice of Right to Cancel

HOME EQUITY LINE OF CREDIT
NOTICE OF RIGHT TO CANCEL

DATE 10/1/2017
LOAN NO. 5931569013
TYPE Equity Line

LENDER: Main Street Bank

BORROWERS/OWNERS Eva St. Clair

ADDRESS 123 Stowes Lane
CITY/STATE/ZIP New Town, MA
PROPERTY 10 Main Street, Unionville, MA

We have agreed to establish an open-end credit account for you, and you have agreed to give us a mortgage/lien/security interest on your home as security for the account. You have a legal right under federal law to cancel this account, without cost, within THREE BUSINESS DAYS after the latest of the following events:

(1)   The opening date of the account, which is 10/1/2017   ; or
(2)   The date you received your Truth in Lending disclosures; or
(3)   The date you received this notice of your right to cancel the account.

If you cancel the account, the mortgage/lien/security interest on your home is also cancelled. Within TWENTY CALENDAR DAYS of receiving your notice, we must take the necessary steps to reflect the fact that the mortgage/lien/security interest on your home has been cancelled. We must return to you any money or property you have given to us or to anyone else in connection with this account.

You may keep any money or property we have given you until we have done the things mentioned above, but you must then offer to return the money or property. If it is impractical or unfair for you to return the property, you must offer its reasonable value. You may offer to return the property at your home or at the location of the property. Money must be returned to the address below. If we do not take possession of the money or property within TWENTY CALENDAR DAYS of your offer, you may keep it without further obligation.

HOW TO CANCEL

If you decide to cancel this account, you may do so by notifying us, in writing, at

Main Street Bank
Unionville, MA

You may use any written statement that is signed and dated by you and states your intention to cancel, or you may use this notice by dating and signing below. Keep one copy of this notice no matter how you notify us because it contains important information about your rights.

If you cancel by mail or telegram, you must send the notice no later than MIDNIGHT of October 5, 2017   (or MIDNIGHT of the THIRD BUSINESS DAY following the latest of the three events listed above). If you send or deliver your written notice to cancel some other way, it must be delivered to the above address no later than that time.

I WISH TO CANCEL

_____   _____
CONSUMER'S SIGNATURE   DATE

The undersigned each acknowledge receipt of two copies each of NOTICE OF RIGHT TO CANCEL.

Each borrower/owner in this transaction has the right to cancel. The exercise of this right by one borrower/owner shall be effective as to all borrowers/owners.

Eva St. Clair 10/1/17   _____
BORROWER/OWNER Eva St. Clair   DATE   BORROWER/OWNER   DATE

_____   _____
BORROWER/OWNER   DATE   BORROWER/OWNER   DATE

Debt Collection

Consumer credit transactions are heavily regulated in an effort to protect consumers and help level the playing field between creditors and debtor consumers. Similarly, when a creditor's agent is collecting a debt owed to the creditor by virtue of an extension of consumer credit, the collection process is subject to regulation. Agents involved in debt collection for consumer debts are directly regulated by a federal statute called the **Fair Debt Collection Practices Act (FDCPA)**.[1] The FDCPA applies only to *agents* of the debtor that are attempting to collect the debt from the consumer.

These agents typically take the form of a collection agency, but others that are collecting consumer debts on behalf of the debtor (such as attorneys) may also be subject to the FDCPA under certain conditions. A creditor that is attempting to collect her own debt is *not* subject to the act. However, both creditors and collection agencies are subject to additional state statutory and regulatory requirements as well.

The FDCPA requires that the collection agency make known certain rights of the debtor in a **validation disclosure** when making the initial inquiry about the debt. This disclosure notice must inform the debtor that he has 30 days to dispute the debt. The law also requires that the collection agency investigate any disputed debt and obtain written verification of the debt from the original creditor.

In addition to requiring validation disclosure, the FDCPA prohibits certain conduct in the course of attempting to collect a debt. First, the law limits the contact that a debt collector may have with third parties such as employers. Second, certain methods are unlawful. Specifically, the FDCPA prohibits collector contact (1) at inconvenient times, such as early-morning or late-night calls, or at inconvenient places, such as the debtor's place of employment or sites of social events; (2) after the collector is informed that the debtor is represented by an attorney; or (3) after the debtor gives written notice that she refuses to pay the debt and requests the agent to cease contact. The FDCPA also prohibits any harassing, intimidating, or misleading tactics by collection agents, such as making threats of incarceration, posing as an attorney or law enforcement agent, or using abusive, degrading language.

Federal statutes that govern consumer debt collection are enforced primarily by the Consumer Financial Protection Bureau (CFPB) and the Federal Trade Commission (FTC). These agencies have the power to impose penalties, issue cease and desist orders, and initiate civil lawsuits to enforce the FDCPA. However, the law also provides individual consumers with a statutory cause of action so that a debtor may sue a collection agent directly for any damages suffered, plus attorney fees incurred in bringing suit. On the state level, state attorneys general often have authority to prosecute collection agents engaged in abusive collection tactics within their state's jurisdiction. In Case 44.2, the CFPB investigates the unlawful collection practices of a law firm that agrees to a consent order.

CASE 44.2 U.S. Consumer Financial Protection Bureau v. Pressler & Pressler LLP, Consent Order, 2016-CFPB-0009

FACT SUMMARY Pressler & Pressler, LLP ("Pressler") is a law firm whose practice was entirely devoted to debt collection, primarily in New Jersey and New York. In response to numerous complaints from consumers concerning Pressler's violation of the Fair Debt Collection Practices Act (FDCPA), the Consumer Financial Protection Bureau (CFPB) investigated Pressler's practices.

The investigation revealed multiple instances of debt-collection efforts in which Pressler employees violated the "False or Unsubstantiated Representations about Owing a Debt" section of the Fair Credit Reporting Act (FRCP). The CFPB found that Pressler had represented, directly or indirectly, expressly or by implication, that consumers owed debts to various clients with certain unpaid

(continued)

---

[1] 15 U.S.C. § 1692 (now Title VII of the Consumer Credit Protection Act).

balances, interest rates, and payment due dates, which were not substantiated by documentation from creditors or were simply false. The investigation also found that from 2009 to 2014, the law firm filed more than 500,000 lawsuits against consumers on behalf of clients who sought payment for debts they purchased from various creditors. This massive litigation mill was powered by an automated claim-preparation system and by non-attorney support staff, who determined which consumers to sue. Actual attorneys generally spent less than a few minutes, sometimes less than 30 seconds, reviewing each case before initiating a lawsuit.

SYNOPSIS OF DECISION AND OPINION

In 2016, the CFPB announced that it had entered into a Consent Order with Pressler whereby Pressler, and its two principal partners—Sheldon Pressler and Gerard Felt—agreed to a civil fine of $1 million. The parties also agreed to halt the practice that caused the filing of inaccurate mass-produced lawsuits targeting consumers in debt in violation of both the Fair Debt Collection Practices Act and the Dodd-Frank Wall Street Reform and Consumer Protection Act, which prohibits unfair and deceptive acts or practices in the consumer financial marketplace.

WORDS OF THE COURT: Documentation Required "In numerous instances the representations set forth in [the CFPB Complaint] were not substantiated at the time the representations were made, including but not limited to where consumers disputed, challenged, or questioned the validity or accuracy of the debt and [Pressler] failed to obtain [documentation from the creditor] before continuing collecting on that account. [Pressler] had knowledge or reason to believe, based on its past course of dealing with its clients' accounts (including factors such as consumer disputes, inaccurate or incomplete information in the portfolio, and contractual disclaimers related to the accounts) that a specific portfolio of clients' accounts might contain unreliable data, but continued to represent that consumers owed the claimed amount on the accounts in question without reviewing [documentation] . . . [Pressler] have unfairly collected or attempted to collect a debt by in many instances relying exclusively on summary data provided by clients without having reviewed supporting documentation underlying the facts [Pressler] asserts. . . . These practices are likely to cause substantial injury to consumers, for example, by imposing costs in defending improperly filed or outright erroneous lawsuits. These injuries are not reasonably avoidable by consumers because, among other things, when a consumer is sued, he or she must defend or otherwise respond to the lawsuit, or else face a default judgment."

Case Questions

1. Although this is an enforcement action against Pressler by the CFPB, do individuals who have been victimized by Pressler have any legal recourse?

2. Why is it relevant that actual attorneys generally spent less than a few minutes, sometimes less than 30 seconds, reviewing each case before initiating a lawsuit?

3. *Focus on Critical Thinking:* Have you, a family member, or a friend ever been contacted by a debt collector? Did the collection agent use intimidation tactics? In your opinion, did he or she violate the FDCPA? Did the debt collector act ethically? Explain.

 THINKING STRATEGICALLY

Negative Online Reviews

PROBLEM: Fake online reviews are a growing problem for many businesses. It's extremely easy to create a new account on Yelp, Google, and other Internet platforms and to leave either a positive or negative review for any business. What should companies do about fake negative reviews?

STRATEGIC SOLUTION: Businesses should consider spending time carefully monitoring their reviews. Sites like Yelp and Google have formal policies for users that leave reviews, so if a business receiving a negative review can explain why the review is against the platform's guidelines, it can ask the platform to remove the review.

In addition, many companies are starting to include terms in their contracts that allow them to sue or penalize consumers for posting negative reviews. However, in December 2016 Congress enacted the Consumer Review Fairness Act (CRFA), which protects people's right to share their honest opinions about a business's products, services, or conduct, in any forum, including social media. Contracts that prohibit honest reviews, or threaten legal action over them, harm people who rely on reviews when making their purchase decisions. Is your company complying?

Businesses should review the terms of their consumer contracts to make sure that such terms comply with the CRFA, which makes it illegal for companies to include standardized provisions that threaten or penalize people for posting honest reviews. For example, in an online transaction, it would be illegal for a company to include a provision in its terms and conditions that prohibits or punishes negative reviews by customers. (The law doesn't apply to employment contracts or agreements with independent contractors. Below are some basic tips for complying with the law.)

What kind of reviews does the law protect? The law protects a broad variety of honest consumer assessments, including online reviews, social media posts, uploaded photos, videos, etc. And it doesn't just cover product reviews; it also applies to consumer evaluations of a company's customer service.

What does the Consumer Review Fairness Act prohibit? In summary, the act makes it illegal for a company to use a contract provision that:

- bars or restricts the ability of a person who is a party to that contract to review a company's products, services, or conduct;
- imposes a penalty or fee against someone who gives a review; or
- requires people to give up their intellectual property rights in the content of their reviews.

What can a company do to protect itself from inappropriate or irrelevant content? The law says it's okay to prohibit or remove a review that:

- contains confidential or private information (e.g., a person's financial, medical, or personnel file information or a company's trade secrets;
- is libelous, harassing, abusive, obscene, vulgar, sexually explicit, or is inappropriate with respect to race, gender, sexuality, ethnicity, or other intrinsic characteristic;
- is unrelated to the company's products or services; or
- is clearly false or misleading.

To make sure your company is complying with the CRFA, (1) review your form contracts, including online terms and conditions; and (2) remove any provision that restricts people from sharing their honest reviews, penalizes those who do, or claims copyright over peoples' reviews, even if you've never tried to enforce it or have no intention of enforcing it.

QUESTION

Check out Section 10 of AirBnB's Terms of Service here: https://www.airbnb.com/terms#sec10 ("Ratings and Reviews"). In your opinion, does Section 10 of AirBnB's user agreement comply with the Consumer Review Fairness Act? Why or why not?

You have a new review!

KEY TERMS

Federal Trade Commission (FTC) p. 835   An agency charged with the broad mandate of preventing unfair and deceptive acts or practices in commercial transactions.

Federal Trade Commission Act (FTCA) p. 835   A statute that created the Federal Trade Commission and prohibited deceptive trade practices.

Bait-and-switch scheme p. 836 When a seller advertises an item for sale at a particularly good price or on favorable terms, but the seller has no intention of actually selling that product at that price or on those terms.

Telephone Consumer Protection Act p. 836 A federal statute regulating telemarketing firms.

Telemarketing and Consumer Fraud and Abuse Prevention Act p. 836 Federal statute that allows consumers to opt out of unwanted calls from telemarketers, bans the use of unsolicited recorded calls and faxes, and prohibits telemarketers from making false representations.

Do Not Call Registry p. 836 A list maintained by the FTC whereby consumers may sign up to be protected from certain unsolicited calls by telemarketers.

Controlling the Assault of Non-Solicited Pornography and Marketing Act of 2003 p. 837 A federal statute that regulates the sending of unsolicited e-mail (spam) by prohibiting certain practices, such as falsifying the "from" name and information in the subject line, and requiring the sender to provide a physical address of the producer of the e-mail. Also called *CAN-SPAM Act*.

Consumer Review Fairness Act (CRFA) p. 837 A federal law designed to protect consumers' ability to share their honest opinions about a business's products, services, or conduct in any forum, including social media.

Food and Drug Administration (FDA) p. 838 The federal agency that regulates the testing, manufacturing, and distributing of foods, medications, and medical devices.

Food, Drug, and Cosmetic Act (FDCA) p. 838 The federal statute that created the Food and Drug Administration and that requires the makers of certain food ingredients, additives, drugs, or medical devices to obtain formal FDA approval before selling the product to the general public.

Federal Odometer Act p. 840 A law that makes it a crime to change vehicle odometers and requires that any faulty odometer be plainly disclosed in writing to potential buyers.

Consumer Financial Protection Bureau (CFPB) p. 840 Independent agency created by the Wall Street Reform and Consumer Protection Act responsible for consumer education, regulation of credit and loan companies, and enforcement of consumer protection laws.

Creditor p. 841 Any party that regularly extends credit and to which a debt becomes owed.

Borrower p. 841 The party to whom credit is extended and who owes the debt.

Fair and Accurate Credit Transactions Act (FACTA) p. 841 Federal legislation that requires credit bureaus to stop reporting any fraudulent account information from the time a consumer alleges identity theft until the conclusion of the investigation.

Consumer Credit Protection Act (CCPA) p. 841 Federal legislation that regulates credit transactions between a creditor and a borrower and provides consumer protections in the areas of disclosure of credit terms, credit reporting, antidiscrimination laws, and collection of debts from consumers; serves as the centerpiece of federal statutory regulation of credit transactions.

Truth in Lending Act (TILA) p. 841 The part of the Consumer Credit Protection Act that requires lenders to disclose to borrower applicants certain information about the loan or terms of credit and mandates uniform methods of computation and explanation of the terms of the loan or credit arrangements.

Fair Debt Collection Practices Act (FDCPA) p. 844 A federal statute that regulates agents of the creditor involved in debt collection for consumer debts and that requires the collection agency to make known certain rights of the debtor.

Validation disclosure p. 844 A notice in which a collection agency, when making initial contact with a debtor, makes known certain rights of the debtor, including the fact that he has 30 days to dispute the debt; required under the Fair Debt Collection Practices Act.

CASE SUMMARY 44.1 Phoenix of Broward, Inc. v. McDonald's Corp., 489 F.3d 1156 (11th Cir. 2007)

Deceptive and Unfair Business Practices

From 1995 to 2001, McDonald's, the fast-food chain, sponsored promotional games including "Monopoly Games at McDonald's," "The Deluxe Monopoly Games at McDonald's," "The Deluxe Monopoly Game," and "Who Wants to Be a Millionaire?" For each of these promotional games, McDonald's conducted an extensive marketing and advertising campaign through which it represented that all customers had a fair and equal chance to win and it specified the odds of winning. The FBI, however, investigated

McDonald's promotional games based on claims that the game pieces required to win the high-value, "million-dollar" prizes were being diverted to family and friends of personnel who had access to these pieces. Yet throughout the FBI's investigation, and even after individuals pleaded guilty to conspiracy charges related to the diversionary practices, McDonald's continued its advertising practices.

CASE QUESTIONS

1. In addition to the FBI, which consumer protection agency of the federal government would also have legal authority to investigate this matter?
2. What legal actions could the consumer protection agency identified in Question 1 take against McDonald's?

CASE SUMMARY 44.2 Barrer v. Chase Bank USA, 566 F.3d 883 (9th Cir. 2009)

Truth in Lending Act

Walter and Cheryl Barrer obtained a credit card with Chase in 2004 and accepted the cardmember agreement. In February 2005, Chase mailed a Change in Terms Notice to the Barrers that notified them of an increase in the annual percentage rate from 8.99 percent to 24.24 percent in certain events, including payment default and persistently late payments. The notice provided a right for the Barrers to reject these terms in writing, but they did not. In April 2005, the Barrers' APR jumped to 24.24 percent. Chase claimed

that it increased the rate because of information obtained from a credit agency about the Barrers being an increased credit risk, even though that condition was not listed in the notice as an event qualifying for a rate increase.

CASE QUESTIONS

1. Do Chase's actions comply with the TILA? Why or why not?
2. Why shouldn't the Barrers be liable for failing to reject the new terms?

CASE SUMMARY 44.3 Myers v. LHR, Inc., 543 F. Supp. 2d 1215 (S.D. Cal. 2008)

Fair Debt Collection Practices Act

Darla Myers owed over $11,000 to an automobile finance company in 2001. LHR was hired to collect the debt, and an LHR agent contacted her with threats of a lawsuit and garnishment of her wages. Ms. Myers negotiated a settlement whereby LHR accepted approximately $3,000 as complete payment for the debt. Myers wire-transferred the money to LHR to satisfy the debt and later received a letter saying the debt was paid in full. Despite this

settlement, Ms. Myers later found out that her settled debt was still reported to the credit agencies by LHR, and this action adversely affected her credit rating.

CASE QUESTIONS

1. Were LHR's actions lawful under the FDCPA? Why or why not?
2. If LHR's actions were not lawful, what could it have done to comply with the act?

CASE SUMMARY 44.4 U.S. v. Facebook, Inc., Case No. 19-cv-2184 (D.D.C. 2019)

Federal Trade Commission Act

In 2012, Facebook, Inc. (Facebook) entered into a consent order with the Federal Trade Commission (FTC),

resolving allegations that the company misrepresented to consumers the extent of data sharing with third-party applications. Among other things, the 2012 FTC order required Facebook to establish a reasonable program to protect user privacy. After it was revealed that the firm Cambridge Analytica had harvested the personal data of millions of people's Facebook profiles without their consent during the 2016 presidential election, the FTC eventually commenced a formal legal action against Facebook on July 24, 2019, in the U.S. District Court for the District of Columbia, alleging that Facebook had violated the 2012 order. On that same day, however, Facebook and the FTC also announced a settlement order in which Facebook agreed to pay a record-breaking $5 billion penalty to the FTC. The settlement order, however, did not mandate any payments to Facebook users; nor did it impose any personal legal liability on Facebook's CEO, Mark Zuckerberg.

CASE QUESTIONS

1. Should Facebook users whose data was harvested by Cambridge Analytica without their consent receive compensation from the $5 billion penalty Facebook agreed to pay to the FTC?
2. Assume Facebook was unaware of what Cambridge Analytica was doing with its users' data. Why should Facebook have to answer for the misdeeds of Cambridge Analytica?

CHAPTER REVIEW QUESTIONS

1. **The purpose of the FTC in relation to consumers is:**
   a. Nonexistent, since the FTC does not apply to consumers.
   b. To prevent unfair or deceptive acts in commercial transactions.
   c. To ensure that the UCC is followed.
   d. To promote interstate commerce.
   e. To ensure fairness in government contracts.

2. **Which of the following is not exempt from the Do Not Call Registry?**
   a. Charitable organizations
   b. Certain political organizations
   c. Businesses seeking commercial contracts
   d. Businesses with which the consumer has past commercial contacts
   e. All are exempt

3. **Johnson helps his neighbor Russell by lending him $1,000 to cover Russell's daughter's tuition bill. Russell fails to pay the money back, and Johnson is forced to sue him to recover the costs. Russell asserts the TILA as a defense because Johnson never gave him a TILA disclosure statement. Who prevails?**
   a. Johnson, because the TILA doesn't apply to this transaction.
   b. Johnson, because Russell had adequate time to cancel the loan.
   c. Russell, because no TILA notice was issued.
   d. Russell, because Johnson did not give him adequate opportunity to cancel.
   e. Neither party, because TILA is a federal law.

4. **Which of the following is an illegal practice wherein a seller advertises a good for an artificially low price but intends to convince buyers to buy a different good?**
   a. Discounting
   b. Bait and switch
   c. Telemarketing
   d. Breach of warranty
   e. All are legal

5. **The Fair Debt Collection Practices Act (FDCPA) prohibits agents of a creditor from which practice(s) when collecting a debt?**
   a. Contacting the debtor at inconvenient times, such as early morning
   b. Posing as an attorney or law enforcement officer
   c. Threatening incarceration as a method to collect the debt
   d. All of the above
   e. None of the above

6. **The Consumer Financial Protection Bureau has the power to investigate complaints by consumers of bait-and-switch ploys.**
   a. True
   b. False

7. **Individual consumers have the right to see their own credit report once every 12 months so long as they pay the cost of the issuance of the credit report.**

   a. True

   b. False

8. **The CAN-SPAM Act does not address spammers who falsify the name of the sender.**

   a. True

   b. False

9. **Victims of odometer tampering are eligible to receive up to triple the amount of their damages.**

   a. True

   b. False

10. **FDA regulations do not apply to the labeling of food packages.**

    a. True

    b. False

 Quick Quiz ANSWERS
Lemon Law 101

1. A lemon is a new or used vehicle that turns out to have serious manufacturing defects that affect its safety, value, or utility.

2. State lemon laws require that an auto manufacturer repurchase a vehicle that has a significant defect that the manufacturer is unable to repair within a reasonable amount of time.

3. It is the manufacturer, not the dealership, that has the obligation to buy back the vehicle in the event it turns out to be a lemon.

CHAPTER REVIEW QUESTIONS: Answers and Explanations

1. **b.** The FTC was created and charged with the task of protecting consumers from unfair and deceptive acts in commercial transactions.

2. **c.** Charitable organizations, certain political organizations, and businesses with which the consumer has past commercial contacts are all permitted to contact consumers.

3. **a.** This is a private transaction that is not subject to TILA disclosures as Johnson is not regularly engaged in the business of lending. Thus, the remaining answers are incorrect.

4. **b.** Bait and switch is an illegal practice in which a seller advertises a good for an artificially low price (the bait) but intends to convince buyers to buy a different good (the switch). Answers *a* and *c* are incorrect because they are not illegal practices. Answer *d* is incorrect because it is unrelated to the price.

5. **d.** Answers *a, b,* and *c* are all prohibited by the FDCPA. Thus, answer *d* is correct.

6. **b. False.** The Federal Trade Commission is the federal agency with the authority to investigate complaints by consumers of bait-and-switch ploys.

7. **b. False.** Under the Fair and Accurate Credit Transaction Act, consumers are entitled to request a free copy of their credit report once every 12 months.

8. **b. False.** Among other things, the CAN-SPAM Act applies to spammers who falsify the name of the sender.

9. **a. True.** Under the Federal Odometer Act, victims of odometer tampering may receive up to triple the amount of their damages.

10. **b. False.** FDA regulations not only apply to drugs but also to the labeling of food packages.

CHAPTER 45

Criminal Law and Procedure

Business owners and managers may face criminal charges for violations of federal food purity laws in daily business operations. In *Thinking Strategically,* we discuss the benefits of creating an effective corporate compliance program as a mechanism to identify misconduct as early as possible, which helps limit the risk of criminal liability.

Learning Objectives

After studying this chapter, students who have mastered the material will be able to:

45-1   Distinguish between criminal law and criminal procedure.

45-2   Compare and contrast criminal law with civil law.

45-3   Articulate the requirements for criminal liability.

45-4   Identify circumstances in which business managers and owners may be liable for criminal violations by a corporation.

45-5   Provide specific examples of white-collar crime laws that may impact a business entity and/or its owners and managers.

45-6   Differentiate between the investigative phase and the adjudication phase in the criminal justice system.

45-7   Explain various constitutional procedural protections afforded to those accused of a crime.

45-8   Articulate the exclusionary rule and how it applies in a business context.

CHAPTER OVERVIEW

One way that the government regulates the practices and operations of business owners and managers is through **criminal law**. This chapter focuses on how criminal law, criminal procedure, and the criminal justice system impact the legal environment of business.

Crime in the United States ordinarily is dealt with by state authorities, predominantly under state statutory law.

While each state has its own system of criminal law, there is an increasing body of federal criminal law. Thus, the federal criminal justice system exists alongside (sometimes overlapping) the state systems. Much of American criminal law is derived from English criminal law, which existed primarily as common law with some statutory mandates. However, in the 1960s, state legislatures began to assemble various statutes addressing criminal culpability and integrating state common law to form more comprehensive criminal codes.

CRIMINAL LAW VERSUS CRIMINAL PROCEDURE

Whereas criminal law defines the boundaries of behavior and prescribes sanctions for violating those boundaries, **criminal procedure** refers to the legal process and safeguards afforded to individuals (and in some cases business entities) during criminal investigations, arrests, trials, and sentencing. *Criminal law* consists of a body of law that, for the purposes of preventing harm to society, defines what conduct is criminal and prescribes the punishment to be imposed for such conduct. *Criminal procedure* sets limits on the government's authority in applying criminal law. Criminal procedure is covered in detail later in this chapter.

LO 45-1

Distinguish between criminal law and criminal procedure.

CRIMINAL LAW AND CIVIL LAW

Recall the distinctions between civil law and criminal law covered in Chapter 1, "Legal Foundations and Thinking Strategically." Civil laws are designed to compensate parties (including businesses) for damages as a result of another's conduct. Criminal statutes are designed to protect society, and the violation of a criminal law results in a penalty to the violator, such as a fine or imprisonment, based on the wrongdoer's level of culpability. It is important to remember that these categories are not mutually exclusive; one can violate a criminal law and commit a civil wrong in the very same act.

LO 45-2

Compare and contrast criminal law with civil law.

For example, suppose that Macduff is an accountant for Shakespeare Book Company (SBC). He steals $100,000 from the business by creating a fake employee on the company's books and secretly paying the fake employee's salary to himself. Upon discovery, SBC notifies the authorities, and Macduff will likely be charged with various criminal offenses, such as grand theft and fraud. If he is convicted, he will likely be incarcerated for an extended period of time. Although sometimes courts order restitution as part of a criminal sentence, SBC also may choose to file a civil lawsuit against Macduff individually in order to recover the losses due to Macduff's commission of the tort of conversion (the civil counterpart of theft). SBC also may be entitled to compensation from Macduff for other incidental expenses it incurred as a result of the theft (e.g., the costs of detecting the theft). If SBC is successful in obtaining a civil judgment against Macduff, the company may then attempt to recover its losses by tapping Macduff's personal assets.

Nearly two-thirds of the states have enacted criminal codes based on the **Model Penal Code (MPC)** adopted by the American Law Institute (ALI) in 1962. The vocabulary and formation of the MPC have been very influential in shaping criminal law notions, even in states where the MPC has not been formally adopted. However, many states have retained certain portions of their common law within their criminal codes as well.

Burden of Proof

One significant difference between a criminal case and a civil case is the **burden of proof**. In a civil case, the plaintiff needs to prove only by a **preponderance of the evidence** that the defendant committed a civil wrong. This means that the fact finder need not be completely convinced that the plaintiff's arguments in the case should prevail. Rather, the fact finder need be convinced only that the defendant's liability was more likely than not to be true for the plaintiff to meet her burden of proof. In criminal cases, where the stakes may involve an individual's liberty, the standard of proof is much higher. In a criminal case, the government must prove its case **beyond a reasonable doubt**. Thus, a fact finder must be convinced that the defendant's criminal liability is not in doubt to a reasonable person.

Criminal Law
• Defines criminal acts and prescribes punishment; protection of society.
Criminal Procedure
• Legal limits on government's authority to apply criminal law that protects citizens (and in some cases corporations).
Civil Law
• Designed to compensate parties who have suffered a loss; lower burden of proof.

CRIMINAL LIABILITY

LO 45-3

Articulate the requirements for criminal liability.

From a legal perspective, a crime has two parts: (1) a physical part, in which the defendant committed an *act* or *omission,* and (2) a mental part, which involves the defendant's subjective *state of mind.* Thus, an analysis of criminal liability involves three fundamental questions: First, did the defendant actually commit the prohibited act? Second, did the defendant have a culpable state of mind? Third, does the law give the defendant a palpable defense (such as a self-defense claim to a homicide charge)?

Act Requirement

The **act requirement**, also called by its Latin name, *actus reus,* requires the government to prove that a defendant's actions objectively satisfied the elements of a particular offense. The act requirement is based on the fundamental criminal law tenet that evil thoughts alone do not constitute a criminal act. Rather, there must be some overt conduct (either an act or an omission), and it must be voluntary. Courts generally follow the rule that an act is voluntary unless it is demonstrated that the defendant acted based on physical compulsion, reflex, or certain physiological or neurological diseases. An *act by omission* occurs when a crime is defined in terms of failure to act. For example, if the chief financial officer fails to disclose data required by federal securities law, she has committed an omission that satisfies the act requirement.

Mental Requirement

The **mental element**, also called by its Latin name, *mens rea,* which translates literally as "guilty mind," requires that the defendant have a requisite degree of culpability with regard to each element of a given crime. The fundamental underpinning is that an act does not make a person guilty unless his mind is guilty. The words contained in a criminal statute to express the guilty mind requirement include *intentionally, knowingly, maliciously, willfully,* and *wantonly.* However, some criminal statutes set the intent requirement at mere recklessness or negligence, rather than actual intent, in determining the level of culpability. Thus, an act or omission in which the defendant's conduct deviated from the standard of conduct so grossly that a reasonable person would judge it as criminal may also satisfy the mental element requirement.

Courts and legislatures have also established certain rules for applying the mental element requirement in cases of mistake. Certain statutes also impose strict liability, whereby

FIGURE 45.1 Excerpt from a Florida Criminal Statute (F.S.A. § 831.02)

Uttering forged instruments

"Whoever utters and publishes as true a false, forged or altered record, deed, instrument or other writing mentioned in § 831.01 (i.e., "letter of attorney, policy of insurance, bill of lading, bill of exchange or promissory note, or an order, acquittance, or discharge for money or other property") knowing the same to be false, altered, forged or counterfeited, with intent to injure or defraud any person, shall be guilty of a felony of the third degree."

---

the mental element is assumed by certain conduct so that the defendant's culpable state of mind need not be proved. Figure 45.1 illustrates the typical language of the act requirement and the mental requirement, using an example from a Florida criminal statute prohibiting forgery.

Defenses

Even when the requisite mental state and criminal act standards are proved, the law provides for certain defenses based on the unique circumstances of the crime. **Self-defense** is an example of a defense to a criminal charge of homicide in which the law recognizes that certain cases necessitate the use of deadly force to repel an attack when the defendant reasonably fears that death or substantial harm is about to occur either to the defendant or to a third party. The rules governing self-defense are complex and vary from state to state, especially on the question of whether the defendant is required to retreat before using deadly force. The defense afforded by the self-defense doctrine is at its height when it involves use of deadly force to repel an attack in the victim's home or place of business.

The other major category of defense is **mental incapacity**. As you may imagine, this defense is very controversial and is sometimes colloquially called the *insanity defense.* That term is potentially misleading because in certain jurisdictions incapacity covers a wide variety of conditions in addition to insanity. Although mental incapacity has a variety of definitions depending on the jurisdiction, the Model Penal Code (MPC) requires the defendant's actions to be related to some type of mental disease or defect. The MPC also specifically rules out any sociopathic personality disorders as the basis for a mental incapacity case.

Less frequently asserted defenses include *duress,* in which a defendant has committed a crime in response to another person's threat to inflict personal injury (threats to property or reputation are insufficient), and *intoxication,* which generally depends on whether the intoxication was voluntary or involuntary. If voluntary, the criminal act is excused only if the defendant was so intoxicated that he could not form the requisite mental intent (guilty mind) to have criminal culpability. If involuntary, the defense is broader but still requires proof that the intoxication rendered the defendant unable to understand that his conduct constituted a crime.

Types of Crimes

Crimes may be classified in several different ways. **Felonies** are crimes that generally carry one year or more of incarceration as the penalty. **Misdemeanors** are crimes that carry up to one year of incarceration as the penalty. Frequently, states also have degrees (or grades) of crimes within each of those categories that further delineate the seriousness of the crime. Thus, a premeditated murder would be referred to as a first-degree felony, whereas shoplifting a shirt may be defined as a second- or third-degree misdemeanor. Many states also have a classification of crimes known as *summary offenses* or *infraction offenses,* which are minor crimes that carry no threat of a jail sentence for first-time offenders.

Crimes are also sometimes classified based on the victim or result of the crime. Crimes in which the perpetrator has used force or violence, such as murder or sexual assault, are classified as *violent crimes.* Crimes that involve offensive or disorderly conduct in public are referred to as *public order crimes.* This category also includes crimes that have no direct victim but that society has judged to be detrimental to public well-being, such as crimes related to narcotics, prostitution, or obscenity. Crimes that involve damage to or stealing of property (such as theft, vandalism, or arson) are usually referred to as *property crimes.* When crimes take place in the business environment, they are classified as *white-collar crimes.*

CRIMINAL LAW AND BUSINESS ENTITIES

LO 45-4

Identify circumstances in which business managers and owners may be liable for criminal violations by a corporation.

While any discussion of criminal law necessarily focuses on the criminal culpability of individuals, business owners and managers should have a fundamental knowledge of how criminal law may be applied to business entities. This knowledge helps business owners and managers to reduce risk and add value to the business by taking affirmative steps to limit criminal culpability for the business and its principals.

The modern trend in criminal law is to expand the scope of criminal statutes to include criminal culpability for corporations and their principals. Courts have allowed liability to exist for corporations so long as the prosecutor can prove that the corporation's agents (not just executive management) were engaged in criminal conduct on behalf of the company.[1] Criminal statutes have embraced the concept that a corporation may be charged with a crime along with, or apart from, its principals or agents. The Model Penal Code (MPC) provides for criminal liability for business entities if any one of the following applies:

1. The criminal act by the business's agent is within the scope of his employment and the statute imposes liability on the business for such an act (e.g., the agent shreds documents related to potentially unlawful conduct, creating liability under obstruction of justice).
2. The criminal omission is the failure to perform a specific duty imposed by law (e.g., the agent fails to make important disclosures in a report to investors).
3. The crime is authorized by one of the corporation's top-level managers (e.g., a chief financial officer orders an internal accountant to file a false corporate tax return).

Congress has specifically included business entities in criminal statutes in areas that impact business, including fraud, obstruction of justice, health and safety requirements, sale of ownership interests (securities law), disclosure requirements, environmental regulations, and antitrust or other anticompetition laws.

Individual Liability for Business Crimes

Congress and state legislatures have also expanded criminal culpability for individual officers and directors (and sometimes majority owners) for corporate crimes committed within the scope of their employment. These principals are often included in criminal statutes that require officers and directors to act as responsible corporate officers in complying with statutes and being diligent about adhering to standards set out in statutes and regulations. Because of the inherent difficulties in terms of proof, most statutes do not require the specific mental intent (guilty mind) that is required for other crimes. However, since the mid-1970s, legislative bodies have begun to impose what amounts to strict liability statutes

---

[1]MPC § 4.01(1).

for corporate officers even when the officer in question did not have any actual knowledge that a crime had taken place.

Responsible Corporate Officers: The *Park* Doctrine

The responsible corporate officer doctrine, commonly referred to as the *Park doctrine,* permits the government to prosecute employees for corporate misconduct when they are in a position of authority and fail to prevent or correct a violation of the Food, Drug, and Cosmetic Act (FDCA). The *Park* doctrine was developed by the U.S. Supreme Court in a famous 1975 case in which the Court held that an individual corporate officer could be guilty of a misdemeanor crime under the FDCA for allowing food to become adulterated while stored in a corporate warehouse. The case centered on John Park, the president of Acme Markets, Inc., a large national retail food chain with approximately 36,000 employees, 874 retail outlets, and 16 warehouses. In 1970, the Food and Drug Administration (FDA) observed and advised Park of unsanitary conditions, including rodent infestation, at Acme's Philadelphia warehouse. In 1971, the FDA found similar conditions at Acme's Baltimore facility. After the violations were not corrected, the government charged Acme and Park with misdemeanors under the FDCA. Although Acme pled guilty, Park argued that he could not possibly have had the requisite knowledge necessary to commit a crime. A jury convicted Park, and eventually the U.S. Supreme Court affirmed the conviction. The Court pointed out the narrowness of the decision (i.e., limited to FDCA violations), but it nonetheless affirmed that corporate agents have a high level of responsibility when it comes to the well-being of the public. The Court rejected Park's argument:

> The requirements of foresight and vigilance imposed on responsible corporate agents are beyond question demanding, and perhaps onerous, but they are no more stringent than the public has a right to expect of those who voluntarily assume positions of authority in business enterprises whose services and products affect the health and well-being of the public that supports them.[2]

Case 45.1 provides an example of a federal court's analysis of individual officer liability under the *Park* doctrine.

CASE 45.1 United States v. DeCoster, 828 F.3d 626 (8th Cir. 2016)

FACT SUMMARY   Jack DeCoster owned Quality Egg, LLC, an Iowa egg production company. Jack's son Peter DeCoster served as the company's chief operating officer. Quality Egg operated six farm sites with 73 barns which were filled with five million egg-laying hens. It also had 24 barns which were filled with young chickens that had not yet begun to lay eggs. Additionally, the company owned several processing plants where eggs were cleaned, packed, and shipped. Jack also owned and operated several egg production companies in Maine, and Peter

worked at those facilities. In 2008, salmonella enteritidis ("salmonella") tests conducted at the Maine facilities came back positive. The DeCosters succeeded in eliminating salmonella from their Maine facilities by following the recommendations of hired consultants, including a poultry disease specialist and a rodent control expert. In its Iowa facility, however, Quality Egg did not test or divert eggs from the market despite receiving multiple positive results from hens indicating a potential for salmonella. Experts hired by Quality Egg recommended

(continued)

---

[2]*United States v. Park,* 421 U.S. 658, 672 (1975).

adopting the same safety measures in Iowa as had been used in Maine. Although the DeCosters claimed they adopted all of the recommendations, the precautions implemented by Quality Egg failed to eradicate salmonella.

In August 2010, federal and state officials determined that a salmonella outbreak had originated at Quality Egg's facilities resulting in approximately 56,000 American consumers falling ill with salmonellosis. In response Quality Egg recalled eggs that had been shipped from five of its six Iowa farm sites between May and August 2010. After a Food and Drug Administration (FDA) inspection of Quality Egg's facilities revealed dangerous conditions that could lead to contamination, the government began a criminal investigation of the company's food safety practices and ultimately filed criminal charges for failing to prevent or correct a violation of the Food, Drug, and Cosmetic Act (FDCA). The DeCosters both pled guilty, as responsible corporate officers of Quality Egg, LLC, for introducing eggs that had been adulterated with salmonella into interstate commerce. The trial court sentenced Jack and Peter to three months' imprisonment. The DeCosters appealed, arguing that their prison sentences were unreasonable and disproportionate because they had no specific knowledge the eggs the company distributed had salmonella.

SYNOPSIS OF DECISION AND OPINION   The U.S. Court of Appeals for the Eighth Circuit affirmed the trial court's decision to sentence the DeCosters to incarceration. The court reasoned that under the FDCA, responsible corporate officer concept, individuals who by reason of their position in the corporation have the responsibility and authority to take necessary measures to prevent or remedy violations of the FDCA and fail to do so, may be held criminally liable as responsible corporate agents, regardless of whether they were actually aware of or intended to cause the violation. The court agreed with the trial court's findings that the DeCosters knew or should have known of the risks posed by the unsanitary conditions at Quality Egg in Iowa, knew or should have known that additional testing needed to be performed before the suspected shell eggs were distributed to consumers,

The U.S. Department of Agriculture is charged with enforcing the Food, Drug, and Cosmetic Act (FDCA).
©Mark Van Scyoc/Shutterstock

and knew or should have known of proper remedial and preventative measures to reduce the presence of salmonella.

WORDS OF THE COURT: Prison Sentence Appropriate   "On this record, the DeCosters' three-month prison sentences are not grossly disproportionate to the gravity of their misdemeanor offenses. When defining the statutory penalties in the FDCA, Congress recognized the importance of placing the burden on corporate officers to protect consumers 'who are wholly helpless' from purchasing adulterated food products which could make them ill. The 2010 salmonella outbreak may have affected up to 56,000 victims, some of whom were hospitalized or suffered long term injuries. For one example, a child hospitalized in an intensive care unit for eight days was saved by antibiotics which damaged his teeth, causing them to be capped in stainless steel."

Case Questions

1. Why is it important in this case that the DeCosters's conduct violated the FDCA?

2. What was the DeCosters's theory of the case on appeal?

3. *Focus on Critical Thinking:* Given what we know about the impact of the salmonella outbreak in 2010, would there be any tort claims against Quality Egg? Against the DeCosters? Explain.

TAKEAWAY CONCEPTS Criminal Law

- Criminal law is based on state and federal laws that started as common law crimes but were codified into statutes based on the Model Penal Code (MPC).
- While some actions involve both criminal and civil liability, *civil* laws protect individuals by redressing injuries, and *criminal* laws protect society as a whole by punishing wrongdoers.
- Criminal liability requires both a bad act (*actus reus*) and a guilty mind (*mens rea*).
- Even when a requisite mental state and bad act are proved, the accused can offer a defense such as mental incapacity, duress, or self-defense to avoid criminal liability.
- Corporations and their managers can be guilty of the crimes of their employees if the crime was committed for some corporate advantage or benefit of the company.
- The responsible corporate officer doctrine, commonly referred to as the *Park doctrine,* permits the government to prosecute employees for corporate misconduct when they are in a position of authority and fail to prevent or correct a violation of the Food, Drug, and Cosmetic Act.

WHITE-COLLAR CRIME

White-collar crimes usually signify criminal violations by corporations or individuals, including fraud, bribery, theft, and conspiracy committed in the course of the offender's occupational duties. Typically, these crimes are set out in state and/or federal statutes.

Fraud

Perhaps the most common white-collar crime is fraud. *Fraud* is a broad general term used to describe a transaction in which one party makes false representations of a matter of fact (either by words or conduct) that are intended to deceive another. In certain cases, active concealment of a material fact (versus an affirmative false representation) may also constitute fraud. The basic elements of criminal fraud are (1) a false representation (or concealment) concerning a material fact and (2) another party that relies on the false misrepresentation of the fact and suffers damages as a result. A *material fact* is one that is essential to the agreement or one that affects the value of the transaction. For example, suppose that Rasputin applies for a loan to start his business. Because his finances are in dire straits, Rasputin submits a false set of tax returns to the bank loan officer. Based on this information, the bank lends Rasputin the money. Rasputin has committed a fraud upon the bank. Bank fraud of this nature is a felony punishable under state and, depending on the bank, federal criminal statutes.

In 1990, Congress passed the **Mail Fraud Act**[3] with the intent of giving federal prosecutors significant leverage in prosecuting white-collar criminals. The statute criminalizes any fraud in which the defrauding party uses the mail or any wire, radio, or television in perpetrating the fraud. This comprehensive approach to criminalizing fraud is based on Congress's authority to regulate mail and interstate commerce. It also covers any organization of a scheme to defraud by false pretenses. For example, in the Rasputin example discussed earlier, suppose that Rasputin sets up an elaborate scheme to fool investors into thinking that he has invented a new product that will bring in several millions of dollars of revenue.

LO 45-5

Provide specific examples of white-collar crime laws that may impact a business entity and/ or its owners and managers.

---

[3]10 U.S.C. § 1341.

He designs a brochure and mails it to several wealthy individuals. At this point, Rasputin has committed mail fraud even though he has not actually induced any investors. The ease of prosecution for mail fraud has made it a primary tool used by prosecutors in white-collar crime investigations.

Another form of fraud is embezzlement. Embezzlement is appropriately categorized as fraud (and not as theft) because it involves fraudulent concealment of financial records to perpetrate theft. Embezzlement occurs when someone in a position of trust creates fraudulent records to disguise the theft. For example, suppose that Rasputin is the controller of WidgetCo. Over the period of a month, Rasputin transfers small amounts of WidgetCo's money to his personal checking account and adjusts the monthly financial statements to indicate that the money is in WidgetCo's account. This act constitutes embezzlement because of the cover-up aspect of the scheme. If Rasputin had come into his office one morning, stolen cash from the safe, and walked out never to return, this would likely constitute theft (not embezzlement) because no scheme was involved.

Ponzi Schemes

A Ponzi scheme is a fraudulent investment operation that pays returns to investors from their own money or money paid by subsequent investors rather than from any actual profit earned. The scheme is named after Charles Ponzi, who became notorious for using the technique in 1903. A Ponzi scheme usually offers returns that other investments cannot match in order to entice new investors. This is generally accomplished in the form of short-term returns that are either abnormally high or unusually consistent. The perpetuation of the returns that a Ponzi scheme advertises and pays requires an ever-increasing flow of money from investors in order to keep the scheme going. The system is destined to collapse because the earnings, if any, are less than the payments. The authorities uncover some schemes before they collapse if an investor suspects that she is a victim and reports the investments to authorities. As more investors become involved, the likelihood of the scheme coming to the attention of authorities increases.

For example, suppose that High Return Investments (HRI) prints advertising brochures that promise a 30 percent return on an investment in just one month—an extraordinary return by any measure. HRI states that it uses a "complex offshore investment strategy that is the result of years of study and testing." No matter how fancy the brochures are, it is difficult to attract any large initial investments without a track record. Thus, HRI convinces a few investors to take the risk with small amounts of money. Instead of investing the money, HRI then takes out a loan and repays the initial investors with the promised 30 percent return one month later. This is where HRI sets the trap: Initial investors now invest larger sums, and new investors want a piece of the action. It is no longer necessary to take out a loan because sufficient capital from eager new investors is flowing into HRI's hands. The cascading effect then allows HRI to pay back any loans used to perpetrate the scheme and take handsome bonus fees for managing the money. HRI covers its tracks by producing false investment statements for its investors showing high returns.

When one or more investors request a withdrawal, there is sufficient cash to pay out. But HRI's scheme cannot last forever. Typically a scheme like HRI's will result in one of two scenarios: (1) the investment company's managers disappear with the investment money or (2) the scheme collapses because too many investors demand their returns at the same time. The second scenario typically happens when investor confidence in the equities markets deteriorates and investors withdraw money from market-based investments in favor of cash and other safer forms. For example, when the financial crisis of 2008 began to shake investor confidence, it unraveled the largest Ponzi scheme ever operated by a single person. Federal prosecutors claim that a 20-year scheme, operated by well-known investment manager Bernard Madoff, cost his investors billions of dollars. In March 2009,

Madoff pleaded guilty to 11 felonies, including fraud and perjury. He was given the maximum sentence of 150 years of incarceration. Madoff's accountant was also charged and cooperated with authorities in exchange for leniency. The Madoff case is discussed in more detail in Chapter 34.

Conspiracy

Conspiracy is an agreement by two or more persons to commit a criminal act. It is itself a punishable offense: All parties to the agreement are subject to prosecution. Because the crime is complete upon agreement, there is a very low threshold for satisfying the criminal act requirement. Conspiracy requires a specific intent to achieve the object of the conspiracy but does not require that the act actually be carried out. The Model Penal Code (MPC) contemplates conspiracy as a crime that requires two guilty minds. Therefore, both parties must actually manifest intent to commit the criminal act for a conspiracy to occur.

Obstruction of Justice

Prosecutors have been increasingly willing to prosecute white-collar criminals under federal laws prohibiting the obstruction of justice[4] for any conduct related to attempting to cover up evidence of wrongdoing. Cover-ups take many forms, including (1) lying to investigators, (2) altering documents, (3) shredding or concealing documents or any media such as videotape, and (4) inducing other witnesses to lie or influencing witnesses to refrain from cooperating with authorities. Note that an obstruction of justice charge may stand independently, and prosecutors need not charge or convict the defendant with the underlying crime. For example, suppose that prosecutors interview Rasputin during the criminal investigation of insider trading at Rasputin's firm and Rasputin lies about his involvement in the insider trading to the authorities. When it is discovered that Rasputin has lied, prosecutors may charge Rasputin with obstruction of justice. Rasputin may be convicted of the obstruction charge even if prosecutors do not have sufficient evidence to charge him with the underlying crime (insider trading).

Racketeer Influenced and Corrupt Organizations Act

The federal Racketeer Influenced and Corrupt Organizations Act[5] (RICO) was enacted in 1970 to provide the government with a powerful tool to fight the rising tide of organized crime. One purpose of the RICO law was to prevent organized crime from infiltrating legitimate business operations. The statute makes it a criminal offense for anyone associated with an enterprise to conduct or participate in its affairs through a pattern of racketeering activity. Although racketeering generally is understood to mean an organized conspiracy to commit the crimes of extortion or coercion, state and federal legislatures have added to the definition by including conduct such as engaging in illegal gambling, narcotics trafficking, and prostitution.

The modern trend is for authorities to use the RICO statute in an expansive manner, including criminal conduct that is not traditionally related to organized crime. Because RICO laws define racketeering in such broad terms, including crimes such as wire fraud, mail fraud, and securities fraud, prosecutors have been increasingly willing to bring RICO cases in white-collar crime and political corruption cases. Although the penalties under RICO are stiff, the real teeth of the law are found in its forfeiture provisions. They allow prosecutors to seize the defendant's personal assets if the government can prove that the

---

[4] 18 U.S.C. § 1001 et seq.

[5] 18 U.S.C. §§ 1961–1968.

assets were obtained using profits from criminal activity. This is a powerful tool because it has the effect of bankrupting the racketeering enterprise while an individual convicted under the statute is incarcerated.

Securities Crimes

In the wake of the financial crisis that began in 2008, the government has become increasingly aggressive about the enforcement of insider trading laws, which are federal securities statutes directed at corporate insiders who have access to certain information that is not available to the general investment public. Insider trading laws prohibit corporate insiders from trading their company's stock based on their insider knowledge. Insiders can be executives, managers, corporate counsel, consultants, certain employees, brokers, and even majority shareholders. In 1988, Congress passed the Insider Trading and Securities Fraud Enforcement Act, which raised the criminal and civil penalties for insider trading, increased the liability of brokerage houses for wrongful acts of their employees, and gave the government more authority to pursue insider trading violations. Insider trading laws and other laws regulate the issuance and trading of certain business ownership interests (such as stocks) and are discussed in detail in Chapter 34, "Regulation of Trading: The Securities Exchange Act of 1934."

Foreign Corrupt Practices Act

The **Foreign Corrupt Practices Act (FCPA)**[6] of 1977 is a criminal statute that was enacted principally to prevent corporate bribery of foreign officials in business transactions. The centerpiece of the FCPA is its antibribery provision. The law prohibits a company and its officers, employees, and agents from giving, offering, or promising anything of value to any foreign (non-U.S.) official with the intent to obtain or retain business or any other advantage. This prohibition is interpreted broadly in that companies may be held liable for violating the antibribery provisions of the FCPA regardless of whether they take any action in the United States. Thus, a U.S. company can be liable for the conduct of its overseas employees or agents even if no money is transferred from the United States and no American citizen participates in any way in the foreign bribery. Specifically, the FCPA prohibits:

> [A]ny domestic concern from mak[ing] use of the mails or any means . . . of interstate commerce corruptly in furtherance of a bribe to any foreign official, or to any person, while knowing that all or a portion of such money or thing of value will be offered, given, or promised, directly or indirectly, to any foreign official, for the purpose of influencing any act or decision of such foreign official . . . in order to assist such domestic concern in obtaining or retaining business for or with, or directing business to, any person.[7]

Foreign officials are any officers or employees of a foreign government, regardless of rank; employees of government-owned or government-controlled businesses; foreign political parties; party officials; candidates for political office; and employees of public international organizations (such as the United Nations or the World Bank). This list can include owner-employees as well. Even if an improper payment is not accepted, just offering it violates the FCPA. Likewise, other FCPA violations include instructing, authorizing, or allowing a third party to make a prohibited payment on a company's behalf; ratifying a payment after the fact; or making a payment to a third party knowing or having reason to know that it will likely be given to a government official. Prohibited payments include not only cash and cash equivalents but also gifts, entertainment, travel, and the like.

---

[6]15 U.S.C. § 78.
[7]15 U.S.C. §§ 78dd-2(a)(1)(3).

One of the recent controversies surrounding the FCPA centers on the meaning of the term *instrumentality*, which is not defined in the statute. In Case 45.2, a federal appellate court considers the appeal of a U.S. business executive convicted in a bribery scheme involving a foreign telephone company.

CASE 45.2 United States v. Esquenazi, 752 F.3d 912 (11th Cir. 2014)

FACT SUMMARY Esquenazi was a co-owner/president of Terra Telecommunications Corp. ("Terra"), a Florida company that purchased phone time from foreign vendors and resold the minutes to customers in the United States. One of Terra's main vendors was Telecommunications D'Haiti, S.A.M. ("Teleco"). In 2001, Terra contracted to buy minutes from Teleco directly. At that time, Teleco's Director General was Patrick Joseph (appointed by then-President Jean-Bertrand Aristide), and its Director of International Relations was Robert Antoine. In October 2001, Terra contacted Teleco about $400,000 in past-due accounts. According to testimony at trial, Antoine agreed to reduce Terra's future bills to Teleco in exchange for receiving from Terra 50 percent of what the company saved. Antoine suggested that Terra disguise the payments by making them to sham companies, which Terra ultimately did. According to Terra employees, Esquenazi was fully aware of the arrangement and shared details of the deal in a meeting with executive management. The following month, Terra began funneling personal payments to Antoine using the subterfuge of sham consulting agreements. All told, while Antoine remained at Teleco, Terra paid him and his associates approximately $822,000. During that time, Terra's bills were reduced by over $2 million.

Soon after, the U.S. Internal Revenue Service (IRS) began to investigate Terra and its relationship with vendors, including Terra. As part of the investigation, Esquenazi admitted he had bribed Teleco officials. The government charged Esquenazi and other Terra officials with several counts of violating the Foreign Corrupt Practices Act (FCPA). Esquenazi pleaded not guilty, proceeded to trial, and was found guilty on all counts. On appeal, Esquenazi argued that his conviction should be reversed because the FCPA did not apply to the Terra-Teleco payments because they were paid directly to Teleco

officials. Esquenazi claimed that Teleco officials did not meet the FCPA definition of "foreign officials." The government countered that Teleco was an "instrumentality" of the Haitian government and therefore Terra's acts of bribery were prohibited by the FCPA.

SYNOPSIS OF DECISION AND OPINION The U.S. Court of Appeals for the 11th Circuit affirmed Esquenazi's conviction. The court rejected Esquenazi's narrow definition of foreign official. Instead, the court adopted the fact-based approach and looked to questions such as who ran the company, who appointed the management, where the company's profits came from, and the extent to which the government was involved in day-to-day decisions. The court cited evidence that 97 percent of the ownership of Teleco was held by the Haitian government and that Teleco was considered a de facto government entity because the Haitian government invested in the enterprise, appointed the board of directors, hired and fired the principals, and exercised a monopoly function.

WORDS OF THE COURT: Evidence of Teleco as Instrumentality "From Teleco's creation, Haiti granted the company a monopoly over telecommunications service and gave it various tax advantages. Beginning in [the] early 1970s, and through the years [Esquenazi was] involved, Haiti's national bank owned 97 percent of Teleco. The company's Director General was chosen by the Haitian President with the consent of the Haitian Prime Minister and the ministers of public works and economic finance. And the Haitian President appointed all of Teleco's board members. The government's expert testified that Teleco belonged 'totally to the state' and 'was considered . . . a public entity.' Although the expert also testified that '[t]here was no specific law

(continued)

that . . . decided that at the beginning that Teleco is a public entity,' he maintained that 'government, officials, everyone consider[ed] Teleco as a public administration.' Construed in the light most favorable to the jury's verdict, that evidence was sufficient to show Teleco was controlled by the Haitian government and performed a function Haiti treated as its own, namely, nationalized telecommunication services."

Case Questions

1. Why is it important to the court's analysis that Antoine set up a sham company and consulting agreements?

2. If Esquenazi had not known about the bribes, would he still be guilty under the FCPA?

3. *Focus on Critical Thinking:* This case was controversial because it was the first time that an appellate court had interpreted the term "foreign official" in the FCPA so broadly. Critics contend that the court inserted its own broad definition instead of using the more narrow definition intended by Congress. Did the court go too far? If Congress had meant to include public/private partnerships in the definition of a foreign official, wouldn't they have added it into the statute? Is this good public policy?

Computer Fraud and Abuse Act

There are three major classes of criminal activity through use of a computer: (1) engaging in unauthorized use of a computer, which might involve stealing a username and password or accessing the victim's computer via the Internet through a backdoor created by a Trojan horse[8] program; (2) creating or releasing a malicious computer program (e.g., computer virus, worm, or Trojan horse); and (3) harassing and stalking in cyberspace.

In a 1983 incident that received substantial media attention, a group of hackers managed to access the computer system at Sloan-Kettering and alter patient files. The incident led to passage of the **Computer Fraud and Abuse Act (CFAA)**,[9] which was amended in 2001 by the USA PATRIOT Act.[10] The law prohibits unauthorized use of computers to commit seven different crimes: (1) espionage, (2) accessing unauthorized information, (3) accessing a nonpublic government computer, (4) fraud by computer, (5) damage to computer, (6) trafficking in passwords, and (7) extortionate threats to damage a computer. The CFAA has stiff criminal penalties and also allows civil actions to be brought against an offender to recover damages.

The CFAA is the primary tool used by the government to prosecute individuals who hack into the computer systems of government and business entities. In 2016, the CFAA was in the headlines after a federal judge sentenced a former scouting director of Major League Baseball's St. Louis Cardinals to nearly four years in prison and to pay $279,038 in restitution for his involvement in a high-tech cheating case. Christopher Correa pled guilty to violating the CFAA for hacking into the player-personnel database and e-mail systems of the Houston Astros. Prosecutors alleged that Correa gained access to the Astros's database using a password similar to that used by a former Cardinals employee who left St. Louis to become the general manager of the Astros. Correa used the password to access hundreds of pages of confidential information about player trade discussions, evaluations, and draft pick alternatives.[11]

---

[8]A Trojan horse is a virus that appears to perform one function yet actually performs another, such as the unauthorized collection, exploitation, falsification, or destruction of data.

[9]18 U.S.C. § 1030.

[10]18 U.S.C. § 2712.

[11]*United States v. Correa,* No. H-15-679 (S.D. Texas 2016).

QUICK QUIZ   White-Collar Crimes

What white-collar crimes are at issue in the following circumstances?

1. WidgetCo applies for a permit to do business in Venezuela. The government official denies the permit, and a WidgetCo executive pays for a lavish meal at a four-
star restaurant while discussing the permit application.

2. InvestCo advertises a return of 15 percent on any investments in its Super Duper
Fund. Even when the market drops dramatically, Super Duper continues to perform at this level for 18 consecutive months. In its disclosures, InvestCo reports
that its auditing firm is headed by an InvestCo officer's son-in-law.

3. WidgetCo and PlankCo agree to illegally fix prices so that the lack of competition
drives the prices of their products artificially high. The companies begin the process to set prices but abandon the plan at the last moment.

4. Evidence exists that WidgetCo's CEO was funneling money from the corporation with the help of several other executive managers. The funds came from an
investment fraud scheme in which each executive played a part to perpetrate the
scheme and use WidgetCo as a front business to help bolster their scheme with
investors.

Answers to this Quick Quiz are provided at the end of the chapter.

THE CRIMINAL JUSTICE SYSTEM

LO 45-6

Differentiate
between the
investigative phase
and the adjudication
phase in the criminal
justice system.

The criminal justice system is best thought of as one process that operates in two phases:
investigation and **adjudication**. This section describes the nuts and bolts of the criminal
justice process. Procedural safeguards that are afforded to those suspected or accused of
crimes constitute *criminal procedure* and are discussed in the next section of this chapter.

Investigation

During the investigation phase, the authorities become aware of an alleged criminal act and
begin an investigation by gathering physical evidence and interviewing witnesses and potential suspects. Because most criminal acts are handled at the state level, most enforcement
of criminal law is conducted by state or local police agencies. Violations of federal laws are
investigated by various federal law enforcement agencies, including the Federal Bureau of
Investigation (FBI). In a business context, investigators from federal regulatory agencies
such as the Securities and Exchange Commission (SEC) or the Internal Revenue Service
(IRS) may also undertake specialized criminal investigation. During this initial stage, investigators may also ask a court to authorize a search warrant in an effort to obtain more evidence. A warrant may be issued based only on **probable cause**.

Once the authorities believe that sufficient evidence creates enough probable cause
to indicate the culpability of a suspect, they will, depending on the circumstances, either
obtain an arrest warrant or, more commonly, arrest the suspect by taking him into physical
custody. If the criminal violation is a minor one, the authorities may simply issue a citation,
whereby the violator may either resolve the charge by paying a fine or contest the charge in
court. If an actual arrest has taken place, the authorities may continue their investigation
by gathering more physical evidence, interviewing new witnesses, and attempting to further
interview the suspect. The investigators then file formal criminal charges against the suspect
and prepare a brief report for a local magistrate and prosecutors.

The suspect, now charged, is referred to as the *defendant* and is formally read the charges
by a magistrate. The magistrate then sets bail (if appropriate) and, if necessary, appoints an

attorney to represent the defendant. Frequently, the prosecutor will review the investigator's report (and sometimes conduct additional investigation) and then decide whether she can prove the charges in a court of law based on available evidence. The prosecutor decides whether to (1) proceed with prosecuting the defendant on the original charge, (2) amend the charges as necessary, or (3) drop the charges altogether due to lack of evidence. The actual title of the prosecutor varies between jurisdictions, but local prosecutors are typically employed by the district attorney, state prosecutors are employed by the state's attorney general, and federal prosecutors work for the U.S. attorney general under the authority of the U.S. Department of Justice.

Adjudication

If the prosecutor elects to proceed with the charges, the defendant is entitled to a *preliminary adjudication.* Some jurisdictions use the *grand jury system,* while others use a preliminary hearing in front of a local magistrate. In each case, the prosecutor presents evidence of the defendant's guilt, and the decision maker (either the grand jurors or the magistrate) determines whether probable cause exists to hold the defendant over for trial. If the prosecutor cannot offer sufficient evidence of probable cause, the charges are dismissed. As a practical matter, very few cases are dismissed at this stage.

The defendant is notified that he is held over for trial through either an *indictment* (in the case of a grand jury) or formal filing of an *information* (in the case of a magistrate). The defendant is then entitled to an arraignment in a state trial court, at which he is informed of the final charges and is asked to enter a plea of guilty, not guilty, or no contest.[12] An overwhelming majority of defendants plead not guilty at this stage, even if they intend to eventually negotiate a guilty plea with the prosecutor. Following the arraignment, the prosecutor and defense counsel typically will enter into a plea-bargaining negotiation. This involves the parties agreeing to concessions from each side that will avoid trial and result in a voluntary plea of guilty or no contest by the defendant. All states also have some type of pretrial intervention for first-time offenders of nonviolent crimes, whereby the defendant typically agrees to fulfill certain conditions (community service, drug rehabilitation, etc.) in exchange for the charges being dismissed at a later date.

TAKEAWAY CONCEPTS The Criminal Justice Process

Investigative Phase	Adjudicative Phase
1. Investigate possible crime.	1. Preliminary adjudication (via grand jury or magistrate, depending on jurisdiction).
2. Interview witnesses.	2. File indictment (known as "information," depending on jurisdiction) *or* drop charges due to insufficient evidence.
3. Obtain search warrants if necessary.	3. The defendant enters a plea and enters plea negotiations if necessary.
4. Obtain arrest warrant or take suspect into custody *or* issue a citation for minor infractions.	4. If no plea agreement is reached, the defendant goes to trial.
5. The defendant is formally charged.	5. Conviction or acquittal of the defendant.
6. The local judicial authority sets bail and appoints defense counsel if necessary.	6. Sentencing (if convicted).

---

[12]In a plea of no contest, sometimes called by its Latin form *nolo contendere,* the defendant does not admit or deny the charges but is willing to accept the sanctions as if guilty.

If a plea agreement cannot be reached, the case proceeds to trial. In a trial, the finder of fact (usually a jury in a criminal trial) weighs the evidence and determines whether the prosecutor has proved the charges against the defendant beyond a reasonable doubt. If the jury finds the defendant guilty, this results in a conviction. If the jury finds the defendant not guilty, this results in an acquittal and the defendant cannot be prosecuted for the same charges again. If the jury is deadlocked (unable to reach a consensus decision), this results in a mistrial and the prosecutor decides whether or not to file charges against the defendant a second time. If the defendant is convicted, he may file an appeal setting out the basis for having the conviction reversed.

CRIMINAL PROCEDURE

LO 45-7

Explain various constitutional procedural protections afforded to those accused of a crime.

Recall from the beginning of this chapter the differences between criminal law and criminal procedure. While criminal law defines the boundaries of behavior and prescribes sanctions for violating those boundaries, *criminal procedure* refers to legal safeguards to protect the rights of individuals (and in some cases business entities) during investigation by the government, arrest, trial, and sentencing. The protections are primarily provided by the U.S. Constitution's Bill of Rights. For purposes of understanding criminal procedure in a business environment, our focus is on protections found in the Fourth and Fifth Amendments. While the Constitution regulates many aspects of criminal procedure, as a practical matter state and federal legislatures also enact statutes and rules setting forth certain procedures that authorities must follow during investigation, arrest, criminal trial, and sentencing. State constitutions may also provide additional criminal procedure protections for a state's citizens. For example, one state may be more apt to require a higher level of probable cause for arrest than is prescribed by the federal rules or courts. Of course, states may not repeal the federal constitutional rights of individuals.

Searches and Arrest

Recall from Chapter 3, "Business and the Constitution," that the Fourth Amendment to the U.S. Constitution protects individuals (and sometimes businesses) from unreasonable search and seizure by government agents and permits warrants to be issued only if probable cause exists. The U.S. Supreme Court has developed a large body of law to guide courts in determining the appropriate boundaries of searches and arrests by authorities.

First, the Court has held that the Fourth Amendment applies to both searches and arrests. However, a warrant is usually required before a search takes place (with certain exceptions). A warrant for arrest is generally not required to take a suspect into custody. Second, the Constitution requires that an impartial magistrate issue a search or arrest warrant only if probable cause has been established. Third, regardless of whether a search or arrest warrant exists, the action taken by authorities must always be reasonable and consistent with constitutional protections. Fourth, the authorities may conduct limited, warrantless searches in certain cases. For example, police may conduct short, pat-down searches even without probable cause when the officer has a reasonable suspicion[13] that criminal activity is taking place or when the officer's safety is an issue.

Expectation of Privacy

A fundamental part of the protections provided by the Fourth Amendment is that its protections are based on whether an individual's reasonable expectation of privacy has been violated by government authorities. The courts have held that individuals have the highest

---

[13]Reasonable suspicion has been described as a standard that is lower than probable cause but "more than just a hunch"; *Terry v. Ohio,* 392 U.S. 1 (1968).

expectations of privacy in their own homes. However, once an individual appears in public (such as driving a car on a public highway), the privacy expectations are diminished and Fourth Amendment protections become more limited in scope. Examples of evidence that is *not* protected under reasonable expectation of privacy include trash that has been set out on the public curb for pickup, any apparently abandoned property, and things a person says or does in public.

In terms of the abandoned property example, note that if the evidence has been disposed of but is still located on the real estate (land) of the owner, then the owner may still have a reasonable expectation of privacy. For example, suppose Scofield is being investigated for tax fraud. The authorities observe Scofield putting out large bags of paper for trash pickup. They wait until midnight and then take the bags from the curbside outside Scofield's residence. When Scofield is brought to trial, the prosecutor introduces the discarded papers as evidence of tax fraud. If Scofield claims his Fourth Amendment rights were violated, it is likely that he will lose that argument because courts have consistently held that public papers disposed of as garbage are abandoned property and not subject to reasonable expectations of privacy. Instead, suppose that the real estate at issue was a country home with a long driveway and that trash collectors actually traveled onto the property to collect the garbage. If the authorities entered the land without a warrant and confiscated the bags of discarded papers, a court may very well find the search to be illegal.

Plain View Doctrine

Courts have held that authorities generally do not commit a Fourth Amendment violation when a government agent obtains evidence by virtue of seeing an object that is in his plain view and the agent has the right to be in the position to have that view. This is called the **plain view doctrine**. For example, suppose that during a routine traffic violation stop, a police officer observes an illegal handgun lying on the seat next to the driver. The officer may then arrest the driver and confiscate the weapon without a warrant because the plain view search is not prohibited by the Fourth Amendment. The plain view doctrine also allows authorities to use simple mechanical devices that are available to the general public, such as flashlights or cameras with telephoto lenses, to enhance their view.

However, courts have limited authorities' ability to obtain information by means of special high-tech devices that are not available to the general public. For example, in a 2001 case, the U.S. Supreme Court held that the use of a thermal imager (a device used to produce images of relative amounts of heat escaping from a structure) by authorities on a public sidewalk outside a residence was not covered by the plain view doctrine and constituted an illegal search. The case involved the use of a device by U.S. Drug Enforcement Agency officials to obtain information on a suspected marijuana-growing operation in a residence owned by Kyllo. The agents obtained a warrant based on the fact that the thermal imager revealed that the garage of the residence was emitting extraordinary levels of heat. Indeed, Kyllo had been using heat lamps to grow marijuana in the garage, and he was eventually convicted at trial. The Supreme Court reversed the conviction on the basis that the thermal search evidence was obtained in violation of the Fourth Amendment. Justice Scalia famously wrote that allowing the authorities to use advanced technology would "leave the homeowner at the mercy of advancing technology—including imaging technology that could discern all human activity in the home."[14] The Court reasoned that because the data could not be obtained through use of the naked eye or basic equipment available to the general public, the action constituted a search even though government authorities had not physically entered the house.

---

[14]*Kyllo v. U.S.*, U.S. 27 (2001).

The courts have adopted a similar position regarding *aerial observations* made by authorities. That is, so long as the plane or helicopter is in public navigable airspace, anything the police can see with the naked eye or basic equipment such as binoculars will be considered in plain view. In *Dow Chemical Co. v. United States*,[15] the Supreme Court ruled that the use of an airplane by government agents to fly over one of Dow's chemical plant complexes for purposes of taking investigative photographs with a zoom lens fit into the plain view exception and did not require a warrant because a zoom lens was readily available for purchase by the public.

Search Incident to Arrest

The search incident to arrest exception allows a law enforcement officer who has lawfully arrested a defendant to search the defendant's person without obtaining a warrant. The primary reasons that justify this exception are (1) protection of the officer/agent and others involved in the booking process and (2) prevention of the destruction of evidence by the defendant. For example, suppose that a federal law enforcement agency arrests the kingpin of a Ponzi scheme. The kingpin is handcuffed and then brought to a booking facility, where one of the agents discovers a small notebook with incriminating notes made by the kingpin. Despite the fact that the agent did not have a warrant, the notebook may be used as evidence against the kingpin discovered in a search incident to arrest.

Electronic Devices   One increasingly important issue faced by law enforcement is the extent to which electronic devices, such as cell phones, fit into current law of unlawful search and seizure as defined by the Fourth Amendment. In Case 45.3, the U.S. Supreme Court considers whether the police need a search warrant to examine contents such as photos and videos from a suspect's cell phone.

CASE 45.3 Riley v. California, 144 S. Ct. 2473 (2014)

FACT SUMMARY   Riley was the driver of a car stopped by a San Diego, California, police officer for a traffic violation that eventually led to his arrest for concealed possession of two loaded handguns found under the seat of his car. Riley was arrested and transported to a booking facility, where police retrieved Riley's cell phone from his pocket. At the police station about two hours after the arrest, a detective specializing in criminal gangs examined the contents of Riley's cell phone. The detective found videos and photographs that connected Riley with a gang-related shooting that had occurred a few weeks earlier.

Based partially on the evidence from Riley's cell phone, the state charged him with attempted murder. The prosecutor also sought an enhanced sentence based on Riley's membership in a criminal street gang. Riley moved to suppress all evidence that the police had obtained from his cell phone, claiming a violation of the Fourth Amendment's warrant requirement. Prosecutors argued that the search of the cell phone was proper because it was incident to a lawful arrest within the guidelines of previous case law. The government argued that the cell phone search was similar to any other method used by individuals to store information (e.g., a wallet) and that cell phones fell into that same category. The trial court denied Riley's motion to suppress the evidence based on the Fourth Amendment, and Riley was convicted at trial. The state

(continued)

---

[15]476 U.S. 227 (1986).

appellate court affirmed Riley's conviction, and Riley appealed to the U.S. Supreme Court, arguing that the evidence obtained from his cell phone was a warrantless search that did not fall into any category of exception.

SYNOPSIS OF DECISION AND OPINION In a unanimous decision, the U.S. Supreme Court reversed the decisions of the lower courts and ruled in favor of Riley. The Court held that the digital era required a rule that individuals have a high level of expectation of privacy in their cell phones because they are capable of storing and accessing a quantity of information, some highly personal, that no person would ever have had on his person in hardcopy form. The Court also reasoned that the search incident to arrest exception to the warrant requirement had two primary purposes: officer safety and prevention of the destruction of evidence. In this case, the search of a cell phone incident to arrest could not be justified on those grounds. As a result, the Court would not extend the warrantless search exception to include cell phones confiscated from an arrested defendant.

WORDS OF THE COURT: No Danger of Harm "Digital data stored on a cell phone cannot itself be used as a weapon to harm an arresting officer or to effectuate the arrestee's escape. Law enforcement officers remain free to examine the physical aspects of a phone to ensure that it will not be used as a weapon—say, to determine whether there is a razor blade hidden between the phone and its case. Once an officer has secured a phone and eliminated any potential physical threats, however, data on the phone can endanger no one."

WORDS OF THE COURT: Importance of Warrant Requirement "Our holding, of course, is not that the information on a cell phone is immune from search; it is instead that a warrant is generally required before such a search, even when a cell phone is seized incident to arrest. Our cases have historically recognized that the warrant requirement is an important working part of our machinery of government, not merely an inconvenience to be somehow 'weighed' against the claims of police efficiency. . . . Modern cell phones are not just another technological convenience. With all they contain and all they may reveal, they hold for many Americans the privacies of life. The fact that technology now allows an individual to carry such information in his hand does not make the information any less worthy of the protection for which the Founders fought. Our answer to the question of what police must do before searching a cell phone seized incident to an arrest is accordingly simple—get a warrant."

Case Questions

1. The Court has held previously that a search incident to arrest may include the defendant's wallet/purse. Is there really a difference between a wallet and a cell phone? What if Riley's wallet had contained incriminating photographs of him? Would the police be required to get a warrant?

2. Why does the Court point out that the warrant requirement is "not merely an inconvenience to be somehow 'weighed' against the claims of police efficiency"? How is that related to Riley's circumstances?

3. *Focus on Critical Thinking:* In what way does this case illustrate the clash between technology and case precedent? What role does stare decisis ("let the decision stand") play in this case?

Search of Business Premises

Courts have been very reluctant to extend reasonable-expectation-of-privacy rights to the workplace. This is particularly true when the business is highly regulated. Remember from our previous discussion on administrative law that certain businesses are classified as *pervasively regulated* and, therefore, are not entitled to full Fourth Amendment protections. Instead, the U.S. Supreme Court has fashioned an exception to the Fourth Amendment warrant requirements that applies when an agency is conducting regularly scheduled inspections pursuant to an administrative rule. Even in cases where courts have held that administrative agencies are required to obtain an administrative warrant to conduct an inspection of a business, the Court has held that agencies are held to a lower standard of probable cause to obtain the warrant than would be required if the government were obtaining a criminal warrant. Table 45.1 summarizes the application of the Fourth Amendment's warrant requirement.

Issue	Example	Business Application
No expectation of privacy	Government searches through a trash can placed out on the public curb of a private house for pickup.	Environmental Protection Agency searches plant of a pervasively regulated business venture (government must still obtain administrative warrant).
Plain view	Police see a weapon on an individual's car seat after a traffic stop.	Government agents use zoom lens photography to obtain information in a tax fraud investigation.
Incident to arrest	Contraband is found in the pocket of an arrestee.	After the operator of a Ponzi scheme is arrested, agents find a notebook with incriminating entries in his suit coat pocket.

Self-Incrimination

The Fifth Amendment provides that no person "shall be compelled in any criminal case to be a witness against himself." This means that individuals have the right not to offer any information or statements that may be used against them in a criminal prosecution. If an individual believes that any statement or testimony may incriminate her in a criminal case, she may decline to testify on Fifth Amendment grounds. Note that the right against self-incrimination also protects those called as witnesses in other types of matters. For example, suppose that in the tax fraud hypothetical case discussed earlier, the government prosecutes Scofield for tax evasion. During the trial, the prosecutor issues a subpoena to Montgomery, Scofield's business partner. If Montgomery believes that any questions asked of him as a witness in Scofield's trial may uncover evidence of his own criminal culpability, Montgomery may refuse to testify at Scofield's trial even though he is not under investigation.

The Fifth Amendment right against self-incrimination also applies while authorities are investigating crimes. In *Miranda v. Arizona,* perhaps the most famous Fifth Amendment case in American legal history, the Supreme Court ruled that custodial interrogations were inherently coercive because of the "pressures which work to undermine the individual's free will to resist and to compel him to speak where he would not otherwise do so freely."[16] Generally, the context is that government authorities are interviewing an individual in the course of a criminal investigation. Although most case law surrounding this right deals with police interrogations of a suspect, business owners and managers should realize that agents of regulatory agencies, such as the Internal Revenue Service, are bound by the same guidelines as agents of police agencies are when interviewing suspects during a criminal investigation. An important element of this protection is that it is limited to custodial interrogations, in which the interviewee has been taken into custody or deprived of his freedom in some significant way. In this event, the authorities are required to give affirmative preinterview warnings to the suspect that he has the right not to make any statements and that any statement that is given may eventually be used as evidence against him in a criminal trial.

For example, suppose that an FBI agent telephones Barrabas and requests a meeting in Barrabas's office. The agent explains that he is investigating a fraud scheme involving government contracts. Barrabas agrees to the meeting, and during the conversation he admits to certain incriminating facts. The admission will likely be admissible as evidence despite the failure of the agent to provide the self-incrimination warning. Because the statement was made voluntarily in a noncoercive setting (Barrabas's office) and because Barrabas could have stopped the interview at any time, the interview may not be considered custodial

---

[16]384 U.S. 436, 441 (1966).

and Barrabas's Fifth Amendment protections are not triggered. Alternatively, if the agent had arrested Barrabas and transported him to a local FBI field office, the agent would be required to give the warnings about self-incrimination.

Production of Business Records

Business records such as letters, memorandums, e-mail exchanges, inventory accounts, financial documents, and the like are often at the heart of cases where government authorities are investigating potential criminal activity in the business environment. Although the U.S. Supreme Court has held that certain business records may be classified as private papers and are protected by the Fifth Amendment, this protection has been severely narrowed over the past several decades. In 1984, the Supreme Court ruled that certain business records of a sole proprietor could be considered private papers because a sole proprietor is a form of business entity that is essentially the alter ego of the individual.[17] The Court reasoned that because there is no legal separation between the business and the sole owner (unlike a corporation, which exists as a separate legal "person"), the owner's records are considered personal and are subject to Fifth Amendment protections. However, the Court also has made clear that records of a corporation are not subject to Fifth Amendment safeguards because that business entity is separate and distinct from its owners and thus does not qualify for self-incrimination protections. In Case 45.4, now considered a landmark case in this area, the U.S. Supreme Court considers where to draw the line between personal and business records.

LANDMARK CASE 45.4 Braswell v. United States, 487 U.S. 99 (1988)

FACT SUMMARY Braswell was the sole shareholder and officer in two companies engaged in brokering (buying and selling) timber, land, oil interests, and machinery. The only other directors in the companies were his wife and his mother. Federal authorities that were investigating Braswell's business subpoenaed his business records. Braswell refused to hand over the documents, claiming that he was asserting his Fifth Amendment right against self-incrimination. Braswell argued that when a business is so small that it is nothing more than a person's "alter ego," the Fifth Amendment safeguards should apply.

SYNOPSIS OF DECISION AND OPINION The U.S. Supreme Court ruled against Braswell and compelled him to hand over the books and records. The Court held that a corporation can act only through its officers and employees. When an officer or employee acts as a records custodian for that company, then he is not entitled to Fifth Amendment protection because he is no longer acting as a private individual but as part of a corporation. The Fifth Amendment protects only private individuals.

WORDS OF THE COURT: Corporate Records "Artificial entities such as corporations may act only through their agents, and a custodian's assumption of his representative capacity leads to certain obligations, including the duty to produce corporate records on proper demand by the Government. Under those circumstances, the custodian's act of production is not deemed a personal act, but rather an act of the corporation. Any claim of Fifth Amendment privilege asserted by the agent would be tantamount to a claim of privilege by the corporation—which of course possesses no such privilege."

(continued)

---

[17] *United States v. Doe,* 465 U.S. 605 (1984).

EXCLUSIONARY RULE

Trial courts are required to exclude presentation of any evidence that is obtained as a result of a constitutional violation. This is known as the *exclusionary rule.* For example, if a law enforcement officer wrongfully searches a suspect's house without first obtaining a search warrant, any evidence obtained in that search may not be used against the suspect if he is arrested and brought to trial. One important exception in the business environment is that the exclusionary rule applies only when violations of the Constitution occur and not when a government agency violates its own internal procedures. For example, suppose that a government agent secretly records a conversation with a suspected tax evader during a meeting in the agent's office. The suspect offers the agent a bribe. However, the agent has violated internal agency rules because he has failed to obtain a supervisor's permission to record any conversations with taxpayers. When the suspect is tried, she asserts that the recording cannot be introduced at trial because it is barred by the exclusionary rule. The U.S. Supreme Court has rejected such an argument and held that the exclusionary rule bars only evidence obtained in violation of a constitutional provision. In this case, an agency rule has been violated but no constitutional violations have taken place and, thus, the exclusionary rule does not apply.[18]

Even evidence that is only indirectly obtained in violation of a defendant's rights is subject to the exclusionary rule because it is considered *fruit of the poisonous tree.* This means that once original evidence is shown to have been unlawfully obtained, all evidence that stems from the original evidence (called *derivative evidence*) is also excluded. For example, suppose an agent of the Securities and Exchange Commission is investigating Falstaff for criminal fraud. The agent illegally searches the handbag of Falstaff's secretary and discovers evidence that Falstaff is concealing incriminating documents in his garage at home. Using the illegally obtained evidence, the agent then obtains a search warrant for Falstaff's home and discovers the incriminating documents. Because the agent's original evidence (obtained from Falstaff's secretary) was obtained in violation of the secretary's constitutional rights, a court would likely hold that the fruit of the poisonous tree doctrine renders the warrant invalid and bars use of all evidence derived from the warrant (the incriminating documents) in a criminal trial against Falstaff.[19]

Good Faith Exception

The exclusionary rule itself is controversial because it tends to benefit guilty parties by excluding key evidence that would help convict them. Legal commentators have filled volumes of journals and written treatises on the topic, but ultimately the exclusionary rule is justified by its proponents on the basis that it acts as a deterrent to violations of the Constitution by government authorities. Proponents argue that the integrity of the judiciary requires that courts not be made a party to lawless invasions of constitutional rights of citizens by permitting unhindered government use of unlawfully obtained evidence.

---

[18]Based on *United States v. Caceres,* 440 U.S. 741 (1979).

[19]See *Silverthorne Lumber Company v. United States*, 251 U.S. 385 (1920).

Nonetheless, the Supreme Court has fashioned several exceptions to the exclusionary rule intended to differentiate between abuse by the authorities of an individual's constitutional rights and those cases where the government has made an innocent mistake in obtaining evidence. Perhaps the most important exception to the rule occurs when the government can show that authorities were acting in *good faith* in obtaining evidence based on a search warrant issued by an authorized judge that was later found to be unsupported by an appropriate level of probable cause. In that case, even though the evidence is derived from a warrant that was granted but that was later found to have been a constitutional violation, the prosecutor may still introduce the evidence yielded from the search so long as the authorities were acting in good faith and with reasonable reliance on the search warrant.

In *Herring v. United States,*[20] the U.S. Supreme Court considered the good faith exception in the context of a police clerical error. The case involved a defendant, Herring, who was arrested after officers were incorrectly informed that an active arrest warrant existed. In fact, no warrant existed and the incorrect information given to the arresting officer was a clerical error. After Herring was arrested, the police searched him incident to arrest and discovered illegal narcotics and a firearm. Herring sought to have the evidence excluded on the basis that it had been obtained without a warrant and only as a result of a wrongful arrest. The government cited the good faith exception because the officers were acting in objectively reasonable reliance on the subsequently invalidated warrant. The U.S. Supreme Court agreed with the government that the good faith exception applied and therefore the evidence should not be excluded. The Court wrote:

> [Herring's] claim that police negligence automatically triggers suppression cannot be squared with the principles underlying the exclusionary rule, as they have been explained in our cases. In light of our repeated holdings that the deterrent effect of suppression must be substantial and outweigh any harm to the justice system, we conclude that when police mistakes are the result of negligence such as that described here, rather than systemic error or reckless disregard of constitutional requirement, any marginal deterrence does not 'pay its way.' In such a case, the criminal should not 'go free because the constable has blundered.'[21]

TAKEAWAY CONCEPTS Criminal Procedure

- The Fourth Amendment requires authorities to obtain a warrant before searching areas where a citizen has a reasonable expectation of privacy.
- Important exceptions to the warrant requirement are the plain view doctrine and search incident to arrest exception.
- The Fifth Amendment protects an individual from involuntary self-incrimination before, during, and after an investigation and trial, but it does not protect a person from disclosing business records made in the person's capacity as a corporate agent. The Fifth Amendment does not protect corporations.
- Anything said during custodial interrogation is presumed to be involuntary unless and until the person has been read the Miranda warning.
- The exclusionary rule bans evidence obtained in violation of the Constitution from being used at trial unless it fits into the good faith exception.

---

[20]555 U.S. 135 (2009).

[21]The Court used this famous "constable has blundered" passage from Judge Benjamin Cardozo's opinion criticizing the federal exclusionary rule, which was not then applicable to the states, from *People v. Defore,* 242 N.Y. 13 (1926). Cardozo would later become an associate justice of the U.S. Supreme Court.

Developing Corporate Compliance Programs

PROBLEM: In this chapter, we discussed the impact of the *Park* doctrine on the criminal liability of executive management and other corporate officers. Given the busy day of a corporate officer, how could one strategically reduce the liability associated with the *Park* doctrine?

STRATEGIC SOLUTION: Create a corporate compliance program as a mechanism to identify misconduct as early as possible, analyze whether the company devotes enough resources to develop and sustain a qualified compliance program, and document the company's efforts to continuously improve areas of weakness. In 2017, the Department of Justice's (DOJ's) Fraud Section released guidance titled *Evaluation of Corporate Compliance Programs*. The DOJ uses these guidelines to evaluate *Park* doctrine liability. While the guidelines cannot provide a one-size-fits-all compliance program, certain key areas help reduce *Park* risks.

- **Gatekeepers:** An essential part of any compliance program is the appointment and training of corporate compliance officers who act as gatekeepers in identifying and controlling misconduct.
- **Autonomy and resources:** A company's compliance department must have autonomy and resources to monitor behavior and regularly meet with management to review performance.
- **Senior and middle management:** The guidelines stress the need for having a compliance officer to create and revise policies and procedures that (1) deter management misconduct and (2) monitor senior management's behavior.
- **Design and accessibility:** Companies are urged to adopt a flexible approach in an ongoing evaluation of their compliance program designed to identify the missing processes required by the current and future business environments and to implement procedures to mitigate risk.
- **Risk assessment:** Corporate compliance programs should include an ongoing risk assessment that collects and analyzes data and then uses those data to make any improvements necessary to deter future misconduct.
- **Training and communications:** The guidelines highlight the need for compliance training generally and for higher levels of training for high-risk and control employees who may be in a position to affect the risk levels at the company.

QUESTIONS

1. Critics of the *Park* doctrine contend that the notion of holding someone strictly liable for a crime where they had no participation or knowledge is unfair and raises public policy concerns. Do you agree? Why or why not?
2. Use your favorite search engine to look up corporate compliance codes for companies that sell products or services that you use. How well does their corporate compliance align with the DOJ guidelines? What changes would you suggest? Why?

KEY TERMS

Criminal law p. 852   The body of law that, for the purpose of preventing harm to society, defines the boundaries of behavior and prescribes sanctions for violating those boundaries.

Criminal procedure p. 853   The body of constitutional protections afforded to individuals and business entities during criminal investigations, arrests, trials, and sentencing.

Model Penal Code (MPC) p. 853   A statutory text adopted by the American Law Institute in 1962 in an effort to bring greater uniformity to state criminal laws by proffering certain legal standards and reforms.

Burden of proof p. 853   The responsibility of producing sufficient evidence in support of a fact or issue and favorably convincing the fact finder of that fact or issue.

Preponderance of the evidence p. 853   The burden of proof used in civil cases, under which the fact finder need be convinced only that the defendant's liability was more likely than not to be true.

Beyond a reasonable doubt p. 853   The heightened burden of proof used in criminal cases, under which a fact finder must be convinced that the defendant's criminal liability is not in doubt to a reasonable person.

Act requirement p. 854   For criminal liability, the requirement that the government prove that a defendant's actions objectively satisfied the elements of a particular offense. Also called *actus reus*.

Mental element p. 854   Known as the guilty mind requirement, criminal statutes require a defendant to have a requisite degree of mental culpability to be convicted.

Self-defense p. 855   A defense to avoid criminal liability whereby the defendant's actions are related to the necessity of using deadly force to repel an attack in which the defendant reasonably feared that death or substantial harm was about to occur either to the defendant or to a third party.

Mental incapacity p. 855   A defense to avoid criminal liability whereby the defendant's actions are related to some type of mental disease or defect.

Felonies p. 855   Crimes that generally carry one year or more of incarceration as the penalty.

Misdemeanors p. 855   Crimes that carry up to one year of incarceration as the penalty.

Mail Fraud Act p. 859   Federal legislation enacted in 1990 that criminalizes any fraud in which the defrauding party uses the mail or any wire, radio, or television in perpetrating the fraud.

Foreign Corrupt Practices Act (FCPA) p. 862   A federal criminal statute enacted principally to prevent corporate bribery of foreign officials in business transactions.

Computer Fraud and Abuse Act (CFAA) p. 864   Federal legislation that prohibits unauthorized use of computers to commit espionage, the accessing of unauthorized information or of a nonpublic government computer, fraud by computer, damage to a computer, trafficking in passwords, and extortionate threats to damage a computer.

Investigation p. 865   The initial phase of the criminal justice process in which authorities become aware of an alleged criminal act and begin gathering physical evidence and interviewing witnesses and potential suspects.

Adjudication p. 865   A phase of the criminal justice system in which the prosecutor, after investigation, elects to proceed with the charges.

Probable cause p. 865   A reasonable amount of suspicion supported by circumstances sufficiently strong to justify a belief that a person has committed a crime.

Plain view doctrine p. 868   A doctrine stating that authorities generally do not commit a Fourth Amendment violation when a government agent obtains evidence by virtue of seeing an object that is in plain view of the agent.

CASE SUMMARY 45.1 Bear Stearns & Co. v. Wyler, 182 F. Supp. 2d 679 (N.D. Ill. 2002)

Production of Business Records

Bear Stearns had done business with Wyler, a Dutch businessman. A venture capitalist and resident of the Netherlands, Wyler kept offices in Toronto and Barbados. After the relationship soured, Bear Stearns sued Wyler for inducing one of its managing directors to make false statements and breach his fiduciary duties. In discovery, Bear Stearns requested that Wyler disclose any business records that related to that fraudulent inducement. Wyler invoked his Fifth Amendment right against self-incrimination.

CASE QUESTIONS

1. Will the court force Wyler to disclose the documents? Are they business records?
2. Does the Fifth Amendment apply in civil suits?

CASE SUMMARY 45.2 Lamb v. Philip Morris, Inc., 915 F.2d 1024 (6th Cir. 1990)

Foreign Corrupt Practices Act

Philip Morris buys tobacco for its cigarettes from all around the world, including from South American growers in Venezuela. Philip Morris entered into a contract with La Fundación del Niño (the Children's Foundation) of Caracas, Venezuela, wherein the cigarette company would give $12.5 million to the charity, which helped poor Venezuelan children. In exchange, the Venezuelan government would put price controls on the country's tobacco crop.

CASE QUESTIONS

1. What criminal law did Philip Morris possibly violate? Why?
2. Should the criminal law object to providing money to poor Venezuelan children and offering work for poor Venezuelan farmers?

CASE SUMMARY 45.3 United States v. Osborn, No. 3:12-cr-00047-M (N.D. Tex. 2012)

Corporate Officer Liability

Apothécure, Inc. and Gary Osborn, the company's owner, president, and chief pharmacist, were charged with distributing misbranded drugs, and violating the FDCA, after the company sold super- and subpotent vials of colchicine, a drug commonly prescribed to treat arthritis and neck and back pain, to a Portland, Oregon, hospital. The hospital administered the drugs to three patients, all of whom died. Osborn was responsible for

Apothécure's employee training and product quality control, but there was no evidence Osborn engaged in illegal conduct. Indeed, the government did not allege that Osborn knew the drugs were illegal.

CASE QUESTIONS

1. What is the government's theory of the case as to why Osborn was charged?
2. Who prevails and why? Explain your answer.

CASE SUMMARY 45.4 State v. Yenzer, 195 P.3d 271 (Kan. Ct. App. 2008)

Exclusionary Rule

The police received information that Yenzer, a fugitive, would be at a local dentist's office the following day. The police arrived at the dentist's office in hopes of capturing Yenzer, but she was not there. The receptionist informed them that Yenzer's appointment had been rescheduled for the next week. The police requested the exact date and time, and the dentist's receptionist complied. The police returned to the office at the rescheduled appointment time and arrested Yenzer when she arrived. Subsequent to her arrest, the police discovered evidence of additional crimes committed by Yenzer and charged her with various felonies. The Health Insurance Portability and Accountability Act (HIPAA) of 1996

prohibits dental offices from disclosing any information (including appointment times) about patients to third parties without the patient's permission. At trial, Yenzer argued that all evidence discovered after the dentist office arrest should be excluded because the arrest was made as a result of a HIPAA violation.

CASE QUESTIONS

1. Is Yenzer's dental appointment time protected by the Fourth Amendment? Why or why not?
2. Did the police go too far in this case by requesting confidential information from the dentist's receptionist? Isn't the exclusionary rule intended to deter unlawful conduct by authorities?

CHAPTER REVIEW QUESTIONS

1. What are the general requirements for criminal liability?
   - I. Preponderance
   - II. Act
   - III. Justice
   - IV. Mental
     - a. I and II
     - b. II and IV
     - c. II and III
     - d. III and IV
     - e. I, II, III and IV

2. Which doctrine was created in a case involving the conviction of an individual executive under the Food, Drug, and Cosmetic Act?
   - a. Miranda
   - b. Park
   - c. Riley
   - d. Braswell
   - e. Rat

3. The U.S. Supreme Court held that the government's use of a zoom lens in a flyover of a chemical company fell into which warrant requirement exception?

a. Search incident to arrest

b. Good faith

c. Plain view

d. Privacy

e. None of the above

4. Greco is arrested for insider trading based on evidence obtained by the government that violates Greco's Fourth Amendment rights. The evidence cannot be used against him at trial based on the:

a. Rights doctrine.

b. Violation rule.

c. Exclusionary rule.

d. Wrongful statute.

e. Securities doctrine.

5. Which amendment requires law enforcement to obtain a search warrant ?

a. First

b. Second

c. Fourth

d. Sixth

e. Eighth

6. A fundamental part of Fourth Amendment protections is based on reasonable expectations of privacy.

a. True

b. False

7. When the police find a defendant's cell phone during a search incident to arrest, they do not need a warrant to search the cell phone for incriminating photos.

a. True

b. False

8. Corporations are fully protected from having to provide self-incriminating business records under the Fifth Amendment.

a. True

b. False

9. The exclusionary rule requires the courts to exclude any evidence obtained in violation of the First Amendment.

a. True

b. False

10. Obstruction of justice charges may be brought even when the government cannot prove the underlying case.

a. True

b. False

 Quick Quiz ANSWERS
White-Collar Crimes

1. FCPA. Buying a lavish meal for foreign government officials is prohibited.
2. Fraud (Ponzi scheme).
3. Conspiracy.
4. RICO.

CHAPTER REVIEW QUESTIONS: Answers and Explanations

1. b. Criminal liability requires both an act (or omission) and the mental element of a guilty mind. The remaining answers are incorrect because preponderance and justice are unrelated to criminal liability.

2. b. Created in *United States v. Park,* the doctrine is cited in the context of holding individual corporate officers liable for certain violations. The

remaining answers are incorrect because they are names of cases unrelated to the *Park* doctrine.

3. c. In *Dow Chemical Co. v. United States,* the Court held that a zoom lens was readily available to the public and therefore could be used to enhance "plain view." Answer *a* is incorrect because no arrest was made. Answer *b* is incorrect because good faith refers to some mistake made by authorities. Answer *d* is not an exception to the warrant requirement.

4. **c.** The exclusionary rule requires that evidence obtained without a warrant and not falling into a warrant exception be excluded from trial. The remaining answers are fictional.

5. **c.** The Fourth Amendment requires law enforcement to obtain a search warrant. The remaining answers are wrong because those amendments are unrelated to the warrant requirement.

6. **a. True.** Fourth Amendment protections center on reasonable expectations of privacy.

7. **b. False.** In *Riley v. California,* the Court ruled that when the police find a defendant's cell phone during a search incident to arrest, they must obtain a warrant to search the cell phone for incriminating photos.

8. **b. False.** In *Braswell v. United States,* the Court held that corporations are not entitled to self-incrimination protection under the Fifth Amendment.

9. **b. False.** The First Amendment is not a criminal procedural protection. The exclusionary rule requires the courts to exclude any evidence obtained in violation of the Fourth, Fifth, or Sixth Amendments.

10. **a. True.** The government need only prove that an individual lied to sustain obstruction of justice.

CHAPTER 46

Insurance Law

Due to the sources of legal liability discussed throughout this textbook, businesses are wise to obtain insurance to cover as many sources of legal risk as possible. At the end of this chapter, you will be presented with a case dealing with an insurance company's decision to settle a claim that involves personal injury.

Learning Objectives

After studying this chapter, students who have mastered the material will be able to:

46-1 Summarize the basic aspects of the insurance business.

46-2 Identify the insurance policies most applicable to businesses.

46-3 Describe the fundamental aspects of an insurance contract.

46-4 Demonstrate the factors that influence insurance pricing.

46-5 Describe the essential aspects of insurance regulation.

CHAPTER OVERVIEW

Individuals and businesses must deal with uncertainty every day. Uncertainty generates risks with respect to events that may or may not occur and that may generate a negative financial impact. In the business world, many activities generate risks. For example, a high-tech firm must live with the risk that it will unintentionally infringe someone else's copyrights. A grocery store should be concerned about the risk that someone might slip and fall in the store. A manufacturer likely will be concerned that its products may injure someone. Accountants and other service professionals should worry that they might overlook something and

be liable to their clients. A restaurateur should be aware of the risk that a fire might destroy the premises and force the business to cease operations for a significant amount of time.

Any of these scenarios could generate a significant financial liability to the business and, in the worse-case scenario, might even cripple or bankrupt the enterprise. Insurance allows businesses to transfer these and other insurable business risks for a fee to a third party known as an *insurance company*. This chapter will provide an overview of the various insurance laws that apply to the relationship between the parties to an insurance contract.

THE INSURANCE BUSINESS

A business may decide to accept a risk without purchasing insurance if it believes it can finance the liability or it believes the risk is too remote. Several factors influence whether a business decides to pay for insurance. One is the potential magnitude of the loss. Another is the probability of the event's occurrence. Generally, the greater the magnitude of the loss and the higher the probability of an event's occurrence, the more likely a business is to purchase insurance and factor that as a cost of doing business.

Some risks are of such a high magnitude that when an event occurs it is deemed catastrophic. For example, the risk of a cruise ship hitting a reef and sinking would be deemed catastrophic because the entire vessel would be lost. Even if the probability of a catastrophic event is low, a business probably will insure against it to avoid the significant potential loss exposure. A useful concept for assessing the magnitude relative to the probability of an event's occurrence is a value known as an **expected loss**. The expected loss arising from an event is the probability of the event multiplied times the magnitude of the loss. The expected loss is represented by the formula:

$$\text{Expected loss} = (\text{Probability}) \times (\text{Magnitude of loss})$$

In the cruise ship example discussed earlier, if the probability of the ship running aground is 1 percent and the magnitude of the loss is $100,000,000 (the value of the ship), then the expected loss is $1,000,000. If the insurance costs slightly more than $1,000,000, the cruise ship company is likely to purchase insurance to cover this risk. The policy will cost more than $1,000,000 because the insurance company must earn a profit for assuming the risk.

Image of the cruise ship *Costa Concordia,* which sunk after it hit a rock near the coast of Italy. The shipwreck was declared a total loss by the insurance company.
©dpa picture alliance archive/Alamy

Insurance essentially is a contract relationship in which the **insured** transfers a specified risk to a third-party **insurer** that aggregates similar risks into a common pool. The contract between these parties allows the insured to transfer the **risk of loss** to the insurer for a price known as a **premium**, paid periodically during the life of the insurance contract. In the event of a loss, the insurer agrees to indemnify, or pay, the insured for the value stated in the insurance policy. The risk of loss is the uncertainty an event will occur that triggers liability or loss of property.

An essential aspect of insurance is that neither the insured nor the insurer knows prior to executing the insurance contract when and how (or even if) the loss will occur. For example, if a restaurateur knows with certainty that a fire will occur in the kitchen, this liability will not be insurable because one of the parties knows it will occur beforehand. The required uncertainty of the risk of loss is defined in insurance law as a **fortuitous** (accidental) event. For an insurance policy to be deemed valid, it must cover risk related to a fortuitous event. Paradoxically, allowing parties to transfer risk through insurance contracts can incentivize parties to engage in riskier behavior. For example, if someone knows his property is fully insured, he might engage in riskier behavior that exposes the property to loss knowing that he will be reimbursed. This is known as a **moral hazard**.

Insurers can reduce moral hazard by requiring the insured to share in the loss exposure. This amount typically is called a **deductible**. In the cruise ship example provided earlier, the insurer may underwrite only a portion of the vessel, such as $80,000,000. This leaves the ship owner to pay a $20,000,000 deductible because the vessel is valued at $100,000,000. In principle, because the cruise ship company knows it will have to co-insure the loss up to the amount of the deductible, it will take appropriate actions to minimize the chances of loss and therefore reduce the moral hazard.

As you learned in Chapters 42 and 45, businesses are exposed to liability if they engage in torts or criminal activities. Another way insurers reduce moral hazard is to deny coverage for intentional torts or crimes. This makes sense from a public policy standpoint, because insurance should not incentivize certain intentional behaviors that cause injury to others.

TAKEAWAY CONCEPTS The Insurance Business

- Two factors that influence a business's decision to pay for insurance are the magnitude of the loss and the probability of the event's occurrence.
- The expected loss arising from an event is the probability of the event multiplied times the magnitude of the loss.
- Insurance essentially is a contract relationship in which the insured transfers a specified risk to a third-party insurer that aggregates similar risks into a common pool.
- The insured transfers the risk of loss to the insurer for a price known as a premium.
- The required uncertainty of the risk of loss is defined in insurance law as a fortuitous (accidental) event.
- When an insured party engages in riskier behavior because he relies on insurance to cover his liability or loss, this is known as a moral hazard.
- Insurers reduce the chance of a moral hazard by including a deductible on a policy and refusing to insure intentional torts and criminal activity.

LO 46-2

Identify the insurance policies most applicable to businesses.

TYPES OF INSURANCE POLICIES

Over the years, the business of insurance developed along different lines corresponding to types of risks. The three main types of risks are personal, property, and liability.

Personal insurance represents policies related to life, health, accident, and disability insurance. In business, sometimes partners insure each other's lives to compensate the partnership in the event a partner dies. These types of policies apply to one individual and are thus personal in nature.

Property insurance covers things like homeowners, renters, automobile, and boat insurance. Businesses take out property insurance to protect assets in the event of loss, damage, or theft. Fire insurance, for example, is a type of property insurance that some businesses purchase. Others take out property insurance on valuable business assets, such as buildings, equipment, inventory, or machinery.

Liability insurance covers any potential insurable business liability. This includes acts of negligence committed by the business and its employees that injure others, property-related torts such as patent infringement, and mistakes made by officers or board members that injure the company and its owners. Often, a business will purchase an insurance policy known as a **commercial general liability (CGL) policy**. A standard CGL policy covers various types of business risks, including bodily injury and property damage, arising from the non-professional negligent acts of employees and injuries sustained within the business premises. Property damage is limited to tangible property and excludes intellectual property and contracts. A few other business risks are covered in the CGL, such as copyright infringement, false advertising, and wrongful eviction.

A significant risk for a sole proprietor or partner is that business liabilities will become personal liabilities. The CGL policy may protect the business to some extent; however, CGL policies contain exclusions for certain types of liabilities or may not cover the total amount of loss exposure. To reduce this risk, some business owners obtain umbrella insurance to cover gaps in their CGL policy coverage or increase the policy limits of their CGL policy.

Businesses that perform professional services, such as banks, accounting firms, and health care companies, add supplementary insurance coverage to their CGL called **professional malpractice insurance**. This type of insurance indemnifies the insured for up to the specified policy limit for the negligent acts performed by professional employees that injure clients. Corporations often purchase an additional type of specialized insurance called **errors and omissions (E&O) liability insurance**. This insurance indemnifies the directors and executive officers of a corporation if they breach any of their fiduciary duties (discussed in Chapter 30) and are found to be personally liable to the corporation due to the breach. Directors and executive officers such as CEOs often negotiate this type of indemnification as part of their agreement to work for the corporation.

TAKEAWAY CONCEPTS Types of Insurance Policies

- The three main types of insurance policy risks are personal, property, and liability.
- Often, a business will purchase an insurance policy known as a commercial general liability (CGL) policy.
- A standard CGL policy covers various types of business risks, including bodily injury and property damage, arising from the nonprofessional negligent acts of employees and injuries sustained within the business premises.
- Professional malpractice insurance indemnifies the insured for up to the specified policy limit for negligent acts performed by professional employees that injure clients.
- Errors and omissions (E&O) liability insurance indemnifies the directors and executive officers of a corporation if they breach any of their fiduciary duties.

INSURANCE CONTRACTS

Insurance contracts fall under the general umbrella of common law contracts. There are a few unique aspects of insurance contracts, however, that will be discussed in this section. First, insurance contracts require that the insured demonstrate they have an **insurable interest**. An insurable interest is an interest by the insured in the value of what is being insured that arises from a financial or legal relationship. Insurable interests arise from property, contracts, and legal liability. For example, insurable interests in property can arise from property or equipment ownership, a lease, an easement, or mineral rights such as water rights.[1] Contract-based insurable interests relate to the rights one has to property owned by someone else. For example, a commercial lease gives the tenant the insurable interest to secure insurance on the commercial real estate. Also, recall from Chapter 14 that a buyer of goods under the UCC has an insurable interest in goods that are being shipped, even if the buyer has not yet acquired title under the contract. Lastly, many business activities have the potential to create liability. The undertaking of activities that give rise to legal

LO 46-3

Describe the fundamental aspects of an insurance contract.

---

[1]See *Alcoa v. Aetna*, 998 P.2d 856 (Wash. 2000).

liability creates an insurable interest from the perspective of the insured to limit the losses from those activities. As discussed earlier, however, insurance companies will not insure liability that arises from intentional behavior such as intentional torts or criminal acts.

The requirement that an insured demonstrate an insurable interest has two policy justifications. The first is to prevent parties from engaging in pure speculative gambling with respect to others' assets or liabilities. The second is to reduce moral hazard. If parties were allowed to take out insurance without demonstrating an insurable interest, they might be incentivized to destroy property or create liability to collect insurance proceeds.

✅ QUICK QUIZ Insurable Interests

Traders such as Michael Burry placed bets that the housing market would collapse.
©AF archive/Alamy

The hit motion picture, *The Big Short,* told the remarkable story of how a few savvy investors were able to profit from the housing *market's* collapse. As detailed in the film, these investors created novel contracts with large Wall Street banks. The contracts essentially required investors to pay premiums in exchange for the *banks'* promise to pay the face value of mortgage-backed bonds that totaled billions of dollars in the event those bonds failed. At the time, few believed the housing market would collapse. Although the investors paid the premiums, they did not own any of the mortgage-backed bonds.

1. Were these contracts a type of insurance? Explain.

2. What would make the contracts fit the definition of insurance?

Answers to this Quick Quiz are provided at the end of the chapter.

An insurer has both a contractual right and a duty to defend any lawsuit alleging claims against the insured that might trigger liability under the policy. This typically is spelled out in the insurance contract. For example, the standard CGL states that "[w]e [the insurer] will pay those sums that the insured becomes legally obligated to pay as damages because of 'bodily injury' or 'property damage' to which this insurance applies. We will have the right and duty to defend the insured against any 'suit' seeking those damages."

Legal defense is an important aspect of liability insurance because the costs of defending a lawsuit can be substantial. It is not unusual for a lawsuit that reaches the jury trial stage to cost several hundred thousand dollars, and in some cases even millions of dollars. Without insurance, these high costs of litigation could devastate or significantly hinder a business. Also, unless the policy states otherwise, the insurer is free to exercise its own judgment regarding whether to settle litigation on behalf of the insured. The insurer therefore reserves the right to settle a case even if the insured objects.

Another important and unique issue related to insurance contracts is the insurer's **right of subrogation**. Once a loss is paid to the insured, subrogation gives the insurer the right to pursue a legal claim against the party who caused the loss to the insured. For example, an insurer pays a homeowner the value of the home after it is destroyed by an arsonist. The insurance company has the right of subrogation to sue the arsonist to collect the extent of the insurance claim. Subrogation also may exist as a contract term in the insurance policy and may allow the insurance company the right to collect from the insured if a claim is paid and the insured obtained payment from the third party who caused the loss.

Case 46.1 deals with Wal-Mart and its subrogation rights under a health insurance policy of an employee who suffered brain damage after a car accident.

CASE 46.1 Administrative Committee of the Wal-Mart Stores, Inc. Associates' Health and Welfare Plan v. James A. Shank et al., 500 F.3d 834 (8th Cir. 2007)

FACT SUMMARY Deborah Shank was a Wal-Mart employee and a member of Wal-Mart's Health and Welfare Plan ("the Plan"), a self-funded employee benefit plan. In May 2000, Shank was severely injured in a car accident and was declared incompetent. Under the terms of the Plan, the Committee paid for Shank's medical expenses related to the accident, a total of $469,216. Shank eventually filed a lawsuit against the parties responsible for her injuries, and in 2002, she obtained a settlement of $700,000. After deducting attorney's fees and costs, the district court placed the remaining $417,477 from the settlement into a special needs trust, with Shank as the beneficiary and her husband, James Shank, as the trustee.

The Plan, however, contained a subrogation and reimbursement clause that granted the Committee first priority over any judgment or settlement Shank received relating to the accident. After the Committee learned of Shank's settlement agreement, it sought to enforce the Plan's reimbursement provision and brought suit against Deborah Shank, James Shank, and the special needs trust. The district court granted summary judgment for the Committee. The Shanks appealed the judgment of the district court.

SYNOPSIS OF DECISION AND OPINION After reviewing the district court's decision, the 8th Circuit appellate court affirmed the trial court upon its review of the subrogation clause in Wal-Mart's employee health care policy.

WORDS OF THE COURT: Subrogation Rights Upheld "In this case, the Plan is clear about the rule of recovery. It states:

> The Plan has the right to recover or subrogate 100 percent of the benefits paid by the Plan on your behalf to the extent of [a]ny judgment, settlement, or any payment made or to be made, relating to the accident.

These rights apply regardless of whether such payments are designated as payment for [m]edical benefits [or] [w]hether the participant has been made whole (i.e., fully compensated for his/her injuries). The Plan has first priority with respect to its right to reduction, reimbursement and subrogation.

"Shank would benefit if we denied the Committee its right to full reimbursement, but all other plan members would bear the cost in the form of higher premiums. . . . Reimbursement and subrogation provisions are crucial to the financial viability of self-funded [health] plans, and, as a fiduciary, the Committee must 'preserve assets to satisfy future, as well as present, claims,' and must 'take impartial account of the interests of all beneficiaries.'

. . .

"The written Plan in this case confers benefits on both parties. Shank contributed premium payments, plus a promise to reimburse the Committee for medical expenses in the event she was injured and received a judgment or settlement from third parties. In exchange, she received the certainty that the Committee would pay her medical bills immediately if she was injured. . . . For these reasons, the judgment of the district court is affirmed."

Case Questions

1. The court relied on the fact that Wal-Mart's health insurance plan was self-funded, which means Wal-Mart was the insurer. Why did this factor matter?

2. After the media reported this story, Wal-Mart dropped its lawsuit against the Shanks and the company changed its subrogation policy. What does this tell you about the ethics of subrogation in health insurance cases?

3. *Focus on Critical Thinking:* Do you agree with the court's decision? Explain.

- Insurance contracts require that the insured demonstrate they have an insurable interest.
- An insurable interest is an interest by the insured in the value of what is being insured that arises from a financial or legal relationship.
- The requirement that an insured demonstrate an insurable interest has two policy justifications: to prevent parties from engaging in pure speculative gambling with respect to others' assets or liabilities and to reduce moral hazard.
- An insurer has both a contractual right and a duty to defend any lawsuit alleging claims against the insured that might trigger liability under the policy.
- Legal defense is an important aspect of liability insurance because the costs of defending a lawsuit can be substantial.
- Once a loss is paid to the insured, subrogation gives the insurer the right to pursue a legal claim against the party who caused the loss to the insured.

INSURANCE PRICING

LO 46-4

Demonstrate the factors that influence insurance pricing.

The amount an insured will receive is controlled by the **principle of indemnity**. The goal of the indemnity principle is to reimburse the insured for the losses sustained and no more. Consequently, an insured can never recover more than the value of the damaged property or the extent of her liability.

To understand how insurance is priced, one must understand how insurers value risk, because this will be reflected in the premiums paid by the insured. Insurers often have access to historical data that allow them to determine the probability of an event occurring. They also may have data on the loss exposure related to these events. Insurers employ **actuaries**, individuals who are trained in mathematics and use statistical models to calculate the probabilities and loss exposure of particular risks. Ultimately, an insurance premium will be determined by the following general formula:[2]

$$\text{Premium} = \text{Losses} + \text{LAE} + \text{UW expenses} + \text{UW profit}$$

Losses represents the estimate of total claims submitted by the insured parties that must be paid out. *LAE* stands for loss adjustment expense and represents additional costs associated with the claims, such as legal defense costs. *UW expenses* are underwriting expenses and are comprised of fees paid to insurance agents and brokers, advertising costs, actuarial costs, and administrative expenses. *UW profit* is the profit that the insurance company must earn to remain in business. All of these items are factored into the price of the premium paid by the insured party.

The insured may take several steps as part of a **risk management program** to minimize the probabilities of a loss or the loss amount should the event occur. Following prudent business practices and maintaining a robust compliance program, for example, can help minimize losses and may be used as a negotiating factor to lower the price of insurance. Several legal techniques can effectively minimize losses. For example, to reduce negligence losses, a service provider may require customers to sign liability waivers. Parties to a manufacturing and distribution contract may limit damages through appropriate drafting techniques, such

---

[2]Geoff Werner, Claudine Modlin, and Willis Towers Watson, *Basic Ratemaking* (2016).

as adding a waiver of consequential damages or lost profits. A seller of goods may disclaim warranties. All of these legal techniques can reduce loss exposure.

The high costs and frequency of litigation, however, will be priced into insurance premiums. Businesses must face the reality that the costs of defending litigation will be spread out among all policyholders. This may lead to high insurance costs in areas of business that are more prone to litigation and liability.

Figure 46.1 provides a breakdown of insurance premiums available to health care companies that employ doctors in Illinois. Notice that certain medical practice areas are more expensive to insure than others. What do you think explains the difference in pricing?

FIGURE 46.1	Insurance Premium Comparison			
MEDICAL SPECIALTY	CODE	$500K/$1.5M	$1M/$3M	$2M/$4M
Internal Medicine-NMRP	80257	27,404	37,688	50,692
Internal Medicine-MRP	80284	33,832	46,688	62,796
Neonatology	83015	71,116	98,888	145,564
Nephrology-NMRP	80260	26,116	35,888	48,268
Nephrology-MRP	80287	29,972	41,288	55,532
Neurology	80261	33,832	46,688	62,796
Neurosurgery-NMRP,NMajS	81045	23,544	32,288	43,428
Neurosurgery-MRP,NMajS	82045	38,972	53,888	72,480
Neurosurgery-No Intracranial Surgery	86027	107,116	149,284	219,748
Neurosurgery	80152	163,684	228,484	346,152
Nuclear Medicine	80262	23,544	32,288	43,428
Obstetrical/Gynecological Surgery	80153	99,400	138,484	203,848
Occupational Medicine	80079	11,976	16,088	21,640
Oncology	80259	23,544	32,288	43,428
Ophthalmology-NS	80263	15,832	21,488	28,900
Ophthalmic Surgery	80114	23,544	32,288	43,428
Oral/Maxillofacial Surgery	86154	23,544	32,288	43,428
Orthopaedics-NMRP,NS	81057	23,544	32,288	43,428
Orthopaedics-MRP,NMajS	82025	33,832	46,688	62,796
Orthopaedic Surgery w/o Spine	86026	76,260	106,084	156,156
Orthopaedic Surgery w/Spine	80154	107,116	149,284	219,748
Otorhinolaryngology-NMRP,NS	80060	11,976	16,088	21,640
Otorhinolaryngology-MRP,NMajS	80291	33,832	46,688	62,796
Otorhinolaryngology: No Elective Plastic	80159	40,260	55,688	74,900
Otorhinolaryngology: Head/Neck	80155	47,972	66,488	92,752
Otorhinolaryngology: Other than Head/Neck	86155	71,116	98,888	145,564
Pathology	80082	15,832	21,488	28,900
Pediatrics-NMRP	80267	17,116	23,288	31,324
Pediatrics-MRP	80293	33,832	46,688	62,796
Physical Med. & Rehab.	80235	11,976	16,088	21,640
Plastic Surgery	80156	71,116	98,888	145,564
Podiatry, No Surgery	86601	15,832	21,488	28,900
Podiatry, Surgery	86602	29,972	41,288	55,532
Psychiatry	80249	15,832	21,488	28,900
Public Health & Preventive Med	80236	11,976	16,088	21,640
Pulmonary Diseases	80269	29,972	41,288	55,532
Radiology-NMRP	80253	29,972	41,288	55,532
Radiology-MRP	80280	33,832	46,688	62,796
Radiology-MajRP	83033	42,832	59,288	79,744
Radiation Oncology	87047	20,976	28,688	38,584

The Practice of Medicine Without Liability Insurance

Many states have statutes that require doctors to carry a minimum amount of medical malpractice liability insurance. Some states, however, have statutes that allow doctors to practice medicine without any liability insurance. For example, a Florida statute[3] allows doctors to practice without insurance if they post the following sign in their office:

Under Florida law, physicians are generally required to carry medical malpractice insurance or otherwise demonstrate financial responsibility to cover potential claims for medical malpractice. YOUR DOCTOR HAS DECIDED NOT TO CARRY MEDICAL MALPRACTICE INSURANCE. This is permitted under Florida law subject to certain conditions. Florida law imposes penalties against noninsured physicians who fail to satisfy adverse judgments arising from claims of medical malpractice. This notice is provided pursuant to Florida law.

Discussion Questions

1. Why would states like Florida allow doctors to practice without carrying malpractice insurance?
2. Why would a doctor and a patient agree to this practice?

TAKEAWAY CONCEPTS Insurance Pricing Factors

- The goal of the indemnity principle is to reimburse the insured for the losses sustained and no more.
- Actuaries are individuals trained in mathematics who use statistical models to calculate the probabilities and loss exposure of particular risks.
- Premiums are calculated using the following formula: Premium = Losses + LAE + UW expenses + UW profit.
- The insured may take several steps as part of a risk management program to minimize the probabilities of a loss or the loss amount should the event occur.

INSURANCE REGULATION

LO 46-5

Describe the essential aspects of insurance regulation.

Insurance is largely governed by state laws and regulations. Congress decided to largely relinquish regulatory control to the states when it passed the McCarran-Ferguson Act.[4] According to that act, "[T]he business of insurance, and every person engaged therein, shall be subject to the laws of the several States which relate to the regulation or taxation of such business."[5] Because most states have passed insurance regulation statutes, this means that insurance law is largely a state law issue. Some states have passed statutes based on a model act developed by the National Association of Insurance Commissioners (NAIC).[6] There is some disparity, however, among the states with respect to insurance regulation statutes. To

---

[3]Florida Statutes § 458.320(7).

[4]15 U.S.C. § 1011 et seq. (1945).

[5]Id. at § 2(a).

[6]The NAIC is an association of the chief regulatory officials of the 50 states. They propose model laws and gather data related to the insurance industry.

the extent that the various state statutes overlap, they empower state insurance regulators, known as *insurance commissioners,* to

1. ensure that consumers are charged fair and reasonable prices for insurance products;
2. protect the solvency of insurers;
3. prevent unfair insurer practices; and
4. guarantee the availability of coverage to the public.[7]

The first objective is achieved through price regulations that prevent insurers from setting artificially high rates and by requiring certain insurance terms to be included in standardized insurance contracts. The second goal is achieved by requiring insurers to maintain adequate capital reserves. The third goal extends to truth-in-advertising laws and good faith obligations. The last objective is met by requiring that certain insurance plans be made available to the public, such as automobile insurance in states where it is legally required. In some cases, insurance regulators require that insurers contribute toward a **residual market plan**, which provides coverage for those who may not be able to obtain insurance through the regular insurance markets.

An important aspect of insurance regulation is the imposition on insurers of a duty of good faith toward the insured. The duty of good faith is not formally defined, but it is generally understood to require insurers to behave reasonably and honestly. An insurer engages in bad faith if it fails to handle a claim in a fair manner, fails to indemnify the insured against loss, or cancels insurance policies without just cause. The courts and state statutes often provide punitive damages to the insured if an insurer engages in bad faith.

In Case 46.2, the Georgia Supreme Court decides a case involving an insured who sued his insurance company for refusing to settle an offer within the policy limits.

CASE 46.2 Cotton States Mutual Insurance Co. v. Brightman, 580 S.E. 2d 519 (2003)

FACT SUMMARY Brightman was seriously injured in August 1992 when a van owned by Martin and driven by Cumbo struck his car as he was turning left at an intersection. Martin had a $300,000 insurance policy with Cotton States Insurance, and Cumbo had a $100,000 policy with State Farm. Brightman offered to settle the case and sent Cotton States the following settlement offer:

> We are willing to give Cotton States Mutual Insurance Company one last chance in which to settle this case for your policy limits of $300,000.00. We will agree to accept your policy limits, contingent upon State Farm Mutual Automobile Insurance Company also tendering its limits of $100,000, for the next ten days. If you have not accepted this offer within ten days from the date of this letter, then it is to be considered irrevocably withdrawn.

Cotton States refused to settle and opted to litigate. A jury then awarded Brightman $1,800,000 in damages. Cotton States paid the policy limit of $300,000, but the remainder of the damages award was assessed against the defendants. Martin sued Cotton States for failing to reasonably settle the claim within the policy limit when it had the opportunity to do so.

SYNOPSIS OF DECISION AND OPINION On appeal, the Georgia Supreme Court held that Cotton States had unreasonably refused to settle the case within the insured's policy limits. The court affirmed the trial court and appellate court and found that Cotton States was liable to the insured for the excess jury award judgment.

(continued)

---

[7]Robert H. Jerry, II, and Douglas R. Richmond, *Understanding Insurance Law* (2012).

WORDS OF THE COURT: Insurer's Duty to Settle

"An insurance company may be liable for the excess judgment entered against its insured based on the insurer's bad faith or negligent refusal to settle a personal claim within the policy limits. Judged by the standard of the ordinarily prudent insurer, the insurer is negligent in failing to settle if the ordinarily prudent insurer would consider choosing to try the case created an unreasonable risk. The rationale is that the interests of the insurer and insured diverge when a plaintiff offers to settle a claim for the limits of the insurance policy. The insured is interested in protecting itself against an excess judgment; the insurer has less incentive to settle because litigation may result in a verdict below the policy limits or a defense verdict.

. . .

"An insurance defense attorney and claims adjuster testified that Cotton States could have offered its $300,000 before the 10-day deadline passed without waiting to see what State Farm would do. In addition, industry experts agreed that, in cases involving multiple defendants and insurance companies, one insurance company can offer its policy limits in response to a demand—'put our money on the table'—and then let the plaintiff negotiate with the remaining insurers. . . .

"[T]here is evidence to support the jury's verdict that Cotton States breached its duty to its insured to settle Brightman's claim.

"Judgment affirmed."

Case Questions

1. Why would an insurance company refuse to settle a claim that is near, or at, the policy limit?

2. Why does an insurer have complete control over the decision to settle a case?

3. *Focus on Critical Thinking:* Was this case correctly decided? Did the insurer exhibit good faith? Explain.

TAKEAWAY CONCEPTS Insurance Regulation

- Insurance is largely governed by state laws and regulations.
- Congress decided to largely relinquish regulatory control to the states when it passed the McCarran-Ferguson Act.
- An important aspect of insurance regulation is the imposition on insurers of a duty of good faith toward the insured.
- An insurer engages in bad faith if it fails to handle a claim in a fair manner, fails to indemnify the insured against loss, or cancels insurance policies without just cause.

 THINKING STRATEGICALLY

Insurer's Duty to Settle a Claim in Good Faith

PROBLEM: Insurer's have a duty to settle claims in good faith, yet, their economic interests can differ from those of an insured client.

STRATEGIC SOLUTION: The following case illustrates this problem and the potential for a bad faith claim against an insurer.

Melissa is a manager at First Indemnity Insurance Co. and has been assigned to oversee a personal injury liability claim brought against an insured customer. The insured customer is Walton's Supermarkets, a national grocery store chain. Several months ago, a customer entered a Walton's grocery store and slipped due to a spill. The case has been in litigation for several months. In the complaint, the plaintiff submitted medical bills totaling $125,000 and statements concerning the treatment and ongoing pain related to a spinal cord injury

Law Offices
John P. Morgan, Esq.

June 11, 2019

Ms. Melissa Crawford
V.P. First Indemnity Insurance Co.

RE: Client settlement offer

Dear Ms. Crawford:

My client is willing to provide First Indemnity Insurance Co. an oportunity to settle this case against your insured for the policy limit of $500,000.00. If you do not accept this offer within 7 business days from the date of this letter the offer will be considered irrevocably withdrawn and we will proceed with litigation and demand a jury trial.

Sincerely,

John P. Morgan

John P. Morgan, Esq.

---

resulting from the fall. Today, Melissa received the letter above from the plaintiff's attorney.

Through her conversations with First Indemnity's outside legal defense counsel, Melissa has learned that the plaintiff's case has roughly a 50 percent chance of winning a jury verdict. The case is uncertain because there is video evidence that the plaintiff negligently ran down the aisle despite the large puddle of brightly colored liquid on the floor. Defense counsel has advised Melissa, however, that due to the serious and permanent nature of the plaintiff's injuries, the potential jury verdict, if the case is won, could reach $2 to $3 million. Melissa now must decide how to respond to the settlement offer letter.

QUESTIONS

1. Would Walton's Supermarkets prefer to settle or litigate the case? Explain.
2. Does First Indemnity have valid reasons to proceed with litigation? Invalid reasons?
3. Does Melissa have to accept the settlement offer? Why or why not?
4. What are the potential legal and financial repercussions if Melissa decides to reject the settlement offer?
5. How would you respond to the letter?

KEY TERMS

Expected loss p. 881   The probability of an event occurring multiplied times the magnitude of the loss.

Insured p. 881   The party that transfers a specified risk to an insurer.

Insurer p. 881   The party that aggregates similar risks into a common pool and agrees to indemnify the insured in the event of a loss.

Risk of loss p. 881   The uncertainty an event will occur that triggers liability or loss of property.

Premium p. 881   The price an insured pays during the life of the insurance contract to transfer the risk of loss to the insurer.

Fortuitous p. 881   The accidental nature of risk of loss required in insurance contracts.

Moral hazard p. 881   When an insured party engages in riskier behavior because he relies on insurance to cover his liability or loss.

Deductible p. 881   The amount the insured is required to share in the loss exposure to reduce moral hazard.

Commercial general liability (CGL) policy p. 882   An insurance policy that covers various types of business risks, including bodily injury and property damage, arising from the nonprofessional negligent acts of employees and injuries sustained within the business premises.

Professional malpractice insurance p. 883   Insurance that indemnifies the insured for up to the specified policy limit for negligent acts performed by professional employees that injure clients.

Errors and omissions (E&O) liability insurance p. 883   Insurance that indemnifies the directors and executive officers of a corporation if they breach their fiduciary duties.

Insurable interest p. 883   An interest by the insured in the value of what is being insured that arises from a financial or legal relationship.

Right of subrogation p. 884   The right of the insurer to pursue a legal claim against the party who caused the loss to the insured.

Principle of indemnity p. 886   Principle that states the insurer will reimburse the insured for no more than the losses sustained.

Actuary p. 886   Individual employed by insurers who is trained in mathematics and uses statistical models to calculate the probabilities and loss exposure of particular risks.

Risk management program p. 886   Steps taken by the insured to minimize the probabilities of a loss or the loss amount should the event occur.

Residual market plan p. 889   An insurance plan that provides coverage for individuals who may not be able to obtain insurance through the regular insurance markets.

CASE SUMMARY 46.1 Balentine v. New Jersey Insurance Underwriting Association, 966 A.2d 1098 (N.J. Super. Ct. App. Div. 2009)

Insurable Interest

Balentine and Gianeta were friends who co-owned a commercial building. After Balentine went bankrupt, they transferred the property to Gianeta. Gianeta allowed Balentine to use the property and gave him authority to manage it. When the building was damaged, Balentine filed an insurance claim that was denied by the insurer. The insurer claimed Balentine had no insurable interest. The court ultimately found in favor of Balentine.

CASE QUESTIONS

1. Why would the insurer deny Balentine's claim?
2. On what grounds would the court find that Balentine had an insurable interest?

CASE SUMMARY 46.2 Eyeblaster, Inc. v. Federal Insurance Co., 613 F.3d 797 (8th Cir. 2010)

CGL—Duty to Defend

David Sefton, a computer user, sued Eyeblaster alleging that Eyeblaster injured his computer, software, and data after he visited an Eyeblaster website. Eyeblaster tendered the defense of the lawsuit to Federal Insurance Co., seeking coverage under a commercial general liability (CGL) policy. Federal denied that it had a duty to defend Eyeblaster, and Eyeblaster brought this action seeking a declaration that Federal owed such a duty. The district court entered summary judgment in favor of Federal, and Eyeblaster appealed. Federal's position was that it owed no coverage under the policy because the policy excluded software and only included tangible property. The appellate court reversed the lower courts and decided that the plain meaning of tangible property includes computers, and the Sefton complaint repeatedly alleged the "loss of use" of his computer. Thus, the claim was within the scope of the general liability policy and Federal owed a duty to defend the lawsuit.

CASE QUESTIONS

1. Why does the CGL only protect tangible property as opposed to intangible property like software?
2. Do you agree with the court's decision? Explain.

Duty to Settle

Dr. Papudesu was sued for medical malpratice. His insurance company settled the case with the defendant, and the doctor objected, arguing that it would injure his reputation and raise his premiums and that the insurance contract required the insurer to litigate the case. The insurance policy stated: "The [insurance] company may make such investigation and settlement of any claim or suit as it deems expedient." The court decided that the contract vested full discretion in the insurer with respect to the issue of settlement. The insurer fully performed its duties in accordance with the unambiguous language of the contract by defending the suit against Dr. Papudesu and by exercising its discretion in investigating and settling that suit in a manner that was deemed expedient and within the policy limits.

CASE QUESTIONS

1. Was the language in the insurance policy vague? Explain your answer.
2. Should insurance companies take the insured party's settlement preferences into account? Explain your answer.

CHAPTER REVIEW QUESTIONS

1. The amount paid by the insured to the insurer for assuming the risk of loss is called the:
   a. Indemnity.
   b. Premium.
   c. Risk of loss.
   d. Subrogation.
   e. Expected loss.

2. Insurers employ _____, individuals trained in mathematics who use statistical models to calculate the probabilities and loss exposure of particular risks.
   a. Adjusters
   b. Attorneys
   c. Actuaries
   d. Underwriters
   e. None of the above

3. If an insurer pays a claim to an insured and the loss arises due to a tort of a third party, the insurer can pursue a legal claim against the third party. This is known as:
   a. Moral hazard.
   b. The principle of indemnity.
   c. Subrogation.
   d. An insurable interest.
   e. None of the above.

4. Which is used by insurers to reduce moral hazard?
   a. Deductible
   b. Premium
   c. Expected loss
   d. Risk of loss
   e. Insurable interest

5. All of the following are used to calculate a premium except:
   a. Losses.
   b. LAE.
   c. UW expenses.
   d. UW profit.
   e. ROA.

6. Individuals and businesses must deal with uncertainty every day.
   a. True
   b. False

7. Businesses always purchase insurance to cover the risk of liability.
   a. True
   b. False

8. The insurer must consult with the insured on accepting a settlement offer.

a. True

b. False

9. Insurers sometimes pay a claim that exceeds an insured's loss of property or liability.

a. True

b. False

10. The expected loss arising from an event is the probability of the event multiplied times the magnitude of the benefit.

a. True

b. False

 Quick Quiz ANSWERS
Insurable Interests

1. These contracts were not a type of insurance. One of the requirements of an insurance contract is an insurable interest, which in this case would arise from the ownership of the mortgage-backed bonds. Because the investors did not own these bonds, they were engaged in pure speculation regarding the decline of the housing market.

2. These contracts would have to have an insurable interest to be considered insurance contracts.

CHAPTER REVIEW QUESTIONS: Answers and Explanations

1. b. The premium is the amount paid by the insured to the insurer for assuming the risk of loss.

2. c. Actuaries are individuals trained in mathematics who use statistical models to calculate the probabilities and loss exposure of particular risks.

3. c. Subrogation allows an insurer to pursue a legal claim against a third party.

4. a. Deductibles are used to reduce moral hazard.

5. e. ROA is not used to calculate a premium.

6. a. True. Individuals and businesses must deal with uncertainty every day.

7. b. False. A business may decide to accept a risk without purchasing insurance if the it believes it can finance the liability or it believes the risk is too remote.

8. b. False. The insurer often reserves the right to decide settlement offers.

9. b. False. The principle of indemnity forbids paying beyond the loss.

10. b. False. The expected loss arising from an event is the probability of the event multiplied times the magnitude of the *loss*.

CHAPTER 47

Environmental Law

Business owners and managers may face environmental law liability when they buy or sell real estate if the land at issue is contaminated even if the buyer had no reason to know about the pollution. In this chapter's *Thinking Strategically*, we examine this issue and provide a solution to reduce liability through environmental due diligence.

Learning Objectives

After studying this chapter, students who have mastered the material will be able to:

47-1 Explain the impact of environmental regulation on business.

47-2 Identify the origins and sources of environmental law.

47-3 Describe the role of the Environmental Protection Agency and state agencies in the implementation and enforcement of environmental laws.

47-4 Explain the role of citizen suits in enforcing environmental regulations.

47-5 Describe the primary objectives and provisions of major federal statutes that protect the environment.

47-6 Provide examples of various industries regulated by air and water pollution laws related to the disposal of waste and hazardous materials.

47-7 Articulate the potential liability of various parties under the federal environmental cleanup statutes.

CHAPTER OVERVIEW

Environmental law is a collection of federal, state, and local laws that protect natural resources and promote a healthier environment for the public at large. Whether it concerns the federal regulation of industrial plants or a city ordinance prohibiting the use of certain pesticides by landscapers within municipal limits, business owners and managers from across the spectrum of commercial sectors encounter environmental law and regulation in their daily operations and their business planning. In this chapter, we discuss the origins, sources, and enforcement mechanisms used in environmental law as well as the primary environmental statutes that apply to business operations.

IMPACT OF ENVIRONMENTAL LAW ON BUSINESS

LO 47-1

Explain the impact of environmental regulation on business.

Business owners and managers all too often assume that environmental law and regulation is a concern only for owners of large industrial plants that produce smokestack pollution or dump waste into rivers. Yet, environmental laws must be thought of as having broad coverage, and understanding environmental law is important in limiting a company's liability and ensuring regulatory compliance. Any assumption that environmental laws are not pertinent to a particular business's operation may be costly in terms of liability and may result in missed opportunities for proactive business planning and risk control.

As the American public becomes increasingly concerned over threats to the environment and related issues such as oil spills and global warming, governments at the federal, state, and local levels have broadened environmental regulation and liability for environmental cleanups. Local businesses such as dry cleaners, bakeries, mechanic shops, gas stations, landscaping firms, contracting firms, and a host of others are now subject to various environmental laws. Liability for environmental cleanup is another concern for business owners and managers if their business operations involve the ownership of land. Certain federal statutes (discussed in detail later in this chapter) create liability for owners of property that is contaminated even if the owner has not contributed to the contamination. This strict liability concept is an important factor when planning a land purchase.

TAKEAWAY CONCEPT Impact of Environmental Law on Business

> Business owners and managers should think of environmental regulation as broad-based and relevant to large and small businesses alike.

ORIGINS AND SOURCES OF ENVIRONMENTAL LAW

LO 47-2

Identify the origins and sources of environmental law.

The origins of environmental protections are primarily based on the common law doctrine of **nuisance**. In a suit for nuisance, an aggrieved party sues to compel a polluter to cease polluting based on the aggrieved party's right to enjoy her property without interference from a third party. Local zoning ordinances are generally designed to prevent nuisance by segmenting a municipality into zones—industrial, residential, and so forth. However, this common law doctrine is a protection of a party's individual property rights. Historically, the federal government has left regulation of the environment to state and local authorities. This has resulted in a patchwork of standards, with some areas of the country allowing heavy industrial pollution and other areas regulating or banning such pollution. Because pollution does not respect state boundaries, federal statutes have become necessary to achieve meaningful environmental protections. Modern environmental protection statutes at both the federal and state levels have largely supplanted any common law protections. In addition, local municipalities often have environmental ordinance standards related to safety and local public policy (such as proper disposal of engine oil or other hazardous waste by a local mechanic).

Environmental protection statutes are wide-ranging, but federal and state statutes that impact businesses are primarily designed to (1) ensure that government agency decisions have the least possible impact on the environment, (2) promote clean air and water through regulation and permits, (3) regulate the use and disposal of solid and hazardous waste, (4) clean up property or waterways that are contaminated with hazardous waste, and (5) protect wildlife and endangered species.

TAKEAWAY CONCEPT Origins and Sources of Environmental Law

Federal and state statutes limit government impact on the environment, promote clean air and water, provide for hazardous waste cleanup, and protect wildlife.

LO 47-3

Describe the role of the Environmental Protection Agency and state agencies in the implementation and enforcement of environmental laws.

GOVERNMENT ENFORCEMENT

Federal environmental laws are primarily administered, implemented, and enforced by the U.S. Environmental Protection Agency (EPA). The EPA, created in 1970, works in tandem with other administrative agencies in handling a broad range of environmental concerns at the federal level. For example, the U.S. Fish and Wildlife Service primarily enforces statutes protecting endangered species. However, if the use of pesticides is responsible for depleting the population of certain endangered species, the EPA will work to use environmental regulation to halt the use of the pesticides. Other agencies that have certain environmental regulation jurisdiction include the Food and Drug Administration (FDA) and the Nuclear Regulatory Commission (NRC).

Like all administrative agencies, the EPA has broad powers to implement and enforce environmental laws by promulgating rules,[1] providing permits, issuing advisory opinions, and investigating potential violations of federal environmental protection statutes, as well as using traditional enforcement tools such as administrative fines and penalties, civil suits, and, in egregious cases, criminal complaints. In addition to the EPA and other federal agencies, each state has its own environmental agency to implement and enforce state environmental statutes. In certain municipalities, a local environmental agency may exist to enforce local ordinances, such as those related to illegal dumping. The name of the agency varies among jurisdictions, but titles such as Department of Environmental Protection or Department of Natural Resources, or some variation of the two, are common. An important feature of many federal environmental laws is that state governments are often mandated to work in conjunction with (or under the supervision of) the EPA when implementing and enforcing federal environmental statutes such as the Clean Water Act.

TAKEAWAY CONCEPT Government Enforcement

- The U.S. Environmental Protection Agency is the primary agency tasked with enforcing federal environmental laws.
- Every state has its own environmental regulation agency to enforce state laws, and local governments often pass environmental ordinances to prevent local hazards (e.g., illegal dumping).

---

[1] Recall from Chapter 43, "Administrative Law," that administrative agencies such as the EPA are authorized by statute to implement binding legal regulations following a rulemaking process.

CITIZEN SUIT PROVISIONS AND WATCHDOG GROUPS

LO 47-4

Explain the role of citizen suits in enforcing environmental regulations.

Perhaps more than in any other area of the law, citizen interest organizations (also called *watchdog groups*) have contributed to the enforcement of environmental statutes and policy. Virtually every major federal environmental statute enacted since 1970 authorizes citizen suits.[2] These citizen interest organizations and individual citizens are statutorily authorized to file a lawsuit against either a polluter who is in violation of environmental statutes or regulations or a government agency or unit (such as the EPA or a municipality) that is not taking legally mandated steps to carry out environmental law enforcement. Individuals and groups derive this authority to file enforcement lawsuits by virtue of **citizen suit provisions** that are a part of many federal and state environmental statutes. When an environmental statute authorizes citizen suits, it generally requires that notice of a citizen suit be given to the agency with jurisdiction over the matter. The statute also allows the agency to decide whether to initiate agency action instead of allowing the citizen suit to go forward. A private citizen or group cannot profit from an enforcement action, and frequently the initiator of the suit is simply seeking a court order that will prevent or require a certain action.

The Sierra Club is an environmental watchdog group that uses citizen suits to bring polluters into compliance with the law.
©Joshua Yospyn/The Washington Post via Getty Images

Typically, citizen suit provisions in environmental law spell out a procedure that gives the appropriate government agency and the polluter specific notice of the complaint and provides a period of time (usually 60 days) for action by the agency or compliance by the violator. If the time period expires without any action, the citizen suit may be filed in court. Citizen suits may not be commenced against a polluter if a government agency is already prosecuting the same violator. Some common initiators of environmental law citizen suits include the Sierra Club, the Natural Resources Defense Council, and the Environmental Defense Fund. Local environmental watchdog groups in different regions of the United States tend to focus on a particular concern unique to the region (e.g., the Spotted Owl Defense League of Oregon).

In Case 47.1, an appellate court analyzes the procedure used in a citizen suit under the Clean Water Act.

CASE 47.1 Friends of the Earth v. Gaston Copper Recycling Corp., 29 F.3d 387 (4th Cir. 2011)

FACT SUMMARY Gaston Copper Recycling ("Gaston") owned a metals smelting facility in South Carolina and operated it until 1995. After 1995, Gaston continued to treat contaminated storm water at the facility and to release this treated water into a lake on its property. However, the lake's water overflow discharged into other waterways and spread pollutants that resulted from the contact of rainwater with scrap metal stored by Gaston on its property. Friends of the Earth ("Friends") is an environmental citizen action group whose members include owners of property affected by the Gaston

(continued)

---

[2]See, e.g., Toxic Substances Control Act, 15 U.S.C. §§ 2618, 2619 (2000); Federal Water Pollution Control Act (Clean Water Act), 33 U.S.C. § 1365 (2000); Clean Air Act, 42 U.S.C. § 7604, 7607 (2000).

pollutants. Although Gaston attempted to solve the problem, the company continued to miss compliance deadlines for reducing the pollutants being discharged into the waterways.

Friends sent Gaston a notice letter that alleged its noncompliance with the statute and named over 300 specific violations committed by Gaston. The Clean Water Act required that this statutory notice be sent prior to bringing a citizen suit. Ultimately, Friends brought a citizen suit, and the trial court imposed a $2.3 million fine on Gaston based on the violations alleged by Friends in the required prelawsuit notice and additional violations that were uncovered during the discovery phase of the litigation. Gaston appealed the trial court's decision, arguing that the imposition of the citizen suit fine was not authorized by the statute because much of the penalty was related to pollutants that were not identified in the original notice letter.

SYNOPSIS OF DECISION AND OPINION The Fourth Circuit Court of Appeals reversed the civil fines imposed by the trial court on Gaston for all violations except the ones that were articulated in Friends's citizen suit notice. The court held that the notice letter provision in the statute has the legislative objective of bringing a polluter into regulatory compliance by means of citizen suit provisions. That objective would be frustrated if courts were to impose civil fines on a polluter based on violations that were unknown to the violator at the time of the notice letter. However, the court upheld several fines that were related to the allegations contained in the notice letter from Friends.

WORDS OF THE COURT: Purpose of the Notice Letter Requirement "This regulation provides, in relevant part, that the notice shall include sufficient information to permit the recipient to identify the specific standard, limitation, or order alleged to have been violated. Notice given by a citizen plaintiff under the Clean Water Act thus must provide the alleged violator with enough information to attempt to correct the violation and avert the citizen suit. . . . Our conclusion is not altered by the fact that when the plaintiffs sent their notice letter, they did not have access to information that they later acquired in discovery in this case. The plaintiffs' lack of information before their suit was filed cannot excuse the deficiencies in the notice letter, because those deficiencies prevented attainment of the legislative objectives of encouraging presuit governmental involvement and securing violator compliance."

Case Questions

1. Did Gaston escape a substantial civil fine based on a statutory technicality?

2. What could Friends have included in the notice letter that might help it prevail in a future case in which the true extent of the violation is unknown?

3. *Focus on Critical Thinking:* Are citizen suit provisions an effective way to achieve environmental objectives? Do citizens have the expertise necessary to make legal or scientific determinations that are inherent in environmental regulation? Should enforcement be left to the government? Why or why not?

TAKEAWAY CONCEPTS Citizen Suit Provisions and Watchdog Groups

- Federal environmental laws are primarily administered, implemented, and enforced by the U.S. Environmental Protection Agency (EPA).
- In addition to the EPA and other federal agencies, each state has its own environmental agency to implement and enforce state environmental statutes.
- Virtually every major federal environmental statute enacted since 1970 authorizes citizen suits allowing citizen interest groups to file a lawsuit against either a polluter who is in violation of environmental statutes or regulations or a government agency or unit (such as the EPA or a municipality) that is not taking legally mandated steps to carry out environmental law enforcement.

NATIONAL ENVIRONMENTAL POLICY ACT

One of the first attempts at comprehensive legislation to address environmental regulation was the **National Environmental Policy Act (NEPA)**, enacted in 1969. The law was intended to serve as a national charter for environmental regulation, but it focuses on planning and prevention rather than on achieving a certain result (such as cleaner water) according to scientific standards. The NEPA established a process that must be followed by federal agencies in making decisions that have the potential to significantly impact the environment. The NEPA also created the Council on Environmental Quality to oversee NEPA procedures and to make periodic progress reports to Congress and the president.

LO 47-5

Describe the primary objectives and provisions of major federal statutes that protect the environment.

NEPA Coverage and Procedures

NEPA procedures are triggered when a federal agency takes any action that reasonably may be considered as having an impact on the environment, such as issuing a permit or license or engaging in rulemaking. The NEPA is also activated when Congress passes a law that requires federal funding (such as federal highway or bridge construction). Note that actions by private individuals, businesses, and state and local governments are not regulated by the NEPA. However, all states have enacted parallel statutes (laws similar to the NEPA statute but covering a wider range of parties) to cover state and local government actions as well.

Procedural Steps

Federal agencies are required to incorporate NEPA procedural steps into their decision-making process at the earliest possible opportunity by identifying the purpose of and need for a promised project, possible alternatives, and the environmental impact of certain actions. Once this step has been accomplished, the agency must categorize the action into one of three classifications based on its level of environmental impact: *categorical exclusion, environmental assessment,* or *environmental impact statement.* Table 47.1 provides a summary of these three categories.

TAKEAWAY CONCEPTS National Environmental Policy Act

- The National Environmental Policy Act (NEPA) of 1969 established a process that must be followed by federal agencies when they are making decisions that may reasonably impact the environment or when Congress passes a law that requires federal funding.
- Federal agencies are required to incorporate NEPA procedural steps into their decision-making process by identifying the purpose of and need for a promised project, possible alternatives, and the environmental impact.
- Once the procedural steps are accomplished, the agency must categorize the action into one of three classifications based on its level of environmental impact: (1) categorical exclusion (little or no potential impact), (2) environmental assessment (unknown impact), or (3) environmental impact statement (potentially significant impact).
- The NEPA process gives public notice and affords consumer interest groups, businesses, and private citizens a chance to influence the agency's decision or directly force compliance via citizen suit provisions.

TABLE 47.1 NEPA Categories

Category	Use	Action
Categorical exclusion (CE)	Used for actions that have little or no potential for significant environmental impact. CE classification also may be mandated by a particular statute, thereby exempting certain actions from any further environmental assessment.	None required.
Environmental assessment (EA)	Used for projects and actions in which the environmental impact is unknown. Actions classified as EA require the agency to produce a public document setting forth the need for the proposed action, alternatives, the environmental impact of the proposed action and its alternatives, and a list of agencies and persons consulted.	The EA is used to determine whether the action requires preparation of a more extensive report called an *environmental impact statement.* If the agency makes a finding of no significant impact based on the EA, the agency may proceed with the proposed action.
Environmental impact statement (EIS)	Used for actions classified as having the potential for significant impact on the environment. If an EA provides evidence that some significant environmental impact is at issue, the agency must prepare a draft of an EIS and publish it for public comment.	The EIS is an expanded form of EA that includes (1) a description of the proposed action, (2) a statement of significant issues and specific forecasting of what environmental risks are involved with the proposed action, (3) alternatives to the actions and an assessment of the environmental risk of the alternatives, (4) financial assessments of the promised actions and alternatives, and (5) plans for reducing or preventing environmental harm. Once the public and interested constituencies have commented on the EIS, the agency revises it as necessary and issues a final EIS. The final EIS also sets out the agency decision on environmental impact and its chosen alternative for pursuing the agency action. As a practical matter, the NEPA process gives public notice and affords consumer interest groups, businesses, and private citizens a chance to influence the agency's decision. The NEPA also contains a citizen suit provision whereby private individuals and organizations may sue a federal agency directly to force compliance with NEPA procedures.

THE CLEAN AIR ACT

LO 47-6

Provide examples of various industries regulated by air and water pollution laws related to the disposal of waste and hazardous materials.

Enacted in 1963, the **Clean Air Act (CAA)**[3] is a complex statute aimed at improving outdoor air quality in the United States. The CAA replaced earlier legislation that had proved ineffective. The law has been amended several times since its original passage, most recently in 1997 to expand its coverage and provide a system of market-based incentives and enforcement options intended to encourage voluntary compliance with clean air standards. As its starting point, the CAA authorized the EPA to establish the National Ambient Air Quality Standards (NAAQS), which set permissible levels of certain air pollutants such as carbon monoxide, lead, and particulate matter (microscopic ash and dirt that are the ingredients for smog). Although the statute itself is multifaceted, its basic structure focuses on **stationary sources of air pollution** (such as an industrial manufacturing plant) and **mobile sources of air pollution** (such as motor vehicles).

---

[3]42 U.S.C. §§ 7401–7671.

Stationary Sources of Air Pollution

An important feature of the CAA is that state legislatures are required to determine the best way to achieve the NAAQS. State governments have a uniquely local understanding of state industries, geography, and demographics and are usually in the best position to decide on a solution. Each state is required to develop a collection of regulations that will help it achieve a reduction in each pollutant to below the maximum level set in the NAAQS. This plan takes the form of a mandated **State Implementation Plan (SIP)**, which must be submitted to the EPA within certain time frames set out in the statute. If the SIP is not acceptable, the EPA may either impose sanctions on the state (such as withholding certain federal funding) or step in to implement its own plan.

SIPs also feature a program for issuing **operating permits** to existing stationary sources that emit pollutants at special levels. Operating permits include information on which pollutants are being released; how much is being released; and steps the source is taking to reduce pollution, including technological requirements and methods to monitor the pollution. SIPs also include the requirements for obtaining a preoperating permit for any new source of pollutants being planned. Preoperating permits require the applicant to show that the construction of a stationary source has incorporated state-of-the-art technology to control the NAAQS pollutants. CAA regulations also require a new source permit when a plant owner makes substantial modifications to an existing stationary source. Sometimes an issue arises as to what constitutes a *modification.* This is an important factor in business planning because certain modifications may trigger additional regulatory measures and permit requirements.

Market-Based Approaches

One relatively controversial part of the CAA is the law's **market-based approach**. This approach was implemented by the 1990 amendments to the CAA and is accomplished through (1) emissions trading via the permitting process and (2) a cap and trade plan intended to achieve lower levels of pollutants that contribute to acid rain.[4] Although the plans have separate procedural systems, they are both considered market-based approaches. Under these approaches, businesses have certain choices as to how they may reach their pollution reduction goals, including pollution allowances that can be traded, bought, and sold. In that same vein, a business may be allowed to expand its pollution output in one area if it is able to offset the increase by reducing another pollutant in greater measure than the one being expanded.

Economic Incentive Theory

The emissions trading scheme embraces the economic incentive theory that overall pollution reduction will result if businesses have an economic and competitive incentive, rather than a mandate, to invest in modern equipment and plants. Proponents argue that this approach will result in businesses investing in more efficient plants that yield clean air units that can then be sold or traded to out-of-compliance buyers. As emitting pollution (and being out of compliance) becomes more expensive, every company will be forced to modernize to stay competitive in the market.

For example, suppose that Citadel Manufacturing Company and Guardian Operations Inc. operate manufacturing plants that emit pollutants regulated by the CAA. Each company obtains a permit to emit 50 units of pollutant X and 50 units of pollutant Y per year. Citadel decides to modernize its plant at a cost of $1 million. The modernization results in a significant reduction in pollutant X, so now Citadel emits only 10 units per year. Guardian,

---

[4]*Acid rain* is a broad term referring to a mixture of wet and dry components from the atmosphere that contains significant amounts of nitric and sulfuric acids. Governmental agencies have concluded that acid rain poses significant threats to the environment and specific ecosystems.

on the other hand, claims it does not have the resources to modernize and its current plant will emit 80 units of pollutant X. In a market-based approach, Guardian may choose to comply by either purchasing 30 units of pollutant X emission credit from Citadel or reducing its use of pollutant Y to offset the additional units of pollutant X. If it chooses to use the offset method, Guardian will have to reduce its use of pollutant Y by at least 31 units (an amount greater than the exceeding pollutant).

In this example, proponents of the market-based approach would point out that (1) this approach does not force burdensome mandates that may bankrupt a company, such as requirements to purchase expensive equipment; (2) eventually Guardian is likely to consider investing in new technology so it will not be dependent on sellers of pollution units; and (3) the overall pollution reduction is the same under this approach as it would be under a mandate approach. Critics of this approach argue that it results in clean air being treated as a commodity rather than as a natural resource. Opponents of market-based solutions argue that the government could achieve greater reductions in pollution through the use of gradual statutory mandates to improve pollution control and government-backed loans to help companies purchase equipment. Figure 47.1 provides a summary of arguments for and against market-based approaches in a point-counterpoint format.

Mobile Sources of Air Pollution

While substantial gains have been made in reducing pollution from motor vehicles over the past few decades, the internal combustion engine remains a significant source of hazardous pollutants. The EPA has issued standards intended to limit motor vehicle emissions through its Transport and Air Quality (TAQ) program. The TAQ program regulates (1) tailpipe emissions, (2) fuel economy, (3) performance standards, and (4) the composition and distribution of fuels, particularly gasoline, used in motor vehicles.

Tailpipe Emissions The CAA initially set the first federal tailpipe emission standards, but it granted California the authority to set even tighter emission standards due to the state's higher-than-average levels of air pollution. The 1990 amendments gave states the choice of either adopting the federal standards or using the California standards, but states may not adopt their own standards. Both the federal and California standards require an inspection and maintenance program to ensure that car manufacturers limit the exhaust emissions of five major pollutants that emit from tailpipes, including hydrocarbons and carbon monoxide. The difference between the two sets of standards is that the California standards have stricter miles-per-gallon (mpg) requirements and lower levels of allowable pollution.

FIGURE 47.1	Point-Counterpoint Summary of Market-Based Approaches

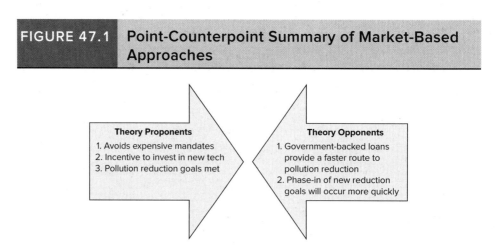

Theory Proponents
1. Avoids expensive mandates
2. Incentive to invest in new tech
3. Pollution reduction goals met

Theory Opponents
1. Government-backed loans provide a faster route to pollution reduction
2. Phase-in of new reduction goals will occur more quickly

Fuel Economy Standards Fuel economy standards set average mpg requirements for motor vehicles and are determined by the year of the motor vehicle's production and its classification (e.g., car versus light truck). These regulations, called the *Corporate Average Fuel Economy (CAFE) standards,* were enacted by Congress in 1975 with the purpose of reducing energy consumption by increasing the fuel economy of cars and light trucks. Regulating the CAFE standards is the responsibility of the National Highway Traffic Safety Administration (which sets the standards) and the EPA (which specifies a required standard calculation method for average fuel economy). The CAFE standards were overhauled in 2007 by the Energy Independence and Security Act,[5] which increased the mandated average for cars from 27.5 mpg to 35.5 mpg by 2020.

Performance Standards The TAQ program also requires that motor vehicle manufacturers obtain a Certificate of Conformity from the EPA that certifies that a vehicle's useful life is at least 10 years or 100,000 miles for passenger cars and up to 365,000 miles for heavy trucks. The useful-life standards are intended to make sure that manufacturers have designed the motor vehicle's emission system to last a certain period of time. Performance standards also include requirements for certain in-vehicle diagnostic systems that allow a mechanic to detect otherwise hidden defects in emission control systems.

Fuel Composition and Distribution The manufacture and transportation of gasoline, diesel fuel, and fuel additives is regulated by the EPA under authority of the CAA. The EPA uses a registration system to ensure that any fuel product is tested and certified as safe for public health and used in compliance with CAA regulations. In addition to requiring a complete ban on the use of lead-based gasoline beginning in 1995, the law also includes a requirement that gasoline components contain certain detergents to reduce emissions.

TAKEAWAY CONCEPTS The Clean Air Act

- The Clean Air Act (CAA) is aimed at improving outdoor air quality based on National Ambient Air Quality Standards (NAAQS) that set permissible levels of certain air pollutants.
- The basic structure of the CAA focuses on pollution from either stationary sources (manufacturing plants) or mobile sources (motor vehicles).
- State legislatures are required to determine the best way to achieve the NAAQS for stationary sources in the form of a mandated State Implementation Plan (SIP) that must be submitted to the Environmental Protection Agency (EPA).
- SIPs also feature a program for issuing (1) operating permits to existing stationary sources that emit pollutants at special levels; (2) preoperating permits for any new source of pollutants being planned; and (3) new source permits for substantial modifications to an existing source.
- A market-based approach embraces an economic incentive theory and was instituted by the 1990 CAA amendments to give businesses a choice of methods for complying with pollution standards.
- The EPA has issued standards intended to limit mobile source emissions through its Transport and Air Quality (TAQ) program, which regulates (1) tailpipe emissions, (2) fuel economy standards, (3) performance standards, and (4) fuel composition and distribution.

---

[5] 542 U.S.C. § 17001 et seq.

WATER POLLUTION CONTROL

The pollution of waterways is one of the biggest challenges facing environmental policy-makers. Waterways take the form of surface water (such as lakes or rivers) or groundwater (subsurface water, such as that used for wells). Because water travels across jurisdictional boundaries and may be subject to various legal property rights,[6] water pollution and conservation regulation are necessarily addressed by a combination of federal, state, and local statutes and rules.

The Clean Water Act

Water quality standards are primarily set by and regulated through the **Clean Water Act (CWA)**,[7] a federal statute implemented and enforced by the EPA in tandem with the U.S. Army Corps of Engineers and state agencies. Much like the CAA, the CWA has been amended in significant ways to stem pollution from industrial, municipal, and agricultural sources. The CWA also contains important enforcement provisions. Any pollution discharge that violates the CWA triggers enhanced penalties if it was a result of gross negligence or willful misconduct.

Water Quality Regulation

Each state sets water quality standards, subject to EPA review, for the navigable waterways within the state's borders. State agencies set scientifically measurable standards consisting of several criteria intended to improve the quality of surface water. The standards are set according to the designated use of the water source. Sources in which the designated uses are swimming or fishing must meet high quality standards. Once the state has set its standards, it must monitor whether its water sources are meeting those standards and disclose the results through a mandatory reporting system. If progress toward achieving the standards is too slow or nonexistent, the state must propose a new strategy to meet the quality standards. The EPA must approve any new strategies and may step in and impose its own strategy if it determines that the state is out of compliance with the CWA.

Permitting   Pollution emission into the waterways from sources such as industrial plants is regulated through the EPA's National Pollution Discharge Elimination System. The system establishes permitting procedures for businesses and individuals that require discharge of some material into a water source in order to operate their facilities. A permit is required regardless of the quality of the receiving water or whether the discharge actually causes pollution. Permits are issued either as individual permits, which are specifically tailored to an individual facility, or as general permits, which cover multiple facilities within a certain category. Individual permits are often issued to business facilities, while general permits are issued for all discharges in a specific geographic area (such as a city-designated development zone).

In order to obtain a permit, existing sources of pollution are required to install the best *practical* pollution control technology. This means that the cost of implementation is given equal weight to that of the effectiveness of pollution control. New applicants for permits are required to employ the best *available* control technology, which means that the permit applicant must install the most technologically advanced control methods on the market, regardless of cost. The EPA has established timetables for existing sources to adopt best available control technology as well.

---

[6]Water rights are also known as *riparian rights.*

[7]733 U.S.C. § 1251 et seq.

Greenwashing

The *Oxford English Dictionary* defines *greenwashing* as "disinformation disseminated by an organization so as to present an environmentally responsible public image," but it was a young, ponytailed environmental activist, Jay Westerveld, who first coined this controversial term in the 1980s. During a trip to the South Pacific, Westerveld noticed a small card in his hotel room. The card was decorated with three green arrows—the universal recycling symbol—and it read as follows: "Save Our Planet: Every day, millions of gallons of water are used to wash towels that have only been used once. You make the choice: A towel on the rack means, 'I will use again.' A towel on the floor means, 'Please replace.' Thank you for helping us conserve the Earth's vital resources." Westerveld promptly questioned the true motives of this "Save Our Planet" policy. Specifically, was the "save the towel" card in his hotel room really about the hotel's commitment to protecting the environment, or was it more about the hotel wanting to save money by having to wash fewer towels?

Collectively, hotels consume massive amounts of energy and water. Take water, for example. Hotels require large amounts of water to provide amenities expected by tourists, such as swimming pools, landscaped gardens, and golf courses. The washing of towels, by contrast, uses up a small amount of water relative to these other uses—but not having to wash as many towels saves the hotel time and money. Westerveld thus coined the term "greenwashing" to describe marketing campaigns designed to manipulate consumers into believing that a company's products, aims, or policies are environmentally friendly.

Today, major multinational firms such as BP, Shell, and ExxonMobil spend millions of dollars in advertising campaigns touting their environmentally friendly policies and their commitment to the environment, but are such companies truly committed to protecting the environment beyond mere compliance with legal standards? Or are they merely greenwashing their corporate image in order to attract customers and increase sales?

Discussion Questions

1. Is greenwashing protected commercial speech under the First Amendment to the U.S. Constitution, or is it an unfair trade practice like fraud? Explain.

2. Should there be a specific law against greenwashing as a matter of public policy? Explain your answer.

3. Who is in the best position to enforce a greenwashing law? The Environmental Protection Agency (EPA)? Consumers? Rival companies? Explain.

Sources: *Oxford English Dictionary Supplement*, Volume 3, p. 664; John Sullivan, "'Greenwashing' Gets His Goat," *Times Herald-Record*, Aug. 1, 2009.

Oil Spills

Largely in response to a 10 million-gallon oil spill that resulted when the *Exxon Valdez* oil tanker ran aground, Congress passed the **Oil Pollution Act (OPA)**[8] in 1990. The OPA increased the EPA's authority to prevent and respond to disastrous oil spills in public water sources. The law also imposed a tax on oil freighters in order to fund the national Oil Spill Liability Trust Fund, which is available to fund up to $1 billion per spill. Energy companies are required to file environmental impact plans with the U.S. Department of Interior, which has oversight authority over all oil drilling. The OPA was intended to promote contingency planning between government and industry to prevent and respond to a spill event. The OPA also increased penalties for noncompliance and broadened the government's response and enforcement authority. The law caps the liability of responsible parties at $75 million per spill, plus removal costs. However, in cases of gross negligence, the cap does not apply.

[8]33 U.S.C. §§ 2702–2761.

Deepwater Horizon **(BP) Oil Spill**   The largest offshore oil spill in U.S. history began on April 20, 2010, after an explosion aboard the BP-controlled oil-drilling platform *Deepwater Horizon.* The *Deepwater Horizon* was situated in the Gulf of Mexico approximately 40 miles southeast of the Louisiana coast. The explosion killed 11 people working on the platform and created an oil spill that the National Oceanic and Atmospheric Administration estimated was leaking almost 5,000 barrels (210,000 gallons) per day. BP tried several methods for controlling the leak, but the logistics of such a deep-sea operation resulted in a number of failed attempts. The gusher continued for nearly three months and resulted in an estimated 4.9 million barrels spilled into the Gulf of Mexico, making it the largest aquatic oil spill in history. The Gulf's coastal communities, whose income comes primarily from fishing and tourism, were devastated. BP faced sharp criticism for its handling of the crisis, and the U.S. Justice Department launched a criminal investigation into the incident. Although BP acknowledged its liability in the accident, the company alleged that other contractors on the oil rig were also negligent in the spill.

Civil Lawsuits   The *Deepwater Horizon* explosion spurred approximately 3,000 lawsuits with over 100,000 named claimants asserting a wide variety of claims, from wrongful death to economic losses resulting from the spill. Most cases were consolidated into a class action lawsuit as a multidistrict litigation (MDL)[9] case and assigned to the U.S. District Court in the Eastern District of Louisiana. In 2012, the court approved a settlement agreement in which BP agreed to pay $7.8 billion to resolve the litigation.

Civil Fines and Criminal Charges   In 2013, two of BP's partners in the oil well agreed to plead guilty to violating the Clean Water Act and the Oil Pollution Act. Deepwater Horizon, Inc., the company that owned the oil-drilling platform, paid $1.4 billion in civil and criminal fines and penalties. Halliburton Co., which had contracted with BP to provide cementing services, pleaded guilty to destruction of critical evidence after the oil spill and paid $200,000 with three years' probation. The U.S. Justice Department also filed suit against various BP executives for manslaughter, obstructing justice, lying to investigators, and obstructing Congress. The government also charged BP, Deepwater Horizon, Inc., and Halliburton Co. with violations of the CWA and the OPA. In Case 47.2, a federal court considers whether BP's actions constituted gross negligence or willful misconduct, which would result in greatly enhanced penalties.

> **CASE 47.2 *In re* Oil Spill by the Oil Rig "Deepwater Horizon" in the Gulf of Mexico, MDL 2179, U.S. District Court, E.D. Louisiana (September 9, 2014)**
>
> **FACT SUMMARY**   The *Deepwater Horizon* was a nine-year-old semisubmersible, mobile, floating, dynamically positioned drilling rig that could operate in waters up to 10,000 feet deep. The rig was owned by Transocean, Inc. and was chartered and operated by BP from March 2008 to September 2013. It was drilling a deep exploratory well roughly 41 miles off the Louisiana coast when high-pressure
>
> *(continued)*

---

[9]The federal rules that govern trials provide for a Judicial Panel for Multidistrict Litigation, which evaluates cases filed in federal courts throughout the United States that are substantially related. The panel has the authority to consolidate these cases into a single trial if it serves the interest of justice.

methane gas from the well expanded into the drilling riser and rose into the drilling rig, where it ignited and exploded, engulfing the platform with 126 crew members on board. Eleven people were killed and 17 others were injured. The *Deepwater Horizon* sank two days after the explosion.

Subsequent investigations revealed that BP managers misread pressure data, failed to administer appropriate tests for integrity of the well, and gave their approval for rig workers to replace drilling fluid in the well with seawater. However, the seawater was not heavy enough to prevent gas that had been leaking into the well from firing up the pipe to the rig and causing the explosion. While acknowledging responsibility for the accident, BP argued that the blame should be fully shared with Transocean, the owner of the *Deepwater Horizon* oil rig, and Halliburton, a contractor that oversaw a critical step in closing up the well. Transocean and Halliburton denied any liability. The government charged BP, Transocean, and Halliburton with, among other charges, violation of the Clean Water Act (CWA) and Oil Pollution Act (OPA). It also asked the court to impose enhanced penalties based on the "recklessness" and "willful conduct" provisions of the CWA and OPA. The impact of such a finding would result in BP being liable for four times the maximum penalties.

SYNOPSIS OF DECISION AND OPINION

Although the case dealt with dozens of legal issues, including maritime law and the common law of torts, the court's conclusion as to BP's liability for willful and reckless conduct was clear. The court ruled that BP had acted with conscious disregard of known risks. The court pointed to the actions of BP employees at the time of the incident and found that they took risks that led to the environmental disaster. In particular, the court ruled that the evidence indicated that the results of a pressure test should have prompted quick action to prevent an impending blowout. The court ruled that the company was reckless and determined that several crucial conversations between BP employees indicated a willful course of conduct that fit squarely into the

statutory definitions of "reckless" or "willful" in the CWA and OPA. The court also found that Transocean's and Halliburton's conduct was negligent but not reckless.

WORDS OF THE COURT: Reckless Conduct
"The Court finds that a prudent well operator in BP's position, knowing what BP knew at the time, would have run a[n integrity test for the cement seal], even if its decision tree concluded otherwise and its drilling and cement contractors did not tell it to do so. The fact that BP did not opt for the [test] when the necessary people and equipment were already on location leads the Court to believe BP's decision was primarily driven by a desire to save time and money, rather than ensuring that the well was secure."

Aftermath: Despite BP's initial promise to appeal, BP, the U.S. Justice Department, and five Gulf Coast states announced that the company agreed to pay a record settlement of $18.7 billion in 2015. According to Reuters news service, BP's cost for the cleanup, environmental and economic damages, and penalties has reached $65 billion.[10]

Case Questions

1. Why did the court find BP liable for enhanced penalties under the CWA and OPA?

2. At the time of the court's decision, BP had already paid $28 billion in cleanup costs and economic claims. Should there be no cap on BP's liability, even if it forces the company into bankruptcy?

3. *Focus on Critical Thinking:* Consider the enhanced penalty provisions in the CWA and OPA. Enhanced penalties are common in criminal statutes to punish conduct and deter behavior that the public considers particularly egregious (e.g., hate crimes). Do violations of environmental laws rise to that standard of egregiousness? Does the public actually benefit from enhanced penalties or, in regard to events such as the *Deepwater Horizon* explosion, is this more of a political reaction to media coverage?

---

[10]Ron Bousso, "BP Deepwater Horizon Costs Balloon to $65 Billion," *Reuters,* Jan. 16, 2018.

Drinking Water

The **Safe Drinking Water Act (SDWA)**[11] is a federal statute that sets minimum quality and safety standards for every public water system and every source of drinking water in the United States. This includes rivers, lakes, reservoirs, springs, and subsurface water wells. The SDWA's standards vary based on the size and usage of the system. The statute requires the EPA to balance both costs and health benefits in setting the standards. Public water agencies are required to test and monitor water sources and systems at various points. A report of the results must be given to the state regulatory agency on a regular basis. The SDWA also requires states to oversee programs to certify that water system operators engage in safe practices and that they have the technical and financial capacity to ensure a consistent supply of safe drinking water as well as the ability to respond quickly to any defects in the water system.

TAKEAWAY CONCEPTS Water Pollution Control

- Water pollution and conservation regulation are addressed by a combination of federal, state, and local statutes and rules.
- Water quality standards are set and regulated through the Clean Water Act (CWA).
- Each state sets water quality standards, subject to EPA review, for the navigable waterways within the state's borders and monitors whether the standards are being met.
- Pollution emission into waterways is regulated through the EPA's National Pollution Discharge Elimination System, which establishes procedures for issuing permits (either individual permits or general permits), which are required regardless of the quality of the receiving water or actual pollution.
- Existing sources of pollution are required to install the best practical control technology, whereas new applicants are required to employ the best available technology in order to obtain a permit.
- Congress increased the EPA's authority to prevent and respond to disastrous oil spills in water sources through the Oil Pollution Act (OPA).
- The Safe Drinking Water Act (SDWA) is a federal statute that sets minimum quality and safety standards for every public water system and every source of drinking water in the United States.

REGULATION OF SOLID WASTE AND HAZARDOUS MATERIALS DISPOSAL

Although hazardous waste was historically within the jurisdiction of state legislatures, several debacles in the early 1970s in which toxic waste was discovered to have polluted community water sources resulted in congressional action in the form of a comprehensive federal statute. Although the handling, proper disposal, and liability for cleanup of abandoned solid waste and hazardous materials are regulated by federal law, states still play a crucial role in enforcement. *Solid waste* generally refers to garbage, refuse, sludge from a

---

[11]42 U.S.C. § 300.

waste treatment plant, and sewage. *Hazardous materials* include chemical compounds and other inherently toxic substances (such as cleaning fluids and pesticides) used primarily in industry, agriculture, and research facilities.

Resource Conservation and Recovery Act

The **Resource Conservation and Recovery Act (RCRA)**[12] is intended to regulate active and future facilities that produce solid waste and/or hazardous materials. The RCRA creates a "cradle-to-grave" procedure for handling waste from its origins to its transportation, treatment, storage, and disposal. Like many other environmental laws, the RCRA establishes reporting requirements and procedures and provides for civil penalties and citizen suits. In egregious cases, the RCRA also includes criminal provisions for the prosecution of intentional violations. The RCRA bans the open dumping of solid waste and authorizes the EPA to set standards for municipal waste landfill facilities. The law specifies special procedures that must be employed for the disposal of certain types of municipal waste, such as refrigerators (which often contain potentially toxic refrigerant solution). The regulations govern the location, design, operation, and closing of a landfill site and require regular testing for groundwater contamination.

Waste that is (or becomes) hazardous is also regulated by the RCRA. The statute regulates both those who generate the pollution and those who transport the waste. A *generator* is defined by the law as any facility whose processes create hazardous waste. A *transporter* is an entity that moves hazardous waste from one site to another via ground, water, or air transportation. These regulations include a mandatory tracking system in which the use of a standardized hazardous waste manifest form establishes a chain of custody for the waste to ensure accountability. The RCRA also imposes a permit system for facilities that treat, store, or dispose of hazardous waste.

Universal waste (e.g., batteries, fluorescent bulbs, and mercury-containing equipment such as thermostats) is included under the RCRA, but the EPA has issued federal rules that make compliance easier for business owners who are disposing of universal waste in the ordinary course of operations. The rules allow universal waste to be transported by common carrier rather than by a more expensive hazardous waste carrier certified by the EPA. Used tires and oil are also covered by the RCRA, and the EPA has established special guidelines for the disposal of motor vehicle waste products by repair and service facilities.

Toxic Substances Control Act

The **Toxic Substances Control Act (TSCA)**[13] is a federal statute that gives the EPA jurisdiction to control risks that may be posed by the manufacture, processing, use, and disposal of chemical compounds. The TSCA's scope is very broad: It covers every chemical substance except pesticides, tobacco, nuclear material, and items already regulated under the Food, Drug, and Cosmetic Act.[14] The TSCA has both reporting and regulatory components. Specifically, the statute provides for (1) an EPA-maintained inventory of every chemical substance that may be legally manufactured in, processed in, or imported into the United States; (2) EPA authority to require companies to conduct specific screening tests that may reveal risks to public welfare; (3) EPA regulation on the use, labeling, and control measures of the substance; (4) record-keeping requirements; and (5) an obligation to report any potential adverse impact that the manufacturer, processor, or importer may become aware of in the course of operations.

---

[12]15 U.S.C. § 2601.

[13]15 U.S.C. § 2601.

[14]The Food, Drug, and Cosmetic Act includes food, food additives, pharmaceuticals, and cosmetics. This law is discussed in detail in Chapter 44, "Consumer Protection."

TAKEAWAY CONCEPTS Regulation of Solid Waste and Hazardous
Materials Disposal

- The Resource Conservation and Recovery Act (RCRA) is intended to regulate active and future facilities that produce solid waste and/or hazardous materials, and it created a "cradle-to-grave" procedure for handling waste.
- The Toxic Substances Control Act (TSCA) is a federal statute that gives the EPA broad jurisdiction to control risks that may be posed by the manufacture, processing, use, and disposal of chemical compounds.
- Federal law regulates the handling, proper disposal, and liability for cleanup of abandoned solid waste and hazardous materials; however, states play a crucial role in enforcement.

LO 47-7

Articulate the potential liability of various parties under the federal environmental cleanup statutes.

COMPREHENSIVE ENVIRONMENTAL RESPONSE, COMPENSATION, AND LIABILITY ACT

The environmental laws that we have discussed so far focus on controlling and reducing existing or new sources of pollution. These laws do nothing to address toxic waste contamination generated prior to the enactment of waste control statutes and then abandoned by the polluter. Faced with this major hurdle to achieving environmental safety for the public, Congress passed the **Comprehensive Environmental Response, Compensation, and Liability Act (CERCLA)**[15] in 1980.

Superfund

The CERCLA is commonly referred to as the **Superfund** because its main provisions center on the notion that cleanup operations for abandoned toxic waste sites (including both land and water sites) are to be funded by a self-sustaining quasi-escrow fund administered by the federal government. Superfund was initially funded by fees and taxes levied on substances that contain hazardous components, primarily in the petroleum and chemical industries. However, the statutory scheme also replenishes the fund by allocating financial responsibility to parties that are statutorily responsible for all or part of the cleanup costs. Therefore, the cleanup of a particularly toxic site could be conducted, and then the EPA could sue a statutorily responsible party for the cleanup costs. Critics of the law argue that the Superfund is consistently underfunded and that taxpayers bear a disproportionate amount of the cleanup costs. Proponents argue that the Superfund model is the most effective way to halt further damage from abandoned toxic waste sites while identifying polluters and assessing financial liability.

In 1986, the CERCLA was amended by the **Superfund Amendments and Reauthorization Act (SARA)**.[16] Although SARA's provisions were primarily clarifications and technical definitional adjustments, the law contained a new requirement for states to establish emergency response commissions to draft emergency procedures for a hazardous chemical accident and to implement them in the event of such an accident. All states must maintain and revise the plan as necessary as well as fund a hazardous materials response unit. The act also requires businesses to disclose the presence of certain chemicals within a community and

---

[15]42 U.S.C. § 9601.
[16]42 U.S.C. § 9601e.

imposes an affirmative obligation to notify authorities of any spills or discharges of hazardous materials. For continuity, this textbook uses the term *Superfund* to refer to all of the provisions of CERCLA and SARA combined.

Removal and Remedial Responses

The Superfund law established a two-front approach to handling hazardous substance cleanup: (1) **removal**, whereby authorization is given for actions to address releases or imminent releases of hazardous materials; and (2) **remedial**, whereby the EPA identifies the most hazardous waste sites and establishes a National Priorities List (NPL) for cleanup. In determining what sites are eligible, the EPA considers the overall potential harm to public health. To date, the EPA has placed over 25,000 sites around the country on the NPL. Once on the NPL, the EPA begins the remedial enforcement process by investigating the site, identifying parties that may be liable for cleanup costs, assessing the toxicity of the site, and determining the best remedial measure to accomplish cleanup. Figure 47.2 provides a map of Superfund sites on the NPL.

Liability of Principally Responsible Parties (PRPs)

The sharpest teeth of the Superfund law are that (1) it is retroactive and, therefore, applies to any disposal made prior to its enactment in 1980 and (2) it imposes broad strict liability standards for cleanup costs on certain businesses and individuals that fit the statute's definition of a *principally responsible party* (*PRP*). The Superfund also specifically imposes joint-and-several liability on PRPs. There are three classes of PRPs:

- Current owners of the site.
- Any owner or operator of the site at the time when the hazardous substances were disposed at the site.
- Any business that accepts hazardous substances for transport to the site and selected the site (such as a waste hauler).

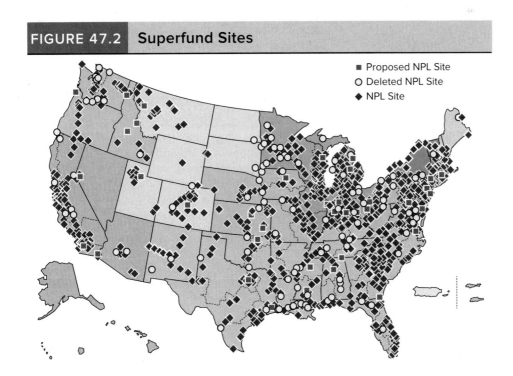

FIGURE 47.2   Superfund Sites

■ Proposed NPL Site
○ Deleted NPL Site
◆ NPL Site

For example, suppose a parcel of commercial real estate is listed on the NPL because the groundwater is contaminated due to a leak in an underground storage tank. The EPA investigates the parcel and finds records of three previous owners: GasCo (which used it for a retail gasoline station); ChairCo (which used it as a furniture storage warehouse); and its current owner, DevelopCo (which is using it for real estate development and has plans to build a retail storefront). The EPA determines that hazardous materials were stored in underground tanks by GasCo. Subject to certain defenses (discussed next), both GasCo and DevelopCo have joint-and-several liability for the cleanup costs. Suppose further that GasCo has been dissolved or liquidated under the bankruptcy law and no longer exists as an entity. Under the Superfund law, the EPA can hold DevelopCo, the parcel's current owner as of the NPL listing, liable for the *full* amount of the cleanup costs even though DevelopCo never contributed to the contamination.

Consent Decrees

Once the EPA has contacted the PRPs, the agency begins negotiations centered on PRP liability and cleanup operations. The parties draft a series of nonbinding agreements to evidence their good faith in moving ahead with the cleanup process. If negotiations result in a settlement being reached before cleanup efforts are commenced or are complete, the EPA and the PRP enter into a binding agreement, called a *consent decree,* that lays out how the cleanup plan will be implemented and who will bear which costs. If the EPA believes the PRP is not negotiating in good faith or is stalling, it may cease negotiations, implement a cleanup plan, and pursue a civil suit against the PRP to recover the entire amount of the cleanup costs. The EPA also may begin enforcement actions against the PRP that may result in civil fines or, in extreme cases, criminal prosecution.

Allocation of Liability

When the EPA enters into a consent decree with a PRP, the PRP has the right to sue third parties such as transporters, other polluters, and municipalities to recover a portion of the cleanup costs related to the polluter's action. However, allocating liability among multiple polluters is a difficult process. In Case 47.3, an appellate court considers the scope of authority and discretion of courts engaged in a Superfund allocation analysis.

CASE 47.3 Goodrich Corp. v. Town of Middlebury, 311 F.3d 154 (2d Cir. 2002)

FACT SUMMARY For decades, two public landfills in Connecticut accepted industrial waste, including municipal solid waste from various municipalities. The EPA declared the landfills to be Superfund sites because they were leaking chemicals and threatening the local water supply. The EPA began the remedial enforcement process by investigating and identifying various principally responsible parties (PRPs) that contributed to the pollution, and it entered into consent decrees for them to contribute to the cost of cleanup. The PRPs, which were all corporations that had disposed of waste in the landfills, formed a coalition to represent their common interests and sued several municipalities for contribution to the cleanup costs. In a long, complicated litigation, a special master was appointed by the court to try to mediate a settlement. The special master came to certain conclusions about which parties contributed how much waste. At trial, the district court did not follow the conclusion of the special master and allocated much of the liability to the municipalities that ran the landfills. The municipalities appealed.

(continued)

SYNOPSIS OF DECISION AND OPINION The U.S. Court of Appeals for the Second Circuit affirmed the district court's ruling. Appellate courts will not overturn a district court's allocation of remediation costs in Superfund cases unless there is an abuse of discretion. It was within the right of the court not to follow all of the findings of the special master and to allocate more costs to the municipalities than recommended by the master. For the court to abuse its discretion, it would have to have committed an error of law or be clearly wrong in its finding of facts. The allocation of costs in such complicated proceedings may produce varying results; the court chose a method of allocation that was proper based on the evidence.

WORDS OF THE COURT: Court's Discretion under CERCLA "Because [CERCLA's] expansive language affords a district court broad discretion to balance the equities in the interests of justice, the appellate court will not overturn the district court's allocation of response costs absent an abuse of that discretion. A district court abuses or exceeds the discretion accorded to it when (1) its decision rests on an error of law (such as application of the wrong legal principle) or a clearly erroneous factual finding, or (2) its decision—though not necessarily the product of a legal error or a clearly erroneous factual finding—cannot be located within the range of permissible decisions. . . . A district court must give 'some deference' to a master's recommendation where the master has 'direct and extensive' knowledge about the particular circumstances of a given case. A district court that extends some deference to the master will consider his recommendation and the factors influencing it, but will not regard the recommendation as the alpha and omega of the analysis. . . . The Federal Rules of Civil Procedure expressly permit a district court to 'modify' a special master's report. . . . [A] plaintiff may recover any necessary costs of response incurred consistent with the national contingency plan. . . . [CERCLA] does not limit courts to any particular list of factors. The court may consider the state of mind of the parties, their economic status, any contracts between them bearing on the subject, any traditional equitable defenses as mitigating factors and any other factors deemed appropriate to balance the equities in the totality of the circumstances."

Case Questions

1. Suppose the coalition sues the companies that transported the waste. Are they liable as PRPs? Why or why not?

2. Why do you believe that the court rejected the special master's report? Do you agree with the court's decision?

3. *Focus on Critical Thinking:* Should courts have broad discretion when engaging in a Superfund allocation analysis? Is the public interest best served by a court deciding the allocation? Why or why not?

Defenses to Liability

As you may imagine, the Superfund law has come under fire by business advocacy groups for its potential to devastate innocent property owners and lenders. As a result, Congress carved out several defenses to liability for parties that meet certain criteria, including secured creditors, innocent landowners, and prospective purchasers.

Secured Creditors Suppose, in the DevelopCo example above, that during the EPA's investigation DevelopCo defaults on its mortgage payments and its financial lender forecloses on the property. Because the lender is now the owner, does that subject the bank to liability under Superfund? Probably not. To protect lenders (such as banks) that have become owners of contaminated property through foreclosure, the Superfund law contains a provision that excludes any such lender from liability for cleanup costs. Lender-owners may avoid liability so long as the lender was (1) an owner by virtue of the contaminated property being used as collateral for a loan and (2) not participating in the management of the facility prior to foreclosure. The EPA has issued specific guidelines to define what activities constitute participating in management.

Innocent Landowners   A current owner of a site that is listed on the NPL may avoid liability for cleanup costs so long as the owner establishes that she purchased the property without knowledge of the contamination. The owner must submit evidence that she conducted *all appropriate inquiries* into the previous ownership, using a reasonable amount of investigation to determine whether any contamination was present. So long as the owner complies with land-use restrictions, takes reasonable steps to limit the impact of the hazardous substances on the general public, and cooperates with government agencies, she may avoid cleanup liability under the statute.

Prospective Purchasers   In 2002, Congress enacted the Small Business Liability Relief Act,[17] which provides a defense to Superfund liability for a party that purchased the property *with knowledge* of the contamination. The statute provides for limited liability so long as the owner agrees to take reasonable steps to limit the impact of the contamination, prevent further contamination, and notify authorities of any imminent or actual pollutant release.

 Quick Quiz Who Has PRP Liability?

The EPA placed a parcel of land known as Noxious Flats on the NPL in 2009 due to contamination caused by chemicals from cleaning solvents and lead paint. Using the information in the following table, determine which parties have PRP liability.

Party	Relationship to Noxious Flats	Hazardous Substance Use
Richmond Industries	Owned the property from 1970 to 1979 and operated an industrial plant.	After using industrial cleaning solvents, stored the used solvents in an underground tank.
Bright Paint Company	Leased the property from Richmond from 1979 to 1985.	Dumped paint production waste into a hole in the ground and buried it.
Warehouse Storage Inc.	Purchased the property from Richmond in 1986 without any environmental investigation; installed concrete over the entire property and built warehouse spaces for lease.	No contamination by Warehouse Storage. Richmond's underground tank ruptured in 1988 and caused groundwater contamination. Warehouse Storage had no knowledge of the contamination.
The Factory Restaurant	Leased the property from Warehouse Storage from 1995 to 2008; built an upscale restaurant as part of a community revitalization project to turn blighted industrial areas into retail and restaurant zones. Lessor hired an environmental service company to survey the property before signing the lease, and no contamination was detected.	No contamination.
First Neighborhood Bank	Foreclosed on Warehouse Storage Inc., which defaulted on its loan in 2008.	None.

Answers to this Quick Quiz are provided at the end of the chapter.

---

[17]42 U.S.C. § 9607(r).

TAKEAWAY CONCEPTS Comprehensive Environmental Response, Compensation, and Liability Act

- If there is an immediate threat of hazardous materials release, the Superfund law requires immediate removal efforts. Local authorities respond pursuant to their Superfund emergency plan.

- In cases of long-term contamination of a land or water site, the Superfund law requires the EPA to determine suitability for placement on the National Priorities List (NPL).

- For sites listed on the NPL, government authorities then investigate the site's chain of ownership to determine any principally responsible parties (PRPs) and assess cleanup alternatives.

- Government officials negotiate with PRPs to determine contributions for cleanup. If an agreement is reached, the parties enter into a binding agreement called a consent decree. If the negotiations fail, the government typically files a Superfund lawsuit to collect cleanup costs from PRPs.

Table 47.2 sets out the major environmental laws discussed in this chapter.

TABLE 47.2	Major Environmental Laws
National Environmental Policy Act (NEPA) of 1969	Establishes a process that must be followed by federal agencies when making decisions that may reasonably impact the environment or when federal funding is involved.
Clean Air Act (most recently amended in 1997)	Improves outdoor air quality based on National Ambient Air Quality Standards that set permissible levels of certain air pollutants. The law focuses on pollution from both stationary sources (manufacturing plants) and mobile sources (motor vehicles).
Clean Water Act	Sets water quality standards and regulates the disposal of pollutants into public waterways.
Resource Conservation and Recovery Act (RCRA)	Regulates active and future facilities that produce solid waste and/or hazardous materials; uses a cradle-to-grave procedure that includes regulations for handling waste from its origins to its transportation, treatment, storage, and disposal.
Comprehensive Environmental Response, Compensation, and Liability Act (CERCLA), commonly referred to as Superfund	Addresses hazardous substance cleanup in two ways: (1) removal (for imminent releases) and (2) remedial (for long-term cleanup projects).

 THINKING STRATEGICALLY

Avoiding Environmental Liability in Land Acquisitions

PROBLEM: A land acquisition by a business entity may result in Superfund liability for the purchasing business even if the acquirer did not contaminate the property.

STRATEGIC SOLUTION: Preserve your status as an innocent landowner under CERCLA by engaging a qualified environmental screening firm as part of an environmental due diligence.

STEP 1: CONTRACT CONTINGENCY

When considering a property for acquisition or lease, the parties are typically under time pressure to sign an agreement of sale or letter of intent. Work with your counsel to develop a contingency clause for the contract that provides you with a period of time for environmental screening. The language "environmental contingency" is important because it helps to document your efforts to make appropriate inquiries into previous ownership as required for innocent landowner status.

STEP 2: TRANSACTION SCREEN

A simple transaction screen can be conducted to provide the buyer with more data on potential environmental problems with the property. This screen (also called an Environmental Phase I) is a minimal, relatively inexpensive assessment that typically consists of (1) record checks for ownership, code violations, or environmental agency actions; (2) an interview with the current site owner; and (3) a site visit for obvious signs of potential environmental liability (such as an aboveground port for an underground tank). If there is any evidence of contamination, advanced assessments (called Phase II and Phase III environmental assessments) that include soil and groundwater testing can be conducted. However, these advanced assessments are more expensive and could impact the cost-benefit analysis for the purchaser.

STEP 3: VERIFY QUALIFICATIONS

It is also important for business owners and managers to be sure that the firms they are hiring are *qualified* within the meaning of federal and state statutory definitions. In order to assert an innocent purchaser defense, the company must have relied on the report of a qualified environmental professional. Federal and state statutes lay out the standards for qualification. To qualify under the EPA standards, an environmental professional must (1) be certified by the federal government to perform environmental inspections, (2) be a licensed engineer or geologist, (3) have at least a bachelor's degree level of education, and (4) have 10 years of relevant work experience.

For example, suppose that Chef Kuo is looking for a new location to expand her restaurant operations. She locates a potential property, but when visiting the site, Kuo notices that it is adjacent to inactive railroad tracks. Kuo recalls an article in the local newspaper that reported on some railroad yards in the area that were contaminated by a toxic substance called PCB that was buried beneath the tracks when they were put down many years ago. Kuo is convinced that this property is ideal for her newest restaurant but is concerned about any potential environmental liability. Yet, at this early stage of the acquisition, she does not wish to invest in an expensive assessment. By using a transaction screen, Kuo will be in a better position to choose whether to abandon the transaction entirely and continue her search or to invest more money in further assessments. These advanced assessments are much more expensive, so Kuo will have to decide if the costs of assessment (and possible remediation) are sufficiently equal to the benefits of putting her restaurant on that site. In any case, Kuo will have accumulated documentation that she qualifies as an innocent landowner under the law.

QUESTIONS

1. What role should the government have in transaction screenings? Although the EPA has established standards for "qualified" environmental firms, how enforceable are those standards as a practical matter? Should environmental firms be required to obtain a permit prior to offering screening services, or should that be left to the consumer?

2. Use your preferred search engine to locate an environmental screening firm near you. What kinds of information do they provide about qualifications, pricing, processes, and experience?

KEY TERMS

Nuisance p. 897   A common law legal action for redressing harm arising from the misuse of one's property that is based on the aggrieved party's right to enjoy his property without interference from a third party.

Citizen suit provisions p. 899   Laws that authorize private individuals or watchdog groups to file environmental enforcement lawsuits.

National Environmental Policy Act (NEPA) p. 901 Federal legislation enacted in 1969 that established a process federal agencies must follow when making decisions that have the potential to significantly impact the environment.

Clean Air Act (CAA) p. 902   Federal legislation enacted in 1963 to improve, strengthen, and accelerate programs for the prevention and abatement of air pollution; focuses on stationary and mobile sources in the United States.

Stationary sources of air pollution p. 902   Fixed-site emitters of air pollutants, including fossil-fueled power plants, petroleum refineries, petrochemical plants, food processing plants, and other industrial sources.

Mobile sources of air pollution p. 902   Nonstationary sources of air pollutants, including automobiles, buses, trucks, ships, trains, aircraft, and various other vehicles.

State Implementation Plan (SIP) p. 903   A mandated state plan for complying with the federal Clean Air Act that is submitted to the Environmental Protection Agency; consists of a collection of regulations that help to achieve a reduction in pollution.

Operating permits p. 903   Licenses issued by authorities to existing stationary sources that allow pollution emission at certain levels.

Market-based approach p. 903   An approach to pollution control that gives businesses a choice of methods based on economic incentives for complying with pollution standards; instituted by the 1990 amendments to the Clean Air Act.

Clean Water Act (CWA) p. 906   Federal legislation that regulates water quality standards and aims to stem water pollution from industrial, municipal, and agricultural sources; implemented and enforced by the EPA.

Oil Pollution Act (OPA) p. 907   Federal legislation enacted in 1990 to streamline and strengthen the Environmental Protection Agency's ability to prevent and respond to catastrophic oil spills in water sources.

Safe Drinking Water Act (SDWA) p. 910   Federal legislation that sets minimum quality and safety standards for every public water system and every source of drinking water in the United States.

Resource Conservation and Recovery Act (RCRA) p. 911   Federal legislation enacted in 1976 to regulate active

and future facilities that produce solid waste and/or hazardous materials.

Toxic Substances Control Act (TSCA) p. 911   Federal legislation that gives the Environmental Protection Agency jurisdiction to control risks that may be posed by the manufacture, processing, use, and disposal of chemical compounds.

Comprehensive Environmental Response, Compensation, and Liability Act (CERCLA) p. 912   Federal legislation enacted in 1980 to create a tax on the chemical and petroleum industries and provide broad federal authority to respond directly to releases or threatened releases of hazardous substances that may endanger public health or the environment. Also called *Superfund.*

Superfund p. 912   Another name for the CERCLA, derived from that act's main provisions whereby cleanup operations for abandoned toxic waste sites are to be funded by a self-sustaining quasi-escrow fund to be administered by the federal government.

Superfund Amendments and Reauthorization Act (SARA) p. 912   A 1986 amendment to the CERCLA that requires that states establish emergency response commissions to draft emergency procedures for a hazardous chemical accident and implement them in the event of such an accident; requires that businesses disclose the presence of certain chemicals within a community; and imposes an obligation on businesses to notify authorities of any spills or discharges of hazardous materials.

Removal p. 913   Under the Superfund law, an approach to handling hazardous substance cleanup whereby authorization is given for actions to address releases or imminent releases of hazardous materials.

Remedial p. 913   Under the Superfund law, an approach to handling hazardous substance cleanup whereby the Environmental Protection Agency identifies the most hazardous waste sites and generates a National Priorities List.

CASE SUMMARY 47.1 Sierra Club v. El Paso Gold Mines, Inc., 421 F.3d 1133 (10th Cir. 2005)

Clean Water Act

El Paso Gold Mines owns 100 acres of land bought in 1968 near Cripple Creek, Colorado. Though El Paso did not engage in mining activity on the land, the land contained a collapsed mine shaft built in 1910. The shaft is connected to a 6-mile-long drainage tunnel that is connected to other old mines that drain into Cripple Creek. A citizens' watchdog group, the Sierra Club, brought suit alleging that El Paso violated the Clean Water Act by discharging pollutants (zinc and manganese) from

a source—the mine shaft—into the creek without a discharge permit.

CASE QUESTIONS

1. Does the Sierra Club have an actionable claim under the Clean Water Act? Why or why not?
2. If El Paso wanted to use the land for mining activity, would the company be required to obtain a permit? If so, what would need to be done in order to obtain the permit?

CASE SUMMARY 47.2 United States v. Southeastern Pennsylvania Transportation Authority, 235 F.3d 817 (3d Cir. 2000)

Superfund

The Paoli Rail Yard covers about 30 acres in Paoli, Pennsylvania, and consists of an electric train repair facility owned by Amtrak and operated by Philadelphia-based Southeastern Pennsylvania Transportation Authority (SEPTA). Prior to Amtrak's acquisition of the property, the site was owned by the Pennsylvania Railroad Company from 1939 until 1967, Penn Central Transportation until 1976, and Conrail until 1982. All previous owners are now defunct. In 1979, a toxic chemical known as PCB was discovered in the rail yard and the EPA declared the yard a Superfund site. The EPA then began the remedial enforcement process and brought an action against potentially responsible parties.

CASE QUESTIONS

1. Do any of the prior owners of the rail yard have PRP liability?
2. Could SEPTA or Amtrak have taken action to avoid liability? Explain.

CASE SUMMARY 47.3 William Paxton v. Wal-Mart Stores, Inc., 176 Ohio App. 3d 364 (2008)

Resource Conservation and Recovery Act

Paxton, a proprietor, intended to set up a recycling facility on one of his properties. He then contracted with Wal-Mart to recycle or dispose of various lamps and bulbs that contained spent mercury and other products that contained lead. Instead of recycling the items, Paxton crushed or shredded them and left them piled on the property. The state determined that there were hazardous waste violations and it filed suit.

CASE QUESTIONS

1. What federal statute(s) could apply to this case? Explain.
2. Citing the RCRA "cradle-to-grave" procedure, do you think Wal-Mart was contributory in violation of the statute? Why or why not?

CASE SUMMARY 47.4 Beverly E. Black and James A. Black v. George Weston & Stroehmann Bakeries, Inc., U.S. Dist. Ct. (W.D.N.Y. 2008)

Clean Air Act

Black, a real estate agent, owned adjacent rental properties in a New York neighborhood. On the same block, Stroehmann Bakeries owned and operated a bakery. Black alleged that the bakery had emitted "noxious discharges" that had coated his properties with mold and mold residue. As a result, Black's properties were discolored, causing a loss of rental income and resale value. An investigation was conducted, and the agency concluded that the bakery was the source of the mold growth found on Black's properties.

CASE QUESTIONS

1. What standard was used to determine whether or not the discharges constituted a violation of the Clean Air Act?
2. What common law doctrine could Black possibly have pursued in an attempt to compel Stroehmann to cease polluting?

Citizen Suits

In the late 1990s, the city of New York confronted growing concerns surrounding the mosquito-borne West Nile virus by implementing an aerial and ground spraying program. The program consisted of spray planes and trucks that would douse the city with malathion, a controversial neurotoxin pesticide, in an attempt to eradicate mosquitoes carrying the potentially fatal virus. The plan was controversial because of the exposure of the general public to the potentially hazardous pesticide. The No Spray Coalition, a group of local organizations and individuals, filed suit to halt the insecticide spraying, alleging that such spraying violated the CWA.

CASE QUESTIONS

1. What would No Spray have to prove in order to have an actionable claim under the CWA?
2. Explain the significance of citizen suit provisions and watchdog groups in the context of this case.

CHAPTER REVIEW QUESTIONS

1. **What agency has the authority to enforce environmental regulations?**
   a. Environmental Protection Agency
   b. Food and Drug Administration
   c. Nuclear Regulatory Commission
   d. All of the above
   e. None of the above

2. **What category does the National Environmental Policy Act (NEPA) use for laws that have no environmental impact?**
   a. Categorical exclusion
   b. Environmental assessment
   c. Environmental impact statement
   d. Non-impact statement
   e. Null and void

3. **The basic structure of the Clean Air Act (CAA) focuses on both stationary and _____ sources of air pollution.**
   a. Fixed
   b. Mobile
   c. Variable
   d. Permanent
   e. Exterior

4. **Cap and trade is an example of what type of approach to controlling air pollution?**
   a. Regulatory
   b. Common law
   c. Permitting
   d. Market-based
   e. Strict liability

5. **The federal law that provides for cleanup operations for abandoned toxic waste using funds from a self-sustaining escrow fund is known as the:**
   a. Cradle-to-Grave Act.
   b. Comprehensive Environmental Response, Compensation, and Liability Act (CERCLA).
   c. Toxic Control Act.
   d. Cleanup Recovery Act.
   e. None of the above.

6. **Environmental regulation exists at the federal, state, and local levels.**
   a. True
   b. False

7. **Citizen suit provisions ban any enforcement action by a citizen until a regulatory agency has acted first.**
   a. True
   b. False

8. **Federal agencies are required to incorporate the Clean Air Act procedural steps into their decision-making process.**
   a. True
   b. False

9. **Under the Oil Pollution Act, recklessness and willful misconduct carry an enhanced penalty.**
   a. True
   b. False

10. **Superfund is an alternate title for the Clean Water Act.**
    a. True
    b. False

1. Richmond Industries is liable as a PRP because it owned the plant at the time of disposal of the cleaning solvents in the underground tank. Note that, under Superfund, it is irrelevant that the disposal was made prior to the Superfund law's enactment (Superfund is retroactive). It is also irrelevant that no actual contamination took place while Richmond owned the parcel.

2. Bright Paint also is liable as a PRP based on the same rationale provided above.

3. Warehouse Storage Inc. probably is not liable as a PRP. No disposal took place under its ownership. The contamination occurred under its ownership, but Warehouse never disposed of any solid waste or hazardous materials.

4. The Factory Restaurant has no liability as a disposer of materials. If the EPA placed Noxious Flats on the NPL while The Factory Restaurant was operating on the site, the business still would be shielded from liability under the Superfund as an innocent lessor because it performed an environmental assessment prior to entering into the lease.

5. First Neighborhood Bank has no liability as a PRP. The bank is shielded because it is a secured creditor that did not actively participate in ownership or operation prior to the foreclosure.

CHAPTER REVIEW QUESTIONS: Answers and Explanations

1. d. All of the agencies listed have jurisdiction over different areas of federal environmental regulation. While the EPA is the primary enforcement agency, it is important to note that other agencies work in tandem with the EPA when an environmental regulation that impacts their jurisdiction is involved (e.g., the NRC for nuclear waste).

2. a. Categorical exclusion is the NEPA category for laws that have no environmental impact. Answers *b* and *c* are incorrect because they are categories used when environmental impact is possible or certain. Answer *d* is incorrect because no such category exists under NEPA.

3. b. The CAA regulates both stationary sources (e.g., industrial plants) and mobile sources (e.g., cars). Answers *a* and *d* are incorrect because both terms are synonyms for *stationary.* Answer *c* is incorrect because no such source exists.

4. d. Cap and trade is an emissions trading scheme based on economic incentives. Answers *a, b,* and *c* are incorrect because they are all examples of non–market-based regulation that is unrelated to cap and trade.

5. b. The Comprehensive Environmental Response, Compensation, and Liability Act (CERCLA) is intended to be a self-sustaining fund for the cleanup of toxic waste sites. Answers *a, c,* and *d* are incorrect because they are fictitious names.

6. a. True. The source of modern environmental law is statutory; the levels are federal, state, and local.

7. b. False. Citizen suit provisions allow enforcement action even before regulatory agency action.

8. b. False. Federal agencies are required to incorporate the NEPA (not the Clean Air Act) procedural steps into their decision-making process.

9. a. True. See the *Deepwater Horizon* case for an example of reckless and willful misconduct.

10. b. False. Superfund is an alternate title for the Comprehensive Environmental Response, Compensation, and Liability Act (CERCLA), not the Clean Water Act.

UNIT EIGHT   Property

CHAPTER 48

Personal Property, Real Property, and Land Use Law

When a business is considering leased-space alternatives to locate its operations, one important strategic objective is planning for expansion while minimizing financial risks. In this chapter's *Thinking Strategically,* we discuss how business owners strategically maximize their leverage by negotiating a subletting clause with an option for an assignment.

Learning Objectives

After studying this chapter, students who have mastered the material will be able to:

48-1   Provide a working definition of property and categories of property.

48-2   Explain the roles of the parties in a bailment relationship.

48-3   Identify the rights that landowners have in real property.

48-4   Give examples of the rights of landlords and tenants.

48-5   Distinguish between an assignment and a sublease and explain how each can be used in business planning objectives.

48-6   Identify the laws that regulate the use of real property by its owners.

CHAPTER OVERVIEW

Laws governing the ownership and use of property have deep historical roots and are an integral part of the American legal system. Business owners and managers regularly encounter property law issues in business planning and operations. Examples include decisions on whether to own or lease certain property, rights of the property owners, landlord-tenant laws, and government restrictions on how property may be used. In this chapter, we categorize various types of property and explain ownership rights, responsibilities, and restrictions. We also examine specific laws governing landlords and tenants as well as governmental regulation of land use.

DEFINITION AND CATEGORIES OF PROPERTY

From a legal perspective, the term *property* is defined broadly as a person's *set of legal rights* over others to use the property exclusively. While the casual meaning of the word *property* is often used in connection with real estate, property law recognizes two distinct categories: tangible property (such as real estate or goods) and intellectual property (such as patents). Laws covering tangible property are discussed in this chapter; intellectual property laws, which also are very important to business owners and managers, are covered in Chapter 50.

LO 48-1

Provide a working definition of property and categories of property.

Tangible Property

Tangible property is property that can be touched and physically possessed. The two forms of tangible property are **personal property** and **real property**. We discuss the law of real property later in this chapter.

Personal Property
Personal property is both tangible and movable. In a business context, goods, vehicles, inventory, and equipment for business operations (e.g., computers) are all examples of personal property. Personal property may be *owned* or *leased.* Leasing, which is governed by state statutory law modeled after the Uniform Commercial Code (UCC), is discussed later in this section. Personal property rights of ownership, possession, and transfer are the subject of a blend of state statutes and common law principles.

The legal term for ownership rights in property is **title**. Normally, title is obtained by a grant of title by the current owner to a new owner, usually through a purchase or gift. Title is thought of as a bundle of rights related to personal property. That is, the titleholder is permitted exclusive use of the personal property and has the rights to sell, lease, or prohibit another from using the property. However, in some instances the law allows a party to take title solely based on *possession.*

Found Articles
Under the common law, the finder's rights depend on the category of the found property. Found property is categorized in one of four ways. First, if the owner intentionally places the property in a certain place and later forgets about it, the property is considered *mislaid.* Second, if the owner unintentionally parts with the property through either carelessness or neglect, it is considered *lost.* Third, if the owner has thrown away or voluntarily forsaken the property, it is considered *abandoned.* Finally, found property is considered *treasure trove* if it is verifiably antiquated and has been concealed for so long as to indicate that the owners are probably dead or unknown. The finder of lost or abandoned property or treasure trove acquires the right to possess the property against the entire world except against the **actual owner**, regardless of the place of the finding. The finder of the mislaid property, however, must turn the property over to the premises owner to safeguard the property for the true owner. The key to determining whether the property is lost (or abandoned or considered a treasure trove) versus mislaid is the element of *involuntariness.* That is, to abandon personal property, one must voluntarily and intentionally give up a known right.

Suppose that Commuter finds a gold wristwatch on a public sidewalk while walking to the train station. She takes the watch to Station Manager, who, after asking each passenger in the area if he or she is the owner of the watch, is unable to find the true owner. Station Manager then keeps the watch from Commuter on the basis that Commuter is not the original owner. Assuming the true owner is not found, a court would likely find that Commuter has title over Station Manager and everyone else except for the original owner.

The ownership rights of found property are the central issue in a surprising number of modern cases. In Case 48.1, a state appellate court analyzes a found property claim.

FACT SUMMARY Robert A. Spann (Spann) lived in his Arizona home until he died in 2001. His daughter, Karen Spann Grande (Grande), became the personal representative of his estate. She and her sister took charge of the house and, among other things, had some repairs made to the home. They also looked for valuables their father may have left or hidden because they knew from experience that he had hidden gold, cash, and other valuables in unusual places in his house. Over the course of seven years, they found stocks and bonds, as well as hundreds of military-style green ammunition cans hidden throughout the house, some of which contained gold or cash.

In 2008, the house was sold "as is" to Sarina Jennings (Jennings). Jennings hired a contractor, Bueghly, to remodel the dilapidated home. Shortly after the work began, an employee of Bueghly's discovered two ammunition cans full of cash in the kitchen wall and found two more cash-filled ammo cans inside other walls in the house. The total amount of cash found by the employee was approximately $500,000.

After the employee reported the find to his boss, Bueghly took possession of the four ammo cans. He did not tell the new owners about the money and hid the cans in his floor safe. Jennings eventually found out from the employee about the cash and contacted the police, who then took protective custody of the cash. Jennings sued Bueghly for, among other things, a court declaration that Bueghly had no right to the money since Jennings was the homeowner. Bueghly filed a counterclaim for a declaration that he was entitled to the found funds as a treasure trove. In the meantime, Grande filed suit on behalf of Spann's estate as the true owner. The cases were consolidated, and the trial court awarded summary judgment in favor of Spann's estate. Jennings appealed.

SYNOPSIS OF DECISION AND OPINION The Arizona Court of Appeals upheld the trial court's decision in favor of Spann's estate. The court determined that the ammunition cans were *mislaid* property because it was undisputed that the Spann estate's representatives did not know that the money was mislaid and did not intend to abandon the funds. Once Grande learned of the discovery, she filed a probate petition to recover the property, which indicates that no abandonment occurred. The court rejected Jennings's argument that a jury could have found that the money had been abandoned because Grande had consciously ignored the possibility that additional large sums of money could be hidden in the home when she sold the house.

WORDS OF THE COURT: Property Not Abandoned "Arizona follows the common law. . . . While personal property of all kinds may be abandoned, the property must be of such a character as to make it clear that it was voluntarily abandoned by the owner. In this connection, it has been said that people do not normally abandon their money; and, accordingly, that found money will not be considered as abandoned, but as lost or mislaid property. . . . Here, it is undisputed that Spann placed the cash in the ammunition cans and then hid those cans in the recesses of the house. He did not, however, tell his daughters where he had hidden the cans before he passed away. His daughters looked for and found many of the ammo cans, but not the last four. In fact, it was not until the wall-mounted toaster oven and bathroom drywall were removed that [the contractor] found the remaining cash-filled cans. As a result, and as the trial court found, the funds are, as a matter of law, mislaid funds that belong to the true owner, Spann's estate."

Case Questions

1. What was each party's (i.e., Grande/Spann's, Jennings's, and Bueghly's) theory of the case as to why they should get the found cash?

2. Why is it important for the court to determine whether the property has been abandoned?

3. *Focus on Critical Thinking:* How could the facts of the case be changed to lead to a conclusion that Jennings should prevail? How could the facts be changed to lead to a conclusion that Bueghly should prevail?

TAKEAWAY CONCEPTS Definition and Categories

- Property is defined broadly as a person's *set of legal rights* over others to use the property exclusively.
- Tangible property is property that can be touched and physically possessed. The two forms of tangible property are personal property and real property.
- Personal property is both tangible and movable. In a business context, goods, vehicles, inventory, and equipment for business operations (e.g., computers) are all examples of personal property.
- The legal term for ownership rights in property is *title*. Normally, title is obtained by a grant of title by the current owner to a new owner, usually through a purchase or gift.

BAILMENTS

In a bailment relationship, although a possessor does not gain title via possession, the non-owner is still a rightful possessor of the goods. A bailment relationship is created when the *bailor* (owner of the property) entrusts a *bailee* to temporarily hold the property, usually for the parties' mutual benefit. If the parties intend to create a bailment relationship, the bailee owes a duty of care and a duty to act reasonably in protecting the property. For example, suppose that Franz brings his gold pocket watch to Max, a jeweler, for repair. Leaving the watch with Max creates a bailment relationship. That is, Franz has entrusted Max with his watch for their mutual benefit (Franz gets his watch fixed; Max earns income). Assume that Max must leave the store in a rush that night and accidentally leaves the door open. The store is burglarized, and Franz's watch is stolen. Max is liable for the cost of the watch due to his breach of the duty of care as bailee. On the other hand, suppose Max locks up the watch in a vault before he leaves, but a burglar with special skills breaks into the vault and takes the watch. In that case, most courts would find that Max has exercised due care and reasonableness and, therefore, is not liable for the theft.[1] Other common examples of bailment relationships are coat check, dry cleaning, and valet parking services.[2]

In Case 48.2, a state appellate court analyzes the limits of bailment liability.

LO 48-2

Explain the roles of the parties in a bailment relationship.

CASE 48.2 Ziva Jewelry v. Car Wash Headquarters, 897 So. 2d 1011 (Ala. 2004)

FACT SUMMARY Smith was employed by Ziva Jewelry, Inc. ("Ziva") as a traveling salesman. In connection with his employment, Smith drove his own car to meet with potential customers and traveled with samples of expensive jewelry, which he typically kept locked in the trunk. In August 2000, while returning from a trade show, Smith stopped at a car wash owned and operated by Car Wash

(continued)

---

[1] Based on examples in Ray A. Brown, *The Law of Personal Property,* 3d ed. (Chicago: Callaghan and Company, 1975).

[2] Note that courts distinguish between a "self-check" parking lot (no bailment) and a valet parking lot, where an agent of the lot *takes physical possession* of the car via keys, etc. (bailment).

Headquarters ("CWH"). Smith left his keys with a CWH employee, watched the car as it went through the tunnel, and observed an employee driving the car a short distance to the drying area. Smith did not alert any CWH employee to the contents of the trunk. After the car was dried, the attendant signaled to Smith that the service was complete. As Smith paid the cashier, someone jumped into Smith's vehicle and drove off. Although the police located Smith's car in just 15 minutes, the jewelry, valued at over $850,000, was gone and was never recovered. Ziva sued CWH, alleging that CWH, as bailee, took possession of Smith's car and of the jewelry inside and that CWH failed to exercise due care to safeguard and return the bailed car and contents to Smith. The trial court granted CWH's motion for a summary judgment on the grounds that no bailment of the jewelry had been created. Ziva appealed.

SYNOPSIS OF DECISION AND OPINION The Supreme Court of Alabama affirmed the trial court's summary judgment in favor of CWH. The court held that Ziva could not establish that CWH expressly or impliedly agreed to take responsibility for the jewelry hidden inside Smith's trunk. Because Ziva acknowledged that the jewelry was not plainly visible, there was no reason for the employees to foresee that the trunk contained expensive jewelry. The court ruled that Ziva could not claim that CWH knew or that it should have reasonably foreseen or expected that it was taking responsibility for over $850,000 worth of jewelry when it accepted Smith's vehicle for the purpose of washing it.

WORDS OF THE COURT: Acceptance by the Bailee "Thus, there is no evidence indicating that CWH expressly or impliedly accepted responsibility for the jewelry in the trunk of Smith's vehicle. Without express or implied acceptance by the purported bailee, a bailment cannot arise."

Case Questions

1. If Smith's car had not been recovered, would CWH be liable as a bailee for the car?

2. When a bailee takes a car as part of a bailment relationship, isn't the bailee also assuming liability for what is inside?

3. *Focus on Critical Thinking:* Is Smith left completely without recourse, or could he advance a different legal theory? If the police determined that the theft was an "inside job" involving CWH employees, how would that impact your analysis?

Leased Personal Property: UCC Article 2A

Businesses often choose to *lease* personal property, especially equipment, rather than purchase it outright. In an equipment lease, the lessor (owner of the property) gives the lessee (the party leasing the property) the exclusive right to possess and use the equipment for a fixed period. The lessee often makes a monthly payment to the lessor, but at the end of the lease term, the equipment is returned to the lessor. As a business matter, leasing is often an attractive alternative because the business can use the equipment on an exclusive basis without the investment required to purchase the equipment. There may also be tax advantages for the lessee in some cases. Examples of equipment that a business may lease are information systems equipment, telephones, furniture, and even heavy machinery used for manufacturing or construction.

Note that leases fall into an area governed by principles of property law and by certain principles of commercial law. Lease agreements are a form of personal property contract and are governed by state statutory laws that are modeled after Article 2A of the Uniform Commercial Code (UCC). Article 2A covers many of the same subjects as the article that governs the sale of goods, such as defining what constitutes a lease agreement, requiring certain lease agreements to be in writing, and allocating the risk of loss (i.e., which party will be responsible if the equipment is destroyed) to one party or the other based on the circumstances of the transaction. Chapter 17, "UCC Article 2A: Lease Contracts," provides a more comprehensive explanation of Article 2A leases.

REAL PROPERTY

Real property ownership is primarily governed by state statutes, although some common law principles still exist. The statutes that regulate the legal relationship between residential landlords and tenants are based on a model act known as the Uniform Residential Landlord-Tenant Act (URLTA). Note that when a landlord leases real property to a business, this is known as a *commercial* landlord-tenant agreement and is not governed by the URLTA. The landlord-tenant relationship is explored more fully later in this chapter.

Ownership Rights

The ownership rights to a parcel (piece) of real property, also called *real estate,* include the land and any structures built upon it as well as plant life and vegetation. The structures are known as the property's *improvements.* The ownership rights also extend to anything that is affixed, known as *fixtures,* to the structure, such as plumbing, heating and cooling systems, and the like. Similar to the ownership rights in personal property, ownership rights in a parcel of real property are thought of as a bundle of rights. This includes the right to sell, gift, lease, and control the property and its improvements. Ownership of real property is typically evidenced by a deed. Traditional property ownership rights are said to extend from "the soil upward into Heaven."[3] Generally, this means that certain rights are attached to the land that fit into four categories: (1) rights related to the *use and enjoyment* of the land, (2) *subsurface* rights, (3) *water* rights, and (4) *airspace* rights.

Use and Enjoyment of the Land

Generally, landowners have the right to use and enjoy the use of their property without interference from others. This interference is known as *nuisance* and occurs when one party creates unreasonable conditions that affect the landowner's use or enjoyment of the property. In many nuisance cases, a residential or business property owner sues a manufacturing company that owns a nearby plant for producing pollutants, making excessive noise, or emitting foul odors. Most courts apply the unreasonableness factor by examining the nature of the parcels of property at issue. In an area that is zoned for heavy industrial use, courts are reluctant to impose liability on a plant owner under the nuisance theory. Areas that are zoned for retail, office, or residential use are more likely to have legal protection from such nuisances.

Subsurface Rights

Landowners have rights to the soil and, most importantly, to any mineral, oil, or natural gas within the soil. These subsurface rights may be severed from the bundle of rights owned by the landowner and sold to a third party.

---

[3]From English common law cases that cite the Latin phrase *cujus est solum, ejus usque ad coelum.*

Water Rights

Also known as *riparian* rights, landowners have the right to reasonable use of any streams, lakes, and groundwater (water contained in soil) that are fully or partially part of their real property. *Reasonable use* means that the landowner is entitled to only as much of the water as she can put to beneficial use upon her land while balancing the rights of others who have riparian rights in the same stream or lake (such as an adjacent landowner).

Airspace Rights

The law contemplates ownership of airspace by drawing an imaginary line emanating from the borders of the property into the sky. Perhaps the most significant exception to this rule is that courts have held that landowners may not use this right to prevent airplane flights over their property.[4] Most airspace rights cases involving businesses arise when one property owner builds a building that somehow interferes with the air rights of another. Consider the dilemma of a resort hotel when faced with a next-door neighbor that builds a building so tall that it blocks the sun from the resort's pool. In Case 48.3, a landmark case in property law, the Florida Supreme Court considers whether a famous Miami Beach resort's airspace rights include solar rights as well.

LANDMARK CASE 48.3 Fontainebleau Hotel v. Eden Roc, 114 So. 2d 357 (Fla. 1959)

FACT SUMMARY The Fontainebleau Hotel was in the process of constructing a 14-story addition to its resort hotel. After completion of 8 stories, one of Fontainebleau's competitors, the Eden Roc Hotel, which owned adjoining property to the Fontainebleau, filed suit asking a court to issue an order prohibiting further construction of the addition. Eden Roc alleged that in the winter months, beginning at 2 o'clock in the afternoon and continuing until sunset, the shadow caused by the new addition would extend over Eden Roc's resort cabanas, main swimming pool, and several designated sunbathing areas. Eden Roc argued that this interference with sunlight and air violated its air rights and was causing Eden Roc to lose profits because its resort was now less desirable for guests wishing to use the pool facilities. Eden Roc also alleged that the construction plan was based on ill will between the owners of the resorts.

SYNOPSIS OF DECISION AND OPINION The Florida Supreme Court ruled in favor of the Fontainebleau based on the general property law rule that property owners may use their property in any reasonable and lawful manner. The court noted that landowners are not obliged to use their property in a way that would prevent injury to a neighbor.

The court also pointed out that modern American courts have consistently rejected the historical English law doctrine of "ancient lights," which provides a right to the free flow of light and air from adjoining land, as unworkable in current commercial life. Therefore, the court held that there is no legal right to the flow of air or light and that there is no cause of action so long as the structure serves a legitimately useful purpose.

WORDS OF THE COURT: Air and Solar Rights "[T]here being . . . no legal right to the free flow of light and air from the adjoining land, it is universally held that where a structure serves a useful and beneficial purpose, it does not give rise to a cause of action . . . even though it causes injury to another by cutting off the light and air and interfering with the view that would otherwise be available over adjoining land in its natural state, regardless of the fact that the structure may have been erected partly for spite."

Case Questions

1. If Eden Roc could prove that the addition was constructed completely out of spite, would this additional fact affect the court's decision?

(continued)

---

[4]*United States v. Causby,* 328 U.S. 256 (1946).

The Florida State Supreme Court ruled that the Fontainbleau Hotel in Miami Beach had the right to construct an addition to its property despite the fact that the addition blocked the sunlight to an adjacent resort hotel.
©AP Images

2. Why is the historical ancient lights doctrine unworkable in modern commercial life?

3. *Focus on Critical Thinking:* The court also notes that individuals are free to build as high as or in any way that they want, provided that doing so does not violate any laws, restrictions, or regulations. If the Fontainebleau had been in violation of any code or regulation, would the outcome of the case have been different? Why or why not?

Forms of Ownership Interests in Real Property

In most cases, real estate owners are entitled to the same general bundle of rights we discussed in the section on personal property. However, because some forms of ownership limit those general rights, it is important to understand the various forms of ownership. These are known as **ownership interests**. There are seven legally recognized interests; however, we will examine four common ownership interests that are important to business owners and managers: (1) fee simple; (2) life estate; (3) leasehold estate; and (4) easements. Table 48.1 provides a summary of real property ownership and an example of each interest.

Sale of Real Property

The most common way for commercial real estate to be transferred is through a sale.[5] Typically, the seller and buyer agree on essential terms about the purchase and enter into

---

[5]Other methods used to transfer (mainly noncommercial) real estate are through a tax sale (for nonpayment of taxes), inheritance, gift, and adverse possession.

TABLE 48.1 Real Property Ownership Rights

Interest	Rights	Example
Fee simple	Highest level of general rights. ■ *Fee simple absolute* (unrestricted rights) ■ *Fee simple defeasible* (restrictions on use or conditions associated with property)	■ Owner of office building. ■ A city grants a contractor an interest in a 1,000-acre city-owned lot on the condition that the contractor build a landfill for public use on a 200-acre portion of the property.
Life estate	Ownership interest that lasts for the lifetime of a particular person.	Life estates are sometimes used as part of a business succession plan designed for the transition of the ownership of a family-owned business from one generation to the next.
Leasehold estate	Least amount of rights because it grants only a qualified right to use the real estate in an exclusive manner for a limited period.	Landlord-tenant agreement (landlord gives the tenant a qualified right to possess and use the real estate for a specified period of years that is often spelled out in a written lease).
Easement	Privilege to use the real estate owned by another that arise from: ■ an express grant ■ implication or necessity, in which a property is landlocked between other properties ■ prescription via adverse possession (discussed in the next section)	Grant given by property owners to utility companies for the privilege to install and maintain gas and water lines.

an agreement of sale for the purchase of real estate. The agreement usually provides for a period devoted to due diligence, specifies a tentative settlement date (also called the *closing date*), and is supported by a cash deposit to be held by an escrow agent. An *escrow agent* is a neutral third party designated to hold a sum of money while the parties fulfill conditions in a contract.

The due diligence period varies based on the complexity of the transaction. During this time, the buyer will (1) arrange for financing through a financial institution or a private lender (such as a relative); (2) conduct an inspection of the property to be sure that the parties are aware of any physical defects, zoning issues, and other items that may affect the use or price of the property; and (3) have an attorney or title agent check to be sure that the seller has clear title to the property and will be able to convey the property without any legal obstacles. The agreement of sale spells out the timelines as well as the rights and obligations of the parties during the due diligence period. After the due diligence period has expired, the parties attend a settlement meeting at which the buyer presents payment and the seller conveys title to the property via a deed.

Adverse Possession

In some cases, a party may gain title to real estate through the doctrine of adverse possession. To gain title to a parcel of property through adverse possession, the acquiring party must demonstrate that she has possessed it in a certain way for a certain period. These requirements are often spelled out in a state's statutory or common law. In general, the requirements are that the party must have met a three-prong test.

1. *Open, notorious, and visible possession:* The true holder of title cannot be relieved of that title unless she can be reasonably expected to know that another person has taken

possession of the real estate and that the adverse possessor intended to assert a claim to its ownership. Examples of cases where courts have held that this prong was satisfied include those in which the adverse possessor had (1) demonstrated that the true owner had actual or imputed knowledge that the adverse party had taken possession of the land; (2) erected a fence or other enclosure around the property; or (3) paid taxes or other maintenance fees in connection with the land.

2. *Exclusive and actual possession:* The adverse possessor must also show that she was in exclusive control of the property and did not share control or possession of the property with the true owner or the public generally. This means that at least a reasonable percentage of the land claimed by the adverse possessor must be in actual use.

3. *Continuous possession:* The adverse possession of the property must be continuous for a period of time set down by state statute or common law. About two-thirds of states require 15 years or longer, but some states allow a shorter period if the adverse possessor pays the taxes on the property. This does not mean that the adverse possessor is required to spend every consecutive day on the property. Rather, it means that the adverse possessor cannot abandon the property for a period. If the owner retakes possession within the prescribed time period, the adverse possessor's use stops, and this prong cannot be satisfied unless the true owner abandons the property again in the future.

In Case 48.4, an appellate court considers a business owner's claim of title to a parcel of property through adverse possession.

CASE 48.4 2 North Street Corporation v. Getty Saugerties Corporation, 68 A.D.3d 1392 (N.Y. App. Div. 2009)

FACT SUMMARY 2 North Street ("2 North") is a corporation that owned a parcel of real estate used for a shopping center and a parking lot. Getty owned the adjacent lot, on which it had operated a gas station. A fence runs close to the boundary line between the properties but lies entirely on Getty's property. A narrow 0.129-acre strip of land exists between the boundary line and the fence. 2 North maintained the strip of land from the time the company purchased the property. For a period of approximately 23 years, 2 North paid a contractor to continuously maintain the strip's grass. The contractor also planted vegetation, removed rubbish and debris, and deposited snow plowed from 2 North's parking lot upon it. Getty never questioned the activities of the contractor, nor did anyone representing Getty grant the contractor permission to perform them. In 2007, 2 North brought an action seeking a declaration that it owned the strip of land through adverse possession. Getty objected on the basis that 2 North's use of the strip was not open and notorious enough to constitute notice to others claiming an adverse and hostile interest in the land. The trial court ruled in favor of 2 North, and Getty appealed.

SYNOPSIS OF DECISION AND OPINION The appellate division of the Supreme Court of New York affirmed the lower court's decision and held in favor of 2 North. The court ruled that 2 North had met its statutory burden of establishing that the character of the possession was hostile under a claim of right, actual, open and notorious, exclusive, and continuous for the statutory period of 10 years. The court was convinced that 2 North initially believed that it owned the strip and exclusively maintained it as its own even though the strip was not included in its deed description. This evidence of 2 North's continuous use and maintenance of the strip exemplified its possession as open and notorious, constituting notice to others that it was claiming an adverse and hostile interest in it.

(continued)

Case Questions

1. Was 2 North's use "notorious" given the fact that it is likely that Getty didn't realize that the strip of land was on its property? What does one have to do to use property in a notorious fashion?

2. How did 2 North satisfy the improvement requirement?

3. *Focus on Critical Thinking:* Should Getty be compensated for the strip of land taken by adverse possession? Should there be an offset for all the money invested by 2 North in maintenance?

LO 48-4

Give examples of the rights of landlords and tenants.

LANDLORD-TENANT LAW

An agreement between a landlord and a tenant for the rental of property is called a **lease** and is an example of the intersection between property law and contract law. As such, the sources of law governing leases range from state statutory protections of residential tenants to common law principles governing certain contracts. While our comprehensive coverage of contracts is in Unit Two, "Contracts, Sales, and Leases" some references to contract law are necessary in a discussion of property law. While statutes that cover residential leases often feature protections for tenants from arbitrary and wrongful acts of the landlord (such as a wrongful eviction), laws that govern the relationship between landlord-tenant agreements in a *commercial lease* (i.e., a lease for property that is to be used for commercial purposes such as a retail store in a shopping center) tend not to offer as much protection for business tenants. This is ordinarily because commercial leases are thought of as negotiated between the parties; because both parties are engaged in business, a degree of sophistication is imputed to the tenant that is not present in a residential lease.

Because many agreements for property between landlords and businesses are documented in the form of a lease, most issues regarding landlord and tenant rights and duties are spelled out in the lease. However, in cases where the parties have not specifically agreed on certain terms, the common law provides a basic set of rules. Because business managers and owners are frequently on the front lines in negotiating a lease, it is important to understand the basic legal framework governing landlord-tenant agreements.

Tenant Rights and Remedies

Fundamentally, tenants have the rights of *possession, quiet enjoyment,* and *habitability.* The right to *possession* simply means that the landlord must deliver the legal right to possess the property to the tenant at the commencement of the lease agreement. In most states, the law requires the landlord to make reasonable efforts to give property access to the tenant by ensuring that any previous tenant has vacated and that the tenant has keys to the premises.[6] *Quiet enjoyment* is the tenant's right to use the premises without interference from the landlord. For example, suppose Barclay leases a retail space to Jimenez. Barclay also owns

---

[6] *Restatement (Second) of Property* § 6.2.

the property next door to the leased property. One week after Jimenez takes possession of the space, Barclay begins to renovate the property next door and allows the contractor to place a construction dumpster in Jimenez's back lot. In this case, Barclay has occupied a part of the property leased to Jimenez and, thus, has breached the tenant's right to quiet enjoyment.

Related to the right of quiet enjoyment is the tenant's right to have the leased space in a reasonable condition, known as the right of *habitability*. Note that the right of habitability is mostly applicable in the residential lease context. Essentially, this is a protection of the tenant's right to occupy leased premises that are not in such an unreasonably poor or unsafe condition that a person cannot live there. Although an increasing number of courts are imposing this common law duty in a commercial context, some courts are still reluctant to protect this right for commercial tenants unless the circumstances are extreme (e.g., the condition of the premises violates a state or local building safety code).[7]

If a landlord breaches a duty or promise to a tenant, a variety of legal alternatives are available to compensate the tenant. These legal alternatives are known as **tenant remedies**. In the case of a violation of the tenant's right of possession, the tenant either may terminate the lease and sue the landlord for damages or may continue the lease and recover damages after the landlord is able to give possession. In the case of violation of the right of either quiet enjoyment or habitability, the tenant generally may choose to terminate the lease and/or sue for damages (particularly if the violation occurs after possession has taken place). In some extreme cases involving a violation of the right of habitability, tenants are permitted to withhold rent and pay the amounts due into escrow until any legal dispute is resolved. If the tenant cannot feasibly use the premises for his intended use because of landlord neglect or inaction, the tenant may claim to have been *constructively evicted* and may vacate the premises and terminate the lease without any further liability to the landlord.

Tenant Duties   For the most part, in a commercial lease context, the tenant's duties under the common law are to pay the rent as agreed upon and to act reasonably in care and use of the property. This duty of reasonableness includes refraining from disturbing other tenants, obeying reasonable landlord rules, complying with health and safety codes, and notifying the landlord when repairs are necessary on the premises.

 QUICK QUIZ Tenant's Rights
Which tenant right is at issue?

1. Tenant calls Landlord to explain that a smell of gas is coming from the heater and that the carbon monoxide detector beeped several times last week.
2. On day 1 of a new lease, Tenant shows up to find that the previous tenant is still living on the premises.
3. One month into a lease, Landlord begins to build a new townhouse directly next door to Tenant's leased space. Landlord also uses part of Tenant's space to store construction materials.

Answers to this Quick Quiz are provided at the end of the chapter.

---

[7] *Restatements (Second) of Property* § 5.1.

Landlord Rights and Remedies

If a tenant violates the duty to pay rent (whether the tenant is using or has abandoned the premises) or the duty to act reasonably in the use of the property, the common law allows several remedies to help the landlord recover damages. Depending on the circumstances, the landlord may keep any security deposit held by the landlord and/or may evict (remove) the tenant from the premises. Most lease agreements typically call for the landlord to hold a certain amount of money to secure the landlord if any damage is committed during the lease term and to give the landlord an option to recover part of any monies owed because of the tenant's abandoning the premises (with or without notice) before the lease term ends. The right of the landlord to keep the security deposit is highly regulated by statute in both residential and commercial real estate leases. At the end of the lease period, the landlord is typically required to return the security deposit to the tenant after subtracting the cost of any damages and giving an itemized list of the claimed damages to the tenant. The landlord must also act within a reasonable time after the end of the lease. The maximum period that the landlord may hold the deposit after the end of the lease is set by state statute and ranges between 15 and 45 days.[8]

In addition to taking action to recover damages via the security deposit, a landlord also may remove the tenant through *eviction*. This is an extreme remedy and may be used only when some significant violation of the tenant's duties has occurred. For example, a tenant that pays rent a few days late one month may not be evicted for violating the duty to pay. To evict a tenant, the landlord must follow statutorily prescribed procedures for eviction. This generally includes filing a lawsuit of eviction at a local court for a summary hearing on the issue. If the court agrees, the landlord is permitted to proceed with the eviction with the assistance of county authorities such as the sheriff's office.

LO 48-5

Distinguish between an assignment and a sublease and explain how each can be used in business planning objectives.

ASSIGNMENT AND SUBLETTING

Absent an agreement to the contrary, the parties in a lease agreement may transfer their interest to a third party. A landlord may sell her property to another party (who must honor the lease agreement) during the lease term, and a tenant may *assign* or *sublet* the premises. If the tenant wishes to transfer his interests (i.e., his right to possess and use the premises) to a third party for the entire remaining length of the term, this is called an **assignment**. The third party in an assignment is known as the *assignee*. If the tenant transfers anything less than the remaining term, this is known as a **sublease**. The third party in a sublease is called a *subleasee*. In both cases, the tenant remains bound to the original lease agreement, and if the assignee or subleasee fails to pay rent, the original tenant is still liable for the payments. The original tenant's liability is extinguished only if the landlord has released the tenant from that obligation. The assignee or subleasee receives the full legal benefits of tenancy, including the right to sue the landlord if the landlord violates any of her duties such as the right to quiet possession (discussed earlier in this section). While landlords often insist that lease agreements contain antiassignment clauses that restrict a tenant's right to assign or sublet, there are certain cases where this right may be a mutually beneficial way to achieve business objectives.

---

[8]For example, in Maryland landlords have 45 days to return security deposits to residential tenants. (See Md. Real Property Code Ann. § 8-203.) Conversely, in Florida landlords have 15 days to return a security deposit if they are not pursuing a damage claim against the tenant. If they are going to impose a claim, they have 30 days to notify the tenant. (See Fla. Stat. § 83.49.)

- A lease is an agreement between a landlord and a tenant for the rental of real estate.

- Generally, statutes are more protective of the tenant in residential leases than in commercial leases.

- Tenants have three basic rights: (1) possession, (2) quiet enjoyment, and (3) habitability. The right of possession is the tenant's right to possess and occupy the property; the right of quiet enjoyment and the right of habitability refer to the tenant's right to have the property be in a safe, livable condition.

- The duties of a tenant are to pay the rent and to act reasonably in his care and use of the property. Acting reasonably includes not disturbing other tenants and notifying the landlord of any needed repairs so that the property remains safe.

- Both the tenant and the landlord have remedies available to them in instances where the other party breaches the lease agreement or does not fulfill her duties.

- Tenants may also assign or sublease their interests in a property. Assignments are for the full term of the original lease, and subleases are for any period less than the full term.

GOVERNMENTAL REGULATION OF LAND USE

LO 48-6

Identify the laws that regulate the use of real property by its owners.

State and local governments frequently pass statutes and ordinances that impose regulation on how a landowner may use a parcel of real estate. These regulations come in several forms, but the two types of regulations that are most crucial in business planning and operations are *zoning ordinances* and *environmental regulations*.

Zoning Ordinances

Zoning is generally done at the local level in the form of local ordinances passed by the county or municipal government. Counties, cities, boroughs, townships, villages, parishes, and the like are all forms of local government that pass ordinances. The power to pass zoning ordinances is well established in the law. Recall our discussion in Chapter 3, "Business and the Constitution," about the government's police powers. When a local government passes a zoning ordinance, it is exercising its *police powers* to advance legitimate objectives of the municipality as a whole. The Supreme Court has recognized such power, but the Court has also set limits on the government's control of private property.[9]

Use Regulation From a business perspective, ordinances, which establish various districts for uses of property, are one of the most important types of zoning regulation. The municipality typically is divided into zones, in each of which only certain use of the land is permitted. These zones include areas for industrial, retail, and residential uses. Some municipalities divide their land uses further, specifying such uses as light industrial, warehouse, and so on.

---

[9]*Village of Euclid v. Ambler Realty Co.*, 272 U.S. 365 (1926).

Enforcement and Appeals   A local administrative agent, such as a zoning officer or building inspector employed by the municipality, typically enforces local use ordinances. A zoning board or commission is often appointed by the local government to handle appeals from decisions of the zoning officer and to consider applications for parties that wish to have an exception to one of the zoning laws. These exceptions are known as *variances.* Local governments vary greatly in their guidelines for permitting a variance, but, typically, the board will permit the variance if it does not harm the surrounding neighborhood or interfere with any local interests.

Limits on Regulation   Courts have ruled that the law sets limits on a local government's right to regulate private property usage through a variety of constitutional protections of property owners. First, if the zoning is so overreaching that it deprives the owner of all economic value of her property, the zoning will be categorized as a taking and the government is required to pay the owner the market value of the property as required in the Constitution's Takings Clause.[10] This is known as the power of **eminent domain** and is discussed in more detail in the next section. Second, under certain circumstances, those affected by a zoning ordinance are entitled to some procedural due process, such as a hearing by the local government.[11] Finally, a zoning law cannot discriminate because doing so violates the Equal Protection Clause of the Fourteenth Amendment. Courts in most states have also generally allowed zoning related to *aesthetics* so long as aesthetics is one factor, not the sole factor, in a municipality's zoning decision.

Environmental Regulations

An increasing concern for business owners and managers is federal, state, and local regulation of land use based on the government's interest in advancing sound environmental policy. In general, governments may impose environmentally based land-use regulations so long as they advance some substantial and legitimate state interest. For example, statutes aimed at preservation of open land areas have been found to be a legitimate government regulation of private property. Courts generally have held that wetland and coastland preservation ordinances that restrict the owner's right to develop, fill, or dredge the land are a legal use of the government's police powers. However, the Supreme Court curtailed this type of regulation by ruling that if the regulation completely depleted all economic value from the property, that act would constitute a government taking under the eminent domain power and trigger the government's obligation to pay compensation to the property owner.

For example, suppose that Developer purchases 20 acres of Florida beachfront property with the intent to develop the acreage into a resort. In response to concerned environmental groups, the state of Florida then passes a statute that restricts development along the coast running from the ocean to 1,000 yards inland. In Developer's case, this would amount to a loss of two prime acres of beachfront property, but Developer would have use of the remaining 18 acres. Developer sues for compensation because its partial loss of revenue was due to the state regulation. Most courts would rule against Developer because the government interest in preserving coastland has been held legitimate in the past and because Developer lost only part of the revenue stream and additional revenue is too speculative. On the other hand, if the state's statute had been more overreaching and resulted in Developer losing *all* economic value of the property, Developer would be entitled to compensation from the government.[12]

---

[10]U.S. Constitution, Fifth Amendment.

[11]U.S. Constitution, Fourteenth Amendment (Due Process Clause).

[12]Based on the facts of *Nollan v. California Coastal Commission,* 483 U.S. 825 (1987).

Of course, apart from understanding environmentally based land-use regulations, business owners and managers also must be knowledgeable about a separate body of federal and state law aimed at broader environmental policies. These broad-based concerns, such as laws that regulate pollution, the operation of factories, and the disposal of solid waste and toxic chemicals, are discussed in detail in Chapter 47, "Environmental Law."

EMINENT DOMAIN

It is important to understand the difference between a legitimate government land-use regulation and a government taking of property that triggers a constitutional requirement to compensate the landowner. The authority of the state and federal government to take private property is called the power of *eminent domain,* which is derived from the Fifth Amendment provision that states: "[N]or shall private property be taken for public use without just compensation."

Procedure

Eminent domain is traditionally invoked using a condemnation proceeding. Once a government has decided that certain real estate is necessary for public use, the government typically begins to negotiate sales agreements with the private property owners of the area(s) to be taken. If the negotiations fail, the government will formally institute a judicial proceeding to condemn the real estate. The court will be sure that procedural rights are being afforded to the property owner and will determine the fair market value of the real estate. Once the court has entered its order, the condemnation is complete, and the government now holds title to the real estate.

Public Use

The Fifth Amendment's phrase *public use* has been the source of controversy. Typically, public use may mean the building of public highways, schools, public hospitals, and other traditional public government functions. However, the U.S. Supreme Court has construed the public use language very broadly for uses outside the traditional uses so long as the government can demonstrate that its actions are rationally related to some conceivable public purpose. This broad construction has been the source of controversy. For example, suppose that the government condemns a blighted area of a city in hopes of developing the condemned area into a thriving example of urban renewal that brings along new retail and office buildings. The plan calls for condemnation of some areas adjacent to the blight that have single-family homes and thriving small, neighborhood businesses. Because the government does not intend to build any facilities for public use, is the taking unconstitutional? The U.S. Supreme Court took up that very issue in Case 48.5 in what was perhaps the most important eminent domain decision since 1954.[13]

CASE 48.5 Kelo v. City of New London, 545 U.S. 469 (2005)

FACT SUMMARY The city of New London devised an economic development plan that was projected to create more than 1,000 jobs and increase tax and other revenue. The plan called for a waterfront conference hotel; a marina; and various retail, commercial, and residential properties. The city's

(continued)

---

[13]The urban renewal interest was first sanctioned by the Court in *Berman v. Parker,* 348 U.S. 26 (1954).

development authority designated a large area composed of adjacent parcels of real estate to be condemned in order to redevelop the property consistent with the redevelopment plan. The city's agent purchased some of the property from willing sellers and gave notice that the city would institute condemnation proceedings via the power of eminent domain to acquire the remaining property from unwilling owners. The city purchased all but nine parcels of real estate and brought condemnations against nine property owners including Kelo, the named plaintiff. Although the city conceded that the condemned properties were not part of the blighted areas (in fact some had recently been renovated), they were condemned simply because of their location in the proposed development area. The lower courts' decisions were mixed, and the U.S. Supreme Court accepted the case on appeal to decide the question of whether the city's plan qualified as a public use within the meaning of the Takings Clause of the Fifth Amendment to the U.S. Constitution.

SYNOPSIS OF DECISION AND OPINION   The Court ruled in favor of the city and articulated guideposts for appropriate use of the Takings Clause. The Court affirmed the principle that the government is not permitted to take one party's private property for the sole purpose of transferring it to another private party and acknowledged that the city would not be able to take the property if the city planned to bestow it to a private development company or individual or if any benefits from the plan would be realized only by private individuals. However, the city's development plan did not contemplate any direct bestowment of property rights upon private individuals or companies. Moreover, even though some of the uses would be private in nature, the Court ruled that the standard to be used is the broader interpretation of the property being used for a public purpose. The Court found that the overall elimination of blight is a legitimate public

purpose and held that the city's plan was a valid exercise of the city's eminent domain power.

WORDS OF THE COURT: Public Purpose "[T]his 'Court long ago rejected any literal requirement that condemned property be put into use for the general public.' Indeed, while many state courts endorsed 'use by the public' as the proper definition of public use, that narrow view steadily eroded over time. Not only was the 'use by the public' test difficult to administer . . . , but it proved to be impractical given the diverse and always evolving needs of society. Accordingly, when this Court began applying the Fifth Amendment to the States at the end of the 19th century, it embraced the broader and more natural interpretation of public use as 'public purpose.' . . . Without exception, our cases have defined [this] concept broadly, reflecting our longstanding policy of deference to legislative judgments in this field. . . Given the comprehensive character of the plan [and] the thorough deliberation that preceded its adoption . . . [it] unquestionably serves a public purpose."

Case Questions

1. How does the Court define "public use"?

2. Would the case have been decided differently if the project built only a large industrial park? Why or why not?

3. *Focus on Critical Thinking:* In dissenting opinions, members of the Court argued that this decision makes all private property vulnerable to being taken and transferred to another private owner (against established principles the Court mentioned earlier) so long as the property is upgraded in some way. Moreover, they argued that this decision is advantageous to large corporations or individuals with political power or connections, while those with few resources are disadvantaged. Do you agree? Why or why not?

TAKEAWAY CONCEPT Eminent Domain

The Fifth Amendment provides state and federal government the authority to take private property for public use and to compensate the owner under the powers of eminent domain.

©valterZ/Shutterstock

Leveraging a Commercial Lease

PROBLEM: When a business is considering leased-space alternatives to locate its operations, one important business objective is planning for expansion while minimizing risks.

To achieve this objective, a business may lease space that is larger than its current needs but needed in the future to implement a 10-year expansion plan. However, the current cash flow of the business may support only a smaller leased area. For example, suppose that the management of Extreme Widget, Inc. (EWI), a manufacturer of high-performance widgets, locates a facility that is 10,000 square feet. Although EWI's current needs and financial ability support only 5,000 square feet, the management team is anxious to secure the space because of its ideal location and competitive rental rate. EWI also is embarking on an expansion plan that will require at least another 5,000 square feet of space over the next five years. EWI's objectives are to (1) secure the 10,000-square-foot parcel, (2) reduce the risk and liability of the added expenses by having alternatives for generating additional revenue to support the additional space until it is needed, and (3) provide EWI with maximum flexibility in case expansion plans must be put on hold.

STRATEGIC SOLUTION: Maximize leverage by negotiating a subletting clause with an option for an assignment.

A strategic method of using the law to help achieve business objectives would be for EWI's management to approach the landlord of the facility and propose the inclusion of a sublease and assignment clause in a five-year lease. The clause could include the following provisions:

■ EWI has the right to negotiate a sublease for up to 5,000 square feet of the facility, with EWI remaining primarily liable to the landlord on the lease.

■ EWI has the option of assigning all or part of the lease so long as the landlord can review the financial condition and creditworthiness of the proposed assignee. The landlord may accept or reject the candidate based on creditworthiness.

■ If the landlord accepts the assignee, EWI remains primarily liable under the lease for a period of one year and then is released from any obligations of the lease.

This solution achieves EWI's objectives by providing maximum flexibility to expand (or contract) while reducing the financial risks associated with leasing 10,000 square feet of property. The landlord also derives a benefit from the agreement because he now has a five-year lease in place for 10,000 square feet and the right to reject any proposed assignee.

QUESTIONS

1. Have you ever signed a lease? If so, was the lease residential or commercial? Did you negotiate the lease, or did you just sign it? Were there any terms that surprised you?

2. If you were negotiating a commercial lease, what terms—other than rent amount—would be most important to your business?

3. Use your favorite search engine to find a sample commercial lease. Do you understand each provision? Is there any risk to using a free sample lease commonly found on the Internet? What would you add or delete to reduce your risk as a tenant?

KEY TERMS

Personal property p. 925   Any movable or tangible object that can be owned or leased (e.g., computers, inventory, furniture, jewelry); includes everything except real property.

Real property p. 925   Land, or anything growing on, attached to, or erected on the land.

Title p. 925   The legal term for ownership in property; confers on the titleholder the exclusive use of personal property and the rights to sell, lease, or prohibit another from using the property.

Actual owner p. 925   The individual who is recognized as having primary or residual title to the property and is, therefore, the ultimate owner of the property.

Ownership interests p. 931   The various forms of real property ownership. Some forms limit the rights that owners of real estate have.

Lease p. 934   A contract in which the terms of an agreement are set out for a person to use someone else's property for a specific period of time (*ch. 17*). An agreement between a landlord and a tenant for the rental of property (*ch. 48*).

Tenant remedies p. 935   The legal alternatives available to tenants as compensation in the event a landlord breaches a lease, including termination of the lease, a suit for damages, and withholding of rent.

Assignment p. 936   When one of the contracting parties transfers their rights under the contract to another party.

Sublease p. 936   A tenant's transfer of her interests to a third party for anything less than the term remaining on the lease.

Eminent domain p. 938   The authority of the state and federal government to take private property.

CASE SUMMARY 48.1 Singer Co. v. Stott & Davis Motor Express, Inc. and Stoda Corp., 79 A.2d 227 (N.Y. App. Div. 1981)

Bailments

Stoda Corporation operated a warehouse used by Singer to store 133 air-conditioner units. Upon storing the goods in the warehouse, officers and managers of Singer inspected the warehouse and observed that it had a network of sprinkler systems. A fire broke out at Stoda's warehouse, the sprinkler system failed to activate, and the fire destroyed all the Singer goods.

Singer sued, claiming Stoda's negligence in storing goods in a warehouse without adequate fire protection breached its bailment duties.

CASE QUESTIONS

1. Who prevails and why?
2. What is the standard duty that the bailee (Stoda) owes to the bailor (Singer)?

CASE SUMMARY 48.2 Chaplin v. Sanders, 676 P.2d 431 (Wash. 1984)

Adverse Possession

In 1957, Hibbard decided to clear his land to open a trailer park. Because there was no clear boundary between Hibbard's property and the adjoining property to the east, Hibbard cleared the property up to a large drainage ditch and installed an access road to the left of the ditch to signify the property line. Hibbard opened a trailer park facility, and later that year, McMurray, the owner of the eastern parcel, had a survey conducted. McMurray informed Hibbard that the access road encroached on his property by 20 feet. Subsequently, Hibbard sold the trailer park to Gilbert and noted in the sales contract that (1) the driveway encroached 20 feet on McMurray's property, (2) Gilbert agreed not to claim ownership of the property, and (3) Gilbert agreed to remove the blacktop if ever requested to do so.

From 1967 to 1976, the property changed ownership several times, but no mention was made of the encroachment or contract provision from the Hibbard-Gilbert sale. In 1976, Sanders purchased the trailer park and was given notice of the encroachment and provision

but mistook the road to which the notice referred. Since the development of the trailer park, the road had been continuously used, and the area between the drainage ditch and road had been maintained by the various trailer park property owners (through means such as planting flowers and mowing the grass) and used by residents for picnics. Sanders also installed underground wiring and surface poles in the area. Two years later, Chaplin purchased the eastern lot from McMurray, had a survey conducted, and had architects design buildings for development based on the true property line from the survey. Washington requires a 10-year period of use to establish adverse possession.

CASE QUESTIONS

1. Are all the elements for adverse possession met so that Sanders now has title to the disputed parcel? Why or why not?
2. What is the appropriate starting time from which to measure ownership to satisfy Washington's statutory requirement for 10 years of possession?

CASE SUMMARY 48.3 Dayenian v. American National Bank and Trust Co. of Chicago, 414 N.E.2d 1199 (III. App. Ct. 1980)

Assignments and Subleases

Dayenian entered into a two-year lease agreement for an apartment with Monticello Realty Corporation on July 14. On October 26 of that year, she signed a portion of the lease headed "Assignment," which stated that she assigned all her rights, title, and interest in the lease to Lambert from December 1 onward but that she was not relieved of any liability under the lease. Lambert accepted this on November 8 by signing a section titled "Acceptance of Assignment." That same day, Monticello Realty executed a portion of the lease entitled "Consent to Assignment," which consented on the condition that Dayenian remain liable for payment of rent. In March of the following year, Lake Shore Drive Development Company mailed Lambert a notice of intent to convert the apartment building to a condominium; the notice provided for a right of first refusal to purchase the apartment if he responded. Lambert never acted upon this notice, and in May the developer entered into a contract to sell the apartment to another party. Dayenian sued, claiming that she should have been given the right of first refusal because she was the tenant of the apartment at the time the notice to convert was sent and that the transfer to Lambert was a sublease.

CASE QUESTIONS

1. Is the transfer an assignment or a sublease? Why?
2. What do the courts examine in making this determination?

CASE SUMMARY 48.4 Amoco Oil Co. v. Jones, 467 N.W.2d 357 (Minn. Ct. App. 1991)

Landlord-Tenant Agreements

Jones operated a gas station, which he leased from Amoco Oil Company under a franchise agreement. The lease was a standard form signed by Jones to obtain the franchise. The lease required Jones to return the premises in substantially the same condition as received, less ordinary wear and tear, and required him to perform necessary upkeep and maintenance on the premises, including clearing sidewalks. Although the lease did not indicate which party was responsible for fire insurance, it did note that Amoco could terminate the lease upon destruction of the premises. Early one morning a no-fault fire broke out, gutting parts of the station and causing $118,850 in damage. After the fire, Amoco terminated the lease and leveled the station. Amoco then sued Jones for not returning the station in substantially the same condition as he received it.

CASE QUESTIONS

1. Does Jones have an obligation to rebuild the gas station? Why or why not?
2. Why would Amoco terminate the lease?

CASE SUMMARY 48.5 Automobile Supply Co. v. Scene-In-Action, 172 N.E. 35 (III. 1930)

Constructive Eviction

Scene-In-Action ("Scene") rented a building from Automobile Supply Co. ("Auto") for Scene's business of manufacturing electrical advertising signs. The space also was used to house administrative offices of the business. Included in the lease was a provision requiring Auto to supply heat to the premises. The heat provision included language to the effect that efficient heat was necessary to keep the building comfortable to produce signs and carry on normal office tasks. Soon after the lease was signed, the building was without heat for several hours on numerous occasions throughout two months. Scene made repeated complaints about the situation to Auto, but Auto failed to fix the problem.

The problems continued, and as the temperature dropped during the height of winter, there were many days when the temperature inside was below 50 degrees. Because of the lack of heat, several Scene's employees would not return to work, claiming they were ill and unable to work in the cold conditions. Unable to carry on business, Scene terminated the lease, claiming it was constructively evicted because it had been deprived of the beneficial use and enjoyment of the premises.

Auto countersued for payments owed, claiming Scene could have vacated the premises earlier but instead stayed and maintained business operations without paying rent. Thus, Scene was not constructively evicted.

CASE QUESTIONS

1. Who prevails and why? Do the conditions support a constructive eviction theory?
2. Suppose that the landlord had made good faith efforts to fix the problem but was unable to for a period of three months. How would that impact your analysis?

CHAPTER REVIEW QUESTIONS

1. **Osterman buys a metal detector and takes it to a public beach. He finds a diamond bracelet near the picnic tables, but there is no one else in sight except a lifeguard. He asks the lifeguard if she owns the bracelet, and the lifeguard replies "no." Who has title to the bracelet?**
   a. Osterman, because title is a bundle of rights.
   b. Osterman, except against the true owner.
   c. The lifeguard, except against the true owner.
   d. The lifeguard, as a bailee.
   e. The city government.

2. **A _____ relationship is created when the owner of personal property entrusts another to temporarily hold the property for the parties' mutual benefit.**
   a. Lease
   b. Title
   c. Possession
   d. Bailment
   e. Trust

3. **Tanner is the owner of Whiteacre. To access the public road, he must cross through Greenacre, a parcel owned by Farmer. Tanner is granted access via a 10-foot-wide strip through Greenacre. What is this access called?**
   a. Trespass
   b. Adverse possession
   c. Tenant right
   d. Easement
   e. None

4. **Fassett is a business executive who travels extensively for work. Harris, her neighbor, often mows Fassett's lawn while she is traveling. Over the course of 20 years, Harris takes care of Fassett's property for periods as long as 11 consecutive months. In a lawsuit by Harris to take Fassett's property through adverse possession, who prevails?**
   a. Harris, because the possession is open, notorious, and visible.
   b. Harris, because the possession is more than 15 years.
   c. Fassett, because Harris is a tenant.
   d. Fassett, because the possession is not continuous.
   e. A court would have to decide.

5. **Which of the following is *not* true concerning zoning ordinances?**
   a. They exist at the federal level.
   b. Exceptions to zoning ordinances are called variances.
   c. Zones typically include areas for industrial and retail use.
   d. They are an exercise of the government's police powers.
   e. All are true.

6. **Tangible property includes personal property, real property, and intellectual property.**
   a. True
   b. False

7. The legal term for ownership rights in property is "fee rights."

a. True

b. False

8. Common examples of a bailment relationship are customers who use coat check services or dry cleaners.

a. True

b. False

9. Tenants have a right of possession, quiet enjoyment, and habitability.

a. True

b. False

10. If a tenant transfers her interest in a lease to a third party for the entire remaining length of the lease's term, this is called a sublease.

a. True

b. False

 Quick Quiz ANSWERS
Tenant's Rights

1. Habitability. The potential for carbon monoxide poisoning leaves the space in an unusable condition.
2. Possession. Landlord has a duty to ensure that the previous tenant has vacated.
3. Quiet enjoyment. The noise and use of Tenant's space for construction is an interference from Landlord.

CHAPTER REVIEW QUESTIONS: Answers and Explanations

1. **b.** The bracelet is mislaid and not abandoned. Thus, the finder has title against everyone except the true owner. Answer *a* is incorrect because a bundle of rights only attaches to the title holder. Answers *c* and *d* are incorrect because the lifeguard has no claim of ownership.

2. **d.** A bailment relationship is created when the owner of real property entrusts a merchant or repair shop with the property (e.g., dropping off a suit at the dry cleaner). Answers *a, b,* and *c* are incorrect because they are unrelated to a bailment relationship.

3. **d.** An easement is a privilege to use the real estate owned by another. Answers *a* and *b* are incorrect because access was granted. Answer *c* is incorrect because this is not a landlord-tenant relationship.

4. **d.** For adverse possession to occur, the possession must be continuous. Therefore, Fassett prevails. Answers *a* and *b* are incorrect because elements of adverse possession are not met. Answer *c* is

incorrect because there is no landlord-tenant relationship.

5. **a.** Zoning ordinances exist at the county and municipal government level only. Answers *b, c,* and *d* are incorrect because each is true.

6. **b.** False. Tangible property includes personal property and real property but *not* intellectual property.

7. **b.** False. The legal term for ownership rights in property is "title."

8. **a.** True. Coat check services or dry cleaners both involve temporary entrustment for the benefit of the owner.

9. **a.** True. Possession, quiet enjoyment, and habitability are part of a tenant's bundle of rights.

10. **b.** False. If a tenant transfers her interest in a lease to a third party for the entire remaining length of the lease's term, this is called an assignment, *not* a sublease.

CHAPTER 49

Wills, Trusts, and Estates

 THINKING STRATEGICALLY

The law of wills, trusts, and estates applies to people from all walks of life. In this chapter's *Thinking Strategically,* we will explore the consequences of the lack of estate planning, using the artist Prince as an example.

Learning Objectives

After studying this chapter, students who have mastered the material will be able to:

49-1	Identify key terms in the law of wills, trusts, and estates.
49-2	Articulate the principle of freedom of disposition.
49-3	Summarize how the probate process works.
49-4	Explain the strategic advantages of trusts.
49-5	Distinguish between estate taxes and inheritance taxes.
49-6	Describe the roles of the Uniform Probate Code and Uniform Trust Code in the development of state law.

CHAPTER OVERVIEW

The law of wills, trusts, and estates is what makes possible the transmission of property rights from one generation to another. In this chapter, we will first define key terms such as *decedent, wills,* and *intestacy,* then explain the existing probate system for transferring decedents' property. After a discussion of the pros and cons of the probate process, we will examine the law of trusts, a popular probate-avoidance device. In this chapter, we discuss key legal terms and basic concepts, including the fundamental principle of freedom of disposition; the pros and cons of the probate system; lifetime transfers such as trusts that can serve as substitutes for wills; and the main sources of state and federal law that apply to wills, trusts, and estates.

KEY TERMS IN WILLS, TRUSTS, AND ESTATES

This section defines some of the key terms and basic concepts discussed in this chapter.

Decedent

A **decedent** is an individual who has died. If the decedent has left a will, he is referred to as a *testator*. If he has not left a will, he is referred to as *dying intestate*. (See the term *intestacy* below.)

LO 49-1

Identify key terms in the law of wills, trusts, and estates.

Estate

An **estate** includes the real and personal property that the decedent owns or has an interest in upon his death. As a result, the estate includes everything a person owns or anything that he could have a legal interest in, including financial investments as individual stocks, bonds, and mutual funds; retirement accounts; personal property such as artwork and other valuables; real property including houses and other real estate; and business interests, including the decedent's interest in such things as personal injury lawsuits and breach of contract lawsuits. An estate can be transferred at death by will or by operation of intestate law if the decedent has failed to leave a valid will.

Last Will and Testament (Will)

A **will** (also referred to as a *last will and testament*) is a legal document in which a person, the *testator,* expresses his wishes as to how his estate is to be distributed at death, and in which the testator appoints an *executor* to manage the estate until its final distribution. A will is thus an estate-planning document that lets one direct how one's assets should be administered; to whom—and under what circumstances—such assets should be distributed; and who should manage such assets after one's death. In addition, people make wills to designate guardianship for minor children, to make charitable bequests, and to specify their funeral arrangements.

To summarize, although the law of wills varies from state to state, there are four main requirements for the formation of a valid will:

1. The will must have been executed with testamentary intent.
2. The testator must have had testamentary capacity.
3. The will must have been executed free of fraud, duress, undue influence, or mistake.
4. The will must have been duly executed through a proper ceremony and signed by at least two to three witnesses. The number of witnesses will depend on the law of the jurisdiction in which the will is executed.

Codicil

Wills are ambulatory, which means that a testator can change his will at any time. In fact, some testators may change their wills several times during their lifetimes. How does a testator change his will? The answer is by means of a **codicil**, which is a separate testamentary document whose purpose is to amend an existing will. Codicils are subject to the same formal requirements as a will, including testamentary capacity, witnesses, and so on. Amendments made by a codicil may alter, explain, add to, subtract from, confirm, or otherwise amend a will in any other way, minor or major, short of complete revocation.

Executor

An **executor** is the person named by the testator in his will to carry out the instructions in the will. Typically, the executor's duties include disbursing property to the beneficiaries

Did you know that the artist Prince died *intestate*, that is, without a will?
©PictureLux/The Hollywood Archive/Alamy

designated in the will, obtaining information on potential heirs, collecting and arranging for payment of debts of the estate, and approving or disapproving creditors' claims. An executor will make sure estate taxes are calculated, necessary forms are filed, and tax payments are made. She will also assist the attorney with the estate. Additionally, the executor acts as a legal conveyor who designates where the donations will be sent using the information left in *bequests*, whether they will be sent to charity or other organizations. In most circumstances, the executor is the representative of the estate for all purposes, and she has the ability to sue or be sued on behalf of the estate. The executor holds legal title to the estate property, but she may not use the title or property for her own benefit unless permitted by the terms of the will.

Intestacy

What if you die without a will? **Intestacy** occurs when the decedent dies without leaving a will or without otherwise fully disposing of his property during his lifetime. By way of example, musical legends Aretha Franklin and Prince (pictured nearby) died without leaving wills. If you die intestate (without a will), your estate is then distributed according to the intestate laws of the state in which you resided. These laws typically are designed to reflect what most people want to happen, such as caring for immediate family. There's no guarantee, however, that the distribution of your assets will reflect your personal wishes.

TAKEAWAY CONCEPTS Key Terms in Wills, Trusts, and Estates

- A decedent is an individual who has died; if the decedent has left a will, he is referred to as a testator.
- An estate refers to all the real and personal property that the decedent owns or has an interest in at the time of his death.
- A will is a legal document in which a person, the *testator,* expresses his wishes as to how his estate is to be distributed at death, and in which the testator appoints an *executor* to manage the estate until its final distribution. A codicil is a testamentary document whose purpose is to amend an existing will.
- Intestacy occurs when a decedent dies without leaving a will or without otherwise fully disposing of his property during his lifetime.

LO 49-2

Articulate the principle of freedom of disposition.

FREEDOM OF DISPOSITION

One of the most important principles in the law of wills is the notion of freedom of disposition. In brief, **freedom of disposition** refers to the fundamental common law principle that says testators should be free to dispose of their property at death in any way they want. The leading justification for freedom of disposition has to do with incentives. Specifically, it is argued that the ability to pass on wealth to heirs of one's choosing creates incentives for individuals to be productive during their lifetime.

But is it fair that some children inherit millions of dollars from their wealthy parents, while others receive small or no inheritances? What limits, if any, should be placed on a testator's freedom of disposition in the name of fairness?

Broadly speaking, there are two competing schools of thought. One view is that freedom of disposition is an artificial or legally created right and should thus be subject to reasonable limits. An alternative view, however, is that freedom of disposition is a natural right and should not be constrained or interfered with by the law.

What about the religious preferences of testators? In Case 49.1, a court grapples with this fundamental dilemma between religious freedom and fairness in the will of Dr. Daniel Shapira. (The symbols of several great religious traditions appear in Figure 49.1.)

FIGURE 49.1   Religious Symbols

CASE 49.1 Shapira v. Union National Bank, Ohio Court of Common Pleas, 315 N.E.2d 825 (1974)

FACT SUMMARY   Daniel Jacob Shapira was the son of David Shapira, M.D. Dr. Shapira conditioned his son's inheritance under his will upon his son's being married to, or marrying within seven years of the testator's death, a Jewish girl with two Jewish parents. The son filed suit in the Ohio Court of Common Pleas, alleging that the condition was unconstitutional based on the premise that the right to marry is protected by the Fourteenth Amendment to the Constitution of the United States.

SYNOPSIS OF DECISION AND OPINION   The Ohio Court of Common Pleas upheld the provisions of the will conditioning the bequest to his sons upon their marrying Jewish girls, ruling that the will did not offend the Constitution. According to the court, the conditions contained in the will were reasonable restrictions, since the testator's unmistakable testamentary plan was for his possessions to be used to encourage the preservation of the Jewish faith.

WORDS OF THE COURT: The Right to Receive Property by Will   "Basically, the right to receive property by will is a creature of the law,

and is not a natural right or one guaranteed or protected by either the Ohio or the United States constitution. . . . This would seem to demonstrate that, from a constitutional standpoint, a testator may restrict a child's inheritance. The court concludes, therefore, that the upholding and enforcement of the provisions of Dr. Shapira's will conditioning the bequests to his sons upon their marrying Jewish girls does not offend the Constitution of Ohio or of the United States."

Case Questions

1. What if the testator had conditioned the inheritance upon his son *not* marrying a Christian girl? Would the outcome of this case be different?

2. What if the testator had imposed a shorter time limit, say one year (instead of seven), but had allowed his son to marry a girl of any religious faith? Would the outcome of this case be different?

3. *Focus on Critical Thinking:* Do you agree with the court's conclusion that "the right to receive property by will is a creature of the law, and is not a natural right"? Why or why not?

Although testators enjoy a broad right of freedom of disposition, they can only transfer those rights that they actually have at the time of death. In Case 49.2, a federal court rejects the intergenerational transfer of property rights that were created many years after the death of a famous testator, movie star Marilyn Monroe.

CASE 49.2 Shaw Family Archives v. CMG Worldwide, 486 F. Supp. 2d 309 (S.D.N.Y. 2007)

FACT SUMMARY Marilyn Monroe left the bulk of her estate to her "method" acting mentor Lee Strasberg. Lee Strasberg died in 1982, leaving his wife Anna Strasberg as the sole beneficiary under his will. Anna Strasberg administered the Monroe estate until 2001, at which time the estate was closed and its intellectual property assets were transferred to a Delaware company, Marilyn Monroe, LLC ("MMLLC").

The Shaw Family Archives is owned by the children of the late photographer Sam Shaw, who took (and owned the copyright for) several of the most famous images of Marilyn Monroe, including several of her standing on the subway grate for the 1955 film *The Seven Year Itch.* (See nearby photo.) MMLLC and its licensing company, CMG Worldwide, brought an action against the Shaw family to stop sales of Marilyn Monroe T-shirts and the commercial licensing of Marilyn Monroe images through the website Shaw Family Archives. Marilyn Monroe's estate alleged that the Shaw Family Archives violated the movie star's publicity rights under Indiana's Right of Publicity Act because it sold T-shirts at a Target store in Indianapolis bearing a photograph of Marilyn Monroe and operated a website through which customers could purchase licenses for the use of her image on various commercial products. Not surprisingly, Indiana is the home of CMG, which controls the publicity rights for numerous other celebrities, both alive and dead—such as James Dean, Ingrid Bergman, and Babe Ruth—and has one of the most sweeping right of publicity statutes in the nation.

The Indiana Right of Publicity Act, which was enacted in 1994, over 30 years after Monroe's death in 1962, created a descendable and transferable right of publicity extending 100 years after a testator's death. Accordingly, CMG moved for summary judgment claiming that Marilyn Monroe's postmortem publicity rights passed to CMG

Iconic photograph of movie star Marilyn Monroe while promoting the film *The Seven Year Itch.*
©Moviestore collection Ltd/Alamy

through a clause of her will. The Shaw Family Archives filed a cross-motion for summary judgment asserting that Marilyn Monroe—a possible domiciliary of either California or New York when she died, but not of Indiana—could not have devised publicity rights she did not own at the time of her death, since no publicity act had yet been enacted in Indiana or in either of Marilyn Monroe's possible domicile states.

SYNOPSIS OF DECISION AND OPINION The United States District Court for the Southern District of New York found in favor of Shaw Family Archives. The court ruled that in 1962, the year Monroe died, New York did not recognize a transferable

(continued)

postmortem right of publicity. Well-settled New York estate law allows testators to devise only the transferable rights they possess at the time of their deaths. Because the court found that the right of publicity did not exist, Monroe did not possess the right when she died; therefore, her will could not have conveyed the right to her heirs. As a result, the heirs of photographer Sam Shaw were therefore free to exploit the many iconic images of Monroe taken by their father.

WORDS OF THE COURT: Postmortem Right of Publicity "MMLLC's case is doomed because both the California and Indiana postmortem right of publicity statutes recognize that an individual cannot pass by will a statutory property right that she did not possess at the time of her death. . . . Thus, even if a postmortem right of publicity in Marilyn Monroe's persona could have been created after her death, [the Indiana Right of Publicity Act does not allow for that right] to be transferred through the will of a 'personality' who, like Ms. Monroe, was already deceased at the time of the statute's enactment."

Case Questions

1. What if Indiana had enacted its Right of Publicity Act in 1963? Would the outcome of the case be the same?

2. The movie *The Seven Year Itch* was distributed by the movie studio 20th Century Fox. Could the movie studio have sued the Shaw family to stop the sales of the merchandise with images of Marilyn Monroe from the film?

3. *Focus on Critical Thinking:* Marilyn Monroe's death was ruled a suicide. In your opinion, should death by suicide result in the forfeiture of the right to transfer one's estate by will? Why or why not?

TAKEAWAY CONCEPTS Freedom of Disposition

- Freedom of disposition is the common law principle that testators should be free to dispose of their property at death in any way they want.
- The freedom of disposition, however, is not absolute, as testators may impose only reasonable conditions in their will.

PROBATE

LO 49-3

Summarize how the probate process works.

When you die, whether or not you leave a will your estate will go through a process called **probate** that manages, settles, and distributes your property according to the terms of your will or by operation of intestate law if no valid will exists. The probate process is governed by state law and will thus vary from state to state, so we paint this process with a broad brush.

When a person dies, someone, usually a family member, may petition a court in the decedent's state of domicile to appoint a personal representative to protect and distribute the property in the decedent's estate.

Probate is the process by which the personal representative assembles and distributes the assets in the decedent's estate to the beneficiaries designated in the decedent's will or to the decedent's heirs as determined by intestacy law if no valid will exists. (If the decedent owned property in other states, a separate, "ancillary" probate might have to be opened—and a personal representative appointed—in each of those states.)

The probate process is also supposed to protect the rights of creditors. The personal representative has a legal obligation to identify and notify the decedent's creditors of the probate proceedings. The creditors of the decedent may then assert their claims against the decedent's estate.

Once the assets of the decedent are assembled and the creditors have been contacted, the estate enters a holding period. During this time, the personal representative has a duty to protect the assets of the estate, but he or she may pay any estate taxes, sell property from the estate to pay creditors, or request property appraisals, if necessary. (*Note:* Because courts have been moving toward treating personal representatives in much the same way as trustees, we will discuss the duties of each after we have examined the law of trusts later in this chapter.)

In addition, any conflicts among the decedent's beneficiaries or heirs are heard and resolved during the probate process. For example, if there is a will that an interested party believes should not be enforced, there may be a will contest, or if there is a dispute about the will's meaning or about the testator's mental capacity when he made the will, there may be litigation.

Once assets have been assembled, creditors paid, and problem areas addressed, the personal representative closes the estate by distributing the remaining property to those entitled to it. Distributions might be to individuals, to charities, to trustees of already existing trusts, or to trustees of trusts created by the decedent's will.

It is worth noting that not all property interests are subject to probate. Property that the decedent held alone or as a "tenant in common" is subject to the system, but most property in the United States is held under "joint tenancy," such as marital property. Moreover, life insurance proceeds on the decedent's life and property in lifetime trusts are all outside of probate.

As a result, if the decedent is survived by a spouse, very little of his wealth may actually be subject to probate. A typical married couple may hold virtually everything (houses, cars, bank accounts, and investments) in joint tenancy. As a result, there may be no need for probate until the surviving spouse dies.

Nevertheless, the probate system is fundamentally important to the entire intergenerational wealth transfer process. Much of the law governing wealth transfer developed in the context of probate. Moreover, it is the ultimate "fail-safe" system. If no other theory authorizes a shift of property from a decedent to another, the probate system comes into play.

TAKEAWAY CONCEPTS Probate

- When you die, whether or not you leave a will, your estate will go through a process called *probate.*
- During the probate process, the decedent's estate will be distributed according to the terms of his will or by operation of intestate law if no valid will exists.

LO 49-4

Explain the strategic advantages of trusts.

THE STRATEGIC ADVANTAGES OF TRUSTS

We now turn to "probate-avoidance devices"—strategic methods of intergenerational wealth transfer that effectively transfer wealth at someone's death but that are not subject to the costly and slow probate system. For this reason, these strategic methods are often referred to as "will substitutes." Principal among them is the trust. This section introduces the trust concept and some terminology.

Trusts

Here are the parties involved in a trust:

- **Trustor** (also called *settlor, grantor,* or *creator*): The person creating the trust.

- **Trustee**: The person or company that holds the legal title to the assets in the trust and is generally responsible for managing and distributing the assets in accordance with the terms of the trust.
- **Beneficiary**: One entitled to receive part or all of the property under the terms of the trust, either now or in the future. A beneficiary can be an individual or an entity.

A **trust** is thus a three-party fiduciary relationship in which the first party, the *trustor,* transfers a piece of property (often but not necessarily a sum of money) to a second party, the *trustee,* for the benefit of a third party, the *beneficiary.* There are two main types of trusts, revocable and irrevocable.

- **Revocable trusts** (or *living trusts*) are created during the trustor's lifetime and generally can be changed or revoked at any time while the trustor is still living. The trustor often serves as trustee during his or her lifetime, but when the trustor dies the trust becomes irrevocable. Living trusts generally do not shelter assets from the U.S. federal estate tax.
- **Irrevocable trusts** are created during the trustor's lifetime or upon his or her death under the terms of a will or another trust. Typically, these types of trusts can't be changed or revoked. For the most part, irrevocable trusts are created for the benefit of individuals or charitable organizations. An irrevocable trust may not be considered part of the taxable estate, so fewer taxes may be due at death.

Because the details of trust law may vary from state to state, and because the circumstances of each person and family are unique, it is essential to talk with an attorney about whether to use a trust for one's estate plan.

Probate Avoidance: Strategic Aspects of Trusts

While trusts are often used as part of a plan to minimize or eliminate estate taxes, there are also other reasons, unrelated to taxes, to establish a trust while you're alive or to create one upon your death. Assets in a trust are transferred outside of the probate system, saving time and court fees, and potentially lowering estate taxes as well. The probate process can be costly and probate records are available to the public, whereas distribution through a trust is private, so avoiding probate may save costs and maintain privacy.

In addition, other strategic benefits of trusts include:

- *Control.* You can specify the terms of a trust precisely, controlling when and to whom distributions may be made. You may also, for example, set up a revocable trust so that the trust assets remain accessible to you during your lifetime while designating to whom the remaining assets will pass thereafter, even when there are complex situations such as children from more than one marriage.
- *Protection against spendthrifts.* A trust can help protect your estate from your heirs' creditors or from beneficiaries who may not be adept at money management.
- *Privacy and probate savings.* Probate is a matter of public record; a trust may allow assets to pass outside of probate and remain private, in addition to possibly reducing the amount lost to court fees and taxes in the process.

Negative aspects of using a trust as opposed to a will and going through probate include up-front legal expenses, the expense of trust administration, and a lack of certain procedural safeguards. Legal protections that apply to probate but do not automatically apply to trusts include provisions that protect the decedent's assets from mismanagement or embezzlement, such as itemized accounting of probate assets. The cost of the trust may eat up to 1 percent or more of the estate per year, versus the one-time probate cost of 1 to 4 percent for probate.

Because the circumstances of each person and family are unique, it is essential to talk with an attorney about the pros and cons of using a trust versus a will for one's estate plan.

Quick Quiz Trusts
Who is whom?

1. Jay-Z and Beyoncé fund an irrevocable trust with $1,000,000 to be administered by their trusted friend Kanye West. The trust states that funds are to be used solely for tuition expenses incurred by their children Blue Ivy, Sir, and Rumi for tuition expenses incurred by them leading to the award of a college degree. The trust also states that all tuition payments are to be made directly to the educational institutions that the children attend. Who are the beneficiaries of this trust, the children or the educational institutions?

2. In the Jay-Z/Beyonce trust, who is the trustee and who is the trustor?

Answers to this Quick Quiz are provided at the end of the chapter.

TAKEAWAY CONCEPTS The Strategic Advantages of Trusts

- A trust is a three-party fiduciary relationship in which the first party (a trustor) transfers a property (often but not necessarily a sum of money) to a second party (the trustee) for the benefit of a third party (the beneficiary).
- There are two main types of trusts, revocable and irrevocable.
- Assets in a trust are transferred outside of the probate system, saving time and court fees, and potentially reducing estate taxes as well.

LO 49-5

Distinguish between estate taxes and inheritance taxes.

DEATH TAXES

As the great statesman and polymath Benjamin Franklin once famously said, nothing in life is certain but "death and taxes." The estate tax, a tax on the transfer of the estate of a deceased person, thus combines both! This tax applies to property that is transferred via a will or according to state laws of intestacy.

Under the federal Tax Cuts and Jobs Act of 2017,[1] estates that exceed $11.2 million are subject to a 40 percent estate tax at the time of death if the death occurs between 2018 and 2025. (For a married couple aggregating their exemptions, an estate exceeding $22.4 million is subject to a 40 percent estate tax at the time of death.) Because of this exemption, it is estimated that only the largest 0.1 percent of estates in the United States will pay the tax. In any case, the estate tax is one part of the unified gift and estate tax system in the United States. The other part of the system, the gift tax, applies to transfers of property during a person's life.

In addition to the federal estate tax, many states have enacted estate and/or inheritance taxes of their own. Figure 49.2 identifies which states have estate taxes and inheritance taxes. The main difference between an estate tax and an inheritance tax is *who* pays the tax. Estate taxes are paid by the decedent's estate before the money is distributed to any heirs or beneficiaries, whereas inheritance taxes are paid by the person who is inheriting the money or assets from the decedent.

" . . . in this world nothing can be said to be certain except death and taxes."—Benjamin Franklin
©typografie/Alamy

---
[1]Pub. L. 115–97.

FIGURE 49.2 | States with Estate or Inheritance Taxes

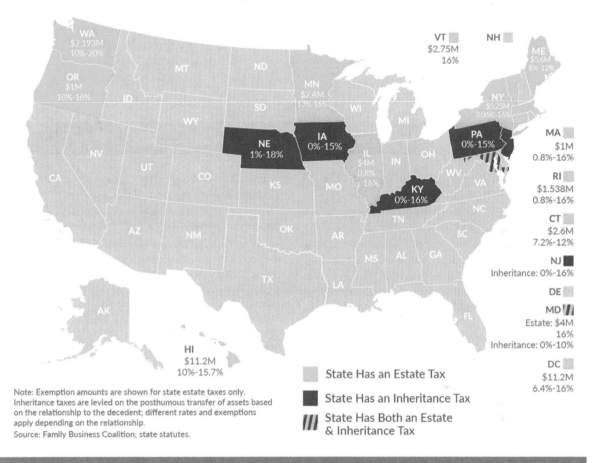

Does Your State Have An Estate or Inheritance Tax?

State Estate & Inheritance Tax Rates & Exemptions in 2018

Note: Exemption amounts are shown for state estate taxes only. Inheritance taxes are levied on the posthumous transfer of assets based on the relationship to the decedent; different rates and exemptions apply depending on the relationship.

Source: Family Business Coalition; state statutes.

State Has an Estate Tax

State Has an Inheritance Tax

State Has Both an Estate & Inheritance Tax

TAX FOUNDATION @TaxFoundation

Either way, these taxes are often the subject of intense political debate. Opponents of the estate tax call it the "death tax." They argue that the government has no right to "double tax" an estate or an inheritance, once upon claiming the wealth, and once upon death. By contrast, supporters of estate and inheritance taxes argue that such taxes are necessary to prevent oligarchy and the concentration of wealth and power. Why does someone like Paris Hilton, for example, deserve to inherit a vast fortune she played no role in creating?

If an asset is left to a spouse or a federally recognized charity, the tax usually does not apply. In addition, a maximum amount, varying year by year, can be given by an individual, before or upon their death, without incurring federal gift or estate taxes: up to $11.18 million was exempt from federal taxation for the estates of persons dying in or after the year 2018.

THE UNIFORM CODES AND THE RESTATEMENTS

The **Uniform Probate Code (UPC)** is a comprehensive model act drafted by National Conference of Commissioners on Uniform State Laws (NCCUSL) governing inheritance and decedents' estates in the United States. The primary purposes of the UPC were to

LO 49-5

Describe the roles of the Uniform Probate Code and Uniform Trust Code in the development of state law.

streamline the probate process and to standardize and modernize the various state laws governing wills, trusts, and intestacy.

Although the UPC was intended for adoption by all 50 states, the original 1969 version of the code was adopted in its entirety by only a handful of states, including Alaska, Arizona, Colorado, Hawaii, Idaho, Maine, Michigan, Minnesota, Montana, Nebraska, New Mexico, North Dakota, South Carolina, South Dakota, and Utah. The remaining states have adopted various portions of the code in a piecemeal fashion.

Even among the adopting jurisdictions, there are variations from state to state, some of which are significant. A person attempting to determine the law in a specific state should check the code *as actually adopted* in that jurisdiction and not rely on the text of the UPC as promulgated by NCCUSL. In Case 49.3, a creditor learns this the hard way.

CASE 49.3 Payne v. Stalley, 672 So. 2d 822 (Fla. Dist. Ct. App. 1995)

FACT SUMMARY Richard M. Wood died while domiciled in Hillsborough County, Florida, on May 30, 1990. Less than two months before Wood died, Priscilla M. Payne and her children ("the Paynes") had obtained a default judgment against Wood in the amount of $1.5 million in a Michigan court. (Wood had previously lived in Michigan, and the lawsuit alleged that he had converted or mishandled securities belonging to the Paynes.) A Michigan lawyer for the Paynes relied on the official text of the Uniform Probate Code but failed to check the actual probate statute as it had been adopted in Florida. As a result, the lawyer missed a filing deadline on the Paynes's claim when Wood's estate was in probate in a Florida court. The probate court eventually rejected the Paynes's claim, and the Paynes then appealed this decision to the Florida District Court of Appeals.

SYNOPSIS OF DECISION AND OPINION The Florida District Court of Appeals affirmed the decision of the probate court, concluding that Florida's probate law—and not the text of the Uniform Probate Code—applied to the facts of the case.

WORDS OF THE COURT: Uniform Probate Code "Although the result seems harsh, we affirm the probate court's order denying [the Paynes's claim]. We cannot rewrite Florida probate law to accommodate a Michigan attorney more familiar with the Uniform Probate Code."

Case Questions

1. Why should the Paynes be penalized for a mistake made by their lawyer?

2. Should Congress adopt a national probate law for the entire United States? Why or why not?

3. *Focus on Critical Thinking:* In reality, Florida had adopted the original 1969 version of the UPC but had not adopted some of the subsequent amendments to the UPC. Given this fact, was the mistake made by the Paynes's lawyer a reasonable one? Explain.

Like the UPC, the **Uniform Trust Code (UTC)** is a comprehensive model act drafted by the NCCUSL governing the creation of trusts in the United States. Although the UTC is not binding, it is used by many states as a model law. As of 2018, 31 states had adopted some substantive form of the UTC, with three others having introduced it into the legislature for adoption.

While the UPC and the UTC offer statutory language and commentary to state legislatures, the Restatement of Property and the Restatement of Trusts provide guidance to courts. Those Restatements, like others you have learned about, are the product of the American Law Institute (ALI), a private organization consisting of a select group of judges, lawyers, and law professors that was initially founded in 1923 to clarify, simplify, and reform the law.

THINKING STRATEGICALLY

©valterZ/Shutterstock

Prince's Vault

PROBLEM: By all accounts the musician Prince was a propulsive, complicated artist; few performers have exacted more control over their art. And yet, surprisingly for an artist who craved absolute authority, Prince left no will. This omission has created some serious problems for his estate, estimated at between $100 million and $300 million before taxes. Several heirs—including a sister and five half siblings, not all of them close, and one who hadn't seen Prince in 15 years—are filing legal challenges in probate. Worse yet, the estate is being supervised by many individuals not of Prince's choosing. Why is this a problem?

During his life, Prince kept a vault of unreleased music and videos—literally, in a Paisley Park basement vault—where they remained until after his death. For example, according to a *Washington Post* report dated April 18, 2018,[2] "The sheer volume of audio and video material is staggering. . . . 'I have everything on tape, man, including all the informal jams,' Prince told *Guitar World* in 1998. 'I used to record something every day,' he told *Rolling Stone* in 2014. 'I always tease that I have to go to studio rehab.'"

Until his untimely death, Prince alone decided what he would share and what he would keep to himself. But he died without a will and did not create a trust during his life, so how will Prince's wishes be carried out after his death? The sheer volume of material in Prince's vault presents many artistic and business challenges. How frequently should his albums or music tracks be circulated? Is it possible to flood the market with too much Prince? Should an artist's unreleased work be distributed at all?

Paisley Park, Prince's private home and production studio.
©Michael S. Williamson/The Washington Post via Getty Images

STRATEGIC SOLUTION: Prince could have used either a trust or a will to plan for and solve these potential problems by (1) identifying ahead of time what actions to take over the contents of his vault or by (2) identifying ahead of time a trusted confidante as the trustee or as the executor of the will, as the case may be, and giving him or her the exclusive power to dispose of the vault. A trust, in particular, might have made a lot of strategic sense for someone like Prince, since a trust may help a trustor avoid the costly and time-consuming probate process altogether. As we noted in this chapter, the probate process can be costly, and probate records are available to the public, whereas distribution through a trust is private, so avoiding probate may save costs and maintain privacy.

QUESTION

During his life, Prince was highly litigious, waging a career-long crusade with his record label, YouTube, bootleggers, and streaming services such as Spotify and

[2]https://www.washingtonpost.com/lifestyle/style/what-would-prince-want-two-years-later-his-estate-is-a-mess-and-his-legacy-unclear/2018/04/18/20136908-3ce9-11e8-8d53-eba0ed2371cc_story.html?utm_term=.232ade0c0b8c

Pandora for sovereignty over his seismic body of work, which included 39 studio albums. (See, for example, this report in *Billboard*: https://www.billboard.com/articles/news/cover-story/7348551/prince-battle-to-control-career-artist-rights. Also, try searching for "Prince" on YouTube, and you will be surprised by how little of his work is available there.) Given this well-documented obsession with control over his work, why did Prince fail to leave a will or use a trust before his death? Specifically, would Prince have wanted to open his Paisley Park home and studio to the public as a museum?

KEY TERMS

Decedent p. 947   An individual who has died. If the decedent has left a will, he is referred to as a *testator*.

Estate p. 947   All the real and personal property that the decedent owns or has an interest in upon his death.

Will p. 947   A legal document in which a person, the *testator*, expresses his wishes as to how his estate is to be distributed at death and in which the testator appoints an executor to manage the estate until its final distribution.

Codicil p. 947   A testamentary document whose purpose is to amend an existing will and is subject to the same formal requirements as a will.

Executor p. 947   The person named by the testator in his will to carry out the instructions in the will.

Intestacy p. 948   When the decedent dies without leaving a will or without otherwise fully disposing of his property during his lifetime.

Freedom of disposition p. 948   The common law principle that testators should be free to dispose of their property at death in any way they want.

Probate p. 951   The process that manages, settles, and distributes a decedent's property according to the terms of a will or by operation of intestate law if no valid will exists.

Trustor p. 952   The person who creates a trust.

Trustee p. 953   The person or company that holds the legal title to the assets in the trust and is generally responsible for managing and distributing the assets in accordance with the terms of the trust.

Beneficiary p. 953   An individual or entity who is entitled to receive part or all of the property under the terms of a will or trust, either now or in the future.

Trust p. 953   A three-party fiduciary relationship in which the first party, the trustor, transfers property to a second party, the trustee, for the benefit of a third party, the beneficiary.

Revocable trust p. 953   A trust created during the trustor's lifetime that can generally be changed or revoked at any time while the trustor is still living.

Irrevocable trust p. 953   A trust created during the trustor's lifetime or upon his or her death under the terms of a will or another trust; these types of trusts cannot be changed or revoked.

Uniform Probate Code (UPC) p. 955   A comprehensive model act governing inheritance and decedents' estates.

Uniform Trust Code (UTC) p. 956   A comprehensive model act governing the creation of trusts.

CASE SUMMARY 49.1 Eyerman v. Mercantile Trust Co., 524 S.W.2d 210 (Mo. Ct. App. 1975)

Freedom of Disposition

A provision in the will of Louise Woodruff Johnston directed her executor to have her historic house in St. Louis's Kingsbury Place neighborhood razed, the land underneath it sold, and the proceeds from the land sale transferred to the residue of the estate. Johnston's beneficiaries did not object to the razing of the home, but the neighbors did object. One month after Johnston's death, they convinced the city government to have Kingsbury Place declared a historic landmark. The neighbors then sought injunctive relief to prevent Johnston's executor from razing the home.

CASE QUESTIONS

1. How would you have decided this case?
2. What if Johnston were a novelist and had requested that her executor burn all her unpublished manuscripts. May an executor refuse to honor such a request?

Intestacy

Henrietta E. Garrett married multimillionaire Walter Garrett. When Walter died in 1895, his will left his vast fortune to his wife. Henrietta, however, died intestate (without a will) in Philadelphia in 1930, leaving an estate of over $17 million, or over $200 million in today's dollars! Nearly 26,000 claims were filed by persons claiming to be Henrietta's heirs. Their testimony covered 390 volumes and over 115,000 pages. Finally, three persons were found to be first cousins of Henrietta. In 1953, after 23 years of litigation, the Supreme Court of Pennsylvania finally ordered the Garrett estate closed.

CASE QUESTIONS

1. Should the law permit intestate succession by remote or distant heirs? Where should the law draw the line?
2. If no heirs had been found in this case, who would have inherited Henrietta's estate: the Commonwealth of Pennsylvania or the United States?

Murdering Heirs

Francis B. Palmer had drafted a will leaving most of his estate to his grandson Elmer E. Palmer. Fearing that his grandfather might change the will, Elmer murdered his grandfather by poisoning him. (At the time, New York had not yet enacted a murdering heir statute.) After he was convicted of murder, the daughters of Francis Palmer sought to invalidate their father's will. They argued that by allowing the will to be executed, Elmer would be profiting from his crime.

CASE QUESTIONS

1. How should the court decide this case?
2. What if Elmer had not been convicted of murder but of manslaughter instead?

State Taxation of Trusts

In 1992, Joseph Lee Rice III established a trust, appointing William B. Matteson as trustee and his three children as beneficiaries. In 1997, of the beneficiaries, Matteson's daughter Kimberly moved to North Carolina, and North Carolina eventually assessed a tax on Kimberly's portion of the trust of more than $1.3 million for the tax years in which she lived in North Carolina. Under the terms of the trust, however, Kimberly had no right to and did not receive any distributions from the trust during the time she resided in North Carolina, and New York was the situs of the trust at all relevant times. Moreover, all of the activities of administering the assets in the trust occurred outside of North Carolina, and all the assets in the trust were also held outside of North Carolina.

CASE QUESTIONS

1. Is the portion of the trust created for the benefit of the trustor's daughter Kimberly subject to taxation in North Carolina?
2. Does it matter whether it is a federal judge or a state court judge who gets to decide this issue?

1. **The personal representative of an estate may not:**
   a. Take possession and control of the decedent's property.
   b. Allocate the expenses of the estate as provided by the will or by law.
   c. Satisfy any obligations or debts of the decedent.
   d. Obtain title to the decedent's property in trust for the benefit of creditors and beneficiaries.
   e. Operate a single proprietorship of the decedent indefinitely if the proprietorship is profitable.

2. **The following are elements of a valid will, except:**
   a. The decedent must have the intention to make a will.
   b. The decedent must have testamentary capacity.
   c. The decedent must affix a seal to the will.
   d. The will must be signed by a number of witnesses.
   e. None of the above.

3. **An amendment to a will is called a:**
   a. Trust.
   b. Codicil
   c. Will substitute.
   d. Will supplement.
   e. None of the above.

4. **Which of the following is a method of avoiding the probate process?**
   a. Intestacy
   b. Revocable trust
   c. Irrevocable trust
   d. Codicil
   e. B and C

5. **A will takes effect:**
   a. When the testator dies.
   b. When the executor ratifies the will.
   c. When the will is signed and sealed.
   d. When the probate court ratifies the will.
   e. When the executor takes possession of the estate.

6. **In the absence of a will, the decedent is said to have died testate, and the decedent's property goes to his heirs by operation of state testate law.**
   a. True
   b. False

7. **A trustee is the person who creates a trust.**
   a. True
   b. False

8. **An executor of an estate is the person named in the decedent's will who administers the estate of the decedent.**
   a. True
   b. False

9. **Estates are not taxable entities under federal tax law.**
   a. True
   b. False

10. **The Uniform Probate Code was enacted by Congress in 1969 to make probate law uniform across the nation.**
    a. True
    b. False

 Quick Quiz ANSWERS
Trusts

1. Most courts would hold that the beneficiaries of the trust are the children, even though the monies from the trust are to be paid directly to the educational institutions.

2. The trustors are Jay-Z and Beyoncé, since they are the ones who created the trust. Kanye is the trustee, since he is the one who will administer the monies in the trust.

CHAPTER REVIEW QUESTIONS: Answers and Explanations

1. e. The executor may not control the estate for an indefinite period of time, while answer choices *a, b, c,* and *d* all describe the duties of the executor.

2. c. A seal is not required to make a valid will, while answer choices *a, b, d,* and *e* all describe the various elements of a valid will.

3. b. An amendment to a will is called a codicil. Answer *b* is incorrect because a trust is a will substitute, while the remaining choices are nonsensical.

4. e. The creation of a trust, whether it be revocable or irrevocable, is a method of avoiding probate. Answer *a* is incorrect because intestacy (dying without a will) triggers the probate process. Choice *d* is incorrect because a codicil is an amendment to a will, and wills—like intestacy—require probate.

5. a. Although a will might be challenged during the probate process, a will takes effect as soon as the testator of the will dies. The remaining answer choices are therefore incorrect.

6. b. False. In the absence of a will, the decedent is said to have died *intestate,* not testate.

7. b. False. A trust is created by a trustor. A trustee is the person or entity who administers the assets in the trust.

8. a. True. An executor is the person named in the decedent's will who administers the estate of the decedent.

9. b. False. Although small estates are exempt from taxation, estates are considered taxable entities under federal law.

10. b. False. The Uniform Probate Code was drafted by a private organization called the National Conference of Commissioners on Uniform State Laws. Although the UPC was intended for adoption by all 50 states, the original 1969 version of the code was adopted in its entirety by only a handful of states. The remaining states have adopted various portions of the code in a piecemeal fashion.

CHAPTER 50

Intellectual Property

THINKING STRATEGICALLY

Intellectual property such as patents, trade secrets, designs, copyrights, and trademarks comprise a significant portion of a company's value. For example, a company like Google is largely valued on its ability to exploit these intangible, knowledge-based assets. Businesses, therefore, must protect these assets through the use of legal means. In the *Thinking Strategically* section you will evaluate the demands made by a trademark cease and desist letter and potential responses to the letter.

Learning Objectives

After studying this chapter, students who have mastered the material will be able to:

50-1 Demonstrate how intellectual capital results in intellectual property.

50-2 Explain the requirements for protecting information as a trade secret.

50-3 Discuss the requirements for obtaining a patent.

50-4 Distinguish among the various theories of copyright infringement.

50-5 Identify the strength of a trademark based on its classification.

CHAPTER OVERVIEW

When the Founding Fathers ratified the Constitution in 1788, they authorized Congress to secure for authors and inventors the exclusive right to their respective writings and discoveries for a limited period of time.[1] This authorized Congress to create a federal system of copyrights and patents. The Founding Fathers did this because they appreciated the fact that a unitary intellectual property system could be a source of wealth creation and social advancement.

Today, many industries, such as biotechnology, software, consumer electronics, and media and entertainment, rely on patents and copyrights to create and sustain value. A study published in the *Harvard Business Review* found that intellectual property represents nearly 70 percent of an average firm's value, a number that has nearly doubled in one decade.[2] This chapter surveys the intellectual property systems, which include trade secrets, patents, copyrights, and

---

[1]U.S. Const. art. I, § 8, cl. 8.

[2]K. Rivet and D. Kline, "Discovering New Value in Intellectual Property," *Harvard Business Review,* January 2000, p. 58.

trademarks. We also discuss how managers can secure and derive value from these knowledge-based rights.

THE RELATIONSHIP BETWEEN INTELLECTUAL CAPITAL AND INTELLECTUAL PROPERTY

LO 50-1

Demonstrate how intellectual capital results in intellectual property.

Intellectual property is an umbrella term for the legal property rights related to trade secrets, patents, copyrights, and trademarks. These rights can emerge from the flow of knowledge. At the beginning of this process is **intellectual capital**, made up of the knowledge, skills, education, training, know-how, and creativity of individuals. These individuals can include employees, partners such as suppliers, independent contractors, and even customers. At this stage, however, intellectual capital is heavily based on **tacit knowledge**, which is highly individualized knowledge that is hard to replicate or even explain. Tacit knowledge, however, can be risky. For example, if the key engineer at a technology company leaves the company, most of the valuable tacit knowledge and human capital associated with that key employee will be lost, and the organization will suffer as a result.

To reduce this risk, organizations develop an intellectual capital management process that translates tacit knowledge into **explicit knowledge** that is recorded and available for the company's interpretation, application, and reproduction. The engineer, for example, may be induced or required by the firm to disclose inventions and describe them in written invention disclosure forms that the company submits for patenting. Or the inventor may be required to create sketches, diagrams, and prototypes in company-owned notebooks and computers.

At this point, explicit knowledge is categorized as an **intellectual asset**, and it may achieve the status of intellectual property when the knowledge is fully secured within any of the intellectual property regimes discussed in this chapter. Once an intellectual asset such as a prototype, business plan, sales pitch, or invention disclosure form is secured as an intellectual property right, it can be used defensively and offensively by strategic managers. A patent, for example, allows a business to prevent another business from replicating the secured technology. Netflix used a patent early in its history to prevent its much larger rival, Blockbuster, from copying its online movie delivery system. Alternatively, a company like Walt Disney can use contracts called **licensing agreements** with external apparel manufacturers to monetize its valuable name and character trademark rights. A license agreement involves an intellectual property owner (the **licensor**) who grants the property user (the **licensee**) permission to use the property in exchange for a fee called a **royalty**. The flow of knowledge within an intellectual capital management system is depicted in Figure 50.1.

The next sections will guide you through the intellectual property rights systems and the various managerial implications associated with each one.

TAKEAWAY CONCEPTS The Relationship between Intellectual Capital and Intellectual Property

- Intellectual property is an umbrella term for the legal property rights related to trade secrets, patents, copyrights, and trademarks.
- Intellectual property is the result of a knowledge flow within an intellectual capital management program.
- The knowledge that resides within employees is tacit knowledge.
- Explicit knowledge is knowledge that is recorded and available for the company's interpretation, application, and reproduction.

FIGURE 50.1 Flow of Knowledge in an Intellectual Capital Management System

Skills, Know-how, Training, Education, Creativity	Prototypes, Business Strategies, Sketches, Blueprints, Designs, Lists, Sales Pitches	Trade Secrets, Patents, Copyrights, Trademarks	License Agreements, Joint Ventures, Mergers and Acquisitions, Litigation
Tacit Knowledge and Intellectual Capital	Explicit Knowledge and Intellectual Assets	Intellectual Property	Strategic Options

LO 50-2

Explain the requirements for protecting information as a trade secret.

PROTECTING TRADE SECRETS

Trade secrets such as processes, formulas, methods, procedures, and lists can be valuable assets that allow companies to obtain a competitive advantage. It is important to understand that many types of trade secrets, business information, and business methods are broader in scope and may not be protectable by patent or copyright laws. In fact, patent applicants generally rely on trade secret law to protect their inventions while patent applications are in progress.

Businesses in various sectors rely on trade secret laws to protect valuable knowledge. Examples of technical and business information material that can be protected by trade secret law include customer lists, designs, instructional methods, sales pitches, manufacturing processes, product formulas, and document-tracking processes. The Coca-Cola Company, for example, uses trade secret law to protect its soft drink syrup recipe. According to the company, the recipe had been stored in a SunTrust Bank vault in downtown Atlanta since 1925 (it has since been moved to the World of Coca-Cola), and only a handful of company executives know the recipe at any given time.

Trade Secret Requirements

The following state common law factors are used by courts to determine whether information constitutes a trade secret:

■ The extent to which the information is known outside the owner's business.

Coca-Cola has protected its famous soft drink formula as a trade secret for more than 125 years.
©Alvin Chan/SOPA Images/LightRocket via Getty Images

- Measures taken by the owner to guard the confidentiality of the information.
- The value of the information to competitors.
- The amount invested in terms of time and money to develop the information.
- The efforts to maintain trade secret confidentiality among employees and third-party vendors (such as auditing firms or suppliers).

Trade secret protections are provided by state statutes and the common law. The model Uniform Trade Secrets Act (UTSA),[3] which has been adopted by 47 states, defines trade secrets as information or articles that are to be kept secret because of their particular value. Under this act, a trade secret includes (but is not limited to) a formula, pattern, compilation, program, device, method, technique, or process that meets the following criteria:

- It derives independent economic value, actual or potential, from not being generally known to, and not being readily ascertainable by proper means by, other persons who can obtain economic value from its disclosure or use.
- It is the subject of efforts that are reasonable under the circumstances to maintain its secrecy.

Businesses' efforts to maintain secrecy include keeping information under lock and key, encrypting information, using password protection, marking sensitive documents as confidential, and requiring employees and outside parties to sign **non-disclosure confidentiality agreements**, contracts that impose a legal duty on the party receiving the information to keep it secret.

Infringement through Misappropriation

Most state statutes use the following definition of **misappropriation** from the UTSA: (1) The acquisition of a trade secret of another by a person who knows or has reason to know that the trade secret was acquired by improper means or (2) any disclosure or use of a trade secret of another without express or implied consent that was knowingly obtained by improper means. A trade secret is obtained through improper means if it is acquired by theft, bribery, misrepresentation, breach or inducement of a breach of a duty to maintain secrecy, or espionage through electronic or other means.

Criminal Sanctions

While the UTSA does not include any criminal sanctions, many states have added separate statutes that make trade secret misappropriation a criminal offense. For example, state prosecutors in California filed charges against several executives and employees of Avant! Corporation after one of Avant!'s competitors sued the firm, in an action brought under California's Trade Secret Act, alleging that Avant! employees had stolen computer code.[4] Ultimately, Avant! accepted a plea bargain from the prosecutor that forced the company and seven individuals to pay $35 million in fines and resulted in incarceration for five of the defendants. The **Economic Espionage Act** is a federal statute passed in 1996 that provides criminal penalties at the federal level for the domestic and foreign theft of trade secrets.

Exclusive Rights for Unlimited Duration

A significant advantage of trade secret protection over other forms of intellectual property (such as patents and copyrights) is that protection for trade secrets does not expire after a fixed period of time. A trade secret owner has the right to keep others from misappropriating

---

[3]The UTSA is a model law drafted by the American Law Institute (ALI) for use by state legislatures.

[4]*Cadence Design Systems, Inc. v. Avant!,* 253 F.3d 1147 (9th Cir. 2002). The parties settled the civil suit for $265 million.

The W Hotels brand successfully introduced the concept of a luxury boutique hotel brand within an existing large corporate hotel chain's operating model. Much of the knowledge surrounding this successful and innovative business is protected by trade secret law.
©Kathy deWitt/Alamy

and using the trade secret for the duration of the firm's existence. Although sometimes the misappropriation is a result of industrial espionage, most trade secret cases involve former employees who have taken their employer's trade secrets for use in a new start-up business or by a new employer.

Trade secret protection endures as long as the requirements for protection continue to be met. The protection is lost, however, if the owner fails to take reasonable steps to keep the information secret. For example, suppose Sam discovers a new method for manipulating images in multimedia works, and he demonstrates his new method to a number of other developers at a multimedia conference. Sam may have lost his trade secret protection for the image manipulation method because he failed to take appropriate steps to keep his method secret.

Trade secret owners have recourse only against misappropriation. Discovery of protected information through independent research or reverse engineering (taking a product apart to see how it works) is not misappropriation.

Case 50.1 involves a case in which Starwood Hotels sued two former executives and Hilton Hotels for trade secret theft related to the W Hotels brand. The opinion is a court order granting Starwood Hotels a preliminary injunction against the parties.

CASE 50.1 Starwood Hotels & Resorts Worldwide, Inc. v. Hilton Hotels Corporation, Ross Klein, and Amar Lalvani, 8:09-CV-03862 (S.D.N.Y. 2009)

FACT SUMMARY In April 2009, Starwood Hotels filed an action against the defendants in a New York federal trial court alleging trade secret theft. Klein and Lalvani were former Starwood senior executives who had helped launch the W Hotels brand. During their long career at Starwood, these individuals gained a great deal of access to confidential information. Hilton Hotels ("Hilton") sought to create a competitor brand modeled after the W Hotels—called Denizen Hotels—and recruited Klein and Lalvani to accomplish this task. Klein, Lalvani, and Hilton were accused of trade secret theft. According to Starwood's complaint, Klein and Lalvani took the following items with them to Hilton as digitally stored files:

- The list containing the names of property owners, developers, and designers who had worked with Starwood to build the W Hotels brand.

- Current and prospective financial and marketing information related to the luxury segment of Starwood's business.

- Site-specific project data related to Starwood properties with details related to costs, fee structures, and termination provisions.

- Marketing and demographic studies that cost Starwood more than $1 million to produce.

- "Brand in a Box" training and operational materials for launching and maintaining a W Hotel.

Starwood had required Klein and Lalvani to sign detailed confidentiality agreements and store confidential data on company-issued computers. Confidential information was kept on password-protected, secure servers.

SYNOPSIS OF DECISION AND OPINION The court issued a preliminary injunction against the defendants to prevent them from using any trade secret–protected information and ceased Hilton's development of the competing Denizen brand of hotels.

(continued)

WORDS OF THE COURT: Injunction Granted "Defendants Hilton, Klein and Lalvani, and their respective officers . . . including without limitation designers, architects, consultants and advisors engaged by Hilton in connection with the Project Global 21 or Denizen Hotels brand . . . are hereby preliminarily [prevented] from knowingly using directly or indirectly in any way the Starwood Information. . . .

"Defendants Hilton, Klein and Lalvani . . . shall cease all further development of the Denizen Hotels brand, including without limitation all internal and external design, branding, development, promotion, programming, staffing, and marketing of the Denizen Hotels brand, including without limitations any discussions or negotiations with prospective owners, developers and/or franchisees relating thereto."

Case Questions

1. Did Starwood have a suitable intellectual capital management program? Why or why not?

2. Was this judgment a favorable outcome for Starwood? Why or why not?

3. *Focus on Critical Thinking:* What other remedies should Starwood obtain? Explain.

TAKEAWAY CONCEPTS Protecting Trade Secrets

- Trade secrets such as processes, formulas, methods, procedures, and lists can be valuable assets that allow companies to obtain a competitive advantage.
- Trade secrets can include information that is broader than what can be protected with patents or copyrights.
- Trade secrets may be independently discovered or reverse engineered without liability.
- A trade secret can be maintained as long as it remains secret.
- Non-disclosure confidentiality agreements are important tools to protect trade secrets.

PATENTS

Patent law in the United States dates back to 1790. It is governed by the Patent Act, which was established by the same Congress that ratified the U.S. Constitution. A **patent** is a statutorily created right that allows an inventor the exclusive right to make, use, license, and sell her invention for a limited amount of time. Patent rights are important for the entire business community but are particularly vital to the manufacturing, technology, and pharmaceutical sectors. Patents are often an important part of these firms' planning because their business model depends on the benefits of obtaining a patent—the full legal protection of their ideas, methods, and inventions. Once a patent is obtained, a competitor is barred from profiting from the patented device or process during the life of the patent. Thus, a patent can be a firm's most important and valuable asset.

It is important for managers to understand the fundamentals and discard the myths regarding patent laws. The most common myth is the assumption that nearly any new idea or invention is patentable. This assumption is *not* true and may be an expensive lesson to learn. To be patented, any invention must meet stringent criteria set down in federal statutes. Another myth is that a patent is always a valuable asset. The fact is that the majority of patents provide little if any value.

LO 50-3

Discuss the requirements for obtaining a patent.

The patent application procedure is often very expensive because one must almost always obtain counsel that specializes in patent law. One intellectual property law firm estimates that legal fees and application fees related to obtaining a patent range from $20,000 for a mechanical tool invention to $30,000 for a software patent.[5]

Even if one is successful in obtaining a patent, enforcing the patent via an infringement lawsuit is an even more expensive undertaking. According to a study in *The Wall Street Journal,* the average cost for enforcing a patent is close to $1.2 million.[6] Although it is not always necessary to go all the way to a trial to enforce the patent, such a significant cost factor must be considered in a company's patent management strategy.

LAW, ETHICS, AND SOCIETY

Patent Trolls or Non-Practicing Entities?

Sometimes a party owns a patent (typically by acquiring it from the inventor) for the sole purpose of collecting licensing fees. These parties use their rights to search for potential infringers and assert their patent with the threat of a lawsuit, even though they are not actually using the patented invention. These entities are not interested in producing or selling any goods. Rather, their sole objective is to profit through the litigation of patent rights. Critics of these entities label them "patent trolls" and argue that they stifle innovation and promote litigation. Proponents refer to them as "non-practicing entities," or NPEs, and view them as owners of valuable property rights who are acting lawfully and who create a market for patented inventions.

Discussion Questions

1. With whom do you agree and why?

2. Universities and companies sometimes create valuable patents and license them. Are universities and companies patent trolls?

Patent Prosecution

Inventors typically seek help from patent attorneys who are skilled and experienced in the patent application process. The application process is called *prosecuting* a patent. Although patent prosecution varies based on the invention, the process typically has three stages. First, the inventors and their patent counsel perform a database search in an attempt to ensure that a similar invention is not protected by an existing patent or technical disclosure known as the **prior art**. Second, the inventor files a provisional application with the U.S. Patent and Trademark Office (USPTO). A provisional patent application discloses the invention in a general way and does not require the formalities necessary for a full (nonprovisional) application. However, a provisional application is wise because it protects the invention and allows the inventor to work on improving the invention over 12 months before a full patent application. Third, once the parties are satisfied that the invention is patentable, the inventor's counsel files a nonprovisional application with the USPTO that is much more comprehensive and typically includes sketches or other supplementary materials. An attorney employed by the USPTO acts as an examiner and reviews the application to determine whether it describes an invention that meets the legal standards for patentability. If the examiner determines that the invention is *not* patentable, the inventor may appeal to the Patent Trial and Appeal Board (PTAB). If the examiner concludes that the invention *is* patentable, he will issue the patent, which gives the inventor the right to enforce the patent against third parties.

---

[5]www.ipwatchdog.com/2015/04/04/the-cost-of-obtaining-a-patent-in-the-us/id=56485/

[6]Dee Gill, "Defending Your Rights: Protecting Intellectual Property is Expensive," *The Wall Street Journal,* September 25, 2000, p. 6.

Types of Patents

There are three types of patents:

- *Utility patents* constitute a broad category that covers the invention of any new and useful process, machine, article of manufacture, or composition of matter or any new and useful improvement. Utility patents also cover software and hardware. The overwhelming majority of patents fall into this category.

- *Design patents* primarily cover the invention of new ornamental designs on articles of manufacture. This category encompasses how a product looks rather than how it functions. Therefore, it is increasingly common to obtain both trademark protection and a design patent for the same product.

- *Plant patents* are the least frequently issued type of patent and cover the invention or discovery of asexually or sexually reproducible plants (such as flowers).

Utility and plant patents last for 20 years from the date of application. Design patents issued before May 13, 2015, have a 14-year term from when they were granted. Design patents filed after this date have a 15-year term that likewise begins on the grant date. The Wright Brothers' flying machine patent is shown in Figure 50.2.

FIGURE 50.2	Wright Brothers' Airplane Patent

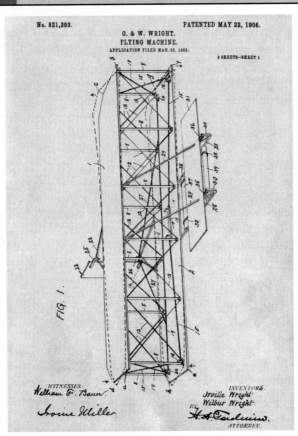

The utility patent issued to the Wright brothers in 1906 for their flying machine began a new era in global commerce.

Patent Eligibility Standards

To meet patent eligibility standards, an invention must be novel and nonobvious and be a proper subject matter for protection under the patent law.

Novelty   An invention or process must be unique and original, and a patent applicant must show that no other identical invention or process exists. The statute delineates the guidelines for this **novelty standard** based on a three-prong test. The first prong is the public use test, which requires that the invention or process not already be in public use. The second prong governs priority for inventors of the same invention or process. The United States recognizes the first-inventor-to-file rule, in which patent rights are granted to the first inventor to file a patent application. The first inventor to file then has priority over other inventors of the same product. The final prong requires a determination by the USPTO that the applicant filed the patent within a reasonable time of the invention. In *Dunlop Holdings v. RAM Golf Corporation,* a landmark case on the issue of public use, a federal appellate court invalidated a patent held by the manufacturer of a specially coated golf ball. The court held that Dunlop's patent on the specially coated ball did not meet the novelty test because there was evidence that the same product had been used by a golf pro 10 years before the patent was issued. The court remarked:

> The only novel feature of this case arises from the fact that [the golf pro] was careful not to disclose to the public the ingredient that made his golf ball so tough. . . . But in this case, although [he] may have failed to act diligently to establish his own right to a patent, there was no lack of diligence in his attempt to make the benefits of his discovery available to the public. . . . [T]he evidence clearly demonstrates that [the golf pro] endeavored to market his golf balls as promptly and effectively as possible. The balls themselves were in wide public use.[7]

Nonobviousness   The **nonobviousness standard** requires that an invention must be something more than that which would be obvious, in light of publicly available knowledge, to one who is skilled in the relevant field. In other words, a patent cannot be granted for minimal improvements that were relatively obvious to those in the field. For example, suppose that Joanna adds a small extender switch to her lawn mower (an existing patented invention) that will make it easier for taller people to turn off the engine. Joanna is not entitled to a new patent because the invention is essentially a minimal (also called *de minimus*) and relatively obvious improvement.

Patentable Subject Matter   Not all processes and inventions that are novel and nonobvious are patentable. The **patentable subject matter standard** prevents laws of nature, natural phenomena, and abstract ideas from being patentable. Albert Einstein's theory of relativity was groundbreaking. It was new and nonobvious beyond question. But should this natural phenomenon be patentable? The patent system was not intended to cover every novel and nonobvious idea. The courts have held that some mathematical algorithms, genetic material, and unapplied ideas are not patentable.

Requirements for Design Patents

Patent laws also protect inventors of any new, original, and ornamental design for an article of manufacture. Design patents are subject to the same requirements as those for utility or business method patents (novelty and nonobvious), and the design must be primarily ornamental (not primarily functional). Design patents are mainly concerned with protecting the appearance of an article. For example, in Figure 50.3, the head dress popularized by the *Dark Knight* movie series received a design patent based on its appearance rather than on any particular function.

---

[7]524 F.2d 33 (7th Cir. 1975).

FIGURE 50.3 | *Dark Knight* Head Dress

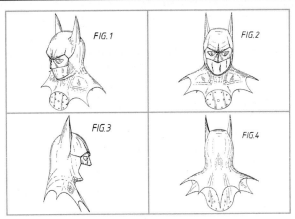

FIG. 1 FIG. 2 FIG. 3 FIG. 4

Source: U.S. Patent and Trademark Office, Patent No. D329,321, filed Oct. 18, 1989, and issued Sept. 15, 1992.

Business Method Patents

Because of the exclusion of certain subject matter from patent protection, courts historically have struggled with the notion of giving patent protection to a process developed by a business in the name of efficiency or some competitive advantage. Some courts have rejected novel, useful, and commercially successful business methods as nonpatentable subject matter. In an attempt to provide guidance to the inventor community, the USPTO issued a 1996 directive that recognizes business method patents but instructs examiners to treat business method applications like any other process claims. In 1998, a federal appeals court helped settle many issues related to business method patents and provided guidance for other courts in the land-mark case of *State Street Bank & Trust Co. v. Signature Financial Group*.[8] The *State Street* court ruled that business methods are patentable as long as they accomplish something practically useful in a novel and nonobvious way. The case also provided a road map for the emerging Internet business community to plan Internet business models in such a way as to be eligible for patent protection. After the *State Street* case, the number of applications for business method patents increased nearly sixfold. However, in Case 50.2, the U.S. Supreme Court significantly narrowed the scope of subject matter eligible for business method patents.

CASE 50.2 Alice Corporation Pty. Ltd. v. CLS Bank International et al., 134 S. Ct. 2347 (2014)

FACT SUMMARY Alice Corporation ("Alice") holds several patents that disclose plans to manage certain forms of financial risk. According to the specification largely shared by the patents, the invention "enables the management of risk relating to specified, yet unknown, future events." The claims at issue relate to a computerized scheme for mitigating "settlement risk"—that is, the risk that only one party to an agreed-upon financial exchange will satisfy its obligation. In particular, the claims

(continued)

---

[8]149 F.3d 1368 (Fed. Cir. 1998). The case involved a challenge to a patent issued to Signature for a process that facilitated a method whereby several mutual funds pooled their investments into a single fund that achieved management cost savings over many other funds.

are designed to facilitate the exchange of financial obligations between two parties by using a computer system as a third-party intermediary. The intermediary creates "shadow" credit and debit records (i.e., account ledgers) that mirror the balances in the parties' real-world accounts at "exchange institutions" (e.g., banks). The intermediary updates the shadow records in real time as transactions are entered, allowing "only those transactions for which the parties' updated shadow records indicate sufficient resources to satisfy their mutual obligations." At the end of the day, the intermediary instructs the relevant financial institutions to carry out the permitted transactions in accordance with the updated shadow records, thus mitigating the risk that only one party will perform the agreed-upon exchange.

CLS Bank International ("CLS") operates a global network that facilitates currency transactions. CLS filed suit against Alice, seeking a declaratory judgment that the patents were invalid. The trial court ruled that the processes were ineligible for a patent because they are directed to the abstract idea of employing a neutral intermediary to facilitate simultaneous exchange of obligations in order to minimize risk. A divided panel of the United States Court of Appeals for the Federal Circuit reversed, holding that it was not "manifestly evident" that the petitioner's claims were directed to an abstract idea. The parties appealed to the U.S. Supreme Court.

SYNOPSIS OF DECISION AND OPINION The U.S. Supreme Court ruled in favor of CLS, holding that the patents were directed to an abstract idea and therefore were invalid because implementing those claims on a computer was insufficient to transform the idea into a patentable invention. The Court applied a two-part test. First, do claims cover an abstract idea? For this case, the Court answered yes, pointing to the concept of intermediated settlement used in Alice's methods. Second, do claims contain an inventive concept sufficient to transform the idea into a patent-eligible application of the idea? On the second question, the Court ruled that the claims did not contain sufficient inventive concept to be patented.

WORDS OF THE COURT: No Evidence of Transformation "Viewed as a whole, [Alice's] method claims simply recite the concept of intermediated settlement as performed by a generic computer. . . . The method claims do not, for example, purport to improve the functioning of the computer itself. Nor do they effect an improvement in any other technology or technical field. Instead, the claims at issue amount to nothing significantly more than an instruction to apply the abstract idea of intermediated settlement using some unspecified, generic computer. Under our precedents, that is not enough to transform an abstract idea into a patent-eligible invention."

Case Questions

1. What was the specific reason for the Court's determination that Alice's business methods were not patentable?

2. What does the Court mean when it states that Alice's methods "simply recite the concept of intermediated settlement as performed by a generic computer"? Why is that relevant?

3. *Focus on Critical Thinking:* Are there any ways that Alice could modify its methods to make them patentable? Explain your answer.

Trade Secret versus Patent

Often, businesses must decide whether to pursue patent rights or to protect their inventions as a trade secret. Several factors are relevant to help managers address this question. The first question is the ease of reverse engineering the invention. Recall that if an invention can be easily reversed engineered, it will lose any trade secret protection and can be used by anyone who is able to reverse engineer it. Inventions that are easily reverse engineered, therefore, might be good candidates for patenting because this exclusivity right will last for 20 years from date of application against anyone who makes, uses, or sells the patented invention, regardless of reverse engineering.

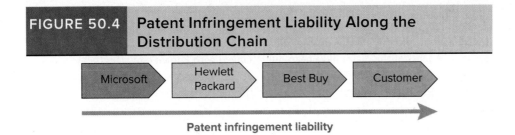

FIGURE 50.4 Patent Infringement Liability Along the Distribution Chain

Microsoft → Hewlett Packard → Best Buy → Customer

Patent infringement liability

Inventions that are difficult to reverse engineer, however, might be best protected as trade secrets. Because the Coca-Cola soft drink syrup recipe is difficult to reverse engineer, it has been preserved as a trade secret since 1925. Another factor is cost. Patents, as mentioned earlier, are expensive and can be difficult to prosecute due to the novelty and nonobviousness standards. Cost may be a deciding factor, and a business without substantial resources would likely have to protect its invention as a trade secret. Lastly, patent applications are published and open to public inspection 18 months after the application date. Unless the business is confident the patent will be issued, a considerable risk is assumed because the trade secret will be lost when the patent application is made available to the public.

Infringement

Infringement is defined in the Patent Act as: "[W]hoever without authority makes, uses or sells any patented invention, within the United States during the term of the patent therefore, infringes the patent." Intent is not a required element to prove infringement. Take the example of Michael, who owns a software patent related to e-mail client technology. If Microsoft integrates this technology without permission into its Outlook e-mail software, everyone to the right in the chain of distribution, all the way to the end user, is liable for patent infringement because they will be making, selling, or using the patented technology. Figure 50.4 demonstrates all the parties in the distribution chain that are liable to Michael for patent infringement. Michael would likely target everyone except the end user for patent infringement damages. The end user is spared because the costs of litigation would outweigh any recovery of damages.

Intent or careless behavior is not a requirement; however, intentional patent infringement is referred to as **willful patent infringement** and merits higher damages due to bad behavior. Anyone who "actively induces infringement" of a patent is considered an infringer as well. Infringement occurs in one of two ways: as literal infringement or through equivalence.

Literal Infringement   The courts have developed three rules for determining whether **literal patent infringement** has occurred. The *rule of exactness* applies when the infringer makes, uses, or sells an invention that is exactly the same as the patent holder's claims in the patent application, thus infringing on the patent. An infringement also occurs if the infringing device does more than is described in the patent application of the protected invention. This literal infringement is known as the *rule of addition*. Under the *rule of omission,* however, when the alleged infringing invention lacks an essential element of the patent holder's claims in the patent application, infringement has not occurred.

Equivalence   The rule of omission is subject to abuse because individuals may avoid infringement liability by omitting an element of the patented device and substituting another element that is substantially similar but not exact. To prevent this abuse, the Supreme Court developed a doctrine that allows courts to find infringement if the invention performs substantially the same function in substantially the same way to achieve the same result. This doctrine, known as the **doctrine of equivalence**, is limited to an evaluation of whether any of the key elements of the claim have been interchanged with known equivalents.

Notice, Enforcement, and Remedies

The Patent Act sets forth appropriate measures that must be taken to properly inform users that an article is patented. This is often done by placing the word "Patent," the abbreviation "Pat.," or the patent number on the specific article. If no marking is identifiable, then the patentee is unable to collect damages from infringers unless they have been properly warned and nonetheless continue to infringe.

In addition to a potential injunction issued by a court ordering the defendant to cease infringing the patent, patent infringers are subject to the following damages:

- *Actual damages:* Examples include profits from lost sales and royalties for any sale made by the infringer.
- *Prejudgment interest:* It is not uncommon for years to pass before an infringer is spotted; thus, revenue from possible sales may have been withheld from the patentee for a long period of time.
- *Attorney fees:* The prevailing party may receive reasonable attorney fees when the infringer has acted in bad faith (i.e., has received notice that the invention is patented and yet continues his infringing conduct).
- *Trebled damages:* Three times the actual damages in cases in which the infringement was willful.

 QUICK QUIZ Patent or Trade Secret?

Tom owns a company that makes bitters for cocktail recipes. His product has an ingredient derived from a shrub native to the Caribbean called *Cascarilla* that gives his bitters a distinctive and pleasant taste.

1. Should Tom protect his recipe with a patent or trade secret? Explain.
2. What are the risks associated with each type of intellectual property?

TAKEAWAY CONCEPTS Patents

- A patent is a statutorily created right that allows an inventor the exclusive right to make, use, license, and sell her invention for a limited amount of time.
- The three main types of patents are utility patents, design patents, and plant patents.
- To be patentable, an invention must be new and nonobvious.
- Several parties in the distribution chain may be liable for patent infringement.
- A utility patent lasts for 20 years from the date of application.
- Anyone who makes, uses, or sells a patented invention during the term of the patent without authorization engages in patent infringement.

COPYRIGHTS

According to one study, the value added by copyright-reliant industries to the U.S. economy amounted to more than $1 trillion and accounted for nearly 7 percent of the U.S. economy.[9] These industries include books, newspapers, motion pictures, recorded music, entertainment, and software.[10] These creative industries and the innovative companies they spawn, such as Netflix, rely on a robust system of copyright laws to survive and thrive.

The federal Copyright Act of 1976[11] allows creators to obtain a **copyright** by having an "original work of authorship fixed in any tangible medium of expression." Protected works include literary works, musical works, dramatic works, choreographic works, motion pictures, sound recordings, and pictorial or graphical works. Works that cannot be protected include ideas, procedures, processes, systems, methods of operation, concepts, principles, and discoveries, no matter how they are explained, illustrated, or described.[12] A work of authorship can be created in various types of media. A book, poem, sheet music, painting, photograph, video game, website, movie, sound recording, and software code are all works that can be protected under copyright.

Required Elements of a Work

To derive copyright protection, a work must meet a three-part test: (1) **originality**, (2) some degree of **creativity**, and (3) fixed in a **durable medium**. The courts have ruled that for a work of authorship to qualify as original, the author must use her own creative capabilities to create the work or medium. In *Feist Publications, Inc. v. Rural Telephone Service,*[13] the landmark case on copyright originality and creativity, the U.S. Supreme Court gave some guidance as to what level of creativity was necessary to meet the originality requirements. The Court ruled that, although compilations of facts such as names and telephone numbers could be copyrightable, there had to be some *creative* element that made the compilation an original work. For example, the White Pages of a telephone directory do not meet the creativity requirement because they are simply arranged alphabetically.

To be protected, a work also must be fixed in a durable medium. This underscores the copyright law's requirement that the work must be more than just an idea or thought process. In fact, the work must be in a tangible format, such as writing, digital, paint, video, and so forth. Copyright protections extend automatically to a work once it is created.

Rights Granted

According to the Copyright Act, the owner of a copyright has the exclusive right to:

- Reproduce work in whole or in part.
- Adapt the work or prepare what are known as "derivatives."
- Distribute copies.
- Perform and display the work.

To illustrate how these rights operate, take the case of author J.K. Rowling, who owns the copyright to the Harry Potter novels. The first right prevents anyone from copying her

---

[9]International Intellectual Property Alliance, *Copyright Industries in the U.S. Economy: The 2013 Report* (2013), p. 2.

[10]Id., 5.

[11]17 U.S.C. § 101 et seq.

[12]Note that ideas, procedures, systems, and the like may be covered by intellectual property protections other than copyright law (e.g., patents or trade secrets).

[13]499 U.S. 340 (1991). This case was the beginning of the phone book battles. Once *Feist* was decided, several different publication companies began to compete with telephone companies for Yellow Pages advertising. This one decision spurred a new niche in the publishing industry.

Author J.K. Rowling retained the copyrights to her blockbuster Harry Potter book series, which has been translated into many languages and remade as a hit movie franchise.
©Samir Hussein/WireImage/Getty Images

books in any form or format (e.g., print or digital). The second right prevents anyone from adapting her novels by creating unauthorized Harry Potter sequels, online games, or comic books. The third right prevents anyone from distributing her novels without permission through e-book or brick-and-mortar retailing. The last right prevents anyone from developing a theatrical rendition of any Harry Potter novel.

The default rule of copyright ownership is that the property owner reserves all rights to the work, hence the term "all rights reserved." However, an **open source license agreement** can be designed that permits others to use and modify copyright-protected software. An open source software license, for example, is used by software developers who prefer open and free access to certain items of software, such as the Linux operating system. The open source license is intended to remove the copyright restrictions that would automatically restrict access to other developers. Similarly, in the online publishing environment, the creators of works such as photographs, videos, or songs may license their work under a **creative commons license** that allows others to adapt, profit from, and copy a work.

Registration and Notice

Although works may be registered with the U.S. Copyright Office, registration is not required for the creator to own the rights. The creation of the work itself automatically confers a copyright on the material. However, registration of the copyright gives its owner the right to bring an infringement action in federal court and the right to collect additional damages from an infringer. Copyright notice is not necessary for works created after 1989. It is a wise practice, however, to place a copyright notice on the work because it limits any defense by an infringer who claims innocent infringement. The copyright notice is the familiar © symbol, "Copr.," or simply "Copyright" accompanied by the year of first publication and the copyright owner's name.

Copyright Infringement

Copyright liability is a major concern for any business. Even a small business that develops a website must ensure that it has the right to use an image "borrowed" from another website. When a copyright owner pursues a party that it believes has infringed its copyright, the owner will pursue one of three theories of infringement that have been developed by the federal courts to analyze copyright infringement cases. The theories are direct, indirect (also known as *contributory*), and vicarious infringement.

Direct Infringement   **Direct infringement** occurs when the copyright owner can prove that she has legal ownership of the work in question and that the infringer copied the work without permission. While the first element is straightforward, the second element is more complex than it appears at first glance. In the context of the copyright protections afforded by law, it is clear that the word *copied* must have an expansive definition rather than a narrow one (e.g., whether *copy* means more than an exact replica). At the same time, of course, the definition cannot be so expansive as to foreclose any works within the same category. To address this issue, courts have developed the *substantial similarity standard*. Under this standard, a copyright holder need only prove that the infringer copied enough elements to make the infringing work substantially similar to the copyrighted work.

Indirect Infringement   **Indirect infringement** (also known as *contributory infringement*) involves three parties: the copyright owner, the direct infringer, and the *facilitator* of the infringement. The theory of indirect infringement holds the facilitator liable for damages. Therefore, before pursuing a theory of indirect infringement, the copyright owner must identify the direct infringer. Normally, for the facilitator to be liable, that party must have knowledge (direct or imputed) of the infringement and contribute to the infringement in some material way. In the famous case of *A&M Records, Inc. v. Napster, Inc.,*[14] a federal appeals court held that Napster's business model of facilitating a peer-to-peer community for the sharing of digital music files constituted contributory infringement because Napster had the ability to locate infringing material listed on its search engines and the right to terminate users' access to the system.

Vicarious Infringement

Vicarious infringement is similar to the indirect infringement theory in that they both involve third parties not involved in actual direct infringement. Vicarious liability is based on agency law (Chapter 37) and can be used as a theory of liability when the infringing party (the agent) is acting on behalf of, or for the benefit of, another party (the principal). In that case, the principal is vicariously liable. The copyright owner will be entitled to remedies against the principal to the same extent as against the direct infringer. Vicarious liability most often occurs when an employee, acting with authority from the employer, commits an act of infringement that benefits the employer (e.g., by using a pirated version of software).

The **No Electronic Theft (NET) Act**[15] of 1997 increased the criminal penalties for violation of the Copyright Act. The NET Act provides for criminal liability for anyone who infringes on a copyright by making a reproduction of or distributing, including by electronic means, one or more copies of a copyrighted work with a total retail value of more than $1,000. Penalties include maximum fines of $250,000 and potential jail time.[16]

Defenses to Infringement Claims

Copyright owners do not enjoy unlimited rights to their work. Rather, the law balances public interests with the property rights of copyright owners. Infringement claims related to copyrighted material are subject to the defenses of fair use, public domain, and the first sale doctrine.

Fair Use

The most common and powerful defense is **fair use**. A landmark case on the fair use defense is *Sony v. Universal City Studios,*[17] in which the U.S. Supreme Court ruled that Sony's manufacturing and selling of Betamax videocassette recorders (VCRs) was not per se infringement. Universal sued Sony on an infringement theory, claiming that consumers were using the Sony product to copy its copyrighted movies. The Court made clear that Congress did not give absolute control over all uses of copyrighted materials. Some uses were permitted, and because the device could still be used for "substantial non-infringing uses," the Court held that Sony was not liable for contributory infringement. Fair use has also been extended to the use of a work for parody, academic, factual reporting, or satirical purposes.[18]

This *fair use exception,* known as the *Sony defense* or the *Betamax doctrine,* was used, unsuccessfully, as the basis for the defense in the *A&M Records v. Napster* case (discussed

---

[14]239 F.3d 1004 (2001).

[15]17 U.S.C. § 506.

[16]A catalyst for this law was a criminal case brought against an MIT student who posted copyrighted software on the web free of charge for anyone to download. The government could not obtain a conviction in the case because the existing law (prior to the NET Act) imposed criminal liability only when the infringement was undertaken for private *financial* gain. The NET Act eliminated the financial gain requirement for a criminal conviction. See *U.S. v. LaMacchia,* 871 F. Supp. 535 (D. Mass. 1994).

[17]464 U.S. 417 (1984).

[18]*Campbell v. Acuff-Rose Music, Inc.,* 510 U.S. 569 (1994).

previously in this chapter). The issue of contributory infringement and fair use was reexamined by the U.S. Supreme Court in Case 50.3.

Fair use in the context of direct infringement includes the following four elements:

1. *The purpose and nature of the use.* This is also called the *transformative* factor because courts analyze whether the work in question has added new expression or meaning to the copyrighted work. If the work centers on the original but creates new information, aesthetics, or insights, the work does not infringe on the copyrighted work. For example, entertainers may use parody for purposes of mocking a particular work because the use is transformative. However, transformative use has its limits. In *Warner Bros.*

CASE 50.3 Metro-Goldwyn-Mayer Studios v. Grokster, Ltd., 545 U.S. 913 (2005)

FACT SUMMARY After the *Napster* decision, a number of other P2P file-sharing communities emerged with a slightly different business model. One firm, Grokster, used a business model whereby it would be *impossible* for Grokster to know if the files being shared were an infringing use. Thus, Grokster argued, no Napster-like imputed liability could attach and no contributor infringement existed. According to Grokster (and many other such firms that were emerging), its business was precisely the same business that Sony was in when selling the Betamax and, thus, Grokster was entitled to the same type of fair use exception—"capable of substantial non-infringing uses"—as was articulated by the Supreme Court in the *Sony* case. When MGM Studios sued Grokster (and others, including StreamCast, the distributor of Morpheus software), both the federal trial court and the federal court of appeals *agreed* with Grokster and allowed Grokster to use the *Sony* exception in its rulings against MGM.

SYNOPSIS OF DECISION AND OPINION The U.S. Supreme Court unanimously held that Grokster *could* be liable for inducing copyright infringement and reversed the court of appeals ruling. The Court specifically ruled that anyone who distributes a device with the intent to promote its use to infringe copyright is liable for the resulting acts of infringement (contributory) by third parties. Although there was some disagreement among the justices about the *Sony* defense, ultimately the Court held that the lower courts had misapplied the *Sony* exception because there was ample evidence that Grokster had acted with intent to cause copyright infringement via the use of its software.

WORDS OF THE COURT: Evidence of Intent "Three features of this evidence of intent are particularly notable. First, each company showed itself to be aiming to satisfy a known source of demand for copyright infringement, the market comprising former Napster users. StreamCast's internal documents made constant reference to Napster, it initially distributed its Morpheus software through an OpenNap program compatible with Napster, it advertised its OpenNap program to Napster users, and its Morpheus software functions as Napster did except that it could be used to distribute more kinds of files, including copyrighted movies and software programs. Grokster's name is apparently derived from Napster, it too initially offered an OpenNap program, its software's function is likewise comparable to Napster's, and it attempted to divert queries for Napster onto its own Web site. Grokster and StreamCast's efforts to supply services to former Napster users, deprived of a mechanism to copy and distribute what were overwhelmingly infringing files, indicate a principal, if not exclusive, intent on the part of each to bring about infringement."

Case Questions

1. Why was the Court so concerned about the OpenNap program offered by StreamCast and Grokster?

2. Why do you think the Court refused to apply the *Sony* exception in this case?

3. *Focus on Critical Thinking:* Is it ethical to obtain music through digital file sharing? Have you ever illegally downloaded music or movies? Does the Court's ruling stifle innovation? Explain your answer.

Entertainment, Inc. v. RDR Books,[19] a court held that a Harry Potter encyclopedia qualified as "slightly transformative," but fair use did not apply because so much of the encyclopedia's text was taken directly from the Harry Potter book series.

Moreover, if the use of the work is to further education or scholarship, courts are more likely to be sympathetic to an assertion of fair use. This does not mean, however, that whole sections of textbooks or copied videotapes may be used without the copyright holder's permission. If the use is for some commercially profitable purpose, this will weigh heavily against the infringer; however, this does not mean that commercial use is a complete bar to assertion of fair use.

2. *The nature of the work itself.* Newsworthy and factual information can be subject to fair use. Courts typically allow more use from nonfiction works (e.g., news stories or biographies) than from fictional works such as novels or plays.

3. *The amount and substantiality of the material used.* Courts analyze the totality of the circumstances regarding the amount of copyrighted material used compared to the entire work at issue. Short phrases and limited use of the copyrighted work are often protected by the fair use defense.

4. *The market effect of the use.* Courts are reluctant to allow fair use as a defense (even if the use meets the other three factors) if a copyright holder demonstrates that the *value* of a copyrighted work will be diminished by allowing its use. Fair use cannot impair the marketability or economic success of the copyrighted work.

Public Domain   A work that is in the *public domain* is not protectable under copyright laws. Works fall into the public domain either because the copyright has expired or because they are published by federal or state governments. Reproductions of classical works in literature, such as Homer's *The Odyssey* or Tolstoy's *War and Peace,* do not require permissions because they are now part of the public domain. Similarly, court cases, government agency correspondence, and statutes are all in the public domain and do not require permission for use.

First Sale   The first sale doctrine allows the owner of a copyrighted work to resell or gift the work to another without permission of the copyright owner. The original work also must be purchased lawfully in order to assert the first sale doctrine as a defense. It is important to note that the first sale doctrine only prevents the copyright owner from the exercise of *distribution* rights and does not allow another to copy the work and distribute it.

TAKEAWAY CONCEPTS Copyrights

- The federal Copyright Act of 1976 allows creators to obtain a copyright by having an "original work of authorship fixed in any tangible medium of expression."
- A copyrighted work must exhibit originality, show some degree of creativity, and be fixed in a durable medium.
- The owner of a copyright has the exclusive right to reproduce the work in whole or in part; to adapt the work or prepare what are known as "derivatives"; to distribute copies; and to perform and display the work.
- Copyright infringement may be direct, indirect, or through vicarious infringement.
- A defense to copyright infringement can be based on fair use, the public domain, or the first sale doctrine.

---

[19]575 F. Supp. 2d 513 (S.D.N.Y. 2008).

LO 50-5

Identify the strength
of a trademark
based on its
classification.

TRADEMARKS

A **trademark** is a nonfunctional, distinctive word, name, shape, symbol, phrase, or combination of words and symbols that helps consumers to distinguish one product or service from another.[20] The Lanham Act[21] is the federal statute that protects an owner's registered trademark from use without the owner's permission. Most case law and legal texts refer to both trademarks and service marks simply as a *mark*. Owners of a mark are called *holders*.

In business terms, marks are typically referred to as *brands* although this concept also encompasses the mental associations consumers have of an offering. The primary objective of trademark protection is to provide the mark holder with a means of preventing others from fooling consumers into buying a product that they erroneously believe is produced by the mark holder. Businesses invest significant resources in their trademarks to build consumer loyalty and to give a unique identity to a particular brand. Designs, color schemes, shapes, and other features all play a role in creating a link and set of associations in the buying public's mind. Trademarks allow consumers to quickly identify a product and distinguish it from similar or competing products. The Lanham Act is designed to prevent business competitors from getting a "free ride" on the shoulders of a more famous brand. For example, if a small economy-car manufacturer could use the name or symbols associated with Rolls-Royce, the smaller company would deprive the mark holder of its investments in the mark and gain name recognition at no cost. Also, the consuming public would suffer from confusion.

The key requirement for a protectable trademark is *distinctiveness* that indicates the product's source. For example, Coca-Cola's name and logo comprise one of the most famous trademarks in the world. Consumers have confidence in the product, and the Coca-Cola trademarks distinguish the product from competing soft drinks. Coca-Cola has protected the name Coca-Cola, the old-style cursive font, and the wavelike ribbon as separate registrations. Other famous marks include McDonald's Golden Arches and Nike's Swoosh. While trademarks typically are associated with products, **service marks** are used to identify business services. Examples of well-known service marks include Starbucks Coffee and Wells Fargo Bank.

Trademarks are a daily part of a consumer's life. Take out your smartphone and see how many registered trademarks you can find. You may see Apple's trademark for the iPhone or Samsung's registered trademark for the Galaxy S. You may also see icons on the screen that allow consumers to distinguish Facebook from Instagram and Pinterest. Want to listen to some music? You can choose between Pandora and Spotify with no difficulty because you recognize their trademarks.

FIGURE 50.5 Hershey's Chocolate Bar Trademark Registration

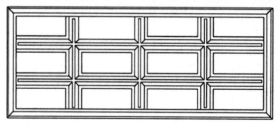

Source: U.S. Patent and Trademark Office, Application No. 77809223, filed August 20, 2009.

---

[20]15 U.S.C. § 1127 (2006).
[21]15 U.S.C. § 1052 (2006).

Trade Dress

Businesses are increasingly eager to extend trademark protection beyond words and symbols to gain protection for a product's shape or the color combination of its packaging. These look-and-feel trademark features are called **trade dress**. Traditionally, courts have allowed trade dress protection for both product design features and product packaging, including textures, shapes, and color combinations, for businesses such as restaurants.[22] More recently, the U.S. Patent and Trademark Office (USPTO) has granted protection to trade dress characteristics so long as the mark holder can prove that the trade dress provides an exclusive association back to the source product or service in the consumer's mind.

A recent trend in strategic business planning is to trademark product design as a form of trade dress. Protecting product design through trademark laws is challenging because the applicant must overcome any notion that the design purpose was to allow the product to function properly rather than as a distinctive trademark. For example, Figure 50.5 is a sketch of a seemingly generic row of rectangles. In its trademark application, the holder describes these rectangles as "a configuration of a chocolate bar that consists of 12 equally-sized recessed rectangular panels arranged in a four panel by three panel format with each panel having its own raised border within a large rectangle." The configuration is the product design of the iconic Hershey's chocolate bar, and the USPTO granted the mark to The Hershey Company in 2012. Hershey was able to convince the USPTO that the rectangles were not essential to the use or purpose of the article. Figure 50.5 shows the sketches submitted by Hershey with its trademark application. Apple is also aggressively registering product designs as trademarks and successfully protected the design of the iPod, iPhone, and iPad, among many others.[23]

Classifications of Trademarks

As discussed earlier, trademark protection is based on distinctiveness. For a trademark to be distinctive, it must identify the source of a particular product (or service for service marks). Courts classify marks based on their level of distinctiveness, and this classification determines their level of legal protection. It is important to note that there is no clear line of demarcation between these classifications. Rather, courts analyze a mark on a case-by-case basis. Simply put, the more distinctive the mark, the more protection the mark has under the Lanham Act.

Arbitrary or Fanciful A mark that has no direct connection to the product is categorized as arbitrary or fanciful. An *arbitrary* mark is a real word being used as part of a mark that has nothing to do with the word's literal meaning (e.g., Uber or Amazon). A *fanciful* mark is one that centers upon a made-up word. For example, Spotify's name and symbol were created by the company's founders and have no obvious connection to streaming music. Therefore, Spotify fits into the fanciful category.

Spotify's logo is an example of a fanciful trademark.
©Jeffrey Blackler/Alamy

Suggestive Marks that suggest the product or service without literally describing it are considered highly distinctive. Courts classify a mark as suggestive if imagination, thought, and perception are required to understand how it is tied to the underlying product or service. For example, the trademark "Under Armour"

---

[22]*Two Pesos, Inc. v. Taco Cabana, Inc.,* 112 S. Ct. 2753 (1992).

[23]See David Orozco and James G. Conley, "The Shape of Things to Come," *The Wall Street Journal,* May 12, 2008.

suggests a product used under something for protection. "Netflix" suggests a web-based movie service. Understanding the actual product, however, requires a leap of imagination, thought, or perception. Suggestive marks are similar to arbitrary marks in that they tend to be highly distinctive and are given a high level of protection.

Descriptive
A descriptive mark is one that makes specific reference to features, qualities, or characteristics of a product or service and is not inherently distinctive. Courts have held that marks such as After Tan (moisturizing lotion for use after sunbathing) and Car Freshener (air deodorizer for cars) are descriptive marks because no leap of imagination is required to connect the mark with the product. Because descriptive marks are not inherently distinctive, they are not protected under the Lanham Act unless they have acquired a **secondary meaning**. Descriptive mark holders must provide evidence that the general public connects the mark with the mark holder's product or service rather than with the ordinary meaning of the term.

A secondary meaning is created when the consuming public primarily associates a mark with a *particular* product rather than with any alternate meaning. For example, Microsoft attempted to protect the term *Windows* as a mark for its operating system for many years. To attain that right, Microsoft was required to show that, for much of the consuming public, the term *Windows* was more often associated with Microsoft's operating system than with the windowing function of its software. Similarly, Twitter's initial application in 2009 to trademark the term *tweet* was rejected because of insufficient evidence of secondary meaning. However, by 2012, Twitter acquired full trademark rights to the term *tweet.*

Recall our discussion of the product design trademark for a Hershey's chocolate bar. Once Hershey overcame the hurdle of proving that the rectangular design was not essential to its function, it still had to prove that the design was a unique link back to the source in the minds of consumers. Well-known elements of branding and design that have been registered by establishing secondary meaning include the robin's egg blue shopping bags and boxes at Tiffany & Co., the shape of the Weber grill, the shape of Hershey's Kiss chocolates, and the yellow roof of a McDonald's restaurant. Often, to prove secondary meaning, the applicant must offer evidence of exclusive use for several years and significant advertising expenditures to build the consumer association with the mark.

Case 50.4 provides insight into an analysis of the secondary meaning requirement.

CASE 50.4 *In re* Hershey Chocolate and Confectionery Corp. (Serial No. 77809223), Trademark Trial and Appeal Board of the USPTO (2012)

FACT SUMMARY The Hershey Chocolate and Confectionery Corporation ("Hershey") filed an application with the USPTO for a trademark to protect the product design of its chocolate bar. The application described the configuration of the candy bar as "twelve (12) equally-sized recessed rectangular panels arranged in a four panel by three panel format with each panel having its own raised border within a large rectangle." The USPTO's Examining Attorney refused registration on two grounds: (1) that the applicant's proposed mark is a functional configuration of the goods and (2) it consists of a nondistinctive configuration of the goods that does not function as a mark under existing trademark law. Hershey appealed the decision, arguing that the candy bar's configuration had nothing to do with functionality and citing marketing surveys as evidence that a sufficient percentage of the consuming public connected the design with the Hershey product.

(continued)

Generic   If the mark does not fall into the arbitrary, fanciful, suggestive, or descriptive with a secondary meaning categories, it is considered generic and cannot be registered as a trademark. For example, the USPTO has denied trademark protection of terms such as *smartphone* or *e-mail.*

Acquiring Rights

Holders acquire rights to trademark protection either through (1) use in commerce or (2) federal registration with the U.S. Patent and Trademark Office (USPTO). Acquiring rights through use in commerce carries a significant risk that the mark holder's rights will not be fully realized nationwide, so most holders opt to register the mark at the federal level. One can apply for federal trademark registration so long as the mark is being used in commerce in more than one state.

A mark holder typically uses the symbol ^{TM} (trademark) or ^{SM} (service mark) to indicate that the mark is not yet registered with the USPTO. However, use of this symbol also indicates that the mark holder considers the mark distinctive enough to be protected and, in some cases, that the application for registration is pending. Once the mark has been approved by the USPTO, it is considered registered and the mark holder can use the symbol ® to indicate completed federal registration nationwide.

A mark may be registered with USPTO only if the holder has a bona fide intent to use the mark in commerce. Once the mark is registered, the mark holder has nationwide rights to its use. However, even with registration, the mark may still be used by anyone who used the mark in commerce *prior* to registration. Different parties can, therefore, have trademark protection simultaneously. For example, if Robert begins to use a trademark for a specialty coffee in his coffee shop in Boston but does not use it in any other market, he has acquired the right to use it in *Boston only* because he was the first to commercialize it. However, if National Coffee Brand (NCB) wants to use the very same trademark, NCB may register it with the USPTO and be entitled to nationwide rights *except* the right to use it in the Boston market.

Applications and the USPTO

Registration of a mark is not automatic. A mark holder must submit to an approval process through the USPTO, which examines the mark for distinctiveness, checks for any similar marks that are already registered, and ensures compliance with trademark registration standards (e.g., secondary meaning for descriptive marks). The Lanham Act also allows the USPTO to reject a mark if it is "immoral, deceptive, or scandalous matter" or may be disparaging to "people, institutions, beliefs, or national symbols."[24] This section of the statute, commonly referred to as *Section 2a,* provides broad authority to the USPTO in evaluating the content of a mark for scandalous material. Some rejections under this section include:

- "Stop the Islamisation of America" (*In re Geller,* 751 F.3d 1355 [Fed. Cir. 2014]).
- "Heeb" (*In re Heeb Media, LLC,* 89 U.S.P.Q.2d 1071 [T.T.A.B. Nov. 26, 2008]).
- "Sex Rod" (*Boston Red Sox Baseball Club L.P. v. Sherman,* 88 U.S.P.Q.2d 1581 [T.T.A.B. Sept. 9, 2008]).
- "Cocaine" in a label for a highly caffeinated soft drink (*In re Kirby,* T.T.A.B. Sept. 22, 2008) as depicted in Figure 50.6.

First Amendment Concerns

A federal appellate court reversed the USPTO's rejection of an application for the name "The Slants" by an Asian-American rock band. In its 2015 decision, *In re Tam,* the U.S. Court of Appeals for the Federal Circuit addressed First Amendment concerns in holding that Section 2a of the Lanham Act was unconstitutional. The case arose after the USPTO

FIGURE 50.6	"Cocaine" Logo Rejected by the USPTO under Section 2a

©ZUMA Press, Inc./Alamy

---

[24] 15 U.S.C. § 1052(a).

rejected the application for The Slants based on the examiner's conclusion that the term was a highly disparaging term for Asian-Americans. The trial court agreed with the USPTO and affirmed its ruling that the mark was appropriately rejected as scandalous. However, the Federal Circuit Court of Appeals reversed the decision, pointing to a U.S. Supreme Court decision that classified trademarks as protected commercial speech. The court analyzed Section 2a under the *Central Hudson* test for government restriction of commercial speech and concluded that, because no substantial government interest exists, the section is unconstitutional. The court summed up its First Amendment analysis as follows:

> Whatever our personal feelings about the mark at issue here, or other disparaging marks, the First Amendment forbids government regulators to deny registration because they find the speech likely to offend others. Even when speech inflicts great pain, our Constitution protects it to ensure that we do not stifle public debate.
> *In re Tam,* 808 F.3d 1321 (Fed. Cir. 2015)

The Supreme Court heard the case and agreed with the appellate court's finding that Section 2a of the Lanham Act is unconstitutional. After the court issued its decision, Pro-Football, Inc., the corporation that owns the Washington Redskins professional football team, used the *Tam* case as the basis for additional appeals concerning the USPTO's cancellation of its registered mark, "Redskins," which the USPTO had found disparaging.[25] In its appeal, Pro-Football successfully cited the appellate court's decision in *In re Tam* as support for its arguments that the cancellation of the "Redskins" mark was unconstitutional.

Maintaining the Mark

After an initial registration period of 10 years, marks registered through the USPTO may be renewed an unlimited number of times so long as the holder continues to pay the registration fee. Unlike a patent or a copyright, trademarks can be renewed and last indefinitely. As such, trademark value can accrue over time and become a substantial asset on a company's balance sheet. Holders that do not maintain the mark through registration renewal risk losing the rights to the mark and can no longer prevent the mark's use by a third party. Additionally, if the holder stops using the mark in commerce for a period of three years, the rights to the mark are lost through abandonment.

Policing the Mark

Mark holders have an obligation to protect their rights by policing their mark. A primary threat to a mark's distinctiveness is the use of the mark by competitors and other third parties. Often, a mark holder will send a **cease and desist letter** to the alleged infringer asking them to discontinue their use of the mark or face potential legal action.

Of particular concern to managers should be the use of the mark as a noun or verb in trade and nontrade publications. If a word becomes generic to the point where it has lost its distinctiveness, the rights are lost through *genericide.* Perhaps the most famous case of genericide is Bayer's loss of the right to protect the mark "aspirin" in 1921. Other well-known mark holders who lost rights to their marks include Otis Elevator in 1950 ("escalator"), King-Seely Thermos Co. in 1963 ("thermos"), and Duncan in 1965 ("yo-yo"). Typically, genericide occurs once the consuming public uses the mark's terminology as a noun or a verb rather than as an adjective to describe a good. When holders of a mark misuse the mark or allow the mark to be misused by others (e.g., advertising agencies), that contributes to the demise of the mark's distinctiveness and therefore its protectability. Companies such as Google, for example, will notify bloggers or journalists if they used the term *google* to imply an Internet search rather than the company or its service.

---

[25] *Pro-Football, Inc. v. Blackhorse,* Memorandum Opinion and Order, No.1:14-cv-01043-GBL-IDD (E.D. Va. 2015).

Trademark Infringement

Infringement occurs when a party uses a protected mark without the mark holder's consent. For a mark holder to prevail on a claim of trademark infringement under the Lanham Act, she has the burden of proving that the infringement would likely cause confusion among reasonable consumers under the **likelihood of confusion** standard. In determining whether a likelihood of confusion exists, many courts apply a balancing test that has largely grown from a model set out by the U.S. Court of Appeals for the Second Circuit in the important infringement case, *Polaroid Corp. v. Polarad Electronics Corp.*[26] The factors considered are:

- the strength of the mark (how famous is it?);
- the similarity between marks;
- the proximity of the products and their competitiveness with each other;
- evidence that the mark holder may be preparing to launch a product for sale in the market of the alleged infringer's product (a technique known in trademark law as *bridging the gap*);
- evidence of actual consumer confusion;
- evidence of bad faith by the infringer;
- the respective quality of the products; and
- the sophistication of consumers in the relevant market.

The application of the *Polaroid* test is not mechanical but rather focuses on the ultimate question of whether, looking at the products in their totality, consumers are likely to be confused.

Trademark Dilution

In addition to bringing an infringement claim under the Lanham Act, holders of famous marks also may enforce their rights via the **Federal Trademark Dilution Act** of 1995,[27] as amended by the Trademark Dilution Revision Act (TDRA)[28] of 2006. In a dilution claim, evidence of consumer confusion is *not* necessary. Dilution occurs either through *blurring* or *tarnishment.* Blurring dilutes the distinctive quality of the mark through its identification with goods that are not alike and may be found regardless of the presence or absence of actual or likely confusion, competition, or actual injury. For example, consider the hypothetical products of Red Bull brand pianos or Google brand tennis shoes. Consumers would not necessarily be confused about the origin, but each dilutes the distinctive quality of a famous mark. Dilution by tarnishment occurs when an association arising from the similarity between a mark or trade name and a famous mark harms the reputation of the famous mark with something that a consumer might find objectionable or unflattering (e.g., Apple brand cigarettes).[29]

The TDRA specifies six nonexhaustive factors for courts to consider in determining whether there is dilution by blurring:[30]

1. The degree of similarity between the mark and the famous mark.
2. The degree of inherent or acquired distinctiveness of the mark.
3. The extent to which the owner of the famous mark is engaging in substantially exclusive use of the mark.
4. The degree of recognition (fame) of the mark.

---

[26]287 F.2d 492 (2d Cir. 1961).

[27]15 U.S.C. § 1125.

[28]Id.

[29]15 U.S.C. § 1125(c)(2)(C) (2006).

[30]15 U.S.C. § 1125(c)(2)(B)(i)–(vi) (2006).

5. Whether use of the mark by the alleged infringer was intended to create an association with the famous mark.

6. Any actual association between the mark and the famous mark.

In addition to setting out statutory blurring standards, the TDRA also requires the mark holder to prove that the mark is famous by offering evidence that it is widely recognized by the general consuming public of the United States. The TDRA provides a powerful legal weapon for trademark holders who cannot prove infringement through consumer confusion. For example, when Facebook sued to prevent Teachbook, a social networking site for secondary school teachers, from using the mark "Teachbook," the court made clear that consumer confusion was not relevant in a dilution claim.[31]

Table 50.1 summarizes intellectual property protections.

TAKEAWAY CONCEPTS Trademarks

- A trademark is a nonfunctional, distinctive word, name, shape, symbol, phrase, or a combination of words and symbols that helps consumers to distinguish one product or service from another.
- The key requirement for a protectable trademark is *distinctiveness* that indicates the product's source.
- Trademarks are classified as arbitrary or fanciful, suggestive, descriptive, or generic.
- Trademark infringement is based on the likelihood of confusion among reasonable consumers.

TABLE 50.1 Intellectual Property Protections

Type	Coverage	Source of Law	Example	Duration
Trade secrets	Secret processes, formulas, methods, procedures, and lists that provide the owner with economic advantage.	State statutes based on Uniform Trade Secret Act and/or state common law	Customer lists with contact information, buying patterns, and credit histories	Life of the owner (entity or individual)
Patents	Inventors, for exclusive rights to make, use, license, or sell an invention.	Federal statute (Patent Act)	Rights to a newly discovered pharmaceutical product	20 years from date of filing, except for design patents (14 years)
Copyrights	Authors and originators of literary or artistic production.	Federal statute (Copyright Act of 1976, as amended)	Rights of a recording artist and writer of a song	*Author:* 70 years from death of the author *Work for hire:* 120 years from date of creation or 95 years from publication
Trademarks, service marks, trade dress	Words, symbols, or phrases that identify a particular seller's product or service and distinguish it from other products and services. Trade dress extends trademark protection to the shape or color scheme of a product.	Federal statute (Lanham Act) and some state and federal common law	Google (trademark); Hilton Hotels (service mark); Hershey chocolate bar's shape (trade dress)	Unlimited so long as the owner actively protects ("polices") the use of the mark

---

[31]*Facebook, Inc. v. Teachbook.com, LLC,* 819 F. Supp. 2d 764 (N.D. Ill. 2011).

Responding to a Cease and Desist Letter

PROBLEM: Brand owners must police their marks to preserve trademark strength and prevent infringement. Some brand owners, however, may legally overreach in their attempt to expand brand power.

STRATEGIC SOLUTION: A cease and desist letter can be an effective low-cost tool to combat intellectual property infringement. Consider the following use of a cease and desist letter to determine if the claim is valid or an abusive tactic designed to shut down competitors.

Vermont T-shirt maker Bo Muller-Moore was asked by a local farmer to create a handmade T-shirt that said "Eat More Kale" on it. Others in the community began asking for the same shirt, and it quickly became Bo's best-selling item. He launched a website (www .eatmorekale.com) and Facebook page to sell his shirts online and expand the reach of his small business. To protect his brand, Muller-Moore decided to file an application with the USPTO to obtain a federal trademark to the "Eat More Kale" slogan. Shortly thereafter, however, his attorney notified him of a letter sent by the fast-food company Chick-fil-A based out of Atlanta. It was a cease and desist letter from Chick-fil-A's attorneys that said:

> Chick-fil-A has continuously and exclusively used its EAT MOR CHIKIN intellectual property in commerce since at least as early as June 19, 1995. Additionally, Chick-fil-A has common law trademark and copyrights and owns numerous U.S. and international trademark and copyright registrations for these and other items of intellectual property. . . .

> It has come to our attention that your client Robert Muller-Moore DBA Eat More Kale has filed on August 31, 2011 a combination use-based and intent-to-use application with the USPTO for Eat More Kale. . . .

> Your client's Eat More Kale mark plays off and imitates Chick-fil-A's valuable EAT MOR CHIKIN intellectual property by using a prefix confusingly similar to Chick-fil-A's federally registered trademarks. Your client's misappropriation of Chick-fil-A's EAT MOR CHIKIN intellectual property, to play off and benefit from the extraordinary fame and goodwill of Chick-fil-A's trademarks, copyrights and popular promotional campaign, is likely to cause confusion of the public and dilutes the distinctiveness of Chick-fil-A's intellectual property and diminishes its value. Such actions constitute trademark infringement, dilution, and unfair competition in violation of federal and state law. . . .

The letter goes on to state that 30 other users of similar marks abandoned their use or trademark applications when Chick-fil-A threatened litigation against them. The marks used by these other merchants included EAT MORE BEEF, EAT MORE BEER, EAT MORE CATFISH, and EAT MORE BURRITOS, among others. Finally, the letter concluded by saying:

> Accordingly, Chick-fil-A hereby demands that your client (1) immediately expressly abandon [the federal trademark application] with the USPTO; and (2) cease and forever desist all plans to expand . . . use of the Eat More Kale mark (3). Please also contact me to arrange for transfer of the <eatmorekale.com> domain name to Chick-fil-A. . . . Please understand that Chick-fil-A's intellectual property is extremely valuable to it, and it will pursue all available remedies. . . .

Bo Muller-Moore was dumbfounded when he received the letter. His attorney informed him that defending this legal action could cost hundreds of thousands of dollars and would require hiring trademark counsel in Atlanta. When he asked his attorney if he could share the cease and desist letter with his customers and followers on Facebook, his attorney replied, "That is not how we attorneys would handle that, however, it is not illegal to do that."

QUESTIONS

1. Does Bo's trademark create likelihood of confusion? Apply the *Polaroid* test to explain your answer.
2. Does Bo's trademark dilute the EAT MORE CHIKIN mark? Why or why not?
3. Why did so many other companies agree to Chick-fil-A's demands?
4. Would you advise Bo to share the cease and desist letter on Facebook? Why or why not?
5. How would you handle this issue?

Intellectual property p. 963   An umbrella term for the legal property rights related to trade secrets, patents, copyrights, and trademarks.

Intellectual capital p. 963   The knowledge, skills, education, training, know-how, and creativity of individuals.

Tacit knowledge p. 963   Highly individualized knowledge that is hard to replicate or even explain.

Explicit knowledge p. 963   Knowledge that is recorded and available for a company's interpretation, application, and reproduction.

Intellectual asset p. 963   Explicit knowledge that is not yet intellectual property.

Licensing agreements p. 963   Contracts that allow intellectual property owners to monetize their intellectual property rights.

Licensor p. 963   The intellectual property owner in a license agreement.

Licensee p. 963   The party who is authorized to use intellectual property in a license agreement.

Royalty p. 963   The fee paid by a licensee to the licensor in a license agreement.

Trade secrets p. 964   Valuable assets such as processes, formulas, methods, procedures, and lists that allow companies to obtain a competitive advantage because they are not generally known and are protected.

Non-disclosure confidentiality agreements p. 965   Contract that imposes a legal duty on the party receiving the information to keep it secret.

Misappropriation p. 965   The improper acquisition or disclosure of a trade secret.

Economic Espionage Act p. 965   A federal statute passed in 1996 that provides criminal penalties for domestic and foreign theft of trade secrets.

Patent p. 967   A statutorily created right that allows an inventor the exclusive right to make, use, license, and sell her invention for a limited amount of time.

Prior art p. 968   The body of preexisting patents or technical disclosures that predate a patent application.

Novelty standard p. 970   A statutory standard to determine whether an invention is unique and original.

Nonobviousness standard p. 970   A standard requiring that an invention must be something more than that which would be obvious, in light of publicly available knowledge, to one who is skilled in the relevant field.

Patentable subject matter standard p. 970   A standard that prevents laws of nature, natural phenomena, and abstract ideas from being patentable.

Willful patent infringement p. 973   Intentional patent infringement that merits higher damages due to bad behavior.

Literal patent infringement p. 973   When an infringer makes, uses, or sells the same thing claimed in a patent or adds something beyond what is claimed.

Doctrine of equivalence p. 974   A doctrine that allows the courts to find patent infringement when an invention, compared with a patented device, performs substantially the same function in substantially the same way to achieve the same result.

Copyright p. 975   A form of protection for an original work of authorship fixed in any tangible medium of expression.

Originality p. 975   Copyright requirement that a work must be the author's own work.

Creativity p. 975   Copyright requirement that a work must have some minimum level of expressive originality.

Durable medium p. 975   Copyright requirement that a work must be in a tangible format, such as writing, digital, paint, video, and so forth.

Open source license agreement p. 976   A license that permits others to use and modify copyright-protected software.

Creative commons license p. 976   A license that allows others to adapt, profit from, and copy a work.

Direct infringement p. 976   A theory of copyright infringement under which the copyright owner proves that she has legal ownership of the work in question and that the infringer copied the work without permission.

Indirect infringement p. 976   A theory of copyright infringement under which a third party has knowledge of the infringement and contributes to it in some material way; also known as *contributory infringement*.

Vicarious infringement p. 977   A theory of copyright infringement in which the infringing party (the agent) is acting on behalf of, or for the benefit of, another party (the principal). In such cases, the principal is vicariously liable.

No Electronic Theft (NET) Act p. 977   A 1997 statute that increased the criminal penalties for violation of the Copyright Act.

Fair use p. 977   A defense against copyright infringement when a product or service has substantial noninfringing uses or when a work is protected due to its parody, academic, factual reporting, or satirical purposes.

Trademark p. 980   A nonfunctional, distinctive word, name, shape, symbol, phrase, or combination of words and symbols that helps consumers to distinguish one product or service from another.

Service marks p. 980   Trademarks used to identify business services.

Trade dress p. 981   Trademarks that include a product's shape or the color combination of its packaging.

Secondary meaning p. 982   A legal requirement whereby descriptive mark holders must provide evidence that the general public connects the mark with the mark holder's product or service rather than with the ordinary meaning of the term.

Cease and desist letter p. 985   A letter sent to alleged infringers asking them to discontinue use of the mark or face potential legal action.

Likelihood of confusion p. 986   Requirement that a mark holder prove that the trademark infringement would likely cause confusion among reasonable consumers.

Federal Trademark Dilution Act p. 986   A federal law enacted in 1995 that permits mark holders to recover damages and prevent others from diluting distinctive trademarks.

CASE SUMMARY 50.1 Harvey Barnett v. Shidler, 338 F.3d 1125 (10th Cir. 2003)

Trade Secret

Harvey Barnett, Inc. is a company that developed a method for surviving in the water that is designed to be taught to infants. The company developed a course in this technique, called *swim-float-swim,* and generates revenue by training and certifying instructors, who then teach the technique to the public at large for a fee. The instructors are trained extensively on the nearly 2,000 procedures necessary to accomplish the technique. All instructors sign a nondisclosure form and an agreement not to compete. When several of the instructors resigned and formed a venture called Aquatic Survival, Barnett filed suit claiming, among other allegations, misappropriation of the swim-float-swim system.

CASE QUESTIONS

1. Does the swim-float-swim technique qualify as a trade secret? Why or why not?
2. What factors would the court use to assess whether the technique is a trade secret? Discuss.

CASE SUMMARY 50.2 *In re* Reed Elsevier, Inc., 2007 WL 1086403 (Fed. Cir. 2007)

Trademarks/Service Marks

Reed Elsevier operated a website that allowed users to identify an attorney using a variety of criteria, including geographic location, practice expertise, and so forth. The website, www.lawyers.com, was first used in commerce by Reed in 1998. Later, Reed applied to have lawyers.com registered as a service mark.

CASE QUESTIONS

1. Is the lawyers.com mark too generic for protection? Why or why not?
2. If the court determines the mark is primarily descriptive, what further obstacle must Reed overcome to obtain protection for the mark?

CASE SUMMARY 50.3 KSR International v. Teleflex, 550 U.S. 398 (2007)

Patents

KSR designs and manufactures auto parts and sells them to auto manufacturers (not consumers). KSR developed and received a patent for a pedal device for Ford vehicles. KSR also sold products to General Motors (GM), and, in order to make the pedal device compatible for GM cars, KSR added an electronic throttle control to the pedal device. Teleflex claimed to have a patent for the pedal device that could be connected to such a throttle and, therefore, sued KSR for patent infringement. KSR defended on the basis that the device produced for GM was simply a combination of two existing products and was not patentable.

CASE QUESTIONS

1. What do you think Teleflex's specific theory of infringement was?
2. Which element of patentability does KSR claim Teleflex is missing in the combined device?

CHAPTER REVIEW QUESTIONS

1. The skills and creativity that are unique to one key employee are an example of:
   a. Explicit knowledge.
   b. An intellectual asset.
   c. Intellectual property.
   d. Tacit knowledge.
   e. A trademark.

2. X Corp. knows about Y Corp.'s patent and decides to make an infringing product that copies the technology claimed in Y Corp.'s patent. X Corp. has engaged in:
   a. Patent infringement.
   b. Willful patent infringement.
   c. Trade secret misappropriation.
   d. Likelihood of confusion.
   e. Contributory infringement.

3. According to the Copyright Act, the owner of a copyright has the exclusive right to:
   a. Reproduce work in whole or in part.
   b. Adapt the work or prepare what are known as "derivatives."
   c. Distribute copies.
   d. Perform and display the work.
   e. All of the above are correct.

4. Coca-Cola has registered the shape of the Coca-Cola bottle as a trademark. This is an example of:
   a. A design patent.
   b. Trade dress.
   c. A derivative.

   d. A logo.
   e. A copyright.

5. Maria transforms a copyrighted work into a parody. It is likely that Maria will be able to assert:
   a. The doctrine of equivalents.
   b. Misappropriation.
   c. Fair use.
   d. Vicarious liability.
   e. Contributory infringement.

6. Utility patents last 10 years from the date of application.
   a. True
   b. False

7. Trademarks last 20 years from the date of filing.
   a. True
   b. False

8. A business strategy can be held as a trade secret.
   a. True
   b. False

9. Descriptive marks can never be federally registered trademarks.
   a. True
   b. False

10. Design patents cover primarily the invention of new ornamental designs on articles of manufacture.
    a. True
    b. False

1. As long as Tom can secure the secrecy of his ingredient with proper controls, such as confidentiality agreements and the use of lock and key or passwords, he may decide to keep the recipe a trade secret. If the information is going to be revealed or is easy to reverse engineer, he may decide to seek a patent.

2. Trade secrets may be reverse engineered or independently discovered by a competitor. A utility patent expires 20 years from the date of application and becomes public domain information after that.

CHAPTER REVIEW QUESTIONS: Answers and Explanations

1. d. Tacit knowledge is individual-specific knowledge that is hard to articulate and reproduce.

2. b. When one knowingly infringes another's patent, this is called willful patent infringement.

3. e. The Copyright Act offers all these rights.

4. b. A product shape can be registered as trade dress.

5. c. Transforming a work into something else, such as a parody, is a factor in the fair use defense.

6. b. False. Utility patents last 20 years from the date of application.

7. b. False. A trademark can be registered and renewed indefinitely.

8. a. True. As long as the business strategy is not generally known, derives value from being secret, and its owner takes reasonable efforts to preserve secrecy, it can be protected as a trade secret.

9. b. False. A descriptive mark can become a federally registered mark if it acquires secondary meaning.

10. a. True. This is what design patents cover.

OVERVIEW AND OBJECTIVES

Two years after opening their family-owned coffee bean roastery, Jim and Annie Clark had become accustomed to long workweeks and bootstrap financing. By 1997, their Black Bear Micro Roastery was finally growing, and the Clarks were hopeful that their new specialty blend, Charbucks, would give their uniquely dark-roasted coffee bean a catchy name to remember.

Soon after launching the new blend, Annie Clark received a phone call from an insistent in-house lawyer at coffee giant Starbucks that threatened the very existence of the Clarks's company. Starbucks claimed that the Charbucks name and label infringed on its trademark, and it demanded that the Clarks cease the use of the Charbucks name and that any existing products with that name be removed from supermarket shelves. But the Clarks insisted that they had been careful to design the label with Black Bear Micro Roastery logos and that the name was tied to the dark-roasting process and not to anything related to the name Starbucks.

Despite their beliefs that no infringement had taken place, the Clarks entered into settlement negotiations to avoid the legal costs associated with defending a trademark lawsuit. After the settlement negotiations failed, Starbucks sued Black Bear Micro Roastery and the stage was set for a coffee war that pitted a multinational powerhouse against a Main Street merchant. This case study emphasizes use of legal insight and business strategy, gives context for evaluating business ethics, and requires the application of trademark law.

Review Legal Concepts

Prior to reading the case, briefly review the following legal concepts that were covered in the textbook: legal insight and business strategy (Chapter 1); business, societal, and ethical contexts of law (Chapter 2); and trademark law (Chapter 50). Think of these areas of the law as you read the case study facts and questions.

---

[1]An earlier version of this case study appeared in the *Journal of Legal Studies Education* (29 J. Legal Stud. Educ. 27). Permission by Sean P. Melvin.

THE BLACK BEAR MICRO ROASTERY

Jim and Annie Clark were native New Englanders who shared a passion for coffee and an entrepreneurial spirit. After three years of research, they launched Black Bear Micro Roastery in 1995 with a mission of creating a unique methodology for roasting gourmet coffee beans through use of advanced technology and the "traditional Yankee work ethic." The company was situated in the Lakes Region of New Hampshire and targeted connoisseur coffee drinkers, primarily in the New England area, who appreciated the micro-roastery approach of producing small, high-quality batches of coffee beans. The beans were sold via mail order, from the Black Bear website, and through New England specialty stores and supermarkets. Eventually, Black Bear also sold its products through its own retail outlet and café in Portsmouth, New Hampshire.

True to their belief in the micro-roastery concept and their entrepreneurial courage, the Clarks invested their life savings in the company. In order to start the business, the couple sold many of their assets and refinanced the mortgage on their home for extra cash. They enlisted their teenage daughters as their labor force and committed to seven-day workweeks. The family business was the centerpiece of their family's livelihood.

As with many start-ups, business for Black Bear was slow and rocky at first. The price of green coffee beans had fluctuated unexpectedly, and the 1997 Teamsters strike at United Parcel Service had eaten into profit margins. Undeterred, Jim and Annie Clark kept the company going until it began to grow ever so slowly. In order to develop a niche in the gourmet coffee market, Black Bear began to develop unique blends with catchy names that were easy to remember. This included blends such as "Country French," "Kenya Safari," and "Mocha Java."

Charbucks

By April 1997, Black Bear had developed a loyal following from which it often solicited feedback and suggestions for new products. One common theme from customers was a desire for a blend with a darker-roasted bean that yielded a richer taste. Responding to that customer demand, Black Bear developed a darker-roasted blend and named it "Charbucks Blend." *Char* was a reference to the new, darker-roasted coffee bean blend.

Charbucks Blend was sold in packaging that showed a picture of a black bear above the printed words "Black Bear Micro Roastery" in large font. The label also informed consumers that the coffee was roasted and "Air Quenched" in New Hampshire, and it contained the catchphrase "You wanted it dark . . . You've got it dark!" There was no similarity between Starbucks's famous logo, a circular shape with the graphic of a mermaidlike siren encompassed by the phrase "Starbucks Coffee," and the Charbucks label except for the partial word *bucks.*

A CALL FROM GOLIATH

It didn't take long for Starbucks to get word of Charbucks Blend. Just four months after making their first sale of the new blend, the Clarks received a call from Starbucks's in-house counsel. In what Annie Clark described as an unmistakably threatening phone call, Starbucks's counsel insisted that Charbucks Blend was a violation of Starbucks's trademark rights and demanded that Black Bear cease the use of the name and take steps to completely remove Charbucks from the marketplace. Starbucks followed up with a formal demand to cease and desist and alleged that Black Bear's use of *Charbucks* was disparaging, diluted Starbucks's mark, and violated federal trademark law.

The Clarks held a family meeting to discuss the matter. While they agreed that they had done nothing wrong, they decided that a trademark battle with Starbucks could bankrupt their family business even if they eventually prevailed in court. The risk was too high, so they decided to pursue negotiations for settlement. They hired an attorney, who sent Starbucks a letter on behalf of Black Bear denying any liability for trademark infringement but also offering to engage in settlement negotiations given the limited time and financial resources that the Clarks had at their disposal.

Starbucks hired outside counsel to negotiate a settlement agreement. In the event that settlement negotiations failed, Starbucks made it clear to Black Bear that it intended to file suit for trademark infringement. The negotiations dragged on for three years, and Black Bear's legal bills were soaring. Starbucks offered to compensate Black Bear for some of its legal expenses and costs of compliance (e.g., changing advertising, removing the products), but the parties could not agree on the amount or on a mutually acceptable public statement.

On July 2, 2001, nearly four years after the first phone call about the dispute, Starbucks filed suit against Black Bear in the U.S. District Court for the Southern

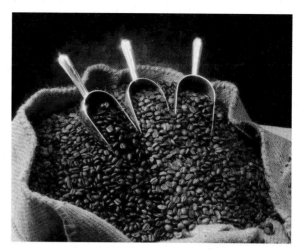

Starbucks sued a small company in a battle over its use of the word "Charbucks." © Greg Kuchik/Getty Images

District of New York, alleging trademark dilution, trademark infringement, and violation of Section 43(a) of the Lanham Act (the federal trademark law). Starbucks demanded both damages and injunctive relief.

Starbucks's Strategy

The Clarks breathed a sigh of relief after learning that Zurich, the insurance carrier that issued Black Bear's general commercial liability insurance policy, determined that their company was covered under the policy for this particular lawsuit and that coverage for their legal defense costs against Starbucks would be provided. This allowed them the opportunity to have their day in court without the fear that Starbucks would use the litigation process to drive Black Bear out of business. Both sides were ordered to mediation, but little progress was made and the case seemed headed for the courtroom.

However, soon after the mediation attempts failed, Starbucks employed a more aggressive litigation strategy. Its outside counsel notified Black Bear's counsel that unless the case was resolved, Starbucks would move to amend the lawsuit to drop a claim for certain damages listed in the original complaint. The impact of this amendment was that Zurich would be able to withdraw coverage for Black Bear's defense on the basis that the remaining claims in the lawsuit were exempt from Black Bear's policy. Still, the Clarks would not settle the claim. Three months later, Starbucks followed through on its promise to amend the complaint, and Zurich soon notified the Clarks of its decision to terminate coverage for defense of the Starbucks case once the amendment was approved by the court. Ultimately, however, the court denied Starbucks's attempt to amend the complaint, finding that the amendment was designed primarily to affect settlement negotiation leverage. Zurich was therefore compelled to continue covering the costs of Black Bear's defense.

In March 2005, a two-day trial was held in the matter of *Starbucks Corp. v. Wolfe's Borough Coffee, Inc., dba Black Bear Micro Roastery* in the U.S. District Court for the Southern District of New York. Starbucks relied primarily on the testimony of its expert, Warren Mitofsky, a scientist who had conducted a consumer survey and concluded that the number-one association of the nature of the name "Charbucks" in the mind of consumers was with the brand Starbucks. However, Mitofsky also conceded that his survey had been conducted entirely by telephone and that any measurement of reaction to the familiarity with other visual cues, such as the Charbucks Blend label, could not be accomplished through a telephone survey. The trial court issued an opinion and order ruling in favor of Black Bear and dismissed all of the counts of Starbucks's complaint. The court held that Starbucks did not meet its burden of proving that *actual dilution* had taken place and that Starbucks could not prevail on the trademark infringement claim because there was no likelihood that consumers would confuse the Charbucks mark with the Starbucks mark.

For the time being, David had battled back against Goliath—but the giant continued the fight in the appellate courts.

The Trademark Dilution Revision Act (TDRA)

In January 2006, Starbucks filed an appeal of the trial court's decision. While the appeal was pending, Congress amended the trademark laws by passing the Trademark Dilution Revision Act (TDRA) of 2006. The TDRA was passed primarily in response to the U.S. Supreme Court's decision in *Moseley v. V Secret Catalogue, Inc.,* in which the Court established the burden of proof for trademark holders by requiring evidence of *actual dilution.* Starbucks then argued that under the TDRA, the test for dilution was substantially easier to meet because the statute rejects actual dilution in favor of a more relaxed *likelihood of dilution* standard. In its appeal, Starbucks contended that the TDRA definition of dilution by blurring and/or tarnishment was directly related to its claims against Black Bear and that the case should now be evaluated in light of changes made by the TDRA.

The appellate wheels of justice were grinding slowly in this case. The appellate court ordered a rehearing by the trial court in light of the TDRA. The trial court again entered a judgment in favor of Black Bear for substantially the same reasons detailed in the first opinion. Not surprisingly, Starbucks appealed.

In a December 2009 opinion, the U.S. Court of Appeals for the Second Circuit handed down its decision and affirmed much of the trial court's ruling. Specifically:

- Although the appellate court agreed with the trial court's conclusion that the Charbucks package design was significantly different in imagery, color, and format from Starbucks's logo and signage, the appellate court also held that the trial court had used the incorrect analytical framework for dilution by blurring as set out in the TDRA. Therefore, the appellate court remanded this one issue back to the trial court.

- The appellate court affirmed the trial court's ruling that Starbucks did not provide sufficient evidence that dilution had occurred through tarnishment because Black Bear's intent was clearly to promote a positive image for its brand of coffee rather than referring to it as a way to harm the reputation of Starbucks's coffees.

- The appellate court also affirmed the trial court's ruling that no infringement had occurred under the federal trademark statute and agreed with Black Bear's argument that the coexistence of the Starbucks mark and Charbucks Blend for 11 years with no report of a single customer becoming confused is a powerful indication that there is no confusion or likelihood of confusion.

Connecting Legal and Ethical Concepts: Questions for Discussion

Chapter 1, "Legal Foundations and Thinking Strategically"

1. What lessons can managers learn from this case in terms of avoiding trademark liability and of decision making when enforcing a trademark?

2. Consider the Charbucks dispute from a cost-benefit perspective. What was the return on Starbucks's investment to pursue Black Bear for trademark infringement? Even if Black Bear's defense was covered by insurance, did the investment of time by the Clarks yield a sufficient return?

3. Apply a strategy that you learned in Thinking Strategically in Chapter 1. What strategy would be helpful in preventing or resolving this dispute?

Chapter 2, "Business, Societal, and Ethical Contexts of Law"

1. Consider Starbucks's litigation strategy. When it used legal maneuvering to attempt to get Zurich to withdraw, was that ethical? Was it a legitimate,

hard-nosed business practice, or did Starbucks use its resources in an attempt to force Black Bear into settlement?

2. Starbucks invests substantial resources in its theme of being a responsible company. On its website, the company announces, "We've always believed that businesses can—and should—have a positive impact on the communities they serve." How does that statement square with its strategy in the Charbucks litigation? Is there any ethical conflict between a company's stated objective to be a good corporate neighbor and its obligation to its stakeholders to protect its intellectual property?

3. Even if Black Bear was legally entitled to use the name "Charbucks," is it ethical to use a name that sounds so close to someone else's famous coffee trademark?

Chapter 50, "Intellectual Property"

1. The TDRA defines blurring as an "association arising from the similarity between a mark and a famous mark that impairs the distinctiveness of the famous mark." How should the trial court rule on the issue of dilution by blurring given the new language in the TDRA?

2. Should the court have given more weight to the testimony of Starbucks's expert? Although the survey was conducted by telephone, shouldn't consumer confusion in the similar sounds (*Charbucks* versus *Starbucks*) be sufficient to show blurring?

3. What legal issues must a famous-mark holder consider in preserving its trademark?

ASSIGNMENT: Find Black Bear a Trademark

Think of several names and a mark that Black Bear could have used for dark-roasted coffee beans instead of Charbucks. You can conduct a preliminary search on the USPTO's website (www.uspto.gov) and on a commercial domain name website such as www.register.com to see if the name or mark is available. Use your knowledge of dilution law to be sure that your trademark is viable and protectable.

Capstone Case Study 2
THE ODWALLA JUICE COMPANY CRISIS

OVERVIEW AND OBJECTIVES

In 1996, a deadly strain of bacteria broke out among residents of some West Coast states and eventually spread into western Canada. When the bacteria was traced to juice products made by the Odwalla Juice Company in California, the company's loyal customers and market analysts were in disbelief. Odwalla had prided itself on being a socially responsible company that was passionate about producing the healthiest juice on the market.

The events that followed the outbreak provide an example of how vastly different areas of the law impact corporate strategy during a corporate crisis and how business ethics principles help drive the decision-making process. The objective of this case study[1] is to attempt to understand legal and ethical implications using a comprehensive and practical approach. In analyzing this case, students hone skills in constructing a business strategy for handling a crisis by (1) spotting the multifaceted legal and ethical challenges of the crisis, (2) recognizing the strengths and weaknesses in Odwalla's responses, and (3) using legal insight and ethical decision-making models to craft a response.

Review Legal Concepts

Prior to reading the case, briefly review the following legal concepts that were covered previously in this textbook: food and drug safety (Chapter 44), product liability (Chapter 42), negligence (Chapter 42), criminal law (Chapter 45), and business ethics (Chapter 2). Think of these areas of the law as you read the case study facts and questions.

THE ODWALLA JUICE COMPANY'S ORIGINS

Odwalla Juice Company was started in 1986 by a group of health-conscious friends living together in the San Francisco Bay area. Starting with a hand juicer and organically grown fruit, the owners produced fresh juice in the back shed of one of the founders' homes and sold their juice by delivering it daily to area restaurants. Perhaps the most essential part of their business model was their claim that their juice was fresh

---

from the fruit, without the pasteurization process that was used by other juice producers. In fact, Odwalla was one of the pioneers of a wider movement in the United States favoring more organic food consumption. Odwalla's founders believed that pasteurization—the process of heating the juice to a certain temperature for purposes of killing any bacteria that had developed during growing, picking, or processing—affected the taste of the juice and was unnecessary. Instead, Odwalla used an acid-based rinsing process to kill bacteria. Producing fresh organic fruit juice as a central component of its business model, Odwalla developed a loyal following of consumers who desired the freshest juice possible, and its sales grew exponentially. By the mid-1990s, Odwalla was selling nearly $90 million worth of juice per year.

"SOIL TO SOUL"

Odwalla's founders were at the forefront of the corporate social responsibility movement that can be traced to the mid-1980s. Indeed, as one of the founders was fond of saying, they embraced a "Zen-like philosophy" in all of their dealings, and community was an important factor in the equation. The company employed a *soil to soul* metaphor to describe its commitment to using fresh organic fruit (soil) to nurture the "body whole" (soul) of its consumers. Odwalla's reputation as a socially responsible, growth-oriented company flourished as it received awards from *Business Ethics* magazine in 1995 for Outstanding Corporate Environmentalism and from *Inc.* magazine in 1996 as Employer of the Year.

CRISIS ON THE COAST

In early October 1996, an outbreak of *E. coli*[2] struck several West Coast states, including California and Washington, and reached into western Canada as well. *E. coli* is a potentially deadly bacterium that develops as a result of contamination of food products or processing. On October 30, 1996, health officials in the state of Washington notified Odwalla that they were investigating a

---

[1]A complete bibliography for this case study may be found in Connect.

[2]For purposes of this case study, *E. coli* is shorthand for *E. coli 0157:H7,* which is the name of a strain of bacteria that lives in the digestive tracts of humans and animals. *E. coli* has been found in uncooked meat, raw milk or dairy products, and raw fruits and vegetables that have not been properly pasteurized or processed.

The Odwalla juice company faced a corporate crisis, which included legal issues and ethical questions, after its product was tied to an *E. coli* outbreak.
©Michael Neelon/Alamy

possible link between the *E. coli* outbreak and Odwalla apple and carrot juice. After learning of the potential link, Odwalla's executive management team had an emergency meeting to discuss their response. Although there was no demonstrable link at this point, Odwalla's executive management team decided to mobilize a voluntary recall of products containing apple or carrot products. This was a major financial commitment involving the removal of Odwalla products from nearly 4,600 retail outlets in seven states in just 48 hours. Odwalla claimed that it spent $6.5 million on the recall effort.

Odwalla's corporate crisis took a tragic turn when, in November 1996, a 16-month-old child died from *E. coli* after drinking Odwalla apple juice. As many as 60 other consumers were hospitalized with *E. coli*–related illnesses in a period of just one month. At the height of the outbreak, government investigators confirmed that

Odwalla products were in fact the source of the *E. coli* contamination. Odwalla implemented a media strategy that included issuing daily statements to the press, holding internal conference calls whereby managers were informed of updates, and setting up a website to disseminate information. Odwalla publicly promised to pay for all medical expenses of injured consumers and to reevaluate its manufacturing process immediately.

FALLOUT

Odwalla's brand name was decimated by the crisis. Immediately after the outbreak, Odwalla's stock price dropped 34 percent, and sales of its juice products fell 90 percent in one month. The outbreak triggered numerous investigations by federal and state authorities. Customers filed negligence lawsuits, claiming that Odwalla had known that the acid-rinse method was ineffective and that scientific studies had shown that the method was effective in killing bacteria that caused *E. coli* only 8 percent of the time. After it had been shown that pasteurization was a widely used practice in the industry (although not required by federal or state laws) and that Odwalla management had ignored its own head of quality assurance's warning about potential contamination sources in the factory, the Food and Drug Administration levied a $1.5 million fine, the largest in the agency's history at that time.

Immediately after the recall, Odwalla was widely praised by the media and commentators for its handling of the crisis. The company decided that, despite mounting financial pressures from lawsuits and fines, no employees would be laid off and that it would continue to donate to community charities. Odwalla hired a public relations firm that constructed a standard explanation that the contamination was unforeseeable and that all appropriate safety measures were in place. The public largely believed Odwalla's explanations because its reputation for social responsibility was ironclad in its consumers' minds. Even the parents of the child whose *E. coli*–related death had ignited the crisis were quoted as saying that they didn't blame the company for her death and that Odwalla had done everything it could have under the circumstances.

However, during the discovery process in one of the lawsuits filed by an injured consumer, it was revealed that Odwalla had more knowledge of a potential health hazard prior to the outbreak than had been previously reported. A report surfaced that indicated that the U.S. Army had rejected Odwalla's proposal to sell its juice in U.S. Army commissaries after an army inspector found uncommonly high levels of bacteria in a sample and concluded that the risk of contamination was extraordinarily high. The army rejection had taken place four months prior to the *E. coli* outbreak. Responding to the army's findings, Odwalla's head of quality assurance recommended that the company add an additional layer of contamination protection by employing a chlorine-based washing system for the fruit. His recommendations were rejected, however, due to management's concern that the chlorine wash would affect the taste of the juice. After the army disclosures were made public, Odwalla settled several lawsuits despite its earlier resistance to a nonlitigation solution.

Soon after the settlement, *The Seattle Times* wrote a scathing editorial about Odwalla's course of action. The editorial predicted that Odwalla would forever be known as "the careless provider of poisoned fruit juice." Odwalla's stock was now trading at its lowest level ever, and the company was incurring massive debt to cover litigation costs and technology upgrades.

ODWALLA TODAY

After the fallout from the *E. coli* crisis, Odwalla invested heavily in quality assurance technology and eventually became an innovator of a "flash-pasteurization" process that killed all bacteria but kept the fresh taste and quality of the juice intact. Just two years after the crisis began, the readers of *San Francisco Magazine* voted Odwalla "Best Brand." Although the company looked poised for a comeback, it had accrued substantial debt and was forced to begin exploring the possibility of merger opportunities. After a merger with East Coast juice maker Fresh Samantha in 2000, Odwalla ended up as part of a large acquisition by the Minute Maid division of the Coca-Cola Company in October 2001. Today, Odwalla remains a subsidiary of Coca-Cola and has over 650 employees. Its management continues to focus on its "soil to soul" model, and Odwalla now features 25 organic products within eight product lines, including smoothies, soy shakes, and food bars.

Connecting Legal and Ethical Concepts: Questions for Discussion

Chapter 2, "Business, Societal, and Ethical Contexts of Law"

1. Is there a disconnect between Odwalla's corporate social responsibility model and its actions or course of conduct? In what ways did Odwalla's course of conduct differ from its stated social goals?

2. Because Odwalla was not specifically required to use the pasteurization process at the time, what ethical considerations factor into the decision on whether or not to use pasteurization?

3. Does the fact that the industry standard at the time was to subject juice to pasteurization impact the ethical decision-making analysis?

Chapter 42, "Torts and Products Liability"

1. Did the manufacturing or *design process* of the juice render it an unreasonably dangerous product under the Restatements? Why or why not?

2. Are there any other ways in which the product could have been defective aside from manufacturing or design?

3. What defenses, if any, could Odwalla use to rebut a claim of a defective product?

Chapter 42, "Torts and Products Liability"

1. Are there any incidents of negligence indicated in the case (either before or after contamination)?

2. In the context of a negligence analysis, what legal duties did Odwalla owe to its consumers? Does it owe any special duty to consumers?

3. Does failing to comply with industry standards at the time of the contamination constitute a breach of duty?

Chapter 44, "Consumer Protection"

1. What federal statute regulates Odwalla's processes and procedures?

2. Because the FDA required no specific pasteurization standards at the time, should Odwalla be fined for failing to use such a system?

3. If Odwalla had not voluntarily recalled the juice, what options did the FDA have in response to the outbreak?

Chapter 45, "Criminal Law and Procedure"

1. Apply the Model Penal Code sections on criminal liability for business entities to the Odwalla case. Do the facts in the case indicate that Odwalla's actions rose to the level of criminal culpability? If yes, what defense, if any, is available to Odwalla?

2. Odwalla's managers consistently issued statements denying that they had any actual or constructive knowledge that Odwalla's processing systems were dangerous. Do any facts in the case study contradict those statements? Are these facts sufficient to establish the elements of criminal intent on the part of the executives who made the denials?

ASSIGNMENT: Devise Odwalla's Strategy

Odwalla ordered a voluntary recall that was expensive and potentially devastating to the company before an affirmative link was found. Assume you were one of the managers at the Odwalla emergency meeting held after the *E. coli* outbreak. What were Odwalla's options? Using what you have learned in Thinking Strategically in Chapter 1, "Legal Foundations and Thinking Strategically," and the ethical decision-making paradigm in Chapter 2, "Business, Societal, and Ethical Contexts of Law," as a starting point, devise a strategy that includes the appropriate balance between (1) representing the best interests of the primary and secondary stakeholders, (2) protecting the company's future, (3) minimizing the risk of public harm, and (4) fulfilling the corporation's commitment to corporate social responsibility.

Capstone Case Study 3
FRAUD UNDER THE ARCHES:
THE MCDONALD'S GAME PIECE SCANDAL

OVERVIEW AND OBJECTIVES

In August 2001, the Federal Bureau of Investigation arrested eight individuals involved in a nationwide scheme to defraud the McDonald's Corporation and its customers by fraudulently manipulating McDonald's promotional prize contests over a period of five years. Although no McDonald's employees were implicated in the scam, the arrests sparked class action litigation by customers and competitors against McDonald's under a variety of legal theories. The events that led up to the arrests and the legal and ethical implications of McDonald's response to the revelations of the fraud are examined in this case study.[1]

Review Legal Concepts

Prior to reading the case, briefly review the following legal concepts that were covered in the textbook: standing (Chapter 5), arbitration (Chapter 5), consumer fraud (Chapter 44), contracts agreement (Chapter 6), unjust enrichment (Chapter 6), agency (Chapter 37 and 38), criminal law (Chapter 45), and business ethics (Chapter 2). Think of these areas of the law as you read the case study facts and questions.

MCDONALD'S PROMOTIONAL GAMES

McDonald's is perhaps the most familiar fast-food restaurant in the world. The business began in 1940 with a restaurant opened by brothers Richard and Maurice McDonald in San Bernardino, California. Their introduction of the "Speedee Service System" in 1948 established the principles of the modern fast-food restaurant. The present company dates its founding to the opening of one of the first McDonald's franchises by Ray Kroc. Eventually, Mr. Kroc purchased the McDonald brothers' shares and began a worldwide expansion. The company was listed on the public stock market in 1965, and there are now more than 32,000 McDonald's restaurants around the world.

Marketing Strategies

One of McDonald's most successful marketing strategies has been to use various cash games of chance based

---

[1]A complete bibliography for this case study may be found in Connect.

on themes from popular television shows such as *Who Wants to Be a Millionaire?* and another promotional cash game based on the popular board game Monopoly. McDonald's operates these games as part of a consolidated national and international advertising and marketing effort. Industry experts have lauded McDonald's games as highly effective in attracting more customers and encouraging more visits by offering the opportunity to win instant prizes ranging from food to cash prizes of $1 million. Each of the promotional games has low-value, midvalue, and high-value prizes. In order to win a prize, a McDonald's customer obtains a game piece, which may be (1) received at a restaurant, either attached to food containers (such as french fry boxes and drink cups) or unattached and handed out separately, (2) found in an advertising insert of a newspaper, (3) received by direct mail, or (4) obtained by requesting a game piece via the mail. Customers have the opportunity to become instant winners or to win by collecting specific game pieces. Low-value prizes include food items and low-dollar cash prizes. High-value prizes include vehicles and cash prizes up to $1 million. Customers can either win the cash prize by obtaining an instant $1 million–winner game piece or by collecting a sufficient number of certain game pieces.

Simon Marketing

Simon Marketing, Inc., an international marketing company headquartered in Los Angeles, was originally hired by McDonald's to develop its highly successful Happy Meal prize and promotional campaigns in the 1980s. Simon eventually became the exclusive company handling McDonald's promotional games, including "Monopoly Game at McDonald's," "Hatch, Match and Win," "When the USA Wins, You Win," and "Who Wants to Be a Millionaire?" In order to claim a high-value prize, the winner was required to redeem the winning game piece through Simon's security procedures. After receiving a game piece claim, Simon would confirm the legitimacy of the game piece and notify McDonald's that the claim was legitimate. McDonald's then distributed the prize to the winner.

In addition to verifying winning game pieces, Simon was also responsible for the printing and distribution of game pieces. As part of its agreement with McDonald's,

The Department of Justice's announcement of arrests related to a fraud scheme involving game pieces from McDonald's Monopoly promotional game sparked legal and ethical challenges for the fast-food giant.

© Tim Boyle/Getty Images

Simon provided security measures to ensure the integrity of promotional games. Simon entrusted its security chief, retired police officer Jerome Jacobson, with the responsibility of ensuring the games' integrity and with disseminating the high-value pieces through legitimate channels.

Arrests and Indictments

In August 2001, the U.S. Attorney's Office filed criminal charges against eight people in Georgia, South Carolina, Florida, Texas, Indiana, and Wisconsin as part of a nationwide investigation into a plot to defraud the public by diverting winning game pieces from various McDonald's cash award giveaways. Dubbed "Operation Final Answer" by government investigators, the Department of Justice alleged that the group had been responsible for more than $20 million worth of winning game pieces that were diverted from proper delivery and then fraudulently claimed by winners

pretending to be legitimate. The ringleader of the plot was 58-year-old Jerome Jacobson, the director of security at Simon Marketing. Jacobson devised a way to remove high-price game pieces prior to their distribution to retail McDonald's restaurants. Jacobson concocted a system of recruiters (none of whom were Simon or McDonald's employees) who solicited others willing to falsely claim that they were legitimate winners of the McDonald's games. Prosecutors alleged that Jacobson sold $1 million prize pieces from the games and charged the fake winner $50,000 in cash plus a commission for the recruiter. On midvalue prizes and luxury vehicle prizes, the recruiters would sell the winning game pieces to other family members or friends. Among those arrested were a husband and wife whose son acted as one of Jacobson's recruiters.

After Jacobson agreed to cooperate with federal authorities in exchange for leniency, the government announced criminal indictments of 51 more individuals involved in the scam. Eventually, Jacobson pleaded guilty and was sentenced to 37 months in prison, assessed $750,000 in fines, and ordered to pay $13.4 million in restitution.

Civil Suits

Two weeks after the government announced the indictment, the first civil lawsuit was filed against McDonald's. By October 2001, so many civil suits had been filed against it that McDonald's asked the federal courts to consolidate all of the litigation into a single proceeding. Lawsuits alleged various claims, including violation of consumer fraud protection laws, unjust enrichment, and breach of contract. In many cases, the plaintiff sought class action[2] status.

In one case filed in an Illinois trial court, a customer sued McDonald's and Simon under the state consumer fraud statute and sought class action status. The plaintiffs alleged that McDonald's and Simon's actions constituted deceptive conduct and omissions of material terms from their promotional games. They pointed to evidence that McDonald's had been made aware of the fraud being conducted by Jacobson but had continued to market its promotional games, including publishing the odds of winning, for at least an additional eight months. However, because of Jacobson's scheme, the

---

[2]A class action lawsuit is a method for conducting a lawsuit in which a large group of persons with a well-defined common interest (class) has a representative of the group litigate the claim on behalf of the larger group, without the need to join every individual member of the class.

plaintiffs alleged that their actual odds of winning a substantial prize were zero.

Other cases centered on a theory of unjust enrichment. In these cases, plaintiffs alleged that McDonald's promotional games were highly successful and resulted in increased revenue for McDonald's and Simon. The plaintiffs pointed to evidence that McDonald's had a spike in sales during certain promotions. They alleged that McDonald's continued to use the promotion even after it knew that the integrity of the game was compromised and, therefore, any profits made were caused by the fraud. Because customers were induced to purchase McDonald's products through the promotion, McDonald's was unjustly enriched by retaining the profits from the products.

McDonald's was also sued by its competitors over the scandal. In *Phoenix of Broward, Inc. v. McDonald's Corporation*,[3] the owner of a Burger King franchise in Fort Lauderdale, Florida, filed suit against McDonald's for false advertising and unfair competition. The owner alleged that McDonald's had enticed customers away from Burger King by employing the promotional game. Because the promotional materials represented that each customer had a fair chance to win the high-value prizes, Phoenix alleged that McDonald's actual knowledge that the game was rigged and its course of conduct, after learning of the FBI investigation, in continuing the promotion constituted unfair competition. Phoenix also claimed that the fraudulent game promotion yielded an unnatural spike in profits for McDonald's and that the Burger King franchise suffered damages as a result of McDonald's conduct.

MCDONALD'S STRATEGY

On the day the Justice Department announced the arrest of Jacobson and seven others, McDonald's announced that it was suspending the game entirely pending an internal investigation of the matter. It also announced a campaign to regain any lost public trust by launching an immediate $10 million promotional giveaway. The promotion allowed customers to win prizes of up to $1 million from promotional game pieces during a weeklong period beginning in late August 2001.

Immediately after the arrests, McDonald's terminated its 25-year relationship with Simon by unilaterally canceling its contract with the agency. The move was devastating to Simon because McDonald's represented two-thirds of the agency's annual revenue.[4] After the

revelations of fraud, Simon's other major client, Philip Morris,[5] which contracted with Simon to run promotional campaigns for its Kraft and Marlboro brands, also terminated its relationship with Simon. In less than one week, the value of Simon's public shares plunged 78 percent, and the company was facing dozens of lawsuits and a criminal investigation.

Aggressive Litigation

McDonald's employed what can aptly be described as an aggressive litigation strategy by vigorously defending lawsuits while also pursuing Simon for reimbursement of the costs being incurred by McDonald's because of the fraudulent act of Simon's employee.

For each case that it defended that was related to the fraud, either McDonald's challenged the *standing* of the plaintiffs to bring an action against McDonald's based on the fraud or it sought a court order to compel *arbitration* based on the published rules of the game.

Phoenix Case

In the *Phoenix* case, McDonald's asserted that Phoenix did not have standing in a case alleging unfair competition because McDonald's actions were unrelated to any provable harm suffered by Phoenix's restaurant. Phoenix alleged that McDonald's misrepresented customers' chances to win high-value prizes but also alleged that as a result of this false advertising, the fraudulent promotion induced customers who would have eaten at Phoenix's Burger King restaurants (and not any other fast-food restaurants) to eat at McDonald's. Ultimately the courts agreed with McDonald's and dismissed the lawsuit, holding that Phoenix's allegations of the link between the false advertising (McDonald's games) and the injury suffered by Phoenix (decrease in Burger King's sales) was too vague to have standing to sue.

Customer Lawsuits

While McDonald's was successful at repelling suits by competitors, its attempts to halt lawsuits by its customers had mixed results. The stakes for customer lawsuits were becoming increasingly high as each plaintiff requested class action status. In each customer case, McDonald's argued that the plaintiff was bound by the terms of the Official Contest Rules published by McDonald's in conjunction with each of its promotional cash giveaway games. The rules included an arbitration clause whereby

---

[3]489 F.3d 1156 (11th Cir. 2007).

[4]In the year prior to the scandal, Simon's annual revenue was $768 million.

---

[5]Philip Morris changed its name to Altria in 2003.

participants in the game promotion agreed to resolve any disputes by final and binding arbitration. The clause called for the arbitration to be held at the regional office of the American Arbitration Association (AAA) located closest to the participant.

In *Popovich v. McDonald's*,[6] a federal district court ruled that the arbitration clause included in the official rules was invalid because the arbitration costs were too prohibitive. Popovich argued that the fees associated with an arbitration proceeding rendered the arbitration agreement an ineffective way to enforce his statutory rights of recovery from McDonald's for its fraudulent conduct. Popovich submitted evidence that, under the AAA rules, his claim would have to be arbitrated using the high-fee *commercial* procedures instead of the much lower-cost *consumer* procedures. In ruling in favor of Popovich, the court held that because Popovich sought $20 million in damages for his potential class action, the fees required by the AAA would be between $48,000 and $126,000. The court concluded that, in the context of this claim, the arbitration costs were prohibitive and the clause was thus unenforceable.

An alternate theory was advanced by the plaintiff in *James v. McDonald's Corp.*[7] In that case, James argued that she should not be forced to arbitrate her claims because she never entered into an agreement to arbitrate her dispute. The plaintiff claimed that she was not aware of the rules, much less any rules that deprived her of a jury trial. She maintained that customers cannot be expected to read every container of food they purchase in order to know that they are entering into a contract. She also argued that, even if she was found to be bound by the rules, the arbitration clause in the rules was invalid because it was overly burdensome due to the high up-front costs required to pursue a claim through the AAA. However, the court ultimately ruled against James, found the arbitration clause to be valid, and refused to allow her lawsuit to go forward in the courts. In rejecting James's claim that the costs were too burdensome, the court pointed out that James had not submitted evidence that she considered applying for a fee waiver from the AAA that could have reduced the fees significantly.

SIMON LAWSUIT AND COUNTERSUIT

Two months after McDonald's terminated its relationship with Simon, its parent company filed a $1.9 billion lawsuit against McDonald's in which the company alleged breach of contract, fraud, and defamation. Simon alleged that, after learning of the nearly yearlong FBI investigation, McDonald's ran a fraudulent campaign to intentionally destroy Simon for its own public relations and financial benefit. The lawsuit also accused McDonald's of orchestrating a smear campaign through McDonald's representatives' contacting other Simon clients and urging them to quit doing business with Simon. Simon alleged that McDonald's abrupt termination of their contract was unwarranted and unlawful and resulted in substantial losses.

McDonald's responded with a $105 million countersuit against Simon for negligence in failing to detect the fraud scheme and for breach of contract. McDonald's contended that its contract with Simon required Simon to repay McDonald's for any losses it incurred as a result of Simon's conduct. Given the losses from the embezzlement and the subsequent giveaway that was required to restore public confidence, McDonald's argued that it was entitled to be reimbursed by Simon.

SETTLEMENTS AND AFTERMATH

After aggressively battling litigants in the courtroom for a year, McDonald's reevaluated its two-front litigation strategy. The company engaged in settlement negotiations with customer lawsuit plaintiffs and was able to structure an agreement with Simon's insurance carrier that ultimately helped settle the class action claims filed against it by various customers. One year later, McDonald's agreed to a final settlement with Simon.

Customer Class Actions

The uncertainties surrounding the arbitration clause and expenses of litigating a class action case resulted in a change in McDonald's strategy. Beginning in April 2002, McDonald's and Simon began to settle the various class action complaints filed by consumers by tapping the proceeds from Simon's liability insurance policies. Eventually, McDonald's settled a similar class action consumer suit filed in Canada.

Simon Litigation

In an August 2003 filing with the Securities and Exchange Commission, McDonald's reported that it had agreed to pay Simon $16.6 million to settle all claims that were raised in the lawsuit.[8] However, in the meantime, Simon had effectively eliminated a majority of its ongoing

---

[6] 189 F. Supp. 2d 772 (2002).

[7] 417 F.3d 672 (7th Cir. 2005).

[8] Simon also sued Philip Morris and Simon Marketing's auditing firms (KPMG, PricewaterhouseCoopers, and Ernst & Young). Each case was settled before trial with a favorable outcome for Simon.

promotion business operations and was in the process of disposing of its assets and settling liabilities related to the fraud. During the second quarter of 2002, the company ceased operations altogether except for attempting to find a buyer for its remaining assets. A September 2009 filing indicated that the company had reduced its workforce to 4 employees (from 136 employees in 2001). Although the company was not successful in finding a buyer for many years, in December 2009, Simon's remaining directors issued public disclosures that they had formed a committee to investigate the potential of an acquisition or combination with another company.

Connecting Legal and Ethical Concepts: Questions for Discussion

Chapter 2, "Business, Societal, and Ethical Contexts of Law"

1. Consider the ethical dilemma of McDonald's if it was approached by government authorities and informed that the promotion's integrity was suspect because of possible embezzlement. However, in order to gather additional evidence, investigators requested that McDonald's take no action until arrests were made. What would be McDonald's ethical duty at this point? If it continued to run the game with knowledge of the fraud, no matter what its motives, wouldn't that expose the company to significant liability?

2. Is there a conflict in this case between McDonald's duties to primary stakeholders and its duties to secondary shareholders?

3. Was McDonald's decision not to discontinue the promotion in the face of ongoing fraud more of a principles-based approach or a consequences-based approach to ethical decision making?

4. Was the use of class action litigation ethically justified in this case? Were the civil suits an attempt to redress harm or a boon for law firms that specialize in class action litigation? Were the plaintiffs more interested in shaking down McDonald's or in justice?

Chapter 5, "Resolving Disputes: Litigation and Alternative Dispute Resolution"

1. In the *Phoenix* case, the court ruled that competitors didn't have standing to sue McDonald's for fraud in the promotional games. Would customers have standing? Explain.

2. Could the arbitration clause used by McDonald's in its rules fit into any of the four grounds for unenforceability under the Federal Arbitration Act?

Chapter 6, "Contracts: Overview, Definition, Categories, and Source of Law"

1. Why did trial courts consider the rules' contractual language binding on participants of the games when it was obvious that most customers hadn't actually read the rules? Had the customers agreed to the terms of the rules contract simply by purchasing a soft drink? Why or why not?

2. Assuming that offer and acceptance are satisfied, what consideration supports a customer-McDonald's contract?

3. Could the inclusion of an arbitration clause by McDonald's in an advertisement amid logos and trademarks be considered bad faith and held invalid as unconscionable?

Chapter 37, "Agency Formation, Categories, and Authority," and **Chapter 38**, "Duties and Liabilities of Principals and Agents"

1. What was the agency status and relationship between McDonald's and Simon? Based on your answer, what duties did the parties owe each other? Were any duties breached?

2. To what extent was Simon liable for the embezzlement scheme of its employee Jacobson? Were Jacobson's actions within the scope of his employment? Why or why not?

Chapter 44, "Consumer Protection"

1. Could McDonald's conduct, specifically its continuing operations after being informed of possible fraud in its promotional games, constitute deceptive advertising and a deceptive sales practice under FTC regulations? Explain.

2. Would your answer to Question 1 be the same if McDonald's halted the promotion as soon as it learned of the FBI investigation? Why or why not?

Chapter 45, "Criminal Law and Procedure"

1. Do Jacobson's actions amount to fraud? Embezzlement? Theft?

2. Ultimately, the government charged Jacobson and his co-conspirators with mail fraud and wire fraud. Why do you think the government did not charge them with embezzlement?

3. Could Simon's executives be held criminally liable for the embezzlement perpetrated by Jacobson? Why or why not?

ASSIGNMENT: Devise a Strategy for McDonald's

Assume you are one of the managers called to a confidential meeting to discuss McDonald's strategy after notification by government authorities that its promotional games were being rigged by a Simon insider. What are McDonald's options? Using what you have learned from Thinking Strategically in Chapter 1, "Legal Foundations and Thinking Strategically," and the ethical decision-making paradigm in Chapter 2, "Business, Societal, and Ethical Contexts of Law" as a starting point, devise a strategy that includes the appropriate balance between (1) representing the best interests of its primary and secondary stakeholders, (2) protecting the future of the company, (3) minimizing the risk of public harm, and (4) addressing factors related to corporate social responsibility. Memorialize your strategy in a two-page memorandum.

APPENDIX A

The Constitution of the United States of America

Preamble

We the People of the United States, in Order to form a more perfect Union, establish Justice, insure domestic Tranquility, provide for the common defence, promote the general Welfare, and secure the Blessings of Liberty to ourselves and our Posterity, do ordain and establish this Constitution for the United States of America.

Article I

Section 1 All legislative Powers herein granted shall be vested in a Congress of the United States, which shall consist of a Senate and House of Representatives.

Section 2 The House of Representatives shall be composed of Members chosen every second Year by the People of the several States, and the Electors in each State shall have the Qualifications requisite for Electors of the most numerous Branch of the State Legislature.

No Person shall be a Representative who shall not have attained to the age of twenty five Years, and been seven Years a Citizen of the United States, and who shall not, when elected, be an Inhabitant of that State in which he shall be chosen.

Representatives and direct Taxes shall be apportioned among the several States which may be included within this Union, according to their respective Numbers, which shall be determined by adding to the whole Number of free Persons, including those bound to Service for a Term of Years, and excluding Indians not taxed, three fifths of all other Persons.[1] The actual Enumeration shall be made within three Years after the first Meeting of the Congress of the United States, and within every subsequent Term of ten Years, in such Manner as they shall by Law direct. The Number of Representatives shall not exceed one for every thirty Thousand, but each State shall have at Least one Representative, and until such enumeration shall be made, the State of New Hampshire shall be entitled to chuse three, Massachusetts eight, Rhode-Island and Providence Plantations one, Connecticut five, New York six, New Jersey four, Pennsylvania eight, Delaware one, Maryland six, Virginia ten, North Carolina five, South Carolina five, and Georgia three.

When vacancies happen in the Representation from any State, the Executive Authority thereof shall issue Writs of Election to fill such Vacancies.

The House of Representatives shall chuse their Speaker and other Officers; and shall have the sole Power of Impeachment.

Section 3 The Senate of the United States shall be composed of two Senators from each State, chosen by the Legislature thereof,[2] for six Years; and each Senator shall have one Vote.

Immediately after they shall be assembled in Consequence of the first Election, they shall be divided as equally as may be into three Classes. The Seats of the Senators of the first Class shall be vacated at the Expiration of the second Year, of the second Class at the Expiration of the fourth Year, and of the third Class at the Expiration of the sixth Year, so that one third may be chosen every second Year; and if Vacancies happen by Resignation, or otherwise, during the Recess of the Legislature of any State, the Executive thereof may make temporary Appointments until the next Meeting of the Legislature, which shall then fill such Vacancies.[3]

---

[1]Changed by the Fourteenth Amendment.

[2]Changed by the Seventeenth Amendment.
[3]Changed by the Seventeenth Amendment.

No Person shall be a Senator who shall not have attained to the Age of thirty Years, and been nine Years a Citizen of the United States, and who shall not, when elected, be an Inhabitant of that State for which he shall be chosen.

The Vice President of the United States shall be President of the Senate, but shall have no Vote, unless they be equally divided.

The Senate shall chuse their other Officers, and also a President pro tempore, in the Absence of the Vice President, or when he shall exercise the Office of President of the United States.

The Senate shall have the sole Power to try all Impeachments. When sitting for that Purpose, they shall be on Oath or Affirmation. When the President of the United States is tried, the Chief Justice shall preside: And no Person shall be convicted without the Concurrence of two thirds of the Members present.

Judgment in Cases of Impeachment shall not extend further than to removal from Office, and disqualification to hold and enjoy any Office of honor, Trust or Profit under the United States: but the Party convicted shall nevertheless be liable and subject to Indictment, Trial, Judgment and Punishment, according to Law.

Section 4 The Times, Places and Manner of holding Elections for Senators and Representatives, shall be prescribed in each State by the Legislature thereof; but the Congress may at any time by Law make or alter such Regulations, except as to the Places of chusing Senators.

The Congress shall assemble at least once in every Year, and such Meeting shall be on the first Monday in December, unless they shall by Law appoint a different Day.[4]

Section 5 Each House shall be the Judge of the Elections, Returns and Qualifications of its own Members, and a Majority of each shall constitute a Quorum to do Business; but a smaller Number may adjourn from day to day, and may be authorized to compel the Attendance of absent Members, in such Manner, and under such Penalties as each House may provide.

Each House may determine the Rules of its Proceedings, punish its Members for disorderly Behaviour, and with the Concurrence of two thirds, expel a Member.

Each House shall keep a Journal of its Proceedings, and from time to time publish the same, excepting such Parts as may in their Judgment require Secrecy; and the Yeas and Nays of the Members of either House on any question shall, at the Desire of one fifth of those Present, be entered on the Journal.

Neither House, during the Session of Congress, shall, without the Consent of the other, adjourn for more than three days, nor to any other Place than that in which the two Houses shall be sitting.

Section 6 The Senators and Representatives shall receive a Compensation for their Services, to be ascertained by Law, and paid out of the Treasury of the United States. They shall in all Cases, except Treason, Felony and Breach of the Peace, be privileged from Arrest during their Attendance at the Session of their respective Houses, and in going to and returning from the same; and for any Speech or Debate in either House, they shall not be questioned in any other Place.

No Senator or Representative shall, during the Time for which he was elected, be appointed to any civil Office under the Authority of the United States, which shall have been created, or the Emoluments whereof shall have been encreased during such time; and no Person holding any Office under the United States, shall be a Member of either House during his Continuance in Office.

Section 7 All Bills for raising Revenue shall originate in the House of Representatives; but the Senate may propose or concur with Amendments as on other Bills.

Every Bill which shall have passed the House of Representatives and the Senate, shall, before it becomes a Law, be presented to the President of the United States; If he approve he shall sign it, but if not he shall return it, with his Objections to that House in which it shall have originated, who shall enter the Objections at large on their Journal, and proceed to reconsider it. If after such Reconsideration two thirds of that House shall agree to pass the Bill, it shall be sent, together with the Objections, to the other House, by which it shall likewise be reconsidered, and if approved by two thirds of that House, it shall become a Law. But in all such Cases the Votes of both Houses shall be determined by Yeas and Nays, and the Names of the Persons voting for and against the Bill shall be entered on the Journal of each House respectively. If any Bill shall not be returned by the President within ten Days (Sundays excepted) after it shall have been presented to him, the Same shall be a Law, in like Manner as if he had signed it, unless the Congress by their Adjournment prevent its Return, in which Case it shall not be a Law.

Every Order, Resolution, or Vote to which the Concurrence of the Senate and House of Representatives may be necessary (except on a question of Adjournment) shall be presented to the President of the United States; and before the Same shall take Effect, shall be approved by him, or being disapproved by him, shall be repassed by two thirds of the Senate and House of Representatives, according to the Rules and Limitations prescribed in the Case of a Bill.

---

[4]Changed by the Twentieth Amendment.

Section 8 The Congress shall have Power To lay and collect Taxes, Duties, Imposts and Excises, to pay the Debts and provide for the common Defence and general Welfare of the United States; but all Duties, Imposts and Excises shall be uniform throughout the United States.

To borrow Money on the credit of the United States;

To regulate Commerce with foreign Nations, and among the several States, and with the Indian Tribes;

To establish an uniform Rule of Naturalization, and uniform Laws on the subject of Bankruptcies throughout the United States;

To coin Money, regulate the Value thereof, and of foreign Coin, and fix the Standard of Weights and Measures;

To provide for the Punishment of counterfeiting the Securities and current Coin of the United States;

To establish Post Offices and post Roads;

To promote the Progress of Science and useful Arts, by securing for limited Times to Authors and Inventors the exclusive Right to their respective Writings and Discoveries;

To constitute Tribunals inferior to the supreme Court;

To define and punish Piracies and Felonies committed on the high Seas, and Offences against the Law of Nations;

To declare War, grant Letters of Marque and Reprisal, and make Rules concerning Captures on Land and Water;

To raise and support Armies, but no Appropriation of Money to that Use shall be for a longer Term than two Years;

To provide and maintain a Navy;

To make Rules for the Government and Regulation of the land and naval Forces;

To provide for calling forth the Militia to execute the Laws of the Union, suppress Insurrections and repel Invasions;

To provide for organizing, arming, and disciplining, the Militia, and for governing such Part of them as may be employed in the Service of the United States, reserving to the States respectively, the Appointment of the Officers, and the Authority of training the Militia according to the discipline prescribed by Congress;

To exercise exclusive Legislation in all Cases whatsoever, over such District (not exceeding ten Miles square) as may, by Cession of particular States, and the Acceptance of Congress, become the Seat of the Government of the United States, and to exercise like Authority over all Places purchased by the Consent of the Legislature of the State in which the Same shall be, for the Erection of Forts, Magazines, Arsenals, dock-Yards, and other needful Buildings;—And

To make all Laws which shall be necessary and proper for carrying into Execution the foregoing Powers, and all other Powers vested by this Constitution in the Government of the United States, or in any Department or Officer thereof.

Section 9 The Migration or Importation of such Persons as any of the States now existing shall think proper to admit, shall not be prohibited by the Congress prior to the Year one thousand eight hundred and eight, but a Tax or duty may be imposed on such Importation, not exceeding ten dollars for each Person.

The Privilege of the Writ of Habeas Corpus shall not be suspended, unless when in Cases of Rebellion or Invasion the public Safety may require it.

No Bill of Attainder or ex post facto Law shall be passed.

No Capitation, or other direct, Tax shall be laid, unless in Proportion to the Census or Enumeration herein before directed to be taken.[5]

No Tax or Duty shall be laid on Articles exported from any State.

No Preference shall be given by any Regulation of Commerce or Revenue to the Ports of one State over those of another: nor shall Vessels bound to, or from, one State, be obliged to enter, clear, or pay Duties in another.

No Money shall be drawn from the Treasury, but in Consequence of Appropriations made by Law; and a regular Statement and Account of the Receipts and Expenditures of all public Money shall be published from time to time.

No Title of Nobility shall be granted by the United States: And no Person holding any Office of Profit or Trust under them, shall, without the Consent of the Congress, accept of any present, Emolument, Office, or Title, of any kind whatever, from any King, Prince, or foreign State.

Section 10 No State shall enter into any Treaty, Alliance, or Confederation; grant Letters of Marque and Reprisal; coin Money; emit Bills of Credit; make any Thing but gold and silver Coin a Tender in Payment of Debts; pass any Bill of Attainder, ex post facto Law, or Law impairing the Obligation of Contracts, or grant any Title of Nobility.

No State shall, without the Consent of the Congress, lay any Imposts or Duties on Imports or Exports, except what may be absolutely necessary for executing its inspection Laws: and the net Produce of all Duties and Imposts, laid by any State on Imports or Exports, shall

---

[5]Changed by the Sixteenth Amendment.

be for the Use of the Treasury of the United States; and all such Laws shall be subject to the Revision and Controul of the Congress.

No State shall, without the consent of Congress, lay any Duty of Tonnage, keep Troops, or Ships of War in time of Peace, enter into any Agreement or Compact with another State, or with a foreign Power, or engage in War, unless actually invaded, or in such imminent Danger as will not admit of delay.

Article II

Section 1 The executive Power shall be vested in a President of the United States of America. He shall hold his Office during the Term of four Years, and, together with the Vice President, chosen for the same Term, be elected, as follows:

Each state shall appoint, in such Manner as the Legislature thereof may direct, a Number of Electors, equal to the whole Number of Senators and Representatives to which the State may be entitled in Congress: but no Senator or Representative, or Person holding an Office of Trust or Profit under the United States, shall be appointed an Elector.

The Electors shall meet in their respective States, and vote by Ballot for two Persons, of whom one at least shall not be an Inhabitant of the same State with themselves. And they shall make a List of all the Persons voted for, and of the Number of Votes for each; which List they shall sign and certify, and transmit sealed to the Seat of the Government of the United States, directed to the President of the Senate. The President of the Senate shall, in the Presence of the Senate and House of Representatives, open all the Certificates, and the Votes shall then be counted. The Person having the greatest Number of Votes shall be the President, if such Number be a Majority of the whole Number of Electors appointed; and if there be more than one who have such Majority, and have an equal Number of Votes, then the House of Representatives shall immediately chuse by Ballot one of them for President; and if no Person have a Majority, then from the five highest on the List the said House shall in like Manner chuse the President. But in chusing the President, the Votes shall be taken by States, the Representation from each State having one Vote; A quorum for this purpose shall consist of a Member or Members from two thirds of the States, and a Majority of all the States shall be necessary to a Choice. In every Case, after the Choice of the President, the Person having the greatest Number of Votes of the Electors shall be the Vice President. But if there should remain two or more who have equal Votes, the Senate shall chuse from them by Ballot the Vice President.[6]

The Congress may determine the Time of chusing the Electors, and the Day on which they shall give their Votes; which Day shall be the same throughout the United States.

No Person except a natural born Citizen, or a Citizen of the United States, at the time of the Adoption of this Constitution, shall be eligible to the Office of President; neither shall any person be eligible to that Office who shall not have attained to the Age of thirty five Years, and been fourteen Years a Resident within the United States.

In Case of the Removal of the President from Office, or of his Death, Resignation, or Inability to discharge the Powers and Duties of the said Office, the Same shall devolve on the Vice President, and the Congress may by Law provide for the Case of Removal, Death, Resignation or Inability, both of the President and Vice President, declaring what Officer shall then act as President, and such Officer shall act accordingly, until the Disability be removed, or a President shall be elected.[7]

The President shall, at stated Times, receive for his Services, a Compensation, which shall neither be increased nor diminished during the Period for which he shall have been elected, and he shall not receive within that Period any other Emolument from the United States, or any of them.

Before he enter on the Execution of his Office, he shall take the following Oath or Affirmation:—"I do solemnly swear (or affirm) that I will faithfully execute the Office of President of the United States, and will to the best of my Ability, preserve, protect, and defend the Constitution of the United States."

Section 2 The President shall be Commander in Chief of the Army and Navy of the United States, and of the Militia of the several States, when called into the actual Service of the United States; he may require the Opinion, in writing, of the principal Officer in each of the executive Departments, upon any Subject relating to the Duties of their respective Offices, and he shall have Power to grant Reprieves and Pardons for Offences against the United States, except in Cases of Impeachment.

He shall have Power, by and with the Advice and Consent of the Senate, to make Treaties, provided two thirds of the Senators present concur; and he shall nominate, and by and with the Advice and Consent of the Senate, shall appoint Ambassadors, other public

---

[6]Changed by the Twelfth Amendment.
[7]Changed by the Twenty-Fifth Amendment.

Ministers and Consuls, Judges of the supreme Court, and all other Officers of the United States, whose Appointments are not herein otherwise provided for, and which shall be established by Law; but the Congress may by Law vest the Appointment of such inferior Officers, as they think proper, in the President alone, in the Courts of Law, or in the Heads of Departments.

The President shall have Power to fill up all Vacancies that may happen during the Recess of the Senate, by granting Commissions which shall expire at the End of their next Session.

Section 3 He shall from time to time give to the Congress Information of the State of the Union, and recommend to their Consideration such Measures as he shall judge necessary and expedient; he may, on extraordinary Occasions, convene both Houses, or either of them, and in Case of Disagreement between them, with Respect to the Time of Adjournment, he may adjourn them to such Time as he shall think proper; he shall receive Ambassadors and other public Ministers; he shall take Care that the Laws be faithfully executed, and shall Commission all the Officers of the United States.

Section 4 The President, Vice President and all civil Officers of the United States, shall be removed from Office on Impeachment for, and Conviction of, Treason, Bribery, or other high Crimes and Misdemeanors.

Article III

Section 1 The judicial Power of the United States, shall be vested in one supreme Court, and in such inferior Courts as the Congress may from time to time ordain and establish. The Judges, both of the supreme and inferior Courts, shall hold their Offices during good Behaviour, and shall, at stated Times, receive for their Services, a Compensation, which shall not be diminished during their Continuance in Office.

Section 2 The judicial Power shall extend to all Cases, in Law and Equity, arising under this Constitution, the Laws of the United States, and Treaties made, or which shall be made, under their Authority;—to all Cases affecting Ambassadors, other public Ministers and Consuls;—to all Cases of admiralty and maritime Jurisdiction;—to Controversies to which the United States shall be a Party;—to Controversies between two or more States;—between a State and Citizens of another State;[8] —between Citizens of different States;—between Citizens of the same State claiming Lands under Grants of different States, and between a State, or the Citizens thereof, and foreign States, Citizens or Subjects.

In all Cases affecting Ambassadors, other public Ministers and Consuls, and those in which a State shall be Party, the supreme Court shall have original Jurisdiction. In all the other Cases before mentioned, the supreme Court shall have appellate Jurisdiction, both as to Law and Fact, with such Exceptions, and under such Regulations as the Congress shall make.

The Trial of all Crimes, except in Cases of Impeachment, shall be by Jury; and such Trial shall be held in the State where the said Crimes shall have been committed; but when not committed within any State, the Trial shall be at such Place or Places as the Congress may by Law have directed.

Section 3 Treason against the United States, shall consist only in levying War against them, or in adhering to their Enemies, giving them Aid and Comfort. No Person shall be convicted of Treason unless on the Testimony of two Witnesses to the same overt Act, or on Confession in open Court.

The Congress shall have Power to declare the Punishment of Treason, but no Attainder of Treason shall work Corruption of Blood, or Forfeiture except during the Life of the Person attainted.

Article IV

Section 1 Full Faith and Credit shall be given in each State to the public Acts, Records, and judicial Proceedings of every other State. And the Congress may by general Laws prescribe the Manner in which such Acts, Records and Proceedings shall be proved, and the Effect thereof.

Section 2 The Citizens of each State shall be entitled to all Privileges and Immunities of Citizens in the several States.

A Person charged in any State with Treason, Felony, or other Crime, who shall flee from Justice, and be found in another State, shall on Demand of the executive Authority of the State from which he fled, be delivered up, to be removed to the State having Jurisdiction of the Crime.

No Person held to Service or Labour in one State, under the Laws thereof, escaping into another, shall, in Consequence of any Law or Regulation therein, be discharged from such Service or Labour, but shall be delivered up on Claim of the Party to whom such Service or Labour may be due.[9]

Section 3 New States may be admitted by the Congress into this Union; but no new State shall be formed or erected within the Jurisdiction of any other

---

[8]Changed by the Eleventh Amendment.

[9]Changed by the Thirteenth Amendment.

State; nor any State be formed by the Junction of two or more States, or Parts of States, without the Consent of the Legislatures of the States concerned as well as of the Congress.

The Congress shall have Power to dispose of and make all needful Rules and Regulations respecting the Territory or other Property belonging to the United States; and nothing in this Constitution shall be so construed as to Prejudice any Claims of the United States, or of any particular State.

Section 4 The United States shall guarantee to every State in this Union a Republican Form of Government, and shall protect each of them against Invasion; and on Application of the Legislature, or of the Executive (when the Legislature cannot be convened) against domestic Violence.

Article V

The Congress, whenever two thirds of both Houses shall deem it necessary, shall propose Amendments to this Constitution, or, on the Application of the Legislatures of two thirds of the several States, shall call a Convention for proposing Amendments, which, in either Case, shall be valid to all Intents and Purposes, as Part of this Constitution, when ratified by the legislatures of three fourths of the several States, or by Conventions in three fourths thereof, as the one or the other Mode of Ratification may be proposed by the Congress; Provided that no Amendment which may be made prior to the Year One thousand eight hundred and eight shall in any Manner affect the first and fourth Clauses in the Ninth Section of the first Article; and that no State, without its Consent, shall be deprived of its equal Suffrage in the Senate.

Article VI

All Debts contracted and Engagements entered into, before the Adoption of this Constitution, shall be as valid against the United States under this Constitution, as under the Confederation.

This Constitution, and the Laws of the United States which shall be made in Pursuance thereof; and all Treaties made, or which shall be made, under the Authority of the United States, shall be the supreme Law of the Land; and the Judges in every State shall be bound thereby, any Thing in the Constitution or Laws of any State to the Contrary notwithstanding.

The Senators and Representatives before mentioned, and the Members of the several State Legislatures, and all executive and judicial Officers, both of the United States and of the several States, shall be bound by Oath or Affirmation, to support this Constitution; but no religious Test shall ever be required as a Qualification to any Office or public Trust under the United States.

Article VII

The Ratification of the Conventions of nine States, shall be sufficient for the Establishment of this Constitution between the States so ratifying the Same.

Done in Convention by the Unanimous Consent of the States present the Seventeenth Day of September in the Year of our Lord one thousand seven hundred and eighty seven and of the Independence of the United States of America the Twelfth. In witness whereof We have hereunto subscribed our Names.

Amendments

[The first 10 amendments are known as the "Bill of Rights."]

Amendment 1 (Ratified 1791)

Congress shall make no law respecting an establishment of religion, or prohibiting the free exercise thereof; or abridging the freedom of speech, or of the press; or the right of the people peaceably to assemble, and to petition the Government for a redress of grievances.

Amendment 2 (Ratified 1791)

A well regulated Militia, being necessary to the security of a free State, the right of the people to keep and bear Arms, shall not be infringed.

Amendment 3 (Ratified 1791)

No Soldier shall, in time of peace be quartered in any house, without the consent of the Owner, nor in time of war, but in a manner to be prescribed by law.

Amendment 4 (Ratified 1791)

The right of the people to be secure in their persons, houses, papers, and effects, against unreasonable searches and seizures, shall not be violated, and no Warrants shall issue, but upon probable cause, supported by Oath or affirmation, and particularly describing the place to be searched, and the persons or things to be seized.

Amendment 5 (Ratified 1791)

No person shall be held to answer for a capital, or otherwise infamous crime, unless on a presentment or indictment of a Grand Jury, except in cases arising in the land or naval forces, or in the Militia, when in actual service in time of War or public danger; nor shall any person be subject for the same offence to be twice put in jeopardy of life or limb; nor shall be compelled in any criminal case to be a witness against himself, nor be deprived of life, liberty, or property, without due process of law; nor shall private property be taken for public use, without just compensation.

Amendment 6 (Ratified 1791)

In all criminal prosecutions, the accused shall enjoy the right to a speedy and public trial, by an impartial jury of the State and district wherein the crime shall have been committed, which district shall have been previously ascertained by law, and to be informed of the nature and cause of the accusation; to be confronted with the witnesses against him; to have compulsory process for obtaining witnesses in his favor, and to have Assistance of Counsel for his defence.

Amendment 7 (Ratified 1791)

In Suits at common law, where the value in controversy shall exceed twenty dollars, the right of trial by jury shall be preserved, and no fact tried by a jury, shall be otherwise re-examined in any Court of the United States, than according to the rules of the common law.

Amendment 8 (Ratified 1791)

Excessive bail shall not be required, nor excessive fines imposed, nor cruel and unusual punishments inflicted.

Amendment 9 (Ratified 1791)

The enumeration in the Constitution, of certain rights, shall not be construed to deny or disparage others retained by the people.

Amendment 10 (Ratified 1791)

The powers not delegated to the United States by the Constitution, nor prohibited by it to the States, are reserved to the States respectively, or to the people.

Amendment 11 (Ratified 1795)

The Judicial power of the United States shall not be construed to extend to any suit in law or equity, commenced or prosecuted against one of the United States by Citizens of another State, or by Citizens or Subjects of any Foreign State.

Amendment 12 (Ratified 1804)

The Electors shall meet in their respective states, and vote by ballot for President and Vice-President, one of whom, at least, shall not be an inhabitant of the same state with themselves; they shall name in their ballots the person voted for as President, and in distinct ballots the person voted for as Vice-President, and they shall make distinct lists of all persons voted for as President, and of all persons voted for as Vice-President, and of the number of votes for each, which lists they shall sign and certify, and transmit sealed to the seat of the government of the United States, directed to the President of the Senate;—The President of the Senate shall, in the presence of the Senate and House of Representatives, open all the certificates and the votes shall then be counted;—The person having the greatest number of votes for President, shall be the President, if such number be a majority of the whole number of Electors appointed; and if no person have such majority, then from the persons having the highest numbers not exceeding three on the list of those voted for as President, the House of Representatives shall choose immediately, by ballot, the President. But in choosing the President, the votes shall be taken by states, the representation from each state having one vote; a quorum for this purpose shall consist of a member or members from two-thirds of the states, and a majority of all the states shall be necessary to a choice. And if the House of Representatives shall not choose a President whenever the right of choice shall devolve upon them, before the fourth day of March next following, then the Vice-President shall act as president, as in the case of the death or other constitutional disability of the President.[10] —The person having the greatest number of votes as Vice-President, shall be the Vice-President, if such number be a majority of the whole number of Electors appointed, and if no person have a majority, then from the two highest numbers on the list, the Senate shall choose the Vice-President; a quorum for the purpose shall consist of two-thirds of the whole number of Senators, and a majority of the whole number shall be necessary to a choice. But no person constitutionally ineligible to the office of President shall be eligible to that of Vice-President of the United States.

Amendment 13 (Ratified 1865)

Section 1 Neither slavery nor involuntary servitude, except as a punishment for crime whereof the party shall have been duly convicted, shall exist within the United States, or any place subject to their jurisdiction.

Section 2 Congress shall have power to enforce this article by appropriate legislation.

---

[10]Changed by the Twentieth Amendment.

Amendment 14 (Ratified 1868)

Section 1 All persons born or naturalized in the United States, and subject to the jurisdiction thereof, are citizens of the United States and of the State wherein they reside. No State shall make or enforce any law which shall abridge the privileges or immunities of citizens of the United States; nor shall any State deprive any person of life, liberty, or property, without due process of law; nor deny to any person within its jurisdiction the equal protection of the laws.

Section 2 Representatives shall be apportioned among the several States according to their respective numbers, counting the whole number of persons in each State, excluding Indians not taxed. But when the right to vote at any election for the choice of electors for President and Vice President of the United States, Representatives in Congress, the Executive and Judicial officers of a State, or the members of the Legislature thereof, is denied to any of the male inhabitants of such State, being twenty-one[11] years of age, and citizens of the United States, or in any way abridged except for participation in rebellion, or other crime, the basis of representation therein shall be reduced in the proportion which the number of such male citizens shall bear to the whole number of male citizens twenty-one years of age in such State.

Section 3 No person shall be a Senator or Representative in Congress, or elector of President and Vice President, or hold any office, civil or military, under the United States, or under any State, who, having previously taken an oath, as a member of Congress, or as an officer of the United States, or as a member of any State legislature, or as an executive or judicial officer of any State, to support the Constitution of the United States, shall have engaged in insurrection or rebellion against the same, or given aid or comfort to the enemies thereof. But Congress may by a vote of two-thirds of each House, remove such disability.

Section 4 The validity of the public debt of the United States, authorized by law, including debts incurred for payment of pensions and bounties for services in suppressing insurrection or rebellion, shall not be questioned. But neither the United States nor any State shall assume or pay any debt or obligation incurred in aid of insurrection or rebellion against the United States, or any claim for the loss or emancipation of any slave; but all such debts, obligations and claims shall be held illegal and void.

Section 5 The Congress shall have power to enforce, by appropriate legislation, the provisions of this article.

Amendment 15 (Ratified 1870)

Section 1 The right of citizens of the United States to vote shall not be denied or abridged by the United States or by any State on account of race, color, or previous condition of servitude.

Section 2 The Congress shall have power to enforce this article by appropriate legislation.

Amendment 16 (Ratified 1913)

The Congress shall have power to lay and collect taxes on incomes, from whatever source derived, without apportionment among the several States, and without regard to any census or enumeration.

Amendment 17 (Ratified 1913)

The Senate of the United States shall be composed of two Senators from each State, elected by the people thereof, for six years; and each Senator shall have one vote. The electors in each State shall have the qualifications requisite for electors of the most numerous branch of the State legislatures.

When vacancies happen in the representation of any State in the Senate, the executive authority of such State shall issue writs of election to fill such vacancies: *Provided,* That the legislature of any State may empower the executive thereof to make temporary appointments until the people fill the vacancies by election as the legislature may direct.

This amendment shall not be so construed as to affect the election or term of any Senator chosen before it becomes valid as part of the Constitution.

Amendment 18 (Ratified 1919; Repealed 1933)

Section 1 After one year from the ratification of this article the manufacture, sale, or transportation of intoxicating liquors within, the importation thereof into, or the exportation thereof from the United States and all territory subject to the jurisdiction thereof for beverage purposes is hereby prohibited.

Section 2 The Congress and the several States shall have concurrent power to enforce this article by appropriate legislation.

Section 3 This article shall be inoperative unless it shall have been ratified as an amendment to the Constitution by the legislatures of the several States, as provided in the Constitution, within seven years from the date of the submission hereof to the States by the Congress.[12]

---

[11]Changed by the Twenty-Sixth Amendment.

[12]Repealed by the Twenty-First Amendment.

Amendment 19 (Ratified 1920)

The right of citizens of the United States to vote shall not be denied or abridged by the United States or by any State on account of sex.

Congress shall have power to enforce this article by appropriate legislation.

Amendment 20 (Ratified 1933)

Section 1 The terms of the President and the Vice President shall end at noon on the 20th day of January, and the terms of Senators and Representatives at noon on the 3d day of January, of the years in which such terms would have ended if this article had not been ratified; and the terms of their successors shall then begin.

Section 2 The Congress shall assemble at least once in every year, and such meeting shall begin at noon on the 3d day of January, unless they shall by law appoint a different day.

Section 3 If, at the time fixed for the beginning of the term of the President, the President elect shall have died, the Vice President elect shall become President. If a President shall not have been chosen before the time fixed for the beginning of his term, or if the President elect shall have failed to qualify, then the Vice President elect shall act as President until a President shall have qualified; and the Congress may by law provide for the case wherein neither a President elect nor a Vice President elect shall have qualified, declaring who shall then act as President, or the manner in which one who is to act shall be selected, and such person shall act accordingly until a President or Vice President shall have qualified.

Section 4 The Congress may by law provide for the case of the death of any of the persons from whom the House of Representatives may choose a President whenever the right of choice shall have devolved upon them, and for the case of the death of any of the persons from whom the Senate may choose a Vice President whenever the right of choice shall have devolved upon them.

Section 5 Sections 1 and 2 shall take effect on the 15th day of October following the ratification of this article.

Section 6 This article shall be inoperative unless it shall have been ratified as an amendment to the Constitution by the legislatures of three-fourths of the several States within seven years from the date of its submission.

Amendment 21 (Ratified 1933)

Section 1 The eighteenth article of amendment to the Constitution of the United States is hereby repealed.

Section 2 The transportation or importation into any State, Territory, or possession of the United States for delivery or use therein of intoxicating liquors, in violation of the laws thereof, is hereby prohibited.

Section 3 This article shall be inoperative unless it shall have been ratified as an amendment to the Constitution by conventions in the several States, as provided in the Constitution, within seven years from the date of the submission hereof to the States by the Congress.

Amendment 22 (Ratified 1951)

Section 1 No person shall be elected to the office of the President more than twice, and no person who has held the office of President, or acted as President, for more than two years of a term to which some other person was elected President shall be elected to the office of the President more than once. But this Article shall not apply to any person holding the office of President when this Article was proposed by the Congress, and shall not prevent any person who may be holding the office of President, or acting as President, during the term within which this Article becomes operative from holding the office of President or acting as President during the remainder of such term.

Section 2 This Article shall be inoperative unless it shall have been ratified as an amendment to the Constitution by the legislatures of three-fourths of the several States within seven years from the date of its submission to the States by the Congress.

Amendment 23 (Ratified 1961)

Section 1 The District constituting the seat of Government of the United States shall appoint in such manner as the Congress may direct:

A number of electors of President and Vice President equal to the whole number of Senators and Representatives in Congress to which the District would be entitled if it were a State, but in no event more than the least populous State; they shall be in addition to those appointed by the States, but they shall be considered, for the purposes of the election of President and Vice President, to be electors appointed by a State; and they shall meet in the District and perform such duties as provided by the twelfth article of amendment.

Section 2 The Congress shall have power to enforce this article by appropriate legislation.

Amendment 24 (Ratified 1964)

Section 1 The right of citizens of the United States to vote in any primary or other election for President or Vice President, for electors for President or Vice President, or for Senator or Representative in Congress, shall not be denied or abridged by the United States or any State by reason of failure to pay any poll tax or other tax.

Section 2 The Congress shall have power to enforce this article by appropriate legislation.

Amendment 25 (Ratified 1967)

Section 1 In case of the removal of the President from office or of his death or resignation, the Vice President shall become President.

Section 2 Whenever there is a vacancy in the office of the Vice President, the President shall nominate a Vice President who shall take office upon confirmation by a majority vote of both Houses of Congress.

Section 3 Whenever the President transmits to the President pro tempore of the Senate and the Speaker of the House of Representatives his written declaration that he is unable to discharge the powers and duties of his office, and until he transmits to them a written declaration to the contrary, such powers and duties shall be discharged by the Vice President as Acting President.

Section 4 Whenever the Vice President and a majority of either the principal officers of the executive departments or of such other body as Congress may by law provide, transmit to the President pro tempore of the Senate and the Speaker of the House of Representatives their written declaration that the President is unable to discharge the powers and duties of his office, the Vice President shall immediately assume the powers and duties of the office as Acting President.

Thereafter, when the President transmits to the President pro tempore of the Senate and the Speaker of the House of Representatives his written declaration that no inability exists, he shall resume the powers and duties of his office unless the Vice President and a majority of either the principal officers of the executive department or of such other body as Congress may by law provide, transmit within four days to the President pro tempore of the Senate and the Speaker of the House of Representatives their written declaration that the President is unable to discharge the powers and duties of his office. Thereupon Congress shall decide the issue, assembling within forty-eight hours for that purpose if not in session. If the Congress, within twenty-one days after receipt of the latter written declaration, or, if Congress is not in session, within twenty-one days after Congress is required to assemble, determines by two-thirds vote of both Houses that the President is unable to discharge the powers and duties of his office, the Vice President shall continue to discharge the same as Acting President; otherwise, the President shall resume the powers and duties of his office.

Amendment 26 (Ratified 1971)

Section 1 The right of citizens of the United States, who are eighteen years of age or older, to vote shall not be denied or abridged by the United States or by any State on account of age.

Section 2 The Congress shall have power to enforce this article by appropriate legislation.

Amendment 27 (Ratified 1992)

No law, varying the compensation for the services of the Senators and Representatives, shall take effect, until an election of Representatives shall have intervened.

APPENDIX B

Uniform Commercial Code (Articles 1, 2, 2a, and 3)

The Uniform Commercial Code (UCC) was developed by the American Law Institute (ALI) and the National Conference of Commissioners on Uniform State Laws (NCCUSL) (now known as the Uniform Law Commission) as a body of rules intended to make the application of law to commercial transactions consistent across 50 states. Like all uniform laws developed by the Uniform Law Commission, the UCC and all changes to the UCC do not become law until officially adopted by the state legislatures. The UCC has been adopted in whole by all but one state legislature, Louisiana, which adopts only certain sections.

Such widespread use of the UCC, even with the minor deviations some jurisdictions make from the official code, makes possible more efficient and more confident transactions across state lines. The UCC can be accessed here: https://www.law.cornell.edu/ucc. The UCC can be also be found on the official website of the Uniform Law Commission at http://uniformlaws .org. Not all states follow the same numbering sequence used in the UCC, so it is always best to check state statutory law before citing the code in any state-specific assignment.

APPENDIX C

Excerpts from the Sarbanes-Oxley Act of 2002

15 U.S.C. § 7241. Corporate Responsibility for Financial Reports

(a) **Regulations required**

The Commission shall, by rule, require, for each company filing periodic reports under section 78m(a) or 78o(d) of this title, that the principal executive officer or officers and the principal financial officer or officers, or persons performing similar functions, certify in each annual or quarterly report filed or submitted under either such section of this title that—

(1) the signing officer has reviewed the report;

(2) based on the officer's knowledge, the report does not contain any untrue statement of a material fact or omit to state a material fact necessary in order to make the statements made, in light of the circumstances under which such statements were made, not misleading;

(3) based on such officer's knowledge, the financial statements, and other financial information included in the report, fairly present in all material respects the financial condition and results of operations of the issuer as of, and for, the periods presented in the report;

(4) the signing officers—

  (A) are responsible for establishing and maintaining internal controls;

  (B) have designed such internal controls to ensure that material information relating to the issuer and its consolidated subsidiaries is made known to such officers by others within those entities, particularly during the period in which the periodic reports are being prepared;

  (C) have evaluated the effectiveness of the issuer's internal controls as of a date within 90 days prior to the report; and

  (D) have presented in the report their conclusions about the effectiveness of their internal controls based on their evaluation as of that date;

(5) the signing officers have disclosed to the issuer's auditors and the audit committee of the board of directors (or persons fulfilling the equivalent function)—

  (A) all significant deficiencies in the design or operation of internal controls which could adversely affect the issuer's ability to record, process, summarize, and report financial data and have identified for the issuer's auditors any material weaknesses in internal controls; and

  (B) any fraud, whether or not material, that involves management or other employees who have a significant role in the issuer's internal controls; and

(6) the signing officers have indicated in the report whether or not there were significant changes in internal controls or in other factors that could significantly affect internal controls subsequent to the date of their evaluation, including any corrective actions with regard to significant deficiencies and material weaknesses.

(b) **Foreign reincorporations have no effect**

Nothing in this section shall be interpreted or applied in any way to allow any issuer to lessen the legal force of the statement required under this section, by an issuer having reincorporated or having engaged in any other transaction that resulted in the transfer of the corporate domicile or offices of the issuer from inside the United States to outside of the United States.

(c) **Deadline**

The rules required by subsection (a) of this section shall be effective not later than 30 days after July 30, 2002.

15 U.S.C. § 7262. Management Assessment of Internal Controls

(a) **Rules required**

The Commission shall prescribe rules requiring each annual report required by section 78m(a) or 78o(d) of this title to contain an internal control report, which shall—

(1) state the responsibility of management for establishing and maintaining an adequate internal control structure and procedures for financial reporting; and

(2) contain an assessment, as of the end of the most recent fiscal year of the issuer, of the effectiveness of the internal control structure and procedures of the issuer for financial reporting.

(b) **Internal control evaluation and reporting**

With respect to the internal control assessment required by subsection (a) of this section, each registered public accounting firm that prepares or issues the audit report for the issuer shall attest to, and report on, the assessment made by the management of the issuer. An attestation made under this subsection shall be made in accordance with standards for attestation engagements issued or adopted by the Board. Any such attestation shall not be the subject of a separate engagement.

18 U.S.C. § 1519. Destruction, Alteration, or Falsification of Records in Federal Investigations and Bankruptcy

Whoever knowingly alters, destroys, mutilates, conceals, covers up, falsifies, or makes a false entry in any record, document, or tangible object with the intent to impede, obstruct, or influence the investigation or proper administration of any matter within the jurisdiction of any department or agency of the United States or any case filed under title 11, or in relation to or contemplation of any such matter or case, shall be fined under this title, imprisoned not more than 20 years, or both.

glossary

ABC test Statutory standard used by many states to determine agency status.

Absolute privilege A defense to a defamation claim whereby the defendant need not proffer any further evidence to assert the defense; provided to government officials, judicial officers and proceedings, and state legislatures.

Acceptance The offeree's expression of agreement to the terms of the offer. The power of acceptance is created by a valid offer.

Accord and satisfaction One party agrees to render a substitute performance in the future known as an accord, and the other party promises to accept that substitute performance to discharge the existing performance as a satisfaction.

ACH transaction An electronic interbank network used to process large batches of direct payments and deposits that are associated with bank accounts.

Acknowledgment form A form commonly used in sales contracts as an acceptance from the seller in response to a purchase order; contains preprinted provisions and has blanks to accommodate the specifics of the transaction. Also referred to as an *invoice.*

Acquisition (takeover) The purchase of one company by another company; such purchase may be of the stock or assets of the acquired entity.

Act requirement For criminal liability, the requirement that the government prove that a defendant's actions objectively satisfied the elements of a particular offense. Also called *actus reus.*

Actual authority Authority granted by a principal to an agent.

Actual damages A fundamental element that must be proved to recover in a negligence lawsuit against a tortfeasor: The injured party must prove that she suffered some physical harm that resulted in identifiable losses.

Actual owner The individual who is recognized as having primary or residual title to the property and is, therefore, the ultimate owner of the property.

Actuary Individual employed by insurers who is trained in mathematics and uses statistical models to calculate the probabilities and loss exposure of particular risks.

Adjudication A phase of the criminal justice system in which the prosecutor, after investigation, elects to proceed with the charges.

Administrative agencies Department, nondepartment, and independent agencies.

Administrative law Refers to both the law made by administrative agencies and the laws and regulations that govern the creation, organization, and operation of administrative agencies.

Administrative law judge (ALJ) The presiding officer in a quasi-judicial administrative hearing.

Affirmative action An action plan designed to maintain equal employment opportunities and to remedy past employment discrimination against women, persons of color, persons with disabilities, and other underutilized protected classes.

Age Discrimination in Employment Act (ADEA) of 1967 A federal statute that prohibits employers from discriminating against employees on the basis of their age once employees have reached age 40.

Agency law The body of laws that govern the relationships created when one party hires another party to act on the hiring party's behalf.

Agent One who agrees to act and is authorized to act on behalf of another, a *principal,* to legally bind the principal in particular business transactions with third parties pursuant to an agency relationship.

Ambiguous terms Contract terms that are vague and indefinite. In contract law, these terms are construed by the court against the interest of the side that drafted the agreement.

American Recovery and Reinvestment Act of 2009 Federal legislation that created a loan program and underlying mandates for corporations most acutely impacted by the financial crisis that began in 2008; also established the Troubled Assets Relief Program (TARP) to administer the loans.

Americans with Disabilities Act (ADA) of 1990 A federal statute that seeks to eliminate discriminatory employment practices against disabled persons; requires that employers with 15 or more employees make reasonable accommodations for a disabled employee in the workplace as long as the accommodations do not cause the employer to suffer an undue hardship.

Answer Defendant's formal response to each paragraph of the complaint.

Anticipatory repudiation Doctrine under which, when one party makes clear that he has no intention to perform as agreed, the nonbreaching party is entitled to recover damages in anticipation of the breach rather than waiting until performance is due. Also called *anticipatory breach.*

Apparent authority When the principal creates a false appearance of an agent possessing authority.

Arbitrary and capricious standard Arbitrariness and capriciousness is found when an agency has taken action that is not based on a consideration of relevant factors, including viable alternatives available to the regulatory agency, or is a result of a clear error of judgment.

Arbitration Method of alternative dispute resolution in which the parties present their sides of the dispute to one or more neutral parties who then render a decision; often involves a set of rules designed to move from dispute to decision quickly.

Article I, Section 8 The main provision of the Constitution that enumerates the limited powers of Congress.

Articles of incorporation The document filed with a state authority that sets in motion the incorporation process; includes the corporation's name and purpose, number of shares issued, and address of the corporation's headquarters.

Articles of organization The document filed to create an LLC; in most states, requires only basic information such as the name of the entity, the location of its principal place of business, and the names of its members. Also called *certificate of organization.*

Asset purchase When a buyer purchases some or all of the target company's assets.

Assignment When one of the contracting parties transfers their rights under the contract to another party.

Assignment for the benefit of creditors (ABC) Form of liquidation that serves as an alternative to bankruptcy and is provided either by state statute, state common law, or a combination of both.

Assumption of the risk A defense to claims of negligence in which the injured party knew that a substantial and apparent risk was associated with certain conduct and the party went ahead with the dangerous activity anyway.

Attachment to the property The requirement that, for a security interest to be enforceable, value must be given, the debtor must have rights in the collateral, and the debtor must authenticate a security agreement that describes the collateral.

Authorization cards Signed statements by employees indicating that they wish to unionize and/or are electing to be represented by an existing union.

Automatic stay A legal prohibition whereby creditors may neither initiate nor continue any debt collection action against the debtor or her property.

Bait-and-switch scheme When a seller advertises an item for sale at a particularly good price or on favorable terms, but the seller has no intention of actually selling that product at that price or on those terms.

Bankruptcy A procedure by which a debtor's assets are reorganized and liquidated by a court order to pay off creditors and free the debtor from obligations under existing contracts.

Bankruptcy estate The debtor's available assets in a bankruptcy proceeding.

Bankruptcy trustee An individual, often an attorney highly skilled in bankruptcy law, appointed in Chapter 7 or Chapter 13 cases and charged with the duty of taking control of the bankruptcy estate and reducing it to cash for distribution, preserving the interests of both the debtor and the creditors.

Bargained-for exchange The aspect of consideration that differentiates contracts from illusory promises by holding that a performance or return promise is bargained for only if it was exchanged for another promise.

Battle of the forms The conflict between the terms written into standardized purchase (offer) and acknowledgment (acceptance) forms, which differ in that one form favors the buyer and the other the seller. The UCC attempts to broker a truce in this battle while keeping the contract of sale intact.

Bench trial Trial without a jury where the judge is both the finder of law and the finder of fact.

Beneficiary An individual or entity who is entitled to receive part or all of the property under the terms of a will or trust, either now or in the future.

Benefit corporation A corporation whose performance is based on social, environmental, and financial performance.

Beyond a reasonable doubt The heightened burden of proof used in criminal cases, under which a fact finder must be convinced that the defendant's criminal liability is not in doubt to a reasonable person.

Bilateral contract A contract where the legal detriment is incurred through mutual promises the parties make to each other.

Bill of Rights The first ten amendments to the United States Constitution.

Black's Law Dictionary The leading legal dictionary.

Blank indorsement An indorsement that consists solely of the indorser's signature.

Blockchain An online peer-to-peer ledger system to account for cryptocurrency transactions.

Blue-sky laws State securities laws designed to protect investors from unsavory issuers selling nothing more than blue sky.

Bona fide occupational qualification (BFOQ) A provision in certain federal antidiscrimination statutes that allows discrimination based on religion, gender, or national origin when it can be shown that such discrimination is reasonably necessary to the business operation.

Borrower The party to whom credit is extended and who owes the debt.

Breach Condition that exists when one party has failed to perform her obligation under a contract. If the breach is material, the nonbreaching party is excused from his performance and can recover monetary damages.

Breach of duty A fundamental element that must be proved to recover a negligence lawsuit against a tortfeasor: The injured party must prove that the tortfeasor failed to exercise reasonable care in fulfilling her obligations.

Burden of proof The responsibility of producing sufficient evidence in support of a fact or issue and favorably convincing the fact finder of that fact or issue.

Business corporation law Often the title for a specific state law that covers such matters as the structure of the corporation, oversight of the activity of the corporation's managers, rights of the principals in the case of the sale of assets or ownership interests, annual reporting requirements, and other issues that affect the internal rules of the business venture.

Business judgment rule A principle that protects corporate officers and directors from liability when they have made an unwise decision that results in a loss to the corporation but they have acted in good faith, had no private financial self-interest, and used diligence to acquire the best information related to the decision.

Business necessity test A defense used to rebut disparate impact claims when a business can prove that a certain skill, ability, or procedure is absolutely necessary to the operation of the business. Discrimination is permitted even if a protected class is adversely affected.

Buyer in ordinary course of business A person who buys goods from a merchant in the business of selling the goods without knowledge that the sale violates the rights of another person.

Buyer in ordinary course of business (BOCB) A person who buys goods in good faith, without knowledge that the sale violates the rights of another person in the goods, and in the ordinary course from a person, other than a pawnbroker, in the business of selling goods of that kind.

Capacity For the formation of a valid contract, the requirement that both parties have the power to contract. Certain classes of persons have only limited powers to contract, including minors and those with mental incapacity.

Case precedent The opinion of an appellate court, which is binding on all trial courts from that point in time onward so that any similar case would be decided according to the precedent.

Cashier's check A check issued by a bank with funds drawn from the bank's own account.

Cause in fact A fundamental element that must be proved to recover in a negligence lawsuit against a tortfeasor: The injured party must prove that, if not for the breach of duty by the tortfeasor, he would not have suffered damages.

Cease and desist letter A letter sent to alleged infringers asking them to discontinue use of the mark or face potential legal action.

Certificate of deposit A written note that indicates a bank has received money as a loan and promises to repay the amount in the future with interest, typically at a higher rate than that offered by a savings account.

Certificate of limited partnership A form filed with the state by a general partner to create a limited partnership.

Certified check A check drawn from a personal account that the bank ensures will clear with sufficient funds.

Certify In labor law, to recognize a collective bargaining unit as a union. The NLRB's certification process occurs when a legally sound election reveals a simple majority of pro-union votes.

Charging of the jury Instructions given by the judge to the jury explaining how to work through the process of coming to a factual decision in the case.

Chattel paper A document issued by a seller that indicates financing terms for the sale of goods and a repayment schedule.

Check Negotiable instrument that is an unconditional order issued to a bank to pay a fixed amount that is in writing and signed by the party undertaking to pay.

Citizen suit Lawsuit brought by any member of the public who is directly affected by a particular agency action (or inaction) against violators of a particular regulation and/or the administrative agency itself for failing to fulfill a duty imposed by a statute.

Citizen suit provisions Laws that authorize private individuals or watchdog groups to file environmental enforcement lawsuits.

Civil laws Laws designed to compensate parties for money lost as a result of another's conduct.

Civil litigation A dispute resolution process in which the parties and their counsel argue their views of a civil controversy in a court of law.

Claims in recoupment A defense in which the amount owed by the obligor is reduced by some amount due to an offsetting claim by the obligor.

Clean Air Act (CAA) Federal legislation enacted in 1963 to improve, strengthen, and accelerate programs for the prevention and abatement of air pollution; focuses on stationary and mobile sources in the United States.

Clean Water Act (CWA) Federal legislation that regulates water quality standards and aims to stem water pollution from industrial, municipal, and agricultural sources; implemented and enforced by the EPA.

Closing arguments Attorneys' summations of the case with the objective of convincing the jury of what theory to decide the case upon, occurring after testimony is completed and evidence has been submitted.

Code of Federal Regulations Publication containing the rules promulgated by federal administrative agencies.

Codicil A testamentary document whose purpose is to amend an existing will and is subject to the same formal requirements as a will.

Collateral The assets a borrower has pledged to secure a loan.

Collective bargaining The process of negotiating terms and conditions of employment for employees in the collective bargaining unit.

Collective bargaining unit An employee group that, on the basis of a mutuality of interests, is an appropriate unit for collective bargaining.

Commerce Clause That part of the Constitution that grants to Congress the power to regulate interstate and foreign commerce.

Commercial general liability (CGL) policy An insurance policy that covers various types of business risks, including bodily injury and property damage, arising from the nonprofessional negligent acts of employees and injuries sustained within the business premises.

Commercial loan Money loaned by a commercial source (e.g., a bank) whereby the debtor agrees to pay back the loan over a certain period of time at a certain rate.

Commercial wires Electronic transfers between businesses that typically involve large sums of money.

Commercially impracticable UCC rule applied when a delay in delivery or nondelivery has been made impracticable by the occurrence of an unanticipated event so long as the event directly affected a basic assumption of the contract.

Commitment device Any method or manner of effectively reducing one's options or choices ahead of time.

Common law Law that has not been passed by the legislature, but rather is made by the courts and is based on the fundamentals of previous cases with similar facts.

Common law contracts Contracts for services or real estate.

Common stock (common shares) A form of equity instrument that entitles the equity owner to payments based on the current profitability of the company.

Community-based nonprofit A tax-exempt entity created for the purpose of serving the community.

Comparative negligence A defense to claims of negligence in which the injured party's conduct has played a factor in the harm suffered and, thus, the proportion of negligence should be divided.

Compensatory damages Damages that are meant to make the injured party whole again. In contract law, they are an attempt to place the nonbreaching party in the position he would have been in had the contract been executed as agreed. Also called *direct* or *actual damages.*

Complaint The first formal document filed with the local clerk of courts when the plaintiff initiates a lawsuit claiming legal rights against another.

Complaint (Discrimination) A form that an aggrieved employee files against his employer with the EEOC that details how the employee was discriminated against.

Compliance department A unit within the organization staffed by lawyers and nonlawyers that helps an organization follow rules and regulations and maintain the company's culture of values and ethics.

Comprehensive Environmental Response, Compensation, and Liability Act (CERCLA) Federal legislation enacted in 1980 to create a tax on the chemical and petroleum industries and provide broad federal authority to respond directly to releases or threatened releases of hazardous substances that may endanger public health or the environment. Also called *Superfund*.

Computer Fraud and Abuse Act (CFAA) Federal legislation that prohibits unauthorized use of computers to commit espionage, the accessing of unauthorized information or of a nonpublic government computer, fraud by computer, damage to a computer, trafficking in passwords, and extortionate threats to damage a computer.

Conciliation negotiations The required attempts by the EEOC to settle a discrimination case instead of filing a lawsuit.

Condition concurrent When each party is required to render performance simultaneously.

Condition precedent A contract term that requires an event to occur before performance under a contract is due.

Condition subsequent A contract term that discharges the parties' obligations if an event occurs after performance under the contract.

Confirmation memorandum A written verification of an agreement. Under the statute of frauds section of the UCC, a merchant who receives a signed confirmation memorandum from another merchant will be bound by the memorandum just as if she had signed it, unless she promptly objects.

Conforming goods Goods bargained for in an agreement.

Consensual lien A lien that a property owner voluntarily grants to a creditor (e.g., a mortgage for real estate).

Consent An agent's agreeing to act for the principal. In the context of agency law, courts apply an objective standard to determine whether the agent did in fact agree to the agency relationship.

Consequential damages Foreseeable losses caused by the breach; may include lost profits.

Consideration The mutual exchange of benefits and detriments; for the formation of a valid contract, the requirement that each party receives something of value (the benefit) from the other and that each party gives up something of value (the legal detriment) to the other, resulting in a bargained-for exchange.

Constitutional law The body of law interpreting state and federal constitutions.

Consumer Credit Protection Act (CCPA) Federal legislation that regulates credit transactions between a creditor and a borrower and provides consumer protections in the areas of disclosure of credit terms, credit reporting, antidiscrimination laws, and collection of debts from consumers; serves as the centerpiece of federal statutory regulation of credit transactions.

Consumer Financial Protection Bureau (CFPB) Independent agency created by the Wall Street Reform and Consumer Protection Act responsible for consumer education, regulation of credit and loan companies, and enforcement of consumer protection laws.

Consumer Review Fairness Act (CRFA) A federal law designed to protect consumers' ability to share their honest opinions about a business's products, services, or conduct in any forum, including social media.

Contract A legally enforceable promise or set of promises.

Contract discharge The subject of how and when a contract is legally terminated.

Controlling the Assault of Non-Solicited Pornography and Marketing Act of 2003 A federal statute that regulates the sending of unsolicited e-mail (spam) by prohibiting certain practices, such as falsifying the "from" name and information in the subject line, and requiring the sender to provide a physical address of the producer of the e-mail. Also called *CAN-SPAM Act*.

Copyright A form of protection for an original work of authorship fixed in any tangible medium of expression.

Corporate governance The process used by corporate officers and directors to establish lines of responsibility, approval, and oversight among key stakeholders and set out rules for making corporate decisions.

Corporate social responsibility (CSR) A broad-based identification of important business and social issues and a critique of business organizations and practices.

Corporate veil The liability protection shareholders, directors, and officers of a corporation have from personal liability in case the corporation runs up large debts or suffers some liability.

Corporation A fictitious legal entity that exists as an independent "person" separate from its principals.

Counsel Another name for an attorney.

Counterclaim Filed when the defendant believes that the plaintiff has caused her damages arising out of the very same set of facts as articulated in the complaint.

Counteroffer An action terminating an offer whereby the offeree rejects the original offer and proposes a new offer with different terms.

Course of dealing How the parties acted in *prior* contracts instead of the specific contract in question.

Course of performance UCC term for the method to show what the parties intended through their own actions in performing the specific contract in question.

Court A judicial tribunal duly constituted for the hearing and adjudication of cases.

Covenant not to compete Type of contract in which one party agrees not to compete with another party for a specified period of time.

Covenant of good faith and fair dealing Common law exception adopted by a minority of states that imposes a duty on every employer to act in good faith and protects employees from terminations without cause that result in unjust treatment.

Cram-down provision A term used in reference to the Chapter 11 provision that allows the debtor to request that the court force the creditors to accept a plan that is fair, equitable, and feasible.

Creative commons license A license that allows others to adapt, profit from, and copy a work.

Creativity Copyright requirement that a work must have some minimum level of expressive originality.

Credit card A card that allows a cardholder to make purchases through an electronic network on credit terms that have been pre-negotiated with the card-issuing bank.

Creditor Any party that regularly extends credit and to which a debt becomes owed.

Criminal law The body of law that, for the purpose of preventing harm to society, defines the boundaries of behavior and prescribes sanctions for violating those boundaries.

Criminal laws Laws designed to protect society that result in penalties to the violator such as fines or imprisonment.

Criminal procedure The body of constitutional protections afforded to individuals and business entities during criminal investigations, arrests, trials, and sentencing.

Cross-claim Filed when the defendant believes that a third party is either partially or fully liable for the damages that the plaintiff has suffered and, therefore, should be involved as an indispensable party in the trial.

Cross-examination The opportunity for the attorney to ask questions in court, limited to issues that were brought out on direct examination, of a witness who has testified in a trial on behalf of the opposing party.

Cryptocurrency A deregulated, decentralized software-based currency that is created using encryption techniques

Cure The right of a seller to replace nonconforming goods before final contract performance is due. If nonconforming goods were delivered in good faith and were considered equal to or superior to what was ordered, the seller may cure after final contract performance is due if the buyer will not suffer injury.

Debit card A card linked to a cardholder's checking account and used at a merchant's point of sale.

Debt A common tool for raising capital that includes promissory notes, bonds, and debentures that offer investors a fixed rate of return, regardless of the profitability of the corporation, with repayment expected after a certain period of years.

Debtor in possession (DIP) A Chapter 11 bankruptcy process in which the debtor generally remains in control of assets and business operations in an attempt to rehabilitate the business entity.

Decedent An individual who has died. If the decedent has left a will, he is referred to as a *testator.*

Deductible The amount the insured is required to share in the loss exposure to reduce moral hazard.

Default When a borrower fails to perform under the contract with the lender.

Default rules Rules that apply when partners have not expressly agreed how to regulate their internal relations with each other.

Defendant The party alleged by the plaintiff to have caused the plaintiff to suffer damages.

Deliberations The process in which a jury discusses, in private, the findings of the court and decides by vote which argument of either opposing side to agree with.

Delist Process by which a reporting company voluntarily changes its status, thereby eliminating reporting and disclosure mandates under the Exchange Act.

Demand note A note that is payable at any time upon the request of the payee.

Deposition Method of discovery where a witness gives sworn testimony to provide evidence prior to trial.

Depositor The person seeking to cash a check.

Depository bank Bank authorized by a depositor to present a check for payment against the drawee bank.

Destination contract Contract that requires the seller to deliver the goods to a specified destination, usually the buyer's location.

Detour When an employee engages in a minor deviation from employment that creates liability for the employer under respondeat superior.

Detrimental reliance Situation in which the offeree acts, based on a reasonable promise made by the offeror, and will be injured if the offeror's promise is not enforced.

Digital wallet Mobile payment app that allows a user to make payments to merchants using a contactless point-of-sale system.

Direct examination The first questioning of a witness during a trial in which the plaintiff's attorney asks questions of the witnesses on the plaintiff's list.

Direct infringement A theory of copyright infringement under which the copyright owner proves that she has legal ownership of the work in question and that the infringer copied the work without permission.

Directors Individuals responsible for oversight and management of the corporation's course of direction.

Disability A physical or mental impairment that substantially limits a person's ability to participate in major life activities.

Disaffirmance The taking of some affirmative action to avoid obligation under a contract; disaffirmance is required when a contract has already been performed or partially performed by the minor.

Discharge In contract law, the removal of all legal obligations under the agreement.

Disclaim When a seller uses language in the contract to remove any of the implied warranties.

Disclosure The underlying premise of all securities regulation in which companies are to release all information, positive or negative, that might bear on an investment decision.

Discovery Process for the orderly exchange of information and evidence between the parties involved in litigation (or in some cases arbitration) prior to trial.

Dishonored Status of an instrument in which the drawee refuses to pay for any reason other than those defined in the UCC related to identification authority and cutoff time.

Disparate impact Theory of employment discrimination in which employee evaluation techniques that are not themselves discriminatory have a different and adverse impact on members of a protected class.

Disparate treatment Theory of employment discrimination predicated on overt and intentional discrimination; includes being treated differently because of one's membership in a protected class.

Dissociation The term used in the RUPA when a partner no longer wishes to be a principal and chooses to leave the partnership.

Dissociation from LLC Process in which an individual member of an LLC exercises the right to withdraw from the partnership.

Dissolution of LLC In the context of an LLC, a liquidation process triggered by an event that is specified in the operating agreement (such as the death of a key member) or by the decision of the majority of membership interests (or the percentage called for in the operating agreement) to dissolve the company.

Diversity of citizenship When opposing parties in a lawsuit are citizens of different states or one party is a citizen of a foreign country, the case is placed under federal court jurisdiction if the amount in controversy exceeds $75,000.

Do Not Call Registry A list maintained by the FTC whereby consumers may sign up to be protected from certain unsolicited calls by telemarketers.

Doctrine of equivalence A doctrine that allows the courts to find patent infringement when an invention, compared with a patented device, performs substantially the same function in substantially the same way to achieve the same result.

Doctrine of stare decisis The principle that similar cases with similar facts under similar circumstances should have similar outcomes.

Dodd-Frank Wall Street Reform and Consumer Protection Act Federal legislation designed to overhaul the regulation of public companies and U.S. financial services and markets *(ch. 35)*. A law enacted in 2010, commonly referred to as *Dodd-Frank,* that made sweeping reforms to the financial regulatory system, including expanded SEC enforcement powers, the creation of a new Financial Stability Oversight Council, and a new bounty plan for whistleblowers *(ch. 36)*.

Draft A written order to pay money signed by the person giving the order (e.g., a check).

Drawee The party who must make a payment as specified to the person receiving the funds in a payment order.

Drawee bank Bank that issues and ultimately pays a check.

Drawer The party issuing the payment order.

Due diligence The pre-closing process in which the acquirer reviews the financial state of the target company and identifies potential or actual legal liabilities of the target.

Durable medium Copyright requirement that a work must be in a tangible format, such as writing, digital, paint, video, and so forth.

Duress The use of any form of unfair coercion by one party to induce another party to enter into or modify a contract; basis for avoiding a contract.

Duty A fundamental element that must be proved to recover in a negligence lawsuit against a tortfeasor: The injured party must prove that the tortfeasor owed him a duty of care.

Duty of care A fiduciary duty owed to shareholders by officers and directors; requires that the fiduciaries exercise the degree of skill, diligence, and care that a reasonably prudent person would exercise under the same circumstances, acting in good faith, and in a manner that is reasonably calculated to advance the best interests of the corporations.

Duty of loyalty A fiduciary duty owed to shareholders by officers, directors, and controlling shareholders; requires that the fiduciaries put the corporation's interests ahead of their own and do not engage in self-dealing or conflicts of interest.

Economic Espionage Act A federal statute passed in 1996 that provides criminal penalties for domestic and foreign theft of trade secrets.

Election A vote by the entire bargaining unit to accept or reject unionization.

Electronic Communications Privacy Act (ECPA) A federal law enacted in 1986 that extends legal protection against wiretapping and other forms of unauthorized interception and explicitly allows employers to monitor employee communications on company equipment as long as this is done in the ordinary course of business or the employee consents to the monitoring.

Eminent domain The authority of the state and federal government to take private property.

Employee agents One of three broad categories of agents; generally, anyone who performs services for a principal if the principal controls what will be done and how it will be done.

Employee Polygraph Protection Act A federal law that prohibits most private sector employers from requiring a polygraph test as a condition of employment.

Employee Retirement Income Security Act (ERISA) A federal law enacted in 1974 consisting of a comprehensive set of laws and regulations that requires employers to make certain disclosures related to investment risk, thus providing transparency for plan beneficiaries.

Employment discrimination Workplace-related discrimination in the hiring process and treatment of employees; encompasses everything from promotions and demotions to work schedules, working conditions, and disciplinary measures.

Employment-at-will doctrine Deep-seated common law principle that an employer has the right to terminate an employee with or without advance notice and with or without just cause, subject to certain exceptions.

Enabling statutes The statutes that create an agency or give the agency explicit authority to implement a statute.

Enforceability The ability of a properly formed contract to be enforceable in a court of law; determined by examining whether the contract is a product of genuine assent and is in writing (under certain circumstances).

Equal Employment Opportunity Commission (EEOC) A five-member federal administrative agency that administers congressional mandates that ensure adequate protection for victims of discrimination; accepts and investigates worker complaints; and, in certain cases, will sue on behalf of employees.

Equal Pay Act of 1963 A federal statute that makes it illegal for employers to pay unequal wages to men and women who perform substantially equal work.

Equal protection The idea that people who are similarly situated should be treated equally.

Equitable relief A type of remedy, including injunctions and restraining orders, that is designed to compensate a party when money alone will not do, but instead forces the other party to do (or not do) something.

Equity Ownership interest in a corporation whereby financial return on the investment is based primarily on the performance of the venture.

Errors and omissions (E&O) liability insurance Insurance that indemnifies the directors and executive officers of a corporation if they breach their fiduciary duties.

Estate All the real and personal property that the decedent owns or has an interest in upon his death.

Ethics The set of moral principles or core values for deciding between right and wrong.

Executive order An order made by the president that carries the full force of law; issued to enforce or interpret federal statutes and treaties.

Executor The person named by the testator in his will to carry out the instructions in the will.

Exempt employees Classification of employees who are not covered by FLSA protections; generally consists of employees whose responsibilities are primarily executive, administrative, or professional.

Exemptions Types of securities or transactions that an issuer may use to sell a security that are not subject to certain Securities and Exchange Commission regulations pertaining to registering securities; intended to assist business ventures seeking smaller amounts of capital from the public investment community.

Expected loss The probability of an event occurring multiplied times the magnitude of the loss.

Expert evaluation Method of alternative dispute resolution in which an independent expert acts as the neutral fact finder; particularly useful for parties involved in a business dispute where the issues are somewhat complex and related to the intricacies of a certain industry or profession.

Expert evaluator The neutral fact finder in expert evaluation who reviews documents and evidence provided by each party and draws on her range of experience and expertise in the industry to offer an opinion on the merits and value of the claim and recommend a settlement amount.

Expiration Method of ending an agency relationship whereby the parties agree to a fixed term for the relationship.

Explicit contracts Contracts where the terms are explicitly defined by the parties.

Explicit knowledge Knowledge that is recorded and available for a company's interpretation, application, and reproduction.

Express acts Acts by which an agency relationship is terminated; can be either simple communication of the desire to terminate the relationship, the expiration of a fixed term, or satisfaction of purpose.

Express authority When a principal makes an affirmative statement that authorizes an agent to act.

Express partnership A partnership in which the principals agree orally or in writing to form an ongoing business relationship.

Express warranty Warranty in which the seller makes a promise regarding the goods or a representation of fact about the goods.

Fair and Accurate Credit Transactions Act (FACTA) Federal legislation that requires credit bureaus to stop reporting any fraudulent account information from the time a consumer alleges identity theft until the conclusion of the investigation.

Fair Debt Collection Practices Act (FDCPA) A federal statute that regulates agents of the creditor involved in debt collection for consumer debts and that requires the collection agency to make known certain rights of the debtor.

Fair Labor Standards Act (FLSA) A federal law enacted in 1938 and intended to cover all employers engaged in interstate commerce; mandates payment of a minimum wage, a maximum 40-hour workweek, overtime pay, and restrictions on children working in certain occupations and during certain hours.

Fair use A defense against copyright infringement when a product or service has substantial noninfringing uses or when a work is protected due to its parody, academic, factual reporting, or satirical purposes.

Family and Medical Leave Act (FMLA) A federal law enacted in 1993 that requires certain employers to give time off to employees to take care of their own or a family member's illness or to care for a newborn or adopted child.

Family limited partnership A limited partnership that is used for estate planning for families of considerable wealth.

Federal courts Courts that adjudicate matters dealing primarily with national laws, federal constitutional issues, and other cases that are outside the purview of state courts.

Federal Odometer Act A law that makes it a crime to change vehicle odometers and requires that any faulty odometer be plainly disclosed in writing to potential buyers.

Federal question Some issue arising from the Constitution, a federal statute or regulation, or federal common law.

Federal Trade Commission (FTC) An agency charged with the broad mandate of preventing unfair and deceptive acts or practices in commercial transactions.

Federal Trade Commission Act (FTCA) A statute that created the Federal Trade Commission and prohibited deceptive trade practices.

Federal Trademark Dilution Act A federal law enacted in 1995 that permits mark holders to recover damages and prevent others from diluting distinctive trademarks.

Federal Unemployment Tax Act (FUTA) A federal law enacted in 1935 that established a state-administered fund to provide payments to workers who have suffered sudden job loss; funded through employment taxes shared by employer and employee.

Federalism The existence of a dual form of government in which there are two levels of government in a single political system: a central or "federal" government as well as multiple regional governments.

Felonies Crimes that generally carry one year or more of incarceration as the penalty.

Fiduciary duties The duties of loyalty, care, and good faith imposed on partners to ensure they are acting in the partnership's best interests.

Finance lease A true lease in which the lessor is not the fundamental supplier of the goods leased, but leases goods to lessees as a means of financing its acquisition from the supplier.

Financial market A highly regulated institution in which people and firms trade securities, commodities, and currencies at prices that reflect supply and demand as well as publicly and privately available information.

Financial Stability Oversight Council (FSOC) An independent body with a board of regulators to address dangerous risks to global financial markets posed by risky investments or the actions of large, interconnected financial institutions.

First-in-time is first-in-right The general rule regarding the timing of UCC-1 filings where the first to file obtains priority.

Fixtures Items that can be detached from real estate, such as cabinetry.

Floating lien A security interest that includes future acquisitions of property (e.g., "all equipment currently owned and hereafter acquired").

Food and Drug Administration (FDA) The federal agency that regulates the testing, manufacturing, and distributing of foods, medications, and medical devices.

Food, Drug, and Cosmetic Act (FDCA) The federal statute that created the Food and Drug Administration and that requires the makers of certain food ingredients, additives, drugs, or medical devices to obtain formal FDA approval before selling the product to the general public.

Forbearance The giving up of a legal right as consideration in a contract.

Force majeure A clause that contemplates uncontrollable acts that will impede performance under the contract.

Foreign Corrupt Practices Act (FCPA) A federal criminal statute enacted principally to prevent corporate bribery of foreign officials in business transactions.

Formal rulemaking Procedures for rulemaking that are used only when Congress has specifically indicated in the enabling statute that the agency rules must be made "on the record after a hearing."

Fortuitous The accidental nature of risk of loss required in insurance contracts.

Fraudulent misrepresentation Situation in which one party has engaged in conduct that meets the standards for misrepresentation and that party has actual knowledge that the representation is not true; basis for avoiding a contract.

Freedom of contract A perspective where courts do not interfere with the contracting process, do not assess the wisdom of the deal, and enforce valid contracts against parties absent evidence of fraud, mistake, oppression, or lack of legal purpose.

Freedom of disposition The common law principle that testators should be free to dispose of their property at death in any way they want.

Freedom of Information Act (FOIA) A statute that gives the public the right to examine a great many government documents.

Frolic When an employee does something purely for her own reasons that are unrelated to employment, which releases the employer from respondeat superior liability.

Frustration of purpose When one party's purpose is completely or almost completely frustrated by supervening events, courts may discharge that party from performance.

Fully disclosed agency When a third party knows the principal's identity.

Genuine assent The knowing, voluntary, and mutual approval of the terms of a contract by each party; required for a contract to be enforceable.

Going-and-coming rule A rule adopted by some courts whereby employers are generally not liable for tortious acts committed by employees while on their way to and from work.

Good faith Honesty in fact and the observance of reasonable commercial standards of fair dealing.

Good faith (HDC) Requirement for HDC status that a holder take the instrument in accordance with honesty in the transaction and reasonable commercial standards.

Good faith buyer Someone who acts honestly and provides reasonable value for the goods.

Goods Tangible personal property that is movable at the time of identification to a contract of sale.

Gratuitous agents One of three broad categories of agents; generally, anyone who acts on behalf of a principal without receiving any compensation.

Grievance In labor law, a complaint filed with or by a union to challenge an employer's treatment of one or more union members.

Guarantor A third party that agrees to be liable to pay a loan only if the debtor actually defaults.

Holder One who has actual physical possession of a negotiable instrument (in bearer form) or is in possession of the instrument (pay to order form) if the instrument was made payable to a specific party.

Holder in due course (HDC) A statutory super status that protects the holder from certain claims by other parties related to the validity of the negotiable instrument.

Holder Rule FTC-promulgated regulation that *preserves* a consumer's rights against an HDC when the transaction involves the consumer entering into credit contracts related to the sale of goods and services.

Horizontal privity Privity of contract issues dealing with the extension of a warranty to someone other than the buyer.

Hostile takeover A transaction in which the board of a target company has no prior knowledge of an acquirer's purchase offer.

Hostile work environment Theory of liability under Title VII for sexual harassment that is of such a severe and crude nature or is so pervasive in the workplace that it interferes with the victim's ability to do the job.

Hung jury A jury that cannot come to a consensus decision on which party should prevail in a case.

Identified to the contract When the parties have specifically identified which goods will be sold to the buyer.

Illusory promise A promise that courts will not enforce because the offeror is not truly bound by his vague promise or because a party cannot be bound by his promise due to the lack of a bargained-for exchange. Promises of gifts and deathbed promises are two examples.

Implied authority Authority that is reasonably necessary to carry out the principal's instructions.

Implied contract Common law exception to at-will employment whereby employees are protected if their at-will status is altered by promises of continued employment that form an implied contract between employer and employee.

Implied contracts Contracts that lack explicit terms and are implied by the parties' behavior or through social custom.

Implied partnership A partnership in which the partners are silent about their partnership status, yet the law considers them partners by virtue of their actions.

Implied warranty Warranty automatically imposed by law on the seller for every sales contract.

Impossibility When the contemplated performance of the obligations becomes objectively impossible and, therefore, is subject to discharge.

Impracticability Discharge arising when performance is not objectively impossible yet performance becomes extremely burdensome due to some unforeseen circumstance occurring between the time of agreement and the time of performance.

Incidental damages Damages that reimburse a buyer's reasonable expenses incurred in handling rightfully rejected goods or in effecting a cover.

Independent contractor One of three broad categories of agents; generally, anyone who performs services for a principal if the principal has the right to control or direct only the result of the work and not the means and methods of accomplishing the result.

Indirect infringement A theory of copyright infringement under which a third party has knowledge of the infringement and contributes to it in some material way; also known as *contributory infringement*.

Indorsement The process of negotiating a check by signing the check and making it payable to someone else.

Informal rulemaking Under the APA, many of an agency's rulemaking duties are carried out through procedures that center on the concepts of notice, public comment, publication of a final rule, and the opportunity to challenge a rule in court.

Injunctive relief A court order to refrain from performing a particular act.

Insider trading When a corporate insider has access to certain information not available to the general investor public and uses that information as the basis for trades in the company's stock.

Insider Trading and Securities Fraud Enforcement Act Legislation passed by Congress in 1988 that raised the criminal and civil penalties for insider trading, increased the liability of brokerage firms for wrongful acts of their employees, and gave the Securities and Exchange Commission more power to pursue violations of insider trading.

Insolvent Condition in which a business venture no longer has adequate assets to maintain its operations and can no longer pay its bills as they become due in the usual course of trade and business.

Inspection The process through which some agencies monitor compliance with administrative regulations.

Installment contract A contract allowing delivery of goods and payments for goods at separate times, with the goods being accepted or rejected separately.

Insurable interest An interest by the insured in the value of what is being insured that arises from a financial or legal relationship.

Insured The party that transfers a specified risk to an insurer.

Insurer The party that aggregates similar risks into a common pool and agrees to indemnify the insured in the event of a loss.

Intellectual asset Explicit knowledge that is not yet intellectual property.

Intellectual capital The knowledge, skills, education, training, know-how, and creativity of individuals.

Intellectual property An umbrella term for the legal property rights related to trade secrets, patents, copyrights, and trademarks.

Intentional torts A category of torts in which the tortfeasor was willful in bringing about a particular event that caused harm to another party.

Interbank network A technology platform used by credit cardholders, merchants, and banks, of which Visa and Mastercard are the largest participants.

Intermediaries Financial institutions that provide services for investors and issuers related to securities transactions.

Interrogatory Method of discovery where one party submits written questions to the opposing party attempting to gather evidence prior to trial.

Intestacy When the decedent dies without leaving a will or without otherwise fully disposing of his property during his lifetime.

Investigation The initial phase of the criminal justice process in which authorities become aware of an alleged criminal act and begin gathering physical evidence and interviewing witnesses and potential suspects.

Investors Individuals or entities seeking a return from their investment based on the perceived value of the security.

Involuntary bankruptcy petition A petition filed in the bankruptcy court against a debtor by a group of three or more creditors with an unsecured aggregate claim of at least $15,775 who claim that the debtor is failing to pay the debt as it comes due.

Irrevocable offers Offers that cannot be withdrawn by the offeror; include offers in the form of an option contract, offers that the offeree partly performed or detrimentally relied on, and firm offers by a merchant under the Uniform Commercial Code.

Irrevocable trust A trust created during the trustor's lifetime or upon his or her death under the terms of a will or another trust; these types of trusts cannot be changed or revoked.

Issuers Institutions and entities that sell issued securities to investors.

Joint-and-several liability When general partners' personal assets are at risk both together (jointly) and separately (severally) for all debts and liabilities of the partnership, regardless of the source of the debt or liability.

Judgment creditor Creditor party that has obtained a court judgment against the debtor.

Judicial lien A lien that arises from a judicial proceeding, most commonly a lawsuit filed by a creditor.

Judicial review The implied power of the courts to declare unconstitutional any law that is inconsistent with the Constitution.

Judiciary The collection of federal and state courts existing primarily to adjudicate disputes and charged with the responsibility of judicial review.

Jurisdiction The legal authority that a court must have before it can hear a case.

Jury selection The process of asking potential jurors questions to reveal any prejudices that may affect their judgment of the facts.

Knockout rule As applied in many states, the view that when a buyer and seller engage in a battle of the forms and different terms are exchanged, both the seller's and buyer's differing terms drop out and UCC gap fillers are substituted to complete the contract.

Labor Management Relations Act A federal law, enacted in 1947 as an amendment to the NLRA, that prohibits requiring employees to join or continue membership in a union as a condition of employment. Also known as the *Taft-Hartley Act.*

Labor-Management Reporting and Disclosure Act A federal law enacted in 1959 that established a system of reporting and checks intended to uncover and prevent fraud and corruption among union officials by regulating internal operating procedures and union matters. Also known as the *Landrum-Griffin Act.*

Lapse of time An event covered under operation of law in which a contract may be terminated once either the offeror's expressed time limit has expired or a reasonable time has passed.

Law A body of rules of action or conduct prescribed by controlling authority and having legal binding force.

Lease A contract in which the terms of an agreement are set out for a person to use someone else's property for a specific period of time (*ch. 17*). An agreement between a landlord and a tenant for the rental of property (*ch. 48*).

Legalese Legal terminology that is characterized by long, complex sentences written in passive voice with many embedded clauses that employ obscure, often archaic, terms.

Legality For the formation of a valid contract, the requirement that both the subject matter and performance of the contract must be legal.

Legislative rules Agency rules that have legal effect and impact the rights of parties.

Lessee The party who acquires the right to the temporary possession and use of goods under a lease.

Lessor The party who owns the leased goods and is making them available for lease.

Letter of intent A special kind of contract that binds the parties to confidentiality and exclusivity obligations during the due diligence phase of a corporate transaction.

Levy A court order that authorizes the local sheriff to take possession of the defendant's personal property on behalf of the judgment creditor in order to preserve the property from being transferred or sold by the debtor.

Libel Written defamation in which someone publishes in print (words or pictures), writes, or broadcasts through radio, television, or film an untruth about another that will do harm to that person's reputation for honesty or subject a party to hate, contempt, or ridicule.

Licensee The party who is authorized to use intellectual property in a license agreement.

Licensing A process through which administrative agencies regulate and administer laws.

Licensing agreements Contracts that allow intellectual property owners to monetize their intellectual property rights.

Licensor The intellectual property owner in a license agreement.

Lien An interest in property that gives the holder of the lien the right to possession of some of a debtor's property if the debtor fails to perform its obligations.

Likelihood of confusion Requirement that a mark holder prove that the trademark infringement would likely cause confusion among reasonable consumers.

Limited liability company (LLC) A form of business entity that offers liability protection for its principals, flexible operation, and pass-through taxation.

Limited partnership Entity that exists by virtue of a state statute that recognizes one or more partners as managing the business while other partners participate only in terms of contributing capital or property.

Line of credit Form of commercial loan that allows the borrower to draw against a predetermined credit limit, as needed, instead of receiving the full loan amount at one time.

Liquidated damages Damages that the parties expressly define in the contract and agree will compensate the nonbreaching party.

Literal patent infringement When an infringer makes, uses, or sells the same thing claimed in a patent or adds something beyond what is claimed.

Living Constitution The progressive view that the meaning of the Constitution is dynamic and flexible.

Lucid Sane; able to think clearly.

Magic words of negotiability The use of the specific terms "pay to the order of," "pay to bearer," or "pay to cash" that are a strict formality required by the UCC if a promise or order is to be considered a negotiable instrument.

Magnetic-ink character recognition (MICR) code The line of digits at the bottom of a check that includes the drawee bank's routing number and the drawer's checking account number.

Mail Fraud Act Federal legislation enacted in 1990 that criminalizes any fraud in which the defrauding party uses the mail or any wire, radio, or television in perpetrating the fraud.

Mailbox rule Principle stating that the acceptance of an offer is effective upon dispatch of the acceptance via a commercially reasonable means and not when the acceptance is received by the offeree; governs common law contracts.

Maker A party who receives a loan and promises to repay it.

Manager-managed LLC LLC management structure in which the members name a designated manager (or authorized representative) who generally has the day-to-day operational responsibilities, while the nonmanaging members are typically investors with little input on the course of business taken by the entity except for major decisions.

Manifest Apparent and evident to the senses. In the context of agency law, courts apply an objective standard to determine whether the principal intended that an agency be created.

Margin When a client of a brokerage firm borrows money to make additional investments and offers securities as collateral.

Market-based approach An approach to pollution control that gives businesses a choice of methods based on economic incentives for complying with pollution standards; instituted by the 1990 amendments to the Clean Air Act.

Material Something that results in a substantial change in the value of the contract or that changes a fundamental basis of the agreement.

Materiality Element in a securities fraud case requiring that a misleading fact be one that an objectively reasonable investor would require in order to make a decision in purchasing a security.

Med-arb Method of alternative dispute resolution whereby the parties begin with mediation and, if mediation fails in a fixed time period, the parties agree to submit to arbitration.

Mediation Method of alternative dispute resolution in which a mediator attempts to settle a dispute by learning the facts of the matter and then negotiating a settlement between two adverse parties.

Member-managed LLC LLC management structure similar to that of a general partnership, with all the members having the authority to bind the business.

Mental element Known as the guilty mind requirement, criminal statutes require a defendant to have a requisite degree of mental culpability to be convicted.

Mental incompetents Category of individuals who have limited capacity to enter into a contract; includes anyone who is unable to understand the nature and consequences of the contract and anyone who is unable to act in a reasonable manner in relation to the transaction when the other party has reason to know of his condition.

Mental incapacity (Criminal law) A defense to avoid criminal liability whereby the defendant's actions are related to some type of mental disease or defect.

Merchant One who is regularly engaged in the sale of a particular good, including anyone who employs a merchant as a broker, agent, or intermediary.

Merchant's firm offer An offer in writing between merchants to buy or sell goods along with a promise without consideration to keep that offer open for a stated amount of time or, if unstated, no longer than three months.

Merchant's privilege A narrow privilege, provided for in the Restatements, that shields a merchant from liability for temporarily detaining a party who is reasonably suspected of stealing merchandise.

Merger When two companies combine to form a new enterprise altogether; neither of the previous companies remains independently.

Mini-trial A condensed version of the case is presented to the top management from both sides, with an expert neutral party conducting the trial, allowing them to see and hear facts and arguments so more meaningful negotiations can take place.

Minimum contacts A defendant's activities within or affecting the state in which a lawsuit is brought that are considered legally sufficient to support jurisdiction in that state's courts.

Minors Category of individuals who have limited capacity to enter into a contract; includes those younger than the majority age of 18. Until a person reaches majority age, any contract entered into is voidable at the minor's option.

Mirror image rule Principle stating that the offeree's response operates as an acceptance only if it is the precise mirror image of the offer.

Misappropriation The improper acquisition or disclosure of a trade secret.

Misdemeanors Crimes that carry up to one year of incarceration as the penalty.

Misfeasance An act by one party that harms or endangers another party.

Misrepresentation Situation in which one party to an agreement makes a promise or representation about a material fact that is not true; basis for avoiding a contract.

Mistake In contract law, an erroneous belief that is not in accord with the existing facts.

Mixed motives Theory of employment discrimination in which the cause of an adverse employment action was motivated by both legitimate and discriminatory motives.

Mobile payment app Software loaded on a mobile device that allows users to track expenses, pay bills, and send money to or receive money from businesses or personal accounts.

Mobile sources of air pollution Nonstationary sources of air pollutants, including automobiles, buses, trucks, ships, trains, aircraft, and various other vehicles.

Model Penal Code (MPC) A statutory text adopted by the American Law Institute in 1962 in an effort to bring greater uniformity to state criminal laws by proffering certain legal standards and reforms.

Model state statutes Statutes drafted by legal experts to be used as a model for state legislatures to adopt in their individual jurisdictions in order to increase the level of uniformity and fairness across courts in all states.

Money damages Sums levied on the breaching party and awarded to the nonbreaching party to remedy a loss from breach of contract.

Moral hazard When an insured party engages in riskier behavior because he relies on insurance to cover his liability or loss.

Morals Generally accepted *standards* of right and wrong in a given society or community.

Mortgage A written document that specifies the parties and the real estate, is filed with a state and/or local government agency, and is intended to give notice to the public and other creditors of the secured party's interest in the real estate collateral.

Motion A request by one party to the court asking it to issue a certain order (such as a motion for summary judgment). Motions may be made by either party before, during, and after the trial.

Mutual assent For the formation of a valid contract, the broad underlying requirement that the parties must reach an agreement using a combination of offer and acceptance and that the assent must be genuine.

Mutual mistake An erroneous belief held by both parties that concerns a basic assumption on which a contract was made.

National Environmental Policy Act (NEPA) Federal legislation enacted in 1969 that established a process federal agencies must follow when making decisions that have the potential to significantly impact the environment.

National Labor Relations Act (NLRA) A federal law enacted in 1935 that provides general protections for the rights of workers to organize, engage in collective bargaining, and take part in strikes and other forms of concerted activity in support of their demands. Also known as the *Wagner Act.*

National Labor Relations Board (NLRB) An independent federal agency created by the NLRA and charged with administering, implementing, and enforcing NLRA provisions, as well as monitoring union elections for fraud and setting guidelines for employers and unions in regard to fair labor practices.

Negligence A category of torts in which the tortfeasor was without willful intent in bringing about a particular event that caused harm to another party.

Negligent hiring doctrine A tort-based theory of employer liability when the employer had reason to know that the employee might cause intentional harm within the scope of employment.

Negotiation Various steps used to transfer a negotiable instrument from party to party through a legally defined process.

No Electronic Theft (NET) Act A 1997 statute that increased the criminal penalties for violation of the Copyright Act.

Nominal consideration Consideration that is stated in a written contract even though it is not actually exchanged.

Non-disclosure confidentiality agreement Contract that imposes a legal duty on the party receiving the information to keep it secret.

Nonconforming goods Goods that fail to match what was bargained for in the contract (e.g., goods of the incorrect quantity or specification).

Nondelegation doctrine The doctrine that Congress may not give an agency so much rulemaking discretion that Congress abdicates its responsibility to exercise "[a]ll legislative Powers" granted in the Constitution.

Nonexempt employees Employees who are protected by the FLSA and other statutes.

Nonfeasance The failure to act or intervene in a certain situation.

Nonlegislative rules Rules that are not legally binding on parties and express an agency's interpretation of a statute or describe the agency's policy views.

Nonobviousness standard A standard requiring that an invention must be something more than that which would be obvious, in light of publicly available knowledge, to one who is skilled in the relevant field.

Nonrestrictive indorsement An indorsement that lacks any type of language that seeks to limit the negotiability of an instrument or conditions to its payment or transfer.

Norms of behavior Well-accepted standards of action given a particular circumstance.

Novation When the parties agree to substitute a third party for one of the original parties to the contract.

Novelty standard A statutory standard to determine whether an invention is unique and original.

Nuisance A common law legal action for redressing harm arising from the misuse of one's property that is based on the aggrieved party's right to enjoy his property without interference from a third party.

Objective intent For an offer to have legal effect, the requirement that, generally, the offeror must have a serious intention to become bound by the offer and that the terms of the offer must be reasonably certain.

Occupational Safety and Health Act (OSHA) A federal law enacted in 1970 that sets forth workplace rules and regulations to promote the safety of workers and prevent workplace injuries.

Offer A promise or commitment to do (or refrain from doing) a specified activity. In contract law, the expression of a willingness to enter into a contract by the offeror's promising an offeree that she will perform certain obligations in exchange for the offeree's counterpromise to perform.

Officers Individuals appointed by the board of directors to carry out the directors' set course of direction through management of the day-to-day operations of the business.

Oil Pollution Act (OPA) Federal legislation enacted in 1990 to streamline and strengthen the Environmental Protection Agency's ability to prevent and respond to catastrophic oil spills in water sources.

Omitted terms Contract terms that are left out or absent. In contract law, courts may supply a reasonable term in a situation where the contract is silent.

Open source license agreement A license that permits others to use and modify copyright-protected software.

Open terms Unspecified terms in a sales contract that do not detract from the validity of the contract so long as the parties intended to make the contract and other specified terms give a basis for remedy in case of breach.

Opening statements Attorneys' presentation at the onset of the trial of their theory of the case and what they hope to prove to the jury.

Operating agreement Document that governs an LLC; sets out the structure and internal rules for operation of the entity.

Operating permits Licenses issued by authorities to existing stationary sources that allow pollution emission at certain levels.

Operation of law (Agency) Method whereby an agency relationship is terminated as provided for in a statute or through certain common law doctrines covering the destruction of essential subject matter, death, bankruptcy, or lack of requisite mental capacity.

Operation of law (contracts) Termination of an offer by the occurrence of certain happenings or events, which generally include lapse of time, death or incapacity of the offeror or offeree, destruction of the subject matter of the contract prior to acceptance, and supervening illegality.

Option contract Contract where offeror agrees to hold an offer open (not enter into a contract with another party) for a certain period of time in exchange for something of value.

Order A written instruction to pay money signed by the person giving the instruction.

Order paper An instrument that is payable to an identified person.

Ordinances Local statutes passed by local legislatures.

Originalism The conservative view that the meaning of the Constitution is fixed and stable. With this view, the only way to change the Constitution is by formally amending it under Article V.

Originality Copyright requirement that a work must be the author's own work.

Originator In a commercial wire, party that sends a payment order to its bank with instructions to send funds to a beneficiary's bank account.

Out of existence Nonstatutory option in which a venture simply ceases operations without paying creditors.

Output contract A contract in which the buyer agrees to buy all the goods that the seller produces for a set time and at a set price and the seller may sell only to that one buyer. The quantity for the contract is the seller's output.

Overtime compensation A higher rate of pay for the hours that nonexempt employees work in excess of 40 hours in one seven-day workweek; calculated at one and one-half times the employee's hourly base rate.

Ownership interests The various forms of real property ownership. Some forms limit the rights that owners of real estate have.

Parol evidence rule Rule of contract interpretation stating that any writing intended by the parties to be the final expression of their agreement may not be contradicted by any oral or written agreements made prior to the writing.

Partially disclosed agency When a third party knows a principal exists but does not know the principal's identity.

Partnership agreement Contract between partners that is meant to supercede the default partnership rules.

Partnership at will A partnership in which the partners agree to continue their association indefinitely.

Party A person or entity making or responding to a claim in a court.

Pass-through entity An entity such as a partnership that pays no level of corporate tax.

Past consideration A promise made in return for a detriment previously made by the promisee; does not meet the bargained-for exchange requirement.

Patent A statutorily created right that allows an inventor the exclusive right to make, use, license, and sell her invention for a limited amount of time.

Patentable subject matter standard A standard that prevents laws of nature, natural phenomena, and abstract ideas from being patentable.

Payable at a definite time An instrument that will be repaid on any given date or range of dates.

Payable to bearer The specification that the person who possesses the negotiable instrument is the party to be paid.

Payable to order Designation on a negotiable instrument that identifies the party to whom payment will be made.

Payable upon demand An instrument that can be presented for payment at any time by its holder.

Payee (Draft) The person who will be paid on a payment order.

Payee (Promissory note) A party who extends credit and is entitled to repayment on the loan.

Pension A retirement benefit in which the employer promises to pay a monthly sum to employees who retire from the company after a certain number of years of service. The amount is ordinarily based on the length of service and the employee's final salary rate.

Perfect a security interest Actions taken by a secured lender to protect its security interest from other creditors who might assert claims against the same collateral.

Perfect tender rule Rule that requires the seller to deliver her goods exactly as the contract requires in quantity, quality, and all other respects or risk the buyer's lawful rejection of the goods.

Personal defenses Any defense of the obligor that would be available if the person entitled to enforce the instrument were enforcing a right to payment under a simple contract; includes defenses associated with formation of a contract and with enforceability. HDCs are immune from this defense.

Personal guarantee Pledge from LLC members of personal assets to guarantee payment obligations of the business venture.

Personal jurisdiction The court's authority over the parties involved in the dispute.

Personal property Any movable or tangible object that can be owned or leased (e.g., computers, inventory, furniture, jewelry); includes everything except real property.

Picketing A union's patrolling alongside the premises of a business to organize the workers, to gain recognition as a bargaining agent, or to publicize a labor dispute with the owner or whomever the owner deals with.

Piercing the corporate veil When the court discards the corporate veil and holds some or all of the shareholders personally liable because fairness demands doing so in certain cases of inadequate capitalization, fraud, and failure to follow corporate formalities.

Plain view doctrine A doctrine stating that authorities generally do not commit a Fourth Amendment violation when a government agent obtains evidence by virtue of seeing an object that is in plain view of the agent.

Plaintiff The party initiating a lawsuit who believes the conduct of another party has caused him to suffer damages.

Portal-to-Portal Act Legislation that provides guidelines for what constitutes compensable work under the FLSA's wage and hour requirements.

Pre-file A legal strategy among lenders that involves filing a UCC-1 financing statement before the security agreement is created and before attachment.

Precedent When courts apply the law of a previous case to current cases with similar facts.

Preexisting duty A duty that one is already legally obligated to perform and, thus, is generally not recognized as a legal detriment.

Preferred stock A form of equity instrument that has less risk than common stock because it has certain quasi-debt features. Preferred stockholders have preference rights over common stockholders in receiving dividends from the corporation.

Premium The price an insured pays during the life of the insurance contract to transfer the risk of loss to the insurer.

Preponderance of the evidence The burden of proof used in civil cases, under which the fact finder need be convinced only that the defendant's liability was more likely than not to be true.

Presentment Process used by a holder to demand that the drawee pay the instrument.

Presentment warranties Warranties made by operation of law by anyone who presents a check for payment.

Pretext A false reason offered to justify an action.

Pretrial conference A meeting between the attorneys for the parties and the judge in the case several weeks prior to trial, with the objectives of encouraging settlement and resolving any outstanding motions or procedural issues that arose during the pleadings or discovery stages.

Primary liability Liability for the amount of the instrument as soon as it is issued; required to be paid as soon as the instrument is presented for payment.

Primary market A financial market in which firms (called *issuers*) raise capital by selling securities to investors.

Principal An agent's master; the person from whom an agent has received instruction and authorization and to whose benefit the agent is expected to perform and make decisions pursuant to an agency relationship.

Principals Owners of a business entity.

Principle of indemnity Principle that states the insurer will reimburse the insured for no more than the losses sustained.

Prior art The body of preexisting patents or technical disclosures that predate a patent application.

Private laws Laws recognized as binding between two parties even though no specific statute or regulation provides for the rights of the parties.

Private loan Money loaned by a private source (e.g., an individual) whereby the debtor agrees to pay back the loan over a certain period of time at a certain rate.

Private placement A securities law provision exempting an issuer from registration where the issuer only accepts investments from those who meet the standards for accredited investors.

Private Securities Litigation Reform Act of 1995 (PSLRA) Federal legislation making it more difficult to pursue litigation under the securities laws that is based solely on commentary by company executives; intended to protect publicly held companies from frivolous litigation.

Privately held corporation A corporation that does not sell ownership interests through sales via a broker to the general public or to financial institutions or investors.

Privity of contract The requirement that a contract with a party is necessary to bring a legal action against that party.

Probable cause A reasonable amount of suspicion supported by circumstances sufficiently strong to justify a belief that a person has committed a crime.

Probate The process that manages, settles, and distributes a decedent's property according to the terms of a will or by operation of intestate law if no valid will exists.

Procedural due process The idea that any government decision to take life, liberty, or property must be made using fair procedures; at a minimum, the government must give a person reasonable notice, a fair hearing, and an opportunity to be heard.

Procedural laws Laws that provide a structure and set out rules for pursuing substantive rights.

Product disparagement statutes Statutes intended to protect the interest of a state's major industries, such as agriculture, dairy, or beef.

Professional malpractice insurance Insurance that indemnifies the insured for up to the specified policy limit for negligent acts performed by professional employees that injure clients.

Promise A written undertaking to pay money signed by the party undertaking to pay.

Promissory estoppel Theory allowing for the recovery of damages by the relying party if the promisee actually relied on the promise and the promisee's reliance was reasonably foreseeable to the promisor.

Promissory note Any type of loan (personal or commercial) in which one party offers to lend a specific amount of money with repayment in the future.

Prosecutorial discretion Agencies have broad discretion as to when and whom to regulate.

Prospectus The first part of the security registration statement prescribed by Securities and Exchange Commission regulations; intended to give investors a realistic view of the issuer's business, risk factors, financial position, financial statements, and disclosures concerning directors, officers, and controlling shareholders.

Protected classes The classifications of individuals that are specified in Title VII, including color, race, national origin, religion, gender, and pregnancy.

Proximate (legal) cause A fundamental element that must be proved to recover a negligence lawsuit against a tortfeasor: The injured party must prove a legally recognized and close-in-proximity link between the breach of duty and the damages suffered.

Public laws Laws derived from a government entity.

Public policy Part of the legality requirement for a valid contract; necessitates that the terms be consistent with public policy objectives.

Public policy exception Most widely accepted exception to the employment-at-will principle; protects an employee from being terminated if the action violates established public policy.

Purchase order A form commonly used in sales contracts as an offer from the buyer; contains preprinted clauses along with blanks to accommodate the specifics of the transaction.

Purchase-money security interest (PMSI) An automatically perfected security interest in consumer goods when a merchant or lender offers financing to a borrower to purchase goods.

Qualified indorsement An indorsement that adds language such as "Without recourse" to limit the indorser's loss exposure due to nonpayment.

Qualified privilege A defense to a defamation claim whereby the defendant must offer evidence of good faith and be absent of malice to be shielded from liability; provided for the media and employers.

Quid pro quo Theory of sexual harassment whereby harasser demands sexual favors as a condition of continued employment or as a prerequisite for a promotion or pay raise.

Ratification (Agency) When a principal affirms a previously unauthorized act of an agent.

Ratification (Contracts) Any act that indicates that a minor intends to be bound by his promise.

Rational basis test Under the rational basis test, a government action is constitutional (1) if its action advances a *legitimate* government objective (such as health, safety, or welfare) and (2) if the action is in some way related to the government's objective.

Real defenses Article 3 defenses that may be asserted against an HDC, including fraud in the essence (e.g., tricking a party into signing a document), bankruptcy, forgery, material alterations of a completed instrument, and infancy (i.e., party is a minor).

Real property Land, or anything growing on, attached to, or erected on the land.

Reasonable accommodations Accommodations, required under the Americans with Disabilities Act, that allow disabled individuals to adequately perform essential job functions.

Reformation Contract modification in which the court rewrites a contract to conform to the parties' actual intentions when the parties have imperfectly expressed their agreement and the imperfection results in a dispute.

Regulation D A securities law provision that exempts an issuer from registration when the issuer is selling the security for limited offers of a relatively small amount of money or offers made in a limited manner.

Rejection An action terminating an offer whereby the offeree rejects the offer outright prior to acceptance.

Relational contracts Contracts involving business relationships that are long term and create strong interdependencies between the contracting parties.

Remand To send a case back to the lower court from which it came for further action consistent with the opinion and instructions of the higher court.

Remedial Under the Superfund law, an approach to handling hazardous substance cleanup whereby the Environmental Protection Agency identifies the most hazardous waste sites and generates a National Priorities List.

Remedies Judicial actions, which can be monetary or equitable, taken by courts that are intended to compensate an injured party in a civil lawsuit.

Removal Under the Superfund law, an approach to handling hazardous substance cleanup whereby authorization is given for actions to address releases or imminent releases of hazardous materials.

Reorganization plan A plan, generally filed by the debtor, that articulates a specific strategy and financial plan for emerging from financial distress; serves as the keystone of a Chapter 11 case.

Representative UCC Article 3 equivalent for *agent.*

Represented person UCC Article 3 equivalent for *principal.*

Repudiate A party repudiates the contract if, before performance, he says or does something that is inconsistent with his performance duties.

Request for admissions A set of statements sent from one litigant to an adversary, for the purpose of determining which facts are in dispute and which facts both parties accept as true.

Request for production A request aimed at producing specific items to help one party discover some important fact in the case.

Requirements contract A contract in which the buyer agrees to buy whatever he needs from the seller during a set period and the buyer may buy only from that one seller. The quantity for the contract is what the buyer requires.

Rescission When the parties agree to cancel the contract.

Rescissionary liability Liability of a wrongdoer to an innocent party whereby the proper legal remedy is to rescind the transaction and restore the parties to their pretransaction positions.

Residual market plan An insurance plan that provides coverage for individuals who may not be able to obtain insurance through the regular insurance markets.

Resource Conservation and Recovery Act (RCRA) Federal legislation enacted in 1976 to regulate active and future facilities that produce solid waste and/or hazardous materials.

Respondeat superior When an employer is liable for the torts committed by an employee acting within the scope of employment.

Restatement (Second) of Contracts A model law that many courts have adopted to govern contracts involving services or real estate.

Restatement (Third) of Agency A set of principles, issued by the American Law Institute, intended to clarify the prevailing opinion of how the law of agency stands.

Restatement of Torts An influential document issued by the American Law Institute (ALI) that summarizes the general principles of U.S. tort law and is recognized by the courts as a source of widely applied principles of law. The ALI has amended the Restatements twice, resulting in the *Restatement (Second) of Torts* and the *Restatement (Third) of Torts.*

Restatements of the Law A collection of uniform legal principles focused in a particular area of the law, which contains statements of common law legal principles and rules in a given area of law.

Restitution A remedy that restores to the plaintiff the value of the performance that he has already rendered to the breaching party and by which the breaching party has been unjustly enriched.

Restrictive indorsement An indorsement that seeks to limit the negotiability of an instrument or impose a condition on the payee.

Reverse merger A transaction in which a privately held company buys a publicly listed shell company.

Reverse takeover When a smaller firm acquires control of a larger or longer-established company and retains the name of the latter for the post-acquisition combined entity.

Revised Model Business Corporation Act (RMBCA) Model act drafted by the American Law Institute and adopted by over half of the states as a template for compiling their own statutes governing corporations.

Revised Uniform Limited Liability Company Act (RULLCA) Model law adopted by 19 states and the District of Columbia related to the formation and organization of Limited Liability Companies.

Revised Uniform Limited Partnership Act (RULPA) A model partnership statute that governs limited partnerships.

Revised Uniform Partnership Act (RUPA) A model partnership statute drafted and occasionally revised by the National Conference of Commissioners on Uniform State Laws. Approximately 40 states have adopted all or substantial portions of the RUPA.

Revocable trust A trust created during the trustor's lifetime that can generally be changed or revoked at any time while the trustor is still living.

Revocation An action terminating an offer whereby the offeror decides to withdraw the offer by expressly communicating the revocation to the offeree prior to acceptance.

Right of subrogation The right of the insurer to pursue a legal claim against the party who caused the loss to the insured.

Right to cover A remedy offered to a buyer to cancel the contract and purchase substitute goods from another vendor.

Right-to-work law A state law prohibiting employers from requiring that employees join a union to continue working and that nonunion employees contribute to certain union costs such as the cost related to collective bargaining.

Rightfully dishonor When a drawee bank fails to pay a check due to an inactive account, insufficient funds, or a stop payment order placed on the check.

Risk management program Steps taken by the insured to minimize the probabilities of a loss or the loss amount should the event occur.

Risk of loss The uncertainty an event will occur that triggers liability or loss of property.

Royalty The fee paid by a licensee to the licensor in a license agreement.

Safe Drinking Water Act (SDWA) Federal legislation that sets minimum quality and safety standards for every public water system and every source of drinking water in the United States.

Sale Transaction that transfers ownership, or *title,* to the goods from the seller to the buyer.

Sales contract Agreement to transfer title to real property or tangible assets at a given price.

Sarbanes-Oxley Act of 2002 (SOX Act) Amendments to the 1933 and 1934 Securities Acts that impose stricter regulation and controls on how corporations do business, through regulation of auditing, financial reporting, and internal corporate governance.

Say-on-pay A vote by shareholders of a company approving or rejecting the compensation of the company's executives.

Scienter Specific intent to deceive, manipulate, or defraud.

Secondary liability Conditional liability that arises only if the primarily liable party fails to pay.

Secondary market A financial market in which investors sell to other investors with the goal of making a profit or preventing a loss.

Secondary meaning A legal requirement whereby descriptive mark holders must provide evidence that the general public connects the mark with the mark holder's product or service rather than with the ordinary meaning of the term.

Secondary sources Sources of law that have no independent authority or legally binding effect but can be used to illustrate a point or clarify a legal issue.

Section 16 Provision of the Securities Act of 1934 that imposes restrictions and reporting requirements on ownership positions and stock trades made by certain corporate insiders named in the statute.

Secured transaction A transaction in which the buyer can retain the goods if the payment obligations are satisfied, but in the event of default, the seller or secured party can repossess the goods. Generally, the secured party must dispose of the goods and apply the proceeds to the outstanding indebtedness. Any surplus proceeds belong to the buyer (*ch. 17*). A financing agreement between a lender (creditor) and a borrower (debtor) in which the borrower pledges assets to secure the loan (*ch. 23*).

Securities Act of 1933 Federal legislation that covers the processes of issuing and reissuing securities to the public; requires registration and certain disclosures and authorizes the Securities and Exchange Commission to oversee the transactions.

Securities and Exchange Commission (SEC) The independent federal administrative agency charged with rulemaking, enforcement, and adjudication of federal securities laws.

Securities Exchange Act of 1934 Federal legislation that regulates the sale of securities between investors after an investor has purchased them from a business entity issuer.

Securities law The body of federal and state laws governing the issuance and trading of equity and debt instruments to public investors.

Securities Litigation Uniform Standards Act of 1998 An amendment to the Securities Act of 1934, intended to prevent a private party from instituting certain lawsuits in federal or state court based on the statutory or common law of any state that punishes "a misrepresentation or omission of a material fact" or the use of "any manipulative device or contrivance" concerning the purchase or sale of a covered security.

Securitization The process of packaging promissory notes and negotiating their sale to investors.

Security agreement An agreement between the borrower and the lender that stipulates the creation of a security interest in the particular property offered as security.

Security interest A legal right granted by a debtor to a creditor over the debtor's property (usually referred to as *collateral*); enables the creditor to have recourse to the property (i.e., retake possession of the property) if the debtor defaults in making payment or in otherwise performing its obligations.

Self-defense A defense to avoid criminal liability whereby the defendant's actions are related to the necessity of using deadly force to repel an attack in which the defendant reasonably feared that death or substantial harm was about to occur either to the defendant or to a third party.

Sentencing guidelines Statutorily prescribed standards for determining the punishment that a convicted criminal should receive on the basis of the nature of the crime and the offender's criminal history.

Separation of powers The existence of multiple power centers within a single level of government.

Service marks Trademarks used to identify business services.

Shareholders The owners of a corporation; act principally through electing and removing directors and approving or withholding approval of major corporate decisions.

Shipment contract Contract that requires the seller to use a third-party carrier to deliver the goods.

Sight draft A draft that is payable at any time upon demand once it is presented to the drawee.

Signature liability Liability that arises by a party's (individual or corporate) authentic signature on the instrument, which may be either primary or secondary depending on the status of the signer.

Slander Oral defamation in which someone tells one or more persons an untruth about another that will harm the reputation for honesty of the person defamed or subject a party to hate, contempt, or ridicule.

Social license to operate The demands on, and expectations for, a business that emerge from neighborhoods, environmental groups, community members, and other elements of civil society.

Social Security Act (SSA) of 1935 A federal law providing a broad set of benefits for workers, including a retirement income; funded by mandatory employment taxes paid into a trust fund by both employer and employee and administered by the federal government.

Sole proprietorship One-person business entity with minimal filing requirements.

Special indorsement An indorsement that specifically identifies the party to whom the instrument is to be payable.

Special relationship In tort law, a heightened duty created between certain parties, such as that of a common carrier to its passengers, innkeepers to guests, employers to employees, businesses to patrons, a school to students, and a landlord to tenants and landowners.

Specific performance An equitable remedy whereby a court orders the breaching party to render the promised performance by ordering the party to take a specific action.

Standing Requirement for any party to maintain a lawsuit against another party necessitating that the party

asserting the claim must have suffered an injury in fact and that harm must be direct, concrete, and individualized.

State appellate courts State-level courts of precedent, concerned primarily with reviewing the decisions of trial courts.

State courts Courts that adjudicate matters dealing primarily with cases arising from state statutes, state common law, or state constitutional law.

State Implementation Plan (SIP) A mandated state plan for complying with the federal Clean Air Act that is submitted to the Environmental Protection Agency; consists of a collection of regulations that help to achieve a reduction in pollution.

State long-arm statute State statute intended to allow a court to reach into another state and exercise jurisdiction over a nonresident defendant due to the defendant's conduct or other circumstances.

State trial courts The first courts at the state level before which the facts of a case are decided.

Statement of qualification Document filed to convert a general partnership to a limited liability partnership.

Stationary sources of air pollution Fixed-site emitters of air pollutants, including fossil-fueled power plants, petroleum refineries, petrochemical plants, food processing plants, and other industrial sources.

Statute of frauds The law governing which contracts must be in writing in order to be enforceable.

Statutory law The body of law created by the legislature and approved by the executive branch of state and federal governments.

Statutory (common law) lien A lien on a debtor's property by virtue of a state statute or state common law.

Statutory safe harbor Statute providing immunity for certain transactions and issuers who meet a good faith criteria.

Stock purchase When a buyer purchases equity interests in a target company from one or more selling shareholders.

Strategically qualified attorneys Attorneys who can work with managers to generate opportunities and create value.

Strict liability A category of torts in which a tortfeasor may be held liable for an act regardless of intent or willfulness; applies primarily to cases of defective products and abnormally dangerous activities.

Strict scrutiny The most stringent standard of judicial review. Whenever a government action impairs a fundamental constitutional right or is based on a suspect classification, courts will uphold the action only if (1) the government's objective is *compelling,* (2) the means chosen by the government to advance that objective are *narrowly tailored* or necessary to achieve that compelling end, and (3) no *less restrictive alternatives* exist.

Strike A concerted and sustained refusal by workers to perform some or all of the services for which they were hired in order to induce the employer to concede certain contract terms during collective bargaining or to engage in fair labor practices.

Strong-arm clause Provision of the Bankruptcy Code that allows the debtor in possession to avoid any obligation or transfer of property that the debtor would otherwise be obligated to perform.

Subject matter jurisdiction The court's authority over the dispute between the parties.

Sublease A tenant's transfer of her interests to a third party for anything less than the term remaining on the lease.

Subordinate agent An agent who is overseen by another agent within an organization.

Substantial impairment Defects in the goods that are substantial in nature.

Substantial performance When one party fails to render perfect performance, yet they have acted in good faith and their breach is not material.

Substantive due process The idea that laws must not be vague, overly broad, or arbitrary.

Substantive laws Laws that provide individuals with rights and create certain duties.

Substitute agreement When the contracting parties discharge their obligations by replacing the original contract with a new agreement.

Successor liability Doctrine that allows a creditor to seek recovery from the purchaser of assets even when the purchaser did not expressly assume such liabilities as part of the purchase.

Summary jury trial An abbreviated trial conducted before a jury and a sitting or retired judge at which attorneys present oral arguments without witness testimony and the decision is nonbinding.

Summons Formal notification to the defendant that she has been named in a lawsuit and that an answer must be filed within a certain period of time.

Superfund Another name for the CERCLA, derived from that act's main provisions whereby cleanup operations for abandoned toxic waste sites are to be funded by a self-sustaining quasi-escrow fund to be administered by the federal government.

Superfund Amendments and Reauthorization Act (SARA) A 1986 amendment to the CERCLA that requires that states establish emergency response commissions to draft emergency procedures for a hazardous chemical accident and implement them in the event of such an accident; requires that businesses disclose the presence of certain chemicals within a community; and imposes an obligation on businesses to notify authorities of any spills or discharges of hazardous materials.

Superior agent An agent who oversees other agents within an organization.

Surety A third party that agrees to be primarily liable to pay a loan.

Systemic risk The possibility that an event at a single firm could trigger severe instability in the entire financial market or the collapse of an entire industry or economy.

Tacit knowledge Highly individualized knowledge that is hard to replicate or even explain.

Tax-deferred retirement savings account A retirement savings plan in which the employee commits to saving a certain percentage of base pay in an account that is controlled directly by the employee. The funds grow tax-free until they are withdrawn.

Telemarketing and Consumer Fraud and Abuse Prevention Act Federal statute that allows consumers to opt out of unwanted calls from telemarketers, bans the use of unsolicited recorded calls and faxes, and prohibits telemarketers from making false representations.

Telemarketing and Consumer Fraud and Abuse Prevention Act Federal statute that allows consumers to opt out of unwanted calls from telemarketers, bans the use of unsolicited recorded calls and faxes, and prohibit telemarketers from making false representations.

Telephone Consumer Protection Act A federal statute regulating telemarketing firms.

Tenant remedies The legal alternatives available to tenants as compensation in the event a landlord breaches a lease, including termination of the lease, a suit for damages, and withholding of rent.

Tender of delivery The UCC obligates the seller to have or tender the goods, give the buyer appropriate notice of the tender, and take any actions necessary to allow the buyer to take delivery.

Tendered When the seller delivers conforming goods to a destination that allows the buyer to take delivery.

Term partnership A partnership in which the partners set a specific future date or event for when the partnership will be disolved.

Termination Method of ending an agency relationship whereby either the principal (revocation) or the agent (renunciation) simply communicates the desire to dissolve the relationship.

Time draft A draft that is payable at a determined future date.

Time note A note that is payable at a definite time.

Title The legal term for ownership in property; confers on the titleholder the exclusive use of personal property and the rights to sell, lease, or prohibit another from using the property.

Title VII The section of the Civil Rights Act of 1964 that serves as the centerpiece of antidiscrimination law; covers a comprehensive set of job-related transactions and prohibits discrimination in the workplace on the basis of an employee's race, color, national origin, gender, religion, or pregnancy. The law applies to any private sector employer with 15 or more full-time employees and to unions, employment agencies, state and local governments, and most of the federal government.

Tort A civil wrong in which one party's action or inaction causes a loss to be suffered by another party.

Tortfeasor One who commits a civil wrong against another that results in injury to person or property.

Tortious conduct The wrongful action or inaction of a tortfeasor.

Toxic Substances Control Act (TSCA) Federal legislation that gives the Environmental Protection Agency jurisdiction to control risks that may be posed by the manufacture, processing, use, and disposal of chemical compounds.

Trade dress Trademarks that include a product's shape or the color combination of its packaging.

Trade libel A tort in which a competitor has made a false statement that disparaged a competing product.

Trade name Name used by a sole proprietor for a business instead of the proprietor's actual name.

Trade secrets Valuable assets such as processes, formulas, methods, procedures, and lists that allow companies to obtain a competitive advantage because they are not generally known and are protected.

Trademark A nonfunctional, distinctive word, name, shape, symbol, phrase, or combination of words and symbols that helps consumers to distinguish one product or service from another.

Transactional contracts Contracts involving business relationships based on short-term impersonal interactions.

Transfer agent A separate company that has custody and record of any investment products.

Transfer warranties Warranties made by operation of law when someone transfers an instrument for consideration.

Treble damages Triple damages; often awarded in fraud cases.

Trial Stage of litigation that occurs when the case cannot be settled, generally taking place in front of a judge as the finder of law and with a jury as a finder of fact.

Triple bottom line A CSR approach that emphasizes not only the conventional creation of economic value (profits), but also a company's creation (or destruction) of environmental and social value.

Troubled Assets Relief Program (TARP) A program established by the American Recovery and Reinvestment Act of 2009 to purchase assets and equity from financial institutions and thereby strengthen the U.S. financial sector.

True lease A contract in which title is never transferred and instead involves granting another party limited-life usage rights to the property.

Trust A three-party fiduciary relationship in which the first party, the trustor, transfers property to a second party, the trustee, for the benefit of a third party, the beneficiary.

Trustee The person or company that holds the legal title to the assets in the trust and is generally responsible for managing and distributing the assets in accordance with the terms of the trust.

Trustor The person who creates a trust.

Truth in Lending Act (TILA) The part of the Consumer Credit Protection Act that requires lenders to disclose to borrower applicants certain information about the loan or terms of credit and mandates uniform methods of computation and explanation of the terms of the loan or credit arrangements.

Turnaround advisor (TA) Individual or group of individual professionals who assist management in the work-out process; also called a *turnaround manager* or *turnaround professional.*

U.S. Courts of Appeal The intermediate appellate courts in the federal system frequently referred to as the *circuit courts of appeal,* consisting of 13 courts, each of which reviews the decisions of federal district courts in the state or several states within its circuit.

U.S. District Courts Courts that serve the same primary trial function as state trial courts, but for issues involving federal matters.

U.S. Supreme Court The ultimate arbiter of federal law that not only reviews decisions of the federal courts but also reviews decisions of state courts that involve some issue of federal law.

UCC sales contracts Contracts dealing with the sale of goods.

UCC-1 financing statement A legal document filed in the state where the borrower resides that indicates a security interest.

Uncertificated securities Securities that are simply recorded as an account with a financial institution.

Unconscionability A defense that may allow a party to potentially avoid a contract on the grounds that she suffered a grossly unfair burden that shocks the objective conscience.

Undisclosed agency When a third party does not know that a principal exists.

Undue influence A defense that gives legal relief to a party who was induced to enter into a contract through the improper pressure of a trusted relationship.

Unenforceable Although a contract may have all the required elements and be considered valid, it may be unenforceable because one party asserts a legal defense to performing the contract.

Uniform Commercial Code (UCC) A model code for the sale of goods.

Uniform Limited Liability Company Act (ULLCA) Early version of a model law adopted by most states related to the formation and organization of Limited Liability Companies.

Uniform Partnership Act (UPA) A model partnership statute that is the RUPA's predecessor.

Uniform Probate Code (UPC) A comprehensive model act governing inheritance and decedents' estates.

Uniform Trust Code (UTC) A comprehensive model act governing the creation of trusts.

Unilateral contract A contract where one party's legal detriment is incurred through the other party's action or inaction rather than through a promise.

Unilateral mistake An erroneous belief held by only one party about a basic assumption in the terms of an agreement.

Unqualified indorsement An indorsement that does not include any language that limits the indorser's non-payment liability.

Unsecured creditor A lender who lacks a security interest in collateral to secure the loan.

Usage of trade Any general practice of method of performance that is specific to a particular trade or industry.

Utilitarian An ethical framework whereby an action is ethically sound if it produces positive results or the least harm for the most people.

Valid When a contract has the required elements, it is called a valid contract.

Validation disclosure A notice in which a collection agency, when making initial contact with a debtor, makes known certain rights of the debtor, including the fact that he has 30 days to dispute the debt; required under the Fair Debt Collection Practices Act.

Value Requirement for HDC status that a holder take a negotiable instrument in exchange for the performance of a preexisting promise.

Value chain activities The different business functions that generate value in most businesses.

Values management A system of business ethics in the workplace that prioritizes moral values for the organization and ensures that employee and manager behaviors are aligned with those values.

Venue A determination of the most appropriate court location for litigating a dispute.

Verdict The final decision of a jury in a case.

Vertical privity Privity of contract issues dealing with parties in the distribution chain.

Vicarious infringement A theory of copyright infringement in which the infringing party (the agent) is acting on behalf of, or for the benefit of, another party (the principal). In such cases, the principal is vicariously liable.

Void When an agreement lacks one of the required elements or has not been formed in conformance with the law from the outset, the contract is considered void.

Void title An invalid title obtained through theft.

Voidable A contract is voidable when the law gives one or more parties the right to cancel an otherwise valid contract under the circumstances.

Voidable title An invalid title obtained through fraud or deceit.

Voidable transfers In bankruptcy proceedings, certain transfers that are considered an unfair advantage of one creditor over another.

Voluntary bankruptcy petition A petition filed in the bankruptcy court by the debtor that includes the names of creditors; a list of debts; and a list of the debtor's assets, income, and expenses.

Warranty A guarantee or promise providing assurance by one contracting party to the other party that specific facts or conditions are true or will happen (*ch. 17*). A seller's promise to a consumer concerning an important aspect of the goods (*ch. 18*).

Warranty liability The legal liability of someone who receives payment on an instrument.

Whistleblower An employee or agent who reports illegal misconduct or a statutory violation by his or her employer to the authorities.

Will A legal document in which a person, the *testator,* expresses his wishes as to how his estate is to be distributed at death and in which the testator appoints an executor to manage the estate until its final distribution.

Willful patent infringement Intentional patent infringement that merits higher damages due to bad behavior.

Winding up After dissolution, the process of paying the debts of the partnership and liquidating and/or distributing the remaining assets.

Withdrawal The term used in the RULPA when a partner no longer wishes to be a principal and chooses to leave the partnership.

Without notice Requirement for HDC status that a holder take an instrument without notice that the instrument was overdue, defective, fraudulent, or subject to a claim by another party.

Workers' compensation State statutes that provide an employee who is injured in the course of employment with a partial payment in exchange for mandatory relinquishment of the employee's right to sue the employer for the tort of negligence; funded through employer-paid insurance policies.

Workout An attempt by a debtor to solve a financial problem through a consensual agreement with creditors outside of a court proceeding.

Written express warranty The type of warranty that triggers coverage under the Magnuson-Moss Warranty Act.

Wrongfully dishonor When a drawee bank fails to cash a check that is properly payable.

***Zippo* standard** The legal framework used by trial courts in determining personal jurisdiction when one party is asserting minimum contacts based on a certain level of Internet activity by the defendant.

A

B

case index

C

George v. Jordan Marsh Co., 781n
GGNSC Batesville, LLC d/b/a Golden Living Center v. Johnson, 675
Giles v. POM Wonderful, LLC, 322
Gilmer v. Interstate/Johnson Lane Corporation, 116
Gimbel v. Signal Companies, Inc., 546–547
Glenn Distributors Corp. v. Carlisle Plastics, Inc., 293–294
Goodman v. Darden, Doman & Stafford Associates, 539
Goodrich Corp. v. Town of Middlebury, 914–915
Goodyear Dunlop Tires v. Brown, 85–86
Goswami v. American Collections Enterprise, Inc., 44
Grande, as Personal Representative of the Estate of Robert A. Spann v. Jennings, et al., 926
Graves v. Warner Brothers, 784n
Greenman v. Yuba Power Products, Inc., 796–800
Griffith v. Mellon Bank, N.A., 346n
Griggs v. Duke Power Co., 748, 752–753
Grimshaw v. Ford Motor Company, 29–31
Gruttinger v. Bollinger, 765n
Gustafson v. Alloyd Co., 591

H

Hadley v. Baxendale, 218
Halifax Corp. v. First Union National Bank, 392
Hammer v. Sidway, 158n
Hannington v. University of Pennsylvania, 686
Harding v. Careerbuilder, LLC, 770
Harley-Davidson Motor Co., v. PowerSports, Inc., 192–193
Harris v. Forklift Systems, Inc., 753n
Harris v. Vector Marketing Corp., 667
Harvey Barnett v. Shidler, 990
Haynes v. Zoological Society of Cincinnati, 704
Hearthstone, Inc v. Department of Agriculture, 210–211
Hebberd-Kulow Enterprises, Inc. v. Kelomar, Inc., 249

Hemlock Semiconductor Operations, LLC v. SolarWorld Industries, 271
Hemmings v. Camping Time RV Centers and Bank of America, 355
Henningsen v. Bloomfield Motors, Inc., 186–187
Hernandez v. Yellow Transportation, 108–109
Herring v. United States, 874
Hill v. Gateway 2000, Inc., 152n
Hively v. Ivy Tech Community College, 746n
Hodges Wholesale Cars and Cleveland Auto Sales v. Auto Dealer's Exchange of Birmingham and Express Drive Away, 257–258
Holder Construction Group v. Georgia Tech Facilities, 205–206
Hooters of America, Inc. v. Phillips, 123
Hornbeck Offshore Services, LLC v. Salazar, 823n
Huntsville Hospital v. Mortara Instrument, 294

I

IBP, Inc. v. Alvarez, 710n
i.Lan, Inc. v. NetScout, 151
Infinite Energy, Inc. v. Thai Heng Chang, 122
In re AppOnline, Inc., 340–341
In re Donald J. Trump Casino Securities Litigation–Taj Mahal Litigation, 596
In re the Dow Chemical Company Derivative Litigation, 539
In re Estate of Joseph M. Silver, 409–410
In re Fehrs, 453
In re Geller, 984
In re Heeb Media, LLC, 984
In re Hershey Chocolate and Confectionery Corp., 982–983
In re High-Tech Employee Antitrust Litigation, 43–44
In re Huffy Corp. Securities Litigation, 633–634
In re Jones, 454
In re Kirby, 984

In re Oil Spill by the Oil Rig "Deepwater Horizon" in the Gulf of Mexico, 908–909
In re Pfautz, 410
In re Piknik Products Co., 410
In re Pillowtex, Inc., 300–301
In re Reed Elsevier, Inc., 990
In re Richie, 454
In re Riverstone National, Inc. Shareholders Litigation, 555
In re Sousa, 451n
In re Spree.com Corp., 496–497
In re Subway Sandwich Marketing and Sales Practices Litigation, 113–114
In re Tam, 984–985
In re The Vantive Corporation Securities Litigation, 598
In re Volkswagen "Clean Diesel" Marketing, Sales Practices, and Products Liability Litigation, 44
In re The Walt Disney Company Derivative Litigation, 676
Integrity Staffing Solutions v. Busk, 711
International Transportation Service v. NLRB, 730n

J

Jacob and Youngs v. Kent, 200–201, 215
Jacq Wilson et al. v. Brawn of California, Inc., 263
James v. Meow Media, Inc., 785–786
Jasper v. H. Nizam, Inc., 693
Jaszczyszyn v. Advantage Health Physician Network, 723–724
Jones v. Royal Administration Services, Inc., 659
Jones v. R. R. Donnelley & Sons Co., 20

K

Kauffman-Harmon v. Kauffman, 20
Kaycee Land and Livestock v. Flahive, 511
Kelley v. Cypress Financial Trading Co., L.P., 445–446
Kelo et al. v. City of New London, 7–8, 939–940
Kirksey v. Grohmann, 508–509

Defendant
    defined, 77
    out-of-state, 85–86
Defenses, criminal liability, 855
Delaware
    chancery courts, 77
    as state of incorporation, 519–520
Deliberations, civil litigation, 111
Delisting process, 605
Delivery, open terms in sales
    contracts, 242
Dell, 255
Demand notes, 331
Department of Labor, U.S., 709,
    710–711, 715
Department of Transportation, U.S.,
    839–840
Depositions, 109
Depositor, 382
Depository bank, 382
Design patents, 970–971
Destination contracts, 259–260, 263
Destruction
    in discharge of contracts, 204
    in termination of offer, 154
Detours, 680
Detrimental reliance, 153
Digital wallets, 387–388
Direct examination, civil
    litigation, 111
Direct infringement, 976
Directors, corporate. *See* Board of
    directors
Disaffirmance, 167
Discharge
    contract. *See* Contract(s),
        discharge
    defined, 373
    negotiable instrument, 373–374
Disclaimer
    defined, 317
    sales warranty, 317, 320
Discovery stage
    civil litigation, 109–110, 122
        exculpatory evidence, 109
        inculpatory evidence, 109
        methods of discovery, 109–110
    in debt collection for secured
        debt, 421
Discretionary courts, 78, 80
Discrimination. *See* Employment
    discrimination

Dishonored instruments, 366–368,
    382–383
Disparate impact (*Griggs* standard),
    748, 752–753
Disparate treatment (*McDonnell
    Douglas* standard), 747–751,
    757–758
Dispute resolution options, 104. *See
    also* Alternative dispute resolution
    (ADR); Civil litigation
Dissociation
    limited liability company (LLC),
        508, 512
    partnership, 490–492
Dissolution
    limited liability company (LLC),
        508–509, 511–512
    partnership, 490–493
District justices, 77
Diversity of citizenship, 84
Doctrine of equivalence, patent,
    973–974
Doctrine of stare decisis, 14–15, 81
Dodd-Frank Wall Street Reform and
    Consumer Protection Act (2010),
    571, 628–631, 641–649
    administrative law courts (ALCs),
        607–608
    CEO pay ratio disclosure rule,
        630, 644–645
    Consumer Financial Protection
        Bureau (CFPB), 642, 643, 647,
        650, 840, 844
    expanded SEC jurisdiction, 629,
        641–642
    Financial Stability Oversight
        Council (FSOC), 629,
        642–644
    moral hazard and clearinghouse
        protections, 648–649
    say-on-pay executive
        compensation, 629, 646
    whistleblower protections,
        630–631, 647–648
Do Not Call Registry, 836
Double jeopardy, 61, 63
Drafts, 329–330
    checks as, 381. *See also* Checks
    defined, 329
    indorsement, 335, 381–382
    parties, 329–330
    types, 330

Drawee
    draft, 329–330, 381
    negotiable instrument, 363–364
Drawee bank, 381
Drawer
    draft, 329–330, 381
    negotiable instrument, 365–366
Drug testing, 727–728
Due diligence, in mergers and acquisi-
    tions (M&A), 551–552, 555
Due process, 64–66
    Fifth Amendment Due Process
        Clause, 61, 63, 64, 83
    Fourteenth Amendment Due
        Process Clause, 58–59, 64, 83
    judicial review standards, 65
    procedural, 64
    substantive, 64
Duncan, David, 623
Durable medium, copyright
    requirement, 975
Duress, 185, 186–192
Duty, 784–788
    assumption of duty, 786–788
    breach of, 784, 789–790
    general duty of reasonable
        conduct, 784
    landowner duty to parties off land,
        786, 787–788
    no general duty to act,
        785–786, 803
Duty-based ethics, 28
Duty of care
    corporation, 530–532
    partnership, 480
Duty of loyalty
    corporation, 530, 532–535
    partnership, 479–480
Duty to disclose
    concealment of material fact,
        183–184
    corporation, 535–536
Duty to mitigate, 222–223

E

eBay, 235–236
Economic Espionage Act (1996), 965
Economic incentive theory, air pollu-
    tion and, 903–90
E-contracts, 150–152
EDGAR, 572–574, 604

Fraudulent liens, 416–418, 424
Fraudulent misrepresentation
  contracts, 182–184
  torts, 779–780
Freedom of contract principle,
  129–130, 201
Freedom of disposition, 948–951, 958
Freedom of Information Act (FOIA),
  642, 824–825
Freedom of religion, First
  Amendment rights, 56–58, 63
Freedom of speech, First Amendment
  rights, 56–58, 63
Friedman, Milton, 32
Frolics, 680–681
Frustration of purpose, in discharge
  of contracts, 207–208
Fully disclosed agency, 677–678

G

Gap fillers, 230–231, 241–242,
  244–245
Garnishment, 420
GE Capital Corporation (GECC), 643
General partnerships, 459, 473–483
  business context, 475–476
  default rules, 475
  dissociation and dissolution,
    490–493
  duties of partners, 478–481,
    496–497
  formation, 473–474, 494–495
  liability, 475–476
  rights of partners, 476–478
Genuine assent, 181
Getting to Yes (Fisher and Ury), 161
Going-and-coming rule, 681
Good faith and fair dealing, 129–130
  business judgment rule and, 519,
    531–532, 539
  contracts, 129–130, 131–132
  employment-at-will doctrine
    exceptions, 692, 695–696
  in holder in due course (HDC)
    status, 347–348
  insurer duty to settle a claim in
    good faith, 890–891, 893
  partnership duty of good faith,
    480–481
  sales contracts, 256–258, 266–267

Goods
  defined, 231, 254
  lease contracts. *See* Lease
    contracts (goods)
  sale of. *See* Sales contracts
  title in identifying, 255
Google, 17, 35, 543, 845–846
Google Pay, 387–388
Gorsuch, Neil, 68
Gratuitous agents, 658, 663
Great Recession, 337
Greenwashing, 907
Grievances, union, 731–732
Griggs standard (disparate impact),
  748, 752–753
Guarantor, creditor rights against
  third parties, 414–415
Guns
  Gun-Free School Zones Act
    (1990), 55
  products liability, 799–800
  Second Amendment rights,
    58–59, 63
Guzmán, Joaquin "El Chapo," 61

H

Hate speech, 57
Hazardous waste control, 912–917
HDC. *See* Holder in due course
  (HDC) status
Health Care and Education
  Reconciliation Act (HCERA,
  2010), 718
Health care benefits, 718–719
Health Insurance Portability and
  Accountability Act (HIPAA), 718
Hedge funds, 642
Hershey's, 980–983
Holder in due course (HDC) status,
  346–356
  consumers and Holder Rule,
    353–356
  defenses, 352, 358
  defined, 346
  protecting, 356
  required conditions, 346–350,
    351, 357–358
    good faith, 347–348
    value, 346–347, 357
    without notice, 348–350

shelter rule, 351
  third-party claims, 352–353
Holder Rule, 353–355
Holding, precedent and, 14
Hopkins standard (mixed motives),
  747–748, 751–752
Horizontal privity, 318, 322, 323
Hostile takeovers, 549–551
Hostile work environment,
  753–754
Housing of soldiers, Third
  Amendment rights, 59, 63
Howey test, 563, 566, 574, 577
Hung jury, civil litigation, 111

I

Identified to the contract, 255
Illusory promises, 159
Implicit knowledge, 963
Implied authority, 674
Implied contracts, 136,
  137–138, 143
  avoiding, 702–703
  in employment-at-will doctrine
    exceptions, 692, 694–695
Implied partnership, 473
Implied warranty, 313–316
  defined, 313
  disclaimer, 317
  fitness for a particular
    purpose, 316
  merchantability, 314–316, 323
  title and noninfringement,
    313–314, 317
Impossibility
  in discharge of contracts,
    204–206, 210
  in discharge of sales contracts,
    270–271, 276
Impracticability
  in discharge of contracts,
    206–207, 210–211
  in discharge of sales contracts,
    270–271, 276
Incapacity
  in discharge of contracts, 204
  in termination of offer, 154
Incidental damages, 283
Incorporation, Bill of Rights, 55–56,
  58–59

Premium, insurance, 881
Preponderance of the evidence
    civil litigation, 111
    criminal law, 853
Presentment
    defined, 366
    negotiable instrument, 366-368,
        376-377
        instruments that are
            dishonored, 366-368
        requirements, 366
Presentment warranties, 370-372
President
    control of administrative
        agencies, 821
    executive orders, 52, 71-72, 821
    overview of powers, 52
Pretext, 750, 770
Pretrial conference, civil
    litigation, 110
Prevention strategy, 6, 16-17
Price, open terms in sales
    contracts, 242
Prima facie case
    age discrimination, 757-758
    defined, 750n
    employment discrimination,
        750, 752
    equal pay, 761
Primary liability, on negotiable
    instruments, 363-365, 377
Primary markets, securities, 561,
    638-639
Primary sources and levels of law,
    7-12
    administrative (regulatory) law,
        7, 10
    common law, 7, 10-11
    constitutional law, 7-9. *See also*
        Constitution, U.S.
    statutory law, 7, 9-10
Prince, 957
Principal
    agency law. *See also* Agency law
        defined, 655
        liability for agent's contracts,
            673-677
        liability for agent's torts,
            679-684
    business entity, 458-459. *See also*
        Business entity

Principally Responsible Parties
    (PRPs), 913-914
Principle of indemnity, 886
Principles-based decision-making,
    27-28
Prior art, 968
Private law, defined, 3
Private loans, sole proprietor, 463
Privately held corporations,
    515-516
Private placements, 583-586
    Rule 504 exemptions from
        registration, 584-585, 586
    Rule 506 exemptions from
        registration, 585, 586
Private property. *See also* Employee
    privacy
    Fifth Amendment (Takings
        Clause) protection, 61, 63
    Fourth Amendment (search and
        seizure) protection, 59-61, 63
    Third Amendment (housing of
        soldiers) protection, 59, 63
Private Securities Litigation Reform
    Act (1995), 592-593, 616
Private Securities Litigation Uniform
    Standards Act (1998), 593
Privity of contract
    defined, 318
    horizontal privity, 318, 322, 323
    vertical privity, 318, 322
Probable cause, 60-61, 865
Probate, 951-952, 953, 955-956
Problem of self-amendment, 67
Procedural due process, 64
Procedural law, defined, 3
Product disparagement statutes, 779
Products liability law, 775, 795-801
    causation and damages, 800-801
    defining "defect," 797-800
    guns and, 799-800
    liability waivers, 801-802
    negligence, 795-796
    strict liability, 796-800
    warranty, 796
Professional corporations, 516
Professional malpractice insurance,
    883, 888
Pro-Football, Inc., 985
Promise
    defined, 327

unconditional, for negotiable
    instruments, 327, 340-341
Promissory estoppel, 160
Promissory notes, 331
Property, 924-945
    definition and categories, 924-925
    personal, 925-929
    real. *See* Real property
    tangible, 925
Prosecutorial discretion,
    administrative agency, 818-819
Prospects, tortious interference,
    782, 803
Prospectus, public offering, 582
Protected classes, 745
Protection of Lawful Commerce in
    Arms Act (PLCAA), 799-800
Proxies, 605, 629
Proximate (legal) cause, 784,
    790-792
    closest-in-proximity, 790-791
    superseding cause, 791-792
Prudential Financial, 643
Public accountability, of
    administrative agencies, 823-825
Public Company Accounting
    Oversight Board (PCAOB), 625
Public corporations, initial public
    offerings (IPOs), 516, 522-523
Public domain, as defense for copy-
    right infringement, 979
Public law, 3
Public offerings
    initial public offerings (IPOs),
        516, 522-523, 561, 638
    misrepresentations in registration
        statement, 588-592
    process steps, 581-583
        postregistration, 583
        preregistration
            documentation, 582
        registration, 582
        waiting period, 582-583
Public policy
    arbitration clauses and, 123
    defined, 172
    in employment-at-will doctrine
        exceptions, 692-694, 703, 704
    legality of purpose in contract
        formation, 172-174
    nondisclosure agreements vs., 175

Punishment, Eighth Amendment
    rights, 62, 63
Punitive damages, 29–31, 757, 792n
Purchase-money security interest
    (PMSI), 404, 405, 410
Purchase orders, 243, 244

Q

Qualified indorsement, 335
Qualified privilege, 777, 778
Quantity, open terms in sales con-
    tracts, 241–242
Quid pro quo theory, 753–754

R

Racketeer Influenced and Corrupt
    Organizations (RICO) Act (1970),
    861–862
Ratification, 167, 675–677
Rational basis test, judicial review, 65
Rawls, John, 29
Reading Pipe case, 200–201, 215
Reagan, Ronald, 821
Real defenses, of holder in due course
    (HDC) status, 352
Real property, 925, 929–941
    assignment, 936–937, 943
    eminent domain, 61, 938,
        939–940
    environmental liability in land
        acquisitions, 916, 917–918
    equitable relief, specific
        performance, 220–221
    equitable remedies
        injunctive relief, 221
        reformation, 221
    governmental regulation of land
        use, 937–939
    landlord duty to parties off land,
        786, 787–788
    landlord-tenant law, 929,
        934–936, 941
    mortgages, 419
    ownership rights, 929–934
    performance assurances, 223–224
    sale of, 931–932
    subletting, 936–937, 943
Reasonable person standard, 147
Reformation, 221
Regulation A, 585, 586

Regulation D, 584–585
Reinstatement, employment
    discrimination, 757
Rejection of offer, 152, 153–154
Relational contracts, 136
Religious Freedom Restoration Act
    (1993), 56–57
Religious tenets, 27–28
Remand, 78
Remediation, of hazardous
    waste, 913
Remedies
    contract law, 217–223, 225
        breach of contract, 214
        duty to mitigate, 222–223
        equitable, 11, 12, 220–221
        money damages, 217–220
    defined, 11, 214, 280–281
    sales contracts, 282–291
        buyer's, 286–290
        limitation of remedies,
        291, 295
        seller's, 282–286
Remedy at equity. *See* Equitable
    remedies
Remington, 799–800
Removal, of hazardous waste, 913
Renunciation, in discharge of negotia-
    ble instrument, 374
Reorganization plan, 448
Representative, 368–369
Represented person, 368–369
Repudiation, 281
Requests for admissions, 109
Requests for production, 109, 122
Requirements contracts, 241–242
Rescission, 201
Rescissionary liability, 591
Residual interest, lease contract
    (goods), 300
Residual market plan, 889
Res ipsa loquitur, 789–790, 804
Resource Conservation and Recovery
    Act (RCRA), 911, 920
Respondeat superior, 679–684
    defined, 679
    independent contractors, 682–683
    intentional torts exception, 682
    negligent hiring doctrine, 682
    physical injury requirement, 679
    scope of employment limitation,
        679–681, 686–687

Restatement (Third) of Agency, 655
*Restatement (Second) of
    Contracts*, 129
Restatement (Second) of Torts,
    775, 796
Restatement (Third) of Torts, 775
Restatements of the Law, defined, 13
Restitution, 218
Restraining orders, 11
Restrictive covenants
    confidentiality/nondisclosure
        agreements, 175, 190–191
    noncompete clauses, 129–130,
        190–191
Restrictive indorsement,
    334–335, 345
Retroactive promotions, employment
    discrimination, 757
Reverse mergers, 546
Reverse takeovers, 546
Revised Model Business Corporation
    Act (RMBCA), 515, 517,
    530, 531
Revised Uniform Limited Liability
    Company Act (RULLCA), 502,
    504–505, 507
Revised Uniform Limited Partnership
    Act (RULPA), 483, 492–493
Revised Uniform Partnership Act
    (RUPA), 474–478, 491–492
Revocable trusts (living trusts), 953
Revocation of offer, 152–153
Rightful dishonor, 382
Right of subrogation, 884–886
Right to cover, 287, 293–294
Right-to-work laws, 729
Riparian rights, of real
    property, 930
Risk capital test, 574
Risk management program,
    886–887
Risk of loss, 881
    defined, 259
    sales contract, 259–264
        destination contracts,
        259–260, 263
        shipment contracts, 259, 260,
        261, 263–265
Roosevelt, Franklin D., 57, 709
Royalty, 963
Rule 504 exemptions, 584–585
Rule 506 exemptions, 585

Trusts, 946-961. *See also* Wills, trusts, and estates
  in probate avoidance, 953
  state taxation of, 959
  terminology, 952-953
  Uniform Trust Code (UTC), 956
Truth in Lending Act (TILA), 841-842, 848
Turnaround advisors (TAs), 429-430, 437-438
Turnaround Management Association (TMA), 437-438
Twenty-first Amendment, 67
Twitter, 982

U

Uber, 661, 683
UCC-1 financing statement, 402-403
UCC sales contracts, 135. *See also* Sales contracts
Uncertificated securities, 404
Unconditional promise, 327, 340-341
Unconscionability, 186-188
Undisclosed agency, 678
Undue influence, 186
Unemployment compensation, 721, 725
Unenforceable contracts, 133
Unenumerated rights, Ninth Amendment protection, 62, 63
Uniform Commercial Code (UCC)
  Article 2 (sale of goods), 135, 228-239. *See also* Sales contracts
  Article 2A (leasing of goods), 229, 298-301, 928. *See also* Lease contracts (goods)
  Article 3 (negotiable instruments), 326-329, 344-348, 363, 380-382. *See also* Negotiable instruments
  Article 4 (interbank transactions), 382, 386, 387
  Article 4A (funds transfers between commercial entities), 386
  Article 9 (secured transactions), 396-398, 399, 402
  defined, 229

introduction, 229
as model statute, 129-130, 229
Section 2-312 (implied warranty of noninfringement), 313-314
Section 2-314 (implied warranty of merchantability), 314-316, 323
Section 2-315 (implied warranty for a particular purpose), 316
Section 2-316(3)(b) (warranty disclaimers), 317
Section 2-318 (horizontal privity), 318, 322, 323
statute of frauds, 136
Uniform Limited Liability Company Act (ULLCA), 502, 504-505
Uniform model laws. *See* Model laws
Uniform Partnership Act (UPA), 474-475
Uniform Probate Code (UPC), 955-956
Uniform Residential Landlord-Tenant Act (URLTA), 929
Uniform Trust Code (UTC), 956
Unilateral contracts, 135, 142, 149
Unilateral mistake, 157
Unions. *See* Labor unions
U.S. Constitution. *See* Constitution, U.S.
U.S. Courts of Appeals, 78, 79, 80
U.S. District Courts, 78-79
U.S. Supreme Court. *See* Supreme Court, U.S.
Universalization test, 28
Unqualified indorsement, 335
Unsecured creditors, 397
UPS, 306-307
Ury, William, 161
Usage of trade, sales contracts, 268
Use regulation, 937
Utilitarianism, 28-29

V

Validation disclosure, 844
Valid contracts, 133
Value, and holder in due course (HDC) status, 346-347, 357
Value chain activities, 129, 131
Value creation strategy, 6, 17-18
Values management, 34-36, 44
Venture capital firms, 522

Venue, 77, 94-95
  change of, 94-95
  forum selection clauses/forum shopping, 88-89, 95, 97, 175-176
Verdict, civil litigation, 111
Vertical privity, 318
Vicarious infringement, 977
Violence Against Women Act (VAWA), 55
Virtual stock exchanges, 567
Virtue ethics, 28
Visa, 385, 390
Voicemail, monitoring employee use of, 726
Voidable contracts, 133, 167
Voidable title, 257
Voidable transfers (bankruptcy), 443-444, 453
Void contracts, 133, 143, 167
Void title, 257
Voir dire, 110-111
Voluntary bankruptcy petition, 444-445
Voluntary personal jurisdiction, 88-89
Voting rights
  board of directors, 528
  partnership, 478

W

Waiting period, public offering, 582-583
Walmart, 34, 386
Walt Disney Company, 17-18
Warranties
  defined, 304
  lease contract (goods), 304
  negotiable instrument warranty liability, 369-372, 377
  products liability, 796
  sales, 312-324
    disclaimers, 317, 320
    express, 313, 319-321
    implied, 313-316
    limitations, 317
    Magnusson-Moss Act regulation, 319-321
    notice of breach, 318-319
    third-party rights, 318-319
    types, 312-316

Warranty liability, negotiable instrument, 369–372, 377
    presentment warranties, 370–372
    transfer warranties, 370
Watchdog groups, 899–900
Water pollution control, 906–910
    drinking water, 910
    oil spills, 123, 822–823, 907–909
Water rights, of real property, 930
Weinstein, Harvey, 175, 756
Wells Fargo, 36–37
Whistleblowers, 698–702
    defined, 647, 650, 698
    Dodd-Frank Act protections, 630–631, 647–648
    False Claims Act protections, 697
    Sarbanes-Oxley Act protections, 627
    separate and independent defense for termination, 700–701
    state versions of False Claims Act, 697–698
    state whistleblower laws, 698–700
    Whistleblower Protection Act (1989), 698

White-collar crime, 859–864
    Computer Fraud and Abuse Act (CFAA), 864
    conspiracy, 861
    Foreign Corrupt Practices Act (FCPA, 1977), 862–864, 876
    fraud, 859–860
    obstruction of justice, 861
    Ponzi schemes, 445n, 616–617, 860–861
    Racketeer Influenced and Corrupt Organizations Act (RICO), 861–862
    securities crimes, 862. *See also* Insider trading
Willful patent infringement, 973
Wills, trusts, and estates, 946–961
    freedom of disposition, 948–951, 958
    inheritance taxes, 954–955
    intestacy, 948, 957, 959
    probate, 951–952, 953
    terminology, 946–948, 952–953
    trusts, 946–961
    Uniform Codes and Restatements, 955–956
Wilson, Woodrow, 57

Winding up, partnership, 492
Wires (electronic funds transfers), 386, 387, 393
Withdrawal, partnership, 490, 492–493
Without notice requirement, in holder in due course (HDC) status, 348–350
Workers' compensation, 719–720, 725, 737–738
Workouts, 429–431
    bankruptcy vs., 430
    models, 430
    turnaround advisors (TAs), 429–430, 437–438
Wrongful dishonor, 382–383

Y

Yelp, 845–846
YouTube, 543

Z

Zippo standard, 90–93, 97–98
Zoning ordinances, 937–938
Zuckerberg, Mark, 64, 494–495, 509–510